MICROSOFT®
Office xp

Introductory Course

Mastering and Using

H. Albert Napier
Philip J. Judd
Bruce McLaren
Benjamin Rand
Susan Lehner
Linda Sourek

**COURSE
TECHNOLOGY**
™
THOMSON LEARNING

Australia • Canada • Mexico • Singapore • Spain • United Kingdom • United States

**COURSE
TECHNOLOGY**

TM

THOMSON LEARNING

Mastering and Using Microsoft® Office XP Introductory Course
by H. Albert Napier, Ph.D. & Philip J. Judd, Bruce McLaren, Benjamin
Rand, Susan Lehner, Linda Sourek

Managing Editor:
Melissa Ramondetta

Development Editor:
Robin M. Romer,
Pale Moon Productions

Product Marketing Manager:
Kim Wood

Product Manager:
Robert Gaggin

Editorial Assistant:
Jodi Dreissig

Production Services:
GEX Publishing Services

Copy Editor:
GEX Publishing Services

Cover Design:
Steve Deschene

Compositor:
GEX Publishing Services

What's New in Office XP

Office XP

- ► Streamlined, flatter look
- ► Multiple task panes containing command shortcuts
- ► Ask A Question Box Help tool
- ► Smart Tags
- ► AutoCorrect Options
- ► Revised Office Clipboard
- ► Paste Options
- ► Route documents for review with tracked changes via e-mail
- ► Speech Recognition
- ► Improved "crash" recovery features
- ► New Search task pane
- ► Digital signatures for documents routed over the Internet

Outlook 2002

- ► Streamlined setup options
- ► Expanded virus protection for e-mail attachments
- ► Calendar color coding
- ► Calendar sharing over the Internet

Word 2002

- ► Multiple text selection using the CTRL key
- ► New task panes to review and apply formatting
- ► New task panes to apply and create styles
- ► Select similarly formatted text with shortcut menu
- ► Revised Mail Merge Wizard
- ► New table styles
- ► Revised Track Changes and Compare Documents features
- ► New drawing tools to create conceptual diagrams
- ► Native Organization Chart drawing tool
- ► Revised watermark creation
- ► New Clear Formatting feature

Excel 2002

- ► Query data directly from Web pages and XML files
- ► Import data from a variety of sources, including databases, OLAP data sources, and SQL Server
- ► Function arguments displayed in ScreenTips as functions entered
- ► Function Wizard uses natural language query to help find best function available
- ► Cut-and-paste function examples from Help into a worksheet
- ► Expanded AutoSum functionality includes commonly used functions such as MIN, MAX, and AVERAGE
- ► Formula evaluator shows results of nested formulas
- ► Formula error checking

- ► Color-coded worksheet tabs
- ► Smart tags for paste, fill, insert, and formula checking
- ► Border drawing to create complex outline borders
- ► AutoRepublish Excel data to the Web
- ► Open and save XML files
- ► Speech playback of cell content
- ► Graphics can be inserted into headers and footers for printing
- ► Merge and unmerge cells with a Format toolbar button
- ► Links Management

PowerPoint 2002

- ► Collaborative online reviews
- ► Print presentation with comment pages
- ► Merge and compare reviewed presentations
- ► Animation schemes with animation and transitions
- ► New animation effects
- ► Motion paths
- ► Better organization charts
- ► New diagram types (cycle, pyramid, radial, Venn)
- ► Task panes for applying slide and presentation formatting
- ► Outline/Slides tab – Thumbnail of slides in Normal view
- ► Print preview
- ► Multiple design templates per presentation
- ► Visible grids for aligning placeholders, shapes, and pictures
- ► Adjustable spacing between grids for more control
- ► Automatic layout for inserted objects
- ► Embedded fonts (characters within presentation or all font characters)
- ► Text AutoFit improvements to automatically adjust layout for charts, diagrams, and pictures
- ► Picture rotation
- ► Play sounds and animation when a presentation is saved as a Web page
- ► Password protection when opening a presentation
- ► Language indicator in status bar

Access 2002

- ► File format compatibility between Access 2000 and Access 2002
- ► Create new copy of saved database
- ► PivotTables and PivotCharts
- ► XML support
- ► Extended support for SQL Server databases through Access Projects
- ► Improved ability to create Data Access Pages
- ► Relative path support for Data Access Pages
- ► Multiple Undo/Replace actions

Napier & Judd

In their over 50 years of combined experience, Al Napier and Phil Judd have developed a tested, realistic approach to mastering and using application software. As both academics and corporate trainers, Al and Phil have the unique ability to help students by teaching them the skills necessary to compete in today's complex business world.

H. Albert Napier, Ph.D. is the Director of the Center on the Management of Information Technology and Professor in the Jesse H. Jones Graduate School of Management at Rice University. In addition, Al is a principal of Napier & Judd, Inc., a consulting company and corporate trainer in Houston, Texas, that has trained more than 120,000 people in computer applications.

Philip J. Judd is a former instructor in the Management Department and the Director of the Research and Instructional Computing Service at the University of Houston. Phil now dedicates himself to consulting and corporate training as a principal of Napier & Judd, Inc.

Philip J. Judd

H. Albert Napier, Ph.D.

Preface

At Course Technology, we believe that technology will change the way people teach and learn. Today millions of people are using personal computers in their everyday lives—both as tools at work and for recreational activities. As a result, the personal computer has revolutionized the ways in which people interact with each other. The *Mastering and Using* series combines the following distinguishing features to allow people to do amazing things with their personal computers.

Distinguishing Features

All the textbooks in the *Mastering and Using* series share several key pedagogical features:

Case Project Approach. In their more than 20 years of business and corporate training and teaching experience, Napier & Judd have found that students are more enthusiastic about learning a software application if they can see its real-world relevance. The textbook provides bountiful business-based profiles, exercises, and projects. It also emphasizes the skills most in demand by employers.

Comprehensive and Easy to Use. There is thorough coverage of new features. The narrative is clear and concise. Each unit or chapter thoroughly instructs on the concepts that underlie the skills and procedures. The text explains not just the *how*, but the *why*.

Step-by-Step Instructions and Screen Illustrations. All examples in this text include step-by-step instructions that explain how to complete the specific task. Full-color screen illustrations are used extensively to provide students with a realistic picture of the software application feature.

Extensive Tips and Tricks. The authors have placed informational boxes in the margin of the text. These boxes of information provide students with the following helpful tips:

▶ *Quick Tip.* Extra information provides shortcuts on how to perform common business-related functions.
▶ *Caution Tip.* This additional information explains how a mistake occurs and provides tips on how to avoid making similar mistakes in the future.
▶ *Menu Tip.* Additional explanation on how to use menu commands to perform application tasks.
▶ *Mouse Tip.* Further instructions on how to use the mouse to perform application tasks.
▶ *Task Pane Tip.* Additional information on using task pane shortcuts.
▶ *Internet Tip.* This information incorporates the power of the Internet to help students use the Internet as they progress through the text.
▶ *Design Tip.* Hints for better presentation designs (found in the PowerPoint chapters).

End-of-Chapter Materials. Each book in the *Mastering and Using* series places a heavy emphasis on providing students with the opportunity to practice and reinforce the skills they are learning through extensive exercises. Each chapter has a summary, commands review, concepts review, skills review, and case projects so that the student can master the material by doing. For more information on each of the end-of-chapter elements, see page ix of the How to Use This Book section in this preface.

Appendices. *Mastering and Using* series contains three appendices to further help students prepare to be successful in the classroom or in the workplace. Appendix A teaches students to work with Windows 2000. Appendix B illustrates how to format letters; how to insert a mailing notation; how to format envelopes (referencing the U.S. Postal Service documents); how to format interoffice memorandums; and how to key a formal outline. It also lists popular style guides and describes proofreader's marks. Appendix C describes the new Office XP speech recognition features.

Microsoft Office User Specialist (MOUS) Certification.
What does this logo mean? It means this courseware has been approved by the Microsoft® Office User Specialist Program to be among the finest available for learning Microsoft Office XP, Microsoft Word 2002, Microsoft Excel 2002, Microsoft PowerPoint® 2002, and Microsoft Access 2002. It also means that upon completion of this courseware, you may be prepared to become a Microsoft Office User Specialist.

What is a Microsoft Office User Specialist? A Microsoft Office User Specialist is an individual who has certified his or her skills in one or more of the Microsoft Office desktop applications of Microsoft Word, Microsoft Excel, Microsoft PowerPoint®, Microsoft Outlook® or Microsoft Access, or in Microsoft Project. The Microsoft Office User Specialist Program typically offers certification exams at the "Core" and "Expert" skill levels. The Microsoft Office User Specialist Program is the only Microsoft approved program in the world for certifying proficiency in Microsoft Office desktop applications and Microsoft Project. This certification can be a valuable asset in any job search or career advancement.

More Information: To learn more about becoming a Microsoft Office User Specialist, visit *www.mous.net*. To purchase a Microsoft Office User Specialist certification exam, visit *www.DesktopIQ.com*.

SCANS. In 1992, the U.S. Department of Labor and Education formed the Secretary's Commission on Achieving Necessary Skills, or SCANS, to study the kinds of competencies and skills that workers must have to succeed in today's marketplace. The results of the study were published in a document entitled *What Work Requires of Schools: A SCANS Report for America 2000*. The in-chapter and end-of-chapter exercises in this book are designed to meet the criteria outlined in the SCANS report and thus help prepare students to be successful in today's workplace.

Instructional Support

All books in the *Mastering and Using* series are supplemented with an **Instructor's Resource Kit.** This is a CD-ROM that contains lesson plans with teaching materials and preparation suggestions, along with tips for implementing instruction and assessment ideas; a suggested syllabus; and SCANS workplace know how. The CD also contains:

- ► Career Worksheets
- ► Evaluation Guidelines
- ► Hands-On Solutions
- ► Individual Learning Strategies
- ► Internet Behavior Contract
- ► Lesson Plans
- ► Portfolio Guidelines

- ► PowerPoint Presentations
- ► Solution Files
- ► Student Data Files
- ► Teacher Training Notes
- ► Test Questions
- ► Transparency Graphics Files

ExamView® This textbook is accompanied by ExamView, a powerful testing software package that allows instructors to create and administer printed, computer (LAN-based), and Internet exams. ExamView includes hundreds of questions that correspond to the topics covered in this text, enabling students to generate detailed study guides that include page references for further review. The computer-based and Internet testing components allow students to take exams at their computers, and also save the instructor time by grading each exam automatically.

MyCourse.com. MyCourse.com is an online syllabus builder and course-enhancement tool. Hosted by Course Technology, MyCourse.com is designed to reinforce what you already are teaching. It also adds value to your course by providing content that corresponds with your text.

MyCourse.com is flexible: choose how you want to organize the material, by date or by class session; or don't do anything at all, and the material is automatically organized by chapter. Add your own materials, including hyperlinks, assignments, announcements, and course content. If you're using more than one textbook, you can even build a course that includes all your Course Technology texts—in one easy-to-use site! Start building your own course today…just go to *www.mycourse.com/instructor*.

Student Support

Activities Workbook. The workbook includes additional end-of-chapter exercises over and above those provided in the main text.

Data Disk. To use this book, students must have the Data Disk. Data Files needed to complete exercises in the text are contained on the Review Pack CD-ROM. These files can be copied to a hard drive or posted to a network drive.

*The availability of Microsoft Office User Specialist certification exams varies by application, application version and language. Visit *www.mous.net* for exam availability.

Microsoft, the Microsoft Office User Specialist Logo, PowerPoint and Outlook are either registered trademarks or trademarks of Microsoft Corporation in the United States and/or other countries.

How to Use This Book

Word 2002

Quick Start for Word

Chapter Overview

This chapter gives you a quick overview of creating, editing, printing, saving, and closing a document. To learn these skills, you create a new document, save and close it, then you open an existing document, revise the text, and save the document with both the same and a different name. This chapter also shows you how to view formatting marks and Smart Tags, zoom the document window, and move the insertion point. In addition, you learn to identify the components of the Word window and create a folder on your hard drive to store your documents. You use these basic skills every time you create or edit a document in Word.

LEARNING OBJECTIVES

- Identify the components of the Word window
- Compose a simple document
- Edit a document
- Save a document
- Preview and print a document
- Close a document
- Locate and open an existing document
- Create a new document
- Close the Word application

Case profile
Today is your first day as a new employee at Worldwide Exotic Foods, Inc., one of the world's fastest growing distributors of specialty food items. The company's mission is to provide customers with an unusual selection of meats, cheeses, pastries, fruits, and vegetables from around the world. You report to Chris Lofton, the Word Processing Department manager, to complete an introduction to the Word 2002 word processing application.

chapter one

Learning Objectives — A quick reference of the major topics learned in the chapter

Case profile — Realistic scenarios that show the real-world application of the material being covered

Chapter Overview — A concise summary of what will be learned in the chapter

Clear step-by-step directions explain how to complete the specific task

Caution Tip — This additional information explains how a mistake occurs and provides tips on how to avoid making similar mistakes in the future

Task Pane Tip — Additional information about using task pane shortcuts

Quick Tip — Extra information provides shortcuts on how to perform common business-related functions

Internet Tip — Information to help students incorporate the power of the Internet as they progress through the text

Mouse Tip — Further instructions on how to use the mouse to perform application tasks

Design Tip — Hints for better presentation designs (found in only the PowerPoint chapters)

WI.10 Word 2002

TASK PANE TIP

You can change the Office Assistant by right-clicking the Office Assistant icon and then clicking Choose Assistant.

Step 3	Switch to	the appropriate disk drive and folder as designated by your instructor
Step 4	Key	Company Profile in the File name: text box
Step 5	Click	Save

After the document is saved, the document name *Company Profile* appears in place of *Document1* on the title bar.

QUICK TIP

The phone line. Since the electric current changed in response.

1.e Previewing and Printing a Document

After you create a document, you usually print it. Before printing a document, you can preview it to see what it will look like when printed. You do not have to preview the document before printing it. However, you can save paper by previewing your document and making any necessary changes before printing it.

To preview the *Company Profile* document and then print it:

INTERNET TIP

You can change the Office Assistant by right-clicking.

| Step 1 | Click | the Print Preview button on the Standard toolbar |

The Print Preview window opens. Your screen should look similar to Figure 1-4.

FIGURE 1-4
Print Preview Window

MOUSE TIP

You also can click the Save Options command on the Tools button.

Print Preview toolbar

Document in Print Preview

DESIGN TIP

The phone line. Since the electric current changed in response to sound, the phone system was known as an analog device.

Quick Start for Word WI.11

When you preview a document, you are verifying that the document text is attractively and appropriately positioned on the page. If necessary, you can change the document layout on the page, key additional text, and change the appearance of the text as you preview it. For now, you should close Print Preview and return to the original view of the document.

| Step 2 | Click | the Close button Close on the Print Preview toolbar |
| Step 3 | Click | the Print button on the Standard toolbar |

You are finished with the *Company Profile* for now, so you can close the document.

1.f Closing a Document

When you use the Word application, you can have as many documents open in the memory of your computer as your computer resources will allow. However, after you finish a document you should close it or remove it from the computer's memory to conserve those resources. To close the *Company Profile* document:

| Step 1 | Click | the Close Window button in the upper-right corner of the menu bar |

When documents are closed from the File menu or the Close Window button on the menu bar, the Word application window remains open. This window is sometimes called the **null screen**. To continue working in Word from the null screen, you can open an existing document or create a new, blank document.

notes
Office 2000 features personalized menus and toolbars, which "learn" the commands you use most often. This means that when you first install Office 2000, only the most frequently used commands appear immediately on a short version of the menus and the remaining commands appear after a brief pause. Commands that you select move to the short menu, while those you don't use appear only on the full menu.

CAUTION TIP

The phone line. Since the electric current changed in response to sound, the phone system was known as an analog device. (Remember that an analogy is a way that things are similar; in other words, the Ishapel of the current flowing on the wire spoken.)

MENU TIP

You can preview a document with the Print Preview command on the File menu. You can print a document with the Print command on the File menu.
To select print options, you must use the Print command. The Print button prints the document based on the options previously selected in the Print dialog box.

chapter one

Full-color screen illustrations provide a realistic picture to the student

Notes — These boxes provide necessary information to assist you in completing the activities

Menu Tip — Additional explanation on how to use menu commands to perform application tasks

End-of-Chapter Material

Concepts Review — Multiple choice and true or false questions help assess how well the student has learned the chapter material

Summary — Reviews key topics discussed in the chapter

Commands Review — Provides a quick reference and reinforcement tool on multiple methods for performing actions discussed in the chapter

Skills Review — Hands-on exercises provide the ability to practice the skills just learned in the chapter

Case Projects — Asks the student to synthesize the material learned in the chapter and complete an office assignment

SCANS icon — Indicates that the exercise or project meets SCANS competencies and prepares the student to be successful in today's workplace

MOUS Certification icon — Indicates that the exercise or project meets Microsoft's certification objectives that prepare the student for the MOUS exam

Internet Case Projects — Allow the student to practice using the World Wide Web

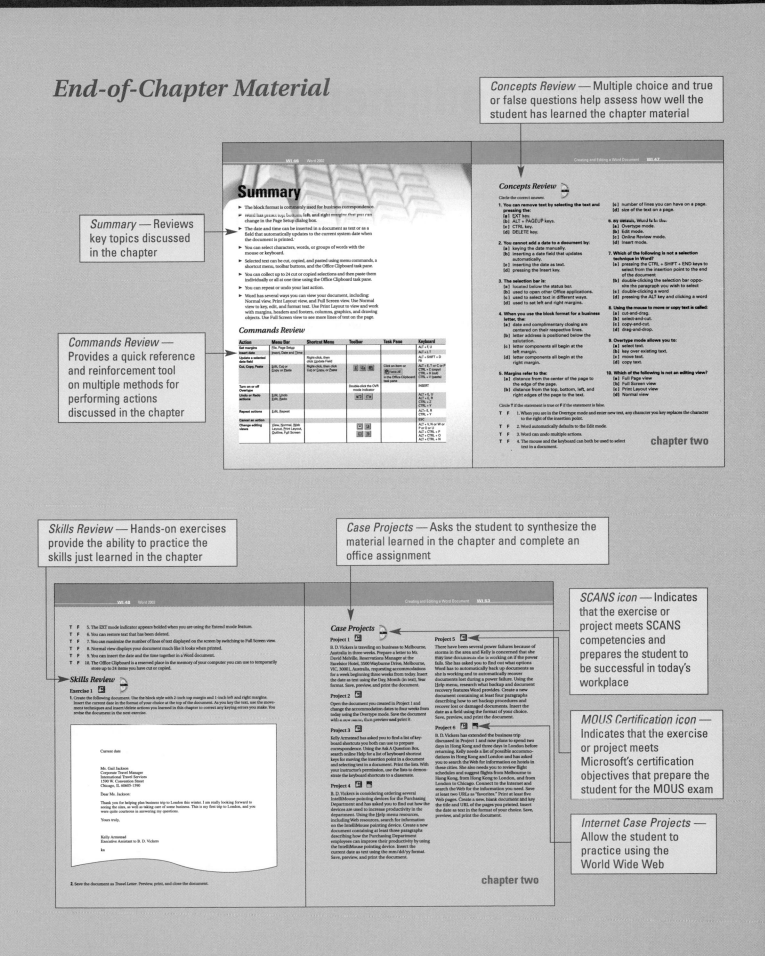

Acknowledgments

We would like to thank and express our appreciation to the many fine individuals who have contributed to the completion of this book.

No book is possible without the motivation and support of an editorial staff. Therefore, we wish to acknowledge with great appreciation the project team at Course Technology: Melissa Ramondetta, managing editor; Robert Gaggin, product manager; and Jodi Dreissig, editorial assistant. Our appreciation also goes to Robin Romer for managing the developmental editing of this series. In addition, we want to acknowledge the team at GEX for their production work, especially Karla Russell, Kendra Neville, Michelle Olson, and Angel Lesiczka.

We are very appreciative of the personnel at Napier & Judd, Inc., who helped to prepare this book. We acknowledge, with great appreciation, the assistance provided by Ollie Rivers and Nancy Onarheim in preparing and checking the many drafts of the Office unit, the Word unit, and the appendices of this book and the Instructor's Manual.

We gratefully acknowledge the work of Linda Sourek and Susan Lehner in writing the PowerPoint unit for this series, Benjamin Rand for writing the Outlook unit and the Excel unit for this series, and Bruce McLaren for writing the Access unit for this series.

Contents

POWERPOINT UNIT   PI 1

Microsoft
Office XP

Getting Started with Microsoft Office XP

Chapter Overview

Microsoft Office XP provides the ability to enter, record, analyze, display, and present any type of business information. In this chapter, you learn about the capabilities of Microsoft Office XP, including its computer hardware and operating system requirements and elements common to all its applications. You also learn how to open and close those applications and get Help.

LEARNING OBJECTIVES

- Describe Microsoft Office XP
- Determine hardware and operating system requirements
- Identify common elements of Office applications
- Start Office applications
- Get Help in Office applications
- Close Office applications

chapter one

notes This book assumes that you have little or no knowledge of Microsoft Office XP but that you have worked with personal computers and are familiar with Microsoft Windows 2000 or Windows 98 operating systems.

1.a What Is Microsoft Office XP?

Microsoft Office XP is a software suite (or package) that contains a combination of software applications you use to create text documents, analyze numbers, create presentations, manage large files of data, and create Web pages.

The **Word 2002** software application provides you with word processing capabilities. **Word processing** is the preparation and production of text documents such as letters, memorandums, and reports. **Excel 2002** is software you use to analyze numbers with worksheets (sometimes called spreadsheets) and charts and to perform other tasks such as sorting data. A **worksheet** is a grid of columns and rows in which you enter labels and data. A **chart** is a visual or graphical representation of worksheet data. With Excel, you can create financial budgets, reports, and a variety of other forms.

PowerPoint 2002 software is used to create a **presentation**, or collection of slides. A **slide** is the presentation output (actual 35mm slides, transparencies, computer screens, or printed pages) that can contain text, charts, graphics, audio, and video. You can use PowerPoint slides to create a slide show on a computer attached to a projector, to broadcast a presentation over the Internet or company intranet, and to create handout materials for a presentation.

Access 2002 provides database management capabilities, enabling you to store and retrieve a large amount of data. A **database** is a collection of related information. A phone book and an address book are common examples of databases you use every day. Other examples of databases include a price list, school registration information, or an inventory. You can query (or search) an Access database to answer specific questions about the stored data. For example, you can determine which customers in a particular state had sales in excess of a particular value during the month of June.

Outlook 2002 is a **personal information manager** that provides tools for sending and receiving e-mail as well as maintaining a calendar, contacts list, journal, electronic notes, and electronic "to do" list. The **FrontPage 2002** application is used to create and manage Web sites.

chapter one

notes For the remainder of this book, Microsoft Office XP may be called Office. Rather than include the words *Microsoft* and *2002* each time the name of an application is used, the text refers to the respective software package as Word, Excel, PowerPoint, Access, or Outlook.

A major advantage of using the Office suite is the ability to share data between the applications. For example, you can include a portion of an Excel worksheet or chart in a Word document, use an outline created in a Word document as the starting point for a PowerPoint presentation, import an Excel worksheet into Access, and merge names and addresses from an Outlook Address Book with a Word letter.

1.b Hardware and Operating System Requirements

You can install Office applications on computers using the Windows 2000, Windows 98, or Windows NT Workstation 4.0 (with Service Pack 6a installed) operating systems. Office XP applications do not run in the Windows 95, Windows 3.x or the Windows NT Workstation 3.5 environments.

You can install Office on a "x86" computer with a Pentium processor, at least 32 MB of RAM for Windows 98 or 64 MB of RAM for Windows 2000, a CD-ROM drive, Super VGA, 256-color video, Microsoft Mouse, Microsoft IntelliMouse, or another pointing device, a 28,800 (or higher) baud modem, and 350 MB of hard disk space. To access certain features you should have a multimedia computer, e-mail software, and a Web browser. For detailed information on installing Office, see the documentation that comes with the software.

1.c Common Elements of Office Applications

Office applications share many technical features that make it easier for Information Technology (IT) Departments in organizations to manage their Office software installations. Additionally, the Office applications share many features that enable users to move seamlessly between applications and learn one way to perform common tasks, such as creating, saving, and printing documents or moving and copying data.

QUICK TIP

Speech recognition features enable users to speak the names of toolbar buttons, menus, menu items, alerts, dialog box control buttons, and task pane items. Users can switch between two modes— Dictation and Voice command—using the Language bar. For more information on using the Speech Recognition features, see Appendix C.

Office applications share many common elements, making it easier for you to work efficiently in any application. A **window** is a rectangular area on your screen in which you view a software application, such as Excel. All the Office application windows have a similar look and arrangement of shortcuts, menus, and toolbars. In addition, they share many features—such as a common dictionary to check spelling in your work, identical menu commands, toolbar buttons, shortcut menus, and keyboard shortcuts to perform tasks such as copying data from one location to another.

notes   You learn more about the common elements of the Office applications in later chapters of this unit or in specific application units.

Figure 1-1 shows many of the common elements in the Office application windows.

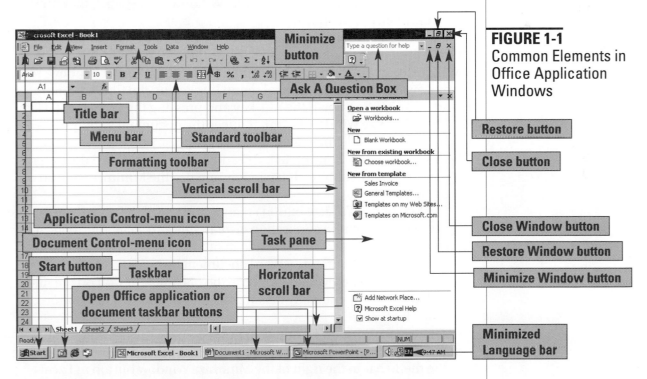

FIGURE 1-1
Common Elements in Office Application Windows

Title Bar

The application **title bar** at the top of the window includes the application Control-menu icon, the application name, the filename of the active document, and the Minimize, Restore (or Maximize), and Close buttons.

The **application Control-menu** icon, located in the upper-left corner of the title bar, displays the Control menu. The Control menu commands manage the application window, and typically include commands such as Restore, Move, Size, Minimize, Maximize, and Close. Commands that are currently available appear in a dark color. You can view the Control menu by clicking the Control-menu icon or by holding down the ALT key and then pressing the SPACEBAR key.

The **Minimize** button, near the right corner of the title bar reduces the application window to a taskbar button. The **Maximize** button, to the right of the Minimize button, enlarges the application window to fill the entire screen viewing area above the taskbar. If the window is already maximized, the Restore button appears in its place. The **Restore** button reduces the application window to a smaller size on your screen. The **Close** button, located in the right corner of the title bar, closes the application and removes it from the computer's memory.

Menu Bar

The **menu bar** is a special toolbar located at the top of the window below the title bar and contains the menus for the application. A **menu** is list of commands. The menus common to Office applications are File, Edit, View, Insert, Format, Tools, Window, and Help. Other menus vary between applications.

The **document Control-menu** icon, located below the application Control-menu icon, contains the Restore, Move, Size, Minimize, Maximize, and Close menu commands for the document window. You can view the document Control menu by clicking the Control-menu icon or by holding down the ALT key and pressing the HYPHEN (-) key.

The **Minimize Window** button reduces the document window to a title-bar icon inside the document area. It appears on the menu bar below the Minimize button in Excel and PowerPoint. (Word documents open in their own application window and use the Minimize button on the title bar.)

The **Maximize Window** button enlarges the size of the document window to cover the entire application display area and share the application title bar. It appears on the title-bar icon of a minimized Excel workbook or PowerPoint presentation. (Word documents automatically open in their own application window and use the Maximize button on the title bar.) If the window is already maximized, the Restore Window button appears in its place.

The **Restore Window** button changes the size of the document window to a smaller sized window inside the application window. It appears in the menu bar to the right of the Minimize Window button in Excel and PowerPoint. (Word documents automatically open in their own application Window and use the Restore button on the title bar.)

The **Close Window** button closes the document and removes it from the memory of the computer. It appears in the menu bar to the right of the Restore Window or Maximize Window button.

Default Toolbars

The **Standard** and **Formatting toolbars**, located one row below the menu bar, contain a set of icons called buttons. The toolbar buttons represent commonly used commands and are mouse shortcuts that enable you to perform tasks quickly. In addition to the Standard and Formatting toolbars, each application has several other toolbars available. You can customize toolbars by adding or removing buttons and commands.

When the mouse pointer rests on a toolbar button, a **ScreenTip** appears, identifying the name of the button. ScreenTips are also provided as part of online Help to describe a toolbar button, a dialog box option, or a menu command.

Scroll Bars

The vertical scroll bar appears on the right side of the document area. The **vertical scroll bar** is used to view various parts of the document by moving or scrolling the document up or down. It includes scroll arrows and a scroll box. The horizontal scroll bar appears near the bottom of the document area. The **horizontal scroll bar** is used to view various parts of the document by moving or scrolling the document left or right. It includes scroll arrows and a scroll box.

Ask A Question Box

The **Ask A Question Box** is a help tool alternative to the Office Assistant that appears on the menu bar of every Office application. The Ask A Question Box is used to quickly key a help question in plain English and then view a list of relevant Help topics.

Task Pane

Office XP includes a **task pane** feature, a pane of shortcuts, which opens on the right side of the application window. The contents of the task pane vary with the application and the activities being performed. For example, task pane shortcuts can be used to create new Office documents, format Word documents or PowerPoint presentations, or perform a Word mail merge. The task pane can be displayed or hidden as desired.

Taskbar

The **taskbar,** located across the bottom of the Windows desktop, includes the Start button and buttons for each open Office document. The **Start button,** located at the left end of the taskbar, displays the Start menu or list of tasks you can perform and applications you can use.

You can switch between documents, close documents and applications, and view other items, such as the system time and printer status, with buttons or icons on the taskbar. If you are using Windows 2000 or Windows 98, other toolbars, such as the Quick Launch toolbar, may also appear on the taskbar.

> **QUICK TIP**
>
> The **Office Assistant** is an interactive, animated graphic that appears in the Office application windows. When you activate the Office Assistant, a balloon style dialog box opens to display options for searching online Help by topic. The Office Assistant may also automatically offer suggestions when you begin certain tasks. You can customize the Office Assistant by changing the animated graphic image or turning on or off various options. Any customization is shared by all Office applications.

chapter
one

1.d Starting Office Applications

You access the Office applications through the Windows desktop. The Windows operating system software is automatically loaded into the memory of your computer when you turn on your computer. After turning on your computer, the Windows desktop appears.

You begin by using the Start button on the taskbar to view the Start menu and open the Excel application. To use the Start button to open the Excel application:

Step 1	*Click*	the Start button ⧉ Start on the taskbar
Step 2	*Point to*	Programs
Step 3	*Click*	Microsoft Excel on the Programs menu

The Excel software is placed into the memory of your computer and the Excel window opens. Your screen should look similar to Figure 1-1.

notes You may sometimes use the keyboard to use Office application features. This book lists all keys, such as the TAB key, in uppercase letters. When the keyboard is used to issue a command, this book lists keystrokes as: Press the ENTER key. When you are to press one key and, while holding down that key, to press another key, this book lists the keystrokes as: Press the SHIFT + F7 keys.

You can open and work in more than one Office application at a time. When Office is installed, two additional commands appear on the Start menu: the Open Office Document command and the New Office Document command. You can use these commands to select the type of document on which you want to work rather than first selecting an Office application. To create a new Word document without first opening the application:

Step 1	*Click*	the Start button ⧉ Start on the taskbar
Step 2	*Click*	New Office Document
Step 3	*Click*	the General tab, if necessary

The New Office Document dialog box on your screen should look similar to Figure 1-2. A **dialog box** is a window that contains options for performing specific tasks.

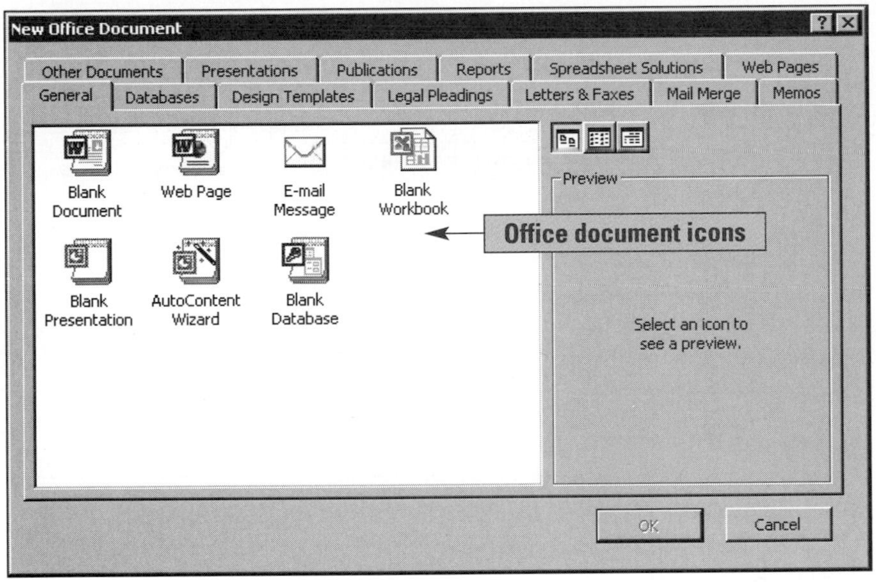

FIGURE 1-2
General Tab in the
New Office Document
Dialog Box

This dialog box provides options for creating different Office documents. **Icons** (or pictures) represent the Office document options; the number of icons available depends on the Office suite applications you have installed. The icons shown here create a blank Word document, a blank Web page (in Word), an e-mail message (using Outlook or Outlook Express), a blank Excel workbook, a blank PowerPoint presentation, a PowerPoint presentation using the AutoContent Wizard, and a blank Access database. You want to create a blank Word document.

Step 4	*Click*	the Blank Document icon to select it, if necessary
Step 5	*Click*	OK

The Word software is placed in the memory of your computer, the Word application window opens with a blank document. Your screen should look similar to Figure 1-3.

M O U S E   T I P

Double-clicking an icon is the same as clicking the icon once to select it and then clicking the OK button.

chapter
one

MENU TIP

The task pane containing shortcuts to create new documents or open existing documents opens by default when you launch a Word, Excel, or PowerPoint application. However, if you create or open another document in the same application, the task pane automatically hides. To display it again, click the Task Pane command on the View menu.

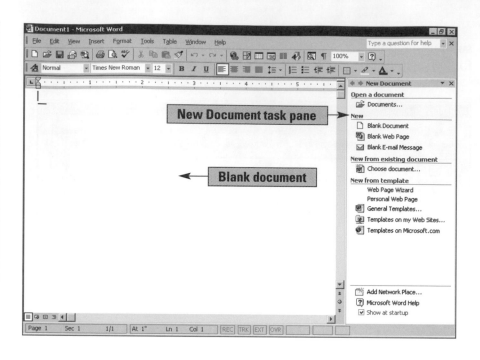

Next you open a blank presentation. To open the PowerPoint application:

| Step 1 | *Open* | the New Office Document dialog box using the Start menu |
| Step 2 | *Double-click* | the Blank Presentation icon |

Your screen should look similar to Figure 1-4.

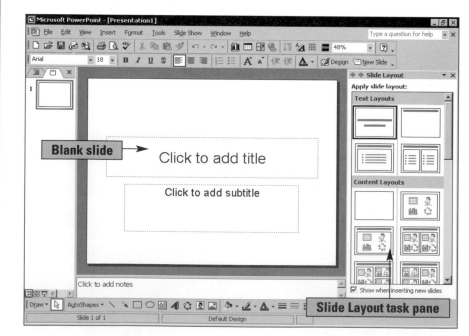

You can also open an Office application by opening an existing Office document from the Start menu. To open an existing Access database:

Step 1	*Click*	the Start button [Start] on the taskbar
Step 2	*Click*	Open Office Document
Step 3	*Click*	the Look in: list arrow in the Open Office Document dialog box
Step 4	*Switch to*	the disk drive and folder where the Data Files are stored
Step 5	*Double-click*	*International Sales*

The Access application window and Database window that open on your screen should look similar to Figure 1-5.

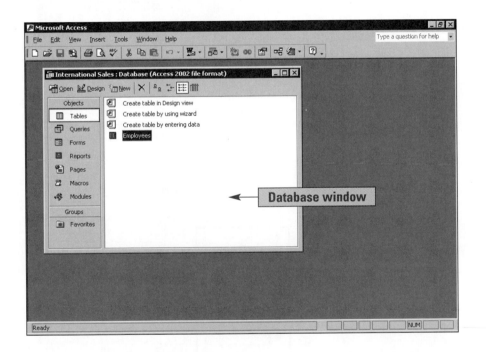

FIGURE 1-5
International Sales
Database in Access
Window

You can switch between open Office documents by clicking the appropriate taskbar button. If multiple windows are open, the **active window** has a dark blue title bar. All inactive windows have a gray title bar. To switch to the Excel workbook and then the Word document:

Step 1	*Click*	the Excel button on the taskbar
Step 2	*Observe*	that the Excel application window and workbook are now visible
Step 3	*Click*	the Word Document1 button on the taskbar
Step 4	*Observe*	that the Word application window and document are now visible

chapter
one

1.e Getting Help in Office Applications

You can get help when working in any Office application in several ways. You can use the <u>H</u>elp menu, the Help toolbar button, or the F1 key to display the Office Assistant; get context-sensitive help with the What's <u>T</u>his command or the SHIFT + F1 keys; or launch your Web browser and get Web-based help from Microsoft. You can also key a help question in the Ask A Question Box on the menu bar.

Using the Ask A Question Box

Suppose you want to find out how to use keyboard shortcuts in Word. To get help for keyboard shortcuts using the Ask A Question Box:

Step 1	*Verify*	that the Word document is the active window
Step 2	*Click*	in the Ask A Question Box
Step 3	*Key*	keyboard shortcuts
Step 4	*Press*	the ENTER key

A list of help topics related to keyboard shortcut keys appears. Your list should look similar to the one shown in Figure 1-6.

FIGURE 1-6
List of Help Topics

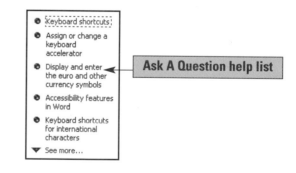

If you want to view the detailed help for any topic, simply click that topic in the list.

| Step 5 | *Press* | the ESC key |
| Step 6 | *Click* | in the document area to deselect the Ask A Question Box |

Using the <u>H</u>elp Menu

The <u>H</u>elp menu provides commands you can use to view the Office Assistant or Help window, show or hide the Office Assistant, connect to the Microsoft Web site, get context-sensitive help for a menu command or toolbar button, detect and repair font and template files, and view licensing information for the Office application. To review the <u>H</u>elp menu commands:

Step 1	*Click*	<u>H</u>elp on the menu bar

The <u>H</u>elp menu on your screen should look similar to Figure 1-7.

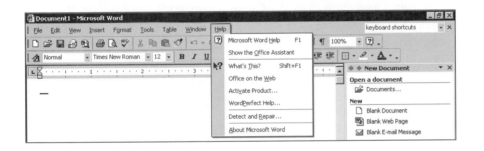

FIGURE 1-7
<u>H</u>elp Menu

Step 2	*Observe*	the menu commands
Step 3	*Click*	in the document area outside the menu to close the <u>H</u>elp menu

Using What's <u>T</u>his?

You can get context-sensitive help for a menu command or toolbar button using the What's <u>T</u>his? command on the <u>H</u>elp menu. This command changes the mouse pointer to a help pointer, a white mouse pointer with a large black question mark. When you click a toolbar button or menu command with the help pointer, a brief ScreenTip help message appears, describing the command or toolbar button. You can quickly change the mouse pointer to a help pointer by pressing the SHIFT + F1 keys.

To view the help pointer and view a ScreenTip help message for a toolbar button:

Step 1	*Press*	the SHIFT + F1 keys
Step 2	*Observe*	the help mouse pointer with the attached question mark
Step 3	*Click*	the Save button 💾 on the Standard toolbar
Step 4	*Observe*	the ScreenTip help message describing the Save button

> **Q U I C K   T I P**
>
> You can click the Help button on the title bar in any dialog box to convert the mouse pointer to a What's <u>T</u>his help pointer.

chapter
one

| Step 5 | *Press* | the ESC key to close the ScreenTip help message |

1.f Closing Office Applications

There are many ways to close the Access, Excel, and PowerPoint applications (or the Word application with a single document open) and return to the Windows desktop. You can:

- double-click the application Control-menu icon on the title bar.
- click the application Close button on the title bar.
- right-click the application button on the taskbar to display a short-cut menu and then click the Close command.
- press the ALT + F4 keys.
- click the Exit command on the File menu to close Office applications (no matter how many Word documents are open).

To close the Excel application from the taskbar:

| Step 1 | *Right-click* | the Excel button on the taskbar |
| Step 2 | *Click* | Close |

You can close multiple applications at one time from the taskbar by selecting the application buttons using the CTRL key and then using the shortcut menu. To close the PowerPoint and Access applications at one time:

Step 1	*Press & hold*	the CTRL key
Step 2	*Click*	the PowerPoint button and then the Access button on the taskbar
Step 3	*Release*	the CTRL key and observe that both buttons are selected (pressed in)
Step 4	*Right-click*	the PowerPoint or Access button
Step 5	*Click*	Close

Both applications close, leaving only the Word document open. To close the Word document using the menu:

Step 1	*Verify*	that the Word application window is maximized
Step 2	*Click*	File
Step 3	*Click*	Exit

Summary

▶ The Word application provides word processing capabilities for the preparation of text documents, such as letters, memorandums, and reports.

▶ The Excel application provides the ability to analyze numbers in worksheets and for creating financial budgets, reports, charts, and forms.

▶ The PowerPoint application is used to create presentation slides and audience handouts.

▶ You use the Access databases to store and retrieve collections of data.

▶ The Outlook application helps you send and receive e-mail and maintain a calendar, "to do" lists, and the names and addresses of contacts—and perform other information management tasks.

▶ One major advantage of using the Office suite applications is the ability to integrate the applications by sharing information between them.

▶ Another advantage of the Office suite applications is that they share a number of common elements such as window features, shortcuts, toolbars, and menu commands.

▶ You can start the Office suite applications from the Programs submenu on the Start menu and from the Open Office Document or New Office Document commands on the Start menu.

▶ To close the Office applications, you can double-click the application Control-menu icon, single-click the application Close button on the title bar, right-click the application button on the taskbar, press the ALT + F4 keys, or click the Exit command on the File menu.

▶ To get help in an Office application, you can click commands on the Help menu, press the F1 key or the SHIFT + F1 keys, or click the Microsoft Help button on the Standard toolbar.

chapter one

Concepts Review

Circle the correct answer.

1. ScreenTips do not provide:
[a] the name of a button on a toolbar.
[b] help for options in a dialog box.
[c] context-sensitive help for menu commands or toolbar buttons.
[d] access to the Office Assistant.

2. To manage a Web site, you can use:
[a] Outlook.
[b] FrontPage.
[c] Excel.
[d] Publisher.

3. The title bar contains the:
[a] document Control-menu icon.
[b] Close Window button.
[c] Standard toolbar.
[d] application and document name.

4. The Excel application is best used to:
[a] prepare financial reports.
[b] maintain a list of tasks to accomplish.
[c] prepare text documents.
[d] manage Web sites.

5. A major advantage of using Office applications is the ability to:
[a] store mailing lists.
[b] analyze numbers.

[c] share information between applications.
[d] sort data.

6. Word processing is used primarily to:
[a] create presentation slides.
[b] analyze numbers.
[c] prepare text documents.
[d] maintain a calendar and "to do" lists.

7. Right-click means to:
[a] press the left mouse button twice rapidly.
[b] place the mouse pointer on a command or item.
[c] press and hold down the right mouse button and then move the mouse.
[d] press the right mouse button and then release it.

8. You cannot close Office XP applications by:
[a] clicking the Exit command on the File menu.
[b] clicking the Close button on the title bar.
[c] right-clicking the application button on the taskbar and clicking Close.
[d] pressing the SHIFT + F4 keys.

Circle **T** if the statement is true or **F** if the statement is false.

T   F   1. You use Excel to create newsletters and brochures.

T   F   2. Word is used to create presentation slides.

T   F   3. The Office Assistant is an interactive graphic used to get online help in Office applications.

T   F   4. Access is used to create and format text.

T   F   5. You can open and work in only one Office application at a time.

T   F   6. When you open multiple documents in an Office application, each document has its own button on the taskbar.

Skills Review

Exercise 1

1. Identify each of the numbered elements of Office application windows in the following figure.

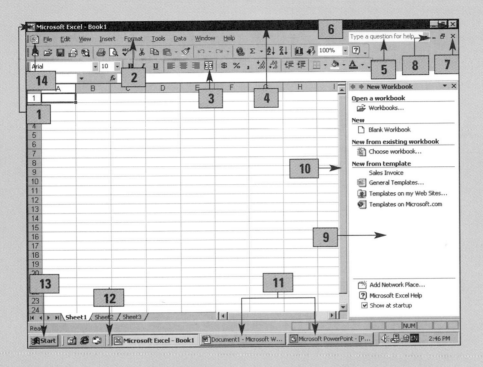

Exercise 2

1. Open the Word application using the Programs command on the Start menu.

2. Close the Word application using the taskbar.

Exercise 3

1. Open the Excel application using the Programs command on the Start menu.

2. Open the PowerPoint application using the Programs command on the Start menu.

3. Open the Access application and the *International Sales* database using the Open Office Document command on the Start menu.

4. Switch to the PowerPoint application using the taskbar button and close it using the Close button on the title bar.

5. Close the Excel and Access applications at the same time using the taskbar.

Exercise 4

1. Create a new, blank Word document using the New Office Document command on the Start menu.

2. Create a new, blank Excel workbook using the New Office Document command on the Start menu.

3. Switch to the Word document using the taskbar and close it using the Close button on the title bar.

4. Close the Excel workbook using the taskbar button.

chapter one

Exercise 5

1. Open the Word application using the Start menu.

2. Show the Office Assistant, if necessary, with a command on the Help menu.

3. Hide the Office Assistant with a shortcut menu.

4. Show the Office Assistant with the Microsoft Word Help button on the Standard toolbar.

5. Search online Help using the search phrase "key text."

6. Click the "Change typing and editing options" link.

7. Review the Help text and then close the Help window.

8. Show the Office Assistant, and then click the Options command on the Office Assistant shortcut menu.

9. Click the Use the Office Assistant check box to remove the check mark and turn off the Office Assistant.

Exercise 6

1. Write a paragraph that describes the different ways to close the Word application.

Exercise 7

1. Open any Office application and use the Ask A Question Box and the keyword "Office Assistant" to search for online Help for information on using the Office Assistant.

2. Write down the instructions for selecting a different Office Assistant graphic image.

Case Projects

Project 1

You are the secretary to the marketing manager of High Risk Insurance, an insurance brokerage firm. The marketing manager wants to know how to open and close the Excel application. Write at least two paragraphs describing different ways to open and close the Excel application. With your instructor's permission, use your written description to show a classmate several ways to open and close the Excel application.

Project 2

You work in the administrative offices of Alma Public Relations and the information management department just installed Office XP on your computer. Your supervisor asks you to write down and describe some of the Office Assistant options. Display the Office Assistant. Right-click the Office Assistant graphic, click the Options command, and view the Options tab in the Office Assistant dialog box. Click the What's This? or Help button on the dialog box title bar and review each option. Write at least three paragraphs describing five Office Assistant options.

Project 3

As the new office manager at Hot Wheels Messenger Service, you are learning to use the Word 2002 application and want to learn more about some of the buttons on the Word toolbars. Open Word and use the What's This? command on the Help menu to review the ScreenTip help for five toolbar buttons. Write a brief paragraph for each button describing how it is used.

Project 4

You are the administrative assistant to the vice president of operations for Extreme Sports, Inc., a sports equipment retailer with stores in several cities in your state. The vice president wants to save time and money by performing business tasks more efficiently. She asks you to think of different ways to perform common business tasks by sharing information between the Office XP applications. Write at least three paragraphs describing how the company can use Word, Excel, PowerPoint, Access, and Outlook to improve efficiency by combining information.

Working with Menus, Toolbars, and Task Panes

Chapter Overview

Office tries to make your work life easier by learning how you work. The personalized menus and toolbars in each application remember which commands and buttons you use and add and remove them as needed. Office has two new tools—task panes and Smart Tags—that provide shortcuts for performing different activities. In this chapter, you learn how to work with the personalized menus and toolbars and how to use task panes and Smart Tags.

LEARNING OBJECTIVES

- ▶ Work with personalized menus and toolbars
- ▶ View, hide, dock, and float toolbars
- ▶ Work with task panes
- ▶ Review Smart Tags

chapter two

2.a Working with Personalized Menus and Toolbars

A **menu** is a list of commands you use to perform tasks in the Office applications. Some of the commands also have an associated image, or icon, which appears to the left of each command in the menu. Most menus are found on the menu bar located below the title bar in the Office applications. A **toolbar** contains a set of icons (the same icons you see on the menus) called "buttons" that you click with the mouse pointer to quickly execute a menu command.

notes

The activities in this chapter assume the personalized menus and toolbars are reset to their default settings. As you learn about menus and toolbars, task panes, and Smart Tags you are asked to select menu commands and toolbar buttons by clicking them with the mouse pointer. You do not learn how to use the menu command or toolbar button, task pane, or Smart Tags to perform detailed tasks in this chapter. Using these features to perform detailed tasks is covered in the individual application chapters.

When you first install Office and then open an Office application, the menus on the menu bar initially show only a basic set of commands and the Standard and Formatting toolbars contain only a basic set of buttons. These short versions of the menus and toolbars are called **personalized menus and toolbars**. As you work in the application, the commands and buttons you use most frequently are stored in the personalized settings. The first time you select a menu command or toolbar button that is not part of the basic set, that command or button is automatically added to your personalized settings and appears on the menu or toolbar. If you do not use a command for a while, it is removed from your personalized settings and no longer appears on the menu or toolbar. To view the personalized menus and toolbars in PowerPoint:

Step 1	*Click*	the New Office Document command on the Start menu
Step 2	*Click*	the General tab in the New Office Document dialog box, if necessary
Step 3	*Double-click*	the Blank Presentation icon
Step 4	*Click*	Tools on the menu bar
Step 5	*Observe*	the short personalized menu containing only the basic commands

The Tools menu on your screen should look similar to Figure 2-1.

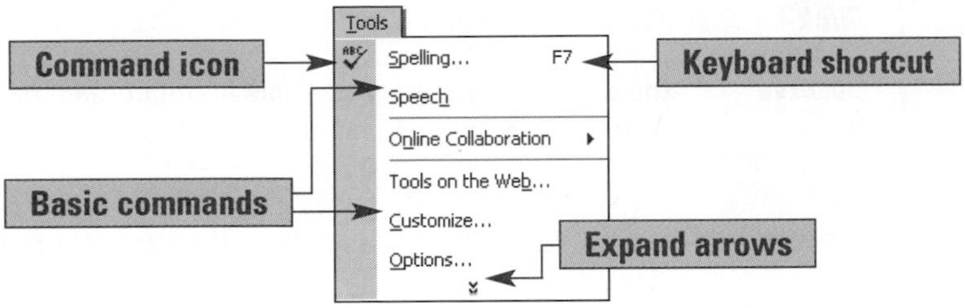

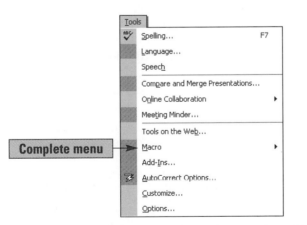

FIGURE 2-1
Personalized Tools Menu

If the command you want to use does not appear on the short personalized menu, you can expand the menu. The fastest way to expand a personalized menu is to double-click the menu command on the menu bar. For example, to quickly expand the Insert menu, you can double-click the Insert command on the menu bar. Another way to expand a menu is to click the Expand arrows that appear at the bottom of the personalized menu when it opens. Finally, after opening a menu, you can pause for a few seconds until the menu automatically expands. To expand the Tools menu:

| Step 1 | *Pause* | until the menu automatically expands *or* click the Expand arrows at the bottom of the menu to expand the menu |

The expanded Tools menu on your screen should look similar to Figure 2-2.

FIGURE 2-2
Expanded Tools Menu

You move a menu command from the expanded menu to the personalized menu simply by selecting it. To add the AutoCorrect Options command to the short personalized Tools menu:

| Step 1 | *Click* | AutoCorrect Options |

chapter
two

Step 2	*Click*	Cancel in the AutoCorrect dialog box to close the dialog box without making any changes
Step 3	*Click*	Tools on the menu bar
Step 4	*Observe*	the updated personalized Tools menu contains the AutoCorrect Options command

The Tools menu on your screen should look similar to Figure 2-3.

FIGURE 2-3
Updated Personalized
Tools Menu

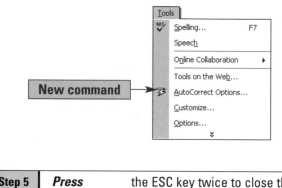

New command

Step 5	*Press*	the ESC key twice to close the menu

The first time you launch most Office applications, the Standard and Formatting toolbars appear on one row below the title bar. In this position, you cannot see all their default buttons. If a toolbar button is not visible, you can resize or reposition one of the toolbars. When the mouse pointer is positioned on a toolbar **move handle** (the gray vertical bar at the left edge of the toolbar), the mouse pointer changes from a white arrow pointer to a **move pointer**, a four-headed black arrow. You can drag the move handle with the move pointer to resize or reposition toolbar. To resize the Formatting toolbar:

Step 1	*Move*	the mouse pointer to the move handle on the Formatting toolbar
Step 2	*Observe*	that the mouse pointer becomes a move pointer

The move pointer on your screen should look similar to Figure 2-4.

FIGURE 2-4
Move Pointer on the
Formatting Toolbar Handle

Move pointer

Step 3	*Click & hold*	the left mouse button
Step 4	*Drag*	the Formatting toolbar to the right as far as you can to view the default buttons on the Standard toolbar

Step 5	*Drag*	the Formatting toolbar to the left as far as you can to view the default buttons on the Formatting toolbar
Step 6	*Release*	the mouse button
Step 7	*Observe*	that you now see three buttons on the Standard toolbar

The buttons that don't fit on the displayed area of a toolbar are collected in a Toolbar Options list. The last button on any toolbar, the Toolbar Options button, is used to display the Toolbar Options list. To view the Toolbar Options list:

Step 1	*Click*	the Toolbar Options button list arrow on the Standard toolbar
Step 2	*Observe*	the default buttons that are not visible on the toolbar

The Toolbar Options list on your screen should look similar to Figure 2-5.

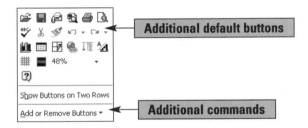

FIGURE 2-5
Toolbar Options List

If you want to display one of the default buttons on a personalized toolbar, you can select it from the Toolbar Options list. To add the Search button to the personalized Standard toolbar:

Step 1	*Click*	the Search button
Step 2	*Observe*	that the Search button is added to the personalized Standard toolbar

When you add another button to the personalized Standard toolbar, one of the other buttons might move out of view. This is because of the limited viewing area of the Standard toolbar in its current position. If you want to view all the menu commands instead of a short personalized menu and all the default toolbar buttons on the Standard and Formatting toolbars, you can change options in the Customize dialog box. To view the Customize dialog box:

Step 1	*Click*	Tools on the menu bar

chapter
two

Step 2	*Click*	Customize

Step 3	*Click*	the Options tab, if necessary

The Customize dialog box on your screen should look similar to Figure 2-6.

FIGURE 2-6
Options Tab in the
Customize Dialog Box

Personalized
menus and
toolbars
options

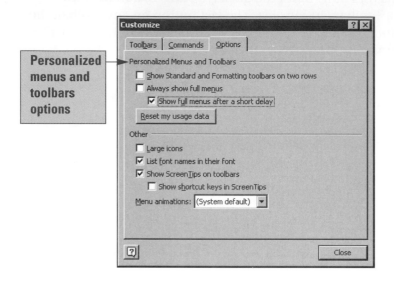

If you reposition the Formatting toolbar below the Standard toolbar, you can view all the default buttons on both toolbars. You can do this by inserting a check mark in the Show Standard and Formatting toolbars on two rows check box. You can insert a check mark in the Always show full menus check box to view the entire set of menu commands for each menu instead of the short personalized menus. If you do not want the short personalized menus to expand automatically when you pause, you can remove the check mark from the Show full menus after a short delay check box. Then, to show the full menu, you have to double-click the menu or click the expand arrows at the bottom of the menu.

You want to show all the Standard and Formatting toolbar buttons and menu commands.

Step 4	*Click*	the Show Standard and Formatting toolbars on two rows check box to insert a check mark

Step 5	*Click*	the Always show full menus check box to insert a check mark

Step 6	*Click*	Close to close the dialog box

Step 7	*Observe*	the repositioned and expanded Standard and Formatting toolbars

| Step 8 | *Click* | Tools to view the entire set of Tools menu commands |
| Step 9 | *Press* | the ESC key to close the Tools menu |

You can return the menus and toolbars to their initial (or **default**) settings in the Customize dialog box. To open the Customize dialog box and reset the default menus and toolbars:

Step 1	*Click*	Tools
Step 2	*Click*	Customize
Step 3	*Click*	the Options tab, if necessary
Step 4	*Remove*	the two check marks you just inserted
Step 5	*Click*	Reset my usage data
Step 6	*Click*	Yes to confirm you want to reset the menus and toolbars to their default settings
Step 7	*Close*	the Customize dialog box
Step 8	*Observe*	that the Tools menu and Standard toolbar are reset to their default settings

2.b Viewing, Hiding, Docking, and Floating Toolbars

Office applications have additional toolbars that you can view when you need them. You can also hide toolbars when you are not using them. You can view or hide toolbars by pointing to the Toolbars command on the View menu and clicking a toolbar name or by using a shortcut menu. A **shortcut menu** is a short list of frequently used menu commands. You view a shortcut menu by pointing to an item on the screen and clicking the right mouse button. This is called right-clicking the item. The commands on shortcut menus vary depending on where you right-click, so that you view only the most frequently used commands for a particular task. An easy way to view or hide toolbars is with a shortcut menu.

notes

Although the PowerPoint application is used to illustrate how to customize toolbars, the same techniques are used to customize toolbars and menus in the Word, Excel, and Access applications.

MOUSE TIP

You can use a command on the Toolbar Options list to place the Standard and Formatting toolbars that currently appear on one row on two rows. You can also place the Standard and Formatting toolbars that appear in two rows back to one row with a command on the Toolbar Options list.

chapter two

To view the shortcut menu for toolbars:

| Step 1 | *Right-click* | the menu bar, the Standard toolbar, or the Formatting toolbar |
| Step 2 | *Observe* | the shortcut menu and the check marks next to the names of displayed toolbars |

Your shortcut menu should look similar to Figure 2-7.

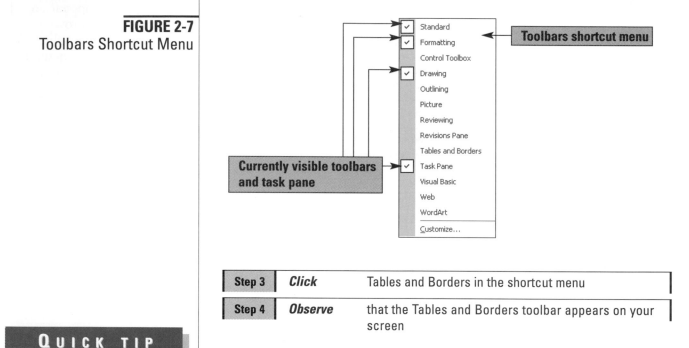

FIGURE 2-7
Toolbars Shortcut Menu

| Step 3 | *Click* | Tables and Borders in the shortcut menu |
| Step 4 | *Observe* | that the Tables and Borders toolbar appears on your screen |

The Tables and Borders toolbar, unless a previous user repositioned it, is visible in its own window near the middle of your screen. When a toolbar is visible in its own window, it is called a **floating toolbar** and you can move and size it with the mouse pointer similar to any window. When a toolbar appears fixed at the screen boundaries, it is called a **docked toolbar**. The menu bar and Standard and Formatting toolbars are examples of docked toolbars because they are fixed below the title bar at the top of the screen. In PowerPoint, the Drawing toolbar is docked at the bottom of the screen above the status bar. You can dock a floating toolbar by dragging its title bar with the mouse pointer to a docking position below the title bar, above the status bar, or at the left and right boundaries of your screen.

To dock the Tables and Borders toolbar below the Standard and Formatting toolbars, if necessary:

| Step 1 | *Click & hold* | the title bar in the Tables and Borders toolbar window |

QUICK TIP

Some of the toolbars that appear on the toolbars shortcut menu vary from one Office application to another.

Step 2	*Observe*	that the mouse pointer becomes a move pointer
Step 3	*Drag*	the toolbar window up slowly until it docks below the Standard and Formatting toolbars
Step 4	*Release*	the mouse button

Similarly, you float a docked toolbar by dragging it away from its docked position toward the middle of the screen. To float the Tables and Borders toolbar, if necessary:

Step 1	*Position*	the mouse pointer on the Tables and Borders toolbar move handle until it becomes a move pointer
Step 2	*Drag*	the Tables and Borders toolbar down toward the middle of the screen until it appears in its own window

When you finish using a toolbar, you can hide it with a shortcut menu. To hide the Tables and Borders toolbar:

Step 1	*Right-click*	the Tables and Borders toolbar
Step 2	*Click*	Tables and Borders to remove the check mark and hide the toolbar

2.c Working with Task Panes

The task pane is a tool with many uses in the Office applications. For example, when you launch Word, Excel, PowerPoint, or Access a new file task pane appears on the right side of the application window. This task pane allows you to create new documents in a variety of ways or open existing documents and replaces the New dialog box found in earlier versions of the Office applications. For example, in the Word application, this task pane is called the New Document task pane and contains hyperlink shortcuts for creating a new document or opening an existing document, creating a blank Web page, sending an e-mail message, choosing an existing document to use as the basis for a new document, and other options. A **hyperlink** is text or a graphic image that you can click to view another page or item. The hyperlink shortcuts in the task pane are colored blue. When you place your mouse pointer on a blue hyperlink shortcut, the mouse pointer changes to a hand with a pointing finger. You can then click the hyperlink shortcut to view the page or option to which the shortcut is linked.

Another way to use a task pane in each of the Office applications is to display the Search task pane and use it to search your local computer

MOUSE TIP

You can dock a floating toolbar by double-clicking its title bar. The toolbar returns to its previously docked position.

You can close a floating toolbar by clicking the Close button on the toolbar's title bar.

QUICK TIP

In Excel, the new file task pane is called the New Workbook task pane; in PowerPoint, it is called the New Presentation task pane; in Access, it is called the New File task pane.

Each Office application also contains specific task panes: for example— you can format text in a Word document, copy and paste data in an Excel worksheet, and apply an attractive design and animation scheme to a PowerPoint presentation—all from special task panes.

chapter
two

system and network for files based on specific criteria such as keywords in the file text, the file's location, the file type, and the file's name. You can also search for Outlook items using the Search task pane.

To view a blank Word document and the Search task pane:

Step 1	**Start**	the Word application using the Start menu
Step 2	**Click**	<u>F</u>ile on the menu bar
Step 3	**Click**	Searc<u>h</u>

The Basic Search task pane is now visible. Your screen should look similar to Figure 2-8.

FIGURE 2-8
Basic Search Task
Pane in Word

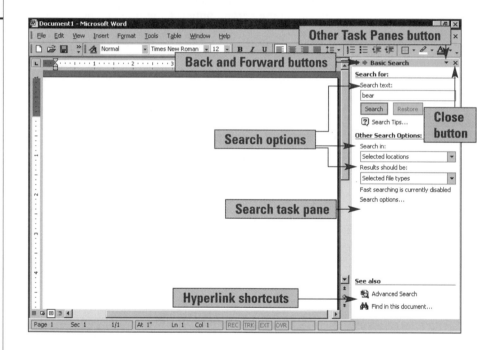

You also can view the Search task pane by clicking the Search button on the Standard toolbar.

When you have multiple task panes open, you can use the Back and Forward buttons on the task pane title bar to switch between the task panes. To switch from the Basic Search task pane to the New Document task pane:

Step 1	**Click**	the Back button 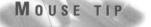 in the Basic Search task pane to view the New Document task pane
Step 2	**Click**	the Forward button in the New Document task pane to view the Basic Search task pane

You can key text in the Search text: text box to look for files containing specific text. You can use the Search in: list to select the locations in which to search, and use the Results should be: list to select the file types to search for. If your search criteria are more complex, you can click the Advanced Search link to view the Advanced Search task pane, where you can set additional search criteria such as file attributes called **properties**, or use operators such as "and" to set multiple criteria or "or" to set exclusive criteria.

A task pane appears docked on the right side of the application window by default. You can "float" the task pane in the application window or dock it on the left side of the application window, as you prefer. Like docking a floating toolbar, when you double-click a task pane title bar, it returns to its last docked or floating position. To float the docked task pane:

Step 1	***Double-click***	the Basic Search task pane title bar
Step 2	***Observe***	the task pane's new position, floating in the application window

Your screen should look similar to Figure 2-9.

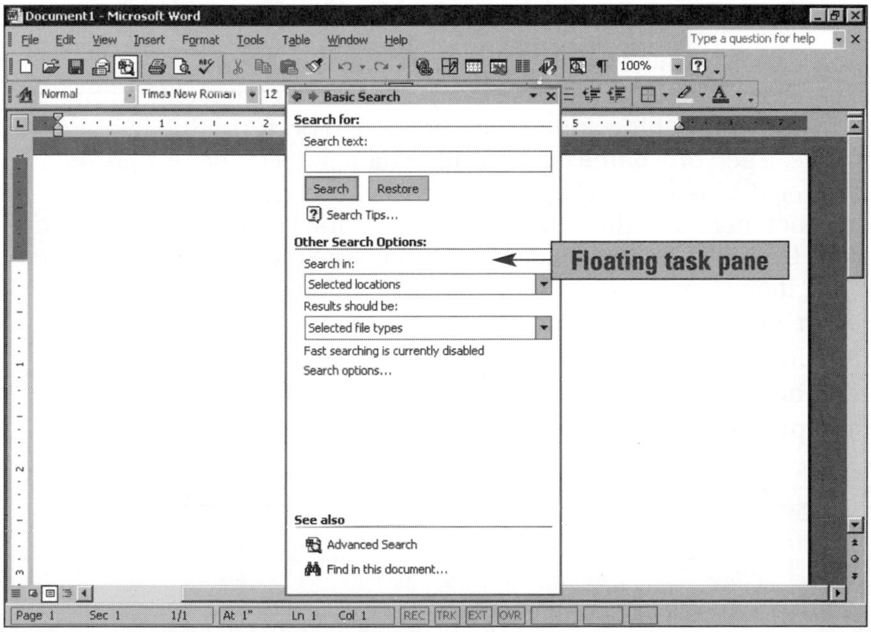

FIGURE 2-9
Floating Task Pane

Step 3	***Double-click***	the Basic Search task pane title bar
Step 4	***Observe***	that the Basic Search task pane returns to its previous docked position

TASK PANE TIP

You can click the Other Task Panes list arrow on the task pane title bar to view a list of different task panes available in the application. Then, you can click one of the task panes in the list to open it. Additionally, some task panes appear automatically as you perform certain activities in an application.

You can also display the last previous visible task pane by using the Task Pane command on the View menu.

MOUSE TIP

You can float a docked task pane by dragging the task pane away from its docked position using the mouse and the task pane title bar. Conversely, you can dock a floating task pane by dragging the task pane to the left or right side of the screen.

You can size a floating task pane by dragging the pane's top, bottom, left, or right borders with the mouse pointer.

You can close the current task pane by clicking the Close button on the task pane title bar. When you close the current task pane, all open task panes are also closed. For example, you currently have the New Document task pane and the Basic Search task pane open. When you close the Basic Search task pane, both task panes are closed. You can view the New Document task pane again with a menu command or toolbar button. To close the Basic Search and New Document task panes and then reopen the New Document task pane:

Step 1	*Click*	the Close button ☒ on the Basic Search task pane title bar
Step 2	*Observe*	that neither the Basic Search nor the New Document task pane is visible
Step 3	*Click*	File on the menu bar
Step 4	*Click*	New

The New Document task pane opens at the right side of the application window.

2.d Reviewing Smart Tags

Smart Tags are labels used to identify data as a specific type of data. You can use Smart Tags to perform an action in an open Office application instead of opening another application to perform that task. For example, a person's name is one kind of data that can be recognized and labeled with a Smart Tag. Suppose you key a person's name in a Word document and then want to create a contact item for that person in your Outlook Contacts folder. You can use a Smart Tag to create the contact item from Word without opening Outlook.

Smart Tags are represented by an action button and a purple dotted line underneath the text. The Smart Tag options are found in the AutoCorrect dialog box. To view the Smart Tag options in the Word application:

Step 1	*Click*	Tools on the menu bar
Step 2	*Click*	AutoCorrect Options
Step 3	*Click*	the Smart Tags tab in the AutoCorrect dialog box

The AutoCorrect dialog box on your screen should look similar to Figure 2-10.

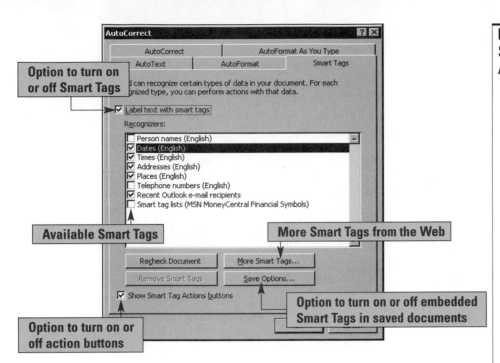

Option to turn on or off Smart Tags

Available Smart Tags

More Smart Tags from the Web

Option to turn on or off action buttons

Option to turn on or off embedded Smart Tags in saved documents

FIGURE 2-10
Smart Tags Tab in the AutoCorrect Dialog Box

You can turn on or off the Smart Tag feature with the Label text with smart tags check box. You can use the Show Smart Tag Actions buttons check box to turn on or off the Smart Tag action buttons. By default, Smart Tags are embedded in a document when it is saved. You can turn off this feature with the Save Options button. You can also remove the Smart Tags or recheck the document using the Remove Smart Tags or Recheck Document buttons. The use of specific Smart Tags and action buttons is covered in more detail in later chapters.

Step 4	*Click*	the Cancel button to close the AutoCorrect dialog box without making any changes
Step 5	*Click*	the Close button ✖ on the title bar to close Word
Step 6	*Close*	the PowerPoint application

chapter
two

Summary

▶ The first time you launch an Office application after installing Office, you see personalized menus that contain basic commands. As you use different commands, they are automatically added to the personalized menu. Commands that are not used for some time are removed from the personalized menus.

▶ The first time you launch an Office application after installing Office, the Standard and Formatting toolbars share a single row below the menu bar. You can reposition the Formatting toolbar to view more or fewer toolbar buttons. The remaining default toolbar buttons that are not visible on the toolbars can be added from the Toolbar Options list. You can turn off or reset the personalized menus and toolbars in the Options tab of the Customize dialog box.

▶ You can hide or view toolbars as you need them by using a shortcut menu. Toolbars can be docked at the top, bottom, or side of the screen, or they can be floating on screen in their own window.

▶ You can open task panes that contain shortcuts to perform various activities; these task panes can be docked at the left or right side of the application window, or they can be floating in the application window. Two examples of a task pane are the New Document and Basic Search task panes.

▶ Smart Tags are labels that identify text or data as a certain type and provide shortcuts to taking certain actions with the text or data.

Commands Review

Action	Menu Bar	Shortcut Menu	Toolbar	Task Pane	Keyboard
Display or hide toolbars	View, Toolbars	Right-click a toolbar, click the desired toolbar to add or remove the check mark	☒ on the toolbar title bar		ALT + V, T
View the New Document task pane	File, New				ALT + F, N
View the Search task pane	File, Search		🔍		ALT + F, H
View the last visible task pane	View, Task Pane	Right-click a toolbar, click Task Pane			ALT + V, K
View the available Smart Tag options	Tools, AutoCorrect Options, Smart Tags tab				ALT + T, A

Concepts Review

Circle the correct answer.

1. A menu is:
- [a] a set of icons.
- [b] a list of commands.
- [c] impossible to customize.
- [d] never personalized.

2. A toolbar is:
- [a] a list of commands.
- [b] always floating on your screen.
- [c] a set of icons.
- [d] never docked on your screen.

3. Which of the following is not an option in the Options tab in the Customize dialog box?
- [a] turning on or off ScreenTips for toolbar buttons
- [b] turning on or off Large icons for toolbar buttons
- [c] adding animation to menus
- [d] docking all toolbars

4. Right-clicking an item on screen displays:
- [a] the Right-Click toolbar.
- [b] animated menus.
- [c] expanded menus.
- [d] a shortcut menu.

5. Double-clicking the menu name on the menu bar:
- [a] resets your usage data.

- [b] floats the menu bar.
- [c] turns off the personalized menus.
- [d] expands a personalized menu.

6. A Smart Tag is:
- [a] a personalized menu.
- [b] displayed by double-clicking an item on your screen.
- [c] automatically expanded when you pause briefly.
- [d] a label used to identify text or data items for shortcut actions.

7. To view all the default buttons on both the Standard and Formatting toolbars at once, you should:
- [a] view the toolbar with a shortcut menu.
- [b] add the View All button to the toolbar.
- [c] reposition the Formatting toolbar on another row below the Standard toolbar.
- [d] drag the Formatting toolbar to the left.

8. The Advanced Search task pane cannot be viewed by clicking a:
- [a] command on a shortcut menu.
- [b] command on the File menu.
- [c] button on the Standard toolbar.
- [d] link on the Basic Search task pane.

Circle **T** if the statement is true or **F** if the statement is false.

T F 1. The Standard and Formatting toolbars must remain on the same row.

T F 2. When updating docked personalized toolbars, some buttons may be automatically removed from view to make room for the new buttons.

T F 3. One way to use a Smart Tag is to create an Outlook contact from a name in a Word document.

T F 4. You cannot add animation to menus.

T F 5. A floating toolbar window can be resized and repositioned using techniques that are similar to those used for any other window.

chapter two

T   F   6. When you open an Office application, the Search task pane is docked at the right side of the application window.

T   F   7. You cannot use keyboard shortcuts to run commands in Office applications.

T   F   8. You cannot turn off the personalized menus and toolbars options.

Skills Review

Exercise 1

1. Open the Word application.

2. Open the Options tab in the Customize dialog box and reset the usage data; show the Standard and Formatting toolbars on one row, and show full menus after a short delay.

3. If necessary, drag the Formatting toolbar to the right until you can see approximately half of the Standard and half of the Formatting toolbar.

4. Add the Show/Hide button to the personalized Standard toolbar using the Toolbar Options list.

5. Add the Font Color button to the personalized Formatting toolbar using the Toolbar Options list.

6. Open the Customize dialog box and reset your usage data in the Options tab.

7. Close the Word application and click No if asked whether you want to save changes to the blank Word document.

Exercise 2   **C**

1. Open the Excel application.

2. Open the Options tab in the Customize dialog box and reset the usage data; show the Standard and Formatting toolbars on one row, and show full menus after a short delay.

3. View the personalized Tools menu.

4. Add the AutoCorrect Options command to the personalized Tools menu.

5. Reset your usage data.

6. Close the Excel application.

Exercise 3

1. Open the PowerPoint application.

2. Display the Basic Search task pane using a menu command.

3. Display the advanced search options.

4. Close the Advanced Search task pane.

5. Close the PowerPoint application.

Exercise 4

1. Open an Office application and verify that the New Document, New Presentation, or New Workbook task pane is docked at the right side of the application window.

2. Float the task pane by dragging it to the center of the application window.

3. Drag the left border of the floating task pane to resize it.

4. Double-click the task pane title bar to dock it in its previous position.

5. Close the task pane.

6. Open the Basic Search task pane using the Search button on the Standard toolbar.

7. Open the New Document task pane using the File menu.

8. Switch between task panes using the Back and Forward buttons on the task pane title bar.

9. Close the task pane.

10. Close the application.

Exercise 5

1. Open the Excel application.

2. View the Drawing, Picture, and WordArt toolbars using a shortcut menu.

3. Dock the Picture toolbar below the Standard and Formatting toolbars.

4. Dock the WordArt toolbar at the left boundary of the screen.

5. Close the Excel application from the taskbar.

6. Open the Excel with the New Office Document on the Start menu. (*Hint:* Use the Blank Workbook icon.)

7. Float the WordArt toolbar.

8. Float the Picture toolbar.

9. Hide the WordArt, Picture, and Drawing toolbars using a shortcut menu.

10. Close the Excel application.

Exercise 6

1. Open the Word application.

2. Turn off the personalized menus and toolbars.

3. Open the Options tab in the Customize dialog box and change the toolbar buttons to large icons and add random animation to the menus.

4. Observe the toolbar buttons and the menu animation.

5. Turn off the large buttons and remove the menu animation.

6. Turn on the personalized menus and toolbars and reset your usage data.

7. Close the Word application.

chapter two

Case Projects

Project 1

As secretary to the placement director for the XYZ Employment Agency, you have been using an earlier version of Word—Word 97. After you install Office XP, you decide you want the Word menus and toolbars to appear on two rows the way they did in the Word 97 application. Use the Ask A Question Box to search for help on "personalized menus." Review the Help topics and write down all the ways to make the personalized menus and toolbars appear on two rows.

Project 2

You are the administrative assistant to the controller of the Plush Pets, Inc., a stuffed toy manufacturing company. The controller recently installed Excel 2002. She is confused about how to use the task panes and asks for your help. Use the Ask A Question Box to search for help on "task panes." Review the topics and write down an explanation of how task panes are used. Give at least three examples of task panes.

Project 3

As administrative assistant to the art director of MediaWiz Advertising, Inc. you just installed PowerPoint 2002. Now you decide you would rather view the complete Standard and Formatting toolbars rather than the personalized toolbars and want to learn a quick way to do this. Use the Ask A Question Box to search for help on "show all buttons." Review the topic and write down the instructions for showing all buttons using the mouse pointer. Open an Office application and use the mouse method to show the complete Standard and Formatting toolbars. Turn the personalized toolbars back on from the Customize dialog box.

Introduction to the Internet and the World Wide Web

Chapter Overview

Millions of people use the Internet to shop for goods and services, listen to music, view artwork, conduct research, get stock quotes, keep up to date with current events, and send e-mail. More and more people are using the Internet at work and at home to view and download multimedia computer files that contain graphics, sound, video, and text. In this chapter, you learn about the Internet, how to connect to the Internet, how to use the Internet Explorer Web browser, and how to access pages on the World Wide Web.

LEARNING OBJECTIVES

- ▶ Describe the Internet
- ▶ Connect to the Internet
- ▶ Use Internet Explorer
- ▶ Use directories and search engines

chapter three

3.a What Is the Internet?

To understand the Internet, you must understand networks. A **network** is simply a group of two or more computers linked by cable or telephone lines. The linked computers also include a special computer called a **server** that is used to store files and programs that everyone on the network can use. In addition to the shared files and programs, networks enable users to share equipment, such as a common network printer.

The **Internet** is a worldwide public network of private networks, where users view and transfer information between computers. For example, an Internet user in California can retrieve (or **download**) files from a computer in Canada quickly and easily. In the same way, an Internet user in Australia can send (or **upload**) files to another Internet user in England. The Internet is not a single organization, but rather a cooperative effort by multiple organizations managing a variety of different kinds of computers.

You find a wide variety of services on the Internet. You can communicate with others via e-mail, electronic bulletin boards called newsgroups, real-time online chat, and online telephony. You can also download files from servers to your computer and search the World Wide Web for information. In this chapter, you learn about using a Web browser and accessing pages on the World Wide Web. Your instructor may provide additional information on other Internet services.

3.b Connecting to the Internet

To connect to the Internet you need some physical communication medium connected to your computer, such as network cable or a modem. You also need a special communication program called a Web browser program (such as Microsoft Internet Explorer) that allows your computer to communicate with computers on the Internet. The Web browser allows you to access Internet resources such as Web pages.

After setting up your computer hardware (the network cable or modem) and installing the Internet Explorer Web browser, you must make arrangements to connect to a computer on the Internet. The computer you connect to is called a **host**. Usually, you connect to a host computer via a commercial Internet Service Provider, such as America Online or another company who sells access to the Internet. An **Internet Service Provider (ISP)** maintains the host computer, provides a gateway or entrance to the Internet, and provides an electronic "mail box" with facilities for sending and receiving e-mail. Commercial ISPs usually charge a flat monthly fee for unlimited access to the Internet and e-mail services.

3.c Using Internet Explorer

A **Web browser** is a software application that helps you access Internet resources, including Web pages stored on computers called Web servers. A **Web page** is a document that contains hyperlinks (often called links) to other pages; it can also contain audio and video clips.

notes The activities in this chapter assume you are using the Internet Explorer Web browser version 5.0 or higher. If you are using an earlier version of Internet Explorer or a different Web browser, your instructor may modify the following activities.

To open the Internet Explorer Web browser:

Step 1	**Connect**	to your ISP, if necessary
Step 2	**Double-click**	the Internet Explorer icon *e* on the desktop to open the Web browser

When the Web browser opens, a Web page, called a **start page** or **home page**, loads automatically. The start page used by the Internet Explorer Web browser can be the Microsoft default start page, a blank page, or any designated Web page. Figure 3-1 shows the home page for the publisher of this book as the start page.

> **CAUTION TIP**
>
> During peak day and evening hours, millions of people are connecting to the Internet, and you may have difficulty connecting to your host computer or to other sites on the Internet.

> **QUICK TIP**
>
> Challenges to using the Internet include the amount of available information, communication speed, the dynamic environment, lack of presentation standards, and privacy/security issues. Evaluate the source and author of information from the Internet and confirm business-critical information from another source.

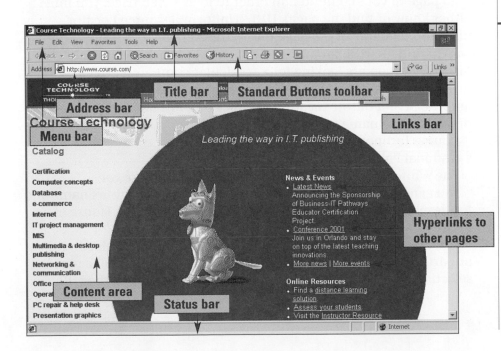

FIGURE 3-1
Internet Explorer Web Browser

chapter
three

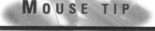
The **title bar** contains the Internet Explorer Web browser Control-menu icon and application name, the title of the current Web page, and the Internet Explorer Web browser Minimize, Restore, and Close buttons. The **menu bar** contains the menu commands you can use to perform specific tasks when viewing the Internet Explorer Web browser window—such as opening a file from your hard disk or printing the current Web page. The **Standard toolbar** contains buttons that provide shortcuts to frequently performed tasks. The **Address bar** contains a text box in which you key the path and filename of the Web page you want to load and a drop-down list of recently loaded Web pages and files. You can click the Go button to load the Web page after keying the page's address in the Address Bar. The **Links bar** is a customizable bar to which you can add shortcuts Web pages you load frequently. The **status bar** displays information about the current Web page. The security zone indicator on the right side of the status bar identifies the security zone you have assigned to the current Web page.

As a Web page loads, the progress bar illustrates the progress of the downloading process. When you place the mouse pointer on a link in the current Web page, its URL appears in the left side of the status bar. The **content area** contains the current Web page. Vertical and horizontal scroll bars appear as necessary so that you can scroll to view the entire Web page after it is loaded.

Loading a Web Page

Loading a Web page means that the Web browser sends a message requesting a copy of the Web page to the Web server where the Web page is stored. The Web server responds by sending a copy of the Web page to your computer. In order to load a Web page, you must either know or find the page's **URL** (Uniform Resource Locator)—the path and filename of the page that is the Web page's address. One way to find the URL for a Web page is to use a search engine or directory. If you are looking for a particular company's Web page, you might find its URL in one of the company's advertisements or on its letterhead and business card. Examples of URLs based on an organization's name are:

Course Technology	*www.course.com*
National Public Radio	*www.npr.org*
The White House	*www.whitehouse.gov*

You can try to "guess" the URL based on the organization's name and top-level domain. For example, a good guess for the U.S. House of Representatives Web page is *www.house.gov*.

You can key a URL directly in the Address bar by first selecting all or part of the current URL and keying the new URL to replace the selection. Internet Explorer adds the "http://" portion of the URL for you. To select the contents of the Address bar and key the URL for the U.S. House of Representatives:

Step 1	*Click*	the contents of the Address bar
Step 2	*Key*	www.house.gov
Step 3	*Click*	the Go button `⟳Go` or press the ENTER key
Step 4	*Observe*	that the home page of the U.S. House of Representatives' Web site opens in your Web browser

Creating Favorites

Web pages are constantly being updated with new information. If you like a certain Web page or find a Web page contains useful information and plan to revisit it, you may want to save a shortcut to the page's URL in the Favorites folder. Such shortcuts are simply called **favorites**. Suppose you want to load the U.S. House of Representatives home page frequently. You can create a favorite that saves the URL in a file on your hard disk. Then at any time, you can quickly load this Web page by clicking it in a list of favorites maintained on the Favorites menu.

The URLs you choose to save as favorites are stored in the Favorites folder on your hard disk. You can specify a new or different subfolder within the Favorites folder and you can change the name of the Web page as it appears in your list of favorites in the Add Favorite dialog box. To create a favorite for the U.S. House of Representatives Web page:

Step 1	*Click*	F<u>a</u>vorites
Step 2	*Click*	<u>A</u>dd to Favorites
Step 3	*Click*	OK
Step 4	*Click*	the Home button `⌂` to return to the default start page

One way to load a Web page from a favorite is to click the name of the favorite in the list of favorites on the F<u>a</u>vorites menu. To load the U.S. House of Representatives home page from the F<u>a</u>vorites menu:

| Step 1 | *Click* | F<u>a</u>vorites |
| Step 2 | *Click* | the United States House of Representatives favorite to load the page |

CAUTION TIP

Any Web page you load is stored in the Temporary Internet Files folder on your hard disk. Whenever you reload the Web page, Internet Explorer compares the stored page to the current Web page either each time you start the browser or each time you load the page. If the Web page on the server has been changed, a fresh Web page is downloaded. If not, the Web page is retrieved from the Temporary Internet File folder and you do not have to wait for the page to download. To view and change the Temporary Internet File folder options (and other options that control how Internet Explorer works), click the Internet <u>O</u>ptions command on the <u>T</u>ools menu.

chapter three

MENU TIP

You can remove a favorite by displaying the Favorites menu, right-clicking the desired favorite shortcut, and then clicking the Delete command on the shortcut menu. You can also open the Organize Favorites dialog box with the Organize Favorites command on the Favorites menu and select and delete a favorite shortcut.

MOUSE TIP

The Links bar provides shortcuts to various Web pages at the Microsoft Web site. You can also add shortcuts to your favorite Web pages by dragging the URL icon from the Address bar to the Links bar. You can reposition the toolbar, the Address bar, and the Links bar by dragging each one to a new location below the title bar.

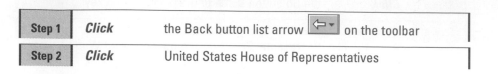

| Step 3 | *Click* | the Home button 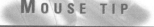 to return to the default start page |

The Back and Forward buttons allow you to review recently loaded Web pages without keying the URL or using the Favorites list. To reload the U.S. House of Representatives home page from the Back button list:

| Step 1 | *Click* | the Back button list arrow ⬅▾ on the toolbar |
| Step 2 | *Click* | United States House of Representatives |

3.d Using Directories and Search Engines

Because the Web is so large, you often need to take advantage of special search tools, called search engines and directories, to find the information you need. To use some of the Web's numerous search engines and directories, you can click the Search button on the Standard toolbar to open the Search list in the Explorer bar. To view the Search list:

| Step 1 | *Click* | the Search button 🔍 Search on the Standard toolbar |
| Step 2 | *Observe* | the search list options |

Search engines maintain an index of keywords used in Web pages that you can search. Search engine indexes are updated automatically by software called **spiders** (or **robots**). Spiders follow links between pages throughout the entire Web, adding any new Web pages to the search engine's index. You should use a search engine when you want to find specific Web pages. Some of the most popular search engines include AltaVista, HotBot, and Northern Light.

Directories use a subject-type format similar to a library card catalog. A directory provides a list of links to broad general categories of Web sites such as "Entertainment" or "Business." When you click these links, a subcategory list of links appears. For example, if you click the Entertainment link, you might then see "Movies," "Television," and "Video Games" links. To find links to Web sites containing information about "Movies," you would click the "Movies" link. Unlike a search engine, whose index is updated automatically, Web sites are added to directories only when an individual or a company asks that a particular Web site be included. Some directories also provide review comments and ratings for the Web sites in their index. Most directories also provide an internal search engine that can only be used to search the directory's index, not the entire Web. You use a directory when you are looking for information on broad general topics. Popular directories include Yahoo and Magellan Internet Guide.

To search for Web pages containing "movie guides":

Step 1	*Key*	movie guides in the Find a Web page containing text box
Step 2	*Click*	the Search button or press the ENTER key
Step 3	*Observe*	the search results (a list of Web pages in the search list)

The search results list consists of Web page titles displayed as hyperlinks. You can click any hyperlink to load that page from the list. To close the Explorer bar and search list:

| Step 1 | *Click* | the Search button [Search] on the Standard toolbar |
| Step 2 | *Close* | Internet Explorer |

The Web's many search tools are all constructed differently. That means you get varying results when using several search engines or directories to search for information on the same topic. Also, search tools operate according to varying rules. For example, some search engines allow only a simple search on one keyword. Others allow you to refine your search by finding phrases keyed within quotation marks, by indicating proper names, or by using special operators such as "and," "or," and "not" to include or exclude search words. To save time, always begin by clicking the search tool's online Help link. Study the directions for using that particular search engine or directory, and then proceed with your search.

QUICK TIP

You can reload pages from the History folder, which stores the Web pages you load for a specific period of time. You set the number of days to store pages on the General tab in the Options dialog box. The default number of days to store pages in the History folder is 20 days. Click the History button on the toolbar to open the History list in the Explorer bar.

CAUTION TIP

After you find the desired information, "let the user beware!" Because the Web is largely unregulated, anyone can put anything on a Web page. Evaluate carefully the credibility of all the information you find. Try to find out something about the author and his or her credentials. Many college or university library Web sites have good tips on how to evaluate online information.

chapter
three

Summary

▶ A network is a group of two or more computers linked by cable or telephone lines, and the Internet is a worldwide "network of networks."

▶ The World Wide Web is a subset of the Internet from which you can download files and search for information.

▶ Other external networks related to the Internet are large commercial networks like America Online, CompuServe, Prodigy, the Microsoft Network and USENET.

▶ To access the Internet, your computer must have some physical communication medium such as cable or dial-up modem, and a special communication program such as Internet Explorer.

▶ An Internet Service Provider (or ISP) maintains a host computer on the Internet. In order to connect to the Internet, you need to connect to the host computer.

▶ You use a Web browser, such as Internet Explorer, to load Web pages. Web pages are connected by hyperlinks that are text or pictures associated with the path to another page.

▶ Directories and search engines are tools to help you find files and Web sites on the Internet.

Commands Review

Action	Menu Bar	Shortcut Menu	Toolbar	Task Pane	Keyboard
Load a Web page	File, Open		🔗 Go		ALT + F, O Key URL in the Address bar and press the ENTER key
Save a favorite	Favorites, Add to Favorites	Right-click hyperlink, click Add to Favorites	Drag URL icon to Links bar or Favorites command		ALT + A, A Ctrl + D
Manage the Standard toolbar, Address bar, and Links bar	View, Toolbars	Right-click the Standard toolbar, click desired command	Drag the Standard toolbar, Address bar, or Links bar to the new location		ALT + V, T
Load the search, history, or favorites list in the Explorer bar	View, Explorer Bar		🔍 Search ⭐ Favorites 🕙 History		ALT + V, E

Concepts Review

Circle the correct answer.

1. A network is:
[a] the Internet.
[b] two or more computers linked by cable or telephone wire.
[c] two or more computer networks linked by cable or telephone lines.
[d] a computer that stores Web pages.

2. Which of the following is not a challenge to using the Internet?
[a] light usage
[b] dynamic environment
[c] volume of information
[d] security and privacy

3. The Address bar:
[a] is a customizable shortcut bar.
[b] contains the search list.
[c] contains your personal list of favorite URLs.
[d] contains the URL of the Web page in the content area.

4. The content area contains the:
[a] Standard toolbar.
[b] status bar.
[c] list of favorites.
[d] current Web page.

5. You can view a list of recently loaded Web pages in the:
[a] Channel bar.
[b] Explorer bar.
[c] Address bar.
[d] Links bar.

6. Search engines update their indexes of keywords by using software called:
[a] Webcrawler.
[b] HTTP.
[c] HotBot.
[d] spiders.

Circle **T** if the statement is true or **F** if the statement is false.

T   F   1. Commercial networks that provide specially formatted features are the same as the Internet.

T   F   2. USENET is the name of the military Internet.

T   F   3. All search engines use the same rules for locating Web pages.

T   F   4. Internet users in Boston or New York can access computer files on computers located in the United States only.

T   F   5. Spiders are programs that help you locate pages on the Web.

T   F   6. A Web page URL identifies its location (path and filename).

chapter three

Skills Review

Exercise 1

1. Open the Internet Explorer Web browser.

2. Open the Internet Options dialog box by clicking the Internet Options command on the Tools menu.

3. Review the options on the General tab in the dialog box.

4. Write down the steps to change the default start page to a blank page.

5. Close the dialog box and close the Web browser.

Exercise 2

1. Connect to the Internet and open the Internet Explorer Web browser.

2. Open the search list in the Explorer bar.

3. Search for Web pages about "dog shows."

4. Load one of the Web pages in the search results list.

5. Close the Explorer bar.

6. Print the Web page by clicking the Print command on the File menu and close the Web browser.

Exercise 3

1. Connect to the Internet and open the Internet Explorer Web browser.

2. Load the National Public radio Web page by keying the URL, *www.npr.org*, in the Address bar.

3. Print the Web page by clicking the Print command on the File menu and close the Web browser.

Exercise 4

1. Connect to the Internet and open the Internet Explorer Web browser.

2. Load the AltaVista search engine by keying the URL, *www.altavista.com*, in the Address bar.

3. Save the Web page as a favorite.

4. Search for Web pages about your city.

5. Print at least two Web pages by clicking the Print command on the File menu and close your Web browser.

Exercise 5

1. Connect to the Internet and open the Internet Explorer Web browser.

2. Load the HotBot search engine by keying the URL, *www.hotbot.com*, in the Address bar.

3. Save the Web page as a favorite.

4. Locate the hyperlink text or picture that loads the online Help page. Review the search rules for using HotBot.

5. Print the HotBot Help page by clicking the Print command on the File menu and close your Web browser.

Exercise 6

1. Connect to the Internet and open the Internet Explorer Web browser.
2. Load the Yahoo directory by keying the URL, *www.yahoo.com*, in the Address bar.
3. Save the Web page as a favorite.
4. Search for Web sites that contain information about restaurants in your city.
5. Print at least two Web pages by clicking the <u>P</u>rint command on the <u>F</u>ile menu and close your Web browser.

Exercise 7

1. Connect to the Internet and open the Internet Explorer Web browser.
2. View the Links bar by dragging the bar to the left using the mouse pointer.
3. Click each shortcut on the Links bar and review the Web page that loads.
4. Drag the Links bar back to its original position with the mouse pointer.

Exercise 8

1. Connect to the Internet and open the Internet Explorer Web browser.
2. Click the History button on the Standard toolbar to load the History list in the Explorer bar.
3. Review the History list and click a hyperlink to a page loaded yesterday.
4. Print the page by clicking the <u>P</u>rint command on the <u>F</u>ile menu, close the Explorer bar, and close the Web browser.

Case Projects

Project 1

Your organization recently started browsing the Web with the Internet Explorer Web browser and everyone wants to know how to use the toolbar buttons in the browser. Your supervisor asks you to prepare a fifteen-minute presentation, to be delivered at the next staff meeting, that describes the Internet Explorer Standard Buttons toolbar buttons. Review the Standard Buttons toolbar buttons and practice using them. Write an outline for your presentation that lists each button and describes how it is used.

Project 2

You are working for a book publisher who is creating a series of books about popular movie actors and actresses from the 1940s and 1950s, including Humphrey Bogart and Tyrone Power. The research director asks you to use the Web to locate a list of movies that the actors starred in. Use the Explorer bar search list and the Yahoo directory search tool to find links to "Entertainment." Click the Entertainment link and close the Explorer bar. Working from the Yahoo Web page, click the Actors and Actresses link. Search for Humphrey Bogart in

chapter three

the Actors and Actresses portion of the database. Link to the Web page that shows the filmography for Humphrey Bogart. Print the Web page that shows all the movies he acted in. Use the History list to return to the Actors and Actresses search page. Search for Tyrone Power, then link to and print his filmography. Close the Internet Explorer Web browser.

Project 3

You are the new secretary for the Business Women's Forum, a professional association. The association's president asked you to compile a list of Internet resources, which she will distribute at next month's lunch meeting. Connect to the Internet, open Internet Explorer, and search for Web pages containing the keywords "women in business" (including the quotation marks) using the AltaVista search engine. To load the AltaVista search engine key the URL, *www.altavista.com*, in the Address bar. From the search results, click the Web page title link of your choice to load the Web page. Review the new Web page and its links. Create a favorite for that page. Use the Back button list to reload the AltaVista home page and click a different Web page title from the list. Review the Web page and its links. Create a favorite for the Web page. Continue loading and reviewing pages until you have loaded and reviewed at least five pages. Return to the default home page. Use the Go To command on the View menu and the History bar to reload at least three of the pages. Print two of the pages. Delete all the favorites you added in this chapter, and then close Internet Explorer.

Using Outlook 2002

Chapter Overview

K eeping pace with today's business world requires important information management skills. Outlook 2002 handles e-mail, contact information, scheduling, tasks list, notes, and more—all organized in one location. In this chapter, you learn how to work with the main Outlook folders—including Inbox, Outbox, Calendar, Contacts, Tasks, and Notes.

LEARNING OBJECTIVES

▶ Identify the components of Outlook
▶ Create, send, and receive e-mail
▶ Insert attachments
▶ Schedule appointments, meetings, and events
▶ Add and edit contacts
▶ Create and update tasks
▶ Create and edit notes
▶ Create folders and shortcuts
▶ Search for and organize items
▶ Save messages in other formats
▶ Save a calendar as a Web page
▶ Use Outlook Today
▶ Close Outlook

Case profile

Walters, Robertson & Associates is an architectural firm with clients and projects around the world. The firm's principals are constantly on the road, meeting with clients, giving presentations, designing buildings, and visiting job sites. You are the project manager of Nakamichi Plaza, a multimillion dollar skyscraper. You coordinate communications between the design team, the project engineers, the contractor, your supervisor, and the Nakamichi Plaza owner.

outlook

notes This text assumes that you have little or no knowledge of the Outlook application. However, it is assumed that you have read Office Chapters 1–3 of this book and that you are familiar with Windows 98 or Windows 2000 concepts, common elements of Office XP applications, and basic Web and Internet skills.

1.a Identifying the Components of the Outlook Window

Outlook manages all sorts of information, including e-mail messages, contact information, appointments and meetings, task lists, and notes. Outlook stores each type of item in a different **folder**. For example, the Inbox stores received e-mail messages, the Contacts folder stores contact information, the Calendar folder stores appointments and meetings, and so forth.

When you start Outlook, a special "page" called **Outlook Today** displays an overview of upcoming items in the Calendar and Tasks folders, and the number of unread or unsent messages in your e-mail folders. To start Outlook and view the Outlook Today page:

MOUSE TIP

You can start Outlook from the Windows desktop by double-clicking the Outlook icon. You also can start Outlook by clicking the Outlook button on the Quick Launch toolbar in the taskbar.

Step 1	*Click*	the Start button [🏁Start] on the taskbar
Step 2	*Point to*	Programs
Step 3	*Click*	Microsoft Outlook

notes If this is the first time Outlook has been opened, you need to follow the setup wizard prompts to configure Outlook. Your instructor may provide additional information about configuring Outlook.

The Outlook application window opens, displaying Outlook Today by default. Your screen should look similar to Figure 1-1. Unless you have used Outlook already, Outlook Today is empty.

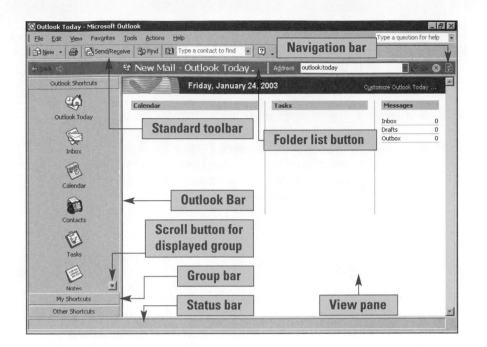

FIGURE 1-1
Outlook Application
Window

The Outlook application window contains a variety of components that appear in every Outlook folder. Table 1-1 lists and describes these components.

Component	Description
Outlook Bar	The **Outlook Bar** provides access to the Outlook folders, the My Documents folder on your computer, and the Favorites folder of Web sites. Click a shortcut icon to display that folder in the Information viewer.
Group bar	**Groups** organize shortcuts to Outlook folders. Click a group bar to display that group.
Standard toolbar	The **Standard toolbar** contains buttons that provide one-click access to commonly used commands, such as printing or creating a new item. Additional buttons appear on this toolbar when you switch to different Outlook folders. For example, the Standard toolbar in the Inbox folder contains buttons to reply to or forward an e-mail message.
Advanced toolbar (not shown)	The **Advanced toolbar** contains buttons for advanced commands, such as Undo or moving between folders. Additional buttons appear on this toolbar depending on which folder of Outlook you are in. For example, the Advanced toolbar in the Calendar folder has a button for planning a meeting.
Status bar	The **status bar** displays useful information such as the number of items in a particular folder.

TABLE 1-1
Components of the Outlook Application Window

outlook

TABLE 1-1
Continued

Component	Description
View pane	The **View pane** is where you view information in Outlook. Depending on the folder you are using, you might see a list of e-mail messages, contacts, or other important items of information.
Navigation bar	The **Navigation bar** helps you move around Outlook by providing Back and Forward buttons, similar to those found in a Web browser. There is also a handy folder list you can use to quickly navigate the various folders you create to keep items organized. The Navigation bar also features a built-in Web toolbar that you can use to view Web pages from within Outlook.

Navigating Outlook

When you work in Outlook, you switch between folders as you perform different tasks. For example, to add to or edit your contact information, you work in the Contacts folder. When you need to read, organize, and compose e-mail messages, you work in one of the message folders, such as the Inbox. To switch between folders in Outlook:

Step 1	*Click*	the Outlook Shortcuts group bar on the Outlook Bar, if necessary
Step 2	*Click*	the Inbox icon
Step 3	*Observe*	that the View pane switches to display the Inbox folder
Step 4	*Click*	the Contacts icon on the Outlook Bar
Step 5	*Observe*	that the View pane displays the Contacts folder

Another way to change folders is to use the Folder list. The Folder list displays Outlook folders in a "tree view," similar to what you see in Windows Explorer. To use the Folder list:

Step 6	*Click*	the Folder list button 📧 Contacts ▾ on the Navigation bar
Step 7	*Click*	Calendar in the Folder list

Using the Navigation bar, you can move back and forth between recently opened folders.

QUICK TIP

If you prefer to work with the Folder list open all the time, click the Push Pin button in the displayed Folder list to "pin" the list in place.

Step 8	*Click*	the Back button ⬅ Back on the Navigation bar twice to return to the Inbox

The Advanced toolbar is not shown in Outlook by default, but it includes buttons for useful commands such as Undo and Redo. To display the Advanced toolbar:

Step 1	*Right-click*	any toolbar in Outlook
Step 2	*Click*	Advanced

The Advanced toolbar appears under the Standard toolbar near the top of the application window.

1.b Creating and Viewing Messages

One of the most common ways of communicating with others is by e-mail. You can use Outlook to send, receive, and organize your messages. The **Inbox** folder is the default destination for incoming messages. The **Drafts** folder stores messages you have started and saved but haven't sent yet. The **Outbox** folder holds messages that you have written and are ready to send the next time you connect to your ISP or mail server. The **Sent Items** folder keeps copies of all messages you have already sent.

If this is the first time Outlook has been used on your computer, you see a message in the Inbox with an introduction to Outlook 2002.

notes For these activities, you can send e-mail messages to yourself or exchange e-mail messages with a classmate. If you are exchanging messages with a classmate, you need his or her e-mail address. When the steps instruct you to key your e-mail address, key your classmate's e-mail address instead of your own. Be sure to have your classmate send you the message as well.

outlook

Creating and Sending an E-mail Message

An e-mail editor is used to compose and send e-mail messages. All e-mail editors feature several common input fields, such as the To, Subject, and Message fields. The **To field** is where you address the e-mail to one or more recipients. The **Subject field** is where you summarize the content or topic of your message. The **Message field** is where you enter the main content of your e-mail message.

Many e-mail editors also use the Cc (courtesy copy) and Bcc (blind courtesy copy) fields for additional addresses. These can be used to send copies of the message to contacts who are not the primary recipients of the message.

E-mail messages can be sent in several formats. The simplest format is **plain text format**, which does not accept any fonts or formatting. Although some people are limited to this type of e-mail, most people can send and receive formats such as Rich Text Format or HTML format. **Rich Text Format (RTF)** includes the ability to use fonts, formatting features such as colored text, bold, italics, and underlining; it even supports bullets and numbered outlines. **HTML format** is basically the same as sending a Web page as an e-mail message. You can take advantage of all the layout and formatting features available in HTML, including pictures and hyperlinks. Almost anyone can view HTML formatted messages.

Outlook includes a built-in e-mail editor, but defaults to use Word as its e-mail editor. Word offers more features to format and check the spelling of your e-mail messages; it also can be used to create messages in RTF and HTML format. When you create a new message, Word opens with a special toolbar that includes the To and Subject fields, and several other buttons used in conjunction with messages. You can move among the fields by clicking in each field, or you can press the TAB key to move forward and the SHIFT + TAB keys to move backward through the fields.

You need to send a message to the engineer who will be working on the Nakamichi Plaza project. To create and send an e-mail message:

Step 1	*Click*	the New Mail Message button [New] on the Standard toolbar

Word opens with the e-mail toolbar. Your screen should look similar to Figure 1-2. You enter the e-mail address for each recipient in the To field located at the top of the message form. If you want to send a message to several recipients, key a semicolon between addresses.

QUICK TIP

Outlook allows you to key name aliases in the recipient boxes in place of the person's e-mail address. A **name alias** is a shortened version of a person's name, like a nickname. You enter name aliases in the Contact folder.

MOUSE TIP

You can click the To button or the Cc button to locate a recipient in the Contacts folder. Click a name in the Name list and then click the To or Cc button to move that person to the corresponding Message Recipients list.

Not ready to send that message you've been working on? You can click the Save button to save the message in the Drafts folder. You can find it later by clicking the My Shortcuts group bar in the Outlook bar, then clicking the Drafts folder button.

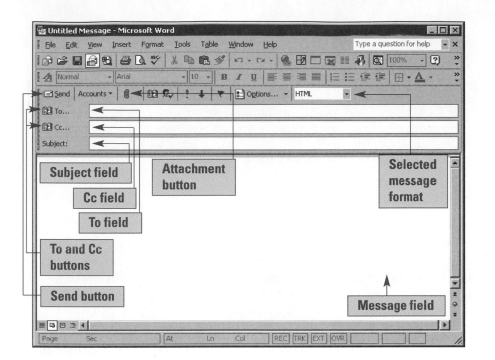

FIGURE 1-2
Word E-mail Editor

QUICK TIP

You can create an electronic **signature** that contains your name and contact information or any text you want to add to all the e-mail messages you send. To create a signature, click Options on the Tools menu, and then click the Mail Format tab. Click Signatures, then click New. You can create different signatures for business or personal correspondence.

Step 2	*Key*	your e-mail address in the To field
Step 3	*Press*	the TAB key twice to move to the Subject: field
Step 4	*Key*	ENGINEER: Oval design for Nakamichi Plaza
Step 5	*Press*	the TAB key to move to the message field
Step 6	*Key*	The design team has proposed using an oval footprint for the Nakamichi Plaza building. Do you see any problems in constructing this shape building?
Step 7	*Press*	the ENTER key twice
Step 8	*Key*	your name
Step 9	*Click*	the Send button ⬛Send

MENU TIP

You can send or send and receive all your messages by clicking the Send All or Send and Receive All subcommand under the Send/Receive command on the Inbox Tools menu from Outlook Today, Inbox, or Outbox.

When you click the Send button, Outlook places your message in the Outbox folder, where it stays until you click the Send/Receive button. If you are using Outlook on a network or are connected to your ISP, the message may be sent automatically. To switch to the Outbox and send the message, if necessary:

| Step 1 | *Click* | the Outbox icon 🔷Outbox in the My Shortcuts group on the Outlook Bar |

outlook

If the message still appears in the Outbox, you need to click the Send/Receive button on the Standard toolbar to send the message.

| Step 2 | *Click* | the Send/Receive button 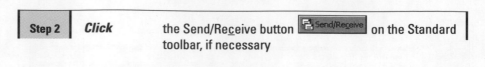 on the Standard toolbar, if necessary |

Outlook sends the message to the recipient.

Receiving Messages

After Outlook sends the message in the Outbox, it retrieves, or **downloads**, any incoming messages that are on the server, and places them in the Inbox. Outlook notifies you that you have received new mail by sounding a tone and opening a dialog box. You can check for new messages even when you don't have any to send by clicking the Send/Receive button on the Standard toolbar in Outlook Today, Outbox, or Inbox.

To receive the ENGINEER: Oval Design for Nakamichi Plaza message:

| Step 1 | *Switch to* | the Inbox |
| Step 2 | *Click* | the Send/Receive button on the Standard toolbar, if necessary, to download the message |

The Nakamichi Plaza message may not appear immediately. If you do not receive the message, wait a few minutes and then try again. When the message appears in the Inbox, you can open it.

Opening and Printing Messages

When you receive an e-mail message, it is placed in your Inbox. You can identify unread messages by the closed yellow envelope icon and the boldface type in the information line. After you have read a message, the envelope icon changes to a white, opened envelope, and the message information is no longer boldface. You can read a message by opening the form in its own message window, or you can activate the preview pane and read the message without opening it.

The ENGINEER: Oval Design for Nakamichi Plaza message should be in the Inbox. To open the message:

| Step 1 | *Observe* | the unread icon to the left of the ENGINEER: Oval Design for Nakamichi Plaza message in the Inbox |

| Step 2 | *Double-click* | the ENGINEER: Oval Design for Nakamichi Plaza message |

The message opens in a separate window. Using the buttons on the Standard toolbar, you can reply to or forward the message, print it, flag it for importance, move it to another folder, or delete it. For now, you want to print a copy of this message for your paper files. To print the message:

| Step 1 | *Click* | the Print button 🖨 on the Standard toolbar in the Message window |

MENU TIP

When you click the Print button on the Standard toolbar in Word, the message automatically prints to the default printer. If you need to select a different printer, or choose other options such as printing multiple copies, click the Print command on the File menu.

Replying to a Message

You often need to respond to a message that you have received. When you reply to a message, Outlook creates a new message that is automatically addressed to the sender. The new message also contains copies of the Message and Subject fields. If you choose to reply to all, then the message is addressed to the sender and all other recipients. In either case, the subject line is prefixed with "RE:" to indicate that the message is a reply. You key your response above the original message to make it easier for the recipient to see your reply. In addition, the reply message you key appears as blue text. To reply to a message:

Step 1	*Click*	the Reply button 🖂 Reply on the Standard toolbar
Step 2	*Verify*	that the insertion point is at the top of the Message field
Step 3	*Key*	Review attached worksheet and return. The worksheet includes a summary of the gross and leasable square footage calculations for each floor.

QUICK TIP

You can print a message without opening it. Select the message In the Inbox, and then click the Print button on the Standard toolbar to print the message to the default printer or click the Print command on the File menu to open the Print dialog box.

Before sending this message, you need to attach a file.

Inserting Message Attachments

In addition to sending a text message, you may want to include an attachment. An **attachment** is a computer file, such as a Word document or an Excel workbook, that you send by e-mail. You want the recipient to review an Excel workbook, so you attach it to your reply message. To attach a file to the message:

| Step 1 | *Click* | the Insert File button 📎 ▾ |

C

The Insert File dialog box opens. This dialog box functions similarly to the Open dialog box.

Step 2	*Switch*	the Look in: location to the Data Disk
Step 3	*Click*	the *Nakamichi Plaza* workbook
Step 4	*Click*	Insert

The attachment appears as an icon in the Attach: text box that's added below the Subject.

Step 5	*Send*	the reply message with its attachment
Step 6	*Close*	the original message

After a few minutes, you can download the RE: ENGINEER: Oval Design for Nakamichi Plaza message with the attached workbook. Messages that have attachments display a paperclip icon next to them. You can open an attachment right from Outlook, as long as you have a program associated with that file type. For example, you need Excel or another spreadsheet application to open and view the attached workbook.

You should always use extreme caution when opening attachments. Message attachments can contain computer viruses that can seriously damage your computer. Computer **viruses** are malicious programs that can, in extreme cases, delete files from your computer. Even messages from people you know may not be safe, as many viruses can create and send e-mail messages to people in your Outlook Contacts list. Before opening any attachment, you should contact the sender and verify its contents, then use antivirus software to scan the attachment for viruses.

To download the message and open the attachment:

Step 1	*Click*	the Send/Receive button ⊞ Send/Receive on the Standard toolbar
Step 2	*Observe*	the paperclip icon next to the reply message with attachment in the Inbox
Step 3	*Click*	the reply message with attachment to select it
Step 4	*Observe*	the reply message in the preview pane

The RE: ENGINEER: Oval Design for Nakamichi Plaza message with attachment on your screen should look similar to Figure 1-3.

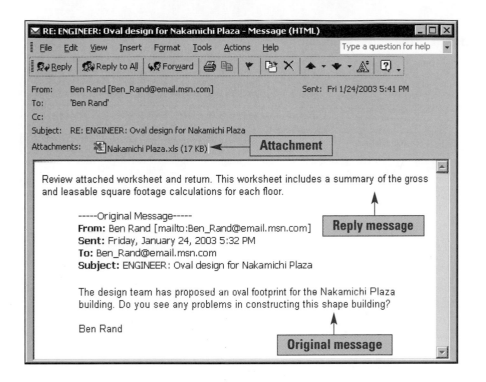

FIGURE 1-3
Message with Attachment

Step 5	*Right-click*	the filename next to Attachments:

Step 6	*Click*	Open

Outlook warns you that this attachment may contain a computer virus. This standard warning appears whenever you open an attachment. Because you know and trust the sender of this attachment—yourself, you open it without scanning it with antivirus software.

Step 7	*Click*	Open it

Step 8	*Click*	OK

Because this attachment is an Excel workbook, Excel starts and opens the workbook.

Step 9	*Review*	the worksheet contents

Step 10	*Close*	Excel without saving the workbook

> **MENU TIP**
>
> You can save one attachment or multiple attachments simultaneously. Click the Save Attachments command on the File menu. To save one attachment, click the attachment filename. To save multiple attachments, click All Attachments, click the appropriate attachments in the Attachments: list box, and then click the OK button.

You can save the attached file to any location using the shortcut menu. To save the workbook attachment:

Step 1	*Right-click*	the filename of the attached file
Step 2	*Click*	Save As
Step 3	*Switch to*	the location where you store your Data Files
Step 4	*Click*	Save
Step 5	*Close*	the e-mail message

In addition to using Outlook for e-mail correspondence, you can employ it to organize your schedule.

1.c Scheduling in the Calendar

The **Calendar** is where you schedule all your appointments, meetings, and events. For each activity, you can enter information beyond its date and time—such as notes, subjects, and reminders. In addition, you can specify how the activity appears in the Calendar by adding color-coded labels; you also can show the time as available or unavailable to others. You can send meeting requests to people who should attend, and accept or decline meeting requests from other people. If you need a paper copy of your calendar, you can print it in a variety of formats.

Scheduling Appointments, Meetings, and Events

An **appointment** is time you schedule personally; unlike a meeting, it usually does not involve other Outlook users or company resources. Next Monday, you are scheduled to conduct several job interviews for potential contractors. To schedule an appointment in the Calendar:

Step 1	*Switch to*	the Calendar folder
Step 2	*Click*	the New Appointment button on the Standard toolbar

The Appointment form on your screen should look similar to Figure 1-4.

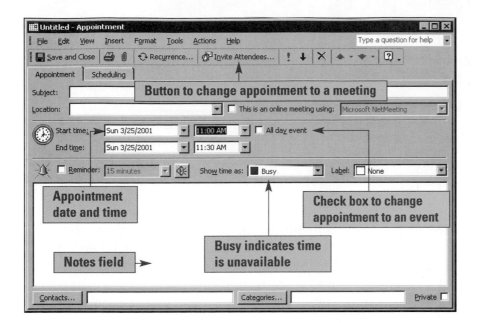

FIGURE 1-4
Appointment Form

Q U I C K   T I P

Natural language dates allow you to key a phrase, such as "tomorrow," "ten days from Thursday," or "two weeks ago," instead of the actual date. Outlook determines the correct date from the phrase.

Step 3	*Key*	Job Interviews in the Subject: field
Step 4	*Press*	the TAB key
Step 5	*Key*	Office in the Location: field
Step 6	*Press*	the TAB key twice to move to the Start time: field
Step 7	*Key*	next Monday
Step 8	*Press*	the TAB key and observe that Outlook enters the correct start date
Step 9	*Verify*	that 8:00 AM is selected as the start time
Step 10	*Press*	the TAB key twice to move to the second End time: field
Step 11	*Key*	9:00 AM
Step 12	*Click*	the notes field
Step 13	*Key*	Conduct job interviews in office.
Step 14	*Click*	the Save and Close button ![Save and Close] on the Standard toolbar

Outlook adds the appointment to your calendar. You can change views in your calendar to view details for a single day, a week, or to get an overview of an entire month. You can switch between day, work week, week, or month views by clicking the appropriate button on the Standard toolbar.

M O U S E   T I P

In Day/Week/Month view, you can create an appointment by dragging to select the length of your appointment, and then keying a subject. Press the ENTER key when you're finished to save the appointment.

Month view doesn't show much detail, but you can position the mouse pointer over any appointment and "hover" (pause for a few seconds) to display a ScreenTip with the full content of the appointment's subject line.

outlook

To change calendar views:

Step 1	*Click*	the Current View button list arrow 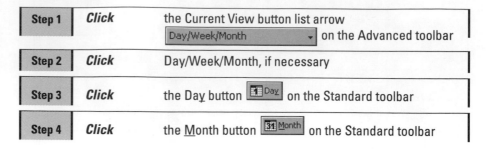 on the Advanced toolbar
Step 2	*Click*	Day/Week/Month, if necessary
Step 3	*Click*	the Day button [1 Day] on the Standard toolbar
Step 4	*Click*	the Month button [31 Month] on the Standard toolbar

Meetings are appointments that involve other Outlook users or company resources such as a conference room or projector. When you schedule a meeting, you invite others via e-mail to find out if they are available at the proposed meeting time. Invitees respond to the e-mail message, indicating whether or not they can attend. As they reply, your meeting form is updated automatically.

 notes You cannot schedule a meeting with yourself. You must work with a classmate to complete the activities for scheduling a meeting.

You want to have a staff meeting on Thursday to review progress on the Nakamichi Plaza project. To schedule a meeting:

Step 1	*Click*	the Work Week button [5 Work Week] on the Standard toolbar
Step 2	*Click*	next Monday in the calendar in the upper-right corner
Step 3	*Double-click*	next Thursday at 10:00 AM in the main view area
Step 4	*Click*	the Invite Attendees button [Invite Attendees...] on the Standard toolbar

The Appointment form changes to a Meeting form, which includes a To field for entering the e-mail addresses of attendees. After you finish filling in details of this meeting, you send it to the attendees by e-mail.

Step 5	*Key*	a classmate's e-mail address in the To... field
Step 6	*Key*	Nakamichi Plaza staff meeting in the Subject: field
Step 7	*Key*	Office in the Location: field
Step 8	*Verify*	that next Thursday 10:00 AM appears in the Start time: field

Step 9	*Select*	10:30 AM in the End time: field
Step 10	*Click*	Important in the Label: list to color code the meeting
Step 11	*Send*	the meeting invitation

After a few minutes, you should receive a meeting invitation from a classmate. A meeting invitation arrives as an e-mail message. The message contains extra buttons so you can accept, decline, mark yourself as tentative, or propose a new time for the meeting. To receive and accept a meeting invitation:

Step 1	*Switch to*	the Inbox
Step 2	*Download*	messages, if necessary
Step 3	*Open*	the Nakamichi Plaza staff meeting message

Your screen should look similar to Figure 1-5.

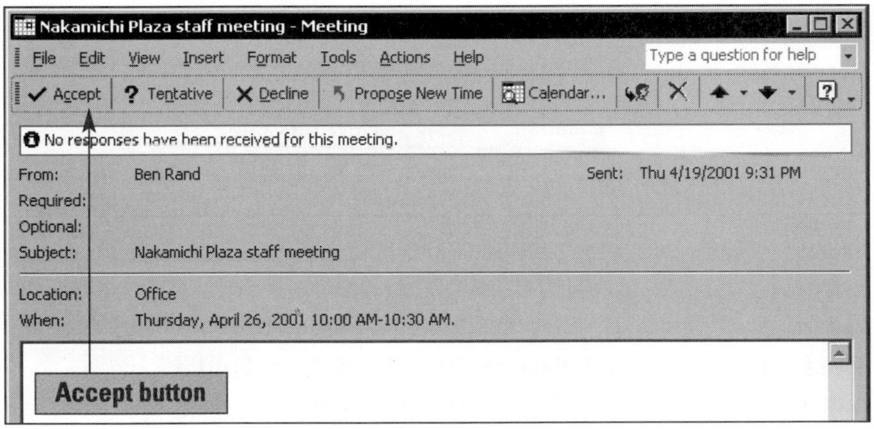

FIGURE 1-5
Meeting Invitation

Step 4	*Click*	the Accept button  ✔ Accept and send the message, if necessary

Your response is returned to the meeting's host. You should receive a response from a classmate. You can review the responses from the open Meeting window. To review responses to the meeting invitation:

Step 1	*Download*	new messages, if necessary
Step 2	*Switch to*	the Calendar folder

MOUSE TIP

You can open any Outlook item for editing by right-clicking the item, and then clicking Open.

outlook

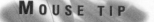
Step 3	*Double-click*	the Nakamichi Plaza staff meeting to open the Meeting window
Step 4	*Observe*	the acceptance in the tally of responses above the To field
Step 5	*Close*	the window

An **event** is an activity that lasts at least one full day; holidays, vacations, and business trips are all events. You schedule an event the same way as an appointment, but you click the All day event check box to insert a check mark. The start and end times options are removed from the Event form. You cannot specify a start and stop time for an all day event. The scheduled event appears as a banner above the appropriate day or days in the calendar.

Next Tuesday, you are scheduled to visit one of the firm's job sites out of town. To schedule an event in your calendar:

Step 1	*Double-click*	the gray area just below Tuesday's date in Work Week view
Step 2	*Observe*	that the new Appointment form opens and that the All day event check box already contains a check mark
Step 3	*Enter*	the following information in the appropriate fields on the Event form: Subject: Nakamichi Plaza site visit Location: New York City Show time as: Out of Office Label: Travel required
Step 4	*Click*	the Save and Close button 🖫 Save and Close on the Standard toolbar

The form closes, and the event appears on the calendar.

A **reminder** is an alarm that alerts you about upcoming appointments, meetings, or events at a preset time. You want to set a reminder before the staff meeting next week. To set a reminder:

Step 1	*Double-click*	the Job interviews appointment to open it
Step 2	*Click*	the Reminder check box to insert a check mark, if necessary
Step 3	*Verify*	that 15 minutes appears in the Reminder: list
Step 4	*Click*	the Save and Close button 🖫 Save and Close on the Standard toolbar

With the reminder set, Outlook will open a Reminder dialog box prior to this meeting.

With your planning for next week complete, your screen should look similar to Figure 1-6. Each item is color coded and shaded, according to the Label: and Show time as: options you selected when you created it.

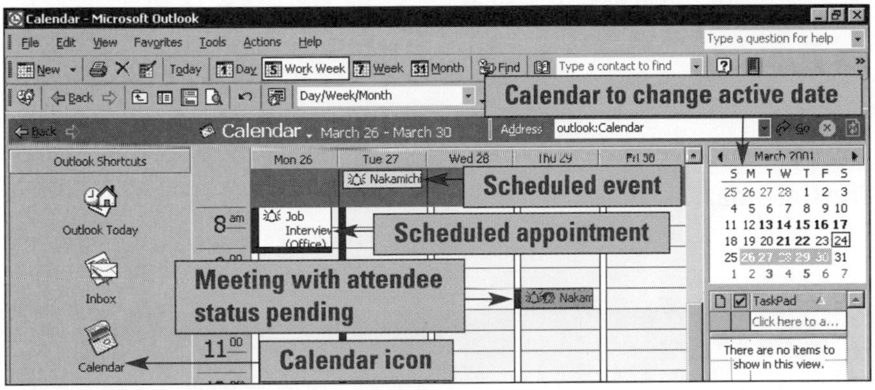

FIGURE 1-6
Calendar in Work
Week View

Printing a Calendar

When you need a paper copy of your calendar, you can print the exact days you need and select from a variety of print styles. To view different print styles and print your calendar for one work week:

| Step 1 | *Click* | the Print button 🖨 on the Standard toolbar |

Your Print dialog box should look similar to Figure 1-7. From this dialog box, you can select a printer and the print style. These options change, depending on what item or folder you are printing. You can print Calendar items in one of several styles, including a day, week, or month view, a tri-fold style, a calendar details style, or a memo style.

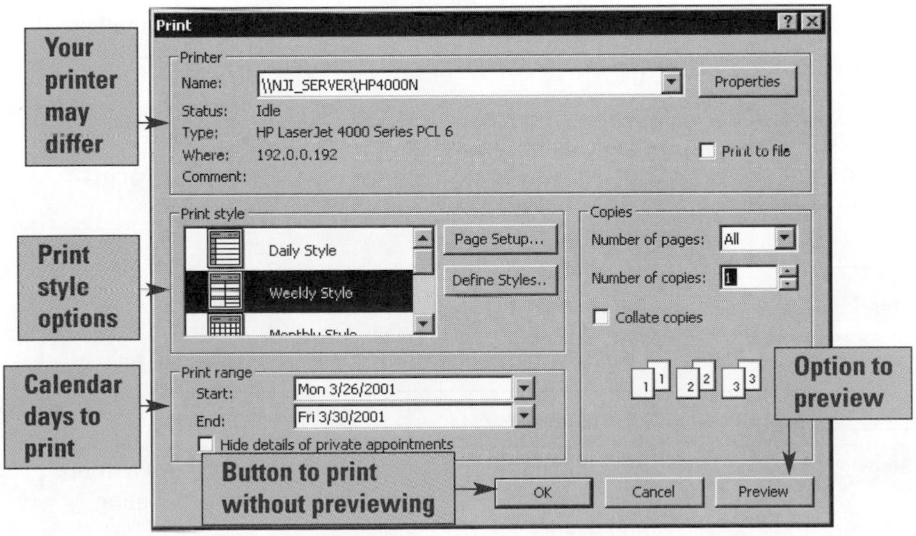

FIGURE 1-7
Print Dialog Box

outlook

Step 2	*Click*	Weekly Style in the Print style list

Before you print, you should preview the printed version to ensure that the output looks as you expect.

Step 3	*Click*	Preview

The Calendar in Weekly Style opens in the Print Preview window. Your screen should look similar to Figure 1-8.

FIGURE 1-8
Calendar in Print Preview

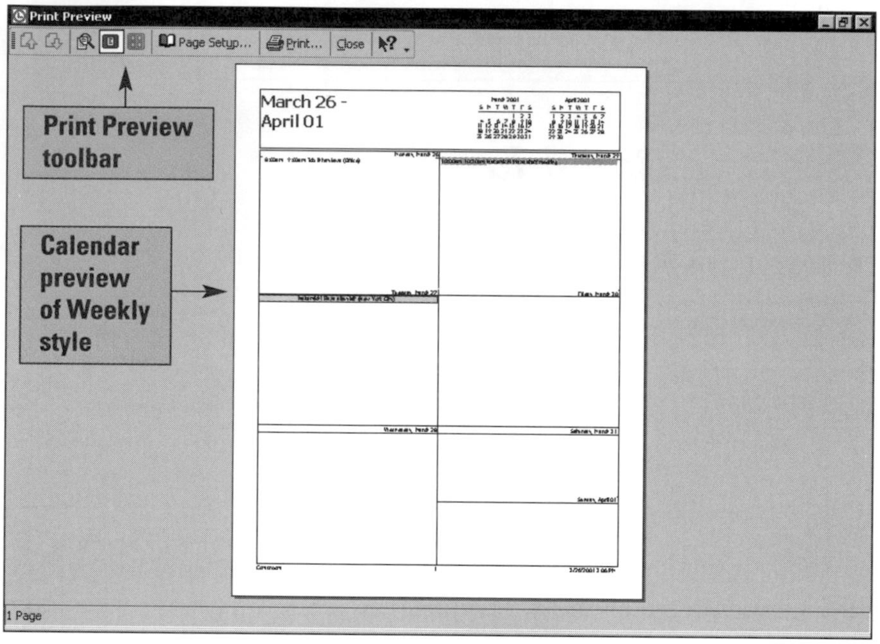

Print Preview toolbar

Calendar preview of Weekly style

March 26 –
April 01

Step 4	*Click*	the Print button Print... on the Print Preview toolbar
Step 5	*Click*	OK

The process for printing in other styles or views is similar. To print the calendar for one month:

Step 1	*Click*	the Print button on the Standard toolbar
Step 2	*Click*	Monthly Style in the Print style list
Step 3	*Preview*	the calendar
Step 4	*Observe*	the calendar for the current month, along with a brief description of the scheduled appointment, meeting, and event

| **Step 5** | *Click* | the Print button on the Print Preview toolbar |
| **Step 6** | *Click* | OK |

1.d Using Contacts

The **Contacts** folder is where you enter and store information about your contacts. A **contact** is an individual with whom you communicate.

Adding a Contact

A contact list is a powerful way to organize all the information about your contacts in a central location. You can store up to nineteen phone numbers, three e-mail addresses, three mailing addresses, a Web site address, a nickname, and the birthdays of both the contact and his or her spouse, among other information. This information is divided into tabs on the Contact form to keep all the information organized. To create a contact:

| **Step 1** | *Switch to* | the Contacts folder |
| **Step 2** | *Click* | the New Contact button 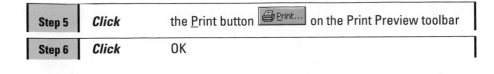 on the Standard toolbar |

The Contact form on your screen should look similar to Figure 1-9. You enter information in fields just as you did on the Appointment form.

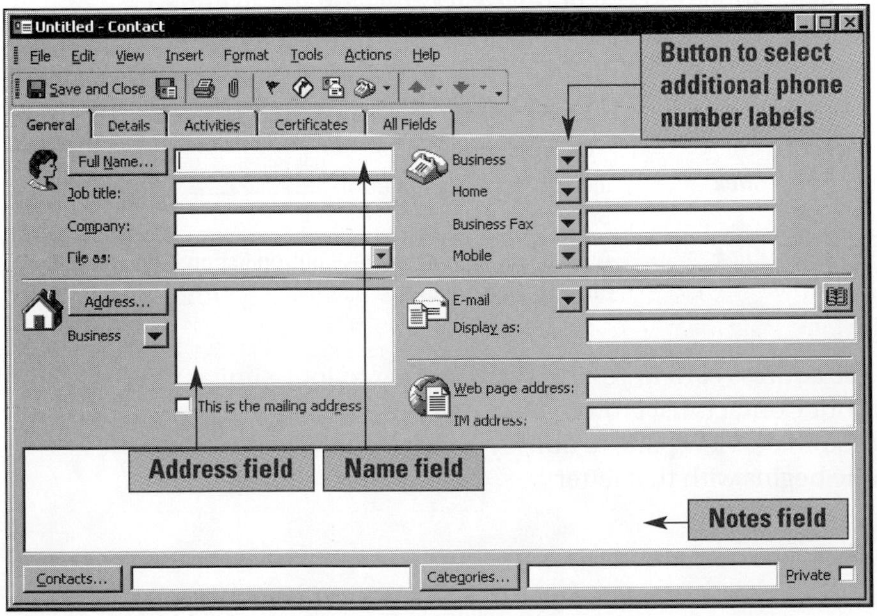

FIGURE 1-9
Contact Form

outlook

Step 3	*Enter*	the following information in the appropriate fields on the General tab:

Full <u>N</u>ame: Osuro Yamato
<u>J</u>ob title: Facilities Development Manager
Co<u>m</u>pany: Nakamichi Enterprises, USA
Business phone
number: (212) 555-4322
E-mail: Osuro@nakamichienterprises.com
<u>W</u>eb page address: www.nakamichienterprises.com

The Details tab is where Outlook stores detailed information about a contact. This information can include data such as the contact's birthday, the name of the contact's spouse, and the department in which the contact works.

Step 4	*Click*	the Details tab
Step 5	*Key*	February 12 in the <u>B</u>irthday field

Outlook prompts you to save the Contact item.

Step 6	*Click*	OK

When you enter a contact's birthday, Outlook automatically adds a recurring event to your calendar to remind you of the birthday. A **recurring event**, **appointment**, or **meeting** is one that reoccurs at a set interval, such as a birthday or anniversary, a monthly haircut, or a weekly meeting. You can double-click the icon in the notes field of Osuro's contact card to open the event without switching to the Calendar folder.

Step 7	*Click*	the <u>S</u>ave and Close button [💾 Save and Close] on the Standard toolbar
Step 8	*Click*	Address Cards in the View button list on the Advanced toolbar, if necessary

The address card in your contact list should look similar to Figure 1-10. As your Contacts list grows, you can use the buttons on the right side of the Contacts view pane to quickly jump to the first contact whose last name begins with that letter.

QUICK TIP

When you enter phone numbers, just key the actual numbers. Outlook automatically inserts the appropriate parentheses and hyphens to properly format the phone number.

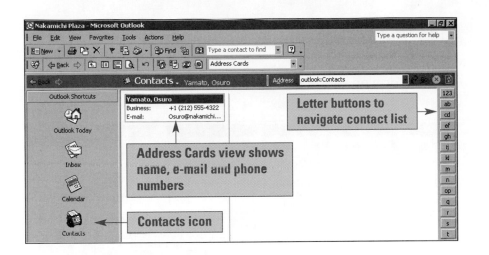

FIGURE 1-10
Contacts Folder in Address
Cards View

You need to enter Osuro's mailing address. You can open the Contact form and make changes at any time. To edit Osuro's contact information:

Step 1	**Double-click**	Osuro's address card
Step 2	**Enter**	the following information in the A̲ddress field, pressing the ENTER key between the two lines: 100 Park Place New York City, NY 10060
Step 3	**Save & Close**	the Contact form

You can edit contact information to keep it up to date.

1.e Creating and Updating Tasks

Many people use a written "to-do" list to keep track of important things they need to get done. Outlook uses the **Tasks folder** to help you create and manage these "to-do" items. You can keep track of whether or not the task is complete. If a task requires a long time to finish, you can track the percentage of completion.

One of the things you need to accomplish today is to review the schematic drawings for the Nakamichi Plaza project. To open the Tasks folder and create a new task:

| Step 1 | **Switch to** | the Tasks folder |

C

outlook

Step 2	*Click*	the New Task button [New] on the Standard toolbar

The Task form on your screen should look similar to Figure 1-11.

FIGURE 1-11
Task Form

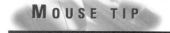

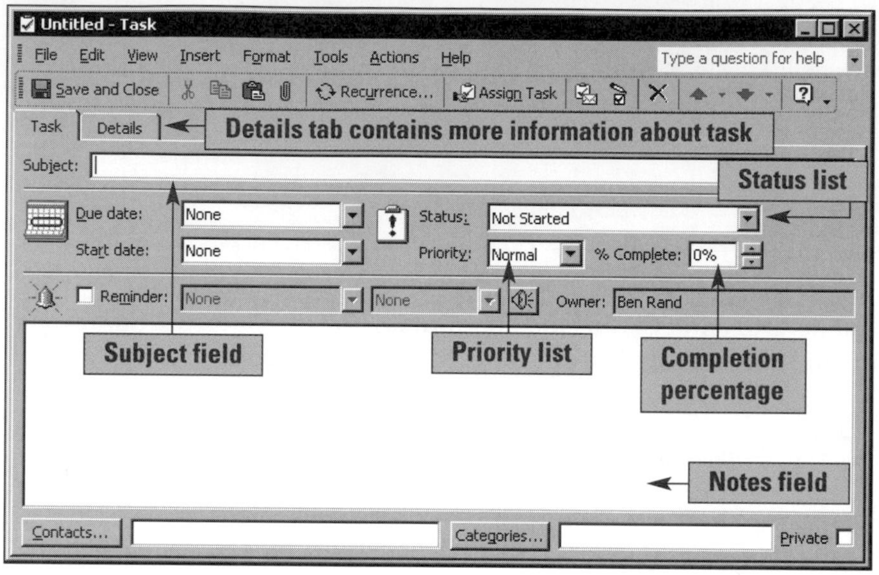

Step 3	*Enter*	the following information in the appropriate fields on the Task tab: Subject: Review Nakamichi Plaza schematics Due date: today
Step 4	*Click*	the Save and Close button [Save and Close] on the Standard toolbar

Outlook adds the task to the list in the Tasks View pane. When you set up the last task, you entered a small amount of information about the task. You can update the task from the task list. To update a task:

Step 1	*Click*	Detailed List in the Current View button list on the Advanced toolbar
Step 2	*Click*	the Status field of the Review Nakamichi Plaza Schematics task to display a list of options
Step 3	*Click*	Waiting on someone else
Step 4	*Click*	the % Complete field of the task
Step 5	*Drag*	across the existing percentage to select it

MOUSE TIP

You can assign tasks to other people, and then track their progress. To assign a task to another person, right-click the task, then click Assign Task. The Task form opens with a To field so you can address and e-mail the task. Upon receiving the task, the recipient has the option to accept or reject the task, or enter the completion status and send it back to you.

QUICK TIP

Tasks also appear on the TaskPad in the Calendar folder. You can create and edit tasks from the TaskPad just as you do in the Tasks lists.

Step 6	*Key*	25
Step 7	*Press*	the ENTER key

Outlook adds the percentage sign.

A **recurring task** is a task that occurs at a set interval. For example, you review the Nakamichi Plaza project budget every week to ensure that the project is on schedule and under budget. Rather than create a new task each week, you can create a recurring task. To create a weekly recurring task:

Step 1	*Double-click*	an empty line in the Task list to open a new Task form
Step 2	*Enter*	Review Nakamichi Plaza budget in the Subject: field
Step 3	*Click*	the Recurrence button Recurrence... on the Standard toolbar

The Task Recurrence dialog box on your screen should look similar to Figure 1-12. In this dialog box, you set the recurrence pattern and the range of recurrence.

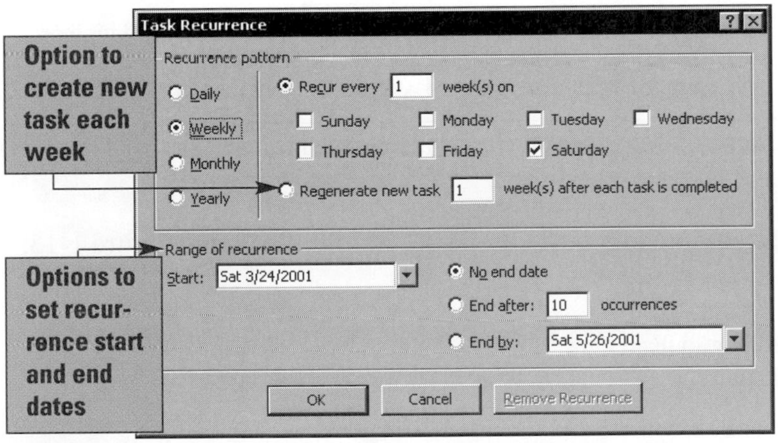

FIGURE 1-12
Task Recurrence Dialog Box

Step 4	*Verify*	that the Weekly option button is selected
Step 5	*Click*	the Regenerate new task option button
Step 6	*Verify*	that 1 appears in the text box

This option creates a new task one week after the previous task is marked complete.

MOUSE TIP

You can check off completed tasks on the Tasks list or the TaskPad in the Calendar. Click the Complete check box in the Tasks list to insert a check mark.

Step 7	*Click*	OK
Step 8	*Save*	the Task form and close it

The Tasks folder enables you to quickly create and organize your to-do list.

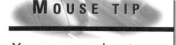

1.f Creating and Editing Notes

Sometimes, you have a quick idea or you need to jot down an important phone number, but don't have time to create a task or a contact. In this case, you can use Notes to store the idea or number. **Notes** are like an electronic form of paper adhesive notes.

During the day, you had several ideas about the Nakamichi Plaza project. You want to record these ideas before you forget them. To switch to the Notes folder and create a note:

Step 1	*Switch to*	the Notes folder
Step 2	*Click*	the New Note button [New] on the Standard toolbar
Step 3	*Observe*	that a yellow note with the current date and time appears
Step 4	*Key*	Check fire exiting requirements for Nakamichi Plaza

The finished note on your screen should look similar to Figure 1-13.

FIGURE 1-13
Finished Note

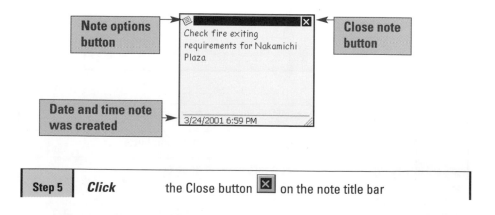

Step 5	*Click*	the Close button [X] on the note title bar

MOUSE TIP

You can use colors to organize your notes. For example, you could use white notes for personal items, blue notes for work items, yellow notes for ideas, and so forth. To change the color of a note, right-click the note or click the Notes Option button on the open note, point to Color, then click a color.

Linking a Note to a Contact

One strategy for organizing information is to link notes or any other item to a contact. Later, when you reopen the Contact form, you see a list of all linked items on the Activities tab. This makes it much simpler to find information related to a specific contact. To link a note to a contact:

Step 1	*Switch to*	the Contacts folder
Step 2	*Right-click*	the Osuro Yamato contact
Step 3	*Point to*	Link
Step 4	*Click*	Items
Step 5	*Click*	Notes in the Look in: list
Step 6	*Click*	the Check fire… note in the Items: list
Step 7	*Click*	OK

The items are linked, although you don't see any changes in the View pane. To review items linked to a contact:

Step 1	*Open*	the Osuro Yamato Contact form
Step 2	*Click*	the Activities tab

Outlook searches for linked items and displays any "hits" in a list.

Step 3	*Save & Close*	the Contact form
Step 4	*Verify*	that the Check fire… note appears in the list

The Activities tab displays any items linked to this contact. You can sort the items by category, such as e-mail, notes, or upcoming tasks/appointments. Double-clicking any of the items opens the item for review or editing.

1.g Customizing Outlook

Outlook features many helpful tools to help you organize items. You can create additional folders to store items. You can search for specific items and then move them between folders. You can categorize items. You can save items in other formats; for example, you can save messages as text files and the Calendar as a Web page.

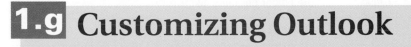

outlook

Creating Offline Folders and Shortcuts

When you download messages from your mail server, they are stored in your computer. **Offline messages** are messages that can be viewed even when you are not connected to the Internet. As messages begin to pile up in the Inbox, you may find it helpful to create additional folders to store messages. You can add folders to Outlook for each type of item.

You want to create a new mail folder for your project and add a shortcut to this folder in the My Shortcuts group. To create a new folder:

| Step 1 | *Click* | the New Contact button list arrow ⬚New ▾ on the Standard toolbar |
| Step 2 | *Click* | Folder |

The Create New Folder dialog box on your screen should look similar to Figure 1-14. In this dialog box, you choose the type of folder you want to create and name it. You want to create a folder within the Inbox named Nakamichi Mail to store e-mail messages.

FIGURE 1-14
Create New Folder
Dialog Box

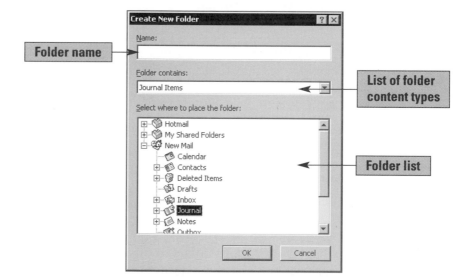

Step 3	*Key*	Nakamichi Mail in the Name: text box
Step 4	*Click*	the Folder contains: list arrow
Step 5	*Click*	Mail and Post Items
Step 6	*Click*	Inbox in the Select where to place the folder: list
Step 7	*Click*	OK

Outlook prompts you to add a shortcut to the new folder on the Outlook Bar.

| Step 8 | **Click** | Yes |

Searching for Messages

You want to move any messages concerning the Nakamichi Plaza project to the Nakamichi Mail folder you just created. Rather than looking through the Inbox for these messages, you can have Outlook search for you. To search for messages:

| Step 1 | **Switch** | to the Inbox folder |

| Step 2 | **Click** | the Find button on the Standard toolbar |

The Find bar appears above the current folder list view.

Step 3	**Key**	Nakamichi in the Look for: text box
Step 4	**Click**	the Search In button
Step 5	**Click**	All Mail Folders
Step 6	**Click**	the Find Now button

A list of all messages containing "Nakamichi" appears in the View pane. Because you started the search from the Journal folder, the entries found by the search temporarily block the display of the journal entry you just created. You can clear the search by clicking the Clear button on the Find bar.

Moving Messages Among Folders

Now that you have located the messages, you can move them into the Nakamichi Mail folder. The simplest way to move messages is to drag them to another folder on the Outlook Bar. To move messages to the Nakamichi Mail folder:

Step 1	**Click**	the ENGINEER message
Step 2	**Press & hold**	the CTRL key
Step 3	**Click**	the RE: ENGINEER message to select a second message
Step 4	**Drag**	the selected messages to the Nakamichi Mail folder in the My Shortcuts Group

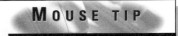

MOUSE TIP

You can add shortcuts to any group. Right-click inside the group and click Outlook Bar Shortcut. Select the folder name in the Folder name: list or double-click the folder in the list box.

You can use the Move To button on the Standard toolbar to move selected items to another folder. When you click the Move To button, a list of folders is displayed from which you can select.

outlook

CAUTION TIP

The messages may not appear to change location while you are viewing the Find results. Switch to the destination folder to verify that the messages were moved.

You can clear the search and then view the messages you moved. To close the Find bar and switch the Nakamichi Mail folder:

Step 1	*Click*	the Clear button on the Find bar to clear the previous search
Step 2	*Click*	the Close button on the Find bar
Step 3	*Switch to*	the Nakamichi Mail folder in the My Shortcuts Group
Step 4	*Observe*	the moved messages

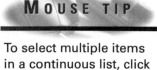

Categorizing Items

Categories provide another way for you to group items, even if they belong to different folders. For instance, many of your contacts, calendar entries, and e-mail messages could be placed into the business category, while others could be placed in a personal category. You can then group or search for items based on categories. **Groups** display items in a folder based on something they have in common, such as the business category and the personal category.

To categorize Osuro's contact as a business item:

Step 1	*Switch to*	the Contacts folder
Step 2	*Double-click*	Osuro's contact to open it
Step 3	*Click*	Categories

The Categories dialog box on your screen should look similar to Figure 1-15. You can add any item to one category or multiple categories. You also can create categories if those provided are insufficient.

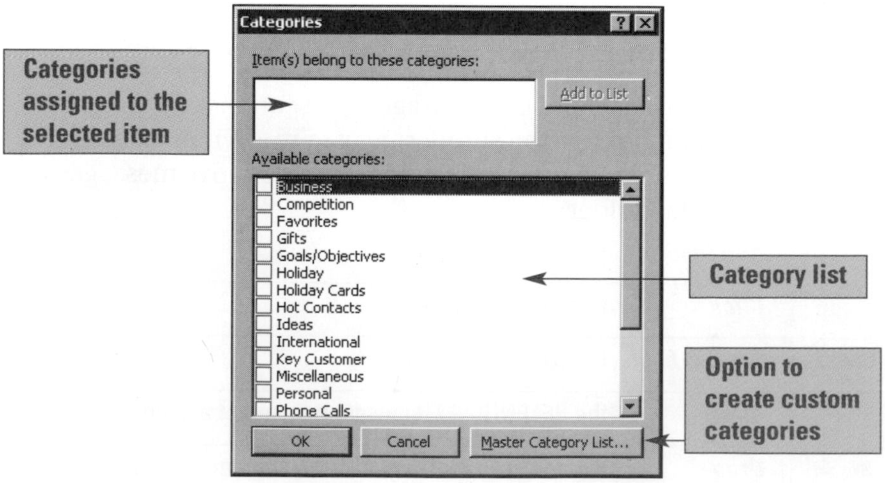

MOUSE TIP

To select multiple items in a continuous list, click the first item, press and hold the SHIFT key, then click the last item in the series. To select multiple items in a noncontiguous list, press and hold the CTRL key while you select the items.

You can open the Categories dialog box by right-clicking any item, and then clicking Categories on the shortcut menu.

FIGURE 1-15
Categories Dialog Box

Categories assigned to the selected item

Category list

Option to create custom categories

Step 4	*Click*	the Business check box to insert a check mark
Step 5	*Click*	OK
Step 6	*Observe*	the assigned category in the Categories text box
Step 7	*Save & Close*	the Contact form

Once your contacts have been assigned to categories, you can change the view to organize items by category. This provides another way for you to organize and locate information. To view your contact list by category:

| Step 1 | *Click* | By Category in the Current View button list on the Advanced toolbar |
| Step 2 | *Click* | the Expand button [+] next to Categories: Business to expand the Business category |

Your screen should look similar to Figure 1-16.

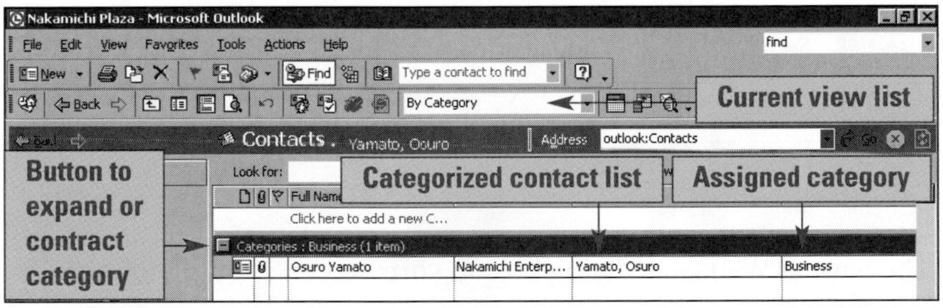

FIGURE 1-16
Contacts Folder Organized by Category

Saving Messages in Other Formats

When you create items in Outlook, you may need to save them to other formats such as text or HTML. Perhaps you want to post a customer's appreciative note on the company intranet, or you need to forward an HTML message to someone using an incompatible e-mail application. In either case you can save a message in another format. To save a message to another format:

| Step 1 | *Switch to* | the Nakamichi Mail folder |

QUICK TIP

You can categorize multiple items at once by holding down the CTRL key as you click the items. Select the category or categories you want to assign to the items, and then click the OK button.

outlook

Step 2	**Click**	the ENGINEER message to select it
Step 3	**Click**	File
Step 4	**Click**	Save As
Step 5	**Switch to**	the Data Files folder in the Save in list
Step 6	**Verify**	that ENGINEER Oval design for Nakamichi Plaza appears in the File name: text box
Step 7	**Verify**	that HTML is selected in the Save as type: list box
Step 8	**Click**	Save to save the message as an HTML file

Saving a Calendar as a Web Page

You can save Calendar entries as Web pages, complete with special formatting. When you have saved a calendar this way, you can post it on the Internet or on a company intranet so others can view it. This also serves as a handy way for you to view your schedule via the Internet even when you can't access your Outlook file.

To save a calendar as a Web page:

Step 1	**Switch to**	the Calendar folder
Step 2	**Click**	File
Step 3	**Click**	Save as Web Page

The Save as Web Page dialog box on your screen should look similar to Figure 1-17.

FIGURE 1-17
Save as Web Page
dialog box

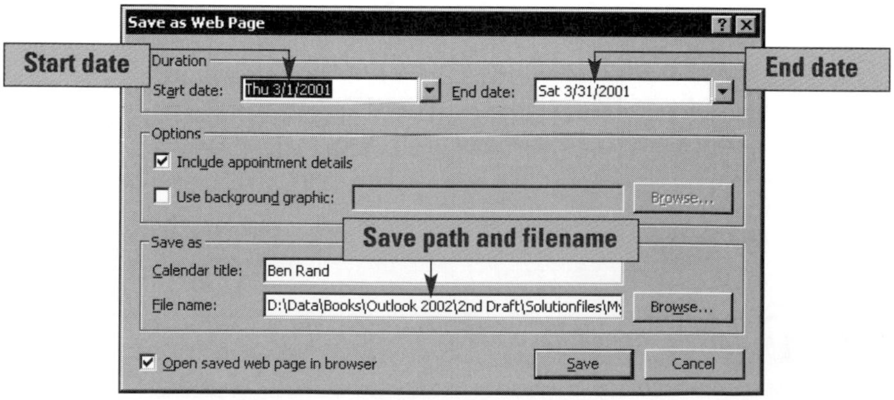

Step 4	***Enter***	the first day of the current month in the Start date: text box
Step 5	***Enter***	the last day of the current month in the End date: text box
Step 6	***Verify***	that the Include appointment details check box contains a check mark
Step 7	***Click***	Browse next to the File name: text box and switch to the Data Disk
Step 8	***Key***	MyCalendar in the File name: text box

Note that the Save as Web Page does not accept spaces in the filename.

Step 9	***Click***	Select
Step 10	***Verify***	that the Open saved web page in browser check box contains a check mark
Step 11	***Click***	Save

QUICK TIP

When you save a Calendar as a Web page, Outlook creates a folder for the Web page that contains the graphic files and other items that make up the Web page.

Your screen should look similar to Figure 1-18. You can click the black triangles in the Appointment and Event Details area to view detailed information.

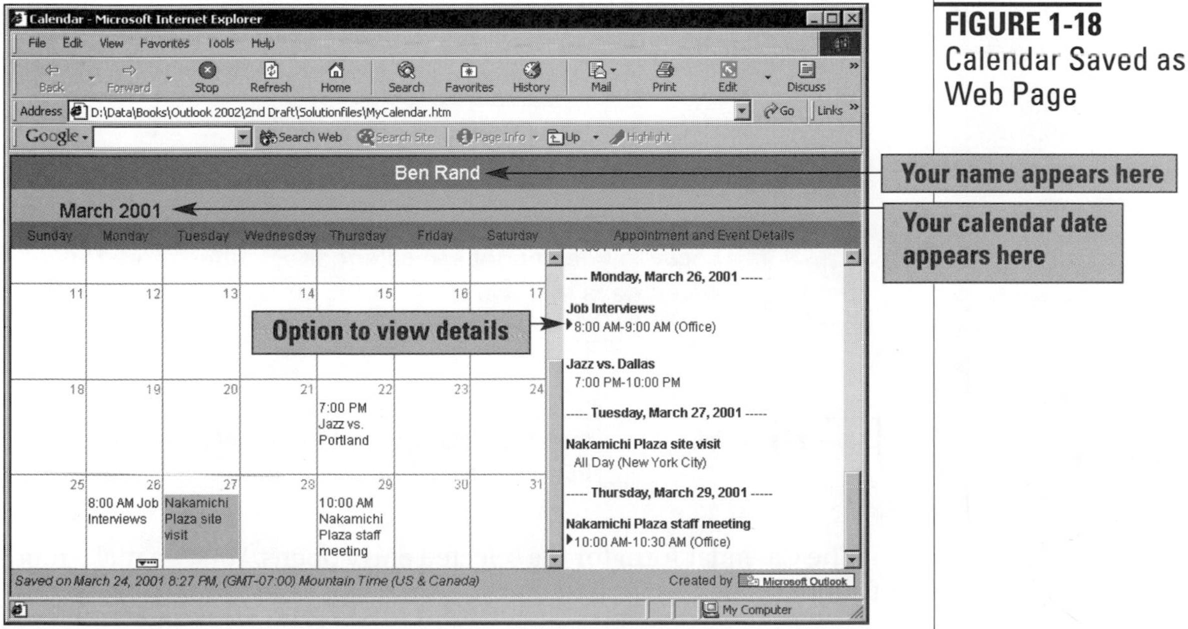

FIGURE 1-18
Calendar Saved as Web Page

Step 12	***Close***	the Web browser

Using Outlook Today

Now that you have created calendar activities, tasks, and messages, Outlook Today provides a helpful overview. Each item in Outlook Today is a hyperlink to that item's form. This makes it easy for you to modify an appointment time, check on details of a task you need to accomplish, or switch to the mail folder with unread messages.

To view items in Outlook Today:

Step 1	*Switch to*	Outlook Today

Your screen should look similar to Figure 1-19.

FIGURE 1-19
Using Outlook Today

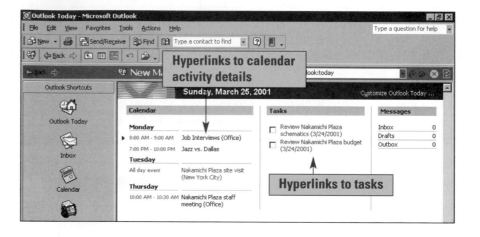

QUICK TIP

You can customize Outlook Today. Click the Customize Outlook Today button in the Outlook Today window. Change any options—including whether the page opens at startup, which message folders appear, how many days of calendar activities are displayed, how tasks are organized, and what style you want to use for the Outlook Today form. Click Save Changes when you finish.

 notes   The calendar activities visible on your screen may vary because you cannot see calendar activities more than seven days in advance.

Step 2	*Click*	the Nakamichi Plaza site visit event listed in the Calendar column

The Calendar form for the selected entry opens. You can make modifications if necessary, and then save and close the form.

Step 3	*Close*	the form

1.h Deleting Items and Exiting Outlook

When you finish your work in Outlook, you should delete items you no longer need. Deleting items moves them to the Deleted Items folder, where they remain until you empty the folder.

To delete items:

Step 1	Switch to	the Inbox
Step 2	Select	the messages you created using the CTRL key
Step 3	Click	the Delete button ☒ on the Standard toolbar
Step 4	Follow	Steps 1 through 3 to delete the Nakamichi Plaza Staff meeting in the calendar
Step 5	Click	Delete without sending a cancellation
Step 6	Click	OK
Step 7	Follow	Steps 1 through 3 to delete the items you created in the Sent Items, Contacts, Notes, Calendar, Tasks, and Journal folders, the Nakamichi Mail folder and shortcut
Step 8	Right-click	the Deleted Items folder
Step 9	Click	Empty "Deleted Items" folder
Step 10	Click	Yes to confirm the deletion

With all the items deleted, you can exit the application. To exit Outlook:

Step 1	Click	the Close button ☒ on the Outlook application window title bar

outlook

Summary

▶ Outlook organizes information in groups and folders. Folders such as the Inbox, Outbox, and Sent Items hold e-mail messages, while the Contacts folder stores contact information, and the Calendar folder holds scheduling information.

▶ You can navigate among Outlook folders using the Outlook Bar or the Folder list on the Navigation bar.

▶ Composing, sending and receiving, and replying to e-mail messages is a critical aspect of business communications.

▶ Attachments are computer files, such as a Word document or Excel workbook, that are sent along with an email message.

▶ All Outlook items can be printed in a variety of styles, including table and memo styles.

▶ Appointments are activities that do not involve other Outlook users or company resources.

▶ Meetings are appointments involving other Outlook users and company resources, such as a conference room or projector. Using Outlook, you can invite attendees and schedule resources.

▶ Events are activities that last for one or more full days.

▶ Contacts include businesses and individuals with whom you communicate. You can store important information—including phone numbers, addresses, e-mail addresses, and detailed information such as birthdays—in your contact list.

▶ Tasks compose a "to-do" list to track progress towards completion of important things you need to accomplish.

▶ Notes provide a place to quickly jot down important items. Notes can be linked to contacts to provide easy reference through the contact list.

▶ You can create folders to organize messages and other items. You can add shortcuts to the Outlook bar for folders you create.

▶ You can have Outlook find items that contain specific keywords.

▶ You can move items, such as messages, to other folders for purposes of organization.

▶ One way to organize contacts is by categories, such as business, personal, or key client.

- You can save Outlook items in other formats, such as saving RTF messages as text or HTML.
- You can save your calendar as a Web page for viewing on an intranet or the Internet.
- Outlook Today provides a quick overview of activities, tasks, and unread messages in Outlook. You can customize the Outlook Today view to display the information you want it to see.
- You should delete any items you no longer need. Deleted items remain in the Deleted Items folder until you empty it.

Commands Review

Action	Menu Bar	Shortcut Menu	Toolbar	Task Pane	Keyboard
Create a new message	File, New, Mail Message	Right-click empty Inbox space, New Mail Message	New		CTRL + SHIFT + M ALT + F, W, M
Reply to a message	Actions, Reply	Right-click message, Reply	Reply		ALT + A, R
Forward a message	Actions, Forward	Right-click message, Forward	Forward		ALT + A, W
Attach a file to a message	Insert, File				ALT + I, L
Print an item	File, Print	Right-click item, Print			CTRL + P ALT + F, P
Create a new appointment	File, New, Appointment	Right-click Calendar, New Appointment	New		CTRL + SHIFT + A ALT + F, W, A
Create a new contact	File, New, Contact	Right-click Contact Information viewer, New Contact	New		CTRL + SHIFT + C ALT + F, W, C
Create a new task	File, New, Task	Right-click Tasks Information viewer, New Task	New		CTRL + SHIFT + K ALT + F, W, T
Create a new journal	File, New, Journal Entry	Right-click Journal Information viewer, New Journal Entry	New		CTRL + SHIFT + J ALT + F, W, J
Create a new note	File, New, Note	Right-click Notes Information viewer, New Note	New		CTRL + SHIFT + N ALT + F, W, N
Save any item	File, Save		Save and Close		CTRL + S ALT + F, S
Edit an item	File, Open, Selected Items	Right-click item, Open			CTRL + O ALT + F, O, S
Exit Outlook	File, Exit	Right-click the application icon, click Close	X		ALT + F4 ALT + F, X
Create a new group		Right-click Outlook Bar, Add New Group			
Create a new folder	File, New, Folder		New, Folder		CTRL + SHIFT + E ALT + F, W, E
Add shortcut to Outlook Bar	File, New, Outlook Bar Shortcut	Right-click Outlook Bar, Outlook Bar Shortcut			ALT + F, W, B

outlook

Concepts Review

Circle the correct answer.

1. Which of the following is *not* a default Outlook folder?
[a] Calendar
[b] Appointments
[c] Inbox
[d] Sent Items

2. The Outlook Bar does *not* display:
[a] shortcuts to Outlook folders.
[b] categories.
[c] shortcuts to other folders on your computer.
[d] hyperlinks to Web pages.

3. Removing a group deletes:
[a] shortcuts to folders.
[b] folders, including any items in those folders.
[c] items in folders.
[d] valuable information from your hard drive.

4. To find saved e-mail messages you have not yet sent, you would look in:
[a] Inbox.
[b] Drafts.
[c] Outbox.
[d] Sent Items.

5. Which statement best describes Outlook Today's functionality?
[a] Outlook Today works like any other folder, storing items you create.
[b] Outlook Today displays upcoming activities, unfinished tasks, and information about unread messages.
[c] Outlook Today downloads and displays world news.
[d] Outlook Today cannot be customized.

6. Notes:
[a] contain many fields to track important information.
[b] track the progress toward completion of an important assignment.
[c] are a good place to permanently store contact information.
[d] are best for quickly jotting down ideas or small bits of information.

7. When items have been linked to a contact, you can find them in the Contact form on the:
[a] General tab.
[b] Details tab.
[c] Activities.
[d] Certificates.

8. Whenever you receive an attachment, you should:
[a] delete the attachment immediately.
[b] open the attachment immediately.
[c] let the attachment sit unopened in the Inbox for a week to weaken the virus.
[d] check with the sender to verify the attachment's contents, and scan the attachment for viruses.

9. Events last at least:
[a] 24 hours.
[b] 12 hours.
[c] 6 hours.
[d] 1 hour.

10. A meeting:
[a] involves only you.
[b] involves other Outlook users or company resources.
[c] cannot occur in your office.
[d] lasts more than a day.

Circle **T** if the statement is true, or **F** if the statement is false.

T F   1. You can reschedule an appointment by dragging the border of the appointment in Calendar view.

T F   2. The TAB key moves the insertion point to the next field on an Outlook form (message, appointment, etc.).

T F   3. The Send button on the Standard toolbar in the Message form sends the messages in the Outbox to the recipient(s) and downloads your messages into the Inbox.

T F   4. You cannot create your own categories.

T F   5. You can select multiple items in any folder by pressing and holding the SHIFT key or the CTRL key.

T F   6. You can create notes in any color you want.

T F   7. Natural language dates let you key phrases, such as "ten days ago," and "in two days" instead of dates.

T F   8. Attachments are computer files you can send with an e-mail message.

T F   9. You cannot customize the Outlook Today view.

T F   10. The Find bar can be used to help you locate items in any folder.

Skills Review

Exercise 1 ⒸC

1. Add at least five classmates to your Contacts.

2. For each contact, include the contact's full name, birthday, e-mail address, and nickname. Enter a note describing something unique about each person.

3. Create a message addressed to these five contacts thanking them for their time. Enter all the addresses in the To field, separating each address with a semicolon.

4. Save the message by clicking the Save button. This places the message in the Drafts folder.

5. Open the Drafts folder in the My Shortcuts group.

6. Open the message by double-clicking it, then click the Send button to move it to the Outbox.

7. Send the message by clicking on the Send/Receive button on the Outbox Standard toolbar, if necessary.

8. Switch to the Sent Items folder, and print a copy of the message you sent.

Exercise 2 ⒸC

1. Use Calendar to schedule a one-hour meeting tomorrow, starting at 10:00 AM.

2. Enter "Review progress on XYZ program beta testing" in the Subject field.

3. Click the Invite Attendees button. Select two people from your contact list to send this message. If necessary, add these contacts to your contact list.

4. Add a message in the notes field inviting these two contacts to the meeting.

5. Send the message.

6. Print a copy of your calendar for tomorrow only using Daily Style.
(*Hint:* Open the Print dialog box.)

outlook

Exercise 3 C

1. You teach computer classes at a local college. Switch to the Tasks folder and create your to-do list.

2. Create a new task to complete a lesson plan on computer basics.

3. Create a task to grade assignments in your advanced Excel class.

4. Set the percentage complete for the grading task to 50%.

5. Create a task to update your parking sticker for next semester.

6. Set the status of the parking task to Not Started.

7. Switch to the Calendar view and observe the tasks In the TaskPad.

8. Click the Complete check box for the parking task to change the status of this task to Completed.

Exercise 4

1. Create a note with the message "MSFT – Buy at 60."

2. Create a note with the message "MSFT – Sell at 65."

3. Create a note with the message "INTC – Sell at 35."

4. Change the color of the MSFT notes to red.

5. Change the color of the INTC note to green.

6. Change the Notes view to By Color.

7. Expand the red color and print the list.

Exercise 5

1. You work in a physician's office. Create a new contact for a patient (using fictional information). Include a phone number and birthday. In the notes field, enter information about two "visits" the contact made to the office.

2. Click the Categories button, then click the Master Category List button. Key "Patients" as a new category and click the Add button. Click OK, then click the Patients category.

3. Create two additional contacts (using fictional information). Include a phone number and birthday. In the notes field, enter information about two "visits" the contact made to the office. Add the Patients category.

4. Switch to the Contacts folder, and change the Contacts view to By Category.

5. Expand the Patients category.

6. Print a list of the contacts in the Patients category. (*Hint:* Select the contacts in the category, and then click the Print only selected rows option in the Print dialog box.)

Exercise 6

1. Create an appointment for the IT manager of your company to attend a training course next Tuesday between 8 AM and 12 PM. Show the time as Out of Office.

2. Create an office safety training meeting one week from Friday starting at 10 AM and lasting for one hour. Invite four employees. (*Hint:* Add four people to your contact list, if necessary.)

3. Create a task to remind yourself to get bagels for the meeting. Set a reminder one hour before the meeting.

4. Create an all-day event for the last Friday of the month at the local amusement park (or another recreational area close to where you live).

5. Compose an e-mail message about the upcoming employee appreciation party. Send it to the same four people you invited to the training meeting.

6. Print a calendar that shows the upcoming events and a task list (*Hint:* Preview the Print style option in the Print dialog box.)

Exercise 7

1. Use Print Preview to preview your contact list. If you don't have anyone in your contact list, create five contacts that include at least a full name and e-mail address.

2. Print all the contacts in Phone Directory Style. (*Hint:* Open the Print dialog box.)

Case Projects SCANS

Project 1

You are the office manager of a small business. Create an e-mail message reminding everyone about the company's efforts to recycle used ink cartridges. Instead of sending the message, save a copy of it as a text file by clicking Save As on the File menu, then changing the Save as type: list to Text Only.

Project 2

Your job is to train employees in the use of Outlook. Connect to the Internet and search the Web for Outlook tips to include in your weekly "Outlook Training Letter." Select one tip and create a short e-mail message with a step-by-step description of your tip. Provide the URL of any sites you used as references for your tip. Send this tip to yourself.

Project 3

You want to send an e-mail message to your state senator. Connect to the Internet and search the Web for the e-mail address of one of the U.S. senators who represent your state. Send the senator a message about an issue you feel is an important concern for people your age. Print a copy of the message you sent.

Project 4

You participate with a group of people who exchange favorite recipes. Find a recipe (on the Internet or at home) and enter it in an e-mail message. Send the message to a classmate, and ask them to reply with a recipe of their own. When you receive this message, forward it to another classmate you know. Print a copy of the e-mail you received.

Project 5

As the project manager on the Nakamichi Plaza project, you send frequent messages to many people. You want to include contact information about yourself with every message you send out. You need to create an electronic signature. Use the Ask A Question Box to research signatures. Use the information you find to create a new signature. Use

the title "Project Manager" for the signature. Enter the signature text to include with outgoing messages. Include your name and title, the company you work for (Walters, Robertson & Associates), and your business phone number (make one up). Verify that your new signature appears in the Use this signature by default box. Create a new message addressed to yourself. In the message, explain how you created the signature. Send the message. Download the message, if necessary, and then print the message you receive.

Project 6

You regularly send status reports of the Nakamichi Plaza project to the same group of contacts. Instead of selecting each contact when you send a report, you decide to create a distribution list—a group of preselected contacts to whom you assign an easy-to-remember name. You can enter this name as the recipient's address in any message, and Outlook automatically sends a copy of the message to each person in the list. Add three people to your contact list, including e-mail addresses. Switch to the Contacts folder and click the New Contact button list arrow on the Standard toolbar, and then click Distribution List. Add three people from your contact list to the new group, and name the group "Nakamichi Group." Create a new message with a project update. Enter Nakamichi Group in the To field and send the message.

Project 7

One way to identify important messages is by adding a flag. Use the Ask A Question Box to learn more about flags. You want to mark all Nakamichi Plaza messages with a flag to remind yourself to follow up. Ask two classmates to send you a message with "Nakamichi Plaza" in the subject field (or send these messages to yourself). Switch to the Inbox folder and then download the messages, if necessary. Right-click each message and click Flag for Follow Up. Assign a different follow-up flag to each message, and then print each message.

Project 8

As the IT manager for your company, you are concerned that people might inadvertently open attachments containing computer viruses. Create a list of tasks that includes the following items: research antivirus programs; research safe e-mail handling procedures for messages that contain attachments; schedule "E-mail attachment procedures" awareness class for company employees; invite employees to meeting. Print your task list using Table Style.

Project 9

Clean-up time! Open each folder and delete all the items you created in Outlook.

Microsoft
Word 2002
Introductory

Quick Start for Word

Chapter Overview

This chapter gives you a quick overview of creating, editing, printing, saving, and closing a document. To learn these skills, you create a new document, save and close it, then you open an existing document, revise the text, and save the document with both the same and a different name. This chapter also shows you how to view formatting marks and Smart Tags, zoom the document window, and move the insertion point. In addition, you learn to identify the components of the Word window and create a folder on your hard drive to store your documents. You use these basic skills every time you create or edit a document in Word.

LEARNING OBJECTIVES

- ▶ Identify the components of the Word window
- ▶ Compose a simple document
- ▶ Edit a document
- ▶ Save a document
- ▶ Preview and print a document
- ▶ Close a document
- ▶ Locate and open an existing document
- ▶ Create a new document
- ▶ Close the Word application

Case profile

Today is your first day as a new employee at Worldwide Exotic Foods, Inc., one of the world's fastest growing distributors of specialty food items. The company's mission is to provide customers with an unusual selection of meats, cheeses, pastries, fruits, and vegetables from around the world. You report to Chris Lofton, the Word Processing Department manager, to complete an introduction to the Word 2002 word processing application.

chapter
one

notes This text assumes that you have little or no knowledge of the Word application. However, it is assumed that you have read Office Chapters 1–3 of this book and that you are familiar with Windows 98 or Windows 2000 concepts.

The illustrations in this book were created using Windows 2000. If you are using the Word application installed on Windows 98, you may notice a few minor differences in some figures. These differences do not affect your work in this book.

1.a Identifying the Components of the Word Window

Before you can begin to work with Word, you need to open the application. When you open the application, a new, blank document opens as well. To open the Word application and a new, blank document:

Step 1	*Click*	the Start button [Start] on the taskbar
Step 2	*Point to*	Programs
Step 3	*Click*	Microsoft Word

When the Word application opens, it contains a blank document with the temporary name *Document1*. Word has many different ways to view a document. The new, blank document is in Print Layout view. However, you want to switch the document to Normal view. Changing document views is discussed in more detail in later chapters. To change the view to Normal view:

Step 1	*Click*	View
Step 2	*Click*	Normal

Your screen should look similar to Figure 1-1, which identifies the specific components of the Word application window.

chapter one

FIGURE 1-1
Word Application Window
with a Blank Document

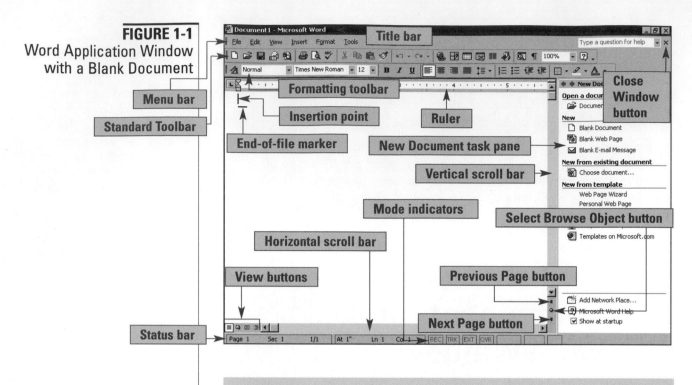

 notes For the activities in this text, you view your documents in Normal view unless otherwise instructed.

Menu Bar

The **menu bar**, located below the title bar, contains nine drop-down menu commands that contain groups of additional, related commands. For example, the File menu contains commands for opening, closing, previewing, and printing files. You can use the mouse or the keyboard to select a command from the menu bar. The activities in this book instruct you to select menu bar commands with the mouse. The Commands Review section at the end of each chapter provides a summary of both mouse and keyboard techniques to select a menu command.

Standard Toolbar

The **Standard toolbar** is located beneath the menu bar and is made up of buttons that represent commonly used commands. For example, the Standard toolbar contains buttons for opening saving, previewing, and printing a file. The Standard toolbar allows you to perform commands quickly by clicking the button that represents that command. You can customize the Standard toolbar (or any other toolbar) by adding or deleting buttons.

Formatting Toolbar

The **Formatting toolbar** is located under the Standard toolbar in Figure 1-1 and is made up of buttons that represent commonly used formats. For example, the Formatting toolbar contains buttons for changing text appearance, such as the font or text alignment.

Ruler

The horizontal **ruler**, located under the Formatting toolbar, provides features you can use to change the tab settings, margins, and indentations in your document.

Insertion Point

The blinking vertical bar in the upper-left corner below the horizontal ruler is the insertion point. The **insertion point** marks the location where text is entered in a document.

End-of-file Marker

The short horizontal line below the insertion point is the **end-of-file marker** that marks the point below which you cannot enter text. This marker moves down as you insert additional lines of text in the document. The end-of-file marker is visible only in Normal view.

Select Browse Object Button

You can use the **Select Browse Object button**, located below the vertical scroll bar, to choose the specific item—such as text, graphics, and tables—you want to use to move or browse through a document.

Previous Page and Next Page Buttons

You use the **Previous Page button** and **Next Page button**, also located below the vertical scroll bar, to move the insertion point to the top of the previous or next page in a multipage document. When you specify a different browse object, the button name changes to include that object, such as Previous Comment or Next Comment. Clicking the buttons moves you to the previous or next browse object specified.

View Buttons

Word has several editing **views**—or ways to look at a document as you edit it. The Normal View, Web Layout View, Print Layout View, and Outline View buttons, located to the left of the horizontal scroll bar, can be used to view and work with your document in a different way. Normal view is the best view for most word-processing tasks, such as keying, editing, and basic formatting. Web Layout view shows how

---

M OUSE TIP

The Standard and Formatting toolbars appear on the same row when you first install Office XP. In this position, only the most commonly used buttons of each toolbar are visible. All the other default buttons appear on the Toolbar Options drop-down lists. As you use buttons from the Toolbar Options drop-down list, they move to the visible buttons on the toolbar, while the buttons you don't use move into the Toolbar Options drop-down list. If you arrange the Formatting toolbar below the Standard toolbar, all buttons are visible. Unless otherwise noted, the illustrations in this book show the Formatting toolbar positioned below the Standard toolbar.

chapter one

your document will look if displayed in a Web browser. Print Layout view shows how your document will look when printed on paper. Outline view displays your document in outline format so you can work on its structure and organization.

Status Bar

The **status bar** appears at the bottom of the screen above the taskbar, and provides information about your document and a task in progress. It indicates the current page number (Page 1), the current section of the document (Sec 1), and the current page followed by the number of pages in the document (1/1). In the center of the status bar you see indicators for the current vertical position of the insertion point measured in inches (At 1"), the current line number of the insertion point on that page (Ln 1), and the horizontal position of the insertion point (Col 1).

There may be up to six mode indicators at the right of the status bar. These indicators provide mouse shortcuts to: record a macro (REC), track changes (TRK), extend a text selection (EXT), type over existing text (OVR), check the spelling and grammar in the document (Spelling and Grammar Status), and change the language. (The Language mode indicator may be blank, depending on the language selections during installation; the Spelling and Grammar Status mode indicator is blank unless the document contains text).

Task Pane

The **New Document task pane**, located on the right side of the application window, gives you the capability of quickly creating a new document or opening an existing document. Word includes task panes for viewing the items on the Clipboard, searching for text, inserting clip art, applying styles and formatting to selected text, displaying formatting properties of selected text, for mail merge, and translating text to another language.

1.b Composing a Simple Document

Chris gives you a short paragraph to key. As you key the text, it is visible on the screen and resides in your computer's memory. Word uses a feature called **word wrap** to automatically move words that do not fit on the current line to the next line. As a result, you can key the text without worrying about how much text fits on a line. You do not press the ENTER key at the end of each line. You press the ENTER key only to end a paragraph or to create a blank line.

The paragraph in Step 1 below contains two intentional errors. Key the text exactly as it appears. If you make additional errors, just continue keying the text. You learn two methods of correcting keying errors in the next section. Remember, do not press the ENTER key at the end of each line. To key the text:

Step 1	*Key*	Worldwide Exotic Foods, Inc. is one of the fastest-growing distributors of specialty food items. Worldwide Exotic Foods branch offices in Chicago, Illinois, Melbourne, Australia, Vancouver, Canada, and London, England, and specializes in supplying high-quality and unusual food products too customers around the world.

Next, you correct any keying errors in the paragraph.

1.c Editing a Document

One of the important benefits of using Word is the ability to easily modify a document by inserting, removing, or editing text without having to key the document again. When you position the mouse pointer in a text area, it changes shape to look like a large "I" and is called the **I-beam**. You use the I-beam to position the insertion point in the text area where you want to correct keying errors or add new text. Recall that the insertion point is the blinking vertical bar that indicates where the next keyed character will appear. The text you just entered contains at least two errors. The first error you should correct is a missing word in the second sentence. To insert the word "has:"

Step 1	*Move*	the I-beam before the "b" in the word "branch" in the second sentence
Step 2	*Click*	the mouse button to position the insertion point

Your screen should look similar to Figure 1-2.

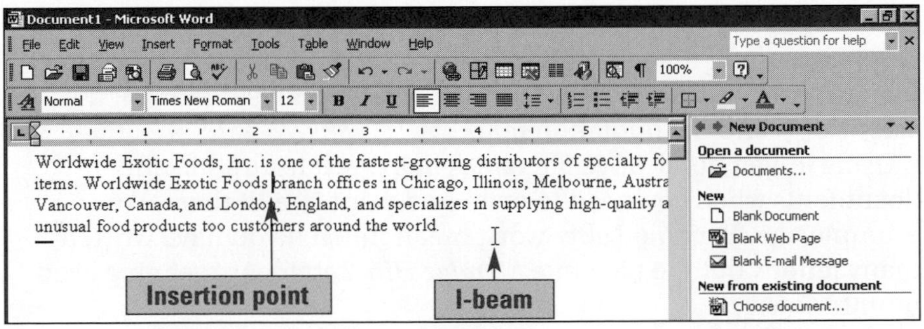

> **CAUTION TIP**
>
> Certain words or phrases may have a red or green wavy line underneath. The red line indicates the word is misspelled or not in the Word English-language dictionary or any custom dictionaries being used. The green line indicates a possible grammar error. Chapter 3 discusses the Spelling and Grammar features.

FIGURE 1-2
Repositioned Insertion Point

**chapter
one**

Document1 - Microsoft Word

File Edit View Insert Format Tools Table Window Help

Normal   Times New Roman   12   B I U

Worldwide Exotic Foods, Inc. is one of the fastest-growing distributors of specialty fo items. Worldwide Exotic Foods branch offices in Chicago, Illinois, Melbourne, Austra Vancouver, Canada, and London, England, and specializes in supplying high-quality a unusual food products too customers around the world.

New Document

Open a document
Documents...

New
Blank Document
Blank Web Page
Blank E-mail Message

New from existing document
Choose document...

Insertion point   **I-beam**

Step 3	*Key*	has
Step 4	*Press*	the SPACEBAR

The second error is an extra letter "o" in the word "too" in the last sentence, which you need to delete. To delete the letter "o":

Step 1	*Move*	the I-beam before the second "o" in the word "too" in the last sentence
Step 2	*Click*	the mouse button to position the insertion point
Step 3	*Press*	the DELETE key
Step 4	*Correct*	any additional errors, if necessary, by repositioning the insertion point and inserting or deleting text

While you are creating or editing a document, every change you make is stored temporarily in your computer's memory. If the power to your computer fails or you turn off the computer, your work is lost. You can prevent such a loss by frequently saving the document to a disk.

1.d Saving a Document

You can save files to a floppy disk, an internal hard disk, or a network server. When you save a file for the first time, it does not matter whether you choose the <u>S</u>ave command or the Save <u>A</u>s command on the <u>F</u>ile menu, or click the Save button on the Standard toolbar. Regardless of which method you use, the Save As dialog box opens—providing a way for you to give your document a new name and specify the disk drive and folder location where you want to save the document.

After you have specified the location for saving your document, you key the name of the document in the File <u>n</u>ame: text box. A filename can have up to 255 characters—including the disk drive reference and path—and can contain letters, numbers, spaces, and some special characters in any combination. Filenames cannot include the following special characters: the forward slash (/), the backward slash (\), the colon (:), the semicolon (;), the pipe symbol (|), the question mark (?), the less than symbol (<), the greater than symbol (>), the asterisk (*), and the quotation mark (").

Using longer descriptive filenames helps you locate specific documents when you need to open and print or edit them. For example, the filename *Letter* won't mean much if you have written many letters, but the filename *Mendez Hire Letter* has meaning even months later.

notes Be sure to check with your instructor if you do not know the disk drive and folder in which to save your documents.

To save your document:

| **Step 1** | *Click* | the Save button 💾 on the Standard toolbar |

The Save As dialog box on your screen should look similar to Figure 1-3.

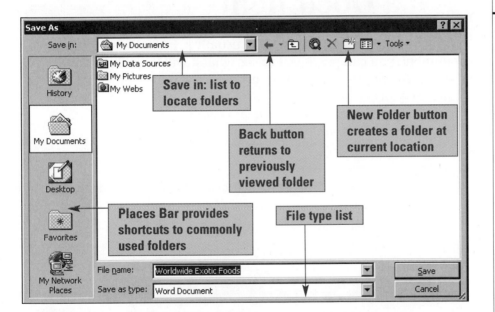

FIGURE 1-3
Save As Dialog Box

You can quickly locate a folder with the Save in: list, move back to the previous viewed folder contents with the Back button, move up one level in the Save in: list, launch the Internet Explorer Web browser and search the Web, delete selected folders or files, create a new folder in the current location, change the viewing options for the folder icons, and change the file type with options in this dialog box. For easier access to commonly used folders, the Save As dialog box also contains a **Places Bar**, which provides shortcuts for opening the My Documents and Favorites folders. You can view any icons on your Windows desktop with the Desktop shortcut in the Places Bar. My Network Places shortcut in the Places Bar allows you to display the computers on your network. The History shortcut on the Places Bar provides access to shortcuts to recently opened folders and files.

| **Step 2** | *Click* | the Save in: list arrow |

INTERNET TIP

You can save your documents as HTML documents (Web pages) by clicking the Save As Web Page command on the File menu or by changing the file type to Web Page in the Save As dialog box.

MENU TIP

To view different save options, click the Options command on the Tools menu, and then click the Save tab in the Options dialog box. Other important Options tabs you should review are User Information, Compatibility, and File Locations.

chapter one

Step 3	**Switch to**	the appropriate disk drive and folder as designated by your instructor
Step 4	**Key**	Company Profile in the File name: text box
Step 5	**Click**	Save

After the document is saved, the document name *Company Profile* appears in place of *Document1* on the title bar.

C **1.e** Previewing and Printing a Document

After you create a document, you usually print it. Before printing a document, you can preview it to see what it will look like when printed. You do not have to preview the document before printing it. However, you can save paper by previewing your document and making any necessary changes before printing it.

To preview the *Company Profile* document and then print it:

| Step 1 | **Click** | the Print Preview button 🔍 on the Standard toolbar |

The Print Preview window opens. Your screen should look similar to Figure 1-4.

FIGURE 1-4
Print Preview Window

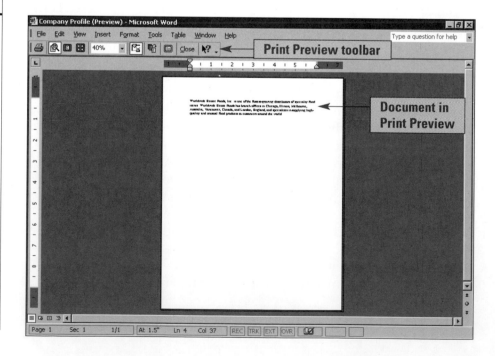

When you preview a document, you are verifying that the document text is attractively and appropriately positioned on the page. If necessary, you can change the document layout on the page, key additional text, and change the appearance of the text as you preview it. For now, you should close Print Preview and return to the original view of the document.

| Step 2 | *Click* | the <u>C</u>lose button Close on the Print Preview toolbar |
| Step 3 | *Click* | the Print button 🖨 on the Standard toolbar |

You are finished with the *Company Profile* for now, so you can close the document.

1.f Closing a Document

When you use the Word application, you can have as many documents open in the memory of your computer as your computer resources will allow. However, after you finish a document you should close it or remove it from the computer's memory to conserve those resources. To close the *Company Profile* document:

| Step 1 | *Click* | the Close Window button ☒ in the upper-right corner of the menu bar |

When documents are closed from the <u>F</u>ile menu or the Close Window button on the menu bar, the Word application window remains open. This window is sometimes called the **null screen**. To continue working in Word from the null screen, you can open an existing document or create a new, blank document.

1.g Locating and Opening an Existing Document

When you want to edit an existing document, you need to open a copy of it from the disk where it is stored. From inside the Word application, you can open a document in three ways: (1) with the <u>O</u>pen command on the <u>F</u>ile menu, (2) with the Open button on the

QUICK TIP

To customize the Places Bar, select the folder you want to add and then click the Add to "My Places" command on the Tools menu in the Save As or Open dialog box. To reposition a shortcut on the Places Bar or to remove a custom shortcut from the Places Bar simply right-click the shortcut and click the desired command on the shortcut menu.

MENU TIP

You can preview a document with the Print Pre<u>v</u>iew command on the <u>F</u>ile menu. You can print a document with the <u>P</u>rint command on the <u>F</u>ile menu.

To select print options, you must use the <u>P</u>rint command. The Print button prints the document based on the options previously selected in the Print dialog box.

chapter
one

Standard toolbar, or (3) with a shortcut on the New Document task pane. Any of these methods opens the Open dialog box. In this dialog box you first select the disk drive and folder where the document is located. Then you can select the specific document you want from a list of documents available at that location.

Chris asks you to open an existing document that contains several paragraphs so that you can see how to scroll and move the insertion point in a larger document. To open an existing document:

Step 1	*Verify*	that the New Document Task Pane is visible
Step 2	*Click*	the link More Documents in the New Document task pane
Step 3	*Observe*	the Open dialog box, which is similar to the Save As dialog box
Step 4	*Click*	the Look in: list arrow to display a list of locations
Step 5	*Switch to*	the disk drive and folder where the Data Files are stored
Step 6	*Double-click*	New Expense Guidelines

The document contains characters you can see as well as characters you cannot see.

Viewing Formatting Marks and Smart Tags

When you create a document Word automatically inserts some characters that you do not see called **formatting marks**. For example, each time you press the ENTER key to create a new line, a paragraph mark character (¶) is inserted in the document. Other formatting marks include tab characters (→) and spaces (·) between words. Sometimes these formatting marks are called **nonprinting characters** because they do not print, but they can be viewed on the screen.

You may want to view the formatting marks to help you edit a document. The Show/Hide button on the Standard toolbar turns on or off the view of formatting marks. To show the formatting marks:

Step 1	*Click*	the Show/Hide button ¶ on the Standard toolbar

Your screen should look similar to Figure 1-5.

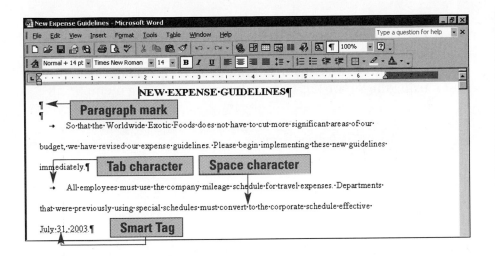

FIGURE 1-5
Formatting Marks and
Smart Tags

CAUTION TIP

If you edit a document and then try to close it without saving, Word opens a message dialog box prompting you to save your changes.

Paragraph marks appear at the end of each paragraph, the tab character at the beginning of each paragraph, and the space indicators between each word. You won't be formatting this document now, so you can hide the formatting marks. To turn off the view of formatting marks:

| Step 2 | *Click* | the Show/Hide button ¶ on the Standard toolbar |

notes The illustrations in this text assume the Smart Tag label and button options in the AutoCorrect dialog box are turned on.

Observe the dotted purple line below the text "July 31, 2003" in the second paragraph. This indicates that the underlined text has a Smart Tag. You can display the Smart Tag Actions button and menu options by simply moving the mouse pointer to the Smart Tag text. To observe the Smart Tag Actions button and menu:

Step 1	*Move*	the mouse pointer to the text "July 31, 2003"
Step 2	*Observe*	the Smart Tag Actions button ⓘ
Step 3	*Move*	the mouse pointer to the Smart Tag Actions button to activate it
Step 4	*Observe*	that the Smart Tag Actions button changes color and a list arrow appears, indicating a drop-down menu is available
Step 5	*Click*	the Smart Tag Actions button list arrow to view the Smart Tag menu

TASK PANE TIP

The New Document task pane closes when you create a new, blank document from the New button on the Standard toolbar or when you open an existing document. To show the New Document task pane you can click the New command on the File menu or, if the New Document task pane was the last task pane closed, you can click the Task Pane command on the toolbar shortcut menu to redisplay the New Document task pane.

To close any task pane, click the Close button on the task pane title bar.

**chapter
one**

Your screen should look similar to Figure 1-6. You can remove the Smart Tag, create an Outlook appointment item or schedule a meeting using Outlook, or view the Smart Tag options in the AutoCorrect dialog box with options in this menu. For now, you do not want to take any action using the Smart Tag, so you close the Smart Tag menu.

FIGURE 1-6
Smart Tag Menu

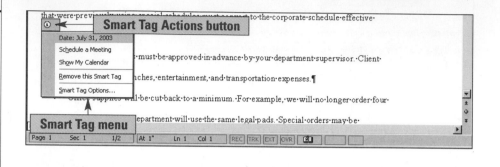

| Step 6 | *Press* | the ESC key or click in the document outside the menu |

Whether or not the formatting marks are visible, you can take a closer look at your document.

Zooming the Document Window

When creating a document, you may want to enlarge your document to read the text more easily or look at a miniature view of an entire page to see how the text is arranged on the page. Resizing the view is called **zooming** the document.

You can zoom a document from 10% to 500% of the actual size. You also can resize the view to show the document's entire width by using the Page Width option. To make the text appear larger on the screen, increase the zoom percentage. To make the text appear smaller on the screen, decrease the zoom percentage. Zooming your document changes only the view on the screen; it does not change the size of characters on the printed document. To zoom the *New Expense Guidelines* document:

Step 1	*Click*	the Zoom button list arrow `100%` on the Standard toolbar
Step 2	*Click*	200%
Step 3	*Observe*	that the Zoom text box indicates 200% and the text is very large
Step 4	*Click*	the Zoom button list arrow `100%` on the Standard toolbar
Step 5	*Click*	Page Width to view the entire width of the document

QUICK TIP

Word displays Smart Tag labels and action buttons if the Smart Tag labels and action buttons features have been turned on. You can turn the Smart Tag labels and action buttons on or off in the Smart Tag tab of the AutoCorrect dialog box.

MENU TIP

You can change the view of your document by clicking the Zoom command on the View menu.

Being able to change the document view is helpful when you are formatting a document. However, when using large zoom percentages or viewing large documents, you might need to scroll to display other parts of your document.

Using the Scroll Bars

When you want to view different parts of a document without moving the insertion point, use the vertical and horizontal scroll bars. Scrolling changes only that part of the document you see in the document window; it does not change your keying position in the document. The scroll bars appear on the right side and bottom of the window above the status bar. The **vertical scroll bar** enables you to scroll up and down in your document. The **horizontal scroll bar** allows you to scroll left and right in your document. A scroll bar has two scroll arrows. A gray shaded area containing a scroll box separates these scroll arrows. The **scroll box** represents your viewing position in the document. For example, if the vertical scroll box appears in the middle of the vertical scroll bar, you are viewing the middle of your document. (Figure 1-1 also identifies the vertical and horizontal scroll bars.) Table 1-1 summarizes how to view a document using the scroll bars.

To Scroll	Do This
Down one line	Click the down scroll arrow
Up one line	Click the up scroll arrow
Down one screen	Click the gray shaded area below the vertical scroll box
Up one screen	Click the gray shaded area above the vertical scroll box
Up or down one page	Click and hold the scroll box on the vertical scroll bar to see the current page number, drag the scroll box to a new page, and release when the ScreenTip shows the page number you want.
End of a document	Drag the vertical scroll box to the bottom of the vertical scroll bar
Beginning of a document	Drag the vertical scroll box to the top of the vertical scroll bar
Right side of document	Click the right scroll arrow
Left side of document	Click the left scroll arrow
Far right side of document	Click the gray shaded area right of the horizontal scroll box
Far left side of document	Click the gray shaded area left of the horizontal scroll box
Beyond the left margin (in Normal view)	SHIFT + Click the left scroll arrow on the horizontal scroll bar
Beyond the right margin (in Normal view)	SHIFT + Click the right scroll arrow on the horizontal scroll bar
To hide the area beyond the left margin (in Normal view)	Click the horizontal scroll box

> **QUICK TIP**
>
> You can change the document zoom by keying a value from 10 to 500 in the text area of the Zoom button. Click the Zoom button text area, key a value, and then press the ENTER key.

TABLE 1-1
Navigating a Document with the Scroll Bars

chapter
one

Moving the Insertion Point

You have already learned how to move the insertion point using the I-beam. You can also use the Next Page, Previous Page, and Select Browse Object buttons to move the insertion point, as explained in Table 1-2. (You must be working in a multipage document to move the insertion point to another page.)

TABLE 1-2
Moving the insertion point

To Move the Insertion Point to	Do This
a new page	Click the Select Browse Object button below the vertical scroll bar and then click the Browse by Page button
the top of the next page	Click the Next Page button below the vertical scroll bar
the top of the previous page	Click the Previous Page button below the vertical scroll bar

You also can use the keyboard to move the insertion point in your document. Table 1-3 summarizes the ways you can do this.

TABLE 1-3
Moving the Insertion Point with the Keyboard

To Move	Press	To Move	Press
Right one character	RIGHT ARROW	**To the top of the next page**	CTRL + PAGE DOWN
Left one character	LEFT ARROW	**To the top of the previous page**	CTRL + PAGE UP
Right one word	CTRL + RIGHT ARROW	**Up one line**	UP ARROW
Left one word	CTRL + LEFT ARROW	**Down one line**	DOWN ARROW
Down one paragraph	CTRL + DOWN ARROW	**Up one screen**	PAGE UP
Up one paragraph	CTRL + UP ARROW	**Down one screen**	PAGE DOWN
Beginning of the line	HOME	**To the beginning of a document**	CTRL + HOME
End of the line	END	**To the end of a document**	CTRL + END
Back to the previous position of the insertion point or to a previous revision	SHIFT + F5	**To go to a specific line or page or section or table or graphic**	F5
To the top of the window	ALT + CTRL + PAGE UP	**To the bottom of the window**	ALT + CTRL + PAGE DOWN

> **QUICK TIP**
>
> If you are using the IntelliMouse pointing device, you can use the scrolling wheel to scroll a document. For more information on using the IntelliMouse pointing device, see online Help.

When instructed to scroll to change the view or move the insertion point to a different location, use one of the methods described in Table 1-1, 1-2, or 1-3.

To move the insertion point:

| Step 1 | *Practice* | using the mouse and keyboard to move the insertion point in the *New Expense Guidelines* document |
| Step 2 | *Close* | the *New Expense Guidelines* document without saving any changes |

Using the Save Command

You can open a copy of an existing document, edit it, and then save it with the same name to update the document on the disk. You want to edit the *Company Profile* document you created earlier. To open the *Company Profile* document:

Step 1	*Click*	the Open button on the Standard toolbar
Step 2	*Switch to*	the appropriate disk drive and folder
Step 3	*Double-click*	*Company Profile*

The file you selected opens in the document window. You edit the document by inserting text. To add an additional paragraph:

Step 1	*Move*	the insertion point to the end of the last sentence
Step 2	*Press*	the ENTER key twice
Step 3	*Key*	Contact us 24 hours a day, seven days a week at our Web site, www.exoticfoods.com.
Step 4	*Press*	the SPACEBAR

Notice that when you press the SPACEBAR after keying the Web site address and period, Word underlines the Web site address *www.exoticfoods.com* and changes the color to blue. This indicates the text is a hyperlink. A **hyperlink** is text or a picture that is associated with the path to another page. For now, you don't want the Web site address text in your document blue and underlined, so you remove the hyperlink formatting by clicking the Undo button on the Standard toolbar or pressing the CTRL + Z shortcut key combination. Then you save the document to update the copy on the disk.

| Step 5 | *Click* | the Undo button ↰ on the Standard toolbar |
| Step 6 | *Click* | the Save button 🖫 on the Standard toolbar |

chapter
one

The copy of the document on disk is updated to include the additional paragraph.

Creating a Folder and Using the Save As Command

Sometimes you may want to keep both the original document and the edited document in different files on the disk. This allows you to keep a backup copy of the original document for later use or reference. To do this, you can save the edited document with a different name. If you want to create a new folder in which to store the modified document, you can create it from Windows Explorer or from inside the Word Save As dialog box.

notes   Check with your instructor, if necessary, for additional instructions on where to create your new folder.

You need to make an additional edit to *Company Profile* by adding the telephone number. This time, after you edit the document you save it to a new location and with a new name so that the document is available both with and without the phone number. To edit the document, create a new folder, and save the document with a new name:

Step 1	*Key*	You may also contact us at (312) 555-1234.
Step 2	*Click*	File
Step 3	*Click*	Save As
Step 4	*Click*	the Create New Folder button in the Save As dialog box
Step 5	*Key*	Completed Files Folder in the Name: text box
Step 6	*Click*	OK to create and open the new folder
Step 7	*Key*	Company Profile Revised in the File name: text box
Step 8	*Click*	Save

You leave this new copy of the document open while you create a new, blank document.

1.h Creating a New Document

From inside the Word application, you can create a new, blank document in two ways: (1) click the New command on the File menu to open the New Document task pane, or (2) click the New Blank Document button on the Standard toolbar. Each document you create in Word is based on a model document called a **template**. When you create a new document using the New Blank Document button on the Standard toolbar, the document is based on the **Normal template**, which is the basic, default Word document model. When you create a document from shortcuts the New Document task pane, you can access a selection of templates for special documents such as letters, memos, and reports.

To create a new, blank document:

Step 1	*Click*	the New Blank Document button on the Standard toolbar

You should have two documents open, *Company Profile Revised* and a blank document. You can switch easily between open Word documents with the <u>W</u>indow command on the menu bar or from the taskbar. To switch to the *Company Profile Revised* document:

Step 1	*Click*	the *Company Profile Revised* taskbar button

You are now viewing the *Company Profile Revised* document. You could work in this document, or return to the new, blank document and work in that document. For now, however, you are finished. When you finish using Word, you should exit or close the application and any open documents.

1.i Closing the Word Application

You can close the Word application without first closing the open documents. If you modify open documents and then attempt to close the Word application without first saving the modified documents, a dialog box prompts you to save the changes you have made.

To close the application:

Step 1	*Click*	<u>F</u>ile
Step 2	*Click*	E<u>x</u>it

The Word application and both open documents close. Because you did not use the blank document, Word did not prompt you to save changes. Also, because you saved the *Company Profile Revised* document after you last modified it, Word closed the document without prompting you to save it.

chapter
one

Summary

- The components of the Word window in Normal view include the title bar, the Standard and Formatting toolbars, the horizontal ruler, the insertion point, the end-of-file marker, the Previous Page and Next Page buttons, the Select Browse Object button, the View buttons, the vertical and horizontal scroll bars and scroll boxes, the status bar, and the New Document task pane.

- Pressing the ENTER key creates a blank line or a new paragraph.

- You can remove text from your document with the DELETE or BACKSPACE key.

- When you create or edit text, changes are temporarily stored in your computer's memory.

- Word wrap is a word processing feature that automatically moves words that do not fit on the current line to the next line.

- To preserve changes to your document, you should save the document frequently.

- Documents must be saved with unique filenames that can be up to 255 characters long, including the disk drive reference and path.

- When you save a document for the first time, you must specify the disk drive and folder where the document will be stored.

- Before printing a document, it is a good practice to preview it to see what it will look like when it is printed.

- You can have as many documents open as your computer's resources allow; however, it is a good practice to close a document when you finish working with it to conserve these resources.

- You can move the insertion point with both the mouse and the keyboard.

- You can view the special formatting marks inserted by Word with the Show/Hide button.

- You can turn on the Smart Tags labels and action buttons in the AutoCorrect dialog box and then view the individual Smart Tag options with the mouse pointer.

- Zooming the document window allows you to increase or decrease the viewing size of the text.

- The vertical and horizontal scroll bars allow you to view different parts of a document without moving the insertion point.

- When all documents are closed, the Word application remains open and you see the null screen.

- To edit an existing document, you can open a copy of the document stored on a disk.

- After opening and editing an existing document, you usually save it again with the same name and in the same location; however, you can save it with a new name or new location.

- You can easily create a new folder for storing documents from the Save As dialog box.

- When you finish using Word, you should close the application.

Commands Review

Action	Menu Bar	Shortcut Menu	Toolbar	Task Pane	Keyboard
Create a new line or end a paragraph					ENTER
Remove a character to the left of the insertion point					BACKSPACE
Remove a character to the right of the insertion point					DELETE
Save a document for the first time or save a document with a new name or to a new location	File, Save As				ALT + F, A F12
Save a document for the first time or save a previously named and saved document	File, Save		🖫		ALT + F, S CTRL + S SHIFT + F12 ALT + SHIFT + F2
Preview a document	File, Print Preview		🔍		ALT + F, V CTRL + F2
Print a document	File, Print		🖨		ALT + F, P CTRL + P CTRL + SHIFT + F12
Close a document	File, Close	Right-click the document taskbar button, click Close	✕ on title bar ✕ on menu bar		ALT + F, C CTRL + W CTRL + F4
Open an existing document	File, Open		📂	Open a document link in New Document task pane	ALT + F, O CTRL + O CTRL + F12 ALT + CTRL + F2
Create a new, blank document	File, New		◻	Blank Document link, Choose document link, or New from template links in New Document task pane	ALT + F, N CTRL + N

chapter one

Action	Menu Bar	Shortcut Menu	Toolbar	Task Pane	Keyboard
Zoom a document	View, Zoom		100% ▼		ALT + V, Z
Show formatting marks	Tools, Options, View tab, All		¶		ALT + T, O, A
Close the Word application	File, Exit	Right-click the application button on the taskbar, click Close	✕ on menu bar		ALT + F, X ALT + F4

Concepts Review

Circle the correct answer.

1. The Standard toolbar appears in the Word application window below the:
   [a] menu bar.
   [b] status bar.
   [c] Formatting toolbar.
   [d] scroll bar.

2. When you are completely finished working with a document you should:
   [a] edit it.
   [b] hide formatting marks.
   [c] key it.
   [d] save it.

3. Zooming the document window:
   [a] shows the formatting marks.
   [b] allows you to delete text.
   [c] moves text to the bottom of the document.
   [d] increases or decreases the viewing size of text.

4. The insertion point:
   [a] is located under the Standard toolbar and contains shortcut buttons.
   [b] indicates the location where text is keyed in a document.
   [c] provides features for changing margins, tabs, and indentations.
   [d] always appears at the bottom of the screen above the taskbar.

5. To preserve any changes to the document currently visible on your screen, it is a good idea to:
   [a] save the document frequently.
   [b] preview the document.
   [c] move the document to the null screen.
   [d] scroll the document.

6. The Select Browse Object button is located:
   [a] below the Formatting toolbar.
   [b] on the menu bar.
   [c] in the lower-left corner of the Word screen.
   [b] below the vertical scroll bar.

7. To save a document for the first time, you can click the:
   [a] Select Browse Object button.
   [b] New Blank Document button.
   [c] Print button.
   [d] Save button.

8. When you key a document that contains errors, you should:
   [a] close the document.
   [b] preview and print the document.
   [c] save the document.
   [d] edit the document.

9. Which of the following characters can be used in a filename?
   [a] period (.)
   [b] asterisk (*)
   [c] pipe symbol (|)
   [d] question mark (?)

10. If you edit a document and then try to close the Word application, Word:
    [a] automatically saves the changes without a message prompt.
    [b] closes without saving any changes to the document.
    [c] opens a message prompt dialog box asking you to save changes.
    [d] requires you to save the changes to the document.

Circle **T** if the statement is true or **F** if the statement is false.

T F   1. If you are creating or editing a document, any changes you make are stored temporarily in your computer's memory.

T F   2. When using Word, you need to press the ENTER key at the end of each line of text to move the insertion point back to the left margin.

T F   3. When you have finished working on a document, Word automatically saves the document to disk.

T F   4. The Formatting toolbar is located below the ruler and consists of buttons that represent commonly used commands.

T F   5. The Save As dialog box opens the first time you save a document.

T F   6. You can create a new document based on an existing document using a shortcut on the New Document task pane.

T F   7. You can view Smart Tag labels, action buttons, and options when the Smart Tag feature is turned on in the Open dialog box.

T F   8. You can use letters, numbers, and some special characters in a filename.

T F   9. When all documents are closed, the null screen appears.

T F   10. You can move the insertion point to the top of individual pages of a multiple page document with the scroll arrows.

notes   The Skills Review exercises sometimes instruct you to create a document. The text you key is shown in italics. Do not format the text with italics unless specified to do so. Your text may word wrap differently from the text shown. Do not press the ENTER key at the end of a line of text to force it to wrap the same way.

Skills Review   SCANS

Exercise 1 C

1. Create a new, blank document using the New Blank Document button on the Standard toolbar and key the following text exactly as shown, including the intentional errors. You correct the text in Exercise 2.

Spreadsheet software is a commmon type of computer application software. Other types of applications include word processing, database management, presentation, communication, and Internet browser.

2. Save the document as *Application Software*. Preview, print, and close the document.

chapter one

Exercise 2   C

1. Open the *Application Software* document you created in Exercise 1 using a shortcut on the New Document task pane.

2. Delete the extra "m" in the word "common" in the first sentence and delete the word "applications" and replace it with the word "software" in the second sentence.

3. Delete the word "Internet" and replace it with the word "Web" in the second sentence.

4. Save the document as *Application Software Revised*. Preview, print, and close the document.

Exercise 3   C

1. Create a new, blank document using a shortcut on the New Document task pane and key the following text exactly as shown, including the intentional errors. You correct the text in Exercise 4.

Word processing provides an individual with an effective and efficient means of preparing documents. You can create documents and quickly make needed changes prior to printing the document. The software allows your to save the document in a file for later use.

2. Save the document as *Word Processing*. Preview, print, and close the document.

Exercise 4   C

1. Open the *Word Processing* document you created in Exercise 3 using the Open button on the Standard toolbar.

2. Delete the words "and efficient" in the first sentence of the first paragraph.

3. Delete the words "the document" and replace them with the word "them" in the second sentence.

4. Delete the character "r" in the word "your" in the last sentence.

5. Save the document as *Word Processing Revised*. Preview, print, and close the document.

Exercise 5   C

1. Create a new, blank document using a shortcut on the New Document task pane and key the following text exactly as shown, including the intentional errors. You correct the text in Exercise 6.

The purchasing department will be ordering employee handboooks for the new employees hired during the month of May. Please determine how many handbooks you need and contact Kelly Armstead at ext. 154 by Monday.

2. Save the document as *Employee Handbooks*. Preview, print, and close the document.

Exercise 6   C

1. Open the *Employee Handbooks* document you created in Exercise 5 using a shortcut on the New Document task pane.

2. Delete the extra "o" in "handboooks" in the first sentence.

3. Insert the word "next" before the word "Monday" in the last sentence.

4. Save the document as *Employee Handbooks Revised*. Preview, print, and close the document.

Exercise 7   C

1. Create the following document, making the noted changes.

> Your monthly sales projection is due on ~~Wednesday~~. Please note that the minimum number of units sold per month must be 1,000. Contact Betty McManners or Jim Davidson if you have any questions about preparing your report.

(margin annotations: "r", "report", "Thursday")

2. Save the document as *Sales Report*. Preview, print, and close the document.

Exercise 8 C

1. Open the *New Expense Guidelines* document located on the Data Disk.

2. Practice using the following keyboard movement techniques to move the insertion point in the document:

   a. Move the insertion point to the end of the document using the CTRL + END keys.

   b. Move the insertion point to the beginning of the document using the CTRL + HOME keys.

   c. Move the insertion point to the word "Foods" in the first line of the first paragraph using the CTRL + RIGHT ARROW keys.

   d. Move the insertion point to the end of the first line of the first paragraph using the END key.

   e. Move the insertion point to the beginning of the first line of the first paragraph using the HOME key.

   f. Move the insertion point to the second paragraph (down one paragraph) using the CTRL + DOWN ARROW keys.

   g. Move the insertion point to the first paragraph (up one paragraph) using the CTRL + UP ARROW keys.

   h. Move the insertion point to the top of the next page using the CTRL + PAGEDOWN keys.

3. Close the document without saving any changes.

Exercise 9 C

1. Create a new, blank document using the method of your choice.

2. Key a paragraph of text describing your favorite hobby.

3. Save the document as *My Favorite Hobby*.

4. Preview, print, and close the document.

5. Open *My Favorite Hobby* document you saved in Step 3.

6. Add a second paragraph further describing why you enjoy the hobby.

7. Open the Save As dialog box.

8. Create a new folder named "Hobby" (check with your instructor, if necessary, to select the appropriate location for the new folder).

9. Save the document in the new Hobby folder with the new name *Why I Enjoy My Hobby*. Preview, print, and close the document.

chapter one

Case Projects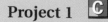

Project 1

Chris Lofton, the Word Processing Department manager at Worldwide Exotic Foods, has asked you to create a new document containing a short paragraph that describes two methods of correcting keying errors, for use in the Word Processing Training Handbook for new employees. Create, save, preview, and print the document.

Project 2

Create a new document for the Word Processing Training Handbook that contains a short paragraph describing the three methods of opening an existing document from inside the Word application. Save, preview, and print the document.

Project 3

If you have not yet done so, read Chapter 1 in the Office Unit in this book to learn more about getting online Help in Office applications. You are working with another new employee at Worldwide Exotic Foods (choose a classmate) to learn how to view, hide, and customize the Office Assistant. Together, review the Office Assistant dialog box options and online Help. Then you and your coworker each create a document and write at least three paragraphs that describe ways to view, hide, and customize the Office Assistant. Save, preview, and print your documents.

Project 4

If you have not yet done so, read Chapter 1 in the Office Unit in this book to learn more about getting online Help in Office applications. Chris asks you to review online Help for several of the buttons on the Standard toolbar and suggests you use the What's This? command on the Help menu to do it. Use the What's This? command on the Help menu to get online Help for three buttons on the Standard toolbar. Create a new document for each button and write one paragraph that describes what the button does and how to use it. Save, preview, and print the documents.

Project 5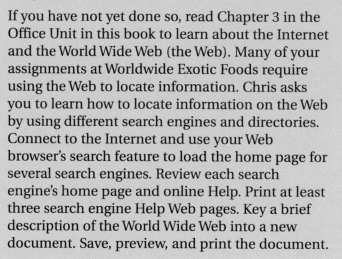

If you have not yet done so, read Chapter 3 in the Office Unit in this book to learn about the Internet and the World Wide Web (the Web). Many of your assignments at Worldwide Exotic Foods require using the Web to locate information. Chris asks you to learn how to locate information on the Web by using different search engines and directories. Connect to the Internet and use your Web browser's search feature to load the home page for several search engines. Review each search engine's home page and online Help. Print at least three search engine Help Web pages. Key a brief description of the World Wide Web into a new document. Save, preview, and print the document.

Project 6

Chris asks you to show several new employees how to print multiple documents at one time from the Open dialog box. Using the various tools available on the Help menu, research how to do this. Create a new document with a short paragraph describing how to print multiple documents from the Open dialog box. Save, preview, and print the document. Using your document as a guide, demonstrate to several coworkers how to print multiple documents at one time from the Open dialog box.

Project 7

Because many of your work assignments at Worldwide Exotic Foods require you to use the Web and your Web browser, Chris wants you to become more familiar with your Web browser's features. Connect to the Internet and load the default home page for your Web browser. Review your Web browser's options to learn how to change the default start page to a page of your choice. With your instructor's permission, change the default start page and close the browser. Open the browser and load the new start page. Reset the option to load the original default start page. Create a new document and key the steps for changing the default start page in your browser. Save, preview, and print the document.

Project 8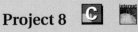

Connect to the Internet and load the home page for a search engine. Use what you learned in Case Project 5 to search for companies on the Web that are similar to Worldwide Exotic Foods. Print at least three Web pages for similar companies. Create a new document and key the names and URLs of the Web pages you found. Save, preview, and print the document.

chapter one

Creating and Editing a Word Document

Chapter Overview

The basic foundation for every document is creating and editing. This chapter discusses these skills in more detail. You learn to insert dates and text and to select, cut, copy, and delete text. In addition, you learn to set margins and page orientation and use different editing views. With these skills, you can produce finished letters and other documents with minimal rekeying and maximum accuracy.

LEARNING OBJECTIVES

- Create a letter
- Select text
- Cut, copy, and paste text
- Switch between editing views

Case profile

B. D. Vickers, the Administrative Vice President of Worldwide Exotic Foods, requests an assistant in the Purchasing Department and you get the assignment. You work with Kelly Armstead, Vickers' executive assistant, in preparing correspondence for the department. The first letter is a reply to someone inquiring about distribution possibilities for the company.

chapter two

notes You should review Appendix B, Formatting Tips for Business Documents, before beginning this chapter.

2.a Creating a Letter

Most organizations follow specific formatting for their letters. A common letter format widely used for both business and personal correspondence is the **block format**. When you create a letter in block format, all the text aligns against the left side of the page. This includes the date, the letter address, the salutation, the body, the complimentary closing, the writer's name, typist's reference initials, and any special letter parts such as an enclosure or subject line. The body of the letter is single-spaced, with a blank line between paragraphs.

Three blank lines separate the date from the letter address information, one blank line separates the letter address information and the salutation, one blank line separates the salutation from the body of the letter, and one blank line separates the body of the letter from the complimentary closing. There are three blank lines between the complimentary closing and the writer's name line. If a typist's reference initials appear below the writer's name, a blank line separates them. If an enclosure or attachment is noted, the word "Enclosure" or "Attachment" appears below the typist's initials with two blank lines separating them. Finally, when keying the letter address information, one space separates the state and the postal code (ZIP+4).

Most companies use special paper for their business correspondence called **letterhead** paper because the organization's name and address are preprinted at the top of each sheet. When you create a business letter, you determine the initial keying position based on the depth of the letterhead information on the paper (most letterheads are between 1 inch and 2 inches deep) and the amount of the letter text. Figure 2-1 illustrates the parts of a block format business letter.

Kelly asks you to create a new letter in the block format. Before you begin keying the text in your letter, you set the appropriate margins and page orientation for the document.

chapter two

FIGURE 2-1
Block Format Business Letter

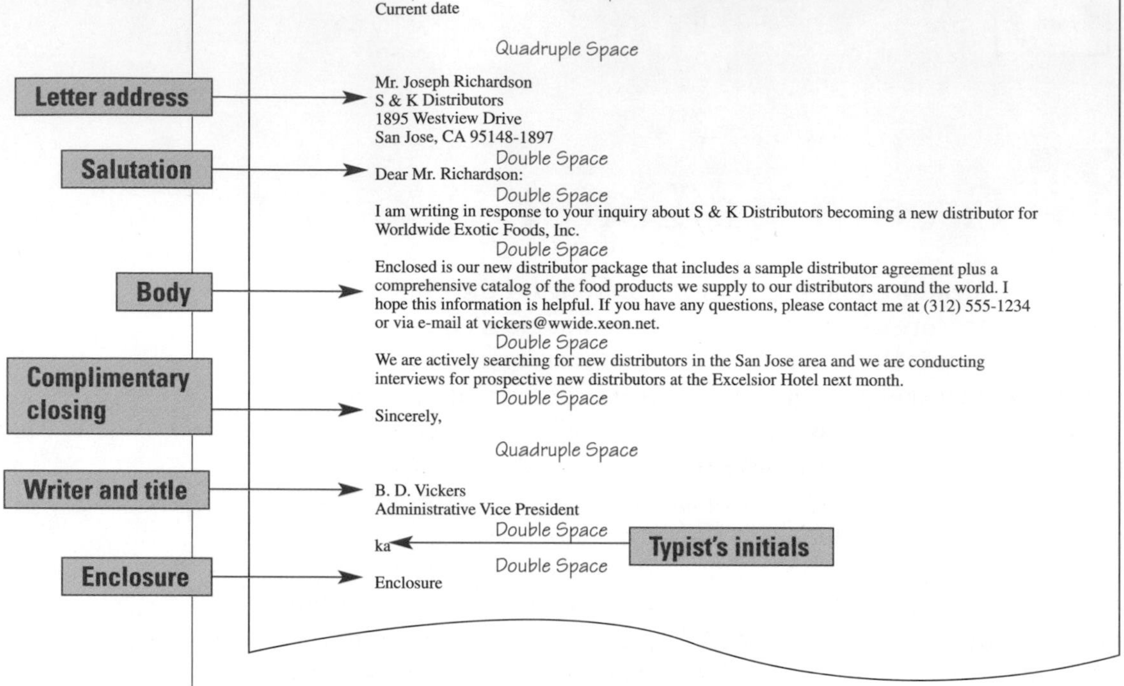
Date
2-inch margin for letterhead
Current date
Quadruple Space
Letter address
Mr. Joseph Richardson
S & K Distributors
1895 Westview Drive
San Jose, CA 95148-1897
Double Space
Salutation
Dear Mr. Richardson:
Double Space
I am writing in response to your inquiry about S & K Distributors becoming a new distributor for Worldwide Exotic Foods, Inc.
Double Space
Body
Enclosed is our new distributor package that includes a sample distributor agreement plus a comprehensive catalog of the food products we supply to our distributors around the world. I hope this information is helpful. If you have any questions, please contact me at (312) 555-1234 or via e-mail at vickers@wwide.xeon.net.
Double Space
We are actively searching for new distributors in the San Jose area and we are conducting interviews for prospective new distributors at the Excelsior Hotel next month.
Double Space
Complimentary closing
Sincerely,
Quadruple Space
Writer and title
B. D. Vickers
Administrative Vice President
Double Space
ka
Typist's initials
Double Space
Enclosure
Enclosure

C

Setting Margins

Margins are the distance from the top, bottom, left, and right edges of the page to the text. All text in a document appears within the margins you specify. When printing on letterhead paper, you must consider the depth of the preprinted letterhead when setting top margins and the amount of letter text when setting left and right margins.

You can change the document margins by clicking the Page Setup command on the File menu to open the Page Setup dialog box. Each margin—Top, Bottom, Left, and Right—has a text box that indicates the current margin setting. You can key a new margin size number in the text box. You also can click the up and down arrow buttons at the right side of each text box to increase or decrease the margin setting. The new margins you set affect the entire document by default. However, you can change the document margins from the position of the insertion point or for a section of a document.

You create the letter shown in Figure 2-1 by first creating a new, blank document and setting the appropriate margins and page orientation. Then you key the letter text. Worldwide Exotic Foods uses letterhead paper that requires a 2-inch top margin.

To create a new, blank document and set the margins:

Step 1	***Create***	a new, blank document, if necessary

notes   For the remainder of this text when you are asked to create a new, blank document or open an existing document, you may use the New Blank Document button or the Open button on the Standard toolbar or a New Document task pane link, whichever you prefer.

For the remainder of this text, a task pane may be shown in the illustrations when appropriate.

Step 2	*Click*	<u>F</u>ile
Step 3	*Click*	Page Set<u>u</u>p
Step 4	*Click*	the Margins tab, if necessary

The dialog box on your screen should look similar to Figure 2-2.

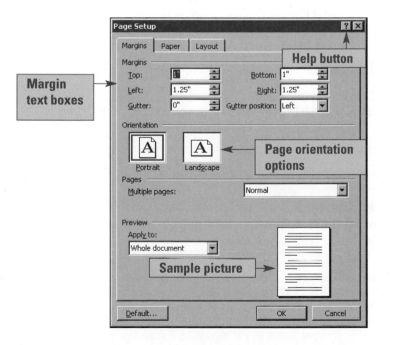

FIGURE 2-2
Page Setup Dialog Box

QUICK TIP

The <u>M</u>ultiple pages: list in the Margins tab of the Page Setup dialog box allows you to set special page orientation used for published material such as books or multi-page reports.

You can use the dialog box Help button to review the options on the Margins and other tabs in this dialog box. The blank document already has 1-inch top and bottom margins, and 1.25-inch left and right margins. These **default** margins are preset in the document. You can change the margins as necessary by keying the correct value in each text box. For this letter, you need to change the top margin to 2 inches, and the left and right margins to 1 inch. You can press the TAB key to quickly select the next option in a dialog box.

chapter two

QUICK TIP

When keying a value for the top, bottom, left, or right margins, it is not necessary to key the inch symbol (").

Step 5	*Key*	2 in the Top: text box
Step 6	*Press*	the TAB key twice
Step 7	*Key*	1 in the Left: text box
Step 8	*Press*	the TAB key
Step 9	*Key*	1 in the Right: text box

Now that you have set the appropriate margins, the next step is to review the page orientation in this same dialog box.

Setting Page Orientation

Page orientation refers to the height and width of a sheet of paper. The default page orientation is **portrait**, which means the paper is taller than it is wide. Most letter documents are printed in portrait orientation. You also can print documents in **landscape** orientation, which means the paper is wider than it is tall. Documents that require more horizontal space such as tabulated reports may be printed in landscape orientation. You can view the current page orientation and change it, if necessary, in the Page Setup dialog box. To view the current page orientation:

| Step 1 | *Observe* | the Portrait and Landscape options in the Orientation group in the Page Setup dialog box |
| Step 2 | *Observe* | the document preview in the lower-right corner of the dialog box |

The default Portrait option is selected and the document preview shows a document that is taller than it is wide. To change the page orientation:

| Step 1 | *Click* | the Landscape option |
| Step 2 | *Observe* | that the document preview in the lower-right corner of the dialog box is now in landscape orientation |

The sample document is now wider than it is tall. Because the standard page orientation for a letter is portrait, you change the page orientation again.

| Step 3 | *Click* | the Portrait option |
| Step 4 | *Observe* | that the document preview in the lower-right corner of the dialog box returns to portrait orientation |

When you change the margins or page orientation you can choose to make those changes for the whole document or for a portion of the document. Because the margins and page orientation are the same for the entire letter, you want the changes to apply to the whole document.

| Step 5 | *Verify* | that Whole document appears in the Apply to: list |
| Step 6 | *Click* | OK to apply the settings and close the dialog box |

After setting the appropriate margins and page orientation, you begin the letter by inserting the current date.

Inserting the Date and Time

Word provides a variety of special options that allow you to insert a date or date and time without keying it. You can insert the date or date and time as text or as a field of information that is automatically updated with the system date. Instead of keying the date manually in the letter, you can have Word insert the date for you. To insert the date:

| Step 1 | *Click* | Insert |
| Step 2 | *Click* | Date and Time |

The Date and Time dialog box opens. Except for the dates, the dialog box on your screen should look similar to Figure 2-3.

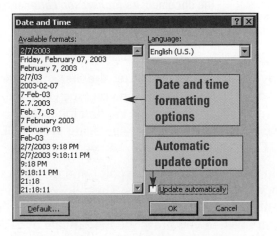

FIGURE 2-3
Date and Time Dialog Box

chapter
two

You can change the format of the date by selecting a format option in the Date and Time dialog box. The Update automatically check box provides an option to insert the date as text or as a date field, which is updated with the current system date whenever the document is printed. The Default button allows you to set a selected date/time format as the default format for all your Word documents. You use the third date/time format option.

Step 3	*Verify*	that the Update automatically check box is blank
Step 4	*Double-click*	the third date format

After the current date is inserted, you are ready to complete the letter by keying the letter text.

Inserting Text

By default, Word is in **Insert mode**, which enters characters at the position of the insertion point. When you insert text within an existing line of text, the text to the right of the insertion point shifts to make room for the new text. You continue with the letter by inserting the letter address, salutation, body, complimentary closing, typist's initials, and enclosure notation you see in Figure 2-1. To complete and save the letter:

Step 1	*Press*	the ENTER key four times
Step 2	*Key*	the remaining letter text as shown in Figure 2-1
Step 3	*Save*	the document as *Richardson Letter* and leave it open

notes   By default, Word capitalizes the first character in the first word of a sentence. When you type your initials, Word automatically capitalizes the first initial. You can manually change it to lowercase by pressing the SPACEBAR and pressing the CTRL + Z keys after you key your initials.

Also, by default, Word changes the color and underlines the path to a Web page or an e-mail address. This allows someone reading the document online to click the e-mail address to open his or her e-mail program. When you press the ENTER key or SPACEBAR after keying an e-mail address, Word changes the e-mail address to a hyperlink. You can remove the hyperlink formatting by clicking the Undo button on the Standard toolbar, by pressing the CTRL + Z keys, or by right-clicking the hyperlink and clicking Remove Hyperlink on the shortcut menu.

When you create a Word document, it is possible to make changes to characters, complete words, or groups of words at the same time by first selecting the text.

2.b Selecting Text

Selecting text is one of the most important word processing techniques. **Selecting** means to highlight one or more characters of text so that you can edit, format, or delete them. Once a character, word, or group of words is selected, Word recognizes the selected text as one unit that you can modify using Word editing features. For example, if you want to underline a group of words for emphasis, you would first select the words and then apply an underline format.

One way to select text is to drag the I-beam mouse pointer across the text. To select text by dragging, click at the beginning of the text, hold down the left mouse button, and move the mouse on the mouse pad in the direction you want to highlight. When the desired text is highlighted, release the mouse button.

The **selection bar** is the vertical area to the far left of the document between the horizontal ruler and the View buttons. When the mouse pointer is in the selection bar, it appears as a right-pointing arrow and you can use it to select text. Figure 2-4 identifies the selection bar and the shape of the mouse pointer when it is in the selection bar.

> ### CAUTION TIP
>
> You should take precautions to back up your work in case of power failure while you are working on a document. You can protect your work by using the AutoRecover feature or the Always create backup copy option. The AutoRecover feature periodically saves a backup copy of a document while you are working on it. The Always create backup copy option saves a backup of your document each time you save it. You can find these options by clicking the Options command on the Tools menu, and then clicking the Save tab in the Options dialog box.

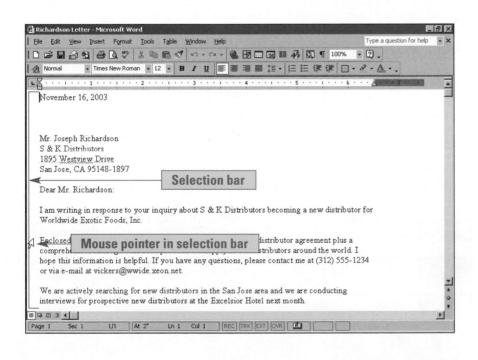

FIGURE 2-4
Selection Bar

chapter
two

Word includes many mouse and keyboard shortcuts for selecting text. Table 2-1 lists some frequently used shortcuts.

TABLE 2-1
Keyboard and Mouse
Shortcuts for Selecting Text

To Select	Do This
a word and the trailing space	Double-click a word
a sentence and the trailing space	Hold down the CTRL key and click inside the sentence
a line of text	Click in the selection bar next to the line
multiple lines of text	Drag in the selection bar next to the lines
a paragraph	Double-click in the selection bar next to the line or triple-click the paragraph
multiple paragraphs	Drag in the selection bar
the document	Hold down the CTRL key and click in the selection bar, or triple-click in the selection bar
a vertical selection of text	Hold down the ALT key and drag the mouse down and left or right
a variable amount of contiguous text	Place the insertion point at the beginning of the text to be selected, move the I-beam to the end of the text to be selected, hold down the SHIFT key, and click the mouse button
multiple areas of a document	Select the first text, then hold down the CTRL key as you select additional text
the text from the insertion point to the end of the document	Press the CTRL + SHIFT + END keys
the text from the insertion point to the beginning of the document	Press the CTRL + SHIFT + HOME keys

Deselecting text means to remove the highlighting. You can deselect text by clicking anywhere in the document area outside the highlighting, by selecting new text, or by pressing a **pointer-movement key** (UP ARROW, DOWN ARROW, LEFT ARROW, RIGHT ARROW) on the keyboard. To select a paragraph of your document by dragging:

Step 1	*Move*	the I-beam before the "E" in "Enclosed" in the second body paragraph
Step 2	*Drag*	down until you have highlighted the entire paragraph and the following blank line
Step 3	*Press*	the RIGHT ARROW key to deselect the text

To compare the dragging selection technique to using the selection bar:

Step 1	*Move*	the mouse pointer into the selection bar before the "E" in "Enclosed" until the mouse pointer becomes a right-pointing arrow
Step 2	*Double-click*	the selection bar
Step 3	*Click*	outside the selected text to deselect it

To select a variable amount of contiguous text using the SHIFT + Click method:

Step 1	*Click*	in front of the "E" in "Enclosed" to position the insertion point
Step 2	*Press & hold*	the SHIFT key
Step 3	*Move*	the I-beam mouse pointer to the end of the word "questions" in the third line
Step 4	*Click*	the mouse button to select the contiguous text beginning with "Enclosed" and ending with "questions"
Step 5	*Deselect*	the text

To select variable amount of noncontiguous text using the CTRL + Click method:

Step 1	*Select*	the text "Enclosed" in the second paragraph
Step 2	*Press & hold*	the CTRL key
Step 3	*Select*	the text "If you have any questions" in the third line of the second paragraph
Step 4	*Continue*	to hold down the CTRL key
Step 5	*Select*	the text "San Jose" in the first line of the third paragraph
Step 6	*Deselect*	the text

After text is selected, you can perform other tasks with the text—such as deleting it, formatting it, replacing it by keying new text, and copying or moving it to another location.

M OUSE TIP

By default, the automatic word selection feature is turned on. When you begin to drag across a second word, the automatic word selection feature quickly selects the entire word and the trailing space. You can turn off this feature in the When selecting, automatically select entire <u>w</u>ord check box on the Edit tab in the Options dialog box. To view the Options dialog box, click the <u>O</u>ptions command on the <u>T</u>ools menu.

Q UICK TIP

You can select text by pressing the F8 key (EXT mode) or holding down the SHIFT key and then pressing a pointer-movement key to turn on **Extend mode** at the location of the insertion point. For example, move the insertion point to the beginning of the word, press the F8 key, then press the CTRL + RIGHT ARROW key to highlight the word. To remove a highlighted selection, press the ESC key and then press a pointer-movement key.

chapter
two

2.c Cutting, Copying, and Pasting Text

You can move, or **cut and paste**, text from one location to another in a Word document. You can duplicate, or **copy and paste**, text from one location to another in a Word document. You also can cut and paste or copy and paste text into a different Word document or into another Office application document.

Cutting and Pasting Using the Office Clipboard Task Pane

You use the Cut command to remove text, the Copy command to duplicate text, and the Paste command to insert the cut or copied text. The Cut and Copy commands collect selected text from your Word document and insert it on the Office Clipboard. The **Office Clipboard** is a reserved place in the memory of your computer that can be used to store text temporarily. The Office Clipboard can hold up to 24 cut or copy actions.

To cut or copy text, you first select the desired text and then click Cut or Copy on the Edit menu or shortcut menu or click the Cut or Copy button on the Standard toolbar. To insert the cut or copied text at a new location in your document, first move the insertion point to the location. Then click the Paste command on the Edit menu or shortcut menu, or click the Paste button on the Standard toolbar. You also can use the Office Clipboard task pane to paste. The Office Clipboard task pane usually appears automatically after you cut or copy a second selection before pasting the first cut or copied selection.

Kelly reviewed the *Richardson Letter* document and wants you to move the third body paragraph to the second body paragraph position. To display the Office Clipboard task pane:

Step 1	*Click*	Edit
Step 2	*Click*	Office Clipboard

The Office Clipboard is currently empty. The next step is to select the text you want to move. You can use a shortcut menu to quickly place the text to the Office Clipboard. To select and cut text:

Step 1	*Select*	the third paragraph beginning with "We are" and the following blank line

Step 2	*Move*	the mouse pointer to the selected text

notes Chapter 1 and the previous sections of this chapter provided step-by-step instructions for repositioning the insertion point. From this point forward, you are instructed to move the I-beam or insertion point to the appropriate position. Review Chapter 1 to see the step-by-step process for repositioning the insertion point, if necessary.

Step 3	*Right-click*	the selected text

A shortcut menu for the selected text appears. Your screen should look similar to Figure 2-5.

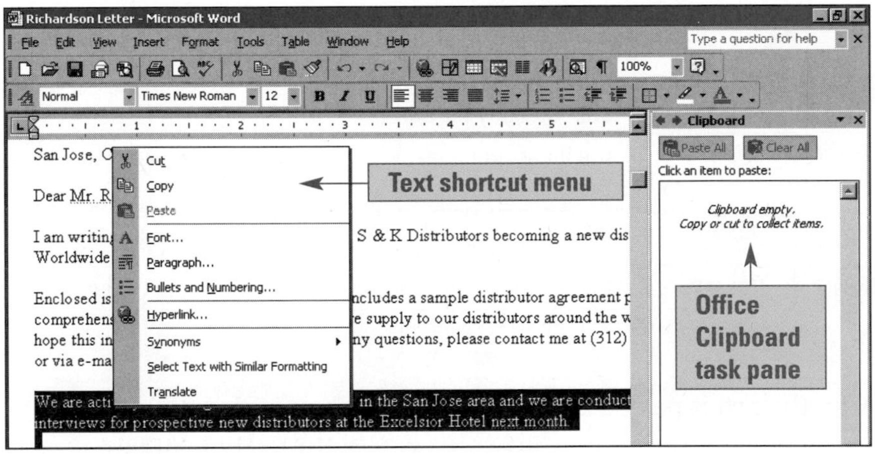

FIGURE 2-5
Text Shortcut Menu

Step 4	*Click*	Cut on the shortcut menu
Step 5	*Observe*	that the third body paragraph no longer appears in the document because it is temporarily stored on the Office Clipboard

TASK PANE TIP

When a task pane is already visible, you can switch to the Office Clipboard task pane with the Other Task Panes button on the task pane title bar.

The Task Pane command on the View menu and the Task Pane command on the toolbar shortcut menu display the last visible task pane. For example, if you open the Office Clipboard task pane and then close it, both the Task Pane command on the View menu and the Task Pane command on the toolbar shortcut menu will redisplay the Office Clipboard task pane.

The Office Clipboard task pane on your screen should look similar to Figure 2-6.

FIGURE 2-6
Text Stored in the Office
Clipboard

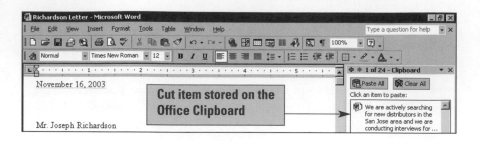

If you have multiple items stored on the Office Clipboard, you can paste all of them at once with the Paste All button. When you move the mouse pointer to an item in the Office Clipboard contents list, the item is selected, a border appears around the item, and a drop-down list arrow appears to the right of the item. To paste an individual item, you can click the item or click the item's drop-down list arrow and click Paste. Once an item is pasted, a dark blue border appears around the item. To paste the individual cut item:

Step 6	*Move*	the insertion point in front of the "E" in "Enclosed" in the second body paragraph
Step 7	*Click*	the individual item in the Click an item to paste: list in the Clipboard task pane
Step 8	*Observe*	that the paragraph is inserted in the new location
Step 9	*Observe*	the dark blue border around the item in the Office Clipboard task pane

After the text is pasted in the document in the new location, the Paste Options Smart Tag icon appears at the end of the pasted paragraph.

Working With Paste Options

The Paste Options Smart Tag feature allows you to control the formatting of the pasted text. You can choose to keep the original formatting, match the destination formatting, keep the text only and remove all formatting, or apply special formatting. Because you are moving text within the same document, you want to keep the original source formatting. To view the Paste Options button menu choices:

Step 1	*Move*	the mouse pointer to the Paste Options icon to activate it
Step 2	*Click*	the Paste Options list arrow to view the menu

Step 3	*Observe*	that the default option is to keep the original source formatting
Step 4	*Press*	the ESC key to close the menu

When you are finished with the Office Clipboard, you can clear it and then close the task pane.

Clearing the Office Clipboard

You can clear the Office Clipboard after you no longer need to paste the items stored there. You can clear all of the items on the Office Clipboard with the Clear All button or you can clear individual items with the Delete command on the individual item's drop-down list.

When the Office Clipboard icon is visible in the taskbar tray, you can right-click it to set Office Clipboard task pane options.

To clear the individual Office Clipboard item:

Step 1	*Move*	the mouse pointer to the item in the Click an item to paste: list in the Clipboard task pane
Step 2	*Click*	the item's list arrow
Step 3	*Click*	Delete
Step 4	*Observe*	that the Office Clipboard is again empty
Step 5	*Close*	the Office Clipboard task pane
Step 6	*Save*	the document as *Revised Richardson Letter*

After reviewing the *Revised Richardson Letter*, Kelly wants to make some additional changes.

Copying and Pasting Using Toolbar Buttons

You do not have to use the Office Clipboard task pane to cut and paste or copy and paste. If you are working with one selection, it may be faster to use the Cut, Copy, and Paste buttons on the Standard toolbar to cut, copy, and paste. Kelly also wants you to copy the letter address and paste it at the end of the document. Before you begin, you add two blank lines at the end of the document. Then you copy the address to the Office Clipboard using the Copy button on the Standard toolbar and paste it using the Paste button.

To copy and paste the address:

Step 1	*Move*	the insertion point to the bottom of the document

---

TASK PANE TIP

You change how the Office Clipboard task pane is displayed by clicking the Options button in the Office Clipboard task pane. One option allows you to turn on or off the automatic display of this task pane as you cut or copy items. Another option allows you to turn on the Office Clipboard but display an icon in the taskbar tray in the lower-right corner of the screen and then close the Office Clipboard task pane so that you have more area in which to view your document. You can still cut or copy multiple items to the Office Clipboard if you elect to show the taskbar tray icon. When you want to view the Office Clipboard task pane, simply double-click the icon.

chapter
two

MENU TIP

You can cut, copy, and paste selected text with the Cut, Copy, and Paste commands on the Edit menu or a shortcut menu.

Step 2	*Press*	the ENTER key twice to insert two blank lines, if necessary
Step 3	*Select*	the four lines of the letter address
Step 4	*Click*	the Copy button on the Standard toolbar
Step 5	*Move*	the insertion point to the bottom of the document
Step 6	*Click*	the Paste button on the Standard toolbar
Step 7	*Observe*	that the letter address is now in two locations in the document
Step 8	*Save*	the *Revised Richardson Letter* document and close it

Not only can you use menu commands and the Office Clipboard task pane to cut, copy, and paste, you can also use the mouse to move or copy text.

Moving and Copying Text with the Mouse

A shortcut method for moving and copying text is called **drag-and-drop**. This method uses the mouse and does not store any items on the Office Clipboard. To move text using drag-and-drop, first select the text and then drag the selection to its new location. To copy text using drag-and-drop, select the text, press and hold the CTRL key, and then drag the text to its new location, releasing the mouse button before you release the CTRL key.

When you are using the drag-and-drop method, the insertion point changes to a small, dashed, gray vertical line. A small box with a dashed, gray border appears at the base of the mouse pointer. If you are copying text, a small plus sign (+) appears below of the mouse pointer.

You open the *Richardson Letter* from the File menu and move the third body paragraph to the second body paragraph position using the mouse pointer. You can quickly open a recently closed document by clicking the document name on the File menu list of recently closed documents. To use the drag-and-drop method to move text:

QUICK TIP

When you open the Save As dialog box and then save the current file with the same name as an existing file, Word opens a dialog box that allows you to replace the existing file, save your changes with a different filename, or merge the changes you made into the existing file.

Step 1	*Click*	File
Step 2	*Click*	the *Richardson Letter* at the bottom of the File menu
Step 3	*Select*	the paragraph beginning with "We are" and the following blank line
Step 4	*Move*	the mouse pointer to the selected text (the pointer is a left-pointing arrow)
Step 5	*Click & hold*	the left mouse button
Step 6	*Observe*	the dashed line insertion point at the tip of the mouse pointer

Step 7	*Drag*	up until the dashed line insertion point is positioned before the word "E" in "Enclosed" in the second body paragraph
Step 8	*Release*	the mouse button
Step 9	*Deselect*	the text

To copy the letter address to the bottom of the document:

Step 1	*Insert*	two blank lines at the bottom of the document
Step 2	*Select*	the letter address
Step 3	*Move*	the mouse pointer to the selected address text
Step 4	*Press & hold*	the CTRL key
Step 5	*Drag*	the selected text to the bottom of the document
Step 6	*Release*	the mouse button
Step 7	*Release*	the CTRL key
Step 8	*Observe*	the copied address text
Step 9	*Close*	the *Richardson Letter* without saving changes

Using Repeat, Undo, and Redo Features

The Repeat, Undo, and Redo features come in handy as you edit documents. The **Repeat** feature allows you to duplicate your last action. The **Undo** feature allows you to reverse a previous action. The **Redo** feature allows you to undo a previously undone action. To repeat the last action, click the Repeat command on the Edit menu or press the CTRL + Y keys. To undo the last action, click the Undo button on the Standard toolbar, click the Undo command on the Edit menu, or press the CTRL + Z keys. To redo the last undone action, click the Redo button on the Standard toolbar. You can undo multiple actions sequentially, beginning with the last action you performed, by clicking the Undo button for each command you want to reverse.

Word has many ways to view a document for editing. The appropriate editing view depends on the kind of editing you are doing.

MOUSE TIP

You can **right-drag** selected text to move or copy it. Select the text you want to move or copy, and then hold down the right mouse button instead of the left mouse button as you drag the text. When you release the mouse button, a shortcut menu containing the Move Here and Copy Here commands appears. Click the appropriate command to paste the selection.

CAUTION TIP

When copying text with drag-and-drop, do not release the CTRL key until you have first released the mouse button. Releasing the CTRL key first causes Word to move the text instead of copying it.

chapter
two

2.d Switching Between Editing Views

You can view documents in several ways for editing: Normal view, Web Layout view, Print Layout view, Full Screen view, Outline view, and Print Preview. The two most commonly used views for entering and editing text are Normal view and Print Layout view. Web Layout view is used to create Web pages, and Outline view is used to create text outlines.

Normal View

Normal view is commonly used for keying, editing, and formatting text. Margins, headers and footers, drawing objects, graphics, and text in column format are not displayed in Normal view. You can switch to Normal view with the Normal command on the View menu or the Normal View button.

Print Layout View

In **Print Layout view**, the document display looks more like the printed page—including headers and footers, columns, graphics, drawing objects, and margins. You also see a vertical ruler in Print Layout view. You can switch to Print Layout view with the Print Layout command on the View menu or with the Print Layout view button. To view a multipage document in Print Layout view:

Step 1	*Open*	the *Vancouver Warehouse Report* located on the Data Disk
Step 2	*Click*	the Print Layout View button to the left of the horizontal scroll bar
Step 3	*Zoom*	the document to Two Pages

Your screen should look similar to Figure 2-7.

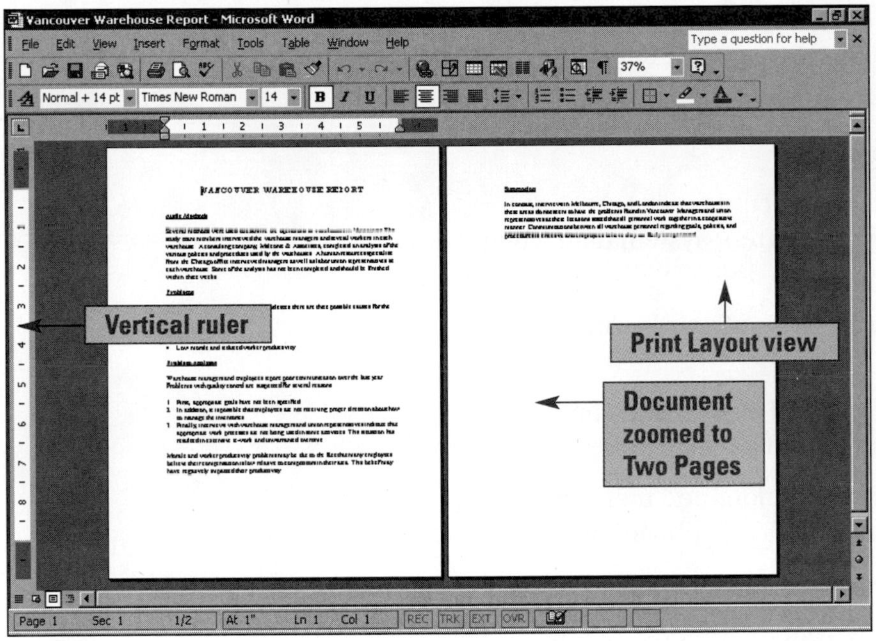

FIGURE 2-7
Print Layout View

Step 4	*Zoom*	the document back to Page Width
Step 5	*Click*	the Normal View button ▣ to the left of the horizontal scroll bar
Step 6	*Close*	the *Vancouver Warehouse Report* document without saving changes

Full Screen View

When you need to maximize the number of text lines you see on your screen, use Full Screen view, which hides the title bar, menu bar, toolbars, scroll bars, status bar, and taskbar. You can switch to Full Screen view with the Full Screen command on the View menu. From Full Screen view, you can switch back to the previous view by clicking the Close Full Screen button on the Full Screen toolbar that appears when in Full Screen view.

MOUSE TIP

You can set margins with the mouse pointer and the horizontal and vertical rulers in Print Layout view. Switch to Print Layout view and point to the margin boundary on the horizontal or vertical ruler. The mouse pointer becomes a black, two-headed move pointer. Drag the boundary to the desired position. If you press and hold the ALT key while dragging, the ruler displays measurements that indicate the margin settings and text area width.

**chapter
two**

Summary

▶ The block format is commonly used for business correspondence.

▶ Word has preset top, bottom, left, and right margins that you can change in the Page Setup dialog box.

▶ The date and time can be inserted in a document as text or as a field that automatically updates to the current system date when the document is printed.

▶ You can select characters, words, or groups of words with the mouse or keyboard.

▶ Selected text can be cut, copied, and pasted using menu commands, a shortcut menu, toolbar buttons, and the Office Clipboard task pane.

▶ You can collect up to 24 cut or copied selections and then paste them individually or all at one time using the Office Clipboard task pane.

▶ You can repeat or undo your last action.

▶ Word has several ways you can view your document, including: Normal view, Print Layout view, and Full Screen view. Use Normal view to key, edit, and format text. Use Print Layout to view and work with margins, headers and footers, columns, graphics, and drawing objects. Use Full Screen view to see more lines of text on the page.

Commands Review

Action	Menu Bar	Shortcut Menu	Toolbar	Task Pane	Keyboard
Set margins	File, Page Setup				ALT + F, U
Insert date	Insert, Date and Time				ALT + I, T
Update a selected date field		Right-click, then click Update Field			ALT + SHIFT + D F9
Cut, Copy, Paste	Edit, Cut or Copy or Paste	Right-click, then click Cut or Copy, or Paste	✂ 📋 📋	Click an item or 📋 Paste All in the Office Clipboard task pane	ALT + E, T or C or P CTRL + C (copy) CTRL + X (cut) CTRL + V (paste)
Turn on or off Overtype			Double-click the OVR mode indicator		INSERT
Undo or Redo actions	Edit, Undo Edit, Redo		↺ ↻		ALT + E, U ALT + E, R CTRL + Z CTRL + Y
Repeat actions	Edit, Repeat				ALT+ E, R CTRL + Y
Cancel an action					ESC
Change editing views	View, Normal, Web Layout, Print Layout, Outline, Full Screen		🔲 🔲 🔲 🔲		ALT + V, N or W or P or O or U ALT + CTRL + P ALT + CTRL + O ALT + CTRL + N

Concepts Review

Circle the correct answer.

1. **You can remove text by selecting the text and pressing the:**
   [a] EXT key.
   [b] ALT + PAGEUP keys.
   [c] CTRL key.
   [d] DELETE key.

2. **You cannot add a date to a document by:**
   [a] keying the date manually.
   [b] inserting a date field that updates automatically.
   [c] inserting the date as text.
   [d] pressing the Insert key.

3. **The selection bar is:**
   [a] located below the status bar.
   [b] used to open other Office applications.
   [c] used to select text in different ways.
   [d] used to set left and right margins.

4. **When you use the block format for a business letter, the:**
   [a] date and complimentary closing are centered on their respective lines.
   [b] letter address is positioned below the salutation.
   [c] letter components all begin at the left margin.
   [d] letter components all begin at the right margin.

5. **Margins refer to the:**
   [a] distance from the center of the page to the edge of the page.
   [b] distance from the top, bottom, left, and right edges of the page to the text.
   [c] number of lines you can have on a page.
   [d] size of the text on a page.

6. **By default, Word is in the:**
   [a] Overtype mode.
   [b] Edit mode.
   [c] Online Review mode.
   [d] Insert mode.

7. **Which of the following is not a selection technique in Word?**
   [a] pressing the CTRL + SHIFT + END keys to select from the insertion point to the end of the document
   [b] double-clicking the selection bar opposite the paragraph you wish to select
   [c] double-clicking a word
   [d] pressing the ALT key and clicking a word

8. **Using the mouse to move or copy text is called:**
   [a] cut-and-drag.
   [b] select-and-cut.
   [c] copy-and-cut.
   [d] drag-and-drop.

9. **Overtype mode allows you to:**
   [a] select text.
   [b] key over existing text.
   [c] move text.
   [d] copy text.

10. **Which of the following is not an editing view?**
    [a] Full Page view
    [b] Full Screen view
    [c] Print Layout view
    [d] Normal view

Circle **T** if the statement is true or **F** if the statement is false.

T   F   1. When you are in the Overtype mode and enter new text, any character you key replaces the character to the right of the insertion point.

T   F   2. Word automatically defaults to the Edit mode.

T   F   3. Word can undo multiple actions.

T   F   4. The mouse and the keyboard can both be used to select text in a document.

chapter two

T F   5. The EXT mode indicator appears bolded when you are using the Extend mode feature.

T F   6. You can restore text that has been deleted.

T F   7. You can maximize the number of lines of text displayed on the screen by switching to Full Screen view.

T F   8. Normal view displays your document much like it looks when printed.

T F   9. You can insert the date and the time together in a Word document.

T F   10. The Office Clipboard is a reserved place in the memory of your computer you can use to temporarily store up to 24 items you have cut or copied.

Skills Review

Exercise 1   C

1. Create the following document. Use the block style with 2-inch top margin and 1-inch left and right margins. Insert the current date in the format of your choice at the top of the document. As you key the text, use the movement techniques and insert/delete actions you learned in this chapter to correct any keying errors you make. You revise the document in the next exercise.

Current date

Ms. Gail Jackson
Corporate Travel Manager
International Travel Services
1590 W. Convention Street
Chicago, IL 60605-1590

Dear Ms. Jackson:

Thank you for helping plan business trip to London this winter. I am really looking forward to seeing the sites, as well as taking care of some business. This is my first trip to London, and you were quite courteous in answering my questions.

Yours truly,

Kelly Armstead
Executive Assistant to B. D. Vickers

ka

2. Save the document as *Travel Letter*. Preview, print, and close the document.

Exercise 2 C

1. Open the *Travel Letter* document you created in Exercise 1 in this chapter.

2. At the end of the street address line, add ", Suite 16A;" in the first sentence, add the word "me" after the word "helping;" in the first sentence, add the word "my" after the word "plan" and delete the word "business;" in the first sentence, delete the word "winter" and replace it with the word "summer."

3. Save the document as *Travel Letter Revised*. Preview, print, and close the document.

Exercise 3 C

1. Create the following document. Use the block style with 2-inch top margin and 1-inch left and right margins. Insert the date as a field at the top of the document. As you key the letter, use the movement techniques and insert/delete actions to correct any keying errors you make. You revise the document in the next exercise.

Current date

Mr. Taylor Schreier
J & H Electronic Wholesalers
4578 Main Street
Cleveland, OH 78433-6325

Dear Mr. Schreier:

Thank you for inquiry about our holiday basket special offers. I am enclosing our most recent holiday catalog that explains and illustrates our special offers.

Please call our Sales Department at (312) 555-5555 when you are ready to place your order.

Yours truly,

P. L. Brown
Marketing Vice President

pb

Enclosure

2. Save the document as *Schreier Letter*. Preview, print, and close the document.

chapter two

Exercise 4   C

1. Open the *Schreier Letter* document you created in Exercise 3 in this chapter.

2. In the first sentence, add the word "your" after the word "for" and delete the word "about" and replace it with the word "regarding."

3. Using the Overtype mode, replace the text "Yours truly," with the text "Sincerely," in the complimentary closing. Delete any extra characters and then turn off the Overtype mode.

4. Save the document as *Schreier Letter Revised*. Preview, print, and close the document.

Exercise 5   C

1. Open the *Employment Application Letter* document located on the Data Disk.

2. Move the second body paragraph to the first body paragraph position using a shortcut menu.

3. Undo the move action.

4. Move the second body paragraph to the first body paragraph position using drag-and-drop.

5. Combine the third body paragraph with the second body paragraph by viewing the formatting marks and deleting the paragraph marks at the end of the second body paragraph and the blank line between the second body paragraph and the third body paragraph. Don't forget to add a space between the two sentences of the revised second body paragraph.

6. Replace the words "Current date" with the current date in the 12 November 2003 format.

7. Save the document as *Employment Application Letter Revised*. Preview, print, and close the document.

Exercise 6   C

1. Open the *Business Solicitation Letter* located on the Data Disk.

2. Change the margins to a 2-inch top margin and 1-inch left and right margins.

3. Delete the word "own" in the first sentence of the first body paragraph. Use the Repeat command on the Edit menu to delete the text "explaining and" in the first sentence of the second body paragraph.

4. Replace the words "Current date" with the current date in the format of your choice.

5. Save the document as *Business Solicitation Letter Revised*. Preview, print, and close the document.

Exercise 7   C

1. Create the following document. Use the block style with 1.5-inch top margin and 1.25 inch left and right margins. Insert the current date in the format of your choice at the top of the document. As you key the letter, use the movement techniques and insert/delete actions to correct any keying errors you make. You revise the document in the next exercise.

Current date

BCH Software Company
4000 Skywalk Way
Ventura, CA 91015-4657

Dear Sir:

Please send by return mail all of products brochures, technical specifications, and price
list for your software related to word processing for IBM PS2/ and IBM-compatible
personal computers.

Additionally, please add your mailing list to update us on any future changes in your
product line.

Sincerely,

B. D. Vickers
Administrative Vice President

ka

2. Save the document as *BCH Software Letter*. Preview, print, and close the document.

Exercise 8   C

1. Open the *BCH Software Letter* document you created in Exercise 7 in this chapter.

2. Edit the document following the proofing notations.

chapter two

Current date

Mr. James Wilson
BCH Software Company
4000 Skywalk Way
Ventura, CA 91015-4657

Dear ~~Sir:~~ ^Mr. Wilson

Please send ^us by return mail all of ^your products brochures, technical specifications, and price list for ~~your~~ software related to ~~word processing~~ ^accounting for IBM PS2/ and IBM-compatible personal computers.

Additionally, please add ^us to your mailing list ~~to update us~~ ^for on any ~~future~~ changes ~~in~~ ^too your product line.

Sincerely,

B. D. Vickers
Administrative Vice President

ka

---

3. Save the document as *BCH Software Letter Revised*. Preview, print, and close the document.

Case Projects

SCANS

Project 1

B. D. Vickers is traveling on business to Melbourne, Australia in three weeks. Prepare a letter to Mr. David Melville, Reservations Manager at the Excelsior Hotel, 3500 Wayburne Drive, Melbourne, VIC, 30001, Australia, requesting accommodations for a week beginning three weeks from today. Insert the date as text using the Day, Month (in text), Year format. Save, preview, and print the document.

Project 2

Open the document you created in Project 1 and change the accommodation dates to four weeks from today using the Overtype mode. Save the document with a new name, then preview and print it.

Project 3

Kelly Armstead has asked you to find a list of keyboard shortcuts you both can use to prepare correspondence. Using the Ask A Question Box, search online Help for a list of keyboard shortcut keys for moving the insertion point in a document and selecting text in a document. Print the lists. With your instructor's permission, use the lists to demonstrate the keyboard shortcuts to a classmate.

Project 4

B. D. Vickers is considering ordering several IntelliMouse pointing devices for the Purchasing Department and has asked you to find out how the devices are used to increase productivity in the department. Using the Help menu resources, including Web resources, search for information on the IntelliMouse pointing device. Create a new document containing at least three paragraphs describing how the Purchasing Department employees can improve their productivity by using the IntelliMouse pointing device. Insert the current date as text using the mm/dd/yy format. Save, preview, and print the document.

Project 5 C

There have been several power failures because of storms in the area and Kelly is concerned that she may lose documents she is working on if the power fails. She has asked you to find out what options Word has to automatically back up documents as she is working and to automatically recover documents lost during a power failure. Using the Help menu, research what backup and document recovery features Word provides. Create a new document containing at least four paragraphs describing how to set backup procedures and recover lost or damaged documents. Insert the date as a field using the format of your choice. Save, preview, and print the document.

Project 6 C

B. D. Vickers has extended the business trip discussed in Project 1 and now plans to spend two days in Hong Kong and three days in London before returning. Kelly needs a list of possible accommodations in Hong Kong and London and has asked you to search the Web for information on hotels in these cities. She also needs you to review flight schedules and suggest flights from Melbourne to Hong Kong, from Hong Kong to London, and from London to Chicago. Connect to the Internet and search the Web for the information you need. Save at least two URLs as "favorites." Print at least five Web pages. Create a new, blank document and key the title and URL of the pages you printed. Insert the date as text in the format of your choice. Save, preview, and print the document.

Project 7

Open the document of your choice. Practice using various selection techniques to select text. Delete and restore text using the Delete key, Undo command and button, and Repeat command. Close the document without saving any changes.

Project 8 C

Worldwide Exotic Foods, Inc. participates in a summer internship program for graduating seniors and has a new group of interns starting the program next week. Margie Montez, the program director, has asked you to prepare a ten-minute presentation on creating business letters using Word 2002. You give the presentation next Thursday, at 3 p.m. Create a new document listing the topics you plan to discuss and the order in which you plan to discuss them. Insert the date and time using the format of your choice. Save, preview, and print the document. Ask a classmate to review the document and provide comments and suggestions on the topics and the organization. With your instructor's approval, schedule a time to give your presentation to your class.

Project 9 C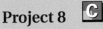

Kelly has subscribed to an e-mail mailing list and gets Word 2002 user tips every day via e-mail. You also would like to subscribe to this kind of mailing list and want to know more about how to do this. Connect to the Internet and search the Web for information on locating and subscribing to mailing lists. Create a new, blank document that lists titles and URLs for pages that provide mailing list information. Insert the date using the Day (in text), Month (in text) and Date, Year format. Save, preview, and print the document.

chapter two

Using the Proofing Tools

Chapter Overview

Documents with misspellings and grammar errors indicate sloppiness and inattention to detail—two traits no company wants to convey. Proofing a document before you print it helps to ensure the document is error-free, allowing readers to focus on its content. Word has several tools to help you proof your documents. In this chapter, you learn to use the Spelling and Grammar, Thesaurus, and AutoCorrect proofing tools. You also learn to create and insert AutoText entries and to find and replace text.

LEARNING OBJECTIVES

- ▶ Check spelling and grammar in a document
- ▶ Use Synonyms and the Thesaurus to replace words
- ▶ Use the AutoCorrect tool
- ▶ Insert text with the AutoText tool
- ▶ Find and replace text

Case profile

Worldwide Exotic Foods requires that all correspondence and documents sent out from the company have accurate spelling and grammar. Kelly Armstead asks you to correct any errors in a letter she keyed before it is printed and mailed.

**chapter
three**

3.a Checking Spelling and Grammar in a Document

Kelly tells you that it is company policy to check the spelling and grammar of any document before you print it. You can check the spelling and grammar in a document with a menu command, a toolbar button, a status bar mode indicator, or a shortcut menu. By default, Word checks the spelling and grammar in your document as you key the text. Using this automatic spelling and grammar tool saves time in editing your document. After you misspell a word or key text that may be grammatically incorrect and then press the SPACEBAR, a wavy red or green line appears below the text. The red line indicates a spelling error and the green line indicates a possible grammar error.

Kelly's letter contains several keying errors. You open the letter and then use the Spelling and Grammar command to correct those errors. To open the letter containing errors:

| Step 1 | *Open* | the *IAEA Letter* document located on the Data Disk |

The wavy red and green lines appear below text that may be misspelled or grammatically incorrect. In this letter the proper names are correct; therefore, you can ignore the wavy red or green lines underneath them if they appear. When necessary, you can add words like proper names to a custom dictionary. *For the activities in this chapter, do not add any words to a custom dictionary.*

There is one grammar error in the letter, indicated by a wavy green line. To correct the grammar error "an" in the second body paragraph:

| Step 1 | *Right-click* | the word "an" |

The Grammar shortcut menu on your screen should look similar to Figure 3-1. The shortcut menu suggestion is to replace the word "an" with "a." You can quickly replace a word by clicking the suggested word in the shortcut menu, or you can display the Grammar dialog box to get more information about the error message. Because this is an obvious error, you can quickly correct it by replacing "an" with "a."

QUICK TIP

You can turn on or off the automatic spelling and grammar checking in the Spelling and Grammar tab of the Options dialog box.

Word can detect text written in many languages other than English when the multiple language features are installed. When you open a document that contains text in other languages or key text in another language, Word uses the spelling and grammar dictionaries, punctuation rules, and sorting rules for that language. For more information on setting up your computer for automatic language detection, see online Help.

MENU TIP

You can right-click a misspelled word or grammar error to correct it. You can also click the Spelling and Grammar command on the Tools menu to correct spelling or grammar errors.

chapter
three

FIGURE 3-1
Grammar Shortcut Menu

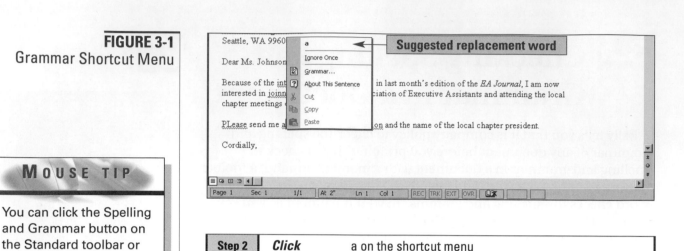

| Step 2 | *Click* | a on the shortcut menu |

Next, you correct the misspellings in the letter. To correct the spelling of the word "intereting" in the first body paragraph:

| Step 1 | *Right-click* | the word "intereting" |

The Spelling shortcut menu on your screen should look similar to Figure 3-2.

FIGURE 3-2
Spelling Shortcut Menu

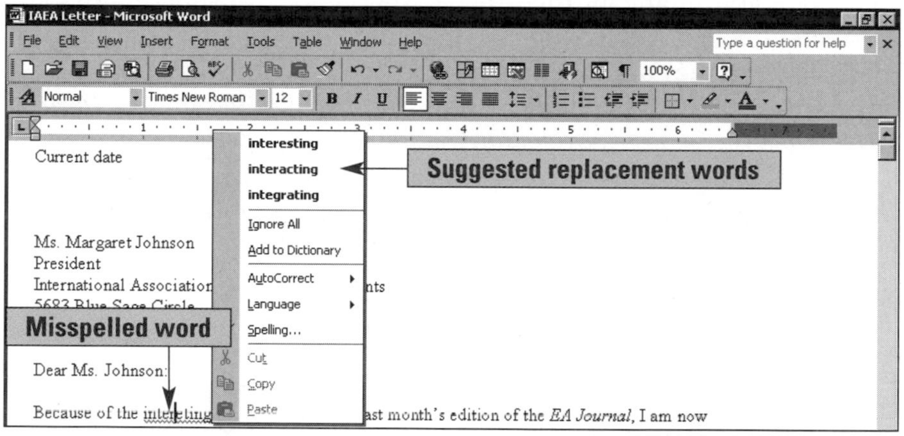

You can click a suggested spelling, ignore the spelling, add the word to a custom dictionary, add the error and suggested replacement word to the AutoCorrect tool, or open the Spelling dialog box. Because the correct spelling is on the shortcut menu, you click it to fix the error.

| Step 2 | *Click* | interesting on the shortcut menu |

You can display the spelling or grammar shortcut menu with the Spelling and Grammar Status mode indicator on the status bar.

To correct the next error, the word "joinng," using the Spelling and Grammar Status mode indicator:

Step 1	*Click*	the word "joinng" to position the insertion point in the word
Step 2	*Double-click*	the Spelling and Grammar Status mode indicator 📖 on the status bar
Step 3	*Click*	joining on the shortcut menu

Another way to correct the spelling and grammar is to use the Spelling and Grammar dialog box. The dialog box shows each spelling or grammar error and provides options for you to correct it. To correct the remaining spelling errors using the Spelling and Grammar dialog box:

Step 1	*Click*	the Spelling and Grammar button ✓ on the Standard toolbar

The Spelling and Grammar dialog box on your screen should look similar to Figure 3-3.

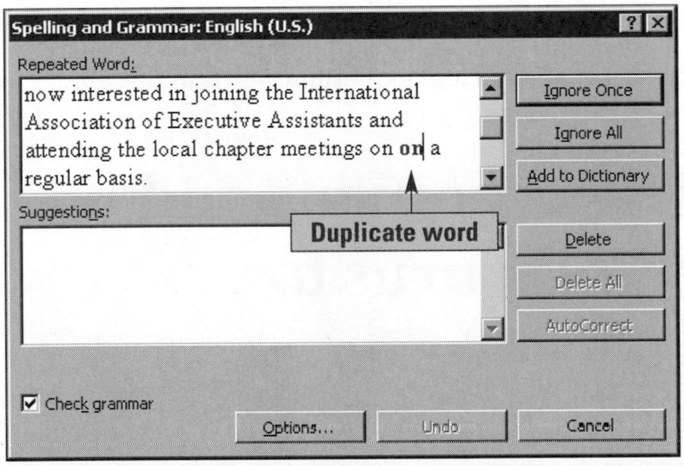

FIGURE 3-3
Spelling and Grammar
Dialog Box

The Spelling and Grammar tool detected the duplicate word "on" in the first body paragraph. You want to delete the duplicate word.

Step 2	*Click*	<u>D</u>elete

Word deletes the extra word and moves to the next spelling error. The word "PLease" appears in the dialog box and Word provides a list of

---

M O U S E   T I P

You can double-click the Spelling and Grammar Status mode indicator to move to the next misspelled or mistyped word in your document.

---

chapter
three

possible corrections in the Sugges<u>t</u>ions: list. Word highlights the most likely suggested correction—"Please"—for the irregular capitalization.

| Step 3 | *Click* | <u>C</u>hange |

The next misspelled word ("app<u>p</u>lication") appears in the dialog box and Word suggests the correct spelling "application."

| Step 4 | *Click* | <u>C</u>hange |

Word highlights the proper name "Armstead." Because this spelling is correct, you can ignore it and proceed to the next error. You can choose to ignore words that are correct but do not appear in the dictionaries. To ignore the remaining suggested errors:

Step 5	*Click*	<u>I</u>gnore Once until the spelling and grammar checking is complete and a dialog box opens, indicating the spelling and grammar check is complete
Step 6	*Click*	OK
Step 7	*Save*	the document as *IAEA Letter Revised* and leave it open

In addition to checking the spelling and grammar, you read Kelly's letter and want to find new words to replace certain words in the letter.

3.b Using Synonyms and the Thesaurus to Replace Words

The **Thesaurus** enables you to replace a selected word with another word that has the same or a very similar meaning, called a synonym. Kelly suggests that you substitute a different word for the word "article" in the first body paragraph of her letter. You decide to use the text shortcut menu to find an appropriate replacement word. To find a synonym:

| Step 1 | *Right-click* | the word "article" in the first body paragraph |
| Step 2 | *Point* | to S<u>y</u>nonyms |

A shortcut menu of replacement words appears along with the <u>T</u>hesaurus command. You decide to replace "article" with "commentary."

Step 3	*Click*	commentary on the shortcut menu
Step 4	*Observe*	that the word "commentary" replaces the word "article"
Step 5	*Save*	the document and leave it open

When you want to look up a variety of possible synonyms, you can use the Thesaurus by selecting a word and opening the Thesaurus dialog box. The <u>T</u>hesaurus subcommand under the <u>L</u>anguage command on the <u>T</u>ools menu or the <u>T</u>hesaurus subcommand under the S<u>y</u>nonyms on the text shortcut menu opens the Thesaurus. In the Thesaurus dialog box you can click the noun, verb, adjective, or adverb form of the selected word and then review a list of synonyms for the word. You can click a word from the list of synonyms and then use it to look up additional synonyms. When you find the replacement word you prefer, you insert it in the document to replace the original selected word.

Another Word proofing tool, AutoCorrect, can automatically correct your keying errors.

3.c Using the AutoCorrect Tool

The **AutoCorrect** tool fixes common errors as you key in the text. For example, if you commonly key "adn" for "and," AutoCorrect corrects the error as soon as you press the SPACEBAR. AutoCorrect also corrects two initial capital letters (DEar), capitalizes the first letter of a sentence, capitalizes the names of days, and corrects errors caused by forgetting to turn off the CAPS LOCK key (aRTICLE). The AutoCorrect tool contains an extensive list of symbols and words that are inserted whenever you type an abbreviation for the symbol or word and then press the SPACEBAR. You can specify certain words as exceptions to this automatic correction.

Marcy Ellison, a purchasing assistant, tells you that the AutoCorrect tool will save you time when you create documents. She suggests you verify that the AutoCorrect tool is turned on. To verify that the AutoCorrect tool is turned on:

Step 1	*Click*	<u>T</u>ools
Step 2	*Click*	<u>A</u>utoCorrect Options
Step 3	*Click*	the AutoCorrect tab, if necessary

QUICK TIP

If AutoCorrect makes a change you do not want, press the CTRL + Z keys or click the Undo button on the Standard toolbar to undo the AutoCorrect action.

chapter
three

The AutoCorrect dialog box on your screen should look similar to Figure 3-4.

FIGURE 3-4
AutoCorrect Dialog Box

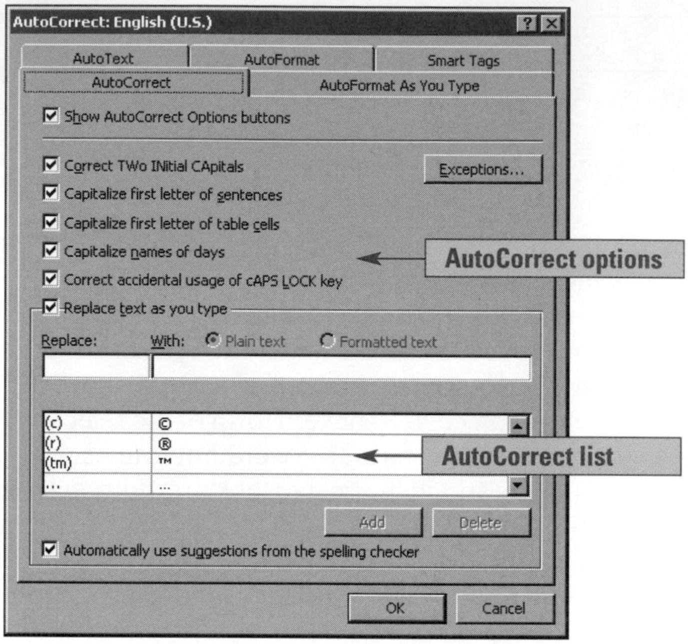

QUICK TIP

AutoCorrect comes with a list of **exceptions**, words or abbreviations that AutoCorrect does not correct automatically. Whenever you key a period (.) in an abbreviation, AutoCorrect may capitalize the next word as if it begins a new sentence. To avoid this, you can set an AutoCorrect exception to ignore capitalization following the period (.) in a specific abbreviation.

If the Automatically add words to list option is turned on in the AutoCorrect Exceptions dialog box, you can backspace over the incorrectly capitalized word and key it again. Word then adds the exception to the list. To keep the AutoCorrect tool from automatically correcting text with mixed upper- and lowercase letters, you can click the INitial CAps tab in the AutoCorrect Exceptions dialog box and add your exception to the list.

Remember that you can use the dialog box Help button to review the all the options on the AutoCorrect tab.

Step 4	*Verify*	that a check mark appears in the Replace text as you type check box
Step 5	*Click*	OK

To test AutoCorrect, you first delete the word "the" before the word "International" in the first body paragraph and then deliberately key the word "teh:"

Step 1	*Select*	the word "the" and following space before the word "International" in the first body paragraph
Step 2	*Press*	the DELETE key
Step 3	*Key*	teh
Step 4	*Verify*	that the word is misspelled
Step 5	*Press*	the SPACEBAR
Step 6	*Observe*	that the word "teh" is automatically corrected to "the" when you press the SPACEBAR

Using AutoCorrect Options

You can control AutoCorrect actions by using the AutoCorrect Options. When you place the mouse pointer over text that has been automatically changed by the AutoCorrect tool, a small blue rectangle appears below the text. If you then move the mouse pointer to the rectangle, the AutoCorrect Options button with a list arrow appears. You click the list arrow to view the AutoCorrect Options menu. To view the AutoCorrect Options button and menu:

Step 1	*Move*	the mouse pointer to the word "the" automatically corrected by the AutoCorrect tool
Step 2	*Observe*	the small blue rectangle
Step 3	*Move*	the mouse pointer to the rectangle
Step 4	*Observe*	the AutoCorrect Options button and list arrow
Step 5	*Click*	the AutoCorrect Options button list arrow to view the menu options

Your screen should look similar to Figure 3-5.

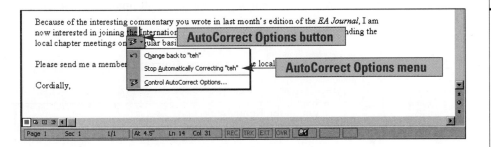

FIGURE 3-5
AutoCorrect Options Menu

You can quickly change text back to the way it was originally keyed, modify the AutoCorrect tool to stop correcting the keyed text, or open the AutoCorrect dialog box and change the AutoCorrect options from this menu. Because you want to maintain the corrected text and continue to automatically correct this particular error in future documents, you can simply close the menu.

| Step 6 | *Click* | in the document area outside the AutoCorrect Options menu to close it |
| Step 7 | *Save* | the *IAEA Letter Revised* document and close it |

Sometimes it is necessary to alter the AutoCorrect tool by adding or removing AutoCorrect items or by setting AutoCorrect exceptions.

**chapter
three**

Customizing AutoCorrect

You can add and delete items in the AutoCorrect list. You can add not only your own common keying errors or misspelled words, but also words and phrases that you would like to insert whenever you key a certain letter combination and press the SPACEBAR. For example, suppose you want to quickly insert the name of your company into a document by keying an abbreviation and then pressing the SPACEBAR. You can add the name of your company and an abbreviation to the AutoCorrect list. Then, when you key the abbreviation and press the SPACEBAR, the company name is inserted in your document. To add the Worldwide Exotic Foods company name to the AutoCorrect list:

Step 1	*Create*	a new, blank document
Step 2	*Key*	Worldwide Exotic Foods, Inc.
Step 3	*Select*	the text (do not include the paragraph mark at the end of the text)
Step 4	*Click*	Tools
Step 5	*Click*	AutoCorrect Options
Step 6	*Click*	the AutoCorrect tab, if necessary
Step 7	*Observe*	that the company name is already entered in the With: text box

Now add an abbreviation for the company name.

Step 8	*Key*	wef in the Replace: text box
Step 9	*Click*	Add
Step 10	*Observe*	that the company name and abbreviation are added to the AutoCorrect list
Step 11	*Click*	OK
Step 12	*Delete*	the selected company name text

You decide to test the abbreviation you added to the AutoCorrect list. To insert the company name using AutoCorrect:

Step 1	*Key*	wef
Step 2	*Press*	the SPACEBAR
Step 3	*Observe*	the company name is automatically inserted

Adding words you key frequently to the AutoCorrect list is a great timesaver. When you no longer need an AutoCorrect entry, you should delete it. You can delete an AutoCorrect entry by selecting the entry in the AutoCorrect tab in the AutoCorrect dialog box and clicking the Delete button. A quick way to delete an AutoCorrect entry is with the AutoCorrect Options button.

To delete the company name from the AutoCorrect list:

Step 1	*Display*	the AutoCorrect Options button
Step 2	*Click*	AutoCorrect Options list arrow to view the options menu
Step 3	*Click*	Stop Automatically Correcting "wef"
Step 4	*Observe*	that the text is returned to its original "Wef"
Step 5	*Verify*	that the entry is removed from the AutoCorrect list
Step 6	*Delete*	the "Wef" text

If you have a large amount of text you key frequently, you can insert it quickly with AutoText.

3.d Inserting Text with the AutoText Tool

An **AutoText** entry is a set of stored text that you can insert in your documents. In this way, it is similar to AutoCorrect; however, AutoText is often used for large amounts of preformatted standard text. Word provides standard AutoText entries or you can create custom AutoText entries.

You review the standard AutoText entries that come with Word, and then create a custom AutoText entry for a letter closing.

Inserting Standard AutoText

Word provides standard AutoText entries, such as complimentary closings or mailing instructions for letters. To view the standard AutoText options:

| Step 1 | *Click* | Insert |
| Step 2 | *Point* | to AutoText |

The standard AutoText menu on your screen should look similar to Figure 3-6.

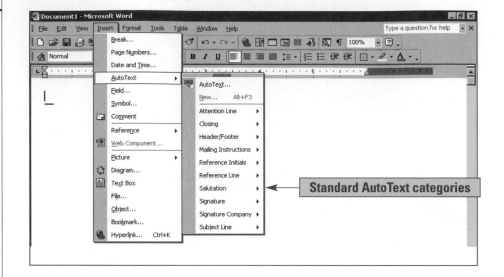

Standard AutoText categories

You can insert the CERTIFIED MAIL mailing instruction in a letter.

Step 3	*Point to*	Mailing Instructions
Step 4	*Click*	CERTIFIED MAIL
Step 5	*Observe*	that the text CERTIFIED MAIL is inserted in the document
Step 6	*Continue*	to explore the standard AutoText entries by inserting an AutoText entry from each AutoText category into the current document and pressing the ENTER key after each insertion
Step 7	*Press*	the ENTER key twice to move the insertion point

In addition to Word standard AutoText, you can create your own custom AutoText entries such as the closing for a letter or standard paragraph text for letters and contracts.

Inserting Custom AutoText

Because you use the same letter closing text for all B. D. Vickers letters, Kelly suggests you create a custom AutoText closing for the letters instead of keying the closing at the end of each letter. To create a custom AutoText entry, first you create and select the text that you want to insert in documents. If you want the text to have a certain format, you must format the text before you select it.

Each AutoText entry must have a unique name. AutoText names can contain spaces and are not case-sensitive. If you name an AutoText entry with uppercase letters, you can insert the entry in the document using lowercase letters. Unless you specify another template, an AutoText entry is saved with the Normal template and is available for all documents created with the Normal template.

You create a custom AutoText complimentary closing for B. D. Vickers that includes the name, your initials, and an Enclosure notation. To create the text for a custom AutoText entry:

Step 1	*Key*	Sincerely,
Step 2	*Press*	the ENTER key four times
Step 3	*Key*	B. D. Vickers
Step 4	*Press*	the ENTER key twice
Step 5	*Key*	your initials and press the SPACEBAR
Step 6	*Press*	the CTRL + Z keys to undo the AutoCorrect capitalization
Step 7	*Press*	the ENTER key twice
Step 8	*Key*	Enclosure

In order for you and Kelly to be able to use the closing you created for B. D. Vickers as custom AutoText, the AutoText entry must be stored in a way that both of you can access it. By default, AutoText entries are created as global entries in the Normal template. The term *global AutoText entry* means that you can use the entry with all documents based on the Normal template.

After you key the text, and format it if necessary, you can turn it into an AutoText entry. To create the AutoText entry:

Step 1	*Select*	all the lines of text (do not select the paragraph mark following Enclosure)
Step 2	*Click*	Insert
Step 3	*Point to*	AutoText
Step 4	*Click*	AutoText

MOUSE TIP

You can view the AutoText toolbar by right-clicking any toolbar and then clicking AutoText.

chapter three

The AutoText tab in the AutoCorrect dialog box on your screen should look similar to Figure 3-7.

By default, Word inserts text from the first line of the selection as the AutoText name. You change this to a more descriptive, brief, unique name for the AutoText entry that will remind you of its content.

Step 5	*Key*	cl (the first two characters of closing) in the Enter AutoText entries here: text box
Step 6	*Click*	Add
Step 7	*Delete*	the selected text

Now you can insert the closing AutoText entry into your document. You can insert a custom AutoText entry by displaying the AutoText dialog box or by keying the name of the entry and pressing the F3 key. You can also key just enough characters for AutoComplete to identify an AutoText entry's unique name and display an AutoComplete tip, then press the F3 key or the ENTER key.

To insert AutoText using the keyboard:

Step 1	*Key*	cl
Step 2	*Press*	the F3 key
Step 3	*Observe*	that the AutoText closing entry is inserted in the document

AutoText can be modified after it is created to add text or formatting.

Editing AutoText Entries

You can easily edit AutoText entries. You need to include B. D. Vickers' job title in the closing AutoText entry. You can edit an AutoText entry by first changing the text, then selecting the changed text, and then adding new AutoText with the same name. To edit the closing AutoText entry:

Step 1	*Move*	the insertion point after the text "B. D. Vickers" in the closing text
Step 2	*Press*	the ENTER key
Step 3	*Key*	Administrative Vice President
Step 4	*Select*	all the lines of the closing, beginning with Sincerely and ending with Enclosure (do not select the paragraph mark following Enclosure)
Step 5	*Click*	Insert
Step 6	*Point to*	AutoText
Step 7	*Click*	AutoText
Step 8	*Click*	cl in the AutoText list
Step 9	*Click*	Add
Step 10	*Click*	Yes to redefine the AutoText entry with Vickers' title

You test the entry by reinserting the closing AutoText. To test the closing entry AutoText:

Step 1	*Delete*	the closing text you just inserted in the document
Step 2	*Key*	cl
Step 3	*Press*	the F3 key

The redefined AutoText closing entry is inserted in the document.

Deleting AutoText Entries

When you no longer need an AutoText entry, you should delete it. To delete an AutoText entry, open the AutoText dialog box. Then click the AutoText name in the AutoText list box and click the Delete button.

QUICK TIP

By default, AutoText entries are automatically saved with the Normal template so they are available for any document created with the Normal template.

MOUSE TIP

You can open the Go To tab in the Find and Replace dialog box by double-clicking the status bar (not a mode indicator). You can also go to specific components of your document with the Select Browse Object button and the Next and Previous buttons located below the vertical scroll bar.

chapter
three

To delete the "cl" AutoText entry:

Step 1	*Open*	the AutoText dialog box
Step 2	*Click*	cl in the AutoText list
Step 3	*Click*	Delete
Step 4	*Click*	OK

The **AutoComplete** tool automatically completes the text of the current date, a day of the week, a month, as well as AutoText entries. As you start to key a date, weekday, month name, or AutoText entry, an AutoComplete tip appears above the insertion point. You press the F3 key or the ENTER key to enter the text or continue keying the text to ignore the AutoComplete suggestion. To enter today's date using AutoComplete:

Step 1	*Move*	the insertion point to a blank line in the document
Step 2	*Key*	the first several characters of the current month name until the AutoComplete tip for the current month appears
Step 3	*Press*	the ENTER key to accept the AutoComplete entry for the current month
Step 4	*Press*	the SPACEBAR
Step 5	*Key*	the day of the month until the AutoComplete tip for the current day and year appears
Step 6	*Press*	the ENTER key to accept the AutoComplete entry for the current day and year
Step 7	*Observe*	the completed current date
Step 8	*Close*	the document without saving

C 3.e Finding and Replacing Text

As you work on existing documents, you may want to move quickly to a certain statement or to each heading in your document. Word can locate a word, a phrase, special characters, or formats each time they occur in a document. You can search for upper- or lowercase text with or without formatting. You can search for whole words or for characters. For example, Word can find the three characters "our" in words such as "hour" or "your" or can find only the whole word "our." Special search operators, such as "?" or "*", enable you to search for text patterns. The

"?" represents any single character. For example, you can use "s?t" to search for three characters beginning with "s" and ending with "t." The "*" represents any series of characters. To search for words ending in "ed" you can use the search pattern "*ed." You can search for words that sound alike but are spelled differently and you can search for all word forms: noun, verb, adjective, or adverb. After Word finds the characters or words, you can edit them manually or replace them with other text automatically.

Finding Text

Kelly asks you to open a document, *Internet Training*, find each instance of the uppercase characters "ISP" as a whole word (so you won't stop at that letter combination in other words), and then bold those characters. To open the document and the Find and Replace dialog box:

Step 1	**Open**	*Internet Training* document located on the Data Disk
Step 2	**Save**	the document as *Internet Training Revised*
Step 3	**Click**	Edit
Step 4	**Click**	Find
Step 5	**Click**	More, if necessary, to expand the dialog box

The Find and Replace dialog box expands to show the options. The dialog box on your screen should look similar to Figure 3-8.

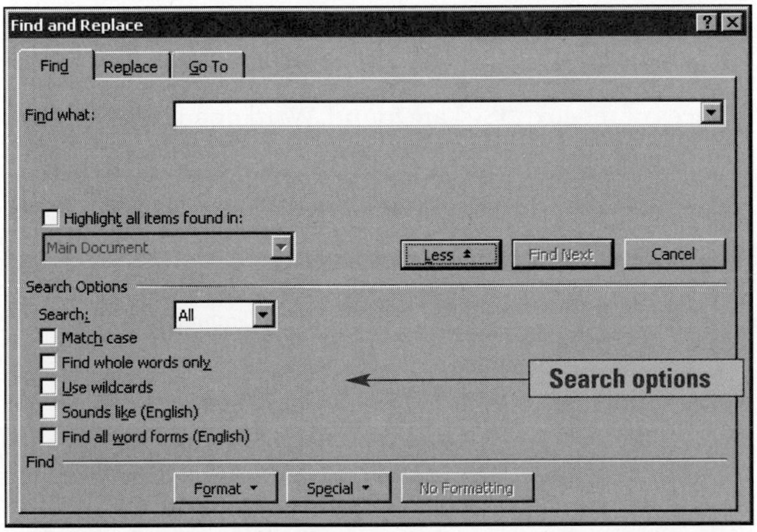

FIGURE 3-8
Find and Replace Dialog Box

Notice that "All" is the default option selected in the Search Options group. This means that Word will search the entire document, regardless

MENU TIP

You can use the Find command on the Edit menu to locate specific text in your document and the Replace command on the Edit menu to replace specified text with new text.

QUICK TIP

You can select all instances of a word or phrase at once with the Highlight all items found in: check box and list.

chapter
three

of the position of the insertion point. You can specify that Word find only text with the exact case by turning on the Match case option.

To find the uppercase characters "ISP" as a whole word and bold each instance:

Step 1	*Key*	ISP in the Find what: text box
Step 2	*Click*	the Match case check box to insert a check mark, if necessary
Step 3	*Click*	the Find whole words only check box to insert a check mark, if necessary
Step 4	*Remove*	the check marks from the remaining check boxes, if necessary
Step 5	*Click*	Less to collapse the dialog box
Step 6	*Click*	Find Next

The first instance of the text "ISP" is selected. When the Find and Replace dialog box opens it becomes the active window and the Word application window becomes inactive (the title bar is gray). To edit or delete the selected text you must activate the Word document window. If the Find and Replace dialog box hides the selected text or the toolbar buttons, you can drag it out of the way by its title bar.

Step 7	*Click*	the Word document window to activate the window (the title bar is blue when the window is active)
Step 8	*Click*	the Bold button **B** on the Formatting toolbar

You continue to find and bold each instance of the text "ISP." When all the instances of the text "ISP" are found, Word opens a confirmation dialog box telling you the search is finished.

Step 9	*Click*	Find Next in the Find and Replace dialog box
Step 10	*Click*	the Bold button **B** on the Formatting toolbar to activate the Word window and format the text in one step
Step 11	*Continue*	to find and bold the text "ISP"
Step 12	*Click*	OK to close the confirmation dialog box when it opens
Step 13	*Click*	Cancel to close the Find and Replace dialog box

Kelly instructs you to find each instance of the phrase "electronic mail" in the *Internet Training Revised* document and change it to "e-mail."

Replacing Text

Often you want to search for a word, phrase, special character, or format and replace it with a different word, phrase, special character, or format. You can have Word replace the text or formatting automatically without adding it manually each time. To replace the phrase "electronic mail" with the word "e-mail" in the *Internet Training Revised* document:

Step 1	*Click*	E̲dit
Step 2	*Click*	R̲eplace
Step 3	*Key*	electronic mail in the Fi̲nd what: text box
Step 4	*Press*	the TAB key to move the insertion point to the next text box
Step 5	*Verify*	that Options: Match Case appears below the Fi̲nd what: text box (the Find whole words only option automatically turns off when you search for multiple words)
Step 6	*Key*	e-mail in the Replace wi̲th: text box
Step 7	*Click*	F̲ind Next and verify that the phrase "electronic mail" is selected
Step 8	*Click*	R̲eplace
Step 9	*Drag*	the dialog box out of the way and scroll to view the selected text, if necessary

The first instance of the phrase "electronic mail" is replaced with the word "e-mail" and Word automatically highlights the next occurrence of the phrase. When Word finds another match, you can replace the phrase by clicking the R̲eplace button. If you want to leave the text unchanged, click the F̲ind Next button to skip that occurrence of the text. If you want to replace every occurrence of the text without reviewing each one, click the Replace A̲ll button. When no more matches exist, a confirmation dialog box opens, informing you that Word finished searching the document.

Step 10	*Click*	R̲eplace
Step 11	*Click*	OK to close the confirmation dialog box
Step 12	*Close*	the Find and Replace dialog box
Step 13	*Save*	the document and close it

With find and replace, you can quickly and easily modify any document.

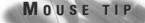

MOUSE TIP

You can close the dialog box and click the Next Find/GoTo or Previous Find/GoTo buttons below the vertical scroll bar to select the next instance of the text or formatting.

QUICK TIP

The Find and Replace dialog box remembers the last search options you set. Always review and turn on or off the search options before each new search. You can also search for and replace formatting as well as text. Always click the No Formatting button to turn off any formatting options set from the previous search before you begin a new search.

chapter
three

Summary

▶ By default, Word checks the spelling and grammar in your document as you type. A wavy red line indicates a misspelled or mistyped word, and a wavy green line indicates a grammar error.

▶ When you display the Spelling and Grammar dialog box, you can choose to ignore the selected word, change it to another word, add the word to a custom dictionary, delete the word from the document, or add the word and its correction to the AutoCorrect list.

▶ The Thesaurus tool and Synonyms command allow you to substitute a word(s) with the same or similar meaning for the word containing the insertion point.

▶ You can display the Word Count toolbar to view the number of pages, words, characters, and other document statistics for the current document.

▶ The AutoCorrect tool is turned on by default and allows you to automatically correct commonly misspelled or mistyped words as you type or insert text by keying an abbreviation for the text and then pressing the SPACEBAR.

▶ The AutoCorrect Options button allows you to manage automatic corrections.

▶ You can add items to the AutoCorrect list and create exceptions to the AutoCorrect list.

▶ The AutoText features allow you to insert standard text such as mailing instructions or create and save custom text and then insert it as needed.

▶ The AutoComplete tool allows you to automatically insert the current month, day of the week, and date by pressing the F3 or ENTER key.

▶ You can quickly find or find and replace text, formatting, and special characters.

Commands Review

Action	Menu Bar	Shortcut Menu	Toolbar	Task Pane	Keyboard
Turn on or off the AutoCorrect tool	Tools, AutoCorrect Options				ALT + T, A
Check spelling and grammar	Tools, Spelling and Grammar	Right-click a word with a wavy red or green line	ABC ✓ ☰✓		ALT + T, S F7 ALT + F7
Substitute words with same or similar meaning	Tools, Language, Thesaurus	Right-click a word, point to Synonyms			ALT + T, L, T
Create, edit, insert, delete custom AutoText entry	Insert, AutoText, AutoText				SHIFT + F7 ALT + I, A, X F3 ENTER ALT + F3
Insert standard AutoText	Insert, AutoText				ALT + I, A
Print AutoText entries	File, Print				ALT + F, P
Find and replace text, formatting, and special characters	Edit, Find or Replace		⚙		ALT + E, F or E CTRL + F CTRL + H
Go to a specific page, section, or line	Edit, Go To		⚙		ALT + E, G CTRL + G
View document statistics	Tools, Word Count				ALT + T, W

Concepts Review

Circle the correct answer.

1. The AutoCorrect tool:
- [a] provides statistics about your document.
- [b] checks for misspelled words as you key text, and underlines them with a wavy red line.
- [c] checks the grammar in the document.
- [d] corrects Caps Lock errors when you press the SPACEBAR.

2. The Thesaurus tool:
- [a] adds new words to the custom dictionary.
- [b] corrects two initial capitalization.
- [c] checks for misspelled words as you key text.
- [d] allows you to substitute words.

3. The Spelling and Grammar tool does not:
- [a] indicate grammatical errors.
- [b] identify words with capitalization problems.
- [c] show you spelling and grammar errors as you key.
- [d] automatically complete dates.

4. The AutoComplete tool:
- [a] presents a tip with contents you can insert by pressing the ENTER key.
- [b] checks the readability of the document.
- [c] checks the spelling in the document.
- [d] checks the grammar in the document.

5. An AutoText entry:
- [a] must have a unique name.
- [b] cannot be saved for future use.
- [c] cannot be changed once it is created.
- [d] replaces text as soon as you press the SPACEBAR.

6. You can create a new AutoText entry with the:
- [a] F3 key.
- [b] AutoText subcommand on the Insert menu.
- [c] AutoComplete tool and the ENTER key.
- [d] INSERT key.

chapter three

7. **Which Find option allows you to avoid search results that include the individual characters of a word inside other words?**
[a] Match case
[b] Find whole words only
[c] Sounds like
[d] Find all word forms

8. **You can check the grammar in your document with the:**
[a] AutoComplete command.
[b] Thesaurus command.
[c] Synonyms command.
[d] Spelling and Grammar status mode indicator.

9. **You can turn on or off the automatic checking of spelling and grammar in the:**
[a] AutoCorrect dialog box.
[b] Options dialog box.
[c] Format dialog box.
[d] AutoText dialog box.

10. **Which option is not available in the Spelling and Grammar dialog box?**
[a] selecting suggested spellings for a word from a list
[b] ignoring the selected word
[c] adding the word to the AutoCorrect list
[d] adding the word to the AutoText list

Circle **T** if the statement is true or **F** if the statement is false.

T F   1. The Spelling and Grammar tool checks the readability of your document.

T F   2. The AutoText tool allows Word to check for spelling errors as you key.

T F   3. The Synonyms command displays words with the same or similar meaning as that of a selected word.

T F   4. You can check the spelling and grammar of your document only with a toolbar button.

T F   5. The Spelling and Grammar tool presents a ScreenTip containing the complete text of the word you are keying.

T F   6. When a word is not found in the dictionaries by the Spelling and Grammar tool, a wavy green line appears underneath it.

T F   7. AutoText names are case-sensitive.

T F   8. You can manage automatic corrections with the AutoCorrect Options button.

T F   9. The AutoCorrect tool automatically corrects commonly misspelled words as they are keyed.

T F   10. You can use the Word Count toolbar to see statistics related to the current document.

Skills Review

Exercise 1

1. Open the *Vancouver Report With Errors* document located on the Data Disk.
2. Correct the spelling errors using the Spelling and Grammar command on the Tools menu.
3. Save the document as *Vancouver Report Revised*. Preview, print, and close the document.

Exercise 2

1. Open the *Solicitation Letter With Errors* document located on the Data Disk.
2. Select the text "Current date" and use AutoComplete to replace it with the actual date.
3. Correct the spelling and grammar errors using the Spelling and Grammar Status mode indicator.

4. Use the Synonyms command to choose another word for "growth" in the first body paragraph.

5. Save the document as *Solicitation Letter Revised*. Preview, print, and close the document.

Exercise 3   C

1. Open the *Personal Letter With Errors* document located on the Data Disk.

2. Select the text "Current date" and use AutoComplete to replace it with the actual date.

3. Correct the spelling and grammar errors using the shortcut menus.

4. Use the Thesaurus tool to select another word for "arrangements" in the last paragraph. (*Hint:* Right-click the word, point to Synonyms, and then click Thesaurus.)

5. Replace the text "Student's name" with your name.

6. Save the document as *Personal Letter Revised*. Preview, print, and close the document.

Exercise 4   C

1. Create a new, blank document.

2. Create an AutoText entry to insert a standard complimentary closing for the letters signed by R. F. Williams. Use the "Sincerely yours" closing text. Add your initials and an Attachment line. Name the AutoText entry "Williams Closing."

3. Insert the "Williams Closing" AutoText entry into a new, blank document using the F3 key or the ENTER key.

4. Save the document as *Williams Closing*.

5. Preview and print the document.

6. Edit the "Williams Closing" AutoText entry to include the job title "Vice President Marketing."

7. Save the document as *Williams Closing Revised*. Preview, print, and close the document.

Exercise 5   C

1. Open the *Client Letter* document located on the Data Disk.

2. Select the text "Current date" and use AutoComplete to replace it with the current date.

3. Insert the "Williams Closing" AutoText entry created in Exercise 4 at the bottom of the document. Add any additional blank lines as necessary.

4. Save the document as *Williams Letter*. Preview, print, and close the document.

Exercise 6   C

1. Print all the current AutoText entries.

2. Delete the "Williams Closing" AutoText entry you created in Exercise 4.

3. Close the Word application to update the Normal template.

Exercise 7   C

1. Open the *Application Letter With Errors* document located on the Data Disk.

2. Select the text "Current date" and use AutoComplete to replace it with the actual date.

3. Move the second body paragraph beginning "Per our conversation" to the first body paragraph position.

chapter three

4. Move the last body paragraph beginning "If you have" and make it the second sentence of the second body paragraph. Delete any extra blank lines, if necessary.

5. Correct the spelling and grammar using the Spelling and Grammar button on the Standard toolbar.

6. Use the Synonyms command to select another word for "department" in the first paragraph.

7. Save the document as *Application Letter Revised.* Preview, print, and close the document.

Exercise 8   C

1. Create the document below just as you see it. Use appropriate margins for a letter to be printed on 2-inch letter-head paper. Correct any spelling or grammar errors as you key using the Spelling and Grammar shortcut menus. Use the AutoComplete and standard AutoText features where appropriate to complete the letter, for example, to enter the current date.

Current date

Ms. Lavonia Jackson
Gift Baskets Galore!
1001 Kirby Drive
Houston, TX 77043-1001

Dear Ms. Jackson:

congratulations on starting your own gift shop. I know you will be successful because of the tremendos the growth of the gift basket market.

We would like to order our holiday gifts from your shop and are lookin forward to receiving your holiday catalog as soon as it is available.

Sincerely,

Tom McGregor
Personnel Manager

mj

2. Save the document as *McGregor Letter*. Preview, print, and close the document.

Exercise 9

1. Open the *British Columbia Report* document located on the Data Disk.

2. Find each occurrence of the text "British Columbia" and replace it with "New York." (*Hint:* Remember to clear any formatting that is set in the dialog box.)

3. Change the left margin to 1 inch.

4. Save the document as *New York Report*. Preview, print, and close the document.

Case Projects

SCANS

Project 1 C

You have been assigned to work in the Legal Department at Worldwide Foods for two weeks. The department manager has asked you to find some way for the three secretaries in the department to save time by using Word to create and proof their documents. Prepare a document describing how the secretaries can use the AutoComplete, AutoText, AutoCorrect, and Find/Replace tools to save time. Include spelling and grammar shortcuts. Use the Spelling and Grammar tool to correct any spelling and grammar errors in your document. Use the AutoCorrect tool to quickly enter symbols and text. Use the Thesaurus tool to replace words with more appropriate or descriptive ones. Use the AutoComplete tool to enter the current date. Save and print the document.

Project 2 C

As Kelly's assistant, you are often called on to solve user problems with the Word application. You received the following list of problems from the secretaries in the Tax Department about the AutoText and AutoCorrect features:

1. How can I store an AutoCorrect entry without its original formatting?
2. My AutoComplete tips are not displaying when I insert AutoText.
3. How can I share AutoText entries with other secretaries in my department?

Using the Office Assistant or Ask A Question Box, research the answers to these questions. Use the keywords "AutoComplete," "AutoText," and "templates" for your search. Create, save, and print a document that describes how to solve these problems. Use the Spelling and Grammar tool to correct any spelling and grammar errors in your document. Use the AutoCorrect tool to quickly enter symbols and text. Use the Thesaurus tool to replace words with more appropriate or descriptive ones. Use the AutoComplete tool to enter the current date. Discuss your proposed solutions with a classmate.

Project 3 C

One of the legal secretaries asks for your help creating AutoCorrect exceptions. Using the Office Assistant or Ask A Question Box, research the AutoCorrect exceptions list tool. Create a new document containing a short paragraph describing how to use this tool. Use the Spelling and Grammar tool to correct any spelling and grammar errors in your document. Use the AutoCorrect tool to quickly enter symbols and text. Use the Thesaurus tool to replace words with more appropriate or descriptive ones. Use the AutoComplete tool to enter the current date. Save and print the document. Open the AutoCorrect dialog box and add two items of your choice to the AutoCorrect Exceptions list.

chapter three

Project 4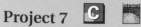

Mark Lee, a human resources consultant, is giving a 30-minute presentation on creating professional resumes at the next meeting of the International Association of Executive Assistants. He asks you to help prepare a list of topics by looking for Web pages that discuss how to create a resume. Connect to the Internet and search the Web for information about writing a resume. Save at least two URLs as "favorites." Print at least two Web pages.

Project 5 [C]

Using the research on creating resumes you prepared in Project 4, create, print, and save a document that Mark can use to prepare his presentation. Use the Spelling and Grammar tool to correct any spelling and grammar errors in your document. Use the AutoCorrect tool to quickly enter symbols and text. Use the Thesaurus tool to replace words with more appropriate or descriptive ones. Use the AutoComplete tool to enter the current date.

Project 6 [C]

B. D. Vickers has noticed that some letters and reports that contain spelling and grammatical errors are being mailed to clients. He asks you to prepare a document describing how to use the Spelling and Grammar tool, which he will give to all administrative assistants and secretaries during a special luncheon next week. Create a new document containing at least four paragraphs outlining how to use the Spelling and Grammar tool *including* custom/special dictionaries and adding a word to the AutoCorrect list during the spell-checking process as well as how to use the various options in the Spelling and Grammar dialog box. Use the Spelling and Grammar tool to correct any spelling and grammar errors in your document. Use the AutoCorrect tool to quickly enter symbols and text. Use the Thesaurus tool to replace words with more appropriate or descriptive ones. Use the AutoComplete tool to enter the current date. Save, preview, and print the document.

Project 7 [C]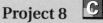

Kelly wants to purchase several reference books for the company library on how to use Microsoft Word. She doesn't have time to check out the local bookstores so she has asked you to look for the books at several online bookstores. Connect to the Internet and search the Web for online bookstores. Load several online bookstore Web pages and search each Web site for books on how to use Microsoft Word. Use the information you gather from the bookstores to prepare a document with a list of books by title. Include the author's name, the price of the book, and the proposed shipping time. Use the Spelling and Grammar tool to correct any spelling and grammar errors in your document. Use the AutoCorrect tool to quickly enter symbols and text. Use the Thesaurus tool to replace words with more appropriate or descriptive ones. Use the AutoComplete tool to enter the current date. Save, preview, and print the document.

Project 8 [C]

B. D. Vickers wants to know something about the readability of the documents the administrative staff is preparing and has asked you to find out which tool in Word can provide that information. Using the Office Assistant or Ask A Question Box, research the readability statistics displayed by the Spelling and Grammar tool. Create a new document with at least three paragraphs describing the readability statistics and formulas. Use the Spelling and Grammar tool to correct any spelling and grammar errors in your document. Use the AutoCorrect tool to quickly enter symbols and text. Use the Thesaurus tool to replace words with more appropriate or descriptive ones. Use the AutoComplete tool to enter the current date. Save, preview, and print the document.

Applying Character Formatting

Chapter Overview

The ability to format text provides a word processing application much of its power. The Word formatting features give you the ability to create professional, unique-looking documents. In this chapter, you learn how to change the appearance of text by changing fonts and font styles and by applying character styles and special effects to text characters. You also learn to copy character formats, review and change text formatting using a task pane, and change the case of text. Finally, you learn to highlight text to be read online in a color and to insert symbols and special characters.

LEARNING OBJECTIVES

- ► Change fonts and font size
- ► Apply font styles, character styles, and special character effects
- ► Change the case of text
- ► Highlight text in a document
- ► Insert symbols and special characters

Case profile

Because of your successful performance in the Purchasing Department, the Marketing Department has requested you to fill in for Elizabeth Chang, the assistant secretary, who is going on a short holiday. Before she left, Elizabeth left several documents for you to format.

chapter four

4.a Changing Fonts and Font Size

You can change the appearance of a document by changing the shape and size of text characters, by changing the spacing between the characters, and by applying special character effects. Changing the appearance of individual text characters or groups of characters is called **character formatting**. You can apply character formatting to text using menu commands, a shortcut menu, toolbar buttons, and with links or commands in the Reveal Formatting task pane.

One of the first formatting choices you make is the type of font and the font size you want to use in a document. A **font** is a set of printed characters with the same size and appearance. A font has three characteristics: typeface, style, and point (font) size.

1. **Typeface** refers to the design and appearance of printed characters. Here are some examples of different typefaces:

   Times New Roman   Courier New
   Arial   *Brush Script MT*

2. **Style** refers to bold or italic print. *Italic print is slanted to the right* and **bold print is darker**.

3. **Point (font) size** refers to the height of the printed characters. There are 72 points to an inch; the larger the point size, the larger the characters. Some common point sizes include:

   8 point   10 point   12 point

A font may be **monospaced**, where all characters occupy an identical amount of horizontal space or **proportional**, where different characters occupy various amounts of horizontal space. Courier is an example of a monospaced font and Times New Roman is an example of a proportional font. Most people who use a word processing application to create text documents use proportional fonts.

There are two main categories of proportional fonts: serif and sans serif. A **serif** is a small line extension at the beginning and end of a character to help the reader's eye move across the text. Serif fonts are often used in documents with a large amount of text. A **sans serif** font is one that does not have the small line extensions on its characters (*sans* is the French word for without). Sans serif fonts are often used for paragraph headings and document titles. The Times New Roman font is an example of a serif font and the Arial font is an example of a sans serif font.

MENU TIP

You can select a font from the Font: list box on the Font tab in the Font dialog box. To open the dialog box, click the Font command on the Format menu or right-click selected text and click Font on the shortcut menu.

The default font and font size in Word are the Times New Roman font and 12-point font size. According to Elizabeth's notes, several changes need to be made to the *Library Bulletin* document. First, the document title should be in Arial font and the entire document should be in 11-point font size.

notes   This book assumes that your computer is connected to a Hewlett-Packard LaserJet printer and you use TrueType fonts. If you have a different printer, make the appropriate selections for your printer.

Changing Fonts

To change the font, first select the text to be changed. For example, if you want to change the font for the entire document, select the entire document. Then select the font you want to use. If the document has not been keyed yet, you can select the font before you key the text. That font selection is then used throughout the document. Currently, the entire *Library Bulletin* document is formatted with the Times New Roman, 10-point font. You begin by opening the document and then changing the font of the title text, "INFORMATION SYSTEMS LIBRARY BULLETIN," to the Arial TrueType font. To change the font:

Step 1	*Open*	the *Library Bulletin* document located on the Data Disk
Step 2	*Select*	INFORMATION SYSTEMS LIBRARY BULLETIN (the title text)
Step 3	*Click*	the Font button list arrow `Times New Roman ▾` on the Formatting toolbar

The font list on your screen should look similar to that in Figure 4-1.

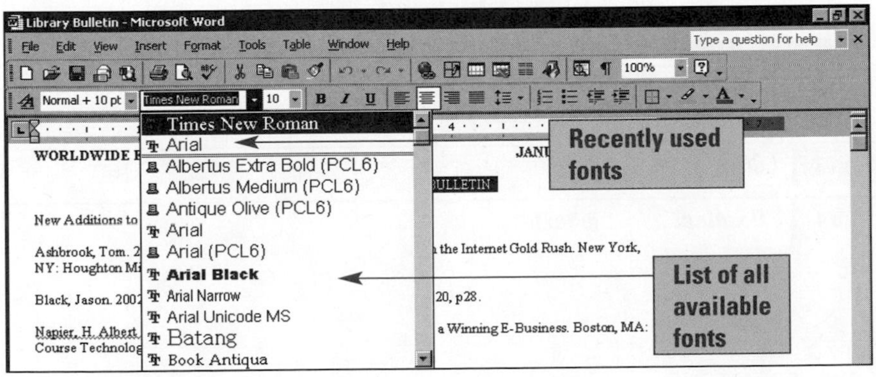

QUICK TIP

Word uses the Times New Roman, 12-point size font as the default font for all documents based on the Normal template. You can change the default font for all new documents based on the Normal template with the Default button in the Font dialog box.

FIGURE 4-1
Font List

chapter
four

Notice that some fonts on the Font list have a symbol to the left of the font name. A "TT" symbol indicates that the font is a **TrueType font** that prints text exactly the way it is displayed on your screen. A printer symbol next to a font indicates that the assigned printer supports the font. A list of the most recently used fonts may appear at the top of the font list, followed by a horizontal double line.

| Step 4 | *Click* | Arial (scroll to view this option, if necessary) |
| Step 5 | *Deselect* | the text |

The document title font is different from the text font, making it distinct. You also can change the font size for your documents.

Changing Font Size

The point (font) size for the text of the entire document is currently 10 point. The *Library Bulletin* document should be in 11 point. To change the point size for the entire document to 11 point:

| Step 1 | *Select* | the entire document |
| Step 2 | *Click* | the Font Size button list arrow 12 ▾ on the Formatting toolbar |

The Font Size list on your screen should look similar to the one in Figure 4-2.

FIGURE 4-2
Font Size List

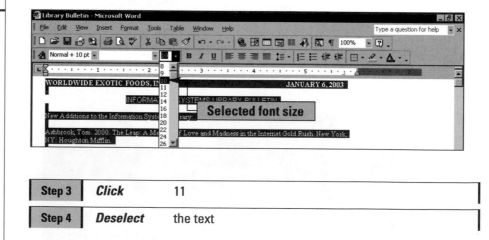

| Step 3 | *Click* | 11 |
| Step 4 | *Deselect* | the text |

The entire document changes to 11-point type. Next, you need to add emphasis to certain text by applying font styles, such as bold and italic.

4.b Applying Font Styles, Character Styles, and Special Character Effects

Elizabeth wants certain words emphasized in the *Library Bulletin* document. You can do this by applying the bold or italic font styles to the text.

Applying the Bold Font Style

Applying the **Bold** style makes the selected text darker than other text to attract a reader's attention. When you apply the Bold style, Word makes the text appear darker on the screen as well as on the printed page.

To add the Bold style to the text "New Additions to the Information Systems Library":

Step 1	*Select*	New Additions to the Information Systems Library (do not select the colon)
Step 2	*Click*	the Bold button **B** on the Formatting toolbar
Step 3	*Deselect*	the text, leaving the insertion point in the paragraph

The text appears darker. The Bold button on the Formatting toolbar is outlined with a border, indicating the Bold style is applied. You remove the Bold style by clicking the Bold button again. The first line of the document contains the company name and date formatted with the Bold style. Elizabeth's notes tell you to remove the bold style. To remove the Bold style:

Step 1	*Select*	the first line of the document using the selection bar
Step 2	*Click*	the Bold button **B** on the Formatting toolbar
Step 3	*Deselect*	the text, leaving the insertion point in the first line

QUICK TIP

You can use keyboard shortcuts to apply font styles. For example, press the CTRL + B keys to apply the Bold style to selected text. Use the Ask A Question Box to view and print a complete list of keyboard shortcuts.

MENU TIP

You can apply the font styles to text on the Fo<u>n</u>t tab in the Font dialog box. You can open the Font dialog box by clicking the <u>F</u>ont command on the F<u>o</u>rmat menu or shortcut menu.

chapter four

The text is no longer bold and the Bold button on the Formatting toolbar no longer has a border.

Applying the Italic Font Style

Italicizing text allows you to emphasize text by slanting it to the right. You apply and remove italic formatting the same way you do bold formatting—in this case, by selecting the text and applying the italic style. Elizabeth's notes indicate the magazine title in which Jason Black's article appears should be italicized. To italicize the magazine title:

Step 1	*Select*	the magazine title "Internet World" in the second item in the list
Step 2	*Click*	the Italic button I on the Formatting toolbar
Step 3	*Deselect*	the text, leaving the insertion point in the title

The magazine title is italicized. The Italic button on the Formatting toolbar has a border, indicating that the italic style is applied to the text.

You can remove the italic style by selecting the formatted text and again clicking the Italic button on the Formatting toolbar.

Applying Underline Formatting

Emphasizing text by placing a line below the text is called **underlining**. You can choose to underline selected letters, selected words, or selected words and the spaces between them. Word also provides a variety of underlines you can use to enhance text.

You want to add a thick single line below the title "New Additions to the Information Systems Library." This underline style is not available by clicking the Underline button on the Formatting toolbar, which formats text and the spaces between the text with a thin single line. Instead, you must open the Font dialog box to see a complete list of underline styles.

A quick way to open the Font dialog box is with a shortcut menu. To apply a thick single underline to text:

Step 1	*Select*	New Additions to the Information Systems Library (do not select the colon)
Step 2	*Right-click*	the selected text
Step 3	*Click*	Font
Step 4	*Click*	the Font tab, if necessary

The Font tab in the Font dialog box on your screen should look similar to Figure 4-3.

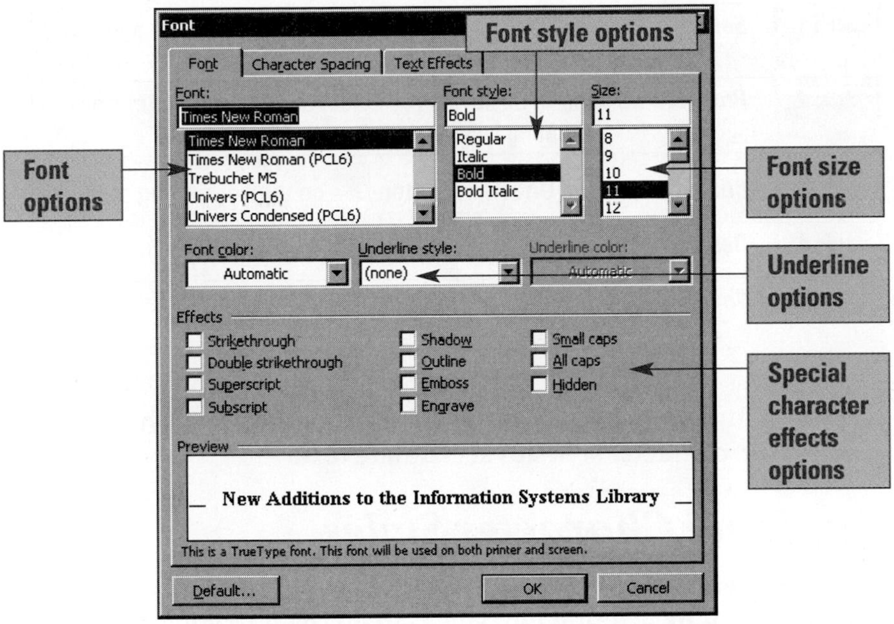

FIGURE 4-3
Font Dialog Box

You can change the font, font style, font size, underlining, underline color, and color of selected text on the Font tab. The Effects group provides options for applying special effects to selected text. The Preview area provides a sample of the formatting options before they are applied to the selected text.

Step 5	*Click*	the Underline style: list arrow
Step 6	*Click*	the thick single line option (the fifth option in the list)
Step 7	*Preview*	the underline formatting in the dialog box
Step 8	*Click*	OK
Step 9	*Deselect*	the text

The text is underlined with a thick single line. The book titles in the first and third items in the list should be underlined. You can add or remove a thin single underline applied to words and spaces with the

chapter
four

Underline button on the Formatting toolbar. To add a thin single underline to both book titles at one time:

Step 1	*Select*	the book title "The Leap: A Memoir of Love and Madness in the Internet Gold Rush"
Step 2	*Press & hold*	the CTRL key as you select the book title "Dot-Commerce: Creating a Winning E-Business"
Step 3	*Click*	the Underline button 𝐔 on the Formatting toolbar
Step 4	*Deselect*	the text
Step 5	*Save*	the document as *Library Bulletin Revised* and leave it open

In addition to using bold, italic, and underlining to emphasize text, you can use character styles to accentuate text.

Applying Character Styles

A **character style** is a collection of character formatting attributes—such as font, font size, and font style—that is given a special name and then applied to selected text by that name. Character styles are applied only to selected text. For example, the Strong character style contains the default Times New Roman font, the default 12-point font size, and the Bold font style. When you want to apply these three formatting attributes to selected text, you can apply all three at once by using the Strong character style.

Elizabeth wants you to apply the Strong character style to the first line of text. You also want to view the nonprinting formatting marks as you format the document. To view the formatting marks and apply the Strong style:

Step 1	*Click*	the Show/Hide button ¶ on the Standard toolbar
Step 2	*Select*	the first line of text
Step 3	*Click*	the Styles and Formatting button 🄰 on the Formatting toolbar

The Styles and Formatting task pane opens. Your screen should look similar to Figure 4-4.

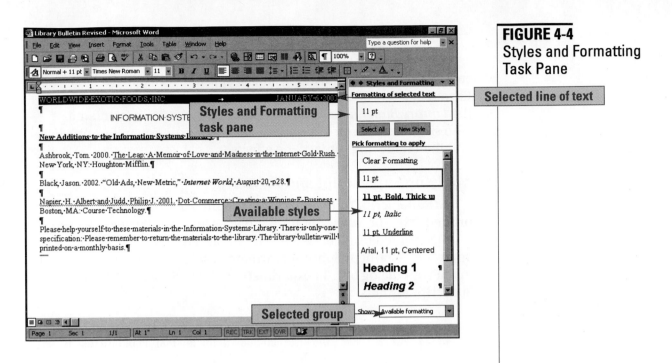

FIGURE 4-4
Styles and Formatting
Task Pane

The Formatting of selected text box in the Styles and Formatting task pane shows you the style applied to the currently selected text. The Pick formatting to apply list allows you to select a group of styles to view: all the default available styles for the current document, only the styles currently being used, or a complete list of styles. You select the group of styles to place in the Pick formatting to apply list with the Show: list. To view a complete list of styles:

Step 1	*Click*	the Show: list arrow in the Styles and Formatting task pane
Step 2	*Click*	All styles to view a complete scrollable list of styles
Step 3	*Scroll*	the Pick formatting to apply list to view the Strong character style
Step 4	*Click*	Strong in the Pick formatting to apply list
Step 5	*Deselect*	the text
Step 6	*Observe*	the formatted text
Step 7	*Close*	the Styles and Formatting task pane

In addition to using character styles to format text, you can use special character effects to add emphasis to text.

**chapter
four**

Applying Special Character Effects

Another way to emphasize text is to add special character effects, such as superscript, subscript, small caps, and strikethrough effects. Elizabeth asks you to add special character effects to specified text in the *Library Bulletin Revised* document. Because you are unfamiliar with special character effects, you decide to experiment by applying and then removing some of the effects.

Applying Superscript and Subscript

The **Superscript** format places text slightly above a line of normal printed text. The **Subscript** format places text slightly below a line of normal printed text. This is ^{superscript}, and this is $_{subscript}$. You can apply Superscript or Subscript formats to selected text in the Font tab in the Font dialog box. To experiment with the Superscript and Subscript formats:

Step 1	*Move*	the insertion point to the left margin before the "B" in "Black"
Step 2	*Key*	1
Step 3	*Select*	the number 1
Step 4	*Click*	Format
Step 5	*Click*	Font
Step 6	*Click*	the Font tab, if necessary
Step 7	*Click*	the Superscript check box to insert a check mark
Step 8	*Click*	OK
Step 9	*Deselect*	the text
Step 10	*Observe*	the [1]Black superscript notation

You apply the Subscript format the same way. To apply the Subscript format:

Step 1	*Move*	the insertion point to the left margin before the "N" in "Napier"
Step 2	*Key*	2
Step 3	*Select*	the number 2
Step 4	*Open*	the Font tab in the Font dialog box
Step 5	*Click*	the Subscript check box to insert a check mark
Step 6	*Click*	OK

Step 7	*Deselect*	the text
Step 8	*Observe*	the $_2$Napier subscript notation
Step 9	*Delete*	the superscript and subscript text
Step 10	*Save*	the document and leave it open

Applying Strikethrough

When you edit a document online, you might want to indicate text that should be deleted. One way to do this is to format the text with the **Strikethrough** effect, which draws a line through selected text. To add the Strikethrough effect to the first sentence of the last paragraph:

Step 1	*Select*	the text "in the Information Systems Library"
Step 2	*Open*	the Font tab in the Font dialog box
Step 3	*Click*	the Strikethrough check box to insert a check mark
Step 4	*Click*	OK

The selected text now has a line through it, indicating it could be deleted from the document. Because you don't want to delete the text, you remove the Strikethrough.

| Step 5 | *Click* | the Undo button 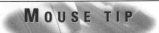 on the Standard toolbar |
| Step 6 | *Deselect* | the text |

Elizabeth indicated that the library name needs to be distinguished from the rest of the text. You decide to apply the Small caps effect.

Applying Small Caps

The **Small caps** effect is a special character effect that displays selected text in all-uppercase characters, where any characters keyed with the SHIFT key pressed display larger than the remaining characters. The Small caps format is appropriate for headings and titles, such as "Information Systems Library." To apply the Small caps effect:

Step 1	*Select*	the text "Information Systems Library" in the first sentence of the last paragraph
Step 2	*Open*	the Font tab in the Font dialog box
Step 3	*Click*	the Small caps check box to insert a check mark

chapter
four

| Step 4 | *Click* | OK |

The text is in all-uppercase characters, with the first character of each word slightly taller than the remaining characters in the word.

| Step 5 | *Continue* | by applying the Small caps effect to each instance of "Information Systems Library" |

The Small caps effect is not visible in the centered title at this time because the text is already in all-uppercase letters.

Applying Character Spacing and Animation Effects

Adding extra spacing between text characters in titles adds variety and interest to a document. **Character spacing** is the amount of white space that appears between characters. You can change the character spacing by scaling the characters to a specific percentage, expanding or condensing the characters a specific number of points, or by kerning. **Kerning** adjusts the space between particular pairs of characters, depending on the font.

You want the title of the *Library Bulletin Revised* document to stand out more, so you scale the text. To scale the title text so that it is stretched horizontally to be 120% of its original width:

Step 1	*Select*	INFORMATION SYSTEMS LIBRARY BULLETIN (the title text)
Step 2	*Open*	the Font dialog box
Step 3	*Click*	the Character Spacing tab
Step 4	*Key*	120 in the Scale: text box
Step 5	*Press*	the ENTER key

The text is "stretched" horizontally to 120% of its original width. Upon her return, Elizabeth plans to attach the *Library Bulletin Revised* document to e-mail messages so recipients can read the document online. She wants you to add animation effects to the *Library Bulletin Revised* document that draw attention to the document's title. To add animation effects:

| Step 1 | *Verify* | that the title text is still selected |
| Step 2 | *Open* | the Font dialog box |

Step 3	**Click**	the Text Effects tab
Step 4	**Click**	Marching Red Ants in the Animations: list box
Step 5	**Click**	OK
Step 6	**Observe**	that a red dashed moving box now appears around the title
Step 7	**Deselect**	the text
Step 8	**Save**	the document and leave it open

The red marching ants will attract immediate attention to the document.

Using the Format Painter

Once you have applied character formatting to text, it's often faster to duplicate that formatting to other text rather than reapplying it each time. Copying formats, rather than recreating them, ensures consistency and saves time. You can copy and paste character formats quickly with the Format Painter button on the Standard toolbar. First place the insertion point in the text that contains the formats to be copied, then click the Format Painter button. When you move the mouse pointer into the typing area, the mouse pointer changes to an I-beam with a paintbrush icon. Drag the Format Painter I-beam across the text you want to format. The Format Painter pastes *all* the formats from the original text.

You want to apply the bold, single underline and font size formats to selected text, and then copy that formatting to unformatted text. To apply multiple character formats:

Step 1	**Select**	the phrase "There is only one specification" in the last paragraph (do not select the colon)
Step 2	**Click**	the Bold button **B** on the Formatting toolbar
Step 3	**Click**	14 in the Font Size button list 12 ▾ on the Formatting toolbar
Step 4	**Click**	the Underline button **U** on the Formatting toolbar
Step 5	**Deselect**	the text leaving the insertion point in the formatted text

MENU TIP

You can repeat formatting you just applied to other text by selecting the text and clicking the Repeat command on the Edit menu. If you applied character formats from the Formatting toolbar, only the last formatting option is repeated. If you applied multiple character formats from the Font tab in the Font dialog box, all the formats are repeated.

chapter four

To copy formats using the Format Painter:

Step 1	*Click*	the Format Painter button on the Formatting toolbar
Step 2	*Observe*	that the mouse pointer is now an I-beam with a paintbrush icon
Step 3	*Drag*	the Format Painter I-beam over the next phrase "Please remember to return the materials to the library" (do not select the period)
Step 4	*Observe*	that when you release the mouse button, the formats are copied to the selected phrase
Step 5	*Save*	the document and leave it open

When necessary, you can quickly modify the formats of similarly formatted text using a shortcut menu to first select the text.

Selecting Similarly Formatted Text

You just checked your e-mail and find a message from Elizabeth with last-minute instructions for formatting the *Library Bulletin Revised* document. Elizabeth asks you to ignore her note to add a single underline to the two multiformatted phrases in the last paragraph. To select the two similarly formatted phrases:

Step 1	*Right-click*	the phrase "There is only one specification"
Step 2	*Click*	<u>S</u>elect Text with Similar Formatting
Step 3	*Observe*	that both phrases are selected
Step 4	*Click*	the Underline button 🔲 on the Formatting toolbar to remove the underline formatting
Step 5	*Deselect*	the text
Step 6	*Save*	the document and leave it open

C Using the Reveal Formatting Task Pane

The Reveal Formatting task pane provides a quick summary of the formatting applied to selected text as well as links to formatting dialog boxes in which you can change the selected text's formatting.

You want to review all the character formats you applied in the *Library Bulletin Revised* document. To display the Reveal Formatting task pane:

Step 1	*Move*	the insertion point to the word "bulletin" in the last sentence
Step 2	*Click*	F**o**rmat
Step 3	*Click*	Re**v**eal Formatting

Your screen should look similar to Figure 4-5.

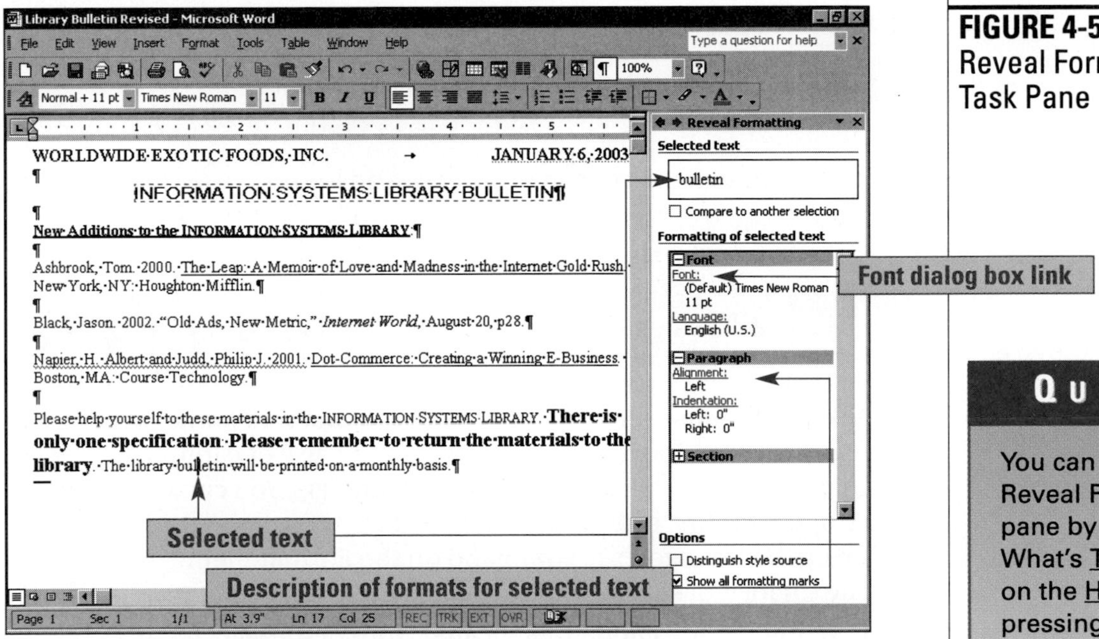

TASK PANE TIP

When a task pane is already displayed, you can view the Reveal Formatting task pane with the Other Task Panes button on the task pane title bar.

FIGURE 4-5
Reveal Formatting
Task Pane

Text you select appears in the Selected text box in the task pane. When you move the mouse pointer to the Selected text box in the task pane, a list arrow appears. You can click this list arrow to view a menu that allows you to select similarly formatted text, format the selected text with the same format as the surrounding text, or clear the formatting.

The Formatting of selected text list box includes links that enable you to open formatting dialog boxes such as the Font dialog box, where you can see a description of the formatting and the formatting applied to selected text. To review some of the text formatting:

QUICK TIP

You can display the Reveal Formatting task pane by clicking the What's **T**his? command on the **H**elp menu or pressing the SHIFT + F1 keys to change the mouse pointer to a Help pointer and then clicking the desired text to display the Reveal Formatting task pane.

Step 1	*Select*	the text "Information Systems Library" in the phrase "New Additions to the Information Systems Library"

**chapter
four**

| Step 2 | *Observe* | the font formatting description in the Formatting of selected text list: (Default) Times New Roman, 11 pt, Bold, Thick underline, English (U.S.), and Small caps effects |

You can change any of these formats from the task pane. To remove the Small caps effects:

Step 1	*Click*	the Effects: link in the Formatting of selected text list in the Reveal Formatting task pane
Step 2	*Click*	the Small caps check box to remove the check mark in the Font dialog box
Step 3	*Click*	OK
Step 4	*Close*	the Reveal Formatting task pane
Step 5	*Save*	the document and leave it open

TASK PANE tip

You can turn on or off the view of formatting marks with the Show all formatting marks check box in the Reveal Formatting task pane.

It's easy to switch between uppercase and lowercase letters after you key text.

4.c Changing the Case of Text

Elizabeth wants you to change the case of the title in the *Library Bulletin Revised* document. **Case** refers to the use of capitalized text characters versus noncapitalized text characters. You can change the case of text by first selecting the text you want to change, and then clicking the Change Case command on the Format menu.

The Change Case dialog box contains five case formats:

1. **Sentence** case capitalizes the first word of the selected text.
2. **lowercase** changes all characters of the selected text to lowercase characters.
3. **UPPERCASE** changes all characters of the selected text to uppercase characters.
4. **Title Case** capitalizes the first character of each word in the selected text.
5. **tOGGLE cASE** changes all uppercase characters to lowercase and all lowercase characters to uppercase for the selected text.

To change the case of the title text:

Step 1	*Select*	the title text "INFORMATION SYSTEMS LIBRARY BULLETIN"
Step 2	*Click*	Format
Step 3	*Click*	Change Case

The Change Case dialog box on your screen should look similar to Figure 4-6.

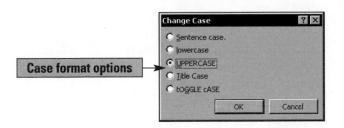
Case format options

FIGURE 4-6
Change Case Dialog Box

Step 4	*Click*	the Title Case option button
Step 5	*Click*	OK
Step 6	*Deselect*	the text

Notice that you can now see the Small cap formatting you applied earlier to the title.

Step 7	*Click*	the Show/Hide button ¶ on the Standard toolbar to turn off the feature
Step 8	*Save*	the document and close it

> **QUICK TIP**
>
> You can turn on or off viewing and printing highlight colors on the View tab in the Options dialog box. Using color to highlight text works best when a document is read on a computer screen. If you print a document with high-lighted text, use a light color.

One way to draw a reviewer's attention to important text in a document being read online is to highlight the text in a special color.

4.d Highlighting Text in a Document

Elizabeth wants to draw attention to the text "Warning! Warning! Warning!" in the *Policy #152* document. To do this, she asks you to highlight the text in color. To highlight the text:

Step 1	*Open*	the *Policy #152* document located on the Data Disk
Step 2	*Select*	the text "Warning! Warning! Warning!"
Step 3	*Click*	the Highlight button list arrow 🖊 on the Formatting toolbar
Step 4	*Click*	Bright Green

chapter
four

| Step 5 | *Observe* | that the text is highlighted in color |
| Step 6 | *Save* | the document as *Policy #152 With Highlighting* and close it |

Another way to enhance text appearance is to insert symbols and special characters into your document.

4.e Inserting Symbols and Special Characters

Symbols and special characters can be inserted into a document using the AutoCorrect feature or the Symbol command on the Insert menu. Elizabeth left instructions for you to complete a new Marketing Department training class announcement by inserting the appropriate symbols and special characters.

First, you need to insert the copyright symbol in the document. To insert the copyright symbol using the AutoCorrect feature:

Step 1	*Open*	the *Quality 2003 Training* document located on the Data Disk
Step 2	*Move*	the insertion point to the end of the "Quality 2003 Training" text in the third line
Step 3	*Key*	(c) to insert the copyright symbol using AutoCorrect
Step 4	*Observe*	the inserted copyright symbol

Special characters such as the en dash (used in inclusive numbers), the nonbreaking space (a fixed space between words that cannot be broken at the right margin), and the em dash (used to insert a break in a thought) as well as the copyright symbol can be inserted from the Special Characters tab in the Symbol dialog box. Elizabeth wants you to replace the hyphen in the first paragraph with an em dash character. To select the hyphen and open the dialog box:

Step 1	*Select*	the hyphen following the word "now" in the last sentence of the first body paragraph
Step 2	*Click*	Insert
Step 3	*Click*	Symbol
Step 4	*Click*	the Special Characters tab, if necessary

The Symbol dialog box on your screen should look similar to Figure 4-7.

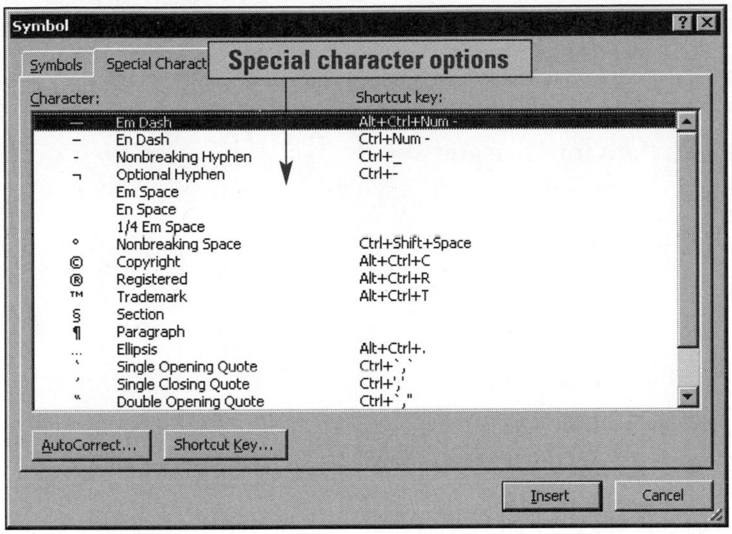

FIGURE 4-7
Symbol Dialog Box

Step 5	*Double-click*	the Em Dash option in the list
Step 6	*Close*	the Symbol dialog box
Step 7	*Observe*	that the em dash replaces the hyphen in the document
Step 8	*Save*	the document as *Quality 2003 With Symbol and Em Dash* and close it

With the Word character formatting features you can make any document look professionally formatted.

QUICK TIP

The **AutoFormat As You Type** feature (in addition to the symbol characters in the AutoCorrect list) automatically formats certain characters as you key them. For example, you can replace ordinals (1st) with superscript (1st), fractions (1/2) with stacked characters ($\frac{1}{2}$), and "straight quotes" with "curly quotes." The automatic formatting is applied when you press the SPACEBAR and is turned on by default.

You can turn off the automatic formatting of characters in the AutoFormat As You Type tab in the AutoCorrect dialog box. The AutoFormat tab in the AutoCorrect dialog box contains options that control how Word automatically formats an entire document. For more information on automatically formatting an entire Word document, see online Help.

**chapter
four**

Summary

▶ Character formatting is used to change the appearance of individual text characters or groups of characters.

▶ A font is a set of printed characters that has the same size and appearance.

▶ A font has three aspects: typeface, style, and point (font) size.

▶ In a monospaced font, all characters occupy the same horizontal space.

▶ In a proportional font, characters occupy different amounts of horizontal space.

▶ A serif is a small line extension at the beginning of a character that helps guide the reader's eyes across the page. Fonts that do not have a serif are called sans serif fonts.

▶ The default font in Word is 12-point Times New Roman.

▶ Bold, italic, and underline formatting can be applied to selected text for emphasis.

▶ You can use the Styles and Formatting task pane to apply character styles to selected text.

▶ Superscript or subscript character formats can be applied to selected characters to position the characters slightly above or below the line of normal text.

▶ You can add animation effects, such as red marching ants, to emphasize text in documents that are to be read online.

▶ Character formats can be copied to new text using the Format Painter button on the Standard toolbar.

▶ The Reveal Formatting task pane contains links and commands you can use to select, review, and change character formatting.

▶ The case of text characters can be changed to Sentence case, lower-case, UPPERCASE, Title Case, or tOGGLE case.

▶ You can apply colored highlights to emphasize text to read online.

▶ You can add symbols and special characters to text.

▶ The AutoFormat As You Type feature automatically formats certain characters such as quote marks, fractions, and ordinals you key when you press the SPACEBAR.

Commands Review

Action	Menu Bar	Shortcut Menu	Toolbar	Task Pane	Keyboard
Change font	Format, Font	Right-click the selected text, click Font	Times New Roman	Click the Font: link in the Reveal Formatting task pane	ALT + O, F CTRL + D CTRL + SHIFT + F, DOWN ARROW
Change font size	Format, Font	Right-click the selected text, click Font	12	Click the Font: link in the Reveal Formatting task pane	ALT + O, F CTRL + SHIFT + P, DOWN ARROW
Apply or remove bold, italic, or underline formatting	Format, Font	Right-click the selected text, click Font	**B** *I* U	Click the Font: link in the Reveal Formatting task pane	ALT + O, F CTRL + B, CTRL + I, CTRL + U
Apply a character style	Format, Styles and Formatting		A, Normal	Click style in the Pick formatting to apply list in the Styles and Formatting task pane	ALT + O, S
Apply or remove superscript or subscript formatting	Format, Font	Right-click the selected text, click Font		Click the Font: link in the Reveal Formatting task pane	ALT + O, F CTRL + = (sub.) CTRL + SHIFT + + (sup.)
Copy formats					CTRL + SHIFT + C CTRL + SHIFT + V
Remove character formatting					CTRL + SHIFT + Z CTRL + SPACEBAR
Repeat formats	Edit, Repeat				ALT + E, R CTRL + Y
Apply character spacing and text animation effects	Format, Font	Right-click the selected text, click Font			ALT + O, F
Select text with similar formatting		Right-click the selected text, click Select Text with Similar Formatting		Click the Selected text list arrow in the Reveal Formatting task pane and then click Select All Text with Similar Formatting	
View the Reveal Formatting task pane	Format, Reveal Formatting Help, What's This				ALT + O, V ALT + H, T SHIFT + F1
Change case	Format, Change Case				ALT + O, E SHIFT + F3
Add highlighting to text			✏		
Insert symbols and special characters	Insert, Symbol				ALT + I, S

chapter four

Concepts Review

Circle the correct answer.

1. **Changing the appearance of individual characters or groups of characters is called:**
   [a] paragraph formatting.
   [b] text formatting.
   [c] character formatting.
   [d] page formatting.

2. **Typeface refers to the:**
   [a] horizontal width of the characters.
   [b] height of the characters.
   [c] design and appearance of the characters.
   [d] slant of the characters.

3. **You can copy character formats by:**
   [a] clicking the Bullets button.
   [b] using the Format Painter button.
   [c] clicking the Numbering button.
   [d] pressing the DELETE key.

4. **The character spacing feature that adjusts the space between pairs of characters is called:**
   [a] kelping.
   [b] spacing.
   [c] underlining.
   [d] kerning.

5. **Which of the following task panes provides a link to the Font dialog box?**
   [a] New Document
   [b] Reveal Formatting
   [c] Styles and Formatting
   [d] Clipboard

6. **Which of the following is not a special font effect in the Font dialog box?**
   [a] Emboss
   [b] Engrave
   [c] Hidden
   [d] Bold

7. **Character spacing options are found in the:**
   [a] Font dialog box.
   [b] AutoCorrect dialog box.
   [c] Formatting dialog box.
   [d] AutoText dialog box.

8. **The Underline button on the formatting toolbar applies the following underline style:**
   [a] Dotted.
   [b] Single, words only.
   [c] Single, words and spaces.
   [d] Double wavy.

9. **Italics emphasizes text by:**
   [a] making the text darker.
   [b] slanting the text to the right.
   [c] placing the text above the baseline.
   [d] slanting the text to the left.

10. **Which of the following is not an option for changing the case of text?**
    [a] Uppercase
    [b] Lowercase
    [c] Triple case
    [d] Sentence case

Circle **T** if the statement is true or **F** if the statement is false.

T F   1. The Italic button on the Formatting toolbar allows you to create text that looks and prints darker than the rest of the text.

T F   2. You can easily select similarly formatted text with a shortcut menu.

T F   3. Subscript formatting places text slightly below a line of normal printed text.

T F   4. Superscript formatting places text slightly above a line of normal printed text.

T F   5. The Format Painter button on the Standard toolbar allows you to copy only one format at a time.

T F   6. The three characteristics of fonts are: typeface, weight, and point (font) size.

T F   7. The Reveal Formatting task pane contains a list of special text characters such as the em dash.

T F   8. Sentence case capitalizes each word of selected text.

T F   9. You cannot turn off the automatic formatting of characters.

T F   10. Font style refers to uppercase and lowercase characters.

Skills Review

Exercise 1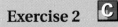

1. Open the *Interoffice Meeting Memo* document located on the Data Disk.

2. Replace the text "Current date" with the actual date.

3. Apply the Bold style the text TO, FROM, DATE, and SUBJECT in the memo form headings. (Do not apply bold formatting to the colons. Don't forget to use the CTRL key to select all the text before you apply the formatting.)

4. Apply the Bold style to the day and time for the meeting in the first paragraph.

5. Single underline the number 20 in the third paragraph.

6. Italicize the topic assignments. (Using the CTRL key, select only the topic assignments. Don't select the names.)

7. Select the similarly formatted topic assignment text using the shortcut menu and change the formatting by removing the italic formatting and adding bold formatting to the topic assignment text.

8. Save the document as *Interoffice Meeting Memo Revised*, and then preview, print, and close it.

Exercise 2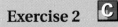

1. Open the *Marketing Department Memo* document located on the Data Disk.

2. Replace the text "Current date" with the actual date.

3. Select the TO: heading text (do not select the colon) and open the Reveal Formatting task pane.

4. Using the Select text box list arrow in the task pane, select all text with similar formatting and then turn off the bold formatting style.

5. Select the entire document and change the font to Arial 12 point.

6. Close the Reveal Formatting task pane.

7. Save the document as *Marketing Department Memo Revised*, and then preview, print, and close it.

Exercise 3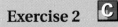

1. Open the *Vancouver Sales Report* document located on the Data Disk.

2. Format the title "VANCOUVER BRANCH OFFICE" with the Strong character style using the Styles and Formatting task pane.

3. Apply the Bold style and underline the column titles. (Don't forget to use the CTRL key to select all the column titles before you apply the formatting.)

chapter four

4. Select all the text except the title and change the font size to 12 point.

5. Save the document as *Vancouver Sales Report Revised,* and then preview, print, and close it.

Exercise 4   C

1. Open the *Commonly Misused Words* document located on the Data Disk.

2. Apply the Bold style to the commonly misused words. (Do not include the example and definition. Don't forget to use the CTRL key to select all the text before you apply the formatting.)

3. Use the shortcut menu to select the similarly formatted definitions text and remove the italic formatting.

4. Save the document as *Commonly Misused Words Revised*, and then preview, print, and close it.

Exercise 5   C

1. Open the *Company Correspondence Memo* document located on the Data Disk.

2. Replace the text "Current date" with the actual date.

3. Change the case of "Memorandum" to all-uppercase.

4. Change the character spacing scale of "MEMORANDUM" to 200%.

5. Apply the Bold style to the text "MEMORANDUM," "TO," "FROM," "DATE," and "SUBJECT." (Do not apply bold formatting to the colons. Don't forget to use the CTRL key to select all the text before you apply the formatting.)

6. Select the text "MEMORANDUM" and change the font to Arial 14 point.

7. Using the CTRL key, select the memo headings using the CTRL key and change the font size to 12 point.

8. Save the document as *Company Correspondence Memo Revised,* and then preview, print, and close it.

Exercise 6   C

1. Open the *Market Research* document located on the Data Disk.

2. Check the spelling and grammar and make the appropriate changes.

3. Insert a superscript number 1 after the word Davidson in the first paragraph.

4. Insert two blank lines at the end of the document and key the following text (including the superscript; do not apply the italic style to the text): [1] *One of the leading market research firms in the country.*

5. Change the case of Vancouver branch in the first paragraph to all-uppercase.

6. Save the document as *Market Research Revised*, and then preview, print, and close it.

Exercise 7   C

1. Open the *Policy #152* document located on the Data Disk.

2. Select the text "Warning! Warning! Warning!" and change the case to uppercase, apply the Bold style, change the font to Arial 24 point, and add the animation effect of your choice.

3. Using the CTRL key, select the text "Only Authorized Personnel" and "May Proceed Beyond This Point," change the case to all-uppercase, and change the font to Arial 14 point bold.

4. Select the remainder of the text and change the font to Arial 12 point.

5. Single-underline only the words in the third sentence beginning "Surveillance."

6. Save the document as *Policy #152 Revised*, and then preview, print, and close it.

Exercise 8

1. Open the *Business Information Management* document located on the Data Disk.

2. Select the entire document and change the font to Arial 12 point.

3. Select the text "BUSINESS INFORMATION MANAGEMENT", apply the Bold style, and change the font size to 18 point.

4. Apply the Bold style and underline the course number and title "BIM 160," then use the Format Painter to copy the formatting to the remaining course numbers and titles.

5. Underline the last two lines below the BIM 240 line.

6. Save the document as *Business Information Management Revised*, and then preview, print, and close it.

Case Projects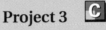

Project 1

Kelly Armstead asks you to show her the different font effect options available in Word. Open an existing document of your choice. Experiment with the special font effects options in the Font dialog box by selecting text and applying special effects formats and animation effects. Create a new Word document listing, describing, and showing the different effects. Use character formats as appropriate. Save, preview, and print the document. With your instructor's permission, give a printed copy of the document to a classmate and, using the document as your guide, show your classmate how to use the different fonts and animation options.

Project 2

Marcy Wainwright, who works in the Purchasing Department, suggests that you could save time in applying character formatting to text by using keyboard shortcuts. You decide to research which keyboard shortcuts to use to apply character formatting. Using the Ask A Question Box, locate, review, and print a list of keyboard shortcut keys that you can use to apply character formatting. Open the document of your choice and apply different character formatting using keyboard shortcuts. Save, preview, and print the document.

Project 3

You have been assigned to key the text of a new client proposal. Because of the proposal format, you want to use special character spacing for some of the proposal titles but aren't certain what character spacing options are available. Using the Ask A Question Box and other Word Help features, research how to use the character spacing options. Create a new document containing at least two paragraphs describing how you can use these character spacing options in the client proposal. Include some sample titles with special character spacing. Use other character formats in the document as appropriate. Save, preview, and print the document.

Project 4

Albert Navarro, in Human Resources, wants to have a "brown bag" lunch seminar for his staff that includes a short presentation on troubleshooting character formatting in documents. He asked Kelly for help and she assigned the presentation to you. Using the Ask A Question Box, search online Help for tips on how to troubleshoot problems with this topic. Create a new document containing at least two paragraphs that describe possible problems and solutions for applying character formatting. Use character formats in the document as appropriate. Save, preview, and print the document. With your instructor's permission, present your troubleshooting tips to several classmates.

chapter four

Project 5 C

The administrative offices are moving to a new floor in the same building and B. D. Vickers asks you to create a letter announcing the move. The letter should contain the department's new address, phone number, fax number, and e-mail address. Create the letter for B. D. Vickers' signature. Set the appropriate margins, use fictitious data, and apply appropriate character formatting features discussed in this chapter to make the text attractive and easy to read. Use different text effects from the Font dialog box. Use other character formats in the document as appropriate. Save, preview, and print the letter.

Project 6 C

Elizabeth left you instructions to create a list of Web sites that are marketing and selling products on the Web. Connect to the Internet, and search the Web for pages that contain information on Web-based marketing and direct sales. Print at least three Web pages. Create a new, blank document and list the title of the Web pages and their URLs. Use character formats in the document as appropriate. Save, preview, and print the document.

Project 7 C

Kelly Armstead needs the mailing addresses or e-mail addresses of the senators and congressional representatives from Illinois. You know that this information is available on the Web. Connect to the Internet, and search the Web to locate the home page for the U.S. Senate and U.S. House of Representatives. Follow the links to the names and addresses of the senators and representatives. Print the appropriate pages. Create a new, blank document and key the information you found. Use character formats in the document as appropriate. Save, preview, and print the document.

Project 8 C

You want to know more about how to use the Reveal Formatting task pane. Using the Ask A Question Box and other Word Help features, research how to use this task pane. Create a new document describing the Reveal Formatting task pane features and how to use them. Save, preview, and print the document.

Setting and Modifying Tab Stops

Chapter Overview

Some information is more clearly presented in columns and rows than in paragraph text. For example, it's easier to compare monthly expenses when the figures are arranged in columns by month and in rows by item. In this chapter, you learn to organize information attractively on the page in rows and columns, using tab stops and tab formatting marks.

LEARNING OBJECTIVES

- ▶ Understand tab stops
- ▶ Set left tab stops
- ▶ Set center tab stops
- ▶ Set decimal tab stops
- ▶ Set right tab stops
- ▶ Set tab stops with leaders

Case profile

The Accounting Department is overwhelmed with special projects and deadlines. Elizabeth Chang was so pleased with your work in the Marketing Department that she recommended you to Bill Wilson, the accounting manager. Bill wants you to create or modify a summary memo to include with the quarterly sales report.

chapter
five

Before beginning the activities in this chapter you should review the Formatting Tips for Business Documents appendix, if you have not already done so.

5.a Understanding Tab Stops

When you need to prepare written communication to someone inside your organization, you can create an interoffice memorandum (or memo) instead of a letter document. Interoffice memorandums generally follow the standard format shown in Figure 5-1. The memorandum should have a 2-inch top margin, 1-inch left and right margins, and the double-spaced heading text TO:, FROM:, DATE:, and SUBJECT: at the beginning of the memorandum, followed by paragraphs that are separated by a blank line. The variable TO:, FROM:, DATE:, and SUBJECT: text that follows each heading should be aligned. You do this with tab stops.

FIGURE 5-1
Standard Interoffice Memorandum

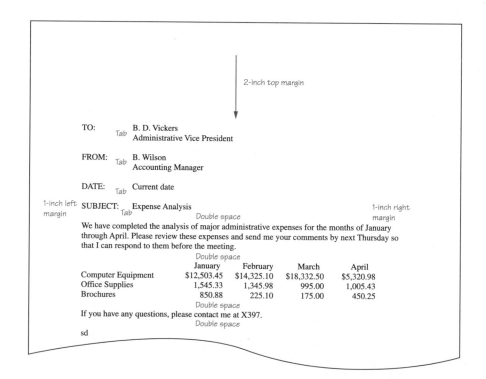

MENU TIP

When Word indents the first line after you press the TAB key, the AutoCorrect Options Smart Tag appears. You can use commands on the AutoCorrect Options drop-down menu to change the indent back to a tab formatting mark or to turn on the feature that automatically sets indents with the TAB and BACKSPACE keys.

After each heading, you insert a **tab formatting mark**, a nonprinting character you key in your document by pressing the TAB key. Each tab formatting mark you insert moves the text to the right of the tab formatting mark to the next tab stop. **Tab stops** are text alignment icons positioned on the horizontal ruler that indicate where text should align. By default, Word documents have tab stops set at every ½ inch. You can also set custom tab stops at any position between the left and right margins for one or more selected paragraphs or the entire document.

Tab stops are part of **paragraph formatting**. This means that only the selected paragraph(s) are affected when you set or modify tabs stops. You must first select the paragraphs for which you want to set custom tab stops. To select a single paragraph, simply move the insertion point into the paragraph. To select multiple paragraphs, use the selection techniques you learned in Chapter 2.

Word has five types of tab stop alignment: Left, Center, Right, Decimal, and Bar. Text is left-aligned at default tab stops and can be left-, center-, right-, or decimal-aligned at custom tab stops. Table 5-1 describes the five tab stop text alignments. For more information on Bar alignment, see online Help.

Tab Stop	Alignment	Icon
Left	Left-aligns text at the tab stop.	⌞
Center	Centers text over the tab stop.	⊥
Right	Right-aligns text at the tab stop.	⌟
Decimal	Aligns text at the decimal character.	⊥
Bar	Inserts a vertical line at the tab stop and aligns text to the right of the line.	❘

TABLE 5-1
Tab Stop Alignment Options

Q U I C K   T I P

To set custom tab stops that affect all the paragraphs in a new document, set the tab stops before you begin keying the first paragraph. When you press the ENTER key to begin a new paragraph, the tab settings are included in the new paragraph.

Bill Wilson asks you to create an interoffice memo to B. D. Vickers, as shown in Figure 5-1. After you create the memo headings, you insert both the tab stops and the tab formatting marks necessary to align the variable heading text. To create the memo:

Step 1	*Create*	a new, blank document
Step 2	*Set*	a 2-inch top margin, and 1-inch left and right margins
Step 3	*Click*	the Show/Hide button ¶ on the Standard toolbar

Your screen should look similar to Figure 5-2.

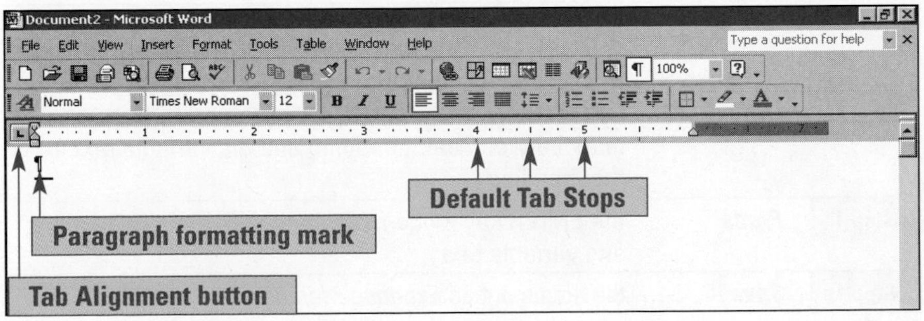

Default Tab Stops

Paragraph formatting mark

Tab Alignment button

FIGURE 5-2
Formatting Marks, Default Tab Stops, Tab Alignment Button

chapter
five

MENU TIP

You can set custom tab stops with the <u>T</u>abs command on the F<u>o</u>rmat menu by specifying where each tab formatting mark is inserted on the page, which tab alignment icon is inserted on the horizontal ruler, and whether leader characters are included.

By default, Word sets tab stops every ½-inch on the horizontal ruler. As you key the heading text, you press the TAB key to insert a tab formatting mark, which moves the insertion point to the next default tab stop on the horizontal ruler. Because you displayed the nonprinting characters, you can see the tab formatting marks when you key them. To view the tab formatting marks and create the memo headings:

Step 1	*Observe*	the paragraph formatting mark at the first line
Step 2	*Observe*	the default tab stops set every ½-inch on the horizontal ruler
Step 3	*Observe*	the Tab Alignment button 🔲 to the left of the horizontal ruler
Step 4	*Key*	TO:
Step 5	*Press*	the TAB key
Step 6	*Observe*	the tab formatting mark
Step 7	*Observe*	that the insertion point moves to the next default tab stop at the ½-inch position on the horizontal ruler

Your screen should look similar to Figure 5-3.

FIGURE 5-3
Insertion Point, Tab Formatting Mark, and Default Tab Stop

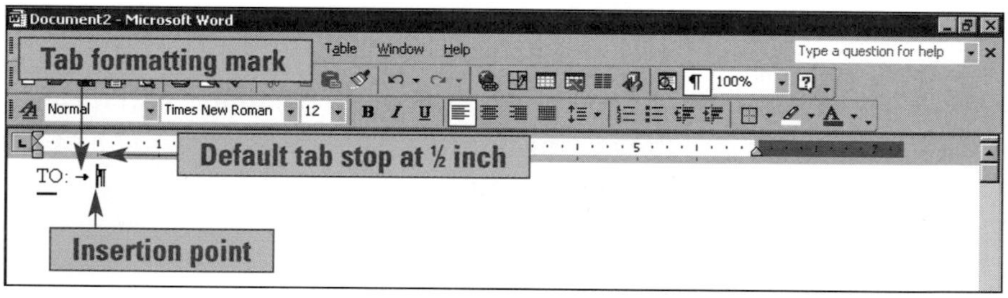

MOUSE TIP

You can set the left, center, right, decimal, and bar tab stops by clicking the Tab Alignment button to the left of the horizontal ruler until the appropriate tab alignment icon appears, and then clicking the appropriate position on the horizontal ruler.

Step 8	*Key*	B. D. Vickers
Step 9	*Press*	the ENTER key
Step 10	*Press*	the TAB key
Step 11	*Key*	Administrative Vice President
Step 12	*Press*	the ENTER key twice
Step 13	*Continue*	to key the remaining headings and variable heading text you see in Figure 5-1, inserting one tab formatting mark between each heading and the variable text for that heading
Step 14	*Press*	the ENTER key twice following the SUBJECT: heading and variable text
Step 15	*Save*	the document as *Expense Memorandum* and leave it open

5.b Setting Left Tab Stops

The variable heading text is not properly aligned because each line shifts to the first available default tab stop setting. To properly align the heading text, you need to add a custom left tab stop to the horizontal ruler for all the heading lines. A **left-aligned tab** stop aligns text along the left at the tab stop position. The quickest way to set custom tab stops is to use the mouse, the Tab Alignment button, and the horizontal ruler. Before you set custom tab stops, you must select the appropriate paragraph or paragraphs, then select the appropriate tab alignment icon with the Tab Alignment button, and finally, click the horizontal ruler to insert the tab stop at the appropriate position. When you click the ruler, the tab alignment icon you select from the Tab Alignment button appears on the ruler, and any default tab stops to the left of the custom tab stop disappear from the ruler. To set a custom left tab stop for all the heading lines at one time:

Step 1	*Select*	the text beginning with the "TO:" paragraph and ending with the "SUBJECT:" paragraph
Step 2	*Click*	the Tab Alignment button ⬚ until the left-aligned tab stop icon appears, if necessary
Step 3	*Move*	the mouse pointer to the 1-inch position on the horizontal ruler
Step 4	*Click*	the horizontal ruler at the 1-inch position
Step 5	*Deselect*	the text, leaving the insertion point in one of the headings

A left-align tab stop icon appears on the horizontal ruler and the variable text in the heading lines aligns at the 1-inch position. Your screen should look similar to Figure 5-4.

> ## CAUTION TIP
>
> By default, the option to increase and decrease indents when the TAB key and BACKSPACE key are pressed is turned on in the Edit tab of the Options dialog box. If you move the insertion point to the beginning of a line of existing text and press the TAB key, Word moves the First Line Indent marker to the next tab stop on the horizontal ruler. If you press the TAB key *before* you key text, Word inserts a tab formatting mark.

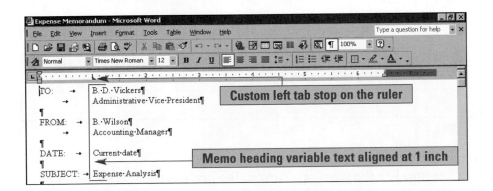

FIGURE 5-4
Custom Left Tab Stop at 1 Inch

You remove tab stops or change the location of tab stops on the horizontal ruler by selecting the appropriate paragraphs and then

chapter
five

QUICK TIP

When you remove custom tab stops, the tab stop settings return to the default settings.

dragging the tab stops with the mouse pointer. To move the custom left tab stop to the 1½-inch position for all the heading paragraphs:

Step 1	*Select*	the heading paragraphs
Step 2	*Position*	the mouse pointer on the left-align tab stop icon at the 1-inch position on the horizontal ruler (the ScreenTip "Left Tab" appears)
Step 3	*Drag*	the left-align tab stop icon to the 1½-inch position on the horizontal ruler

The variable text in each heading paragraph shifts to the 1½-inch position. You remove a tab stop by dragging it completely off the ruler. To remove the custom tab stop at the 1½-inch position:

Step 1	*Verify*	that the heading paragraphs are still selected
Step 2	*Drag*	the tab icon at the 1½-inch position down off the horizontal ruler
Step 3	*Observe*	that the tab stops on the horizontal ruler indicate the ½-inch default settings and the variable heading text is no longer properly aligned

You set custom tab stops for individual paragraphs just as you do multiple paragraphs. To set a left tab stop for the first heading paragraph only:

Step 1	*Click*	in the heading paragraph beginning "TO:" to position the insertion point (this selects the paragraph)
Step 2	*Verify*	the Tab Alignment button **L** is set for a left tab stop
Step 3	*Click*	the 1-inch position on the horizontal ruler
Step 4	*Observe*	that the first line of the first paragraph *only* moves right and aligns at the new custom tab stop position
Step 5	*Set*	a 1-inch left-aligned custom tab stop for the remaining heading paragraphs
Step 6	*Deselect*	the text
Step 7	*Save*	the document

You now key the paragraph text in the body of the memo and then organize the expense analysis data in columns using tab formatting characters and tab stops on the horizontal ruler.

5.c Setting Center Tab Stops

C

Center-aligned tab stops center text over the tab stop, which is appropriate for creating column headings. Figure 5-1 includes text in five columns separated by tab formatting marks. The last four columns include column headers. You key the first body paragraph and the column headings. To key the first body paragraph:

Step 1	*Key*	the first body paragraph from Figure 5-1 on the second line following the SUBJECT: heading line
Step 2	*Press*	the ENTER key twice

Next you set custom center-aligned tab stops for the expense analysis column headings and key the headings.

Step 3	*Click*	the Tab Alignment button until the center-aligned tab icon ⊥ appears
Step 4	*Click*	the 2.5-, 3.5-, 4.5-, and 5.5-inch positions on the horizontal ruler to insert the center-aligned tab icons
Step 5	*Press*	the TAB key
Step 6	*Key*	January
Step 7	*Press*	the TAB key
Step 8	*Key*	February
Step 9	*Press*	the TAB key
Step 10	*Key*	March
Step 11	*Press*	the TAB key
Step 12	*Key*	April
Step 13	*Press*	the ENTER key

When you press the ENTER key to create a new paragraph, Word remembers the previous paragraph tab stop settings. Because you use different tab stop settings for the text you key in the columns, you should remove the center-aligned tab icons from the ruler for this paragraph. To remove the center-aligned tab icons:

Step 1	*Drag*	each tab stop for the current paragraph off the ruler
Step 2	*Save*	the document and leave it open

**chapter
five**

C 5.d Setting Decimal Tab Stops

You want the expense data to align on the decimal point in each column when you key the data in the columns. This makes reading columns of numbers easier. A **decimal tab** stop aligns numbers at the decimal point. If a number does not contain a decimal point, it is aligned at the rightmost position. Decimal tabs do not affect text. To set decimal tab stops and enter the expense data text in columns:

Step 1	Click	the Tab Alignment button until the decimal-aligned tab icon appears
Step 2	Press & hold	the ALT key while you click the horizontal ruler at the 2.61-, 3.61-, 4.61-, and 5.61-inch positions to insert the decimal-aligned tab stops
Step 3	Key	Computer Equipment
Step 4	Press	the TAB key
Step 5	Key	$12,503.45
Step 6	Press	the TAB key
Step 7	Key	$14,325.10
Step 8	Press	the TAB key
Step 9	Key	$18,332.50
Step 10	Press	the TAB key
Step 11	Key	$5,320.98
Step 12	Press	the ENTER key

When you press the ENTER key, the next paragraph retains the tab stop settings from the previous paragraph. These tab stops are appropriate for the remaining rows of data. To create the remaining lines:

Step 1	Key	Office Supplies
Step 2	Press	the TAB key
Step 3	Observe	that the insertion point moves to the tab stop position and aligns on the decimal point of the number above it
Step 4	Continue	to add the remaining two lines of tabbed text and the rest of the memo, as shown in Figure 5-1
Step 5	Save	the document and close it

Bill asks you to update the Accounting Department telephone extension list and add the revision date at the right margin below the phone numbers. You can use a right-aligned tab stop to add the date.

5.e Setting Right Tab Stops

A **right-aligned tab** stop is appropriate for text that should be aligned at the right of the tab stop, such as a date at the right margin of a document. To position the date at the right margin, set a right-aligned tab stop, press the TAB key, and then key or insert the date. To set a right tab stop and right-align the date on the first line:

Step 1	**Open**	the *Telephone List* document located on the Data Disk
Step 2	**Move**	the insertion point to the bottom of the document and add two new blank lines
Step 3	**Click**	the Tab Alignment button to the left of the horizontal ruler until the right-aligned tab icon ⌐ appears
Step 4	**Click**	the 5½-inch position on the horizontal ruler to insert the right-aligned tab icon
Step 5	**Drag**	the right-aligned tab icon to the 6-inch position (the right margin)

Your screen should look similar to Figure 5-5.

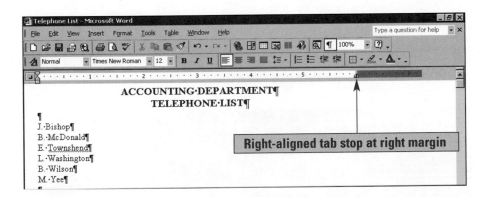

FIGURE 5-5
Right-Aligned Tab Stop

Step 6	**Press**	the TAB key
Step 7	**Key**	today's date
Step 8	**Observe**	that as you key the date the text flows left from the tab stop position
Step 9	**Save**	the document as *Telephone List Revised* and leave it open

chapter
five

Bill asks you to position each employee's name at the left margin and telephone number at the right margin in the telephone list document. He also wants you to insert a dotted or dashed line between the employee's name at the left margin and their extension at the right margin to help guide the reader's eye across the page. You can use right-aligned tab stops with tab leaders to do this.

C 5.f Setting Tab Stops with Leaders

Documents that have a large amount of white space between columns of text, such as a table of contents or a phone list, can be difficult for a reader's eye to follow across the page from column to column. **Tab leaders** are dashed or dotted lines you can add to a tab stop to provide a visual guide for readers as they follow the text from column to column. You add a leader character to a tab stop in the Tabs dialog box. Before you open the Tabs dialog box to set tab stops and add leaders, you must remember to select the appropriate paragraphs to be formatted. To set a right-aligned tab stop at the 6-inch position and add the second leader style:

Step 1	*Select*	the lines of text beginning with "J. Bishop" and ending with "M. Yee"
Step 2	*Click*	F<u>o</u>rmat
Step 3	*Click*	<u>T</u>abs

The Tabs dialog box on your screen should look similar to Figure 5-6.

FIGURE 5-6
Tabs Dialog Box

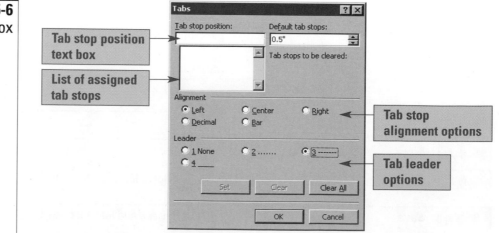

You can use the dialog box Help button to review the options in the dialog box. You set tab stops in the dialog box by keying the tab stop position and selecting an alignment option. Then, you can select a leader style.

Step 4	*Key*	6 in the Tab stop position: text box
Step 5	*Click*	the Right option button
Step 6	*Click*	the 2 .... leader option button
Step 7	*Click*	OK

With the tab stops and leader set, you can enter the tab formatting marks and telephone extensions for each item. To key the telephone extensions list:

Step 1	*Move*	the insertion point to the end of the J. Bishop text
Step 2	*Press*	the TAB key
Step 3	*Observe*	the leader characters that appear from the J. Bishop text to the tab stop
Step 4	*Key*	X388
Step 5	*Press*	the DOWN ARROW key to move the insertion point to the end of the B. McDonald text
Step 6	*Continue*	to key the telephone extensions to the document, pressing the TAB key between the name and extension B. McDonald, X391 E. Townshend, X402 L. Washington, X455 B. Wilson, X397 M. Yee, X405
Step 7	*Hide*	the nonprinting formatting marks
Step 8	*Save*	the document and close it

No matter what type of document you create, tab stops enable you to precisely align text in columns.

M OUSE TIP

You can use the Click and Type feature in Print Layout view or in Web Layout view to set a left tab stop anywhere in the document. Move the I-beam to the desired location. When you see the left-alignment icon next to the I-beam, double-click the document to insert a left tab stop at that position. When using the Click and Type feature to set multiple tab stops on the same text line, you can set center- and right-aligned tab stops as well.

chapter
five

Summary

▶ You can reposition and organize text in columns by setting tab stops on the horizontal ruler and inserting tab formatting marks in the text.

▶ Tab formatting marks are nonprinting characters you key in your document by pressing the TAB key.

▶ Tab stops are text-alignment icons positioned on the horizontal ruler that indicate where text should align.

▶ Left-aligned tab stops position text at the tab stop and then flow the text to the right.

▶ Right-aligned tab stops position text at the tab stop and then flow the text to the left.

▶ Center-aligned tab stops are appropriate for column headings; they position text at the tab stop and then flow the text left and right as necessary to center it at the tab stop.

▶ Decimal-aligned tab stops are appropriate for columns of numbers containing decimal points; they align the numbers on their decimal points.

▶ To assist the reader's eye in following text from column to column, you can add leader characters to a tab stop.

Commands Review

Action	Menu Bar	Shortcut Menu	Toolbar	Task Pane	Keyboard
Set custom tab stops	Format, Tabs		Click the Tab Alignment button to select an alignment icon, then click the horizontal ruler at the appropriate position		ALT + O, T

Concepts Review

SCANS

Circle the correct answer.

1. Which of the following is not a tab stop alignment?
[a] Left
[b] Right
[c] Justify
[d] Decimal

2. To align text along the right margin by setting a tab stop on the horizontal ruler, select the:
[a] Left alignment icon.
[b] Justify alignment icon.
[c] Right alignment icon.
[d] Center alignment icon.

3. You can insert a tab formatting mark by pressing the:
[a] ENTER key.
[b] TAB key.
[c] HOME key.
[d] END key.

4. To quickly set custom tab stops that affect one paragraph, first:
[a] select the entire document.
[b] select multiple paragraphs.
[c] move the insertion point to the paragraph.
[d] click the horizontal ruler then select the paragraph.

5. The default tab stops are positioned every:
[a] ½ inch.
[b] 1 inch.
[c] ¾ inch.
[d] ¼ inch.

6. To assist the reader's eye in following text from column to column, you can add:
[a] length to the line.
[b] less space between the characters.
[c] leader characters.
[d] lending characters.

7. To view the tab formatting marks in a document, click the:
[a] Show Tabs button.
[b] Show/Hide button.
[c] Format Marks button.
[d] Tab Alignment button.

8. You can manually enter the tab stop position, change the default tab stop settings, and add leaders to tab stops with the:
[a] Format, Paragraph commands.
[b] Insert, Tabs commands.
[c] Tools, Options commands.
[d] Format, Tabs commands.

Circle **T** if the statement is true or **F** if the statement is false.

T   F   1. The default setting for tab stops is every ½ inch.

T   F   2. You can set tab stops with the mouse and the horizontal ruler.

T   F   3. The Tab Alignment button has four alignment settings.

T   F   4. Use a center-aligned tab stop to position text at the right margin.

T   F   5. Use a left-aligned tab stop to start a new paragraph.

T   F   6. When you create text column headings, you can use the decimal-aligned tab stop to center the headings over the column.

T   F   7. You cannot remove tab stops with the mouse pointer.

T   F   8. Tab leader characters can be added by clicking the Tab Alignment button.

chapter five

Skills Review

SCANS

Exercise 1 C

1. Create a new, blank document and key the text in columns below, inserting a tab formatting mark between the text in each column.

	2001	2002	2003
Division 1	$200,000	$90,000	$180,000
Division 2	212,000	205,000	79,000
Division 3	140,000	400,000	120,000
Division 4	304,000	107,000	105,000
Division 5	201,000	148,000	195,000

2. Use right-aligned tab stops to align the numbers.

3. Use center-aligned tab stops to align the column headings.

4. Save the document as *Division Data*, and then preview, print, and close it.

Exercise 2 C

1. Open the *Media Memo* document located on the Data Disk.

2. Replace the text "Current date" with the actual date.

3. Set the appropriate margins for an interoffice memorandum.

4. Insert tab formatting marks in the heading paragraphs so you can align the variable heading text.

5. Set a left-aligned tab stop at 1 inch on the horizontal ruler for all the heading paragraphs to align the variable heading text.

6. Insert a new line below R. F. Jones and then insert a tab formatting mark and key "Media Buyer" as the title.

7. Insert a new line below B. Wilson and then insert a tab formatting mark and key "Accounting Manager" as the title.

8. Check the spelling of the document.

9. Save the document as *Media Memo Revised*, and then preview, print, and close it.

Exercise 3 C

1. Create a new, blank document and key the text in columns below, inserting a tab formatting mark between the text in each column.

Branch	Cheese	Meat	Produce
Chicago	$55,900	$125,000	$77,000
Vancouver	33,000	7,890	15,000
London	22,500	12,500	18,000
Melbourne	34,333	40,100	48,550

2. Use right-aligned tab stops to align the numbers.

3. Use center-aligned tab stops to align the column headings.

4. Save the document as *Branch Sales*, and then preview, print, and close it.

Exercise 4 C

1. Open the *Vendor Phone List* document located on the Data Disk.

2. Select the four lines of text and set a right-aligned tab stop with the leader of your choice at the 6-inch position on the horizontal ruler.

3. Insert a new line at the top of the document and remove the right-aligned tab stop from the horizontal ruler.

4. Insert a tab formatting mark, key "Vendor" as the column title, insert a tab formatting mark, and key "Phone List" as the column title.

5. Set two center-aligned tab stops on the horizontal ruler to center the column titles attractively over their respective columns.

6. Use the CTRL key to select both column headings and underline them.

7. Save the document as *Vendor Phone List Revised*, and then preview, print, and close it.

Exercise 5 C

1. Create a new, blank document and key the text in columns below, inserting a tab formatting mark between the text in each column.

Sales District	Telephone	Supplies	Misc.
A	$1,450.25	$744.33	$225.45
B	1,645.33	525.88	214.55
C	985.22	275.90	243.89
D	1,112.98	210.66	423.67
E	1,967.34	678.23	313.56

2. Use decimal-aligned tab stops to align the telephone, supplies, and miscellaneous expense numbers.

3. Use center-aligned tab stops to align the column headings and the sales district numbers.

4. Use the CTRL key to select the column headings and bold them.

5. Save the document as *Sales District Expenses*, and then preview, print, and close it.

Exercise 6 C

1. Create a new, blank document and key the following text in columns, inserting a tab formatting mark between the text in each column.

Item	Budget	Actual	Variance
Executive Secretaries	$1,234,000	$1,145,000	$(89,000)
Administrative Assistants	289,500	364,800	75,300
Equipment	850,000	730,000	(120,000)
Telecommunications	365,000	340,500	(24,500)
Miscellaneous	65,000	50,000	(15,000)

2. Use the appropriate tab stops to center the column headings and align the budgeted, actual, and difference numbers.

3. Use the CTRL key to select the column headings and italicize them.

4. Save the document as *Budget Variance*, and then preview, print, and close it.

chapter five

Exercise 7   C

1. Open the *Regional Expenses Memo* document located on the Data Disk.

2. Replace the text "Current date" with the actual date.

3. Select the heading paragraphs and then set a left-aligned tab stop at 1½ inches on the horizontal ruler.

4. Move the left-aligned tab stop to 1 inch.

5. Insert the following columnar text separated by tab stops below the first body paragraph of the memo. Use center-aligned tab stops for the column titles. Use decimal-aligned tab stops for the direct sales, employee, and all other numbers. Remember to add a single blank line before and after the columnar text. Apply bold formatting to all the column titles.

Region	Direct Sales	Employee	All Other
Central	$42,000.50	$2,210.00	$12,825.98
Eastern	32,545.78	3,412.44	7,890.66
Midwest	53,897.75	3,508.34	8,454.88
Mountain	49,154.33	6,974.76	5,221.44
Southern	34,675.21	11,242.88	15,111.75
Western	40,876.21	8,417.77	10,445.29

6. Save the document as *Regional Expenses Memo Revised*, and then preview, print, and close it.

Exercise 8   C

1. Create the following interoffice memorandum.

Bold the memo headings

TO: D. Ingram
           Sales Director

FROM: B. Wilson
           Accounting Manager

DATE: Current date

SUBJECT: Sales Summary   Replace "Summary" with "Analysis"

I have completed the sales analysis you requested and the data appear below.

Sales Representative	April	May	June
Davis, Stephen	$65,000	$45,000	$78,000
McCarthy, Rachel	45,000	58,000	76,000
Mills, Cheryl	95,000	99,000	92,000

Please contact me at X397 if you have any questions.

sd

2. Key the current date in the memorandum using AutoComplete.

3. Set appropriate margins for an interoffice memorandum.

4. Set the appropriate tab stops for the memo headings and the text in columns.

5. Apply bold formatting to the TO:, FROM:, DATE:, and SUBJECT: headings.

6. Save the document as *Ingram Memo*, and then preview, print, and close it.

Case Projects

Project 1

Bill Wilson asks you to prepare an interoffice memorandum from him to all regional sales managers advising them of the semiannual sales meeting to be held in two weeks in the main conference room at corporate headquarters in Chicago. Everyone attending the meeting must contact you to arrange hotel accommodations, rental cars, and airline tickets. Use character and tab formatting features to make the memo interesting to read and professional in appearance. Save, preview, and print the document.

Project 2

You are preparing a sales analysis for Bill Wilson to take to the semiannual sales conference and you would like to change the default tab stop position from every ½ inch to every ¼ inch. Using the Ask A Question Box and the keyword "tabs" search for help topics on changing the default tab stop position in a document. Create an interoffice memorandum to Bill Wilson from yourself with the subject line "Default Tabs." Add at least two body paragraphs describing how to change the default tab settings. Save, preview, and print the document.

Project 3

Benji Hori, one of the accounting assistants, asks you if there is a way to vary the alignment of text in a single line. He needs to create a document with the document title, date, and page number all on the same line. He wants the document title left-aligned, the date center-aligned, and the page number right-aligned. If necessary, look up the "Troubleshoot paragraph formatting" topic in

online Help using the Ask A Question Box and review how to align text differently on the same line. Create a sample document with the title "Quarterly Sales Report" left aligned, the current date center-aligned, and the text "Page Number" right-aligned. Save, preview, and print the document. With your instructor's permission, show a classmate how to align text differently on the same line.

Project 4

Before you begin keying a new accounting report for Bill Wilson, you want to practice setting and removing tab stops in a document. Open an existing document that contains tab stops and tab formatting marks. Remove all the tab stops for the entire document at one time. Explore using left-, center-, right-, and decimal-aligned tab stops to make the document easier to read. Save the document with a new name, and then preview and print it.

Project 5

Bill Wilson is planning an auto trip to Houston, Texas, and he asks you to use the Web to look up the mileage and print driving instructions and a city-to-city trip map from Chicago to Houston. Using the Internet, locate Web pages that help you plan auto trips by calculating the mileage and creating driving instructions and maps from city to city. Save and print the driving instructions and trip map. Create an interoffice memorandum to Bill outlining the mileage and driving instructions. Save, preview, and print the memorandum.

chapter five

Project 6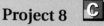

Katrina Levy, one of the accounting assistants, asks you for help. She has an old document with tab stops set differently for each paragraph. She wants to remove all the tab stops for the entire document at one time, but isn't certain how to do this. Open the Tabs dialog box and use the dialog box Help button to get more information about the Clear and Clear All buttons. Using the Ask A Question Box and the keywords "clear tabs," search online Help for information on clearing all the tab stops in a document. Create an interoffice memorandum to Katrina describing how to clear all the tab stops in the document at one time. Save, preview, and print the memo.

Project 7

Kelly Armstead called to ask you how to find someone's e-mail address using the Web. Connect to the Internet, and search for Web pages that allow you to search for e-mail addresses. Print at least three pages. Create an interoffice memorandum to Kelly listing the Web pages you can use to search for e-mail addresses. Save, preview, and print the memo.

Project 8

Bill Wilson is attending a meeting with the branch vice presidents to discuss the quarterly sales figures. He wants you to create a document he can hand out at the meeting. Using fictitious data for the Chicago, London, Melbourne, and Vancouver branches, create a document with two columns for branch names and total sales data for each branch. Use tab stops with leaders to organize the data attractively on the page. Save, preview, and print the document.

Formatting Paragraphs

Chapter Overview

Poorly arranged and formatted text can distract readers from the information in a document. When text is attractively spaced and positioned on the page, readers can concentrate on the document content. In this chapter, you use bullets and numbering, borders and shading, line spacing, alignment and indentation, and page breaks to format and position paragraph text. In addition, you use two other features to position paragraphs in a document: headers and footers, and outlining.

LEARNING OBJECTIVES

- ▶ Add bullets, numbering, borders, and shading
- ▶ Set line and paragraph spacing
- ▶ Align and indent paragraphs
- ▶ Insert page breaks
- ▶ Create and modify headers and footers
- ▶ Apply paragraph styles
- ▶ Create outlines

Case profile

After completing your assignment in the Accounting Department, you are asked to return to the Purchasing Department to help Kelly Armstead create and format the department's correspondence and reports. You begin by formatting the new audit report from the Melbourne branch office.

chapter six 6

For this chapter, the Define styles based on your formatting feature is turned off in the AutoFormat As You Type tab in the AutoCorrect dialog box.

Before beginning the activities in this chapter you should review the Formatting Tips for Business Documents appendix, if you have not already done so.

6.a Adding Bullets, Numbering, Borders, and Shading

There are several ways to format text paragraphs to make them stand out in a document. You can precede lists of text paragraphs with special symbols called bullets, or with numbers. You also can add a border to a paragraph and add shading to a paragraph. All of these formats add interest and emphasis to paragraphs.

Adding Bullets and Numbering

The *Melbourne Audit Report* document contains two groups of short paragraphs to which Kelly wants you to add bullets and numbers. To begin, you open the document and set the appropriate margins for an unbound report. To open the document, set the margins, and add bullets to the first groups of paragraphs:

Step 1	*Open*	the *Melbourne Audit Report* document located on the Data Disk
Step 2	*Set*	2-inch top and 1-inch left and right margins consistent with an unbound report document
Step 3	*Click*	the Show/Hide button ¶ on the Formatting toolbar
Step 4	*Select*	the three paragraphs beginning with "Insufficient quality control" and ending with "Poor communication"
Step 5	*Click*	the Bullets button ☰ on the Formatting toolbar
Step 6	*Deselect*	the text
Step 7	*Observe*	that the paragraphs are moved to the right, are preceded by bullet symbols, and include a tab formatting mark that moves the paragraph text ¼ inch from the bullet

Numbered lists are used to organize items sequentially. You want to create a numbered list from the second group of paragraphs. To create a numbered list:

Step 1	*Select*	the three paragraphs beginning with "Appropriate goals…" and ending with "Employees are not…"
Step 2	*Click*	the Numbering button on the Formatting toolbar
Step 3	*Deselect*	the paragraphs
Step 4	*Observe*	that the paragraphs are moved to the right, are preceded by numbers, and include a tab formatting mark that moves the paragraph text ¼ inch from the number

Your screen should look similar to Figure 6-1.

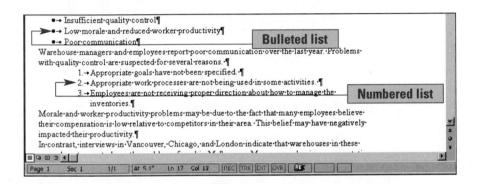

Step 5	*Save*	the document as *Melbourne Audit Report Revised* and leave it open

Another way to add emphasis is with borders and shading.

Adding Borders and Shading

Kelly reviews the *Melbourne Audit Report Revised* and decides that you should add a title to the report. She suggests you emphasize the title by adding a border and shading to it. To add the report title:

Step 1	*Move*	the insertion point to the top of the document
Step 2	*Press*	the ENTER key twice to add two blank lines at the top of the document
Step 3	*Move*	the insertion point to the first blank line
Step 4	*Key*	Melbourne Audit Report and format it with the 14-point font size

MENU TIP

To change the bullet or numbering style, you can click the Bullets and Numbering command on the Format menu, click the appropriate tab, and select a different bullet or numbering style.

FIGURE 6-1
Bulleted and Numbered Paragraphs

MOUSE TIP

You can apply border formatting to selected paragraphs with the Border button on the Formatting toolbar.

C

chapter
six

To add a border around the report title text:

Step 1	*Select*	the "Melbourne Audit Report" title text but do not select the paragraph mark
Step 2	*Click*	F<u>o</u>rmat
Step 3	*Click*	<u>B</u>orders and Shading
Step 4	*Click*	the <u>B</u>orders tab, if necessary

The Borders and Shading dialog box on your screen should look similar to Figure 6-2.

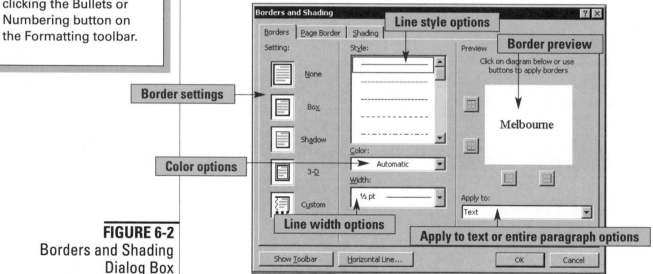

FIGURE 6-2
Borders and Shading
Dialog Box

You can quickly apply or remove a border to either selected text or to an entire paragraph—from margin to margin—by clicking an option in the Setting: list and then clicking the Text or Paragraph option in the Appl<u>y</u> to: list. You also can set the border style, color, and width before you apply the border formatting. Because you selected only the text (not including the paragraph mark) in the title paragraph, you apply a 1½ point box border to the selected text. To apply the border:

Step 1	*Click*	the Bo<u>x</u> setting
Step 2	*Click*	the <u>W</u>idth: list arrow
Step 3	*Click*	1 ½ pt
Step 4	*Verify*	that Text appears in the Appl<u>y</u> to: list
Step 5	*Observe*	the border in the Preview area

You can also apply shading in this dialog box. Because the document will be printed on a black-and-white printer, you can apply gray shading to the title for additional emphasis. To apply light gray shading to the report title:

Step 1	*Click*	the Shading tab
Step 2	*Click*	the Gray-12.5% square on the Fill color grid (the fourth square in the first row)
Step 3	*Verify*	that Text appears in the Apply to: list
Step 4	*Observe*	that the text in the Preview area has a border and shading
Step 5	*Click*	OK
Step 6	*Deselect*	the text
Step 7	*Save*	the document and leave it open

To make the document easier to read, you can add more white space between the lines of text by adjusting the line and paragraph spacing.

6.b Setting Line and Paragraph Spacing

Line spacing indicates the vertical space between lines of text. The default setting for line spacing in Word is single spacing. The paragraph text in letters and memorandums is usually single-spaced. Double spacing is most often used for long reports so that they are easier to read. Also, the line spacing in documents in progress is often greater than single spacing, so reviewers can use the extra white space to write their comments and proofing notations. **Paragraph spacing** refers to the additional points of white space above and below a paragraph.

After reviewing your progress on the *Melbourne Audit Report Revised* document, Kelly suggests that spacing the report text 1.5 times single spacing and adding 6 points of additional white space after each paragraph would enable her supervisor and other reviewers to read it more easily. To space the report:

| Step 1 | *Select* | all the body text below the title document |
| Step 2 | *Click* | the Line Spacing button list arrow [icon] on the Formatting toolbar |

CAUTION TIP

If you select an entire paragraph including the paragraph mark or if you move the insertion point to a single paragraph, Word selects the entire paragraph for formatting. If you then open the Borders and Shading dialog box, the default option is to apply the borders and shading to the entire paragraph— from margin to margin.

MENU TIP

You can change the line or paragraph spacing for selected paragraphs by clicking the Paragraph command on the Format menu or a shortcut menu and then setting line or paragraph spacing options on the Indents and Spacing tab of the Paragraph dialog box.

chapter
six

Your screen should look similar to Figure 6-3.

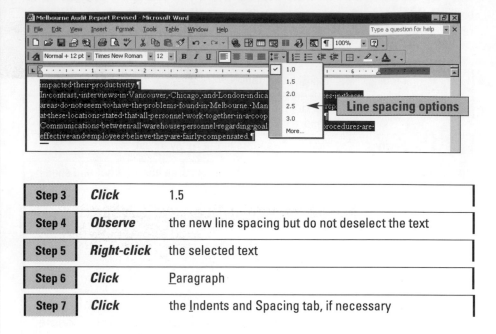

Step 3	*Click*	1.5
Step 4	*Observe*	the new line spacing but do not deselect the text
Step 5	*Right-click*	the selected text
Step 6	*Click*	Paragraph
Step 7	*Click*	the Indents and Spacing tab, if necessary

The Paragraph dialog box on your screen should look similar to Figure 6-4. You can set horizontal alignment, line spacing, and paragraph spacing in this dialog box. Line spacing options available in the Paragraph dialog box include: At Least, which sets a minimum line spacing that adjusts for larger font sizes and graphics; Exactly, which sets a fixed line spacing that will not adjust; and Multiple, which sets the line spacing as a percentage of the single line space.

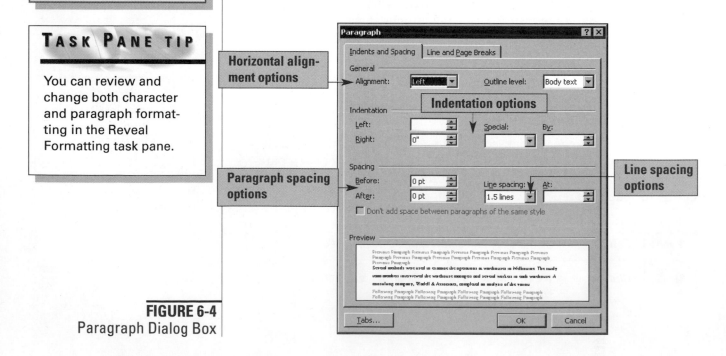

Step 8	*Key*	6 in the Aft<u>e</u>r: list box in the Spacing group
Step 9	*Click*	OK
Step 10	*Move*	the insertion point to the top of the document
Step 11	*Observe*	the additional white space between paragraphs
Step 12	*Save*	the document and leave it open

Next, you add to the text's readability by aligning and indenting paragraphs.

6.c Aligning and Indenting Paragraphs

Vertical alignment affects how the text is placed on the page in relation to the top and bottom margins. **Horizontal alignment** affects how the text is placed on the page in relation to the left and right margins. Sometimes it is useful to move text away from the left margin to set it off from the text that follows it. This is called **indenting** text. You can indent the first line, all the lines, or all lines *except* the first line of a paragraph.

Kelly and her supervisor have reviewed the *Melbourne Audit Report Revised* and they have a few final suggestions for making the report more attractive and easier to read. First, Kelly wants you to create a sample cover page document for the report. Next, she wants you to modify the report by centering the title paragraph between the left and right margins and then indenting the first line of each paragraph, indenting one of the paragraphs from both the left and right margins, and repositioning the bulleted and numbered lists at the left margin.

Aligning Paragraphs Vertically and Horizontally

Reports sometimes have a single cover page that provides the reader the name and date of the report and other important information. You can create a cover page as a separate document or you can create it as the first page of the report document. Because Kelly is undecided about using a cover page, she asks you to create a sample page as a separate document containing the report name and today's date centered vertically and horizontally on the page. You align text vertically on the page by changing the alignment options in the Layout tab of the Page Setup dialog box.

To create a cover page document with vertically aligned text:

| Step 1 | *Create* | a new, blank document |

chapter
six

Step 2	*Set*	1-inch top, left, and right margins
Step 3	*Key*	Melbourne Audit Report
Step 4	*Press*	the ENTER key three times
Step 5	*Insert*	today's date
Step 6	*Format*	the text with the bold, 20-point font size
Step 7	*Click*	File
Step 8	*Click*	Page Setup
Step 9	*Click*	the Layout tab
Step 10	*Click*	the Vertical alignment: list arrow

The Page Setup dialog box on your screen should look similar to Figure 6-5.

FIGURE 6-5
Layout Tab in the Page
Setup Dialog Box

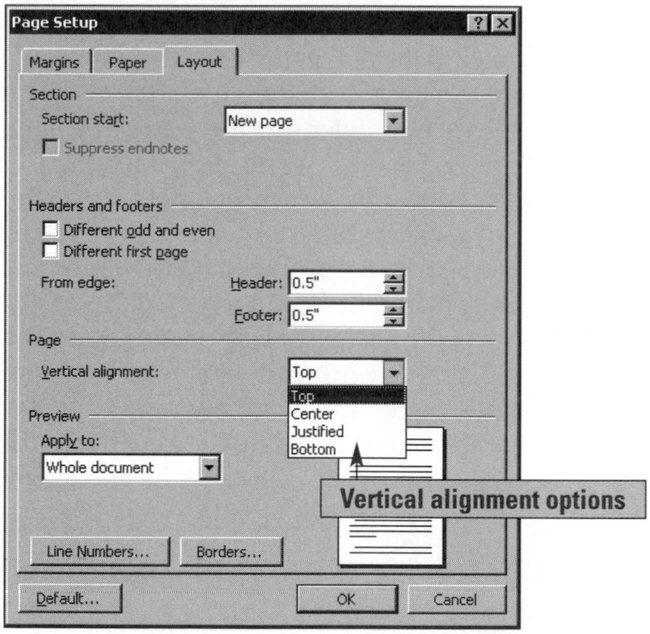

The **Top** vertical alignment option aligns text with the top margin. The **Center** vertical alignment option allows you to center the text between the top and bottom margins. This option is good for creating report title pages. The **Bottom** vertical alignment option aligns the text at the bottom margin, leaving the extra white space at the top of the page. The **Justified** vertical alignment option distributes full-page text evenly between the top and bottom margins by adding additional line spacing.

| Step 11 | *Click* | Center |

Step 12	*Click*	OK
Step 13	*Switch to*	Print Layout view, if necessary
Step 14	*Zoom*	to Whole Page
Step 15	*Observe*	that the text is centered between the top and bottom margins

The four horizontal text alignment options are Left, Center, Right, and Justify. The default horizontal text alignment is left. **Left alignment** lines up the text along the left margin and leaves the right margin "ragged," or uneven. **Right alignment** lines up the text along the right margin and leaves the left margin "ragged." **Center alignment** centers the text between the left and right margins and leaves both margins "ragged." **Justified alignment** aligns the text along both the left and right margins; Word adjusts the spaces between words so that each line is even at both margins. The quickest way to change the alignment of selected paragraphs is to use the alignment buttons on the Formatting toolbar.

Center alignment is appropriate for single line paragraphs, such as cover page text, report titles, and paragraph headings. To center the cover page text horizontally:

Step 1	*Select*	all the lines of text
Step 2	*Click*	the Center button ▤ on the Formatting toolbar
Step 3	*Deselect*	the text
Step 4	*Observe*	that the cover page text is centered both vertically and horizontally between the margins
Step 5	*Zoom*	back to 100%
Step 6	*Switch to*	Normal view
Step 7	*Save*	the document as *Melbourne Audit Report Sample Cover Page* and close it

You are ready to modify the alignment in the report.

Kelly asks you to center-align the title paragraph and use justified alignment for all the body text paragraphs in the document except the bulleted and numbered paragraphs.

To center the title paragraph:

Step 1	*Move*	the insertion point to the title paragraph
Step 2	*Click*	the Center button ▤ on the Formatting toolbar

MENU TIP

You can change horizontal alignment by clicking the Alignment: list arrow on the Indents and Spacing tab in the Paragraph dialog box and selecting the appropriate alignment format.

chapter
six

The title paragraph is centered between the left and right margins. To justify all the paragraphs *except* the bulleted and numbered paragraphs:

Step 1	*Select*	all the body text paragraphs *except* the bulleted and numbered paragraphs, using the CTRL key
Step 2	*Click*	the Justify button on the Formatting toolbar
Step 3	*Deselect*	the paragraphs and scroll the document to verify that the paragraphs are justified
Step 4	*Save*	the document and leave it open

Now you want to indent the individual paragraphs.

Indenting Paragraphs

Indenting, or moving text away from the margin, helps draw attention to that text. Word indentation options position some or all lines of a paragraph to the right of the left margin (or to the left of the right margin). Indenting is part of paragraph formatting, which means only selected paragraphs are indented. The other paragraphs in the document remain unchanged.

There are four types of indents: first line, left, right, and hanging. A **First Line Indent** moves the first line of a paragraph to the right or the left. A **Left Indent** moves all the lines of a paragraph to the right, away from the left margin. A **Right Indent** moves all lines of a paragraph to the left, away from the right margin. A **Hanging Indent** leaves the first line of the paragraph at the left margin and moves the remaining lines to the right, away from the left margin. Hanging Indents are often used to create bulleted lists, numbered lists, and bibliographies.

The easiest way to indent selected paragraphs is to drag the First Line, Hanging Indent, or Left Indent marker to the desired location on the horizontal ruler.

You can use the First Line Indent marker on the horizontal ruler to indent just the first line of a paragraph, leaving the remaining lines in their original position. You often see first-line indents in long text documents, such as books and reports. You decide to indent the first line of each body text paragraph in the report. To indent the first line of the first paragraph of the report with the First Line Indent marker:

Step 1	*Move*	the insertion point to the first body text paragraph
Step 2	*Move*	the mouse pointer to the First Line Indent marker ▽ on the horizontal ruler

Your screen should look similar to Figure 6-6.

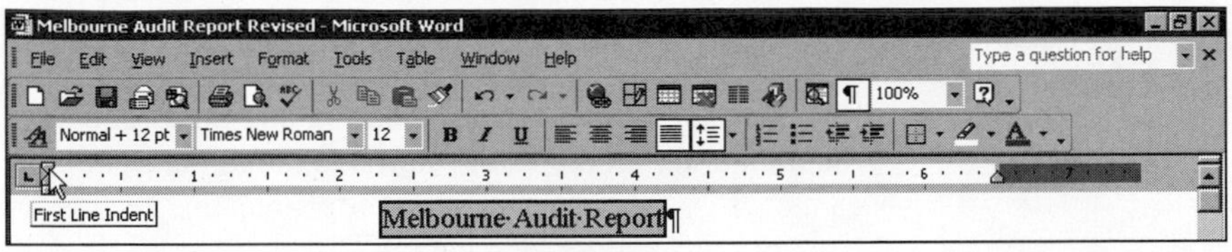

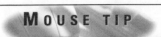

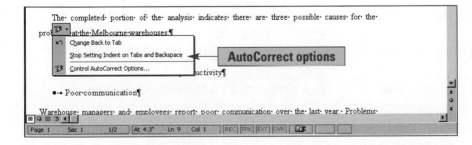

| Step 3 | *Drag* | the First Line Indent marker to the ¼-inch position on the horizontal ruler |
| Step 4 | *Observe* | that the first line of the paragraph is indented to the ¼-inch position |

Another way to move the First Line Indent is with the TAB key. To indent the first line of the next paragraph using the TAB key:

Step 1	*Move*	the insertion point in front of the "T" in "The" in the second body paragraph
Step 2	*Press*	the TAB key
Step 3	*Observe*	that the first line is indented to the ¼-inch position

In addition, the First Line Indent marker on the ruler is positioned at ¼ inch and the AutoCorrect Options button appears. To review the AutoCorrect Options:

| Step 1 | *Move* | the mouse pointer to the AutoCorrect Options button to view the list arrow |
| Step 2 | *Click* | the AutoCorrect Options button list arrow to view the menu |

Your screen should look similar to Figure 6-7.

You can change the indent back to a simple tab formatting mark, turn off the automatic indentation feature, or view additional AutoCorrect Options. You want to change the indent back to a tab.

FIGURE 6-6
First Line Indent Marker

M O U S E   T I P

You can increase and decrease the left indent for selected paragraphs by clicking the Increase Indent and Decrease Indent buttons on the Formatting toolbar.

M E N U   T I P

You can indent paragraphs from the left or right margins by keying the indent positions on the Indents and Spacing tab in the Paragraph dialog box.

FIGURE 6-7
AutoCorrect Options Menu

chapter
six

Step 3	**Click**	Change Back to Tab
Step 4	**Observe**	that a tab formatting mark is inserted and the First Line Indent marker on the ruler returns to the left margin

The AutoCorrect Options button appears again. If desired, you can remove the tab formatting mark and replace it with a First Line Indent with a command on the AutoCorrect Options menu. To change the tab formatting mark back to an indent:

Step 1	**Display**	the AutoCorrect Options menu
Step 2	**Click**	Redo First Indent
Step 3	**Observe**	that the tab formatting mark is replaced with a First Line Indent
Step 4	**Continue**	to indent the first line of the each paragraph (except the bulleted and numbered paragraphs) by dragging the First Line Indent marker to the ¼-inch position on the ruler
Step 5	**Save**	the document and leave it open

You can modify an indent for selected paragraphs by dragging the indent markers to a new position on the horizontal ruler. You can remove an indent by dragging the indent markers back to the left margin. Kelly wants the numbered and bulleted paragraphs to be positioned at the left margin. When you applied the bullets and numbering formatting, Word indented the paragraphs with a Hanging Indent. To position the paragraphs at the left margin, you can drag the Left Indent marker, which moves all components of the indent marker, to the left until the First Line Indent marker is positioned at the left margin. This retains the Hanging Indent but repositions the first line of each paragraph at the left margin. To move the indents:

Step 1	**Select**	the bulleted paragraphs
Step 2	**Move**	the mouse pointer to the Hanging Indent marker ⌂ on the horizontal ruler
Step 3	**Drag**	the left tab stop off the Hanging Indent marker
Step 4	**Drag**	the Left Indent marker ▢ to the left until the First Line Indent marker is at the left margin
Step 5	**Observe**	that the bulleted paragraphs are repositioned at the left margin
Step 6	**Select**	the numbered paragraphs
Step 7	**Follow**	Steps 2 through 4 to position the numbered paragraphs at the left margin

| Step 8 | *Observe* | that the numbered paragraphs are repositioned at the left margin |
| Step 9 | *Deselect* | the text |

Sometimes it is preferable to indent a paragraph from both the left and the right to draw the readers' attention to the paragraph or to set off quoted material. After reviewing your changes, Kelly asks you to indent the paragraph beginning "Morale…" 1 inch from the left and right margins. First you need to remove the First Line Indent from the paragraph. To remove the First Line Indent and then indent the paragraph from both the left and right margins:

Step 1	*Move*	the insertion point to the "Morale…" paragraph
Step 2	*Drag*	the First Line Indent marker ▽ back to the left margin to remove the First Line Indent
Step 3	*Observe*	that the paragraph is no longer indented
Step 4	*Drag*	the Left Indent marker ▢ to the right to the 1-inch position on the horizontal ruler
Step 5	*Observe*	that all the lines of the paragraph are indented 1 inch from the left margin
Step 6	*Move*	the mouse pointer to the Right Indent marker △ on the ruler

Your screen should look similar to Figure 6-8.

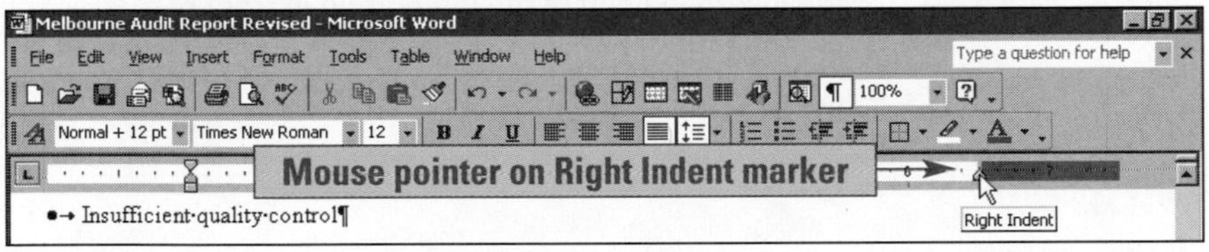

Step 7	*Drag*	the Right Indent Marker △ to the left 1 inch from the right margin
Step 8	*Observe*	that the paragraph is indented from both the left and right margins
Step 9	*Save*	the document and leave it open

Another way to control the arrangement of paragraphs on each page is to control where the text ends on one page and begins on the next page.

CAUTION TIP

It's easy to drag the First Line, Hanging, or Left Indent markers on the ruler beyond the document's left margin. In Normal view, if you can still see the indent marker, drag it back to the appropriate position and then click the scroll box on the horizontal scroll bar to reposition the screen. If you can no longer see the indent markers, switch to Print Layout view, drag the indent markers to the right, and then return to Normal view.

FIGURE 6-8
Right Indent Marker

chapter
six

C 6.d Inserting Page Breaks

Word determines how much text will fit on a page based on the margins, font, font size, and paper size. A **page break** identifies where one page ends and another begins. There are two types of page breaks: a soft, or automatic, page break and a hard, or manual, page break. Word inserts an **automatic page break** when a page is full of text. In Normal view, an automatic page break appears as a dotted horizontal line from the left to the right margins. You can create a **manual page break** at any point on a page; a manual page break appears as a dotted horizontal line from the left to right margins with the words "Page Break" in the center. Manual page breaks are used to force paragraphs to the next page.

Adjusting the line and paragraph spacing in the *Melbourne Audit Report Revised* document causes an automatic page break to occur immediately above the next-to-last paragraph. This forces the last two paragraphs—containing just a few lines of text—to the second page. Kelly decides that she wants to more evenly distribute the text by moving the paragraph beginning "Morale…" to the second page. Changing the position of the page breaks in a document is called **repagination**. To repaginate the document, you cannot move or delete the automatic page break Word inserted. Instead, you must insert a manual page break above the automatic page break. Word then repaginates the entire document from the position of the manual page break.

To insert a manual page break before the "Morale…" paragraph:

Step 1	*Scroll*	to view the automatic page break, a single dotted line, below the "Morale…" paragraph
Step 2	*Move*	the insertion point to the left margin in front of the "M" in "Morale", if necessary
Step 3	*Click*	Insert
Step 4	*Click*	Break

The Break dialog box on your screen should look similar to Figure 6-9.

QUICK TIP

The quickest way to insert a manual page break is to move the insertion point where you want to insert the page break and press the CTRL + ENTER keys.

CAUTION TIP

If you add or remove pages, edit text, or replace formatting, any manual page breaks you inserted may then be incorrect. You can move a manual page break by dragging it to a new position with the mouse pointer. You can delete a manual page break by selecting it and pressing the DELETE key or by moving the insertion point to the left margin below the dotted line and pressing the BACKSPACE key.

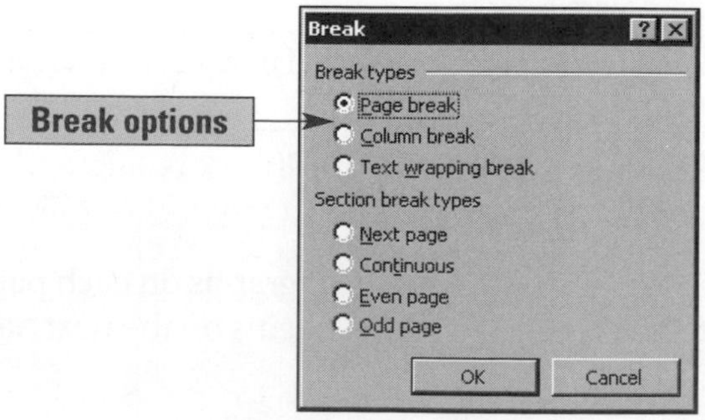

FIGURE 6-9
Break Dialog Box

Break options →

The default option, <u>P</u>age Break, is already selected.

Step 5	*Click*	OK
Step 6	*Observe*	the manual page break above the "Morale…" paragraph
Step 7	*Observe*	that Word repaginated the document and removed the automatic page break
Step 8	*Save*	the document and leave it open

To wrap up the *Melbourne Audit Report Revised* document, Kelly asks you to add page numbers in a footer and the department name and today's date in a header.

6.e Creating and Modifying Headers and Footers

Sometimes you need to have short, one-line paragraphs appear at the top or the bottom of document pages. For example, perhaps you want to include the date and preparer's name at the top of each page of a report and the document filename and page number at the bottom of each page. You use header text and footer text to position these short, one-line paragraphs at the top or bottom of a page above or below the top and bottom margins and body text area. **Header** text, often called **headers**, appears at the top of each page and **footer** text, also called **footers**, appears at the bottom of each page. You can specify that headers or footers print on every page or only on certain pages. For example, you can create headers and footers for every page except the first page or for even- or odd-numbered pages. You can view headers and footers in Print Layout view or Print Preview, but not in Normal view.

Inserting Page Numbers

Page numbers are always inserted at the top or bottom of a document in a header or footer. One way to insert and format page numbers is to first create the header or footer and then use buttons on the Header and Footer toolbar to insert and format the page numbers. A quick way to insert page numbers is to click the Page N<u>u</u>mbers command on the <u>I</u>nsert menu, select header or footer, specify the horizontal alignment, indicate whether to show the number on the first page, and select a number format.

Kelly asks you to insert a center-aligned page number in a footer on all pages of the document. To insert the page number:

Step 1	*Move*	the insertion point to the top of the document
Step 2	*Click*	<u>I</u>nsert
Step 3	*Click*	Page N<u>u</u>mbers

The Page Numbers dialog box on your screen should look similar to Figure 6-10.

FIGURE 6-10
Page Numbers Dialog Box

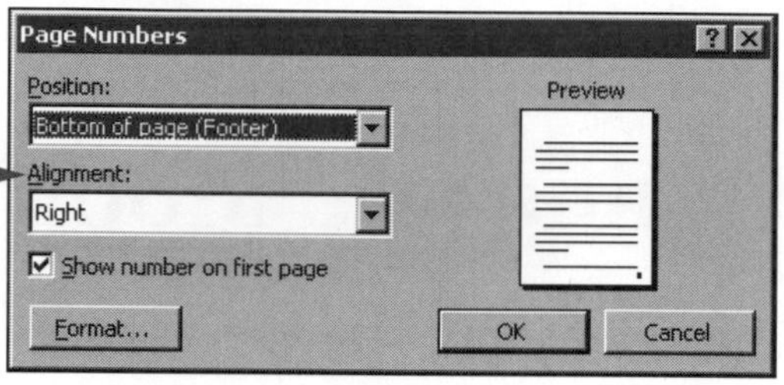

Page number position and alignment options →

Page Numbers ? X

Position:
Bottom of page (Footer) ▼

Alignment:
Right ▼

☑ Show number on first page

Format...   OK   Cancel

Preview

C A U T I O N   T I P

Be careful when working in large documents that contain both manual and automatic page breaks. Adding text, changing margins, or inserting and deleting manual page breaks results in repagination. When Word repaginates a document, it cannot move or delete your manual page breaks, which may result in pagination errors. To be sure the pagination is correct, always use Print Preview to review the pagination of documents before printing them.

You select the position of the page numbers and their alignment in this dialog box. You also can turn on or off the page number on the first page and change the number format in this dialog box.

Step 4	*Verify*	that Bottom of page (Footer) appears in the <u>P</u>osition: list
Step 5	*Click*	the <u>A</u>lignment: list arrow
Step 6	*Click*	Center
Step 7	*Click*	the Show number on first page check box to insert a check mark, if necessary
Step 8	*Click*	OK

Word switches to Print Layout view so you can see the footer.

Step 9	*Scroll*	to view the page numbers in the footer on both pages then return to the top of the document

Now you want to create the header.

Creating and Modifying a Header

Kelly asks you to insert the department name and today's date at the top of every page. You do this in a header. To create the header:

Step 1	*Click*	View
Step 2	*Click*	Header and Footer

Your screen should look similar to Figure 6-11.

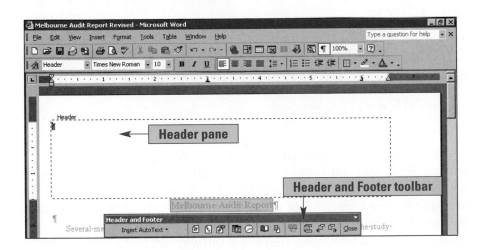

FIGURE 6-11
Header Pane in Print Layout View

The Header pane is visible and contains the insertion point. The Header and Footer toolbar automatically appears. You can use buttons on the Header and Footer toolbar to insert and format page numbers, insert the date and time, and switch between the Header and Footer panes among other tasks.

The horizontal ruler displays a center tab stop set at the 3-inch position and a right tab stop set at the 6-inch position. These are default tabs set for the Header and Footer panes. Because you want to insert today's date at the right margin, you do not need the center tab stop and you need to reposition the right tab stop at the right margin.

Step 3	*Drag*	the Center tab stop off the ruler to remove it
Step 4	*Drag*	the Right tab stop to the right margin to reposition it
Step 5	*Key*	Purchasing Department in the Header pane at the left margin
Step 6	*Press*	the TAB key
Step 7	*Click*	the Insert Date button on the Header and Footer toolbar to insert today's date

chapter
six

Step 8	*Observe*	that the department name and today's date are inserted in the header
Step 9	*Click*	the Close button [Close] on the Header and Footer toolbar
Step 10	*Zoom*	the document to Whole Page and observe the completed header and footer
Step 11	*Switch to*	Normal view
Step 12	*Save*	the document and close it

You can quickly apply multiple paragraph formats at once with paragraph styles.

6.f Applying Paragraph Styles

Kelly is pleased with the formatting of the *Melbourne Audit Report Revised* document and wants you to reformat a similar document. She needs this document reformatted quickly and suggests you try using built-in paragraph formatting, called styles, to reformat it. A **paragraph style** contains multiple formatting attributes, such as line spacing, alignment, and indentations, that affect the way text looks on the page. When you use a style, you can quickly apply the multiple paragraph formatting attributes at one time.

Your first step is to open the *Chicago Draft* document and then set the appropriate margins for an unbound report document. You then use a paragraph style to automatically format the title, the body text, paragraph headings, and the bulleted and numbered lists. Like character styles, you can quickly apply paragraph styles using the Styles and Formatting task pane. To set the appropriate margins and view the Styles and Formatting task pane:

Step 1	*Open*	the *Chicago Draft* document located on the Data Disk
Step 2	*Set*	a 2-inch top margin and 1-inch left and right margins, consistent with an unbound report document
Step 3	*Click*	the Styles and Formatting button [icon] on the Formatting toolbar to view the Styles and Formatting task pane
Step 4	*Show*	All styles, if necessary

To format the report title:

Step 1	*Move*	the insertion point to the top of the document, if necessary
Step 2	*Point to*	Title in the Pick formatting to apply list in the Styles and Formatting task pane (scroll to the bottom of the list to view this style)
Step 3	*Observe*	the ScreenTip that defines the formatting attributes contained in the style
Step 4	*Click*	the Title style in the Pick formatting to apply list in the Styles and Formatting task pane
Step 5	*Observe*	that the title text is centered, bolded, and changed to the 16-point font

To format the body text:

Step 1	*Select*	all the body text below the title
Step 2	*Click*	Body Text 2 in the Pick formatting to apply list in the Styles and Formatting task pane

To format the paragraph headings "Audit Methods," "Issues," "Issues Analyses," and "Summation":

Step 1	*Select*	the four paragraph headings, using the CTRL key
Step 2	*Click*	the Heading 3 style in the Pick formatting to apply list in the Styles and Formatting task pane

To format the bulleted and numbered lists:

Step 1	*Select*	the three paragraphs beginning "Outstanding management style" and ending "High morale and increased worker productivity"
Step 2	*Click*	the List Bullet style in the Pick formatting to apply list in the Styles and Formatting task pane
Step 3	*Select*	the paragraphs beginning "First, appropriate goals..." and ending "Finally, interviews..."
Step 4	*Click*	the List Number style in the Pick formatting to apply list in the Styles and Formatting task pane
Step 5	*Select*	the bulleted and numbered lists using the CTRL key
Step 6	*Double-space*	the lists using the Formatting toolbar
Step 7	*Close*	the Styles and Formatting task pane

MENU TIP

You can create custom list styles using options in the List Styles tab in the Bullets and Numbering dialog box. To view this tab, click the Bullets and Numbering command on the Format menu or a shortcut menu.

MOUSE TIP

You can apply paragraph styles (including list styles containing bullets, numbering, font, and other formats) with the Style button on the Formatting toolbar.

QUICK TIP

You can add spacing before and after a paragraph by applying a style such as the Body Text style that contains additional spacing formats.

chapter
six

| Step 8 | **Save** | the document as *Chicago Audit Report With Styles* and close it |

Now that you have finished the *Chicago Audit Report With Styles* document, Kelly wants you to organize the text paragraphs in another document as an outline.

6.g Creating Outlines

QUICK TIP

You can create an outline using headings styles in Outline view. For more information on using Outline view, see online Help.

An outline, also called an outline numbered list, is a way to structure information logically. You can use an outline to organize the ideas and information into topics and subtopics for a large document, such as a report, proposal, or presentation. An **outline** consists of heading and body text paragraphs organized by level or importance. Body text is paragraph text below an outline heading. Major headings are called level one headings. Each major heading can have subheadings, called level two headings. Each level two heading can have its own subheadings at level three, and so forth. An outline is also a good way to construct multilevel lists. Using an outline numbered list is an easy way to indent paragraphs and add numbering. Kelly wants you to add paragraph numbering to a report and then create a formal topic outline for a business presentation.

Outlining Paragraphs

Numbered text paragraphs are often used in reports and proposals when it is useful to structure the report or proposal information logically. Kelly's supervisor is traveling to London on business next week and will be meeting with the London branch manager to discuss a research report on stores in the London branch. Kelly asks you to add paragraph numbering to the research report. To open the document and add paragraph numbering:

Step 1	**Open**	the *London Research* document located on the Data Disk
Step 2	**Select**	the entire document
Step 3	**Click**	Format
Step 4	**Click**	Bullets and Numbering
Step 5	**Click**	the Outline Numbered tab

You can select different numbering options for an outline in this tab. Your dialog box should look similar to Figure 6-12.

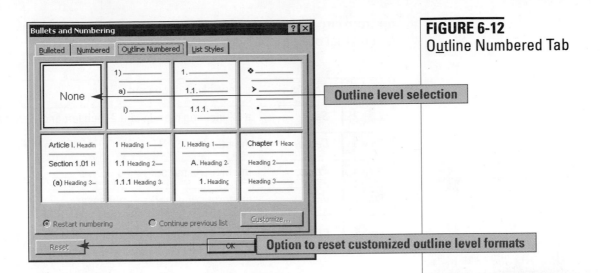

FIGURE 6-12
Outline Numbered Tab

Outline level selection

Option to reset customized outline level formats

Step 6	**Double-click**	the third option in the first row (1, 1.1, 1.1.1)
Step 7	**Deselect**	the text and review the new paragraph numbering

You can use the TAB key to demote outline numbered paragraphs to the next-lower outline level and the SHIFT + TAB keys to promote outline numbered paragraphs to the next-higher level. Paragraphs 3 and 4 are subparagraphs of paragraph 2, so you need to demote the paragraphs to the next-lower level. To demote paragraphs 3 and 4:

Step 1	**Select**	paragraphs 3 and 4
Step 2	**Press**	the TAB key
Step 3	**Deselect**	the paragraphs and observe the new subparagraph numbering (2.1 and 2.2)
Step 4	**Save**	the document as *London Research Revised* and close it

Creating a Formal Topic Outline

When you need to create a formal topic outline, you can use a modified Outline Numbered format. A short formal topic outline has a 1½-inch top margin and 2-inch left and right margins with an uppercase, centered title followed by three blank lines. Each major heading is numbered with Roman numerals followed by a period. The numerals are decimal aligned on the periods (for example, the I. and IV. heading numbers are aligned on the period). You double-space before and after each major heading. The subheadings are single-spaced and the number for each new subheading level (A., 1.) begins immediately below the text of the previous heading.

While in London, Kelly's supervisor will be making a presentation to a group of clients. She wants you to create a formal topic outline for the presentation. Kelly will expand the outline later by adding the

QUICK TIP

In some dialog boxes, you can double-click certain options to select them and close the dialog box in one step.

C

chapter
six

appropriate body text and formatting. To create the margins and title of a formal outline:

Step 1	*Create*	a new, blank document
Step 2	*Set*	a 1½-inch top margin and 2-inch left and right margins
Step 3	*Center*	the title "PRESENTATION OUTLINE" on the first line
Step 4	*Press*	the ENTER key four times
Step 5	*View*	the formatting marks, if necessary
Step 6	*Click*	the Align Left button on the Formatting toolbar to move the insertion point to the left margin

Next you select and customize an Outline Numbered format. To create and customize the formal outline:

Step 1	*Open*	the Outline Numbered tab in the Bullets and Numbering dialog box
Step 2	*Click*	the second outline option (1, a, i) in the first row
Step 3	*Click*	Reset to return the second outline option to its default formatting settings, if necessary
Step 4	*Click*	Customize

Your dialog box should look similar to Figure 6-13.

FIGURE 6-13
Customize Outline
Numbered List Dialog Box

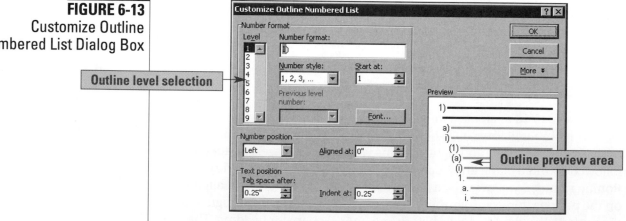

You can change the number format, number style, and number or text positioning for each level in a formal outline in this dialog box. To conform to the formatting standards for a formal topic outline, you must change the number style to Roman numerals for level one, uppercase alphabetic characters for level two, and Arabic numbers for level three. The character following the number to must be changed to a period. The level one number alignment must be changed to right-aligned so that the numbers align on the period at the end of each number. The indentation for levels two and three must be modified to line up the number with the text above it. You modify the outline format for level one:

Step 5	*Verify*	that 1 is selected in the Le*v*el list
Step 6	*Click*	the *N*umber style: list arrow
Step 7	*Click*	I, II, III, …
Step 8	*Click*	in the Number f*o*rmat: text box
Step 9	*Replace*	the closing parenthesis with a period
Step 10	*Change*	the N*u*mber position to Right
Step 11	*Change*	the *A*ligned at: text box to .25
Step 12	*Change*	the Ta*b* space after: text box to .4 inch
Step 13	*Change*	the *I*ndent at: text box to .5 inch
Step 14	*Observe*	the changes to the level one heading in the Preview

You repeat the same series of actions for the level two headings. To modify the level two indentations, numbering style and following character:

Step 1	*Click*	2 in the Le*v*el list
Step 2	*Change*	the *N*umber style to A, B, C, …
Step 3	*Replace*	the closing parenthesis with a period in the Number f*o*rmat: text box
Step 4	*Change*	the *A*ligned at: text box to .4 inch
Step 5	*Change*	the Ta*b* space after: text box to .75 inch
Step 6	*Change*	the *I*ndent at: text box to 1.2 inch

To modify the level three indentations, numbering style, and following character:

Step 1	*Click*	3 in the Le*v*el list
Step 2	*Change*	the *N*umber style to 1, 2, 3, …

**chapter
six**

Step 3	*Change*	the closing parenthesis to a period
Step 4	*Change*	the Aligned at: text box to .75 inches
Step 5	*Change*	the Indent at: text box to 1.45 inches
Step 6	*Click*	OK

The indented first number appears. When you press the ENTER key, the next heading line is automatically created with the next number at the same level. To double-space between the major heading and any subheadings, you can insert a New Line formatting mark that adds a blank line without outline numbers by pressing the SHIFT + ENTER keys. A **New Line formatting mark** creates a new line inside an existing paragraph formatting mark. You then press the ENTER key to create a new paragraph and begin the next numbered heading line. You promote or demote headings by clicking the Increase and Decrease Indent buttons on the Formatting toolbar or by pressing the TAB and SHIFT + TAB keys before you key the text.

To key the first heading:

Step 1	*Key*	MARKETING FORECAST
Step 2	*Press*	the SHIFT + ENTER keys to insert a New Line formatting mark (small return arrow) at the end of the MARKETING FORECAST heading and move the insertion point to a new line
Step 3	*Press*	the ENTER key to move the insertion point to the next line and continue the outline numbers

The next outline heading is automatically numbered at the same level, as the previous heading which is level one. However, you now want to key level two headings. You demote the insertion point to the next level.

Step 4	*Click*	the Increase Indent button 📋 on the Formatting toolbar to move the insertion point to the next level and insert the A. outline number
Step 5	*Key*	Projected Sales
Step 6	*Press*	the ENTER key
Step 7	*Key*	Sales Stars!
Step 8	*Press*	the ENTER key

Next, key the level three headings below "Sales Stars!"

Step 9	*Press*	the TAB key
Step 10	*Key*	Wilson, Betancourt, and Fontaine, pressing the ENTER key after each heading
Step 11	*Key*	Lu
Step 12	*Press*	the SHIFT + ENTER keys to insert a New Line formatting mark
Step 13	*Press*	the ENTER key

The next heading is level one. To promote the insertion point and key the second level one heading:

Step 1	*Click*	the Decrease Indent button [icon] twice on the Formatting toolbar
Step 2	*Key*	ADVERTISING CAMPAIGN
Step 3	*Press*	the SHIFT + ENTER keys to insert a New Line formatting mark
Step 4	*Press*	the ENTER key to create the next heading line
Step 5	*Press*	TAB key to demote the insertion point to level two
Step 6	*Key*	Media Budget
Step 7	*Press*	the ENTER key
Step 8	*Press*	the TAB key to demote the insertion point
Step 9	*Key*	TV, Radio, and Web banners, pressing the ENTER key after each heading
Step 10	*Press*	the SHIFT + TAB keys to promote the insertion point
Step 11	*Key*	Print Ads
Step 12	*Press*	the ENTER key
Step 13	*Press*	the TAB key to demote the insertion point
Step 14	*Key*	Newspapers and Magazines pressing the ENTER key after Newspapers
Step 15	*Switch to*	Print Layout view, if necessary
Step 16	*Zoom*	the document to see all of the text
Step 17	*Zoom*	the document back to 100%
Step 18	*Save*	the document as *Presentation Outline* and close it

Outlines provide a quick way to organize thoughts and topics.

chapter
six

Summary

▶ When applying paragraph formatting, you must select the paragraph or paragraphs to be formatted before you select the formatting option.

▶ Bullets, numbering, borders, and shading can add emphasis to paragraphs and draw a reader's attention to the paragraphs.

▶ You can select different line spacing options such as Single, Double, and 1.5 from the Line spacing: list in the Paragraph dialog box or from the Line Spacing button on the Formatting toolbar.

▶ You can add spacing before and after a paragraph by setting paragraph spacing options in the Paragraph dialog box.

▶ Paragraphs can be aligned vertically between the top and bottom margins and horizontally between the left and right margins.

▶ Paragraphs can be indented with options in the Paragraph dialog box, buttons on the Formatting toolbar, and by dragging the indent markers on the horizontal ruler. Indentation options include First Line, Hanging, Left, and Right Indents.

▶ Word inserts automatic page breaks whenever text fills a page. Although you cannot delete an automatic page break, you can insert manual page breaks to change the pagination of a document.

▶ Headers and footers position text such as names, dates, and page numbers, at the top and bottom of specific pages.

▶ You can apply paragraph styles to one or more paragraphs with options in the Styles and Formatting task pane.

▶ An outline is a way of organizing the ideas and information presented in a long document or presentation. You can create an outline by adding outline numbers to paragraphs, by setting custom outline numbering formats and keying the outline text, by using heading styles in Outline view, or by using outline paragraph numbering in the Paragraph dialog box.

Commands Review

Action	Menu Bar	Shortcut Menu	Toolbar	Task Pane	Keyboard
Apply or remove bullets and numbering to lists	Format, Bullets and Numbering	Right-click the selected text or at the insertion point, click Bullets and Numbering		Click the List link in the Bullets and Numbering group in the Reveal Formatting task pane	ALT + O, N Key a number, press the SPACEBAR or TAB key, and key the text Key an asterisk, press the SPACEBAR or TAB key, and key the text
Add borders and shading to text and entire paragraphs— from margin to margin	Format, Borders and Shading				ALT + O, B
Change line and paragraph spacing	Format, Paragraph	Right-click selected paragraph(s), click Paragraph		Click the Spacing link in the Paragraph group in the Reveal Formatting task pane	ALT + O, P CTRL + 1 (single) CTRL + 2 (double) CTRL + 5 (1.5)
Change vertical alignment	File, Page Setup			Click the Layout link in the Section group in the Reveal Formatting task pane	ALT + F, U
Change horizontal alignment	Format, Paragraph	Right-click selected paragraph(s), click Paragraph		Click the Alignment link in the Paragraph group in the Reveal Formatting task pane	ALT + O, P CTRL + L (Left) CTRL + E (Center) CTRL + R (Right) CTRL + J (Justify)
Indent paragraphs	Format, Paragraph	Right-click selected paragraph(s), click Paragraph	Drag the indent marker on the horizontal ruler	Click the Indentation link in the Paragraph group in the Reveal Formatting task pane	ALT + O, P CTRL + M (from Left) CTRL + T (Hanging)
Insert page breaks	Insert, Break				ALT + I, B CTRL + ENTER
Create headers and footers	View, Header and Footer		Various on the Header and Footer toolbar		ALT + V, H
Insert page numbers	Insert, Page Numbers				ALT + I, U
Apply paragraph styles	Format, Styles and Formatting		Normal	Click the style in the Pick a formatting to apply list in the Styles and Formatting task pane	ALT + O, S
Create an outline numbered list	Format, Bullets and Numbering				ALT + O, N
Remove formatting from selected text	Edit, Clear, Formats			Click Clear Formatting in the Pick a formatting to apply list in the Styles and Formatting task pane (Show Formatting in use)	ALT + E, A, F CTRL + Q (paragraph formatting) CTRL + SPACEBAR (character formatting)

chapter six

Concepts Review

SCANS

Circle the correct answer.

1. The default line spacing is:
[a] Justified.
[b] Single.
[c] Double.
[d] Center.

2. You can quickly apply a combination of formats to a paragraph by applying a paragraph:
[a] template.
[b] style.
[c] task pane.
[d] dialog box.

3. A page break:
[a] moves all the lines of a paragraph to the right of the left margin.
[b] centers text between the left and right margins.
[c] identifies where one page ends and another begins.
[d] adds emphasis to paragraphs.

4. Numbered lists are used to:
[a] align paragraphs vertically on the page.
[b] align paragraphs horizontally on the page.
[c] organize paragraphs logically.
[d] create headers and footers.

5. You cannot indent selected paragraphs by:
[a] dragging an indent marker on the horizontal ruler.
[b] clicking the Increase Indent button.
[c] keying the indent position in the Paragraph dialog box.
[d] keying the indent position in the Font dialog box.

6. A hanging indent moves:
[a] all the lines of a paragraph to the right.
[b] all the lines of a paragraph to the left.
[c] only the top line.
[d] all lines except the top line.

7. A header appears at the:
[a] bottom of every page.
[b] left margin of the first page.
[c] top of every page.
[d] the right margin of every page.

8. Page numbers are always inserted:
[a] in headers or footers.
[b] only on the first page.
[c] at each new paragraph.
[d] with the Break command on the Insert menu.

9. An outline is:
[a] always double-spaced.
[b] only created in Outline view.
[c] used to organize paragraphs logically.
[d] a way to quickly apply a combination of formats to paragraphs.

10. When document text aligns at the left margin and has a ragged right margin, the text is:
[a] center-aligned.
[b] left-aligned.
[c] right-aligned.
[d] justified.

Circle **T** if the statement is true or **F** if the statement is false.

T   F   1. The default horizontal alignment is left alignment.

T   F   2. You can set line spacing with the mouse and the horizontal and vertical ruler.

T   F   3. Paragraph spacing allows you to add additional white space before and after a paragraph.

T   F   4. Justified alignment means that text is aligned only along the left margin.

T   F   5. The only way to indent a paragraph is to press the TAB key.

T   F   6. A paragraph can be indented from the right margin.

T   F   7. You can add borders and shading to text in paragraph or to the entire paragraph.

T   F   8. You can set, modify, or delete automatic page breaks.

T   F   9. Headers and footers are visible in Normal view.

T   F   10. When applying paragraph formatting to an entire document that has already been keyed, only the first paragraph must be selected.

notes   For the remainder of this text, when you open a letter or memo document from the Data Disk or key a new document from a figure, replace the text "Current date" with the actual date using the AutoComplete feature or the Date and <u>T</u>ime command on the <u>I</u>nsert menu.

Skills Review

SCANS

Exercise 1 **C**

1. Open the *Expense Guidelines* document located on the Data Disk.

2. Set a 2-inch top margin and 1-inch left and right margins, as appropriate for an unbound report document.

3. Format the "Expense Guidelines" title to change the case to uppercase and apply bold, 14-point, centered alignment formats.

4. Add a 2¼ pt box border and Gray-10% shading to the Expense Guidelines title text. (*Hint:* Do not apply the formats to the entire paragraph.)

5. Justify the body paragraphs between the left and right margins.

6. Double-space the body paragraphs.

7. Indent the first line of each paragraph using the TAB key.

8. Save the document as *Expense Guidelines Revised*, and then preview and print it.

9. Remove the First Line Indents from all the body paragraphs *except* the first body paragraph by dragging the First Line Indent marker back to the left margin.

10. Create a numbered list using all the body paragraphs *except* the first body paragraph.

11. Save the document as *Expense Guidelines Numbered List*, and then preview and print it.

12. Change the numbered list to a bulleted list.

chapter six

13. Create a footer containing your name at the left margin and the current date at the right margin.

14. Save the document as *Expense Guidelines With Bullets and Footer*, and then preview, print, and close it.

Exercise 2 C

1. Open the *Interoffice Training Memo* located on the Data Disk.

2. Change the margins to the appropriate margins for an interoffice memorandum.

3. Set a tab stop to line up the heading paragraphs.

4. Change the case of the To, From, Date, and Subject headings to uppercase. (*Hint:* Don't forget to use the CTRL key to select all the items before you change the case.)

5. Change the line spacing for all the body paragraphs to 1.5 using the Formatting toolbar.

6. Indent the two paragraphs beginning "Samantha" and "Steve" ½ inch from both the left and the right margins.

7. Select the two indented paragraphs and add six points of spacing after the selected paragraphs by opening the Paragraph dialog box and changing the Spacing After: option to 6 pt.

8. Save the document as *Interoffice Training Memo Revised* and then preview and print it.

9. Remove the left and right indents from the two indented paragraphs and use outline numbering to number all the body paragraphs. The two paragraphs beginning "Samantha" and "Steve" are subparagraphs of the first body paragraph.

10. Save the document as *Interoffice Training Memo With Outline Numbering*, and then preview, print, and close it.

Exercise 3 C

1. Open the *District C Sales Decline* document located on the Data Disk.

2. Set a 2-inch top margin and 1.5-inch left and right margins.

3. Double-space and justify the entire document.

4. Single-space all the stores paragraphs *except* store A5.

5. Create a bulleted list with the stores paragraphs.

6. Save the document as *District C Sales Decline With Bulleted List*, and then preview and print it.

7. Change the bulleted list to a numbered list.

8. Save the document as *District C Sales Decline With Numbered List*, and then preview, print, and close it.

Exercise 4 C

1. Open the *Expense Guidelines* document located on the Data Disk.

2. Set the appropriate margins for an unbound report document.

3. Center-align the "Expense Guidelines" title, format it with the 14-point bold font, and delete the two blank lines that follow it.

4. Apply the Body Text paragraph style to the body paragraphs.

5. Indent the first line of each body paragraph ¼ inch using the First Line Indent marker on the horizontal ruler.

6. Save the document as *Expense Guidelines With Body Text*, and then preview and print it.

7. Remove the Body Text formatting from the body paragraphs. (*Hint:* Display the Formatting in use options in the Styles and Formatting task pane and clear the formatting.)

8. Justify all the paragraphs including the title paragraph vertically between the top and bottom margins.

9. Save the document as *Expense Guidelines With Vertical Justification*, and then preview, print, and close it.

Exercise 5 [C]

1. Open the *Vancouver Draft* document located on the Data Disk.

2. Set the appropriate margins for an unbound report document.

3. Apply the Body Text style to the entire document.

4. Center-align and format with Times New Roman 14 point bold the title "Vancouver Warehouse Report."

5. Justify the body paragraphs between the left and right margins.

6. Apply the Small caps effect and bold formatting to the paragraph heading "Audit Methods."

7. Copy the Small caps effect and bold formatting to the "Problems," "Problem Analyses," and "Summation" paragraph headings using the Format Painter.

8. Create a bulleted list with the three paragraphs beginning "Poor Communication" and then center-align the list.

9. Create a numbered list with the three paragraphs in the Problem Analyses section beginning "First," and ending with "Finally,".

10. Create a footer and insert the current date at the right margin using a button on the Header and Footer toolbar.

11. Save the document as *Vancouver Draft Revised*, and then preview, print, and close it.

Exercise 6 [C]

1. Open the *Vancouver Draft Revised* document you created in Exercise 5.

2. Select the entire document.

3. Press CTRL + Q to remove the paragraph formatting.

4. Press CTRL + SPACEBAR to remove the character formatting.

5. Remove the Body Text style. (*Hint:* View the Formatting in use in the Styles and Formatting task pane and clear the formats.)

6. Triple-space the document.

7. Insert the page number in the center position in a footer on each page.

8. Create a manual page break above the "Summation" paragraph.

9. Save the document as *Vancouver Draft With Triple Spacing*, and then preview, print, and close it.

Exercise 7 [C]

1. Open the *Sales Opportunities* document located on the Data Disk.

2. Change the text "Introduction," "Types of Stores," "Shopper Personalities," and "Conclusion" to all caps, bold, and Arial 14 point. (*Hint:* Use the CTRL key to select all the text before formatting it.)

3. Select the text beginning with "The Mall" and ending with "The Gourmet Store" and add bullets.

4. Select the text beginning with "The Sale Hunter" and ending with "The Catalog Shopper" and add bullets.

5. Create a header with your name at the right margin.

chapter six

6. Insert a manual page break above the "Types of Stores," "Shopper Personalities," and "Conclusion" paragraphs.

7. Save the documents as *Sales Opportunities Revised*, and then preview, print, and close it.

Exercise 8

1. Create a new, blank document and key the following text in a formal topic outline using customized outline numbering. Do not apply the italic formatting.

> *Using the Proofing Tools*
>> *Using the Spelling and Grammar Command*
>> *Using the Thesaurus Command*
>> *Using AutoCorrect*
>>> *Customizing AutoCorrect*
>>> *Setting AutoCorrect Exceptions*
> *Creating and Applying Frequently Used Text*
>> *Inserting Standard AutoText*
>> *Inserting Custom AutoText*
>> *Editing, Saving, Printing, and Deleting AutoText*
> *Inserting Dates with AutoComplete*

2. Save the document as *Proofing Topics*, and then preview, print, and close it.

Case Projects

Project 1

Kelly asks you how to use different indent options using the Paragraph dialog box instead of the indent markers on the horizontal ruler. Using the Ask A Question Box, find and review information on indenting paragraphs. Create a new interoffice memorandum to Kelly with at least four paragraphs describing how to use the different indent options using the Paragraph dialog box, the indent markers on the horizontal ruler, and the Indent buttons on the Formatting toolbar. Save, preview, and print the document.

Project 2

B. D. Vickers believes you can purchase and print postage over the Internet. Connect to the Internet, and search the Web for pages containing information about purchasing and printing postage on the Web. Create a favorite or bookmark for the home page at each site you visit. Create an interoffice memorandum to B. D. Vickers describing how to purchase and print postage from pages on the Web. Save, preview, and print the document.

Project 3

One of the new employees in the Purchasing Department is having a problem creating evenly spaced lines in a document that contains large text characters on various lines. Using the Ask A Question Box, search for help topics on setting line spacing for this type of document. Create a new unbound report document with a title and a numbered list of instructions on how to change the line spacing to create evenly spaced lines with mixed-size characters. Save, preview, and print the document. With your instructor's permission, demonstrate these instructions to a classmate.

Project 4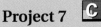

Kelly asks you to prepare an interoffice memorandum to all Purchasing Department employees reminding them of the annual purchasing conference to be held in three weeks in Vancouver. All employees who plan to attend the conference must contact her no later than next Thursday to arrange for someone to handle their responsibilities while they are at the conference. Use character and paragraph formatting features to make the memo interesting to read and professional in appearance. Save, preview, and print the document.

Project 5

You must complete Project 2 before beginning Project 5.

Kelly tells you that Word provides a special toolbar you can use to open your Web browser and load Web pages from inside Word. View the Web toolbar using the toolbar shortcut menu. Use the Favorites button to display a Web page with information about purchasing and printing postage on the Web. Create an interoffice memorandum to Kelly describing how to view and use the Web toolbar. Save, preview, and print the document.

Project 6

Kelly wants you to create a one-page cover sheet for an audit report on the Melbourne branch that she is completing. She wants the title of the report to contain B. D. Vickers name and title and the current date triple spaced, in a 16-point font, and centered vertically and horizontally on the page. Create the cover sheet for Kelly, and then save, preview, and print it.

Project 7

Kelly asks you to present some troubleshooting tips on indenting text at the next meeting of the International Association of Executive Assistants. Using the Ask A Question Box, review how to indent text. Create a new document containing a list of at least five indenting troubleshooting tips. Save, preview, and print the document. With your instructor's approval, demonstrate these troubleshooting tips to several classmates.

Project 8

You want to know more about how to use the keyboard to create bulleted and numbered lists automatically. Using the Ask A Question Box to research how to create bulleted and numbered lists automatically. Create a new document and practice creating bulleted and numbered lists automatically with the fictitious data of your choice. Save, preview, and print the document.

chapter six

Previewing and Printing a Document

Chapter Overview

Previewing documents before printing them enables you to find errors you might otherwise not notice until you print. You can fix any problems you find right in Print Preview, whether they are text edits or formatting changes. In this chapter, you learn how to edit a document in Print Preview and set print options.

Case profile

Worldwide Exotic Foods requires all employees to preview their documents and make necessary changes before printing to prevent reprinting and keep costs down. Kelly Armstead needs your help in previewing, editing, and printing a document she created previously. The printed document—an analysis report—then will be duplicated and distributed to the branch managers.

**chapter
seven**

7.a Using Print Preview

Print Preview displays your document onscreen exactly as it will print on paper. When viewing a document in Print Preview, you can see one or more pages of your document. Headers, footers, margins, page numbers, text, and graphics can also be seen in Print Preview.

The document Kelly asks you to finalize and print is an *Analysis Report*. To open and preview a document:

MENU TIP

You can click the Print Preview command on the File menu to see how your document looks before it is printed.

Step 1	**Open**	the *Analysis Report* document located on the Data Disk
Step 2	**Verify**	that the insertion point is at the top of the document
Step 3	**Click**	the Print Preview button 🔍 on the Standard toolbar
Step 4	**Click**	the One Page button 🄱 on the Print Preview toolbar to view only the first page of the document, if necessary

The first page of the *Analysis Report* document appears in Print Preview. Your screen should look similar to Figure 7-1.

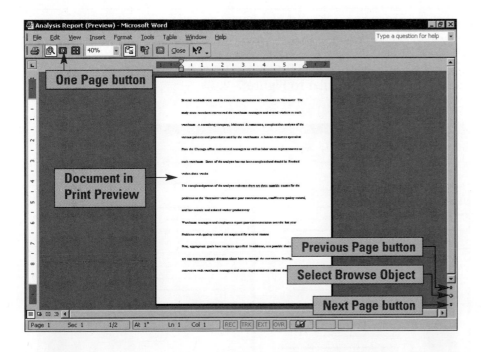

FIGURE 7-1
Print Preview

When only one page of a multiple-page document is viewed, you can use the vertical scroll bar or the Previous Page and Next Page buttons located below the vertical scroll bar to scroll between the pages.

chapter
seven

| Step 5 | *Click* | the Next Page button ⬇ below the vertical scroll bar to view the second page of the document |
| Step 6 | *Click* | the Previous Page button ⬆ below the vertical scroll bar to return to the first page |

The One Page button on the Print Preview toolbar displays a single page at a time. You can use the Multiple Pages button on the Print Preview toolbar to view two or more small, thumbnail-sized pages. When you view several thumbnail-sized pages at one time, you can compare how the text appears on subsequent pages and where the page breaks occur. To view both pages of the *Analysis Report* document side by side:

Step 1	*Click*	the Multiple Pages button 🔳 on the Print Preview toolbar to open the Multiple Pages grid
Step 2	*Point to*	the second square in the top row of the grid
Step 3	*Observe*	the 1 × 2 Pages notation at the bottom of the grid
Step 4	*Click*	the second square in the top row
Step 5	*Observe*	both pages of the document displayed side by side
Step 6	*Observe*	the dark blue border around the first page

The dark border indicates the active page of the document. Your screen should look similar to Figure 7-2.

FIGURE 7-2
Thumbnail Pages

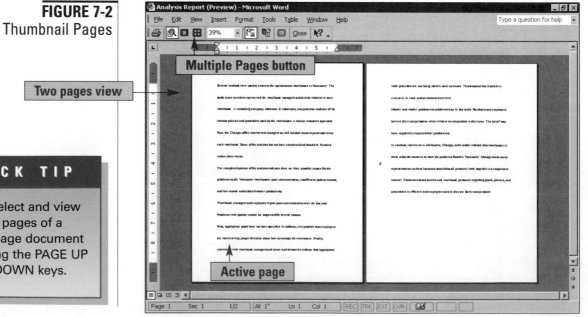

You can zoom individual pages when viewing more than one page by first making a page the active page. To activate a page, you simply click it with the mouse pointer.

Step 7	*Click*	page 2
Step 8	*Observe*	the dark blue border around the page
Step 9	*Click*	page 1

You also can edit your document in Print Preview. You can key text, apply formatting, set tab stops and paragraph indents, and change margins in Print Preview. For easier viewing, you can magnify, or zoom, a portion of the document with the zoom pointer or the Zoom button on the Print Preview toolbar.

The **Magnifier** button on the Print Preview toolbar is a toggle switch that turns on or off the zoom pointer. By default, the Magnifier button and the zoom pointer are turned on when you Print Preview a document. When the Magnifier button is turned on and the mouse pointer is positioned on a selected page, it changes into the zoom pointer. If multiple pages are displayed, you should first select a page by clicking it and then position the mouse pointer on it.

To view single pages and zoom the first page:

Step 1	*Click*	the One Page button  on the Print Preview toolbar
Step 2	*Move*	the mouse pointer to the beginning of the first paragraph on the page
Step 3	*Observe*	that the mouse pointer changes into a zoom pointer (a magnifying glass with a plus sign in the middle)

Your screen should look similar to Figure 7-3.

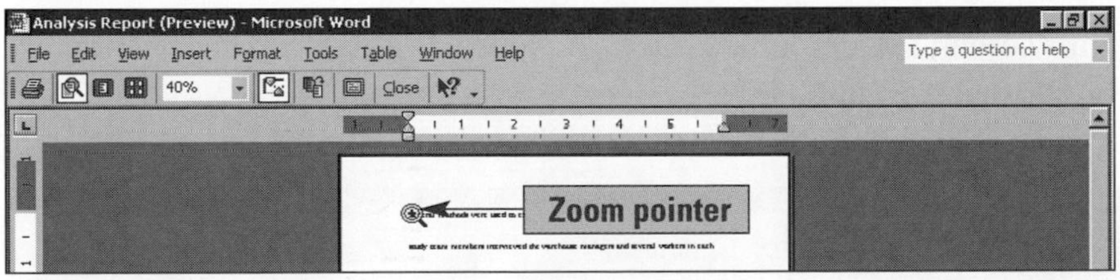

| Step 4 | *Click* | the paragraph with the zoom pointer |
| Step 5 | *Observe* | that the document is zoomed to 100% and you are viewing the portion of the first paragraph you clicked |

M O U S E T I P

You can show additional toolbars in Print Preview with the toolbar shortcut menu or you can customize the Print Preview toolbar by clicking the Toolbar Options list arrow and then pointing to <u>A</u>dd or Remove Buttons.

M E N U T I P

You can close the Print Preview of the current document with the taskbar shortcut menu. This does not close the document. It returns you to previous Normal or Print Layout view.

FIGURE 7-3
Zoom Pointer

chapter
seven

| Step 6 | *Observe* | that the mouse pointer is still the zoom pointer (a magnifying glass with a minus sign in the middle) |
| Step 7 | *Click* | the document with the zoom pointer |

The document is zoomed to one page. You need to change the margins for the *Analysis Report* document. Because the document is in Print Preview, you can make the change here. The same formatting features that are available in Normal and Print Layout views are available in Print Preview. To set the margins for an unbound report:

Step 1	*Open*	the Margins tab in the Page Setup dialog box
Step 2	*Set*	the appropriate margins for an unbound report
Step 3	*Observe*	the new margins

To key or format selected text in Print Preview, you must first have an insertion point and an I-beam. When you turn off the Magnifier button, the insertion point appears and the mouse pointer becomes an I-beam when you position it over the document. To see the insertion point and the I-beam and zoom the document to 75%:

Step 1	*Click*	the Magnifier button 🔍 on the Print Preview toolbar to turn off the zoom pointer
Step 2	*Move*	the mouse pointer to the top of the page
Step 3	*Observe*	that the mouse pointer is an I-beam and the small, flashing insertion point appears at the top of the document
Step 4	*Click*	the Zoom button list arrow 42% on the Print Preview toolbar
Step 5	*Click*	75%

Your screen should look similar to Figure 7-4. You can see the text well enough to edit it.

FIGURE 7-4
Document Zoomed to 75%

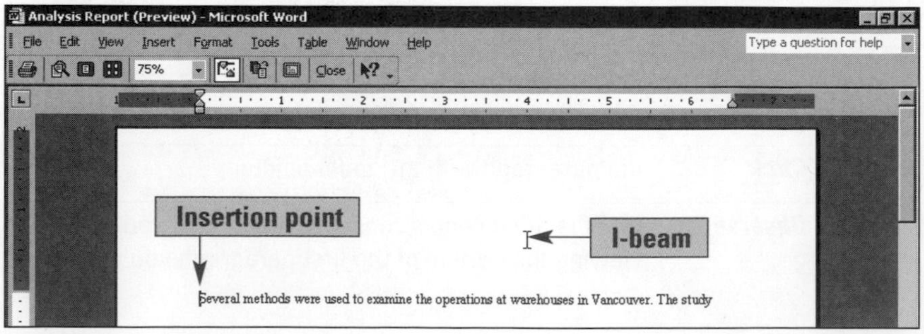

You want to indent the first line of all the paragraphs. You can show the horizontal and vertical rulers in Print Preview and then indent individual paragraphs or you can select the entire document, open the Paragraph dialog box, and indent all the paragraphs at the same time. To indent the first line of each paragraph ½ inch from the left margin:

Step 1	*Select*	the entire document
Step 2	*Open*	the Indents and Spacing tab in the Paragraph dialog box
Step 3	*Click*	the Special: list arrow
Step 4	*Click*	First line
Step 5	*Key*	.5 in the By: text box, if necessary
Step 6	*Click*	OK
Step 7	*Deselect*	the text

You want to zoom the document back to two pages so you can see your changes.

Step 8	*Click*	the Zoom button list arrow `42%` ▾ on the Print Preview toolbar
Step 9	*Click*	Two Pages
Step 10	*Observe*	the indented paragraphs
Step 11	*Zoom*	the first page to 75%

The *Analysis Report* document should have a title. You can key and format that title when the Magnifier button is turned off and you see the insertion point and the I-beam. To key and format a title:

Step 1	*Insert*	a blank line at the top of the first page
Step 2	*Move*	the insertion point to the new blank line
Step 3	*Key*	Analysis Report
Step 4	*Select*	the title text using the I-beam
Step 5	*Format*	the title text with bold, 14-point font using a shortcut menu and the Font dialog box
Step 6	*Center*	the title text using a shortcut menu and the Paragraph dialog box
Step 7	*Deselect*	the title text

chapter
seven

Step 8	*Zoom*	the first page to One Page
Step 9	*Insert*	page numbers centered at the bottom of each page

Your screen should look similar to Figure 7-5.

FIGURE 7-5
New Title, Indented
Paragraphs, Page
Numbers

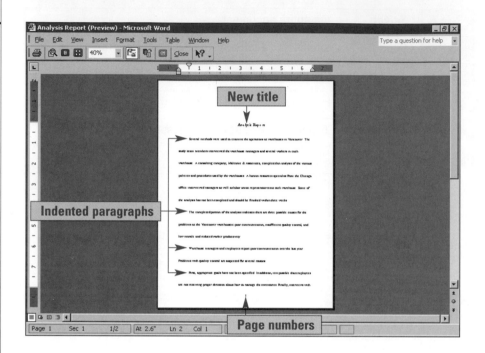

You can close Print Preview and save the document.

Step 10	*Click*	the <u>C</u>lose button Close on the Print Preview toolbar
Step 11	*Save*	the document as *Revised Analysis Report* and leave it open

The document looks good with the correct margins, paragraph indentation, and title. You're ready to print it.

C 7.b Printing a Document

After you correct the margins and paragraph indentations, you are ready to print the document. Before you print it, however, you may need to change the paper size, paper orientation, or paper source. You can change these options in the Page Setup dialog box. Word provides a list of common paper sizes from which to choose, including Letter (8½ × 11 in), Legal (8½ × 14 in), and Executive (7½ × 10½ in).

You can also choose a paper **orientation** (the direction text is printed on the paper): Portrait or Landscape. **Portrait orientation** means that the short edge of the paper is the top of the page. **Landscape orientation** means that the long edge of the paper is the top of the page. To review the current settings in the Page Setup dialog box:

Step 1	*Open*	the Page Setup dialog box

Step 2	*Click*	the Paper tab

The dialog box on your screen should look similar to Figure 7-6.

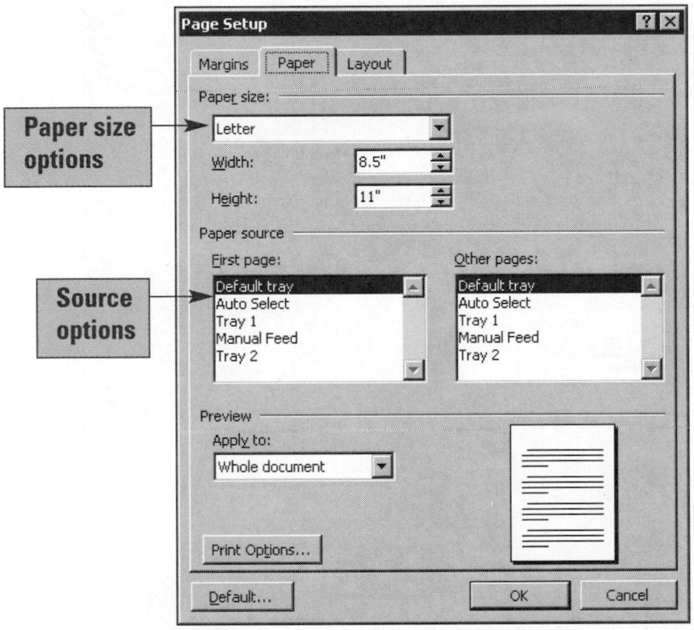

FIGURE 7-6
Paper Tab in the Page Setup Dialog Box

The Paper size: list box provides a list of preset paper sizes. You can also select a Custom size from the list, and then specify the paper dimensions in the Width: and Height: text boxes. By default, the paper size is Letter (8½ × 11 in). By default, the paper size settings apply to the whole document. You can change this option with the Apply to: list. As you change the options, the Preview area shows a sample of the document. You close the dialog box without making changes.

Step 3	*Click*	Cancel

Printing is usually your final activity in document creation. You can print a document by clicking the Print button on the Print Preview toolbar or the Standard toolbar. However, when you click the Print

**chapter
seven**

button, you do not get an opportunity to change the print options in the Print dialog box.

The Print command on the File menu opens the Print dialog box that contains options and print settings you can modify before printing a document. To set the print options for the *Revised Analysis Report*:

Step 1	*Click*	File
Step 2	*Click*	Print

The Print dialog box on your screen should look similar to Figure 7-7.

FIGURE 7-7
Print Dialog Box

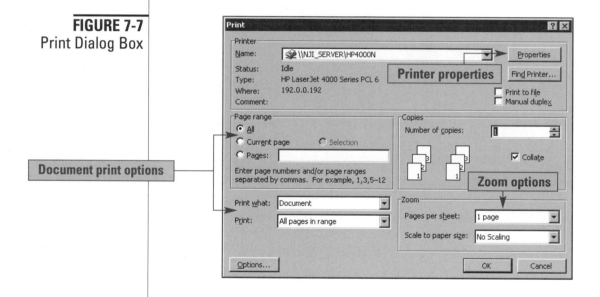

By default, Word prints one copy of your entire document. The Print what: list box provides a list of items you can print other than your document. For example, to print a list of AutoText entries stored in the Normal template, select AutoText entries from this list.

You can specify the number of copies to print in the Number of copies: text box. The Page range group contains options for printing All pages, the Current page that contains the insertion point, the Selection of highlighted text, or the Pages you specify by page number. The Print: list box allows you to print only odd or even pages in a selected page range. By default, Word **collates** or prints copies of a multiple-page document in binding order as it prints. You can turn off the collating option by removing the check mark from the Collate check box.

Printing your document to a file is helpful if you want to print on a higher-quality printer at a different location or on a computer that does not have the Word program. You can print your document to a file on a disk rather than send it to a printer by inserting a check mark in the Print to file check box.

Sometimes you need to print on both sides of a sheet of paper. You can use the Manual duple$\underline{x}$ option to do that. For more information about printing on both sides of a sheet of paper or on folded paper, see online Help.

Text can be scaled to fit multiple pages on one sheet of paper or scaled to fit to various paper sizes in the Zoom group. Use this feature to scale larger documents to fit smaller paper or print several miniature document pages on one sheet of paper.

Selecting a Printer

The active printer is identified in the <u>N</u>ame: list box. You can select from a list of available printers by clicking the list arrow and clicking the printer you want to use. You can view the properties such as default paper size, default page orientation, or graphics resolution for the selected printer with the <u>P</u>roperties button.

Step 1	*Click*	<u>P</u>roperties

The Properties dialog box opens. Except for the printer name, which may be different, your dialog box should look similar to Figure 7-8.

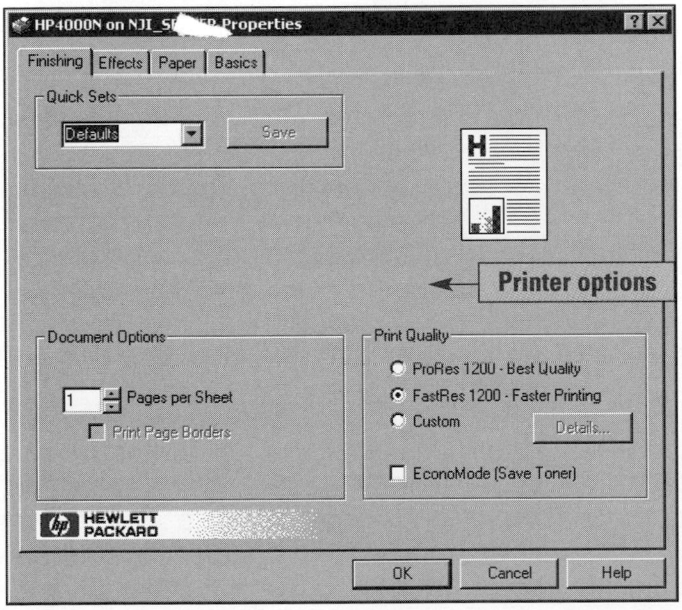

FIGURE 7-8
Printer Properties
Dialog Box

After reviewing the printer properties, you can cancel the Properties dialog box.

Step 2	*Click*	Cancel

chapter
seven

Kelly asks you to check the print options available for your printer.

Setting Print Options

You can specify a number of different print options by clicking the Options button in the Print dialog box or by clicking the Print tab in the Options dialog box. To review print options:

Step 1	*Click*	Options

The Print tab from the Options dialog box on your screen should look similar to Figure 7-9.

FIGURE 7-9
Print Tab from the Options
Dialog Box

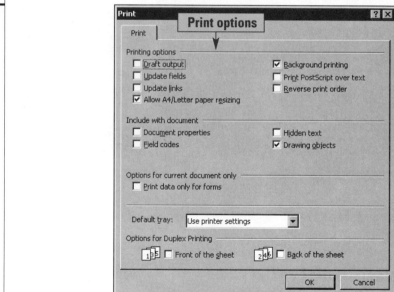

Step 2	*Review*	the options in the Print tab using the dialog box Help button
Step 3	*Close*	the Print (Options) and Print dialog boxes
Step 4	*Print*	the document
Step 5	*Save*	the document and close it

The printed *Revised Analysis Report* is ready to be duplicated and distributed to the Worldwide Exotic Foods branch managers.

Summary

▶ To save time and money, preview your document before printing to avoid printing a document that contains errors.

▶ You can view one page or multiple pages of your document in Print Preview.

▶ Print Preview displays headers, footers, margins, page numbers, text, and graphics.

▶ You can edit a document by keying text, applying formatting, setting tab stops, indenting paragraphs, and changing margins in Print Preview.

▶ You can turn off the Magnifier button in Print Preview and then key and edit text in the document.

▶ Documents can be zoomed in Print Preview by turning on the Magnifier button and clicking the document with the mouse pointer or by using the Zoom button on the Print Preview toolbar.

▶ You can set print and page setup options in the Print and Page Setup dialog boxes before you print your document.

▶ The Print button on the Print Preview or Standard toolbars prints the document without allowing you to review the settings in the Print dialog box. The Print command on the File menu opens the Print dialog box and allows you to confirm or change print options before printing a document.

Commands Review

Action	Menu Bar	Shortcut Menu	Toolbar	Task Pane	Keyboard
Preview a document	File, Print Preview		🔍		ALT + F, V CTRL + F2
View multiple pages in Print Preview			▦		
View one page in Print Preview			▤		
Magnify a document in Print Preview			🔍		
Print a document	File, Print		🖨		ALT + F, P CTRL + SHIFT + F12 CTRL + P

chapter seven

Concepts Review

Circle the correct answer.

1. **By default, Print Preview displays your document:**
   [a] in two pages.
   [b] in multiple pages.
   [c] exactly as it will print on paper.
   [d] in Landscape orientation.

2. **The Magnifier button:**
   [a] scrolls to a new page.
   [b] shows the horizontal and vertical rulers.
   [c] shows two pages side by side.
   [d] allows you to zoom your document with the mouse pointer.

3. **You set the default print orientation in the:**
   [a] printer Properties dialog box.
   [b] Page Setup dialog box.
   [c] Page Layout dialog box.
   [d] Options dialog box.

4. **The default paper size and orientation is:**
   [a] 11 × 18 inch, Portrait.
   [b] 8½ × 12 inch, Landscape.
   [c] 8½ × 11 inch, Portrait.
   [d] A4, Portrait.

5. **To key or format selected text in Print Preview, you must use the:**
   [a] zoom pointer.
   [b] horizontal ruler.
   [c] I-beam.
   [d] Magnifier button.

6. **When Word collates a printed document, it:**
   [a] saves the document to a file.
   [b] prints AutoText entries.
   [c] prints copies of multiple-page documents in binding order.
   [d] scales larger documents to fit on smaller paper.

7. **The actions of the Next and Previous buttons in Print Preview are controlled by the:**
   [a] vertical scroll bar.
   [b] Magnifier button.
   [c] Zoom button.
   [d] Select Browse Object button.

8. **To key text in your document from Print Preview, you first:**
   [a] minimize the window.
   [b] view multiple pages.
   [c] zoom the document.
   [d] turn off the Magnifier button.

9. **You can view and change print options by clicking the:**
   [a] Printer command on the File menu.
   [b] Options command on the Tools menu.
   [c] Print Options command on the Print Preview menu.
   [d] Set Print Options button in the Print dialog box.

10. **The Print dialog box contains all of the following options except:**
    [a] Print to file.
    [b] Collate copies.
    [c] Set the paper orientation.
    [d] Print selected text.

Circle **T** if the statement is true or **F** if the statement is false.

T   F   1. To print only the page that contains the insertion point, you should select the <u>A</u>ll option in the Print dialog box.

T   F   2. To print the entire document that you are currently editing, you should select the Curr<u>e</u>nt Page option in the Print dialog box.

T   F   3. If you type "1-4" in the Pages text box in the Print dialog box, Word prints only pages 1 and 4 of the document.

T   F   4. The Letter (8½ × 11 in) paper size is the default paper size.

T   F   5. It is not possible to print only odd or even pages.

T   F   6. You can change margins, tab stops, or paragraph indents in Print Preview.

T   F   7. The Print button on the Print Preview toolbar opens the Print dialog box.

T   F   8. By default, Word prints copies of a multiple-page document in binding order as it prints.

T   F   9. You can view additional toolbars in Print Preview.

T   F   10. It is possible to scale text to fit multiple pages on one sheet of paper or to fit various paper sizes.

Skills Review

Exercise 1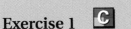

1. Open the *Vancouver Warehouse Report* document located on the Data Disk.

2. Print Preview the document.

3. Print only page 2 and close the document.

Exercise 2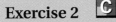

1. Open the *Analysis Report* document located on the Data Disk.

2. Print the entire document using the Print button on the Standard toolbar in Normal view and close the document.

Exercise 3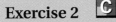

1. Open the *Interoffice Meeting Memo* document located on the Data Disk.

2. Print Preview the document.

3. Apply bold formatting to the meeting day and time in the first body paragraph in Print Preview.

4. Save the document as *Interoffice Meeting Memo Edited*.

5. Print the document from Print Preview and close the document.

chapter seven

Exercise 4

1. Open the *New Expense Guidelines* document located on the Data Disk.

2. Print Preview the document.

3. Format the title with the Arial, 16-point font in Print Preview and leave the insertion point in the title paragraph.

4. Save the document as *New Expense Guidelines Revised*.

5. Print only the current page from Print Preview and close the document.

Exercise 5

1. Open the *Research Results* document located on the Data Disk.

2. Print Preview the document.

3. Change the top margin to 2 inches and the left and right margins to 1 inch in Print Preview.

4. Create numbered paragraphs with the last two single spaced paragraphs in Print Preview using a shortcut menu and the Bullets and Numbering dialog box.

5. Horizontally justify all the paragraphs in the document using a shortcut menu and the Paragraph dialog box.

6. Save the document as *Research Results Revised*.

7. Print the document from Print Preview and close the document.

Exercise 6

1. Open the *Understanding The Internet* document located on the Data Disk.

2. Print pages 1 and 3 in Normal view and close the document.

Exercise 7

1. Open the *Understanding The Internet* document located on the Data Disk.

2. Print Preview the document.

3. View the document in multiple pages with 4 pages on 2 rows.

4. Remove the bold, italic formatting and apply bold, small caps effect to the side (paragraph) headings in Print Preview. (*Hint:* After selecting and formatting the first bold, italic paragraph heading, use the CTRL + Y shortcut keys to copy the formatting to the other bold, italic paragraph headings.)

5. Save the document as *The Internet And The Web*.

6. Switch to Normal view and print pages 2, 4, and 6.

7. Use the Zoom options in the Print dialog box to print the entire document with two pages per sheet of paper and close the document.

Exercise 8

1. Create the following document.

TO: Marketing Department

FROM: J.D. Collins

DATE: Current date

SUBJECT: Holiday Gift Baskets

There will a meeting on Tuesday, October 2 at 1:00 p.m. to discuss how to introduce our
line of holiday gift baskets. Please bring any ideals you have to the meeting.

ke

(handwritten annotations: "be", "Wednesday", "new", "ideas")

2. Use the default margins and set the appropriate tab stops for the memo headings.

3. Print Preview the document.

4. Change the margins to the appropriate margins for an interoffice memorandum in Print Preview.

5. Change the font for the entire document to Arial, 12 point in Print Preview.

6. Apply bold formatting to the memo heading text "TO," "FROM," "DATE," and "SUBJECT" (do not include the colons) in Print Preview.

7. Save the document as *Holiday Gift Baskets*.

8. Print the document from Print Preview and close the document.

Case Projects

Project 2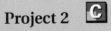

Kelly wants you to review setting different print options and then create a memo to all summer interns describing the print options and how to set them. Using the Ask A Question Box, review setting print options. Create a new interoffice memorandum to all summer interns containing at least three paragraphs that describes how to use at least three print options. Save, preview, and print the document.

Project 2

Dale Metcalf, a purchasing agent, asks you how to view and change the properties for his printer, which is the same model as your printer. Open the Print dialog box and review the Properties for your printer. Create an unbound report document containing at least four paragraphs that describes the properties set for your printer. Save, preview, and print the document. With your instructor's permission, use the unbound report document as a guide to demonstrate viewing and changing printer properties to one of your classmates.

chapter seven

Project 3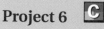

You recently read an article in the company newsletter that describes Internet newsgroups (online discussion groups) and would like to know more about how to participate in them. Connect to the Internet and search for Web pages that contain information on newsgroups. Save at least two Web pages as favorites or bookmarks. Print at least two Web pages. Create an unbound report containing at least five paragraphs that describes newsgroups and how to subscribe to them. Use vertical and horizontal alignment, line spacing, and indentation options to give the report a professional appearance. Save, preview, and print the report.

Project 4

B. D. Vickers needs to purchase several new laser printers for the Worldwide Exotic Foods and wants you to review the models that are currently available and make a recommendation. Connect to the Internet and search the Web for vendors who sell laser printers. Review information on two printers from at least three vendors. Create an interoffice memorandum to B. D. Vickers recommending one of the printers. Include each vendor's name and the printer price in the memo. Save, preview, and print the memo.

Project 5

You are having lunch with Bob Garcia, the new administrative assistant, and he describes several problems he has when printing documents. He frequently gets a blank page at the end of his documents, sometimes the text runs off the edge of the page, he gets a "too many fonts" error when he prints a document, and occasionally the printed text looks different from the text on his screen. You offer to look into the problems and get back to him. Using the Ask A Question Box, search for troubleshooting tips for printing documents and find suggested solutions to Bob's problems. Write Bob a memo that describes each problem and suggests a solution to that problem. Save, preview, and print the memo.

Project 6

Kelly wants a document she can use to train new employees how to set print options. She also wants to train the new employees to use the Zoom options in the Print dialog box. Open the Options dialog box and click the Print tab. Use the dialog box Help button to review each of the print options. Open the Print dialog box and review the Zoom options. Create an unbound report document titled "Print Options" and describe each of the options on the Print tab and the Print Zoom feature. Save, preview, and print the document. Attach a sample of a two-page document printed on one sheet of paper using the Zoom options.

Project 7

You just purchased a new printer, but do not know how to set up it and define it as your default printer. Using the Ask A Question Box, research how to set up a new printer and define it as the default printer. Write Kelly Armstead a memo that discusses the process. Save, preview, and print the memo.

Project 8

The Melbourne branch office manager is ill and B. D. Vickers wants to send flowers using a shop that accepts orders on the Web but isn't certain how to do this. Connect to the Internet, and search for Web pages with information about ordering and paying for flowers for international delivery to Melbourne, Australia. Print at least three Web pages. Create a memo to B. D. Vickers that describes how to order and pay for flowers on the Web. Save, preview, and print the memo. Attach the Web pages you printed to the memo.

Printing Envelopes and Labels

Chapter Overview

Every business depends on its correspondence. Letters and packages need to be sent daily. Each needs an envelope or mailing label before it can be mailed. In this chapter, you create, format, and print envelopes and labels.

LEARNING OBJECTIVES

▷ Print envelopes
▷ Print labels

Case profile

Kelly Armstead asks you to help print envelopes and labels for items that need to be mailed today. Worldwide Exotic Foods uses the U.S. Postal Service (USPS) guidelines for envelopes and mailing labels that do not have a corresponding letter. Otherwise, they follow the punctuation and case of the corresponding letter address. You create an envelope that does not have a corresponding letter, an envelope for an existing letter, an envelope and label from a list of addresses, and a sheet of return address labels for B. D. Vickers.

chapter eight

notes Because different printers have varying setup requirements for envelopes and labels, your instructor may provide additional printing instructions for the activities in this chapter.

C 8.a Printing Envelopes

Printing addresses on envelopes is a word processing task that almost everyone must perform at one time or another. Envelopes do not use the standard 8.5-inch × 11-inch paper on which you normally print letters and reports. A standard Size 10 business envelope is 4⅛ inches × 9½ inches, and a standard short Size 6¾ envelope is 3⅝ inches × 6½ inches. To create envelopes, you can open an existing letter and let Word identify the letter address as the envelope delivery address, or you can key the envelope delivery address in a blank document.

You can create an individual envelope by first creating a blank document. To create an envelope from a blank document:

QUICK TIP

Before you begin the activities in this chapter, you should review Appendix B, Formatting Tips for Business Documents, if you have not already done so.

Step 1	*Create*	a new, blank document, if necessary
Step 2	*Click*	Tools
Step 3	*Point to*	Letters and Mailings
Step 4	*Click*	Envelopes and Labels
Step 5	*Click*	the Envelopes tab, if necessary

The Envelopes and Labels dialog box on your screen should look similar to Figure 8-1.

FIGURE 8-1
Envelopes and Labels
Dialog Box

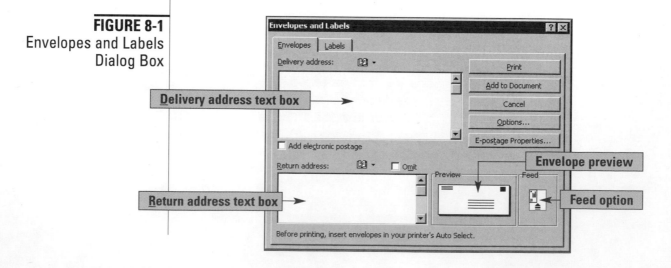

You key the delivery address in the Delivery address: text box. You can edit or key the return address in the Return address: text box, which contains information from the User Information tab in the Options dialog box. If you are using envelopes with a preprinted return address, you can omit printing the return address by inserting a check mark in the Omit check box. The Feed image illustrates how to insert envelopes in the current printer. You click the Options button to change envelope size, print the Delivery point barcode, add character formatting to the address text, select manual or tray feed for blank envelopes, or change the feed position. You send the envelope directly to the printer with the Print button. The Add to Document button attaches the envelope to the current document for saving and printing.

Word automatically formats the text you key in the Delivery address: text box with the Envelope Address style and the return address with the Envelope Return style. The Envelope Address style contains the sans serif Arial font with a 12-point font size. You key the delivery address using the USPS guidelines (see Appendix B). To key the envelope text:

Step 1	*Verify*	that the insertion point is in the Delivery address: text box
Step 2	*Key*	MS ELAINE CHANG 719 EAST 35TH STREET ST PAUL MN 55117-1179

Because Worldwide Exotic Foods uses preprinted envelopes for all correspondence, you omit the return address. Then you select the envelope size.

Step 3	*Click*	the Omit check box to insert a check mark, if necessary
Step 4	*Click*	Options
Step 5	*Click*	the Envelope Options tab, if necessary

The Envelope Options dialog box on your screen should look similar to Figure 8-2. You can select the envelope size in the Envelope size: list box. Options for using the Facing Identification Mark (FIM-A) and Delivery point barcode to speed mail delivery are in the If mailed in the USA group. For a more detailed explanation of these two codes, see online Help. You can also change the font and position of the envelope addresses. You change the envelope size.

> **QUICK TIP**
>
> You can change the font of the delivery or return address in the Envelopes and Labels dialog box by selecting the text and then opening the Font dialog box with a shortcut menu.

chapter eight

FIGURE 8-2
Envelope Options
Dialog Box

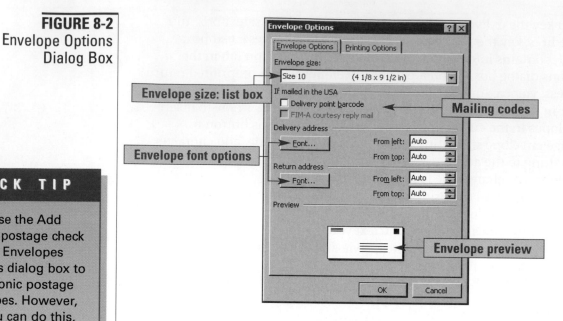

Step 6	*Click*	the Envelope size: list arrow
Step 7	*Click*	Size 6¾ (3⅝ × 6½ in), if necessary
Step 8	*Observe*	that the sample envelope now displays the 6¾ size

You also set printing options in this dialog box. The current options
are set for your printer. You can specify envelope rotation, face up or
down, and manual or tray feed on this tab. You accept the current
printing options and envelope size. To review print options:

Step 1	*Click*	the Printing Options tab
Step 2	*Observe*	the different Feed method options
Step 3	*Click*	OK

To print the envelope, you may have to manually feed a blank
envelope or blank sheet of paper in your printer. If your instructor
tells you to print the envelope, follow your printer's envelope setup
instructions and print the envelope by clicking the Print button in the
Envelopes and Labels dialog box. Otherwise you cancel the Chang
envelope by closing the Envelopes and Labels dialog box.

| Step 4 | *Click* | Close |

Another way to create an envelope is to open a document that
contains a list of frequently used delivery addresses, move the insertion

point to one of the addresses, and open the Envelopes and Labels dialog box. Word enters the delivery address for you. To open an address list document and create an envelope:

Step 1	*Open*	the *Envelope And Label List* document located on the Data Disk
Step 2	*Move*	the insertion point to the address for Elaine Fitzsimmons (scroll to view this address)
Step 3	*Click*	Tools
Step 4	*Point to*	Letters and Mailings
Step 5	*Click*	Envelopes and Labels

The Envelopes tab in the Envelopes and Labels dialog box opens with Elaine Fitzsimmons' address in the Delivery address: list box. Unless instructed to print the Fitzsimmons envelope by your instructor, you close the dialog box by canceling it.

| Step 6 | *Click* | Cancel |
| Step 7 | *Close* | the document without saving any changes |

When you open an existing letter and then open the Envelopes and Labels dialog box, Word selects the letter address exactly as it appears in the document and places it in the Delivery address: text box. B. D. Vickers' letter to Ms. Neva Johnson needs an envelope. To create and format an envelope for an existing letter:

Step 1	*Open*	the *Johnson Letter* document located on the Data Disk
Step 2	*Open*	the Envelopes tab in the Envelopes and Labels dialog box
Step 3	*Observe*	that the letter address is automatically placed in the Delivery address: text box
Step 4	*Click*	the Omit check box to remove the check mark, if necessary
Step 5	*Select*	all the text in the Return address: text box or move the insertion point to the text box if it is blank
Step 6	*Key*	B. D. Vickers Administrative Vice President Worldwide Exotic Foods, Inc. Gage Building, Suite 2100 Riverside Plaza Chicago, IL 60606-2000
Step 7	*Click*	Options and click the Envelope Options tab, if necessary

chapter eight

Step 8	*Click*	the Envelope <u>s</u>ize: list arrow
Step 9	*Click*	Size 6¾ (3⅝ × 6½ in), if necessary
Step 10	*Observe*	the envelope preview
Step 11	*Click*	OK

To add an envelope to the letter document so that you can edit or print both at the same time:

Step 1	*Click*	<u>A</u>dd to Document

A confirmation dialog box opens, asking whether you want to save the new return address as the default return address for all future envelopes. If you click the <u>Y</u>es button, Word adds the return address information to the User Information tab in the <u>T</u>ools, <u>O</u>ptions dialog box. You do *not* want to change the default return address.

Step 2	*Click*	<u>N</u>o

The envelope is added as Page 0 at the top of the document with a (Next Page) section break separating the envelope from the document. **Section breaks** divide your document into differently formatted parts. To view the envelope and letter in Print Layout view:

Step 1	*Verify*	that the insertion point is in the envelope text
Step 2	*Switch to*	Print Layout view

Your screen should look similar to Figure 8-3.

FIGURE 8-3
Envelope in Print
Layout View

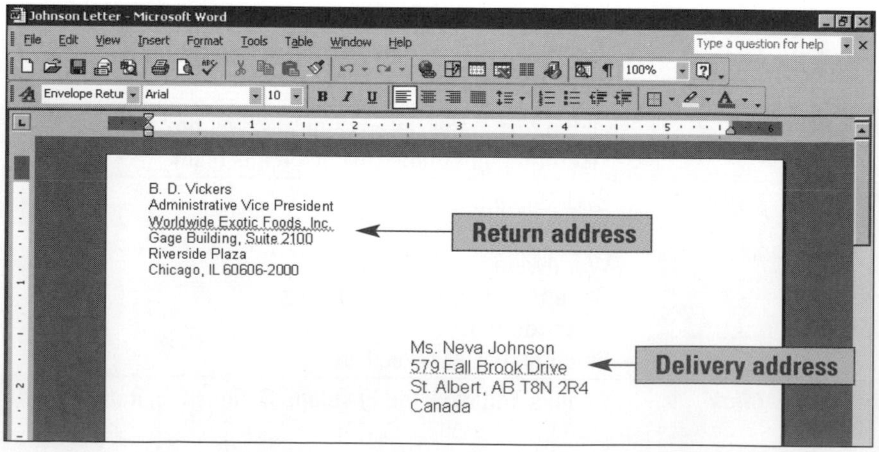

| Step 3 | *Scroll* | to view both the envelope and the letter, and then scroll to view just the envelope |

If necessary, you can reposition the delivery address in Print Layout view by moving the frame that Word inserts around the address. A **frame** is a box added to text, graphics, or charts that you drag to reposition these items on a page. To view the frame:

| Step 1 | *Move* | the insertion point before the "M" in "Ms." in the delivery address |

The frame around the delivery address appears. Your screen should look similar to Figure 8-4. You reposition the delivery address on the envelope by dragging and then deselecting the frame.

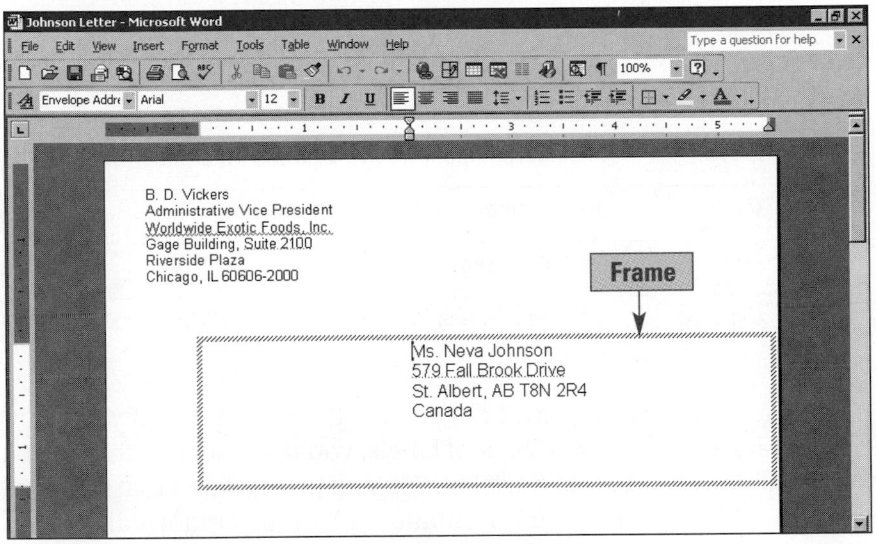

FIGURE 8-4
Frame Around the
Delivery Address

Step 2	*Position*	the mouse pointer on the frame border (the mouse pointer becomes a move pointer)
Step 3	*Drag*	the frame ½ inch to the right
Step 4	*Click*	outside the frame
Step 5	*Observe*	the new position of the delivery address
Step 6	*Switch to*	Normal view
Step 7	*Save*	the document as *Johnson Letter With Envelope* and close it

Kelly also wants you to create a mailing label for an oversized envelope and to create a sheet of return address labels for B. D. Vickers.

chapter
eight

C   **8.b** Printing Labels

You can create many different types of labels in many different sizes, such as mailing labels, name tags, file folder labels, and computer diskette labels, with the Envelopes and Labels command on the Tools menu. Word has built-in label formats for most types of labels. If you are not using a standard label, you can specify a similar label format, or you can create a custom label format.

Printing Individual Labels

When you need just one label, you create it and then specify which label on a sheet of labels to use on the Labels tab in the Envelopes and Labels dialog box. Kelly asks you to create an individual label in the first row and first column on a sheet of Avery 5160 - Address labels. To create an individual label:

Step 1	*Open*	the *Envelope And Label List* document located on the Data Disk
Step 2	*Move*	the insertion point to the address for Debbie Gonzales
Step 3	*Open*	the Envelopes and Labels dialog box
Step 4	*Click*	the Labels tab
Step 5	*Observe*	that the address is inserted in the Address: text box

The default option is to print a full page of the same label. If you want to print a single label from a sheet of labels, you must specify the exact row and column position of the label. You can print a label that includes the return address in the User Information tab of the Options dialog box by inserting a check mark in the Use return address check box. As with envelopes, clicking the Options button enables you to select a label format or printer. Now you specify the label size and position.

Step 6	*Click*	the Single label option button
Step 7	*Verify*	that both the Row: and Column: text boxes contain 1, to print the label in the first row and first column of the sheet
Step 8	*Click*	Options

The Label Options dialog box on your screen should look similar to Figure 8-5. The Printer information group contains options for selecting a Dot <u>m</u>atrix or <u>L</u>aser and ink jet printer, as well as <u>T</u>ray options. You use the Label <u>p</u>roducts: list box to select an Avery or other label product list. The Product n<u>u</u>mber: list box contains the list of label products by product number. The Label information group contains a description of the format for the label selected in the Product n<u>u</u>mber: list box. Use the <u>D</u>etails button to display margins, height, and width for the selected label. You also can change the pitch (the space between the labels) and the number of labels in each row or column with the <u>D</u>etails button. Custom labels can be created and saved with the <u>N</u>ew Label button. When you create and save a custom label, it is added to the Product n<u>u</u>mber: list.

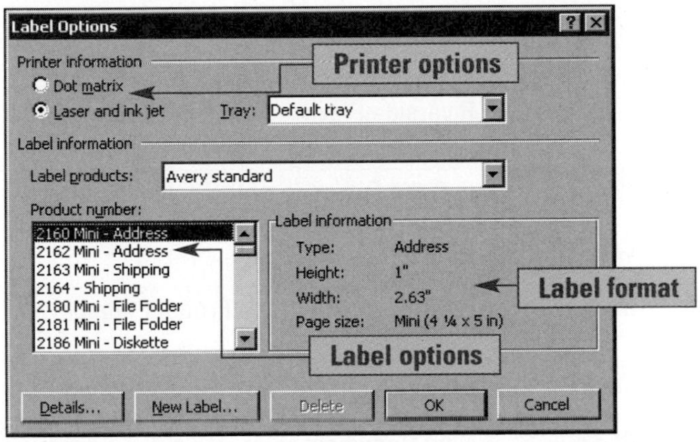

FIGURE 8-5
Label Options Dialog Box

Step 9	*Verify*	that Avery standard is in the Label <u>p</u>roducts: list box
Step 10	*Click*	5160 - Address in the Product n<u>u</u>mber: list box (scroll to view this option)
Step 11	*Observe*	that the label type, height, and width appear in the Label information group
Step 12	*Click*	OK

You are ready to print the label, if instructed to do so. Otherwise, cancel the Gonzales label by canceling the dialog box.

| Step 13 | *Click* | Cancel |
| Step 14 | *Close* | the document without saving any changes |

Next you create a sheet of return address labels for B. D. Vickers.

QUICK TIP

To quickly locate all the Avery standard labels in each numerical series, simply key the first number of the series. For example, to find the 5160 - Address label, key "5" when viewing the Product n<u>u</u>mber: list in the Label options dialog box. Word scrolls the list to the series of labels that begins "5". You then can manually scroll all the labels in the 5XXX series to find the 5160 - Address label.

chapter eight

CAUTION TIP

The Word spelling checker does not work in the Envelopes and Labels dialog box so you should proof the address information you key very carefully.

QUICK TIP

You can use the AutoText feature to quickly insert an address in the Envelopes and Labels dialog box. Simply create the address and store it as AutoText. Then, open the Envelopes and Labels dialog box, key the AutoText name, and press the F3 key.

Printing a Sheet of Return Address Labels

The label product you use for B. D. Vickers' return address labels is the Avery 5260 - Address label. To create the labels you create a new, blank document, open the Labels tab in the Envelopes and Labels dialog box and key the address, select label options, and add the labels to the document. To create a sheet of address labels:

Step 1	*Create*	a new, blank document, if necessary
Step 2	*Open*	the Labels tab in the Envelopes and Labels dialog box
Step 3	*Verify*	that the insertion point is in the Address: text box
Step 4	*Key*	B. D. Vickers Administrative Vice President Worldwide Exotic Foods, Inc. Gage Building, Suite 2100 Riverside Plaza Chicago, IL 60606-2000
Step 5	*Verify*	that the Full page of the same label option is selected
Step 6	*Click*	Options
Step 7	*Click*	5262 - Address in the Product number: list box (scroll to view this option)
Step 8	*Click*	OK
Step 9	*Click*	New Document to create a document with labels

The new document containing a sheet of return address labels appears. Your screen should look similar to Figure 8-6.

FIGURE 8-6
Sheet of Labels for B. D. Vickers

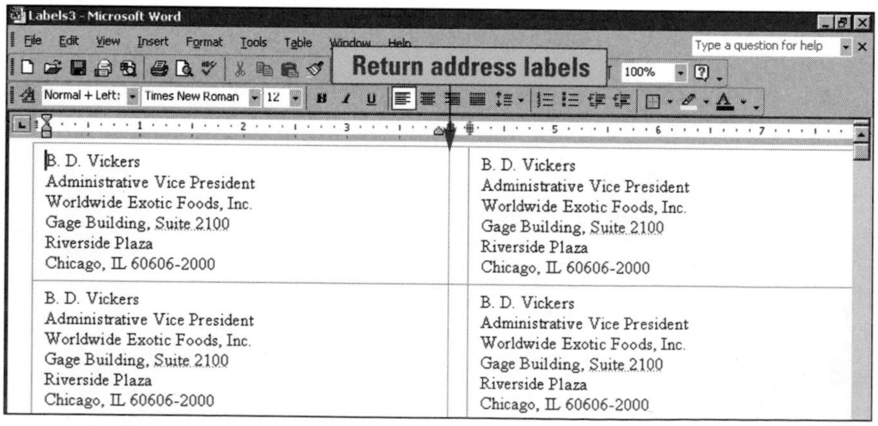

Word organizes label text in a series of columns and rows called a **table**. Each intersection of a column and row is called a **cell**. Each cell of the table represents a label that contains B. D. Vickers' return address. If you save the new label document, you can use it later to create more labels.

| Step 10 | *Save* | the document as *Return Address Labels* and close it |

Because you saved the new label document, you can use it later to create more labels whenever B. D. Vickers runs out.

**chapter
eight**

Summary

▶ You can send an envelope or a sheet of labels directly to a printer or you can add them to the current document. An individual label must be sent directly to the printer.

▶ You can create an envelope or label by keying the delivery address in the Envelopes or Labels dialog box or by selecting the delivery address in a document.

▶ When you create an individual envelope for a letter that is open, Word creates the delivery address from the letter address.

▶ Word inserts a frame or box around the delivery address on an envelope document that enables you to reposition the delivery address.

▶ Word adds the default return address from data found in the User Information tab of the Options dialog box, which you can change or omit.

▶ You can create a full sheet of the same label, or create individual labels at a specific position on the label sheet.

▶ You can select from a list of commonly used Avery labels, or you can create your own custom labels.

Commands Review

Action	Menu Bar	Shortcut Menu	Toolbar	Task Pane	Keyboard
Create an individual envelope, label, or sheet of the same label	Tools, Letters and Mailings, Envelopes and Labels				ALT +T, E, E

Concepts Review

Circle the correct answer.

1. To print a single label you must:
[a] open a document that contains the label address.
[b] specify the column and row on the label sheet.
[c] change the return address in the User Information dialog box.
[d] use a name tag label format.

2. A Size 10 business envelope is:
[a] 3⅝ × 6½ inches.
[b] 4⅛ × 9½ inches.
[c] 3⅝ × 9½ inches.
[d] 4⅛ × 6½ inches.

3. Labels are created and displayed in:
[a] table format.
[b] column format.
[c] Landscape orientation.
[d] only Print Preview.

4. You can modify the font, style, and size of addresses in the Envelopes and Labels dialog box with the:
[a] Font command on the menu bar.
[b] CTRL + Z keys.
[c] Font command on the shortcut menu.
[d] Change Formatting button in the Envelopes and Labels dialog box.

5. To reposition the delivery address for an envelope:
[a] view the envelope in Print Preview.
[b] drag the default frame to a new location.
[c] delete the return address.
[d] change the return address on the User Information tab in the Options dialog box.

6. The default formatting style that Word uses when you key the envelope delivery address is:
[a] Normal.
[b] Envelope Address.
[c] Heading 1.
[d] Envelope Return.

7. When you create a custom label, it is added to the:
[a] Label products list.
[b] Product number list.
[c] Label options list.
[d] Tray list.

Circle **T** if the statement is true or **F** if the statement is false.

T   F   1. You can create file labels in the Envelopes and Labels dialog box.

T   F   2. The return address can be omitted when creating envelopes.

T   F   3. You can send an envelope directly to a printer or save it with the letter for printing later.

T   F   4. If you save an envelope with the letter, Word places the envelope at the bottom of the letter.

T   F   5. The USPS approved envelope format is mixed case with punctuation.

T   F   6. You cannot create custom labels.

T   F   7. Envelopes and labels must be printed on a laser printer.

T   F   8. The Details button in the Labels tab allows you to change the margins, pitch, and number of labels on a sheet.

chapter eight

T   F   9. The default envelope font is Times New Roman, 10 point.

T   F   10. You can specify envelope rotation, face up or face down, and manual or tray feed in the Labels Options dialog box.

Skills Review

Exercise 1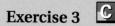

1. Create envelopes for each of the addresses below. Use the Times New Roman, 12-point font and the open punctuation, uppercase delivery address format. Create each envelope as a separate document.

Mr. Thomas Williams   *Ms. Barbara Robins*
Williams Products Company   *Sunrise Orange Growers*
293 East Road   *698 Orange Grove Drive*
Houston, TX 77024-2087   *Miami, FL 33153-7634*

2. Use the Size 10 (4⅛ × 9½ in) envelope size.

3. Omit the return address.

4. Save the Williams envelope as *Williams Envelope*. Save the Robins envelope as *Robins Envelope*.

5. Preview and print the envelopes and close the documents.

Exercise 2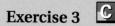

1. Create envelopes for each of the addresses below. Use the Arial 12-point font and open punctuation, uppercase delivery address format. Create each envelope as a separate document.

Mr. Alex Pyle   *Ms. Alice Yee*
Office Supplies, Inc.   *Raceway Park*
20343 Blue Sage Drive *632 Raceway Drive*
Shreveport, LA 71119-3412   *Sebring, FL 33870-2156*

2. Use the Size 6¾ (3⅝ × 6½ in) envelope size.

3. Omit the return address.

4. Save the Pyle envelope as *Pyle Envelope*. Save the Yee envelope as *Yee Envelope*.

5. Preview and print the envelopes and close the documents.

Exercise 3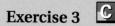

1. Create a sheet of labels for the following address. Use the Avery 5160 label product for laser printers.

Ms. Ramona Mendez
Southwest Services, Inc.
3426 Main Street
Dallas, TX 72345-1235

2. Format the address in the USPS style.

3. Add the labels to a new document.

4. Save the document as *Mendez Labels*, and then preview, print and close it.

Exercise 4 C

1. Open the *Envelope And Label List* document located on the Data Disk.

2. Create a sheet of Avery 5260 product laser labels for John Delany as a new document.

3. Save the document as *Delany Labels*, and then preview, print, and close it.

Exercise 5 C

1. Open the *Wilson Advertising Letter* document located on the Data Disk.

2. Create a Size 10 envelope.

3. Key your name and address as the return address.

4. Add the envelope to the document.

5. Do not save the new return address as the default return address.

6. Reposition the delivery address ½ inch to the right.

7. Save the document as *Wilson Advertising Letter With Envelope*, and then preview, print, and close it.

Exercise 6 C

1. Open the *Wilson Advertising Letter* document located on the Data Disk.

2. Create a sheet of return labels using the Avery 5160 product for laser printers.

3. Format the labels with Times New Roman 10-point font and the uppercase and open punctuation style. (*Hint:* Remove the punctuation, select the address, right-click the address, and click <u>F</u>ont.)

4. Add the labels to a new document.

5. Save the label document as *Wilson Labels*, preview and print the label document, and close both documents.

Exercise 7 C

1. Create a sheet of nametag labels using the Avery 5362 product for laser printers. Add the labels to a new document.

2. Key the following names into the labels (*Hint:* Press the TAB key to move to the next label):
   Janice Greene
   Frances Carmichael
   Carlos Armondo
   Sarah Winters
   Felix Martinez

3. Select the entire document and change the font to Arial 20 point.

4. Apply the bold and center align formats.

5. Save the document as *Name Tags*, and then preview, print, and close it.

chapter eight

Exercise 8 C

1. Create the following letter. Set the appropriate margins for a block-style letter.

Current date

Mr. Raul Rodriguez
Rodriguez Food Suppliers
355 Allen Drive
Houston, TX 77042-3354

Dear Mr. Rodriguez:

Congratulations on starting your own business. Given the growth of the specialty food industry, I
know you will be successful.

Please send me a catalog explaining and illustrating your product lines. I hope we can do
business together.

Yours truly,

Davita Washington
Purchasing Agent

ka

---

2. Create a Size 6¾ (3⅝ × 6½ in) envelope and format the delivery address in the approved USPS format.

3. Omit the return address.

4. Add the envelope to the document.

5. Save the document as *Solicitation Letter With Envelope.*

6. Create a sheet of return address labels using the Avery 2160 product for laser printers.

7. Add the labels to a new document.

8. Save the document as *Rodriguez Labels,* preview and print the sheet of labels, and close the documents.

Case Projects

Project 1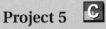

One of the Purchasing Department employees frequently creates return address labels and wants to be able to do this more quickly. You suggest using the AutoText feature. Create an AutoText entry for B. D. Vickers' return address. Using this AutoText entry, create a sheet of return address labels. Save, preview, and print the labels.

Project 2

You have been asked to add the POSTNET code and FIM-A code to an envelope. Using the Ask A Question Box, search online Help for information about these two codes. Create an unbound report document that describes these two codes and explains how to insert them on an envelope. Save, preview, and print the document. Attach a sample envelope with the codes inserted.

Project 3

Kelly Armstead wants to know how to print just the envelope attached to a document. Using the Ask A Question Box, research how to print only the envelope when it is attached to a document. Create an interoffice memorandum to Kelly explaining how to do this. Save, preview, and print the memorandum. Then, open an existing document with an attached envelope and print only the envelope, following the instructions in your memo to Kelly.

Project 4

At next week's "brown bag" lunch and training session for the Purchasing Department clerical staff, the discussion topic is "Printing Envelopes and Labels." You are presenting information on inserting an address from an electronic address book. Use the Ask A Question Box to locate information on your topic. Create an unbound report document that describes techniques for doing this. With your instructor's permission, explain the process to a group of classmates.

Project 5

The Purchasing Department is having an "open house" holiday celebration and B. D. Vickers asks you to create a letter inviting three top Chicago-area distributors. Using fictitious data, create three letters in the block format with appropriate margins inviting each distributor. Attach an envelope in the approved USPS format to each letter. Save, preview, and print each document.

Project 6

Several important clients and their families are visiting the Chicago office next week and you have been asked to prepare a list of Chicago-area sites and facilities the families can enjoy during their visit. Connect to the Internet, and search for Chicago-area sites of interest to visitors. Print at least five Web pages. Create an interoffice memorandum to B. D. Vickers that describes the sites of interest. Save, preview, and print the memorandum.

Project 7

You have been asked to find out how to automatically add the company graphic logo to the return address each time you create an envelope. Use the Ask A Question Box to research how to do this. Create an interoffice memorandum to Kelly Armstead that describes how to add a graphic logo to the return address automatically. Save, preview, and print the memorandum.

Project 8

Worldwide Exotic Foods is going to sponsor an evening at a sports event for Chicago-area youth groups and you need to prepare a list of possible events. Connect to the Internet, and search for sports events in the Chicago area. Print at least three Web pages. Create an interoffice memorandum to Kelly Armstead that lists the sports events and Web site URLs. Save, preview, and print the memorandum.

chapter eight

Working with Columns, Pictures, Diagrams, and Charts

LEARNING OBJECTIVES

▶ **Create and use newspaper columns**
▶ **Insert pictures**
▶ **Create diagrams**
▶ **Create and modify a data chart**

Chapter Overview

Columns are used in many documents—from annual reports to brochures to newsletters. Often pictures, diagrams, and charts are added to documents to help explain a topic and to create an interesting and attractive format. In this chapter, you learn how to format text into columns, insert a picture, draw a diagram, and create a chart.

Case profile

Jody Haversham, in the Human Resources Department, asks you to help out for a few days. The Human Resources Department distributes the company newsletter each month. Jody assigns you the task of formatting the company newsletter for September. Jody wants the newsletter to be one page of text that includes a title and newspaper-style body text. Jody also asks you to insert appropriate pictures, a diagram, and a chart to add interest and draw attention to some aspects of the newsletter.

chapter
nine

9.a Creating and Using Newspaper Columns

So far, you've worked with documents that are a single column, which extends from the left to the right margin. You can also create multicolumn documents, such as advertising brochures or newsletters, using **newspaper-style columns**, which divide a document into two or more vertical columns placed side-by-side on a page. When you format a document with columns, text fills the length of the first column before flowing into the next column. You can create two, three, four, or more newspaper-style columns of equal or unequal width for an entire document or for selected text in a document.

The Columns button on the Standard toolbar displays a grid from which you specify the number of equally spaced columns you want. By default, the Columns button applies column formatting to the whole document. To apply column formatting to a portion of the document, first select the text to be formatted and then select the number of columns from the Columns button grid. Word automatically inserts a continuous section break before and, if necessary, after the selected text in columns.

You begin by opening the newsletter draft document Jody prepared earlier and then you format the document text in columns. To format the text in columns, you first select the text. To open the September newsletter and format the text in columns:

Step 1	*Open*	the *September Newsletter* document located on the Data Disk
Step 2	*Select*	the text beginning "Happy Birthday!" to the end of the document
Step 3	*Click*	the Columns button 📑 on the Standard toolbar
Step 4	*Move*	the mouse pointer to the second column indicator on the grid
Step 5	*Observe*	the text "2 Columns" at the bottom of the grid
Step 6	*Click*	the second column indicator on the grid

Word creates the newspaper-style columns and automatically switches to Print Layout view, if necessary. You can view multiple columns in Print Layout view or Print Preview but not in Normal view. When the text in the first column reaches the bottom of the page, the remaining text shifts automatically to the next column. This can create uneven columns lengths. For example, the second column in the *September Newsletter* document is not as long as the first column.

chapter nine

To view the columns:

Step 1	*Deselect*	the text
Step 2	*Zoom*	the document to Whole Page to view the two newspaper-style columns

Your screen should look similar to Figure 9-1.

FIGURE 9-1
Text in Columns

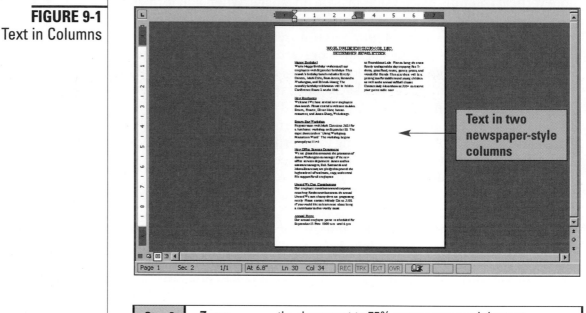

Step 3	*Zoom*	the document to 75% so you can read the text

Although the two-column format looks great, you decide to see how the document looks with other column formats.

Revising the Column Layout

The Columns dialog box provides a variety of formatting options that save you time creating newspaper-style columns. The five preset newspaper-style column formats are: One column, Two columns, Three columns, Left column, and Right column. The One, Two, and Three column formats create even column widths. The Left and Right column formats create uneven column widths. You can also add a horizontal line as a divider between the columns. To revise the column structure:

Step 1	*Move*	the insertion point into the two-column text, if necessary
Step 2	*Click*	Format
Step 3	*Click*	Columns

The Columns dialog box on your screen should look similar to Figure 9-2.

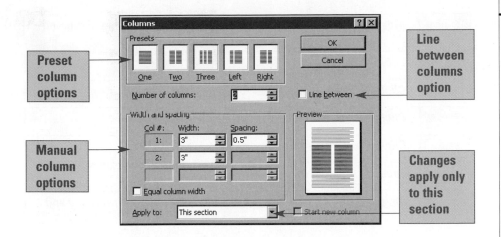

FIGURE 9-2
Columns Dialog Box

MOUSE TIP

You can change column widths by dragging the column indicator on the horizontal ruler with the mouse.

You try two newspaper-style columns with uneven widths.

Step 4	*Click*	Left in the Presets group
Step 5	*Click*	OK
Step 6	*Zoom*	the document to Whole Page and review the columns

The text is in a narrow left and a wide right column. You prefer two evenly spaced columns but want to add a vertical line between them. To change the column structure and add the line:

Step 1	*Open*	the Columns dialog box
Step 2	*Click*	Two in the Presets group
Step 3	*Click*	the Line between check box to insert a check mark
Step 4	*Click*	OK

To make the newsletter more attractive, you can balance the column length.

Modifying Column Text Alignment

You can modify the text alignment within the columns by balancing the column length. To balance column length, you can insert manual column breaks that force text into the next column. Manual column breaks are inserted with an option in the Break dialog box. Manual column breaks can be deleted and reinserted, if necessary, as you

QUICK TIP

Move the insertion point to the desired position and press the CTRL + SHIFT + ENTER keys to insert a column break.
 Word cannot remove a manual column break when it applies a different column format to text. To reformat columns, you should remove any manual column breaks by moving the insertion point to the right of the column break and pressing the BACKSPACE key.

chapter
nine

MENU TIP

You can also balance column length by inserting a continuous section break at the end of each column. To insert a continuous section break, click the Break command on the Insert menu.

continue to edit the document. To insert a manual column break in the *September Newsletter* document:

Step 1	*Move*	the insertion point to the left margin of the paragraph "United We Care Contributions"
Step 2	*Click*	Insert
Step 3	*Click*	Break
Step 4	*Click*	the Column break option button
Step 5	*Click*	OK
Step 6	*Zoom*	the document to 100%
Step 7	*Save*	the document as *September Newsletter Revised* and leave it open

To make the *September Newsletter Revised* document more interesting to readers, Jody asks you to add an appropriate picture to the Happy Birthday! and Annual Picnic paragraphs.

C 9.b Inserting Pictures

Word comes with a set of pictures you can access from the Clip Organizer. You can import pictures into the Clip Organizer from other sources, or you can insert pictures in your document from disk files without first importing them into the Clip Organizer.

notes Your Clip Organizer might contain different pictures than the ones used in this chapter. If necessary, you can substitute pictures from those available in your Clip Organizer in the activities in this chapter.

Jody tells you that there are some great pictures in the Clip Organizer. You begin by opening the Clip Organizer using a button on the Drawing toolbar and then searching for the appropriate images. To display the Drawing toolbar and open the Clip Organizer:

MOUSE TIP

You can insert pictures from the Clip Organizer by clicking the Insert Clip Art button on the Drawing toolbar. You can insert pictures from your hard drive, network drive, or a diskette by clicking the Insert Picture button on the Drawing toolbar.

Step 1	*Click*	the Drawing button [icon] on the Standard toolbar to view the Drawing toolbar
Step 2	*Observe*	the Drawing toolbar, which, by default, is docked at the bottom of the window above the status bar
Step 3	*Click*	the Insert Clip Art button [icon] on the Drawing toolbar

The Add Clips to Organizer dialog box may open. If you have additional picture, motion, or sound files located on your hard drive, you can catalog those files into the folders you specify and have the files appear in the Clip Organizer.

Step 4	*Click*	Later to close the Add Clips to Organizer dialog box, if necessary
Step 5	*Observe*	the Insert Clip Art task pane

Your screen should look similar to Figure 9-3.

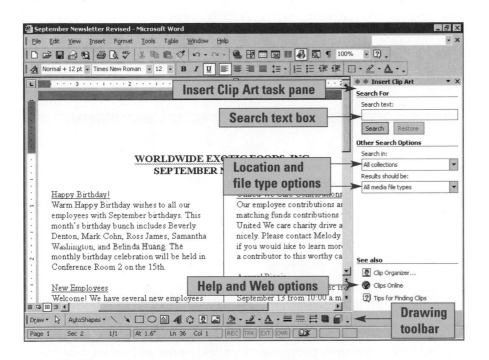

MENU TIP

You can insert pictures located on your hard drive, network drive, or a diskette by clicking Insert, pointing to Picture, and clicking From File.

FIGURE 9-3
Drawing Toolbar and Insert Clip Art Task Pane

QUICK TIP

The Drawing toolbar also contains buttons you can use to draw lines and arrows, rectangles and squares, ovals and circles, and other shapes such as WordArt text, special charts, and AutoShapes.

Clip Organizer picture, sound, and motion clips are stored in different folders, called catalogs or collections. Each picture, sound, or motion clip is associated with a series of keywords that help identify the clip. One way to locate suitable pictures in the Clip Organizer is to search for them by keyword. You can enter a keyword in the Search text: text box, select the collection in which to search from the Search in: list, and then select the type of file for which to search in the Results should be: list. To search for an appropriate birthday picture using the keyword "birthday":

Step 1	*Key*	birthday in the Search text: text box in the Insert Clip Art task pane
Step 2	*Verify*	that All collections appears in the Search in: list box in the Insert Clip Art task pane

TASK PANE TIP

You can insert pictures from the Clip Organizer using the Insert Clip Art task pane by clicking Insert, pointing to Picture, and then clicking Clip Art.

Step 3	*Verify*	that All media file types appears in the Results should be: list box in the Insert Clip Art task pane
Step 4	*Click*	the Search button in the Insert Clip Art task pane
Step 5	*Observe*	that the Results: grid containing clips appears in the Insert Clip Art task pane (it may take a few seconds for the clips to appear)
Step 6	*Scroll*	the Results: grid in the Insert Clip Art task pane to see the available clips
Step 7	*Point to*	the first picture in the Results: grid in the Insert Clip Art task pane

When you move the mouse pointer to a picture, sound, or motion clip icon in the Results: grid, a list arrow and a ScreenTip containing the associated keywords, file type, and file size appear. Your screen should look similar to Figure 9-4.

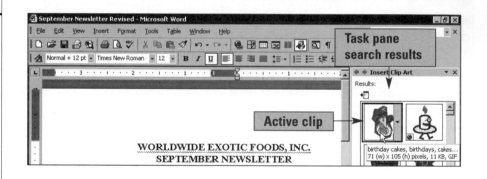

FIGURE 9-4
Search Results in Clip Art
Task Pane

You can insert a selected picture or other clip in your document, copy it to the Office Clipboard, delete it from the Clip Organizer, move it to another collection, add or edit the keywords associated with the file, and view a picture's properties by clicking the list arrow.

A quick way to insert a picture is to drag it from the Insert Clip Art task pane into your document. To drag the birthday picture of your choice into the *September Newsletter* document:

Step 1	*Drag*	the birthday picture of your choice from the Insert Clip Art task pane to the left margin of the "Warm Happy..." paragraph in the first column
Step 2	*Close*	the Insert Clip Art task pane
Step 3	*Observe*	that the picture is inserted into the document as a selected object and that the Picture toolbar may appear

TASK PANE TIP

In addition to importing pictures from other sources, you can go directly to a special Web page containing additional pictures and import them directly into the Clip Organizer with the Clips Online link in the Insert Clip Art task pane. You can get online Help for the Clip Organizer by clicking the Tips for Finding Clips

MOUSE TIP

When a picture object is selected, the Picture toolbar may appear automatically. If it does not appear, you can display it with a command on the toolbar shortcut menu. The Picture toolbar has buttons you use to edit the picture.

Your screen should look similar to Figure 9-5.

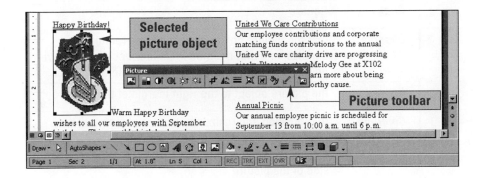

FIGURE 9-5
Selected Picture Object
and Picture Toolbar

A Word document has a text "layer" in which the text and pictures appear and additional "layers" that allow you to position pictures and other objects in front of or behind the text. The default is for pictures to be inserted in the same "layer" as the text, or **in line** with the text, which means that the picture is on the same line as text that appears before or after it. When a picture is in line with text, you can position it with the alignment buttons on the Formatting toolbar, just as you would text. You can size a picture object proportionally by dragging a corner sizing handle. If you want to size a picture object proportionally while maintaining its center position, press and hold the CTRL key as you drag a corner sizing handle.

Now that the birthday picture is inserted in the text, you need to reposition and resize it. A picture object is automatically selected when it is inserted. You deselect a picture object by clicking in the document outside the picture object; you select a picture for editing, sizing, or repositioning by clicking the picture object. A selected picture object that is in line with the text has a border and eight sizing handles around the border. You can size a picture object with the mouse by dragging a sizing handle. To deselect and then select and size the birthday picture object:

Step 1	*Click*	in the document outside the picture object to deselect it
Step 2	*Click*	the picture object to select it
Step 3	*Drag*	the picture object's lower-right corner sizing handle diagonally up approximately ½ inch

You want to position the picture at the right margin of the paragraph and then let the text wrap down the left side of the picture. To edit the text wrapping and reposition the picture object:

| Step 1 | *Verify* | that the picture object is still selected |

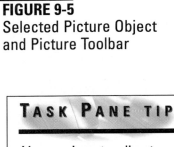

TASK PANE TIP

You can insert a clip at the insertion point by clicking the clip in the Insert Clip Art task pane.

MENU TIP

You can format a selected picture (including the text wrapping) with the Picture command on the Format menu or the Format Picture command

QUICK TIP

You can delete a picture, by selecting the picture and pressing the DELETE key.

Step 2	*Click*	the Text Wrapping button 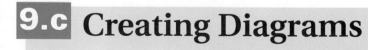 on the Picture toolbar
Step 3	*Click*	<u>S</u>quare
Step 4	*Observe*	that the picture object now has clear round sizing handles, and that the mouse pointer becomes a move pointer when placed on the selected picture object
Step 5	*Drag*	the picture object to the right margin of the paragraph
Step 6	*Continue*	to reposition and resize the picture object until the picture object is attractively positioned at the right margin and the text wraps attractively down the left side of the picture
Step 7	*Deselect*	the picture object

Your screen should look similar to Figure 9-6.

FIGURE 9-6
Resized and Repositioned
Picture

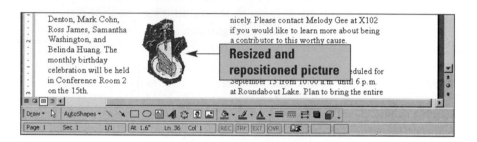

Step 8	*Display*	the Insert Clip Art task pane and search for an appropriate picture for a "picnic"
Step 9	*Drag*	the picture to the "Our annual employee picnic…" paragraph
Step 10	*Wrap*	the text around the picture using the <u>S</u>quare option
Step 11	*Resize*	and reposition the picture attractively in the paragraph
Step 12	*Save*	the document and leave it open
Step 13	*Close*	the Insert Clip Art task pane

Jody wants you to add a diagram to a paragraph.

C 9.c **Creating Diagrams**

Diagrams and organization charts are often used instead of, or in addition to, text to explain complex relationships and ideas. For example, cycle diagrams show a process with a continuous cycle, radial diagrams illustrate relationships to and from a central core

MOUSE TIP

When you want text to wrap around or through a picture, you use the Text Wrapping button on the Picture toolbar to select the <u>S</u>quare, <u>T</u>ight, Behind Text, or In Front of Wrapping style. When you select one of these options, you can reposition the picture by dragging it to a new location with the mouse pointer.

element, pyramid diagrams show foundation-based relationships, Venn diagrams illustrate areas that overlap between elements, and a target diagram shows steps toward a goal. An organization chart illustrates hierarchical relationships between people in an organization. You use the Insert Diagram or Organization Chart button on the Drawing toolbar to turn on the drawing canvas and insert special diagrams. To insert a Venn diagram:

| Step 1 | *Move* | the insertion point to the end of the Brown Bag Workshop paragraph |

| Step 2 | *Click* | the Insert Diagram or Organization Chart button  on the Drawing toolbar |

Your Diagram Gallery dialog box should look similar to Figure 9-7.

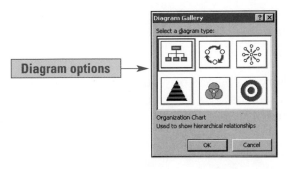

FIGURE 9-7
Diagram Gallery Dialog Box

| Step 3 | *Double-click* | the Venn Diagram icon (the second icon in the second row) |

The Diagram toolbar appears and the drawing canvas contains the components of a Venn diagram. Your screen should look similar to Figure 9-8.

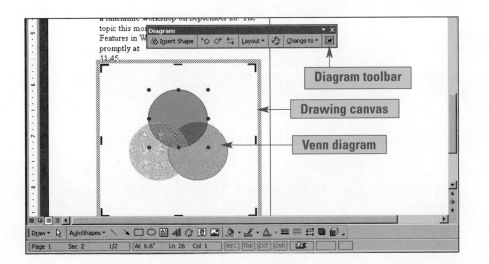

FIGURE 9-8
Drawing Canvas and Venn Diagram

chapter
nine

You resize the diagram so you can better position it. To size the diagram from its center to approximately ⅙ its original size:

Step 1	*Click*	the Layout button 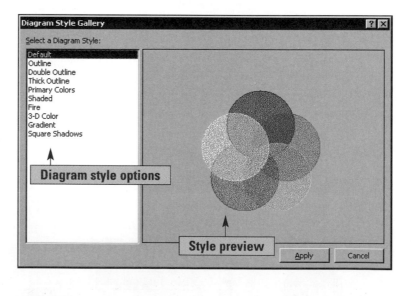 on the Diagram toolbar
Step 2	*Click*	Scale Diagram
Step 3	*Observe*	the drawing canvas round sizing handles
Step 4	*Press & hold*	the CTRL key
Step 5	*Drag*	the lower-right sizing handle diagonally up and to the left to size the diagram to approximately ⅙ its original size

You can choose from a variety of diagram styles. To change the diagram format to remove the fill color and modify the line color:

| Step 1 | *Click* | the AutoFormat button  on the Diagram toolbar |

The Diagram Style Gallery dialog box on your screen should look similar to Figure 9-9. You select a style for your diagram from a variety of outline and fill styles in this dialog box.

FIGURE 9-9
Diagram Style Gallery
Dialog Box

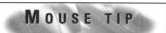

| Step 2 | *Double-click* | 3-D color in the Select a Diagram Style: list |

You now move the diagram into the "layer" behind the text and reposition it.

Step 3	*Click*	the Text Wrapping button on the Diagram toolbar
Step 4	*Click*	Behind Text
Step 5	*Drag*	the diagram to the center of the paragraph (place the mouse pointer on the diagram's border to see the move pointer)
Step 6	*Deselect*	the diagram
Step 7	*Observe*	that the diagram is visible behind the paragraph text

To finish the newsletter document you insert a chart comparing the actual employee and corporate contributions to the United We Care charity to the contribution goals.

9.d Creating and Modifying a Data Chart

C

Microsoft Graph is a supplementary application that comes with Office. With this application you can present numerical information as a **chart**, which is a pictorial representation of data or the relationship between sets of data. Common chart styles include bar charts, pie charts, and line charts.

Creating a Chart

You can create a Word chart by selecting data keyed in a table and then importing it into a chart datasheet or by keying the data directly into the chart datasheet. Jody gives you the data in Table 9-1, which you key into a chart datasheet.

Label	Data
Employee Contributions	100,000
Corporate Contributions	50,000
Contribution Goal	250,000

TABLE 9-1
Chart Data

To insert the data chart below the "Our employee contributions…" paragraph in the second column:

Step 1	*Move*	the insertion point to the end of the paragraph
Step 2	*Press*	the ENTER key

chapter
nine

Step 3	*Click*	<u>I</u>nsert
Step 4	*Click*	<u>O</u>bject
Step 5	*Click*	the <u>C</u>reate New tab in the Object dialog box, if necessary

Your Object dialog box should look similar to Figure 9-10.

FIGURE 9-10
<u>C</u>reate New Tab in the
Object Dialog Box

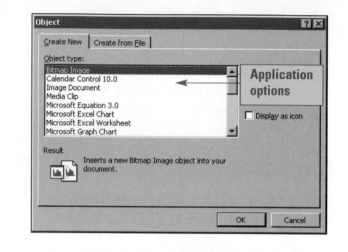

Step 6	*Double-click*	Microsoft Graph Chart in the <u>O</u>bject type: list (scroll to view this option, if necessary)

Word displays a chart based on the sample data contained in the datasheet. Your screen should look similar to Figure 9-11.

FIGURE 9-11
Sample Chart and
Datasheet

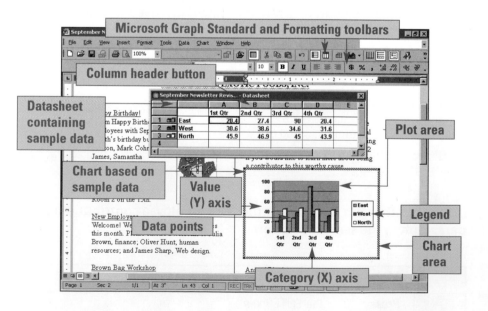

A datasheet is similar to a Word table and contains columns (A, B, C, etc.) and rows (1, 2, 3, etc.). The intersection of a column and row is called a cell. For example, cell A1 is at the intersection of column A and row 1. The unnumbered row immediately below the column header buttons is used to enter text labels for the columns. The remaining rows contain data and row labels for that data. The unlettered column immediately to the right of the row header buttons is used to enter text labels for the rows. You activate a cell to enter text or numbers by clicking the cell with the mouse pointer, which becomes a large white plus sign pointer when positioned in the datasheet. The active cell has a dark black border around it.

You can replace the sample data by keying new data in each cell or by deleting the sample data before you key the new data. To enter data in a cell, you activate the cell, key the data, and then press the ENTER key. To key the chart labels:

Step 1	*Click*	the first cell in column A (currently contains "1st Qtr")
Step 2	*Key*	Contributions
Step 3	*Press*	the ENTER key
Step 4	*Click*	the first cell in row 1 (currently contains East)
Step 5	*Key*	Employee
Step 6	*Press*	the ENTER key to enter the text and move the active cell indicator down to row 2
Step 7	*Key*	Corporate
Step 8	*Press*	the ENTER key to enter the text and move the active cell indicator down to row 3
Step 9	*Key*	Goal
Step 10	*Press*	the ENTER key

You follow the three-step process to enter the contribution values. To enter the values in column A:

Step 1	*Enter*	100,000 in the second cell in row 1 (currently contains 20.4)
Step 2	*Enter*	50,000 in the second cell in row 2 (currently contains 30.6)
Step 3	*Enter*	250,000 in the second cell in row 3 (currently contains 45.9)

MOUSE TIP

You can widen a column by placing the mouse pointer on the right boundary between column header buttons and dragging the boundary to the right or left.

QUICK TIP

You can move the datasheet out of the way, if necessary, by dragging its title bar.

QUICK TIP

Both Word charts and Excel charts are created using the Microsoft Graph features. This means that all the chart creation and editing features available in Excel are also available in Word when you open the Microsoft Graph application.

chapter
nine

CAUTION TIP

Be careful when you use the double-click method to edit a chart object. Because the chart objects are positioned so closely, it's easy to accidentally double-click an adjacent object instead of the intended object. An alternative to double-clicking an object is to use the Chart Objects and Format Objects buttons on the Microsoft Graph Standard toolbar to select an object and open its formatting dialog box or to right-click an object and click the Format (selected object) command.

MOUSE TIP

You can select individual chart objects by clicking the Chart Objects button list arrow on the Microsoft Graph Standard toolbar and selecting a chart item from the list. Then you can open the formatting dialog box for that object by clicking the Format Object button on the Microsoft Graph Standard toolbar.

You can delete the remaining sample data or simply hide the columns. To hide columns B–D and view the chart in the newsletter document:

Step 1	*Double-click*	the Column B, C, and D header buttons
Step 2	*Observe*	the changes to the chart
Step 3	*Click*	in the document outside the chart area and datasheet
Step 4	*Observe*	the chart

Jody reviews the newsletter and suggests you modify the chart. To change the chart type to a simple column chart, remove the plot area color, and change the column colors.

Modifying a Data Chart

Microsoft Graph inserts a chart into a Word document as an embedded object. An **embedded object** must be edited with the tools of the application in which it was created, sometimes called the **source application**. To edit the embedded chart, you can double-click it to open Microsoft Graph and then edit each chart item, called a chart object—such as the legend, the data points (columns), the plot area, or the Category (X) or Value (Y) labels. To modify individual chart objects, you can double-click the object or right-click the object to open its formatting dialog box.

To modify the embedded chart:

Step 1	*Double-click*	the chart object to open Microsoft Graph
Step 2	*Click*	the Chart Type button list arrow 📊 on the Microsoft Graph Standard toolbar
Step 3	*Click*	Column Chart (first item in the third row)
Step 4	*Right-click*	the gray plot area
Step 5	*Click*	Format Plot Area to open the Format Plot Area dialog box

The Format Plot Area dialog box on your screen should look similar to Figure 9-12.

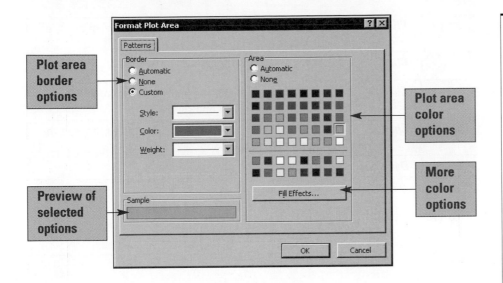

FIGURE 9-12
Format Plot Area Dialog Box

Step 6	*Click*	the Non<u>e</u> option button above the color grid in the Area group
Step 7	*Click*	OK
Step 8	*Double-click*	the Employee data series (blue column) to open the Format Data Series dialog box
Step 9	*Click*	the Patterns tab, if necessary

The Format Data Series dialog box on your screen should look similar to Figure 9-13.

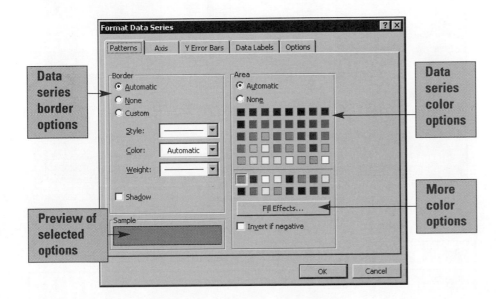

FIGURE 9-13
Format Data Series
Dialog Box

chapter
nine

Step 10	*Click*	the Red square (first color in the third row) in the Area color grid
Step 11	*Click*	OK
Step 12	*Change*	the Corporate data series (maroon column) to Blue (sixth color in the second row)
Step 13	*Change*	the Goal data series (yellow column) to Green (fourth color in the second row)
Step 14	*Deselect*	the chart

To view the completed newsletter document:

| Step 1 | *Print Preview* | the document |

The previewed document on your screen should look similar to Figure 9-14.

FIGURE 9-14
Completed Document

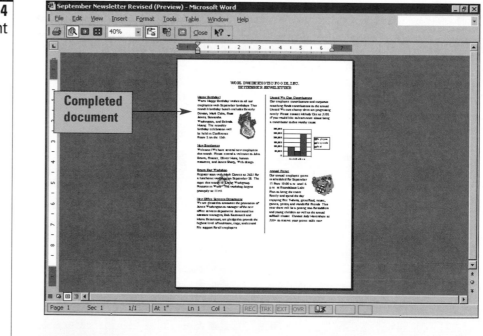

Step 2	*Close*	Print Preview
Step 3	*Close*	the Drawing toolbar
Step 4	*Save*	the document and close it

The September newsletter is completely formatted. Jody will have the newsletter copied and then distribute it appropriately.

Summary

▶ Newspaper-style columns are appropriate for documents such as brochures or newsletters.

▶ When you use newspaper-style columns, the text fills the length of the first column before flowing to the next column.

▶ Newspaper-style columns can be created for an entire document or a section of a document.

▶ You can select text and create columns from the selected text, or you can insert a section break and then create columns for the text in a specific section.

▶ Text columns can be viewed in Print Layout view or Print Preview, but cannot be viewed in Normal view.

▶ You can create columns of unequal width by using one of the two preset unequal-width column options or by specifying the exact column width in the Columns dialog box.

▶ A vertical divider line can be added between columns.

▶ You can insert pictures from the Clip Organizer using the Insert Picture button on the Drawing toolbar.

▶ You can insert and edit diagrams with the Insert Diagram or Organization Chart button on the Drawing toolbar.

▶ You can create a data chart object in Word using the Microsoft Graph application.

▶ You enter data into a chart by keying the data into the datasheet.

▶ A chart is inserted into a Word document as an embedded object that must be edited with options in Microsoft Graph, the source application.

▶ You can select individual chart items, called chart objects, and then format them.

Commands Review

Action	Menu Bar	Shortcut Menu	Toolbar	Task Pane	Keyboard
Create newspaper columns	Format, Columns		🖿		ALT + O, C
Insert a column break	Insert, Break				ALT + I, B CTRL + SHIFT + ENTER
Insert a picture	Insert, Picture, Clip Art Insert, Picture, From File		🖾 🖼	Drag a picture from the Results: section of the Insert Clip Art task pane into the document	ALT + I, P, C ALT + I, P, F

chapter nine

Action	Menu Bar	Shortcut Menu	Toolbar	Task Pane	Keyboard
Text wrapping for selected picture	Format, Picture	Right-click picture, click Format Picture			ALT + O, I
View the Drawing toolbar	View, Toolbars, Drawing	Right-click any toolbar, click Drawing			ALT + V, T
Insert a diagram	Insert, Diagram				ALT + I, G

Concepts Review

Circle the correct answer.

1. **The Columns dialog box contains all of the preset options for creating columns except:**
   [a] Right.
   [b] Center.
   [c] Left.
   [d] Two.

2. **Which task pane is used to insert pictures, sound, and motion clips?**
   [a] Insert Media Clips
   [b] Insert Picture Art
   [c] Insert Clip Art
   [d] Insert Clip Media

3. **Word presents collections or catalogs of picture, sound, and motion clips in the:**
   [a] Clip Organizer.
   [b] Media Organizer.
   [c] Art Organizer.
   [d] Picture Organizer.

4. **When you use the Columns button to create newspaper-style columns, the columns are formatted into:**
   [a] unequal column widths.
   [b] equal column widths.
   [c] vertical column widths.
   [d] justified column widths.

5. **To balance columns of uneven length, you should insert a(n):**
   [a] page break.
   [b] even page section break.
   [c] column break.
   [d] line break.

6. **Which of the following is not a text wrapping option for picture objects?**
   [a] Near
   [b] Square
   [c] Tight
   [d] Behind Text

7. **The diagram that illustrates the relationship to and from a central element is:**
   [a] Venn.
   [b] Pryamid.
   [c] Radial.
   [d] Cycle.

8. **A datasheet is a(n):**
   [a] embedded object.
   [b] source application.
   [c] worksheet of columns and rows.
   [d] picture object.

9. **You can use sizing handles to:**
   [a] format picture objects.
   [b] position text in newspaper-style columns.
   [c] change the size and shape of picture objects.
   [d] embed picture objects.

10. **The drawing canvas is used to:**
    [a] position picture objects in line with the text.
    [b] control the position of drawing objects such as diagrams.
    [c] insert data charts.
    [d] wrap text around picture objects.

Circle **T** if the statement is true or **F** if the statement is false.

T F   1. With default newspaper-style columns, text fills one column before flowing to the next column.

T F   2. Columns appear on the screen only in Print Layout view.

T F   3. You can redistribute text in columns by inserting a manual page break.

T F   4. A chart is a pictorial representation of numerical data or the relationship between sets of numerical data.

T F   5. The Microsoft Graph application is used to create charts in a Word document.

T F   6. You can view vertical lines between columns in Normal view.

T F   7. You can create a manual column break with the CTRL + SHIFT shortcut keys.

T F   8. Diagrams and charts are used to help readers understand complex relationships and ideas.

T F   9. A datasheet consists of rows, columns, and cells, and is similar to a Word table.

T F   10. You can size a picture object proportionally while maintaining its center position by pressing the CTRL key while dragging a corner sizing handle.

Skills Review

Exercise 1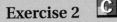

1. Open the *Legislative Update* document located on the Data Disk.

2. Select all the text below the second title line "LEGISLATIVE UPDATE."

3. Format the selected text with two columns of even width.

4. Insert column breaks so that the columns are approximately the same length.

5. Add a vertical line between the columns.

6. Switch to Normal view and select the two lines of title text.

7. Expand the character spacing in the title text by 0.5 points. (*Hint:* Use the Character Spacing tab in the Font dialog box.)

8. Save the document as *Legislative Update With Columns*, and then preview, print, and close it.

Exercise 2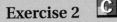

1. Create a new, blank document.

2. Center and bold the title "Targeted Sales by Department" in 14-point Times New Roman font and press the ENTER key twice.

3. Display the Drawing toolbar.

4. Insert a Target diagram.

5. Click the outside ring of the target to select it and then change the color to red. (*Hint:* Click the Fill Color button list arrow on the Drawing toolbar and click red on the color grid.)

6. Change the color of the middle ring to black and the center ring to white.

chapter nine

7. Click the "Click to add text" text box for the outside ring and key "A=1M." Key "B=2M" as the middle ring text and "C=3M" as the center ring text. Size the diagram appropriately.

8. Save the document as *Target Diagram*, and then preview, print, and close it.

Exercise 3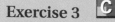

1. Open the *Announcements* document located on the Data Disk.

2. Find all instances of underlined text and replace it with no underline and Small caps effect. (*Hint:* use the Format button in the Find and Replace dialog box to find and replace formatting.)

3. Format the entire document in two columns of uneven width using the Right preset option.

4. Replace the "For Sale:" text with an appropriately sized and positioned picture.

5. Save the document as *Announcements Revised*, and then preview, print, and close it.

Exercise 4

1. Create a new, blank document.

2. Center the title "Radial Diagram" in Arial, 14-point, bold font and press the ENTER key twice.

3. Display the Drawing toolbar.

4. Insert a Radial diagram.

5. Add two additional elements. (*Hint:* Click the Insert Shape button on the Diagram toolbar once for each additional element you wish to add.)

6. Change the format to Primary Colors. (*Hint:* Use the AutoFormat button on the Diagram toolbar.)

7. Add the centered text of your choice formatted with the white color to each of the diagram elements. Click an element, click the Font Color button list arrow on the Drawing toolbar and click white in the color grid, then key the text. Reposition the diagram attractively below the heading text.

8. Save the document as *Radial Diagram*, and then preview, print, and close it.

Exercise 5

1. Open the *Chicago Warehouses Audit* report located on the Data Disk.

2. Select the body text (not the title) and format it in two columns of even width.

3. Insert a manual column break at the paragraph beginning "A consulting company…." to balance the columns.

4. Insert a vertical line between the columns.

5. Save the document as *Chicago Warehouses Audit With Columns*, and then preview, print, and close it.

Exercise 6

1. Open the *Travel Services* document located on the Data Disk.

2. Create newspaper-style columns for the body text beginning with "Pink Beach" paragraph heading.

3. Insert, size, and position (including wrapping the text attractively) an appropriate picture for each of the paragraphs.

4. Insert a manual column break as needed to balance the columns attractively.

5. Save the document as *Travel Services Revised*, and then preview, print, and close it.

Exercise 7 C

1. Open the *Office Technology Society* document located on the Data Disk.

2. Create three columns of equal width for the body text (do not include the title) and insert appropriate manual column breaks. Add a vertical line between the columns.

3. Insert, format, and size the diagram of your choice and position it behind the text in column 2.

4. Save the document as *Office Technology Society Revised*, and then preview, print, and close it.

Exercise 8 C

1. Open the *Training Commitment* document located on the Data Disk.

2. Move the insertion point to the second blank line following the second body paragraph.

3. Insert a data chart using the following data. Key the text "Employees" as the heading in the first cell below column A. Hide columns B–D.

Label	Data
Sales and Marketing	35
Accounting	50
Information Technology	125
All Other	130

4. Format the data chart as a Column Chart, change the Plot Area to white, change the data points to the colors of your choice.

5. Add data label values to the chart. Click the Chart Options command on the Chart menu and select the Value option on the Data Labels tab.

6. Position the chart legend below the Category (x) axis. Click the Chart Options command on the Chart menu and select the Bottom option on the Legend tab.

7. Center the chart object. After clicking in the document to close the Microsoft Graph application, click the chart to select it, and then click the Center button on the Formatting toolbar.

8. Save the document as *Training Commitment With Chart*, and then preview, print, and close it.

Case Projects

Project 1 C

You are the secretary for the local chapter of the Office Technology Society and you prepare a quarterly newsletter for all chapter members. Create a newsletter titled "OFFICE TECHNOLOGY BULLETIN" with two newspaper-style columns of body text containing fictitious data for the following paragraph headings: *Membership Drive*; *New Members*; *Annual Conference*; *User Tips for Word 2002*; and *Hot Internet Sites*. Add a line between the columns. Add an appropriate picture, sized and positioned attractively at the bottom of column 2. Save, preview, and print the document.

Project 2 C

Bill Martin, another administrative assistant to B. J. Chang, is having trouble preparing the monthly employee newsletter. He does not know how to change column widths or balance the column text so that the newsletter has an attractive appearance and he asks you for help. Create an interoffice memorandum to Bill describing how to use the Ask A Question Box to troubleshoot problems with columns. Include two paragraphs explaining how to change column widths and balance column text. Save, preview, and print the memorandum.

chapter nine

Project 3 C

Your new assignment in the Human Resources Department is to fill in for the corporate librarian while she is at a conference. Joe Beck in the Finance Department requests a list of investment-oriented online magazines and newsletters. Using the Internet and Internet search tools, search for investment-oriented online newsletters and magazines. Print at least two Web pages for each type. Create an interoffice memo to Joe describing the results of your search. Use two evenly spaced columns separated by a line for the Web page descriptions. Add an appropriate picture or diagram to the memo. Attach the Web pages you printed.

Project 4 C

Bill Martin drops by your desk to tell you about the different diagrams he discovered in Word. You want to experiment with creating these diagrams and then tell Kelly Armstead and Jody Haversham about them. Create a new, blank document. Display the Drawing toolbar, and explore creating at least three different diagrams and formatting them with buttons on the Diagram toolbar and the Drawing toolbar. Save, preview, and print the document.

Project 5 C

Chris Lofton, the manager of the Word Processing Department, calls and asks you to present a brief "brown bag" seminar on tips and tricks for inserting, sizing, positioning (including text wrapping) pictures in Word documents. Create an outline of the topics you will present at the seminar. Save, preview, and print the outline. Then, with your instructor's permission, use the outline to show several classmates how to insert, size, and position pictures in a Word document.

Project 6 C

The Human Resources Department is helping a neighborhood civic association to hold its annual fund-raising bake sale by providing clerical support for the association. You are asked to create a flyer that can be copied and posted at Create an 8½ × 11-inch flyer using fictitious data announcing the bake sale. Include appropriately sized and positioned pictures in the flyer. Save, preview, and print the flyer.

Project 7 C

Bill Martin calls and asks you for help. B. J. Chang wants a list of Web-based training classes covering office technology topics and Bill is not familiar with the WWW. You agree to search for the Web sites and write a memo to Chang. Using the Internet and Internet search tools, search for Web sites providing online classes in office technology topics. Print at least three Web pages. Write an interoffice memorandum to B. J. Chang describing the results of your search. Use columns and pictures to make the memo more interesting. Save, preview, and print the memorandum. Attach the Web pages to the memorandum.

Project 8 C

Your recent "brown bag" seminars for the word processing staff have been so well received that Chris Lofton, the manager of the Word Processing Department, asks you to prepare another seminar on inserting data charts into a Word document. Create a new, blank document and create a Word table containing fictitious data. Select the data and insert a Microsoft Graph data chart below the table. Experiment with modifying the chart using different chart types and experiment with the options in the Chart Options dialog box. Also experiment with ways to format the different chart objects and then close the document without saving it. Create an outline of the topics you will present at the seminar. Save, preview, and print the outline. With your instructor's permission, use the outline to show several classmates how to create and format charts in a Word document.

Creating Basic Tables

Chapter Overview

Certain columnar data included in a document, such as budgets and price lists, needs to be organized in a logical manner so that it is easier to read and understand. You could use tabs to organize this data, but usually it is simpler to place it in a table. In this chapter, you learn how to create and edit tables.

LEARNING OBJECTIVES

- ▶ Create and format tables
- ▶ Modify tables
- ▶ Position tables
- ▶ Apply AutoFormats to tables

Case profile

The Marketing and Sales Departments at Worldwide Exotic Foods, Inc. are getting ready for the busy holiday shopping season and need assistance preparing correspondence and reports. You are assigned to handle the work overflow for both departments. You begin by creating a letter containing a table of data for the media budget.

chapter ten

C 10.a Creating and Formatting Tables

R. D. Jacobson, the media director for the Marketing Department, gives you a page of handwritten notes and asks you to use the notes to create a letter to the advertising agency that develops the media buying plans for Worldwide Exotic Foods. The letter contains the media budget for this year's holiday season. Jacobson's executive assistant, Maria Betancourt, suggests you use a table to organize the budget data in the letter. You begin by creating a new, blank document and keying part of text. To create the letter:

Step 1	*Create*	a new, blank document
Step 2	*Set*	the appropriate margins for a block format letter
Step 3	*Key*	the current date, letter address, salutation, and first two body paragraphs shown in Figure 10-1

FIGURE 10-1
Completed Dynamic Advertising Letter

Current date

Ms. Sue Wong
Account Executive
Dynamic Advertising Agency
3268 West International Blvd.
Dallas, TX 75211-1052

Dear Ms. Wong:

Please extend our thanks and congratulations to everyone at the Dynamic Advertising Agency who works on the Worldwide Exotic Foods, Inc. account. Because of the outstanding media program developed by your team last year, we experienced exceptional holiday sales.

We anticipate holiday sales for this year to exceed last year. Therefore, we are increasing this year's media budget by 20%. The budget is detailed below:

Worldwide Exotic Foods, Inc. Media Budget			
Branch Office	**Holiday Baskets**	**Beverage Baskets**	**Gift Certificates**
Chicago	$133,175	$55,321	$11,500
London	74,768	46,987	10,589
Melbourne	97,509	30,890	1,561
Vancouver	458,321	138,079	15,345

We can discuss these budget figures in detail at our media program meeting next week.

Sincerely,

R. D. Jacobson
Media Director

xx

| Step 4 | *Press* | the ENTER key twice |

The next part of the letter contains the table of information. A **table** is a grid organized into columns and rows. A **column** is a set of information that runs down the page. A **row** runs across the page. A **cell** occurs at the intersection of a column and row. First, you create the table grid and key the data in the table cells. Then, you can add or remove the table border and format the text using the same formatting features you use for the body text.

The Insert Table button on the Standard toolbar displays a grid from which you select the number of rows and columns for the table, simply by dragging the mouse pointer down and across the grid. To create a table with five rows and four columns:

Step 1	*Click*	the Insert Table button  on the Standard toolbar
Step 2	*Move*	the mouse pointer to the upper-left square in the grid
Step 3	*Observe*	the text "1 × 1 Table" at the bottom of the grid, indicating that one row and one column are selected
Step 4	*Drag*	the mouse pointer down five rows and across four columns (until you see 5 × 4 Table at the bottom of the grid)
Step 5	*Release*	the mouse button to create the table
Step 6	*Scroll*	to view the table, if necessary
Step 7	*Save*	the document as *Dynamic Advertising Letter* and leave it open

The insertion point automatically appears in the first cell of the table. Whenever the insertion point is in the table, column markers also appear on the horizontal ruler. Word inserts table nonprinting formatting marks, called **end-of-cell** and **end-of-row marks**, in the table. You use these formatting marks to select cells, rows, and columns.

| Step 8 | *Click* | the Show/Hide button ¶ on the Standard toolbar to view the table formatting marks |

Your screen should look similar to Figure 10-2.

chapter
ten

FIGURE 10-2
Table Grid, Column Markers, and Formatting Marks

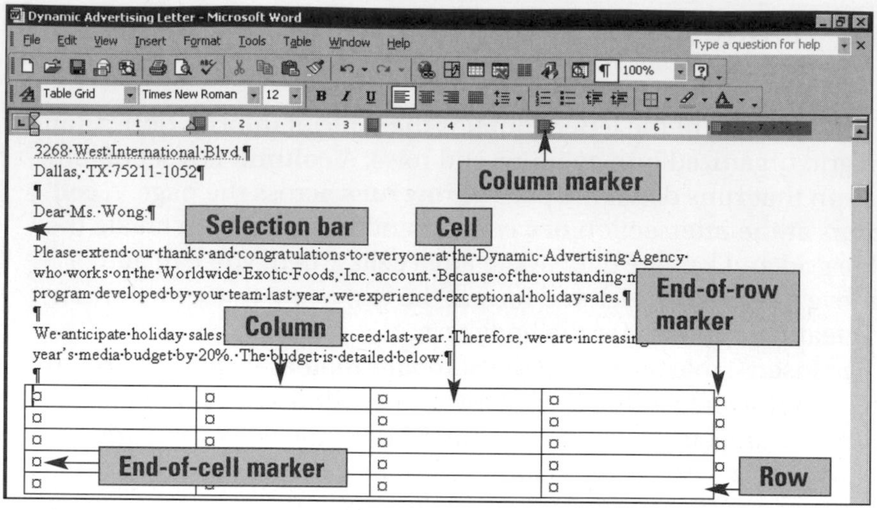

CAUTION TIP

By default, the table is created with thin, black borders that print. If you do not want to print a border, you can easily remove it. Just move the insertion point inside the table, open the Borders and Shading dialog box, and click the None preset option on the Borders tab.

To key text in a table you must move the insertion point from cell to cell.

Moving the Insertion Point in a Table

You can use the I-beam and the keyboard to move the insertion point from cell to cell in a table. You do not press the ENTER key. Pressing the ENTER key creates a new paragraph inside the table cell. To move the insertion point with the I-beam, just click in the appropriate cell.

To use the keyboard, press the appropriate ARROW key, press the TAB key to move one cell to the right, or press the SHIFT + TAB keys to move one cell to the left. Table 10-1 lists methods for moving the insertion point in a table using the keyboard.

TABLE 10-1
Table Movement Keys

Location	Keys	Location	Keys
One cell down	DOWN ARROW	**First cell in a row**	ALT + HOME
One cell right	TAB (RIGHT ARROW, if the cell is empty)	**Last cell in a row**	ALT + END
One cell left	SHIFT + TAB (LEFT ARROW, if the cell is empty)	**First cell in a column**	ALT + PAGE UP
One cell up	UP ARROW	**Last cell in a column**	ALT + PAGE DOWN

To move the insertion point in the table:

Step 1	***Click***	the middle of the first cell in the second row
Step 2	***Press***	the UP ARROW key

Step 3	*Continue*	to practice moving the insertion point in the table, using Table 10-1 as your guide
Step 4	*Move*	the insertion point to the first cell (upper-left corner) in the table

You are ready to key the text in the table.

Keying Text in Tables

You key the column headings in the first row of the table, called the **heading row**, and then key the media budget data in the following rows. As you key the numbers, do not attempt to align them in the cells; you do that later. If you accidentally press the ENTER key while keying data in a cell, press the BACKSPACE key to remove the paragraph mark and blank line from the cell.

To key the column headings:

Step 1	*Verify*	that the insertion point is in the first cell in the first row
Step 2	*Key*	Branch Office
Step 3	*Press*	the TAB key
Step 4	*Key*	Holiday Baskets
Step 5	*Press*	the TAB key
Step 6	*Key*	Beverage Baskets
Step 7	*Press*	the TAB key
Step 8	*Key*	Gift Certificates
Step 9	*Press*	the TAB key

The insertion point moves to the first cell in the second row. Now you can key the rest of the data for the table.

Step 10	*Key*	Chicago
Step 11	*Press*	the TAB key
Step 12	*Continue*	to key the remaining data in the Branch Office, Holiday Baskets, Beverage Baskets, and Gift Certificates columns for the Chicago, London, Melbourne, and Vancouver branches, as shown in Figure 10-1 (do not align the budget amounts at this time)
Step 13	*Save*	the document and leave it open

MENU TIP

You can point to the Select command on the Table menu and then click Table, Column, Row, or Cell to select all or part of the table containing the insertion point.

QUICK TIP

You can use the SHIFT + Click and CTRL + Click methods to select contiguous and noncontiguous rows, columns, and cells in the same way you do body text.

chapter
ten

In addition to moving the insertion point from cell to cell, you also select cells, rows, and columns to format or delete the contents or to insert or delete the cells, rows, and columns.

Selecting Cells, Rows, and Columns

Before you can format the table contents, you must select the cells that contain the text. If you move the mouse pointer to the lower-left corner of a cell, to the selection bar to the left of a row, or to the top of a column, the mouse pointer becomes a selection pointer. You can also select parts of a table with the keyboard. Table 10-2 lists mouse pointer and keyboard selection techniques.

TABLE 10-2
Table Selection Methods

Selection	Mouse	Keyboard
Cell	Move the mouse pointer inside the left boundary of a cell and click	Move the insertion point to the cell and press the SHIFT + END keys
Several cells	Drag across the cells with the selection pointer or the I-beam	Move the insertion point to the first cell, press and hold the SHIFT key, and then press the UP, DOWN, LEFT, or RIGHT ARROW key
Column	Move the mouse pointer to the top of the column until it becomes a vertical selection pointer, then click (or hold down the ALT key and click) a cell in the column with the I-beam pointer	Move the insertion point to the first cell in the column, hold down the SHIFT key, and press the ALT + PAGE DOWN keys
Row	Click the selection bar at the left of the row, or double-click any cell in a row with the selection pointer	Move the insertion point to the first cell in the row, hold down the SHIFT key, and press the ALT + END keys
Table	Drag to select all rows or all columns (including the end-of-row marks) with the selection pointer	Move the insertion point to any cell, press the NUMLOCK key on the numeric keypad to turn off the Number Lock feature, and press the ALT + 5 keys (the 5 key on the numeric keypad).

QUICK TIP

You can delete both the contents of a table and the table grid. To delete the contents of a cell, row, or column, simply select the cell, row, or column and press the DELETE key. To delete the entire table grid or a cell, row, or column, you must use a menu command. First move the insertion point to the table column, row, or cell, point to the Delete command on the Table menu, and click Table, Columns, Rows, or Cells.

To select a row, column, and cell in the table:

Step 1	*Move*	the mouse pointer to the left of the first row in the selection bar
Step 2	*Click*	the selection bar
Step 3	*Move*	the mouse pointer to the top of the second column (the mouse pointer becomes a small black selection pointer)

Step 4	*Click*	the column with the selection pointer
Step 5	*Move*	the mouse pointer just inside the left cell boundary in last cell in the last row (the mouse pointer becomes a small black selection pointer)
Step 6	*Click*	the cell with the selection pointer
Step 7	*Continue*	to select cells, rows, columns, and the entire table, using Table 10-2 as your guide
Step 8	*Move*	the insertion point to the first cell in the first row

You are ready to format the table text.

Changing Cell Formats

You format text in a table just as you do in the body of a document. To help distinguish the column labels from the rest of the data, you can shade, bold, and center them. You also can use the alignment buttons on the Formatting toolbar to align the numbers in their cells.

To bold and center the column headings and right-align the numbers:

Step 1	*Select*	the first row containing the column headings
Step 2	*Click*	the Bold button **B** on the Formatting toolbar
Step 3	*Click*	the Center button ▣ on the Formatting toolbar
Step 4	*Click*	any cell to deselect the row
Step 5	*Select*	the cells that contain the budget numbers
Step 6	*Click*	the Align Right button ▣ to align the numbers to the right
Step 7	*Deselect*	the cells
Step 8	*Save*	the document and leave it open

Later you shade the cells. To complete the table contents you need to add the heading row.

10.b Modifying Tables

Once you create a table, you often need to modify it by inserting rows or columns for additional data, or deleting unused rows and columns. For the table in the letter, you need to insert a row at the top of the table for the table heading, a row at the bottom of the table for the column totals, and a column at the right of the table for the row totals.

CAUTION TIP

When you select all or part of a table and then press the DELETE key, only the contents in the selected part of the table are deleted. To use the DELETE key to delete an entire table, you must also select a portion of the text or a blank line above or below the table before you press the DELETE key.

QUICK TIP

You can set tab stops on the horizontal ruler to align text and numbers in cells in the same way you use tab stops to align text and numbers in the body of a document. Select the cells, set the tab alignment you want, and then click the horizontal ruler where you want to insert the tab stop.

To insert a tab formatting mark in a cell, press the CTRL + TAB keys.

**chapter
ten**

Inserting Rows and Columns

MENU TIP

To insert a row or column, you can click the Insert command on the Table menu to insert the rows or columns above or below a selected row and left or right of a selected column. You also can use a shortcut menu to insert rows or columns.

To insert rows or columns, first select the number of rows or columns you wish to insert. For example, to insert two rows, select two rows in the table. The new row you insert retains the formatting from the original row. If you don't specify where you want to insert rows or columns, Word automatically inserts rows above the selected row and inserts columns to the left of the selected column.

You want to add a row at the top of the table in which you can key a heading for the table. To add a new row at the top of the table using the Table menu:

Step 1	*Move*	the insertion point to any cell in the first row
Step 2	*Click*	Table
Step 3	*Point to*	Insert
Step 4	*Click*	Rows Above

A new row is inserted at the top of the table.

A table heading in the first row helps identify the data in the table. Currently the first row has four cells, one for each column. You only need one cell for a table heading.

MOUSE TIP

You can use the Insert Table button on the Standard toolbar to insert rows and columns. When you select a table row, the Insert Table button on the Standard toolbar becomes the Insert Rows button. When you select a cell or column, the Insert Table button becomes the Insert Cell or Insert Column button.

Merging Cells

You can combine, or **merge**, cells vertically or horizontally by first selecting the cells to be merged and then clicking the Merge Cells command on the Table menu or a shortcut menu. You also can divide, or **split**, cells vertically or horizontally. Before you key and format the table heading, you want to merge the five cells in the first row into one cell. To merge the cells in the first row:

Step 1	*Select*	the first row, if necessary
Step 2	*Right-click*	the selected row
Step 3	*Click*	Merge Cells

The first row of the table now contains one large cell. To create the two-line table heading:

Step 1	*Key*	Worldwide Exotic Foods, Inc.
Step 2	*Press*	the ENTER key to create a new line in the cell
Step 3	*Key*	Media Budget

| Step 4 | *Observe* | that the two-line table heading is centered and bold, and the row height increases to accommodate the second line of the heading |

Using AutoFit to Change Column Width

Once the table contents are complete, you want to resize the widths to fit the data. A quick way to resize the table is to use the <u>A</u>utoFit options on the T<u>a</u>ble menu. You can have Word size or fit each column to match the column's contents. This method creates a column width that accommodates the widest cell contents in that column. Word also can resize the entire table to fit within the document margins or format rows for uniform height and columns for uniform width.

To have Word automatically fit the entire table with evenly distributed columns (columns with the same width):

Step 1	*Verify*	that the insertion point is in the table
Step 2	*Click*	T<u>a</u>ble
Step 3	*Point to*	<u>A</u>utoFit
Step 4	*Click*	Auto<u>F</u>it to Contents

You decide to see how the table looks without a border and with shaded column label cells.

Adding Borders and Shading to Tables

Borders and shading can make a table more attractive and easier to read. When you create a table using the Insert Table button on the Standard toolbar or <u>I</u>nsert Table command on the T<u>a</u>ble menu, Word adds a border around each cell in the table. You can modify or remove this border and add shading from the Borders and Shading dialog box. To open the Borders and Shading dialog box:

Step 1	*Right-click*	the table
Step 2	*Click*	<u>B</u>orders and Shading
Step 3	*Click*	the <u>B</u>orders tab, if necessary

The border options for tables appear in the <u>B</u>orders tab. You can select one of the five preset border options or customize the table border. If you remove the table's printing border, the table appears with light gray gridlines. These nonprinting **gridlines** provide a visual

QUICK TIP

To insert a column at the end of the table, first select the end-of-row marks just like you select a column. When you add a new column, the overall size of the table doesn't change but the column widths adjust to accommodate the new column.

You can easily add as many rows to a table as you need by pressing the TAB key to create each new row as you key the data. You also can quickly insert multiple rows at the end of a table by moving the insertion point to the blank line immediately below the table, clicking the Insert Rows button on the Standard toolbar, and specifying the number of rows to add.

MENU TIP

You can split a cell vertically and horizontally by first selecting the cell and then clicking the S<u>p</u>lit Cells command on the T<u>a</u>ble menu.

chapter
ten

guide as you work in a table. The nonprinting gridlines can be turned on or off with the Show Gridlines or Hide Gridlines commands on the Table menu. You remove the border and view the nonprinting gridlines.

| Step 4 | *Click* | the None preset border option in the Setting: group |
| Step 5 | *Click* | OK |

The light gray nonprinting gridlines should appear. However, if the gridlines were previously turned off they do not appear. To turn on the gridlines, if necessary, and Print Preview the document:

Step 1	*Click*	Table
Step 2	*Click*	Show Gridlines, if necessary
Step 3	*Print Preview* the document	
Step 4	*Observe*	that the light gray gridlines do not print
Step 5	*Close*	Print Preview

The information in the table was easier to read with the default border. To reapply the default border and add shading to the column label row:

Step 1	*Open*	the Borders tab in the Borders and Shading dialog box
Step 2	*Click*	the Grid option
Step 3	*Click*	OK
Step 4	*Select*	the second row, which contains the column heading text
Step 5	*Open*	the Shading tab in the Borders and Shading dialog box
Step 6	*Click*	the Gray-10% square on the color grid (the third square in the first row)
Step 7	*Click*	OK
Step 8	*Deselect*	the row

 ## 10.c Positioning Tables

You can horizontally align a table in relation to the edge of the page, the margins, or column boundaries. Tables can also be vertically aligned in relation to the top and bottom of the page, the top and bottom margins, or the top and bottom of a paragraph. The Table tab in the Table Properties dialog box provides options for positioning a table on the page. To position the table using the Table Properties dialog box:

Step 1	*Right-click*	the table
Step 2	*Click*	Table Properties
Step 3	*Click*	the Table tab, if necessary

Your Table Properties dialog box should look similar to Figure 10-3.

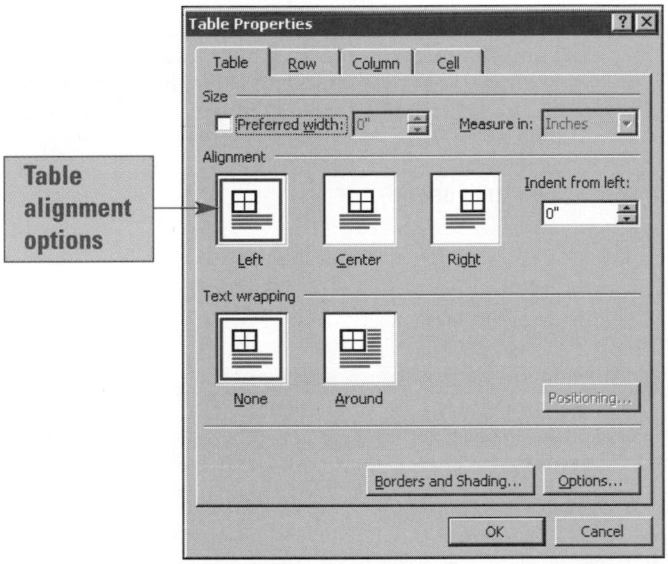

Table alignment options →

FIGURE 10-3
Table Properties
Dialog Box

MOUSE TIP

You can quickly align a table at the left or right margin or center the table by selecting the entire table *including the end-of-row marks* and clicking an alignment button on the Formatting toolbar.

| Step 4 | *Click* | the Center alignment option |
| Step 5 | *Click* | OK |

The table is centered between the left and right margins. The table is complete and you need to finish the letter. To key the remaining body text and closing:

Step 1	*Move*	the insertion point to the blank line below the table
Step 2	*Press*	the ENTER key
Step 3	*Key*	the last body paragraph, closing, and your initials, using Figure 10-1 as your guide
Step 4	*Save*	the document

MENU TIP

When you have a long table that flows over to another page, you can repeat the heading row of the table on each page by moving the insertion point to the heading row and clicking the Heading Rows Repeat command on the Table menu.

chapter
ten

Maria asks you to reformat the table.

C 10.d Applying AutoFormats to Tables

One way to quickly format a table is to apply a Table AutoFormat, also called a table style, which is a table format that includes preset borders and shading. Many of the automatic formats can be modified by turning on or off special formatting for the heading row, the first and last column, and the last row. To apply a Table AutoFormat:

Step 1	*Click*	anywhere inside the table to position the insertion point
Step 2	*Click*	Table
Step 3	*Click*	Table AutoFormat

Your Table AutoFormat dialog box should look similar to Figure 10-4.

FIGURE 10-4
Table AutoFormat
Dialog Box

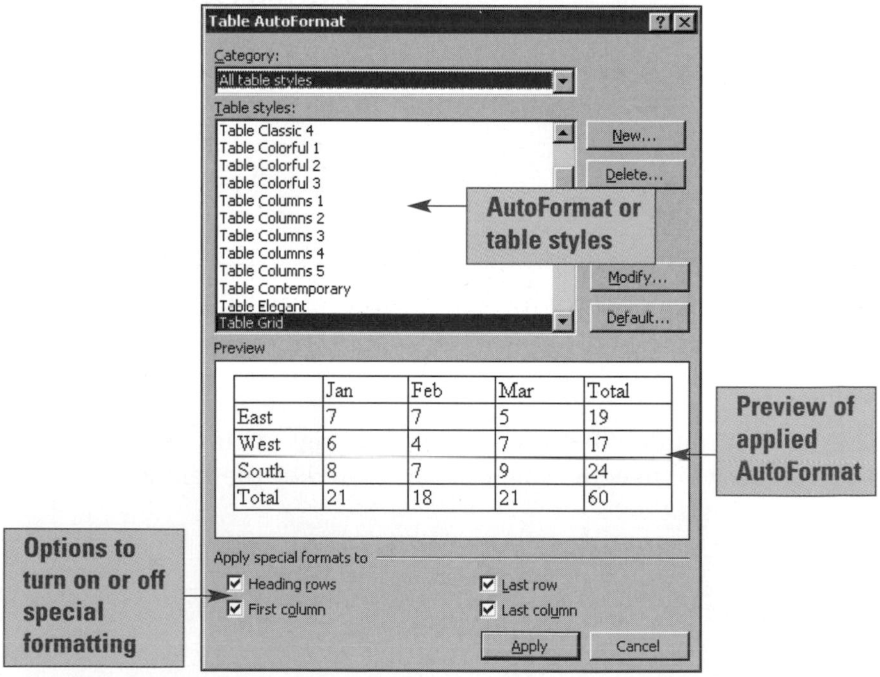

Table AutoFormat

Category:
All table styles

Table styles:
Table Classic 4
Table Colorful 1
Table Colorful 2
Table Colorful 3
Table Columns 1
Table Columns 2
Table Columns 3
Table Columns 4
Table Columns 5
Table Contemporary
Table Elegant
Table Grid

New...
Delete...
Modify...
Default...

AutoFormat or table styles

Preview

	Jan	Feb	Mar	Total
East	7	7	5	19
West	6	4	7	17
South	8	7	9	24
Total	21	18	21	60

Preview of applied AutoFormat

Apply special formats to
☑ Heading rows   ☑ Last row
☑ First column   ☑ Last column

Apply   Cancel

Options to turn on or off special formatting

You can select from a variety of automatic formats or styles in the Table styles: list and then preview what the document table would look like with the selected AutoFormat (table style) applied. To apply special formatting to the heading rows, first column, last row, or last column, you click the appropriate check box.

Step 4	*Click*	Table 3D effects 3 in the Table styles: list
Step 5	*Observe*	the table preview
Step 6	*Preview*	several other table styles

You want to use the Table Classic 3 style with heading row and first column formatting. To apply the Table Classic 3 style:

Step 1	*Click*	Table Classic 3 in the Table styles: list
Step 2	*Click*	the Heading rows and First column check boxes to insert check marks and remove any check marks from the Last row and Last column check boxes, if necessary
Step 3	*Observe*	the table preview
Step 4	*Click*	Apply

The table will look better centered between the left and right margins. To quickly center the table horizontally:

Step 1	*Select*	the entire table (including the end-of-row marks)
Step 2	*Click*	the Center button ▤ on the Formatting toolbar
Step 3	*Deselect*	the table
Step 4	*Save*	the document as *Dynamic With Table AutoFormat* and close it

The AutoFormats provide a variety of looks that you can use to quickly format a table.

chapter
ten

Summary

▶ Data in a Word document can be placed in a table so that it is easier to read and understand.

▶ A table is a grid organized into rows and columns.

▶ A column is a set of information that runs down a page, and a row is a set of information that runs across a page.

▶ A cell is the intersection of a column and a row.

▶ You can format text in table cells just as you format paragraph text.

▶ You can merge multiple cells into one cell.

▶ You can use the mouse or keyboard to move the insertion point between cells in a table.

▶ You can select cells, rows, and columns in a table; you can then format them, insert and delete rows or columns, or shift cells.

▶ You can change the widths of one or more columns in a table with the mouse or use the AutoFit commands on the Table menu.

▶ You can view nonprinting gridlines when working in a table.

▶ You can add printable borders and gridlines to a table.

▶ Word has many automatic table formats you can apply to an existing table.

Commands Review

Action	Menu Bar	Shortcut Menu	Toolbar	Task Pane	Keyboard
Create a table	Table, Insert, Table or Draw Table		▦		ALT + A, I, T or W
Delete a table or columns, rows, or cells	Table, Delete, Table, or Columns or Rows or Cells	Right-click selected table component, click Delete			ALT + A, D, T or C or R or E
Insert rows, columns, or cells in a table	Table, Insert, Columns to the Left or Columns to the Right or Rows Above or Rows Below or Cells	Right-click selected table component, click Insert	▦ ▦ ▦		ALT + A, I, L or R or A or B or E
Merge cells	Table, Merge Cells	Right-click selected cells, click Merge Cells	▦		ALT + A, M
Split cells	Table, Split Cells	Right-click cell, click Split Cells	▦		ALT + A, P
Change column width for selected column(s)	Table, Table Properties Table, AutoFit, AutoFit to Contents or AutoFit to Window or Fixed Column Width or Distribute Rows Evenly or Distribute Columns Evenly		Drag the column boundary or the column marker on the horizontal ruler		ALT + A, R ALT + A, A, F or W or X or N or Y

Action	Menu Bar	Shortcut Menu	Toolbar	Task Pane	Keyboard
Add borders and shading to a table	Format, Borders and Shading	Right-click table, Borders and Shading			ALT + O, B
Show or hide Table Gridlines	Table, Show Gridlines				ALT + A, G
Align text horizontally and vertically		Right-click cell, click Cell Alignment			
Position a table on the page	Table, Table Properties	Right-click a table, click Table Properties			ALT + A, R
Repeat a heading row on all pages of the table	Table, Heading Rows Repeat				ALT + A, H
Apply a Table AutoFormat	Table, Table AutoFormat				ALT + A, F

Concepts Review

SCANS

Circle the correct answer.

1. A table:
 [a] is a grid organized in columns and rows.
 [b] must be created with a button on the Standard toolbar.
 [c] cannot be formatted with character formats like bold and paragraph formats like borders and shading.
 [d] is created without a printable border.

2. You cannot change the width of a column in a table by:
 [a] pressing the TAB key.
 [b] dragging a row boundary between two rows.
 [c] clicking the Column Width command on the Table menu.
 [d] dragging a column boundary on the horizontal ruler.

3. When you create a new table, the insertion point automatically appears:
 [a] in the last cell.
 [b] below the table.
 [c] in the first cell.
 [d] in the second row.

4. A cell is:
 [a] a set of information that runs down a page.
 [b] a set of information that runs across the page.
 [c] the intersection of a column and row.
 [d] a grid of columns and rows.

5. You cannot move the insertion point in a table with the:
 [a] I-beam.
 [b] TAB key.
 [c] UP ARROW and DOWN ARROW keys.
 [d] SPACEBAR.

6. To select a cell using the keyboard, press the:
 [a] SHIFT + ALT keys.
 [b] ALT + END keys.
 [c] SHIFT + END keys.
 [d] ALT + 5 keys.

7. To delete a table grid, you must:
 [a] press the F8 key.
 [b] use a menu command.
 [c] use a shortcut menu.
 [d] press the DELETE key.

chapter ten

8. Combining cells is also called:
   [a] splitting them.
   [b] deleting them.
   [c] merging them.
   [d] formatting them.

9. The best way to align the numbers 973, 734, 1,034 in a table column is to:
   [a] left-align the numbers.
   [b] justify the numbers.
   [c] right-align the numbers.
   [d] center the numbers.

10. To automatically resize column widths so that all the columns in the table have enough space for the largest cell in the column, use the:
    [a] AutoFit to Height command.
    [b] AutoFit to Width command.
    [c] AutoFit to Size command.
    [d] AutoFit to Contents command.

Circle **T** if the statement is true or **F** if the statement is false.

T   F   1. A table column contains text in a vertical arrangement down the page.

T   F   2. To delete a table's contents, first select the table and then press the DELETE key.

T   F   3. Rows can be inserted above or below the selected rows.

T   F   4. Cells can be merged horizontally but not vertically.

T   F   5. To move the insertion point to the next cell, press the ENTER key.

T   F   6. You set tab stops for table cells in the same manner as body text.

T   F   7. The default table border cannot be removed or modified.

T   F   8. Nonprinting gridlines can provide a visual guide when you are working in a table.

T   F   9. The ALT + TAB keys move the insertion point one cell to the left.

T   F   10. Before you format the contents of a table, you must first select the cells, rows, or columns to be formatted.

Skills Review

Exercise 1

1. Create a new, blank document.

2. Change the top margin to 1½ inches and the left and right margins to 1 inch.

3. Create a 5 × 4 Table and key the following text in the table.

Branch	2001	2002	2003
Chicago	300,000	100,000	210,000
London	323,000	306,000	89,000
Melbourne	250,000	500,000	130,000
Vancouver	405,000	108,000	206,000

4. AutoFit the table to its contents.

5. Center and bold the column headings.

6. Right-align the numbers in their cells.

7. Insert a new first row, merge the cells, and key the following heading text in the new row.
Worldwide Exotic Foods, Inc.
Annual Beverage Sales
($000)

8. Bold and center the heading text.

9. Add 10% gray shading to the column headings.

10. Add a grid border to the table.

11. Save the document as *Annual Sales Data*, and then preview and print it.

12. Apply the Table AutoFormat of your choice and center the table horizontally.

13. Save the document as *Annual Sales With AutoFormat*, and then preview, print, and close it.

Exercise 2   C

1. Open the *Regional Deli Sales* document located on the Data Disk.

2. Insert a row between North and East regions using the Insert Rows button on the Standard toolbar.

3. Key the following text in the row: Central, 28,975.33, 54,333.45, and 78,125.54.

4. Insert a column at the end of the table. (*Hint:* View and select the end-of-row marks and insert a column to the left.)

5. Key "Beverages" in the first cell of the column.

6. Key the following text in the column: $30,456.78, 11, 300.56, 23,678.99, 97,234.55, and 59,112.45. (*Hint:* Use the DOWN ARROW to move to the next cell in the column.)

7. Right-align the numbers in the cells.

8. Adjust the column widths by dragging the column boundaries with the mouse pointer so that each column is just wide enough for the largest cell contents. (*Hint:* Place the mouse pointer on the right column boundary until it changes shape to a sizing pointer and then drag the boundary to the left.)

9. Center and bold the heading row.

10. Insert a new row at the top of the table, merge the cells, and then key, bold, and center the following text in the row: Regional Deli Sales.

11. Center the table between the left and right margins using the Table Properties dialog box.

12. Save the document as *Regional Deli Sales Revised*, and then preview, print, and close it.

Exercise 3   C

1. Create a new, blank document.

2. Create 5×4 Table and key the following text in the cells. Use the TAB key to insert a new row at the bottom of the table each time you need one.

Pastries	June	July	August
Éclairs	1,500	3,000	2,600
Danish	7,800	5,600	9,300
Croissants	13,000	15,000	10,500
Butter Biscuits	30,000	45,000	26,450
Lemon Tarts	5,600	3,500	3,450
Truffle Torte	850	1,200	635
Raspberry Charlotte Torte	1,300	1,475	2,300
Sweet Pretzels	75,000	65,000	80,000
German Chocolate Brownies	125,000	150,000	210,000

chapter ten

3. Size the columns attractively using the mouse. (*Hint:* Drag a right column border to the left or right to size a column.)

4. Bold and center the column headings.

5. Insert a new row at the top of the table, merge the cells, and key the following as boldfaced centered heading text.
   Vancouver Branch
   Pastries Sales

6. Remove the grid border from the table.

7. Add Gray-12.5 % shading to the top row.

8. Center the table between the left and right margins using the mouse pointer. (*Hint:* Select the entire table *including the end-of-row marks* and click the Center button.)

9. Save the document as *Vancouver Pastries Sales*, and then preview, print, and close it.

Exercise 4   C

1. Create a new, blank document.

2. Create a 1×4 Table and key the data below. Use the TAB key to add additional rows as you key the data.

District	Selling	Employee	Overhead
Central	$49,100.60	$12,421.00	$13,921.99
Eastern	41,756.72	5,523.42	8,992.33
Midwest	64,871.86	4,819.89	9,655.76
Mountain	59,256.36	7,085.07	6,332.99
Southern	45,817.32	12,253.57	16,322.86
Western	51,857.52	9,528.88	11,661.30

3. Select the first row, and then bold and center the text.

4. AutoFit the table to the contents.

5. Right-align the numbers.

6. Insert a row at the top of the document, merge the cells, and key the following title text in bold Arial 14-point font.
   Worldwide Exotic Foods, Inc.
   District Expense Report
   Fourth Quarter

7. Add a 1½-point grid border to the table.

8. Align the table at the right margin.

9. Save the document as *District Expense Report*, and then preview, print, and close it.

Exercise 5   C

1. Open the *Adjusted Costs Memo* document located on the Data Disk.

2. Create a 7×4 Table with no border below the memo body text.

3. Merge the cells in the first row.

4. Key the following heading text (boldface and centered) in two lines in the first row.
   EXECUTIVE SUPPORT DIVISION
   Adjusted Costs for Second Fiscal Quarter

5. Key the following data in the remaining rows.

Item	Budgeted	Actual	Difference
Executive Secretaries	$2,455,000	$2,256,000	-$199,000
Administrative Assistants	390,600	475,900	85,300
Equipment	960,000	840,000	-120,000
Telecommunications	476,000	450,600	-25,400
Miscellaneous	76,000	60,000	-16,000

6. Right align the numbers.

7. Underline and center the column heading text in the second row.

8. AutoFit the table to the contents.

9. Shade the Difference column with 10% gray.

10. Center the table between the left and right margins.

11. Save the document as *Adjusted Costs Memo Revised*, and then preview, print, and close it.

Exercise 6 C

1. Create a new, blank document and insert the text "TRIVIA INFORMATION ABOUT SELECTED STATES" centered in 14-point Times New Roman font at the top of the document.

2. Create a 2×2 Table on two lines below the title and key the following information in 12-point Times New Roman font in the table. Use the TAB key to add additional rows to the end of the table as necessary.

Arkansas	The Natural State
Arizona	Grand Canyon State
Colorado	Centennial State
Connecticut	Constitution State
Nebraska	Cornhusker State
New Mexico	America's Land of Enchantment
Texas	The Lone Star State
Washington	The Evergreen State

3. Change the first column width to 1.5 inches and the second column width to 3.5 inches. (*Hint:* Select the column and change the width on the Column tab in the Table Properties dialog box.)

4. Center the table between the left and right margins.

5. Center the contents of each column.

6. Add 10% gray shading to each alternate row beginning with the first row. (*Hint:* You can use the CTRL key to select multiple, noncontiguous rows.)

7. Save the document as *State Trivia*, and then preview, print, and close it.

Exercise 7 C

1. Open the *Burns Letter* document located on the Data Disk.

2. Insert a row at the top of the table, merge the cells, and key the following text.
Vancouver Office Expense Report
Second Quarter

3. Select the first two rows and the first column cells, bold and center the contents, and add 12.5% gray shading. (*Hint:* Use the CTRL key to select the table rows and cells before formatting them.)

4. Right-align the numbers and key "$" before each number in the first and last rows.

chapter ten

5. Center the table horizontally between the left and right margins.

6. Save the document as *Burns Letter With Formatted Table*, and then preview, print, and close it.

Exercise 8

1. Create a new, blank document.

2. Add the title "NEW TELEPHONE LIST" centered in 14-point Times New Roman font at the top of the page.

3. Create a 2×2 Table on the third line below the table and key the following text in 12-point Times New Roman font in the table.

NAME	*EXTENSION*
Maria Sanchez	*X3316*
Michael Chin	*X3201*
Susan Hernandez	*X3455*
Marshall Collins	*X4453*
Frances Robinson	*X3233*

4. Add a blank row at the bottom of the table and merge the cells.

5. Key the following information in a bulleted list in the new row.
- *Fax Number (713) 555-3456*
- *Dial 0 for the operator*
- *Dial 9 for an outside line*
- *Dial 8 for long distance calls*

6. Modify the bulleted list hanging indent so that the bullets are at the left margin of the row.

7. Center the table between the left and right margins.

8. AutoFit the table to the contents.

9. Italicize the table column headings.

10. Save the document as *New Telephone List*, and then preview, print, and close it.

Case Projects

SCANS

Project 1

A Marketing Department coworker, Ella Cohen, wants to know how to insert information from a database or other data source into a Word document as a table. Use the Ask A Question Box to locate online Help topics about inserting information from other applications. Write an interoffice memorandum to Ella describing the process. Save, preview, and print the memo.

Project 2

R. D. Jacobson asks you to create an interoffice memo to five Vancouver sales representatives advising them of the profit (sales minus expenses) for the third quarter on the Extravaganza Basket product. Use a table to present the data for the five sales representatives by listing the sales, expenses, and profit for each. Use fictitious data. Format and position the table attractively on the page. Save, preview, and print the memo.

Project 3

Maria Betancourt does not understand the concept of Word fields, such as the formula field or date and time field, and asks for your help. Use the Ask A Question Box to search online Help for information on Word fields. Print and review the information. Open the Options dialog box and use the Help button to review the Field options in the View tab. Create an interoffice memorandum to Maria describing Word fields and how to use the options on the View tab to view the fields. Use a table to organize the information about the View tab options. Save, preview, and print the memo.

With your instructor's permission, use the memo as a guide to describe Word fields to a classmate. Then open a document that contains a date and time or formula field and demonstrate how to use the View tab field options.

Project 4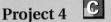

R. D. Jacobson asks you to help locate a list of firms that provide Web-based advertising. Connect to the Internet, and search for companies that provide advertising services on the Web. Print at least five home pages. Create an interoffice memorandum to R. D. Jacobson listing your Web sources and a brief description of their services. Organize your Web source list in an attractively formatted and positioned table. Save, preview, and print the memo.

Project 5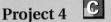

Create letter and an accompanying envelope to the president of WholeSale Food Distributors from M. D. Anderson, Sales Director, advising the president of the first quarter sales data for five products. Use an attractively formatted and positioned table to itemize the product sales for January, February, and March. Use fictitious data. Save, preview, and print the letter.

Project 6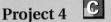

You have been asked to present a 15-minute brown bag luncheon presentation on mouse and keyboard selection techniques with Word tables.

Create a new document and use a table to organize your ideas for the presentation. Save, preview, and print the document. Then, with your instructor's permission, use the document to demonstrate the table selection techniques to a classmate.

Project 7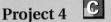

R. D. Jacobson assigns you to write a memorandum to all Sales and Marketing Department employees advising them how to save a Word document to the company FTP site on the Internet. Use the Ask A Question Box to research how to save a Word document to an FTP site. Create a memorandum that describes an FTP site and provides step-by-step instructions on how to save a document to an FTP site. Use a table to organize the steps. Save, preview, and print the document.

Project 8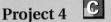

During lunch, Maria Betancourt tells you that the Tables and Borders toolbar is a great tool. You want to explore using it. Create a new, blank document and display the Tables and Borders toolbar by clicking the Tables and Borders button on the Standard toolbar. Use the What's This? Help pointer to review the buttons on the toolbar. Explore using each of the buttons. Create a new document with a table that lists each button and what it does. Save, preview, and print the document.

chapter ten

Using Templates and Wizards

Chapter Overview

Templates help reduce the time you need to format documents you create repeatedly, such as schedules, fax cover sheets, or reports. Word has several built-in templates you can use to create new documents or you can create a custom template. Additionally, Word has several step-by-step processes called wizards you can use to create special documents. This chapter shows you how to use built-in templates and wizards, as well as how to create and modify custom templates.

LEARNING OBJECTIVES

▶ **Create a document using a template**
▶ **Create a custom template**
▶ **Create a document using a wizard**

Case profile

The public affairs officer, Viktor Winkler, handles investor and customer inquiries from around the world. Winkler's assistant is out of the office for two weeks and you are chosen to be her replacement. Winkler asks you to prepare several documents using both templates and wizards.

chapter eleven

11.a Creating a Document Using a Template

Every document you create in Word is based on a template. A **template** is a master document or model that contains any text, formats, styles, and AutoText that you want to include in a particular kind of document. Templates enable you to prepare documents more quickly because they supply many of the settings that you would otherwise need to create—such as margins, tabs, alignment, and formatted nonvariable text. Each time you click the New Blank Document button on the Standard toolbar you create a new document based on the Normal template. Another example of a template is a letter template that contains the margin settings for a block-format letter, the date field, and a standard closing that includes the writer's signature area.

There are two types of templates: global templates and document templates. The Normal template is an example of a **global template**, which means its settings are available for all documents. **Document templates** supply settings that affect only the current document and help you format letters, faxes, memos, reports, manuals, brochures, newsletters, and special documents, such as Web pages. Word provides many built-in document templates and you can easily create your own.

notes It is assumed that the Word templates used in the activities and exercises in this chapter are already installed on your computer. See your instructor if the templates are not installed.

Viktor Winkler sends many faxes in response to customer and investor inquiries. He asks you to create a fax cover sheet. A quick way to do this is to base your new cover sheet document on one of the Word fax templates.

To create a fax cover sheet based on a template:

Step 1	*Click*	File
Step 2	*Click*	New to view the New Document task pane
Step 3	*Click*	the General Templates link in the New Document task pane
Step 4	*Click*	the Letters & Faxes tab

TASK PANE TIP

You can click the *Templates on Microsoft.com* link in the New Document task pane to download templates from the Microsoft Office Template Gallery. You can also click the Templates on my Web Sites link to access templates stored on a Web server.

QUICK TIP

To use settings from another template, you can load it as a global template and attach it to your document. For more information on using and attaching global templates, see online Help.

chapter eleven

The Templates dialog box on your screen should look similar to Figure 11-1.

FIGURE 11-1
Letters & Faxes Tab in the
Templates Dialog Box

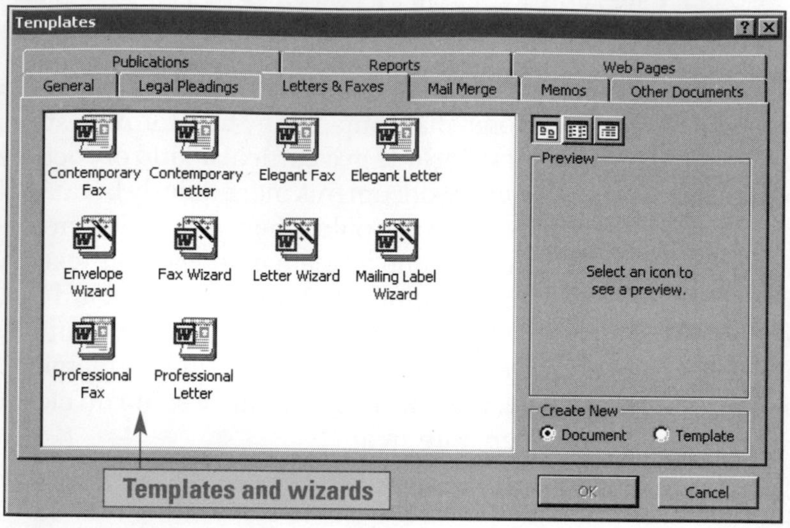

QUICK TIP

You can create a new document based on a template or a new custom template based on another template using the Templates dialog box. To create a new custom template based on an existing template, first click the template icon on which you wish to base the new custom template and then click the Template option button.

You can select several different letter or fax templates on the Letter & Faxes tab. You want to use the Contemporary Fax template.

Step 5	*Double-click*	the Contemporary Fax icon
Step 6	*Observe*	that a new document is created based on the Contemporary Fax template and Word switches to Print Layout view
Step 7	*Zoom*	the document to Page Width, if necessary

Your screen should look similar to Figure 11-2.

FIGURE 11-2
Document Based on the
Contemporary Fax
Template

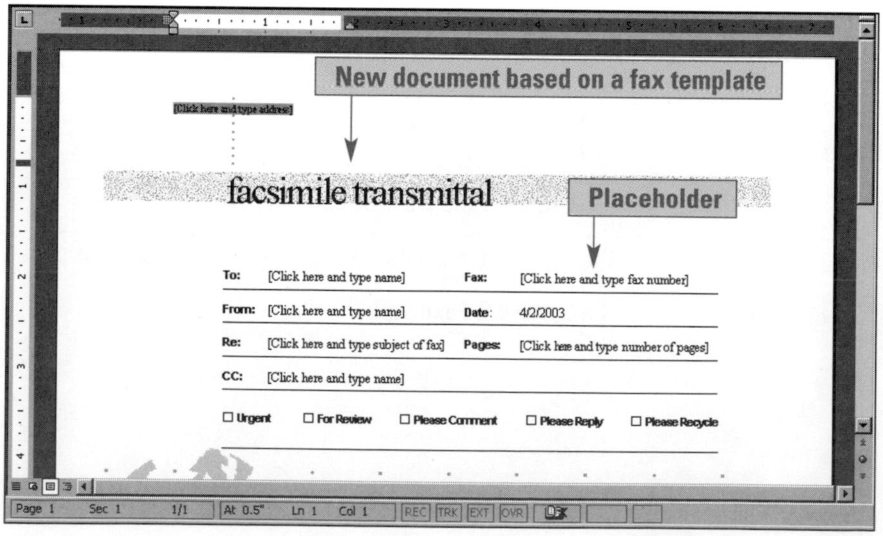

The document is preformatted with graphics, text boxes, heading text, lines, and placeholders. **Placeholders** are areas in which you key the variable information. All you need to do to complete the fax is to key the appropriate variable information in the [Click here and type…] placeholders. After you click a variable text placeholder to select it, you key the appropriate text. You can press the F11 key to move to the next placeholder. To key the company name and address and other variable text:

QUICK TIP

You can press the SHIFT + F11 keys to move back to a previous placeholder.

Step 1	*Observe*	that the current date already appears in the Date: placeholder because the date area contains a Date field
Step 2	*Click*	the address placeholder text box in the upper-left corner of the document
Step 3	*Key*	Worldwide Exotic Foods, Inc. Gage Building, Suite 1200 Riverside Plaza Chicago, IL 60606-2000
Step 4	*Press*	the F11 key to select the next placeholder
Step 5	*Key*	John Washington, Software Inc.
Step 6	*Press*	the F11 key
Step 7	*Key*	311-555-0098 in the Fax: placeholder
Step 8	*Press*	the F11 key
Step 9	*Key*	Viktor Winkler in the From: placeholder
Step 10	*Press*	the F11 key twice
Step 11	*Key*	Speaking Engagement in the Re: placeholder
Step 12	*Press*	the F11 key
Step 13	*Key*	2 in the Pages: placeholder
Step 14	*Press*	the F11 key
Step 15	*Press*	the Delete key to delete the CC: placeholder
Step 16	*Press*	the F11 key
Step 17	*Key*	X in the Urgent placeholder check box
Step 18	*Select*	the Notes: text below the check box placeholders (do not select the word and colon "Notes:")
Step 19	*Key*	I am happy to accept your invitation to speak at the Software Inc. executive committee luncheon tomorrow. Attached is a draft of my speech.
Step 20	*Save*	the document as *Washington Fax* and close it

chapter
eleven

During the day, Viktor Winkler asks you to create several fax cover sheets for him. It takes several minutes to create each cover sheet using the fax template. To save time, you decide to create a custom fax cover sheet template that already contains the company name, address, and Viktor Winkler's name.

11.b Creating a Custom Template

You can create your own templates by making changes to the current document and saving it as a template. You can also use one of the Word templates as a basis for your custom template.

You use the Contemporary Fax template as the basis for the Winkler fax template. To create a custom template:

Step 1	*Open*	the Letters & Faxes tab in the Templates dialog box
Step 2	*Click*	the Template option button to create a new template based on another template
Step 3	*Double-click*	the Contemporary Fax icon

A template document named Template1 – Fax Coversheet opens. You can replace the placeholders with text that never changes. To add text to the template:

Step 1	*Click*	the address placeholder text box in the upper-right corner of the document
Step 2	*Key*	Worldwide Exotic Foods, Inc. Gage Building, Suite 1200 Riverside Plaza Chicago, IL 60606-2000
Step 3	*Press*	the F11 key three times
Step 4	*Key*	Viktor Winkler
Step 5	*Delete*	the Notes: text (do not delete the word and colon "Notes:")

Next you customize the heading text at the top of the document.

| Step 6 | *Select* | the text "facsimile transmittal" near the top of the document |
| Step 7 | *Key* | Fax Cover Sheet |

Like a document, you need to save the changes you made to the template. To save the template:

Step 1	**Open**	the Save As dialog box
Step 2	**Observe**	that Save in: location defaults to the Templates folder
Step 3	**Observe**	that the file type is Document Template
Step 4	**Save**	the template as *Winkler Fax Template* and close it

The next time Viktor asks for a fax cover sheet, you can create one quickly based on the *Winkler Fax Template* template. To test the custom template:

Step 1	**Open**	the General tab in the Templates dialog box
Step 2	**Observe**	the new *Winkler Fax Template* template icon
Step 3	**Click**	the Document option button, if necessary
Step 4	**Double-click**	the *Winkler Fax Template* template icon
Step 5	**Create**	a one-page fax to Beryl Davis, 311-555-7890, for review with a note confirming receipt of the new brochure listing government offices in the Chicago area
Step 6	**Save**	the fax as *Davis Fax* and close it

When you no longer use a template, you can delete it by opening the Templates dialog box, right-clicking the template icon, and clicking Delete. Your fax assignments for Viktor are complete so you want to delete the template. To delete the *Winkler Fax Template* template:

Step 1	**Open**	the General tab in the Templates dialog box
Step 2	**Right-click**	the *Winkler Fax Template* icon
Step 3	**Click**	Delete
Step 4	**Click**	Yes to confirm the deletion, if necessary
Step 5	**Cancel**	the Templates dialog box

You can also modify the Normal template to change the default settings. Common defaults that users change are the font style, font size, and margin settings. Viktor Winkler uses the same margins and fonts for all public affairs correspondence. You can create a custom template

---

TASK PANE TIP

A link to the most recently used templates is added to the New from template section of the New Document task pane.

QUICK TIP

Another quick way to create a template is to use an existing document. Simply open the document, make any necessary changes or deletions, then save the document as a template by changing the file type to Document Template in the Save as type: list box in the Save As dialog box.

The nonvariable portion of a template is called **boilerplate text** or **fixed text**.

chapter
eleven

for Viktor Winkler's correspondence or you can modify the margins and font settings in the Normal template so that every document you create contains the preferred margin and font settings.

Changing the Normal Template

The Normal template contains default formats and settings that are appropriate for most common documents. If, like Viktor Winkler, you use a different font and margins in most documents you create, it would be easier to modify the Normal template rather than to manually change the font and margins for each new document. One way to change the Normal template settings is to open the Normal template, change the settings, and then save the template with the changes. The most common changes to the Normal template are to the font and font size and margin settings. These changes can be made to the Normal template from the Font and Page Setup dialog boxes.

To change the default font in the Normal template from Times New Roman 12 point to Arial 12 point, the top margin to 2 inches, and the left and right margins to 1 inch:

Step 1	*Create*	a new, blank document, if necessary
Step 2	*Open*	the Fo_n_t tab in the Font dialog box
Step 3	*Change*	the font to Arial
Step 4	*Click*	Default
Step 5	*Click*	Yes to confirm the font change to the Normal template
Step 6	*Open*	the Margins tab in the Page Setup dialog box
Step 7	*Change*	the top margin to 2 inches and the left and right margins to 1 inch
Step 8	*Click*	Default
Step 9	*Click*	Yes to confirm the font change to the Normal template

After you modify a template, you should test it to make sure the new settings appear correctly. You verify the changes to the Normal template.

Step 10	*Switch to*	Print Layout view, if necessary
Step 11	*Create*	a new, blank document
Step 12	*Observe*	the new margin settings and the new font

Step 13	*Repeat*	Steps 2 through 9 to return the font and margin settings to Times New Roman font, 1-inch top margin and 1.25-inch left and right margins
Step 14	*Close*	all open documents without saving changes

Another quick way to create special documents is to use a wizard.

11.c Creating a Document Using a Wizard

A **wizard** is a series of dialog boxes that take you through a step-by-step process to create a document. You can choose from several different Word wizards that help you create letters, legal documents, calendars, resumes, and other documents. Viktor Winkler asks you to create an attractive calendar for the month of December (current year) that he can put on the employees bulletin board. He suggests you use the Calendar Wizard to quickly do this. You select a document wizard in the Templates dialog box.

To create a calendar for the month of December:

Stop 1	*Open*	the Templates dialog box
Step 2	*Click*	the Other Documents tab
Step 3	*Click*	the Document option button, if necessary
Step 4	*Double-click*	the Calendar Wizard icon

The first wizard dialog box opens. As you work through the wizard steps, you can use the Next> button to go forward to the next step, the Back> button to go back to a previous step, the Cancel button to stop the wizard process, and the Finish button to complete the wizard process. You go to the next step.

Step 5	*Click*	the Next> button

The second wizard dialog box on your screen should look similar to Figure 11-3.

chapter
eleven

FIGURE 11-3
Second Calendar Wizard
Dialog Box

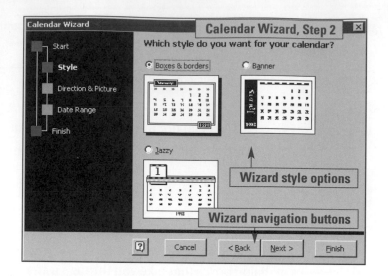

In this and subsequent dialog boxes, you select the options necessary to create a December calendar in landscape orientation.

Step 6	*Click*	the B<u>a</u>nner option button, if necessary
Step 7	*Click*	the <u>N</u>ext> button
Step 8	*Click*	the <u>L</u>andscape option button, if necessary
Step 9	*Click*	the N<u>o</u> option button, if necessary
Step 10	*Click*	the <u>N</u>ext> button
Step 11	*Click*	the Start: month list arrow
Step 12	*Click*	December
Step 13	*Click*	the Start: year spin box arrow to select the current year
Step 14	*Change*	the End: month and year to December and the current year
Step 15	*Click*	the <u>N</u>ext> button
Step 16	*Click*	the <u>F</u>inish button
Step 17	*Print Preview*	the calendar document
Step 18	*Save*	the calendar document as *December Calendar* and close it

Wizards and templates make it simple to create consistently formatted
documents quickly, letting you focus on the content of your documents.

Summary

▶ A template is a model document. The default model is the Normal template.

▶ You can modify the Normal template by opening it and making changes to it. Also, you can change the font, font size, and margin settings in the Normal template in the Font and Page Setup dialog boxes.

▶ Word has many letter, fax, Web page, and other templates you can use to create your own documents.

▶ You can create a custom template by example from other Word documents or by using a Word template as the basis for the new custom template.

▶ A wizard is a step-by-step series of dialog boxes you can use to create special documents, such as a fax cover sheet.

Commands Review

Action	Menu Bar	Shortcut Menu	Toolbar	Task Pane	Keyboard
Base a document on a Word template	File, New			Click the General Templates link in the New Document task pane	ALT + F, N
Create a template from a Word document	File, Save As (change the file type to Document Template)				ALT + F, A
Go to the next field in a document based on a Word template					F11
Go to the previous field in a document based on a Word template					SHIFT + F11
Base a document on a Word wizard	File, New			Click the General Templates link in the New Document task pane	ALT + F, N

Concepts Review

Circle the correct answer.

1. **You can access Word templates by clicking a link in the:**
   [a] Save As dialog box.
   [b] New Document task pane.
   [c] New Document dialog box.
   [d] New Template task pane.

2. **To move from placeholder to placeholder in a document based on a template, press the:**
   [a] F12 key.
   [b] F10 key.
   [c] F11 key.
   [d] F13 key.

chapter eleven

3. **The template that contains the default margin and formatting settings for a basic Word document is the:**
   [a] Fax template.
   [b] Document template.
   [c] Wizard template.
   [d] Normal template.

4. **A template is a:**
   [a] place to store documents.
   [b] tool to apply multiple formats at once.
   [c] model document.
   [d] step-by-step series of dialog boxes.

5. **A wizard is a:**
   [a] template.
   [b] way to apply multiple formats at one time.
   [c] task pane.
   [d] step-by-step process to create a document.

6. **Two basic types of templates are:**
   [a] global and fax.
   [b] fax and letter.
   [c] document and fax.
   [d] global and document.

7. **A template does not include:**
   [a] styles.
   [b] formatting.
   [c] text.
   [d] task panes.

8. **You can download additional templates from the Microsoft Office:**
   [a] Web Warehouse.
   [b] Style Gallery.
   [c] Template Gallery.
   [d] Internet Gallery.

Circle **T** if the statement is true or **F** if the statement is false.

T F 1. A global template's settings are available for all documents.

T F 2. Placeholders are areas in a document based on a template that cannot be used for text.

T F 3. You can change the margins and font in the Normal template just once.

T F 4. Each time you click the New Blank Document button on the Standard toolbar, you are creating a document based on the Contemporary Document template.

T F 5. Any Word document (.doc file extension) that is saved in the Microsoft Office\Templates folder can be used as a template.

T F 6. You can use buttons in each wizard dialog box to move forward to the next wizard step or back to the previous wizard step.

T F 7. When you no longer need a custom template, you can delete it from the Templates dialog box.

T F 8. You can create a custom template by saving a Word document with the Document Template file type or by basing the custom template on an existing template.

Skills Review

Exercise 1

1. Use the Resume Wizard located on the Other Documents tab in the Templates dialog box to create your own professional style resume. Select the wizard options you desire as you go through the wizard dialog boxes.

2. Save the document as *My Personal Resume*, and then preview, print, and close it.

Exercise 2 ⓒ

1. Use the Mailing Label Wizard on the Letters & Faxes tab in the Templates dialog box to create a page of the same Avery 5260-Address mailing labels for the following address.

Mr. James Daniels
President
Nevada Lumber
1177 Wickshire Street
Reno, NV 89501-4899

2. Save the document as *Daniels Mailing Labels*, and then preview, print, and close it.

Exercise 3 ⓒ

1. Use the Elegant Fax template on the Letters & Faxes tab in the Templates dialog box to create a fax cover sheet with the following information.

Company Name	*Worldwide Exotic Foods, Inc.*
To	*Becky Hardcastle*
From	*Yourself*
Company	*Hardcastle Specialties*
Date	*Current Date*
Fax #	*311-555-2345*
# of pages	*1*
Phone #	*311-555-2346*
Sender reference	*None*
Re:	*Order # 56A5678*
Your reference	*None*
Please reply	*X*
Notes/Comments	*The captioned order was shipped to your Denver warehouse on March 15. Please confirm receipt of the order.*
Return Address	*Gage Building, Suite 1200*
	Riverside Plaza
	Chicago, IL 60606-1200

2. Save the document as *Hardcastle Fax*, and then preview, print, and close it.

Exercise 4 ⓒ

1. Use the Calendar Wizard on the Other Documents tab in the Templates dialog box to create a March calendar for the current year in the Jazzy format and in Portrait orientation.

2. Save the document as *March Calendar*, and then preview, print, and close it.

Exercise 5 ⓒ

1. Use the Contemporary Memo template on the Memos tab in the Templates dialog box as the basis for a custom template.

2. Key "Ben Adams" in the CC: placeholder and your name in the From: placeholder.

3. Save the document with the Document Template file type in the location specified by your instructor with the filename *Custom Memo Template*.

4. Preview, print, and close the template.

chapter eleven

Exercise 6 [C]

1. Use the *Custom Memo Template* you created in Exercise 5 (if you have not created the template, do so now) to create a new memo. Use the following information in the memo.

To:	*Alex Cruz*
Re:	*Vacation*
Text	*Your vacation scheduled for May 5-10 is approved. Please see Marla about getting another staff member to cover your client calls while you are out.*

2. Save the memorandum as *Cruz Memo*, and then preview, print, and close it.

Exercise 7 [C]

1. Create a new fax cover sheet based on the Professional Fax template and insert the following information.

Return Address	*Gage Building, Suite 1200*
	Riverside Plaza
	Chicago, IL 60606-1200
Company Name	*Worldwide Exotic Foods, Inc.* (resize the cell to avoid word wrap)
To	*B. J. Chang*
From	*Bill Martin*
Fax #	*312-555-1345*
# of pages	*1*
Phone #	*312-555-1346*
Date	*Current Date*
Re:	*Sales Meeting*
CC:	*None*
Urgent	*X*
Comments	*I cannot attend the next sales meeting and I am sending Barbara Belville in my place. She will make the quarterly sales results presentation for me.*

2. Save the document as *Chang Fax*, and then preview, print, and close it.

Exercise 8 [C]

1. Open the *Marketing Memo* document located on the Data Disk.

2. Remove all the variable information such as the addressee, reference, and text information and replace the current date with the date field. (*Hint:* Insert the date as a field.)

3. Save the document with the Document Template file type as *Marketing Memo Template* in the location specified by your instructor, and then preview, print, and close the template.

4. Create a new memo document using the *Marketing Memo Template* and the fictitious data of your choice.

5. Save the new document as *Marketing Memo Document*, and then preview, print, and close it.

Case Projects SCANS

Project 1 [C]

Viktor Winkler's assistant, Bob Thackery, returns from vacation and is impressed with the documents you have created. He wants to know how to use the built-in templates and how to create custom templates.

Use the Ask A Question Box to research using built-in templates and creating custom templates. Write Bob an interoffice memorandum based on a memo template explaining how he can create documents with built-in and custom templates. Save, preview, and print the memo.

Project 2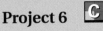

The Human Resources Department frequently receives unsolicited resumes from people around the world who want to work for Worldwide Exotic Foods. Company policy is to thank the sender for the resume and advise them that their resume will be kept on file for six months. If a position becomes available, the sender will be contacted to arrange for an interview. To save time in responding to unsolicited resumes, B. J. Chang asks you to create a block format custom letter template with B. J. Chang's signature line. The only variable data keyed in documents based on this new custom template is the letter address and the name portion of the salutation. The date, the "Dear" portion of the salutation, the body text, the closing, the signature line, and the typist's initials are fixed text in the template. Create, save, preview, and print the template. Then, create two letters, including attached envelopes to fictitious persons using the new custom letter template. Save, preview, and print the letters and envelopes.

Project 3

Viktor Winkler needs a list of government Web sites containing information of interest to Worldwide Exotic Foods, Inc. management and employees. Connect to the Internet, and search the Web for government Web pages of interest. Print at least five Web pages. Use a report template of your choice to create a report on the Web sites you found. Save, preview, and print the report.

Project 4

The chairman wants to nominate you to represent Worldwide Exotic Foods, Inc. at an international foods symposium next month in New York. He asks you to prepare an up-to-date resume to be submitted with the nomination. Use the resume template of your choice to create a professional-looking resume. Save, preview, and print the resume.

Project 5

Viktor Winkler wants to include current U.S. government international travel warnings in a bulletin he wants faxed to each branch office and posted in the employee lounge area to warn traveling employees. He asks you use the Internet to locate the government page where international warnings are posted and then print the page. Create a document using an appropriate template and list the travel warnings you printed out. Save, preview, and print the document.

Project 6

To save time in creating interoffice memos, Lydia Cruz asks you to create a human resources interoffice memorandum template. She wants you to use the Professional Memo template as the basis for the custom template but she does not want the page number at the bottom of the page. Create the custom memo template, making any other changes to styles, layout, and formatting you think appropriate. Save, preview, and print the document.

Project 7

Viktor Winkler is so impressed with your work with templates and the amount of time you have saved by using them. He asks you to go to the Microsoft Office Template Gallery Web site and check the kinds of Word templates available there. Use a Word template to create a document describing what you find at the Web site. With your instructor's permission, download two new templates and create a new document based on each template. Save, preview, and print the documents.

Project 8

Jody Haversham calls to ask for your help. She needs a list of expert information exchange Web sites to post in the employee cafeteria. Use the Internet to locate expert information exchange Web sites such as Ask.com. Then use an appropriate template to create a document listing at least four expert information Web sites. Save, preview, and print the document.

chapter eleven

Comparing and Merging Documents

Chapter Overview

It is common to edit documents and keep track of the changes made and to compare and combine different documents. In this chapter, you edit a document, track your editing changes, and then insert an internal document notation called a comment. Next you compare your edited document with a similar document and merge both documents into a new, third document. Finally, you preview the resulting document as a Web page and then save it as a Web page.

LEARNING OBJECTIVES

- ▶ Track changes to a document
- ▶ View and edit comments
- ▶ Compare and merge documents
- ▶ Convert documents into Web pages

Case profile

After your successful two weeks assisting Viktor Winkler, the Human Resources Department asks you to spend a few days updating a document to be saved as a Web page. Your first assignment is to edit an existing document in a way that your supervisor can review the original document and the changes you have made.

chapter twelve 12

12.a Tracking Changes to a Document

To make it easier to review changes to documents, you can use the Track Changes feature. The Track Changes feature enables a reviewer to suggest changes to a document by actually keying the changes into the document. Then the document with changes can be reviewed online or in printed hard copy. When the document is reviewed online the changes can be accepted or rejected either individually or all at once. When reviewing the tracked changes to a document online, the reviewer can choose to view all the changes at once, or limit the kind of changes that are displayed. For example, you might want to see only the additions and deletions first without viewing any formatting changes. Some of the tracked changes are displayed inline with the original text and others are displayed in the document margin in a balloon-style notation.

Setting the Track Changes Options

You can determine the formatting style for tracked changes by setting options in the Track Changes tab of the Options dialog box or in the Track Changes dialog box. Your supervisor asks you to make some revisions in the *About the Internet* document and track your changes. Before you edit the document, you need to review the Track Changes options. To review the Track Changes options:

Step 1	*Create*	a new, blank document, if necessary
Step 2	*Right-click*	the TRK mode indicator on the status bar
Step 3	*Click*	Options

You set the formatting for the type of mark and the color for inserted text and reformatted text in this dialog box. You also can turn on or off the use of the balloon-style notations and specify their size and position. If you are printing the balloons, you can specify the paper orientation. Finally, you can indicate which lines are changed by positioning a mark at the margin of the changed line. The Track Changes dialog box on your screen "remembers" the last setting changes.

You want any text you insert to be changed to red and any reformatted text to have a double underline. You also want the balloons in the right margin and the changed lines mark to be positioned at the left margin of the line. To set the Track Changes options:

| Step 1 | *Click* | Color only in the Insertions: list, if necessary |

chapter
twelve

Step 2	*Click*	Red in the Color: list, if necessary
Step 3	*Click*	Double underline in the Formatting: list, if necessary
Step 4	*Insert*	check marks in the Use balloons in Print and Web Layout and Show lines connecting to text check boxes, if necessary
Step 5	*Key*	2.5" in the Preferred width: text box, if necessary
Step 6	*Click*	Inches in the Measure in: list, if necessary
Step 7	*Click*	Preserve in the Paper orientation: list, if necessary
Step 8	*Click*	the Left border in the Mark: list, if necessary

The Track Changes dialog box on your screen should look similar to Figure 12-1.

FIGURE 12-1
Track Changes Dialog Box

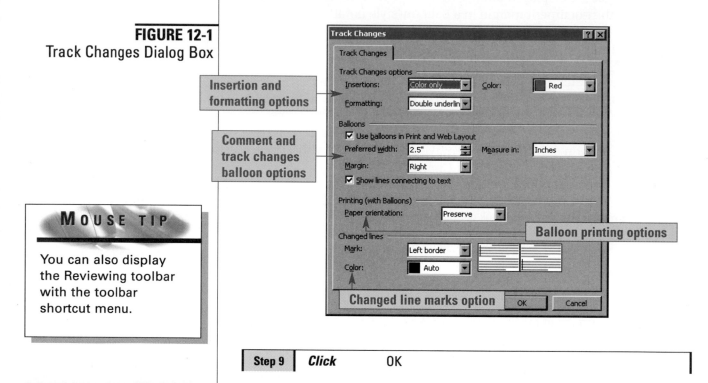

Step 9	*Click*	OK

Tracking Changes

You can use the Track Changes command on the Tools menu to display the Reviewing toolbar and turn on the Track Changes feature. You can also use the TRK mode indicator on the status bar to turn on or off the Track Changes feature and to turn on the Reviewing toolbar. You use buttons on the Reviewing toolbar to manage the Track Changes process.

You can preview a document with tracked changes in several ways: Final mode shows how the document would look with all the editing changes; Final Showing Markup mode shows deleted text in balloons and inline inserted text and all formatting changes applied; Original mode shows the original unedited document; and Original Showing Markup mode shows the original document with inline deleted text and inserted text and formatting changes in balloons. You use the Display for Review button on the Reviewing toolbar to select your reviewing option.

To turn on the Track Changes feature and begin modifying the document:

Step 1	*Open*	the *About the Internet* document located on the Data Disk
Step 2	*Double-click*	the TRK mode indicator on the status bar
Step 3	*Observe*	the bolded TRK mode indicator on the status bar and the Reviewing toolbar
Step 4	*Dock*	the Reviewing Toolbar below the Formatting toolbar, if necessary

When you are editing or reviewing a document with tracked changes, you should use the Final Showing Markup view. To change the reviewing display:

Step 1	*Click*	the Display for Review button list arrow
		[Final Showing Markup ▾] on the Reviewing toolbar
Step 2	*Click*	Final Showing Markup, if necessary

To edit the document:

Step 1	*Switch to*	Print Layout view, if necessary
Step 2	*View*	the nonprinting formatting marks, if necessary
Step 3	*Zoom*	the document to 75%
Step 4	*Delete*	the "Introduction to the Internet" paragraph heading
Step 5	*Bold*	the text "World Wide Web" in the first body paragraph
Step 6	*Replace*	the word "computer" in the last line of the first body paragraph with "multimedia"
Step 7	*Select*	all of the paragraph headings using the CTRL key
Step 8	*Change*	the formatting to Small caps effect
Step 9	*Move*	the insertion point to the top of the document
Step 10	*Observe*	the tracked changes, including the single vertical lines at the left margin that indicates changes

chapter
twelve

Your screen should look similar to Figure 12-2.

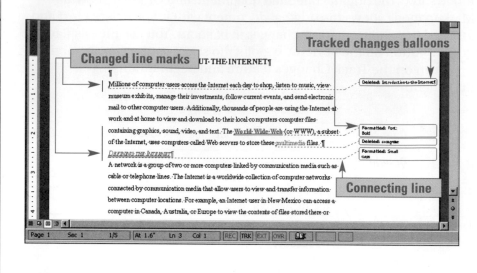

| Step 11 | *Save* | the document as *Internet With Tracked Changes* and leave it open |

Accepting or Rejecting Tracked Changes

You can accept or reject individual changes or all changes with the Accept Change and Reject Change/Delete Comment buttons on the Reviewing toolbar. You also can use a shortcut menu to accept or reject individual changes. Your supervisor reviews all your changes and approves them. To accept all the changes:

Step 1	*Click*	the Accept Change button list arrow [icon] on the Reviewing toolbar
Step 2	*Click*	Accept All Changes in Document
Step 3	*Double-click*	TRK mode indicator on the status bar to turn off the Track Changes feature
Step 4	*Turn off*	the view of formatting marks, if necessary
Step 5	*Save*	the document as *Internet With Accepted Changes* and leave it open

Your supervisor asks you to insert an internal document notation that can be viewed by others when they read the document online.

12.b Viewing and Editing Comments

A **comment** is an internal notation in a document. Comment text is displayed in a balloon, if the balloon feature is turned on. Otherwise, the comment text is keyed in the Reviewing Pane. Your supervisor wants you to add a comment to the document title reminding employees to call the Human Resources Department for a list of new training classes. To add the comment to the document:

Step 1	*Zoom*	the document to 100%, if necessary
Step 2	*Move*	the insertion point to the end of the title text "ABOUT THE INTERNET"
Step 3	*Click*	the New Comment button on the Reviewing toolbar
Step 4	*Scroll*	the document horizontally to view the Comment balloon containing the insertion point
Step 5	*Key*	Call the Human Resources Department for a list of new training classes.

Your screen should look similar to Figure 12-3.

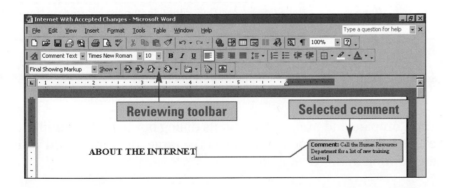

The insertion point remains in the Comment balloon. If you move the insertion point to another position in the document, you can move it back into the Comment balloon simply by clicking inside the balloon. You can select, edit, and format text or add and delete text in a Comment balloon just as you would in the body of a document.

After reading the comment you decide to edit the comment text to add the Human Resources Department telephone extension. To edit the comment text:

Step 1	*Insert*	the text "X299" between the words "Department" and "for" in the Comment balloon

MOUSE TIP

You can edit or delete a selected comment by clicking the New Comments button list arrow on the Reviewing toolbar. You also can delete an individual comment or all document comments by clicking the Reject Change/Delete Comment button on the Reviewing toolbar.

To view and edit a comment in Normal view, turn on the Reviewing Pane with the Reviewing Pane button on the Reviewing toolbar.

FIGURE 12-3
Comment Balloon and Text

MENU TIP

You can insert a comment by using the Comment command on the Insert menu. You can delete an individual comment by right-clicking the comment balloon and clicking Delete Comment.

chapter
twelve

| Step 2 | **Save** | the document as *Internet With Edited Comment* and close it |

Your supervisor wants you to merge your document with a similar document she created earlier.

12.c Comparing and Merging Documents

When merging two documents, Word compares the documents and then uses the Track Changes feature to illustrate the changes. Word identifies the document to be compared and merged as the **current document** (the document that is open) and the **target document** (the document you choose for comparison). During the comparison and merging process, you can choose one of three locations in which to merge the documents and display the document differences: into the current document; into the target document; or into a new, third document. You make the choice when you open the Compare and Merge Documents dialog box using the Compare and Merge Documents command on the <u>T</u>ools menu.

To compare and merge the documents:

Step 1	**Open**	the *Supervisors Document* document located on the Data Disk
Step 2	**Click**	<u>T</u>ools
Step 3	**Click**	Compare and Merge <u>D</u>ocuments

The Compare and Merge Documents dialog box, which is similar to the Open dialog box, opens. You select the target document and your merge option in this dialog box.

Step 4	**Switch to**	the disk drive and folder where your files are stored
Step 5	**Click**	the *Internet With Edited Comment* filename (do not double-click)
Step 6	**Click**	the <u>M</u>erge button list arrow to view the merge options
Step 7	**Click**	Merge into <u>n</u>ew document
Step 8	**Observe**	that a new, third document containing tracked changes opens
Step 9	**Scroll**	the document to review all the suggested changes

You review the tracked changes with your supervisor who suggests you reject the change from "multimedia" to "computer" and the title change, but accept all the remaining changes. To reject the "multimedia" deletion, the "computer" insertion, and the title change:

Step 1	*Right-click*	~~multimedia~~
Step 2	*Click*	Reject Deletion
Step 3	*Reject*	the "computer" insertion using the shortcut menu
Step 4	*Reject*	both title changes using the shortcut menu
Step 5	*Click*	the Accept Change button list arrow on the Reviewing toolbar
Step 6	*Click*	Accept All Changes in Document
Step 7	*Hide*	the Reviewing toolbar
Step 8	*Save*	the document as *Compared and Merged Internet* and leave it open
Step 9	*Close*	the *Supervisors Document* document without saving changes

Your supervisor wants you to save the document as a Web page so that other employees can view it via the company intranet.

notes It is assumed you have read Chapter 3 in the Office unit before starting this section. It is also assumed that you are using the Internet Explorer Web browser. If you are using a different browser, your instructor may modify the following activities.

12.d Converting Documents into Web Pages

You can quickly convert an existing Word document to a Web page to be later uploaded to a Web server and then viewed by others on a local intranet or on the Internet using a Web browser. You do this by simply saving the document as a Web page. Before you save a Word document as a Web page, it is a good idea to first preview it in your Web browser to see how it will look.

C

chapter twelve

To preview the *Compared and Merged Internet* document in a Web browser:

Step 1	*Click*	File
Step 2	*Click*	Web Page Preview
Step 3	*Observe*	that the Internet Explorer Web browser opens and contains the document
Step 4	*Maximize*	the Internet Explorer window, if necessary
Step 5	*Scroll*	to review the document
Step 6	*Move*	the mouse pointer to the Comment notation following the document title
Step 7	*Observe*	the ScreenTip containing the Comment text
Step 8	*Close*	the Internet Explorer window

The document is formatted for viewing as a Web page, so you can save it. To save the document as a Web page:

Step 1	*Click*	File
Step 2	*Click*	Save As Web Page

The Save As dialog box opens and the file type is changed to Web Page. Before you save the document you can create a descriptive page title that appears in the title bar of the Web browser when the page is viewed. To change the page title:

Step 1	*Click*	the Change Title button
Step 2	*Key*	About the Internet in the Page title: text box in the Set Page Title dialog box
Step 3	*Click*	OK
Step 4	*Save*	the Web page as *About the Internet Web Page* and close it

It's easy to compare and merge different documents, accept or reject the differences, and then preview and save the resulting document as a Web page.

Summary

▶ The Track Changes feature makes it easier to review document changes either online or in hard copy.

▶ Tracked changes are identified by different formatting or by balloon-style notations in the margin.

▶ You can change the formatting style of tracked changes in the Track Changes tab of the Options dialog box or in the Track Changes dialog box.

▶ You can turn on the Track Changes feature with a menu command, a button on the Reviewing toolbar, or the TRK mode indicator on the status bar.

▶ When reviewing a document that contains tracked changes, you can accept or reject changes with buttons on the Reviewing toolbar or with a shortcut menu.

▶ A comment is an internal document note that appears in a balloon-style notation.

▶ You can compare and merge two documents by merging the changes into the currently open document, the target document (the document being compared to), or a new, third document.

▶ When you compare and merge two documents, the differences are shown as tracked changes.

▶ You can preview a Word document as a Web page to see how it will look when viewed in a Web browser before saving it as a Web page.

▶ You can easily convert an existing Word document into a Web page by saving it as a Web page.

chapter twelve

Commands Review

Action	Menu Bar	Shortcut Menu	Toolbar	Task Pane	Keyboard
Set the Track Changes options	Tools, Options	Right-click the TRK mode indicator on the status bar, click Options	Click the Options command on Show list		ALT +T, O
Turn on the Track Changes feature	Tools, Track Changes	Right-click the TRK mode indicator on the status bar, click Track Changes	Double-click the TRK mode indicator on the status bar		ALT +T, T CTRL + SHIFT+ E
Select a tracked change			In Normal view: drag to select the changed text In Print Layout or Web Layout view: click or right-click the tracked change balloon		
Accept tracked change		Right-click change, click Accept (Insertion or Deletion or Formatting Change)			
Reject tracked change		Right-click change, click Reject (Insertion or Deletion or Formatting Change)			
Create a comment	Insert, Comment				ALT + I, M
View the Reviewing Pane (View and edit comments in Normal view)					
Edit a comment in Print Layout or Web Layout view			Click Edit Comment on the list		Key, delete, and edit comment text inside the balloon-style notation or in the Reviewing Pane
Delete a comment		Right-click the comment balloon and click Delete Comment	Click Delete Comment on the list		
Compare and Merge documents	Tools, Compare and Merge Documents				ALT +T, D
Preview an existing Word document as a Web page	File, Web Page Preview				ALT + F, B
Save an existing Word document as a Web page	File, Save as Web Page				ALT + F, G

Concepts Review

Circle the correct answer.

1. You can turn on or off the Track Changes feature by double-clicking the:
[a] Turn On/Off Track Changes button.
[b] TRK mode indicator.
[c] OVR mode indicator.
[d] Insert Track Changes button.

2. You can manage tracked changes and comments with buttons on the:
[a] Track Changes toolbar.
[b] Comments and Changes toolbar.
[c] Reviewing toolbar.
[d] Compare and Merge Documents toolbar.

3. You cannot see the track change balloon in:
[a] Print Layout view.
[b] Web Layout view.
[c] Print Preview.
[d] Normal view.

4. A comment is a(n):
[a] tracked change.
[b] internal document notation.
[c] formatting option.
[d] target document.

5. To edit comments in Normal view, you must:
[a] display the Reviewing Pane.
[b] click the comment balloon.

[c] turn on the Edit Comment feature in the Options dialog box.
[d] first compare the document to another document.

6. When comparing and merging two documents, Word illustrates the changes with the:
[a] Comment feature.
[b] Compare feature.
[c] Track Changes feature.
[d] Merge feature.

7. When comparing and merging two documents, the document you choose for comparison is called the:
[a] comparison document.
[d] original document.
[c] current document.
[d] target document.

8. Before you save an existing Word document as a Web page, it is a good idea to first:
[a] format the document.
[b] compare the document to another document.
[c] track changes to the document.
[d] preview the document as a Web page in your Web browser.

Circle **T** if the statement is true or **F** if the statement is false.

T F 1. You can view and change the options for formatting and displaying tracked changes in the Options or Track Changes dialog box.

T F 2. You can change the view of tracked changes with the Display for Review or Show buttons on the Track Changes toolbar.

T F 3. You can use a shortcut menu to delete a comment in Print Layout view.

T F 4. The Track Changes dialog box "remembers" its previous settings.

T F 5. To view tracked changes in Normal view, you can display the Reviewing Pane.

T F 6. When comparing and merging two documents, the document that is open is called the original document.

chapter twelve

T   F   7. You can merge two documents into a new, third document.

T   F   8. When you save a Word document as a Web page, Word creates a new folder containing special Web browser instructions associated with the Web page.

Skills Review

Exercise 1

1. Open the *Preparing For A Speech* document located on the Data Disk.

2. Preview the document as a Web page.

3. Scroll to review the document, and then close the Web browser.

4. Center the document title and apply Arial, bold formatting.

5. Using the CTRL key, select the paragraph headings "Overcoming Fear" and "Make Your Talk Interesting," and apply Arial, bold formatting.

6. Using the CTRL key, select all the paragraphs following the "Overcoming Fear" paragraph heading and all the paragraphs following the "Make Your Talk Interesting" paragraph heading.

7. Create bulleted lists from the selected paragraphs.

8. Select all the text below the document title and change the line spacing to 1.5 lines.

9. Preview the document as a Web page, review the new look and the improved readability, and close the Web browser.

10. Save the document as a Web page with the title "Speaking Tips" and the filename *Preparing For A Speech*, and then preview, print, and close it.

Exercise 2

1. Open the *Security Policy* document located on the Data Disk and view the document in Print Layout view.

2. Open the Track Changes dialog box using the TRK mode indicator on the status bar.

3. Change the insertion formatting option to Italic, Bright Green; change the balloon position to the Left margin; change the Paper orientation for printing with balloons to Force Landscape (to print in Landscape orientation without changing the document orientation); and view the changed line mark at the Right border.

4. Turn on the Track Changes feature and display the Reviewing toolbar using the TRK mode indicator on the status bar.

5. Change the Warning! line to bold, uppercase.

6. Delete the word "clearance" in the first line of the body paragraph; change the security level from "8" to "10"; and change "this level" in the second line to "this area."

7. Turn off the Track Changes feature.

8. Save the document as *Security Policy With Tracked Changes*, and then preview, print, and close it. (*Hint:* Click Yes if warned that the margins in section 1 are outside the printable area of the page.)

Exercise 3

1. Open the *Security Policy With Tracked Changes* document you created in Exercise 2. If you have not completed Exercise 2, do so now.

2. Switch to Print Layout view, if necessary, and hide the Reviewing toolbar.

3. Right-click the document title tracked change balloon and accept the change.

4. Use the shortcut menu method to accept the "clearance" deletion, the "level" deletion, and the "area" insertion.

5. Use the shortcut menu method to reject the "8" deletion and the "10" insertion.

6. Save the document as *Security Policy With Accepted Changes*, and then preview, print, and close it.

Exercise 4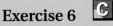

1. Open the *Vancouver Warehouse Report* document located on the Data Disk and switch to Print Layout view, if necessary.

2. Change the Track Changes options to view all insertions with Color only in Red; formatting changes with a single Underline; balloons at the Right margin; changed line marks at the Left border; and change the Printing (with Balloons) paper orientation option in the Track Changes dialog box to Force Landscape, if necessary.

3. Compare the current document to the *London Warehouse Report* target document located on the Data Disk and merge the changes into the current document.

4. Select Final using the Display for Review button on the Reviewing toolbar and review how the document would look if all changes were accepted then switch back to the Final Showing Markup display.

5. Reject all the formatting changes *except the numbered list change* with the shortcut menu.

6. Accept all the remaining changes with the Accept Change button on the Reviewing toolbar.

7. Save the document as *Vancouver Warehouse Report With Accepted Changes*, and then preview, print, and close it.

Exercise 5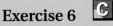

1. Open the *Winter Schedule* document located on the Data Disk.

2. Preview the document as a Web page.

3. Italicize the two lines beginning "Dates:" and set left-aligned tab stops for the two lines at 1.5, 3, and 4.5 inches on the horizontal ruler using the mouse pointer. (*Hint:* When changing the formatting for multiple areas of the document in the same way, don't forget to use the CTRL key to select the multiple areas.)

4. Select the document title and the three paragraph headings and apply Arial, bold formatting.

5. Change the document title font size to 14 point.

6. Preview the document as a Web page and observe the different formatting.

7. Save the document as a Web page with the title "Winter Schedule" and the filename *Winter Schedule Web Page*; print, and close it.

Exercise 6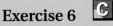

1. Open the *Automation Society* document located on the Data Disk.

2. Switch to Normal view and display the Reviewing toolbar, if necessary.

3. Change the Printing (with Balloons) paper orientation option in the Track Changes dialog box to Force Landscape, if necessary.

4. Insert a comment containing the following after the document title using the New Comment button on the Reviewing toolbar. (*Hint:* In Normal view, the Reviewing Pane opens when you insert the comment. Key the comment text in the Reviewing Pane at the position of the insertion point, then click the Reviewing Pane button on the Reviewing toolbar to close the Reviewing Pane.)

Jody, please review this document and give me a call at X367 if you have any questions or comments.

chapter twelve

5. Observe the red comment icon at the end of title text.

6. Save the document as *Automation Society With Comment*, and then preview and print it.

7. Switch to Print Layout view and observe the comment balloon.

8. Edit the comment to replace "Jody" with "Helen" and "X367" with "X450."

9. Save the document as *Automation Society With Edited Comment*, and then preview, print, and close it.

Exercise 7 C

1. Open the *Policy #152* document located on the Data Disk.

2. Compare the current document to the *Security Policy With Accepted Changes* document you created in Exercise 3 and merge the changes to a new, third document. If you have not completed Exercise 3, do so now.

3. Reject the title formatting change and accept all the remaining changes.

4. Save the document as *Compared And Merged Security Policy*, and then preview, print, and close it.

5. Close the *Policy #152* document.

Exercise 8 C

1. Open the *Compared And Merged Security Policy* document you created in Exercise 7. If you have not completed Exercise 7, do so now.

2. Preview the document as a Web page and then close the Web browser.

3. Make formatting changes you feel are appropriate to make the document more attractive or easier to read in the Web browser.

4. Save the document as a Web page with the title "Security Policy" and the filename *Security Policy Web Page*; and then print and close it.

Case Projects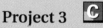

Project 1 C

One of the Purchasing Department employees has a new assignment that requires him to compare and then merge two documents. He asks for your help. Using the Ask A Question Box, search online Help for information on comparing and merging documents. Then create a document containing at least two paragraphs that describe the compare and merge process. Save, preview, and print the document.

Project 2 C

Your supervisor has asked you to make a short presentation on how to use the Track Changes feature at the next staff meeting. Use the Ask A Question Box to review online Help topics related to tracking changes. Then create an outline of the topics you plan to cover. Save, preview, and print the outline. With your instructor's permission, use your outline to demonstrate the Track Changes feature to two classmates.

Project 3 C

Kelly Armstead calls you for help. She has displayed the Reviewing toolbar and wants to know how to use each of the buttons. She is also curious about how to use the TRK mode indicator on the status bar. Using the What's This? Help tool and the Ask A Question Box, review the Reviewing toolbar and the TRK mode indicator online Help topics. Then write Kelly an interoffice memo containing a brief explanation of the toolbar buttons and mode indicator. Save, preview, and print the memo.

Project 4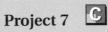

At next week's "brown bag" lunch and training session for the Purchasing Department clerical staff, the discussion topic is "Saving a Word Document as a Web Page" and you have been asked to make the presentation. Use the Ask A Question Box to locate information on your topic. Create an outline containing information for your presentation. Save, preview, and print the outline. With your instructor's permission, use the outline to describe the process of previewing and saving a Word document as a Web page to a group of classmates.

Project 5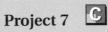

Marcia Davenport, in the Finance Department, needs to make changes to an existing document and then send the document to her supervisor for review online. Her supervisor wants to see both the original document and Marcia's changes and then be able to accept or reject the changes as he is reviewing the document online. Neither Marcia nor her supervisor knows where to start with this project, so she calls you. Create an interoffice memorandum to Marcia describing how to change the Track Changes options, how to turn on the Track Changes features, and how to accept or reject changes using both the toolbar and shortcut menu method while the document is being reviewed online. Save, preview, and print the memo.

Project 6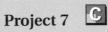

Your supervisor asks you to find out what different compare and merge software programs might be available. Using the Internet and the keywords "compare and merge" search for other software vendors that offer file compare and merge software. Print at least three Web pages. Create an interoffice memorandum to your supervisor describing three different compare and merge software applications including vendor name and URL, package features, and package prices. Save, preview, and print the memo and attach the three printed Web pages.

Project 7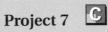

Chris Lofton calls and requests your help. Several of his new Word Processing Department employees are having problems using the comment, tracked changes, and compare and merge documents features. The most common problems include:

1. Word not tracking all the changes made to a document.
2. Problems rejecting changes made to a bullet list.
3. Comment text not appearing in a ScreenTip.
4. Merging changes into the wrong document.

Using online Help, troubleshoot problems working with comments, tracked changes, and comparing and merging documents. Then create an interoffice memorandum to Chris, which details each problem and its possible solution. Save, preview, and print the document.

Project 8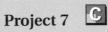

While attending the monthly meeting of the Administrative Assistants Group, you overhear two other attendees discussing Office "document libraries." You want to know more about document libraries, so you decide to check online Help. Using the Ask A Question Box, review the online Help topics related to document libraries. Then create a report-style document containing at least three paragraphs describing document libraries and how you might use them when working with Word documents. Save, preview, and print the document.

chapter twelve

Integrating Word with Other Office Applications

LEARNING OBJECTIVES

- ▶ Use Excel data in a Word document
- ▶ Share data with PowerPoint
- ▶ Use Access tables or queries in a Word document
- ▶ Create and modify charts using data from other applications

A very important feature of the Word application is the ability to integrate data with other Office applications. This means you can create documents with the application most suited to that information, such as analyzing and calculating numerical data in Excel, and then use that same information in other application documents. In this chapter, you learn to use Excel, PowerPoint, and Access data in Word documents.

Case profile

Marisa DaFranco, the executive assistant to the chairperson, asks for your help in preparing documents for the third quarter sales meeting. Working with Marisa, you combine information from Excel worksheets, PowerPoint slide show presentations, and Access database information with Word documents.

chapter thirteen

13.a Using Excel Data in a Word Document

The Excel application is designed to analyze and perform calculations on numerical data rather than prepare text documents. You enter data in Excel **workbooks** that contain **worksheets** consisting of columns and rows similar to Word tables. Then you use Excel special features, which are more flexible and comprehensive than Word table features, to analyze and format the numerical data. When you have a large set of numerical data that includes calculations, you should use an Excel worksheet instead of a Word table to take advantage of Excel's special features.

It is possible to enter, format, and calculate numerical data in an Excel worksheet and then integrate that data into a Word document in several ways. You can:

1. Insert an Excel file into a Word document.
2. Copy and paste Excel worksheet data or a chart into a Word document.
3. Embed Excel data or a chart in a Word document.
4. Link Excel data or a chart in a Word document.
5. Import Excel data into a Microsoft Graph Chart datasheet and place the chart object in a Word document.

When you **insert** an Excel file into a Word document, the data is placed in a Word table that must be edited with Word table features.

When you use the <u>C</u>opy and <u>P</u>aste commands, the data are pasted into a Word table. Neither option maintains a link to the original Excel data—that is, the Word document includes a copy of the data, but it does not maintain any connection to the Excel workbook. Any changes you make to the data in the Word document do *not* appear in the original Excel workbook. Use the insert or copy and paste option when you want to include Excel data in a Word document in a table format, and when you want to edit the data with Word editing features. Do not use these options if you want to edit the data with Excel editing features or if you want to edit the data in the original Excel workbook.

When you **embed** Excel data, you place a copy of the data in a Word document as an object that you can edit only with Excel menu commands and toolbar buttons. However, the embedded data maintains no link or connection with the original Excel workbook. Any changes you make to the data in the Word document do *not* appear in the original Excel workbook. Use the embed method when you want to include Excel data in a Word document and want to edit the data with the Excel features (instead of Word features) without affecting the original Excel data.

QUICK TIP

When sharing data between Excel and Word, Excel is usually the **source**, or originating application and Word is usually the **destination**, or target application. However, you can embed and link Word text into an Excel work-sheet. For example, you can paste Word text such as a date into the Excel formula bar; or, you can "paste link" a lengthy piece of text from a Word document into a worksheet cell or paste Word text into a text box on a worksheet.

chapter thirteen

When you **link** Excel worksheet data to a Word document, the data are displayed in the Word document but stored and edited in the Excel workbook. You must make any changes to the data in the original Excel workbook. When you open the Word document, the data is automatically updated to reflect the changes in the original Excel workbook. Use the link method when the Excel workbook data changes frequently.

notes The activities in this chapter assume you are familiar with the Excel, PowerPoint, and Access applications. Your instructor may provide additional information about these applications before you begin these activities.

Copying and Pasting Excel Data into a Word Document

To include Excel data in a Word document and then edit the data with Word editing features, you can copy the data from an Excel worksheet and then paste it into a Word document. You use this method to paste data from an Excel worksheet located in the *Worldwide Exotic Foods Sales Report* workbook into the *Worldwide Memo* document. To open the Excel and Word files:

Step 1	*Open*	the *Worldwide Memo* document located on the Data Disk
Step 2	*Move*	the insertion point to the end of the document
Step 3	*Open*	the Excel application and the *Worldwide Exotic Foods Sales Report* Excel workbook located on the Data Disk and maximize the Excel window, if necessary
Step 4	*Click*	the Sales Data sheet tab, if necessary

You want to use the data in the group of cells (called a **range**) that start in cell A1 and end in cell F10. To copy the worksheet data to the Office Clipboard:

Step 1	*Move*	the insertion point to cell A1 (the cell pointer becomes a large white plus pointer)
Step 2	*Drag*	down and to the right to cell F10 to select the range of cells A1:F10
Step 3	*Right-click*	the selected range of cells
Step 4	*Click*	Copy

The Excel data is stored on the Office Clipboard and the Clipboard task pane may appear. To switch to the Word application and paste the data into the *Worldwide Memo* document in Word's default table format:

Step 1	*Click*	the *Worldwide Memo* document button on the taskbar
Step 2	*Display*	the Clipboard task pane, if necessary
Step 3	*Click*	the Worldwide Exotic Foods, Inc. copied item in the Click an item to paste: list in the Clipboard task pane
Step 4	*Observe*	the Excel data pasted into the Word document

To reformat the table with Word's commands and features:

Step 1	*Turn on*	the gridlines, if necessary
Step 2	*Double-click*	the right boundary of the Branch, Meat, Cheese, Produce, Beverage, and Total columns in the table to AutoFit each column's width
Step 3	*Right-align*	the dollar values in the cells
Step 4	*Right-align*	the Meat, Cheese, Produce, Beverage, and Total column headings
Step 5	*Delete*	the blank row below the three table heading rows
Step 6	*Merge*	the three table heading rows
Step 7	*Center*	the table horizontally
Step 8	*Hide*	the gridlines
Step 9	*Click*	the Clear All button [Clear All] on the Clipboard task pane
Step 10	*Click*	the Close button [X] on the Clipboard task pane title bar
Step 11	*Move*	the insertion point to the end of the document, if necessary
Step 12	*Scroll*	to view the table, if necessary

Your screen should look similar to Figure 13-1.

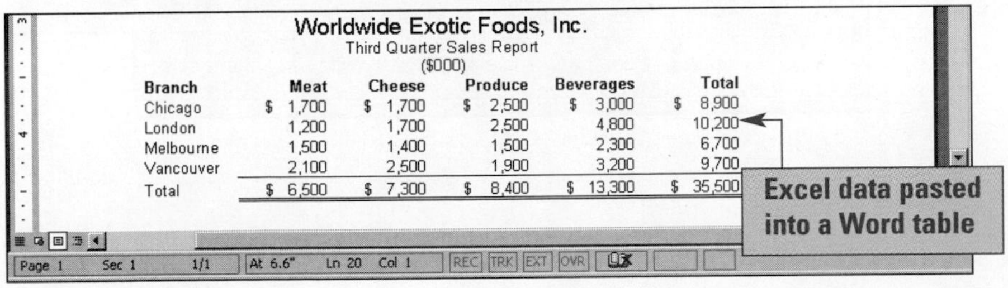

Worldwide Exotic Foods, Inc.					
Third Quarter Sales Report					
($000)					
Branch	Meat	Cheese	Produce	Beverages	Total
Chicago	$ 1,700	$ 1,700	$ 2,500	$ 3,000	$ 8,900
London	1,200	1,700	2,500	4,800	10,200
Melbourne	1,500	1,400	1,500	2,300	6,700
Vancouver	2,100	2,500	1,900	3,200	9,700
Total	$ 6,500	$ 7,300	$ 8,400	$ 13,300	$ 35,500

Excel data pasted into a Word table

Page 1   Sec 1   1/1   At 6.6"   Ln 20   Col 1   REC TRK EXT OVR

FIGURE 13-1
Excel Data Pasted into a Word Table

chapter thirteen

| Step 13 | *Save* | the document as *Worldwide Memo With Pasted Data* and close it (leave the Excel application and workbook open) |

Embedding Excel Worksheet Data in a Word Document

Sometimes you need to share data between Excel and Word but still want to edit the data with the Excel menus and toolbars. In this case, you insert the Excel worksheet data into the Word document as an embedded object. Embedding leaves the data in its original Excel format and you must edit it with Excel features.

You need to reopen the *Worldwide Memo* document and then copy and paste the Excel data into it as an embedded object using the Paste Special command. To create an embedded object:

Step 1	*Open*	the *Worldwide Memo* document located on the Data Disk
Step 2	*Move*	the insertion point to the end of the document
Step 3	*Switch to*	the Excel application and worksheet using the taskbar
Step 4	*Copy*	the selected range A1:F10
Step 5	*Switch to*	Word and the document using the taskbar
Step 6	*Click*	Edit
Step 7	*Click*	Paste Special

The Paste Special dialog box on your screen should look similar to Figure 13-2.

MENU TIP

You can embed Excel worksheet data in a Word document with the Object command on the Insert menu. You can also use the Copy and Paste Special commands on the Edit menu.

CAUTION TIP

Remember that simply pasting Excel data into a Word document places the data in a Word table. To create an embedded Excel object, use the Paste Special command not the Paste command, Clipboard task pane, or Paste button.

FIGURE 13-2
Paste Special Dialog Box

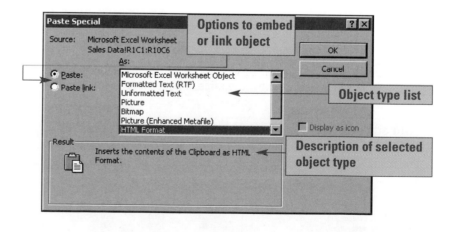

The eight data types allow you to embed or link the Excel worksheet data in the Clipboard as an Excel object, data in a table, pictures, or HTML format. You can click a data type in the As: list box and view its description in the Result box. The Display as icon option inserts an icon representing the worksheet data in the Word document. Double-clicking the icon in the destination document displays the worksheet data. To embed the worksheet data:

Step 1	*Click*	the Paste: option button, if necessary
Step 2	*Double-click*	Microsoft Excel Worksheet Object in the As: list box
Step 3	*Observe*	the embedded Excel object in the document
Step 4	*Click*	the embedded Excel object to select it
Step 5	*Observe*	the eight sizing handles on the object's border
Step 6	*Center*	the selected object horizontally using the Formatting toolbar
Step 7	*Deselect*	the object
Step 8	*Save*	the document as *Worldwide Memo With Embedded Data* and leave it open

You can edit an embedded worksheet object by double-clicking the object to view the Excel menu bar, toolbars, and worksheet grid. When you edit an embedded object, you are editing the data *only* in the Word document (although you use the Excel features). You are *not* editing the data in the original Excel source workbook.

You need to update the London meat expense in the worksheet object and then verify that no changes are made to the data in the Excel source file. To edit the embedded worksheet object:

Step 1	*Double-click*	the Excel embedded object to view the Excel features
Step 2	*Observe*	the Excel menu bar and toolbars and the data in an Excel worksheet grid
Step 3	*Observe*	that the title bar indicates you are still working in the Word application

To turn off the gridlines and edit the data in cell B7:

Step 1	*Click*	Tools
Step 2	*Click*	Options and click the View tab, if necessary

QUICK TIP

When you embed data or a chart from an Excel worksheet in a Word document, the entire workbook is embedded. When you activate the embedded Excel object for editing, you can view different worksheets by clicking the individual sheet tabs.

MENU TIP

You can edit a selected embedded Excel object by pointing to the Worksheet Object command on the Edit menu and clicking Edit. You can also right-click an embedded Excel object, point to Worksheet Object, and click Edit.

chapter thirteen

Step 3	Click	the Gridlines check box to remove the check mark
Step 4	Click	OK
Step 5	Click	cell B7 (column B and row 7) to make it the active cell
Step 6	Key	2500
Step 7	Press	the ENTER key
Step 8	Observe	the recalculated totals in cells F7, B10, and F10
Step 9	Click	anywhere in the document outside the embedded worksheet object to deselect it

The data in the worksheet object have changed. To verify that no changes have been made to the original Excel workbook:

Step 1	Switch to	the Excel application and workbook using the taskbar
Step 2	Observe	that the gridlines still appear and that the data in B7 and the totals in F7, B10, and F10 did not change
Step 3	Switch to	the Word application and document using the taskbar
Step 4	Save	the document and close it

Linking Excel Worksheet Data to a Word Document

When you link data between an Excel worksheet and a Word document, the Word destination file contains only a reference, or pointer, to the data—although the data are visible in the document. The data exist only in the Excel source file. When you edit linked data, you actually open the source application and file and do all your editing in the source file. When you change data in the source file, the data displayed in the destination file are updated.

You want to insert a linked Excel object in the *Worldwide Memo* document and then edit the original source worksheet to update the linked document. To begin:

Step 1	Open	the *Worldwide Memo* document located on the Data Disk
Step 2	Move	the insertion point to the end of the document
Step 3	Switch to	the Excel application and workbook using the taskbar
Step 4	Save	the workbook as *Sales Report 2*

Step 5	*Select*	the range A1:F10, if necessary
Step 6	*Copy*	the selected range
Step 7	*Switch to*	the Word application and document using the taskbar

To paste the Excel data as a linked object:

Step 1	*Open*	the Paste Special dialog box
Step 2	*Click*	the Paste link: option button
Step 3	*Double-click*	Microsoft Excel Worksheet Object in the As: list
Step 4	*Observe*	that a linked Excel worksheet object appears in the *Worldwide Memo* document
Step 5	*Center*	the object

By default, any changes you make to the source Excel worksheet are updated automatically in the Word document each time you open the document. However, you can require that the linked Excel object be updated manually. This allows you more control over whether or not to show the most current changes in the original Excel worksheet when you open the Word document. When you no longer want the Excel object to be linked to the original Excel workbook, you can break the link. If the original Excel workbook is moved to a new location, you can redirect the link. You make these changes in the Links dialog box.

You want to be able to control the updating process for the linked Excel object. To change the link status:

Step 1	*Right-click*	the linked Excel object
Step 2	*Point to*	Linked Worksheet Object
Step 3	*Click*	Links to open the Links dialog box

Except for the location of the Excel workbook file, the Links dialog box on your screen should look similar to Figure 13-3.

chapter thirteen

FIGURE 13-3
Links Dialog Box

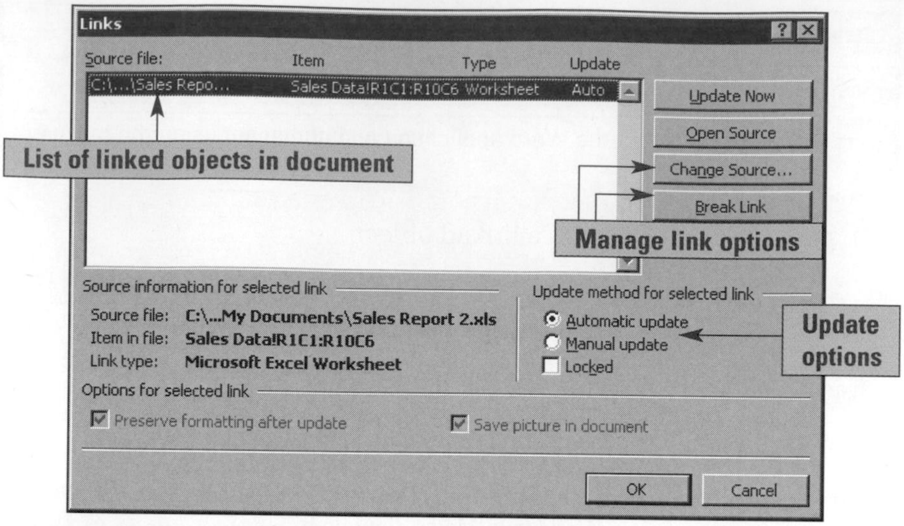

MENU TIP

You can manage the Excel links in a Word document by selecting the linked object, clicking the Edit command, pointing to Linked Worksheet Object, and then clicking the desired subcommand.

Step 4	***Click***	the Manual update option button
Step 5	***Click***	OK
Step 6	***Save***	the document as *Worldwide Memo With Linked Data* and close it

MOUSE TIP

You can open the Excel application and source workbook file by double-clicking a linked Excel object.

The Excel object in the *Worldwide Memo With Linked Data* is a reference to the *Sales Report 2* Excel source workbook file. The data does not exist in Word document and cannot be edited in the Word document.

Marisa asks you to change the Vancouver branch produce sales to $2,500 in the *Sales Report 2* Excel workbook and then update the *Worldwide Memo With Linked Data* document. To edit the Excel workbook:

Step 1	***Switch to***	the Excel application and workbook using the taskbar
Step 2	***Click***	cell D9 to make it the active cell
Step 3	***Key***	2500
Step 4	***Press***	the ENTER key to enter the data in the cell
Step 5	***Save***	the workbook and close the Excel application and the workbook
Step 6	***Open***	the *Worldwide Memo With Linked Data* document
Step 7	***Right-click***	the linked Excel object
Step 8	***Click***	Update Link
Step 9	***Observe***	that the value for Vancouver's produce is updated to $2,500

Step 10	*Deselect*	the linked Excel object
Step 11	*Save*	the document as *Worldwide Memo With Edited Linked Data* and close it

In addition to using Excel data in Word, you can share data between PowerPoint and Word.

13.b Sharing Data with PowerPoint

The PowerPoint application provides tools for creating slides and audience handout materials for presentations. You can integrate a PowerPoint presentation with Word in several ways. You can copy and paste PowerPoint information into Word documents, or you can embed or link PowerPoint slides into a Word document just as you can with Excel worksheet data or charts. You can send PowerPoint items, such as slides, notes pages, or an outline to Word to be edited or printed. In addition, you can create a PowerPoint presentation from a Word outline.

Creating a PowerPoint Presentation from a Word Outline

You can create a Word outline using outline level headings and then send that outline to PowerPoint to create slides. When you send a Word outline to PowerPoint, the Level 1 heading formatted text creates a new Text slide containing a bulleted list. The remaining lower-level headings create the individual bulleted text items on the slide.

You can create an outline in Outline view by selecting text and then applying an outline level heading to the text or by using toolbar buttons to demote or promote selected text to different outline levels. To open a Word document and view it in Outline view:

Step 1	*Open*	the *Worldwide Outline* document located on the Data Disk
Step 2	*Click*	the Outline View button  to switch to Outline view
Step 3	*Observe*	that the Outlining toolbar opens
Step 4	*Dock*	the Outlining toolbar below the Formatting toolbar, if necessary

Your screen should look similar to Figure 13-4.

chapter
thirteen

FIGURE 13-4
Document in Outline View

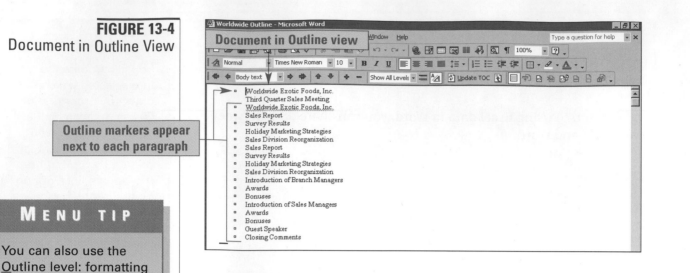

Outline markers appear next to each paragraph

There are 18 short paragraphs in the document. Paragraphs 1–2, 7–11, 14, and 17–18 will be used to create new slides. Paragraphs 3–6, 12–13, and 15–16 will be used to create bulleted list text. To apply the outline level headings to the text:

Step 1	*Select*	paragraphs 1–2, 7–11, 14, and 17–18 using the CTRL key
Step 2	*Click*	the Outline Level button list arrow [Level 1 ▼] on the Outlining toolbar
Step 3	*Click*	Level 1
Step 4	*Select*	paragraphs 3–6, 12–13, and 15–16, using the CTRL key
Step 5	*Click*	the Outline Level button list arrow [Level 1 ▼]
Step 6	*Click*	Level 2
Step 7	*Deselect*	the text

Now that the Word document is properly formatted with outline level headings, you are ready to create a PowerPoint presentation by sending the Word document to PowerPoint. To send the Word document to PowerPoint:

Step 1	*Click*	File
Step 2	*Point to*	Send to
Step 3	*Click*	Microsoft PowerPoint
Step 4	*Observe*	that the PowerPoint application opens in Normal view and contains Text slides based on the Word outline

Your screen should look similar to Figure 13-5.

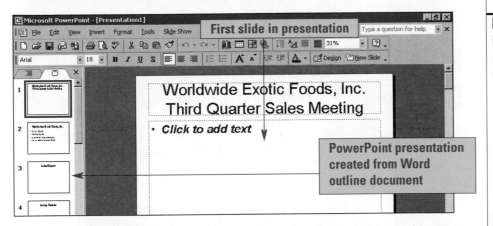

PowerPoint creates a new bulleted list text slide for each topic formatted with the Level 1 outline heading and a bulleted list detail item for text formatted with the Level 2 outline heading. You edit text on a PowerPoint slide just like you edit text in Word. You can change the general format of a slide, called the slide layout, if necessary. The general format or layout of the first slide should be a Title Slide. To convert the first text slide to a Title Slide, you open the Slide Layout task pane and then click the Title Slide layout format. You work with task panes in PowerPoint in the same way you work with them in Word.

To change the slide layout:

Step 1	*Click*	F<u>o</u>rmat
Step 2	*Click*	Slide <u>L</u>ayout
Step 3	*Click*	the Title Slide layout (first layout, first row) in the Text Layouts group in the Apply slide layout: section of the Slide Layout task pane
Step 4	*Observe*	the change to the layout of the text on the slide
Step 5	*Close*	the Slide Layout task pane
Step 6	*Click*	the Next Slide button ⬇ below the vertical scroll bar
Step 7	*Observe*	that the second slide is in the Text slide layout and has title text (the Word Level 1 text) and four bullet items (the Word Level 2 text that immediately follows the Level 1 text)
Step 8	*Review*	the remaining slides using the Next Slide button ⬇
Step 9	*Scroll*	the vertical scroll bar to view the first slide

M E N U   T I P

You can also bring a Word outline into PowerPoint by clicking the <u>O</u>pen command on the PowerPoint <u>F</u>ile menu (or the Open button on the Standard toolbar), and then changing the Files of type: list to All Outlines. Switch to the appropriate disk drive and folder and open the Word outline. For more information, see PowerPoint online Help.

**chapter
thirteen**

QUICK TIP

You can link or embed individual slides or an entire presentation to a Word document with options in the Object dialog box. To embed or link a single slide from a PowerPoint presentation into a Word document, select the slide icon in PowerPoint Normal or Slide Sorter view, use the Copy and Paste Special commands, and then Paste or Paste Link the slide object.

To make the slides more attractive, you can use PowerPoint features to format the text, add a color-coordinated design theme to the slides, insert graphic images, and so forth. For now, you save the presentation.

Step 10	*Save*	the presentation as *Worldwide Sales Meeting* and leave the presentation open
Step 11	*Close*	the *Worldwide Outline* document without saving any changes

Sending a PowerPoint Presentation to Word

Another way to integrate a PowerPoint presentation with Word is to send part of a presentation to Word. Marisa wants a copy of the *Worldwide Sales Meeting* presentation in a format suitable for manually adding notations about how to format and enhance the presentation. She asks you to send the *Worldwide Sales Meeting* presentation to Word to create the document she needs. To send the *Worldwide Sales Meeting* presentation to Word:

Step 1	*Switch to*	the PowerPoint application and presentation using the taskbar
Step 2	*Click*	File
Step 3	*Point to*	Send To
Step 4	*Click*	Microsoft Word

The Send To Microsoft Word dialog box on your screen should look similar to Figure 13-6.

FIGURE 13-6
Send To Microsoft Word
Dialog Box

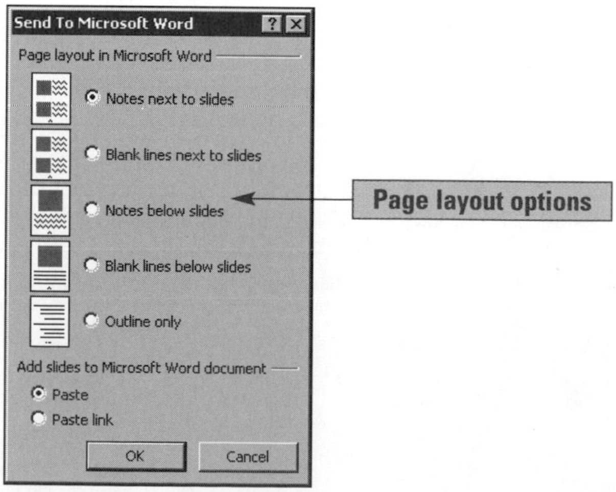

This dialog box has options for the Word document format as well as for whether to embed or link the slides to the Word document. You select the Blank lines next to slides format and embed the slides.

Step 5	*Click*	the Blank lines next to slides option button
Step 6	*Click*	the Paste option button, if necessary
Step 7	*Click*	OK

In a few seconds, the application creates a Word document that contains a large table. Each row is used to display an individual slide. The first column contains the slide number, the second column contains the embedded slide object, and the third column contains the blank lines.

Step 8	*Switch to*	Print Layout view and zoom the document to Whole Page
Step 9	*Observe*	that the embedded slide objects are inserted into a table
Step 10	*Zoom*	to 100% view and switch to Normal view
Step 11	*Save*	the document as *Worldwide Sales Meeting Notes* and close it
Step 12	*Close*	the PowerPoint application and presentation

You also can integrate data stored in an Access table or query with a Word document.

13.c Using Access Tables or Queries in a Word Document

Data in an Access database is maintained in **Access tables**. An **Access query** is a subset of an Access table that meets specific criteria. For example, an Access table may include data for all sales representatives and an Access query created from that table may include only the sales representatives from a specific division. Data from an Access table or query can be inserted into a Word document. You also can use an Access database table or query as the data source in the mail merge process or import a Word document converted to a text file into the Access application.

chapter thirteen

Inserting an Access Query into a Word Document

Worldwide Exotic Foods, Inc. maintains information about its branch office vice presidents and sales managers in an Access database. You want to add a list of the vice presidents to an interoffice memorandum created by Marisa. To open the memorandum:

| Step 1 | *Open* | the *Confidential Memo* document located on the Data Disk |
| Step 2 | *Move* | the insertion point to the end of the document |

Next you need to get the data from the Access database. To insert an Access query:

| Step 1 | *Display* | the Database toolbar using the toolbar shortcut menu and dock it below the Formatting toolbar, if necessary |
| Step 2 | *Click* | the Insert Database button  on the Database toolbar |

The Database dialog box on your screen should look similar to Figure 13-7.

FIGURE 13-7
Database Dialog Box

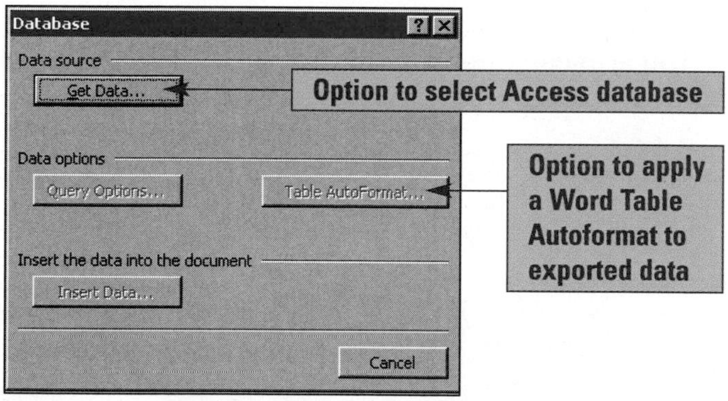

Database

Data source
Get Data... — **Option to select Access database**

Data options
Query Options...   Table AutoFormat... — **Option to apply a Word Table Autoformat to exported data**

Insert the data into the document
Insert Data...

Cancel

You insert the Vice President query data in the *Worldwide Sales* database located on the Data Disk.

| Step 3 | *Click* | the <u>G</u>et Data button |

The Select Data Source dialog box, which is very similar to the Open dialog box, opens.

Step 4	*Switch to*	the Data Disk
Step 5	*Click*	Access Databases in the Files of type: list
Step 6	*Double-click*	*Worldwide Sales*
Step 7	*Double-click*	Vice President Query in the Select Table dialog box

The Access table data will be inserted into the Word document as a Word table. You can either format the table after it is inserted, using table formatting features, or apply a Table AutoFormat now. To apply a Table AutoFormat and insert the data:

Step 1	*Click*	the Table AutoFormat button
Step 2	*Double-click*	Colorful 2 in the Formats: list box
Step 3	*Click*	the Insert Data button in the Database dialog box

The Insert Data dialog box opens from which you select which data records to insert.

Step 4	*Click*	the All option button, if necessary
Step 5	*Click*	OK in the Insert Data dialog box to insert all the records
Step 6	*Observe*	that the Access query data appear in your document as a formatted Word table
Step 7	*AutoFit*	the table to the window using the table shortcut menu
Step 8	*Save*	the document as *Confidential Memo With Vice President Data* and close it
Step 9	*Hide*	the Database toolbar

Exporting Access Data to Word

You can also send (or **export**) an Access table or query to Word for formatting or to use as a data source in a Word mail merge. When you export Access table or query data to a Word document, Access creates a Rich Text Format (.rtf) file (a text file containing the formatting) and stores the file in the default document folder specified in the File Locations tab in the Options dialog box or in the folder that is open when the data is exported.

**chapter
thirteen**

The *Worldwide Sales* database includes information on sales managers that you want to send to a Word document. To specify the destination folder, open the database, and send the query data to Word:

Step 1	*Open*	the Access application and the *Worldwide Sales* database located on the Data Disk
Step 2	*Click*	Queries in the Objects bar, if necessary
Step 3	*Select*	the Sales Managers Query, if necessary
Step 4	*Click*	the OfficeLinks button list arrow [icon] on the Access Database toolbar
Step 5	*Click*	Publish It with Microsoft Word

In a few seconds, the Sales Managers Query data is sent to Word as a Rich Text Format file named *Sales Managers Query*. (The file is stored in the last opened folder or the default documents folder.)

Step 6	*View*	the new *Sales Managers Query* document using the taskbar, if necessary
Step 7	*Center*	the table horizontally
Step 8	*Save*	the document as *Worldwide Sales Managers* as a Word document type and close it
Step 9	*Close*	the Access application and database
Step 10	*Delete*	the *Sales Managers Query* (.rtf) document from the default documents folder or the folder that was open when the data was exported

Access and Excel also can supply the data when you create charts in Word.

C 13.d Creating and Modifying Charts Using Data from Other Applications

You can use data from Excel or Access to create charts in Word. To do this, you can import Excel data into the Microsoft Graph datasheet or export Access to Word and use the resulting table to create a chart. Marisa wants you to create a document that shows a chart of the third quarter pastries sales. You import the data from an Excel worksheet into the Microsoft Graph datasheet and create a chart based on the imported data.

To create a new document and create a chart:

Step 1	*Create*	a new, blank document
Step 2	*Key*	Pastries Sales
Step 3	*Format*	the text as 14-point, bold, Times New Roman, center-aligned
Step 4	*Press*	the ENTER key twice
Step 5	*Click*	Insert
Step 6	*Click*	Object
Step 7	*Click*	the Create New tab
Step 8	*Double-click*	Microsoft Graph Chart in the Object type: list

The datasheet opens and contains sample data. You replace the sample data with the imported data. To import the data from the Excel worksheet:

Step 1	*Click*	the Import File button 📇 on the Standard toolbar

The Import File dialog box, which is quite similar to the Open dialog box, opens.

Step 2	*Switch to*	the Data Disk
Step 3	*Double-click*	the *Quarterly Pastries Sales* Excel workbook filename on the Data Disk

The Import Data Options dialog box on your screen should look similar to Figure 13-8.

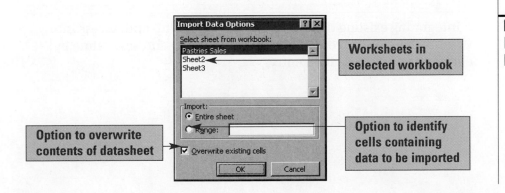

Worksheets in selected workbook

Option to overwrite contents of datasheet

Option to identify cells containing data to be imported

FIGURE 13-8
Import Data Options
Dialog Box

chapter thirteen

You specify the worksheet and data range to import in this dialog box. The data you want to import begins in cell A5 (column A, row 5) and ends in cell D9 (column D, row 9) in the Pastries Sales worksheet in the workbook. The group of cells beginning in A5 and ending in D9 is called a range and is written as A5:D9.

Step 4	*Click*	Pastries Sales in the Select sheet from workbook: list, if necessary
Step 5	*Click*	the Range option button
Step 6	*Key*	A5:D9 in the Range: text box
Step 7	*Click*	the Overwrite existing cells check box to insert a check mark, if necessary
Step 8	*Click*	OK
Step 9	*Observe*	that the pastries sales data replaces the sample data in the datasheet
Step 10	*Click*	the View Datasheet button 🖩 to hide the datasheet
Step 11	*Deselect*	the chart object and return to the document

You can format the chart object by double-clicking it to activate the Microsoft Graph application and then selecting individual chart objects for formatting. For this document, however, all that's left to do is to finish sizing it so that all the Category (X) labels are visible. To resize the chart object:

Step 1	*Select*	the chart object, if necessary
Step 2	*Drag*	the middle-right sizing handle to the right until three months (July, August, September) appear in the Category (X) axis
Step 3	*Deselect*	the chart object
Step 4	*Save*	the document as *Pastries Sales With Chart* and close it

Integrating existing data from Excel, PowerPoint, and Access into Word documents increases document flexibility and saves time by eliminating duplicate data entry.

QUICK TIP

You can copy an existing Excel chart in an Excel workbook and then embed or link the chart in a Word document by using the Paste Special command.

Summary

▶ You can insert an Excel worksheet into a Word document as a Word table and you can copy and paste Excel data into a Word document as a Word table.

▶ Embedding data in a Word document inserts a copy of the data in its original source format and the data must be edited with the source application features.

▶ Linking data in a Word document places a reference or pointer in the Word document, but the data continue to reside in the source application and must be edited in the source application.

▶ A PowerPoint presentation can be based on an imported Word outline created with outline level headings.

▶ You can send a PowerPoint presentation to Word to create notes or handout materials.

▶ Data from a database application, such as Access, can be inserted into a Word document as a Word table.

▶ You can open an Access database and publish a selected table or query to a Rich Text Format document.

▶ You can import Excel data into the Microsoft Graph datasheet to create a chart in Word.

Commands Review

Action	Menu Bar	Shortcut Menu	Toolbar	Task Pane	Keyboard
Insert Excel worksheet data as a Word table	Edit, Copy Edit, Paste Insert, File	Right-click selected worksheet range, click Copy Right-click at insertion point, click Paste	🖻 🖺	Use the Clipboard task pane features to paste copied Excel data into a Word document Use the Paste Options features to set the formatting for a pasted object	ALT + E, C ALT + E, P ALT + I, L CTRL + C CTRL + V
Create hyperlinks between Word and Office documents	Insert, Hyperlink				ALT + I, I CTRL + K
Embed Excel worksheet data into a Word document	Insert, Object Edit, Copy Edit, Paste Special, Paste				ALT + I, O ALT + E, C ALT + E, S, P
Link Excel worksheet data to a Word document	Edit, Paste Special, Paste Link	Right-drag and click Link Excel object here			ALT + E, S, L
Manage links to Excel linked object in a Word document	Edit, Linked Worksheet Object	Right-click object, point to Linked Worksheet Object			ALT + E, O
Manually update a selected linked Excel object	Edit, Update	Right-click object, click Update Link			ALT + E, D F9

chapter thirteen

Commands Review

Action	Menu Bar	Shortcut Menu	Toolbar	Task Pane	Keyboard
Create a blank embedded Excel object	Insert, Object				ALT + I, O
Apply outline level heading formatting to selected text	Format, Paragraph				ALT + O, P
Create a PowerPoint presentation from a Word outline	File, Send To, Microsoft PowerPoint				ALT + F, D, P
Import a Word outline to create a PowerPoint slide show	From PowerPoint: File, Open, All Outlines				ALT + F, O, O
Link a PowerPoint presentation to a Word document	Edit, Copy Edit, Paste Special				ALT + E, C ALT + E, S
Send a PowerPoint presentation to Word	From PowerPoint: File, Send To, Microsoft Word				ALT + F, D, W
Import an Access table or query into a Word document					
Send an Access table or query to Word	From Access: File, Save As/Export				ALT + F, A

Concepts Review

SCANS

Circle the correct answer.

1. **You can link Excel worksheet data to a Word document with the:**
   [a] Copy and Paste buttons on the Standard toolbar.
   [b] Copy and Paste Special commands.
   [c] Link button on the Standard toolbar.
   [d] Link command on the Edit menu.

2. **When you insert an Excel file into a Word document, the data are:**
   [a] linked.
   [b] embedded.
   [c] hyperlinked.
   [d] placed in a Word table.

3. **To edit data in an embedded Excel worksheet object in a Word document, you use the:**
   [a] Excel menu bar and toolbars in Word.
   [b] Excel menu bar and toolbars in Excel.
   [c] Word menu bar and toolbars in Word.
   [d] Word menu bar and toolbars in Excel.

4. **When you link data maintained in another Office application to Word, the Word document:**
   [a] cannot be edited.
   [b] contains a copy of the actual data.
   [c] contains a hyperlink.
   [d] contains a reference to the original source document and application.

5. **You can use the drag-and-drop method to embed Excel worksheet data in a Word document by:**
   [a] dragging Excel data to the Word button on the taskbar while pressing the CTRL key.
   [b] displaying both applications side-by-side and dragging Excel data into the Word application window while pressing the ALT key.
   [c] dragging Excel data to the Word button on the taskbar while pressing the SHIFT key.
   [d] dragging Excel data to the Word button on the taskbar while pressing the SPACEBAR.

6. **When you want to insert a blank embedded Excel object in a Word document, you can click the:**
   [a] Object command on the Insert menu.
   [b] Create Worksheet button on the Formatting toolbar.
   [c] Import Excel command on the File menu.
   [d] Office Links button on the Word Standard toolbar.

7. **When you create a PowerPoint presentation from a Word outline, the Word outline must be:**
   [a] linked to a PowerPoint presentation.

   [b] formatted with outline level formats.
   [c] copied to PowerPoint first.
   [d] sent to PowerPoint with the Send Word command on the File menu.

8. **If you use the Paste command to place Excel data in a Word document, you create a(n):**
   [a] Word table.
   [b] embedded Excel object.
   [c] linked Excel object.
   [d] hyperlink.

Circle **T** if the statement is true or **F** if the statement is false.

T   F   1. When you link an Excel worksheet object to a Word document, the data must be edited in the Word application with Excel features.

T   F   2. If you want to modify the data only in the Word document using the source application's tools, you should embed the data.

T   F   3. When you paste Excel data into a Word document, the data is placed in a Word table.

T   F   4. To have data in the destination application automatically reflect changes made in the source application, you should embed the data.

T   F   5. You can send a PowerPoint presentation to Word to create speaker notes and handout materials.

T   F   6. When you embed data, any changes you make to the original data are reflected in the embedded object.

T   F   7. An Access query is a subset of an Access table.

T   F   8. You can import Access data into a Microsoft Graph datasheet.

Skills Review

Exercise 1   **C**

1. Open the *Vancouver Sales Memo* document located on the Data Disk.

2. Open the Excel application and the *Vancouver Branch Sales* workbook located on the Data Disk.

3. Copy the Sales Report data in the range A1:F10 and paste the data into a Word table below the body paragraph using the Clipboard task pane.

4. AutoFit the Meat, Cheese, Produce, Beverages, and Total columns.

5. Right-align the dollar values and the Meat, Cheese, Produce, Beverages, and Total column headings.

6. Delete the blank row below the three rows of table titles.

7. Center the table horizontally.

8. Save the document as *Vancouver Sales Memo With Pasted Data*, and then preview, print and close it.

9. Close the Excel application and workbook.

chapter thirteen

Exercise 2 ⒞

1. Open the *Vancouver Sales Memo* document located on the Data Disk.

2. Open the Excel application and the *Vancouver Branch Sales* workbook located on the Data Disk.

3. Save the workbook as *Modified Vancouver Branch Sales*.

4. Copy the Sales Report data in the range A1:F10 and paste the data as a linked object below the body paragraph using the Paste Special dialog box.

5. Center the object.

6. Change the object's update option to manual.

7. Save the document as *Vancouver Sales Memo Revised*, and then preview, print, and close it.

8. Edit Excel worksheet to right-align the column headings in cells B5:F5 using the Align Right button on the Formatting toolbar and change the sales figures for Meat to 1,000 for North, 800 for South, 1,300 for East, and 900 for West.

9. Save the workbook and close the Excel application.

10. Open the *Vancouver Sales Memo Revised* and update the linked object.

11. Preview, print, and close the Word document without saving changes.

12. Close Excel and the workbook.

Exercise 3 ⒞

1. Open the *Australia Outline* document located on the Data Disk.

2. Switch to Outline view.

3. Format paragraphs 2-4, 7, 9, and 14 with outline heading Level 1.

4. Format paragraphs 5-6, 8, 10-13, and 15-17 with outline heading Level 2.

5. Save the document as *Formatted Australia Outline*, and then preview and print it.

6. Send the Word outline document to PowerPoint to create a presentation.

7. Change the layout of the first slide to Title Slide.

8. Save the presentation as *Australia Highlights*.

9. Print the presentation slides and close PowerPoint and the presentation. (*Hint:* Click Print on the File menu to open the Print dialog box.)

10. Close the Word document without saving any changes.

Exercise 4 ⒞

1. Open the *Vancouver Sales Memo* document located on the Data Disk.

2. Open the Excel application and the *Vancouver Branch Sales* workbook located on the Data Disk.

3. Copy the Sales Report data in the range A1:F10 and embed the object below the body paragraph using the Paste Special dialog box.

4. Center the embedded object horizontally.

5. Save the document as *Vancouver Sales Memo With Embedded Data*, and then preview and print it.

6. Edit the embedded Excel object to remove the bold formatting from the District, Meat, Cheese, Produce, Beverages, and Total headings using the Formatting toolbar. (*Hint:* Remember to double-click the object to activate it for editing.)

7. Select the three table heading rows and italicize the heading text. (*Hint:* Drag down across the row 1, 2, and 3 buttons at the left of the activated worksheet object to select the rows and then use the Formatting toolbar to italicize the text in the rows.)

8. Click outside the object to deselect it.

9. Save the document as *Vancouver Sales Memo With Edited Data*, and then preview, print, and close it.

Exercise 5 [C]

1. Open the PowerPoint application and the *Australia Highlights* presentation you created in Exercise 3.

2. Send the presentation to Word and use the Blank lines next to slides and Paste options.

3. Save the Word document as *Australia Handout*, and then preview, print, and close it.

4. Close the PowerPoint application and presentation.

Exercise 6 [C]

1. Open the *District A Sales Decline* document located on the Data Disk.

2. Double-space the document. Center and single-space the Store A1–Store A4 paragraphs.

3. Save the document as *Modified Sales Decline*.

4. Open the Excel application and open the *District A Sales Report* workbook located on the Data Disk.

5. Copy the District A Sales Report data in the range A1:H11 and paste the data as an embedded worksheet object below the document text.

6. Edit the embedded object to change the sales figures for Store A5 to 68,000 for November, 59,100 for December, 57,850 for January, 59,150 for February, 58,000 for March, 67,100 for April, and 66,900 for May.

7. Save the document, and then preview, print, and close it.

8. Close the Excel application and workbook without saving any changes.

Exercise 7 [C]

1. Open Access and the *London Personnel* database located on the Data Disk.

2. Publish the Employees table to a Word document.

3. Edit the Word table to apply the Table AutoFormat of your choice editing features.

4. Save the document as *London Personnel* as a Word document type, and then preview, print and close it.

Exercise 8 [C]

1. Create a new, blank document.

2. Key "Third Quarter Bread Sales" as the title and apply 14-point, bold, center-aligned formatting.

3. Insert two blank lines after the title.

4. Create a Microsoft Graph Chart object and import the data from the *Third Quarter Bread Sales* workbook, Sales Unit worksheet, cell range A1: D4. Overwrite the sample data in the datasheet.

5. Edit the chart as desired and widen the chart object as necessary.

6. Save the document as *Third Quarter Bread Sales Chart*, and then preview, print, and close it.

Case Projects

Project 1 [C]

Marisa DaFranco calls to tell you that whenever she double-clicks a linked Excel object in one of her Word documents, see gets a "cannot edit" error message. Using the Ask A Question Box, research troubleshooting linked and embedded objects. Create a memo to Marisa telling her how to solve the problem. Save and print the memo.

Project 2 [C]

Margaret Nguyen, the administrative assistant to the vice president of marketing, asks you to create a PowerPoint presentation announcing the new holiday sales campaign and then send it to her in a memo for her review. She will format the slides in the presentation after reviewing it. Create a new Word outline using outline heading level formatting and

chapter thirteen

containing fictitious sales campaign topics. Then create a PowerPoint slide presentation from the outline. Save and print the presentation slides. Create a memo to Margaret from inside Word and attach the presentation file. Save and print the memo.

Project 3

Chris Lofton, the word processing manager, asks you to give a short presentation to the word processing specialists on the difference between embedding and linking objects. Use online Help to review the explanation of linked objects and embedded objects. Then create a Word outline of the topics you plan to cover in the presentation using outline level formatting. Send the Word outline to PowerPoint to create a presentation. Format the presentation as desired and print it. Send the PowerPoint presentation to Word using an output format of your choice. Save and print the Word document. With your instructor's permission, open the PowerPoint presentation and, using the presentation and the Word handout document, explain the difference between linked and embedded objects to a group of classmates.

Project 4

Jody Haversham asks for your help in managing the linked Excel objects in her documents. She has linked objects to source application files that have been moved to a new location, linked objects that are updated automatically when she wants to update them manually, and linked objects that she no longer wants linked to the source file. Using the Ask A Question Box, search for and review topics related to linked objects. After reviewing the topics, write Jody a memo providing some suggestions to help her manage linked objects. Save and print the memo.

Project 5

Kelly Armstead has a Word document that contains a list of contact names and addresses. She wants to import the Word information into her Outlook Contacts folder. Use online Help to research how to do this, then write Kelly a memo describing what she needs to do. Save and print the memo.

Project 6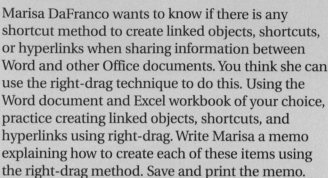

Marisa DaFranco wants to know if there is any shortcut method to create linked objects, shortcuts, or hyperlinks when sharing information between Word and other Office documents. You think she can use the right-drag technique to do this. Using the Word document and Excel workbook of your choice, practice creating linked objects, shortcuts, and hyperlinks using right-drag. Write Marisa a memo explaining how to create each of these items using the right-drag method. Save and print the memo.

Project 7

The Vancouver branch manager wants to review the data in the *Vancouver Branch Sales* workbook. He asks you to e-mail the data. Open the *Vancouver Branch Sales* workbook and copy the range A1:F10 to the Clipboard. Create a new memo in Word. Address it to the Vancouver branch manager using a fictitious e-mail address. Add appropriate subject and message text and paste the copied data into a Word table. Save and print the memo.

Project 8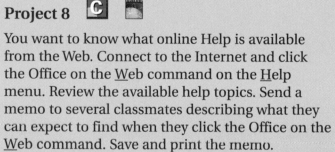

You want to know what online Help is available from the Web. Connect to the Internet and click the Office on the <u>W</u>eb command on the <u>H</u>elp menu. Review the available help topics. Send a memo to several classmates describing what they can expect to find when they click the Office on the <u>W</u>eb command. Save and print the memo.

Microsoft
Excel 2002
Introductory

Quick Start for Excel

S preadsheet applications, such as Excel, help you organize and analyze information, especially information involving numbers. In this chapter, you learn about the components of the Excel window, and you perform simple tasks to become more familiar with how Excel works. You open a workbook file, navigate a workbook, select cells, work with worksheets, save your work, preview and print a workbook, and create a new workbook based on a predesigned template.

LEARNING OBJECTIVES

- Identify the components of the Excel window
- Locate and open an existing workbook
- Navigate a worksheet
- Select cells, columns, and rows
- Insert, reposition, and delete worksheets
- Save a workbook
- Preview and print a worksheet
- Close a workbook
- Create a new workbook from a template
- Exit Excel

Case profile

Luis Alvarez owns a computer store called Super Power Computers. His business has grown from a single location to a medium-sized chain of outlets spread out over several states. Luis employs several hundred people, and his business is divided into several departments to handle sales, inventory, delivery, technical support, accounting, and personnel. As an administrative assistant, you use Excel to organize and prepare a sales report for Luis.

chapter one

notes This text assumes that you have little or no knowledge of the Excel application. However, it is assumed that you have read Office Chapters 1–3 of this book and that you are familiar with Windows 98 or Windows 2000 concepts.

The illustrations in this unit were created using Windows 2000. If you are using the Excel application installed in Windows 98, you may notice a few minor differences in some figures. These differences do not affect your work in this unit.

1.a Identifying the Components of the Excel Window

A **spreadsheet** is a computer file specifically designed to organize data by using special containers, called **cells**. Cells are organized into rows and columns to create a **worksheet**. A collection of worksheets is called a **workbook** and is saved as an Excel file.

Before you can begin to work with Excel, you must open the application. When you open the application, a new, blank workbook opens as well. To open Excel and a new, blank workbook:

Step 1	*Click*	the Start button 🔲**Start** on the taskbar
Step 2	*Point to*	Programs
Step 3	*Click*	Microsoft Excel

Within a few seconds, Excel starts. Your screen should look similar to Figure 1-1.

**chapter
one**

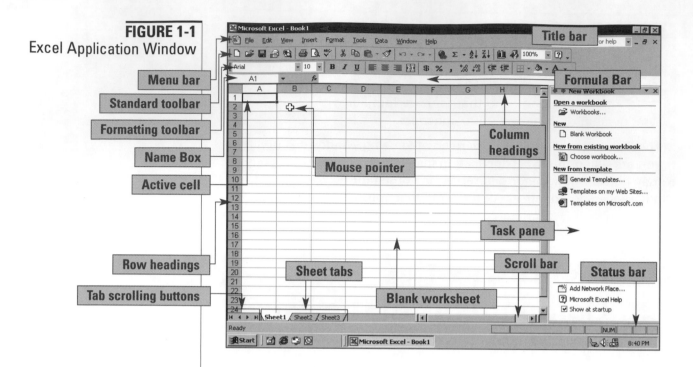

FIGURE 1-1
Excel Application Window

- Menu bar
- Standard toolbar
- Formatting toolbar
- Name Box
- Active cell
- Row headings
- Tab scrolling buttons
- Title bar
- Formula Bar
- Column headings
- Mouse pointer
- Task pane
- Scroll bar
- Status bar
- Sheet tabs
- Blank worksheet

Worksheets

Each new workbook contains three worksheets, similar to pages in a notebook. You switch between worksheets by clicking the **sheet tabs** near the bottom of the Excel window. Each worksheet can be named and color-coded individually. When you click a sheet tab, you make that worksheet the **active worksheet**, and any values you key are entered on that worksheet. The active sheet tab appears to be in front of the other tabs, with the sheet tab name in bold.

Worksheets are divided into columns and rows. **Columns** run vertically up and down a worksheet. **Rows** run horizontally from left to right across a worksheet. Across the top of each worksheet you see **column headings**, which are lettered from A to Z, AA to AZ, and so on to column IV (256 columns in total). On the left side of each worksheet are **row headings**, which are numbered from 1 to 65,536 (the maximum number of rows in a worksheet).

Cells are the containers where values are stored. **Values** include numbers, text, hyperlinks, formulas, and functions. A **cell reference** is the column letter and row number that identifies a cell; for example, cell A1 refers to the cell at the intersection of column A and row 1. Each cell can contain up to 32,000 characters. When you click a cell, it becomes the **active cell**, and a thick border surrounds it. Any values you enter are stored in the active cell.

When you move your mouse pointer over a worksheet, it changes to a large, white cross. This mouse pointer changes shape depending on what you are doing.

Task Pane

The **New Workbook task pane** helps you work faster by providing helpful shortcuts. Using the New Workbook task pane, you can quickly open recently used workbooks, create new workbooks from templates, or search for templates on the Microsoft Web site, *Microsoft.com.* There are other task panes to help you complete specific types of tasks, such as when you need to paste information from the Clipboard or when you need to search your computer for a certain file.

Top of the Window

The **title bar** displays the application name as well as the current workbook name. The default name for the blank workbook that appears when you start Excel is "Book1." On the right side of the title bar are the Minimize, Maximize/Restore, and Close buttons. The **menu bar**, located below the title bar, features drop-down menu commands that contain groups of additional, related commands. The activities in this book instruct you to select menu bar commands with the mouse; if you prefer, however, you can press the ALT key plus the underlined letter in the menu command to open the menu, then press the underlined letter in the command on the menu. In addition, many menu commands have an associated keyboard shortcut. For example, to open a file, you could click the File menu, then click Open; you could press the ALT + F keys, then press the O key; or you could press the CTRL + O keys. The Commands Review section at the end of each chapter summarizes both the mouse and keyboard techniques used to select a menu command.

The **Standard toolbar**, located beneath the menu bar, provides easy access to commonly used commands, such as Save, Open, Print, Copy, and Paste, as well as to many other useful commands. The **Formatting toolbar**, shown below the Standard toolbar in Figure 1-1, provides easy access to commonly used formatting commands, such as Style, Font, Font Size, Alignment, Fill Color, and Font Color. The **Name Box**, located beneath the Formatting toolbar, displays the current cell or cells. Use the **Formula Bar**, to the right of the Name Box, to create and edit values. The Formula Bar becomes active whenever you begin keying data into a cell. When the Formula Bar is active, the Enter, Cancel, and Edit Formula buttons appear.

**chapter
one**

notes   Office XP features personalized menus and toolbars, which "learn" the commands you use most often. This means that when you first install Office XP, only the most frequently used commands appear immediately on a short version of the menus, and the remaining commands appear after a brief pause. Commands that you select move to the short menu, while those you don't use appear only on the full menu.

The Standard and Formatting toolbars appear on the same row when you first install Office XP. When they appear in this position, only the most commonly used buttons of each toolbar are visible. All the other default buttons appear on the Toolbar Options drop-down lists. As you use buttons from the Toolbar Options list, they move to the visible buttons on the toolbar, while the buttons you don't use move into the Toolbar Options list. If you arrange the Formatting toolbar below the Standard toolbar, all buttons are visible. Unless otherwise noted, the illustrations in this book show the full menus and the Formatting toolbar on its own row below the Standard toolbar.

Bottom of the Window

The **tab scrolling buttons** allow you to navigate through the sheet tabs, or worksheets, contained in your workbook. The right- and left-pointing triangles scroll one tab to the right or left, respectively. The right- and left-pointing triangles with the vertical line jump to the first and last sheet tabs in the workbook, respectively. Scrolling the sheet tabs does not change your active worksheet. The **status bar** at the bottom of the Excel window indicates various items of information, such as whether the NUM LOCK or CAPS LOCK feature is active. If you select a range of cells containing numbers, the sum of the selected cells is displayed on the status bar.

Luis, the company president, would like you to review the workbook he has been using to track regional sales.

C

1.b Locating and Opening an Existing Workbook

MOUSE **TIP**

Click the Open button on the Standard toolbar to open the Open dialog box.

When you want to edit an existing workbook, you need to open it from the disk where it is stored. You can open several workbooks at a time. Luis asks you to review the *Super Power Computers – Q1 Sales* workbook he has created.

notes If you do not know where your Data Files are stored, check with your instructor to find out the location.

To open an existing workbook:

| Step 1 | *Click* | the Workbooks or More workbooks link in the Open a workbook section of the New Workbook task pane |

The Open dialog box on your screen should look similar to Figure 1-2, although your file list might differ.

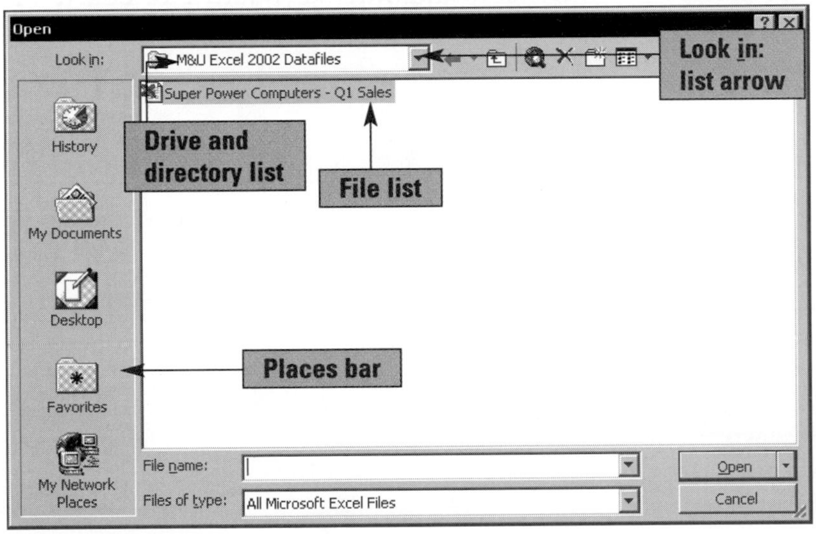

Drive and directory list

File list

Places bar

Look in: list arrow

FIGURE 1-2
Open Dialog Box

Step 2	*Click*	the Look in: list arrow
Step 3	*Switch to*	the disk drive and folder where your Data Files are stored
Step 4	*Double-click*	*Super Power Computers – Q1 Sales* in the file list

The *Super Power Computers – Q1 Sales* workbook opens, and the New Workbook task pane closes until you need to use it again. Luis created this workbook to keep track of sales for the first quarter of 2003.

chapter
one

1.c Navigating a Worksheet

In Excel, data you enter is placed in the active cell. Recall that the active cell is the cell with the thick black border around it. When you want to make a cell active, position the mouse pointer over the cell you want to activate, and then click the cell. To activate a cell using the mouse:

Step 1	*Point to*	cell B6
Step 2	*Click*	cell B6
Step 3	*Verify*	that cell B6 is active by looking in the Name Box

You can use the ARROW keys and other keyboard shortcuts to move the active cell. Table 1-1 summarizes some of the keyboard shortcuts for moving around in Excel.

TABLE 1-1
Using the Keyboard to
Navigate a Workbook

To Move	Press
Up one cell	the UP ARROW key
Down one cell	the DOWN ARROW key
Right one cell	the TAB key or the RIGHT ARROW key
Left one cell	the SHIFT + TAB keys or the LEFT ARROW key
To first active cell of the current row	the HOME key
To last active cell of the current row	the END key and then the ENTER key
Down one page	the PAGE DOWN key
Up one page	the PAGE UP key
To cell A1	the CTRL + HOME keys
To last cell containing data in a worksheet	the CTRL + END keys or the END key and then the HOME key
To edge of the last cell containing a value or to the edges of a worksheet	the CTRL + ARROW keys

You also can move around a workbook using the keyboard. To navigate a workbook using the keyboard:

Step 1	*Press*	the CTRL + HOME keys to move to cell A1
Step 2	*Press*	the CTRL + END keys to move to the last cell containing data in the worksheet
Step 3	*Press*	the HOME key to move to the first cell in the current row

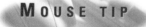

MOUSE TIP

You can scroll through a worksheet by clicking the scroll arrows to scroll one row or column at a time; drag the scroll boxes to scroll several rows or columns.

| Step 4 | *Press* | the CTRL + PAGE DOWN keys to move to Sheet2 |
| Step 5 | *Press* | the CTRL + PAGE UP keys to return to the Sales Report Data worksheet |

You also can switch to another worksheet by using the mouse. To switch to another worksheet by using the mouse:

| Step 1 | *Click* | the Sheet2 sheet tab |
| Step 2 | *Click* | the Sales Report Data sheet tab |

Throughout the remainder of this book, you are instructed to activate a particular cell or worksheet. Use your mouse to click the cell or sheet tab, or use your favorite keyboard shortcut, whichever you prefer.

1.d Selecting Cells, Columns, and Rows

Selecting cells is a fundamental skill used when working in Excel. You select cells for editing, for moving, for copying, for formatting, or as references in formulas. To select cells by using the mouse:

Step 1	*Click*	cell B3, *but do not release* the mouse button
Step 2	*Drag*	the pointer to cell D5
Step 3	*Release*	the mouse button

You have selected a range of cells. A **range** is any group of contiguous cells. To refer to a range, you specify the cells in the upper-left and lower-right corners. In this step, you selected the range B3:D5. As you select the range, the status bar displays the sum of all cells in the selected range containing numerical values, and the Name Box displays a running count of rows and columns in your selected range. In this example, the Name Box indicated 3R x 3C, indicating that three rows and three columns were being selected. As soon as you release the mouse button to close your selection, the Name Box displays the group's active cell reference. The first selected cell, B3, remains unshaded to indicate that it is the active cell in the group. Your screen should look similar to Figure 1-3.

M O U S E   T I P

With the IntelliMouse pointing device, you can use the scrolling wheel to scroll a worksheet. For more information on using the IntelliMouse pointing device, see online Help.

Q U I C K   T I P

The AutoCalculate feature displays the sum of a selected range in the status bar. To display different calculations, such as the average, minimum, or maximum value of a range, right-click the status bar, then click the appropriate calculation in the shortcut menu.

chapter
one

FIGURE 1-3
Selected Range

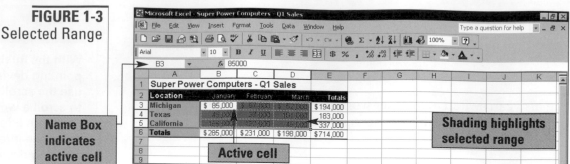

Name Box indicates active cell

Active cell

Shading highlights selected range

QUICK TIP

While working in a selection, press the ENTER key to move the active cell down one cell. Press the TAB key to move the active cell to the right. Press the SHIFT + TAB keys to move the active cell to the left.

You also can use keys to select cells. Holding down the SHIFT key allows you to select cells by pressing only the ARROW keys. Pressing the CTRL key in combination with the ARROW keys causes the selection to jump to the last cell containing data. If the cells in the direction you specify are blank, the selection moves to the limits of the worksheet. To select cells using keys:

Step 1	*Activate*	cell B4
Step 2	*Press & hold*	the SHIFT key
Step 3	*Press*	the RIGHT ARROW key twice to select cells C4 and D4
Step 4	*Release*	the SHIFT key
Step 5	*Press & hold*	the SHIFT + CTRL keys
Step 6	*Press*	the UP ARROW key
Step 7	*Release*	the SHIFT + CTRL keys to select the range B2:D4
Step 8	*Click*	any cell in the worksheet to deselect the range

You often want to apply formatting to an entire column or row, or several columns or rows at once. You can drag to select multiple columns or rows with the mouse, or you click while pressing the SHIFT or CTRL keys. To select an entire row or column, or to select several rows or columns:

MOUSE TIP

Many situations require the use of multiple, nonadjacent ranges. For example, to select cells in columns A and C, select the cells in column A, press and hold the CTRL key, then select the cells in column C.

Step 1	*Click*	the number 3 in the row 3 heading at the left of the worksheet to select row 3
Step 2	*Drag*	across the column headings for columns B, C, and D to select columns B, C, and D
Step 3	*Click*	the column E heading
Step 4	*Press & hold*	the SHIFT key
Step 5	*Click*	the column B heading to select columns B through E

You can also quickly select an entire worksheet at once. To select an entire worksheet:

| Step 1 | **Click** | the Select All button located to the left of column A and above row 1 |
| Step 2 | **Activate** | cell A1 to deselect the worksheet |

QUICK TIP

Press the CTRL+ A keys to select an entire worksheet.

Now that you can easily select cells and navigate a worksheet, you are ready to organize a workbook.

1.e Inserting, Repositioning, and Deleting Worksheets

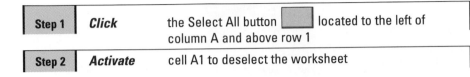

C

By default, Excel creates new workbooks that contain three worksheets. You can add or delete worksheets from your workbook at any time. You also can change the order of worksheets as you further refine your workbook design.

Inserting a Worksheet

You need to add a new worksheet to the workbook. To add a new worksheet to a workbook:

Step 1	**Right-click**	the Sales Report Data sheet tab
Step 2	**Click**	Insert
Step 3	**Verify**	that the Worksheet icon in the Insert dialog box is selected
Step 4	**Click**	OK

A new worksheet is inserted to the left of the active worksheet.

Copying and Moving a Worksheet

You need to create a second copy of the Sales Report Data worksheet for second quarter data. To copy a worksheet:

| Step 1 | **Right-click** | the Sales Report Data sheet tab |
| Step 2 | **Click** | Move or Copy |

MENU TIP

You can insert a new worksheet by clicking the Worksheet command on the Insert menu.

QUICK TIP

To have Excel insert more or fewer than three worksheets in each new workbook, click the Options command on the Tools menu to open the Options dialog box. On the General tab, enter the number of worksheets in the Sheets in new workbook: text box.

chapter one

The Move or Copy dialog box on your screen should look similar to Figure 1-4.

FIGURE 1-4
Move or Copy Dialog Box

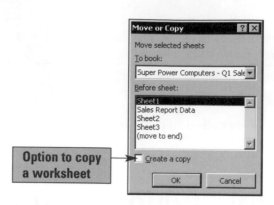

Option to copy
a worksheet

Step 3	*Click*	the Create a copy check box to insert a check mark
Step 4	*Click*	OK

The active worksheet is copied and a new worksheet, called Sales Report Data (2) appears to the left of Sheet1.

You can reorganize your worksheets by dragging sheet tabs to a new location. In your workbook, the Sales Report Data worksheet should appear first, followed by the Sales Report Data (2) worksheet. To move a worksheet:

Step 1	*Point to*	the Sheet1 sheet tab
Step 2	*Press & hold*	the left mouse button

The pointer changes to an arrow with a small rectangle attached to it to indicate that you are moving a sheet tab, and a small black triangle appears at the left of the sheet tab to indicate the tab's position.

Step 3	*Drag*	the Sheet1 sheet tab to the right of the Sales Report Data sheet tab

As you drag, the small black triangle moves with the pointer to indicate the worksheet's new position, and the sheet tabs scroll left. Your screen should look similar to Figure 1-5.

QUICK TIP

To copy a worksheet, press and hold the CTRL key while you drag the sheet tab.

MOUSE TIP

Right-click a tab scroll button to display a menu of sheet tabs. Click any of the listed worksheets to scroll to and activate that worksheet.

FIGURE 1-5
Moving a Sheet Tab

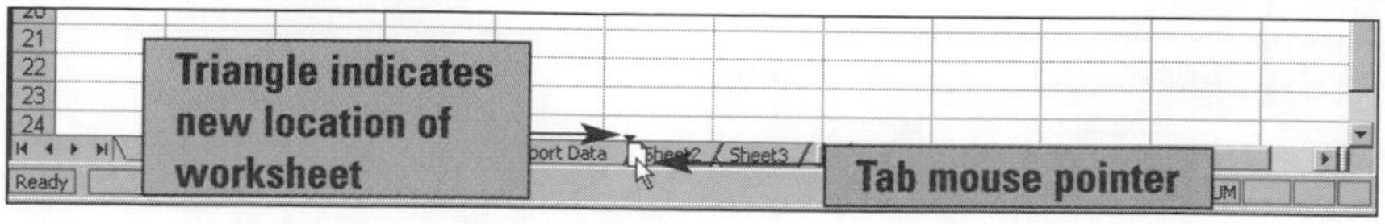

Triangle indicates new location of worksheet

Tab mouse pointer

Step 4	*Release*	the mouse button

The sheet tab moves to the new location.

Step 5	*Follow*	Steps 1 through 4 to position the Sales Report Data (2) sheet tab to the right of the Sales Report Data sheet tab

Deleting a Worksheet

You can also delete worksheets that you no longer need. To delete a worksheet:

Step 1	*Right-click*	the Sheet1 sheet tab
Step 2	*Click*	<u>D</u>elete
Step 3	*Click*	the Sales Report Data sheet tab

1.f Saving a Workbook

The first rule of computing is: Save Your Work Often! The second rule of computing is: Follow the first rule of computing. There are two distinct saving operations: Save and Save As.

Managing Files and Folders

To keep your work more organized, you decide to create a new folder. You can do this from the Open or Save As dialog box. To create a new folder:

Step 1	*Click*	<u>F</u>ile
Step 2	*Click*	Save <u>A</u>s
Step 3	*Click*	the Save <u>i</u>n: list arrow
Step 4	*Switch to*	the appropriate disk drive and folder, as designated by your instructor
Step 5	*Click*	the Create New Folder button in the Save As dialog box
Step 6	*Key*	your name as the name of the folder (Example: Kylie)
Step 7	*Click*	OK

chapter
one

The folder is created in the current location and listed in the Save in: list box.

Using the Save As Command

When you use the Save As command, you provide a filename and specify the disk drive and folder location where the workbook should be saved. A filename can have as many as 255 characters, including the disk drive reference and path, and can contain letters, numbers, spaces, and some special characters in any combination. If you use the Save As command on a previously saved workbook, you actually create a new copy of the workbook, and any changes you made appear only in the new copy.

You also can use the Save As command to save a workbook file in another format, such as HTML for the Internet, or for use in another spreadsheet or accounting application. First, you save the workbook to a different format to send to someone using a different spreadsheet application. To save a workbook in a different file format:

Step 1	*Verify*	that the Save As dialog box is still open
Step 2	*Click*	the Save as type: list arrow
Step 3	*Scroll*	the list to find WK4 (1-2-3)
Step 4	*Click*	WK4 (1-2-3)

This is the format for Lotus 1-2-3 workbooks.

Step 5	*Select*	All of the text in the File name: text box
Step 6	*Key*	Super Power Computers - Q1 Sales WK4 Format
Step 7	*Click*	Save

A warning message appears telling you that some of the workbook's features may not save correctly in the new format. Although Excel does its best to translate the workbook into another format, not everything transfers correctly. For more information about a specific format's limitations, click Help.

Step 8	*Click*	Yes

You have now created a copy of your Excel formatted workbook. Next, you want to save the workbook back to Excel format. To save the workbook with a new filename in Excel format:

Step 1	*Open*	the Save As dialog box
Step 2	*Key*	Super Power Computers – Q1 Sales Revised in the File name: text box
Step 3	*Click*	Microsoft Excel Workbook in the Save as type: list box

The Save As dialog box on your screen should look similar to Figure 1-6.

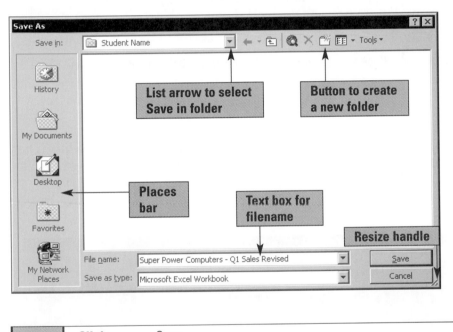

FIGURE 1-6
Save As Dialog Box

Step 4	*Click*	Save

The workbook is saved to your folder as *Super Power Computer – Q1 Sales Revised*. Notice that the title bar includes the new filename.

Using the Save Command

When you want to save changes to a previously named workbook without creating a copy, you use the Save command. No dialog box opens, but the changes are saved to your workbook, and you go back to work. To modify your workbook and save the changes:

Step 1	*Delete*	the Sheet2 and Sheet3 sheet tabs

chapter
one

| Step 2 | *Click* | the Save button 🖫 on the Standard toolbar |

No dialog box opens because you have already named the workbook.

1.g Previewing and Printing a Worksheet

Luis asks you to print a copy of the Q1 Sales figures. Before you print a worksheet, preview it to ensure that you are printing the right information. To preview the worksheet:

| Step 1 | *Click* | the Sales Report Data sheet tab, if necessary |
| Step 2 | *Click* | the Print Preview button 🔍 on the Standard toolbar |

Your Print Preview might appear in color or in black and white. The Print Preview toolbar appears at the top of the window. The status bar indicates the number of pages that print. Your screen should look similar to Figure 1-7.

FIGURE 1-7
Print Preview Window

Print Preview toolbar

Number of pages that print

Preview: Page 1 of 1

| Step 3 | *Click* | the Print button on the Print Preview toolbar |
| Step 4 | *Click* | OK to send the worksheet to the default printer |

1.h Closing a Workbook

When you finish working with a workbook, you can close it without closing the Excel application. If you have modified the workbook you are closing, Excel prompts you to save your work. To close the *Super Power Computers – Q1 Sales Revised* workbook:

| Step 1 | *Click* | the Close Window button on the right side of the menu bar |
| Step 2 | *Click* | Yes to save any changes, if prompted |

Excel displays the next open workbook, if there is one. If no workbooks are open, you see a blank workspace. You can quickly reopen a saved workbook from a folder that you created. To open a workbook from a folder:

Step 1	*Click*	the Open button on the Standard toolbar
Step 2	*Click*	the Look in: list arrow
Step 3	*Click*	the folder with your name (the folder you created in the previous section)
Step 4	*Double-click*	*Super Power Computers – Q1 Sales Revised*

The workbook opens. Next you create a new workbook from a template.

1.i Creating a New Workbook from a Template

A **template** is a workbook into which formatting, settings, and formulas are already inserted. When you create a new workbook, you are actually creating a new workbook based on Excel's default workbook template, which contains three blank worksheets. You can create a new workbook based on another template. You can choose from additional templates provided with Excel, or you can create your own.

CAUTION TIP

Be careful when clicking the Print button on the Standard toolbar. It immediately sends the file to the printer using the current page setup options. You may not be aware of the current print area or even which printer will print the file.

TASK PANE TIP

You can open a workbook by clicking the More workbooks link in the Open a workbook section in the New Workbook task pane.

MENU TIP

Click the Close command on the File menu to close the workbook.

chapter
one

CAUTION TIP

You must use the New command on the File menu, which displays the New Document task pane, to access the New dialog box. Clicking the New button on the Standard toolbar opens a new, blank worksheet based on the default template.

You need to create a blank invoice to bill customers of Super Power Computers. To create a new workbook based on the Invoice template:

Step 1	*Click*	File
Step 2	*Click*	New

The New Workbook task pane opens.

Step 3	*Click*	the General Templates link in the New from template section in the New Workbook task pane

The Templates dialog box opens.

Step 4	*Click*	the Spreadsheet Solutions tab
Step 5	*Click*	the Sales Invoice template icon

You should see a preview of the template in the Preview box. Your dialog box should look similar to Figure 1-8.

FIGURE 1-8
Creating a New Workbook from a Template

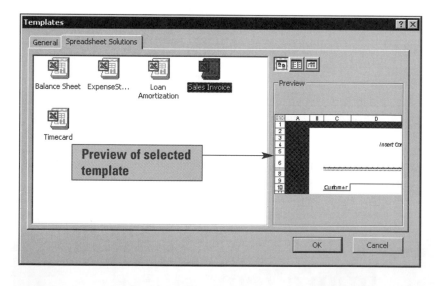

MENU TIP

Click the Exit command on the File menu to close the Excel application.

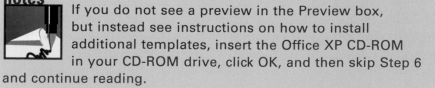

notes
If you do not see a preview in the Preview box, but instead see instructions on how to install additional templates, insert the Office XP CD-ROM in your CD-ROM drive, click OK, and then skip Step 6 and continue reading.

| Step 6 | *Click* | OK |

A new workbook, based on the Sales Invoice template, opens. The title bar identifies this workbook as "Sales Invoice1." Changes you make to this workbook do not affect the template itself. Your screen should look similar to Figure 1-9.

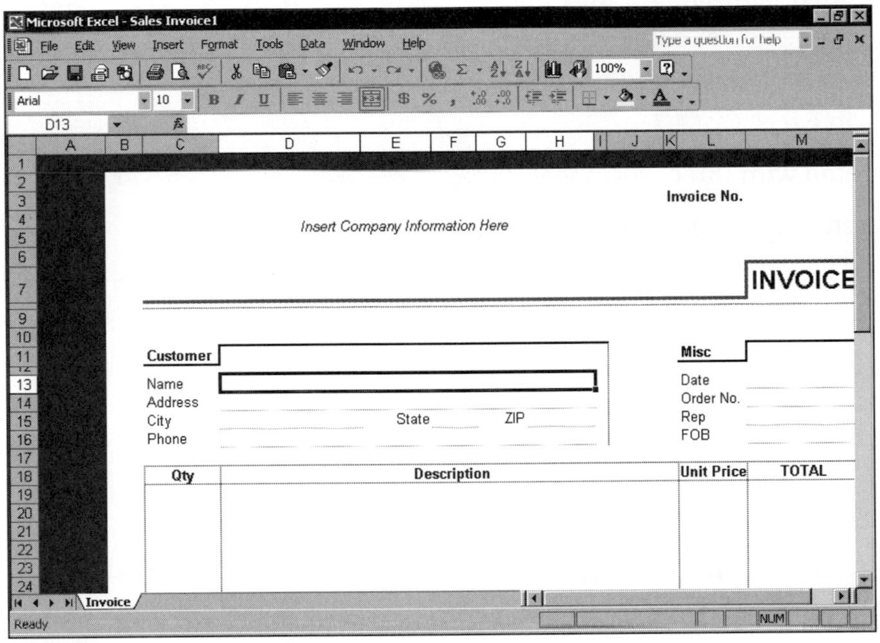

FIGURE 1-9
New Invoice Workbook

The new workbook looks very different from the workbooks you have seen thus far. Gridlines and column and row headings are turned off to reduce the amount of distracting elements in the template.

| Step 7 | *Scroll* | the worksheet to familiarize yourself with it |

Super Power Computers generates many invoices every day. By using this template, you save yourself a lot of time and effort.

1.j Exiting Excel

When you finish working in Excel, you should exit the application. You are prompted to save any modified workbooks that remain open. If you change your mind about exiting, click the Cancel button. To exit Excel:

| Step 1 | *Click* | the Close button ☒ on the Excel title bar |
| Step 2 | *Click* | No if prompted to save any changes to open workbooks |

CAUTION TIP

Some templates and workbooks contain macros that have been written by other users to automate certain routine tasks in the workbook. Unfortunately, some macros, known as macro viruses, are programmed to do malicious things. Whenever you open a workbook containing macros, you will receive a warning about the possibility of macro viruses. Excel cannot tell you whether the macros will do anything harmful; rather, it simply alerts you to the fact that the workbook contains macros. If you have downloaded a workbook from the Internet and are not sure of its origin, you should take a cautious approach and disable the workbook macros. The data will remain intact, even though the macros are disabled.

chapter
one

Summary

▶ A worksheet is an electronic spreadsheet. A workbook is a collection of worksheets.

▶ Cells are containers in worksheets for text, numerical values, and formulas that calculate data. Cells are organized into rows and columns. A cell reference identifies a particular cell through a combination of the column letter and the row number.

▶ You can open multiple workbooks in Excel.

▶ By default, new workbooks are created with three worksheets.

▶ You can use keyboard shortcuts such as the HOME key, the CTRL + HOME keys, the TAB key, and the SHIFT + TAB keys to navigate around a worksheet. You can also use the mouse to activate a cell or to scroll to other cells.

▶ You can select cells with the mouse by pressing and holding the left mouse button as you drag across cells. Select cells with the keyboard by pressing and holding the SHIFT key plus the ARROW keys, and other shortcut keys, such as the CTRL, HOME, and END keys. Select columns and rows by clicking the column and row headers.

▶ You can organize worksheets by inserting, moving, copying, or deleting worksheets.

▶ You can create new folders to organize your work from within the Open and Save As dialog boxes.

▶ You can use the Save As command when you want to make a copy of an existing workbook or save a workbook in a different file format.

▶ You can use the Save command to save a new workbook or to save changes to a previously named workbook.

▶ You should preview worksheets before you print them.

▶ Templates are used to start a new workbook with preset formatting, data, and formulas.

▶ When you close a new or modified workbook, Excel reminds you to save your work.

▶ When you close the Excel application, Excel reminds you to save any unsaved workbooks.

Commands Review

Action	Menu Bar	Shortcut Menu	Toolbar	Task Pane	Keyboard
Open a workbook	File, Open	Right-click empty Excel workspace, click Open	🗁	More workbooks link in New Workbook task pane	CTRL + O ALT + F, O
Create a new workbook	File, New	Right-click empty Excel workspace, click New	🗋	Blank workbook link in New Workbook task pane	CTRL + N ALT + F, N
Insert a worksheet	Insert, Worksheet	Right-click sheet tab, click Insert			ALT + I, W
Move or copy a worksheet	Edit, Move or Copy Sheet	Right-click sheet tab, click Move or Copy			ALT + E, M
Delete a worksheet	Edit, Delete Sheet	Right-click sheet tab, click Delete			ALT + E, L
Save a workbook	File, Save		💾		CTRL + S CTRL + F12 ALT + F, S
Save As	File, Save As				ALT + F, A F12
Create a new folder from Open or Save As dialog box		Right-click blank area in dialog box, point to New, click Folder	📁		
Preview a worksheet	File, Print Preview		🔍		ALT + F, V
Print a worksheet	File, Print		🖨		ALT + F, P CTRL + P CTRL + Shift + F12
Close a workbook	File, Close		✕		CTRL + F4 ALT + F, C CTRL + W
Close multiple workbooks	Press and hold the SHIFT key, then File, Close All				SHIFT + ALT + F, C
Create a new workbook based on a template	File, New	Right-click empty Excel workspace, click New		General Templates link in New Workbook task pane	ALT + F, N
Exit Excel	File, Exit	Right-click application icon, click Close	✕		ALT + F4 ALT + F, X

Concepts Review

SCANS

Circle the correct answer.

1. Excel worksheets contain:
- [a] 30 rows.
- [b] 256 rows.
- [c] 20,000 rows.
- [d] 65,536 rows.

2. Excel worksheets contain:
- [a] 30 columns.
- [b] 256 columns.
- [c] 20,000 columns.
- [d] 65,536 columns.

3. Excel workbooks use the three-letter filename extension:
- [a] doc.
- [b] txt.
- [c] htm.
- [d] xls.

chapter one

4. The status bar displays:
[a] text and formulas you are entering.
[b] results of the formula you are entering.
[c] important worksheet and system information.
[d] the filename of your workbook.

5. The active cell is identified by a:
[a] thick black border.
[b] change in the font color.
[c] shaded cell background.
[d] thin dashed border.

6. To save changes to a workbook without creating a new copy, use the:
[a] Save As command.
[b] Open command.
[c] More workbooks command.
[d] Save command.

7. To change the active worksheet:
[a] click the title bar.
[b] click the sheet tab.
[c] press the RIGHT ARROW key.
[d] click and drag the scroll bar at the bottom of the worksheet window.

8. To select nonadjacent ranges, you drag across the second range while you press and hold the:
[a] CTRL key.
[b] SHIFT key.
[c] CAPS LOCK key.
[d] ALT key.

9. To select adjacent cells using only the keyboard, you would use the ARROW keys as you press and hold the:
[a] CTRL key.
[b] SHIFT key.
[c] TAB key.
[d] ALT key.

10. To select an entire column or row:
[a] key the column letter or row number.
[b] press and hold the CTRL key, then key the column letter or row number.
[c] click the column or row header.
[d] key the column letter or row number in the Name Box.

Circle **T** if the statement is true or **F** if the statement is false.

T F 1. Excel can open many workbooks at once.

T F 2. Cells can contain numbers, text, or formulas.

T F 3. Rows run vertically down the worksheet.

T F 4. You can select menu items using only keyboard shortcuts.

T F 5. The Formula Bar displays the row and column number of the active cell.

T F 6. Columns run vertically down the worksheet.

T F 7. Clicking a tab scroll button changes the active worksheet.

T F 8. Pressing the CTRL + HOME keys closes the Excel application and saves any open workbooks.

T F 9. You cannot open a file unless it is saved on your computer.

T F 10. The Save and Save As commands do exactly the same thing.

Skills Review

Exercise 1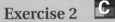

1. Start Excel.

2. Open the *Sweet Tooth Q1 2003 Sales* workbook located on the Data Disk.

3. Copy Sheet1 to a new worksheet.

4. Save the workbook as *Sweet Tooth Q1 2003 Sales Revised,* and print it.

5. Close the workbook.

Exercise 2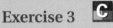

1. Open the *Region Sales Summary* workbook located on the Data Disk.

2. Save the workbook as *Region Sales Summary Revised*.

3. Change the worksheet order to: East, West, North, South.

4. Activate the East sheet tab.

5. Activate cell A1, if necessary.

6. Save your changes, and print the worksheet.

7. Close the workbook.

Exercise 3

1. Create a new workbook using the *ExpenseStatement* template.

2. Use Print Preview to preview the printed worksheet.

3. Print the worksheet.

4. Save the workbook as *My Expense Statement*, and print it.

5. Close the workbook.

Exercise 4

1. Open the *2003 Sales Projections* workbook located on the Data Disk.

2. Delete all the sheet tabs for the year 2002.

3. Switch between worksheets to locate the store whose projected sales total will be the greatest.

4. Select the cells containing data for that store.

5. Save the workbook as *2003 Sales Projections Revised*, and print it.

6. Close the workbook.

chapter one

Exercise 5   C

1. Open the *Half Marathon Mile Splits* workbook located on the Data Disk.

2. Select cells B3:B9 and D3:D9.

3. Delete the Sheet2 and Sheet3 worksheets from the workbook.

4. Save the workbook as *Half Marathon Mile Splits Revised*, and print it.

5. Close the workbook.

Exercise 6   C

1. Create a new, blank workbook.

2. Insert a new worksheet.

3. Move the new worksheet so it is the last worksheet in the workbook.

4. Save the workbook as *4 Blank Sheets* in a new folder named "Practice."

5. Close the workbook.

6. Open the workbook *4 Blank Sheets* located in the Practice folder.

7. Reorganize the worksheets in the following order: Sheet4, Sheet3, Sheet2, Sheet1.

8. Save the workbook as *4 Blank Sheets Revised* in the Practice folder.

9. Close the workbook.

Exercise 7   C

1. Open the *State Capitals* workbook located on the Data Disk.

2. Use Print Preview to preview the printed worksheet.

3. Print the worksheet.

4. Save the workbook as *State Capitals WK4 Format* in Lotus 1-2-3 format.

5. Close the workbook without saving any additional changes.

Exercise 8   C

1. Open the *2002 Sales Report* workbook located on the Data Disk.

2. On the Southwest Division 2002 sheet tab, select all of the data except the two title lines by using the mouse or keyboard.

3. On the Southeast Division 2002 sheet tab, select column C.

4. On the Northwest Division 2002 sheet tab, select row 9.

5. On the Northeast Division 2002 sheet tab, select cells B8:C8.

6. Save the workbook as *2002 Sales Report Revised*, and print it.

7. Close the workbook.

8. Exit Excel.

Case Projects

Project 1

You work for a large company with many offices spread throughout the United States and Canada. To facilitate information sharing between offices, your company stores many files on an FTP server. Your job is to train new employees how to open files on the company's FTP server. Using the Ask A Question Box, research how to open workbooks on an FTP server, then create a Word document and write at least two paragraphs explaining how to do this. Save your document as *Open an Excel Workbook on an FTP Server* and print it. Close the document and exit Word.

Project 2

You work as an office manager. You decide to reorganize the company's workbook files by date. To do this, you need to create folders for the last five years. Use the Open or Save As dialog box in Excel to create a new folder called "Project 2." Inside that folder, create a new folder for each of the last five years.

Project 3

You would like to find out more about Excel's keyboard shortcuts, particularly as they apply to navigating worksheets. Use online Help to search for keyboard shortcuts, then look for a topic "Move and scroll within worksheets." Copy and paste this list into a Word document and save the document as *Excel Worksheet Navigation Shortcuts*. Print the document, then close it.

Project 4

You work for a mortgage company, and it is your job to calculate amortization tables for clients. You'd like to use a template, but aren't sure how to start. You notice a Templates on Microsoft.com link in the New Workbook task pane, and decide to investigate. Click the link, locate a *Loan Calculator* template for Excel, and download it. Open the template in Excel, then preview and print a copy of the template. Save the workbook as *Loan Calculator*.

chapter one

Entering and Editing Data in a Worksheet

Chapter Overview

With Excel, you can store numerical data in a variety of formats. You can also store text data such as names and Social Security numbers. In this chapter, you learn how to enter and edit data in a worksheet. You also learn to use the Undo and Redo commands to help you when you make the inevitable mistake, how to zoom in on a worksheet, and how to name and color sheet tabs.

LEARNING OBJECTIVES

- ▶ Create new workbooks
- ▶ Enter text and numbers in cells
- ▶ Edit cell contents
- ▶ Use Undo and Redo
- ▶ Change the Zoom setting
- ▶ Rename a sheet tab
- ▶ Change a sheet tab color

Case profile

To keep track of employees at Super Power Computers, each store uses an employee name list workbook. This workbook stores important information such as the name, hourly wage, and phone number of each employee. A new store has just opened in Kansas City, and you need to provide them with this workbook.

chapter two

2

2.a   Creating New Workbooks

In Chapter 1, you learned how to create a new workbook based on a template, a special type of Excel file. You also learned that Excel automatically creates a new, blank workbook when you start the application. In this section, you learn to create new, blank workbooks and to create new workbooks from existing workbooks, similar to using a template file.

Creating a New, Blank Workbook

When you start Excel, a new workbook is created for you automatically. However, you may need to create additional workbooks while you are working in Excel. To create a new blank workbook:

Step 1	*Start*	Excel
Step 2	*Click*	the Blank Workbook link in the New Workbook task pane

A new workbook is created in Excel.

Step 3	*Close*	both of the blank workbooks

Creating a Workbook Based on an Existing Workbook

Instead of starting a new workbook, you decide to create the new workbook from an existing workbook file, and then add the data you need to change. The New Workbook task pane provides a quick shortcut for this task. To create a new workbook from an existing workbook file:

Step 1	*Click*	<u>F</u>ile
Step 2	*Click*	<u>N</u>ew
Step 3	*Click*	the Choose workbook link in the New Workbook task pane
Step 4	*Select*	*Super Power Computers – Blank Employee List* from the Data Disk
Step 5	*Click*	<u>C</u>reate New

A new file is created from the existing workbook. Excel assigns the new workbook the same filename as the original workbook with a "1" at the end of the filename, as you can see in the title bar.

MOUSE TIP

You can click the New button on the Standard toolbar to create a new workbook.

chapter
two

| Step 6 | *Save* | the workbook as *Super Power Computers – Kansas City Employee List* |

C 2.b Entering Text and Numbers in Cells

You can enter numbers, letters, and symbols into the active cell. When you enter data in a cell, Excel recognizes the type of data you are entering. For example, if you enter your name in a cell, Excel knows that this is a text value and therefore cannot be used in numerical calculations. Date and time values are special cases of numerical data. When you enter this type of data, Excel automatically converts the value you key into a special numerical value, which makes it easier for Excel to use in calculations.

When you've finished entering data in a cell, you need to accept the entry by pressing the ENTER key, the TAB key, or any of the ARROW keys, or by clicking the Enter button next to the Formula Bar or another cell in the worksheet. Before accepting the entry in a cell, you can change your mind by pressing the ESC key, and the cell's content reverts to the way it was before you began entering or editing the data.

Entering Text

You receive the employee information from the new Kansas City store, as shown in Table 2-1. The first row of data has already been entered in the workbook you opened. These values are **column labels**, identifying the data stored in each column.

TABLE 2-1
Super Power Computers
Employee Data

Name	Wage	Phone
Jared Wright	$9.00	(816) 555-3456
Kaili Muafala	$9.00	(816) 555-9254
Jenna McGregor	$16.00	(816) 555-0012
Monica Chambers	$11.50	(816) 555-1827
Baka Hakamin	$12.75	(816) 555-4637
Homer Hansen	$14.00	(816) 555-8822

To enter text in a worksheet:

| Step 1 | *Activate* | cell A2 |
| Step 2 | *Key* | Jared Wright |

Your screen should look similar to Figure 2-1.

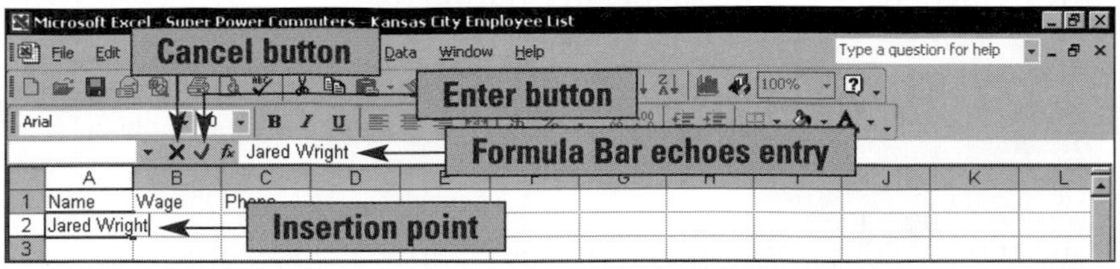

FIGURE 2-1
Entering Data

As you enter data, the status bar displays the word "Enter." The Formula Bar displays the contents of the active cell, while the cell itself shows the results of any formula entered in the cell. In the case of numbers or text, no calculation takes place, so you see exactly what you enter. As you enter or edit data in a cell, the Cancel and Enter buttons appear next to the Formula Bar, the mouse pointer changes to an I-beam pointer to indicate that you are entering a value in a cell, and a blinking **insertion point** appears in the cell to indicate where the next character that you key will go.

| Step 3 | *Press* | the ENTER key |

When you press the ENTER key, the entry is accepted, and the active cell moves down one row by default.

| Step 4 | *Follow* | Steps 2 and 3 to add each name listed in Table 2-1 to column A of your worksheet |

You can use any of the navigation keys to complete data entry in one cell and then move to another.

Entering Numbers

You enter number values directly into the active cell, the same way you enter text values, or date and time values. To enter numerical values:

Step 1	*Activate*	cell B2
Step 2	*Key*	$9.00
Step 3	*Click*	the Enter button ☑ on the Formula Bar

Excel recognizes the number you entered as currency. It shows the number in the cell with a dollar sign, but in the Formula Bar, the number is displayed without the dollar sign and the trailing zeros.

MENU TIP

You can change the default behavior of the ENTER key by using the Options dialog box. Click the Options command on the Tools menu. On the Edit tab, locate the Move selection after Enter check box. To turn the behavior off, remove the check mark. To force the active cell in a different direction, select a new direction from the Direction: list box.

chapter
two

You can no longer see the full value in cell A2. The data (Jared's name) is still there; it is just hidden. You learn how to adjust column widths to display more characters in Chapter 4.

| Step 4 | *Enter* | the rest of the data in the Wage column in Table 2-1 |

Some types of data, although numeric in appearance, aren't really intended to be used in mathematical calculations. Examples of these special types of numbers include phone numbers and Social Security numbers. When you enter numbers mixed with other characters, such as parentheses, dashes, and so on, Excel automatically treats the cell value as a text value.

Step 5	*Key*	(816) 555-3456 in cell C2
Step 6	*Press*	the ENTER key
Step 7	*Enter*	the rest of the data in the Phone column in Table 2-1

Your worksheet should look similar to Figure 2-2.

FIGURE 2-2
Super Power Computers
Employee Data

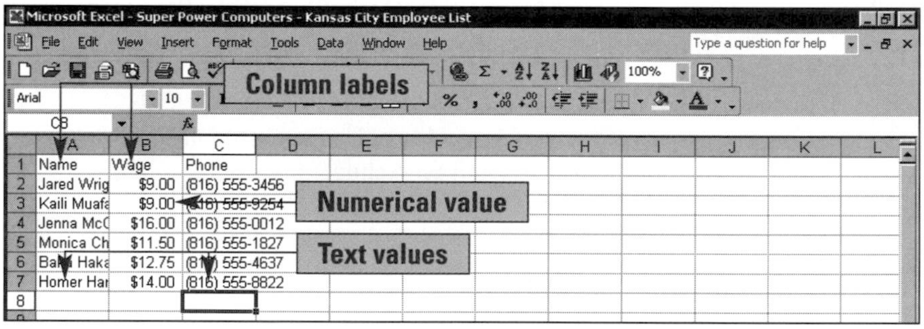

In general, entering data into cells is a simple process: activate the cell, enter the data, and accept the entry.

2.c Editing Cell Contents

Excel provides many ways to edit the contents of a cell. You receive updated information from the Kansas City store, and you need to modify your worksheet. To completely replace a cell's value:

| Step 1 | *Activate* | cell A7 |
| Step 2 | *Key* | Ross Phillips |

Step 3	*Press*	the TAB key
Step 4	*Key*	$13.00 in cell B7
Step 5	*Press*	the ENTER key

Editing in the Active Cell

Often, you need to revise only part of an entry. To edit in the active cell:

| Step 1 | *Double-click* | cell B4 |

The entry in cell B4 changes to display only the number 16 without the dollar sign and trailing zeros, and the blinking insertion point appears in the cell.

| Step 2 | *Drag* | the I-beam pointer $\mathcal{I}$ over the 6 to select it |

Your screen should look similar to Figure 2-3. The 6 in cell B11 is **selected**. Anything you key replaces the selected text.

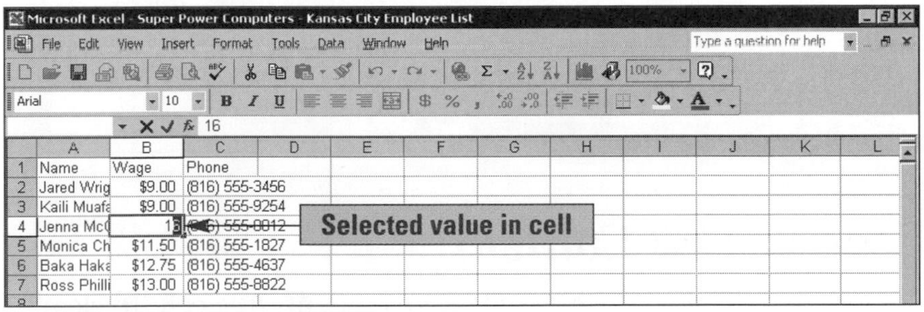

FIGURE 2-3
Editing in the Active Cell

| Step 3 | *Key* | 7.25 |
| Step 4 | *Press* | the ENTER key |

The wage for Jenna should be $17.25.

Editing in the Formula Bar

An alternative to editing directly in the cell is to use the Formula Bar. You can edit the contents of the active cell in the Formula Bar by either moving the insertion point to where you want to make changes or highlighting the text you want to change and then keying new text.

C A U T I O N   T I P

Although the rekeying method is the fastest way to edit a cell, be careful when taking this approach. The previous contents of the cell are replaced with any new data you enter.

Q U I C K   T I P

Sometimes it is difficult to select text precisely with the mouse. Try this: Click to position the insertion point at the start of your selection, then press and hold the SHIFT key while you press the right ARROW key to move across the text.

---

chapter
two

To edit in the Formula Bar:

Step 1	*Activate*	cell C3
Step 2	*Click*	to the left of 4 in the Formula Bar
Step 3	*Press*	the DELETE key

Pressing the DELETE key deletes the character to the right of the insertion point. Pressing the BACKSPACE key deletes the character to the left of the insertion point.

| Step 4 | *Key* | 8 |
| Step 5 | *Click* | the Enter button ✔ on the Formula Bar |

Your worksheet should look similar to Figure 2-4.

FIGURE 2-4
Modified Worksheet

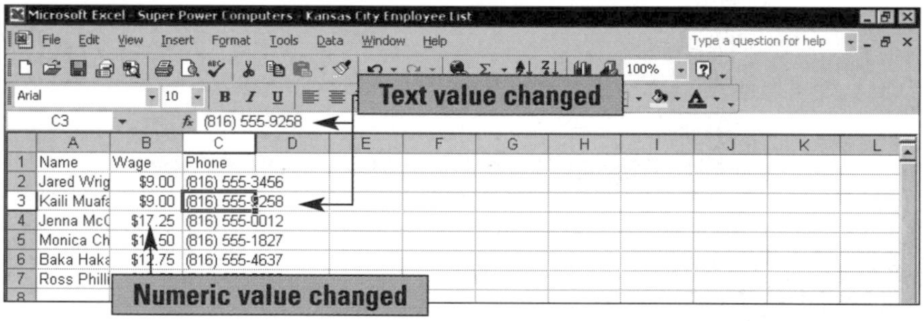

Clearing Cell Content

Sometimes you need to delete all of the contents in a cell. To clear cell content:

| Step 1 | *Drag* | to select cells A7:C7 |
| Step 2 | *Press* | the DELETE key |

The contents of cell A7:C7 are deleted. In the next section you learn to use the Undo and Redo tools. Do *not* save your workbook at this point.

2.d Using Undo and Redo

The **Undo** command reverses your previous action or actions. The **Redo** command reinstates the action or actions you undid. You can Undo and Redo one action at a time, or you can select a number of actions to Undo and Redo from a list of up to 16 previous actions. To undo the last action, click the Undo button on the Standard toolbar. The Redo button is not active until you have used Undo. Click the Redo button to undo the last Undo command.

You realize that you changed the value in cell C3 by mistake. Rather than reentering the data, you can use Undo. To use the Undo and Redo commands:

Step 1	*Click*	the Undo button 🔙 on the Standard toolbar

The contents of cells A7:C7 return.

Step 2	*Click*	the Redo button 🔜 to change the value back again
Step 3	*Click*	the Undo button 🔙 on the Standard toolbar to restore the contents again

You can use the Undo list to quickly Undo several commands at once. To use the Undo list:

Step 1	*Change*	the value in cell C4 to (816) 555-1200
Step 2	*Change*	the value in cell A4 to Lori Jones

You have performed two actions, both data entry. The Undo list allows you to select multiple actions to Undo.

Step 3	*Click*	the Undo button list arrow 🔙▾ on the Standard toolbar
Step 4	*Move*	the pointer down the list, selecting the top two "Typing" actions
Step 5	*Click*	the second "Typing" action

Cells A4 and C4 return to their previous values. The Redo list functions in the same way as the Undo list.

chapter two

| Step 6 | **Save** | the workbook |

2.e Changing the Zoom Setting

If you use a small monitor or worksheets containing a lot of data, it may be hard to read or see the data you want to see. The Zoom setting allows you to **zoom**, to increase or decrease, the viewable area of your worksheet. Zooming in magnifies cells, making them appear much larger. Zooming out makes cells appear smaller, allowing you to see more of the worksheet. You can zoom in to 400% or out to 10%. To zoom in on the worksheet:

| Step 1 | **Click** | the Zoom button list arrow 100% ▼ on the Standard toolbar |
| Step 2 | **Click** | 200% |

Your worksheet zooms in to 200%, or twice the default size. You can select any of the preset Zoom options, or key a custom Zoom setting.

Step 3	**Click**	in the Zoom button text box 200% ▼ on the Standard toolbar
Step 4	**Key**	125
Step 5	**Press**	the ENTER key
Step 6	**Save**	the workbook

C 2.f Renaming a Sheet Tab

An organized workbook is one in which information is logically grouped and easy to find. Each store's staff comprises sales representatives and technicians. By separating employee data for each group onto different sheet tabs, your workbook will be more organized. Naming each sheet tab makes it much easier to find the data. To name a sheet tab:

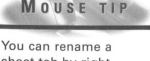
| Step 1 | **Double-click** | the Sheet1 sheet tab |
| Step 2 | **Key** | Sales Reps |

Step 3	*Press*	the ENTER key

Step 4	*Rename*	Sheet2 as Technicians

2.g Changing a Sheet Tab Color

To make it even easier to identify sheet tabs, you can color-code the tabs to make them stand out. To change a sheet tab color:

Step 1	*Right-click*	the Sales Reps sheet tab

Step 2	*Click*	Tab Color

The Format Tab Color dialog box on your screen should look similar to Figure 2-5.

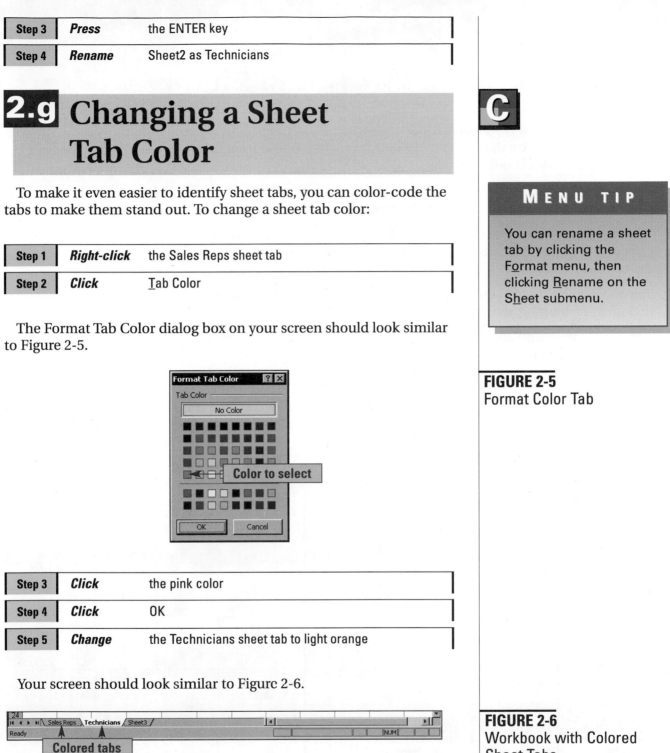

Step 3	*Click*	the pink color

Step 4	*Click*	OK

Step 5	*Change*	the Technicians sheet tab to light orange

Your screen should look similar to Figure 2-6.

Step 6	*Save*	the workbook and close it

The employee name list workbook for the new Kansas City store is ready to be used.

C

MENU TIP

You can rename a sheet tab by clicking the Format menu, then clicking Rename on the Sheet submenu.

FIGURE 2-5
Format Color Tab

FIGURE 2-6
Workbook with Colored Sheet Tabs

chapter
two

Summary

▶ You can create new, blank workbooks by clicking the Blank Workbook link in the task pane.

▶ You can create a new workbook based on an existing workbook by clicking the New command on the File menu, then clicking the Choose workbook link in the New Workbook task pane.

▶ You enter data by keying the information directly into the active cell or in the Formula Bar. You can enter text and numbers in a variety of formats.

▶ You edit data by keying new data in a cell, double-clicking a cell to edit directly in the cell, or pressing the F2 key and using the Formula Bar to edit the cell's contents.

▶ You can use the Undo list to quickly undo as many as 16 actions at once, including formatting, data entry, editing, and deletion.

▶ The Zoom command zooms a worksheet in and out, making it easier to read or display more data at one time.

▶ You can rename and recolor worksheet tabs to make it easier to find data.

Commands Review

Action	Menu Bar	Shortcut Menu	Toolbar	Task Pane	Keyboard
Create a new workbook	File, New	Right-click Null application window, click New	⬜	Blank workbook link in New Workbook task pane	CTRL + N ALT + F, N
Create a new workbook based on another workbook				Choose workbook link in New Workbook task pane	
Edit a cell					F2
Accept a cell entry			✓		ENTER
Cancel a cell entry			✕		ESC
Undo the previous action	Edit, Undo		↺		CTRL + Z ALT + E, U
Redo an undo action	Edit, Redo		↻		CTRL + Y ALT + E, R
Zoom	View, Zoom		100% ▾		ALT + V, Z
Rename a worksheet tab	Format, Sheet, Rename	Right-click sheet tab, click Rename			ALT + O, H, R
Change a worksheet color tab	Format, Sheet, Tab Color	Right-click sheet, tab, click Tab Color			ALT + O, H, T

Concepts Review

Circle the correct answer.

1. To cancel an entry in a cell, press the:
[a] TAB key.
[b] ENTER key.
[c] ESC key.
[d] DELETE key.

2. To accept an entry in a cell:
[a] press the CTRL + ALT + ESC keys.
[b] stop keying and wait for the previous value to return.
[c] press the ESC key.
[d] press the ENTER key.

3. You can undo or redo:
[a] as many as 1 operation.
[b] as many as 10 operations.
[c] as many as 16 operations.
[d] an unlimited number of operations.

4. When you activate a cell containing data and begin keying new data, the new data:
[a] is added to the end of the old data.
[b] is added in front of the old data.
[c] is rejected since there is already data in the cell.
[d] replaces the old data.

5. Pressing the DELETE key when the insertion point is blinking in a cell or in the Formula Bar:
[a] deletes the entire value.
[b] deletes one character to the right.
[c] deletes one character to the left.
[d] does nothing.

6. Pressing the BACKSPACE key when the insertion point is blinking in a cell or in the Formula Bar:
[a] deletes the entire value.
[b] deletes one character to the right.
[c] deletes one character to the left.
[d] does nothing.

7. Which of the following values would be treated as a text value?
[a] 111-22-3333
[b] 11,122,333
[c] 111.22333
[d] $111,223.33

8. When you make a mistake while entering data, you should immediately:
[a] save the workbook.
[b] close the workbook without saving your changes.
[c] reopen the workbook.
[d] use the Undo command.

9. Which of the following is not an option when using the Zoom command?
[a] 200%
[b] 50%
[c] Selection
[d] 1%

10. The default action that occurs when you press the ENTER key when entering cell data is to:
[a] accept the entry and move the active cell down one.
[b] accept the entry and move the active cell to the left.
[c] discard the changes and revert the cell's contents back to the way they were.
[d] accept the entry and move the active cell to the right.

chapter two

Circle **T** if the statement is true or **F** if the statement is false.

T   F   1. The Undo command can undo any command in Excel.

T   F   2. If you rename a sheet tab, you cannot change its color.

T   F   3. To edit a cell entry, you must double-click it first.

T   F   4. You cannot use the Undo command until you have first used the Redo command.

T   F   5. You can zoom in to 1600% using the Zoom button on the Standard toolbar.

T   F   6. When you create a new workbook from an existing workbook, a number is added to the end of the filename.

T   F   7. Pressing the ESC key is a valid means of accepting an entry in a cell.

T   F   8. The Cancel and Enter buttons do not appear on the Formula Bar until you are entering data in a cell.

T   F   9. The insertion point appears while you are editing a cell to indicate where the next character you key will go.

T   F   10. Using any of the navigation keys is a valid way of accepting data entry in a cell.

Skills Review

SCANS

Exercise 1   C

1. Create a new workbook and enter the data below on Sheet1. Enter the text "TIME SHEET" in cell A1. (*Hint:* Enter the dates with forward slashes and the times with colons. Use 24-hour clock times, as shown in the table.)

TIME SHEET		
Date	Start Time	End Time
5/10/2003	8:00	17:00
5/11/2003	8:05	16:30
5/12/2003	8:00	16:55

2. Save the workbook as *Time Sheet*, and print it.

3. Close the workbook.

Exercise 2   C

1. Create a new workbook based on the *Employee Time Sheet* workbook located on the Data Disk.

2. Save the workbook as *Employee Time Sheet Revised*.

3. Change the value in cell A2 to your name.

4. Change the start time for 5/10/2003 to 8:15.

5. Change the end time for 5/12/2003 to 17:35.

6. Enter the following data in row 7:

   5/13/2003   8:45   17:00

7. Save your changes, and print the worksheet.

8. Close the workbook.

Exercise 3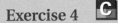

1. Create a new workbook based on the *Employee Time Sheet Revised* workbook that you created in Exercise 2.

2. Save the workbook as *Multiple Employees Time Sheets*.

3. Rename Sheet2 as "Lori Jones."

4. Rename Sheet3 as "Kaili Muafala."

5. Rename Sheet1 as your name.

6. Change the sheet tab color of each worksheet to a different color.

7. Save your changes, and print the worksheet.

8. Close the workbook.

Exercise 4

1. Create a new workbook and enter the data below on Sheet1. Enter the label "CHECKBOOK TRANSACTIONS" in cell A1.

CHECKBOOK TRANSACTIONS			
Date	Description	Credit	Debit
10/12/2003	Paycheck	1542.90	
10/14/2003	Groceries		142.57
10/20/2003	Bonus	300.00	
10/21/2003	House payment		842.50

2. Save the workbook as *Checkbook Transactions*, and print it.

3. Close the workbook.

Exercise 5

1. Create a new workbook based on the *Checkbook Transactions* workbook that you created in Exercise 4.

2. Change cell A1 to read "PERSONAL CHECKBOOK TRANSACTIONS."

3. Save the file as *Personal Checkbook Transactions*.

4. Delete the four transactions found in cells A3 through D6.

5. Save and print the workbook, then close it.

chapter two

Exercise 6   C

1. Create a new workbook and enter the data below on Sheet1. Enter the label "STATE CAPITALS" in cell A1.

STATE CAPITALS	
State	Capital City
Utah	Salt Lake City
Delaware	Dover
California	Los Angeles
Arizona	Tempe
New York	Albany
Florida	Miami
Texas	Dallas
Colorado	Denver

2. Rename Sheet1 as "Capitals."

3. Recolor the Capitals sheet tab to red.

4. Save the workbook as *State Capitals*, and print it.

5. Close the workbook.

Exercise 7   C

1. Create a new workbook based on the *State Capitals* workbook that you created in Exercise 6.

2. Save the workbook as *Corrected State Capitals*.

3. Display the Web toolbar, if necessary, by clicking the <u>V</u>iew menu, pointing to <u>T</u>oolbars, then clicking Web.

4. Search the Web for a list of state capitals.

5. Correct any errors you find in the workbook.

6. Rename the Capitals sheet tab as "Corrected Capitals," and change the sheet tab color to green.

7. Save and print the workbook, then close it.

Exercise 8   C

1. Use the Internet to search for movie times in your area.

2. Create a new workbook with column headings for "Movie Title," "Time," and "Theater."

3. Record the start times for at least five different movies you would like to see.

4. Save the workbook as *Movie Times*, and print it.

5. Close the workbook.

Case Projects

Project 1

You are the office manager of a small business. One of your duties is to keep track of the office supplies inventory. Create a workbook using fictitious data for at least 20 items. Include a column for each of the following: name of item, current amount in stock, and estimated price. Save the workbook as *Office Supplies Inventory*, and print and close it.

Project 2

As the payroll clerk at a college bookstore, you must calculate the hours worked by each student employee during the week. Create a new workbook based on the workbook *Employee Work Hours* located on the Data Disk. In row 1 of columns B, C, D, E, and F, list the days Monday through Friday. List the number of hours that each student works each day. Save the workbook as *Employee Work Hours Revised*, and then print and close it.

Project 3

You are a teacher who uses Excel to record student scores. Create a workbook containing 15 fictitious student names with five assignment columns and a total column. Record data indicating each student's scores for the five assignments. Switch to Sheet2 to enter data from another class. Enter 15 more student names and five assignment columns. Record new data as you did before. Rename Sheet1 as "Class 1" and Sheet2 as "Class 2." Change the color of the two sheet tabs to red. Save the workbook as *Student Scores*, and then print and close it.

Project 4

You are thinking of investing money in the stock market. Connect to the Internet and search the Web to find the most current stock price of five companies in which you are interested. Create a new workbook to record the company name, company stock ticker symbol, current share price, yesterday's share price, and the date. Rename the worksheet as "Stocks." Save the workbook as *Stock Prices*, and then print and close it.

Project 5

You make purchasing recommendations for computer systems to your boss. Connect to the Internet and search the Web to obtain prices for systems offered by at least three different vendors. Create a new workbook to record the vendor name, Web address, system price, processor speed, amount of RAM, hard drive size, and monitor size. When you enter a Web address, Excel automatically formats it with blue text and underline. Rename the sheet tab with today's month and day; for example, Jan 4. Save the workbook as *Computer Prices*, and then print and close it.

Project 6

You are planning a road trip. Connect to the Internet and search the Web to find the driving distance from your city to at least five other cities you would like to visit. (*Hint:* Search for the keywords "driving directions.") Create a new workbook to record the starting city, destination city, and driving distance. Save the workbook as *Road Trip*, and then print and close it.

Project 7

You are working on a statistics project. Over the next five days, count the number of students attending each of your classes. Create a new workbook. In row 1, enter the dates you used for your survey. In column A, enter the class names. Enter the data you collected each day for each class. Save the workbook as *Attendance Statistics*, and then print and close it.

Project 8

You are a runner training for a marathon. You keep track of your progress by recording the date, mileage, and time of your runs. Create a new workbook to record fictitious data. Rename Sheet1 as "Week 1," Sheet2 as "Week 2," and Sheet3 as "Week 3." Give each sheet tab a different color. On the Week 1 worksheet, record fictitious data for one week. Save the workbook as *Running Log*, and then print and close it.

chapter two

Building Worksheets

Chapter Overview

M ost worksheets do much more than store data. Data needs to be analyzed, calculated, and presented. To perform most of this work, functions and formulas work tirelessly behind the scenes, calculating and recalculating every time data is changed in your worksheets. Reorganizing worksheets by moving and copying data is a regular task. In this chapter, you learn how to accomplish this efficiently.

LEARNING OBJECTIVES

▸ Create and revise formulas
▸ Use cut, copy, and paste
▸ Copy formulas with relative, absolute, and mixed cell references
▸ Use basic functions
▸ Use the Insert Function dialog box
▸ Use 3-D references in formulas

Case profile

One of your duties at Super Power Computers is to calculate sales commissions and bonuses and send this information back to the store managers. Excel makes this simple by allowing you to use formulas to do the calculations. You can also use specialized Excel functions, which help you use your time more effectively. You can then copy and paste the formulas to quickly build your worksheets.

chapter three

3.a Creating and Revising Formulas

Formulas provide much of the true power of a spreadsheet. A **formula** is a mathematical expression that calculates a value. Some formulas are simple, such as those that add, subtract, multiply, and divide two or more values; for example, 2+2. Other formulas can be very complex and include a sequence of **functions**, or predefined formulas. All formulas require **operands**, which can be either values or references to cells containing values. Most formulas require **operators** to indicate the type of calculation that will take place. Common mathematical operators include + for addition, – for subtraction, * for multiplication, / for division, and ^ for exponentiation.

Following Formula Syntax and Rules of Precedence

Formulas follow a syntax. The **syntax** is the proper structure, or order, of the elements (operands and operators) in a formula. Excel follows the **rules of precedence**: it evaluates formulas from left to right, first evaluating any operations between parentheses, then any exponentiation, then multiplication and division, followed by addition and subtraction. Consider the following examples: 5+2*3 and (5+2)*3. In the first formula, 2*3 is calculated first and then added to 5, giving a result of 11. In the second example, 5+2 is calculated first and then multiplied by 3, giving a result of 21.

Entering Formulas

The real power of formulas lies in their ability to use cell references. Using cell references allows you to quickly change values, leaving the formula intact. Sales representatives at Super Power Computers are paid a commission based on the total sales. You need to calculate the sales commission for each employee. To enter a formula:

| Step 1 | *Open* | the *Super Power Computers - Bonus* workbook located on the Data Disk |
| Step 2 | *Save* | the workbook as *Super Power Computers - Bonus Revised* |

This workbook contains sales data from each of the Super Power Computer stores.

| Step 3 | *Activate* | cell D4 on the Store #1 worksheet |

chapter three

All formulas begin with an equal sign = to indicate to Excel that the following expression needs to be evaluated.

| Step 4 | *Key* | =c4*0.05 |

You do not have to capitalize column references. Excel performs this task for you automatically when you enter a formula.

| Step 5 | *Click* | the Enter button ☑ on the Formula Bar |

This simple mathematical formula multiplies the value in cell C4 by 0.05 and displays the result, $1,726.55. The Formula Bar displays the formula, not the calculated result. Your screen should look similar to Figure 3-1.

FIGURE 3-1
Formula Displayed in the
Formula Bar

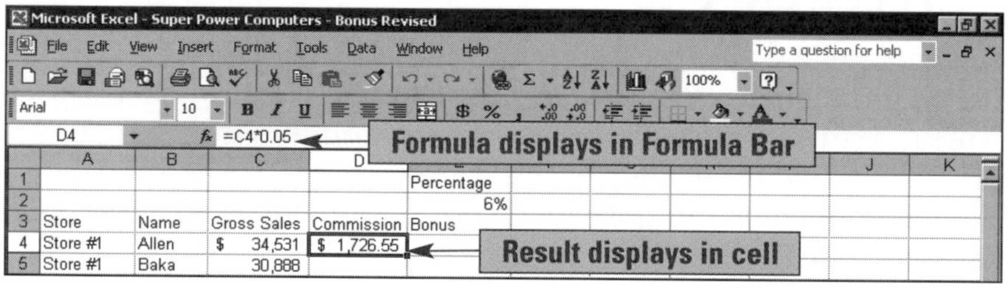

Editing Formulas Using the Formula Bar

Because Super Power Computers has had a good year, the sales commission has been increased to 6%. You can edit the formula to reflect this change. To edit a formula:

Step 1	*Verify*	that cell D4 is the active cell
Step 2	*Drag*	to select 5 in the Formula Bar
Step 3	*Key*	6
Step 4	*Press*	the ENTER key

Cell D4 displays the new result of the calculation, $2,071.86.

| Step 5 | *Save* | the workbook |

QUICK TIP

The blue box that appears around cell C4 is called a **range finder**. It highlights cells that are referenced in a formula.

3.b Using Cut, Copy, and Paste

Moving and copying data helps you organize and prepare worksheets quickly. When data is moved, or **cut**, from a worksheet, it is removed from its original location and placed on the **Clipboard**, which holds data temporarily. To finish moving the data that you cut to another location, you **paste** it from the Clipboard. When data is **copied**, the original data remains in place and a copy of the data is placed on the Clipboard. Data that you cut or copy stays on the Clipboard until you cut or copy more data, or until you exit Excel.

Copying Data Using Copy and Paste

The formula you added to cell D4 needs to be copied for each employee. To copy data using copy and paste:

Step 1	*Activate*	cell D4
Step 2	*Click*	the Copy button on the Standard toolbar
Step 3	*Click*	cell D5
Step 4	*Click*	the Paste button list arrow on the Standard toolbar
Step 5	*Click*	Formulas

This is the default command if you simply click the Paste button. Clicking Values in the list would paste the value from cell D4 instead of the formula.

Step 6	*Press*	the ESC key to end the Copy command

The formula in the Formula Bar has changed to reflect that this cell is in row 5 instead of in row 4. In other words, the formula references cell C5 instead of cell C4.

Copying Data Using the Fill Handle

Using the fill handle, you can quickly copy the contents of a cell to adjacent cells. The fill handle is the small black square that appears in the lower-right corner of a selected cell. To copy a formula using the fill handle:

Step 1	*Activate*	cell D5, if necessary

chapter
three

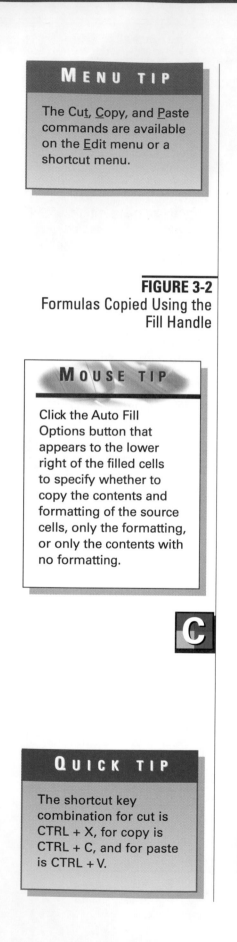

MENU TIP

The Cut, Copy, and Paste commands are available on the Edit menu or a shortcut menu.

MOUSE TIP

Click the Auto Fill Options button that appears to the lower right of the filled cells to specify whether to copy the contents and formatting of the source cells, only the formatting, or only the contents with no formatting.

QUICK TIP

The shortcut key combination for cut is CTRL + X, for copy is CTRL + C, and for paste is CTRL + V.

| Step 2 | *Drag* | the fill handle to cell D17 |

Make sure you drag only to cell D17 and not to cell D18.

| Step 3 | *Release* | the left mouse button |

The formula is copied to cells D6:D17. Your screen should look similar to Figure 3-2.

FIGURE 3-2
Formulas Copied Using the Fill Handle

![Microsoft Excel screenshot showing the Super Power Computers - Bonus Revised workbook with formulas copied using the fill handle. Cell D5 contains =C5*0.06. Columns show Store, Name, Gross Sales, Commission, and Bonus data with labels for Fill handle and Auto Fill Options button.]

C *Moving Data Using Cut and Paste*

When you cut data from cells, a flashing border surrounds the selected area. The status bar provides instructions about how to select a destination cell. The destination can be on another worksheet or even another open workbook. To move data by using cut and paste:

Step 1	*Select*	the range E1:E2
Step 2	*Click*	the Cut button on the Standard toolbar
Step 3	*Activate*	cell F1
Step 4	*Click*	the Paste button on the Standard toolbar

The Cut command in Excel differs from that in other programs, such as Microsoft Word. Excel does not remove the selected text until you take one of two actions: (1) complete the move by selecting a destination and performing the Paste command or (2) press the DELETE key. If you press the DELETE key instead of completing the Paste operation, you do not place the data on the Clipboard; it is removed permanently. If you change your mind before pasting or deleting, press the ESC key to cancel the cut operation.

Using Drag-and-Drop to Cut, Copy, and Paste

Another way to move and copy data is to use **drag-and-drop**. To drag selected cells, click the selection border using the left mouse button. Hold the left mouse button down as you *drag* the cells to a new location. The mouse pointer changes to a four-headed arrow pointer, indicating the cells are being moved. Then *drop* them by releasing the left mouse button. To move data by using drag-and-drop:

Step 1	**Select**	cells A3:E19
Step 2	**Move**	the pointer over the border of your selection
Step 3	**Drag**	the range to cells A1:E17

A ScreenTip and a range outline guide you in moving the cells. Your screen should look similiar to Figure 3-3.

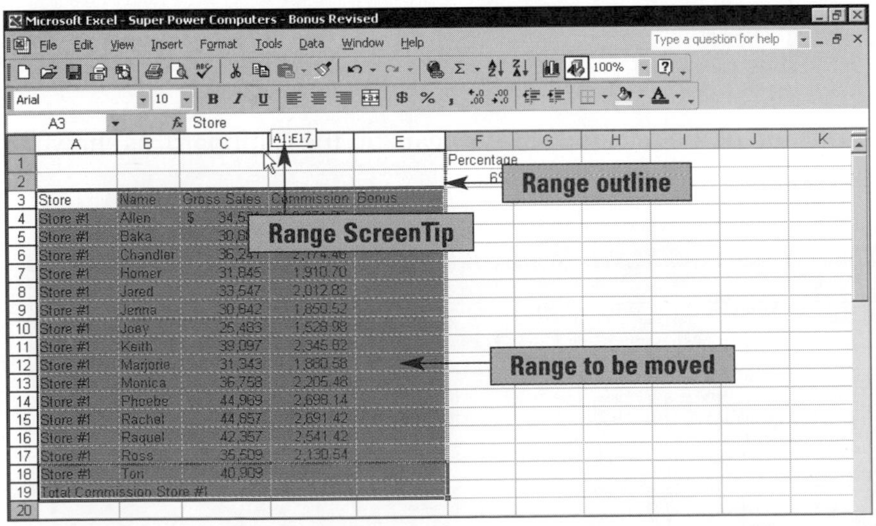

CAUTION TIP

When moving data with drag-and-drop, Excel prompts you if the move will overwrite data. However, Excel does *not* warn you of this when copying using drag-and-drop, and it overwrites any data in the target cells.

FIGURE 3-3
Dragging and Dropping to Copy Cells

Step 4	**Release**	the mouse button

chapter
three

TASK PANE TIP

If a task pane is already visible, you can click the Other Task Panes list arrow at the top of the open task pane, then click Clipboard to open the Office Clipboard.

You can use a similar process to copy data. To copy data using drag-and-drop:

Step 1	***Select***	cell D15
Step 2	***Press & hold***	the CTRL key
Step 3	***Move***	the pointer over the border of your selection
Step 4	***Observe***	the plus sign in the mouse pointer, indicating that you are creating a copy of the selected data
Step 5	***Drag***	the selection to cell D16
Step 6	***Release***	the mouse button and the CTRL key

C

Using the Office Clipboard to Paste Data

MOUSE TIP

To move data from one worksheet to another using drag-and-drop, press and hold the ALT key as you drag the range onto the new sheet tab. To copy data to another worksheet using drag-and-drop, press and hold the CTRL + ALT keys as you drag the range onto the new sheet tab.

Every time you cut or copy a piece of data, it replaces the data that was previously on the Clipboard. Office has its own Clipboard, called the Office Clipboard, which holds up to 24 items from any open application. You can then select the item you want and paste it into another Office document. You need to activate the Office Clipboard before you can collect cut or copied items on it. To activate the Office Clipboard:

Step 1	***Click***	Edit
Step 2	***Click***	Office Clipboard
Step 3	***Observe***	that the Clipboard task pane opens
Step 4	***Copy***	the range F1:F2

A portion of the selected data appears on the Clipboard, as shown in Figure 3-4.

FIGURE 3-4
Clipboard Items

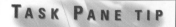

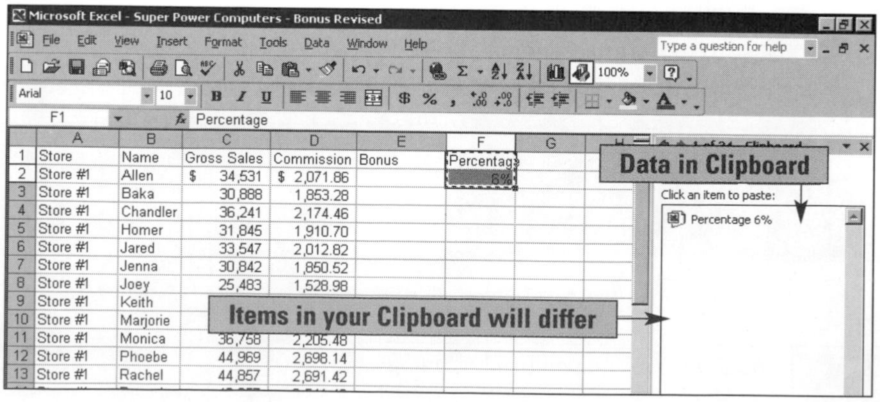

 **Step 5** | *Activate* | cell F1 on the Store #2 sheet tab

The top item on the Office Clipboard is the last item cut or copied.

Step 6 | *Point to* | Percentage 6% in the Clipboard task pane

A list arrow appears. If you click the list arrow, a submenu opens with <u>P</u>aste and <u>D</u>elete on it. Clicking the item on the Clipboard is the same as clicking the list arrow and then clicking <u>P</u>aste.

Step 7 | *Click* | the Percentage 6% Clipboard item

A copy of your data is placed in cells F1:F2 on the Store #2 worksheet.

Step 8 | *Click* | the Close button on the Clipboard task pane title bar

Step 9 | *Save* | the workbook

3.c Copying Formulas with Relative, Absolute, and Mixed Cell References

Excel uses three types of cell references: absolute, relative, and mixed. When you copy a formula containing a **relative reference**, the references change relative to the cell from which the formula is being copied. If cell C1 contains the formula =A1+B1 and is copied to cell D2, the formula changes to =B2+C2. Cell D2 is one row down and one row over from cell C1; the references B2 and C2 are correspondingly one row down and one row over from cells A1 and B1. When you copied the formulas in column D earlier in this chapter, you copied relative references, so the formulas were automatically updated to reflect the new row they were copied to.

When you need a formula to refer to a specific cell, no matter where the formula is copied, you use an **absolute reference**. Absolute cell references prefix the column and row with a dollar sign ($). A better way to set up the formula in column D is to use an absolute reference to cell F2, so that if the sales commission must be adjusted, it only has to be changed in one place. The formula for cell D2 would be **=C2*F2**.

chapter three

QUICK TIP

To change a relative cell reference to an absolute or mixed reference, position the insertion point within the cell reference in the Formula Bar, then press the F4 key to cycle through the cell references.

When this formula is copied, the first, relative, reference changes, while the second, absolute, reference does not. To edit the formula and add an absolute reference:

Step 1	*Click*	the Store #1 sheet tab
Step 2	*Enter*	=C2*F2 in cell D2
Step 3	*Use*	the fill handle to copy cell D2 to cells D3:D16

The formula as well as its format is pasted into cell D3:D16. You don't want to copy the formatting.

Step 4	*Click*	the Auto Fill Options button ▦ on the worksheet
Step 5	*Click*	Fill Without Formatting
Step 6	*Observe*	that the dollar signs disappear from cell D3:D16
Step 7	*Click*	cell D3

Note in the Formula Bar that the relative reference in the formula was correctly updated to the proper row number, while the absolute reference remained fixed on cell F2.

Step 8	*Save*	the workbook

In addition to absolute and relative references, Excel uses mixed references. A **mixed cell reference** maintains a reference to a specific row or column. For example, to maintain a reference to column A while allowing the row number to increment, use the mixed reference $A1. To maintain a reference to a specific row number while allowing the column letter to increment, use the mixed reference A$1.

C 3.d Using Basic Functions

Functions are predefined formulas that reduce complicated formulas to a function name and several required arguments or operands. An **argument** is some sort of data, usually numeric or text, that is supplied to a function. For example, to find the average of a series of numerical values, you must divide the sum by the number of values in the series. The AVERAGE function does this automatically when you supply the series of values as arguments. Arguments can be supplied to functions by keying the value in directly, or by using cell references. You can use formulas, or even other functions, as some or all of the arguments of a function.

To enter a function in a cell, you key the = sign, the name of the function, and then any required and/or optional arguments used by the function enclosed in parentheses. If the function is part of a longer formula, you key the = sign only at the beginning of the formula. The first function you learn about, the **SUM** function, uses the following syntax:

=**SUM**(**number1**, number2, …)

Required arguments are listed in bold. Certain functions, such as the SUM function, allow you to supply as many optional arguments as you like, indicated by the ellipses (…).

notes
Throughout this book function names are capitalized to distinguish them from other text. Function names are not actually case-sensitive, so =count, =Count, and =COUNT are all valid ways to enter the function name.

Using the SUM Function

The SUM function, which adds two or more values, is one of the most commonly used functions. You need to add the total amount to be paid in sales commissions. To start keying the SUM function:

Step 1	*Activate*	cell D17

Step 2	*Key*	=SUM(

The Argument ScreenTip appears with the syntax of the formula you've started entering. You can enter individual values separated by commas, enter a range, or simply select cells. You select a range of cells.

Step 3	*Drag*	to select cells D2:D16

Your screen should look similar to Figure 3-5. The range D2:D16 is the number1 argument of the SUM function.

chapter
three

FIGURE 3-5
Using the SUM Function

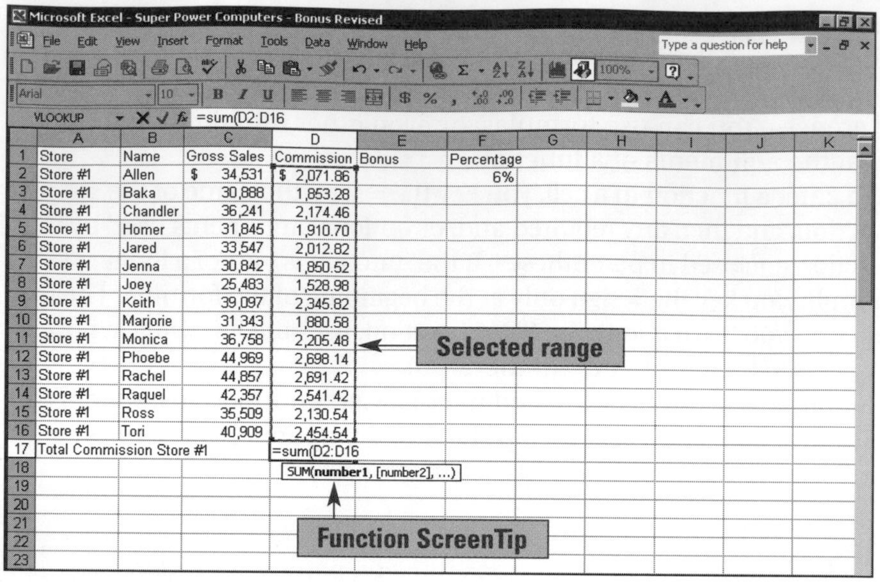

| Step 4 | *Click* | the Enter button ☑ on the Formula Bar |

The total commission for Store #1, $32,350.56, appears in cell D17.
Note in the Formula Bar that the end parenthesis was automatically
added when you accepted the entry. If you want to sum the values in a
second range, separate each range with a comma. For example, to
sum the ranges A3:D3 and A14:D14, the SUM function would be
written as =SUM(A3:D3, A14:D14).

Entering Functions Using the AutoSum Command

To quickly insert commonly used functions, you can use the
AutoSum button on the Standard toolbar. When you use the AutoSum
button, Excel inserts the selected function and scans cells above and
to the left for arguments. If it detects a continuous series of cells
containing values, the reference is selected and added as an argument.
To enter the SUM function using the AutoSum button:

Step 1	*Click*	the Store #2 sheet tab
Step 2	*Click*	cell D17
Step 3	*Click*	the AutoSum button list arrow Σ ▾ on the Standard toolbar

Five common functions are listed on the AutoSum button list.

Step 4	*Click*	Sum

The range D2:D16 is automatically selected, and the function =SUM(D2:D16) is inserted in cell D17.

Step 5	*Press*	the ENTER key
Step 6	*Observe*	that the result, $35,396.04, appears in cell D17
Step 7	*Save*	the workbook

3.e Using the Insert Function Dialog Box

Excel provides many more functions in addition to the five listed on the AutoSum button. The Insert Function dialog box helps you enter values or cell references for each of the required arguments in the correct order. For convenience, Excel divides functions into categories, such as statistical, date and time, and financial. In this section you preview a few of the many functions available.

Using the Date Function DATE

Date and time values are calculated in Excel by using special values called **serial numbers**. A value of 1 represents the first day that Excel can use in calculations, January 1, 1900. Hours, minutes, and seconds are portions of a day, so 12:00 PM is calculated using a value of .5. Most of the time, you enter the actual date, such as 1/1/1900, and Excel hides the serial value by formatting the cell with a date or time format. At times you may need to convert a given date to its serial number. For example, you need to update your workbook every 60 days, so you want to add the update date to the workbook. You can do this by using the DATE function to change the date to its serial value, and then adding 60 to the result. The **DATE** function returns the serial number value of a date. Its syntax is as follows:

=DATE(year, month, day)

The required arguments, year, month, and day, must be supplied as individual values. To calculate this date using the DATE function:

Step 1	*Activate*	cell C22 on the Store #1 worksheet

chapter three

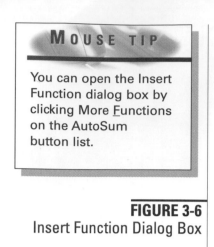

MOUSE TIP

You can open the Insert Function dialog box by clicking More <u>F</u>unctions on the AutoSum button list.

Step 2	*Key*	Updated
Step 3	*Press*	the TAB key
Step 4	*Click*	the Insert Function button 𝒇ₓ on the Formula Bar

The Insert Function dialog box displays a list of Function categories and function names. Your dialog box should look similar to Figure 3-6.

FIGURE 3-6
Insert Function Dialog Box

Step 5	*Click*	the Or select a <u>c</u>ategory: list arrow
Step 6	*Click*	Date & Time

The Select a function: list changes to an alphabetical list of all the functions in the Date & Time category.

Step 7	*Click*	Date in the Select a functio<u>n</u>: list
Step 8	*Click*	OK

The Function Arguments dialog box opens, and guides you through the entry of each argument of the selected function. A description of the function is located in the middle of the dialog box. Each text box is an argument of the function. If the name of the argument is in bold, then it is a required argument. The Year text box is selected, as indicated by the blinking insertion point. A description of the selected argument appears below the function description. See Figure 3-7.

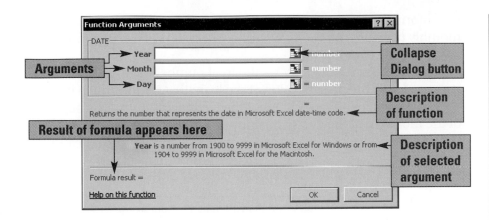

FIGURE 3-7
Function Arguments

QUICK TIP

The name of the function you are working with—in this case, DATE—appears in the Name box in the worksheet.

Step 9	*Key*	2003 in the Year text box
Step 10	*Press*	the TAB key to move to the Month text box
Step 11	*Key*	5 in the Month text box
Step 12	*Press*	the TAB key to move to the Day text box
Step 13	*Key*	1 in the Day box
Step 14	*Observe*	the formula result at the bottom of the dialog box
Step 15	*Click*	OK

Next, you need to add 60 to the result of the function. To add a formula to a function:

Step 1	*Press*	the F2 key
Step 2	*Key*	+60
Step 3	*Press*	the ENTER key

The result of the formula, 6/30/2003, appears in cell D22.

Using the Financial Function PMT

Financial functions are used to calculate values for all types of investments and loans, as well as to calculate depreciation of assets. The **PMT** function is used to calculate the payment of a loan based on constant payments and a constant interest rate.

Luis Alvarez, the owner of the Super Power Computers chain of stores, is considering borrowing some money to expand its headquarters, and he wants to get his managers' opinions on the loan, so you want to include

MOUSE TIP

If you cannot see the cells you want to add as arguments, click the Collapse Dialog button in the text box of the selected argument to shrink the dialog box to a single line. Click the button again to restore the dialog box to its normal size.

chapter three

this information in the workbook. You need to calculate how much monthly payments on the loan will be. The syntax of the PMT function is:

$$=PMT(\textbf{rate,nper,pv,}fv,type)$$

Rate is the interest rate, *nper* is the total number of payments for the loan, and *pv* is the present value of the loan; that is, how much is owed. *Fv* (future value) and *type* (whether the payment is due at the beginning of the month or at the end of the month) are both optional arguments because they have default values of 0 for *fv* and 0 for *type*, indicating payment will be made at the end of the month. To use the PMT function:

Step 1	*Activate*	cell E3 on the Financial worksheet
Step 2	*Click*	the Insert Function button 📊 on the Formula Bar
Step 3	*Click*	the Or select a <u>c</u>ategory: list arrow
Step 4	*Click*	Financial
Step 5	*Double-click*	PMT in the Select a functio<u>n</u>: list

Instead of keying arguments into the Function Arguments dialog box, you can click cells on the worksheet.

| Step 6 | *Drag* | the Function Arguments dialog box title bar to move the dialog box so you can see row 3 |
| Step 7 | *Click* | cell A3 |

Because the interest rate is expressed in terms of a year, you must divide the rate by 12, and supply this result as the rate argument.

Step 8	*Key*	/12
Step 9	*Press*	the TAB key to move to the Nper text box
Step 10	*Click*	cell B3
Step 11	*Press*	the TAB key to move to the Pv text box
Step 12	*Click*	cell C3
Step 13	*Click*	OK

The monthly payment for this loan is calculated at $3,945.94. It appears in parentheses and in red because it is a negative value (an expense to the company). This is common accounting notation.

Using the Logical Function IF

Logical functions test data using a true/false evaluation. Think of a true/false evaluation is as a yes/no choice. For example, bonuses are paid to a Super Power Computer's sales representative if his or her sales are greater than $37,500. The question "Are the total sales for this employee greater than or equal to $37,500?" has only two answers, "Yes" or "No."

The **IF** function is used to evaluate whether a given statement is true. If the logical test is true, the function returns one value; otherwise, it returns a different value. The IF function has the following syntax:

=IF(logical_test,value_if_true,value_if_false)

The first argument identifies the logical test. The second argument indicates the formula's value if the logical test is true. The last argument identifies the formula's value if the logical test is false. Sometimes it is easier to create logical functions by writing them in statement form first:

> **If** sales are greater than or equal to 37,500, **then** the bonus is 500, **else** (otherwise) the result is 0.

Now, you can put your sentence into something resembling function syntax:

> =IF(sales>=37500, then bonus is 500, else bonus is 0)

Finally, create your formula using named ranges, cell references, or values. To use the IF function:

MENU TIP

To open the Insert Function dialog box, click the Function command on the Insert menu.

Step 1	*Activate*	cell E2 on the Store #1 worksheet
Step 2	*Click*	the Insert Function button fx on the Formula Bar
Step 3	*Double-click*	the IF function in the Logical category
Step 4	*Key*	C2>=37500 in the Logical_test text box
Step 5	*Press*	the TAB key
Step 6	*Key*	500
Step 7	*Press*	the TAB key
Step 8	*Key*	0
Step 9	*Click*	OK

Because the value in cell C2 ($34,531) is less than 37500, the value of cell E2 evaluates to 0.

| Step 10 | *Copy* | the formula in cell E2 to cells E3:E16 |

QUICK TIP

If you see #NUM! in a cell, then you used an unacceptable argument in a function requiring a numeric argument. This error also arises if a formula produces a number too large (greater than $1*10^{307}$) or too small (less than $-1*10^{307}$) to be represented in Excel.

chapter three

3.f Using 3-D References in Formulas

Cell references are used in formulas to ensure that when a data value changes, the formula recalculates and displays the new result automatically. The simple formula =A1+B1, for example, links to cells A1 and B1 to calculate the sum of the values contained in those cells. **Linking** formulas link to the cells on another worksheet. The linked formulas maintain a connection to the worksheet that holds the original formula.

In complex workbooks with many worksheets, you may need to perform calculations that use cell references from several worksheets. This type of cell reference is called a **3-D reference**. 3-D references span not only columns and rows, but worksheets as well.

You need to find the minimum and maximum commissions for all four stores. The syntax of the MAX and MIN functions is similar to that of the SUM function:

=**MAX**(**number1,** *number2, …*)
=**MIN**(**number1,** *number2, …*)

To add the MAX function to a worksheet using 3-D references:

Step 1	*Click*	cell B19 on the Store #1 worksheet
Step 2	*Key*	Maximum commission
Step 3	*Press*	the TAB key twice
Step 4	*Click*	the AutoSum button list arrow Σ ▾ on the Standard toolbar
Step 5	*Click*	Max
Step 6	*Press & hold*	the SHIFT key
Step 7	*Click*	the Store #4 sheet tab

This selects all the worksheets from Store #1 to Store #4.

Step 8	*Select*	the range D2:D16

In the formula, you see the 3-D reference =MAX('Store #1:Store #4'!D2:E16). The worksheet names are enclosed by apostrophes (') and separated from the cell references by an exclamation point (!).

| Step 9 | **Click** | the Enter button ☑ on the Formula Bar |

The result, 2936.46, is correctly identified as the highest value among the selected cells on the four store worksheets.

To add the MIN function to a worksheet using 3-D reference:

Step 1	**Click**	cell B20 on the Store #1 worksheet
Step 2	**Key**	Minimum commission
Step 3	**Press**	the TAB key twice
Step 4	**Click**	the AutoSum button list arrow ∑ ▾ on the Standard toolbar
Step 5	**Click**	Min
Step 6	**Press & hold**	the SHIFT key
Step 7	**Click**	the Store #4 sheet tab
Step 8	**Select**	the range D2:D16
Step 9	**Click**	the Enter button ☑ on the Formula Bar

The result, 1506.66, is correctly identified as the lowest value among the selected cells on the four store worksheets.

| Step 10 | **Save** | the workbook and close it |

Your workbook is ready for distribution to the four stores.

QUICK TIP

The functions presented in this chapter are only a small sample of the many functions offered in Excel. Take time to explore the functions using the Insert Function dialog box, or use Ask A Question Box to look up detailed help about any function you want to learn more about.

chapter
three

Summary

▶ You can create formulas to calculate values. Formulas can use cell references to update information whenever the referenced cell's data changes.

▶ All formulas have a syntax; when Excel calculates results, it follows the rules of precedence.

▶ Functions are built-in formulas used to perform a variety of calculations. Most functions require arguments, which you can supply as values, cell references, or even formulas.

▶ You use the cut, copy, and paste operations to move or copy information.

▶ Use the Office Clipboard to store up to 24 items. These items can be pasted into other workbooks, or even into documents created in other applications.

▶ You can drag selection borders to move data. Press the CTRL key and drag selection borders to copy data. Press the ALT key to move or copy data to another worksheet.

▶ Relative cell references change relative to the source cell when copied.

▶ Absolute cell references always refer to the same cell when a formula is copied. Absolute cell references use the dollar sign ($) in front of the column and row identifiers: A1.

▶ Mixed cell references always refer to a specific row or column when the formula is copied. Mixed references use the dollar sign ($) in front of either the row or column identifier: $A1 or A$1.

▶ Insert Function and the Function Palette work together as a function wizard, providing helpful information to guide you through the construction of complex formulas.

▶ Basic functions, such as SUM, MAX, and MIN, can be inserted by using the AutoSum button.

▶ Date and time functions, including DATE, allow you to perform calculations using dates.

▶ Financial functions, such as PMT, allow you to calculate values for investments and loans.

▶ Logical functions, such as IF, test data using a true/false evaluation. The calculated result depends on the result of the evaluation.

▶ Formulas can use 3-D cell references—cell references from other worksheets or other workbooks.

Commands Review

Action	Menu Bar	Shortcut Menu	Toolbar	Task Pane	Keyboard
Cut	Edit, Cut	Cut	✂		CTRL + X ALT + E, T
Copy	Edit, Copy	Copy	📋		CTRL + C ALT + E, C
Paste	Edit, Paste	Paste	📋	Click item in palette in Office Clipboard task pane	CTRL + V ALT + E, P
Insert common functions using AutoSum			Σ ▾		
Insert Function	Insert, Function		*fx*		SHIFT + F3 ALT + I, F
Cycle reference type between absolute, mixed, and relative					F4

Concepts Review

SCANS

Circle the correct answer.

1. To copy a selection while dragging, press and hold the:
   [a] SHIFT key.
   [b] END key.
   [c] CTRL key.
   [d] ALT key.

2. To copy a selection to another worksheet, press and hold the:
   [a] SHIFT + CTRL keys.
   [b] CTRL + ALT keys.
   [c] SHIFT + ALT keys.
   [d] CTRL + SPACEBAR keys.

3. Which of the following cell references is an absolute reference?
   [a] A1
   [b] $A1
   [c] A1
   [d] A$1

4. Copying the formula =A1+B1 from cell C1 to cell E3 would make what change to the formula?
   [a] =A1+B1
   [b] =A1+C3
   [c] =B3+C1
   [d] =C3+D3

5. Copying the formula =$A1+B$2 from cell C1 to cell E3 would make what change to the formula?
   [a] =$A3+D$2
   [b] =$A1+B$2
   [c] =$A2+E$2
   [d] =$A3+C$2

6. Identify the type of reference for the row and column of the following cell reference: X$24.
   [a] absolute, absolute
   [b] absolute, relative
   [c] relative, absolute
   [d] relative, relative

7. The DATE function returns the:
   [a] serial value of a date.
   [b] current date.
   [c] current time.
   [d] current system status.

8. The proper syntax for an IF formula is:
   [a] =IF(condition,value_if_false,value_if_true).
   [b] =IF(condition,value_if_true,value_if_false).
   [c] =IF(value_if_true,value_if_false,condition).
   [d] =IF(value_if_false,value_if_true,condition).

chapter three

9. Which of the following formulas returns the value 60?

[a] =10*2+4

[b] =(10*2)+4

[c] =10*(2+4)

[d] =10+(2*4)

10. All formulas start with:

[a] @.

[b] the keyword "Formula".

[c] =.

[d] $$.

Circle **T** if the statement is true or **F** if the statement is false.

T   F   1. The Formula Arguments dialog box displays the results of the formula as you add values for each of the arguments.

T   F   2. A good way to create a logical formula is to write it out in statement form first.

T   F   3. Skipping optional arguments in a function is acceptable.

T   F   4. Changing the order of required arguments in a function is acceptable, as long as they are all there.

T   F   5. The formula =(5+5)*2 gives the same result as the formula =5+5*2.

T   F   6. Formulas are only updated when you press the F9 key.

T   F   7. You can use the F4 key to cycle through cell reference options when editing formulas.

T   F   8. As soon as you cut data from a worksheet, it disappears, whether you paste it somewhere else or not.

T   F   9. A cut-and-paste operation is the same as dragging a selection border to another location.

T   F   10. The Office Clipboard provides access to only the last eight items copied or cut.

notes   Several of the following Skills Review exercises introduce functions not covered in the chapter. Use the Insert Function tool to guide you through the use of new functions. For additional information, use online Help.

Skills Review

SCANS

Exercise 1   C

1. Create a new workbook.

2. Enter "Test Scores" in cell A1.

3. Using the values 100, 121, 135, 117, 143, 122, 125, 118, 111, and 135, use statistical functions (*Hint:* check the Statistical function category) to perform the following tasks:

a. Determine the minimum value.

b. Determine the maximum value.

c. Find the average value by opening the Insert Function dialog box, double-clicking Average in the Statistical category, dragging to select the numbers you entered, then clicking OK.

d. Find the 50th percentile by opening the Insert Function dialog box, double-clicking Percentile in the Statistical category, dragging to select the numbers you entered, typing 0.5 in the K box, then clicking OK.

e. Count the number of items by opening the Insert Function dialog box, double-clicking Count in the Statistical category, dragging to select the numbers you entered, then clicking OK.

4. Save the workbook as *Test Scores.* Print and close the workbook.

Exercise 2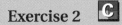

1. Create a new workbook.

2. Enter "Enter a Date:" in cell A2.

3. Enter "Is it a Friday?" in cell A4.

4. The WEEKDAY function, in the Date & Time category, returns a number indicating a day of the week for a given date, 1 = Sunday, 2 = Monday, and so on. In cell A5, create a formula using an IF statement that determines whether any given date since January 1, 1900 in cell A3 is a Friday. If the date is a Friday, the formula should return "Yes." If not, the formula should return "No."

5. Enter several dates in cell A3 until you find one that is a Friday. Cell A5 should show the value "Yes."

6. Save the workbook as *Day Finder.* Print and close the workbook.

Exercise 3

1. Create a new workbook.

2. Enter "The Quick Brown Fox" in cell A2.

3. In cell A3, enter "Jumped Over the Lazy Dog."

4. Use text functions to perform the following tasks:

a. Join the content of cells A2 and A3 in cell A6. To do this, insert the CONCATENATE function from the Text category. Click cell A2 as the first argument, key " " (quotation mark, a space, and another quotation mark) as the second argument, then click cell A3 as the third argument.

b. In cell A8, convert the value of cell A6 to uppercase. To do this, insert the UPPER function from the Text category, and click cell A6 as the argument.

c. In cell A10, locate the character position of the letter "Q" in cell A6. To do this, insert the FIND function from the Text category, enter "Q" as the first argument, and click cell A6 as the second argument.

5. Save the workbook as *Text Practice.* Print and close the workbook.

Exercise 4

1. Open the *Depreciation Calculator* workbook located on the Data Disk.

2. In cell B12, a financial function called SLN has been entered using relative cell references. This formula was copied to cells C12:K12, resulting in errors. Change the cell references in cell B12 to absolute references.

3. Copy the revised formula in cell B12 to cells C12:K12.

4. In cell L12, total cells B12:K12.

5. Save the workbook as *Depreciation Calculator Revised.* Print and close the workbook.

chapter three

Exercise 5   C

1. Create a new workbook.

2. Enter "Year" in cell A1 and "Roman" in cell B1.

3. Enter the following numbers in column A: 1900, 1941, 1999, 2000, 2010.

4. In column B, use the ROMAN function from the Math & Trig category to convert the numbers to ROMAN numerals by using the cells in column A as the argument.

5. Save the workbook as *Roman Conversion*. Print and close the workbook.

Exercise 6   C

1. Create a new workbook.

2. Using the RAND function in the Math & Trig category, generate five random numbers in column A. The RAND function takes no arguments, so simply enter the function in each cell.

3. In column B, create a formula to generate whole numbers between 1 and 100 using the RAND and ROUND functions. To do this, open the Insert Functions dialog box, double-click the ROUND function in the Math & Trig category, type RAND()*100 in the Number argument box, and enter 0 as the Num_digits argument.

4. Save the workbook as *Random Numbers*. Print and close the workbook.

Exercise 7   C

1. Enter the following data in a new workbook on the Sheet1 worksheet:

Employee Name	Current Wage	Proposed Wage	Increase per Month
Mark Havlaczek	$7.50	$8.00	
Roberta Hernandez	$8.25	$9.00	
Loren Mons	$12.00	$13.00	
Total Increase (all stores)			

2. Rename the Sheet1 worksheet to "Downtown Store."

3. Enter the following data on the Sheet2 worksheet:

Employee Name	Current Wage	Proposed Wage	Increase per Month
Eric Wimmer	$8.25	$8.85	
Micah Anderson	$7.75	$8.50	
Allyson Smith	$9.50	$10.35	

4. Rename the Sheet2 worksheet "Uptown Store."

5. On the Downtown Store worksheet, create a formula in cell D2 that calculates how much *more* each employee will make per month as a result of the proposed wage increase. Assume that each employee works 168 hours per month. (*Hint:* Subtract the Current Wage from the Proposed Wage, then multiply the result by 168.)

6. Copy the formula to cells D3:D4.

7. Copy the formulas in cells D2:D4 on the Downtown Store worksheet to the same cells on the Uptown Store worksheet.

8. In cell D5 on the Downtown Store worksheet, "enter = sum(".

9. Press and hold the SHIFT key, then click the Uptown Store worksheet.

10. Select cells D2:D4 and press the ENTER key.

11. Save the workbook as *Proposed Wage Increase*. Print and close the workbook.

Exercise 8

1. Open the *Proposed Wage Increase* workbook you created in Exercise 7.

2. Using drag-and-drop, move cells D1:D5 on the Downtown Store worksheet to G1:G5.

3. Using cut and paste, move cells C1:C4 on the Downtown Store worksheet to E1:E4.

4. Using your choice of move commands, move cells B1:B4 on the Downtown Store worksheet to cells C1:C4.

5. Repeat Steps 2 through 4 on the Uptown Store worksheet.

6. On the Downtown Store worksheet, activate cell G5.

7. Change the cell reference D2:D4 in the Formula Bar to G2:G4.

8. Save the workbook as *Proposed Wage Increase Revised.* Print and close the workbook.

Case Projects

Project 1

You work for an insurance company processing accident claims. One of your tasks is to determine how many days have elapsed between the date of an accident and the date that a claim was filed. You know that Excel stores dates as numbers, so you must be able to create a formula that calculates this information. Use the Ask A Question Box to look up more information about how Excel keeps track of dates. Can you figure out the trick? Create a workbook with column labels for Accident Date, Claim Filed Date, and Elapsed Days. Enter two fictitious accident dates and two corresponding claim filed dates. Save the workbook as *Claim Lapse Calculator,* and then print and close it.

Project 2

You are a college entrance administrator. To gain admittance to your school, a prospective student must score in the 80th percentile on the school's entrance exam. In a new workbook, use the RAND function in the Math & Trig category to generate a list of 100 random test scores between 30 and 100.

Once you've generated the random scores, copy and paste the values over the formulas in the scores column to keep them from changing. (*Hint:* Use Copy, Paste Special.) Use statistical functions to find the average test score, the median test score, and the 80th percentile of the scores. Use an IF function with the PERCENTILE function to display "Yes" if the score is higher than the 80th percentile, or "No" if the score is lower than the 80th percentile. Save the workbook as *College Entrance Exam Scores,* and then print and close it.

Project 3

Connect to the Internet and search the Web to locate a timeline showing major events of the twentieth century. Create a workbook to record the date and a description of the event. Include at least one event from each decade of the twentieth century. Do not include more than three events from any decade. Save the workbook as *20th Century Timeline,* and then print and close it.

chapter three

Project 4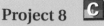

Connect to the Internet and search the Web to locate information about current events. Create a workbook to list the date(s) of the event, the place, and a brief description of the event. Save the workbook as *Current Events*, and then print and close it.

Project 5

The CONVERT function is used to convert units of measurement from one system to another. You work as a lab technician in a bioengineering firm, and you need to convert temperatures from Fahrenheit to Celsius and to Kelvin. Create a workbook with 10 Fahrenheit temperatures in column A. In column B, use the CONVERT function to convert the temperatures to Celsius. In column C, convert from Celsius to Kelvin. Save the workbook as *Temperature Conversion*, and print and close it. (*Hint:* If the CONVERT function is not available, enable it by clicking the Tools menu, then clicking Add-Ins. Click the Analysis ToolPak check box, then click OK.)

Project 6

You are considering a loan for $8,000 to buy a car. The loan will be paid back in 36 months at an interest rate of 6.5%. Calculate the monthly payment using the PMT function. Then, calculate the amount of interest and principal for each payment of the loan using the IPMT and PPMT functions. Save the workbook as *Car Loan Payments*, and then print and close it.

Project 7

Use the Ask A Question Box to locate and print a list of conversion units.

Project 8

You are the personnel manager of a large bookstore. Each employee is given one week (five days) of vacation after he or she has been employed for at least six months (180 days). After that time, one day of vacation is added for every 45 days the employee works. Create a new workbook that will calculate the number of vacation days an employee has earned by subtracting the employee's hire date from today's date. (*Hint:* Use the TODAY function to automatically insert today's date.) Save the workbook as *Holiday Calculator*, and then print and close it.

Enhancing Worksheets

Chapter Overview

Worksheets hold and process a lot of data. The goal of well-designed worksheets is to provide information in a clear, easy-to-read fashion. Thoughtful application of formatting styles can enhance the appearance of your worksheets on-screen and in printed documents. In this chapter, you explore how to format worksheets and cell data, and how to filter a list of data so that only relevant data appears. You also learn to extend the power of pasting far beyond simply copying data from one location to another.

LEARNING OBJECTIVES

- ▶ Create worksheet and column titles
- ▶ Format cells, rows, and columns
- ▶ Use Paste Special
- ▶ Define and apply styles
- ▶ Manipulate rows, columns, and cells
- ▶ Filter lists using AutoFilter

Case profile

One of your jobs at Super Power Computers is to prepare last year's quarterly sales reports for distribution. The workbook must be easy to use and logically present the information so that company managers can quickly summarize the data and report to the president.

chapter four

4.a   Creating Worksheet and Column Titles

Titles provide a clear indication of what type of information can be found on the worksheet. You can add titles to a worksheet or column to indicate the type of information in each column.

Merging and Splitting Cells

To add visual impact, titles are often centered at the top of a worksheet. To do this quickly, you can use the Merge and Center command. To merge cells and create a worksheet title:

Step 1	*Open*	the *Super Power Computers - Quarterly Sales Report 2002* workbook on the Data Disk
Step 2	*Save*	The workbook as *Super Power Computers - Quarterly Sales Report 2002 Revised*

This workbook contains a summary of 2002 sales on the Sales Summary worksheet. The Source Data worksheet contains the raw data from the stores. The error message ####### indicates that a numerical value is too long to display using the current column width. You increase the width of the column later in this chapter.

Step 3	*Select*	the range A1:F1
Step 4	*Click*	the Merge and Center button ⊞ on the Formatting toolbar

The selected cells are merged into a single cell whose cell reference is the cell in the upper-left corner of the selection—in this case, cell A1—and the contents of cell A1 are centered in the new cell.

Step 5	*Repeat*	Steps 3 and 4 twice to merge and center cells A2 and A3 across the ranges A2:F2 and A3:F3

You didn't mean to center the data in cell A3.

Step 6	*Click*	cell A3
Step 7	*Click*	the Merge and Center button ⊞ on the Formatting toolbar

CAUTION TIP

If you use the Merge and Center command on multiple cells that contain data, all the data will be lost except that in the upper-left cell in the selected area.

The data in cell A3 is no longer centered across cells A3:F3. Your worksheet should look similar to Figure 4-1.

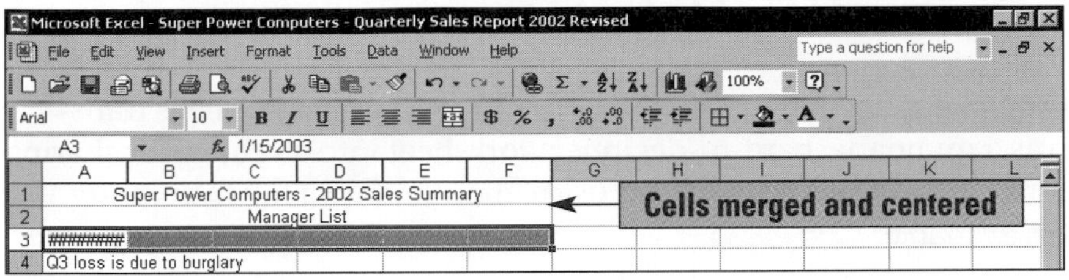

Using AutoFill to Create Column Titles

The **AutoFill** command creates a series of values. AutoFill can automatically increment numerical values, cells containing a mixture of text and numbers, days of the week, months of the year, and even custom series you define. To use AutoFill to add column labels:

Step 1	*Activate*	cell B5
Step 2	*Move*	the pointer over the fill handle
Step 3	*Drag*	the fill handle to cell E5

As you drag the fill handle, a ScreenTip displays the new values being added. Your screen should look similar to Figure 4-2. Excel correctly identifies the quarter numbers and increments them as you drag.

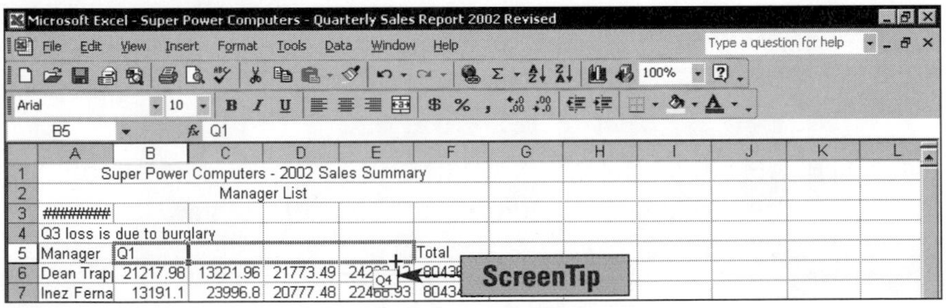

| Step 4 | *Release* | the mouse button |

When you release the mouse button, the column headings Q1 through Q4 appear in cells B5:E5.

| Step 5 | *Save* | the workbook |

FIGURE 4-2
AutoFill Numbers

MENU TIP

Not all fill options are available when you drag to use the AutoFill feature. To see additional AutoFill options, use the Edit menu, Fill, Series command to open the Series dialog box.

MOUSE TIP

Click the AutoFill Options button on the screen to change how the cells are filled when you drag the fill handle.

---

chapter
four

4.b Formatting Cells, Rows, and Columns

Careful application of formatting to rows, columns, and cells transforms a mundane, hard-to-decipher worksheet into a vehicle for sharing information. In this section, you learn about many of the formatting tools available.

Applying AutoFormats to Worksheets

AutoFormats are predefined combinations of shading, cell borders, font styles, and number formatting that quickly give worksheets a stylized look. To apply AutoFormats:

Step 1	*Select*	the range A5:F10
Step 2	*Click*	F<u>o</u>rmat
Step 3	*Click*	<u>A</u>utoFormat

The AutoFormat dialog box displays a list of available AutoFormat styles and should look similar to Figure 4-3.

FIGURE 4-3
AutoFormat Dialog Box

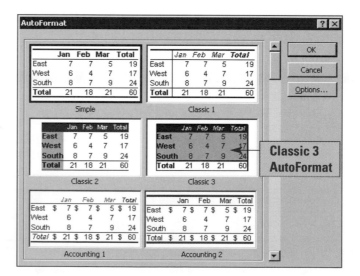

Step 4	*Click*	the Classic 3 AutoFormat
Step 5	*Click*	OK
Step 6	*Click*	any cell in the worksheet to deselect the range

The AutoFormat is applied to the selected area. You don't like the way the AutoFormatted worksheet looks, so you format it yourself.

| Step 7 | *Click* | the Undo button 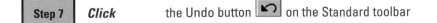 on the Standard toolbar |

Applying Fonts and Font Styles

A **font** is a set of printed characters that share a common typeface. A **typeface** is the design and appearance of the font in printed form. The **style** refers to whether the font is displayed with *italic*, **bold**, an underline, or normal print. The **point size** refers to the print height. You can also add **effects**, such as strikethrough, superscripts, and subscripts. Some common typefaces include the following:

Arial   Times New Roman   Courier New   Book Antiqua

To maintain consistency in its documents, Super Power Computers has selected the Impact font style, set to point size 14, for worksheet titles. To change the font and font size:

Step 1	*Select*	cell A1
Step 2	*Click*	the Font button list arrow `Arial` on the Formatting toolbar to display the available fonts
Step 3	*Click*	Impact (or another font if Impact is not available on your system)
Step 4	*Click*	the Font Size button list arrow `10` on the Formatting toolbar
Step 5	*Click*	14

Usually, when you increase the font size in a cell, the row height automatically increases to accommodate the larger font; however, when you increase the font size in a merged cell, it does not. You adjust this later in this chapter. You decide to make the Total label stand out more.

| Step 6 | *Change* | the font in cell A10 to Arial Black |

Another way to add emphasis is to change the font color. To change the font color:

| Step 1 | *Activate* | cell A1 |

CAUTION TIP

To make your worksheets look as professional as possible, avoid using more than three or four fonts. Too many fonts may look comical and detract from an otherwise well-designed layout.

MENU TIP

Click the Cells command on the Format menu, then click the Font tab to choose a font, font size, font style, and font color.

chapter four

| Step 2 | *Click* | the Font Color button list arrow 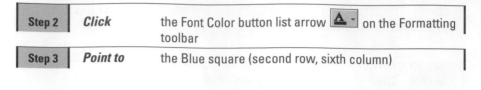 on the Formatting toolbar |
| Step 3 | *Point to* | the Blue square (second row, sixth column) |

A ScreenTip displays the color name under the pointer.

| Step 4 | *Click* | the Blue square |

You can also use bold, italics, or underlining to draw attention to or emphasize certain cells. To change the font style:

Step 1	*Select*	the range B5:F5
Step 2	*Click*	the Bold button **B** on the Formatting toolbar
Step 3	*Select*	the range A6:A10
Step 4	*Click*	the Italic button *I* on the Formatting toolbar

Modifying the Alignment of Cell Content

You can change the alignment of values within a cell. The default horizontal alignment in a cell is for text values to be left-aligned, and numbers, dates, and times to be right-aligned. The default vertical alignment is for data to be aligned at the bottom of a cell. Typically, column labels are centered in the column, while row labels are left-aligned. To change the alignment of cells:

| Step 1 | *Select* | the range B5:F5 |
| Step 2 | *Click* | the Center button  on the Formatting toolbar |

Applying Number Formats

Understanding how and when to apply number formats is very important. Using the extensive set of number formats in Excel, you can display numerical values such as times, dates, currency, percentages, fractions, and more. When you apply a numerical format to a value, the manner in which the value is displayed may vary dramatically, but the actual value held by the cell remains the same. Table 4-1 illustrates how a common numerical value of 1054.253 would be displayed with different number formats applied.

TABLE 4-1
Comparing Number
Formats

Category	Description	Default Display (Value = 1054.253)
General	No specific number format	1054.253
Number	Default of two decimal places; can also display commas for thousand separators	1054.25
Currency	Default of two decimal places, comma separators, and $ (the U.S. dollar sign)	$1,054.25
Accounting	Aligns currency symbol, displays two decimal places and comma separators	$ 1,054.25
Date	Displays serial equivalent of date	11/19/1902
Time	Displays serial equivalent of time	11/19/1902 6:00 AM
Percentage	Multiplies value by 100 and displays the result with % sign	105425%
Fraction	Displays decimal portion of value as a fraction	1054 1/4
Scientific	Displays the number in scientific notation	1.05E+03

The comma format automatically sets the numerical display to two decimal places, inserts a comma when needed for thousands, millions, and so on, and adjusts the alignment of the cell(s) to line up on the decimal. To change the formatting to the comma format:

Step 1	*Select*	the range B6.E10

Step 2	*Click*	the Comma Style button [,] on the Formatting toolbar

The cells are updated to display the new formatting, including a slight, automatic column width adjustment to accommodate the extra formatting. (You format the Total column later in this chapter.)

Currency style is commonly used when dealing with money. There are several ways to adjust currency style, including changing the font color to red for negative numbers. You can also insert other symbols, such as those for the euro (E) and the yen (¥). To use currency style:

Step 1	*Verify*	that the range B6:E10 is still selected

Step 2	*Click*	the Currency Style button [$] on the Formatting toolbar

chapter
four

This looks fine, but you want the negative values to stand out even more. To adjust the currency format, you use the Format Cells dialog box. To change formatting using the Format Cells dialog box:

Step 1	*Click*	Format
Step 2	*Click*	Cells

The Format Cells dialog box opens. Each tab contains a different category of formatting options that you can apply to selected cells.

Step 3	*Click*	the Number tab, if necessary
Step 4	*Click*	Currency in the Category: list

The Number tab in the Format Cells dialog box permits you to change a variety of options for each of the available number formats. When the Currency category is selected, you can choose how negative numbers are displayed. The dialog box on your screen should look similar to Figure 4-4.

QUICK TIP

When you activate a cell containing a date or time format, the Formula Bar displays the date or time value, not the serial, or number, value. To view the serial value of a date, you must change the cell's format to a number format.

FIGURE 4-4
Format Cells Dialog Box

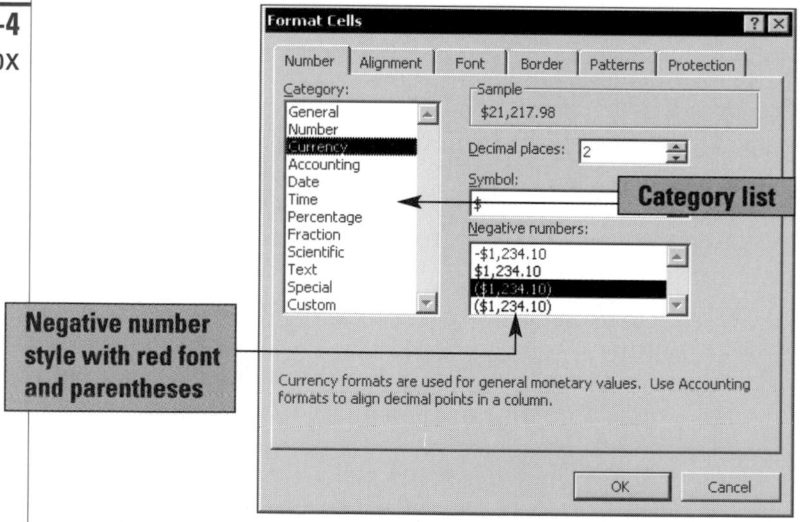

Step 5	*Click*	the fourth item in the Negative numbers: list, red text and parentheses
Step 6	*Click*	OK

The loss in cell D8 is now easy to see.

Adjusting the Decimal Place

You can adjust the number of decimal places displayed in all number formats except General, Date, Time, and Text. To change the number of decimal places displayed in a cell:

| Step 1 | *Verify* | that the range B6:E10 is still selected |
| Step 2 | *Click* | the Decrease Decimal button  on the Formatting toolbar twice |

The data in the selected cells is rounded to the nearest whole dollar. Although the cells display rounded numbers, the original value is stored in each cell and appears in the Formula Bar when the cell is active.

Indenting, Rotating, and Wrapping Text in a Cell

To give more visual appeal to your worksheets, you can indent, rotate, or wrap values in a cell. The employee names would be easier to distinguish if they were indented in the cells. To indent cell content:

| Step 1 | *Select* | the range A6:A9 |
| Step 2 | *Click* | the Increase Indent button on the Formatting toolbar |

Sometimes rotating text is a good way to make it stand out. To rotate text in a cell:

Step 1	*Select*	the range B5:E5
Step 2	*Right-click*	the selected range
Step 3	*Click*	Format Cells
Step 4	*Click*	the Alignment tab

Your dialog box should look similar to Figure 4-5. The Alignment tab is used to control various alignment settings, including rotation.

MOUSE TIP

To increase the indent more, click the Increase Indent button on the Formatting toolbar again. To decrease the indent, click the Decrease Indent button on the Formatting toolbar.

chapter
four

FIGURE 4-5
Alignment Tab in the
Formal Cells Dialog Box

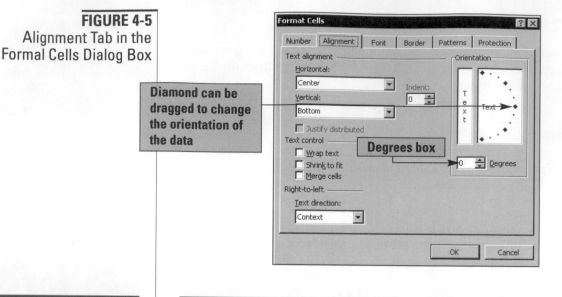

Diamond can be dragged to change the orientation of the data

Degrees box

Step 5	*Drag*	the red diamond in the Orientation box up until the Degrees box displays 45
Step 6	*Click*	OK

The column labels rotate 45 degrees, and the row height increases to display the rotated value.

When data is too long for the column width, it is displayed as long as neighboring cells are empty. You can adjust the column width, but this isn't always desirable for long entries. Instead, you can use wrapping to maintain column width, while displaying all the data entered in a particular cell. **Wrapping** allows longer cell entries to continue to the next "line" within a single cell. To turn on text wrapping:

Step 1	*Activate*	cell A4
Step 2	*Open*	the Alignment tab in the Format Cells dialog box
Step 3	*Click*	the Wrap text check box
Step 4	*Click*	OK

The text is wrapped to fit within the column width. The row height might adjust automatically. If not, you adjust it later.

Applying Cell Borders and Shading

Cell borders and shading are two of the more dramatic visual effects available to enhance your worksheets. Borders can be used to separate row and column labels from data. Shading can be used to emphasize important cells. Although you see grid lines on your screen, the default for printed worksheets is for no grid lines to appear. If you want grid lines to appear on your printed pages, you need to apply a border. Borders can be applied to a range of selected cells or to individual cells. To add a border:

Step 1	**Select**	the range B6:E9
Step 2	**Click**	the Borders button list arrow ⊞ ▾ on the Formatting toolbar
Step 3	**Click**	the All Borders button ⊞

The All Borders command applies a border to all edges surrounding and within the selection. Your screen should look similar to Figure 4-6.

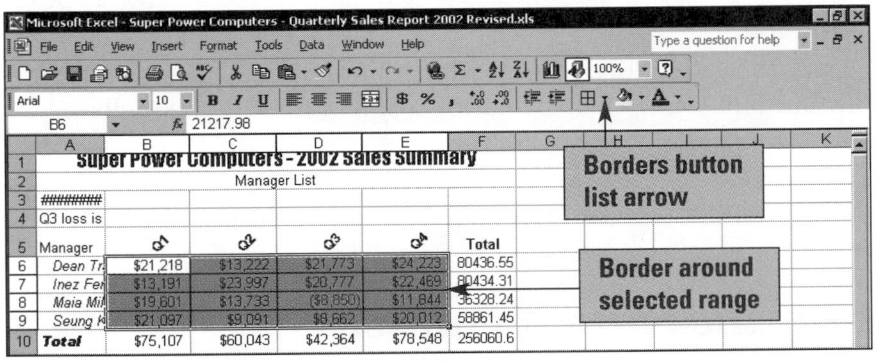

QUICK TIP

You are not limited to the 12 choices appearing on the Borders list button. Use the Borders tab in the Format Cells dialog box to select different line styles, change line colors, and choose additional border options, such as inserting diagonal lines and applying borders to only the inside of a selection.

FIGURE 4-6
All Borders Added to the Selection

One way you can make row 5, which contains the column labels, stand out is to use a "reverse text" effect. To create this effect, you apply a dark fill color to the cells, then change the font color to white. To add shading to a cell:

Step 1	**Select**	cells A5:F5
Step 2	**Click**	the Fill Color button list arrow 🪣 ▾ on the Formatting toolbar
Step 3	**Select**	the Blue square (second row, sixth column)
Step 4	**Click**	the Font Color button list arrow A ▾ on the Formatting toolbar
Step 5	**Select**	the White square (last row, last column)
Step 6	**Activate**	cell A1 to deselect the cells

chapter four

Drawing Cell Borders

You can also draw cell borders exactly where you want them. To draw cell borders:

Step 1	Click	the Borders button list arrow ▦ ▾ on the Formatting toolbar
Step 2	Click	<u>D</u>raw Borders to display the Borders toolbar
Step 3	Click	the Line Style button list arrow [━━━━━ ▾] on the Borders toolbar to drop down a list of line styles
Step 4	Click	the double-line style
Step 5	Drag	across the bottom of cells B9:E9

A double-line is added to the bottom of the cells. To deactivate the Draw Border button, click the button again or turn off the toolbar.

| Step 6 | Click | the Close button ☒ on the Borders toolbar |

Using the Format Painter

The Format Painter copies formats from one cell to another. To use the Format Painter:

Step 1	Select	the range E6:E10
Step 2	Click	the Format Painter button  on the Standard toolbar
Step 3	Select	the range F6:F10

The currency formatting and borders from cells E6:E10 are copied to cells F6:F10.

Clearing Formats

Occasionally, you need to remove formatting from a cell or cells, while maintaining the data in the cell. To clear formatting from cells:

| Step 1 | Activate | cell A10 |

Step 2	*Click*	E̲dit
Step 3	*Point to*	Clea̲r
Step 4	*Click*	F̲ormats

All formatting is removed from the cell, and the font is changed to the default style of 10-point Arial.

Step 5	*Save*	the workbook

4.c Using Paste Special

The Paste S̲pecial command provides you with extra options when you copy or move data in Excel. The best quarter for each manager is listed in row 12. To create the column labels for this data, you copy and transpose the names listed in column A to row 12. To use the Paste Special command:

Step 1	*Copy*	cells A6:A9
Step 2	*Right-click*	cell B12
Step 3	*Click*	Paste S̲pecial

The Paste Special dialog box should look similar to Figure 4-7.

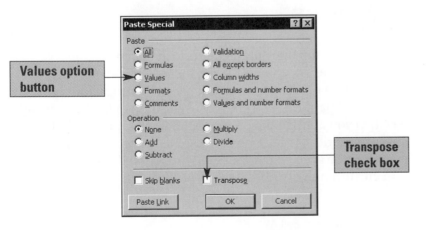

FIGURE 4-7
Paste Special Dialog Box

chapter
four

The Paste Special dialog box contains options for pasting data, formulas, and formats in cells. Some of these options are explained in Table 4-2.

TABLE 4-2
Paste Special Options

Paste Option	Description
All	Pastes content and formulas from source cell
Formulas	Pastes only formulas from source cell
Values	Pastes only values from source cell, converting formulas into latest result
Formats	Pastes only formats from source cell, leaving content of destination cell in place
Operation (add, subtract, multiply, divide)	Performs operation on value from source cell with value of destination cell to create new value without a formula

Step 4	*Click*	the Values option button
Step 5	*Click*	the Transpose check box to insert a check mark
Step 6	*Click*	OK
Step 7	*Press*	the ESC key to end the Copy command

The names are transposed to row 12 without the formatting from the source cells.

C 4.d Defining and Applying Styles

To create a consistent corporate identity, many companies use certain styles whenever a workbook is created. **Styles** can cover a variety of settings, such as number format, alignment settings, font type, cell borders, and cell patterns. You already used some of the built-in styles in Excel when you applied the comma and currency number styles. In addition to numerical styles, you can also define your own styles, which can then be applied to other cells and copied into other workbooks. To create a new style:

QUICK TIP

To create a style from a previously formatted cell, select the cell, then open the Style dialog box. The format settings for the style of the cell you selected will be listed in the dialog box.

Step 1	*Activate*	cell A2
Step 2	*Click*	Format
Step 3	*Click*	Style

The Style dialog box opens, displaying the settings for the Normal style, as shown in Figure 4-8. To create a new style, type a new style name in the Style name: box, then modify the settings as necessary.

| Style name list box |
| Option to merge style from another workbook |

| Step 4 | *Key* | Worksheet Subtitle in the Style name: text box |
| Step 5 | *Click* | Modify |

The familiar Format Cells dialog box opens.

Step 6	*Click*	the Font tab
Step 7	*Click*	Impact in the Font: list
Step 8	*Click*	12 in the Size: list
Step 9	*Click*	the Color: list arrow
Step 10	*Click*	the Red square (third row, first column)

You can apply alignment options, borders, and numerical formats to your style as well.

Step 11	*Click*	the Alignment tab
Step 12	*Click*	the Horizontal: list arrow
Step 13	*Verify*	that Center is selected

This command centers the value in the cell. It was already selected because you applied the Merge and Center command to cell A2 earlier. When the style is applied to cell A2, it centers, the value in the merged cell. If the style is applied to a cell that isn't merged, it centers the data only in the cell you apply the style to.

MOUSE TIP

You can copy styles from workbook to workbook by using the Format Painter. Open both workbooks. In the source workbook, select a cell with the formatting style you want to copy, and click Format Painter. Switch to the target workbook, then click the cell to which you want to apply the formatting. The style is automatically transferred to the Style list of the target workbook.

QUICK TIP

You can copy styles from workbook to workbook by using the Copy and Paste commands. Open both workbooks, copy the cell in the source workbook containing the desired style, then use the Paste Special command and select the Formats option to paste it into the target workbook.

chapter
four

| Step 14 | *Click* | OK to close the Format Cells dialog box |
| Step 15 | *Click* | OK to close the Style dialog box and apply the style to the active cell |

To apply this style to other cells in this workbook, activate the cell(s), reopen the Style dialog box, select the style you wish to apply, then click OK. A real advantage of using named styles is that when you modify a named style, all cells with that style applied are updated automatically.

4.e Manipulating Rows, Columns, and Cells

As you organize worksheets, you will find many occasions when you need to insert a few cells into a list—or entire rows or columns—to add new information to a worksheet. You may also need to delete cells, rows, or columns.

Inserting and Deleting Rows and Columns

You decide to insert a blank row above row 5. To insert a new row:

| Step 1 | *Right-click* | the row 5 heading |
| Step 2 | *Click* | Insert |

The data in row 5 and below is shifted down to accommodate the new row. When a column is inserted, all data is shifted to the right.

Upon reviewing your worksheet, you realize that you don't need the extra row after all. To delete rows or columns:

| Step 1 | *Right-click* | the row 5 heading |
| Step 2 | *Click* | Delete to delete the newly added row |

Changing Column Width and Row Height

If the data in a cell is too long for the column width, Excel allows the value to spill over into the next cell, as long as the neighboring cell is empty. If the neighboring cell contains data, Excel shows only the first part of the data. By changing the column width, you can show more or less data.

MOUSE TIP

To remove a style, select the style name in the Style dialog box, then click the Delete button.

MENU TIP

You can insert a new row by clicking Rows on the Insert menu. You can insert a new column by clicking Columns on the Insert menu.

QUICK TIP

To insert multiple rows, select the number of rows you want to insert, then right-click the row heading and click Insert.

As you adjusted the font height, or turned on the wrap text feature, you may have noticed that the row height increased to show the data in the cell. Although this change is generally automatic, sometimes you need more precise control of the row height.

You need to resize rows 1 and 2 to accommodate the larger font size. To AutoFit a row to the largest point size:

Step 1	***Double-click***	the boundary between row headings 1 and 2
Step 2	***Double-click***	the boundary between row headings 2 and 3

Rows 1 and 2 increase in height to fit the entries in cells A1 and A2. You also might need to adjust the height of row 4 if it did not automatically resize to accomodate the wrapped text in cell A1.

Step 3	***Double-click***	the boundary between row headings 4 and 5, if necessary

Next you need to adjust column widths to display the widest entries. To manually change the column width:

Step 1	***Right-click***	the column A heading
Step 2	***Click***	Column Width
Step 3	***Key***	15 in the Column width: text box
Step 4	***Click***	OK

You can also use the AutoFit feature to automatically adjust the width to fit the longest entry in the column. To AutoFit a column to the longest entry:

Step 1	***Move***	the mouse pointer over the boundary between the column B and column C headings
Step 2	***Double-click***	the boundary

The column automatically resizes so it is wide enough to display the value in cell B12, the widest entry in column B.

Step 3	***Repeat***	Step 2 to AutoFit columns C, D, and E

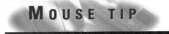

QUICK TIP

To change the width of several columns at once, select them before opening the Column Width dialog box.

MOUSE TIP

To change the formatting in a newly inserted row or column, click the Insert Options button that appears after you insert the row or column.

MENU TIP

To adjust the width of a column, click Format, point to Columns, then click Width. To AutoFit the row height, select AutoFit instead of Height.

To adjust the height of a row by using menus, click Format, point to Row, then click Height. To AutoFit the row height, select AutoFit instead of Height.

chapter
four

Now you need to decrease the height of row 4. To manually adjust the height of a row:

Step 1	*Right-click*	the row 4 header
Step 2	*Click*	Row Height
Step 3	*Key*	25.5 in the Row height: text box
Step 4	*Click*	OK

The row height decreases to fit the entry in cell A4.

Inserting and Deleting Cells

In some instances, you may need to insert extra cells without inserting an entire row or column. The Store Data worksheet has an error in column D. The data in rows 27–37 should actually be in rows 28–38. To insert extra cells:

Step 1	*Click*	the Store Data sheet tab
Step 2	*Scroll*	the Store Data worksheet so you can view rows 27–38
Step 3	*Right-click*	cell D27
Step 4	*Click*	Insert

The Insert dialog box opens.

| Step 5 | *Verify* | that the Shift cells down option button is selected |
| Step 6 | *Click* | OK |

The data in column D below row 26 shifts down one cell.

| Step 7 | *Enter* | 1104 in cell D27 |

Hiding and Unhiding Rows and Columns

You can hide columns and rows when extraneous data does not need to be displayed. To hide a row or column:

| Step 1 | *Right-click* | the column D heading on the Store Data sheet tab |

| Step 2 | *Click* | Hide |

Column E slides left, hiding column D. To unhide a column or row:

Step 1	*Select*	both column headings surrounding column D
Step 2	*Right-click*	either column heading
Step 3	*Click*	Unhide

Column D reappears.

Freezing and Unfreezing Rows and Columns

When working with large worksheets, it can be helpful to keep row and column labels on the screen as you scroll through your worksheet. The Freeze Panes command freezes the rows above and the columns to the left of the active cell and prevents them from scrolling off the screen. The Store Data worksheet contains more data than will fit on the screen at once. To freeze the columns and row headings:

Step 1	*Activate*	cell A5
Step 2	*Click*	Window
Step 3	*Click*	Freeze Panes

A thin, black line appears on your workbook, indicating that the rows above row 5 are frozen and will not scroll with the rest of your worksheet. This black line will not print when you print the worksheet.

| Step 4 | *Press & hold* | the DOWN ARROW key until your worksheet begins scrolling down |

The worksheet scrolls, but the column labels stay fixed at the top of the worksheet. When you no longer need the frozen panes, you can unfreeze them. To unfreeze panes:

| Step 1 | *Click* | Window |
| Step 2 | *Click* | Unfreeze Panes |

 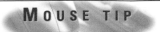
chapter four

Step 3	*Save*	the workbook

The panes are removed, permitting normal worksheet scrolling.

4.f Filtering Lists Using AutoFilter

Excel is often used to store lists of data, similar to a database table. The Store Data sheet tab in your workbook contains a list of sales data. Sometimes, you want to look at data that meets some criteria. **Filtering** a list allows you to screen out any data that does not meet your **criteria**, or conditions that you specify. You can apply more than one filter so as to reduce the list even more. When you apply a filter, only the data meeting the specified criteria are displayed. While the filter remains on, you can format, edit, chart, and print the filtered list. When you have finished, turn the filter off and the rest of the records in the list will appear.

The AutoFilter command offers a fast, easy way to apply multiple filters to a list. To apply AutoFilter:

Step 1	*Activate*	any cell in the list
Step 2	*Click*	<u>D</u>ata
Step 3	*Point to*	<u>F</u>ilter
Step 4	*Click*	Auto<u>F</u>ilter

The filter list arrow appears next to each column label. Clicking any of these arrows displays a list of AutoFilter options.

Step 5	*Click*	the Filter list arrow next to Store in cell A4
Step 6	*Click*	Store #2

The list is filtered for any entries in column A that contain "Store #2"; your screen should look similar to Figure 4-9. The filter list arrows of the filtered columns and the row headings appear in blue. All other entries are hidden.

CAUTION TIP

The active cell must be within the continuous table of data, and not elsewhere in the worksheet for AutoFilter to be able to find the data to filter.

MOUSE TIP

You can filter for a secondary criteria by clicking the list arrow next to a second column label.

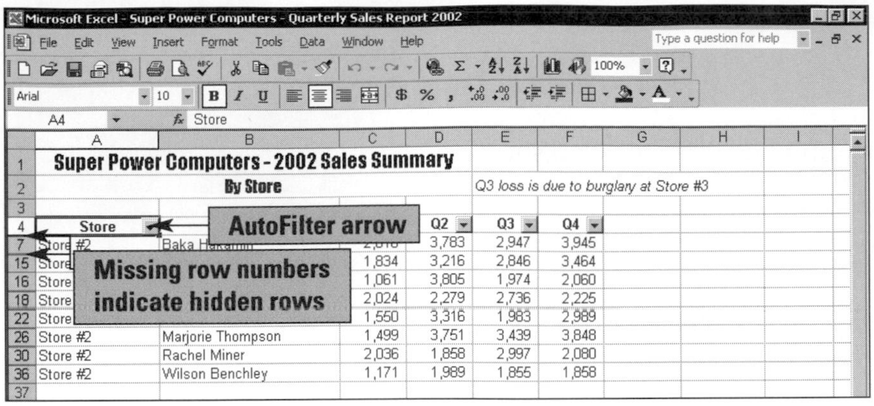

FIGURE 4-9
Applying AutoFilter to a List

When you want to display all of the records again, use the Show all command. To clear the filters:

| Step 1 | *Click* | the Filter list arrow next to Store in cell A4 |
| Step 2 | *Click* | (All) to restore the entries |

When you have finished filtering a list, you can turn off AutoFilter. To turn off AutoFilter:

Step 1	*Click*	Data
Step 2	*Point to*	Filter
Step 3	*Click*	AutoFilter
Step 4	*Save*	the workbook and close it

Your formatted worksheets are much easier to read than the unformatted worksheets were.

M E N U T I P

You can also clear the filters by pointing to Filter on the Data menu, and then clicking Show All.

chapter
four

Summary

▶ You can use the Merge and Center command to create worksheet titles.

▶ AutoFill fills in series of numbers, alphanumeric combinations, and day and month names.

▶ Judicious use of fonts and font styles can enhance a worksheet's appearance and make it easier to read.

▶ Align cell contents to enhance visual clarity. The default for text is left-alignment. For numeric entries, such as currency, dates, and times, the default is right-alignment.

▶ Number formats change how cells' numerical contents are displayed. Excel detects date, time, and currency entries and formats the cell accordingly.

▶ Rotate text to add visual interest or to decrease the width of a column. Indent text to provide visual breaks or to indicate that a list has a certain hierarchical structure. Use the alignment tab of the Format Cells dialog box to apply these settings.

▶ Borders and shading can add major visual impact to worksheets.

▶ Format Painter enables you to copy formats to other cells.

▶ You can clear cell contents, formats, or both using the Clear command on the Edit menu.

▶ AutoFormat applies stylized formatting to a selection of cells.

▶ Paste Special includes many options for pasting. Use Paste Special to paste only formats, to paste only values, to perform calculations automatically, or to transpose data from rows to columns.

▶ You can create and modify styles to reuse throughout a worksheet and in other workbooks.

▶ You can insert and delete rows and columns as needed to organize worksheets.

▶ You can change column width and row height to display more or less data.

▶ You can insert and delete cells by shifting the remaining cells up, down, left, or right when necessary to maintain surrounding information.

▶ You should hide columns and rows when extraneous data does not need to be displayed. Unhide them when you want to display the data again.

▶ You can freeze columns and rows to prevent them from scrolling along with the worksheet.

▶ You can use AutoFilter to display only data belonging to a certain category.

Commands Review

Action	Menu Bar	Shortcut Menu	Toolbar	Task Pane	Keyboard
Merge and Center			[icon]		
AutoFill Series	Edit, Fill, Series				ALT + E, I, S
AutoFormat	Format, AutoFormat				ALT + O, A
Format cells	Format, Cells	Right-click selected range, Format Cells			CTRL + 1 ALT + O, E
Font Color	Format, Cells, Font tab		**A**		ALT + O, E
Bold	Format, Cells, Font tab		**B**		ALT + O, E CTRL + B
Italics	Format, Cells, Font tab		*I*		ALT + O, E CTRL + I
Underline	Format, Cells, Font tab		U		ALT + O, E CTRL + U
Align cell contents	Format, Cells, Alignment tab		[align icons]		ALT + O, E
Apply number formats	Format, Cells, Number tab		$ % , .00 .0		ALT + O, E
Rotate text	Format, Cells, Alignment tab				ALT + O, E
Increase/decrease indent	Format, Cells, Alignment tab		[indent icons]		ALT + O, E
Add borders	Format, Cells, Borders tab		[border icon]		ALT + O, E
Add shading to cells	Format, Cells, Patterns tab		[shading icon]		ALT + O, E
Use Format Painter			[painter icon]		
Clear formats	Edit, Clear, Formats				ALT + E, C, F
Apply AutoFormat	Format, AutoFormat				ALT + O, A
Paste Special	Edit, Paste Special	Right-click cell, Paste Special			ALT + E, S
Define or Merge Format Style	Format, Style				ALT + O, S ALT + '
Insert rows	Insert, Rows	Right-click row, Insert			ALT + I, R
Insert columns	Insert, Columns	Right-click column, Insert			ALT + I, C
Delete rows and columns	Edit, Delete	Right-click row or column, Delete			ALT + E, D
Change column width	Format, Columns, Width Format, Columns, AutoFit Selection				ALT + O, C, W ALT + O, C, A

chapter four

Action	Menu Bar	Shortcut Menu	Toolbar	Task Pane	Keyboard
Change row height	Format, Rows, Height Format, Rows, AutoFit Selection				ALT + O, R, H ALT + O, R, A
Insert cells	Insert, Cells	Right-click cell, Insert			ALT + I, E CTRL + SHIFT + + (plus key)
Delete cells	Edit, Delete	Right-click cell, Delete			ALT + E, D
Hide rows or columns	Format, Row, Hide Format, Column, Hide				ALT + O, R, H ALT + O, C, H
Unhide rows or columns	Format, Row, Unhide Format, Column, Unhide				ALT + O, R, U ALT + O, C, U
Freeze/unfreeze rows and columns	Window, Freeze Panes Window, Unfreeze Panes				ALT + W, F
Use AutoFilter	Data, Filter, AutoFilter				ALT + D, I, F

Concepts Review

Circle the correct answer.

1. Which of the following commands can you use to copy formatting only from one selection to another?

[a] Copy, Paste Special (Formats option)

[b] Copy, Paste

[c] Cut, Paste

[d] Paste Special, Copy

2. To apply multiple changes to a font, use the _____ tab of the Format Cells dialog box.

[a] Font

[b] Border

[c] Patterns

[d] Number

3. To apply custom border styles, use the _____ tab of the Format Cells dialog box.

[a] Font

[b] Border

[c] Patterns

[d] Number

4. To insert a cell in the middle of existing data:

[a] click Format, then click Add Cells.

[b] right-click the row header, then click Insert.

[c] right-click the column header, then click Insert.

[d] right-click the cell where you want a new blank cell to appear, then click Insert.

5. To prevent a row from scrolling, you should:

[a] hide the row.

[b] freeze the row.

[c] insert a new row.

[d] filter the list.

6. AutoFill can be used to fill series of:

[a] day names.

[b] month names.

[c] alphanumeric combinations.

[d] All of the above.

7. To maintain a set column width while still displaying all of a cell's content, you must:
[a] indent the text.
[b] rotate the text.
[c] edit the content until it fits.
[d] wrap the text.

8. Using the Font tab of the Format Cells dialog box, you can:
[a] change numerical style settings.
[b] add borders to cells.
[c] change the alignment of text in a cell.
[d] change font settings, such as font, size, style, and color.

9. Cell A1 contains a value of .25. If the currency style is applied to cell A1, the cell displays:
[a] 25%.
[b] 0.25%.
[c] $0.25.
[d] 2.50E-01.

10. Cell A2 contains a value of 45.26 and has been formatted to display 0 decimal places. What is displayed in cell A2?
[a] $45.26
[b] $45.00
[c] 45
[d] 45%

Circle **T** if the statement is true or **F** if the statement is false.

T F 1. To delete a range of cells, you must first delete the rows or columns that contain the cells.

T F 2. You can apply a border diagonally across a cell (or cells).

T F 3. AutoFilter has certain preset categories, but does not automatically add categories based on the data in your worksheet.

T F 4. Increasing the font size automatically increases the row height.

T F 5. Rotating text automatically adjusts the row height.

T F 6. AutoFill cannot fill a series of values containing a mixture of text and numbers, such as "Apollo 11."

T F 7. The Merge and Center command merges only the value in the upper-left cell of your selection.

T F 8. Changing a cell's number format alters the actual value of the cell.

T F 9. You can create your own cell styles.

T F 10. You can copy styles created in one workbook to another workbook.

Skills Review

Exercise 1 **C**

1. Open the *Project Expense Log* workbook located on the Data Disk.

2. Change the numeric format of column A to the MM/DD/YY date format.

3. Change the number format of column C to Currency Style.

4. Merge and center cell A1 across cells A1:C1.

5. Center the column labels in row 3.

6. Turn on AutoFilter and filter the Place column for Phoenix, AZ.

7. Save the workbook as *Project Expense Log Revised*. Print and close the workbook.

chapter four

Exercise 2   C

1. Open the *Wage Increase* workbook located on the Data Disk.

2. Use the Format Cells dialog box to format the column labels as follows:

　a. Change the font to Times New Roman.

　b. Increase the font size to 12.

　c. Change the font color to blue.

　d. Change the font style to bold.

　e. Turn on Wrap Text.

3. Center the column labels.

4. Make cells A7:D7 bold and add a Gray-25% shade.

5. Add a thick bottom border to cells A1:D1.

6. Indent cell A7.

7. Adjust the column widths using AutoFit.

8. Hide the row containing Micah Anderson.

9. Delete the range A4: D4.

10. Insert cells above the range A3: D3.

11. Enter the following in row 3: Jared Wright, 8.50, 8.75.

12. Copy the formula from cell D2 to cell D3.

13. Change the format of the range B3: D3 to Accounting with two decimal places and no dollar sign.

14. Save the workbook as *Wage Increase Revised*. Print and close the workbook.

Exercise 3   C

1. Open the *Number Formatting* workbook on the Data Disk.

2. Apply the List 1 AutoFormat to the data.

3. Use the number format indicated by each column label to format the columns. Use the default settings unless otherwise directed.

　a. In the Number column, select the Use 1000 Separator (,) check box in the Number format settings.

　b. In the Date column, set the Date type to 3/14/2001. (Excel converts numbers into dates, starting with 1 equal to 1/1/1900.)

　c. In the Time column, set the Time type to 3/14/2001 1:30 PM. (*Hint:* If you don't have this format, set it as 3/14/01 1:30 PM.)

　d. In the Fraction column, set the Fraction type to Up to two digits (21/25). (*Hint:* Because many of the numbers are whole numbers, no fraction will appear in this column in the worksheet, but the numbers will move to the left side of the cell to allow proper alignment of fractions when needed.)

4. Save the workbook as *Number Formatting Revised*. Print and close the workbook.

Exercise 4   C

1. Create a new workbook.

2. Enter the data as shown in the table below:

Important Dates of World War II	
Date	**Event**
9/1/1939	Germany invades Poland
6/14/40	German troops occupy Paris
7/10/40	Battle of Britain begins
6/22/1941	German troops invade Russia
12/7/1941	Japan attacks U.S. forces at Pearl Harbor, Hawaii
12/8/1941	U.S. declares war on Japan
12/11/1941	U.S. declares war on Germany and Italy
6/4/1942	Battle of Midway starts (turning point of Pacific war)
1/23/1943	Casablanca Conference decides on Cross Channel Invasion of Continental Europe
7/10/43	Allies invade Sicily
6/6/1944	D-Day Allied invasion of Western Europe commences in France
5/7/1945	Germany surrenders to Allies at Reims, France
7/16/1945	U.S. tests 1st atomic bomb in New Mexico
8/6/1945	U.S. drops atomic bomb on Hiroshima, Japan
8/9/1945	U.S. drops atomic bomb on Nagasaki, Japan
8/14/1945	Japan agrees to surrender
9/2/1945	Japan formally surrenders in Tokyo Bay

3. Merge and center the title in the range A1: B1.

4. Bold and center the titles in the range A2: B2.

5. Change the format of the Date column to the Month DD, YYYY format.

6. Format cell A1 with a black fill and white text.

7. Format the text in cell A1 as bold and increase the font size to 16 points.

8. Format row 2 with a dark gray fill and white text.

9. Use AutoFit to adjust the column widths.

10. Save the workbook as *WWII*. Print and close the workbook.

Exercise 5   C

1. Open the *WWII* workbook you created in Exercise 4.

2. Change the width of column B to 45.

3. Turn on wrap text with column B selected.

4. Left align cells A3:A19.

chapter four

5. Italicize cells A3, A7, A13, A14, and A19.

6. Activate cell A1, then save the workbook as *WWII Revised*. Print and close the workbook.

Exercise 6   C

1. Open the *New Computer Prices* workbook located on the Data Disk.

2. Change the title in row A1 to 16 point, bold text.

3. Merge and center cell A1 across A1:G1.

4. Bold and center the titles in row 3.

5. Resize columns A–G to fit.

6. Format column C with Currency Style and no decimal places.

7. Change the data in columns E and F to right-aligned. (Do not right-align the column labels.)

8. Save the workbook as *New Computer Prices Formatted*. Print and close the workbook.

Exercise 7   C

1. Open the *Employee Time 1* workbook located on the Data Disk.

2. Insert a new column to the left of column A, on the Revised Data worksheet.

3. Move all of the data (including the column heading) under Project to the new column A.

4. Delete the empty column C.

5. Change column C to Number format with two decimal places.

6. Increase the width of column A to show the project names in full.

7. Bold and center the column labels.

8. Move the title in cell B1 to cell A1, make the title bold, then merge and center it across columns A through C.

9. Delete the blank rows 2, 3, and 4 under the worksheet title.

10. Freeze the column labels. (*Hint:* Freeze rows 1 and 2.)

11. Save the workbook as *Employee Time 2*. Print and close the workbook.

Exercise 8   C

1. Create a new workbook, and then enter "Title" in cell A1.

2. Change the Font style to Times New Roman, font size 16, and color blue.

3. Fill the cell with the light turquoise color.

4. Create a new style "Title" based on cell A1.

5. Enter "Column Heading" in cell A2.

6. Rotate the text 45 degrees.

7. Change the alignment to center, horizontally and vertically.

8. Add a left and right dashed style border.

9. Create a new style "Column Heading" based on cell A2.

10. Key 1 in cell A5, and key 2 in cell B5.

11. Select A5:B5, then drag the fill handle to cell E5.

12. Save the workbook as *Cell Styles*. Print and close the workbook.

Case Projects

Project 1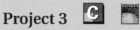

You work in a large bank. You are frequently asked about the current exchange rate for U.S. dollars relative to a variety of foreign currencies. Connect to the Internet and search the Web for a site that reports currency exchange rates. Create a new workbook to keep track of recent updates. Include the URL of the site(s) you find in the workbook, which will allow you to access these sites easily later. Record the date and currency exchange rate for converting U.S. dollars into the euro currency and the currencies of at least six countries, including those of Japan, Germany, France, and the United Kingdom. Apply currency formats displaying the appropriate currency symbol for each country (if available). Set up your workbook so that you can monitor the changes in exchange rates over time. Center and bold column labels, and italicize row labels. Make sure your worksheet has a formatted title. Save the workbook as *Foreign Currency Exchange*, and then print and close it.

Project 2 C

Your mom, a quilter, has come to you with an interesting project. She needs to organize her quilt pattern, but because of the number of pieces, it's very difficult to keep track of everything. You know that Excel can shade cells in different colors. That gives you an idea. Can you use shading and borders to create a fun geometrical pattern? Don't be afraid to modify column widths and row heights to achieve a more artistic pattern. Save your workbook as *Quilt*, and then print and close it.

Project 3 C

You are an instructor at a community college who teaches working adults about Excel. Several of your students have asked you for additional resources. Connect to the Internet and use the Web toolbar to search for Excel books. Create a new worksheet that lists the title, author name, and ISBN number for each book. Add a fourth column that lists the URL where you found the information about each book. (*Hint:* To copy the URL of the current Web page, click in the Address or Location box in your browser window, click Copy on the Edit menu, then paste this into your worksheet.) Add a title to your worksheet and format it nicely. Save the workbook as *Excel Books*, and then print and close it.

Project 4 C

You are the manager of a pizzeria. Create a worksheet with fictitious data that shows how many pizzas were sold last month. Calculate the total sales, figuring that each pizza sold for $8.00. Show the following column headings: Overhead, Labor, Ingredients, Advertising, and Profit. Calculate the amount spent in each category, figuring 15% for overhead, 30% for labor, 25% for ingredients, 10% for advertising, and the remainder for profit. Format the column labels to stand out from the rest of the data, and add a worksheet title. Save the workbook as *Pizzeria*, and then print and close it.

chapter four

Project 5

You plan on selling your car soon and want to find out how much it is worth. Connect to the Internet and use the Web toolbar to search for used car prices. Try finding a listing for your car and two other cars built the same year. (*Hint:* Search for "Blue Book values.") Create an Excel worksheet listing your car and the two cars you found. List the trade-in value of the cars you selected. Format the workbook nicely. Save the workbook as *Blue Book Values*, and then print and close it.

Project 6

You are a major sports fan. Create a workbook with column headings for Team Name, City, and Sport, then list as many pro sports teams as you can think of. Use the Internet to help you. When you finish the list, add AutoFilter to the list so you can filter the list by city or sport. Hide the row of the team you dislike the most. Format the worksheet nicely and add a worksheet title. Save the workbook as *Sports Teams*, and then print and close it.

Problem 7

You are a busy salesperson who is constantly visiting clients in your car, and who therefore, depends on a cellular phone. You want to see if your usage in the last year warrants changing your cellular calling plan. Create a worksheet with columns for local and long-distance minutes. Randomly generate numbers for each month between 0 and 400 for local air time, and numbers between 0 and 150 for long-distance air time. Copy the formula cells, then use the Paste Special command to paste only the values (not the formulas) in the same cells. Add a worksheet title and format the column headings with bold. Change the font color of any monthly total over 400 minutes to red. Save the workbook as *Cell Phone*, and then print and close it.

Project 8

Create a new workbook, enter some data, and then copy the workbook's contents using the Paste Special command. Paste Special provides many ways to copy data from one cell to another. Use the Ask A Question Box to learn about each option. Write a four-paragraph document explaining each of the options. Save the document as *Paste Special Options.doc*, and then print and close it.

Previewing and Printing Worksheets and Workbooks

Chapter Overview

When data needs to be changed or located in a workbook, the Find and Replace commands are at your service. AutoCorrect can simplify data entry and reduce spelling errors by correcting mistakes as you key. Prior to printing, it's a good idea to check for spelling errors. Excel provides many options to help you print exactly what you want. For example, you can print selections, worksheets, or entire workbooks. You also can set up headers and footers using pre-defined styles, or create custom headers and footers. In addition, you can modify page breaks and margin settings to print sheets to fit every need.

LEARNING OBJECTIVES

▶ Use Find and Replace
▶ Check spelling
▶ Set print options and print worksheets
▶ Print an entire workbook

Case profile

Every six months, Super Power Computers holds a long-range planning session. In this meeting, the company president, Luis Alvarez, reviews the accomplishments of the last six months and notes the company's progress toward previously set goals. Goals for the next six months are revised and set. You have prepared a calendar in Excel for 2003 that each participant in the meeting can use for notes.

chapter five

C

5.a Using Find and Replace

The Find command locates data and formats in a cell value, formula, or comment. Your calendars are ready to print, but you reread the worksheet, and you realize that the year displayed on each of your calendars is "02" instead of "03." To find and replace items:

Step 1	**Open**	the *12 Month Calendars* workbook located on the Data Disk
Step 2	**Save**	the workbook as *12 Month Calendars Revised*
Step 3	**Click**	Edit
Step 4	**Click**	Find
Step 5	**Click**	Options >> to expand the dialog box to show search options

CAUTION TIP

If the Options button shows two arrows pointing to the left (Options <<), then the dialog box is already expanded.

The Find tab in the Find and Replace dialog box on your screen should look similar to Figure 5-1. This tab provides many options for finding data. You want to search only this worksheet, by rows, and for data entered directly into a cell; it doesn't matter whether you look in Formulas or in Values. The search options are fine in this case. You enter the search text.

FIGURE 5-1
Find and Replace Dialog Box

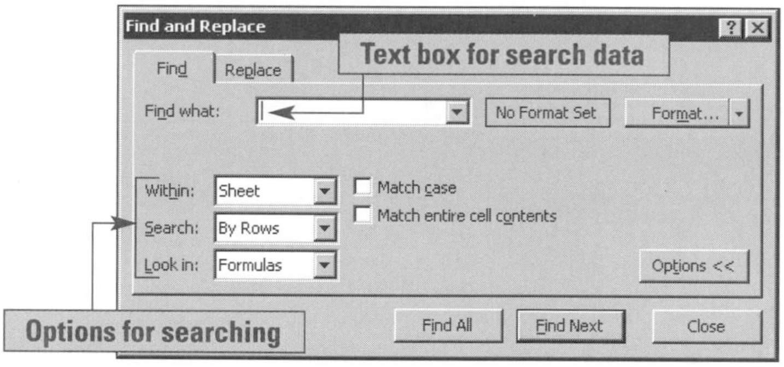

Step 6	**Key**	02 in the Find what: text box
Step 7	**Click**	the Format button list arrow
Step 8	**Click**	Choose Format From Cell
Step 9	**Click**	cell A1

A preview of the format appears to the left of the Format button.

Step 10	**Click**	Find All

At the bottom of the Find and Replace box, a list of cells appears. Each item in this list is a hyperlink to that cell, and you can click any link to jump directly to a cell containing the found item. You want to replace each of these with "03" formatted with bold. The Replace command finds and replaces individual instances or all instances of a given value.

Step 11	*Click*	the Replace tab
Step 12	*Key*	03 in the Replace with: text box
Step 13	*Click*	the Format list arrow in the Replace with: section
Step 14	*Click*	Format
Step 15	*Click*	Bold in the Font style: list on the Font tab
Step 16	*Click*	OK
Step 17	*Click*	Replace All
Step 18	*Click*	OK in the dialog box that opens to tell you that 12 replacements have been made
Step 19	*Click*	Close

The dates are now correct and formatted with bold.

Step 20	*Save*	the workbook

5.b Checking Spelling

Before you print a worksheet, you should proofread it and check the spelling. Excel provides two ways to check the spelling in a worksheet: AutoCorrect and the spell checker.

Using AutoCorrect

AutoCorrect checks your spelling as you go and automatically corrects common typos, such as "teh" for "the." You can turn AutoCorrect into a powerful helper by adding your own commonly used abbreviations in place of longer words or phrases. You decide to set up an abbreviation in AutoCorrect. To set AutoCorrect options:

Step 1	*Click*	Tools
Step 2	*Click*	AutoCorrect Options
Step 3	*Click*	the AutoCorrect tab, if necessary

chapter
five

Your AutoCorrect dialog box should look similar to Figure 5-2.

FIGURE 5-2
AutoCorrect Dialog Box

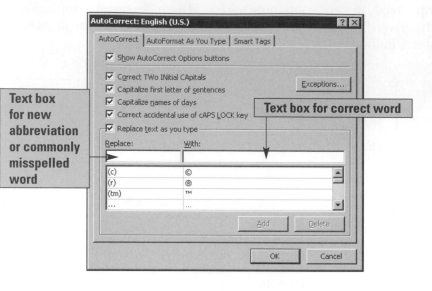

QUICK TIP

Take a quick scroll through the list of AutoCorrect items. You'll be surprised at some handy shortcuts, such as (tm) for the ™ symbol.

CAUTION TIP

If someone has already added "spc" to the AutoCorrect list, the list scrolls to the entry and the Add button is not available. Skip Step 6.

Step 4	*Key*	spc in the Replace: text box
Step 5	*Key*	Super Power Computers in the With: text box
Step 6	*Click*	Add

Now, whenever you key "spc" it will automatically be replaced with "Super Power Computers."

Step 7	*Click*	OK
Step 8	*Insert*	two rows at the top of the worksheet
Step 9	*Key*	spc in cell A1
Step 10	*Press*	the ENTER key
Step 11	*Merge*	and center cell A1 across columns A:O

Another Super Power Computers employee created a style for worksheet titles and copied the style to this workbook, so you can apply it to the title.

Step 12	*Apply*	the Worksheet Title style to cell A1
Step 13	*Save*	the workbook

Checking Spelling

Excel features a powerful spell checker that flags words that are not in the built-in dictionary and suggests alternate spellings. The spell checker does not find words that are spelled correctly but used incorrectly—for example, it will not flag "there" as misspelled when you should have used "their"—so always proofread your worksheets for errors, in addition to running a spell check. To spell check a worksheet:

| Step 1 | Click | the Spelling button on the Standard toolbar |

The spell checker starts at the active cell and checks the active worksheet row by row until it reaches the end of the worksheet. If the active cell is not at the top of the worksheet, Excel asks if you want to start at the top. The Spelling dialog box opens when the spell checker locates a word it doesn't recognize. Suggested corrections appear in the Suggestions: list box, as shown in Figure 5-3. Excel locates the misspelled word, "Wedensday" in the March calendar. The first suggestion in the Suggestions: list box is selected and is correct.

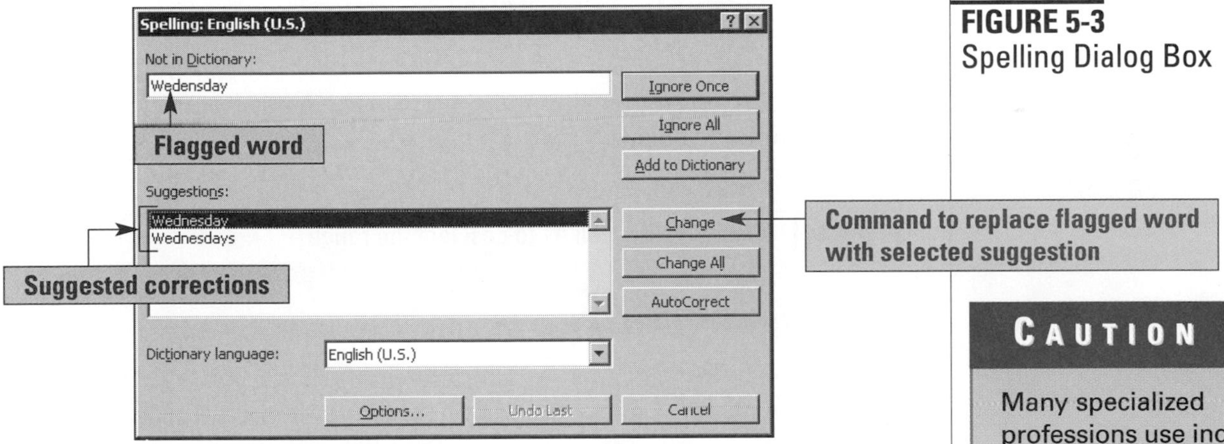

| Step 2 | Click | Change to replace the misspelled word with the selected suggestion |

There are no more spelling errors in the worksheet, so a dialog box opens, telling you that the spell check is complete.

| Step 3 | Click | OK |
| Step 4 | Save | the workbook |

MENU TIP

You can run the spell checker by clicking the Spelling command on the Tools menu.

QUICK TIP

To spell check multiple worksheets, select the sheet tabs of each sheet you want to check, then click the Spelling button.

FIGURE 5-3
Spelling Dialog Box

CAUTION TIP

Many specialized professions use industry-specific vocabularies that may not be included in the Excel dictionary. Proper names are also not included in the Excel dictionary. Click Ignore Once or Ignore All to skip these items.

chapter five

C | 5.c Setting Print Options and Printing Worksheets

Excel provides many options for formatting and printing your worksheets. You can change the margins and the orientation, add headers, footers, and print titles, or print multiple ranges or worksheets. You can also set a specific print area.

Setting the Print Area

By default, Excel prints all data on the current worksheet. If you need to print only a portion of a worksheet, however, you can define a print area by using the Set Print Area command. To set the print area:

Step 1	*Select*	the range A1:011
Step 2	*Click*	File
Step 3	*Point to*	Print Area
Step 4	*Click*	Set Print Area

This action defines a print area covering the worksheet title and the months January-03 and February-03.

Step 5	*Click*	cell A1 to deselect the range

Changing Margins

When the data is not situated properly on the page, you can adjust the margins, or align the data centered on the page. You can change margins in the Print Preview window or in the Page Setup dialog box. To change margins in Print Preview:

Step 1	*Click*	the Print Preview button 🔍 on the Standard toolbar
Step 2	*Click*	the Margins button on the Print Preview toolbar

Your screen should look similar to Figure 5-4. The dotted lines indicate the margins and the header/footer locations. You can change these margins by dragging the lines.

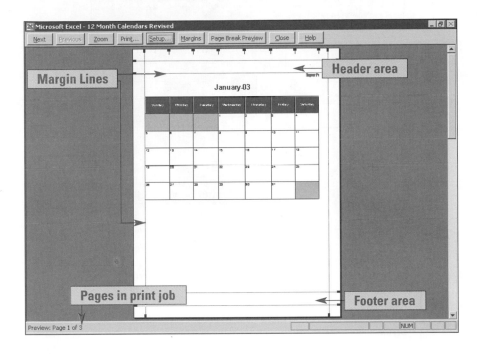

FIGURE 5-4
Adjusting Margins in Print Preview

MENU TIP

You can click the Print Preview command on the File menu to preview a document.

MOUSE TIP

Drag the scroll box in the vertical scroll bar in the Print Preview window to move to another page.

QUICK TIP

Zoom in to the worksheet to get more precise control.

Step 3	*Move*	the mouse pointer over the left margin line so that it changes to a double-headed arrow
Step 4	*Drag*	the margin line to the right, observing that the status bar indicates the width (in inches) of the margin
Step 5	*Release*	the mouse button when the status bar displays approximately "Left Margin: 1.00"
Step 6	*Click*	the Margins button on the Print Preview toolbar to turn off the margin lines

You also can precisely set margins in the Page Setup dialog box. To adjust the margins using the Page Setup dialog box:

| Step 1 | *Click* | the Setup button on the Print Preview toolbar |
| Step 2 | *Click* | the Margins tab |

chapter five

Your dialog box should look similar to Figure 5-5.

Step 3	**Double-click** the Right: text box to select the current margin setting
Step 4	**Key** 1
Step 5	**Click** OK

The right margin is now 1 inch. Luis wants the calendar to print two months to a page and sideways.

Changing Scaling and Page Orientation

The Page Setup dialog box provides many settings through which you can arrange the page, including scaling and orientation. Scaling a document allows you to fit a report to a certain number of pages. To scale the print area:

Step 1	**Click** the Setup button on the Print Preview toolbar
Step 2	**Click** the Page tab
Step 3	**Click** the Fit to: option button

The Page tab in the Page Setup dialog box on your screen should look similar to Figure 5-6. The Fit to option automatically fits your print area to the number of pages you specify.

MENU TIP

You can open the Page Setup dialog box by clicking the Page Setup command on the File menu.

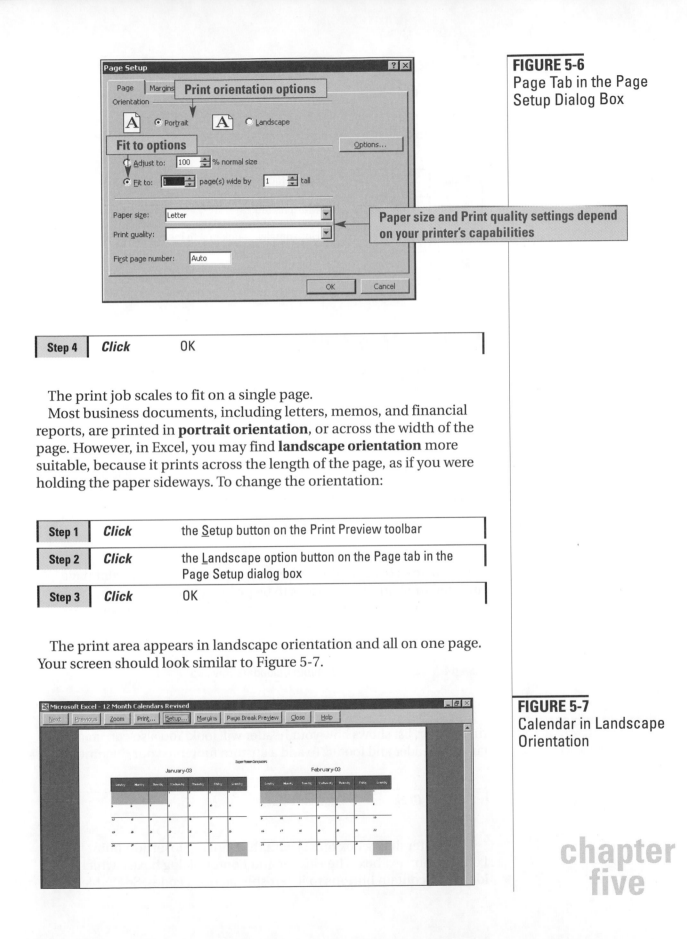

FIGURE 5-6
Page Tab in the Page
Setup Dialog Box

| Step 4 | *Click* | OK |

The print job scales to fit on a single page.

Most business documents, including letters, memos, and financial reports, are printed in **portrait orientation**, or across the width of the page. However, in Excel, you may find **landscape orientation** more suitable, because it prints across the length of the page, as if you were holding the paper sideways. To change the orientation:

Step 1	*Click*	the Setup button on the Print Preview toolbar
Step 2	*Click*	the Landscape option button on the Page tab in the Page Setup dialog box
Step 3	*Click*	OK

The print area appears in landscape orientation and all on one page. Your screen should look similar to Figure 5-7.

FIGURE 5-7
Calendar in Landscape
Orientation

chapter
five

Centering the Page Horizontally and Vertically

You can use the Page Setup dialog box to center the print area vertically and horizontally on the page. To center a print area on the page:

Step 1	*Click*	the Setup button on the Print Preview toolbar
Step 2	*Click*	the Margins tab
Step 3	*Click*	the Horizontally check box to insert a check mark
Step 4	*Click*	the Vertically check box to insert a check mark
Step 5	*Click*	OK to center the print area on the page

Setting Headers and Footers

A **header** appears above the top margin of every page you print. A **footer** appears below the bottom margin of every page you print. Excel has several predefined headers and footers, using common options such as the page number, filename, and date. To add a header:

Step 1	*Click*	the Setup button on the Print Preview toolbar
Step 2	*Click*	the Header/Footer tab
Step 3	*Click*	the Header: list arrow

The Header: list contains preset headers to print the current page number, total number of pages to be printed, worksheet name, company name, date, filename, and user name, as well as several variations and combinations of these elements.

| Step 4 | *Click* | 12 Month Calendars Revised |

This choice prints the filename as the header. The mini-preview above the Header: list shows how your header will look. You also can create a custom header and footer. To add a custom footer to your document:

| Step 1 | *Click* | Custom Footer |

The Footer dialog box opens with the blinking insertion point in the Left section: text box. The Header and Footer dialog boxes, which look identical, contain buttons to insert special print codes. See Table 5-1.

QUICK TIP

For more information about options on any tab of the Page Setup dialog box, click the Help button in the upper-right corner to activate the What's This? feature. Click any setting or control in the dialog box to obtain an explanation of the control's function.

To	Use	Code Inserted
Change the text font	A	
Insert a page number	#	&[Page]
Insert the total number of pages		&[Pages]
Insert the current date		&[Date]
Insert the current time		&[Time]
Insert the workbook path and filename		&[Path]&[File]
Insert the workbook filename		&[File]
Insert the worksheet name		&[Tab]
Insert a picture		&[Picture]
Format a picture		

TABLE 5-1
Header and
Footer Buttons

Step 2	*Key*	your name in the Left section: text box
Step 3	*Click*	in the Right section: text box
Step 4	*Click*	the Date button
Step 5	*Click*	in the Center section: text box
Step 6	*Click*	the Page Number button
Step 7	*Press*	the SPACEBAR
Step 8	*Key*	of
Step 9	*Press*	the SPACEBAR
Step 10	*Click*	the Total Pages button

QUICK TIP

Text you key in the Left section: text box will be left aligned, text in the Center section: text box will be center aligned, and text in the Right section: text box will be right aligned.

The Footer dialog box on your screen should look similar to Figure 5-8.

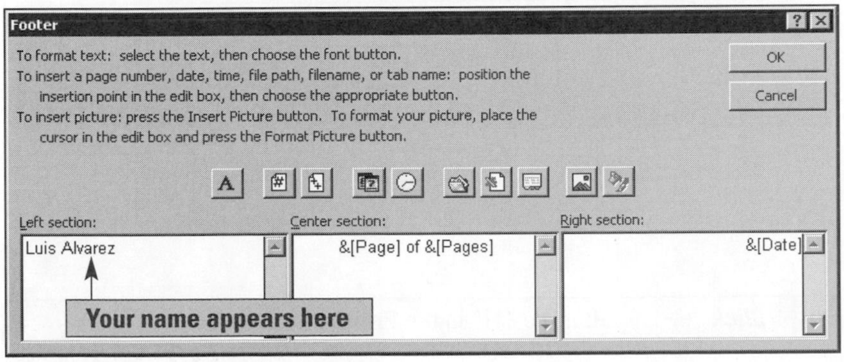

FIGURE 5-8
Footer Dialog Box

chapter
five

QUICK TIP

You can suppress the display of cell errors when printing. In the Page Setup dialog box, click the Sheet tab, then click the Cell errors as list arrow, and choose an option from the list.

Step 11	*Click*	OK

Your footer appears in the Footer: list box, and the mini-preview below the Footer: list box shows what the footer will look like.

Step 12	*Click*	OK to apply the header and footer

The preview shows that one page of the calendar with two months on it will print. However, you need all 12 months to print.

Step 13	*Click*	the Close button on the Print Preview toolbar

Setting Multiple Print Ranges

To print more than one area of a worksheet, you can specify multiple ranges in the Page Setup dialog box. You key a comma between each range to separate them. To set multiple print ranges:

Step 1	*Click*	File
Step 2	*Click*	Page Setup
Step 3	*Click*	the Sheet tab, if necessary

MENU TIP

When you open the Page Setup dialog box from the File menu as opposed to the Print Preview toolbar, a few extra options are enabled, such as the Print area: text box and the Print titles section.

The dialog box on your screen should look similar to Figure 5-9.

FIGURE 5-9
Sheet Tab in the Page Setup Dialog Box

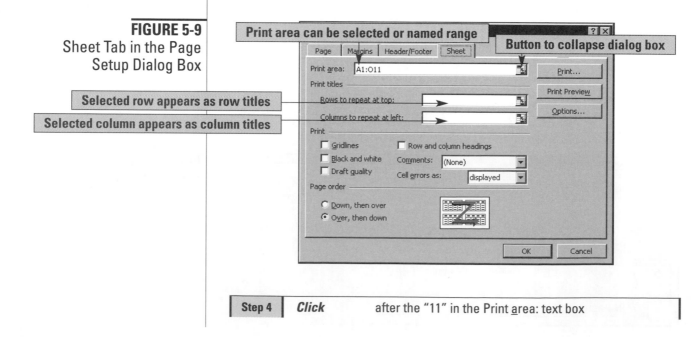

Step 4	*Click*	after the "11" in the Print area: text box

A flashing border in your worksheet indicates the current print area.

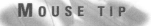

Step 5	Key	, (a comma)
Step 6	Click	the Collapse dialog box button
Step 7	Select	A13:O21
Step 8	Click	the Expand dialog box button
Step 9	Click	Print Preview in the Page Setup dialog box
Step 10	Click	the Next button on the Print Preview toolbar
Step 11	Click	the Close button on the Print Preview toolbar

Two pages are now set to print. There is another way to print more than one page at a time.

Inserting and Removing Page Breaks

To quickly print all the data on a worksheet, you can use Page Break Preview. When a worksheet contains data that will print on more than one page, you may need to adjust the position of page breaks so that information appears on the correct page. Because you have already defined a print area and set the print setting to Fit to, first you need to clear those settings. To clear the print area and change the Fit to option:

Step 1	Click	File
Step 2	Point to	Print Area
Step 3	Click	Clear Print Area
Step 4	Open	the Page tab in the Page Setup dialog box
Step 5	Key	6 in the box next to tall
Step 6	Click	OK

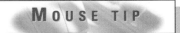

Your print job fits on six pages, two months per page. To change to Page Break Preview:

Step 1	Click	View
Step 2	Click	Page Break Preview
Step 3	Click	OK to close the Welcome to Page Break Preview dialog box, if necessary

chapter
five

Your screen should look similar to Figure 5-10. Dashed blue lines represent the automatic page breaks in Excel. A light gray page number indicates the order in which pages will print. You can drag the page break to a new location to change how pages are printed.

FIGURE 5-10
Page Break Preview Mode

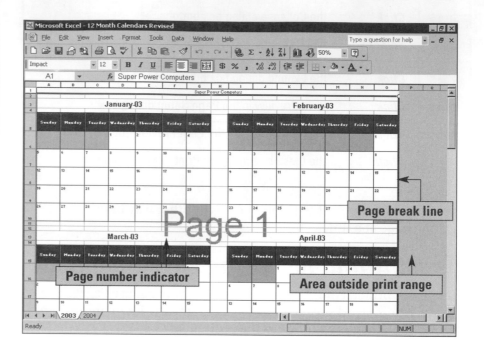

QUICK TIP

You must set page breaks separately for each worksheet in a workbook.

Because of differences in printer margins, the exact row number you use may differ in the steps that follow.

MENU TIP

You can click Remove Page Break on the Insert menu to remove a page break.

| Step 4 | **Scroll** | the worksheet until you see the dashed line, near row 22 |
| Step 5 | **Drag** | the dashed blue page break line from near row 22 to row 11 |

The dashed blue line changes to a solid blue line, representing a manually adjusted page break.

CAUTION TIP

The dashed blue page break lines may be difficult to see due to the blue heading formatting. View column H as you scroll to observe the lines.

Step 6	**Follow**	Steps 4 and 5 to manually position a page break at rows 21, 31, and 41
Step 7	**Activate**	cell A52
Step 8	**Click**	Insert
Step 9	**Click**	Page Break

In Normal view, the page breaks appear as dotted black lines. To switch back to Normal view:

Step 1	*Click*	<u>V</u>iew
Step 2	*Click*	<u>N</u>ormal

Check to make sure that your calendar will now print two months per page.

Step 3	*Click*	the Print Preview button 🔍 on the Standard toolbar
Step 4	*Click*	the down scroll arrow five times to scroll through the preview
Step 5	*Drag*	the scroll box back to the top of the scroll bar
Step 6	*Close*	Print Preview

The worksheet title, "Super Power Computers," appears on page 1, but not on the rest of the pages. You can set a print title to appear on each page.

Setting Print Titles

Print titles are useful when you need column or row labels to appear on every printed page. You set print titles from the Page Setup dialog box, but this command is not available when you open the dialog box with the Print Preview window open. To create print titles:

Step 1	*Open*	the Sheet tab in the Page Setup dialog box
Step 2	*Click*	in the <u>R</u>ows to repeat at top: text box
Step 3	*Select*	row 1 in your worksheet
Step 4	*Click*	Print Previe<u>w</u> in the Page Setup dialog box
Step 5	*Scroll*	through the pages to verify that the title repeats on every page
Step 6	*Close*	Print Preview

chapter
five

Printing a Worksheet

Now that you have adjusted the page setup options and set the page breaks, you are ready to print. To print a worksheet:

Step 1	*Click*	File

Step 2	*Click*	Print

The Print dialog box on your screen should look similar to Figure 5-11.

FIGURE 5-11
Print Dialog Box

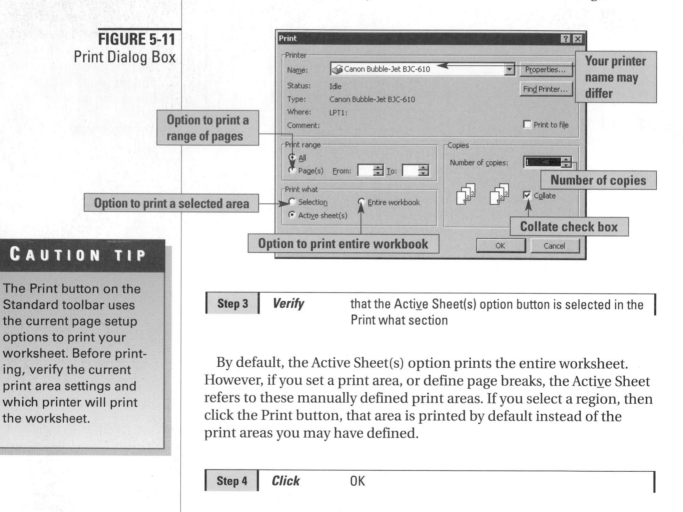

Option to print a range of pages

Option to print a selected area

Option to print entire workbook

Your printer name may differ

Number of copies

Collate check box

CAUTION TIP

The Print button on the Standard toolbar uses the current page setup options to print your worksheet. Before printing, verify the current print area settings and which printer will print the worksheet.

Step 3	*Verify*	that the Acti<u>v</u>e Sheet(s) option button is selected in the Print what section

By default, the Active Sheet(s) option prints the entire worksheet. However, if you set a print area, or define page breaks, the Acti<u>v</u>e Sheet refers to these manually defined print areas. If you select a region, then click the Print button, that area is printed by default instead of the print areas you may have defined.

Step 4	*Click*	OK

The 2003 worksheet prints, two months per page.

Until now, you have been working with areas on only one worksheet. In the next section, you learn how to print multiple worksheets.

5.d Printing an Entire Workbook

Luis wants everyone to have a 2004 calendar at the meeting as well. It is just for reference, so it can be printed six months to a page. When you print multiple worksheets, each worksheet has its own page break settings. To print the entire workbook:

Step 1	*Click*	the 2004 sheet tab
Step 2	*Switch to*	Page Break Preview
Step 3	*Drag*	the vertical page break line to the right of column O
Step 4	*Drag*	the horizontal page break near row 22 to below row 29
Step 5	*Right-click*	cell A40
Step 6	*Click*	Remove Page Break
Step 7	*Remove*	the other page break at row 50
Step 8	*Switch to*	Normal view
Step 9	*Click*	File
Step 10	*Click*	Print
Step 11	*Click*	the Entire workbook option button in the Print what section
Step 12	*Change*	the Number of copies text box to 2
Step 13	*Click*	Preview
Step 14	*Verify*	that the pages will print as desired
Step 15	*Verify*	that your instructor wants you to print two copies of all eight pages
Step 16	*Click*	the Print button on the Print Preview toolbar
Step 17	*Click*	OK
Step 18	*Save*	the workbook and close it

You're all set for the meeting!

CAUTION TIP

When you print multiple worksheets, remember to check the page breaks on every page.

QUICK TIP

The Collate check box in the Print dialog box organizes the order of your print job. Select it when you are printing more than one copy of a multiple-page worksheet to print a complete copy of the document before starting the next copy.

chapter five

Summary

▶ The Find and Replace commands enable you to locate and change data.

▶ AutoCorrect corrects common spelling errors as you type. Add AutoCorrect entries to replace abbreviations with long words, titles, or phrases.

▶ You should always spell check workbooks before printing them. Remember that the spell checker does not detect incorrect usage, such as "your" for "you're." Always proofread your document after spell checking it.

▶ You can define print areas by clicking the File menu, pointing to Print area, and then clicking Set Print Area.

▶ You can set margins by dragging them in Print Preview or by using the Margins tab in the Page Setup dialog box.

▶ You can use the Page tab in the Page Setup dialog box to set scaling options and to change the orientation of the page.

▶ You can use the Margins tab in the Page Setup dialog box to select page centering options.

▶ You can use the Header/Footer tab to add a header or footer to a printed worksheet.

▶ You can set multiple print ranges on the Sheet tab in the Page Setup dialog box.

▶ You can manually adjust page breaks in Page Break view.

▶ You can select rows and columns to repeat on every printed page on the Sheet tab in the Page Setup dialog box.

▶ You can print a workbook by clearing print areas, then selecting the Entire Workbook option in the Print dialog box.

Commands Review

Action	Menu Bar	Shortcut Menu	Toolbar	Task Pane	Keyboard
Find	Edit, Find				ALT + E, F CTRL + F
Replace	Edit, Replace				ALT + E, E CTRL + H
Add AutoCorrect entries	Tools, AutoCorrect options				ALT +T, A
Check spelling	Tools, Spelling				ALT +T, S F7
Set print area	File, Print Area, Set Print Area				ALT + F,T, S
Clear print area	File, Print Area, Clear Print Area				ALT + F,T, C
Preview the workbook to be printed	File, Print Preview		🔍		ALT + F, V
Set print options	File, Page Setup				ALT + F, U
View page breaks	View, Page Break Preview				ALT +V, P
Switch to Normal view	View, Normal				ALT +V, N
Print	File, Print		🖨		CTRL + P ALT + F, P

Concepts Review

SCANS

Circle the correct answer.

1. To create multiple ranges for printing, press and hold the:
[a] SHIFT key while selecting ranges.
[b] END key while selecting ranges.
[c] CTRL key while selecting ranges.
[d] ALT key while selecting ranges.

2. To set centering options for a printed report, open the Page Setup dialog box and use the:
[a] Page tab.
[b] Margins tab.
[c] Header/Footer tab.
[d] Sheet tab.

3. To set a page to print in landscape orientation, open the Page Setup dialog box and use the:
[a] Page tab.
[b] Margins tab.
[c] Header/Footer tab.
[d] Sheet tab.

4. When you include the print formula "&[Page]" in a header or footer, it prints:
[a] "&[Page]" on every page.
[b] the total page count on every page.

[c] the current page number on each page.
[d] a box where you can write in the page number by hand.

5. In Normal view, page breaks are indicated by a:
[a] heavy blue line.
[b] heavy black line.
[c] dotted black line.
[d] thin blue line.

6. In Page Break Preview view, default page breaks are indicated by a:
[a] dotted blue line.
[b] heavy black line.
[c] solid blue line.
[d] thin blue line.

7. Replace can replace values in which of the following?
[a] chart objects
[b] comments
[c] formulas
[d] chart objects, comments, and formulas

chapter five

8. You set up page breaks on Sheet1 of a work-book and select Entire workbook from the Print dialog box. Sheet2 doesn't print correctly. What should you do?
   [a] Click the Print button again to see whether the problem goes away.
   [b] Check to see whether the printer is working properly.
   [c] Clear the print area.
   [d] Use Page Break Preview mode to check the page breaks on both worksheets.

9. To set collating options for a print job, you use the:
   [a] Page Setup dialog box.
   [b] Page Break Preview.
   [c] Print dialog box.
   [d] Options button in the Page Setup dialog box.

10. When you manually adjust page break lines, Page Break Preview displays a:
   [a] dotted blue line.
   [b] heavy black line.
   [c] solid blue line.
   [d] thin blue line.

Circle **T** if the statement is true or **F** if the statement is false.

T   F   1. You should always preview before you print.

T   F   2. Clicking the Print button on the Standard toolbar opens the Print dialog box.

T   F   3. The dotted black page preview lines cannot be turned off.

T   F   4. You must select named ranges by opening the Page Setup dialog box from the File menu.

T   F   5. Once you change page break locations, you can't undo them.

T   F   6. You can see page breaks only in Page Break Preview mode.

T   F   7. You should always proofread your worksheet in addition to checking spelling.

T   F   8. Headers and footers must use the same font.

T   F   9. AutoCorrect can be used to replace a shortcut with a longer word or phrase.

T   F   10. You need to set footer options for each page in your printed report.

Skills Review

Exercise 1   ©

1. Open the *24 Month Calendar* workbook located on the Data Disk.

2. Select the Jan-03, Feb-03, Jun-03, and Jul-03 calendars.

3. Set the print area with these ranges selected.

4. Preview the worksheet.

5. Print the worksheet if instructed to do so.

6. Change the view to Normal view.

7. Activate cell A1.

8. Save the workbook as *24 Month Calendar Revised* and close it.

Exercise 2 [C]

1. Open the *Sales Rep Data* workbook located on the Data Disk.

2. Add a custom header "Sales Rep Data" using 16-point, bold text, and center it in the header area.

3. Use Page Break Preview to set page breaks after every 30 rows. Pull down the top page break to prevent the two blank rows from printing.

4. Center the print area horizontally, and set row 3 to repeat at the top of each page.

5. Preview your print job, and print the worksheet if instructed to do so.

6. Save the workbook as *Sales Rep Data Revised* and close it.

Exercise 3

1. Open the *Cookie Sales* workbook located on the Data Disk.

2. Replace all instances of the word "chip" with the work "chunk."

3. Use the Replace command to change all cells containing "Totals" to "Total" formatted with 12-point red font.

4. Run the spell checker.

5. Set the print area to cover all the data in the worksheet.

6. Change the print orientation to landscape.

7. Use the Fit to: option to print all of the data on one page.

8. Set the print options to center the data vertically and horizontally.

9. Print the worksheet if instructed to do so.

10. Save the workbook as *Cookie Sales Revised* and close it.

Exercise 4 [C]

1. Open the *Home Loan* workbook located on the Data Disk (click OK if a dialog box opens warning you about macros).

2. Switch to the Loan Amortization Table worksheet.

3. Use Page Break Preview to print 50 payments per page. Insert new page breaks as necessary.

4. Print the worksheet if instructed to do so.

5. Save the workbook as *Home Loan Revised* and close it.

Exercise 5 [C]

1. You will be distributing the *24 Month Calendar Revised* to all employees in your company. Write a step-by-step description explaining how to print only the January-03 calendar. Save the document as *Printing a Calendar*. Include the following instructions:

a. Explain how to add **2003** as the header for the printed report.

b. Explain how to print the calendar in Landscape orientation.

2. Print your document or e-mail it to a classmate. Have your classmate follow your directions *exactly* and print the report. See how well he or she was able to follow your instructions.

3. Save and close the *Printing a Calendar.doc* document.

chapter five

Exercise 6

1. Open the *Sweet Tooth Q2 2003 Sales* workbook located on the Data Disk.

2. Set print options to print the worksheet centered horizontally and vertically using Portrait orientation.

3. Print the worksheet.

4. Set print options to print the worksheet centered horizontally, but not vertically, using Landscape orientation.

5. Print the worksheet.

6. Save the workbook as *Sweet Tooth Q2 2003 Sales Revised* and close it.

Exercise 7

1. Open the *Sweet Tooth Q3 2003 Sales* workbook located on the Data Disk.

2. Change the top and bottom margins to 3 inches.

3. Create a custom footer displaying the filename on the left, the date in the center, and the time on the right.

4. Print the worksheet.

5. Save the workbook as *Sweet Tooth Q3 2003 Sales Revised* and close it.

Exercise 8

1. Open the *Sweet Tooth 2003 Sales* workbook located on the Data Disk.

2. Add the abbreviation "sw" to the AutoCorrect list. Replace the abbreviation with "Sweet Tooth."

3. Use the AutoCorrect abbreviation "sw" to add "Sweet Tooth" to cell A1 on each of the worksheets.

4. Set the print scale to 150% on all four worksheets.

5. Set the print options on all four worksheets to print in Landscape orientation, with a 2-inch top margin, and centered horizontally.

6. Print the worksheet if instructed to do so.

7. Save the workbook as *Sweet Tooth 2003 Sales Revised* and close it.

Case Projects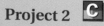

Project 1

Your job is to train employees in the use of Excel. Search the Internet for Excel tips to include in your weekly "Excel Training Letter." Select one tip and create a Word document of at least two paragraphs describing it. Provide the URL of any sites that you used as references for your tip. Save the document as *Excel Training Letter.doc* and then print and close it.

Project 2

As part of your job, you track inventory at a used car dealership. You must record the number of cars sold by type per month. Create a worksheet providing fictitious sales data on at least four different types of cars for a period of four months. Set page breaks to print each month's data on a separate page. Center the data horizontally on each page. Print the worksheet title and column labels on each page. Save the workbook as *Car Sales* and close it.

Project 3

You're an office manager for a busy construction company. You have a lot of names, phone numbers, and addresses to manage. You keep the data for each state on separate worksheets. Create a new workbook. At the top of each worksheet create the following column headings: Last Name, First Name, Address, City, State, Zip, Phone number. On each worksheet, enter fictitious data for at least five people from the same state. Include a footer on each page with your company's name. Print the entire workbook in landscape orientation. Save the workbook as *Phone List* and close it.

Problem 4

You are a travel agent. To stay competitive, you use the Internet to find out about your competitors' offers. Connect to the Internet, and use the Web toolbar to locate at least three Web sites offering five- to seven-night packages to Cancun, Mexico. Print pages showing information about each of these packages. Create a workbook listing the name of each package, and enter the Web address where you located the vacation package. Save the workbook as *Vacation to Cancun*. Print it in an attractive format, and then close it.

Problem 5

You are interested in increasing your productivity while using Excel. Using the Ask A Question Box, search for the topic "keyboard shortcuts." Print one of the pages containing keyboard shortcuts for any of the shortcut key categories. Instructions for printing are included on each page in the Help file.

Problem 6

You need to purchase a workgroup class laser printer (16+ pages a minute, 600 dpi or better) for your publishing company. Connect to the Internet and search the Web for a review of this type of printer. Create a workbook and list your findings on three of the printers. Be sure to include the manufacturer, model, pages per minute, dpi if higher than 600, cost, and the Web address where you found the review. Save the workbook as *Workgroup Printer*, print it in an attractive format, and close it.

Project 7

In order to be better organized, you decide to create a daily planner. Create a worksheet that breaks the day into one-hour segments, starting from when you get up in the morning and ending when you go to bed at night. Fill in the planner with your usual schedule for seven days. Print the worksheet(s) in an attractive format. Save the workbook as *Daily Planner* and close it.

Project 8

You are the accounts manager of a graphic design company. Create a list of 10 clients who owe your company money. Use fictitious client names and amounts due (between $500 and $2,000). Add a column indicating how many days the account is overdue. Print the worksheet it in an attractive format. Save the workbook as *Overdue Accounts* and close it.

chapter five

Creating Charts and Sharing Information

Chapter Overview

Charts offer a great way to summarize and present data, providing a colorful, graphic link to numerical data collected in worksheets. Graphics can add visual interest to your worksheet. Creating such an explicit relationship helps other people analyze trends, spot inconsistencies in business performance, and evaluate market share. Sharing information electronically is an essential task. In this chapter, you learn how to create and modify charts, add graphics, add comments to worksheets, use the Web Discussion feature, and save Excel documents as Web pages.

LEARNING OBJECTIVES

- ▶ Use the Chart Wizard to create a chart
- ▶ Format and modify a chart
- ▶ Insert, resize, and move a graphic
- ▶ Work with embedded charts
- ▶ Preview and print charts
- ▶ Use workgroup collaboration
- ▶ Use Go To

Case profile

Each quarter, Super Power Computers' regional managers meet with the company president, Luis Alvarez, to review sales figures and set goals for the next quarter. You have collected data from each of the regional offices and are now ready to compile a report for the meeting. You decide to use charts to show the company's final sales figures.

chapter six

6.a Using the Chart Wizard to Create a Chart

A chart provides a graphical interface to numerical data contained in a worksheet. Almost anyone can appreciate and understand the colorful simplicity of a chart. The data found in the *Super Power Computers - Sales Data Q1 2003* workbook represents Super Power Computers' sales for the first quarter. Your job is to create and format a chart for use in tomorrow's sales meeting. To open the workbook and save it with a new name:

Step 1	*Open*	the *Super Power Computers - Sales Data Q1 2003* workbook located on the Data Disk
Step 2	*Save*	the workbook as *Super Power Computers - Sales Data Q1 2003 Revised*

The Chart Wizard walks you step by step through a series of four dialog box boxes to quickly create a chart. You can create charts as separate workbook sheets called **chart sheets**, or you can place them directly on the worksheet page as **embedded charts**. One type of chart, called a column chart, helps you compare values across categories. To create a chart using the Chart Wizard:

Step 1	*Activate*	cell A5 on the Summary worksheet
Step 2	*Click*	the Chart Wizard button  on the Standard toolbar

The Chart Wizard dialog box on your screen should look similar to Figure 6-1. In Step 1, you select the type of chart you want to create from the list of chart types on the left side of the dialog box. You click a chart type on the left to display chart subtypes on the right side of the dialog box. A description of the chart subtype appears below the preview box. You want to create a three-dimensional chart, which is an interesting visual alternative to two-dimensional charts.

chapter
six

FIGURE 6-1
Step 1 of the Chart Wizard

FIGURE 6-1
Step 1 of the Chart Wizard

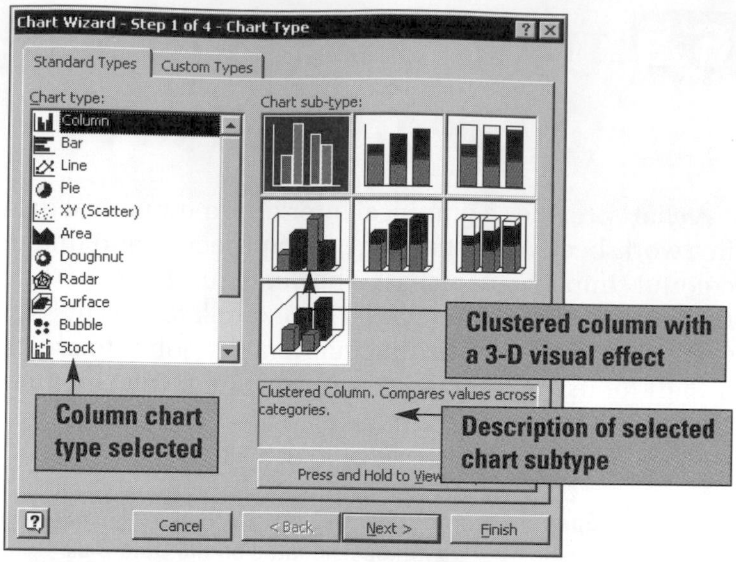

QUICK TIP

By default, data is plotted with the longest edge along the *x*-axis—in this case, the column labels. If the chart doesn't show the data the way you expected, click the other option button in the Series in: section in Step 2 of the Chart Wizard to reverse the way data is plotted in the chart—in this case, by row labels.

MOUSE TIP

You can change a chart to a different type at any time. Right-click the chart you want to change, click Chart type on the shortcut menu, select a new chart type and subtype, then click the OK button.

Step 3	*Verify*	that Column is selected in the Chart type: list
Step 4	*Click*	the Clustered column with a 3-D visual effect from the Chart sub-type: box (first column, second row)
Step 5	*Click*	Next >

In Step 2 of the Chart Wizard, you select or modify the chart's source data. A preview of the selected data appears at the top of the Data Range tab. Notice the flashing border surrounding the chart data in the worksheet behind the Chart Wizard.

| Step 6 | *Click* | Next > |

The Titles tab in Step 3 of the Chart Wizard on your screen should look similar to Figure 6-2.

FIGURE 6-2
Step 3 of the Chart Wizard

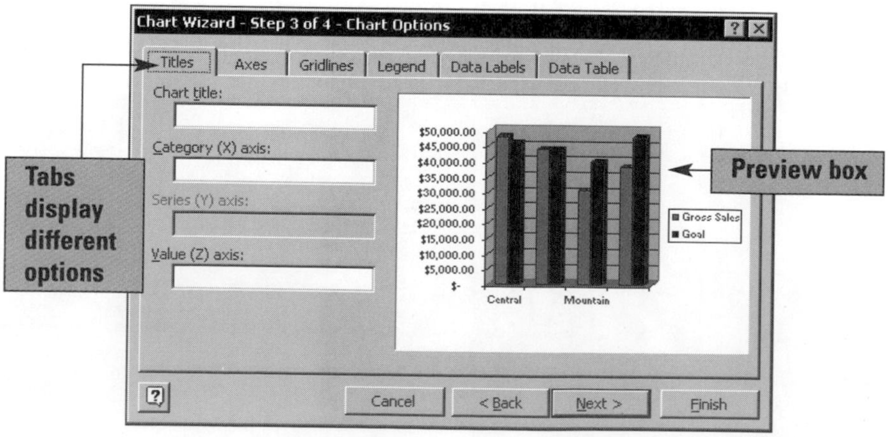

You enter chart options such as titles, legends, and data labels. The tabs vary depending on the chart type you selected.

| Step 7 | *Click* | in the Chart title: text box |
| Step 8 | *Key* | Gross Sales by Region |

Change your mind while using the Chart Wizard? Step backward at any time by clicking the < Back button. Make any changes, then click the Next > button to continue. The wizard leaves all other settings intact.

The title you just keyed appears in the Preview box after a few seconds.

Step 9	*Press*	the TAB key to move to the Category (X) axis: text box
Step 10	*Key*	Region Name
Step 11	*Click*	the Legend tab
Step 12	*Click*	the Bottom option button
Step 13	*Click*	Next >

The dialog box on your screen should look similar to Figure 6-3. In Step 4 of the Chart Wizard, you specify the location of the new chart. You can create the chart as a new sheet or as an object in another worksheet.

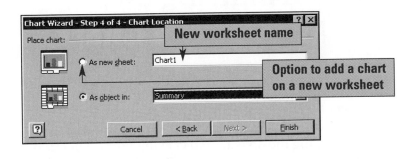

FIGURE 6-3
Step 4 of the Chart Wizard

Step 14	*Click*	the As new sheet: option button
Step 15	*Key*	Gross Sales by Region Chart in the As new sheet: text box
Step 16	*Click*	Finish

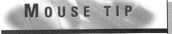

You can change the location of a chart by right-clicking the chart and clicking Location.

The chart appears on a new worksheet in your workbook, and the Chart toolbar appears. Your screen should look similar to Figure 6-4.

chapter
six

FIGURE 6-4
Chart Created with
Chart Wizard

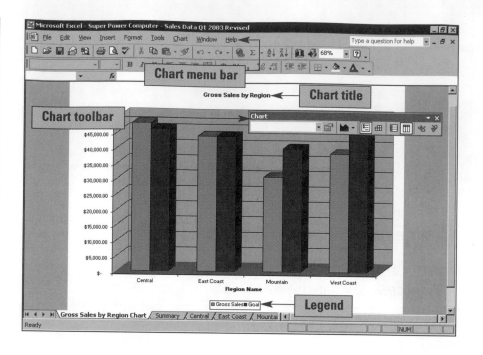

MENU TIP

Do you use a certain type of chart most of the time? You can change the default chart type. First, create a chart. Click Chart Type on the Chart menu, select the type of chart and the subtype that you use most often, then click the Set as default chart button.

When you create a chart, the Chart toolbar appears, and the Chart menu replaces the Data menu in the menu bar. The Chart menu bar and toolbar contain chart-specific tools to help you create and modify charts.

6.b Formatting and Modifying a Chart

Every element of a chart, such as the title, legend, and plot area, is considered an object. An **object** is a graphical element added to a worksheet that you can manipulate by moving, resizing, or reformatting it. Each chart object can be formatted by double-clicking or right-clicking the object, then clicking Format *object* (where *object* is the name of the selected object). The Format dialog box displays options unique to each object.

Some of the more important chart objects are defined here. The **legend** is the key used to identify the colors assigned to categories in a chart. **Tick marks** are small marks on the edges of the chart that delineate the scale or separate the data categories. **Data points** represent the numerical data in your worksheet. In the current chart type, the data points are represented by horizontal columns. Data points, however, can also be represented by bars, columns, pie slices, and a variety of other shapes and marks. A **data series** represents all related data points in a set. On your chart, the Gross Sales columns are a data series, as are the Goal columns. A **data label** displays the actual value of each data point on the chart. The **plot area** of a chart is the area that includes only the chart itself.

MOUSE TIP

To select a data point in a chart, click it, then click it again. Do not double-click the data point.

Changing Chart Fonts

You can change font settings for all text on the chart simultaneously, or you can select individual text objects and then customize their font settings. You want the title to stand out from the other elements of the chart. To change fonts for individual objects:

Step 1	*Move*	the mouse pointer over the Chart Title object at the top of the chart to display the ScreenTip
Step 2	*Right-click*	the Chart Title object
Step 3	*Click*	Format Chart Title
Step 4	*Click*	the Font tab in the Format Chart Title dialog box, if necessary
Step 5	*Click*	Impact in the Font: list
Step 6	*Click*	20 in the Size: list
Step 7	*Click*	the Color: list arrow
Step 8	*Click*	the Blue square (second row, sixth column)
Step 9	*Click*	the Patterns tab
Step 10	*Click*	the Automatic option button in the Border section
Step 11	*Click*	OK
Step 12	*Press*	the ESC key to deselect the Chart Title object

The chart title is now formatted with your selections. Next, you format one of the axes.

Formatting the Axes

You can modify both axes of the chart. The **category axis**, sometimes called the *x*-axis, is the axis along which you normally plot categories of data. This axis runs horizontally along the bottom of many chart types. The **value axis**, or *y*-axis, usually runs vertically along the left side of a chart, and is the axis along which you plot values associated with various categories of data.

Excel gives you full control over the scale of the axes, the number format, and the appearance of the axis labels. You decide to modify the number format of the value axis by dropping the decimal amount. To modify the value axis scale:

Step 1	*Right-click*	the value axis along the left side of the chart
Step 2	*Click*	Format Axis

chapter
six

MOUSE TIP

You can quickly format Chart Area fonts. For example, suppose all text on the chart should be bold. Click the Chart Area to select it, then click the Bold button on the Formatting toolbar. All text items are bolded.

Step 3	*Click*	the Number tab in the Format Axis dialog box
Step 4	*Click*	the down spin arrow in the Decimal places: text box twice to set it to 0
Step 5	*Click*	OK

Your screen should look similar to Figure 6-5.

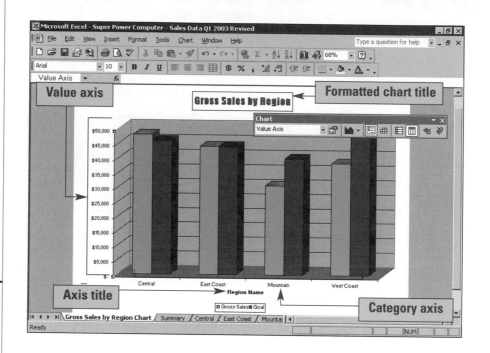

FIGURE 6-5
Changing Value
Scale Options

Adding a Data Table to a Chart

A **data table** displays the actual data used to create the chart. For small data sets, you may find it helpful to show this information on the chart worksheet. To add a data table to the chart:

CAUTION TIP

If the Chart toolbar is not displayed, right-click any toolbar, then click Chart.

Step 1	*Click*	the Data Table button ⊞ on the Chart toolbar

The data table is added beneath the value axis. Your screen should look similar to Figure 6-6.

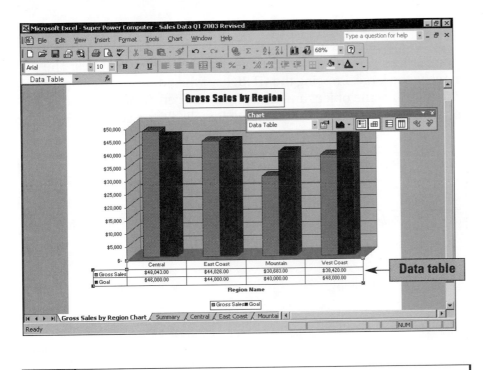

FIGURE 6-6
Adding a Data Table to
a Chart

MOUSE TIP

You can add data labels by right-clicking the data series, clicking the Data Labels tab, selecting an option button, then clicking the OK button.

QUICK TIP

When a chart object is selected, you can cycle to other chart objects by pressing the ARROW keys.

Step 2	**Save**	the workbook

The Gross Sales by Region chart is complete. Next, you insert the company logo on the chart.

6.c Inserting, Resizing, and Moving a Graphic

You can insert other types of objects into a chart. For example, you can place text, lines, or pictures to further enhance your chart. To insert an object into a chart:

Step 1	**Click**	the Drawing button on the Standard toolbar to display the Drawing toolbar, if necessary
Step 2	**Click**	the Insert Picture From File button on the Drawing toolbar

The Insert Picture dialog box opens.

chapter
six

QUICK TIP

To insert clip art, click the Insert Clip Art button on the Drawing toolbar. To insert other types of objects, click the Object command on the Insert menu.

Step 3	*Click*	*SPC Logo* on the Data Disk
Step 4	*Click*	In<u>s</u>ert

The image object is inserted in your chart. The Picture toolbar might appear. The small circles around the image are **sizing handles**. The image is too large. Pressing the CTRL key while dragging a sizing handle resizes the object uniformly from the center of the object. As you drag the object handle, the Name Box displays a scale percentage.

Step 5	*Press & hold*	the CTRL key
Step 6	*Drag*	the lower-right sizing handle up and to the left
Step 7	*Release*	the mouse button when the object is approximately 45% of its original size

MOUSE TIP

To resize an object proportionally from the edge, press and hold the SHIFT key while you drag a selection handle.

To move the object:

Step 1	*Move*	the mouse pointer over the image object
Step 2	*Drag*	the object to position it to the left of the chart title

The chart on your screen should look similar to Figure 6-7.

FIGURE 6-7
Inserting and Positioning a Chart Object

QUICK TIP

To delete a chart object, select it and then press the DELETE key.

Step 3	*Press*	the ESC key to deselect the logo
Step 4	*Save*	the workbook

6.d Working with Embedded Charts

Embedded charts are charts placed directly into a worksheet, rather than on a separate sheet tab. You decide to create an embedded chart in your workbook. To create an embedded chart:

Step 1	*Select*	the range A5:B8 on the Central worksheet
Step 2	*Click*	the Chart Wizard button ▦ on the Standard toolbar
Step 3	*Click*	Pie in the Chart type: list
Step 4	*Click*	Finish

The default chart type is an embedded chart, so there is no need to click all the way through the Chart Wizard. The chart is embedded in your worksheet, but it needs a little work. To resize and move an embedded chart:

| Step 1 | *Verify* | that the chart is still selected |

Sizing handles appear around the edges of the chart when it is selected.

Step 2	*Drag*	the sizing handle in the middle of the left edge of the chart object
Step 3	*Release*	the mouse button near the divider line between columns D and E
Step 4	*Position*	the mouse pointer anywhere in the white chart area (ScreenTip displays Chart Area)
Step 5	*Drag*	the chart object so that the chart is vertically centered next to the worksheet data

Your screen should look similar to Figure 6-8.

QUICK TIP

To delete an embedded chart, select the chart, and then press the DELETE key.

chapter
six

FIGURE 6-8
Resizing and Moving an Embedded Chart

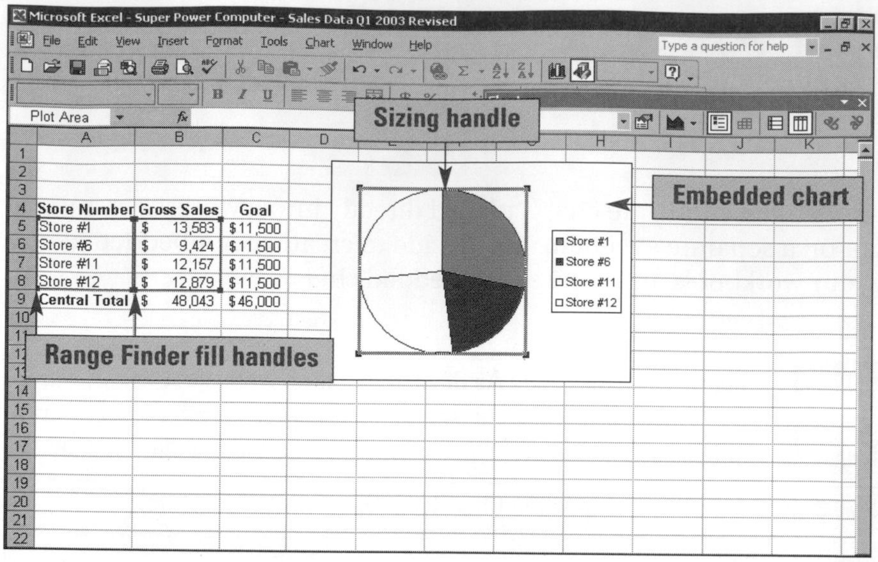

QUICK TIP

If you have an object selected within the chart, you may need to press the ESC key a few times until a cell in the worksheet becomes active.

The data you charted is surrounded by colored boxes, called **Range Finder**. You can use Range Finder to adjust the data used by the chart. You don't want to include the total row in the chart. To modify the chart using Range Finder:

Step 1	***Position***	the mouse pointer over one of the Range Finder fill handles at the bottom of row 8

The pointer changes to a double-headed arrow.

Step 2	***Drag***	the fill handle up to just below row 7

The chart displays only three sets of data.

Step 3	***Press***	the ESC key to deselect the chart
Step 4	***Save***	the workbook

C

6.e Previewing and Printing Charts

Before you print your chart for the meeting, you should preview it in Print Preview to make sure that everything looks the way you expected. You can preview a chart, change print setup options, and print the chart from the Print Preview window.

Printing Chart Sheets

Printing charts on separate worksheets is very similar to printing any worksheet data. To preview the chart sheet, change chart printing options, and print a chart:

Step 1	*Click*	the Gross Sales by Region Chart sheet tab
Step 2	*Click*	the Print Preview button on the Standard toolbar
Step 3	*Click*	the Setup button on the Print Preview toolbar
Step 4	*Click*	the Chart tab in the Page Setup dialog box

The Scale to fit page option scales the chart until either the height or the width of the chart hits a page margin. The Use full page option scales the chart until both the height and the width touch the page margins on all sides of the page.

Step 5	*Click*	the Scale to fit page option button
Step 6	*Click*	OK
Step 7	*Click*	the Print button on the Print Preview toolbar
Step 8	*Click*	OK

Printing an Embedded Chart

You have a few choices to make when printing embedded charts. One option is to print the chart by itself. Another option is to print the chart as part of the worksheet, and the final option is to exclude the chart from printing at all. By default, an embedded chart prints as part of the worksheet, as long as it is not specifically excluded from a print area. If Print Preview does not show a chart you expected to print, try clearing the print area, or adjusting the page breaks in Page Break Preview. When you select a chart, Excel assumes that you want to print only the chart.

Because of all these print options, it is especially important that you preview the document before printing it when you work with embedded charts. To preview the worksheet with the embedded chart:

Step 1	*Click*	the Central sheet tab

QUICK TIP

You can print an embedded chart by itself or with the data on the worksheet. To print an embedded chart by itself, select the chart by clicking it once, then click the Print Preview button on the Standard toolbar.

Step 2	*Click*	the Print Preview button on the Standard toolbar
Step 3	*Click*	the Print button on the Print Preview toolbar
Step 4	*Click*	OK
Step 5	*Save*	the workbook

C 6.f Using Workgroup Collaboration

Sharing information electronically is no longer an option; it's an essential part of doing business. To effectively communicate with colleagues and coworkers, you can use comments, engage in Web discussions, and publish pages to a Web server for periodic review.

You need to send the workbook with the finished charts to the regional managers for their comments and suggestions.

Adding and Editing Comments

You can add comments to any cell to provide a simple, effective way to share explanatory information with others. Comments can highlight important cells or explain complex formulas. To add a comment:

Step 1	*Right-click*	cell C9 on the Central sheet tab
Step 2	*Click*	Insert Comment
Step 3	*Key*	Consider revising goal in Q2 to $52,500
Step 4	*Click*	cell C9 to close the comment

A small red triangle appears in the upper-right corner of cells containing comments. To read comments:

| Step 1 | *Move* | the mouse pointer over cell C9 |

The yellow comment note that appears on your screen should look similar to Figure 6-9.

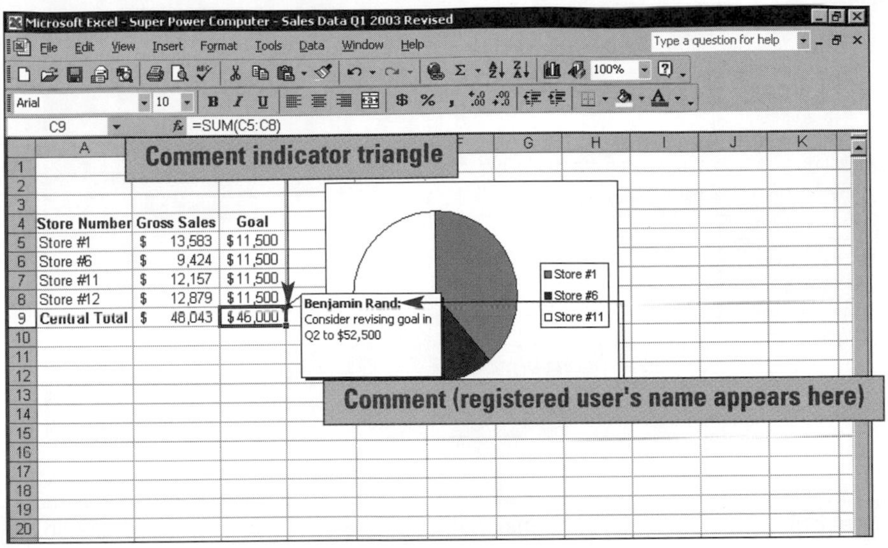

FIGURE 6-9
Reading a Comment

You can add or modify the text in a comment. To edit a comment:

Step 1	*Right-click*	cell C9
Step 2	*Click*	Edit Comment
Step 3	*Select*	$52,500
Step 4	*Key*	$54,000
Step 5	*Click*	cell C9

Inserting Hyperlinks

Another helpful collaboration tool is the ability to insert hyperlinks in a document. A **hyperlink** is a link to another place in the current workbook, to another file on your computer or on your network, or to a Web page, or it can be a mailto link. When clicked, a **mailto link** automatically starts a new message using the user's default e-mail program. To insert a hyperlink in a document:

Step 1	*Right-click*	cell A1 on the Summary worksheet
Step 2	*Click*	Hyperlink
Step 3	*Click*	E-mail Address in the Link to: list

The Insert Hyperlink dialog box on your screen should look similar to Figure 6-10. When you click an option in the Link to: list, the dialog box options change. When you clicked the E-mail Address option, the dialog box provides text boxes to enter an e-mail address and a message subject.

chapter
six

FIGURE 6-10
Insert Hyperlink
Dialog Box

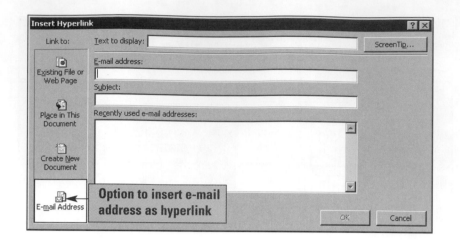

Option to insert e-mail address as hyperlink

Step 4	**Key**	your e-mail address (or a fictitious e-mail address) in the E-mail address: text box
Step 5	**Key**	Review Chart in the Subject: text box
Step 6	**Select**	the text in the Text to display: text box
Step 7	**Key**	Contact me in the Text to display: text box
Step 8	**Click**	OK

The hyperlink appears in cell A1 as blue, underlined text. When you click this link, your e-mail program opens with the e-mail address you added in the Insert Hyperlink dialog box in the To text box (in this case, it's your e-mail address). To test the link:

Step 1	**Click**	the Contact me hyperlink in cell A1
Step 2	**Observe**	the message window with your e-mail address in the To text box
Step 3	**Close**	your e-mail program without sending a message or saving changes to the message

Creating and Responding to Discussion Comments

Discussions allow users to post and respond to comments made by other users. For example, one user might post a question about how to perform a certain task in Excel. Other users can then respond to the question.

MOUSE TIP

To delete a hyperlink, right-click the link, then click Remove Hyperlink on the shortcut menu.

You display the Web Discussions toolbar to create and respond to topics. For a new topic you enter a subject and message, and then post the topic to the discussion server, where other users can log in, read, and respond to the topic. To create and post a discussion comment:

Step 1	*Click*	Tools
Step 2	*Point to*	Online Collaboration
Step 3	*Click*	Web Discussions to display the Web Discussions toolbar
Step 4	*Click*	the Insert Discussion about the Workbook button on the Web Discussions toolbar
Step 5	*Key*	Review Sales Figures in the Discussion Subject: text box
Step 6	*Press*	the TAB key to move to the message text box
Step 7	*Key*	Please review sales figures for your region and respond with any corrections.
Step 8	*Click*	OK
Step 9	*Click*	the Close button Close to close the Web Discussions toolbar

Previewing and Saving a Workbook or a Worksheet as a Web Page

You post the Gross Sales chart on the company's intranet to allow other employees to see the company's progress. You can save a workbook in HTML format for publication on the Web. To preview a workbook as a Web page:

Step 1	*Click*	the Gross Sales by Region Chart sheet tab
Step 2	*Click*	File
Step 3	*Click*	Web Page Preview

A copy of your workbook appears in HTML format in your Web browser. Your screen should look similar to Figure 6-11.

chapter
six

FIGURE 6-11
Previewing a Workbook as
a Web Page

G:\Documents and Settings\Benjamin Rand.BEN-II\Local Settings\Temp\ExcelWebPagePreview\Super Po - Microsoft Interne...

File   Edit   View   Favorites   Tools   Help

← Back   →   ⊗   🔄   🏠   🔍 Search   📁 Favorites   🕘 History   🖨 ▾ 📧 ▾ 📄

Address   C:\Documents and Settings\Katherine Pinard.W2000\Local Settings\Temp\ExcelWebPagePreview\Super Power Computer - Sal ▾   🔗 Go   Links »

Gross Sales by Region

- $50,000
- $45,000
- $40,000
- $35,000
- $30,000
- $25,000
- $20,000
- $15,000
- $10,000

« < > »   Gross Sales by Region Chart | Summary | Central | East Coast | Mountain | West Coast | Source Data

My Computer

INTERNET TIP

It's a good idea to avoid using spaces and uppercase letters in filenames for pages intended for the Web because many Web servers cannot properly handle them.

| Step 4 | *Close* | your Web browser |

You want to publish only the chart page. To save the chart worksheet as a Web page:

Step 1	*Click*	File
Step 2	*Click*	Save As Web Page
Step 3	*Click*	the Selection: Chart option button
Step 4	*Key*	sales_data_chart in the File name: text box
Step 5	*Click*	Save

The chart is saved and ready to be uploaded to a Web server. You can save your page directly to a Web server by clicking the Publish button instead of the Save button in the Save As dialog box.

C   6.g   Using Go To

A quick way to select cells is to use the Go To command. Using Go To, you can select ranges, named ranges, and cells based on certain characteristics, such as selecting all cells that contain formulas.

To use Go To:

Step 1	*Click*	the Central sheet tab
Step 2	*Click*	Edit
Step 3	*Click*	Go To

The Go To dialog box opens. You can enter a range, select a named range, or click the Special button to locate cells that share common characteristics.

| Step 4 | *Click* | Special |

The Go To Special dialog box on your screen should look similar to Figure 6-12. It provides additional search options.

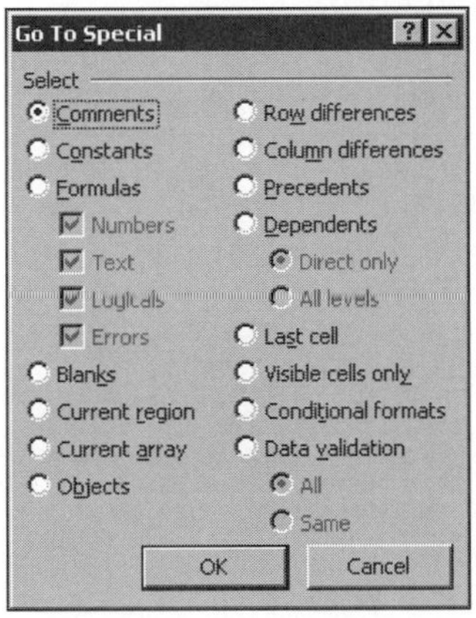

FIGURE 6-12
The Go To Special
Dialog Box

| Step 5 | *Click* | the Formulas option button |
| Step 6 | *Click* | OK |

All of the cells containing formulas on the Central worksheet are highlighted.

| Step 7 | *Save* | and close the workbook |

You can use Go To to find and select cells or ranges based on content.

chapter
six

Summary

► The Chart Wizard enables you to create a chart. You can create a new default chart by pressing the F11 key.

► Charts can be placed on a separate chart tab, or they can be embedded in a worksheet. A chart location can be changed at any time.

► Charts contain many types of objects, including titles, legends, data tables, and plot areas. Each of these objects can be formatted independently.

► You can change formatting elements for all chart objects at any time by using the Format dialog box.

► You can add a data table to a chart to show the actual data used to create the chart.

► Drawing objects, such as pictures or text boxes, can be inserted into a chart. Drag selection handles to resize them. Drag entire objects to new locations.

► You can move and resize embedded worksheets as you like.

► It is a good idea to preview charts before printing them so you can set print options. Embedded charts can be printed separately or as part of the active worksheet.

► Comments enable you to highlight important cells or explain formulas. You can edit existing comments.

► Hyperlinks can be added to cell content to provide easy links to Web pages, files, or e-mail addresses.

► Discussion comments can be added to any file if you have a connection to a discussion server.

► Workbooks or worksheets can be previewed and saved as Web pages.

► Go To enables you to find and select cell ranges or cells based on the type of content.

Commands Review

Action	Menu Bar	Shortcut Menu	Toolbar	Task Pane	Keyboard
Use the Chart Wizard	Insert, Chart				ALT + I, H
Create a default chart					F11 ALT + F1
Format a selected chart object	Format, Selected (chart object name)	Right-click chart object, Format (chart object name)	Select object from the Chart Objects list box, ; double-click object		ALT + O, E CTRL + 1
Change chart type	Chart, Chart Type	Right-click chart, Chart Type			ALT + C, T
Change chart options	Chart, Chart Options	Right-click chart, Chart Options			ALT + C, O
Show the Chart toolbar	View, Toolbars, Chart				ALT + V, T
Add a data table to a chart					
Show the Drawing toolbar	View, Toolbars, Drawing				ALT + V, T
Insert a picture	Insert, Picture, From File				ALT + I, P, F
Insert clip art	Insert, Picture, Clip Art				ALT + I, P, C
Insert an object	Insert, Object				ALT + I, O
Preview a chart	File, Print Preview				ALT + F, V
Print a chart	File, Print				CTRL + P ALT + F, P
Add a comment	Insert, Comment	Right-click, Insert Comment			ALT + I, M
Edit a comment	Insert, Edit Comment	Right-click comment, Edit Comment			ALT + I, E
Delete a comment	Insert, Delete Comment	Right-click comment, Delete Comment			ALT + I, M
Insert a hyperlink	Insert, Hyperlink	Right-click text Hyperlink			ALT + I, I CTRL + K
Remove a hyperlink		Right-click hyperlink, Remove Hyperlink			
Insert discussion comments	Tools, Online Collaboration, Web Discussions				ALT + T, N, W
Preview a worksheet as a Web page	File, Web Page Preview				ALT + F, B
Save a worksheet as Web Page	File, Save As Web Page				ALT + F, G
Use Go To	Edit, Go to				ALT + E, G CTRL + G

chapter six

Concepts Review

Circle the correct answer.

1. A data label:
[a] displays the name of a chart object when the mouse pointer is over that object.
[b] displays the actual data used to create a chart.
[c] is a key used to identify patterns, colors, or symbols associated with data points on a chart.
[d] displays the value of a data point on a chart.

2. A legend:
[a] displays the name of a chart object when the mouse pointer is over that object.
[b] displays the actual data used to create a chart.
[c] is a key used to identify patterns, colors, or symbols associated with data points on a chart.
[d] can show the value of a data point on a chart.

3. A mailto link opens:
[a] a Web browser.
[b] a Web page.
[c] a new e-mail message and addresses it.
[d] none of the above.

4. A data point:
[a] represents a series of data.
[b] represents a single value.
[c] identifies the colors assigned to categories in a chart.
[d] separates the data categories.

5. Which of the following does *not* bring up the Format (chart object) Properties dialog box?
[a] double-click (chart object)
[b] right-click (chart object), select Format (chart object)

[c] select object, click Edit, click Format (chart object)
[d] click the Chart Objects list arrow on the Chart toolbar to select the chart object, then click the Format (chart object) button on the Chart toolbar

6. The F11 shortcut key allows you to:
[a] create an embedded chart.
[b] choose whether to use the Chart Wizard.
[c] create a default chart sheet chart.
[d] create either an embedded chart or a chart sheet chart.

7. The Chart Wizard allows you to:
[a] create either an embedded chart or a chart sheet chart.
[b] create only an embedded chart.
[c] create only a chart sheet chart.
[d] edit an existing chart.

8. If you change your mind while using the Chart Wizard, you can click the:
[a] Cancel button and start over.
[b] Finish button, delete the chart, and start over.
[c] Next button.
[d] Back button.

9. To change the location of a chart, right-click the chart and click:
[a] Chart Type.
[b] Source Data.
[c] Chart Options.
[d] Location.

10. The value axis of a chart represents:
[a] the actual data values of each category.
[b] the categories of data.
[c] nothing.
[d] the chart height and width.

Circle **T** if the statement is true or **F** if the statement is false.

T   F   1. Charts make data easier to understand.

T   F   2. Embedded charts cannot be moved on the worksheet.

T   F   3. A data point is a graphical means of displaying numerical data.

T   F   4. The Go To command is one way to select all cells that contain formulas.

T   F   5. The Format (chart object) dialog box is the same no matter which object is selected.

T   F   6. Hyperlinks cannot be linked to files on your computer.

T   F   7. The Use Full Page print option scales a chart in both directions to fill the entire page.

T   F   8. You can't print an embedded chart by itself.

T   F   9. Web Page Preview is a good way to see what your workbook will look like as a Web page.

T   F   10. You do not need access to a discussion server to add comments to a discussion.

Skills Review

Exercise 1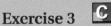

1. Open the *Sales Data* workbook located on the Data Disk.

2. Using the data on the Summary tab, create a new Clustered Column chart with a three-dimensional effect.

3. Title the chart "Sales by Region."

4. Insert the chart on a new chart sheet called "Sales by Region Chart."

5. Print the Sales by Region Chart.

6. Switch to the Source Data worksheet, then use the Go To command to highlight all cells containing a formula.

7. Save the workbook as *Sales Data Revised* and close it.

Exercise 2

1. Open the *Sales Data Revised* workbook that you created in Exercise 1.

2. Look at the embedded chart on the West Coast tab, then find two other types of charts that present the data in a clear manner.

3. Find two types of charts that make it more difficult to understand the data.

4. Using Microsoft Word, write at least two paragraphs describing why certain types of charts worked well to illustrate the data and why others did not. Try to discern from the chart type description what type of information is needed for each type of chart and why your data did or did not work.

5. Save the document as *Chart Types.doc* and then print and close it. Close the workbook.

Exercise 3

1. Open the *Exports by Country* workbook located on the Data Disk.

2. Activate cell A2.

3. Create a line with markers chart using the Chart Wizard.

4. Title the chart "Exports by Country."

chapter six

5. Add "2003" to the Category (X) axis.

6. Create the chart as an object on Sheet1.

7. Preview and print your chart as part of the worksheet. (*Hint:* Move the chart or change the paper orientation as necessary.)

8. Use Go To to select the last cell in the worksheet.

9. With your instructor's permission, connect to the Internet, and search the Web for a picture of a flag of one of the countries used in your chart. Be sure to verify that the image is one you can use for free.

10. In your Web browser, right-click the picture, then click Save Picture As and save the picture.

11. Insert the picture on your chart.

12. Save the workbook as *Exports by Country Chart,* print the chart sheet, and then close the workbook.

Exercise 4   C

1. Open the *Exports by Country Chart* workbook that you created in Exercise 3.

2. Add the following data to row 5: Japan, $6,438,945.00, $2,345,743.00, $5,098,760.00, $3,198,245.00.

3. Select the chart and use the Range Finder to add Japan's data to the chart.

4. Save the workbook as *Exports by Country Chart Revised,* print the chart sheet, and close the workbook.

Exercise 5   C

1. Open the *Expenses* workbook located on the Data Disk. Activate cell A2.

2. Create a Bar of Pie type chart using the Chart Wizard (in the Pie chart type category). This type of chart uses a selected number of values from the bottom of a list of values to create a "breakout" section. In this case, the breakout section is the category Taxes.

3. Title the chart "Expenses."

4. Show the percentage data labels.

5. Create the chart as an embedded chart.

6. Save the workbook as *Expenses Chart,* print the worksheet, and close the workbook.

Exercise 6   C

1. Open the *Computer Comparison* workbook located on the Data Disk.

2. Create a new chart, using the Line – Column on 2 Axes custom type of chart. (*Hint:* Click the Custom Types tab in Step 1 of the Chart Wizard.)

3. Title the chart "Computer Price/Speed Comparison."

4. Title the *x*-axis "System."

5. Title the *y*-axis "Price."

6. Title the secondary *y*-axis "Speed."

7. Create the chart as a new sheet.

8. Preview the Web page, then save the chart sheet as a Web page called *computer_comparison_chart.htm.*

9. Save the workbook as *Computer Comparison Chart,* print the chart sheet, and close the workbook.

Exercise 7

1. Open the *Computer Comparison Chart* workbook that you created in Exercise 6.

2. Show the data table on the chart.

3. Click the Athlon 1.2 GHz data point two times to select it (do not double-click it). Drag the data point handle at the top-middle of the data point down until the value reads $2,650.

4. Modify the value of the PIII 1 GHz data point to $2,400 by dragging the data point handle.

5. Print the chart.

6. Add comments in cells B3 and B5 indicating that the value of each of these cells was changed.

7. Save the workbook as *Computer Comparison Chart Revised*.

8. Print the chart sheet and the worksheet, and then close the workbook.

Exercise 8

1. Open the *Class Attendance* workbook located on your Data Disk.

2. Create a new chart with the Chart Wizard.

3. Use the Custom Types tab to select the Colored Lines chart type.

4. Title the chart "Class Attendance."

5. Put the chart on a new sheet called "Attendance Chart."

6. Change the area fill of the Chart Area to Automatic (white).

7. On the data page, include a hyperlink to your favorite search engine.

8. Print the chart, save your workbook as *Class Attendance Chart*, and close it.

Case Projects

Project 1

As the entertainment editor for a local newspaper, you publish a weekly chart of the top five films based on their box office revenues for the week. Connect to the Internet and use the Web toolbar to search the Web for information on the top five movies from the last week. Create a worksheet listing each of the titles and showing how much each film grossed in the last week. Add another column to show total revenues to date for each film. Insert comments next to two of the films indicating whether you want to see the film, or what you thought of it if you have already seen it. Create a chart that best illustrates the data. Save the workbook as *Box Office*, and then print and close it.

Project 2

Use the Ask A Question Box to find out how to add a text box to a chart. Create a Word document and use your own words to describe step by step how to accomplish this task. Save the document as *Adding a Text Box to a Chart.doc,* and print and close it.

Project 3

As the owner of a mall-based cookie store, you want to track your cookie sales by type and month to determine which cookies are bestsellers and what the best time of the year is for cookie sales. Create a worksheet with 10 types of cookies (examples: chocolate chip, oatmeal, walnut, peanut butter). Include fictitious data for cookie sales for

each type of cookie during the past 12 months. Create charts showing overall cookie sales by month and overall cookie sales by type. With your instructor's permission, connect to the Internet and search the Web for a picture of your favorite type of cookie. Verify that the file you want to use is an image you can use for free, then save the picture, and then insert it on your chart. Save the workbook as *Cookie Sales,* and print and close it.

Project 4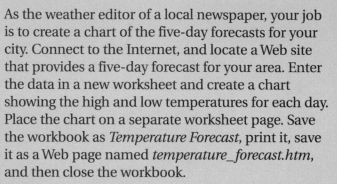

Connect to the Internet and use the Web toolbar to search the Web for different types of charts. Look for charts showing sales volume, stock prices, or percentages of sales by category. Create a workbook containing hyperlinks to five different charts. Save your workbook as *Charts on the Web,* and print and close it.

Project 5

Stock price charts are usually displayed using a high-low-close style chart, which requires three columns of data. Connect to the Internet and use the Web toolbar to search the Web for stock prices for three companies whose products you use. Locate price histories for the last five days for each stock, including the high, low, and closing prices for each day. Create a High Low Close chart (stock category) for each company, showing the price plotted against the date. Save the workbook as *High Low Close,* and print and close it.

Project 6

Create a worksheet showing one month's expenses for at least 10 expense categories in your

household (estimate your expenses or supply fictitious data). Create a three-dimensional pie chart, and separate the largest expense from the pie. Use data labels to display the label and value of each expense. Save the workbook as *Family Expenses,* and print and close it.

Project 7

As the weather editor of a local newspaper, your job is to create a chart of the five-day forecasts for your city. Connect to the Internet, and locate a Web site that provides a five-day forecast for your area. Enter the data in a new worksheet and create a chart showing the high and low temperatures for each day. Place the chart on a separate worksheet page. Save the workbook as *Temperature Forecast,* print it, save it as a Web page named *temperature_forecast.htm,* and then close the workbook.

Project 8

You are interested in finding out how the government spends the money in its budget. Connect to the Internet, and search the Web for a site that shows where the government spends tax revenue. Create a new workbook and pie chart showing the information you find. Include at least five categories. If you have access to a discussion server, set up a discussion and include a comment about your budget findings. Have classmates add comments to the discussion. Save your workbook as *Government Spending,* and print and close it.

Microsoft
PowerPoint 2002
Introductory

Quick Start for PowerPoint

Chapter Overview

This chapter introduces you to the components of your working environment—the PowerPoint application window. First, you create a presentation using the AutoContent Wizard. Then, you navigate through the presentation and among the various view options of PowerPoint. Next, you create a new presentation using a design template. This simple presentation consists of a title slide and a bullet slide. You save, check spelling, change the design template, print, and finally close the presentation.

LEARNING OBJECTIVES

- Explore the PowerPoint window
- Create a presentation from the AutoContent Wizard
- Navigate in PowerPoint
- Close a presentation
- Create a presentation from a design template
- Save a presentation
- Check spelling
- Apply a design template
- Print slides
- Exit PowerPoint

Case profile

Teddy Toys, a toy manufacturing company located in Boise, Idaho, manufactures toys for all ages, from infants to grandparents, for distribution internationally as well as within the United States. Although it manufactures a wide range of toys, Teddy Toys is proudest of its line of quality teddy bears.

You are the administrative assistant to Sandra Hill, the new products manager at Teddy Toys. Ms. Hill has asked you to prepare a presentation that will be given to key personnel within the company in the next couple of weeks.

chapter one

notes This text assumes that you have little or no knowledge of the PowerPoint application. However, it is assumed that you have read Office Chapters 1–3 of this book and that you are familiar with Windows 98, Windows 2000 or Windows ME concepts.

The figures in this book were created using Windows 98. If you are using the PowerPoint application installed on Windows 2000 or Windows ME, you may notice a few minor differences in some figures. These differences do not affect your work in this book.

1.a Exploring the PowerPoint Window

When you start PowerPoint, a new document window opens with a blank slide displayed. You can begin creating a new presentation by keying text on the slide, or you can create a presentation based on a template or wizard. You also have the option of opening an existing presentation. To start the PowerPoint application and explore the PowerPoint window:

Step 1	*Click*	the Start button  on the taskbar
Step 2	*Point to*	Programs
Step 3	*Click*	Microsoft PowerPoint

The application opens with the PowerPoint window displayed. Your screen should look similar to Figure 1-1.

The Microsoft PowerPoint application **title bar** at the top of the window indicates the application you are using and the name of the presentation file currently on the screen. Once you save a presentation file, the actual filename replaces the word "Presentation1" in the title bar. At the extreme left of the title bar are the application icon and name, and at the extreme right are the Minimize, Maximize or Restore, and Close buttons for the PowerPoint application window.

The **menu bar**, located below the title bar, contains the majority of commands you use to work on your presentation, organized into menus.

At the extreme left of the menu bar is the Document Control-menu icon, and at the extreme right is the document Close Window button.

MENU **TIP**

You can start PowerPoint by clicking the New Office Document command on the Start menu to start a new presentation or by clicking the Open Office Document command on the Start menu to open an existing presentation.

MOUSE **TIP**

The Standard and Formatting toolbars appear on the same row when you first install Office XP. In this position, only the most commonly used buttons of each toolbar are visible. All the other default buttons appear on the Toolbar Options lists. As you use buttons from the Toolbar Options lists, they move to the visible buttons on the toolbar; the buttons you don't use move into the Toolbar Options list. If you arrange the Formatting toolbar below the Standard toolbar, all buttons are visible. The illustrations in this book show the Formatting toolbar positioned below the Standard toolbar.

chapter one

FIGURE 1-1
PowerPoint Window

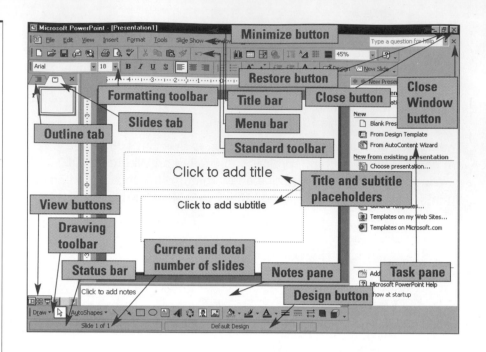

Below the menu bar are the **Standard toolbar** and the **Formatting toolbar**, which contain buttons for easy access to the most commonly used commands of the application. If you do not know what a toolbar button does, simply point to it; a yellow rectangular box called a **ScreenTip** appears with the name or a brief description of the button.

Below the Formatting toolbar, the current presentation is displayed in Normal view. A **task pane** at the right contains hyperlink shortcuts to common actions, such as creating a new presentation or choosing a design template. A **hyperlink** is text or a graphic that you click to view another page or item.

At the bottom of the window is the **status bar**, which, depending on the view, contains the current slide number and the total number of slides (Slide 1 of 1), the current presentation design template (*Default Design*), and the Spelling Status button (book icon with a check mark or an x mark) when PowerPoint is or has completed spell checking your presentation.

Just above the status bar is the **Drawing toolbar**, which contains buttons and list boxes you can use to create and manipulate text and shapes.

Located below the Outline tab and Slides tab, just above the Drawing toolbar, are the three **view buttons**: Normal View, Slide Sorter View, and Slide Show. You can switch between views by clicking the appropriate view button or by choosing the appropriate command on the View menu. Normal view is the PowerPoint default view. It combines four working areas of your presentation: a slide pane in the middle, an outline/slides pane at the left that includes both an Outline tab (where text is displayed in outline format) and a Slides tab (where miniature slides are displayed), a notes pane (where speaker notes are displayed) directly below the slide pane (where text and graphics are displayed on the slide), and a task pane (that provides easy access to many PowerPoint options) at the right.

When PowerPoint starts, it opens a new, blank PowerPoint presentation, which defaults to a blank title slide. A title slide is a slide based on one of many **layouts** (predesigned combinations of placeholders), available in PowerPoint to save you time in creating a presentation. Usually the first slide you create in a new presentation is one that contains a title and subtitle to introduce your topic. The Slides tab displays a miniature of the slide, and the slide pane displays a larger, more detailed version.

Because this is a new presentation, the slide does not yet contain any text or graphics, but the title slide layout does contain two placeholders. **Placeholders** are objects on a slide that hold text, charts, tables, organization charts, clip art, or other objects. They indicate what information is to be keyed in that location on the slide. Each PowerPoint layout contains a different combination of placeholders to make it easier to position and key information. Placeholders display eight sizing handles (four corner handles and four middle handles).

1.b Creating a Presentation from the AutoContent Wizard

The AutoContent Wizard is a welcome guide to anyone who is asked to plan, prepare, and give a presentation, especially for the first time. The wizard asks you questions and then provides an appropriate "look" for a particular type of presentation, along with starter text and suggestions on content and organization. The AutoContent Wizard lets you create a presentation in any of the following categories: General, Corporate, Project, Sales/Marketing, or the Carnegie Coach. Each category provides several presentation ideas and suggestions related to that category. To access the AutoContent Wizard:

| Step 1 | *Click* | the From AutoContent Wizard link in the New Presentation task pane |

The AutoContent Wizard dialog box opens, displaying a description of the wizard and a diagram illustrating the steps it guides you through.

| Step 2 | *Click* | <u>N</u>ext > |

QUICK TIP

The Language Bar may be displayed in the window. The Language Bar enables you to spell check in different languages and to use speech and handwriting options. You can click the Minimize button on the Language Bar to place it in the tray on the taskbar.

C

QUICK TIP

You do not have to key data in every placeholder on a slide because the information does not print or appear on the actual slide. If you want to delete a placeholder, click the placeholder's selection border, and then press the DELETE key.

chapter
one

QUICK TIP

The Office Assistant (a Help feature that can answer your questions) is hidden unless you need it for a specific activity. The Office Assistant may pop up at various times, indicating presentation design tips as well as software shortcuts. If that happens, just hide it by right-clicking the Office Assistant, and then clicking <u>H</u>ide.

Step 3	*Click*	<u>P</u>rojects
Step 4	*Click*	Project Overview in the list box, if necessary
Step 5	*Click*	<u>N</u>ext >
Step 6	*Verify*	that the On-<u>s</u>creen presentation is selected
Step 7	*Click*	<u>N</u>ext >
Step 8	*Key*	Welcome to PowerPoint in the <u>P</u>resentation title: text box
Step 9	*Remove*	the check marks from <u>D</u>ate last updated and <u>S</u>lide number check boxes, if necessary
Step 10	*Click*	<u>N</u>ext >
Step 11	*Click*	<u>F</u>inish

The Project Overview presentation displays in Normal view. The Outline tab displays the text for each slide in outline format. Your screen should look similar to Figure 1-2.

FIGURE 1-2
Project Overview
Presentation in Normal View

CAUTION TIP

Based on the user information in the Options dialog box, the text on your slide may be different.

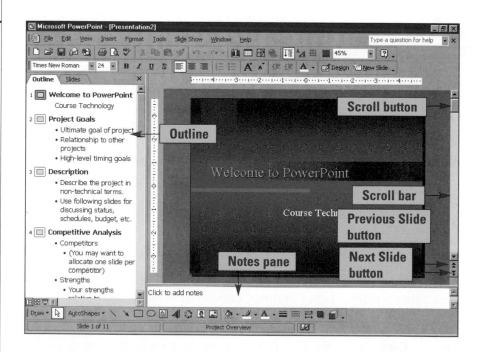

When you create a presentation using a template or wizard, the slides often contain sample text that you can customize for your own purposes.

1.c Navigating in PowerPoint

To work in PowerPoint, you need to move among various slides in a presentation so that you can add and edit text, make formatting changes, and review your work. You also need to switch among different views in the PowerPoint application so you can work effectively on various aspects of your presentation, such as organizing ideas or adding text and graphics.

Navigating Through a Presentation

To view the slides in a presentation in Normal view, you can click the Previous Slide and Next Slide buttons, drag the scroll box located at the right of the slide pane, or press the PAGE UP and PAGE DOWN keys. You can also check the status bar to tell which slide you are viewing and how many slides are in your presentation (such as Slide 1 of 11).

To view slides in Normal view:

Step 1	*Press*	the HOME key to display Slide 1, if necessary
Step 2	*Click*	the Next Slide button ⮁ below the vertical scroll bar to view Slide 2
Step 3	*Press*	the PAGE DOWN key to view Slide 3
Step 4	*Drag*	the scroll box down on the vertical scroll bar to the right of the slide to view Slide: 6 of 11
Step 5	*Press*	the HOME key to return to the first slide in the presentation

Navigating Among PowerPoint Views

You can view a presentation using one of three main PowerPoint views: Normal view, Slide Sorter view, Slide Show; and also in Notes Page view. **Normal view**, the default view that opens when you start PowerPoint, provides a combined look at your presentation: the slide pane in the center shows the currently selected slide in detail, the outline/slides pane at the left gives you a bird's-eye view of several slides in outline text and thumbnail slide formats, the notes pane below the slide pane displays speaker notes for the current slide, and the task pane at the right displays links to PowerPoint tasks. Normal view is good for creating a presentation because you can see the actual slide as you create it. The Normal View button is outlined in blue because that is the current view.

Slide Sorter view displays miniature representation of all the slides in a presentation on screen at one time. This view is excellent for rearranging, copying, or deleting slides, as well as for changing the

chapter one

way slides appear on the screen and the speed at which they appear during a visual display of the presentation on the computer screen. To switch to Slide Sorter view:

| Step 1 | *Click* | the Slide Sorter View button 🔲 to the left of the horizontal scroll bar in the outline/slides pane |
| Step 2 | *Click* | Slide 7 to select it |

A selection border appears around the slide you selected. Your screen should look similar to Figure 1-3.

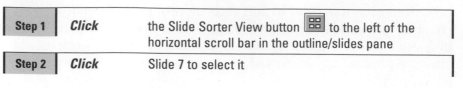
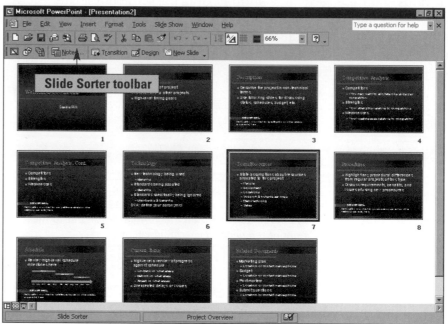

Notes Page view displays a miniature version of the current slide with a pane for keying speaker notes that can be printed and used by the presenter during a presentation. A small notes pane is displayed below the slide pane in Normal view for keying speaker notes. There is no Notes Page View button. To access Notes Page view, click the Notes Page command on the View menu. To switch to Notes Page view:

| Step 1 | *Click* | View |
| Step 2 | *Click* | Notes Page |

Notes Page view opens. Your screen should look similar to Figure 1-4.

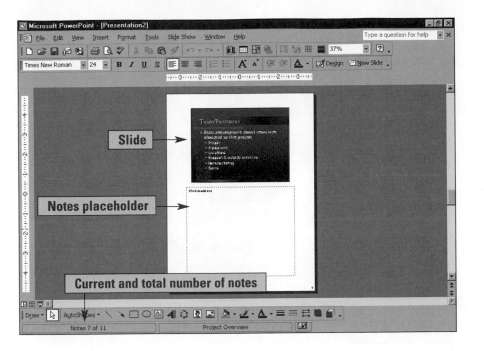

FIGURE 1-4
Notes Page View

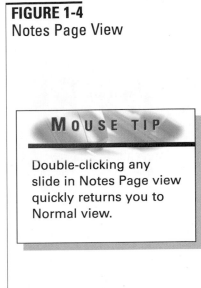

MOUSE TIP

Double-clicking any slide in Notes Page view quickly returns you to Normal view.

Step 3	*Click*	the Next Slide button ⬇ below the vertical scroll bar to view the notes pane for a different slide
Step 4	*Click*	the Zoom button list arrow `50%` on the Standard toolbar
Step 5	*Click*	66% to zoom in to read the speaker notes more easily

Slide Show displays all the slides in a presentation, sized to fill your screen, one after another at the speed you choose. The process is similar to projecting your own slides, assembled in a slide carousel, on a screen and moving to the next slide by clicking a button. When you switch to Slide Show view using the Slide Show button, the slide show runs, beginning with the currently selected slide. To start the slide show, beginning with Slide 6:

| Step 1 | *Display* | Slide 6 (Technology) |
| Step 2 | *Click* | the Slide Show (from current slide) button 🖥 to the left of the horizontal scroll bar |

Your slide should look similar to Figure 1-5.

MENU TIP

You can display a slide show by clicking the Slide Sho<u>w</u> command on the <u>V</u>iew menu or by clicking the <u>V</u>iew Show command on the Sli<u>d</u>e Show menu. These commands start the slide show from Slide 1, regardless of which slide is currently selected.

chapter
one

FIGURE 1-5
Technology Slide in Slide Show

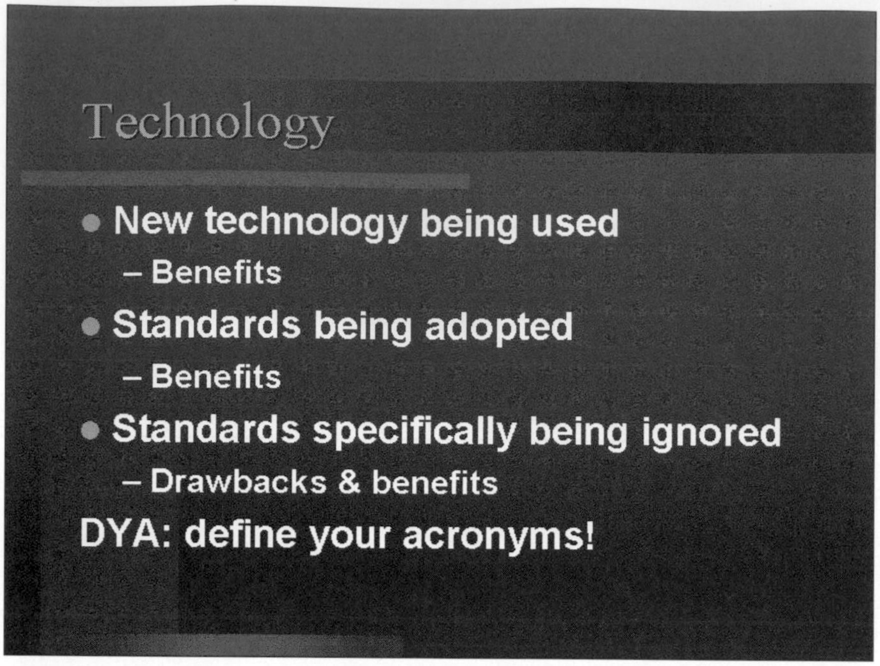
Technology
New technology being used
– Benefits
Standards being adopted
– Benefits
Standards specifically being ignored
– Drawbacks & benefits
DYA: define your acronyms!

QUICK TIP

You can start a slide show from Normal view by pressing the F5 key; no matter which slide is selected, the slide show starts from Slide 1.

CAUTION TIP

If you click the application Close button instead of the Close Window button, you exit PowerPoint.

Step 3	***Click***	the left mouse button to progress through the rest of the slides until you return to your previous view

1.d Closing a Presentation

PowerPoint allows you to have as many presentations open as your computer resources can handle. Each open presentation displays a separate presentation button on the taskbar. However, it is a good idea to close any presentations you are not using to free memory and allow the computer to run more efficiently. To close the *Project Overview* presentation:

Step 1	***Click***	the Close Window button on the menu bar
Step 2	***Click***	No if you are prompted to save the presentation

notes

The presentation design templates used in this book include the PowerPoint 2002 design templates. If the designs do not appear immediately, you need to install them from the Office XP CD-ROM before continuing this chapter.

1.e Creating a Presentation from a Design Template

PowerPoint provides many templates of presentation designs to help you set up a particular, consistent look for a presentation. **Design templates**, like blueprints, contain a master design that determines the overall look of a presentation—the color scheme that coordinates the colors on the slide so they complement each other; coordinating fonts, font styles, and font sizes; graphical elements to enhance the presentation; and the placeholder arrangement and alignment for various slide layouts within the presentation. You can create a presentation using a design template, or you can apply a design template to an existing presentation. To create a new presentation using a design template:

Step 1	*Click*	File
Step 2	*Click*	New

The New Presentation task pane displays shortcuts to creating a new presentation.

Step 3	*Click*	the From Design Template link under New in the New Presentation task pane

The Slide Design task pane opens. It displays design template previews organized as follows: Used in This Presentation (any previously used design templates for the existing presentation), Recently Used (any design templates recently selected for use in any presentation), and Available For Use (all available design templates). To see the name of a template, you point to the preview until a ScreenTip appears. When you point to a preview, a selection frame surrounds it and it displays a list arrow. If you click a preview, you automatically apply the design template to all slides. If you click the list arrow, you can elect to apply the template to all slides, only to selected slides, or to change the size of the previews so they are easier to view.

Step 4	*Point to*	each design template until its name appears in a ScreenTip
Step 5	*Scroll*	through the previews until you see the Crayons preview
Step 6	*Click*	the Crayons preview

chapter
one

The Crayons design template is applied to the presentation. By default, PowerPoint assigns a title slide layout to the first slide in any new presentation. Your screen should look similar to Figure 1-6.

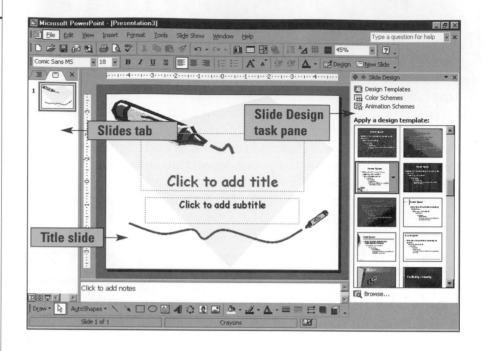

Title Slides

The **title slide**, usually the first slide in a presentation, introduces the topic of the presentation. The goal of a title slide is to grab the audience's attention, set the tone, and prepare the audience for what is to follow. Title slides can also be used to differentiate between sections of a presentation. To enter text on a title slide:

Step 1	*Click*	the "Click to add title" placeholder
Step 2	*Key*	Teddy Toys
Step 3	*Click*	the "Click to add subtitle" placeholder
Step 4	*Key*	Focusing on the Future
Step 5	*Click*	outside the slide area to deselect the placeholder
Step 6	*Click*	the Slide Show button ⬜ to view the title slide on a full screen
Step 7	*Click*	on the screen until you return to Normal view

Bullet Slides

Bullet slides or **Text slides** are used to group related topics or items together, list items, emphasize important information, or summarize key points. In the Teddy Toys presentation, for example, you can use a bullet slide to list the sales meeting agenda. **Bullets** are symbols that guide the reader's eye to the start of each item in a list, helping to emphasize important material. To add a new bullet slide:

Step 1	*Click*	the New Slide button 🖰 New Slide on the Formatting toolbar

notes The text assumes you have checked the Show when inserting new slides check box at the bottom of Slide Layout task pane.

The Title and Text slide layout, which is formatted for bullets, is automatically selected for the new slide. The Slide Layout task pane opens, in case you want to choose a different layout. A bulleted list or text slide appears in Normal view. The Slide Layout task pane displays 31 layouts in the Apply slide layout: section arranged in the following categories: Text Layouts, Content Layouts, Text and Content Layouts, and Other Layouts. **Layouts** are predesigned slide layouts that contain placement for titles, bulleted lists, text, charts, objects, clip art, and media clips. Instead of designing each slide manually, you can simply choose a layout that fits your needs.

Step 2	*Click*	the "Click to add title" placeholder
Step 3	*Key*	Agenda
Step 4	*Click*	the "Click to add text" placeholder
Step 5	*Key*	Mission statement
Step 6	*Press*	the ENTER key
Step 7	*Key*	the remaining bullets, including the intentional errors, pressing the ENTER key after each bullet except the last: Current products New products Future opportunities Current marrket status Projected marrket share
Step 8	*Click*	outside the slide area

DESIGN TIP

Using too many bullets lessens their effectiveness because the audience cannot quickly isolate the topics being discussed. Limit the number of bullets on any one slide to six or fewer, with each line containing no more than six to eight words.

Be sure to use parallel syntax when starting each bullet item to provide consistency throughout the slide. If the first bullet begins with an action verb, such as *highlight*, then all succeeding bullets should begin with an action verb, such as *discuss, introduce, compare,* and so forth.

TASK PANE TIP

You can insert a specific new slide from the Slide Design task pane by clicking the list arrow for the slide layout you desire, and then clicking Insert New Slide.

chapter
one

Your screen should look similar to Figure 1-7.

FIGURE 1-7
Agenda Text Slide with
Bullets

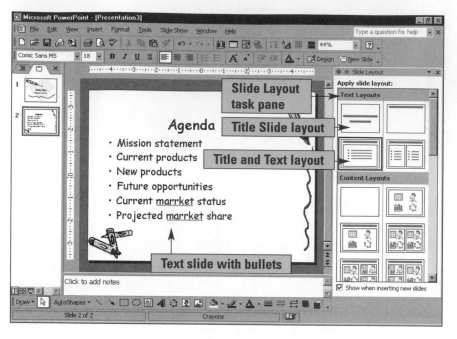

QUICK TIP

The AutoCorrect feature
automatically checks for
common keying errors
after you press the
SPACEBAR, ENTER, or
TAB key, or key any
punctuation mark after
a word, and makes the
correction automatically
using entries stored in
the AutoCorrect dialog
box. You can add words
you commonly misspell
to the AutoCorrect
dialog box by clicking
AutoCorrect Options on
the Tools menu.

CAUTION TIP

Filenames cannot
include the following
special characters: the
forward slash (/), the
backward slash (\), the
colon (:), the semicolon
(;), the pipe symbol (|),
the question mark (?),
the less than symbol (<),
the greater than symbol
(>), the asterisk (*), and
the quotation mark (").

1.f   Saving a Presentation

The first time you save a presentation, you can use either the Save
command or the Save As command on the File menu. Both
commands open the Save As dialog box. After you have saved a
presentation, use the Save command to save the presentation with the
same name to the same location, or use the Save As command to give
the same presentation a different name or to specify a new disk drive
and folder location. To save the *Teddy Toys* presentation:

notes Be sure to check with your instructor if you do not
know on which disk drive and in which folder to save
your presentations.

| Step 1 | *Click* | the Save button 💾 on the Standard toolbar |

The Save As dialog box on your screen should look similar to Figure 1-8.

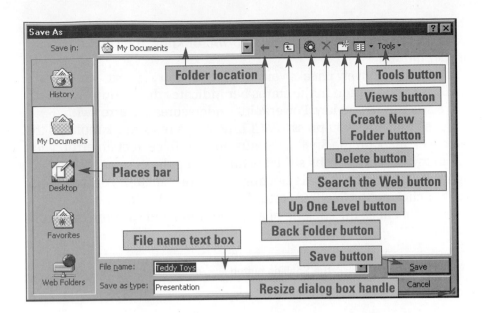

FIGURE 1-8
Save As Dialog Box

> **QUICK TIP**
>
> You can save a slide as a graphic so you can insert it as an image in any software program. In the Save As dialog box, click the Save as type: list arrow and select the graphic format of your choice.

In the Save As dialog box, the File name: text box suggests a filename based on the first text that appears in the presentation. You can use this name or key a different name of up to 255 characters, including the drive and path. Characters can include letters, numbers, spaces, and some special characters in any combination.

Step 2	*Key*	Teddy Toys in the File name: text box, if necessary
Step 3	*Verify*	that Presentation appears in the Save as type: list box
Step 4	*Switch to*	the appropriate disk drive and folder
Step 5	*Click*	Save

Your presentation is saved and the filename, *Teddy Toys*, appears in the title bar. PowerPoint adds a .ppt extension to the presentation filename. This extension may also appear in the title bar. The *Teddy Toys* presentation is used throughout the PowerPoint chapters to introduce new slide types and concepts.

1.g Checking Spelling

After you create or edit a presentation, you should save the presentation, check spelling in the presentation, and then resave the presentation with the corrections. Even after you spell check a presentation, it is still necessary to proofread it because the spell

> **MOUSE TIP**
>
> The Save As dialog box can be resized to display more files at one time by dragging the lower-right corner of the dialog box (or any border). You can customize the Places bar to change the order of the folders by right-clicking the desired folder and then clicking either Move Up or Move Down. You can also remove or rename a folder and display folders as large or small icons.

chapter
one

checker does not correct grammatical errors, the use of the wrong word (for example, *from* instead of *form*), or know the spelling of proper names.

PowerPoint actively checks your spelling as you key text, while the Spelling Status button in the status bar indicates that action. If you make an error as you key, PowerPoint underscores the error with a wavy red line once you press SPACEBAR, and a red x mark replaces the red check mark on the Spelling Status button. To correct an error, you can manually correct it by selecting and keying the correct spelling, by right-clicking the error and selecting the correct spelling, or by double-clicking the Spelling Status button and selecting the correct spelling. To check the spelling of a presentation and save the changes:

| Step 1 | *Click* | the Spelling button on the Standard toolbar |

When spell-checking a presentation, you can click the Ignore button if the spelling is correct in the Not in Dictionary: text box, or select the correct word in the Suggestions: list box and click the Change button. If the spell checker stops at a word that is spelled incorrectly but offers no suggestions for replacement, key the correct word in the Change to: text box and then click the Change button.

| Step 2 | *Correct* | the text as needed |
| Step 3 | *Click* | OK when PowerPoint has completed spell checking the entire presentation |

Saving Changes to a Presentation

Once you save a presentation, you can make changes to it by editing, formatting, and adding slides. You then resave the presentation and all the changes automatically save. To save changes to a presentation:

| Step 1 | *Click* | the Save button 🖫 on the Standard toolbar to save your changes to the presentation |

1.h Applying a Design Template

After you have created a presentation with a design template, you have the option of changing the design template to one that better fits the needs of your presentation. Because design templates change the color, background, font, and formatting of all slides in a presentation, you can easily change the look of your presentation by changing the design template as often as you like. You can use more than one design template in a presentation by applying a design template only to selected slides.

To apply a design template to an entire presentation:

Step 1	*Click*	the Slide Design button [⧉ Design] button on the Formatting toolbar
Step 2	*Scroll*	through the design previews in the Available For Use section of the Slide Design task pane
Step 3	*Click*	the Quadrant design
Step 4	*View*	Slides 1 and 2 and observe the changes in the slides
Step 5	*Save*	the *Teddy Toys* presentation

1.i Printing Slides

PowerPoint provides different options for printing slides in a presentation. At this time, you want to print the presentation as slides and then as a handout. Printing all the slides in a presentation, one per page, is the default printing option, with each slide printing on a separate sheet of paper. By clicking the Print button on the Standard toolbar, your presentation automatically prints without displaying the Print dialog box.

To print all slides in the presentation:

| Step 1 | *Click* | the Print button [🖨] on the Standard toolbar |

A **handout** displays multiple slides per page at a reduced size, to provide a convenient copy of your presentation for audience members. To print as a handout with two slides per page:

| Step 1 | *Click* | <u>F</u>ile |
| Step 2 | *Click* | <u>P</u>rint |

MENU TIP

You can display the Slide Design task pane by clicking the Slide Design command on the F<u>o</u>rmat menu or by right-clicking the slide background (not a placeholder) and then clicking Slide <u>D</u>esign.

C

DESIGN TIP

Good design is vital to good presentations because the layout, focus, balance, consistency, typeface, and color create appeal and readability that aid in comprehension and retention. Design creates first impressions, sets the tone, and motivates you to read, buy, or learn. It also establishes the credibility of the presentation's message.

chapter one

The Print dialog box opens with various printing options. The dialog box on your screen should look similar to Figure 1-9.

FIGURE 1-9
Print Dialog Box

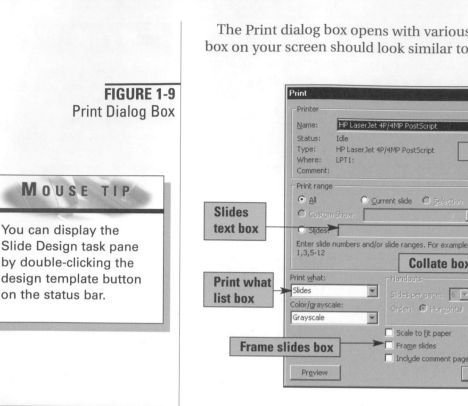

Step 3	*Click*	Handouts in the Print what: list box
Step 4	*Click*	the Slides per page: list arrow in the Handouts box
Step 5	*Click*	2 as the number of slides per page
Step 6	*Click*	OK

1.j Exiting PowerPoint

When you have completed all work in PowerPoint, you should exit the application. Any open documents close when you exit PowerPoint. If you haven't saved, you are prompted to save your changes. To exit PowerPoint and close any open documents:

| Step 1 | *Click* | the application Close button ☒ on the PowerPoint title bar |

Because you didn't make any changes since you last saved *Teddy Toys*, the presentation closes, the PowerPoint application exits, and the Windows desktop appears.

Summary

▶ The PowerPoint default window includes the menu bar, Standard toolbar, Formatting toolbar, view buttons, scroll bars, Drawing toolbar, status bar, outline/slides pane, slide pane, notes pane, and task pane.

▶ You can work on a presentation in Normal view, Slide Sorter view, Notes Page view, and Slide Show. Normal view, the default view, combines an outline/slides pane, a slide pane, and a task pane.

▶ The task pane provides hyperlink shortcuts to common tasks, such as creating a new presentation, changing the design template, or changing slide layout.

▶ The AutoContent Wizard provides templates with text and suggestions on content and organization to help you start creating a presentation.

▶ Presentation design templates enable you to enhance your presentation by including a professionally designed background, color scheme, font appearance, and graphic elements.

▶ PowerPoint provides 31 layouts for help in creating different slide layouts, such as title slides and bulleted lists.

▶ For the first slide of a new presentation, PowerPoint uses the Title Slide Layout.

▶ Title slides are used as the first slide or as section dividers within a presentation.

▶ For the second slide of a presentation, PowerPoint uses the Title and Text Layout.

▶ Bullet slides include a title and a list of numbered or bulleted items. Bullets are symbols used to emphasize text that is listed.

▶ After creating a presentation, you should save it for future use.

▶ The Spelling feature displays errors as you key text and enables you to spell check a presentation for typographical errors.

▶ Proofreading is an essential part of preparing any presentation because spell checking does not find all types of errors.

▶ You can change the presentation design template of a presentation after it has been created.

▶ You can print one slide per page or print a handout page with two slides per page.

▶ Closing a presentation frees computer resources and enables the computer to run more efficiently.

▶ When you finish working in PowerPoint, you should exit the application.

chapter one

Commands Review

Action	Menu Bar	Shortcut Menu	Toolbar	Task Pane	Keyboard
Display the task pane	View, Task Pane	Right-click any toolbar, click Task Pane			ALT + V, K
Create a new presentation	File, New		(icon)	Blank Presentation, From Design Template, or From AutoContent Wizard links in New Presentation task pane	CTRL + N ALT + F, N
Display the New Presentation task pane	File, New	Right-click any toolbar, click Task Pane		Other Task Panes list arrow, click New from Existing Presentation	ALT + F, N
View the next slide			Drag scroll box down one slide		PAGE DOWN
View the previous slide			Drag scroll box up one slide		PAGE UP
Display the first slide					HOME
Display the last slide					END
Display Normal view	View, Normal		(icon)		ALT + V, N
Display Slide Sorter view	View, Slide Sorter		(icon)		ALT + V, D
Display Notes Page view	View, Notes Page				ALT + V, P
Display Slide Show	View, Slide Show Slide Show, View Show		(icon)		ALT + V, W ALT + D, V F5
Add a new slide	Insert, New Slide	Right-click slide layout, click Insert New Slide	New Slide	Click list arrow on slide layout in Slide Layout task pane, click Insert New Slide	CTRL + M ALT + I, N ALT + N
Display the Slide Layout task pane	Format, Slide Layout	Right-click empty area on slide, click Slide Layout		Click Other Task Panes list arrow, click Slide Layout	ALT + O, L
Apply a layout				Click a slide layout in Apply slide layout: section in Slide Layout task pane	
Display the Slide Design task pane	Format, Slide Design	Right-click empty area on slide, click Slide Design	Design	Click Other Task Panes list arrow, click Slide Design-Design Templates	ALT + O, D
Apply a design template			Double-click design template button in status bar	Click a design template in Apply a design template: section in Slide Design task pane	
Save a presentation	File, Save File, Save As		(icon)		CTRL + S ALT + F, S F12
Check the spelling in a presentation	Tools, Spelling	Right-click word with wavy red line	(icon), Double-click Spelling Status icon in status bar		F7 ALT + T, S
Print a presentation	File, Print		(icon)		CTRL + P ALT + F, P
Close a presentation	File, Close		(icon)		CTRL + F4 ALT + F, C
Exit PowerPoint	File, Exit	Right-click PowerPoint button on the taskbar, click Close	(icon)		ALT + F, X ALT + F4

Concepts Review

SCANS

Circle the correct answer.

1. Most commands can be found on the:
[a] menu bar.
[b] Standard toolbar.
[c] Formatting toolbar.
[d] Drawing toolbar.

2. The PowerPoint window displays which of the following toolbars by default?
[a] Outlining toolbar, Standard toolbar, and Clipboard toolbar
[b] Standard toolbar, Formatting toolbar, and Drawing toolbar
[c] Picture toolbar, Formatting toolbar, Drawing toolbar
[d] Standard toolbar, Formatting toolbar, and WordArt toolbar

3. You cannot navigate through a PowerPoint presentation in Normal view by:
[a] pressing the PAGE UP and PAGE DOWN keys.
[b] dragging the scroll box.
[c] clicking the Previous Slide and Next Slide buttons.
[d] pressing the F5 key.

4. A combination view consisting of an outline pane, a slide pane, and a task pane is the:
[a] Slide Sorter view.
[b] Notes Page view.
[c] Normal view.
[d] Slide Show.

5. Presentation designs that regulate the formatting and layout for the slide are called:
[a] blueprints.
[b] placeholders.
[c] design templates.
[d] design plates.

6. You can create a new presentation by doing any of the following *except*:
[a] pressing the Ctrl + N keys.
[b] clicking File, Open.
[c] clicking File, New.
[d] clicking the New button on the Standard toolbar.

7. Objects on a slide that hold text are called:
[a] textholders.
[b] layouts.
[c] object holders.
[d] placeholders.

8. The type of slide used to introduce a topic and set the tone for a presentation is called a:
[a] title slide.
[b] bullet slide.
[c] graph slide.
[d] table slide.

9. What type of symbols are used to identify items in a list?
[a] graphics
[b] bullets
[c] markers
[d] icons

10. To exit the PowerPoint application, you can:
[a] double-click the document Control-menu icon.
[b] click the application Close button.
[c] click the Close Window button.
[d] click the application Minimize button.

chapter one

Circle **T** if the statement is true or **F** if the statement is false.

T   F   1. You can create a presentation from within PowerPoint or use the New Office Document command on the Start menu.

T   F   2. The title bar of PowerPoint contains the name of the application—Microsoft PowerPoint—as well as the name of the active presentation.

T   F   3. To begin a new presentation, you must close all current presentations.

T   F   4. When you add a new slide, PowerPoint provides 51 layout designs from which to choose.

T   F   5. A title slide can be used only as the first slide in any presentation.

T   F   6. A bullet slide should include as many bullets as necessary to fill the slide.

T   F   7. After initially saving a presentation, you should use the S̲ave command to give your presentation a new name.

T   F   8. As you work in PowerPoint, you should save periodically to avoid losing your work.

T   F   9. *Midwest Sales Report** is a valid filename for saving a PowerPoint presentation.

T   F   10. Clicking the Print button automatically prints the presentation.

notes In subsequent chapters, you build on the presentations you create below. Therefore, it is advisable to complete all Skills Review exercises and Case Projects and to use the filenames suggested before going on to the next chapter. It is a good idea to save three presentations per one disk so that you do not run out of disk space.

Skills Review

Exercise 1 ▣

1. Create a new presentation using the Layers design template.

2. Use the Title Slide layout for the first slide. The title should read "PowerPoint"; the subtitle should read your name.

3. Add a new slide using the Title and Text layout. The slide title should read "PowerPoint Defined." The bullet should read "PowerPoint is an easy-to-use presentation graphics application that allows you to create slides that entertain, motivate, convey, persuade, sell, or inform."

4. Save the presentation as *PowerPoint*.

5. Spell check, proofread, and resave the presentation, and then print the presentation as a two-slides-per-page handout and close it.

Exercise 2

1. Create a new, blank presentation.

2. Use the Title Slide layout for the first slide. The title should read "Why Microsoft Office Professional?"; the subtitle should read "Are You Ready?"

3. Apply the Shimmer design template to the presentation.

4. Add a new slide using the Title and Text layout. The slide title should read "What is Office Professional?" Key the following as separate bullets: "Word," "Excel," "PowerPoint," "Access," and "Outlook."

5. Save the presentation as *Office*.

6. Spell check, proofread, and resave the presentation, and then print and close it.

Exercise 3

1. Create a new presentation using the Curtain Call design template.

2. Use the Title Slide layout for the first slide. The title should read "Designing a Presentation"; the subtitle should read your name.

3. Add a new slide using the Title and Text layout. The slide title should read "Dale Carnegie Presentation Tips." Key the following as separate bullets: "Plan," "Prepare," "Practice," and "Present."

4. Save the presentation as *Design*.

5. Spell check, proofread, and resave the presentation, and then print the presentation as a two-slides-per-page handout and close it.

Exercise 4

1. Create a new, blank presentation.

2. Use the Title Slide layout for the first slide. The title should read "Precision Builders"; the subtitle should read "Builders of Distinction."

3. Apply the Cliff design template to the presentation.

4. Add a new slide using the Title and Text layout. The slide title should read "Why Precision Builders?" Key the following as separate bullet items: "Quality craftsmanship," "Quality materials," "Dedicated personnel," and "Excellent reputation."

5. Save the presentation as *Precision Builders*.

6. Spell check, proofread, and resave the presentation, and then print and close it.

Exercise 5

1. Create a new presentation using the Maple design template.

2. Add a Title slide with the title "S & L Nature Tours" and the subtitle "Enjoying the Outdoors While Promoting Good Health."

3. Add a Title and Text slide with the title "National Park Tours" and the following bullets: "Glacier National Park," "Yellowstone National Park," "Rocky Mountain National Park," and "Teton National Park."

4. Save the presentation as *Nature Tours*.

5. Spell check, proofread, and resave the presentation, and then print the presentation as a two-slides-per-page handout and close it.

chapter one

Exercise 6 C

1. Create a new presentation using the Eclipse design template.

2. Add a Title slide with the title "Health in the New Millennium" and the subtitle "Are You Ready to Reduce Stress in Your Life?"

3. Add a Title and Text slide with the title "Good Health Helps Everyone." Add the following bullets: "Eat a balanced diet," "Drink plenty of water," "Exercise regularly," "Visit your doctor periodically," "Reduce the level of stress," and "Enjoy life."

4. Save the presentation as *A Healthier You*.

5. Spell check, proofread, and resave the presentation, and then print and close it.

Exercise 7 C

1. Create a new presentation using the Satellite Dish design template.

2. Add a Title slide with the title "Buying A Computer" and the subtitle "A Guide to Selecting the Perfect Computer for Your Needs."

3. Add a Title and Text slide with the title "Getting Started."

4. Add the following bullets: "What do I need to do on the computer?"; "How much can I afford?"; "Where should I purchase the computer?"; and "Where can I find information about computers?"

5. Save the presentation as *Buying A Computer*.

6. Spell check, proofread, and resave the presentation, and then print the presentation as a two-slides-per-page handout and close it.

Exercise 8 C

1. Create a new presentation using the Ocean design template.

2. Add a Title slide with the title "Leisure Travel" and the subtitle "You Deserve a Great Vacation."

3. Add a Title and Text slide with the title "Vacation Packages for Everyone." Add the following bullets: "Spring Rafting Package," "Summer Hiking Package," "Fall Get-A-Way Package," "Winter Ski Package," "Canada's Splendor Package," and "Land Down Under Package."

4. Save the presentation as *Leisure Travel*.

5. Spell check, proofread, and resave the presentation, and then print and close it.

Case Projects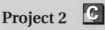

SCANS

Project 1

You have been asked to explain to your fellow assistants how to create a presentation using Web templates. Using online Help, review information on creating presentations using templates from the Web. Print the "Select from templates on a web site" and the "Select from templates on Office Update" topics.

Project 2 C

You work in the Human Resources Department of Communicate Corporation. You have been selected to give a presentation to train employees on proper telephone usage. Apply a presentation design template of your choice to create a title slide introducing the topic and a Title and Text slide defining the subject matter and topics to be covered. Save the presentation as *Communicate*. Spell check and proofread the presentation, and then print the presentation as a two-slides-per-page handout.

Project 3

You work for Souner & Associates, a software training company. You are to give a sales presentation to a group of office managers that contains information about why they should hire your organization. Apply a presentation design template of your choice to create a Title slide introducing your company and a Title and Text slide displaying training classes offered. Spell check the presentation, and then save it as *Souner*. Print the presentation as a two-slides-per-page handout.

Project 4

Create a realistic presentation about the company you work for or an organization with which you are familiar. Choose an occasion on which it might be appropriate to create a PowerPoint presentation for this company or organization. Consider what your message will be, who your audience will be, and what medium you will use to present your topic. To help you accomplish this, you can use the Office Assistant to access Presentation tips from Dale Carnegie Training®. Apply a presentation design template of your choice and begin with a Title slide and a Title and Text slide. Use your company or organization name and any other information that pertains to the presentation. Save the presentation as *My Presentation*. Spell check and then print the presentation.

Project 5

You have just accepted a full-time summer job at your local zoo. One of your job responsibilities is to create a presentation that entices grammar school children to visit the zoo during the summer as well as the regular school season. Decide what areas of the zoo, and possibly any special attractions, that would be of interest. Apply a presentation design template of your choice and begin with a Title and a Title and Text slide. Save the presentation as *Zoo*. Print the presentation as a two-slides-per-page handout.

Project 6

Your employer has asked whether or not you think your department should upgrade from your existing PowerPoint software to PowerPoint 2002. Connect to the Internet and visit the Microsoft PowerPoint page at *http://www.microsoft.com/office/powerpoint*. Search for new features in PowerPoint 2002. Use the presentation design of your choice to create a PowerPoint Title and Text slide itemizing some of the new features you found. Print the slide and close the presentation without saving it.

Project 7

As a consumer education instructor, part of your curriculum is to educate students on how to purchase a new car. Decide how you plan to introduce this topic to a class of 15- and 16-year-old students. Connect to the Internet and search the Web to find out current information on the best-selling new cars this past year. Based on your research, create a new presentation consisting of a Title slide and a Title and Text slide. Save the presentation as *Cars,* and print it.

Project 8

You are a teaching assistant at Millennium University. Your lead professor is teaching an Introduction to the Internet class for college freshmen. You and another teaching assistant (choose a member of your PowerPoint class to work with) must gather the information and create a PowerPoint presentation for the professor to use in his class. Decide on the topics to be covered in this eight-week course. Connect to the Internet to search the Web for new Internet topics that you feel should be covered. Download and use a presentation design template that you find on the Internet. Save the presentation as *Internet*, and print it.

chapter one

Editing and Formatting Slides

Chapter Overview

The process of creating a presentation usually spans more than one work session and involves modifying slide text so it conveys information effectively and captures viewer attention. In this chapter, you learn about opening an existing presentation, adding a slide, working with next-level bullets, editing and formatting text, using the slide master, and printing an individual slide.

LEARNING OBJECTIVES

- ▶ Open a presentation and add a slide
- ▶ Work with bulleted text
- ▶ Work with slides in the outline/slides pane
- ▶ Edit and format text on slides
- ▶ Modify the slide master
- ▶ Print an individual slide

Case profile

Today you are asked to continue working on the *Teddy Toys* presentation. Ms. Hill would like you to list the current products produced by Teddy Toys to help the personnel at the meeting understand how the new product she plans to introduce fits in the Teddy Toys family.

chapter two

2.a Opening a Presentation and Adding a Slide

When you complete a presentation, you save and close it. If you want to edit or add to that presentation at a later time, you open it from the location where it was saved. When you add a slide to a presentation, the slide is inserted after the current slide. To open an existing presentation and add a slide:

Step 1	*Click*	the Open button  on the Standard toolbar
Step 2	*Display*	the folder or drive containing your work
Step 3	*Double-click*	the *Teddy Toys* presentation
Step 4	*Display*	the last slide in the presentation in the slide pane
Step 5	*Click*	the New Slide button on the Formatting toolbar

A Title and Text slide displays in Normal view, and the Slide Layout task pane opens. PowerPoint automatically applies this slide layout to the new slide. The Slide Layout task pane opens to facilitate changing the slide layout.

Step 6	*Click*	the "Click to add title" placeholder
Step 7	*Key*	Mission Statement
Step 8	*Click*	the "Click to add text" placeholder
Step 9	*Key*	Teddy Toys strives to manufacture toys that are developmentally appropriate, safe, guaranteed to last, and fun for the youth market.
Step 10	*Save*	the *Teddy Toys* presentation

2.b Working with Bulleted Text

Much of the text in a PowerPoint presentation is formatted in bullets rather than paragraphs. Bulleted text is easy to scan, so viewers can grasp the main points on a slide while the speaker elaborates as necessary. You can format slide text in up to five available bullet levels. Each level is indented further than the previous bullet level, uses a smaller font size, and displays a different bullet symbol. First-level or major

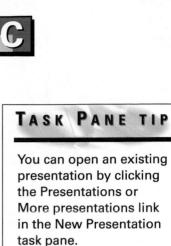

TASK PANE TIP

You can open an existing presentation by clicking the Presentations or More presentations link in the New Presentation task pane.

MOUSE TIP

You can open an existing presentation by clicking the Search button on the Standard toolbar, which opens the Search task pane and allows you to locate a presentation by having the computer search Everywhere, in My Computer, Web Folders, or Outlook.

chapter
two

bullets introduce an idea. Second-level or minor bullets support or provide additional information about the first-level bullet. Third-, fourth-, and fifth-level bullets provide additional information about each previous bullet level. Second-level through fifth-level bullets are also known as **next-level** bullets because they are demoted one or more levels. A first-level bullet, or any bullet that is at a higher level than another existing bullet, is also known as a **previous-level** bullet. To avoid filling a slide with overly detailed information at several font sizes, you should avoid using too many bullet levels.

When you create a new supporting bullet level, you demote the bullet by moving the selected paragraph to the next (lower) bullet level. **Demoting** (indenting) moves the bullet down one level to the right. When you want to create a higher bullet level, you promote the bullet by moving the selected paragraph to the previous (higher) bullet level. **Promoting** moves the bullet up one level to the left. To add first- and second-level bullets:

Step 1	*Click*	the New Slide button [New Slide] on the Formatting toolbar
Step 2	*Click*	the "Click to add title" placeholder
Step 3	*Key*	Introducing Baby Teddy
Step 4	*Click*	the "Click to add text" placeholder
Step 5	*Key*	Great new addition to the family
Step 6	*Press*	the ENTER key
Step 7	*Press*	the TAB key to demote the text to the second-level bullet position
Step 8	*Key*	Targeted for the infant market
Step 9	*Press*	the ENTER key
Step 10	*Key*	Safest & softest Teddy available
Step 11	*Press*	the ENTER key

On this line, you plan to key a first-level bullet, so you need to move this bullet position to the first-level position. Pressing the SHIFT + TAB keys or clicking the Decrease Indent button moves a bullet from its existing level to the previous level.

Step 12	*Press & hold*	the SHIFT key as you press the TAB key
Step 13	*Key*	Potential for a teen bear
Step 14	*Save*	the *Teddy Toys* presentation

Your screen should look similar to Figure 2-1.

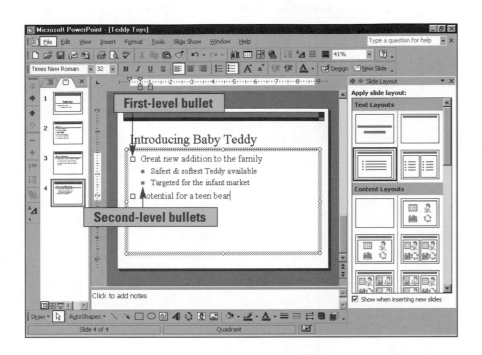

FIGURE 2-1
Introducing Baby
Teddy Slide

2.c Working with Slides in the Outline/Slides Pane

The outline/slides pane is useful for working with text and organizing slides in a presentation. You can add slides in either tab of this pane, and you can edit and format slide text in the Outline tab. The Slides tab is excellent for rearranging slides (though you can also rearrange slide order in the Outline tab), and the Outline tab lets you expand or collapse your view of a slide to see more or less of the text it contains. These choices make it easier to concentrate on organizing the ideas in your presentation rather than focusing on details like graphics and formatting. To add a slide in the Outline tab:

Step 1	*Click*	the Outline tab in the Outline/Slides pane
Step 2	*Click*	after the Introducing Baby Teddy text
Step 3	*Click*	the New Slide button [New Slide] on the Formatting toolbar
Step 4	*Key*	Current Products and press the ENTER key
Step 5	*Press*	the TAB key and key Family bears

Q U I C K   T I P

The current bullet level is retained when you press the ENTER key until you promote or demote the level by pressing the TAB key or the SHIFT + TAB keys, clicking the Increase Indent or Decrease Indent button on the Formatting toolbar, or clicking the Demote or Promote button on the Outlining toolbar.
   Pressing the CTRL + ENTER keys moves you from the first text placeholder on a slide to the next. When you press the CTRL + ENTER keys from the last text placeholder on the slide, you add a text slide to your presentation.

chapter
two

<table>
<tr><td>Step 6</td><td>*Press*</td><td>the ENTER key and then the TAB key to create a second-level bullet</td></tr>
<tr><td>Step 7</td><td>*Key*</td><td>Papa Teddy and press the ENTER key</td></tr>
<tr><td>Step 8</td><td>*Key*</td><td>Mama Teddy and press the ENTER key</td></tr>
<tr><td>Step 9</td><td>*Press & hold*</td><td>the SHIFT key as you press the TAB key</td></tr>
<tr><td>Step 10</td><td>*Key*</td><td>Action bears and press the ENTER key</td></tr>
<tr><td>Step 11</td><td>*Press*</td><td>the TAB key</td></tr>
<tr><td>Step 12</td><td>*Key*</td><td>the following second-level bullets under Action bears:
Dancing Teddy
Sport Teddy
Rock & Roll Teddy</td></tr>
<tr><td>Step 13</td><td>*Save*</td><td>the *Teddy Toys* presentation</td></tr>
</table>

You decide to rearrange the slides in your presentation to improve the flow of information. To move slides in the outlines/slides pane:

<table>
<tr><td>Step 1</td><td>*Click*</td><td>the Slides tab located on the outline/slides pane</td></tr>
<tr><td>Step 2</td><td>*Point to*</td><td>Slide 5 until the ScreenTip displays: Current Products</td></tr>
<tr><td>Step 3</td><td>*Drag*</td><td>the Current Products slide to above Slide 4, the Introducing Baby Teddy slide</td></tr>
<tr><td>Step 4</td><td>*Release*</td><td>the mouse button when a horizontal line representing the slide appears above Slide 4</td></tr>
<tr><td>Step 5</td><td>*Click*</td><td>the Outline tab located on the outline/slides pane</td></tr>
<tr><td>Step 6</td><td>*Scroll*</td><td>to view the Teddy Toys title slide icon</td></tr>
<tr><td>Step 7</td><td>*Click*</td><td>the Expand All button on the Standard toolbar</td></tr>
</table>

The Expand All button is a toggle that expands to show slide titles and bullet text, and also collapses to show only slide numbers and titles.

<table>
<tr><td>Step 8</td><td>*Click*</td><td>the Expand All button to display the bullets</td></tr>
</table>

MOUSE TIP

You can move a selected slide in the Outline tab by clicking the Move Up or Move Down buttons on the Outlining toolbar until the slide is at a new location.

QUICK TIP

You can add a slide from the outline/slides pane by clicking immediately to the right of the slide title text on the Outline tab and then pressing the ENTER key, or by clicking on or between thumbnail images on the Slides tab and then pressing the ENTER key.

You can double-click a slide icon in the Outline tab to collapse a single bullet family, and double-click it again to expand a single bullet family.

MENU TIP

If the Outlining toolbar is not displayed, right-click any toolbar, and then click Outlining.

Rearranging Bullets in the Outline Tab

You may often need to rearrange bullets after keying them so that they follow a more logical sequencing of topics. Moving bullets is easy in the Outline tab. You can also use the Outlining toolbar in Normal view. To move a bullet:

Step 1	**Display**	the Outlining toolbar if necessary
Step 2	**Click**	the Introducing Baby Teddy slide icon in the Outline tab
Step 3	**Click**	the bullet symbol to the left of the "Targeted for the infant market" bullet in the Outline tab
Step 4	**Click**	the Move Down button ⬇ once on the Outlining toolbar

Your screen should look similar to Figure 2-2.

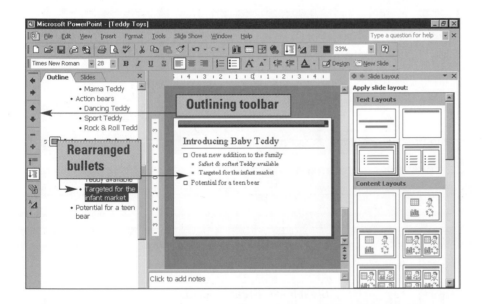

MOUSE TIP

When working in the outline pane, or on a slide in Normal view, you can move a bullet by selecting the entire bullet and dragging it to a new position. To select an entire bullet, point to the bullet before the bullet text you want to move. When the I-beam pointer changes to a four-headed arrow, click to select it, and then drag the selected bullet to its new position.

FIGURE 2-2
Slide with
Rearranged Bullets

QUICK TIP

The Undo feature enables you to undo your last action. If you decide you do not want to undo what you just did, click the Redo button. The Redo button reverses the Undo.

2.d Editing and Formatting Text on Slides

While working on a presentation, you often want to change the look of text on a slide. You can change the spacing between lines and paragraphs, alignment of text, indents, and type of bullets. Although you can edit and format a slide on the Outline tab of the outline/slides pane, it may be more convenient to make these changes in the slide pane, where your view of the slide is larger.

C

chapter
two

CAUTION TIP

As you work, periodically save your presentation by clicking the Save button on the Standard toolbar or by pressing the CTRL + S keys. Saving frequently ensures that you do not lose your work if there is a power outage, computer error, or human error.

To switch to the Slides tab and edit and format text on an existing slide:

Step 1	*Click*	the Slides tab
Step 2	*Click*	Slide 1 in the Slides tab
Step 3	*Click*	at the end of the "Focusing on the Future" subtitle on the title slide

A hatch-marked border with eight sizing handles appears around the subtitle text placeholder, and the insertion point appears, indicating that the placeholder is active. The insertion point is positioned just to the right of the text and is blinking to indicate that new text will be keyed here. Your slide should look similar to Figure 2-3.

FIGURE 2-3
Selected Text Placeholder

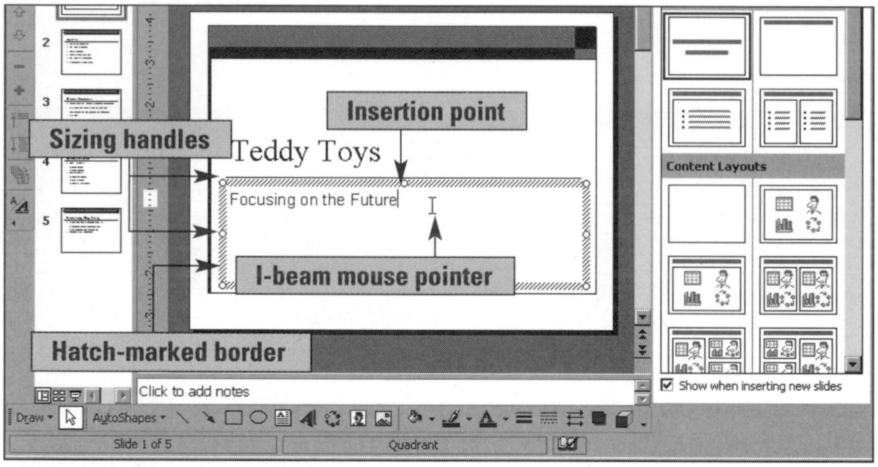

Step 4	*Press*	the ENTER key
Step 5	*Press*	the TAB key
Step 6	*Key*	Great Ideas, Great Products

QUICK TIP

You can further increase your view by switching to the Slides tab in the outline/slides pane; this makes more room for the slide pane and also lets you use the Slides tab to quickly navigate through your presentation. To make even more room for the slide pane, you can close the outline/slides pane by clicking the Close button. You can click the Normal View (Restore Panes) button to the left of the horizontal scroll bar to restore the outline/slides pane.

Before you can edit text in a text placeholder, the placeholder must be active or selected. A hatch-marked border with eight sizing handles around a placeholder indicates it is selected. To edit or format some of the text in a placeholder, you select just the text to which you want to apply changes. To select an entire placeholder, you can hold down the SHIFT key and click anywhere in an inactive placeholder including the existing text, or you can click any border of an active placeholder.

Step 7	*Drag*	to select "Great Ideas, Great Products"
Step 8	*Click*	the Decrease Font Size button [A▾] on the Formatting toolbar to reduce the size of the text to the next size smaller

Changing Text Alignment

Changing **alignment** adjusts the horizontal position of text on a slide. For example, the title and subtitle text placeholders on the Quadrant design template use left alignment. Four types of alignment options—left, center, right, and justify—are available.

If the insertion point appears in the placeholder, you must click in the paragraph or select the paragraphs you want to align. To change the alignment of the title and subtitle text:

Step 1	*Click*	the Teddy Toys title text placeholder
Step 2	*Click*	the Center button [≣] on the Formatting toolbar
Step 3	*Click*	outside the placeholder to deselect it
Step 4	*Press & hold*	the SHIFT key
Step 5	*Click*	the subtitle text placeholder

The placeholder is selected, but the insertion point does not appear. When you change the alignment, both paragraphs in the subtitle change.

Step 6	*Click*	the Align Right button [≣] on the Formatting toolbar
Step 7	*Click*	the Undo button [↰] to change back to left alignment

Changing Line Spacing

Depending on the number of lines on a slide, you may want to either increase or decrease the line spacing to fit more lines on a slide, make the lines stand out more, or fill more of the slide. **Line spacing** is a measurement of space between lines of text on a slide. **Paragraph spacing** refers to the spacing between paragraphs. Changes to the line spacing on a slide affect the amount of white space between the lines of a paragraph. **White space** is the empty space on a slide between

QUICK TIP

You can select individual lines of text or you can select the entire placeholder. To select individual lines of text or individual characters, you drag the mouse pointer across the desired text in an active placeholder; the text you selected is then highlighted.

CAUTION TIP

If an insertion point appears within a text placeholder when you attempt to change alignment, you only change the alignment for the line containing the insertion point.
If the placeholder is selected but the insertion point does not appear, any alignment changes you make affect all the paragraphs in the placeholder.

chapter two

lines or surrounding lines of text and is intended to aid the readability of the text. To change the line spacing of bulleted text on a slide:

Step 1	*Display*	the Mission Statement slide
Step 2	*Press & hold*	the SHIFT key
Step 3	*Click*	anywhere in the bullet text placeholder to select the entire placeholder
Step 4	*Click*	Format
Step 5	*Click*	Line Spacing

The Line Spacing dialog box opens, with options for changing the line spacing and spacing before and after paragraphs. Line spacing increases or decreases the amount of space between all lines of text. The Before and After paragraph spacing options increase or decrease the amount of space before or after paragraphs only, not between the lines within a paragraph.

Step 6	*Drag*	the Line Spacing dialog box to the right so you can see the bullet on the Mission Statement slide
Step 7	*Key*	1.25 in the Line spacing box
Step 8	*Click*	Preview

If the Line Spacing dialog box obscures your view of the slide, drag the title bar so you can see the effect these line spacing changes have on the text.

Step 9	*Click*	OK

The AutoFit Options button may appear on your slide and display the following options: AutoFit Text to Placeholder, Stop Fitting Text to This Placeholder, Split Text Between Two Slides, Continue on a New Slide, Change to Two-Column Layout, and Control AutoCorrect Options. When the AutoFit Text to Placeholder option is activated, you can set the text size to change automatically to fit the placeholder.

Step 10	*Display*	the Introducing Baby Teddy slide

QUICK TIP

If you want to change the line spacing or paragraph spacing of all the bulleted text on a slide, you must first select the bulleted text placeholder or select the text within the box. If you see the blinking insertion point, you are changing the line spacing between only two bullets instead of between all the bullets.

QUICK TIP

The AutoFit Options button is a Smart Tag, an Office feature that appears when you complete certain actions, such as autofitting text to a placeholder, to enable you to make further modifications if desired. Other Smart Tags include the AutoCorrect Options button, the Paste Options button, and the Automatic Layout Options button.

Step 11	*Press & hold*	the SHIFT key
Step 12	*Click*	anywhere in the bullet text placeholder to select the entire bullet placeholder
Step 13	*Open*	the Line Spacing dialog box
Step 14	*Key*	0.4 in the Before paragraph box
Step 15	*Click*	Preview to view the changes
Step 16	*Click*	OK
Step 17	*Save*	the *Teddy Toys* presentation

Changing Bullet Symbols

A **bullet symbol** is a design element that sets off each bullet point in a list. PowerPoint enables you to use symbols, pictures, font characters, numbers, and letters as bullet symbols. You can keep the bullet symbol styles determined by the presentation design, or change their color and size, or even select a different bullet symbol. The Formatting toolbar provides a quick method for displaying or hiding bullet symbols and numbers. The Format menu provides additional symbols and bullet customization. To change the bullets from symbols to numbers:

Step 1	*Display*	the Agenda slide
Step 2	*Select*	the entire bullet text placeholder
Step 3	*Click*	the Numbering button on the Formatting toolbar
Step 4	*Display*	the Introducing Baby Teddy slide
Step 5	*Select*	the entire bullet text placeholder
Step 6	*Click*	Format
Step 7	*Click*	Bullets and Numbering
Step 8	*Click*	the Numbered tab in the Bullets and Numbering dialog box, if necessary
Step 9	*Double-click*	the first example in row 2 to display capital letters A. B. C.
Step 10	*Save*	the *Teddy Toys* presentation

chapter
two

C 2.e Modifying the Slide Master

The **slide master** is an element of a template that controls the formatting, color, and graphic elements for all the slides in a presentation based on that template. Making changes to a slide master enables you to make formatting changes—such as font style, placeholder positions, bullet styles, background design, and color scheme—to all slides (except title slides) in a presentation automatically, instead of manually changing each one. Global title slide formatting is controlled by a **title master**, to guarantee consistent formatting across multiple title slides in a presentation. The information stored in the title and slide masters is based on the design template. You work with the title master in a future chapter. For now, you want to use the slide master to make some simple formatting changes. To change the bullets on the slide master:

Step 1	*Point to*	the Normal View button located to the left of the horizontal scroll bar
Step 2	*Press & hold*	the SHIFT key until the ScreenTip displays: Slide Master View
Step 3	*Click*	the Slide Master View button

Your screen should look similar to Figure 2-4.

FIGURE 2-4
Slide Master View

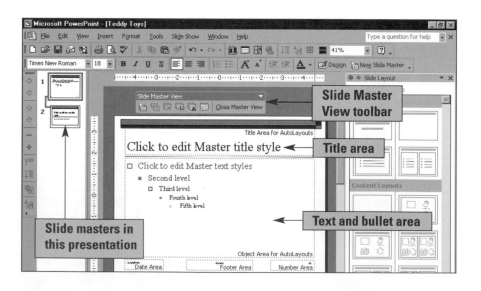

The slide master template displays placeholders for the title, bullet, date, footer, and slide number areas. It displays existing formats in terms of font, point size, alignment, color scheme, graphic elements, and bullet symbols dependent on the design template used. The Slide

Master View toolbar is displayed in the slide master, with options for inserting a new slide master, inserting a new title master, deleting a master, preserving a master, renaming a master, accessing the Master Layout dialog box, and closing the master view.

Adding Graphical Bullets to the Slide Master

You can add graphical bullets to your presentation to enhance the look of your text slides. Graphical bullets are more colorful and more interesting in shape than the default bullet symbols. When you change bullets on the slide master, bullet symbols change on all text slides in the presentation. To add a graphical bullets to the slide master:

Step 1	*Right-click*	in the first-level bullet text
Step 2	*Click*	Bullets and Numbering
Step 3	*Click*	the Bulleted tab, if necessary
Step 4	*Click*	Picture
Step 5	*Double-click*	the bullet example that is a brown split circular shape (ScreenTip displays: bullets, global marketing)
Step 6	*Right-click*	in the second-level bullet text
Step 7	*Click*	Bullets and Numbering
Step 8	*Click*	Customize
Step 9	*Click*	Wingdings in the Font: list box
Step 10	*Double-click*	the star bullet in the ninth row, twelfth column
Step 11	*Click*	the first brown color in the Color: list
Step 12	*Click*	OK
Step 13	*Click*	the Slide Show button ⊟ located to the left of the horizontal scroll bar and progress through the slide show
Step 14	*View*	the bullet symbols on each slide until you return to the slide master

The changes you've made to the slide master are applied throughout the presentation. The bullet symbols change only on the text slides that follow the slide master. If you make individual changes to bullets on a slide, that slide follows the individual changes and does not follow the slide master.

MENU TIP

You can display the slide master by pointing to the Master command on the View menu, and then clicking the Slide Master command on the submenu.

MOUSE TIP

You can close the slide master by clicking the Close Master View button on the Slide Master View toolbar; you then return to the previous view.

chapter
two

MENU TIP

You can reapply the slide master by clicking the Slide Layout command on the Format menu, and then clicking the Text list arrow in the Slide Layout task pane, and then clicking Reapply Layout.

MOUSE TIP

You can close slide master view by clicking the Normal View button located to the left of the horizontal scroll bar.

Your changes to the slide master are saved and you return to Normal view. As you observed during the slide show, when you change bullets on an individual slide, you override the slide master. You can reapply the slide master formatting to any slide. To close the slide master and reapply the current master styles:

Step 1	*Click*	the Close Master View button Close Master View on the Slide Master View toolbar
Step 2	*Display*	the Agenda slide
Step 3	*Right-click*	a blank area of the slide (not on a placeholder)
Step 4	*Click*	Slide Layout
Step 5	*Click*	the Title and Text layout list arrow in the Slide Layout task pane
Step 6	*Click*	Reapply Layout
Step 7	*Display*	the Introducing Baby Teddy slide
Step 8	*Click*	the Title and Text layout list arrow
Step 9	*Click*	Reapply Layout
Step 10	*Save*	the *Teddy Toys* presentation

2.f Printing an Individual Slide

CAUTION TIP

If you want to print transparencies, check your printer and see if it accepts transparencies. If so, determine what types of transparencies work with your printer model.

PowerPoint provides different options for printing a presentation. If you want to print only a single slide, you can use the Print command on the File menu. In addition, you can print a range of slides using the Slides: text box in the Print dialog box by clicking the Slides: option button, and then keying the range of slides, such as 2-3. You also can print a slide as an overhead transparency by placing a transparency in your printer when you print your slides. To print an individual slide:

Step 1	*Display*	the Current Products slide
Step 2	*Click*	File
Step 3	*Click*	Print to open the Print dialog box
Step 4	*Click*	the Current slide option button
Step 5	*Click*	OK
Step 6	*Save*	the *Teddy Toys* presentation and close it

Summary

▶ PowerPoint enables you to add slides at any point in the presentation.

▶ First-level bullets introduce a topic and second-level bullets provide additional information regarding first-level bullets.

▶ The Outline tab in the outline/slides pane allows you to create, edit, rearrange, and add slides easily.

▶ The Slides tab in the outline/slides pane allows you to add and rearrange slides.

▶ The sequence or order of slides in a presentation can be changed in the outline/slides pane.

▶ Changes may be made to any presentation design to personalize the look of the presentation.

▶ Alignment changes the position of text within a text placeholder.

▶ Left, center, right, and justify are four types of alignment for positioning text.

▶ Increasing or decreasing line spacing changes the space between lines of text on a slide.

▶ White space is the empty space on a slide that aids readability.

▶ The slide master controls settings for the formatting, color, and graphic elements such as bullets on all slides in a presentation.

▶ You can move indents by dragging the first-line indent marker, bullet text marker, or left indent marker on the horizontal ruler.

▶ You reapply the formatting of the slide master to any slide by reapplying the current master styles of the slide layout.

▶ You can print a single slide or selected slides by clicking Print on the File menu.

Commands Review

Action	Menu Bar	Shortcut Menu	Toolbar	Task Pane	Keyboard
Open an existing presentation	File, Open		📂	Click desired presentation in the Open a presentation section in New Presentation task pane	CTRL + O ALT + F, O
Add a slide from outline/slides pane					Click after slide title on Outline tab, press ENTER Click between thumbnail images on Slides tab, press ENTER

chapter two

Action	Menu Bar	Shortcut Menu	Toolbar	Task Pane	Keyboard
Create a next-level bullet			[→ button]		TAB
Return to a previous-level bullet			[← button]		SHIFT + TAB
Change line spacing on a slide	Format, Line Spacing				ALT + O, S
Display the ruler	View, Ruler				ALT + V, R
Undo a previous action	Edit, Undo		[undo button]		CTRL + Z ALT + E, U
Redo previous Undo	Edit, Redo		[redo button]		CTRL + Y ALT + E, R
Access the slide master	View, Master, Slide Master		SHIFT + [button]		ALT + V, M, S
Display the Slide Layout task pane	Format, Slide Layout	Right-click empty area on slide, click Slide Layout		Other task panes list arrow, click Slide Layout in Slide Layout task pane	ALT + O, L
Reapply the master styles		Click the slide layout list arrow, then click Reapply Layout		Click list arrow on slide layout, click Apply to Selected Slides or Apply Layout in Slide Layout task pane	
Print an individual slide	File, Print, Current slide				ALT + F, P, C CTRL + P

Concepts Review

Circle the correct answer.

1. To open an existing presentation, click:
[a] File, New.
[b] File, Open.
[c] Insert, New Presentation.
[d] File, Add a New Presentation.

2. To promote a bullet up one previous level, press the:
[a] TAB key.
[b] ENTER key.
[c] SHIFT key.
[d] SHIFT + TAB KEYS.

3. Which of the following is not a Smart Tag?
[a] AutoCorrect Options button
[b] AutoFit Options button
[c] Automatic Layout Options button
[d] AutoDelete Options button

4. The bullets order can be changed in the Outline tab by:
[a] clicking the Move Up or Move Down buttons.
[b] dragging the tab marker to its new location.
[c] dragging the indent markers to their new location.
[d] clicking the Collapse or Expand buttons.

5. You can tell that a text placeholder is selected when:
[a] a dotted border with eight selection handles appears surrounding the text.
[b] a hatch-marked border with eight small sizing handles appear surrounding the text.
[c] the text placeholder is shaded.
[d] a solid black border with eight selection handles appears surrounds the text.

6. Line spacing is the amount of white space:
[a] between lines of text.
[b] before and after paragraphs.
[c] between the characters of a line.
[d] between words of a line.

7. Alignment refers to the:
[a] length of the line.
[b] horizontal position of a line on the page.
[c] vertical space between the lines of text.
[d] size of the characters in a line.

8. Which of the following is *not* used to position text on a slide?
[a] tabs
[b] alignment
[c] line spacing
[d] font color

9. If you want all the slides in the presentation to be formatted with the same new bullet symbol, use:
[a] a presentation design template.
[b] the slide master.
[c] the add a slide option.
[d] the slide layout option.

10. Reapplying the current master styles to a slide:
[a] changes the formatting on all slides.
[b] reverts formatting changes to the styles on the slide master.
[c] adds an identical slide.
[d] removes any inserted or drawn objects on a slide.

Circle **T** if the statement is true or **F** if the statement is false.

T   F   1. Second-level bullets are the exact same size as first-level bullets.

T   F   2. Much of the text in a PowerPoint presentation is formatted in paragraphs.

T   F   3. Bullets can be moved by clicking the Move Up or Move Down button on the Outlining toolbar.

T   F   4. When applying a particular presentation design, you must apply this design to each slide individually.

T   F   5. You can add a slide from the Outline/Slides pane by clicking immediately to the right of the slide title text, on the Outline tab and then pressing the TAB key.

T   F   6. You can select an entire placeholder by holding down the CTRL key and then clicking anywhere in the placeholder.

T   F   7. Increasing or decreasing line spacing aids in readability.

T   F   8. Paragraph and line spacing change the spacing between lines of type within a paragraph.

T   F   9. The slide master displays placeholders and formatting for titles and text on all slides in a presentation except the title slide.

T   F   10. PowerPoint does not allow you to print an individual slide.

Skills Review

SCANS

Exercise 1 [C]

1. Open the *PowerPoint* presentation you created in Chapter 1, and add a Title and Text slide at the end of the presentation.

2. The title of the new slide should read "The Views of PowerPoint" and the bullets should read "Normal View," "Slide Sorter View," "Notes Page View," and "Slide Show."

chapter two

3. Move the Slide Show bullet up two levels in the Outline tab so that it appears as the second bullet.

4. Use the slide master to change the first-level bullet to a Picture bullet using any bullet symbol with the following ScreenTip: bullets, romanesque, web bullets.

5. Save, spell check, and proofread the presentation, then resave if necessary.

6. Print only the new slide, and then close the presentation.

Exercise 2 C

1. Open the *Office* presentation you created in Chapter 1, and add a Title and Text slide at the end of the presentation.

2. The title should read "Why Use Office Professional?" The bullets should read "Share files on the Internet," "Use speech recognition technology," "Use IntelliSense™ technology," and "Use e-mail based collaboration." Use the Symbol command on the Insert menu to insert the trademark symbol in the third bullet.

3. Using the slide master, change the bullet symbol of the first-level bullet to the Microsoft Windows symbol (last Wingdings symbol) from the Wingdings font list under the Customize section in the Bullets and Numbering dialog box.

4. Using the slide master, change the size of the new bullet to 75%.

5. Using the Line Spacing dialog box, change the paragraph spacing on the bullet text of the Why Use Office Professional? slide to 0.5 lines before the paragraph.

6. Save, spell check, and proofread the presentation, then resave if necessary.

7. Print the presentation as a three-slides-per-page handout, and then close the presentation.

Exercise 3 C

1. Open the *Design* presentation you created in Chapter 1, and add a Title and 2 Column Text slide at the end of the presentation.

2. The title should read "Presentation Fonts." The first-level bullet item in the first text placeholder on the left should read "Serif Fonts." Key the following next-level bullets: "Serious messages," "Ease of reading," and "Large amounts of text." The first-level bullet in the second text placeholder on the right should read "Sans Serif Fonts." Key the following next-level bullets: "Lighthearted messages," "Cleaner look," and "Titles and headlines."

3. Change the line spacing of the bullets in each text placeholder to 1.5.

4. Display the Dale Carnegie Presentation Tips slide.

5. Edit the text slide in the Outline tab by adding the following next-level bullets under each of the first-level bullets: Under the first-level bullet "Plan" add the next-level bullet "Define audience, purpose, and medium"; under the first-level bullet "Prepare" add the next-level bullet "Establish positive mindset and prepare structure of presentation"; under the first-level bullet "Practice" add the next-level bullet "Review, rehearse, get feedback"; under the first-level bullet "Present" add the next-level bullet "Build rapport with audience."

6. Change the first-level bullet on the slide master to a Picture bullet. Adjust bullet size as necessary.

7. Change the next-level bullet on the slide master to a Customized bullet. Adjust bullet size as necessary.

8. View the presentation as a slide show.

9. Save, spell check, and proofread the presentation, then resave if necessary.

10. Print only slides two and three, and then close the presentation.

Exercise 4   C

1. Open the *Precision Builders* presentation you created in Chapter 1, and add a Title and Text slide at the end of the presentation.

2. The title should read "Our Motto" and the bullet should read "Precision Builders wants to work with you to build the home of your dreams at a price that will not shatter your dreams."

3. Change the line spacing of the bullet to 1.25 lines on the Our Motto slide.

4. Display the Precision Builders title slide and change the alignment of the subtitle to align right.

5. Reapply the layout of the current master of a Title and Text slide to the Our Motto slide.

6. Save, spell check, and proofread the presentation, then resave if necessary.

7. Print the presentation as a three-slides-per-page handout, and then close the presentation.

Exercise 5   C

1. Open the *Nature Tours* presentation you created in Chapter 1, and add a Title and Text slide at the end of the presentation.

2. The title should read "Available Tours." The first-level bullet should read "Each tour is available at beginning, intermediate, and expert levels." The next-level bullets should read "Hiking," "Biking," "Rafting," and "Horseback riding."

3. Using the slide master, change the bullet symbol for the first- and next-level bullet using a Picture bullet.

4. Using the slide master, change the line spacing of the bullet text to 1.1; 0.0 spacing before and after paragraphs.

5. If necessary, change the size of the bullet and/or increase or decrease the size of the text on the master.

6. Save, spell check, and proofread the presentation, then resave if necessary.

7. Print only the new slide, and then close the presentation.

Exercise 6   C

1. Open the *A Healthier You* presentation you created in Chapter 1, and add a Title and Text slide at the end of the presentation.

2. The title should read "Balanced Diet at a Glance" and the bullets should read "Carbohydrates," "Proteins," "Fats," "Minerals," "Vitamins," and "Fiber."

3. Using the Outline tab or the Normal View, move the Fats bullet to the end of the bullet list.

4. Using the slide master, change the paragraph spacing of the bullet text to increase the spacing before the paragraphs.

5. Display the Good Health Helps Everyone slide.

6. Add the following first-level bullet as the first bullet: "Basic common sense rules."

7. Demote the remaining bullets to next-level bullets.

8. Save, spell check, and proofread the presentation, then resave if necessary.

9. Print the presentation as a three-slides-per-page handout, and then close the presentation.

chapter two

Exercise 7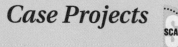

1. Open the *Buying A Computer* presentation you created in Chapter 1, and add a Title and 2 Column Text slide at the end of the presentation.

2. The title should read "Reasons to Buy a Computer." The first-level bullet item in the first text placeholder on the left should read "Family essentials." Key the following next-level bullets: "Family budgets," "Address book," "School homework," and "Personal e-mail." The first-level bullet in the second text placeholder on the right should read "Family enjoyment." Key the following next-level bullets: "Internet surfing," "Computer games," "Web page design," and "Holiday cards."

3. Change the bullet symbols on the slide master.

4. Rearrange the order of the bullets in order of your priority.

5. Display the Getting Started slide. Add the following first-level bullet as the first bullet: "Ask yourself the following:"

6. Demote the remaining bullets to next-level bullets.

7. Save, spell check, and proofread the presentation, then resave if necessary.

8. Print Slides 2 and 3 as a two-slides-per-page handout, and then close the presentation.

Exercise 8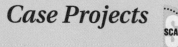

1. Open the *Leisure Travel* presentation you created in Chapter 1, and add a Title and Text slide at the end of the presentation.

2. The title should read "Leave Everything to Us." The first-level bullet should read "We do all the work." The next-level bullets should read "Travel arrangements," "Hotel accommodations," "Restaurant reservations," "Golf tee times," and "Sight-seeing tours." Add another first-level bullet that reads "You will be pampered and relaxed."

3. Change the bullet size on the Leave Everything to Us slide.

4. Change the alignment of the title on the slide master.

5. Change the bullet symbols on the Vacation Packages for Everyone Slide to a lettering style, and change the lettering color.

6. Save the presentation, print only the slides with changes, and then close the presentation.

Case Projects

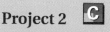

Project 1

An administrative assistant in the next department has asked you how to remove the bullets in front of the bullet text. Using online Help, review information on removing bullets or numbering from text on a text slide. Create a simple text slide to summarize the information you find so your coworker can refer to it again. Print the new slide, remembering to spell check and proofread your work first.

Project 2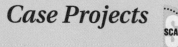

You have been asked to add a Title and Text slide to the *Communicate* presentation you created in the previous chapter. This slide should provide information about the first bullet on the previous text slide. Make any formatting decisions with regard to alignment, line spacing, and bullet symbols. Save the presentation, and print the new slide.

Project 3 ©

As you work toward your goal of selling your Souner & Associates training program to prospective clients, you need to begin "selling them" early in the presentation. Add a Title and Text slide to the *Souner* presentation you created in the previous chapter, detailing what your organization can provide. Make any formatting decisions with regard to alignment, line spacing, and bullet symbols. Make some of the changes to the slide master. Save the *Souner* presentation, and print the presentation as a four-slides-per-page handout.

Project 4 ©

Open the *My Presentation* presentation you created in the previous chapter. As this is the project on which you are working independently, all decisions are entirely up to you. You should edit your previous slides and add another slide to your presentation. Keep in mind your message, audience, and medium as you work. Make any formatting decisions with regard to alignment, line spacing, and bullet symbols. Make some of the changes to the slide master. It may be necessary to change your presentation design template to set the tone of your topic. Save *My Presentation,* and print the new slide.

Project 5 ©

Open the *Zoo* presentation you created in the previous chapter, and add a Title and 2 Column Text slide that can be added to the presentation concerning possible zoo events, occasions, important dates, or animal facts. Make any formatting decisions with regard to alignment, line spacing, and bullet symbols. Make some of the changes to the slide master. Save and print the presentation as a three-slides-per-page handout.

Project 6 ©

You cannot find an appropriate design template for your presentation. So, you decide to connect to the Internet and visit the Microsoft Home Page at *http://www.microsoft.com* to search for information on downloading new presentation design templates. Print the Web pages.

Project 7 © 🌐

As you continue building the *Cars* presentation you created in the previous chapter, add a Title and Text slide on how to purchase a new car. This slide should summarize the locations to use for finding out as much as you can about your particular car choice. Connect to the Internet to search the Web for current information about the car you plan to buy. Make any formatting decisions with regard to alignment, line spacing, and bullet symbols. Make some of the changes to the slide master. Save *Cars,* and print the presentation as a three-slides-per-page handout.

Project 8 © 🌐

You and your partner continue to work on the *Internet* presentation you created in the last chapter. Add a Title and Text slide at the end of the presentation that highlights one of the topics you chose earlier. Connect to the Internet to search the Web for your research. Make any formatting decisions with regard to alignment, line spacing, and bullet symbols. Make some of the changes to the slide master. Save and print the new slide.

chapter two

Working with Clip Art, Pictures, and WordArt

Chapter Overview

You can enhance the slides in your presentation by adding clips and WordArt and by changing the layout of individual slides. You also can insert a variety of pictures and other art files from Clip Organizer, a floppy or Zip disk, a network drive, or the Internet. WordArt is a feature you can use to create special text effects, such as unusual alignment, stretching, and 3-D. In this chapter, you also learn to change the layout of a slide, so that it best suits your purposes as you develop a presentation.

Case profile

Ms. Hill has sent you to a workshop on creating effective presentations. At that workshop, you learn that adding graphic images to slides in a presentation supports the text or data on the slide. In addition, you learn that images should be added only if they add value to the message; they should not overwhelm the message. You decide to add images and WordArt to your *Teddy Toys* presentation and to change the layout of some slides to present information more effectively.

chapter
three

3.a Adding Clip Art Images to Slides

You can add clip art images to the slides in your presentation to enhance, emphasize, or convey an idea graphically. You can obtain clip art images in the Microsoft Clip Organizer or from a disk, hard drive, network folder, CD-ROM, or the Internet. Methods for adding clip art images from all these sources are presented throughout this chapter.

Images can be categorized as drawn or bitmapped. **Drawn pictures** (also known as **vector drawings**) are created using a sequence of mathematical statements that create lines, curves, rectangles, and other shapes. Windows Metafile images, which end with the .wmf extension, are one example of drawn pictures that can be edited extensively in PowerPoint. Most images in the Microsoft Clip Organizer Gallery are drawn pictures. **Bitmap pictures** (also known as **raster images**) are comprised of a series of small dots. Bitmap pictures can be flipped or rotated, but they cannot be ungrouped to isolate and modify individual parts of the image. Editing of bitmaps must be accomplished by using a paint or graphics editing program. Examples of bitmap pictures are those that end with .bmp, .png, .jpg, or .gif.

notes

Depending on your installation of Microsoft Office, the Microsoft Clip Organizer may display different categories and clip art images than displayed in this text. All images used within this chapter can be found on the Data Disk. If you don't see an image used in this chapter in the Clip Organizer, obtain it from the Data Disk.

Inserting Clip Images from the Microsoft Clip Organizer

The Microsoft Clip Organizer contains a wide variety of pictures, photographs, sounds, and video clips that improve the appearance of your slides. Images in the Clip Organizer are organized by category so they are easy to access. You can find an image by using the Search text: text box in the Insert Clip Art task pane or browsing the Microsoft Clip Organizer. The Clip Organizer also lets you import clips from other sources, as well as search the Web for online clips. Microsoft provides a site on the Internet, Microsoft Design Gallery Live, which provides new clips to review and download to your Clip Organizer.

You can add a clip to a slide that contains a Clip Art placeholder or a Content placeholder, or to any slide. Depending on your settings in the AutoFormat As You Type tab in the AutoCorrect dialog box, inserting an

DESIGN TIP

Although graphic images can increase the effectiveness of a presentation, remember to be selective. Allow the images to enhance, not overtake, your message.

CAUTION TIP

Many Internet sites offer free clip art images for you to use in presentations. Others contain copyrighted images that require you to obtain permission before using.

chapter
three

FIGURE 3-1
Insert Clip Art Task Pane

image in a slide containing text or content placeholders, rather than on a blank slide, results in the layout of that slide automatically changing to accommodate the clip art image. If this happens, the Smart Tag, the Automatic Layout Options button, appears at the bottom right on the inserted image. Click the button to Undo Automatic Layout, Stop Automatic Layout of Inserted Objects, or Control AutoCorrect Options. To add a blank slide and then add a clip image:

Step 1	*Open*	the *Teddy Toys* presentation you modified in Chapter 2, and display the last slide in the presentation
Step 2	*Close*	the Outlining toolbar, if necessary
Step 3	*Display*	the Slide Layout task pane
Step 4	*Click*	the list arrow on the Blank layout in the Content Layouts section of the Slide Layout task pane
Step 5	*Click*	Insert New Slide
Step 6	*Click*	the Insert Clip Art button  on the Drawing toolbar
Step 7	*Click*	Later, if a dialog box opens, asking if you want to organize and catalog all media files

The Insert Clip Art task pane opens, providing you with options for searching for clip art by topic, searching for clip art within folders, searching different media types, accessing the Clip Organizer, Clips Online, and Tips for Finding Clips. Your screen should look similar to Figure 3-1.

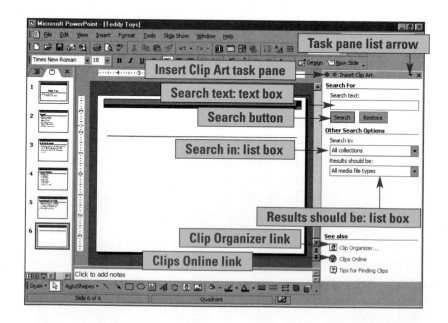

| Step 8 | *Click* | the Clip Organizer link at the bottom of the Insert Clip Art task pane and click <u>L</u>ater, if necessary |

The Microsoft Clip Organizer dialog box opens with a Collection List task pane that includes My Collections, Office Collections, and Web Collections folders. These folders organize your clip images.

| Step 9 | *Click* | the plus sign to the left of the Office Collections folder |
| Step 10 | *Click* | the Sports folder |

The Microsoft Clip Organizer window on your screen should look similar to Figure 3-2.

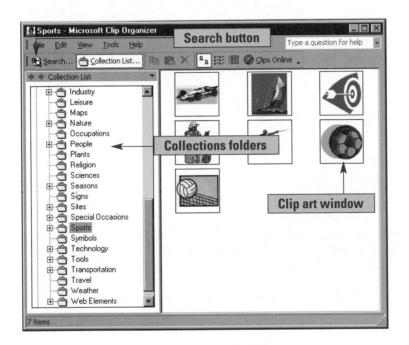

FIGURE 3-2
Microsoft Clip
Organizer Window

Step 11	*Point to*	the soccer ball image (ScreenTip displays: soccer, soccer balls)
Step 12	*Click*	the list arrow on the soccer ball image
Step 13	*Click*	<u>C</u>opy
Step 14	*Click*	the Close button ⊠ on the Clip Organizer window title bar
Step 15	*Click*	<u>Y</u>es to the Would you like these to remain on the clip-board after Clip Organizer shuts down? question
Step 16	*Click*	the Paste button 🗋 on the Standard toolbar

chapter
three

The clip art image is automatically aligned at the center of the slide. If you know what type of clip art you want to find in the Clip Organizer, you can speed the search by defining a specific category and media type. To add images using the Search text: text box in the Insert Clip Art task pane:

Step 1	*Key*	bear in the Search text: text box on the Insert Clip Art task pane
Step 2	*Click*	All media file types in the Results should be: list box, if necessary
Step 3	*Click*	Search
Step 4	*Scroll*	through the Results: list box
Step 5	*Click*	the panda bear identified by the ScreenTip as animals, bears, cartoons, leisure

3.b Moving and Resizing an Image

Images are graphic objects that can be moved, resized, edited, and copied. You can **move** an image by pointing anywhere inside the image's border and sizing handles (the mouse pointer changes to a four-directional arrow) and dragging. In order to work with an image, it must be selected. When an image is selected, eight sizing handles surround it, a rotate handle appears at the top center of the picture, and the Picture toolbar is displayed. To move the bear image:

Step 1	*Click*	the bear image to select it, if necessary
Step 2	*Observe*	that the image displays sizing handles, indicating that it is selected
Step 3	*Point to*	the middle of the image or anywhere inside the image's borders and sizing handles
Step 4	*Drag*	the bear image to the lower-right corner of the slide
Step 5	*Drag*	the soccer ball image to the lower-left corner of the slide

Your screen should look similar to Figure 3-3.

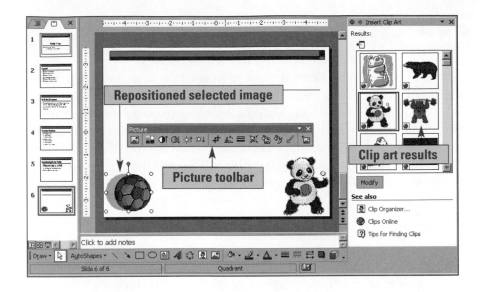

FIGURE 3-3
Clip Art Placement

INTERNET TIP

You can click the Clips Online link in the Insert Clip Art task pane to access more images on the Web. You can insert images from the Internet into a slide by right-clicking the image, clicking Copy, right clicking an area on the PowerPoint slide, and then clicking Paste.

You can **resize** (change the size of) an image by using the Format Picture dialog box or by dragging any sizing handle (pointer becomes a double-headed arrow). If you drag a middle handle, you resize only in one direction, changing the proportions of the image. If you drag a corner handle, you maintain the image's original proportions. You can resize to exact measurements by accessing the Format Picture dialog box, where you specify the width, height, and scale of the image. To resize an image using the Format Picture dialog box:

Step 1	*Right-click*	the bear image
Step 2	*Click*	Format Picture
Step 3	*Click*	the Size tab of the Format Picture dialog box
Step 4	*Key*	1.75 in the Height: text box

TASK PANE TIP

You can insert an image in a specific location on the slide by dragging the image from the Insert Clip Art task pane search results area to the desired location.

You decide to lock the aspect ratio of a picture and set resizing to be relative to the original picture size. The **aspect ratio** is the relationship between the height and the width of an object. When you maintain the aspect ratio while resizing an object, you change the height and width simultaneously; if the height changes, the width changes automatically in proportion to the height.

Step 5	*Verify*	that the Lock aspect ratio and Relative to original picture size check boxes contain check marks
Step 6	*Click*	OK and position the bear in the lower-right corner

**chapter
three**

3.c Editing Clip Art Images

Clip art images can be customized to fit your presentation design, slides, and words. Suppose you want to use a clip art image, but the colors within the image clash with those colors used on the presentation design. Or, suppose you want to use part of the clip art image, not the entire image; or the image directs the eye away from the words you want to reinforce, instead of toward them. To remedy such situations, you can edit or modify the image.

Recoloring an Image

Recoloring an image changes its original colors. When you edit a clip art image, you can recolor selected parts of the image, so you have a great degree of control over its appearance. To add and recolor an image:

Step 1	*Click*	Modify in the Insert Clip Art task pane

The Results: box closes and the Search text: text box and Other Search Options section appear.

Step 2	*Key*	tops in the Search text: text box
Step 3	*Click*	Search
Step 4	*Scroll*	down to the image of a spinning top with a purple background (ScreenTip displays: households, playthings)
Step 5	*Click*	the spinning top image in the Results: list box
Step 6	*Click*	the Recolor Picture button ▨ on the Picture toolbar
Step 7	*Drag*	the Recolor Picture dialog box if it obscures the image you are recoloring
Step 8	*Click*	the turquoise color list arrow in the New: list box
Step 9	*Click*	the darker green color (sixth from left)
Step 10	*Click*	the reddish-brown color list arrow below the turquoise color
Step 11	*Click*	the white color
Step 12	*Click*	the red color list arrow
Step 13	*Click*	the white color
Step 14	*Scroll*	down to the purple color
Step 15	*Change*	the purple color to the lighter green color (fifth from left)

The Recolor Picture dialog box on your screen should look similar to Figure 3-4.

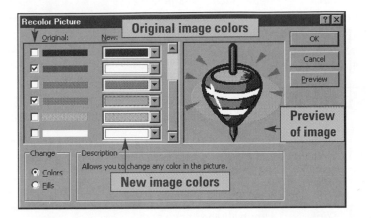

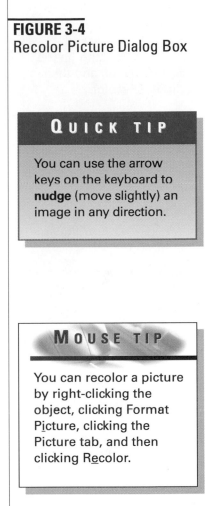

FIGURE 3-4
Recolor Picture Dialog Box

> **Q U I C K   T I P**
>
> You can use the arrow keys on the keyboard to **nudge** (move slightly) an image in any direction.

> **M O U S E   T I P**
>
> You can recolor a picture by right-clicking the object, clicking Format Picture, clicking the Picture tab, and then clicking Recolor.

Step 16	*Change*	the pink color to black
Step 17	*Click*	Preview to view the effect of the intended changes
Step 18	*Remove*	the check mark from the pink color check box in the Original: column to return to the original color
Step 19	*Click*	OK
Step 20	*Resize*	the spinning top image to approximately 1 inch high and 1 inch wide using the Format Picture dialog box
Step 21	*Reposition*	the spinning top image to the upper-right corner of the slide

Cropping an Image

Cropping an image trims or cuts part of an image or object so that you can use only part of it. Cropping an image enables you to trim or cut off a portion of that image along its vertical and/or horizontal edges so that you can see only a portion of it. You can also **outcrop** an image by increasing the size of the padding around the picture, giving it more white space around the image. You decide to add another image to this slide and crop the image so that you only use the portion of the image you need for this slide. To insert and crop an image:

Step 1	*Click*	Modify in the Insert Clip Art task pane
Step 2	*Key*	puzzles in the Search text: text box
Step 3	*Click*	Search

**chapter
three**

Step 4	*Scroll*	to the puzzle pieces image (ScreenTip displays: games, households, jigsaws, puzzles)
Step 5	*Click*	the puzzles image
Step 6	*Click*	the Crop button on the Picture toolbar
Step 7	*Move*	the mouse pointer to the lower-left corner of the puzzle piece image until the mouse pointer shape changes
Step 8	*Drag*	the lower-left corner of the puzzle piece image to the right until only the yellow puzzle piece is displayed in the dotted rectangle
Step 9	*Release*	the mouse button
Step 10	*Crop*	the puzzle piece image to just above and just below the yellow puzzle piece
Step 11	*Click*	outside the image area

The image on your screen should look similar to Figure 3-5.

FIGURE 3-5
Cropped Puzzle Piece Image

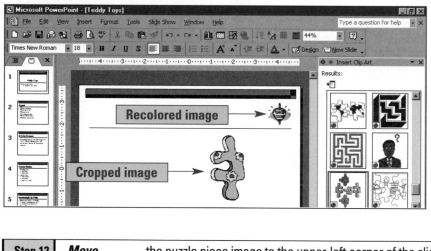

| Step 12 | *Move* | the puzzle piece image to the upper-left corner of the slide |
| Step 13 | *Save* | the *Teddy Toys* presentation |

Flipping and Rotating an Image

When viewing a presentation, the eye goes to the top of the slide first, then works from left to the right and down in a Z pattern. When an image points off the slide, the eye follows the direction of the image off the slide. To avoid having the audience work to bring their eyes back to the rest of the slide once they have been guided off, it is best to flip the image so that it points into the slide. You realize that the bike image points away from the text, so you need to adjust it. You can **flip** an image to change its vertical or horizontal direction. You can also **rotate** an image to change its angle.

To flip and rotate an image:

Step 1	*Select*	the puzzle piece image, if necessary
Step 2	*Click*	the D_raw button Dr_aw ▾ on the Drawing toolbar
Step 3	*Point to*	Rotate or Fli_p
Step 4	*Click*	Flip H_orizontal
Step 5	*Point to*	the rotate handle above the center of the picture
Step 6	*Drag*	the rotate handle to the right slightly
Step 7	*Resize*	the puzzle piece image to approximately 2 inches high and 1 inch wide
Step 8	*Resize*	the soccer ball image to approximately 1.2 inches high and 1.4 inches wide
Step 9	*Save*	the *Teddy Toys* presentation

3.d Inserting Images from Another Source

You can insert images of any graphics format, such as .bmp, .gif, .png, or .jpg, on a slide. The images can be stored on other folders on your computer's hard drive, diskettes, a network server, or the Internet. You can add more than one image at a time if the images are located in the same path location. To add multiple images from another source:

Step 1	*Add*	a new slide with the blank layout at the end of the presentation
Step 2	*Click*	the Insert Picture button 🖼 on the Drawing toolbar
Step 3	*Click*	the Look i_n: list arrow, and switch to the drive or folder where the Data Files are stored
Step 4	*Select*	the *blocks.wmf* graphics file
Step 5	*Press & hold*	the CTRL key
Step 6	*Select*	the *lightbulb.wmf* graphics file
Step 7	*Click*	In_sert
Step 8	*Move*	the light bulb image to the upper-right corner of the slide
Step 9	*Resize*	the light bulb image to approximately 1.5 inches high and 1.3 inches wide

QUICK TIP

You can restore a cropped picture to its original dimensions by clicking the Re_set button on the Picture tab in the Format Picture dialog box.

DESIGN TIP

When possible, rotate or flip an image so that it points or leads the eye to the text message. Images should not face off the page, because they draw attention away from your message.

chapter
three

Step 10	*Rotate*	the light bulb image down and to the right
Step 11	*Resize*	the blocks image to approximately 3.0 inches high and approximately 3.75 inches wide
Step 12	*Reposition*	the blocks image to the center of the slide, if necessary
Step 13	*Save*	the *Teddy Toys* presentation

C 3.e Changing the Layout of Individual Slides

Once you have inserted a slide using a particular layout, you are not tied forever to that layout. You can change the layout of a slide at any time using the Slide Layout task pane. To change the slide layout:

Step 1	*Verify*	that the last slide in the presentation is active
Step 2	*Display*	the Slide Layout task pane, if necessary
Step 3	*Click*	the Title Only layout slide under Text Layouts in the Apply slide layout: section
Step 4	*Key*	We Welcome New Ideas in the title placeholder

Your screen should look similar to Figure 3-6.

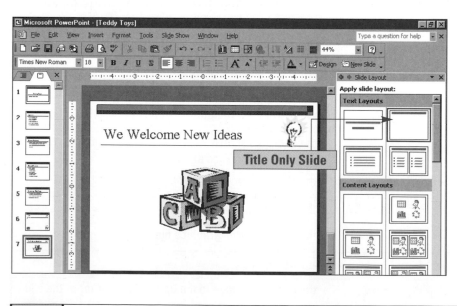

FIGURE 3-6
Slide with New Layout

| Step 5 | *Save* | the *Teddy Toys* presentation |

QUICK TIP

You can resize an image to enlarge it so that you can crop the image to a finer degree. You can then resize it to the exact size you want the image to be on your slide.

MOUSE TIP

You can rotate an image at 90-degree angles by clicking the Rotate Left button on the Picture toolbar.

3.f Adding Animated Clip Images

Animated clips or **motion clips** are clip images, usually in GIF format, that show movement or motion. The Clip Organizer includes motion clips, as does the Design Gallery Live on the Internet. In addition, you can search the Internet for animated clip images and insert the clips on your slide. You only see the animation during the slide show.

To add an animated clip image and position it on a slide:

Step 1	*Display*	the slide which contains the bear, top, puzzle piece and soccer ball
Step 2	*Delete*	the bear image in the lower-right corner of the slide
Step 3	*Click*	the Insert Picture button on the Picture or Drawing toolbar
Step 4	*Switch to*	the drive or folder where the Data Files are stored
Step 5	*Double-click*	the *horse.gif* image file
Step 6	*Resize*	the rocking horse image so that it is approximately 2 inches high and 2.6 inches wide
Step 7	*Reposition*	the rocking horse image to the center of the slide, if necessary
Step 8	*Click*	the Insert Picture button on the Picture or Drawing toolbar
Step 9	*Switch to*	the drive or folder where the Data Files are stored
Step 10	*Double-click*	the *present.gif* image file
Step 11	*Drag*	the present image to the lower-right corner of the slide
Step 12	*Resize*	the present image so that it is approximately 1.75 inches high and 2 inches wide
Step 13	*Flip*	the present image horizontally
Step 14	*Click*	the Slide Show button to view the animation
Step 15	*Save*	the *Teddy Toys* presentation

MENU TIP

You can add an image by clicking the <u>P</u>icture command on the <u>I</u>nsert menu, and then clicking <u>F</u>rom File.

MOUSE TIP

You can add an image stored on disk, hard drive, or network drive, or an image you have scanned and saved, to a PowerPoint slide by clicking the Insert Picture button on the Picture toolbar or the Drawing toolbar.

chapter three

3.g Adding an Image to the Slide Background

Consistency throughout a presentation creates a sense of unity, a feeling among the audience that the slides belong together, and works to reinforce the intended goal of the presentation. To accomplish this, you can add an image to the slide master so that it appears on the background of all the slides for that slide master. As you have learned, a slide master controls the font, size, color, style, and alignment for the titles and main text on your slides. It also determines the location of placeholders, background colors, and objects. If you add an image to the slide master, the image appears on the backgrounds of all slides in a presentation except for the title slides (there is a separate title master for the title slides in a presentation). To add an image to the slide master:

Step 1	**Switch to**	Slide Master view
Step 2	**Click**	the Insert Picture button 🖼 on the Picture or Drawing toolbar
Step 3	**Double-click**	the *teddybear.wmf* image file
Step 4	**Resize**	the teddy bear image until it is 1.5 inches high
Step 5	**Move**	the teddy bear image to the lower-right corner of the slide master
Step 6	**Flip**	the teddy bear image so it faces the center of the slide

Your screen should look similar to Figure 3-7.

FIGURE 3-7
Bear Image on
Slide Master

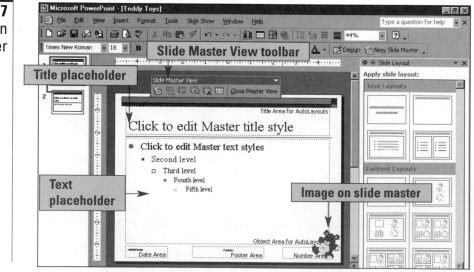

Step 7	Run	the slide show to verify that the teddy bear image does not overlap any object on the slides (ignore the placement of the teddy bear on the slide containing the animated present image)
Step 8	Resize	or move the teddy bear image as needed
Step 9	Switch to	Normal view
Step 10	Save	the *Teddy Toys* presentation

Omitting Background Graphics

A **background graphic** is any image or pattern in a background fill on a slide. PowerPoint provides an option that enables you to omit or hide a background graphic on an individual slide or selected slides. When you hide a background graphic on an individual slide, all graphics from the design template are also hidden. To hide the background graphics on a slide:

Step 1	Display	the slide that contains the animated clip images, if necessary
Step 2	Right-click	a blank area on the slide
Step 3	Click	Background
Step 4	Click	the Omit background graphics from master check box in the Background dialog box
Step 5	Click	Apply

The teddy bear image, the horizontal line, and the bar object across the top are no longer displayed.

| Step 6 | Save | the *Teddy Toys* presentation |

3.h Adding WordArt to a Slide

WordArt enables you to enhance a string of text by using the Insert WordArt button on the Drawing toolbar. WordArt enhances text by shadowing, skewing, rotating, and stretching, as well as applying a predefined shape to the text. To add WordArt to a slide:

| Step 1 | Click | the Insert WordArt button 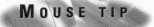 on the Drawing toolbar |

MOUSE TIP

You can hide background graphics by right-clicking the slide, clicking Background, and then clicking the Omit background graphics from master check box to add a check mark.

CAUTION TIP

If you click the Apply to All button in the Background dialog box, the background graphics are hidden on all the slides in the presentation.

chapter
three

> **QUICK TIP**
>
> To add a custom background image to a slide, such as a picture you have saved to disk, click Background on the Format menu, click the Background fill color list arrow, click Fill Effects, click the Picture tab, click Select Picture, switch to the drive or folder that contains the file, select the file, and then click the Insert button.

The WordArt Gallery dialog box opens, with several styles of WordArt from which to choose.

Step 2	***Double-click***	the yellow and orange WordArt style in the third row, first column

The Edit WordArt Text dialog box opens. Here you can key, edit, and format the text you want the WordArt object to display.

Step 3	***Key***	Our Toys Rock, Spin, and Amaze! in the Text: text box in the Edit WordArt Text dialog box

The dialog box on your screen should look similar to Figure 3-8.

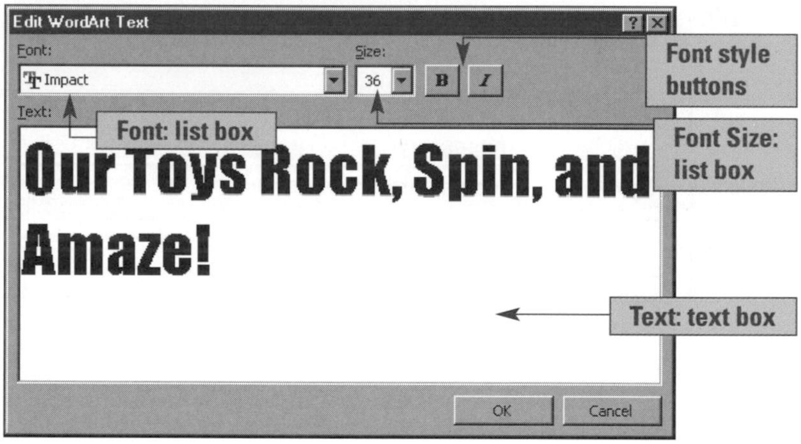

FIGURE 3-8
Edit WordArt Text Dialog Box

Step 4	***Click***	OK
Step 5	***Drag***	the rocking horse image to a position above the WordArt object

> **MENU TIP**
>
> You can insert a WordArt object by pointing to the Picture command on the Insert menu and then clicking WordArt.

Editing a WordArt Object

WordArt objects can be resized and moved just like other objects. You can edit WordArt text using the WordArt toolbar, which opens when a WordArt object is selected, or you can make your changes in the Edit WordArt dialog box. To edit the WordArt object using the Edit WordArt dialog box:

Step 1	***Double-click***	the Our Toys Rock, Spin, and Amaze! WordArt object
Step 2	***Click***	immediately to the left of the letter S in Spin

Step 3	*Press*	the ENTER key
Step 4	*Click*	the Size: list arrow
Step 5	*Click*	48
Step 6	*Click*	the Font: list arrow
Step 7	*Click*	Times New Roman
Step 8	*Click*	the Bold button
Step 9	*Click*	OK
Step 10	*Reposition*	the WordArt object at the center of the slide

<table>
<tr><td colspan="3" align="center">QUICK TIP</td></tr>
<tr><td colspan="3">The Edit WordArt dialog box allows you to key, edit, and format the text in a WordArt object.</td></tr>
</table>

You can format WordArt using the WordArt toolbar, or you can make your changes in the Format WordArt dialog box. To format the WordArt object with different colors using the WordArt toolbar:

Step 1	*Verify*	that the WordArt object is selected and that the WordArt toolbar is displayed
Step 2	*Click*	the Format WordArt button 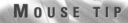 on the WordArt toolbar
Step 3	*Click*	the Colors and Lines tab, if necessary
Step 4	*Click*	the Fill Color: list arrow
Step 5	*Click*	Fill Effects
Step 6	*Click*	the Color 1: list arrow on the Gradient tab
Step 7	*Click*	the brown color (ScreenTip displays: Follow Shadows Scheme Color)
Step 8	*Click*	the From center option button in the Shading Styles box
Step 9	*Click*	the variant style at the right in the Variants box
Step 10	*Click*	OK twice to return to the slide

<table>
<tr><td colspan="3" align="center">MOUSE TIP</td></tr>
<tr><td colspan="3">You can right-click any toolbar and click WordArt to display the WordArt toolbar.

You can access the Edit WordArt Text dialog box by right-clicking the WordArt object and clicking Edit Text, or by clicking the Edit Text button on the WordArt toolbar.

You can change the color of the WordArt object by right-clicking the WordArt object and clicking Format WordArt.</td></tr>
</table>

Changing the shape of a WordArt object adds interest to the artistic text. In addition, you can create different moods simply by changing the shape of the WordArt object. To change the WordArt shape:

Step 1	*Select*	the WordArt object, if necessary
Step 2	*Click*	the WordArt Shape button on the WordArt toolbar
Step 3	*Click*	the Double Wave 2 shape in the third row, last column
Step 4	*Run*	the slide show

chapter
three

Your completed slide should look similar to Figure 3-9.

FIGURE 3-9
Completed Slide with
Edited WordArt

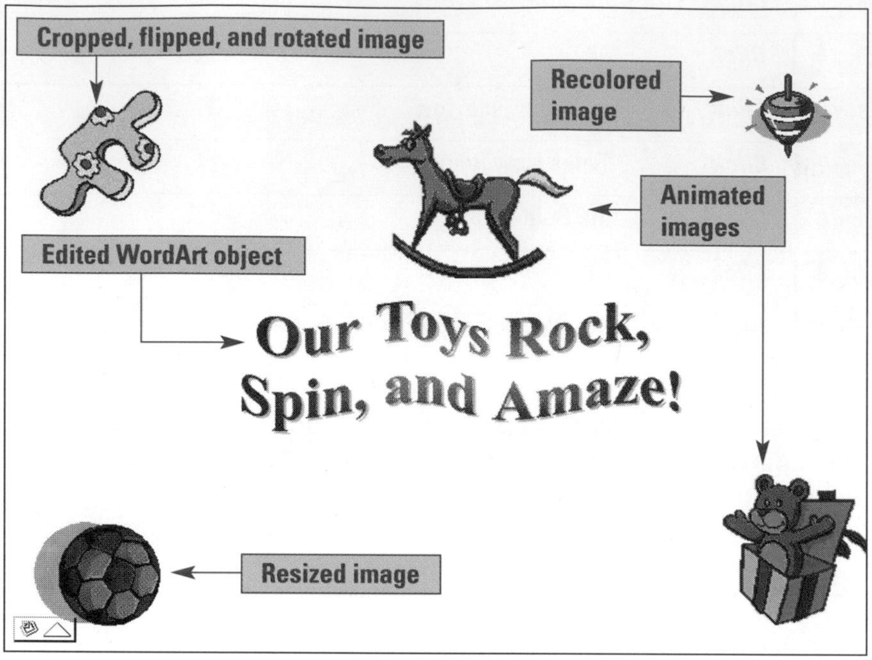

Cropped, flipped, and rotated image

Recolored image

Animated images

Edited WordArt object

Our Toys Rock, Spin, and Amaze!

Resized image

MENU TIP

You can change the color of the selected WordArt object by clicking the WordArt command on the Format menu.

QUICK TIP

If you decide to change the original WordArt design you selected, click the WordArt Gallery button on the WordArt toolbar and select a design from the gallery of 30 WordArt designs.

| Step 5 | *Save* | the *Teddy Toys* presentation and close it |

Summary

- The Microsoft Clip Organizer contains a wide variety of pictures, photographs, sounds, and video clips, organized by category.

- Images are objects that can be moved, resized, deleted, recolored, cropped, and copied.

- Images (with the exception of bitmap images) can be converted into Microsoft Office drawing objects that can be moved, resized, deleted, colored, flipped, rotated, and cropped.

- Limit the number of clip images per slide to eliminate the possibility of the audience being distracted.

- Resizing an image by dragging the corner handles maintains its original proportions.

- Resizing an image by dragging the middle handles distorts the image's original proportions.

- To resize an image to exact specifications, use the Format Picture dialog box.

- Recoloring an image changes the original colors.

- Recoloring of bitmap images is accomplished in a paint or picture editing program, not PowerPoint.

- Cropping an image is done when you want to use only a portion of the image.

- Outcropping an image is used when you want to add padding or white space around the image.

- Flipping an image changes its vertical and/or horizontal direction.

- Images can be added from other folders, clip art packages, and the Internet.

- Slide layouts can be changed at any time.

- Animated clip images show movement or motion in the slide show.

- Images that are placed on the slide master can be hidden on individual slides.

- Clip art images can be added to any slide in a presentation, as well as to the slide master.

- WordArt is used to shape, skew, and change the appearance of a string of text.

chapter three

Commands Review

Action	Menu Bar	Shortcut Menu	Toolbar	Task Pane	Keyboard
Display the Insert Clip Art task pane	Insert, Picture, Clip Art; Insert, Object, Microsoft Media Gallery			Other Task Panes list arrow, and then click Slide Layout	ALT + I, P, C ALT + I, O
Insert an image from the Clip Organizer		Click the list arrow, click Insert; Drag the clip to the slide; Right-drag the clip, click Copy Here		Click the Clip Organizer on the Insert Clip Art task pane	
Insert an image from another source	Insert, Picture, From File			Click the Clips Online link on the Insert Clip Art task pane	ALT + I, P, F
Move a selected image			Drag the middle of the image		
Resize a selected image	Format, Picture, Size; Format, Object, Size	Right-click image, Format Picture, Size; Format, Object, Size	Drag a sizing handle		ALT + O, I ALT + O, O
Delete a selected image					DELETE
Recolor a selected image	Format, Picture, Picture, Recolor	Right-click image, Format Picture, Picture, Recolor; Double-click the image, Picture, Recolor			ALT + O, I, ALT + E
Crop a selected image	Format, Picture, Picture	Right-click image, Format Picture, Picture			ALT + O, I
Rotate an image	Draw button on Drawing toolbar, Rotate or Flip	Drag rotate handle on object			ALT + R, P, L or R
Flip an image	Draw button on Drawing toolbar, Rotate or Flip				ALT + R, P, H or V
Change slide layout		Click the slide layout list arrow, click Apply to Selected Slides or Apply Layout		Click a slide layout in the Apply slide layout: section	
Omit background graphics from slide master	Format, Background, Omit background graphics from master	Right-click slide background, click Background, click Omit background graphics from master check box			ALT + O, K, ALT + G
Insert a WordArt image	Insert, Picture, WordArt				ALT + I, P, W
Edit text of a selected WordArt object	Edit, Text	Right-click WordArt object, Edit Text Double-click the WordArt image	Edit Text...		ALT + E, X ALT + X
Change the WordArt shape					
Format selected WordArt object	Format WordArt	Right-click WordArt object, Format Word Art			ALT + O, O

Concepts Review

Circle the correct answer.

1. **The Microsoft Clip Organizer allows you to:**
   [a] add slides to a presentation.
   [b] add picture, sound, and motion clips to a slide.
   [c] spell check your presentation.
   [d] add WordArt images to a slide.

2. **When an image is selected, it displays:**
   [a] six boxes and a rotate handle.
   [b] eight sizing handles and a rotate handle.
   [c] six middle handles and a rotate handle.
   [d] two corner handles and a rotate handle.

3. **When you want to resize an image from the center and keep it proportioned, press the:**
   [a] SHIFT key.
   [b] CTRL key.
   [c] ALT key.
   [d] SPACEBAR.

4. **After moving a clip art image to a particular location on the slide, you can immediately reverse the action by doing all of the following** *except*:
   [a] clicking the Redo button.
   [b] clicking the Undo button.
   [c] clicking the Undo Move Object command on the Edit menu.
   [d] pressing the CTRL + Z keys.

5. **A good design practice when adding clip art images to your slides is to:**
   [a] add as many clip art images as you desire.
   [b] resize the image so it takes up as much space as your text.
   [c] be sure to place at least one clip art image per slide.
   [d] add clip art sparingly and only if it relates to your topic.

6. **To delete an image, you must first:**
   [a] move the image to a new location.
   [b] resize the image.
   [c] select the image.
   [d] double-click the image.

7. **What term describes dragging a handle of an image?**
   [a] copying
   [b] selecting
   [c] resizing
   [d] moving

8. **What term describes the separation of a clip art image into different parts so that it becomes a Microsoft Office drawing?**
   [a] grouping
   [b] ungrouping
   [c] regrouping
   [d] embedding

9. **What is the term for changing the direction in which a clip art image faces?**
   [a] crop
   [b] flip
   [c] group
   [d] align

10. **You can change the layout of a slide by:**
    [a] right-clicking the slide and then clicking Background.
    [b] clicking Edit, Change Layout.
    [c] clicking the desired layout on the Slide Layout task pane.
    [d] clicking Format and then clicking Slide Design.

chapter three

Circle **T** if the statement is true or **F** if the statement is false.

T   F   1. Clip art and WordArt should be used only to enhance the goal of a presentation.

T   F   2. Images in the Microsoft Clip Organizer are arranged by category so they are easy to access.

T   F   3. The Picture toolbar may appear when you insert an image from the Microsoft Media Gallery.

T   F   4. Selecting the image and dragging it to a new location is the same as moving an image.

T   F   5. To resize an image from the center while maintaining its original proportions, you should press the ALT key when you drag to resize.

T   F   6. Once an image is added to a slide, you cannot remove it.

T   F   7. By design, images should face off the slide, away from the text.

T   F   8. The slide master enables you to create consistency in your presentation by adding images so they appear on all slides in your presentation, except the title slide.

T   F   9. The layout of a slide can never be changed once you have saved it in your presentation.

T   F   10. WordArt contains only five styles to display your text.

Skills Review

Exercise 1

1. Open the *PowerPoint* presentation you modified in the previous chapter, and display a slide that could benefit from clip art images.

2. Access the Microsoft Clip Organizer, and select a category that pertains to the topic of the slide.

3. Add a clip art image to the slide, and then resize and move the image as needed. (When you add the image to the text slide, the layout of the slide may automatically change to a text and clip art layout, and the bullet text readjusts to fit the new text placeholder if the Automatic layout for inserted objects feature is activated.)

4. If necessary, flip the image so it faces the text.

5. Add a blank slide at the end of the presentation for a WordArt object.

6. Use the WordArt style in the fourth row, third column.

7. Add the following text: "PowerPoint Presentations," pressing the ENTER key between the words.

8. Change the WordArt font to Impact and the Font size to 48.

9. Resize the WordArt object to approximately 2.5 inches high and 6.5 inches wide, and position it at the center of the slide.

10. Run the slide show.

11. Save the presentation, print the slides containing images and WordArt only, and then close the presentation.

Exercise 2

1. Open the *Office* presentation you modified in Chapter 2.

2. Use the Search For clips feature to find an image for one of your text slides. Make sure the clip art image enhances and complements the text on the slide. You may want to consider searching for computers, software, or technology.

3. Recolor the clip art image to match the design template, if necessary.

4. Add a blank slide at the end of the presentation for a WordArt object.

5. Use the first WordArt style in the first row, first column. Add the following text: "Office XP Is Here"

6. Change the WordArt font to Times New Roman, Bold, and the font size to 60.

7. Change the shape of the WordArt object to Stop.

8. Change the WordArt fill color to Pale Blue and the WordArt line color to White or Dark Blue. Resize the WordArt object as needed.

9. Browse the Microsoft Clip Organizer, and then add an image from the People, Groups category of the Office Collections to the WordArt slide.

10. Reposition and resize the image as necessary to complement the WordArt image on the slide.

11. Run the slide show.

12. Save the presentation, print only the slides containing images and WordArt, and then close the presentation.

Exercise 3

1. Open the *Design* presentation you modified in Chapter 2.

2. Add a blank slide at the end of the presentation for a WordArt object.

3. Use the WordArt style in the third row, fifth column.

4. Add the following text: "Design and You"

5. Change the WordArt font to Comic Sans MS and the font size to 60, and then resize the WordArt object as needed.

6. Search for "ideas" in the Microsoft Clip Organizer, select the light bulb image (*lightbulb.wmf*), and add it to the slide master.

7. Resize the image and place it in the lower-right corner.

8. Save the presentation, print only the slides containing images and WordArt, and then close the presentation.

Exercise 4

1. Open the *Precision Builders* presentation you modified in Chapter 2.

2. Display the Why Precision Builders? slide, and change the layout to the Title, Text, and Clip Art layout.

3. Double-click the clip art placeholder, and search for an appropriate image that depicts carpentry and complements the presentation design template.

4. Resize, move, rotate, or flip the image as needed.

5. Resize the bullet placeholder to avoid word wrapping of any bullet text.

6. Add a blank slide at the end of the presentation for a WordArt object.

7. Use the WordArt style in the fourth row, first column.

8. Add the following text: "Distinctive Designs"

9. Change the WordArt font to Book Antiqua and the font size to 60.

10. Change the color of the fill to the Parchment texture in Fill Effects.

11. Resize the WordArt object as needed.

12. Save the presentation, print only the slides containing images and WordArt, and then close the presentation.

Exercise 5

1. Open the *Nature Tours* presentation you modified in Chapter 2.

chapter three

2. Using the Clip Organizer or the Design Gallery Live on the Internet, find photographic image of any park, and copy and paste it on one of the slides.

3. Resize, move, rotate, or flip the image as needed.

4. Add a clip art image to the slide master. Resize, move, rotate, or flip the image as needed.

5. Make any adjustments to bullet placeholders to aid readability.

6. Add a blank slide at the end of the presentation for the following WordArt object: "Are You Ready for a Great Tour?"

7. Change the WordArt font, size, and colors to match the design template.

8. Resize the WordArt object as needed.

9. Save the presentation, print only the slides containing images and WordArt, and then close the presentation.

Exercise 6 Ⓒ

1. Open the *A Healthier You* presentation you modified in Chapter 2.

2. Use the Search feature to add an appropriate clip image or images to one of the slides.

3. Resize, move, recolor, crop, rotate, or flip the image as needed.

4. Add a blank slide at the end of the presentation for the following WordArt object: "A Healthy Body is a Happy Body"

5. Change the WordArt font, size, and colors to match the design template.

6. Add the exercise animated GIF image (*exercise.gif*) from the Data Disk to the WordArt slide.

7. Resize the WordArt object as needed.

8. Save the presentation, print only the slides containing images and WordArt, and then close the presentation.

Exercise 7 Ⓒ

1. Open the *Buying A Computer* presentation you modified in Chapter 2.

2. Add a computer clip art image or an appropriate image to a slide of your choice.

3. Add an animated clip image to a different slide of your choice.

4. Resize, move, recolor, crop, rotate, or flip the images as appropriate.

5. Add a blank slide at the end of the presentation for the following WordArt object: "The World at Our Door"

6. Change the WordArt font, size, and colors to match the design template.

7. Resize the WordArt object as needed.

8. Save the presentation, print only the slides containing images and WordArt, and then close the presentation.

Exercise 8 Ⓒ

1. Open the *Leisure Travel* presentation you modified in Chapter 2.

2. Add a blank slide at the end of the presentation for the following WordArt object: "Make the World Your Playground"

3. Change the WordArt font, size, and colors to match the design template. Resize the WordArt object as needed.

4. Add an image related to world travel to the WordArt slide.

5. Omit the background graphics from the master on the WordArt slide.

6. Use the Search for clips feature to find an image relating to world travel, and then add this image to the slide master.

7. Modify and move the images as appropriate.

8. Save the presentation, print only the slides containing images and WordArt, and then close the presentation.

Case Projects

Project 1

You have been asked by an assistant in the Personnel Department to explain how to connect to the Design Gallery Live Web site, where you can preview and download additional clips. Access the Microsoft Design Gallery Live Web site and download a few clips so you can explain the procedure correctly to the other assistant. Create a PowerPoint text slide listing the steps needed to access the Design Gallery Live. Print the slide.

Project 2

You decide to add Microsoft Clip Organizer images to the *Communicate* presentation you modified in Chapter 2. Use the Search for clips feature, and be selective with the clip images. Resize and move the images as needed. Recolor or crop as needed. Add a WordArt slide at the end of the presentation. Run the slide show and save the presentation. Print the slides with WordArt or clip images only.

Project 3

As you look over the *Souner* presentation you modified in the previous chapter, you feel you need to incorporate an image of cooperation between clients and your company to strengthen your message. You decide to add an appropriate clip image to one of the existing slides. The image you portray should be positive and encourage the spirit of teamwork. You also decide to add a new slide at the end of the presentation consisting of a WordArt object. Be as creative as possible. Run the slide show and save the presentation. Print the slides with WordArt or clip images only.

Project 4

You determine that there are several options you can pursue to enhance your independent presentation, *My Presentation,* that you modified in Chapter 2. You can let the software help you find appropriate images by using the Search for clips feature, you can ask coworkers if they have clip art images you can add, you can access the Internet and copy and paste clip images or animated clip images to enhance your slides, or you can create a WordArt object. Decide what option(s) to pursue and make whatever editing changes necessary to give your presentation a professional touch. Save and print the presentation.

Project 5

Because you work for a zoo, the *Zoo* presentation you modified in Chapter 2 should definitely include appropriate clip images on several of the slides. Remember that the audience of this presentation is children. Be selective and remember not to overload the slides with clip images. Make all decisions regarding placement, size, color, and rotation of the images. If possible, change the layout of one of the slides with clip art to a Title, Text, and Clip Art layout. Add an image to the slide master. Save and print the new slides.

Project 6

You are taking a class at the local community college and are assigned to a group that will be conducting a class discussion on multiculturalism in the workplace. Access the PowerPoint home page through the Office on the Web command on the Help menu. Search for clip images that best illustrate the term multicultural. Download one or more clip images, and add the clip images to a PowerPoint slide. Print the slide containing the clip art images.

chapter three

Project 7

You want to dress up the *Cars* presentation you modified in Chapter 2 by adding clip art images to a slide or slides of the presentation. Use the Microsoft Design Gallery Live on the Internet to download clip images. Access different automobile sites on the Web, and copy and paste photographic images to add to your slides. Search the Internet for animated clip images related to cars. Add one or two animated images to the slides. Make all formatting decisions regarding the images. If possible, make changes to the slide master. Add WordArt to a new slide or an existing slide. Save the presentation, and print only the slides with WordArt or clip art images.

Project 8

You and your partner want to use the most recent and high-tech images available for your presentation. Connect to the Internet and search the Web for clip images and animated images to download that relate to the *Internet* presentation you modified in Chapter 2. The two of you also investigate bringing in clip images from other sources such as different clip software and scanned images. Make all formatting decisions regarding the images. If possible, make changes to the slide master. Add WordArt to a new slide or an existing slide. Save the presentation, and print only the slides with WordArt or clip art images.

Using Drawing Tools

Chapter Overview

In this chapter, you learn how to use the drawing tools in PowerPoint to create shapes. You learn to use the AutoShapes tool to create more sophisticated shapes, such as stars, squiggly lines, and arrows. By creating your own art elements on a slide, you can grab the audience's attention, control the focus of the audience on a word or a point, and enhance interest.

LEARNING OBJECTIVES

- ▶ Add AutoShapes to slides
- ▶ Use the Office Clipboard
- ▶ Work with multiple objects
- ▶ Format shapes
- ▶ Add text to shapes
- ▶ Order and group objects

Case profile

Reading through the material you received when you attended the workshop on design, you notice that several example slides include simple graphics, such as stars, rectangles, and arrows. Looking at your *Teddy Toys* presentation, you determine that adding shapes to some slides will help your audience follow the presentation and remember the important points.

chapter
four

4.a Adding AutoShapes to Slides

Shapes are objects you create using the Drawing toolbar. You can add one or more shapes to a slide to add visual interest, direct the flow of information, or help the audience notice and retain important information. The Drawing toolbar contains tools for drawing and modifying shapes to create the greatest visual impact. **AutoShapes** are ready-made shapes—squares, rectangles, hearts, stars, callouts, flowchart symbols, lines, arrows, and so on—that are available in PowerPoint at the click of a button. These shapes are organized into submenus located on the AutoShapes menu. When you click the AutoShapes button, you see a list of commands, such as Lines or Connectors. Pointing to a command displays a submenu of related AutoShapes. These submenus can be dragged onto a slide as separate toolbars.

notes

PowerPoint displays the Drawing toolbar by default. If the Drawing toolbar is not displayed, right-click any toolbar, and then click Drawing on the shortcut menu.

It is a good idea to display the ruler, grid, and guides to assist you in placing and drawing your shapes. The ruler helps you to draw or move an object to a precise location or size. The grid and guides are nonprinting lines that help you draw, align, and move objects with a great degree of control. The **horizontal** and **vertical guides** divide the slide area into four equal parts, providing another visual reference when drawing and positioning shapes and other objects. To add a blank slide and display the ruler, grid, and guides:

Step 1	*Open*	the *Teddy Toys* presentation you modified in Chapter 3 and display the last slide
Step 2	*Add*	a new slide with the Blank layout
Step 3	*Display*	the ruler if necessary
Step 4	*Click*	View
Step 5	*Click*	Grid and Guides
Step 6	*Verify*	that the Snap objects to grid check box contains a check mark
Step 7	*Verify*	that the spacing is 0.083 in the Spacing text box under Grid settings
Step 8	*Click*	the Display grid on screen and Display drawing guides on screen check boxes to add check marks

| Step 9 | *Click* | OK |

Your screen should look similar to Figure 4-1.

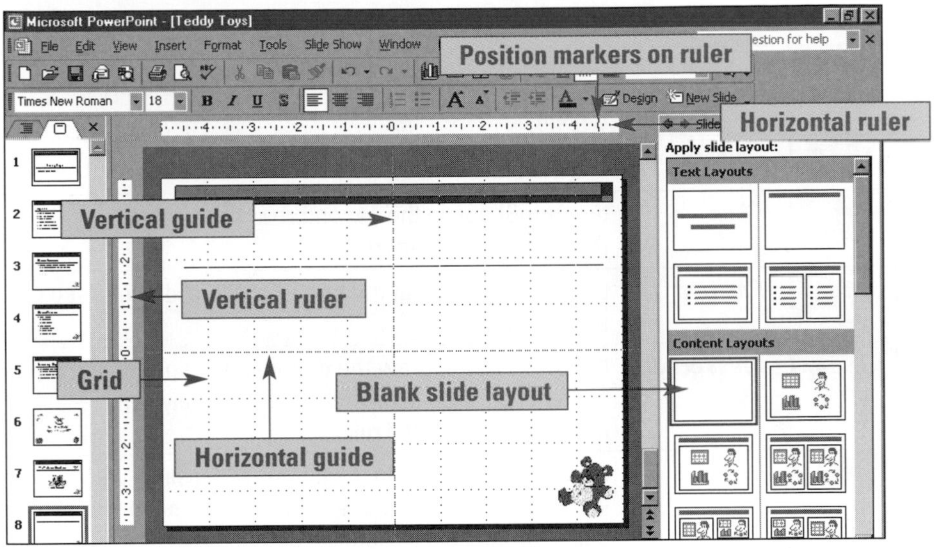

MENU TIP

To change the spacing between gridlines in the grid, click Grid and Guides on the View menu, then key a different number in the Spacing text box. The smaller the number, the closer the gridlines are set, allowing you more control when placing the objects or snapping them to the grid.

FIGURE 4-1
Blank Slide with Ruler, Guides, and Grid

MOUSE TIP

When moving any shape, you can hold down the ALT key to position the shape in a precise location.
    You can show or hide the grid by clicking the Show/Hide Grid button on the Standard toolbar.

Drawing Shapes

To draw shapes, you click a shape button, position the mouse, and then drag to create the desired shape. If you click a shape button and then click the slide (instead of dragging), you insert a default-sized, proportionally shaped object at that location. If you click a shape button, position the mouse, and then drag, you determine the size of the object. To draw shapes using the grid and guides:

DESIGN TIP

The default color of a drawing shape is based on the color scheme of the Presentation design template.

Step 1	*Click*	the AutoShapes button AutoShapes ▼ on the Drawing toolbar
Step 2	*Point to*	Flowchart
Step 3	*Click*	the AutoShape in the first row, first column (ScreenTip displays: Flowchart: Process)
Step 4	*Position*	the mouse pointer at the center of the slide (intersection of guides)
Step 5	*Press & hold*	the CTRL + SHIFT keys
Step 6	*Drag*	to draw the AutoShape from the center of the slide to approximately the 1-inch mark on the horizontal ruler
Step 7	*Drag*	the process shape to the left side of the slide resting on the horizontal guide and to the right of the first vertical grid line (see Figure 4-2 for placement)

chapter four

The process shape is filled with green (the default color based on the design template) and is selected displaying the eight sizing handles and the rotate handle. When an AutoShape is selected, it displays eight sizing handles, a rotate handle, and an adjustment handle that allows you to alter the shape of the AutoShape.

Step 8	**Click**	the AutoShapes button AutoShapes ▾ on the Drawing toolbar
Step 9	**Point to**	Flowchart
Step 10	**Click**	the AutoShape in the second row, third column (Flowchart: Document)
Step 11	**Position**	the mouse pointer at the center of the slide (intersection of guides)
Step 12	**Press & hold**	the SHIFT key to draw the document shape from the center of the slide to the right approximately to the 2-inch mark on the horizontal ruler
Step 13	**Move**	the document shape to the center of the slide, with the lower middle handle of the shape resting on the vertical and horizontal guides (see Figure 4-2 for placement)
Step 14	**Add**	the Flowchart: Preparation shape in the third row, second column to the right side of the slide resting on the horizontal guide
Step 15	**Size**	the preparation shape to approximately 1.3 inches high and 2.3 inches wide using the Format AutoShape dialog box
Step 16	**Save**	the *Teddy Toys* presentation

Your screen should look similar to Figure 4-2.

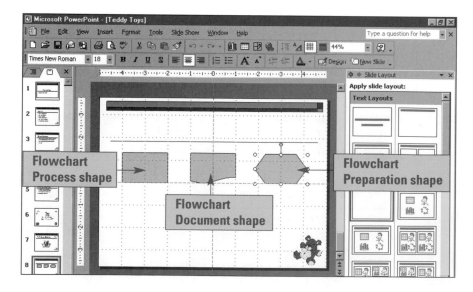

FIGURE 4-2
Slide with Flowchart AutoShapes

4.b Using the Office Clipboard

The Office Clipboard enables you to copy up to 24 items so you can paste them to different locations. You can copy objects to a new place on a slide, to different slides, and between other Office XP applications.

Copying Objects

When you want the same object to appear in more than one place in your presentation, you copy that object. Copying is actually a two-step process that involves copying the object and then pasting it onto the slide. If you copy more than one object without pasting it, the objects are placed on the Office Clipboard so that you can choose which object you want to paste. To copy shapes:

Step 1	*Select*	the process shape (the flowchart shape at the left)
Step 2	*Click*	the Copy button 📋 on the Standard toolbar
Step 3	*Click*	the document shape (the flowchart shape at the center)
Step 4	*Click*	the Copy button 📋 on the Standard toolbar

The Office Clipboard task pane appears with the two copied flowchart shapes. Your task pane should look similar to Figure 4-3.

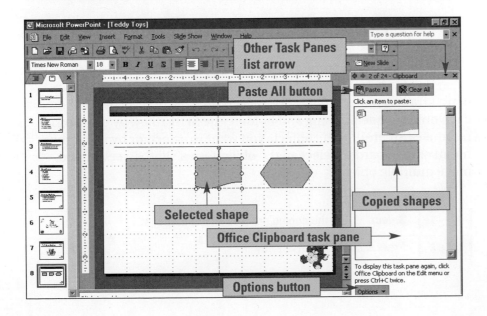

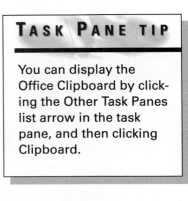

FIGURE 4-3
Office Clipboard Task Pane

chapter four

The Office Clipboard icon may appear in the taskbar if that option has been activated. The icon in the taskbar displays the number of copied items in the Office Clipboard and enables you to access the Office Clipboard in any Office application.

Step 5	*Copy*	the preparation shape

The third shape is automatically placed in the Office Clipboard. When you point to each item on the Office Clipboard task pane, it displays a list arrow with options for pasting or deleting the item.

Pasting Objects

When you **paste** an object, you complete the copy process by placing the copied object in a different location. When a copy of an object is pasted on the same slide as the original object, it is positioned slightly below and to the right of the original object. If the copied object is pasted on a different slide, it is positioned at the location of the original copied object. Once you've pasted an object, you can move it to the desired location. To paste Clipboard objects:

Step 1	*Click*	the process shape on the Office Clipboard (third shape from the top)
Step 2	*Click*	each of the remaining shapes on the Office Clipboard

4.c Working with Multiple Objects

When working with multiple shapes and other objects on a slide, you often need to select more than one object at a time to delete, move, copy, arrange, or align them. You select multiple objects by clicking each object while pressing and holding the SHIFT key, by drawing a marquee box around the objects you want to select, or by using the menu or keyboard to select all the objects on a slide. To select and move multiple objects:

Step 1	*Select*	the copied process shape at the left
Step 2	*Press & hold*	the SHIFT key

Step 3	*Click*	each remaining copied shape on the slide
Step 4	*Drag*	the selected shapes down to a position directly above the last horizontal grid line and to the right of the first vertical grid line

Your screen should look similar to Figure 4-4.

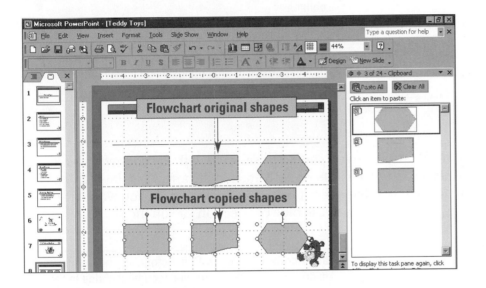

FIGURE 4-4
Slide with Repositioned Flowchart Shapes

Connecting Shapes

PowerPoint includes AutoShapes that let you add connector lines between shapes on your slide. Connector AutoShapes move with the shape to which they are attached. You can change the color, style, shape, and thickness of any Connector AutoShape to achieve a particular visual effect. When you use Connector AutoShapes (straight, elbow, or curved) to connect AutoShapes, **connection sites** (nonprinting colored dots) appear on the shapes to help you connect them successfully. Once you click a Connector AutoShape tool and then point to an existing shape on a slide, the shape displays four blue connection sites. After a successful connection, the connection sites display in red indicating that you have locked or attached the connector line to the shape. If the connection is not successful, the connection sites remain blue and the end of the connector line displays a green circle, indicating that the site is unlocked.

MOUSE TIP

The Paste All button at the top of the Office Clipboard task pane pastes a copy of every object in the clipboard onto your slide or document. The Clear All button removes all objects from the Office Clipboard.

DESIGN TIP

Using Connector AutoShapes instead of simple lines to connect objects provides you with greater flexibility and control.

chapter
four

MOUSE TIP

You can copy and paste by clicking the Copy and Paste buttons on the Standard toolbar, or by right-clicking the object, clicking Copy, then right-clicking, and clicking Paste.

Right-dragging enables you to move or copy an object quickly using the right mouse button; you decide whether to move, copy, or cancel your action after you release the mouse button.

You can hold down the CTRL key and drag the mouse to copy an object. You must release the mouse button before you release the CTRL key.

MENU TIP

You can select all objects on a slide by clicking the Select All command on the Edit menu.

CAUTION TIP

When you drag to copy an object, the object is not placed on the Office Clipboard.

To connect the flowchart shapes:

Step 1	*Click*	the AutoShapes button  on the Drawing toolbar
Step 2	*Point to*	Connectors
Step 3	*Click*	the Straight Arrow Connector in the first row, second column
Step 4	*Point to*	the middle-right handle of the first process shape
Step 5	*Drag*	from the rightmost middle blue connection site on the process shape to the leftmost middle blue connection site on the document shape to the right
Step 6	*Release*	the mouse

The connector arrow should be selected with the connection sites displayed in red. If either or both ends of the arrow display a green circle, then the shape is not connected to the arrow. You would then drag the green circle to the blue connection site on the shape.

Step 7	*Draw*	another Straight Arrow Connector from the rightmost middle connection site of the document shape in the center of the slide to the leftmost middle connection site of the preparation shape at the right
Step 8	*Click*	the Curved Arrow Connector AutoShape in the third row, second column of the Connectors category
Step 9	*Drag*	from the rightmost middle connection site on the preparation shape at the right of the slide to the top middle connection site on the process shape in the lower-left corner of the slide

Two yellow diamonds appear that enable you to reshape the curved line. The shaping diamonds or adjustment handles can be dragged to change the shape of the line.

| Step 10 | *Draw* | another Curved Arrow Connector AutoShape from the bottom middle connection site of the process shape in the lower-left corner of the slide to the bottom-middle connection site of the document shape in bottom center of the slide |
| Step 11 | *Draw* | the Elbow Arrow Connector (second row, second column) AutoShape from the top-middle connection site of the document shape in bottom center of the slide to the rightmost connection site of the preparation shape in the lower-right corner of the slide |

| Step 12 | *Save* | the *Teddy Toys* presentation |

Your screen should look similar to Figure 4-5.

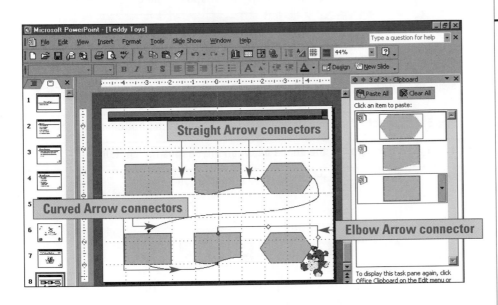

FIGURE 4-5
Shapes with Connector
Lines

> **M O U S E   T I P**
>
> You can select multiple
> objects on a slide by
> drawing a marquee box
> encompassing the
> objects.
>   You can size and scale
> an AutoShape by right-
> clicking the shape, click-
> ing Format AutoShape,
> and then clicking the
> Size tab.

Aligning Objects with Other Objects

Even with the help of the grid and guides, it can be difficult to align two or more objects by dragging them separately. When objects are aligned, it is easier for the audience to follow the directional flow of the slide. You can **align** objects on the same line at the left, right, center, top, bottom, or middle. You also can distribute the shapes so that the space between the shapes is even. To align objects:

Step 1	*Select*	the three flowchart shapes at the center of the slide
Step 2	*Click*	the D<u>r</u>aw button Draw ▾ on the Drawing toolbar
Step 3	*Point to*	<u>A</u>lign or Distribute
Step 4	*Click*	Align <u>M</u>iddle
Step 5	*Select*	the three flowchart shapes at the bottom of the slide
Step 6	*Align*	the three shapes at the middle

> **Q U I C K   T I P**
>
> Selected objects display
> eight handles—four
> middle handles and four
> corner handles—and a
> rotate handle. Lines and
> arrows, however, dis-
> play only two handles,
> one at each end.

Objects can be aligned on a slide, but the spacing between the objects may or may not be even. Depending on the message of the slide, you can distribute the spacing between the objects to appear evenly both horizontally and vertically. To distribute space between objects, you need to have three or more objects. The space is distributed evenly

**chapter
four**

between objects based on the amount of space between the first and last objects. To distribute space evenly between objects:

Step 1	*Select*	the three flowchart shapes at the center of the slide
Step 2	*Click*	the Draw button Draw ▾ on the Drawing toolbar
Step 3	*Point to*	Align or Distribute
Step 4	*Click*	Distribute Horizontally to evenly distribute the space between the three shapes
Step 5	*Select*	the three flowchart shapes at the bottom of the slide
Step 6	*Distribute*	the space between the shapes horizontally
Step 7	*Save*	the *Teddy Toys* presentation

4.d Formatting Shapes

You can format shapes to improve their appearance by changing fill color, line color and style, shadow style, and 3-D effects. You can format shapes individually, or you can format one shape and use the Format Painter to apply those formats to any other shapes with the simple click of a button.

Changing Fill and Line Colors

By default, drawing shapes and basic AutoShapes use colors from the current design template. AutoShapes from the More AutoShapes dialog box, however, do not use the design template colors because they are predesigned shapes with predetermined colors similar to clip art images. You can change the fill color of shapes and AutoShapes to solid colors, gradients, textures, and patterns. You can even fill a shape with a picture. PowerPoint provides 24 preset gradients if you want to use a specific look instead of creating your own gradients. **Gradients** are shaded variations of a color or combination of colors. To change the fill colors of the flowchart shapes:

Step 1	*Select*	the first process shape at the left of the slide
Step 2	*Click*	the Fill Color button list arrow 🪣 ▾ on the Drawing toolbar
Step 3	*Click*	Fill Effects

The Fill Effects dialog box on your screen should look similar to Figure 4-6.

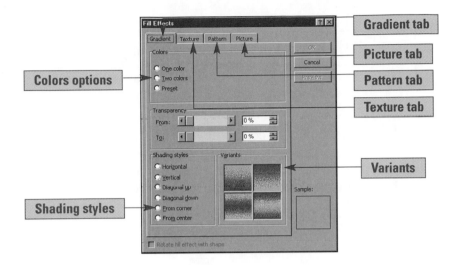

QUICK TIP

When aligning objects, the object you select first is the anchor object. The other objects will be aligned to that first selected object.

FIGURE 4-6
Fill Effects Dialog Box

Step 4	*Click*	the Gradient tab if necessary
Step 5	*Click*	Preset in the Colors box
Step 6	*Click*	the Preset colors: list arrow
Step 7	*Click*	Parchment
Step 8	*Click*	From center in the Shading styles box
Step 9	*Click*	the leftmost Variants example
Step 10	*Click*	OK

MOUSE TIP

You can align objects at the same time you are copying them, by holding down the SHIFT and CTRL keys while you drag; in other words, if you copy to the left or right, the objects are aligned horizontally; if you copy up or down, the objects are aligned vertically.

Applying Special Effects

The Drawing toolbar makes it easy to add shadow and 3-D effects to images. When objects are formatted to be **three-dimensional (3-D)**, they appear raised instead of flat. The shadow effect casts a gray shadow near the shape just as a shadow appears when the sun shines on an object. Textures also add to a three-dimensional look. To add shadow and 3-D effects:

MENU TIP

You can size and scale an AutoShape by clicking the Format AutoShape command on the Format menu, and then clicking the Size tab.

| Step 1 | *Click* | the Shadow Style button  on the Drawing toolbar |
| Step 2 | *Click* | the style in the first row, first column (ScreenTip displays: Shadow Style 1) |

chapter
four

After applying a shadow effect, you decide to change to a 3-D effect. When you apply a 3-D effect to a shape, the shadow effect is automatically removed.

Step 3	*Click*	the 3-D Style button 🔲 on the Drawing toolbar
Step 4	*Click*	the style in the first row, second column (ScreenTip displays: 3-D Style 2)

You can change the thickness, color, and style of lines and arrows, and the style and shape of the arrowheads. You cannot change their fill colors, because these objects are comprised only of length and width of line. To change the thickness, color, and style of the line and arrow:

Step 1	*Select*	the first connector arrow
Step 2	*Click*	the Line Style button ▤ on the Drawing toolbar
Step 3	*Click*	the 4½ pt example
Step 4	*Click*	the Line Color button list arrow 🖉▾ on the Drawing toolbar
Step 5	*Click*	the brown color (ScreenTip displays: Follow Shadows Scheme Color)
Step 6	*Click*	the Arrow Style button ⇄ on the Drawing toolbar
Step 7	*Click*	the double arrow style (ScreenTip displays: Arrow Style 7)
Step 8	*Click*	Undo to return to the single arrow style
Step 9	*Save*	the *Teddy Toys* presentation

Using the Format Painter

The **Format Painter** allows you to copy the formatting attributes of shapes and text boxes without going through the trouble of applying the same set of attributes to each. You can use the Format Painter to "paint" or copy any combination of fill color, line color, line thickness, font, font size, font style, and 3-D effects from one object to another. To use the Format Painter, you select the object whose formatting you want to copy, click or double-click the Format Painter button on the Standard toolbar, and then click the object to which you want to copy the formatting. If you click the Format Painter button one time, you can paint the formatting to one object. If you double-click the Format Painter button, you can paint until you turn off the feature by clicking the Format Painter button again or by clicking the slide background.

To use the Format Painter:

Step 1	*Select*	the first process shape at the left of the slide
Step 2	*Click*	the Format Painter button 🖌 on the Standard toolbar
Step 3	*Click*	the document shape located to the right of the process shape
Step 4	*Verify*	that the document shape is still selected
Step 5	*Double-click*	the Format Painter button 🖌 on the Standard toolbar
Step 6	*Click*	each of the remaining shapes
Step 7	*Click*	the Format Painter button 🖌 to turn it off
Step 8	*Click*	the first connector arrow
Step 9	*Double-click*	the Format Painter button 🖌 on the Standard toolbar
Step 10	*Click*	each of the remaining connector lines to paint their color and thickness
Step 11	*Click*	the Format Painter button 🖌 to turn it off
Step 12	*Save*	the *Teddy Toys* presentation

Changing the Shape of an AutoShape

Once you have added an AutoShape to a slide, you may decide a different shape better fits your needs. You can change the shape of an AutoShape easily. Any formatting you have applied to the shape remains after you have changed the shape. You can change the shape of multiple shapes by selecting each shape and then applying the change to all at one time. To change the shape of selected AutoShapes:

Step 1	*Select*	the process shape in the lower-left corner of the slide and the document shape in the bottom center of the slide
Step 2	*Click*	the Draw button [Draw ▾] on the Drawing toolbar
Step 3	*Point to*	Change AutoShape
Step 4	*Point to*	Flowchart
Step 5	*Click*	the AutoShape in the first row, second column (ScreenTip displays: Change Shape to Flowchart: Alternate Process)

> **QUICK TIP**
>
> To change line options, including line color, thickness, and arrowhead direction, select the object and then use the Line Color button list arrow, Line Style button, and Arrow Style button on the Drawing toolbar to make your changes.

**chapter
four**

Step 6	*Select*	the process shape at the left of the slide and the preparation shape in the lower-right corner of the slide
Step 7	*Change*	the selected shapes to the shape in the third row, first column (ScreenTip displays Change Shape to Flowchart: Terminator)
Step 8	*Resize*	the terminator shapes to 1.3 inches high and 2 inches wide using the Format AutoShape dialog box
Step 9	*Save*	the *Teddy Toys* presentation

C 4.e Adding Text to Shapes

In addition to adding text to placeholders, you can add text to shapes, AutoShapes, and text boxes. You can format text on a shape just as you do text in a text placeholder, to modify its font, size, style, alignment, or color.

Adding Text to AutoShapes

Just as you can add text to a slide and format it, you can add text to a shape or an AutoShape. You do so by selecting the shape and then keying the text. To add text to an AutoShape:

Step 1	*Select*	the first terminator shape at the left of the slide
Step 2	*Key*	Discover What the Consumer Wants
Step 3	*Click*	outside the shape to deselect it

The text is too long for the shape, but you change that later in the chapter. Your screen should look similar to Figure 4-7.

FIGURE 4-7
AutoShape with
Unwrapped Text

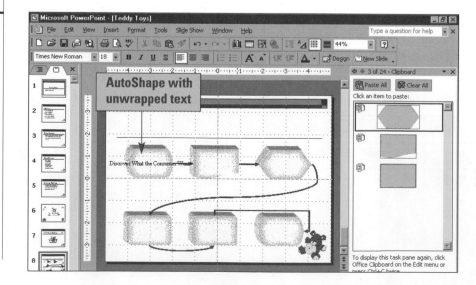

You can format the text within a shape by changing the font, size, and color. If you have text that is too large to fit a shape, you can change the size of the text to fit the AutoShape or you can change the size of the AutoShape to fit the size of the text. You also can word wrap the text within the AutoShape. **Word wrap** is the adjusting of text to fit horizontally in the AutoShape. If the text added to an AutoShape is too long to fit within the horizontal limits of the shape, it automatically wraps to continue to the next line. In addition, you can change the anchor point of the text within the AutoShape. An **anchor point** is the point in the AutoShape to which you want to anchor the text, relative to the selection border. Anchor points are Top, Middle, Bottom, Top Centered, Middle Centered, and Bottom Centered. To format and wrap the text:

MENU TIP

You can format an object by clicking the AutoShape command on the Format menu.

Step 1	*Select*	the first terminator shape (do not click in the text area)
Step 2	*Click*	the Font Color button list arrow [A▾] on the Drawing toolbar
Step 3	*Click*	the brown color (ScreenTip displays: Follow Shadows Scheme Color)
Step 4	*Click*	the Font button list arrow [Comic Sans MS ▾] on the Formatting toolbar
Step 5	*Click*	Comic Sans MS
Step 6	*Double-click*	the first terminator shape
Step 7	*Click*	the Text Box tab in the Format AutoShape dialog box
Step 8	*Verify*	that the Text anchor point: list box displays Middle
Step 9	*Click*	the Word wrap text in AutoShape check box to add a check mark
Step 10	*Click*	OK
Step 11	*Key*	one line of the following text in each box, starting with the second flowchart shape: Produce the Product Price Correctly Promote the Product as New or Improved Create a Page to Link with Home Page Sell the Product

CAUTION TIP

Be careful to select the AutoShape instead of clicking inside the text in the AutoShape. You make changes to the entire text in the AutoShape when the AutoShape is selected. You make changes only to the word when the insertion point is flashing in that word.

You decide to use the Format Painter to format the remaining text boxes so that you don't have to manually change the font, size, color, and word wrap alignment of each.

chapter four

Step 12	*Format*	all the AutoShapes using the Format Painter so that they match the formatting of the first terminator shape at the left of the slide

Your screen should look similar to Figure 4-8.

FIGURE 4-8
Slide with Changed
Shapes and Wrapped Text

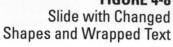

AutoShapes changed
with wrapped text

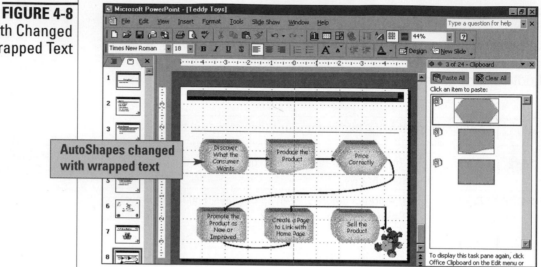

Adding a Text Box

You can add additional text objects to a slide without keying text into a layout placeholder or AutoShape. To add text to a slide without using a placeholder, you use the Text Box button on the Drawing toolbar. You can use the Text Box button to draw a text box by dragging on top of a shape or other object or by dragging on the blank area of a slide. You can move, resize, edit, format, and rotate text boxes to help convey the message of your slide. To add and format a text box:

Step 1	*Click*	the Text Box button ▦ on the Drawing toolbar
Step 2	*Click*	at the vertical guide directly below the first horizontal grid line
Step 3	*Click*	the Center button ▤ on the Formatting toolbar
Step 4	*Key*	Marketing Strategies for Future Toys

Step 5	*Click*	the selection border of the text box to select the entire text box
Step 6	*Click*	the Increase Font Size button  on the Formatting toolbar until the Font Size button list box displays 32
Step 7	*Change*	the color of the font to dark brown
Step 8	*Change*	the font to Comic Sans MS
Step 9	*Run*	the slide show from the beginning of the presentation
Step 10	*Save*	the *Teddy Toys* presentation

4.f Ordering and Grouping Objects

When a slide contains several shapes and other objects, you may find it easier to manipulate all the objects to achieve the look you want. A large image may obscure a smaller one, hiding it completely instead of providing the framing effect you hoped for. Or, you may find you have moved several objects into a perfect combination and then have to repeat your work one object at a time because you want to flip the objects so they face the other way. Ordering and grouping are two techniques that make it easier to work with multiple objects so they complement instead of compete with each other on a slide.

Ordering Objects

On a PowerPoint slide, each object resides on its own invisible plane. The **order**, or layering position, of each object is determined by the order that the objects were drawn or copied onto the slide. If three objects are added to the slide, there are three planes, each succeeding one placed atop the previous one. You can change the order of objects to create a layered effect, such as using a solid box as a background for a graphic. PowerPoint provides options for sending objects to the back, to the front, backward one layer, or forward one layer. To change the order of objects:

Step 1	*Display*	the We Welcome New Ideas slide
Step 2	*Click*	the Rectangle button ▢ on the Drawing toolbar
Step 3	*Draw*	a rectangle over the blocks clip art image

MOUSE TIP

If you want to rotate a text box, drag the green rotate handle of the text box; the text rotates with the text box.

If you want to rotate just the text within a text box, select the text box, right-click the text box, click Format Text B<u>o</u>x, click the Text Box tab on the Format Text Box dialog box, and then click the Rotate text within AutoShape by 90° check box to add a check mark.

CAUTION TIP

When you click to draw a text box, the text box expands to accommodate the text. When you drag to draw the text box instead, the text box has a definite width and the keyed text wraps to fit the text box.

chapter
four

Step 4	*Resize*	the rectangle shape to 4 inches high and 6 inches wide
Step 5	*Click*	the Fill Color button list arrow ▣▾ on the Drawing toolbar
Step 6	*Click*	Fill Effects
Step 7	*Click*	the Two colors option button in the Colors box on the Gradient tab
Step 8	*Click*	the Color 1: list arrow
Step 9	*Click*	the brown color (ScreenTip displays: Follow Shadows Scheme Color)
Step 10	*Click*	the From center option button in the Shading styles box
Step 11	*Click*	the rightmost Variants example
Step 12	*Click*	OK
Step 13	*Click*	the Draw button [Draw ▾] on the Drawing toolbar
Step 14	*Point to*	Order
Step 15	*Click*	Send to Back

The rectangle shape is placed behind the blocks image. It provides an attractive backdrop for the blocks.

Grouping Objects

Grouping is a feature that allows you to take two or more objects and group them so they behave as one. When you group objects, you can than manipulate that one object easier than the separate objects. For example, you can rotate, flip, resize, or scale a grouped object as if it were a single object. To align and group objects and make final positioning changes:

Step 1	*Select*	both the rectangle shape and the blocks image
Step 2	*Align*	both objects at the center and at the middle
Step 3	*Click*	the Draw button [Draw ▾] on the Drawing toolbar
Step 4	*Click*	Group

| Step 5 | *Reposition* | the grouped shape so that it is centered horizontally below the ruled line using the grid and guides for placement |

When you are finished using the drawing tools, you may want to remove the grid and guides. You can hide or display the grid by clicking Show/Hide Grid button on the Standard toolbar. You decide to hide both the grid and guides before saving and closing the presentation. To hide the grid and guides:

Step 1	*Right-click*	the slide background
Step 2	*Click*	Grid and Guides
Step 3	*Click*	the Display grid on screen and the Display drawing guides on screen check boxes to remove the check marks
Step 4	*Click*	OK

Your screen should look similar to Figure 4-9.

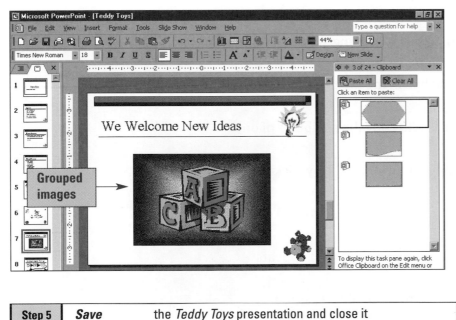

FIGURE 4-9
Completed We Welcome New Ideas Slide

| Step 5 | *Save* | the *Teddy Toys* presentation and close it |

The drawing tools enable you to add visual appeal to any presentation.

chapter
four

Summary

▶ You can draw shapes on a slide to grab the audience's attention, control the focus of the audience, and add visual appeal.

▶ Displaying the ruler, grid, and guides helps to position objects on slides more precisely.

▶ Using the SHIFT key in combination with drawing tools lets you draw straight lines, circles, and squares.

▶ AutoShapes are common shapes that you can draw for use in a slide.

▶ You can change fill and line colors of drawing shapes and line colors of lines and arrows.

▶ Shadow effects and 3-D effects may be added to drawing and AutoShape objects.

▶ The Office Clipboard allows you to copy up to 24 objects and paste them into different programs as well as different slides in PowerPoint.

▶ You can copy and paste multiple objects using the Office Clipboard.

▶ You can select multiple shapes for moving, copying, or deleting by holding down the SHIFT key as you click each one.

▶ Objects can be aligned on the same line at the top, middle, bottom, left, center, or right.

▶ The Format Painter feature allows you to copy the attributes of one object onto another object.

▶ You can add text to any AutoShape or drawing shape by clicking the shape and keying the text.

▶ You can add text to any part of a slide using the Text Box tool on the Drawing toolbar.

▶ You can arrange the order of objects, so that one object appears behind or in front of another.

▶ Grouping allows you to work with two or more objects as if they were one single object, to facilitate flipping, resizing, moving, and formatting.

Commands Review

Action	Menu Bar	Shortcut Menu	Toolbar	Task Pane	Keyboard
Display ruler	View, Ruler				ALT + V, R
Display grid	View, Grid and Guides		▦		ALT + V, I CTRL + G SHIFT + F9
Display guides	View, Grid and Guides		▦		ALT + V, I CTRL + G ALT + F9
Draw a rectangle			▭		
Draw a square			SHIFT + ▭		
Draw an oval			⬭		
Draw a circle			SHIFT + ⬭		
Draw a line			◹		
Draw a straight line			SHIFT + ◹		
Draw an arrow			↘		
Draw a straight arrow			SHIFT + ↘		
Resize shape		Double-click shape, click Size tab, change Height and Width	⬊		
Delete a selected shape					DELETE
Add AutoShapes	Insert, Picture, AutoShapes		AutoShapes ▾		ALT + I, P, A ALT + U
Display the Office Clipboard	Edit, Office Clipboard			▾ on task pane, then click Clipboard	ALT + E, B
Select all objects	Edit, Select All	SHIFT + Click each object, or draw a marquee box around all objects			ALT + E, L CTRL + A
Duplicate objects	Edit, Duplicate Edit, Copy, then Edit, Paste	Right-click object, Copy, then right-click, Paste; Right-drag, then Copy Here; CTRL + drag the left mouse		Click item on Clipboard task pane; or click list arrow on item and click Paste	ALT + E, I ALT + E, C, then ALT + E, P CTRL + D
Change fill and line colors	Format, AutoShape	Right-click object, Format AutoShape; Double-click object			ALT + O, O
Align selected objects	Draw, Align or Distribute				ALT + R, A
Distribute space between selected objects	Draw, Align or Distribute				ALT + R, A
Format Painter			⬧		

chapter four

Action	Menu Bar	Shortcut Menu	Toolbar	Task Pane	Keyboard
Add text to selected drawings and AutoShapes		Right-click shape, click Add Text			Key text in selected object
Change selected AutoShape	Draw, Change AutoShape				ALT D + C
Insert a text box	Insert, Text Box				ALT + I, X
Order selected objects	Draw, Order	Right-click, Order			ALT + R, R
Group selected objects	Draw, Group	Right-click, Grouping, Group			ALT + R, G
Ungroup object	Draw, Ungroup	Right-click, Grouping, Ungroup			ALT + R, U

Concepts Review

Circle the correct answer.

1. Rulers, grids, and guides:
[a] help position objects on the slide.
[b] print on the slide.
[c] cannot be turned on or turned off.
[d] automatically appear when drawing shapes.

2. When you want to draw a perfectly shaped object, use the mouse and the:
[a] SHIFT key.
[b] CTRL key.
[c] ALT key.
[d] SPACEBAR.

3. If you release the mouse button before releasing the SHIFT key when you draw a square, the square will:
[a] be larger.
[b] be smaller.
[c] not be at the center of the slide.
[d] not be a perfect square.

4. The AutoShapes menu provides you with:
[a] clip art that is related to your presentation.
[b] any shape you want to add on a slide.
[c] commonly found shapes.
[d] fancy text to place on your slide.

5. Which option changes the fill color of an object back to the default color?
[a] fill colors
[b] patterns
[c] Automatic fill
[d] template

6. Special effects that can be applied to drawing shapes include all of the following *except*:
[a] 3-D shadows.
[b] rotating.
[c] gradient fills.
[d] copying.

7. When selecting multiple objects to format, you can select all objects at one time by pressing the:
[a] ALT + A keys.
[b] SHIFT + ENTER keys.
[c] CTRL + A keys.
[d] CTRL + SHIFT keys.

8. To place one object in front of another object, use the:
[a] Align and Distribute feature.
[b] Order feature.
[c] Duplicate feature.
[d] Rotate or Flip feature.

9. Which of the following is true of using the Text Box tool?

[a] You can create text anywhere on the slide.

[b] You can move the text box after you have keyed the text.

[c] You can format the text size and style easily.

[d] You can only have one text box on a slide.

10. To add text to a slide without using the standard placeholders, use the:

[a] AutoShapes tool.

[b] Drawing tool.

[c] Line tool.

[d] Text Box tool.

Circle **T** if the statement is true or **F** if the statement is false.

T   F   1. Grids and guides are nonprinting lines to help you place and position objects on a slide.

T   F   2. After drawing a perfect shape, you must release the mouse after releasing any other keys.

T   F   3. PowerPoint limits you to six colors for fill and line color changes.

T   F   4. Shadows and 3-D effects can be added to enhance the AutoShape object.

T   F   5. You can draw a marquee box around multiple objects to select them all at once.

T   F   6. You can duplicate an object by dragging the object to a new location on the slide.

T   F   7. You can copy objects by dragging them while holding down the CTRL key.

T   F   8. The Text Box tool enables you to type text anywhere on the slide area.

T   F   9. Gradients require the selection of two or more colors.

T   F   10. Grouping allows you to place certain shapes in categories that are easily accessed.

Skills Review

Exercise 1   C

1. Open the *PowerPoint* presentation you modified in Chapter 3, and display the Slide Master view.

2. Add the 16-Point Star from the Stars and Banners AutoShapes category.

3. Resize the star AutoShape so it is approximately 0.5 inch high by 0.5 inch wide, and move it to the lower-right corner of the slide master.

4. Change the AutoShape fill to gradient fill using the gray color (Follow Accent and Followed Hyperlink Scheme Color) for the first color and the beige color (Follow Background Scheme Color) for the second color.

5. Use the From center shading style and the variant on the right.

6. Add the 3-D Style 5 to the AutoShape, and reposition the star, if necessary.

7. Add a blank slide at the end of the presentation.

8. Add the Bevel Shape from the Basic Shapes AutoShapes category (fourth row, third column). Draw or resize the bevel shape so that it is approximately 3.8 inches high by 6 inches wide.

9. Center the shape on the slide.

10. Key "PowerPoint will help sell your products and ideas" in the bevel shape. Change the font to Times New Roman, 44 point, bold, and italic.

chapter four

11. Format the bevel shape so that the text wraps within the shape.

12. Save the presentation, print only the slides with changes, and then close the presentation.

Exercise 2   [C]

1. Open the *Office* presentation you modified in Chapter 3, and add the Down Ribbon (third row, second column) from the Stars and Banners AutoShapes category to Slide 1.

2. Resize the Down Ribbon to approximately 1 inch high by 6 inches wide.

3. Add the following text to the AutoShape: "Software for the Future." (*Hint:* Press the ENTER key after the word "for" so the text wraps to the next line.) Change the fill color of the ribbon shape to match the color scheme of the slide, and change the font, font color, and font size as appropriate.

4. Select all three objects on the slide, and align them at their centers.

5. Add a blank slide at the end of the presentation.

6. Add two arrows from the Block Arrows AutoShapes category: a Curved Right Arrow, a Curved Left Arrow—each arrow should be 4 inches high by 1.5 inches wide—and a Curved Up Arrow, and a Curved Down Arrow—each arrow should be 1.5 inches high by 4 inches wide. Change the fill color of one of the arrows using a gradient or a texture fill effect. Then use the Format Painter to apply this fill coloring to the remaining three arrows.

7. Flip and position the arrows around the center section of the slide.

8. Add a text box with the following text: "All Roads Lead to Office XP"; use word wrap in the text box, and resize the text box until the text displays on three lines. Change the text size to 44 point, change the text color and font, and position the text box in the center of the slide.

9. Key "Excel" in the Curved Right Arrow, key "Word" in the Curved Left Arrow, key "PowerPoint" in the Curved Down Arrow, and key "Access" in the Curved Up Arrow.

10. Save the presentation, print only the slides with changes, and then close the presentation.

Exercise 3   [C]

1. Open the *Design* presentation you modified in Chapter 3, and add the Up Ribbon AutoShape from the Stars and Banners AutoShapes to Slide 1.

2. Align the ribbon shape on top of your name. Send the ribbon shape to the back so your name appears on top of the shape. Resize, move, and recolor the shape and text box as needed.

3. Add the 24-Point Star AutoShape from the Stars and Banners AutoShapes category to the slide with the WordArt object or any slide. Resize the star shape to approximately 5 inches high by 5.5 inches wide. Change the fill color to black (ScreenTip displays: Follow Accent Scheme Color).

4. Change the star shape to a 3-D effect. Drag the star shape and position it over the word "Design" of the WordArt object or any text object. Then send the star shape to the back. (*Hint:* Change the text color if you cannot read the text after the star shape is sent behind the text.)

5. Select and group the star shape with the WordArt object or the text object.

6. Add a blank slide at the end of the presentation. Omit the background graphics from this slide only.

7. Draw an oval approximately 2.5 inches high by 3.5 inches wide. Then key "Ovals and Circles Give a Feeling of Indecision" in the oval shape.

8. Format the shape to wrap the text.

9. Add the 3-D Style 2 to the oval. Change the fill color to black (ScreenTip displays: Follow Accent Scheme Color), and change the font of the text to Tahoma, 24 point, bold.

10. Draw a rectangle approximately 2.5 inches high by 3 inches wide, and key "Rectangles and Squares Relate to Rigidity" in this shape.

11. Add the Isosceles Triangle shape from the Basic Shapes AutoShapes category, resize it to approximately 4 inches high by 4 inches wide, and key "Triangles Allow All Ideas to be Considered" in it.

12. Use the Format Painter to copy the attributes of the oval shape to both the rectangle and the triangle shapes.

13. Position all three shapes attractively on the slide.

14. Save the presentation, print only the slides with changes, and close it.

Exercise 4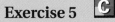

1. Open the *Precision Builders* presentation you modified in Chapter 3, and add the 5-Point Star from the Stars and Banners AutoShapes category to the slide with the WordArt object.

2. Resize the star shape to approximately 0.75-inch high by 0.75-inch wide.

3. Change the fill color of the star shape to the Parchment Texture in the Fill Effects dialog box.

4. Add a shadow effect to the star, and then recolor the shadow for greater visibility on the slide. (*Hint:* Use the Shadow Color button on the Shadow Settings toolbar.)

5. Position the star shape so that it is in the upper-left corner of the slide.

6. Make six copies of the star, and place them on the slide as you desire.

7. Add a blank slide at the end of the presentation, create a text box, and key the following: "Decisions Before Building a Home" in the text box.

8. Change the font to 36 point, and center the text within the text box.

9. Add the Flowchart Decision shape from the Flowchart AutoShapes.

10. Resize the shape to approximately 1.75 inches high and 3 inches wide, and add a shadow effect.

11. Change the font to Tahoma, 20 point, and word wrap the text.

12. Make three more copies of the decision shape.

13. Key the following text in the respective AutoShapes: "Location?"; "Split-level or Ranch?"; "Number of Bedrooms?"; and "Number of Bathrooms?"

14. Reposition, align, and distribute the space between the AutoShapes attractively on the page.

15. Save the presentation, print the slide with changes only, and then close the presentation.

Exercise 5

1. Open the *Nature Tours* presentation you modified in Chapter 3, and add a Title Only slide at the end of the presentation. The title should read "Special Tours."

2. Using the Basic Shapes AutoShapes category, add the Sun and the Moon shapes to the Title Only slide.

3. Using the Text Box tool, create two separate text boxes. Key "For the Early Risers" in one box and "For the Night Owls" in the other.

4. Rotate the text boxes and format the text in regard to font style, size, and color.

5. Format the shapes in regard to color, size, and placement on the slide.

6. Align the Sun and Moon images and their appropriate text boxes.

chapter four

7. Group the Sun and its appropriate text box. Repeat for the Moon and its text box.

8. Add an AutoShape from the More AutoShapes dialog box to any slide. Resize, recolor, and/or move the AutoShape.

9. Save the presentation, print only the slides with the changes, and then close the presentation.

Exercise 6   C

1. Open the *A Healthier You* presentation you modified in Chapter 3, and add the Heart AutoShape to the slide master.

2. Resize the Heart AutoShape, add a gradient fill effect to change the color of the heart, and use a 3-D effect.

3. Position the heart attractively on the slide master. If necessary, move the text placeholders on the slide master if the text overlaps with the heart shape.

4. Add a blank slide at the end of the presentation. Add an AutoShape of your choice, and key "Reduce Your Stress" in the AutoShape.

5. Add at least four copies of another AutoShape to this slide, and key "Relax" in each AutoShape.

6. Format the color and size of the AutoShapes. Use 3-D styles or shadows, if desired. Use the Format Painter.

7. Position the shapes attractively on the slide. Format the font, font size, and font color of the text.

8. Save the presentation, print only the slides with changes, and then close the presentation.

Exercise 7   C

1. Open the *Buying A Computer* presentation you modified in Chapter 3, and add a Title Only slide at the end of the presentation.

2. Key the title "Places to Buy a Computer" on the slide.

3. Add various computer and other AutoShapes to this slide indicating at least four types of places to purchase your computer (for example, retail store, Internet, computer catalog, computer outlet). Format the AutoShapes with regard to size, color, and 3-D effect.

4. Key each different place in an AutoShape. (*Hint:* Word wrap the text, if necessary.)

5. Use the Straight Arrow Connector from the Connectors AutoShapes category to connect the AutoShapes in the order that you would prefer to begin shopping for your computer. Change the arrow thickness and color, if appropriate.

6. Save the presentation, print only the slides with changes, and then close the presentation.

Exercise 8   C

1. Open the *Leisure Travel* presentation you modified in Chapter 3, and add a Title Only slide at the end of the presentation. The title should read "Your Season – Your Choice."

2. Add an appropriate AutoShape to the center of the slide. Change the color of the shape.

3. Key "Anywhere – Anytime" in the shape. Wrap the text and format the text as desired.

4. Add an appropriate Cloud AutoShape, and then make three copies of the cloud shape.

5. Key the name of one season (Summer, Fall, Winter, and Spring) into each of the cloud shapes.

6. Add appropriate fills to each of the cloud shapes to depict that season.

7. Format the font within the clouds as desired.

8. Save the presentation, print only the slides with changes, and then close the presentation.

Case Projects

Project 1

You are not quite sure you understand the difference between grouping and regrouping objects. You decide to access the online Help feature to determine the difference. Click Show All in the Help window, and then print the "Group, ungroup, or regroup objects" Help topic.

Project 2 C

Looking at the *Communicate* presentation, you decide that in addition to using clip images on some of the slides, you also could use AutoShapes that resemble the cartoon balloons or a phone or a sound file. Open the *Communicate* presentation you modified in Chapter 3, and add a blank slide using AutoShapes and text to encourage courteous telephone answering. Add AutoShapes to any slide where you feel the shape enhances the slide message. Change colors and size to fit the presentation. Save the presentation, and print only the slides with the AutoShapes.

Project 3 C

Open the *Souner* presentation you modified in Chapter 3, and view the presentation, looking for places where you may want to add an AutoShape. When finished, add AutoShapes to a slide or slides to help deliver the theme of the training organization. Add a blank slide at the end of the presentation incorporating AutoShape objects, lines or arrows, or text boxes. Make color, size, and font enhancements. If possible, duplicate an AutoShape object to add interest to your slide. Align shapes and order shapes as needed. Add 3-D or shadows to the shapes to enhance them. View the slide show. Save the presentation and print only the slides with the AutoShapes.

Project 4 C

You decide to view your *My Presentation* presentation to see where you can enhance it by adding AutoShapes. You want to add a text box inside an AutoShape to describe your company's service or product. Open the *My Presentation* presentation you modified in Chapter 3, and add a new blank slide or enhance an existing slide or slides. Be careful not to let the AutoShape become the dominant part of your presentation. If appropriate, consider adding an AutoShape or text box to the slide master. Rotate text boxes and shapes as needed to attract attention to that section of the slide. Save the presentation, and print only the slides with AutoShapes.

Project 5 C

You try to think of creative ways to show the paths to certain areas in the zoo. You decide that using the flowchart symbols and connecting lines would be a great way to help children find the zoo exhibits. Open the *Zoo* presentation you modified in Chapter 3, and add the appropriate AutoShapes to accomplish the task. Add 3-D and various fill effects to the AutoShapes to help enhance their interest to the children. Change the color and thickness of the arrows. Use the guides to place the shapes. Save the presentation, and print only the slide or slides with AutoShapes.

Project 6 C 🌐

You want to use clip art, WordArt, and AutoShapes to enhance slides, guide the eye through a slide, and bring attention to a concept on a slide. You also want to learn more about design tips that you can apply to your presentations. Connect to the Internet and search the Web for design tips. Be sure to check out the fonts available for specific moods or tones and additional clip art or images that can be downloaded for future use. Create a presentation consisting of a title slide, a text slide with several design tips, a slide illustrating several new fonts, and a slide with clip art or images accessed via the Internet. Include drawing shapes or AutoShapes in your presentation. Print the presentation.

chapter four

Project 7 C

You decide to incorporate some drawing shapes in the *Cars* presentation. You want to add shapes to display the different types of places that students can find information about new and used cars. Open the *Cars* presentation you modified in Chapter 3, and add text to some of the AutoShapes, as well as individual text boxes. To create interest on some of your existing slides, add shapes and send them behind some of the text already in your presentation. Resize, color, and align shapes as desired on each slide. If possible, add a shape to the slide master. Save the presentation, and print only the slides with the AutoShapes.

Project 8 C

In your *Internet* presentation, you and your partner discuss how to handle the lecture on search engines. Connect to the Internet to search the Web for information about the various search engines. Open the *Internet* presentation you modified in Chapter 3. Add AutoShapes to show why you would or should use a particular search engine on the Internet. You may need to create a new slide for each search engine you research. Format your AutoShapes and drawing shapes to fit the design and color scheme of your *Internet* presentation. Save the presentation, and print only the slides with the AutoShapes.

Working with Tables

Chapter Overview

When you need to present quantitative or relational information in a presentation, you may want to use a table. Tables display data in tabular format. In this chapter, you learn how to add, edit, and position a table on a slide. You also learn to format a table to make important information stand out.

LEARNING OBJECTIVES

► Create a table on a slide
► Add and delete rows and columns
► Format a table

Case profile

To alert employees to a host of upcoming Teddy Toys products, Ms. Hill asks you to include a slide containing several pieces of information. She wants the slide to display the names of new products in development, their team leaders, and the expected date they will be on the market. Because Teddy Toys is proud of their products and production teams, you want to display that information in a format that is compelling and easy to comprehend.

chapter
five

5.a Creating a Table on a Slide

When creating a presentation it is important to anticipate your audience's needs and convey information so that they grasp it quickly and easily. Organizing information into a table enables them to see at a glance the information being conveyed.

The easiest way to create a table is to add a table slide to the presentation. A table slide contains a table placeholder that you complete by specifying the size of the table and then entering the information. You can insert an existing Word table or an Excel worksheet onto a PowerPoint slide. If you insert a table created in another software program, you must use that program to make editing and formatting changes to the table. To add a table slide at the end of the presentation:

Step 1	*Open*	the *Teddy Toys* presentation you modified in Chapter 4 and display the last slide
Step 2	*Click*	the <u>N</u>ew Slide button [New Slide] on the Formatting toolbar
Step 3	*Click*	the Title and Table layout in the Other Layouts area of the Slide Layout task pane

Your screen should look similar to Figure 5-1.

FIGURE 5-1
Slide with Table Placeholder

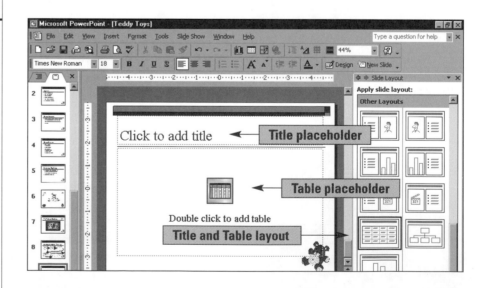

At the top of the new slide is a title placeholder, and at the center is a table placeholder. To add a title and insert the table:

Step 1	*Key*	New Product Production in the "Click to add title" placeholder

Step 2	**Double-click** the table placeholder

The Insert Table dialog box opens. Here you specify how many rows and columns you want in your table. You can key the desired numbers, or you can click the spin arrows until the boxes display the desired numbers.

Step 3	**Key**	3 in the Number of <u>c</u>olumns: text box
Step 4	**Key**	4 in the Number of <u>r</u>ows: text box
Step 5	**Click**	OK

A table appears on your slide with three columns and four rows, forming twelve cells, as shown in Figure 5-2. The Tables and Borders toolbar may appear and obscure the table. If necessary, drag the toolbar out of the way.

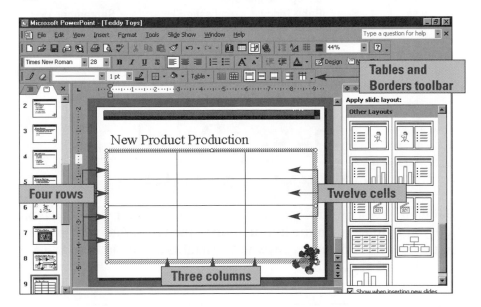

A **cell** is the intersection of a column and a row. Lines, called **borders**, separate the columns and rows. Above and to the left of the table, the ruler is displayed to help work in the table. Unless the data in your table is self-explanatory, you should begin a table by keying column headings in the first row. **Column headings** identify the contents of each column. PowerPoint automatically capitalizes the first word in a new cell. You can turn off automatic capitalization by clicking <u>A</u>utoCorrect Options on the <u>T</u>ools menu, and then removing the check mark in the Capitalize first letter of table <u>c</u>ells check box.

The remaining rows contain information related to the column headings. To enter column headings:

Step 1	**Click**	in the first cell, if necessary

TASK PANE TIP

You can create a table by clicking any Content Layout or Text and Content Layout in the Slide Layout task pane and then clicking the Table icon on the placeholder.

FIGURE 5-2
Created Table

MOUSE TIP

The Tables and Borders toolbar displays when a table is selected. Or, you can right-click any toolbar, and then click Tables and Borders.

QUICK TIP

The maximum number of rows and columns you can specify in the Insert Table dialog box is 25. You add additional rows when working in the table by pressing the TAB key at the end of the last row.

chapter
five

Step 2	*Key*	New Product
Step 3	*Press*	the TAB key
Step 4	*Key*	Team Leader
Step 5	*Press*	the TAB key
Step 6	*Key*	Target Date
Step 7	*Press*	the TAB key

The headings are complete. By default, they are aligned at the left and at the top of the cells. To enter table data:

Step 1	*Key*	the following, pressing the TAB key after each entry except the last entry:		
		Baby Teddy	Leslie Skylar	September 15
		Teddy Wagon	Juan Ortiz	October 31
		Rocking Horse	Ran Un	December 1
Step 2	*Save*	the *Teddy Toys* presentation		

5.b Adding and Deleting Rows and Columns

Sometimes when you reach the end of a table, or after viewing a table slide, you want to add more information to the table. You can insert additional rows or columns anywhere in a table at any time. To add a row at the end of the table:

Step 1	*Move*	the insertion point to the last cell of the existing table, if necessary
Step 2	*Press*	the TAB key

A new row is created. The table is now too long for the slide; you fix this later in the chapter.

Step 3	*Key*	the following, pressing the TAB key after each entry, except the last entry:		
		Toddler Bike	Sara Jackson	May 5

The new row and text have been added to the existing table. You also can add or delete rows and columns anywhere within a table, not just at an outer edge. First you select the row or column below or to the right of where you want to insert the new item. When you make the insertion, the item is inserted above or to the left of the row or column you selected. To add a column to a table:

Step 1	***Click***	outside the table object
Step 2	***Move***	the mouse pointer slightly above the Team Leader column until you see a solid black down arrow

Your screen should look similar to Figure 5-3.

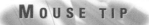

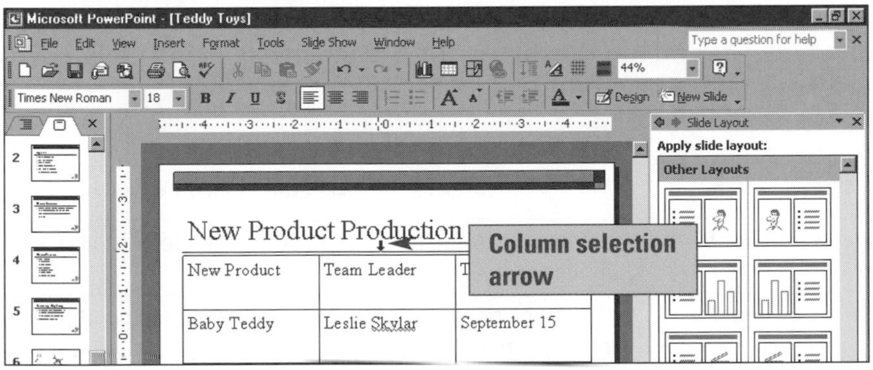

FIGURE 5-3
Table with Column Selection Arrow

Step 3	***Right-click***	the top of the column to select the Team Leader column
Step 4	***Click***	Insert Columns

A new column is inserted to the left of the column you selected.

You can delete rows and columns from a table when you no longer need the information. To delete a row or column, you must first select it. To delete a column:

Step 1	***Right-click***	the selected column
Step 2	***Click***	Delete Columns
Step 3	***Save***	the *Teddy Toys* presentation

MOUSE TIP

If the rulers do not appear above and to the left of the slide, you can right-click any area of the slide that does not contain a placeholder or object and then click Ruler.

MENU TIP

If the rulers do not appear above and to the left of the slide, you can click the Ruler command on the View menu.

C   5.c Formatting a Table

After you complete a table, you can format it to change its appearance. Perhaps you want to make it larger or smaller. Perhaps the column headings do not stand out distinctly enough for quick reference and should be bolded, italicized, or shaded, or the column widths are too narrow or too wide for your purposes. Or, you may not want to see borders surrounding all cells, so you need to remove some or all of them. And, just like other text in PowerPoint, you can change font, font size, font style, and alignment to make the most of your information.

Resizing a Table

A table created in PowerPoint is an object. As such, it can be resized and moved using the same methods you use on other objects, such as clip art images and AutoShapes. When selected, a table displays eight sizing handles. To resize the table:

Step 1	Click	the table to display the sizing handles, if necessary
Step 2	Scroll	down to view the lower-right sizing handle of the table, if necessary
Step 3	Point to	the lower-right sizing handle until the mouse pointer changes to a double-tipped black arrow
Step 4	Drag	the sizing handle up and to the left until the vertical ruler guide reaches the 2.5-inch mark and the horizontal ruler guide reaches the 3-inch mark

Do not be concerned if the text wraps unattractively within the cell. You correct this later in the chapter.

Moving a Table

Often, you need to reposition a table on a slide to improve its appearance. Because the table is an object, you move the table object as you would any object—by selecting and dragging it to the desired location. To move the table:

Step 1	Select	the table object, if necessary
Step 2	Position	the mouse on the selection border on the left, right, top, or bottom of the table
Step 3	Verify	that the mouse pointer changes to a four-directional arrow

| Step 4 | Drag | to the right approximately 0.25 inch and down approximately 0.25 inch, being sure not to cover the teddy bear graphic |

The table is positioned more attractively on the slide. Your screen should look similar to Figure 5-4.

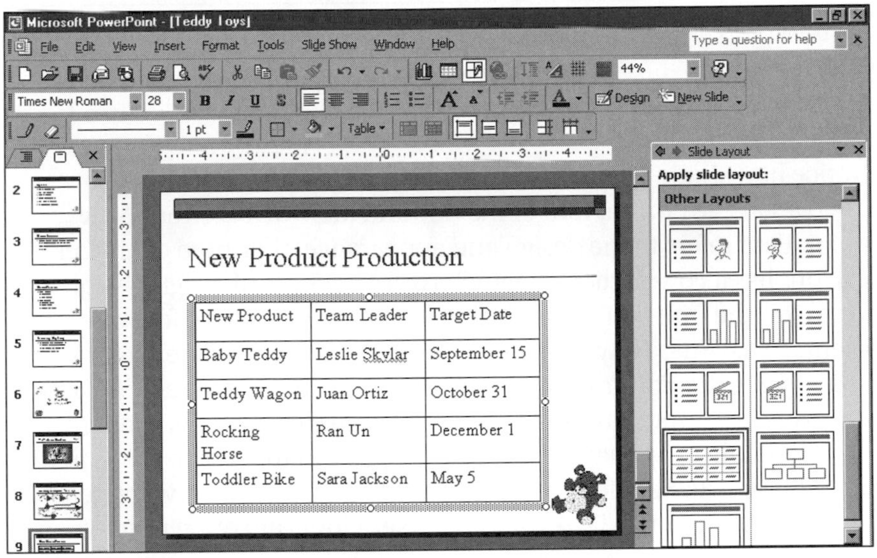

FIGURE 5-4
Resized and Moved Table

MOUSE TIP

To insert a row between two existing rows in a table, position the insertion point in the row below where you want the new row to appear, right-click the row, and then click Insert Rows.

| Step 5 | Save | the *Teddy Toys* presentation |

Changing Text and Cell Formatting

You can change formatting in any or all cells in a table to help guide the viewer's eye to important information. Because tables display information in a relational manner—the information in rows relates to the information in the column headings—you want to make sure the audience can quickly identify the column headings, especially in tables containing several rows. You can make text stand out by italicizing, bolding, shading, increasing font size, and/or changing text alignment. To format the cells containing the column headings:

Step 1	Drag	to select the column headings
Step 2	Click	the Italic button I on the Formatting toolbar
Step 3	Click	the Bold button B on the Formatting toolbar
Step 4	Right-click	the selected row

QUICK TIP

You can add a new cell, row, or column by splitting a cell, row, or column vertically or horizontally using the Draw Table button on the Tables and Borders toolbar.

You can merge any cell with the adjacent cell, if you want to join two or more cells to create one cell, by erasing the line between the cells. Click the Eraser button on the Tables and Borders toolbar, and then click the line to be erased.

chapter
five

Step 5	*Click*	Bord<u>e</u>rs and Fill
Step 6	*Click*	the Fill tab in the Format Table dialog box
Step 7	*Click*	the Fill <u>c</u>olor: list arrow
Step 8	*Click*	the green color, sixth color from the left in the first row
Step 9	*Click*	the Semi<u>t</u>ransparent check box to add a check mark
Step 10	*Click*	OK
Step 11	*Click*	outside the column headings to deselect them

DESIGN TIP

You can make column headings stand out by applying bold and/or italics, shading the row, changing the font, or increasing the size of the column headings.

Serif fonts are good choices for text-heavy documents that are viewed at close range, because the serifs help guide the eye from one character to the next. Sans serif fonts are excellent for titles, subtitles, and short passages of text because from a distance, each character does not appear to run together. When creating a presentation, experiment with different fonts from the Font button list on the Formatting toolbar to find one that suits your presentation.

Notice how shading attracts the eye to the information within the shaded area. The current font of the title and table text is Times New Roman. **Font** refers to the design and appearance of printed characters. Each font has its own unique characteristics in terms of weight, height, and stroke. The font you choose helps set the mood or tone for your presentation. Times New Roman is a serif font. **Serifs** are fine cross strokes that appear at the bottom and the top of a letter. **Sans serif** means without serifs. Sans serif fonts have no cross strokes, are clean, modern looking, and very simple in appearance. Using an appropriate font also aids in the readability of text. Serif fonts are often used to guide the eye when reading large amounts of normal sized text. Sans serif fonts are often used when the text is going to be read at a distance or as headline text. To change the font style of selected table text:

Step 1	*Select*	the column headings
Step 2	*Change*	the font to Arial Narrow
Step 3	*Deselect*	the cells
Step 4	*Save*	the *Teddy Toys* presentation

Changing Indents and Setting Internal Margins

Each cell in a table has an indent marker. An **indent marker** enables you to change the position of the first line of text in a column, the second line (if there is any), or all the lines within a cell. Indent markers for the currently selected cell are displayed on the ruler that appears above the table. You can set a new indent for the current cell by moving the indent marker.

The indent markers on the Quadrant presentation template are at the extreme left edge of each column. You want to position the table text away from the left edge of the cell throughout your table. To achieve this, you could set new indents for each cell.

To move the existing indents:

Step 1	*Click*	in the New Product cell

The horizontal ruler highlights the active column in white and displays indent markers for the columns. The first line indent marker (top triangle) shows the indent position of the first line of text in the cell. The bottom triangle shows the indent position of the second and any following lines of a paragraph in a cell. The left indent marker (rectangle box) shows the indent position of all lines of text in a cell.

Step 2	*Drag*	the left indent marker ⬜ to the 0.5 inch mark on the ruler

If your goal is to position text in all columns in the same way, creating internal margins is quicker than setting new indents because you can set the internal margin of several cells at one time by selecting the cells first and then changing the internal margin—unlike an indent, which must be applied individually to cells.

Step 3	*Click*	the Undo button ↰ on the Standard toolbar
Step 4	*Right-click*	the table selection border
Step 5	*Click*	Borders and Fill
Step 6	*Click*	the Text Box tab

The Text Box tab in the Format Table dialog box has options for text alignment, internal margins, and rotating text. The dialog box on your screen should look similar to Figure 5-5.

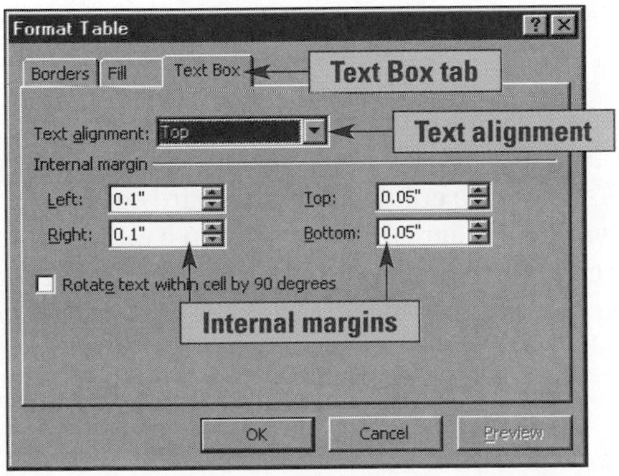

FIGURE 5-5
Format Table Dialog Box

MOUSE TIP

You can change fills and borders by right-clicking the selected row, column, or table, and then clicking Borders and Fill.

MENU TIP

You can make changes to the font, font style, font size, font color, and font effects of slide text by clicking the Font command on the Format menu.

chapter
five

CAUTION TIP

Be careful not to click in the white area of the ruler. If you do, you set a tab for that column. If you set a tab and no longer want it, simply drag it down off the ruler.

QUICK TIP

To center only the contents of one cell or a row, you can select the cell or row and click the desired alignment button.

Instead of changing the alignment of text or numbers in a table, you can set a tab by clicking the Tab button at the left of the horizontal ruler to display the type of tab you want, and then clicking the ruler where you want to set the tab. After the tab is set, hold down the CTRL key, press the TAB key to the desired tab, and key your data.

Step 7	*Key*	0.2 in the Left: text box and the Right: text box under Internal margin
Step 8	*Click*	OK
Step 9	*Click*	outside the table object

Changing Text Alignment

Alignment refers to the position of text within a cell. **Horizontal alignment** refers to the horizontal position of text within a cell. **Vertical alignment** refers to the vertical position of text within a cell. To change horizontal alignment in a table:

| Step 1 | *Select* | the table object |
| Step 2 | *Click* | the Center button ▤ on the Formatting toolbar |

All of the table text is now center aligned. To change the horizontal alignment of a column and a cell:

Step 1	*Point*	slightly above the Target Date column until you see a solid black down arrow
Step 2	*Click*	the top of the column (the entire column should be selected)
Step 3	*Click*	the Align Right button ▤ on the Formatting toolbar
Step 4	*Click*	in the Target Date cell
Step 5	*Click*	the Center button ▤ on the Formatting toolbar
Step 6	*Drag*	to select the first column text, excluding the column heading
Step 7	*Click*	the Align Left button ▤ on the Formatting toolbar

The text below the column heading in the first column is aligned at the left, the Target Date column text is aligned at the right, and the New Product and Target Date column headings are centered.

Text can be vertically aligned within a cell in a table, at the top, center, or bottom of the cell. You want the text in the cells to be vertically centered so that there is equal space above and below the text within the cells.

To change vertical alignment:

Step 1	*Click*	the Tables and Borders button ⊞ on the Standard tool-bar to display the Tables and Borders toolbar, if necessary
Step 2	*Click*	the Table button [Table ▾] on the Table and Borders toolbar
Step 3	*Click*	Select Table
Step 4	*Click*	the Center Vertically button ▤ on the Tables and Borders toolbar
Step 5	*Click*	outside the table

The table text is vertically aligned within the cells. Your screen should look similar to Figure 5-6.

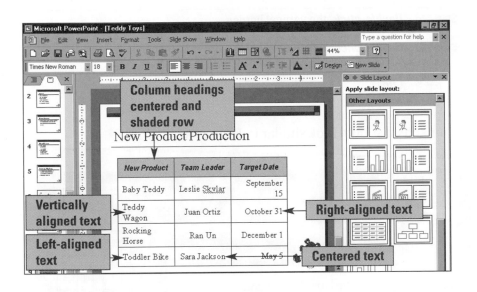

FIGURE 5-6
Table with Text Aligned Vertically and Horizontally

Adjusting Column Width and Row Height

After completing any table, you may need to adjust column width and/or row height to improve the table's appearance and readability. **Column width** refers to the horizontal size of a cell or column, and **row height** refers to the vertical size of a cell or row. You can drag row and column borders to quickly change column width and row height within a table. You can adjust the row height of one row, or the width of one column, and then use the Distribute Rows Evenly or Distribute Columns Evenly buttons on the Tables and Borders toolbar to automatically make the row heights even or the column widths even.

chapter
five

The heights of the rows on the table you just created are equal, but you want the height of the first row to be larger so it stands out more than the rest of the rows. To change row height of the first row:

| Step 1 | *Position* | the mouse pointer on the horizontal border between the New Product and Baby Teddy rows until it changes to the row resizing arrow |
| Step 2 | *Drag* | the resizing arrow down approximately two marks on the vertical ruler |

Double-clicking the vertical border of a column automatically resizes that column to the longest item within the column.

Step 3	*Position*	the mouse pointer on the vertical border after the New Product column
Step 4	*Double-click*	the vertical border
Step 5	*Double-click*	the vertical border after the Team Leader and Target Date columns
Step 6	*Click*	outside the table

Your screen should look similar to Figure 5-7.

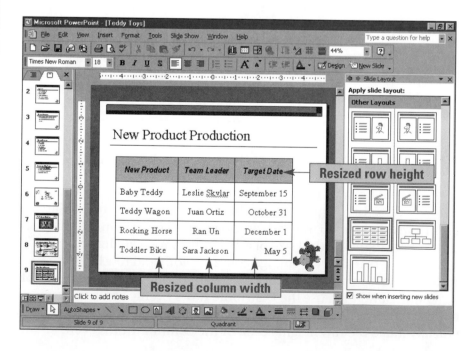

FIGURE 5-7
Table with Row Height and Column Width Changes

Each of the three column widths automatically adjusts to fit the longest item within the column.

Removing and Adding Borders

As you have learned, **borders** are lines that delineate or set off rows, columns, selected cells, or an entire table. PowerPoint provides the versatility to create any desired arrangement of borders or no borders at all. To change borders:

Step 1	*Select*	the table object
Step 2	*Click*	the Border button list arrow ▫▾ on the Table and Borders toolbar
Step 3	*Click*	the No Border button in the first row, last column

The border button now displays nonprinting gridlines and no borders. If you position the mouse pointer over the button, the ScreenTip displays No Border. The Border button displays the last selected border style as its ScreenTip.

Step 4	*Click*	outside the table to view the table without the borders
Step 5	*Select*	the table object
Step 6	*Click*	the Border button list arrow ▫▾ on the Tables and Borders toolbar
Step 7	*Click*	the Outside Borders button in the first row, first column
Step 8	*Select*	the column headings
Step 9	*Click*	the Border button list arrow ▫▾ on the Tables and Borders toolbar
Step 10	*Click*	the Bottom Border button in the second row, second column
Step 11	*Click*	outside the table
Step 12	*Reposition*	the table so the right edge does not overlap the teddy bear image

chapter
five

Your screen should look similar to Figure 5-8.

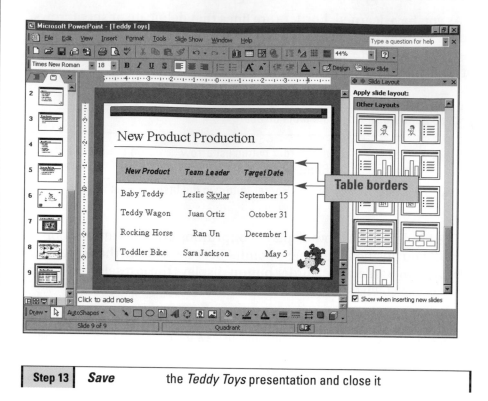

Step 13	**Save**	the *Teddy Toys* presentation and close it

The table slide you added to the presentation makes it easy for the employees to determine what the new products are, who is responsible for the product, and when they will be ready for market.

Summary

▶ You can create a table on any slide in a PowerPoint presentation.

▶ The easiest way to create a table in PowerPoint is to add a new slide based on the table layout and then double-click the table placeholder on the new slide.

▶ You can insert an existing Word or Excel table in a PowerPoint slide.

▶ You can add or remove table borders to separate the columns and rows, one column or one row, or selected columns or rows.

▶ You can easily add a row or column at the end of a table or within the body of a table.

▶ You can easily delete columns or rows in a table.

▶ You can format all attributes of a table, including the font, font size, font style, alignment, borders, shading, column widths, and row heights.

▶ You can size table objects in PowerPoint by dragging the sizing handles with the mouse.

▶ You can easily adjust column widths or row heights by dragging the borders.

▶ The goal of column headings is to enable viewers to quickly identify the items in their respective columns.

▶ Cell, column, or row text can be horizontally and vertically aligned.

▶ Borders can be removed or added to cells, rows, or columns in a table, or to the entire table itself.

▶ Dragging the table object to a new position easily moves tables.

Commands Review

Action	Menu Bar	Shortcut Menu	Toolbar	Task Pane	Keyboard
Add a table	Insert, Ta_b_le	Right-click, Slide Layout, click Title and Table layout Double-click table placeholder	Table ▾ , Insert Table	Click Title and Table layout under Other Layouts on the Slide Layout task pane, or click any Content layout on the Slide Layout task pane, then click the Insert Table icon	ALT + I, B

chapter five

Action	Menu Bar	Shortcut Menu	Toolbar	Task Pane	Keyboard
Add a row to a table		Right-click a row, Insert Rows	Table ▾ , Insert Rows Above or Insert Rows Below		ALT + A, A or B
Delete a row in a table		Right-click the row beneath the desired rows, Delete Rows	Table ▾ , Delete Rows		ALT + A, W
Add a column to a table		Right-click a selected column, Insert Columns	Table ▾ , Insert Columns to the Left or Insert Columns to the Right		ALT + A, L or R
Delete a column from a table		Right-click a selected column, Delete Columns	Table ▾ , Delete Columns		ALT + A, C
Change table text font	Format, Font	Right-click selected text, Font	Comic Sans MS		ALT + O, F
Select a row		Drag across the row to select it	Table ▾ , Select Row		ALT + A, T
Select a column		Drag down the column to select it, or click just above the column to select it	Table ▾ , Select Column		ALT + A, O
Select the entire table	Edit, Object	Right-click the table, Select Table, SHIFT + click table, or drag over entire table text	Table ▾ , Select Table		ALT + E, O ALT + A, S
Indent text within a column	Format, Table, Text Box tab	Drag indent marker on ruler in selected cell; Right-click cell, Borders and Fill, Text Box tab			ALT + O, T ALT + A, E
Change horizontal alignment of table text	Format, Table, Text Box tab	Right-click cell, row, column, or table, Borders and Fill, Text Box tab			ALT + O, T ALT + A, E
Change vertical alignment of table text	Format, Table, Text Box tab	Right-click cell, row, column, or table, Borders and Fill, Text Box tab			ALT + O, T ALT + A, E
Change column width		Drag border between columns, or double-click border between columns to AutoFit text to longest item			
Change row height		Drag border between rows			
Change table borders and fill	Format, Table, Borders or Fill tab	Right-click cell, row, column, or table, Borders and Fill, Borders or Fill tab	Table ▾ Borders and Fill		ALT + O, T ALT + A, E
Move a table			Drag the selection border		

Concepts Review

SCANS

Circle the correct answer.

1. Material consisting of relational information is best presented as a:
[a] title slide.
[b] text slide.
[c] table slide.
[d] drawing slide.

2. Which of the following statements is false?
[a] You can insert a Word table or an Excel worksheet on a PowerPoint slide.
[b] You can edit a table by double-clicking the table and using Microsoft Word's creating and editing capabilities.
[c] You can draw a table within PowerPoint.
[d] You can create a table by clicking any Content layout in the Slide Layout task pane.

3. A cell is defined as:
[a] a rectangular marker.
[b] a text box.
[c] the intersection of a column and a row.
[d] a border style.

4. To add a new row at the end of a table, you can position the insertion point in the last cell and:
[a] click the Insert Rows button on the Standard toolbar.
[b] press the ENTER key.
[c] press the TAB key.
[d] press the CTRL + ENTER keys.

5. To insert a row within a table, you position the insertion point:
[a] in the row above where you want to insert the new row, right-click the table, and click Insert Rows.
[b] in the row below where you want to insert the new row, right-click the table, and click Insert Rows Above.

[c] anywhere in the row where you want to insert the new row, right-click the table, and click Insert Rows.
[d] anywhere in the row where you want to insert the new row, click Format, Table, Row tab, and then click the Insert Row check box.

6. You format a simple table object by:
[a] right-clicking the table, and then clicking Edit Document Object.
[b] double-clicking the table.
[c] clicking the Edit subcommand of the Document Object command on the Edit menu.
[d] right-clicking the table, and then clicking the desired option.

7. The size of a table:
[a] is determined by the number of columns and rows.
[b] is determined by the presentation design and cannot be changed.
[c] is dependent on the intended look desired by the creator.
[d] cannot exceed 10 rows and 10 columns.

8. Which of the following enables viewers to quickly identify the items in the columns of a table?
[a] column names
[b] column headings
[c] row identifiers
[d] column markers

chapter five

9. To adjust the width of table columns, you:

[a] click the Column width command on the Format menu.

[b] drag the vertical line between two columns.

[c] right-click the table, and then click Column width.

[d] double-click the table and select the Column tab.

10. Which of the following statements concerning tables is not true?

[a] Individual cells can be aligned.

[b] Individual columns can be aligned.

[c] Individual rows can be aligned.

[d] Nonadjacent columns can be aligned at the same time.

Circle **T** if the statement is true or **F** if the statement is false.

T F 1. A table slide displays data organized into columns and rows.

T F 2. Tables can be created in Word and Excel and inserted in PowerPoint slides.

T F 3. You can insert rows in a table only by clicking the Insert Rows command on the Table menu.

T F 4. Pressing the ENTER key within a cell of a table adds another row.

T F 5. Table border lines can be added or removed by right-clicking the table and clicking Borders and Fill.

T F 6. You can automatically adjust the width of any column to its longest item by double-clicking the column's right border.

T F 7. Shading in a table attracts the eye to the text or information within the shaded area.

T F 8. You can change the vertical and horizontal alignment of cells, rows, and columns.

T F 9. Column headings help viewers to quickly identify items within respective columns.

T F 10. Once a table is created, it cannot be repositioned.

Skills Review

Exercise 1 [C]

SCANS

1. Open the *PowerPoint* presentation you modified in Chapter 4, and add a table slide at the end of the presentation. The title should read "Slide Types."

2. Create a table consisting of two columns and four rows using the following information:

Slide Type	Function
Title	Introduce topic
Bullet	Summarize or prioritize
Table	Establish relationship between data

3. Add shading and bold the column headings. (Try to match one of the colors in the presentation design.)

4. Vertically center the text in the entire table, and change the font size to 24 point.

5. Increase the width of column 2 by decreasing the width of column 1.

6. Remove any indents in the column heading cells, and center the column headings horizontally.

7. Add an internal margin of 0.25 inches to all cells in the table.

8. Select the last three rows (do not include the column headings), and change the font to Times New Roman.

9. Reduce the height of rows 2, 3, and 4 by approximately 0.25 inch. (*Hint:* Change one row, then select the three rows, and then click the Distribute Rows Evenly button on the Tables and Borders toolbar.)

10. Resize and reposition the table to enhance the appearance of the slide.

11. Save the presentation, spell check it, resave if necessary, print the table slide, and close the presentation.

Exercise 2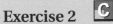

1. Open the *Office* presentation you modified in Chapter 4, and add a table slide at the end of the presentation. The title should read "Microsoft Office XP."

2. Create a table using the Content layout consisting of two columns and six rows using the following information:

Software	Application
Word	Word processing
Excel	Worksheets
Access	Databases
PowerPoint	Presentations
FrontPage	Web site creation and management tool

3. Change the font size of the column headings to 28 point, Bold, Center Align.

4. Increase the row height of the column headings by approximately 0.25 inch, and vertically center the text.

5. Add an internal margin of 0.25 inch to the left and right margin for both columns.

6. Adjust the width of the columns, making column 1 narrower than column 2.

7. Italicize the names of the software in column 1, excluding the column heading.

8. Remove the existing table borders, add an outside border to the table, add a bottom border to the column headings, and add a right column border to column 1.

9. Resize and reposition the table attractively on the slide.

10. Save the presentation, spell check it, resave if necessary, print the table slide, and close the presentation.

Exercise 3 C

1. Open the *Design* presentation you modified in Chapter 4, and add a table slide at the end of the presentation. The title should read "Basic Color Tips."

2. Create a table consisting of two columns and six rows using the following information:

Color	Message
Blue	Security, relaxation, conservatism
Red	Power, passion, competition
Black	Directness, force
Green	Intelligence, development
Purple	Entertainment, royalty

3. Resize the columns to the longest item in each column.

4. Apply bold formatting to the column headings, and change the size to 26 point. (*Hint:* You can key 26 in the Font Size text box.)

5. Add the following row so that it appears above the "Purple" row:

Gray	Neutral

chapter five

6. Remove all the borders around the table.

7. Add an Inside Horizontal Border to the selected table.

8. Add a Bottom Border to the last row of the table.

9. Resize and reposition the table for readability and to insure that the entire table appears on the slide.

10. Vertically align the text to the bottom in the entire table.

11. Save the presentation, spell check it, resave if necessary, print the table slide, and close the presentation.

Exercise 4   C

1. Open the *Precision Builders* presentation you modified in Chapter 4, and add a table slide at the end of the presentation. The title should read "Quality Materials."

2. Create a table consisting of four columns and six rows using the following information:

Materials	Ranch	Two-story	Townhome
Brick	X	X	X
Hardwood floors	X	X	X
Ceramic baths	X	X	X
Two-story foyer		X	X
Thermal windows	X	X	X

3. Bold and italicize the column headings.

4. Adjust the width of the types of homes columns so that they are even.

5. Add shading (try to match one of the colors in the presentation design) to the column headings, and change the text color, if necessary.

6. Horizontally center columns 2, 3, and 4, and vertically center the column headings.

7. Vertically align all rows at the bottom, except the column headings.

8. Delete the row containing information about a Two-story foyer.

9. Resize and reposition the table, if necessary.

10. Save the presentation, spell check it, resave if necessary, print the table slide, and close the presentation.

Exercise 5   C

1. Open the *Nature Tours* presentation you modified in Chapter 4, and add a table slide at the end of the presentation. The title should read "Let Your Legs Do the Work."

2. Enter the following table text, pressing the ENTER key at the breaks shown:

Leg Tours	Locations
Hiking	Grand Canyon, Rocky Mountains, Glacier National Park, Lake Tahoe
Walking	Sonoran Desert, Maine Coast, Hawaiian Islands
Mountain climbing	Tetons, Seven Summits, High Sierras, Mount Olympus

3. Adjust column widths so that column 2 is wider than column 1.

4. Change the font, font size, style, and vertical and horizontal alignment of the column headings.

5. Align the text in the columns as necessary.

6. Resize the table, if necessary.

7. Save the presentation, spell check it, resave if necessary, print the table slide, and close the presentation.

Exercise 6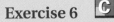

1. Open the *A Healthier You* presentation you modified in Chapter 4, and add a table slide at the end of the presentation. The title should read "Food Pyramid Guide."

2. Enter the following table text:

Food Group	Servings Per Day
Breads, Cereal, Rice, & Pasta	6 – 11
Vegetables	3 – 5
Fruits	2 – 3
Milk, Yogurt, & Cheese	2 – 3
Meat, Poultry, Fish, Dry Beans, Eggs, & Nuts	2 – 3
Fats, Oil, Sweets	use sparingly

3. Adjust column widths for ease of readability and appearance.

4. Add shading and determine where to place borders to enhance the table.

5. Change the border lines of the table to 2 ¼ point, and use an appropriate border color that matches the presentation.

6. Format the text within the table with regard to font style, font size, and alignment.

7. Adjust the row height of the column headings.

8. Change the vertical and horizontal alignment where necessary for readability.

9. Indent the text from the border for column 1.

10. Resize the table, if necessary.

11. Save the presentation, spell check it, resave if necessary, print the table slide, and close the presentation.

Exercise 7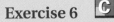

1. Open the *Buying A Computer* presentation you modified in Chapter 4, and add a table slide at the end of the presentation. The title should read "Computer Essentials."

2. Enter the following table text:

What minimum options do I need?				
Processor	RAM	MHz	Hard Drive	Drives
Celeron	64MB	500	6.5GB	3 ½"
Pentium III	128MB	700	15GB	3 ½" (Press the ENTER key)
				250MB ZIP (Press the ENTER key)
				CD-ROM

3. Select the first row ("What minimum options do I need?") and merge the cells. (*Hint:* Use the Tables and Borders toolbar.)

4. Adjust the column widths for optimal readability.

5. Change the font, font size, style, and/or alignment of the first row.

6. Format the text within the table.

7. Add or remove borders and/or shading to improve the appearance of the table.

chapter five

8. Resize the table to fit attractively on the slide.

9. Save the presentation, spell check it, resave if necessary, print the table slide, and close the presentation.

Exercise 8

1. Open the *Leisure Travel* presentation you modified in Chapter 4, and add a table slide at the end of the presentation. The title should read "All-Inclusive Package Teasers."

2. Enter the following table text:

Pkg. #	Destination	# of Days	Approx. Cost*
1224	Aruba	7	$2,000
1335	Puerto Vallarta	6	$1,150
1129	St. Thomas	5	$1,500

3. Adjust column widths as necessary.

4. Horizontally and vertically align text as desired.

5. Add another row anywhere after the column headings row, and key the following:

1546	Cancun	5	$1,350

6. Resize and reposition the table.

7. Add a row at the bottom of the table, merge the cells, and key the following text: "*Average price quoted for the given number of days."

8. Reduce the font size and change the vertical alignment of the last row (the footnote) to center.

9. Remove the borders around the last row.

10. Save the presentation, spell check it, resave if necessary, print the table slide, and close the presentation.

Case Projects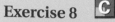

Project 1

You decide that you want to learn more about the Draw Table button and the Eraser button on the Tables and Borders toolbar. You are particularly interested in how to use the buttons on an existing table, what type of tables you can draw with the Draw Table mouse pointer, and how to erase lines. Use the Ask A Question Box to find information on the Draw Table button and Eraser button. Using the information you find, create a presentation that consists of only a table slide using the Draw Table and Eraser buttons to draw rows and columns. Arrange the information you find from the online Help in a table format. Print the table slide.

Project 2

Your manager is concerned about the reaction of callers to the employees they deal with on the telephone. She believes that there is a correlation between the phone etiquette of employees and customers' needs, concerns, and expectations being satisfied. She asks you to create a checklist of basic phone etiquette employees should perform when talking to customers. Open the *Communicate* presentation you modified in Chapter 4, and add a table slide to your presentation that conveys at least three actions employees should do when receiving calls. Add shading and borders as you desire. Change alignment, fonts, font size, etc., as appropriate. After completing the table slide, you should make any adjustments necessary to aid readability. Spell check and save the presentation. Print the table slide.

Project 3

Because the owner of Souner & Associates believes that variety and a continuous offering of courses will satisfy most potential clients' needs, your manager wants you to add a table slide to the *Souner* presentation that indicates course offerings for the current month. Open the *Souner* presentation you modified in Chapter 4, and add a table that includes at least four classes that are being offered and indicate whether or not they are being offered each week. Change the borders within the table. After completing the table slide, make any adjustments necessary to aid readability. Spell check and save the presentation. Print the table slide.

Project 4

You have informed your employer that you think a table slide should be added to your presentation to best display additional information concerning your topic. Open the *My Presentation* presentation you modified in Chapter 4, and add a table slide. You want to display your data attractively in rows and columns for this presentation. After completing the table slide, make any adjustments necessary to aid readability. Be sure to spell check and save the *My Presentation* presentation. Print the table slide.

Project 5

The zoo has several special exhibits and showings scheduled for the current month. They are especially proud of the births of Chi Lo, the first panda ever born at the zoo, and Tweeky, the new son of Zelda, one of the female hippopotamuses, which occurred during the first week of the month. In addition, the newly renovated ape house and bird aviary are done and will open to the public the second and third week of the month. You need to add this information to your *Zoo* presentation. Open the *Zoo* presentation you modified in Chapter 4, and create a table slide that displays these special events and the dates of the events. Make any formatting decisions with regard to text alignment, borders and shading, and fonts. Save the presentation, and print the table slide.

Project 6

There are several very good integrated software suites on the market today. You are curious how they compare with each other. Connect to the Internet and search the Web for information that compares Microsoft Office with the latest Lotus SmartSuite and Corel WordPerfect Suite. Print the information you find. Create a new presentation consisting of a title and table slide that compares the three suites. View the slide show, save the presentation with an appropriate filename, and print the presentation.

Project 7

You have just read an article relating the survival rate of car drivers and passengers in car accidents. The article has indicated that the fate of drivers and passengers in some accidents is dependent on the safety features found in the cars on the highway today. You found the article to be extremely interesting and want to share this information with your fellow students. Connect to the Internet and search the Web for current information about your car's safety features. Open the *Cars* presentation you modified in Chapter 4, and add a table slide to your presentation that lists several of the safety features you found and their descriptions. Make any formatting decisions with regard to alignment of text, column widths, typeface, type size, and table size. Replace the presentation fonts for this presentation. Save the presentation and print the table slide.

Project 8

You and your partner decide that a table slide would be a good way to display several of the terms and their definitions that you found while searching the Internet. Open the *Internet* presentation you modified in Chapter 4, and add a table slide at the end that displays the top six terms you found vital to understanding the Internet. If necessary, connect to the Internet and search the Web for appropriate terms. Make any formatting changes to shading, typeface, font size, column widths, and table size to improve the readability and appearance of the table. Save the presentation, and print the table slide.

chapter five

Working with Charts

Chapter Overview

Charts are important tools in PowerPoint; they present complex data in a simple, graphical form that an audience can easily understand. You might use a chart to compare results such as monthly product sales or to identify trends such as weather patterns. Like a table, a chart organizes data, but it also interprets the data as a visual picture, so the audience gets the message without having to read every number. In this chapter, you learn how to create chart slides and how to work with different types of charts. You also learn how to edit and format a chart to convey your information most effectively.

Learning Objectives

- Add a chart to a slide
- Work with a datasheet
- Format a chart
- Add a pie chart to a slide
- Format a pie chart

Case profile

To present the current market status of Teddy Toys, Ms. Hill wants you to include two charts in the *Teddy Toys* presentation. First, she would like you to create a graph depicting sales within each of Teddy Toys' four product areas over the last two years. In addition, two of Teddy Toys' competitors hold a significant portion of the toy market, with Teddy Toys coming in as the leader. To highlight the need to maintain Teddy Toys' position in the marketplace, Ms. Hill wants you to create a slide that compares the market share among all three top toy manufacturers.

chapter six

6.a Adding a Chart to a Slide

To add a chart to a presentation, you can create a chart from scratch in PowerPoint or you can insert an existing chart that you created in another program, such as Word or Excel. You can create a chart in PowerPoint using **Microsoft Graph**, a charting program shared by the Office suite of products. In Microsoft Graph, you can quickly create almost any type of chart, including column, bar, line, pie, XY (scatter), area, doughnut, radar, surface, bubble, stock, cylinder, cone, and pyramid charts. Within each chart type available in Microsoft Graph, you can choose from at least two or three subtypes. If one of these standard chart types does not meet your needs, you can choose a custom chart type.

You can create a chart in any slide, or you can use one of the layouts in the New Slide task pane that contains a chart placeholder. To add a chart using a chart layout slide at the end of a presentation:

Step 1	*Open*	the *Teddy Toys* presentation you modified in Chapter 5 and display the last slide in the presentation
Step 2	*Click*	the <u>N</u>ew Slide button  on the Formatting toolbar
Step 3	*Scroll*	to the Other Layouts area of the Slide Layout task pane
Step 4	*Click*	the Title and Chart layout in the Other Layouts area of the Slide Layout task pane

Your screen should look similar to Figure 6-1.

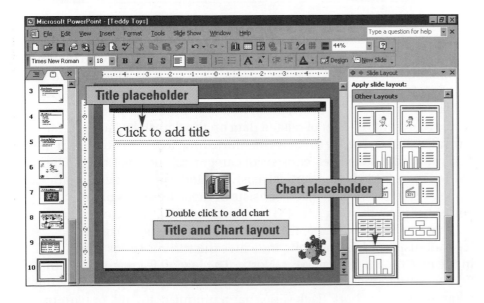

TASK PANE TIP

You can add a chart to a PowerPoint slide by clicking one of the Content layouts in the Slide Layout task pane and then clicking the Insert Chart icon.

You can also create a chart by clicking any Content Layout or Title and Text and Content Layout in the Slide Layout task pane and then clicking the Insert Chart icon on the placeholder.

FIGURE 6-1
Slide with Chart Placeholder

**chapter
six**

To add a title and create the chart:

Step 1	*Click*	the "Click to add title" placeholder
Step 2	*Key*	Market Status
Step 3	*Double-click*	the chart placeholder

Microsoft Graph opens and displays a default chart on the slide and a **datasheet**, a worksheet that is linked to your new chart. It contains default data that you replace with the your own data. Your screen should look similar to Figure 6-2.

FIGURE 6-2
Default Chart with Datasheet

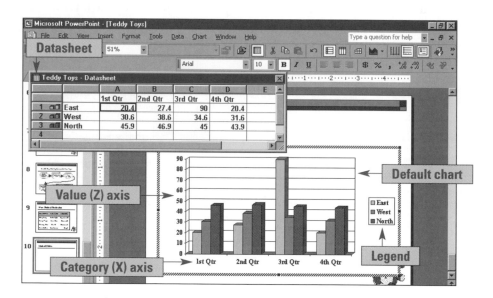

The data in the datasheet is depicted visually in the chart. When you create a new chart, Microsoft Graph displays the datasheet with **default data**, sample data that it uses to draw the sample chart. Once you enter or edit information in the datasheet, the chart changes accordingly. In the chart, each data series is represented by a different color. A **data series** represents one set of related data on the datasheet, such as 1st Qtr sales. The **Category (X) axis** (the horizontal axis), created from the first row in the datasheet, consists of categories, such as 1st Qtr. The **Value (Y) or (Z) axis** (the vertical axis), created from the actual data values keyed in the datasheet, consists of measurements of the categories listed on the Category (X) axis, such as sales. If the chart is a 3-D chart, you have a Value (Z) axis instead of a Value (Y) axis. A **legend**, displayed on the right, indicates the various series being used in the chart, such as East, West, North. The legend is created from the first column in the datasheet. The columns for one category represent a data series in a chart. Each series has a unique color, fill, or pattern and is represented in the chart legend. You can plot one or more data

series in a chart, with the exception of pie charts, which have only one data series. A **data point** represents one data series in a chart, such as one slice of a pie or one column in a series of columns.

6.b Working with a Datasheet

On the datasheet, columns are identified by letters, and rows are identified by numbers. In the first column and first row of the datasheet are sample labels for the data. When you replace the default labels with your own, you replace the sample column labels with text descriptions of the data categories in your chart and the sample row names with descriptions of the data values. You enter labels and data in cells, as you do in Microsoft Excel, though there are some important differences in the entry process.

Deleting Default Data

Before entering data in a datasheet, you delete the default data. You could delete this information one cell at a time, but doing so is time consuming and may leave you with undesired cells. Deleting individual cell contents clears only the data; the empty cell, row, or column still remains, which may cause the chart to produce gaps between the data series. To delete the data and the empty rows or columns, it's better to select all the data at once and then delete it. The datasheet contains a Select All button in the upper-left corner of the datasheet that you can click to select all the rows and columns in the datasheet. To delete all the default data from the datasheet:

| Step 1 | *Click* | the Select All button in the upper-left corner of the datasheet |

The datasheet on your screen should look similar to Figure 6-3.

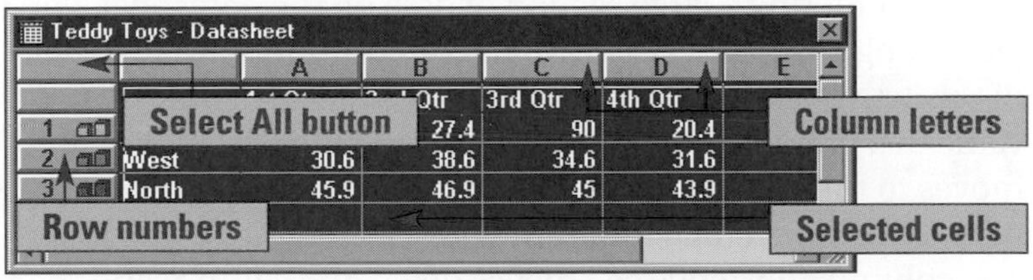

| Step 2 | *Press* | the DELETE key to delete the existing default data |

> **CAUTION TIP**
>
> If you drag and select the text in a datasheet, or delete the text cell by cell, your chart may contain large blank areas without columns or bars. Click the Select All button to ensure that you delete all previous text.

FIGURE 6-3
Datasheet with Selected Cells

chapter
six

Keying Chart Data

You key data in a datasheet just as you key data into an Excel worksheet. After keying data in a cell, you complete your entry and move to a different cell by pressing the TAB key, the ENTER key, or any of the ARROW keys. If you wish to return to a previous cell, you can press the SHIFT + TAB keys, the LEFT ARROW key, the SHIFT + ENTER keys, or the UP ARROW key. As in an Excel worksheet, a cell is identified by a cell address, which represents the intersection of the lettered column and numbered row; cell A1, for example, is the cell located at the intersection of column A and row 1. The datasheet in Microsoft Graph also contains cells to the left of column A and above row 1 for text that identifies the data; these cells are not represented by a cell address. To key data into a datasheet:

Step 1	*Click*	the cell in the first row immediately below the column A indicator
Step 2	*Key*	Last Year
Step 3	*Press*	the TAB key
Step 4	*Key*	This Year
Step 5	*Click*	the cell immediately to the right of the row 1 indicator and to the left of cell A1
Step 6	*Key*	the following, pressing the ENTER key after each entry: Family Bears Action Bears Sports Clothes Toys

Notice that the column labels, Last Year and This Year, are displayed on the Category (X) axis, and the row labels, Family Bears, Action Bears, Sports Clothes, and Toys, are displayed in the legend on the chart beneath the datasheet.

When entering a large section of data on the datasheet, you can preselect a range of cells. **Preselecting a range** temporarily changes the path of the active cell to make it easier to key quickly. After keying the first value in a preselected range and pressing the ENTER key, the active cell moves to the next cell in the range. This enables you to complete the data entry more efficiently. If the preselected range includes more than one column, the active cell moves down one column and then to the top of the next. To preselect a range, enter values in the range and then close the datasheet:

Step 1	*Drag*	from the center of cell A1 to cell B4 to select eight cells

---

QUICK TIP

You can use keyboard shortcuts to move around the datasheet quickly. For example, press the CTRL + HOME keys to move to the first data cell in the datasheet (cell A1). For more information on keyboard shortcuts, see Microsoft Graph online Help.

MOUSE TIP

You can close the datasheet window by clicking the Close button on the datasheet window or by double-clicking the Control-menu icon in the datasheet title bar.

You can display or close the datasheet at any time by clicking the View Datasheet button on the Standard toolbar.

| Step 2 | *Key* | the following, pressing the ENTER key after each value:
25000
30000
15000
50000
28000
32000
12000
45000 |

| Step 3 | *Observe* | how the chart builds to reflect the data you are entering |

The columns on the chart represent the data series from the values in the datasheet.

| Step 4 | *Click* | the View Datasheet button 🖼 on the Standard toolbar to close the datasheet |

Notice that the Value (Z) axis displays a range of numbers based on the values in the datasheet. This represents the sales for each year. The Category (X) axis displays Last Year and This Year categories of comparison. The chart displays a different colored column or bar for each of the four major product areas. The legend displays a colored key box indicating each specific product. To close the Microsoft Graph application and view the chart slide:

| Step 1 | *Click* | outside the chart object |

Your screen should look similar to Figure 6-4.

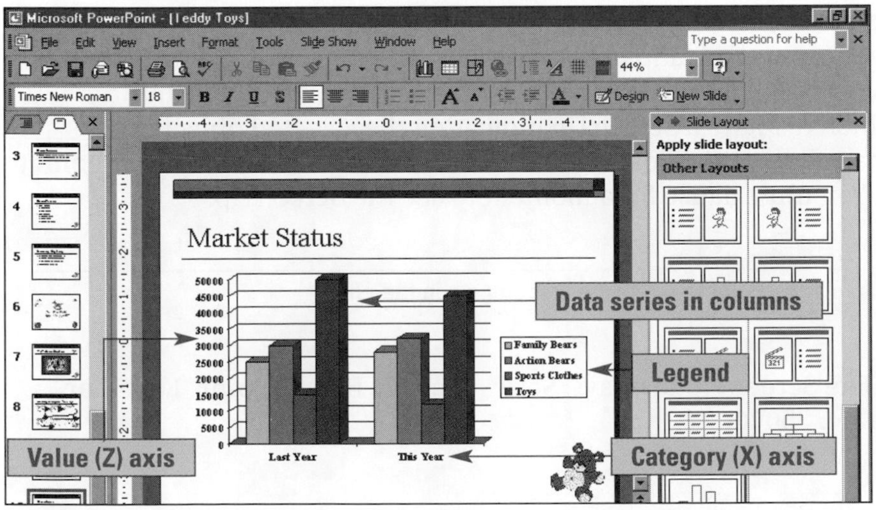

MOUSE TIP

You can adjust column width in a datasheet by dragging the border between the column letters to the desired width, or by double-clicking the border between the column letters.

MENU TIP

You can display or hide the datasheet at any time by clicking the Datasheet command on the View menu in Microsoft Graph.

FIGURE 6-4
Column Chart Slide

chapter
six

| Step 2 | *Save* | the *Teddy Toys* presentation |

6.c Formatting a Chart

A chart is an embedded object. An **embedded object** is an object that was created in a different program and must be opened in that program to make editing and formatting changes. Therefore, if you need to edit the information in a datasheet or format the chart on a slide, you must open Microsoft Graph. Microsoft Graph provides its own set of toolbars for editing and formatting charts. Some toolbar buttons are available when the chart is selected, and other buttons are available when the datasheet is displayed.

You can format a chart by changing the chart type, chart and series colors, number and text format, legend placement, axes titles, and data labels. A chart is actually made up of individual objects, such as columns or bars, gridlines, and a legend; to make formatting changes, you open Microsoft Graph, select the object you want to modify, and then make the necessary changes. To open Microsoft Graph:

| Step 1 | *Double-click* | the chart object |

Microsoft Graph opens, and the chart is ready to be edited or formatted. The selection border and eight sizing handles surrounding the chart indicate it is selected.

| Step 2 | *Close* | the datasheet, if necessary |

You must select a chart object to format it. You can select chart objects by clicking them or by selecting them from the Chart Objects list box on the Standard toolbar in Microsoft Graph. Immediately to the right of the Chart Objects list box is a Format Object button, which displays a ScreenTip indicating the selected object on the chart. ScreenTips identify each section of the chart when you point to it. You must pause for a moment to see the ScreenTip.

| Step 3 | *Point to* | the first column in the chart |

The ScreenTip displays: Series "Family Bears" Point "Last Year" Value: 25000.

| Step 4 | *Point to* | each chart object and observe its ScreenTip |

M E N U   T I P

You can edit the selected legend object by clicking the Se<u>l</u>ected Legend command on the F<u>o</u>rmat menu.

Formatting a Chart Legend

The **legend** on a chart is an object that identifies the patterns, fills, or colors that are assigned to the categories or data series. The legend on the Teddy Toys slide contains the four products with their respective colored box indicating each series. Legends, like all objects, can be enhanced to improve readability and comprehension. To format and move the legend:

| Step 1 | *Double-click* | the Legend object |

The Format Legend dialog box opens, with options for changing fill and border colors, fonts, font styles, font sizes, font colors, and placement of the legend on the chart.

Step 2	*Click*	the Patterns tab, if necessary
Step 3	*Click*	the Sha<u>d</u>ow check box to insert a check mark
Step 4	*Click*	the pale orange color in the fifth row, second column under Area
Step 5	*Click*	the Font tab
Step 6	*Click*	Italic in the F<u>o</u>nt style: list box
Step 7	*Click*	16 in the <u>S</u>ize: list box
Step 8	*Click*	the Placement tab
Step 9	*Click*	the <u>B</u>ottom option button
Step 10	*Click*	OK
Step 11	*Save*	the *Teddy Toys* presentation

M OUSE **TIP**

You can edit the legend object by right-clicking the Legend object and then clicking F<u>o</u>rmat Legend. You also can edit a selected legend by clicking the Format Legend button on the Standard toolbar in Microsoft Graph.

You can move the legend by dragging it to a new location. (Be careful not to drag a sizing handle, or you will resize the legend.)

Changing the Chart Display

The chart display shows how your current chart plots the data from the datasheet. You can change the chart display to display by rows or by columns. You use the By Column display when you want the columns on the datasheet to represent the data series in the chart. You use the By Row display when you want the rows on the datasheet to represent the data

chapter
six

series in the chart. The chart compares each product's sales for last year and each product's sales for this year. To change the chart display:

Step 1	*Click*	the By Column button 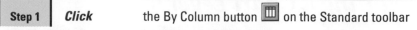 on the Standard toolbar

The legend and the Category (X) axis labels are reversed, and the chart now compares each product's last year's sales with this year's sales. Comparing all product sales for last year with all product sales for this year gives a better picture of how sales have changed in the marketplace, so you change the display back to By Row.

Step 2	*Click*	the By Row button ▦ on the Standard toolbar

Changing the Chart Type

When you create a chart in Microsoft Graph, the default chart type, a column chart, is created. You can change to any chart type available in Microsoft Graph, including column, bar, line, pie, XY (scatter), area, doughnut, radar, surface, bubble, stock, cylinder, cone, and pyramid charts. Each type is best for presenting a particular type of information. Column and bar charts, for example, are most effective when the goal is to show changes in data over a period of time or comparisons among items. Line charts are most effective when the goal is to show trends over a period of time. Cone, pyramid, or cylinder charts create a dramatic 3-D effect when showing changes in data over a period or time or when comparing data. Stock charts are most effective when the goal is to display high-low-close ratings of stocks. To change the chart type:

Step 1	*Click*	the Chart Type button list arrow ◪▾ on the Standard toolbar
Step 2	*Click*	various chart types to view your chart in different forms

Generally, the choices on the left of the Chart Type list are 2-D examples, whereas the choices in the middle are 3-D choices. After viewing different chart types, you want to return to your original 3-D column chart. The 3-D column chart found in the Chart Type list displays 3-D columns, but it also displays 3-D walls and floors around the columns. You decide to return to your original column chart.

Step 3	*Click*	Chart

Step 4	*Click*	Chart Type
Step 5	*Click*	the Standard Types tab, if necessary

The Chart Type dialog box opens with the Standard Types tab displaying the chart types in the column on the left and previews of various sub-types on the right. The dialog box on your screen should look similar to Figure 6-5.

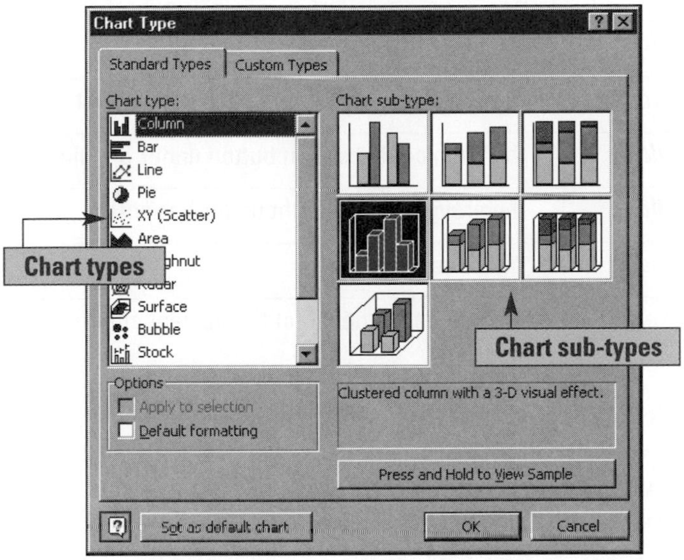

FIGURE 6-5
Chart Type Dialog Box

Step 6	*Click*	Column in the Chart type: list
Step 7	*Click*	the Clustered column with a 3-D visual effect in the second row, first column in the Chart sub-type: list
Step 8	*Click*	OK

Formatting a Data Series

A data series in a chart can be formatted by changing the border and fill styles and colors, the depth and width, the shape, and the data labels. You can add different types of fill effects to each different series. Gradients are shaded colors that are usually comprised of two colors blending from one color to the other. You can use various shading styles, patterns, or solid fill colors. Textures reflect fills that represent a realistic effect, such as bubbles or wood fills. When you change a series color and fill, the legend reflects that change in the legend key box. When you change the fill of a data series, you select the entire series. If you select only one of the columns in the series, the changes only affect that column.

DESIGN TIP

Decide what you want to display before choosing a type of chart. If you want to show comparisons or changes in data over a period of time, use variations of an area, column, or bar chart. If you want to show trends over a period of time, use variations of a line chart. If you want to show pieces of a whole, use a pie chart.

CAUTION TIP

If you inadvertently select a series before opening the Chart Type dialog box, Microsoft Graph may indicate that certain chart types cannot be combined with other chart types. Make sure that only the chart is selected; deselect any column if necessary.

To format a data series with a different fill color and gradient:

Step 1	Double-click	the Toys series column for either year
Step 2	Click	the Patterns tab in the Format Data Series dialog box, if necessary
Step 3	Click	Fill effects in the Format Data Series dialog box
Step 4	Click	the Gradient tab, if necessary
Step 5	Click	the Two colors option button under Colors
Step 6	Click	the Color 1: list arrow under Colors
Step 7	Click	the Dark Red color in the second row, first column
Step 8	Click	the From center option button under Shading styles
Step 9	Click	the preview on the right under Variants
Step 10	Click	OK twice
Step 11	Press	the ESC key to deselect the current chart objects

After previewing a gradient fill effect, you decide to add a texture fill effect and a pattern fill to the Sports Clothes and Action Bears data series to see which effect you want to use. To format a data series with texture and pattern fill effects:

Step 1	Double-click	the Sport Clothes series column for either year
Step 2	Click	Fill effects in the Format Data Series dialog box
Step 3	Click	the Texture tab
Step 4	Click	the Papyrus texture in the fourth row, first column
Step 5	Click	OK twice
Step 6	Double-click	the Action Bear series column for either year
Step 7	Click	Fill Effects
Step 8	Click	the Pattern tab
Step 9	Click	the Solid diamond pattern (last row, last column)

Step 10	*Click*	OK twice
Step 11	*Press*	the ESC key

All the columns display different fill effects, from solid, to pattern, to texture, to gradient. Your screen should look similar to Figure 6-6.

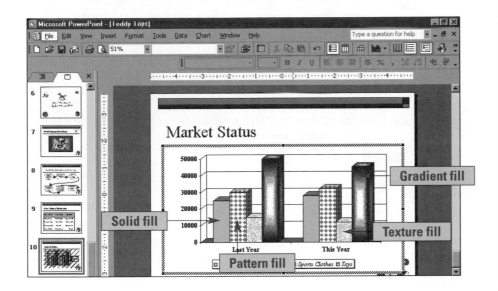

FIGURE 6-6
Columns with Different
Fill Effects

MOUSE TIP

You can change the chart type by right-clicking the series, plot area, or chart area in a chart and then clicking Chart Type.

From a design point of view, the columns in a chart should have a consistent look. For example, if you use a gradient fill effect, then all columns in the chart should use that same effect. To format a data series with a solid fill color:

CAUTION TIP

When accessing the Format Data Series dialog box, be sure to double-click—do not click twice. If you click twice, you may select only one of the columns. To be safe, be sure that all columns of a series are selected before making changes.

Step 1	*Double-click*	the Toys series column for either year
Step 2	*Click*	the Patterns tab, if necessary
Step 3	*Click*	the medium brown color in the sixth row, third column under Area
Step 4	*Click*	OK
Step 5	*Double-click*	the Sports Clothes series column for either year
Step 6	*Change*	the series color to the pale orange color in the fifth row, second column under Area
Step 7	*Double-click*	the Action Bears series column for either year
Step 8	*Change*	the series color to the green color in the sixth row, second column under Area
Step 9	*Save*	the *Teddy Toys* presentation

**chapter
six**

Formatting the Value Axis

The Value (Z) axis displays numbers corresponding to the values listed on the datasheet. You can format a Value (Z) axis to display currency to indicate that the numbers represent sales in terms of dollars or to add or remove decimals. In addition, you can also format a Value (Z) axis to change the scale minimum, maximum, or interval units. This affects how the data series is displayed according to the chart data. You have the option of changing the scale, font, font size, style and color, and the alignment of the Value (Z) axis.

To change the format of the numbers on the Value (Z) axis to include a $, a comma, and no decimal places:

Step 1	**Double-click**	any number on the Value (Z) axis to open the Format Axis dialog box
Step 2	**Click**	the Number tab
Step 3	**Click**	Currency in the Category: list box
Step 4	**Key**	0 in the Decimal places: text box
Step 5	**Verify**	that a $ symbol appears in the Symbol: list box
Step 6	**Click**	OK

Adding titles to the axes in a chart helps the audience to clearly understand the categories and measurements being displayed. You want to add a title to the Value (Z) axis to indicate that the dollar amounts are in thousands. The Value (Z) axis title appears on the slide in a horizontal format. The more you add to a chart, the smaller the columns become. You can rotate the Value (Z) axis title to increase the size of your columns. There is no need to add a Category (X) axis title at this time because the labels, Last Year and This Year are self-explanatory. To add a title to the Value (Z) axis and rotate it:

Step 1	**Click**	Chart
Step 2	**Click**	Chart Options
Step 3	**Click**	the Titles tab, if necessary

Your screen should look similar to Figure 6-7.

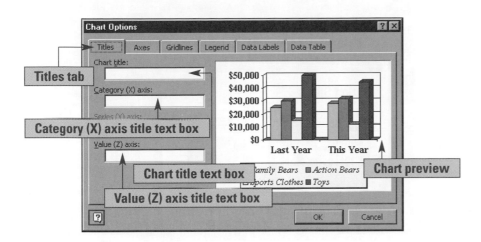

FIGURE 6-7
Chart Options Dialog Box

QUICK TIP

You can change the orientation of the Value axis title by clicking anywhere on the Orientation dial or by dragging the red orientation diamond or the Text arm in the Chart Options dialog box.

Step 4	*Click*	in the Value (Z) axis: text box
Step 5	*Key*	Total Sales
Step 6	*Click*	OK
Step 7	*Right-click*	the Value Axis Title (Total Sales)
Step 8	*Click*	Format Axis Title
Step 9	*Click*	the Alignment tab
Step 10	*Key*	90 in the Degrees: text box
Step 11	*Click*	OK
Step 12	*Click*	outside the chart object
Step 13	*Save*	the *Teddy Toys* presentation

Your screen should look similar to Figure 6-8.

MOUSE TIP

You can display labels and values by right-clicking the series, clicking Format Data Series, and then clicking the Data Labels tab.

chapter
six

FIGURE 6-8
Formatted Column
Chart Slide

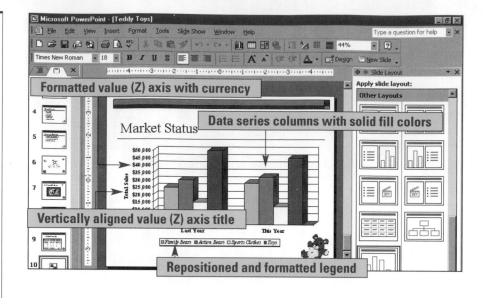

C 6.d Adding a Pie Chart to a Slide

Column and bar graphs are most effective for showing the relationship among groups of data, trends, or time changes. When you want to show the relationship of parts the whole, pie charts are the best choice. In addition, a pie chart is useful when you want to emphasize a major component of a series; say, for example, you want to show the sales for only one quarter or one area. To add a pie chart to a slide at the end of a presentation:

> ### QUICK TIP
>
> When you key data for a pie chart, you can key the pie slice data in the first column, column 0. The values are keyed directly to the right of each slice label. When completed, click the By Column button on the Standard toolbar.

Step 1	*Display*	the column chart slide, if necessary
Step 2	*Add*	a new slide based on the Title and Chart layout
Step 3	*Key*	Market Share in the title placeholder
Step 4	*Double-click*	the chart placeholder

The default column chart with default data appears every time you add a chart to a slide. You need to delete the default data and key in your own data for a pie chart. To delete the sample data from the datasheet and enter new data:

| Step 1 | *Click* | the Select All button in the upper-left corner of the datasheet to select the contents of the datasheet |

Step 2	*Press*	the DELETE key
Step 3	*Click*	the cell immediately below the column A indicator
Step 4	*Key*	Andy's Amusements and press the TAB key
Step 5	*Key*	Gary's Games in cell B0 and press the TAB key
Step 6	*Key*	Teddy Toys in cell C0
Step 7	*Click*	cell A1
Step 8	*Key*	the following values, pressing the TAB key after each value: 75000 90000 120000
Step 9	*Close*	the datasheet

The data you just keyed in the datasheet reflects total sales from last year for each of three toy manufacturers. When you create a chart in Microsoft Graph, it is automatically displayed as a column chart. To display the data in a different chart type, you must change the chart type. Because you keyed data for only one data series, you decide to change the column chart to a pie chart. To change the default chart to a pie chart:

| Step 1 | *Click* | the Chart Type button list arrow [icon] on the Standard toolbar |
| Step 2 | *Click* | the 3-D Pie Chart button in the fifth row, second column |

6.e Formatting a Pie Chart

After you create a pie chart, you have many options for enhancing its appearance. You can display names of series, categories, values, and percentages instead of using a legend for clarity. The pie may be rotated, tilted, resized, and moved to make it easier for the audience to interpret the data. Individual pie slices (as well as the entire pie) can be pulled out for emphasis and the border and fill colors can be changed to match the presentation design. Two-dimensional and three-dimensional pies create different effects.

DESIGN TIP

Data labels can be displayed on a column or bar chart, but they sometimes are too large and difficult to read. A legend displays better on a column chart, whereas data labels display better on a pie chart.

As a general design rule, a pie chart should contain no more than seven slices. Too many slices cause a pie chart to lose its effectiveness. If you find that your series of information consists of more than seven values, consider using a different type of chart to display your data.

MENU TIP

You can access the 3-D View dialog box by clicking the 3-D View command on the Chart menu in Microsoft Graph.

---

chapter
six

Hiding a Legend and Displaying Data Labels

Instead of displaying a legend with a pie chart, it is usually more effective to use data labels and values. Legends tend to take up a lot of room on a pie chart, and the eye has to travel off the pie to see the label for the slices. **Data labels** can be set to display series names, category names, values, percentages, or any combination.

The pie chart displays three colored slices representing the three toy manufacturers. You can display data labels and percentages for each, so that the audience readily identifies each competitor and its market share. To hide the legend and display labels and percentages:

Step 1	*Click*	the Legend button 🖼 on the Microsoft Graph Standard toolbar to hide the legend
Step 2	*Click*	Chart
Step 3	*Click*	Chart Options
Step 4	*Click*	the Data Labels tab
Step 5	*Click*	the Category name and Percentage check boxes
Step 6	*Click*	OK
Step 7	*Click*	outside the chart area

Your screen should look similar to Figure 6-9.

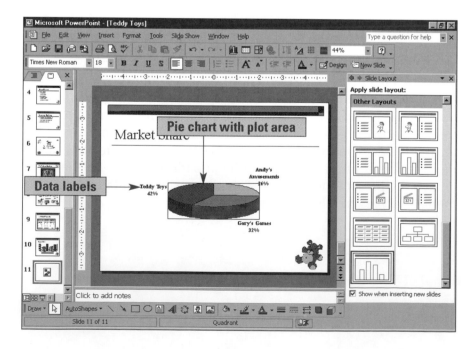

FIGURE 6-9
Pie Chart with Data Labels

Rotating and Tilting a Pie Chart

After creating a pie chart, the slices and labels can be rotated so they fit better in the chart slide area. You can tilt and change the height of the pie to create a different 3-D visual effect. You decide to change the tilt and rotation of the Teddy Toys pie slice to emphasize that Teddy Toys holds a large slice of the current market. To change the 3-D view options:

Step 1	***Double-click***	the pie chart object
Step 2	***Close***	the datasheet, if necessary
Step 3	***Right-click***	the chart area (ScreenTip displays: Chart Area)
Step 4	***Click***	3-D <u>V</u>iew

The 3-D View dialog box on your screen should look similar to Figure 6-10. This dialog box contains options for rotating, tilting, and changing the base height.

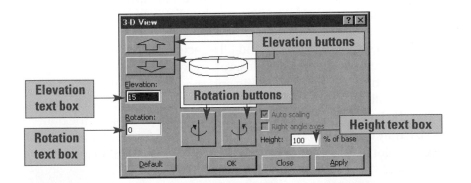

Step 5	***Drag***	the 3-D View dialog box so that you can see the pie chart
Step 6	***Click***	the Up arrow button to change the elevation (tilt) of the pie to 35
Step 7	***Click***	Apply and observe the change
Step 8	***Click***	the Left rotate button until the <u>R</u>otation: text box displays 150
Step 9	***Click***	Apply and observe the change
Step 10	***Click***	OK
Step 11	***Save***	the *Teddy Toys* presentation

FIGURE 6-10
3-D View Dialog Box

chapter
six

Pulling Out a Pie Slice

You can pull out an individual slice to emphasize the importance of that particular slice, or data point. To select one slice of a pie chart object, you click once to select the data series (entire pie), and then again to select just that data point (one slice). If you select the pie instead of one slice, you pull out all the slices of the pie. As you pull out a slice, or all the slices, you might need to adjust the labels and percentages so that you can read them. The size of the labels and percentages may change depending on how you pull out the slices. To pull out a slice:

| Step 1 | *Click* | the Teddy Toys slice twice to select it; do not double-click the slice |
| Step 2 | *Drag* | the Teddy Toys slice to the right approximately 0.5 inch |

Formatting the Plot Area of a Pie Chart

The plot area of a chart is the area of a chart that graphically displays statistical data being plotted. The plot area border line can be formatted with a different style, color, and weight, while the plot border area can be formatted with different fill colors and fill effects. You resize the plot area by dragging one of the corner handles. You move the plot area by dragging the selection border. Although resizing and moving the plot area is very helpful, you still have the option of moving and resizing the entire chart object on the PowerPoint slide. When you resize the pie object, the data labels size may change. To change the size of the pie in the plot area, remove the plot area border, and make any final plot area adjustments:

Step 1	*Click*	the plot area border line (ScreenTip displays: Plot Area)
Step 2	*Drag*	any corner handle to increase the size of the pie chart so that it fits better in the chart area
Step 3	*Resize*	the plot area as necessary to make sure all labels and percentages fit in the chart area
Step 4	*Drag*	the plot area border to center the pie object in the chart area
Step 5	*Select*	the plot area border, if necessary
Step 6	*Press*	the DELETE key to delete the Plot Area border
Step 7	*Click*	any data label to select all of the labels
Step 8	*Change*	the font size to 20 point

| Step 9 | *Click* | outside the chart area |

The pie chart on your slide should look similar to Figure 6-11.

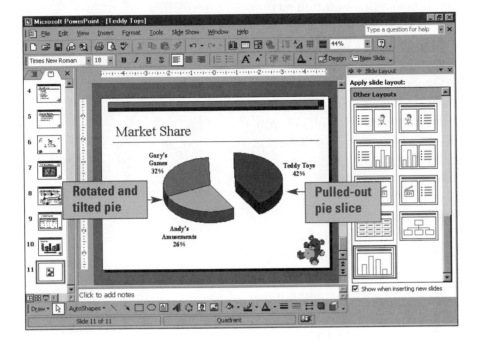

| Step 10 | *Save* | the *Teddy Toys* presentation and close it |

The pie chart clearly shows the Teddy Toys' market share.

MOUSE TIP

You can edit the selected plot area by right-clicking the plot area and then clicking F_ormat Plot Area.

You can also edit the selected plot area by selecting the plot area and then clicking the Format Plot Area button on the Standard toolbar in Microsoft Graph.

FIGURE 6-11
Completed Market Share Pie Chart

MENU TIP

You can edit the selected plot area by clicking the Se_lected Plot Area command on the F_ormat menu.

QUICK TIP

You can select all data labels by clicking one data label. However, if you select all the data labels and then click only one data label, only that data label is selected.

chapter
six

Summary

► You can add a chart slide to a presentation to illustrate statistical and quantitative information in a graphical representation so that the audience can quickly interpret your message.

► You create a chart in PowerPoint using Microsoft Graph, a program that comes with PowerPoint.

► You can insert an existing chart that you created in another program, such as Word or Excel, in a PowerPoint slide.

► Because a chart in a PowerPoint slide is an embedded object, you edit and format it using the program in which it was created.

► A data series represents one set of related data on the datasheet, such as one set of columns on a chart.

► A data point represents only one item in a data series, such as one column in a series of columns or one slice in a pie chart.

► The datasheet is used to key values in the form of rows and columns, similar to a Microsoft Excel worksheet, to create a chart that reflects those values.

► When keying data in the datasheet, preselecting a range temporarily changes the path of the active cell, to make it easier to key quickly.

► The Select All button on the datasheet is used to select all the default data before deleting it.

► The category (X) axis on a chart displays the categories being measured.

► The value (Y) or (Z) axis displays a scale based on the values that are entered on the datasheet.

► When working on three-dimensional charts, the value (Y) axis displays as value (Z).

► A chart legend is a chart object that identifies the patterns, fills, or colors that are assigned to the categories or data series on a chart.

► Depending on the chart type, rows and columns can be switched to display data differently.

► Depending on the type of data you want to project, you can choose many different types of charts including column, bar, line, pie, XY, area, doughnut, radar, surface, bubble, stock, cylinder, cone, or pyramid.

► Column and bar charts show changes in data over a period a time or show comparisons among individual items.

► Line charts show trends over a period of time.

► Pie charts are best for displaying the relationship of parts to the whole.

► Cone, pyramid, or cylinder charts add a dramatic 3-D effect when showing changes in data over time or when comparing data values.

► Stock charts are most effective for showing the high-low-close ratings of stocks.

▶ You can format the Value (Y) or Value (Z) axis to display currency, to represent dollar amounts, change the axis scale, change the text alignment, and change the font.

▶ Titles can be added to a chart and rotated on the axes for clarity.

▶ Labels and values or percentages should be used instead of a legend to identify the series on a pie chart.

▶ You can rotate and tilt the pie chart to create a different visual effect.

▶ You can cut a slice of the pie or explode the entire pie for emphasis.

▶ The colors of individual slices of a pie can be changed.

▶ The plot area displays the actual chart series such as columns, bars, lines, and pie slices.

▶ The plot area can be used to resize the chart within the chart area, and the plot area border can be deleted.

Commands Review

Action	Menu Bar	Shortcut Menu	Toolbar	Task Pane	Keyboard
Add a chart	Insert, Chart Insert, Object, Microsoft Graph Chart	Double-click chart placeholder	📊	Click Title and Chart layout on the Slide Layout task pane under Other Layouts, or click any Content layout on the Slide Layout task pane and then click the Insert 📊 Chart icon	ALT + I, H ALT + I, O
Edit the selected legend	Format, Selected Legend	Right-click legend, Format Legend Double-click legend			ALT + O, E CTRL + 1
Change the chart display	Data, Series in Rows or Series in Columns		📊 📋		ALT + D, R ALT + D, C
Change the chart type	Chart, Chart Type	Right-click series, plot area, or chart area, then Chart Type	📈 ▾		ALT + C, Y
Format the selected data series	Format, Selected Data Series	Right-click series, Format Data Series Double-click the series object	🖼		ALT + O, E CTRL + 1
Format the selected axis	Format, Selected Axis	Right-click axis, Format Axis Double-click the axis	🖼		ALT + O, E CTRL + 1
Add axis titles	Chart, Chart Options	Right-click plot area or chart area, Chart Options			ALT + C, I
Display labels and percentages	Chart, Chart Options, Data Labels	Right-click plot area or chart area, Chart Options, Data Labels Double-click the pie object, Data Labels			ALT + C, I
Format the selected data labels	Format, Selected Data Labels	Right-click the data labels, Format Data Labels Double-click any data label	🖼		ALT + O, E CTRL + 1
Rotate, tilt, and change the pie height	Chart, 3-D View	Right-click the plot area or chart area, 3-D View			ALT + C, V
Cut a pie slice		Drag the selected pie slice			
Format a selected slice	Format, Selected Data Point	Right-click selected slice, Format Data Point Double-click selected slice	🖼		ALT + O, E CTRL + 1
Format selected plot area	Format, Selected Plot Area	Right-click the plot area, Format Plot Area Double-click plot area	🖼		ALT + O, E CTRL + 1

chapter six

Concepts Review

Circle the correct answer.

1. A chart slide is created by using Microsoft:
[a] Word.
[b] Excel.
[c] Table.
[d] Graph.

2. The name of the form used to input chart values is:
[a] AutoForm.
[b] Microsoft Graph Chart.
[c] Microsoft Excel.
[d] Datasheet.

3. The values entered in a datasheet are displayed on the:
[a] (X) axis.
[b] (Y) or (Z) axis.
[c] legend.
[d] title area.

4. Which of the following formatting options allows you to display dollar signs on the Value axis?
[a] Number
[b] Date and Time
[c] Currency
[d] Percentage

5. Titles can be added to all of the following except the:
[a] (Y) or (Z) axis.
[b] (X) axis.
[c] chart.
[d] gridlines.

6. Charts should be used to display statistical data on a slide to show all of the following *except*:
[a] comparisons.
[b] parts of a whole.
[c] trends.
[d] a bulleted list.

7. A pie chart best displays statistical data using which of the following?
[a] trends over time
[b] comparisons of ten products
[c] comparisons of parts to the whole
[d] comparisons of many different categories of data

8. All of the following may appear near each slice of the pie *except*:
[a] titles.
[b] percentages.
[c] values.
[d] category names.

9. To pull out a slice of a pie:
[a] right-click the selected slice.
[b] drag the selected slice.
[c] double-click the selected slice.
[d] press the CTRL + X keys.

10. The part of a chart slide that holds the actual series objects (columns, bars, pie slices, and so on) created from the datasheet, is the:
[a] plot area.
[b] chart area.
[c] category axis.
[d] legend.

Circle **T** if the statement is true or **F** if the statement is false.

T   F   1. In a chart, a series represents one set of related data.

T   F   2. Double-clicking a chart in PowerPoint enables you to make formatting changes to the chart.

T   F   3. A legend displays the series color and the series name.

T   F   4. All column charts display a Value (Z) axis.

T   F   5. The (X) axis displays the values that were keyed on the datasheet.

T   F   6. A legend should always be used in a pie chart.

T   F   7. You should have as many slices on a pie chart as you desire.

T   F   8. You can display values, percentages, series name, or category name, but not all at one time on a pie chart.

T   F   9. The reason you pull out a slice is usually to emphasize that particular slice of the pie chart.

T   F   10. The plot area of a pie chart is the only element of the chart that cannot be changed.

Skills Review

Exercise 1   C

1. Open the *PowerPoint* presentation you modified in Chapter 5, and add a chart slide at the end of the presentation with the title "Comparing Slide Types."

2. Clear the datasheet of sample data, and complete the chart using the information below:

	Accounting	Marketing
Title	15	30
Bullet	35	50
Table	25	15
Chart	60	40

3. Change the chart to display By Column.

4. Change the location of the legend to the top.

5. Change the color of the Accounting column to display a texture that complements the presentation design and the color of the Marketing column to display a texture that complements the presentation design.

6. Add the following title to the Value axis: "number of slides".

7. Rotate the Value axis title to 90 degrees.

8. Save the presentation, print the chart slide, and then close the presentation.

Exercise 2   C

1. Open the *Office* presentation you modified in Chapter 5, and add a chart slide at the end of the presentation with the title "Daily Office Use."

2. Clear the datasheet of sample data, and complete the chart using the information below:

Word	Excel	PowerPoint	Access	Outlook
80	65	50	40	35

3. Change the chart to a 3-D pie.

4. Hide the legend, and display data labels with category names and percentages.

5. Rotate the pie to 130 degrees.

6. Tilt or elevate the pie to 40 degrees.

7. Remove the plot area border.

8. Pull out the PowerPoint slice.

chapter six

9. Resize the pie chart within the chart area so you can read all the data labels.

10. Save the presentation, print the chart slide, and then close the presentation.

Exercise 3   C

1. Open the *Design* presentation you modified in Chapter 5, and add a chart slide at the end of the presentation with the title "Design Element Frequency."

2. Clear the datasheet of sample data, and complete the chart using the information below:

Clip Art	*100*
AutoShapes	*75*
Music	*50*
Videos	*25*

3. Change the chart to a 3-D horizontal bar chart.

4. Change the chart to display By Column.

5. Hide the legend.

6. Change the bar fill to either a gradient fill or a texture fill to match the presentation design.

7. Change the wall colors to enhance the bars, and then change the gridline color, if necessary.

8. Add the following title to the Value (Z) axis: "Percentage Used in Presentations."

9. Resize and reposition the chart as needed.

10. Save the presentation, print the chart slide, and then close the presentation.

Exercise 4   C

1. Open the *Precision Builders* presentation you modified in Chapter 5, and add a chart slide at the end of the presentation with the title "New Homes Built This Year."

2. Clear the datasheet of sample data, and complete the chart using the information below:

Ranch Homes	*Townhomes*	*Two-story Homes*
8	*5*	*10*

3. Change the chart to a 3-D pie chart.

4. Tilt or elevate the pie to 35 degrees.

5. Rotate the pie to 260 degrees.

6. Pull out the Ranch Homes slice of the pie.

7. Hide the legend, and display data labels with category names and percentages.

8. Change the color of all the slices to match the presentation design.

9. Remove the plot area border.

10. Resize and reposition the chart as needed.

11. Resize the labels for readability.

12. Save the presentation, print the chart slide, and then close the presentation.

Exercise 5 [C]

1. Open the *Nature Tours* presentation you modified in Chapter 5, and add a chart slide at the end of the presentation with the title "National Park Visitors."

2. Complete the chart using the information below:

	1998	1999	2000
Glacier	150000	175000	160000
Yellowstone	200200	195000	175000
Rocky Mountain	95000	105000	100000
Teton	75000	80000	85000

3. Select a column chart using cylinders, cones, pyramids, or any other chart type.

4. Add commas (thousands' separators), 0 decimals to the Value axis.

5. Add an appropriate title to the Value axis.

6. Change the font, font style, font color, and font size for the axes labels.

7. Format the legend, and change the position of the legend on the chart.

8. Resize and reposition the chart as needed.

9. Save the presentation, print the chart slide, and then close the presentation.

Exercise 6 [C]

1. Open the *A Healthier You* presentation you modified in Chapter 5, and add a chart slide at the end of the presentation with the title "Books on Nutrition."

2. Complete the chart using the information below:

Diets and You	15000
Today's Foods	35000
Eating Wisely	30000

3. Decide on the type of chart you want to use to show the relationship between the different books on nutrition.

4. Make changes regarding size, position, font, and so forth to the chart.

5. Add the following chart title: "Copies Sold."

6. Save the presentation, print the chart slide, and then close the presentation.

Exercise 7 [C]

1. Open the *Buying A Computer* presentation you modified in Chapter 5, and add a chart slide at the end of the presentation with the title "Home Computer Prices."

2. Complete the chart using the information below:

	1997	1998	1999	2000	2001
Home PCs	3000	2400	1800	1550	1200

3. Use a line chart to show the trend over the past five years.

4. Change the line color and weight.

5. Change the line marker—style, color, shape, and size.

6. Display the legend and format it in regard to location, size, color, and so forth.

chapter six

7. Display currency on the Value axis.

8. Resize and reposition the chart as needed.

9. Save the presentation, print the chart slide, and then close the presentation.

Exercise 8

1. Open the *Leisure Travel* presentation you modified in Chapter 5, and add a chart slide at the end of the presentation with the title "Future Cruises."

2. Complete the chart using the information below:

	2001	2002	2003
Aruba	45	50	30
Cancun	50	52	48
Puerto Vallarta	40	30	25
St. Thomas	30	40	30

3. Select an appropriate chart to show future bookings for cruises.

4. Decide whether to compare the years or the locations.

5. Display the legend and format it in regard to location, size, color, and so forth.

6. Add a title on the Value axis.

7. Make any other formatting changes to the chart.

8. Resize and reposition the chart as needed.

9. Save the presentation, print the chart slide, and then close the presentation.

Case Projects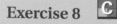

Project 1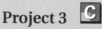

You want to import a Microsoft Excel chart into a PowerPoint slide. Access the Microsoft Graph online Help, and find information on importing a Microsoft Excel chart. In addition, you want to find out what other file formats Microsoft Graph can import. Print all information, as well as any linked information.

Project 2

Communicate Corporation wants employees to know the typical types of customer calls that are handled daily so they can anticipate what to expect when the phone rings. Your manager wants you to create a chart slide for the *Communicate* presentation you modified in Chapter 5 that compares the types of telephone calls received on a daily basis. You decide which chart type best fits your data. Make any formatting changes in regard to size, color, shape, font, and so forth. Save the presentation, print the chart slide, and close the presentation.

Project 3

Souner & Associates has been very successful during the past few years. However, the owners want to see how their training company compares with the competition. They ask you to create a chart slide for the *Souner* presentation you modified in Chapter 5 that compares the number of training classes held by Souner & Associates with three competitors for the past year. It is your decision to select an appropriate chart type that reflects your company's position and share in the market. Enhance the chart by formatting and customizing various parts of the chart. Remember that your chart should match your presentation design. Save the presentation, print the chart slide, and close the presentation.

Project 4

As you continue working on your own presentation, you find that a chart slide helps to display and present your data. Create a chart slide for the *My Presentation* you modified in Chapter 5 that provides additional information concerning your topic. Think about comparing, showing trends, or displaying parts of a whole when you create the chart slide. You can select any chart type you desire to present your data. Make any formatting changes you feel necessary. Save the presentation, print the chart slide, and close the presentation.

Project 5

As the season progresses, you want to compare the attendance figures for various exhibits at the zoo. This will help determine staffing needs for next year. Add a chart to the *Zoo* presentation you modified in Chapter 5 listing at least four exhibits and comparing the visitors' attendance. Make the chart as attractive as possible; however, the data must be clearly expressed. Save the presentation, print the chart slide, and close the presentation.

Project 6

You have been using PowerPoint for a few weeks, and you want to find out more information regarding Microsoft Graph Chart. Connect to the Internet and search the Web for new features about Microsoft

Graph Chart. Print the information you find. Create a presentation consisting of a title slide and one or two charts displaying the information you discovered. Save, print, and close the presentation.

Project 7

In the *Cars* presentation that you modified in Chapter 5, you want to compare the sales of the most popular cars on the market today. Connect to the Internet and search the Web for the most popularly sold cars and their current selling prices. You decide on the type of chart slide to add to your presentation. Make any formatting changes and enhancements to help display your message. Save the presentation, print the chart slide, and close the presentation.

Project 8

As an example of how people use various sites on the Internet, you and your partner want to add a chart slide comparing the number of hits (visits) per site in a given period of time. You each choose three Internet sites, and track the number of hits for a two-week period. After that time, you compile your data and show each Internet site and its number of hits. Enhance the chart slide as needed to present your findings in the *Internet* presentation you modified in Chapter 5. Save the presentation, print the chart slide, and close the presentation.

chapter six

Preparing and Running a Slide Show

Chapter Overview

A slide show is a PowerPoint slide presentation that can be viewed on a computer screen or projected onto a large screen by a specially designed projection device connected to the computer. Although you can output PowerPoint slides for use in a slide projector or an overhead projector, running a slide show in PowerPoint lets you control the transition of slides and even add special effects. In this chapter, you learn to run a slide show in PowerPoint, add transitions and animation schemes to slides, enhance transitions with special effects, and set timings to run the slide show automatically.

LEARNING OBJECTIVES

▶ Run a slide show
▶ Apply transition effects and animation schemes
▶ Rehearse presentations
▶ Prepare slide shows for delivery
▶ Create a new blank presentation from existing slides

Case profile

During a meeting with your boss, Ms. Hill, you review the various media options available for the presentation you have been working on for her. Ms. Hill tells you that there will be less than twenty people at the initial presentation. She has learned that the room is equipped with an overhead projection system. Because Ms. Hill has a laptop computer she can use with the overhead projection system, you suggest that she run the presentation as a slide show in PowerPoint.

chapter seven

7.a Running a Slide Show

You decide to run the slide show of the *Teddy Toys* presentation as it is so you can determine what transitions to add to the slides as they appear on the screen. To run a slide show:

Step 1	*Open*	the *Teddy Toys* presentation you modified in Chapter 6 and display Slide 1
Step 2	*Click*	the Slide Show (from current slide) button 

After the "Starting slide show" message appears briefly, the current slide fills the screen. Your screen should look similar to Figure 7-1.

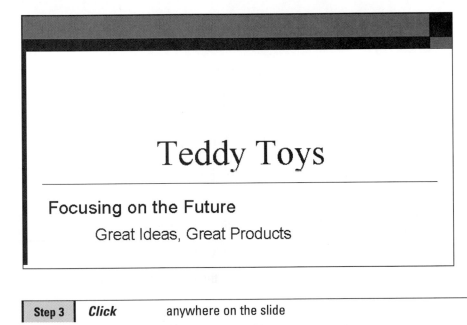

Step 3	*Click*	anywhere on the slide

The second slide appears. Each time you click or press certain keys, the next slide appears. As you progress through the slide show, pay careful attention to how each slide comes on to the screen.

Step 4	*Press*	the PAGE DOWN key to display the next slide
Step 5	*Press*	the RIGHT ARROW key to display the next slide
Step 6	*Press*	the DOWN ARROW key to progress to the next slide
Step 7	*Key*	N to progress to the next slide
Step 8	*Press*	the SPACEBAR to progress to the next slide

MENU TIP

You can run a slide show from the beginning by clicking the Slide Show command on the View menu or by clicking the View Show command on the Slide Show menu.

FIGURE 7-1
Title Slide in Slide Show

MOUSE TIP

You can start a slide show presentation from your desktop by right-clicking the presentation filename and then clicking Show or by double-clicking a PowerPoint presentation saved as a PowerPoint Show (.pps).

QUICK TIP

You can start the slide show from the first slide by pressing the F5 key.

chapter
seven

You also can press one of several keys to move to previous slides in a presentation. To move to a previous slide in Slide Show:

Step 1	*Press*	the PAGE UP key to move to the previous slide
Step 2	*Press*	the LEFT ARROW key
Step 3	*Press*	the UP ARROW key
Step 4	*Key*	P
Step 5	*Press*	the BACKSPACE key
Step 6	*Press*	the END key to move to the last slide
Step 7	*Press & hold*	both mouse buttons for two seconds to move to the first slide
Step 8	*Press*	the ESCAPE key to end the slide show

Working with Slide Show Options

As you view a slide show, you can click an onscreen icon to open a shortcut menu displaying controls, commands, and options for use during the slide show. To display this shortcut icon initially during a slide show, you simply move the mouse slightly on the screen; the icon then remains on the screen until the slide show ends. This shortcut menu also appears when you right-click anywhere on the screen during a slide show. To display the shortcut icon in Slide Show:

Step 1	*Start*	the slide show from the beginning
Step 2	*Point*	anywhere on the screen
Step 3	*Click*	the shortcut icon at the lower-left corner of the screen

The shortcut menu on your screen should look similar to Figure 7-2.

FIGURE 7-2
Shortcut Menu in Slide Show

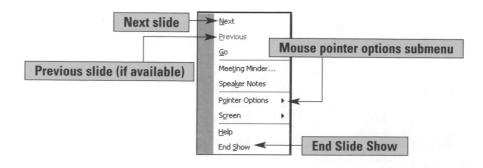

You can move from slide to slide during a presentation by clicking the Next, Previous, and Go commands on this shortcut menu. You also can navigate through a slide show to any desired slide according to its title by clicking the By Title command on the Go submenu.

By default, the mouse pointer in Slide Show appears as an arrow. You can, however, hide the mouse pointer or change the mouse pointer shape to a pen you can use to temporarily write or draw on the slide as it is being viewed in a slide show. To use the pen pointer during a presentation:

Step 1	*Point to*	Pointer Options
Step 2	*Click*	Pen
Step 3	*Press & hold*	the SHIFT key
Step 4	*Draw*	a line under the title text

Pressing the SHIFT key constrains the line you draw to a straight line. Any marks you draw while in slide show appear only in slide show and only while the current slide is displayed. The marks you make are removed as soon as you move to a different slide or end the slide show. You also can remove pen marks on the current slide by pressing the E key. In addition, you can change the color of the pen. To draw circles with a different pen color:

Step 1	*Click*	the shortcut icon
Step 2	*Point to*	Pointer Options
Step 3	*Point to*	Pen Color
Step 4	*Click*	Red
Step 5	*Draw*	a circle around the word "Focusing" and the word "Products"

Your screen should look similar to Figure 7-3.

QUICK TIP

To move to the first slide in the slide show, you can press the HOME key. To move to the last slide, you can press the END key. To progress to a particular slide within a presentation, you can press the key of the number of the slide + ENTER. To end the slide show, press the ESCAPE or HYPHEN key.

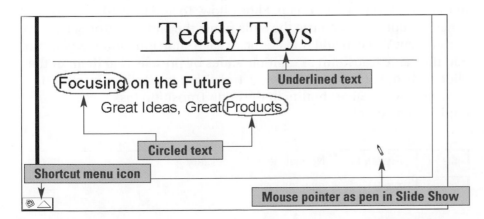

FIGURE 7-3
Pen Options in Slide Show

chapter
seven

To use keyboard shortcuts to remove the line and circles and change the mouse pointer back to the arrow shape:

Step 1	*Press*	the E key to remove all the pen marks
Step 2	*Press*	CTRL + A to change the mouse pointer from a pen to an arrow
Step 3	*Press*	the ESCAPE key to return to Normal view

7.b Applying Transition Effects and Animation Schemes

A slide show visually reinforces the ideas, comments, solutions, or suggestions you are presenting. By using creative techniques to move from slide to slide, such as transition effects and animation schemes, you also are conveying to the audience that you and your company use the most creative and innovative methods to achieve your goals.

Applying Transitions

When you run a slide show, each slide replaces the previous slide whenever you click the mouse button or press a key to change slides. You may, however, want to add special effects when moving from one slide to the next in the slide show. **Transitions** are special display effects used to introduce a slide during the slide show. Transitions determine how the display changes as the user progresses from one slide to another. Examples of transitional effects include a slide that wipes down across the screen, a slide that is formed out of a set of blinds closing, and a slide that appears as a spoke turns clockwise, exposing more and more of the slide as the spoke turns.

You can add slide transitions and animation schemes to slides in any of the PowerPoint views except Slide Show. To add transitions and times to slides, you can use the Slide pane, the Slides tab, or Slide Sorter view. You can add transitions to each slide individually, you can add the same transition to multiple slides by preselecting them in the Slides tab, or you can add the same transition to all slides by clicking the Apply to All Slides button in the Slide Transition task pane. To apply transition effects:

Step 1	*Switch to*	Normal view, if necessary
Step 2	*Click*	Sli<u>d</u>e Show

Step 3	*Click*	Slide Transition
Step 4	*Verify*	that the AutoPreview check box at the bottom of the Slide Transition task pane contains a check mark
Step 5	*Click*	the first effect (Blinds Horizontal) in the Apply to selected slides: list box in the Slide Transition task pane

Your screen should look similar to Figure 7-4.

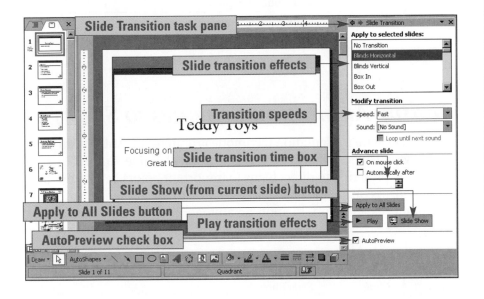

FIGURE 7-4
Slide Transition Task Pane

TASK PANE TIP

You can access the Slide Transition task pane when the task pane is open by clicking the Other Task Panes list arrow in the task pane and then clicking Slide Transition.

The slide in Normal view illustrates the effect. To view the effect again, click the transition effect in the Apply to selected slides: list box or click the Play button at the bottom of the Slide Transition task pane. You can try other effects from the Slide Transition effects list in the same way.

Step 6	*Click*	Blinds Vertical
Step 7	*Continue*	to view the remaining transitions, scrolling when necessary
Step 8	*Click*	Newsflash

In addition to changing the transition effect, you can change the speed of the transition effect in the Speed: list box under Modify transition in the Slide Transition task pane. To apply a transition speed to all the slides:

Step 1	*Click*	Slow in the Speed: list

MENU TIP

You can access the Slide Transition task pane by clicking the Slide Transition command on the Slide Show menu. You can access the Slide Design task pane to change animation schemes by clicking the Animation Schemes command on the Slide Show menu.

chapter
seven

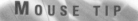
You like this speed. To apply this transition effect to all slides in the presentation:

Step 2	*Click*	the Apply to All Slides button in the Slide Transition task pane
Step 3	*Display*	Slide 1, if necessary
Step 4	*Click*	the Slide Show button [Slide Show] in the Slide Transition task pane
Step 5	*View*	each slide in the presentation until you reach the end of the slide show
Step 6	*Save*	the *Teddy Toys* presentation

Adding Animation Schemes to Slides

Another useful presentation technique is animation. **Animation** is special visual effects that you can add to parts of a slide. Animation effects enable the presenter to direct focus to important points as they are being presented, to control the flow of information to the audience, or to capture the audience's attention. To apply an animation scheme to a text slide:

Step 1	*Display*	Slide 2
Step 2	*Click*	Slide Show
Step 3	*Click*	Animation Schemes

The Slide Design-Animation Schemes task pane opens. Your screen should look similar to Figure 7-5.

FIGURE 7-5
Animation Schemes in Slide Design Task Pane

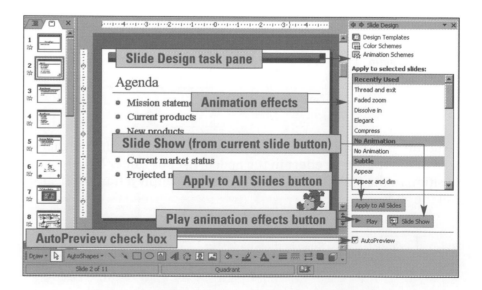

The task pane displays a list box of animation schemes that can be applied to the current slide or to all slides in the presentation. The animation schemes in the Apply to selected slides: list box enable you to pick schemes from the following categories: Recently Used, No animation, Subtle animation, Moderate animation, and Exciting animation.

| Step 4 | *Click* | Elegant in the Moderate category |

A ScreenTip displays when you point to an animation effect indicating the exact Slide Transition, Title, and/or Body effects. If an animation scheme also changes the slide transition, that transition replaces any previously applied transition. You can see the slide transition and animation scheme by clicking the Play button at the bottom of the Slide Design task pane or by clicking the effect in the animation schemes list again.

Step 5	*Click*	several effects in each category and observe the different animation schemes
Step 6	*Click*	the Slide Show button [Slide Show] in the Slide Design task pane, and view the animation effects for the current slide
Step 7	*Click*	to view each bullet item

Because the default for progressing through slides is manual progression, you have to click the mouse or press the SPACEBAR, the ENTER key, the PAGE DOWN key, or an ARROW key to see each effect.

Step 8	*Press*	the ESCAPE key after viewing the bullets on the slide to end the slide show
Step 9	*Click*	Elegant in the Moderate category
Step 10	*Click*	the Apply to All Slides button in the Slide Design task pane
Step 11	*Run*	the slide show from the beginning, clicking to progress through each slide and then return to Normal view
Step 12	*Save*	the *Teddy Toys* presentation

7.c Rehearsing Presentations

There are four steps involved in creating presentations: plan, prepare, practice, and present. **Planning** involves establishing the goal of the presentation and researching information to find the essential

chapter
seven

TASK PANE TIP

You can access the Slide Design - Animation Schemes task pane when the task pane is open by clicking the Other Task Panes list arrow in the task pane and then clicking Slide Design - Animation Schemes.

DESIGN TIP

Setting times manually is a good option if you plan to run a slide show automatically, without a presenter. The audience gets to read each slide as it is presented, and after a preset period of time, the next slide automatically appears on the screen.

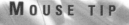

MOUSE TIP

You can add animation schemes to a slide or slides of a presentation by clicking the Design button on the Formatting toolbar and then clicking Animation Schemes in the Slide Design task pane.

facts or concepts to support or establish that goal. **Preparing** involves using presentation graphics software to provide the medium to display that goal. **Practicing** involves learning the material, equipment, and software to present the information. **Presenting** involves the actual conveying of information in an effective and effective manner. PowerPoint provides you with the tools necessary to prepare and practice presentations.

A PowerPoint feature that aids in rehearsing and presenting is the ability to set timings for your slides. When you set **timings** for slides, the slides in the presentation progress from one to the other automatically when running a slide show. You do not have to click the mouse, press the SPACEBAR, or otherwise manually advance the slides. This way, the presenter is not tied to a computer console and can walk around the room while the slides progress when new topics, points, or ideas are being discussed. You can manually set what you consider appropriate timings for the slides and then rehearse the presentation, or you can work with PowerPoint to set timings while you rehearse.

Setting Slide Times Manually

Setting times manually is advisable when you know you have only so many minutes available in which to give a presentation. In this way, when you practice your presentation, you work within the allotted time frame established for each slide.

To manually set slide times in a slide show, you can be in either Normal or Slide Sorter view. In Normal view, you select the slide or slides in the Slides tab. In Slide Sorter view, you can see all the slides of the presentation and then "guesstimate" how long it will take to go over the information on each slide. The time for each slide can be set independently of the others or all slides can be set for the same time.

notes For purposes of practice, you set minimal times in this chapter. This enables you to view the effects quickly.

To manually set times for individual slides and view the slide show:

Step 1	*Click*	the Other Task Panes list arrow in the Slide Design task pane
Step 2	*Click*	Slide Transition
Step 3	*Display*	Slide 1
Step 4	*Key*	2 in the Automatically after text box
Step 5	*Click*	anywhere on the slide in Normal view

Notice that the time "00:02" appears in the Automatically after text box in the Advance Slide area.

Step 6	*Select*	every even-numbered slide (press and hold the CTRL key as you click each even-numbered slide) in the Slides tab
Step 7	*Key*	4 in the Automatically after text box
Step 8	*Click*	anywhere on the slide in Normal view
Step 9	*Select*	the remaining odd-numbered slides
Step 10	*Key*	2 in the Automatically after text box
Step 11	*Click*	anywhere on the slide in the Normal view
Step 12	*Press*	the F5 key to start the slide show from the beginning

You can now view the slide show from the beginning without clicking the mouse. If you were planning to make this presentation, you could rehearse your comments and see whether you needed to lengthen or shorten any timings.

| Step 13 | *Click* | to end the slide show, if necessary |

Setting Slide Times During Rehearsal Mode

You can also set timings while you rehearse a presentation. It is important to practice timings with the material so that your words match the flow of the presentation. This can be very difficult if you plan to orally present the material with the slide show running with preset times. You need to be extremely familiar with the material and practice it many times to successfully match your words, ideas, and timing with that of the preset times. You can use rehearsal mode to accurately determine the length of a presentation. To set timings while rehearsing:

| Step 1 | *Click* | Sli<u>d</u>e Show |
| Step 2 | *Click* | <u>R</u>ehearse Timings |

The first slide and the Rehearsal toolbar appear. Your screen should look similar to Figure 7-6. The Rehearsal toolbar includes a Next button for progressing to the next slide, a Pause button to stop the clock, the time spent on each slide, a Repeat button to rehearse a slide again, and the time spent on the total presentation.

DESIGN TIP

Animation schemes work well with title and text slides because each part of the slide can be introduced by itself.

CAUTION TIP

Setting times to a slide show should only be done after much practice by a presenter who is sure of the time required for each slide. Inexperienced presenters often have more success by manually progressing through a presentation.
Do not click the Apply to All Slides button in the Slide Transition task pane unless you want the same time applied to all the slides.

MOUSE TIP

You can start rehearsing timings in Slide Sorter view by clicking the Rehearse Timings button on the Slide Sorter toolbar.

chapter
seven

FIGURE 7-6
Rehearsal Toolbar in
Slide Show

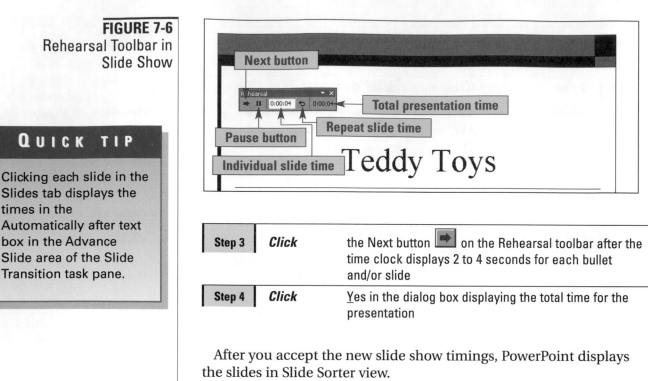

Next button

Total presentation time

Repeat slide time

Pause button

Individual slide time

Teddy Toys

| Step 3 | *Click* | the Next button  on the Rehearsal toolbar after the time clock displays 2 to 4 seconds for each bullet and/or slide |
| Step 4 | *Click* | Yes in the dialog box displaying the total time for the presentation |

After you accept the new slide show timings, PowerPoint displays the slides in Slide Sorter view.

The times displayed below the slides in Slide Sorter view for your presentation are the times you set during your rehearsal. Your screen should look similar to Figure 7-7, though your times may vary. You can rehearse the material again at any time and set new times.

FIGURE 7-7
Slide Sorter View with
Rehearsal Times

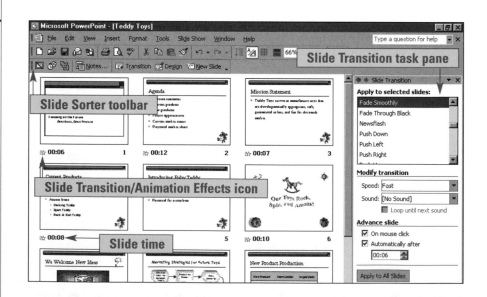

Slide Sorter toolbar

Slide Transition task pane

Slide Transition/Animation Effects icon

Slide time

To cycle through all the slides quickly, you decide to change the times for all the slides to 4 seconds. To apply the same time to all the slides:

| Step 1 | *Key* | 4 in the Automatically after text box |

Step 2	*Click*	the Apply to All Slides button in the Slide Transition task pane
Step 3	*Run*	the slide show
Step 4	*Save*	the *Teddy Toys* presentation

7.d Preparing Slide Shows for Delivery

Slide Sorter view is a good view for adding transitions, animation schemes, and times. In addition, this view is ideal for rearranging and managing the slides in your presentation. Because your presentations may consist of many slides, it is easier to move, copy, hide, and delete the slides when they are displayed in Slide Sorter view than when in Normal view.

Changing the Order of Slides

Moving a slide from one location to another within a presentation, or from one presentation to another, is a common task when managing presentations. After practicing a presentation or giving a presentation for the first time, you may need to rearrange slides to match your flow of thought or maintain a logical progression. In Slide Sorter view, you can move the slide miniatures as you would any object to rearrange them. To change the order of slides in Slide Sorter view:

Step 1	*Select*	any slide in the presentation
Step 2	*Drag*	the selected slide to the right of the next slide
Step 3	*Drag*	the last slide to the left of the first slide of the presentation
Step 4	*Click*	the Undo button [↰] on the Standard toolbar twice

As you drag the slide, a vertical line and the Move arrow are displayed to the right of the slide to indicate where the slide will be repositioned. When you release the mouse button, the move is complete.

C

QUICK TIP

You can undo an action by pressing the CTRL + Z keys. You can redo an action by pressing the CTRL + Y keys.

C

QUICK TIP

You can select multiple slides in Slide Sorter view by holding down the SHIFT or CTRL key and clicking each slide. The SHIFT key enables you to select slides in a continuous order, whereas the CTRL key enables you to select slides individually, in no particular order.

You can select all slides in Slide Sorter view by pressing the CTRL + A keys.

chapter
seven

Copying Slides in Slide Sorter View

Copying slides in Slide Sorter view involves the same techniques as copying any object. You can use the menu, toolbar, and mouse methods to copy slides within a presentation. To copy a slide in Slide Sorter view:

Step 1	*Right-click*	any slide in the presentation
Step 2	*Click*	Copy
Step 3	*Right-click*	to the right of the last slide in the presentation
Step 4	*Click*	Paste

You have created a copy of the slide. The copied slide has the same transition and time as the original slide.

Deleting Slides

When viewing a presentation in Slide Sorter view, you may decide that a slide or slides do not work well within the presentation or are no longer necessary to the goal of the presentation. When that happens, you need to delete slides. Again, because the miniature slides are objects, you delete them just as you would delete any object. To delete slides in the Slide Sorter view:

Step 1	*Select*	the copied slide and the Our Toys Rock, Spin, and Amaze! slide
Step 2	*Press*	the DELETE key

Hiding Slides

Sometimes you may need to give a presentation to two different groups. Because the groups are different, you may not want to show all the slides in each presentation. When this happens, it is not necessary to delete the slide or slides for the next group. Instead, you can **hide** a slide or slides for a particular presentation. Then, if you wish to use the entire presentation again, you simply show or **unhide** the slide or slides.

To hide slides in Slide Sorter view:

| Step 1 | *Select* | the New Product Production and the Introducing Baby Teddy slides |
| Step 2 | *Click* | the Hide Slide button 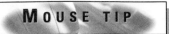 on the Slide Sorter toolbar |

An icon displays under the lower-right corner of each slide with a diagonal line covering the slide number, indicating that the slide is hidden.

| Step 3 | *Run* | the slide show from the beginning and observe that the hidden slides do not appear |

To show or unhide slides in Slide Sorter view:

Step 1	*Select*	the hidden slides, if necessary
Step 2	*Click*	the Hide Slide button 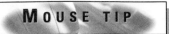 on the Slide Sorter toolbar
Step 3	*Save*	the *Teddy Toys* presentation

Removing Transitions, Animation Effects, and Timings

Transitions, animations, and timings can be removed while in Slide Sorter or Normal view using the Slide Design and Slide Transition task panes. To remove transitions, animations, and timings:

Step 1	*Click*	the Slide Transition button [Transition] on the Slide Sorter toolbar
Step 2	*Click*	No Transition in the Apply to selected slides: list box in the Slide Transition task pane
Step 3	*Click*	the Automatically after check box to remove the check mark
Step 4	*Click*	the Apply to All Slides button in the Slide Transition task pane
Step 5	*Click*	the Other Task Panes list arrow in the Slide Transition task pane
Step 6	*Click*	Slide Design - Animation Schemes
Step 7	*Click*	No Animation in the No Animation section in the Apply to selected slides: list box
Step 8	*Click*	the Apply to All Slides button in the Slide Design task pane
Step 9	*Save*	the *Teddy Toys* presentation

MOUSE TIP

You can copy a slide by right-dragging the slide and clicking Copy, or by holding down the CTRL key, dragging the slide to a new location, releasing the mouse button then the CTRL key.

You can copy a slide by clicking the Copy and Paste buttons on the Standard toolbar.

If you move, copy, delete, or hide a slide and then change your mind, you can click the Undo button on the Standard toolbar.

MENU TIP

You can delete a slide by clicking the Delete Slide command on the Edit menu.

You can hide and unhide a slide by clicking the Hide Slide command on the Slide Show menu.

chapter seven

7.e Creating a New Blank Presentation from Existing Slides

You can create a new presentation by moving or copying existing slides from another presentation and then saving the new presentation. Any slide copied or moved from one presentation to another is formatted based on the design template of the destination presentation. To create a new presentation from existing slides:

Step 1	*Verify*	that the presentation is in Slide Sorter view
Step 2	*Click*	the New button on the Standard toolbar to create a new, blank presentation
Step 3	*Key*	Teddy Toys Products in the title placeholder
Step 4	*Key*	Striving for Customer Satisfaction in the subtitle placeholder
Step 5	*Click*	the Slide Design button on the Formatting toolbar
Step 6	*Click*	the Crayons design template
Step 7	*Click*	the Slide Sorter View button
Step 8	*Click*	Window
Step 9	*Click*	Arrange All

The presentations are arranged side by side. This makes it easier to copy slides. Your screen should look similar to Figure 7-8.

FIGURE 7-8
Side-by-Side Presentations in Slide Sorter View

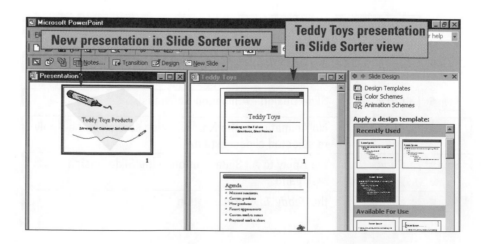

Step 10	*Click*	in the Teddy Toys window to activate the Teddy Toys presentation
Step 11	*Select*	the following Mission Statement, Current Products, Introducing Baby Teddy, and We Welcome New Ideas slides
Step 12	*Drag*	the selected slides to the new presentation window (see Figure 7-9 for placement)

When you drag to copy, the mouse pointer displays a rectangle at the lower-right corner of the mouse and a + sign at the upper-right corner of the mouse. This indicates that you are copying, not moving the slides. A vertical guide indicates the position of the moved or copied slide or slides. Your screen should look similar to Figure 7-9.

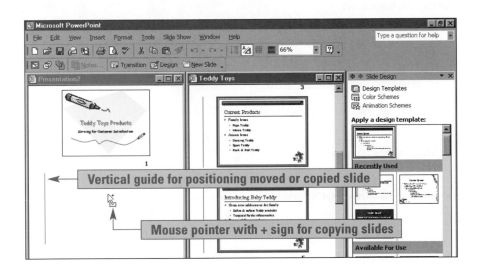

FIGURE 7-9
Mouse Pointer for Copying Slides

MOUSE TIP

You can copy or move a slide or slides from one presentation to another in Slide Sorter view by selecting the slide or slides you want to copy or move and then right-clicking the selected slide or slides and then clicking <u>C</u>opy or Cu<u>t</u>. To paste the copied or cut slide or slides in a different presentation, right-click in front of the slide where you want to place the moved or copied slide or slides, and then click <u>P</u>aste.

| Step 13 | *Release* | the mouse button when a vertical guide appears in the new presentation window under the title slide |

Because your newly created presentation used the Crayons design template, the copied slides no longer retain the formatting of the Quadrant design template. A Smart Tag, the Paste Options button, appears in the newly created presentation that enables you to <u>K</u>eep Source Formatting (the Quadrant design template formatting) or Use <u>D</u>esign Template Formatting (the Crayons design template formatting).

| Step 14 | *Save* | the new presentation as *Teddy Toys Products* |
| Step 15 | *Close* | both presentations |

Copying slides from an existing presentation is a quick way to create a new presentation.

chapter
seven

Summary

▶ A slide show is a computer-based slide presentation that can be viewed on a computer monitor or projected onto a large screen.

▶ Transitions are special effects that introduce slides in Slide Show.

▶ PowerPoint offers a variety of effects for transitions.

▶ You can change the speed at which a transition appears from slow to medium or fast.

▶ Animations are special visual effects that can be added to parts of the slides.

▶ Animation schemes allow the presenter to focus on important points, control the flow of information, and capture the audience's attention.

▶ Setting times to the slides in a presentation can be done before rehearsing the presentation or as you rehearse the presentation.

▶ Setting times to the slides in a presentation allows the presentation to run in Slide Show without clicking the mouse.

▶ You can create a new presentation using slides in an existing presentation.

▶ You can move, copy, hide, and delete slides in Slide Sorter view.

▶ You can move and copy slides from one presentation to another.

Commands Review

Action	Menu Bar	Shortcut Menu	Toolbar	Task Pane	Keyboard
View slide show from the beginning	Slide Show, View Show; View, Slide Show				ALT + D, V ALT + V, W F5
View slide show from current slide			🖥	Slide Show on Slide Design-Animation Schemes or Slide Transition task pane	
Move to the next slide in the slide show		Right-click slide, Next	, Next		PAGE DOWN, RIGHT or DOWN ARROW, N, SPACEBAR, ENTER
Move to the previous slide in the slide show		Right-click slide, Previous	, Previous		PAGE UP, LEFT or UP ARROW, P, BACKSPACE
End a slide show		Right-click slide, End Show	, End Show		ESCAPE, HYPHEN

Action	Menu Bar	Shortcut Menu	Toolbar	Task Pane	Keyboard
Display the Slide Transition task pane	Slide Show, Slide Transition	Right-click empty area on slide, Slide Transition		⏷ , Slide Transition	ALT + D, T
Set transitions	Slide Show, Slide Transition	Right-click slide in Slide Sorter view, Slide Transition	⬚ Transition on Slide Sorter toolbar	ALT + D, T	
Display the Slide Design-Animation Schemes task pane	Slide Show, Animation Schemes	Right-click empty area on slide, Slide Design, then click Animation Schemes on the Slide Design task pane; Right-click slide in Slide Sorter view; Animation Schemes		⏷ , Slide Design - Animation Schemes	ALT + D, C
Add animation schemes	Slide Show, Animation Schemes				ALT + D, C
Set times to slides rehearsing	Slide Show, Rehearse Timings		⬚ on Slide Sorter toolbar		ALT + D, R
Set times to slides before rehearsal	Slide Show, Slide Transition	Right-click slide in Slide Sorter view, Slide Transition			ALT + D, T
Move slides in Slide Sorter view	Edit, Cut; position cursor; Edit, Paste	Right-click slide, Cut; right-click, Paste; Right-drag slide, Move	✂ 📋		ALT + E, T; then ALT + E, P CTRL + X; then CTRL + V
Copy slides in Slide Sorter view	Edit, Copy; position cursor; Edit, Paste	Right-click slide, Copy, right-click, Paste; Right-drag slide, Copy	📋 📋		ALT + E, C; then ALT + E, P CTRL + C; then CTRL + V
Hide and unhide slides in Slide Sorter view	Slide Show, Hide Slide	Right-click slide, Hide Slide	🔲		ALT + D, H
Delete selected slides in Slide Sorter view	Edit, Delete Slide	Right-click slide, Delete Slide			ALT + E, D DELETE
Delete selected slide in Normal view	Edit, Delete Slide				ALT + E, D DELETE

Concepts Review

SCANS

Circle the correct answer.

1. You cannot advance slides in Slide Show with:
 [a] the mouse button.
 [b] the ENTER key.
 [c] the SPACEBAR.
 [d] the ESCAPE key.

2. Slide show options available to the presenter include all of the following except:
 [a] navigation commands.
 [b] Pointer Options.
 [c] End Show.
 [d] Transitions command.

3. You can show the shortcut menu during the slide show by:
 [a] clicking the title area of the current slide.
 [b] right-clicking the current slide.

 [c] clicking the Shortcut button on the Formatting toolbar.
 [d] clicking the Shortcut icon at the bottom right of the slide.

4. Special effects that are applied to a slide to introduce the slides in a presentation are called:
 [a] animation schemes.
 [b] transitions.
 [c] special effects.
 [d] predesigned effects.

chapter seven

5. The best view for setting transition effects for all slides in a presentation is:
 [a] Outline view.
 [b] Transition view.
 [c] Notes Pages view.
 [d] Normal view.

6. You would use animation schemes to:
 [a] show bullet items as they are discussed.
 [b] add times to selected slides.
 [c] add clip art images to your slides.
 [d] customize animation effects.

7. Which of the following is not a transition effect?
 [a] Blinds Vertical
 [b] Fade Through Black
 [c] Dissolve
 [d] Blinds Diagonal

8. Which of the following features allows you to view slides in a slide show without manually advancing each slide?
 [a] adding transitions
 [b] setting slide times
 [c] adding build effects
 [d] setting animation schemes

9. To select several nonadjacent slides in Slide Sorter view or in the Slides tab:
 [a] CTRL + Click each slide.
 [b] SHIFT + Click each slide.
 [c] CTRL + SHIFT click each slide.
 [d] ALT + Click each slide.

10. Which of the following does *not* allow you to add times to the slides in a presentation?
 [a] Slide Transition button
 [b] Rehearse Timings button
 [c] Slide Show menu
 [d] Animation Schemes list box

Circle **T** if the statement is true or **F** if the statement is false.

T F   1. The shortcut icon in Slide Show is located at the lower-right corner of the screen.

T F   2. Slide shows should be center stage in your presentation.

T F   3. Using a variety of transition effects on each slide of the presentation contributes to the cohesiveness of your presentation.

T F   4. Transition effects control the flow of information in a presentation.

T F   5. Slide shows are a visual medium; therefore, sound is never used.

T F   6. You must apply transition effects, slide times, and animation schemes to only one slide at a time.

T F   7. The speed of transition effects can be adjusted from slow, to medium, and fast.

T F   8. There are only a few animation schemes that can be applied to your slides.

T F   9. After rehearsing timings, you are given an option of accepting or rejecting the rehearsed times.

T F 10. Hidden slides are hidden in both Slide Show and Slide Sorter view.

Skills Review

Exercise 1

1. Open the *PowerPoint* presentation you modified in Chapter 6.

2. Using the Slide Transition task pane, apply a transition effect to all the slides.

3. Add an animation scheme to any title and text slides by accessing the Slide Design–Animation Schemes task pane and selecting an animation scheme.

4. Set times to the slides in the presentation using the Rehearse Timings button in Slide Sorter view.

5. Run the slide show. Save and close the presentation.

Exercise 2 Ⓒ

1. Open the *Office* presentation you modified in Chapter 6.

2. Use the Slide Transition task pane to select the Wipe Right effect, and apply that effect to all the slides in the presentation.

3. Use the Animation Schemes list box to apply the Wipe animation effect to the title and text slides in your presentation.

4. Add different slide times to slides in the presentation.

5. Run the slide show. Save and close the presentation.

Exercise 3 Ⓒ

1. Open the *Design* presentation you modified in Chapter 6.

2. Use the Slide Transition task pane to apply the Wheel Clockwise, 1 Spoke effect, using medium speed, to all the slides in the presentation.

3. Use the Animation Scheme list box to apply the Spin animation effect to the title and text slides in your presentation, and then observe the change in the slide transitions.

4. Add the same slide times to all slides in the presentation by selecting all slides and using the slide time text box.

5. Move the Basic Color Tips slide to the fourth position (before the WordArt slide).

6. Run the slide show. Save and close the presentation.

Exercise 4 Ⓒ

1. Open the *Precision Builders* presentation you modified in Chapter 6.

2. Add the Box Out effect for the transition to each of the slides in the presentation.

3. Add the Zoom animation scheme to the title and the two title and text slides in the presentation.

4. Add different slide times to slides in the presentation.

5. Hide the WordArt slide.

6. Run the slide show.

7. Show the WordArt slide.

8. Save the presentation. With the *Precision Builders* presentation still open, create a new presentation.

9. Apply the Balance design template to the new presentation.

10. Add the title "Builders of Distinction." Add the subtitle: "Your Name, President."

11. Using Slide Sorter view, arrange the windows to view both presentations, and copy the three slides with clip art and AutoShapes from the *Precision Builders* presentation to the new presentation, keeping the Balance design template.

12. Add transitions to the slides in the new presentation. Run the slide show.

13. Save the new presentation as *Distinctive Designs*. Close both presentations.

Exercise 5 Ⓒ

1. Open the *Nature Tours* presentation you modified in Chapter 6, and display the slides in Slide Sorter view.

2. Add a transition effect to all of the slides in the presentation.

3. Move the WordArt slide to the right of the title slide.

4. Add an animation scheme to one or more title and text slides.

5. Add times to the slides in the presentation using the Rehearse Timings button.

6. Hide the AutoShapes slide.

7. Run the slide show.

8. Change the pen color in Slide Show, and use the pen on various slides in the slide show.

9. Unhide the hidden slide.

10. Run the slide show. Save and close the presentation.

chapter seven

Exercise 6 C

1. Open the *A Healthier You* presentation you modified in Chapter 6, and display the slides in Slide Sorter view.

2. Add transitions to all the slides and an animation scheme to the title and text slides in the presentation.

3. Add different slide times to slides in the presentation using the Slide Transition task pane.

4. Make two copies of any slide in the presentation, and place one copy at the beginning of the presentation and one copy at the end of the presentation.

5. Run the slide show.

6. Delete the copied slides.

7. Move the WordArt slide to the right of the title slide.

8. Run the slide show. Save and close the presentation.

Exercise 7 C

1. Open the *Buying A Computer* presentation you modified in Chapter 6.

2. Add transitions to all the slides in the presentation.

3. Add an animation scheme to the title and text slides.

4. Add the same slide times to slides in the presentation.

5. Rearrange the slides in a different but logical sequence.

6. Run the slide show. Save and close the presentation.

Exercise 8 C

1. Open the *Leisure Travel* presentation you modified in Chapter 6, and display the slides in Slide Sorter view.

2. Add a slow transition to all the slides.

3. Add times to slides in the presentation using the Rehearse Timings button.

4. Rearrange the slides in a different but logical sequence.

5. Run the slide show.

6. Save the *Leisure Travel* presentation, and keep it open.

7. Create a new presentation, and save it as *Travel Ideas*.

8. Add the title "Travel Ideas" and the subtitle "By (press ENTER) Leisure Travel."

9. Copy the two slides with WordArt and AutoShapes from the *Leisure Travel* presentation to the *Travel Ideas* presentation.

10. Apply a presentation design template to the *Travel Ideas* presentation.

11. Add a transition to all the slides in the *Travel Ideas* presentation, and run the slide show.

12. Save the *Travel Ideas* presentation, and close both presentations.

Case Projects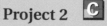

Project 1

Your immediate supervisor has asked you about the Custom Shows command on the Slide Show menu. Using online Help, search for information about Custom Shows. Print the information you find, including all the linked information.

Project 2 C

The Director of Human Relations has asked to see the *Communicate* presentation you modified in Chapter 6 displayed as a slide show. You decide to add transition and animation effects to the presentation. Experiment with different effects to find the one that best fits the presentation. After completing the effects, practice setting times to the slides using the presentation-rehearsal method so that you can show her how to set times for the slides and make a decision as to whether or not she would prefer the slide show to run automatically or manually. Save the presentation.

Project 3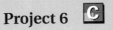

Your employer informs asks you to add different transitions to the *Souner* presentation you modified in Chapter 6 and she wants those transitions to be obvious to the audience. Your employer understands that you can assign times to the slides so that they automatically progress as she presents the material. She asks you not to add times. Because she is not that comfortable with the process, she wants to manually progress through the slide show. She also wants to use more than one method for progressing through the slides. Review the various methods of viewing the next and previous slides. When you are done reviewing, add transition to all the slides and an animation scheme to the text slides. Save the presentation.

Project 4

You just learned about transitions, animation schemes, and times for slide shows, and you want to practice what you learned on your *My Presentation* presentation you modified in Chapter 6. As you practice, review the various transition and animation schemes. Remember to use the same effect on all slides for consistency. Rearrange the slides in a different but logical sequence. Hide a slide of your choice. Practice giving the presentation using the Rehearsal Mode feature. Save the presentation.

Project 5

Children's Day is rapidly approaching. Your employer wants to welcome the children by presenting the information in the *Zoo* presentation you modified in Chapter 6. There will be a projection system hooked up to a computer in the room where children will view the presentation. You want to add some special effects to the presentation. Add transitions, an animation scheme, and times to the *Zoo* presentation. If necessary, rearrange the order of the slides. Save the presentation.

Project 6

You are excited about what you have learned so far about slide shows, and you want to know more. Connect to the Internet and search the Web for the words "slide show" to find more information about this medium for presentation. View a slide show of your choice, and print at least one or two slides of the selected presentation.

Project 7

As an instructor, you realize that it is very important to keep the students' attention as you present information. After learning about slide transitions, you find it extremely important to add slide transitions so the students keep their attention focused on the *Cars* presentation you modified in Chapter 6. You decide to add transitions to all the slides in the presentation as well as an animation scheme to many of the slides. Connect to the Internet and search the Web for slide shows of other presentations to determine how to make your presentation stand out. Save the presentation.

Project 8

Your professor asks to see the *Internet* presentation you modified in Chapter 6. You and your partner think that adding transitions and an animation scheme to the title and text slides will further impress the professor with what you have done thus far. Both you and your partner are comfortable with transitions and animation, but you want to find more information about slide shows. You connect to the Internet and search the Web for additional research. Make sure that the transitions and animations you select fit the goal of the presentation. The professor wants the presentation to be interesting, but the transition effects should not overpower the topic presented. This presentation will be used for two different level classes. Your professor wants you to create a new presentation from the existing slides and save it as *Internet Level II*. Apply a different presentation design and hide at least two slides in the *Internet Level II* presentation. Save the presentation.

chapter seven

Preparing, Previewing, and Printing Presentation Documents

Chapter Overview

There are many ways to ensure the success of your PowerPoint presentations with helpful support materials. In this chapter, you learn how to create and customize speaker notes for presenters and handouts for audience members. You also learn to preview all types of presentation materials, such as individual slides, outlines, notes pages, and audience handouts, to ensure they look the way you want when printed. Finally, you learn about the different options you have for printing these materials.

LEARNING OBJECTIVES

- ► **Prepare speaker notes**
- ► **Prepare audience handouts**
- ► **Preview a presentation**
- ► **Print presentation documents**

Case profile

Ms. Hill gives you some individual notes for certain slides in the *Teddy Toys* presentation. She wants you to create notes pages to accompany her presentation. In addition, she wants you to distribute handouts that display the slides, the name of the presentation, and her name so that members of the meeting have a hard copy of the presentation to which they can refer during the presentation.

chapter eight

8.a Preparing Speaker Notes

Speaker notes consist of information the presenter needs to remember during a presentation. **Notes pages** are printouts that contain a picture of a slide along with the speaker notes for that slide, so a presenter can quickly refer to them during a presentation as each slide appears in the slide show. The audience sees the slides in the presentation, while the presenter glances at the printed notes page. In PowerPoint, a notes pane automatically accompanies each slide in Normal view, allowing you to key notes for each slide. You can key speaker notes either in Notes Page view, which displays a small miniature of the slide in the top section and a large notes pane, or in the notes pane located below the slide pane in Normal view. You edit and format the notes in a notes page in the same way that you work with any other text box or placeholder on a slide. To change to Notes Page view and create speaker notes for a slide:

Step 1	*Open*	the *Teddy Toys* presentation you modified in Chapter 7 and display Slide 1 in Normal view
Step 2	*Click*	View
Step 3	*Click*	Notes Page

Notes Page view displays a reduced view of the slide at the top of the page with a notes pane below it for any notes regarding this slide. The **notes pane** is a text box where you key the lecture or speaker notes for the first slide. Your screen should look similar to Figure 8-1.

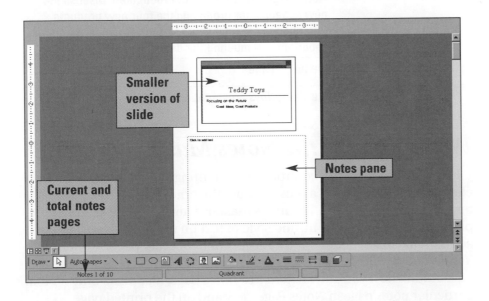

FIGURE 8-1
Notes Page View

chapter
eight

MENU TIP

You can access Notes Page view by clicking the Notes <u>P</u>age command on the <u>V</u>iew menu.

You can open the Notes Layout dialog box in Notes Page view by clicking the Notes <u>L</u>ayout command on the F<u>o</u>rmat menu.

You can open the Zoom dialog box by clicking the <u>Z</u>oom command on the <u>V</u>iew menu.

INTERNET TIP

Speaker notes can be used for a different purpose for presentations that you broadcast over the Internet. When you save a presentation as a Web page, you can display speaker notes on the screen below each slide; the effect is similar to viewing a presentation in Normal view. These notes can give your viewing audience the background and details that they would receive during a live presentation.

It is advisable to zoom in so that you can see the text as you key.

Step 4	*Click*	the Zoom button list arrow on the Standard toolbar
Step 5	*Click*	75%
Step 6	*Click*	the "Click to add text" placeholder
Step 7	*Key*	Thank all participants for attending the meeting.
Step 8	*Press*	the ENTER key twice
Step 9	*Key*	Be sure to show the new Baby Teddy and distribute one to each of the participants. Indicate that they will be able to pick up additional bears for their sales reps when they leave the meeting.
Step 10	*Click*	the Next Slide button  on the vertical scroll bar
Step 11	*Click*	the "Click to add text" placeholder for Slide 2
Step 12	*Key*	Briefly highlight what will be covered in today's meeting. Remind participants that old, current, and new products are what determine market share.
Step 13	*Continue*	to key the following notes text in the notes pages: Notes page 3 (Mission Statement): Reiterate that the mission statement guides everything done at Teddy Toys. Teddy Toys wants parents to believe, and rightfully so, that any toy manufactured by Teddy Toys can be trusted to be appropriate for the intended ages, that no harm will come to their children when playing with the toys, that the toys will last, and that the fun will continue from their first child to their last child. Notes page 8 (New Product Production): Discuss the new schedule for producing the four new products. Introduce the team leaders and emphasize the importance of meeting the deadlines.
Step 14	*Spell check*	the notes pages
Step 15	*Save*	the *Teddy Toys* presentation

Working with the Notes Master

Just as the slide master controls the formatting, color, and graphic elements for the slides in a presentation, the notes master serves as a template for notes pages. The **notes master** determines the layout of the placeholders, typeface, font, and style of text on the page, as well as any additional items the presenter wants printed on every page. Additional items you can add are clip art images, text, headers and footers, and page numbers. If you add an item to a notes page, it appears only on that particular notes page in Notes Page view and on the printed page.

However, if you add an item to the notes master, it appears on every notes page in Notes Page view and on every printed page.

To add text and an image on the notes master:

Step 1	***Click***	View
Step 2	***Point to***	Master
Step 3	***Click***	Notes Master
Step 4	***Scroll***	to the top of the notes master

Your screen should look similar to Figure 8-2. The Notes Master View toolbar appears. You can click the Notes Master Layout button to open the Notes Master Layout dialog box. Here you can redisplay any deleted placeholders. Clicking the Close Master View button closes Notes Master view and returns you to Notes Page view.

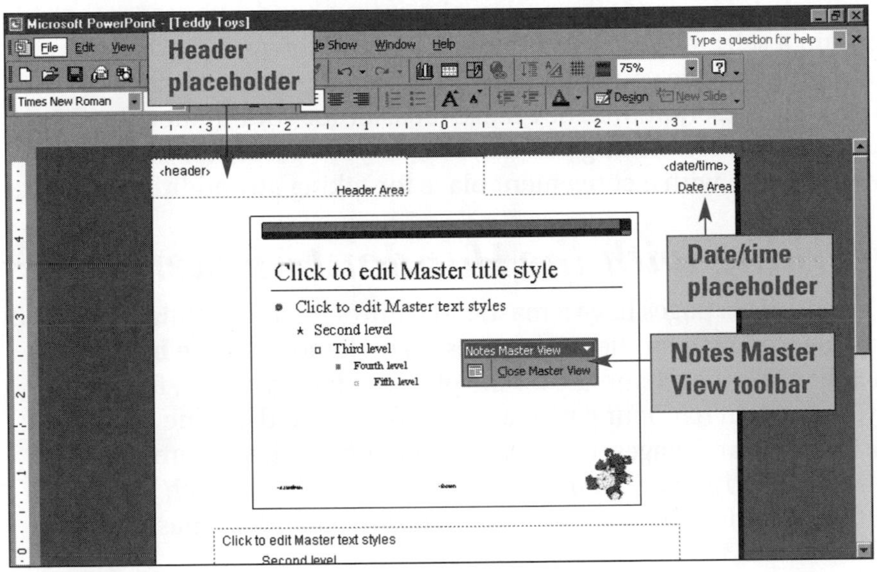

FIGURE 8-2
Notes Master View with Notes Master View Toolbar

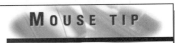

Step 5	***Click***	the <header> text placeholder in the Header Area text box
Step 6	***Key***	Teddy Toys
Step 7	***Scroll***	to the bottom of the notes master
Step 8	***Click***	the <footer> text placeholder in the Footer Area text box
Step 9	***Key***	Sandra Hill
Step 10	***Click***	the Insert Picture button on the Drawing toolbar

QUICK TIP

You can navigate through the notes pages by pressing the PAGE UP or PAGE DOWN key to move to the previous or next page, and the HOME or END key to move to the first or last page.

MOUSE TIP

When working in Notes Master view, you can open a Notes Master Layout dialog box to display or hide placeholders for the Slide image, the Body, the Date, the Page number, and the Header or Footer. If you inadvertently delete any placeholders in Notes Master view, you can redisplay them by clicking the appropriate check box in the Notes Master Layout dialog box.

MOUSE TIP

You can open the Notes Layout dialog box by right-clicking outside the slide area and notes text area in Notes Page view and then clicking Notes Layout.

Step 11	*Switch to*	the Data Disk
Step 12	*Double-click*	the *teddybear.wmf* graphics file
Step 13	*Drag*	the teddy bear image to the upper-right corner of the notes master
Step 14	*Flip*	the teddy bear image horizontally so it faces the miniature slide
Step 15	*Click*	the Close Master View button Close Master View on the Notes Master View toolbar
Step 16	*Save*	the *Teddy Toys* presentation

MENU TIP

You can add a header or footer, page numbers, and dates to a notes page or handout master by clicking the Header and Footer command on the View menu, then clicking the Notes and Handouts tab and making the appropriate selections. If you add a header or footer, page number, date, or fixed text to a notes or handout master, that information appears on each notes page or handout that you print.

8.b Preparing Audience Handouts

PowerPoint provides the option of printing **handouts**, pages that contain a selected number of miniature slides of your presentation. Handouts provide your audience with reference materials during and after your presentation. They make it easier for your audience to concentrate on watching and listening to your presentation and provide them with a convenient place for taking any additional notes.

Working with the Handout Master

Just as notes pages have a master to control the formatting, color, and graphic elements for the notes pages, so do handouts. The **handout master** serves as a template for the placeholders, typeface, font, and style of text on handout pages, as well as on printed outline pages. You can add clip art images, text, headers and footers, page numbers, and other items to a handout master. These items print on each handout, but do not print on each slide. To add text to a handout master:

Step 1	*Point to*	the Slide Sorter View button
Step 2	*Press & hold*	the SHIFT key until the ScreenTip displays Handout Master View
Step 3	*Click*	the Handout Master View button
Step 4	*Click*	the Show positioning of 6-per-page handouts button on the Handout Master View toolbar, if necessary

The handout master displays with a Handout Master View toolbar. Your screen should look similar to Figure 8-3. The toolbar contains buttons for printing two, three, four, six, or nine slides per page, as well as an outline layout. The outline layout displays only the text of a presentation in an outline format, excluding any design templates or graphic images. It provides a quick reference to the title and bullet text items displayed on slides in a presentation. The handout master contains placeholders for a header, footer, date, and page number.

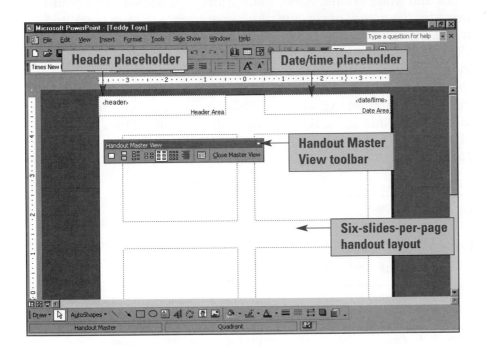

FIGURE 8-3
Handout Master with Handout Master View Toolbar

To add text to all pages of the handout:

Step 1	*Click*	the <header> text placeholder in the Header Area text box
Step 2	*Key*	Teddy Toys
Step 3	*Click*	the <date/time> text placeholder in the Date Area text box
Step 4	*Click*	Insert
Step 5	*Click*	Date and Time
Step 6	*Click*	the Update automatically check box so that the presentation displays the current date each time it is opened and printed
Step 7	*Double-click*	the fourth date format
Step 8	*Click*	the Close Master View button ⟨Close Master View⟩ on the Handout Master View toolbar
Step 9	*Save*	the *Teddy Toys* presentation

chapter eight

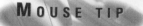
8.c Previewing a Presentation

Most PowerPoint presentations are designed to display in color in Normal view. However, when you print handouts and/or slides to a black and white printer, PowerPoint prints in grayscale. PowerPoint provides the option of viewing slides in grayscale or pure black and white, instead of color, while working on slides in Normal view. The Color/Grayscale button on the Standard toolbar displays options for viewing a presentation in grayscale or black and white when the design template may appear too dark while keying or formatting. To view a presentation in grayscale or black and white, you can be in any view except Slide Show. When viewing slides in Slide Show, slides are always displayed in color. To view a presentation in black and white in Normal view:

Step 1	*Display*	Slide 1 in Normal view
Step 2	*Click*	the Color/Grayscale button ▣ on the Standard toolbar
Step 3	*Click*	Grayscale
Step 4	*Click*	the Next Slide button ⬇ on the vertical scroll bar to view each of the slides
Step 5	*Run*	the slide show to view the slides in color
Step 6	*Click*	the Close Grayscale View button Close Grayscale View on the Grayscale View toolbar

Working in Print Preview

Before sending any PowerPoint presentation to the printer, you can **preview** it to see how the presentation will look in printed form. When you preview a presentation, you have many different options for viewing and printing presentation materials, such as slides, handouts, notes pages, and an outline.

You can make a few global changes to a presentation in Print Preview, such as adding a header or footer and changing the scale of a presentation to fit on the paper, but you cannot edit other presentation elements in the Print Preview window. This view is most useful for viewing different output formats and making sure your printed presentation looks the way you want. If your computer is connected to a color printer, your presentation appears in color; you can change options in print preview to color, grayscale, or pure black and white. If your computer is connected to a black and white printer, your preview appears in grayscale or pure black and white. The Color (On Black and White Printer) option in Print Preview displays the presentation in black and white. You want to preview the slides before printing. To preview a presentation as slides:

Step 1	*Display*	Slide 1, if necessary
Step 2	*Click*	the Print Preview button  on the Standard toolbar

The Print Preview window opens and displays the title slide. You can navigate in Print Preview by clicking the Previous Page and Next Page buttons on the Print Preview toolbar. You can print slides, handouts, notes pages, and an outline view directly from this window. You can add a Header or Footer, Scale to Fit Paper, Frame Slides, Print Hidden Slides, Include Comment Pages, and change the Printing Order in the Options list box in the Print Preview window. When previewing handouts, notes pages, or an outline view of your presentation, you can change the page orientation from portrait to landscape.

Your screen should look similar to Figure 8-4.

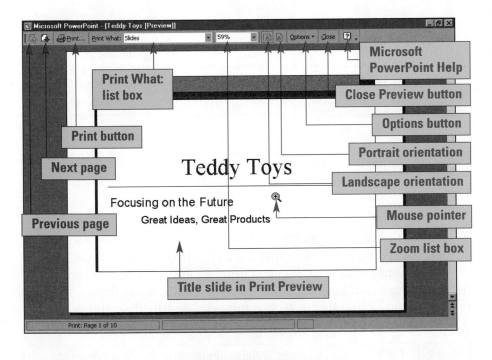

Step 3	*Verify*	that Slides is selected in the Print What: list on the Print Preview toolbar
Step 4	*Click*	the Next Page button  on the Print Preview toolbar to view the second slide in Print Preview

MENU TIP

You can change the slide colors to grayscale or pure black and white by clicking the Color/Grayscale command on the View menu in Normal view and then clicking Grayscale or Pure Black and White.

You can preview a presentation by clicking the Print Preview command on the File menu.

FIGURE 8-4
Teddy Toys Title Slide in Print Preview

chapter
eight

FIGURE 8-5
Notes Page in Print Preview

You decide to preview notes pages, handouts, and an outline view of the *Teddy Toys* presentation to see how the final printed copies will look. To preview notes pages, handouts, and an outline view:

Step 1	*Click*	Notes Pages in the Print What: list on the Print Preview toolbar

Your screen should look similar to Figure 8-5.

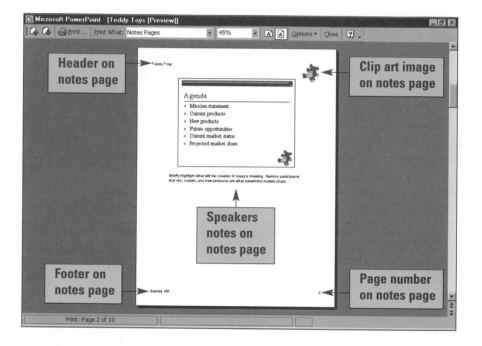

Step 2	*Navigate*	through all the notes pages in the preview window, viewing the header, footer, page number, and graphic on each notes page

The text Teddy Toys appears on each notes page in the upper-left corner, the teddy bear image appears in the upper-right corner, and the name Sandra Hill and the page number appear at the bottom of the page. Page numbers appear by default on the notes pages. This text prints on each notes page, but not on the individual slides.

Step 3	*Click*	Handouts (6 slides per page) in the Print What: list

Your screen should look similar to Figure 8-6. Slides display two across and three down.

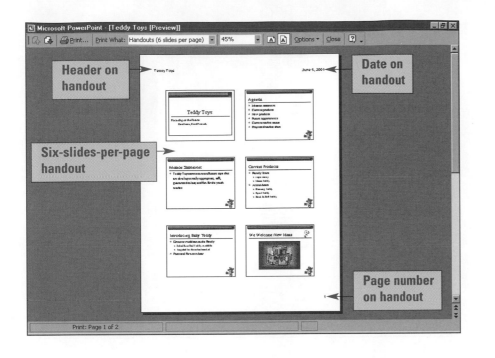

FIGURE 8-6
Handouts Page in Print Preview

Step 4	*Click*	the Options button ⌐Options ▾⌐ on the Print Preview toolbar
Step 5	*Click*	Frame Slides if it is not checked to display a thin border around each miniature slide
Step 6	*Navigate*	through the two pages of the handout

The text Teddy Toys appears on each handouts page in the upper-left corner, the date appears in the upper-right corner, and the page number appear at the bottom of the page. Page numbers appear by default on the handouts pages. This text prints on each handouts page, but not on the individual slides.

| Step 7 | *Click* | Outline View in the Print What: list on the Print Preview toolbar |

Your screen should look similar to Figure 8-7. Outline View displays the same settings as the handouts page. The handout master determines the text and objects placed on both the handout pages and the outline view pages.

**chapter
eight**

FIGURE 8-7
Outline View in Print
Preview

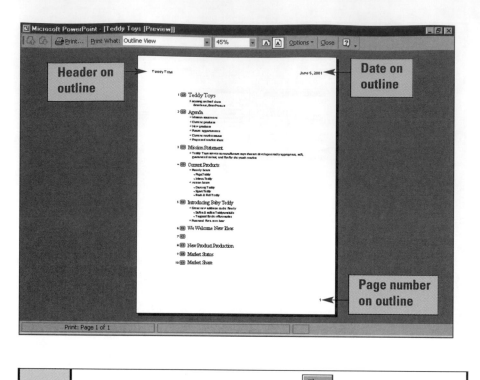

MENU TIP

You can change the
orientation of slides,
notes pages, handouts,
and outlines in Normal
view by clicking the
Page Set<u>u</u>p command
on the <u>F</u>ile menu.

QUICK TIP

You can change the
page orientation of
notes pages, handouts,
and outlines in Print
Preview, but not the
orientation of slides.

Step 8	*Click*	the <u>C</u>lose Preview button Close on the Print Preview toolbar

Changing Page Orientation

Page orientation refers to the vertical or horizontal position of the
printed page. In **portrait orientation**, the page is printed across the short
edge, or top, of the page; this is the common orientation for documents
that are narrower than they are wide. In **landscape orientation**, the page
is printed across the long edge, or the side. Landscape is the default
orientation for slides because you can fit more text across a landscape
page than a portrait page. However, you can change the presentation
from landscape to portrait orientation. When you do, your slides may
need to be readjusted so that all items fit appropriately on the slides. To
change the orientation of a presentation:

Step 1	*Click*	<u>F</u>ile
Step 2	*Click*	Page Set<u>u</u>p
Step 3	*Click*	the <u>P</u>ortrait option button in the Slides section under Orientation
Step 4	*Click*	OK
Step 5	*Run*	the slide show and notice the placement and distortion of objects on each slide

You decide to return the presentation to landscape orientation.

Step 6	*Open*	the Page Setup dialog box
Step 7	*Click*	the Landscape option button in the Slides section under Orientation
Step 8	*Click*	OK

Print Preview allows you to change the orientation of notes pages, handouts, and outline view to provide another format for your presentation output. To change the orientation in Print Preview:

Step 1	*Click*	the Print Preview button ▣ on the Standard toolbar
Step 2	*Click*	Outline View in the Print What: list on the Print Preview toolbar, if necessary
Step 3	*Click*	the Landscape button ▣ on the Print Preview toolbar and observe the change
Step 4	*Close*	the Print Preview window

8.d Printing Presentation Documents

The Print dialog box provides options for printing your presentation in different forms. You can print in grayscale or pure black and white, include animations, scale to fit the paper, frame the slides, print hidden slides, and include comment pages. You can print all slides, the current slide, a selection, a custom show, a range of slides, audience handouts, notes pages, and an outline. PowerPoint provides options for printing more than one copy and for collating. In addition, the Print dialog box provides a Preview button that opens Print Preview.

Printing Selected Slides

In some situations, you may want to print only selected slides of your presentation. You can print the current slide, a specific slide, or a range of slides. The default orientation for slides is landscape. To print selected slides:

| Step 1 | *Click* | File |
| Step 2 | *Click* | Print |

chapter eight

The Print dialog box on your screen should look similar to Figure 8-8.

FIGURE 8-8
Print Dialog Box

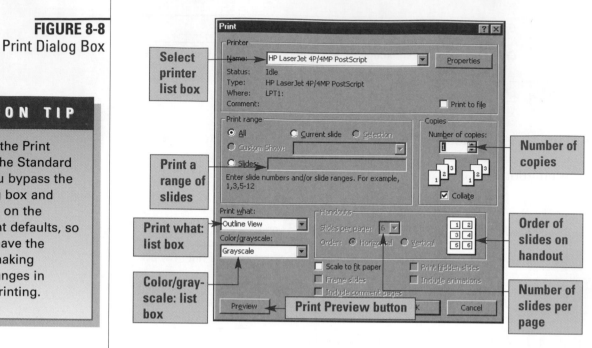

CAUTION TIP

If you click the Print button on the Standard toolbar, you bypass the Print dialog box and print based on the current print defaults, so you don't have the option of making specific changes in regard to printing.

QUICK TIP

You can open the Print dialog box by pressing the CTRL + P keys.

Step 3	*Click*	the Slides: option button in the Print range box
Step 4	*Key*	4,8 in the text box
Step 5	*Verify*	that Slides appears in the Print what: list box
Step 6	*Click*	Preview to view the slides
Step 7	*Click*	the Print button [Print...] on the Print Preview toolbar
Step 8	*Click*	OK

Slides 4 and 8 print one slide per page.

Printing an Outline View

For situations when you want to print primarily the slide text of a presentation, PowerPoint includes a feature for printing an Outline View. An **Outline View** lists all slides in the presentation without displaying backgrounds, colors, or clip art images. The default orientation for outlines is portrait. To print an outline:

| Step 1 | *Click* | the Print button [Print...] on the Print Preview toolbar |

Step 2	*Click*	the <u>A</u>ll option button in the Print range box, if necessary
Step 3	*Click*	Outline View in the Print <u>w</u>hat: list box
Step 4	*Click*	Pr<u>e</u>view
Step 5	*Change*	the orientation to Portrait
Step 6	*Click*	the <u>P</u>rint button 🖨 <u>P</u>rint... on the Print Preview toolbar
Step 7	*Click*	OK

An outline prints, displaying all slides in the presentation. Notice that Teddy Toys, the current date, and the page number are printed on each page of the outline. Any edits to a handouts master also appear on the printed outline for the same presentation.

Printing Notes Pages

Each notes page prints with a small slide at the top and your lecture or speaker notes at the bottom. The default orientation for notes pages is portrait. To print notes pages:

Step 1	*Click*	the <u>P</u>rint button 🖨 <u>P</u>rint... on the Print Preview toolbar
Step 2	*Click*	the Sl<u>i</u>des: option button in the Print range box
Step 3	*Key*	1-3, 8 to print notes pages for Slides 1 through 3, and 8
Step 4	*Click*	Notes Pages in the Print <u>w</u>hat: list box
Step 5	*Click*	Pr<u>e</u>view
Step 6	*Verify*	that the orientation is Portrait
Step 7	*Click*	the <u>P</u>rint button 🖨 <u>P</u>rint... on the Print Preview toolbar
Step 8	*Click*	OK

Any text keyed in the header and/or footer areas of the notes master, along with any images, print on the notes pages. The page number appears at the lower-right corner by default.

Printing an Audience Handout

Handouts can be printed in layouts of two, three, four, six, or nine slides per page. When you decide to print handouts, you have the option of printing the slides in order horizontally or vertically. Two slides per page print one above the other in portrait orientation or side by side in landscape orientation. Three slides per page print down the left side of the page with horizontal lines to the right for taking notes in portrait orientation and three slides across the page with horizontal lines below. Four slides print two slides side by side in two columns. Six slides print two slides side by side in three rows in portrait orientation, and three slides side by side in two rows in landscape orientation. Nine slides print three slides across and three slides down. The default orientation for handouts is portrait. To print an audience handout:

Step 1	*Click*	the Print button 🖨 Print... on the Print Preview toolbar
Step 2	*Click*	the All option button in the Print range box
Step 3	*Click*	Handouts in the Print what: list box

When you want to print four, six, or nine slides per page, you have the option of changing the order of the slides. You can print the slides on a handout in order horizontally across the page or vertically down the page.

Step 4	*Click*	the Slides per page: list arrow in the Handouts box
Step 5	*Click*	6 as the number of slides per page, if necessary
Step 6	*Click*	Horizontal for the Order so the handout slides print in order across the page, if necessary
Step 7	*Click*	the Frame slides check box to insert a check mark, if necessary, to put a frame around each slide on the handout
Step 8	*Click*	Preview and verify that the orientation is Portrait
Step 9	*Click*	the Print button 🖨 Print... on the Print Preview toolbar
Step 10	*Click*	OK
Step 11	*Close*	the Print Preview window

Two pages print with six slides on the first page and four slides on the second page. The slides are in order from left to right across the page. Each handout displays Teddy Toys, the current date, and automatic page numbers.

| Step 12 | *Save* | the *Teddy Toys* presentation and close it |

Ms. Hill will distribute the handout you created to the meeting attendees.

Summary

► Speaker notes contain information that a presenter can refer to during a presentation.

► Speaker notes can be keyed in Notes Page view or in the notes pane below the slide in Normal view.

► A notes master allows you to add text or clip art images that print on each notes page.

► Audience handouts display miniature slides printed on paper in two, three, four, six, or nine slides per page.

► The Handout Master Layout dialog box displays placeholders for the date, page number, header, or footer that appears on printed handouts.

► You can access the handout master to add text or clip art images that print on each audience handout.

► Print Preview allows you to preview how a presentation will actually look when it is printed. You can preview slides, handouts, outlines, and notes pages.

► A presentation can be viewed in color, grayscale, or black and white.

► You can change orientation of slides, handouts, outlines, and notes pages in the Page Setup dialog box.

► You can navigate in Notes Page view using the previous and next slide buttons on the scroll bar.

► Portrait orientation refers to the paper being printed across the short edge, or top, of the page.

► Landscape orientation refers to the paper being printed along the long edge, or side, of the page.

► By default, slides in a presentation print in landscape orientation.

► By default, notes pages, handouts, and outlines print in portrait orientation.

► You can change the page orientation of notes pages, handouts, and outlines in the Print Preview window.

► The Print dialog box provides several options for printing, including printing selected slides, outlines, notes pages, and handouts.

► You can print an entire presentation based on the current print defaults by clicking the Print button on the Standard toolbar.

chapter eight

Commands Review

Action	Menu Bar	Shortcut Menu	Toolbar	Task Pane	Keyboard
Add a notes page	View, Notes Page				ALT + V, P
Change the Zoom control	View, Zoom		50%		ALT + V, Z
Display the notes master	View, Master, Notes Master				ALT + V, M, N
Display the handout master	View, Master, Handout Master		SHIFT + ⊞		ALT + V, M, D
Preview a presentation	File, Print Preview		🔍		ALT F, V CTRL + P, ALT + E
Preview a slide in grayscale or black and white	View, Color/Grayscale, Grayscale or Pure Black and White		▣		ALT + V, C, G ALT + V, C, U
Change page orientation	File, Page Setup				ALT + F, U
Change page orientation in Print Preview window for notes pages, hand-outs, outlines			🅰 🅰		
Print selected slides	File, Print, Slides				ALT + F, P, ALT + I
Print an outline	File, Print, Print what: Outline View				ALT + F, P, ALT + W
Print notes pages	File, Print, Print what: Notes Pages				ALT + F, P, ALT + W
Print handouts	File, Print, Print what: Handouts				ALT + F, P, ALT + W

Concepts Review

Circle the correct answer.

1. Which of the following provides a way to print out speaker notes with a miniature slide on a printed page?

[a] audience handout

[b] notes page

[c] Outline view

[d] slides with animation

2. Which of the following provides a printed copy of your presentation with horizontal lines for taking notes?

[a] audience handout

[b] notes page

[c] Outline view

[d] slides with animation

3. The handout master contains placeholders for all of the following *except* the:

[a] header.

[b] footer.

[c] title.

[d] page number.

4. Which of the following provides a printed copy of your presentation without the slide or clip art images?

[a] audience handouts

[b] notes pages

[c] outlines

[d] slides

5. **When printing handouts, you cannot print:**
   [a] two slides per page.
   [b] three slides per page.
   [c] six slides per page.
   [d] ten slides per page.

6. **Previewing a presentation before printing provides a(n):**
   [a] audience handout.
   [b] printed copy of all the slides.
   [c] actual representation of how slides will appear when printed.
   [d] color notes page.

7. **In the Print Preview window, you cannot change the page orientation of:**
   [a] slides.
   [b] handouts.
   [c] notes pages.
   [d] outlines.

8. **The default page setup orientation for slides in PowerPoint is:**
   [a] portrait.
   [b] landscape.

   [c] vertical.
   [d] sideways.

9. **To print only Slides 5 and 12 in a presentation, click the:**
   [a] All option button in the Print dialog box.
   [b] Current slide option button in the Print dialog box.
   [c] Custom Show option button in the Print dialog box.
   [d] Slides option button in the Print dialog box.

10. **To bypass the Print dialog box when printing individual slides or an entire presentation, use:**
    [a] the CTRL + P keys.
    [b] File, Print.
    [c] the Print button.
    [d] File, Print Preview.

Circle **T** if the statement is true or **F** if the statement is false.

T   F   1. Notes page text can be only one sentence long per slide.

T   F   2. The purpose of the notes page is to aid the presenter when delivering the presentation.

T   F   3. Audience handouts can only be printed for an even number of slides.

T   F   4. Placeholders cannot be restored on a master once they have been deleted.

T   F   5. You can preview a presentation only to see how the slides look in color.

T   F   6. When printing an outline, clip art images do not print for each slide.

T   F   7. When printing a presentation, printing audience handouts and outlines can use less paper than printing the entire presentation as slides.

T   F   8. Audience handouts can be printed either across or down the page when printing more than three slides per page.

T   F   9. You can add the current date, page number, header, or footer to the audience handouts.

T   F   10. You cannot change the default orientation for printing notes pages, handouts, and outlines.

chapter eight

Skills Review

SCANS

Exercise 1 C

1. Open the *PowerPoint* presentation you modified in Chapter 7.

2. Create the following notes page for the title slide: "Welcome everyone. Inform them that your goal today is to get them to appreciate PowerPoint, the popular presentation graphics software program."

3. Print the notes page for the title slide.

4. Prepare an audience handout using the six-slides-per-page option.

5. Add your name in the header area.

6. Add the name of the presentation in the footer area.

7. Preview the handout for the presentation, and then print the audience handout for the *PowerPoint* presentation using the six-slides-per-page option. Save and close the presentation.

Exercise 2 C

1. Open the *Office* presentation you modified in Chapter 7.

2. Add your name to the footer area and the current date on the handout master.

3. Add an appropriate clip art image to the handout master.

4. Preview and print the outline for the *Office* presentation.

5. Print an audience handout using the two-slides-per-page option. Save and close the presentation.

Exercise 3 C

1. Open the *Design* presentation you modified in Chapter 7.

2. Create the following notes page for the title slide: "Creating a presentation takes careful planning. Remember to keep the interest of the audience and the objective of the presentation in mind while you create each slide."

3. Create the following notes page for the WordArt slide: "Design is an important factor in every presentation. However, there are three main focus points of every presentation—the Audience, the Audience, the Audience."

4. Select the text box on the notes master, and change the font to Times New Roman 16 point.

5. Add an appropriate AutoShape to the notes master.

6. Preview and print the notes pages for Slides 1 and 5. Save and close the presentation.

Exercise 4 C

1. Open the *Precision Builders* presentation you modified in Chapter 7.

2. Add your name to the footer area on the handout master.

3. Add the name of the presentation to the header area on the handout master.

4. Select the four-slides-per-page layout.

5. Add an appropriate AutoShape to the top right of the handout master.

6. Preview and print the audience handout using the four-slides-per-page layout with the vertical option. Save and close the presentation.

Exercise 5

1. Open the *Nature Tours* presentation you modified in Chapter 7.

2. Preview the presentation in grayscale and then close the Grayscale view.

3. Create a notes page that contains relevant text for each of the even-numbered slides in the presentation.

4. Add an appropriate clip art image to the notes master. Add your name to the footer area on the notes master.

5. Change the page orientation of the notes pages to Landscape.

6. Preview and print only the even-numbered notes pages. Save and close the presentation.

Exercise 6

1. Open the *A Healthier You* presentation you modified in Chapter 7.

2. Prepare an audience handout to print three slides per page.

3. Add the title of the presentation in the header area. Add your name in the footer area.

4. Add an AutoShape to the handout master.

5. Verify that the page orientation of the handouts is Portrait.

6. Preview and print the handout with frames. Save and close the presentation.

Exercise 7

1. Open the *Buying A Computer* presentation you modified in Chapter 7.

2. Add the name of the presentation and the current date to the top of the handout master and your name to the footer area.

3. Select the nine-slides-per-page layout.

4. Add a computer clip art image to the handout master.

5. Preview and print the outline and the handout for the presentation. Save and close the presentation.

Exercise 8

1. Open the *Leisure Travel* presentation you modified in Chapter 7.

2. Preview the presentation in grayscale, pure black and white, and then in color.

3. Add the name of the presentation and the current date to the top of the handout master and your name to the footer area.

4. Change the page orientation for notes, handouts, and outline to Landscape.

5. Add an appropriate clip art image to the handout master.

6. Preview and print the audience handout using the four-slides-per-page option. Save and close the presentation.

Case Projects

SCANS

Project 1

One of your coworkers is having problems using the notes and handout masters. You remember how to create notes pages, but you need to use the Ask A Question Box and online Help to search for information on using the notes and handout master. Print a copy of help topics including any additional links for notes and handout masters.

Project 2

Your employer is new to presenting to a large audience. She asks you to provide notes pages for every even-numbered slide in the *Communicate* presentation you modified in Chapter 7. Create notes pages for each slide with information relevant to that slide. Add the title of the presentation in the header and your name in the footer area on the notes master. Preview and print the notes pages for all the even-numbered slides. Save the presentation and close it.

Project 3

The owners of Souner & Associates are masters when it comes to presenting slide show presentations. They want to make it easy for the audience to take notes during their upcoming slide show presentation. They ask you to create a handout that prints three slides per page so audience members can take notes next to each slide during the presentation. Prepare the handouts for the *Souner* presentation you modified in Chapter 7, including a clip art image and/or text on the handout master. Change the page orientation to landscape for the handout. Preview and print the handouts horizontally in the three-slides-per-page layout. Save the presentation and close it.

Project 4

While working on your own presentation, you decide that it might be beneficial to create a few notes pages for slides that need some clarification or reminders for the speaker. You also want to print an outline displaying a brief overview of the slides in the presentation. Create notes pages, an audience handout, and an outline for *My Presentation* you modified in Chapter 7. Add text and/or clip art images to your master. Preview and print the notes pages, handouts, and the outline. Save the presentation and close it.

Project 5

You work on the *Zoo* presentation you modified in Chapter 7 with enthusiasm, and you want to show your employer a quick overview of the slides. Instead of printing each slide of the presentation on a full sheet of paper, you decide to print a handout displaying the best layout for the number of slides in your presentation. Add text and/or clip art images to the handout master. Preview and print the audience handout in both portrait and landscape orientation. Save the presentation and close it.

Project 6

You are interested in finding out new information about PowerPoint. Connect to the Internet and search the Web for current articles on PowerPoint 2002. Create a presentation consisting of at least three slides detailing the new features you found. Print the presentation as an outline and as an audience handout with three slides per page. Add text and clip art images as needed to the handout master. Save and close the presentation.

Project 7

You are getting close to finishing the details of your *Cars* presentation you modified in Chapter 7. You know that it would be helpful for your students to have a printed copy of the presentation you plan to give. You decide to add appropriate clip art images to the handout master to add some interest for the students. You also want to print one of the most interesting slides on a full page for the students. Preview and print the audience handout and any slide of interest. Save the presentation and close it.

Project 8

Your professor wants to distribute the entire *Internet* presentation you modified in Chapter 7 to his class. Because he expects the class to take notes on the handout of the presentation, hc asks you to find a layout that accommodates lines next to the slides so that students have room to write notes. He also wants the current semester, year, course name, and his own name to appear on the handout. The pages should be numbered as well. In addition, the professor wants an outline of the presentation for his files. It is up to you and your partner to add clip art images to the masters and print the requested handouts. Save the presentation and close it.

Microsoft
Access 2002
Introductory

Quick Start for Access

Chapter Overview

Database applications help you store vast amounts of information for use in decision making. In this chapter, you learn about the purpose of the Access application, become familiar with its menus and toolbars, and view some of its objects, including a table, a form, a query, a report, and a data access page.

LEARNING OBJECTIVES

▶ Define Access
▶ Open the Access application
▶ Identify the components of the Access window
▶ Identify Access objects
▶ Exit Access

Case profile

You work for Online University (OLU), an educational organization that has been in business for the past 10 years. The for-profit company offers classes over the Internet, by correspondence, and in person for students all over the world. As the database administrator, you are responsible for creating and managing one of the company's databases, which must include accurate information about its courses, students, instructors, and staff members. You use Access to create and maintain this database.

chapter one

To start Access and open an Access database:

Step 1	*Click*	the Start button ▣Start on the taskbar
Step 2	*Point to*	Programs
Step 3	*Click*	Microsoft Access

The Microsoft Access application and the New File task pane open. Your screen should look similar to Figure 1-1.

FIGURE 1-1
Access Application Window and New File Task Pane

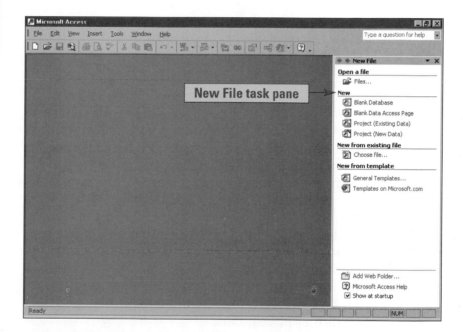

MENU TIP

Office XP features personalized menus, which "learn" the commands you use most often. This means that when you first install Office XP, only the most frequently used commands immediately appear on short versions of the menus and the remaining commands appear after a brief pause. Commands that you click move to the short menu, while those you don't use appear only on the full menu. Unless otherwise noted, the illustrations in this book show the full menus.

1.c Identifying the Components of the Access Window

When you look at Figure 1-1, some parts of the Access window may seem familiar, because they are similar to other Office applications. However, other parts are unique to Access, such as some toolbar buttons and menu options.

Task Pane

The **New File task pane** lets you accomplish the most common Access startup commands. The New File task pane appears when you start Access, or you can display it with the New command on the File

notes This text assumes that you have little or no knowledge of the Access application. However, it also assumes that you have read Office Chapters 1–3 of this book and that you are familiar with Windows 98 or Windows 2000 concepts.

The figures in this book were created using Windows 98. If you are using the Access application installed on Windows 2000, you may notice a few minor differences in some figures. These differences do not affect your work in this book.

1.a Defining Access

Access is a database application. A **database** is a collection of records and files organized for a particular purpose. For example, you could use a database to store information about your friends and family, including their addresses and phone numbers. Access, however, is more powerful than a simple database because it uses a **relational database management model**, which means you can relate each piece of information to other pieces of information by joining them. For example, suppose you have a table of information whose rows represent customers and whose columns represent information about customers such as their names, addresses, and telephone numbers. In another table, you have information about the orders that these customers place with your company. You can join the customer and order information from these two tables by creating a relationship. This way, you don't need to reenter customers' information every time they place orders.

Access makes it easy to view and edit data through on-screen forms that resemble paper forms. You can quickly find the data you need by requesting information with a query. Access creates sophisticated reports to display information on the screen or on paper. Access has many automated tools (called wizards) for building the parts of your database, called objects. Database objects include tables, queries, forms and reports.

1.b Opening the Access Application

Before you can work with Access, you must open the application. When you start Access, you see the New File task pane providing options to create a new database or open an existing one. You open one of OLU's existing Access databases, *mdbOnlineU1-*, so that you can better understand how to use its powerful features.

QUICK TIP

Join means matching rows from the two tables that have identical customer numbers, and *relationship* refers to the formal way that Access keeps these rows together.

**chapter
one**

menu. The New File task pane lets you open an existing database, create a new blank database, or create a database by using a Database Wizard. The task pane appears on the right of the Access window and organizes commands for a particular task.

Opening a Database File

You use the New File task pane to create a copy of an existing database. To create a new database from an existing database:

Step 1	**Verify**	that the New File task pane is open in the Access window
Step 2	**Click**	the Choose file link in the New from existing file section in the New File task pane

The New from Existing File dialog box opens.

Step 3	**Click**	the Look in: list arrow
Step 4	**Switch to**	the drive and folder that contains the Data Disk

notes   Be sure to check with your instructor if you do not know on which disk drive and from which folder you are to retrieve and save your databases.

Your dialog box should look similar to Figure 1-2. The folders, files, and file extensions depend on your computer's configuration.

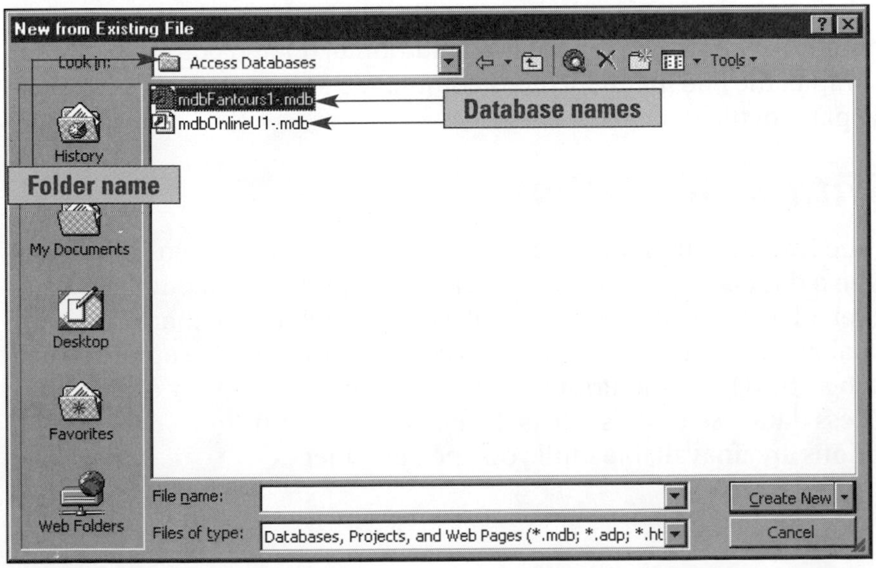

TASK PANE TIP

The New File task pane lists existing databases you used recently. If you want to open a database that is not listed, click the More files link. This link exists only if you have previously opened a database in this installation of Access. You can then locate a database on your hard drive or network. The New File task pane closes when you click the Close button on its title bar.

New from Existing File dialog box

Look in: Access Databases   Tools

mdbFantours1-.mdb
mdbOnlineU1-.mdb ← **Database names**

Folder name

History
My Documents
Desktop
Favorites
Web Folders

File name:
Files of type: Databases, Projects, and Web Pages (*.mdb; *.adp; *.ht

Create New
Cancel

FIGURE 1-2
New from Existing File
Dialog Box

chapter one

Step 5	**Click**	*mdbOnlineU1-*
Step 6	**Click**	Create New

Access makes a copy of the database, naming it *mdbOnlineU1-1*, and closes the New File task pane. The **Database window** in the middle of the Access program window contains all objects of your database. In this case, you see the tables in the database. Your screen should look similar to Figure 1-3.

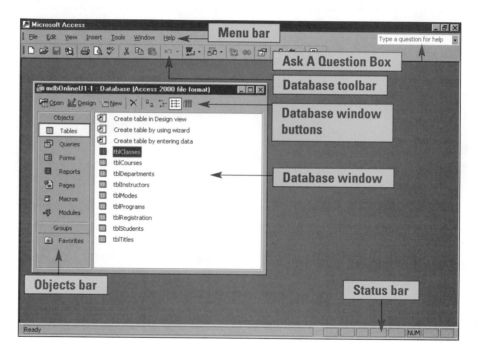

FIGURE 1-3
mdbOnlineU1-1 Database Window

Quick Tip

To maintain the original contents of the sample databases used in each chapter, you create a duplicate database from an existing file. Access adds a digit to the end of the existing filename and creates the copy in the folder that contains the original database.

Menu Bar

The **menu bar**, located below the title bar, has drop-down menu commands that contain groups of additional, related commands. For example, the File menu includes commands for previewing and printing parts of the database.

Database Toolbar

The Database toolbar appears below the menu bar when you first open a database. As you access different objects in that database, other, object-specific toolbars replace the Database toolbar. The Database toolbar contains features common to all Office applications, such as the Open and Print buttons. It also contains many of the Access database tools, such as the Relationships button. Grayed options are unavailable until you open an object.

Menu Tip

To customize the toolbars, click the View menu, point to Toolbars, and then click Customize. You can then choose the toolbars you want Access to display when you open the application.

Ask A Question Box

The Ask A Question Box appears on the right side of the menu bar. When you key a phrase in this text box, Access searches its online Help files for information relating to this phrase. You then click the topic that matches your interest. You also can get online Help by clicking Help on the menu bar and then clicking Microsoft Access Help. When you're working with a dialog box, you can get context-sensitive help by pressing the F1 key or by clicking the Help button.

Status Bar

The **status bar** at the bottom of the Access window indicates the condition of the open database, such as READY. Other areas of the status bar indicate such features as NUM LOCK or CAPS LOCK. As you work with databases, the status bar is helpful when you are editing data in tables or forms—the status bar shows you a description of the selected field. It also tells you when you are in overtype mode by displaying OVR in the status bar.

Objects Bar

Access **objects** are the parts of the database. Tables, forms, and reports are all objects. Most databases contain tables to store data, forms to view and edit data, and reports for displaying information to users. Access manages the objects in your database by displaying them in the Database window.

Each object type relates in some way to the data stored in the database and how you view that data. The Objects bar on the left of the Database window shows each object type (tables, queries, forms, reports, data access pages, macros, and modules). Note that an object type appears in the Objects bar even if the database itself does not contain an object of that type. When you click an object type, Access displays all objects of that type in the Database window.

The buttons in the Database window let you manipulate each object. After you highlight an existing object in the Database window, you can open that object in **Normal view** (to see the contents of the object) or in **Design view** (to see the structure of the object). You can use the buttons in the Database window to create a new object of that type or to delete the highlighted object. The final four buttons let you choose how objects appear in the Database window (as large or small icons, as a list, or with details).

MENU TIP

You can get context-sensitive help on menu options. Select an option and then press the F1 key to see a related help topic. This is particularly helpful when you deal with properties of objects in later chapters.

MOUSE TIP

When you work with Access objects, you can press the SHIFT + F1 keys to switch to the What's This? Help pointer, then click any on-screen item, such as a button or field, to see a brief explanation.

---

chapter
one

MOUSE TIP

Double-clicking the object is the same as clicking the object and then clicking the Open button on the Database toolbar.

QUICK TIP

This book uses the Leszynski naming convention (LNC) for databases and database objects. The following prefixes indicate the kind of database object you're working with:

tbl: table
qry: query
frm: form
rpt: report
mcr: macro
dap: data access page
mdb: database

Tables contain information about specific topics. For example, the tblStudents table contains OLU's student information. When you open your database, the tables appear by default in the Database window.

1.d Identifying Access Objects

Access displays objects in the Database window. The most frequently used objects are the table, form, query, report, and data access page. More advanced Access objects include macros and modules.

Tables

Tables are at the heart of every database; when you create a database, you most often start by creating tables. **Tables** store information in records and fields. **Records** are groups of entries that Access stores in rows. For example, a row stores information about one student. **Fields** are categories of specific information (such as first name, last name, and phone number) that Access stores in columns.

To open the *mdbOnlineU1-1* tblStudents table by using the Objects bar:

Step 1	*Click*	Tables  on the Objects bar in the Database window, if necessary
Step 2	*Double-click*	tblStudents

The tblStudents table opens. Your screen should look similar to Figure 1-4.

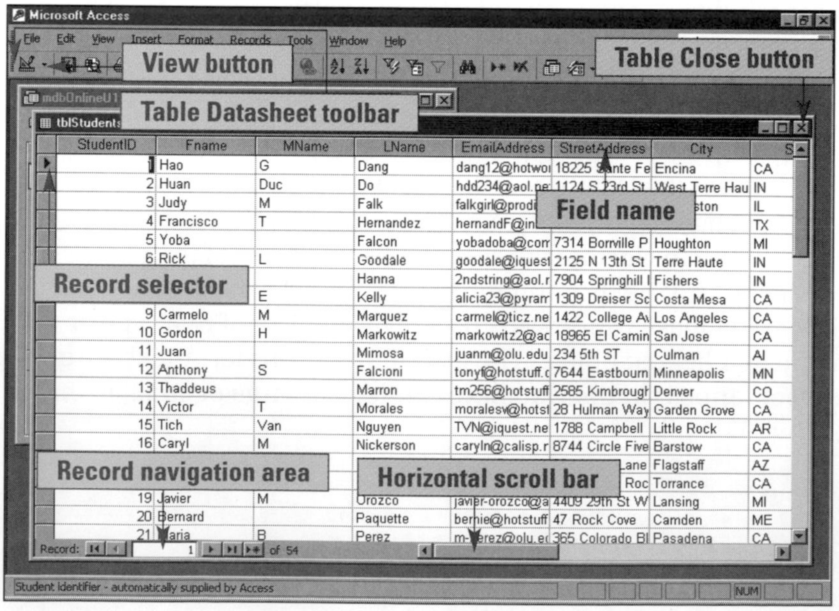

FIGURE 1-4
tblStudents Table in Datasheet View

Figure 1-4 shows the parts of an Access table. Notice that the **Table Datasheet toolbar** is now the current toolbar; it contains tools for working with the Access table. The status bar message about the Student identifier field shows the description for that field. The **record selector** lets you select or highlight an entire record in a table. Record selector symbols include a triangle, which points to the current record; an asterisk, which shows a new blank record; a pencil, which tells you that you are editing a record; and a null symbol, which indicates the record is locked and cannot be changed.

Record navigation buttons let you move from one record to the next. The middle two buttons move one record at a time in the direction of each arrow. The first button on the left moves to the first record in the table. The fourth button on the right moves the insertion point to the last record. The **New Record button** adds a new, blank record to the table. The **Specific Record box** indicates the number value of the current record as related to the rest of the records in the table. Finally, the **horizontal scroll bar** lets you view the rest of the fields. These navigational tools work the same for all database objects.

After you examine the table, you should close it before viewing other Access objects. To close the tblStudents table:

Step 1	*Click*	the Close button ☒ on the table title bar

Once you create a table, you often create a form to enter, view, and edit data values.

Forms

A **form** is a convenient way to enter or find information in tables. Although you can enter information directly into a table, using a form is easier. The form displays a template for each field that you tab through as you enter data. If you add a blank record, the template shows empty fields while you enter data in them. Labels identify the type of information you are entering. You can also use forms to search or review your data.

To look at the parts of an Access form:

Step 1	*Click*	Forms ⊞ Forms on the Objects bar in the Database window
Step 2	*Double-click*	frmStudents

chapter
one

Your screen should look similar to Figure 1-5.

The field names on a form are called **labels**. These are the same fields found in the tables used to generate the form. A **value** is the data entered and contained in a single field in a single record. For example, a student's last name, such as Dang, is a value.

After you finish looking at the layout of a form, you should close it to avoid cluttering the desktop. To close the frmStudents form:

Step 1	Click	the Close button ☒ on the frmStudents title bar

After creating a form, you use it to enter data in one or more Access tables. You can then locate specific data by using queries.

Queries

One of the most powerful features of Access is the **query**, which lets you request information from a table. Access then uses your questions to generate a subset of the data in your database. The data may be drawn from multiple tables. Before you open a query, let's discuss the different views that are available in Access.

You can display each object in Access in different views. These **views** let you work with your database in different ways. The views can be grouped according to their use.

Some views show the data. **Datasheet view** displays records in a row-and-column format, similar to a table, and lets you see many records at the same time. **Design view** lets you design and modify elements of your database, such as its tables, queries, forms, reports, and macros. **Form view** displays records in a layout you design to make data entry easy.

The database developer, or database specialist who creates a database application, uses other views when designing the objects. **SQL view** shows the SQL programming for the limiting factors of a query.

Print Preview shows how a report looks when printed. **Layout Preview** shows a small portion of the data in a report before printing.

Opening a Query in Design View

If you double-click a query object to open it, you open the results of the query. Because you want to look first at the design of a query, you must click the Design button in the Database window. To open an Access query:

Step 1	*Click*	Queries [⊞ Queries] on the Objects bar in the Database window

This database has only one query; thus, clicking Queries on the Objects bar and selected it by default.

Step 2	*Click*	the Design button [✎ Design] in the Database window

Your screen should look similar to Figure 1-6.

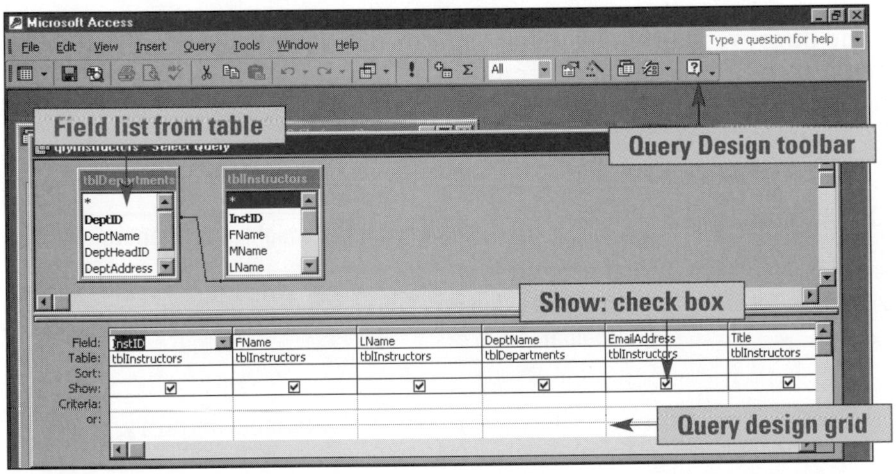

FIGURE 1-6
qryInstructors Query in
Design View

Figure 1-6 shows the parts of a query. Notice that the current toolbar changes to the Query Design toolbar, which contains tools that you use only for an Access query.

The query title bar indicates the name (here, qryInstructors) and type of query (here, Select Query). The default query type is **select query**, which you use when you want to view a set of records for examination or modification. The **field list** contains all the fields from the table or query being used in the query. In designing a query, you may select fields from different tables and use as many fields in your query as you wish.

The **design grid** resembles a table and contains the criteria used in the query. The **Field: row** is the top row of the design grid and contains

---

MOUSE TIP

To open a query quickly in Design view, right-click the query name, and then click <u>D</u>esign view.

MOUSE TIP

When the query is open in Design view, clicking the View button on the Query Design toolbar switches you to Datasheet view. Conversely, when the query is open in Datasheet view, clicking the View button on the Query Datasheet toolbar switches you to Design view.

chapter
one

MOUSE TIP

The choices for the View button vary with the type of object. For most objects, you can choose Design view to see the underlying structure of the object and change the design. For most objects, you can also choose Datasheet view to see records in table format. For reports, you can choose Print Preview view to see how the report will appear when printed.

QUICK TIP

Sorting information lets you view the same information from a different perspective.

MENU TIP

To sort on a field, right-click the field, and then click the sort option of your choice.

fields used in the query. The **Table: row** indicates the name of the tables on which your query is based. The **Sort: row** indicates whether the records are sorted on a particular field. The **Show: check box** indicates the field is shown in query results. If you remove the check mark from the Show: check box for a field, that field does not appear in the query results. This is useful if you want to query on a certain field but do not want that field to show in the results. You use the **Criteria: row** to determine which records appear in the query results. This is a limiting feature such as "Indiana" or "<25." Finally, the **or: row**, used in sorting the information, is similar to the Criteria: row.

You can see the results of a query by switching to Datasheet view.

Switching Between Object Views

You can easily switch views of query objects by clicking the appropriate View button on the Query Design toolbar. You also can switch views by clicking the appropriate command on the View menu. To see the query results by switching to Datasheet view:

| Step 1 | *Click* | the View button list arrow 🔲 ▾ on the Query Design toolbar |
| Step 2 | *Click* | Datasheet View |

The query results are displayed in table form. The OLU instructors are listed in alphabetical order and sorted according to their department code. You also can sort the data by using any other field, such as the LName (last name) field. To sort on the LName field:

| Step 1 | *Click* | the LName column heading to highlight the entire column |
| Step 2 | *Click* | the Sort Ascending button ↓ on the Query Datasheet toolbar |

After looking at the sorted query results, you close the query.

| Step 3 | *Click* | the Close button ⊠ on the query title bar |

Because you changed this query's design, Access asks whether you want to save changes. In this case, you don't want to save the changes.

| Step 4 | *Click* | No |

After performing a query, you might want to view the information in a report.

Reports

A **report** is an organized presentation, designed for printing, of the information in your tables or queries. You can create a report from a single table or from a query of two or more tables. A report can also process data and can automatically calculate and show subtotals and totals. Finally, inserting graphic elements and using formatting techniques often improve the readability and attractiveness of reports.

To open the rptStudents report:

Step 1	**Click**	Reports [Reports] on the Objects bar in the Database window
Step 2	**Double-click**	rptStudents

Your screen should look similar to Figure 1-7.

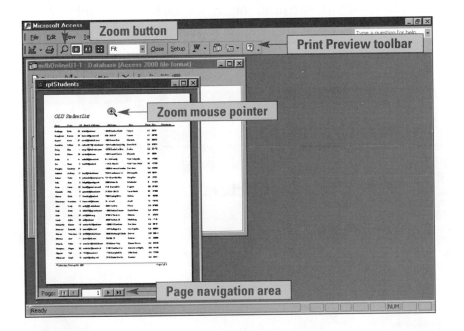

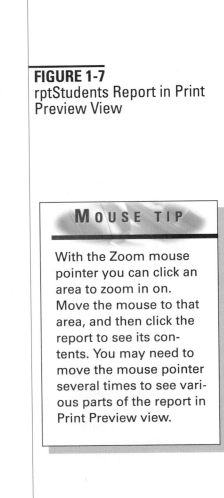

MOUSE TIP

With the Zoom mouse pointer you can click an area to zoom in on. Move the mouse to that area, and then click the report to see its contents. You may need to move the mouse pointer several times to see various parts of the report in Print Preview view.

The Print Preview toolbar is the current toolbar; it contains tools used by Access reports. For example, the **Zoom** button lets you magnify a particular area of the report. The report is in Print Preview view, which lets you see what the report looks like when printed. This saves you time and paper, as you can determine if you need to make any changes or corrections before you print.

After you look at the report preview, you close it. To close the rptStudents report:

Step 1	**Click**	the Close button [X] on the report title bar

**chapter
one**

Data Access Pages

A **data access page (DAP)** lets you extend the database by creating Hypertext Markup Language (HTML) pages that display data from an Access database. HTML is used to create the pages that you might see on the Web or on an intranet. (An **intranet** is a private Web site for an organization and is not accessible to users outside that organization.) Written for use on an intranet or the Internet, HTML pages let you share information with others in any location.

Data access pages are stored as an HTML file, not a database file. To work properly, a DAP must be configured to connect to the folder and database that contains the data that the DAP displays. The DAP lets others who do not have Access installed on their computers browse the information. You can e-mail a DAP to your coworkers using **Outlook**, the Microsoft e-mail and personal information application. Access and Outlook can share information, which is not always true with other e-mail applications.

DAPs are more than Internet packaging for Access; they are a convenient way to interact with Access data. People with whom you share your data can view, sort, and print the data, even if they do not have Access on their computers. To open a DAP, click Pages on the Objects bar of the Database window and then double-click the DAP you want to open. Figure 1-8 shows a data access page for OLU instructors.

CAUTION TIP

You must have Internet Explorer version 5.0 or later installed on your computer to view the contents of a data access page on the Web. Data access pages do not work with Netscape Navigator or earlier versions of Internet Explorer.

FIGURE 1-8
daplnstructors Data Access Page in Preview Mode

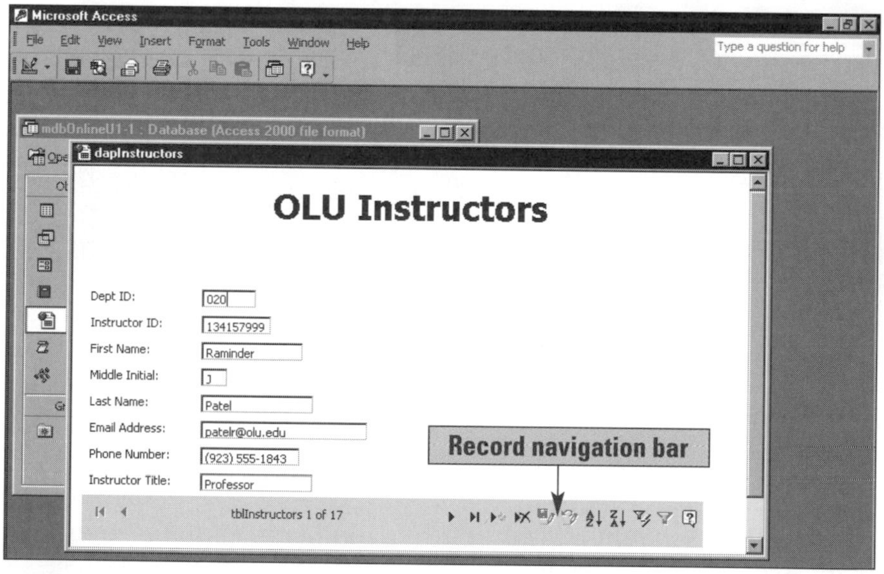

QUICK TIP

Compacting the database is not the same as compressing the database into a .zip file with WinZip or another compression utility.

Figure 1-8 shows the parts of a DAP. (This DAP is not included on the Data Disk.) Some tools are unavailable at this time because the page is being viewed in **Preview mode**, which lets you browse records but not enter information or make changes. The DAP's navigation bar lets you view the records included in the DAP.

In Design view, you can create and edit a DAP using the **Web Editing toolbar**, which includes tools for modifying the text, background, and placement of objects on the DAP. The **Page Design toolbar** lets you add, delete, group, and sort the fields that you choose for your HTML file. Finally, the **Toolbox** has the tools you need to build the fields for the HTML page.

Macros

An Access **macro** is a set of one or more actions that perform a particular operation, such as opening a form or printing a report. A **macro group** is a collection of related macros stored together under a single macro name. You can automate certain activities by including the actions in a macro connected to a command button you can click. A command button is a button on a form; when clicked, it causes some action to take place.

Modules

Modules are programs written in the Visual Basic language, which other Office applications use. With Visual Basic, you can program all aspects of your Access database, including your own tables, forms, reports, and queries. Although writing programs is a challenge at first, modules can provide your database with incredible functionality. For example, you can use a module to check the accuracy of information keyed into your database or to check for redundant data.

1.e Exiting Access

As you make changes to the records in your tables, Access automatically saves them. In other words, you do not have to save changes you make to the *values* in your database. However, if you change the *design* of any database objects after you last saved them, Access asks if you want to save these changes before exiting. When saving your database, Access can automatically compact the database (reduce its file size) to save space on your hard drive. The smaller file size also makes it easier to transfer the database to other locations on your network. Note that compacting the database is not the same as compressing the database into a .zip file with WinZip or another compression utility.

To exit Access:

Step 1	*Click*	File
Step 2	*Click*	Exit

The *mdbOnlineU1-1* database and the Access application close. Because you did not make any changes to the database, Access does not prompt you to save changes to any objects in the database.

CAUTION TIP

If you turn off your computer without exiting Access, you may damage your database. Always save your work and exit Access before you turn off your computer.

If you are using a database located on a removable storage medium such as a floppy disk, Zip disk, or CD-ROM, be sure to close the database before removing the disk.

QUICK TIP

You can automatically compact a database when closing it. Click the Options command on the Tools menu, click the General tab, and then click the Compact on Close check box. You also can compact the database manually when needed.

MENU TIP

You can close the database without exiting Access by using the Close command on the File menu.

---

chapter
one

Summary

▶ A database is a collection of related information. An example of a database is a list of students and their contact information.

▶ The New File task pane lets you open an existing database, create a new blank database, or use the Database Wizard to create a new database based on a template.

▶ Access uses objects such as tables, queries, forms, reports, and data access pages. These objects all relate to the data stored in the database.

▶ The most common Access views are Design view and Datasheet view. In Design view, you create the look of the database. In Datasheet view, you see the data.

▶ A table contains data in columns (fields) and rows (records) called a datasheet. A field in a datasheet contains one type of information, such as customers' phone numbers. A record in a datasheet contains all fields for one item, such as for one customer.

▶ You use Access forms to enter, update, search, or review data in tables.

▶ An Access query lets you ask questions about your data. A query shows you specific data that you want to work with.

▶ Access reports enable you to share database information in printed form.

▶ A data access page (DAP) lets you create an interactive HTML page using the information stored in your Access database. This tool lets you share your database with others who may not have Access installed on their computers.

▶ Macros are programs that let you customize the database and automate tasks that you perform regularly.

▶ Modules are advanced programs written in Visual Basic that let you automate tasks that you perform regularly.

▶ When you exit Access, changes to the data in your database are saved automatically. You should always exit Access before turning off your computer.

Commands Review

Action	Menu Bar	Shortcut Menu	Toolbar	Task Pane	Keyboard
Open an existing database	<u>F</u>ile, <u>O</u>pen			Click the More files link in the in the Open a file section in the New File task pane	ALT + F, O CTRL + O
Create a new database from existing file				Click the Choose file link in the New from exiting file section in the New File task pane	
Open an object in the Database window	<u>V</u>iew, Database Objects	Right-click object, click <u>O</u>pen Double-click object			ALT + V, J
Get help	<u>H</u>elp				F1
Close an object	<u>F</u>ile, <u>C</u>lose	Right-click object, click <u>C</u>lose	✕		ALT + F, C
Display the New File task pane	<u>F</u>ile, <u>N</u>ew	Right-click toolbar, click Task Pane			ALT + F, N CTRL + N
Exit Access	<u>F</u>ile, E<u>x</u>it	Right-click application button on taskbar, click <u>C</u>lose	✕		ALT + F, X ALT + F4

Concepts Review

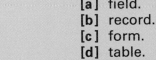

Circle the correct answer.

1. A database is a:
 [a] tool for editing files.
 [b] way to automate common tasks.
 [c] collection of related information.
 [d] link to the World Wide Web.

2. Access has menus and toolbars that:
 [a] learn what you do.
 [b] are the same for all objects.
 [c] are exactly the same as those in other Office products.
 [d] never change.

3. In Datasheet view, you can:
 [a] design tables and forms.
 [b] view data in rows and columns.
 [c] preview your printed reports.
 [d] establish criteria for which records appear.

4. Which of the following is not an Access database object?
 [a] table
 [b] data access page
 [c] query
 [d] command button

5. A category of information, such as last name or phone number, is called a:
 [a] field.
 [b] record.
 [c] form.
 [d] table.

6. Which record selector symbol points to the current record in a table?
 [a] check mark
 [b] asterisk
 [c] null symbol
 [d] triangle

7. To enter, update, search, or review data quickly and easily, use a:
 [a] form.
 [b] table.
 [c] report.
 [d] query.

8. You can switch between Design view and Datasheet view by clicking the:
 [a] Queries object tab.
 [b] <u>S</u>witch command on the <u>V</u>iew menu.
 [c] View button, then click a view option.
 [d] query title bar.

chapter one

9. A data access page lets you:
  [a] know who can access data.
  [b] create a Web page using your database.
  [c] edit an HTML page.
  [d] select a page to print.

10. Modules are:
  [a] a selection of tables linked together in a relationship.
  [b] programs written in Visual Basic.
  [c] object tabs.
  [d] a group of records.

Circle **T** if the statement is true or **F** is the statement is false.

T F   1. An example of a table is a list of customers and their addresses and phone numbers.

T F   2. You can open more than one database file at a time in Access.

T F   3. You cannot make a copy of an existing database in Access.

T F   4. Access automatically opens a blank database when you start the application.

T F   5. Tables store information in rows of records and columns of fields.

T F   6. Layout Preview shows a small portion of data in a report before printing.

T F   7. You can use the Zoom mouse pointer to zoom in on particular area in Design view.

T F   8. You can use a query to print a report in Access.

T F   9. A macro forces Access to perform one task at a time.

T F   10. If you create a data access page, you can share your database with others, even if they don't use Internet Explorer.

notes   The Skills Review Exercises and Case Projects in each chapter are designed to be completed in the order presented. You should work through each exercise or project before moving onto the next one.

Skills Review

SCANS

Exercise 1

1. Start the Access application.

2. Observe the four active buttons in the Database toolbar that are not grayed out.

3. Use What's Is? command on the Help menu to explore and then briefly describe of the function of each active button.

4. Close the New File task pane.

Exercise 2

1. Use the New command on the File menu to display the New File task pane.

2. Click the Choose file link in the New from existing file section in the New File task pane.

3. Switch to the drive and folder that contains the Data Disk.

4. Create a new copy of the *mdbFanTours1-* database on your computer; Access saves it as *mdbFanTours1-1*.

5. Close the database.

Exercise 3

1. Open the *mdbFanTours1-1* database that you created in Exercise 2.

2. Open the tblProspects table in Datasheet view.

3. Move to the last record in the table by using the navigation buttons.

4. Scroll horizontally to view all fields in the record, including the last field.

5. Close the table. Close the database.

Exercise 4

1. Open the *mdbFanTours1-1* database that you modified in Exercise 3.

2. Open the frmProspects form.

3. Press the TAB key to move to the next field.

4. Press the TAB key repeatedly to move to the StreetAddress field.

5. Close the form. Close the database.

Exercise 5

1. Open the *mdbFanTours1-1* database that you modified in Exercise 4.

2. Open the qryProspects query in Design view.

3. In the design grid, review the design for this query: the fields and tables used, criteria, sort order, and whether to show the State field in the query results.

4. Switch to Datasheet view to see the query results.

5. Close the query. Close the database.

Exercise 6

1. Open the *mdbFanTours1-1* database that you modified in Exercise 5.

2. Open the tblProspects table in Datasheet view.

3. Sort the list in ascending order by the students' first names.

4. Close the table without saving the changes to the table layout. Close the database.

Exercise 7

1. Open the *mdbFanTours1-1* database that you modified in Exercise 6.

2. Open the rptProspects report.

3. Preview the report.

4. Click the Print button in the Print Preview toolbar to print the report.

5. Close the report. Close the database.

chapter one

Exercise 8

1. Open the *mdbFanTours1-1* database that you modified in Exercise 7.

2. Open tblProspects in Datasheet view.

3. Use the toolbar shortcut menu to verify which toolbar(s) are in use.

4. Switch to Design view by clicking on the Design View button, and then verify which toolbar(s) are in use.

5. Close the table and verify which toolbar(s) are in use. Close the database.

Case Projects

Project 1

Your supervisor at Fantastic Sports Tours, Inc. (FST) asks you to write an introduction to Access databases, using *mdbFantours1-1* as an example. New employees at Fantastic Sports Tours plan to use your introduction to learn the basics of Access databases. In a Word document, write two or three paragraphs defining terms every Access user should know. Explain the meaning and provide an example of each term. Save and print the document.

Project 2

Create a new document for the Fantastic Sports Tours Employee Handbook that contains one or two paragraphs about how to use the Database window while working in Access, including the Objects bar and the buttons in the Database window. Use Word to create, save, and print the document.

Project 3

To increase efficiency, your supervisor at Fantastic Sports Tours asks you to create a chart of Microsoft Access keyboard shortcuts. Use the Ask A Question Box to review the Access shortcut keys. In a Word document, list each shortcut command and the action it performs. Save and print the document.

Project 4

Your colleague, who works for another company, tells you about the Northwind sample database packaged with Microsoft Access. You can load this database from the Help menu under Sample Databases. Open the *Northwind* database and describe what appears on the screen when the database first opens. (If you do not have the *Northwind* database, you can install it from the Office XP CD-ROM by running the *Setup* program.)

Project 5

You decide to create a notebook for your department that outlines the features of Access. Create a new document for your notebook that identifies the Database toolbar and lists the name and purpose of each button on the toolbar. (*Hint:* Use the What's This command on the Help menu to obtain online Help for the buttons.) Use Word to create, save, and print the document.

Project 6

You decide to include information about the Access views in your Access notebook. Write two paragraphs explaining the purpose and features of two views. Use Word to create, save, and print the document.

Project 7

Your supervisor at Fantastic Sports Tours asks you to show several new employees how to open a database. Using the Ask A Question Box, research how to open a database. In Word, create a new document and write one or two paragraphs describing how to open an existing database in Access. Save and print the document. Then demonstrate to your coworkers how to open a database in Access.

Project 8

Connect to the Internet and load the home page for a search engine. Search for companies on the Web that are similar to Fantastic Sports Tours. Print at least three Web pages for similar organizations.

Planning a New Database

Chapter Overview

In this chapter, you learn and apply principles of effective database design. You then create the database by adding tables. You also learn how to modify a database table by choosing field types, changing field layouts, modifying field properties, and rearranging fields. Then you learn how to use an input mask to control how data is entered into a field and how to create a lookup field to get categorical data from another source. Finally, you import data into a new table.

LEARNING OBJECTIVES

▶ Determine appropriate data inputs and outputs
▶ Create and save a new database
▶ Create a table using the Table Wizard
▶ Create a table in Design view
▶ Modify a table in Design view
▶ Use the Input Mask Wizard
▶ Create a lookup field
▶ Import data into a table

Case profile

The provost of Online University, Constance Tucker, asks you to design and create an Access database that tracks students and courses for the institution and maintains current instructor and employee information. You plan a database for Online University to maintain this information. In particular, you must design tables for each part of the university and decide on field names, data types, and special properties.

chapter two

2.a Determining Appropriate Data Inputs and Outputs

Before you create a database, it is a good idea to take some time to plan its design. Start by describing the inputs and outputs of your database. The **input** for a database is the information that you enter into the database. The **output** is the information that the database provides.

To determine the purpose of the Online University database, you talk with department managers to find out the kind of information they want to include and how they want to work with the database.

Deciding What Tables Are Necessary

List the subjects or types of information you want the database to cover. Types of information can include student, class, and instructor information. You store each type of information in a table. Be sure to dedicate each table to only one subject, and don't duplicate information within a table or between tables. The only exception to the rule about not duplicating information occurs when you use a common field (such as StudentID or ClassID) to link related tables.

Storing each type of information in a separate table reduces your workload, because you go to only one place to add or update that type of information. Storing each type of information in a separate table also avoids duplicating records and entering the same information more than once. For example, suppose you store a student's information in one table and the student's classes in another table. When the student changes a class, you need modify only the class information, not the student information.

Constance asks you to include three types of information in the Online University database: course, student, and instructor information. Although Online University offers hundreds of classes, ranging from accounting to technology, they fit into only a few departments. This fact simplifies data entry and data maintenance. You perform data maintenance whenever you add, delete, or change data in your database.

In the preliminary database, you need five tables: one for student information (tblStudents), one for departments (tblDepartments), one for courses in each department (tblCourses), one for class offerings (tblClasses), and one for student registrations (tblRegistration).

Determining the Essential Fields

Each table contains information about a subject (such as students); each record in the table contains specific information about one student (in this example), and each field in the table contains specific facts (such as a phone number) about that student. After planning you determine the necessary fields for the five tables, as listed in Table 2-1.

Required Table	Purpose of Table	Necessary Fields
Students	Hold information about each student	*StudentID*, FirstName, MiddleName, LastName, Address, City, StateOrProvince, PostalCode, PhoneNumber, EmailName, Major
Departments	Hold information about each department	*DeptID*, DeptName, DeptAddress, DeptPhone
Courses	Hold information about each course in the OLU catalog	*DeptPrefix*, *CourseNumber*, CourseTitle, CourseDescription, Credits, NonCredit, RevisionDate
Classes	Hold information about each class offering	*ClassID*, *DeptPrefix*, *CourseNumber*, SemesterCode, DeliveryMode, ClassRoom, ClassLocation, ClassInstructorCode
Registration	Hold information about student registrations for each class	*StudentID*, *ClassCode*, DateEnrolled, Grade

TABLE 2-1
Tables and Fields for the OLU Database

QUICK TIP

It is customary to name tables using the plural form, such as Students.

Table 2-1 shows primary key fields in boldface and common fields in italics. In a relational database, common fields link tables. Linking enables you to use information from two tables at the same time.

Each table must have a unique identifier field called the **primary key**. No two records in one table can have the same primary key value. The primary key value helps you identify each unique record. In this chapter, you develop the Students and Departments tables.

Understanding the Leszynski Naming Convention

The Leszynski naming convention (LNC) uses a prefix tag before an object's name to identify the type of database object. At a glance, you know that an electronic file is a database if its filename begins with *mdb*, the Access database filename extension. The tags let you sort objects by type for documentation purposes and help you understand the structure of your data names. You can determine whether a field comes from a table or a query.

Tags for Database Window Objects

Table 2-2 lists the LNC tags corresponding to database objects.

CAUTION TIP

When determining the fields for a table, keep in mind four principles: (1) relate each field to the subject of the table, (2) omit any calculated data, (3) include all the information you need, and (4) store information in small bits (e.g., *last name* and *first name* as separate fields).

Prefix	Object	Prefix	Object
tbl	Table	dap	Data Access Page
qry	Query	mcr	Macro
frm	Form	bas	Module (Visual Basic)
rpt	Report		

TABLE 2-2
LNC Prefixes for Basic Database Objects

chapter
two

Field Names in Tables

For consistency, it is helpful to use a convention for naming fields within tables. Access requires you to surround field names with square brackets in expressions if the field name includes a space to avoid embedded blank characters in field names. In this book, field names consist of one or more capitalized words without spaces. For example, the FirstName field represents the first name of an individual. However, avoiding spaces in table names is not necessary.

Control Tags

LNC includes additional prefix tags for controls in forms and reports. A **control** displays information in a form or report. The information can be the value of a field (from a table or query) or it can represent artwork (lines, rectangles, and images). Table 2-3 lists the LNC control prefixes. For example, the StudentID field that appears in a text box control in a form might be named txtStudentID.

TABLE 2-3
LNC Prefixes for Access Controls

Prefix	Control	Prefix	Control
lbl	Label	opt	Option button
cht	Chart	grp	Option group
chk	Check box	brk	Page break
cbo	Combo box	shp	Rectangle
cmd	Command button	sub	Subform/subreport
fra	Frame	txt	Text box
lin	Line	tgl	Toggle button
lst	List box		

2.b Creating and Saving a New Database

The **Database Wizard** guides you step-by-step through the process of creating a database. Access includes a number of sample databases, such as those for contact, order, or personal information. If you create a database of similar information, you can use the wizard to choose a sample database. Access then creates all the tables and fields (as well as forms and reports) necessary for that type of database. You can change the information to suit your needs. The Database Wizard saves you time when creating common types of databases.

QUICK TIP

Microsoft follows this field name convention in the *Northwind* sample database that comes with Access; however, the *Northwind* database does not follow the LNC convention for database objects such as tables, queries, and so forth.

CAUTION TIP

Name all objects *before* you begin building forms and reports; changing names is difficult after you incorporate fields from tables and queries. The LNC provides documentation and is particularly useful to database developers.

Using the Database Wizard

Access comes with 10 Database Wizard templates, from Asset Tracking to Time and Billing. These templates contain the instructions for the wizard to produce a full set of database objects, including menus, for your application. To create a database using the Database Wizard:

Step 1	*Verify*	that the New File task pane is displayed
Step 2	*Click*	the General Templates link in the New from template section in the New File task pane
Step 3	*Click*	the Databases tab
Step 4	*Click*	Contact Management
Step 5	*Click*	OK
Step 6	*Switch to*	the appropriate drive and folder
Step 7	*Key*	mdbContactManagement2-1 in the File name: text box
Step 8	*Click*	Create

The Database Wizard asks a series of questions about your database. Armed with your answers, Access then creates the appropriate data objects for that database. To accept all default answers:

Step 1	*Click*	Next > to continue
Step 2	*Click*	Next > to accept the three tables and all fields
Step 3	*Select*	Standard style for screen displays, if necessary
Step 4	*Click*	Next >
Step 5	*Click*	Corporate style for the printed reports, if necessary
Step 6	*Click*	Next >
Step 7	*Click*	Next > to accept the default name for the database, Contact Management
Step 8	*Click*	Finish to complete the creation of the database and its objects

Access creates a complete database with four tables, seven forms, two reports, and one module, and displays the main switchboard form (menu). The switchboard provides a simpler interface for interacting with the database. Your screen should look similar to Figure 2-1.

MENU TIP

You can open the New File task pane by clicking the New command on the File menu.

INTERNET TIP

You can find additional templates at the Microsoft.com Web site.

CAUTION TIP

Be sure to check with your instructor if you do not know on which disk drive and in which folder you are to save your database.

TASK PANE TIP

If you are already working in Access, you can create a new database by clicking the New button on the Database toolbar and then clicking the Blank Database link in the New section in the New File task pane.

chapter
two

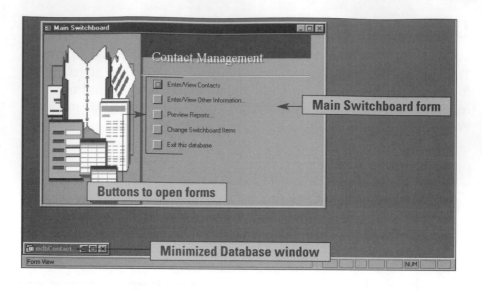

FIGURE 2-1
Finished Database and
Main Switchboard Form

CAUTION TIP

The Database window is
behind the main switch-
board form in the
Access window, or it is
minimized, depending
on the settings in your
installation of Access.

A filename can have
up to 255 characters,
including the disk drive
reference and path, and
any combination of let-
ters, numbers, spaces,
and special characters.

Filenames cannot
include forward slash (/),
backward slash (\),
colon (:), semicolon (;),
pipe symbol (|), ques-
tion mark (?), less than
symbol (<), greater than
symbol (>), asterisk (*),
quotation mark ("), and
period (.).

QUICK TIP

Access automatically
saves the database con-
tents whenever you open
another database, close
a database, or close
Access. You use the Save
command on the File
menu to save objects
within the database.

| Step 9 | *Maximize* | the mdbContact Management database window, if necessary |
| Step 10 | *Click* | the buttons on the Objects bar to observe the mdbContact Management database objects that were created |

Creating a Blank Database

If the database you want to create is not similar to one of the sample databases, you can start with a blank database. You have more flexibil-ity when you start with a blank database. You use the Table Wizard later in this chapter when creating tables. To create a new database:

| Step 1 | *Click* | File |
| Step 2 | *Click* | New |

The New File task pane opens. When you create a new, blank file, Access automatically closes the database currently open. In Access, you can have only one database open at a time.

| Step 3 | *Click* | the Blank Database link in the New section in the New File task pane |

The File New Database dialog box opens. Whenever you create a new database file, Access requires you to name the database file before con-tinuing. In the File name: text box, you can see the temporary name, for example *db1*, that Access assigns the database. You can switch to the location where you want to store your file (a folder on your hard disk or network server) and then accept the name or key another filename.

Step 4	**Switch to**	the appropriate drive and folder
Step 5	**Key**	mdbOnlineU2-1 in the File name: text box
Step 6	**Click**	Create

The *mdbOnlineU2-1* Database window opens. A blank database contains no objects. You create the first table using the Table Wizard.

2.c Creating a Table Using the Table Wizard

Creating a table involves defining the structure for each field stored in the table. Access provides three options: You can open an empty table and then enter data, use the Table Wizard, or create a table in Design view. The **Table Wizard** lets you create a table by choosing from a list of commonly used table templates. For this database, you create tables using both the Table Wizard and Design view. The tblStudents table is similar to one of the wizard's templates. To create the tblStudents table using the Table Wizard:

| Step 1 | **Double-click** | Create table by using wizard in the Database window |
| Step 2 | **Click** | Students in the Sample Tables: list (scroll to view this option) |

Your screen should look similar to Figure 2-2.

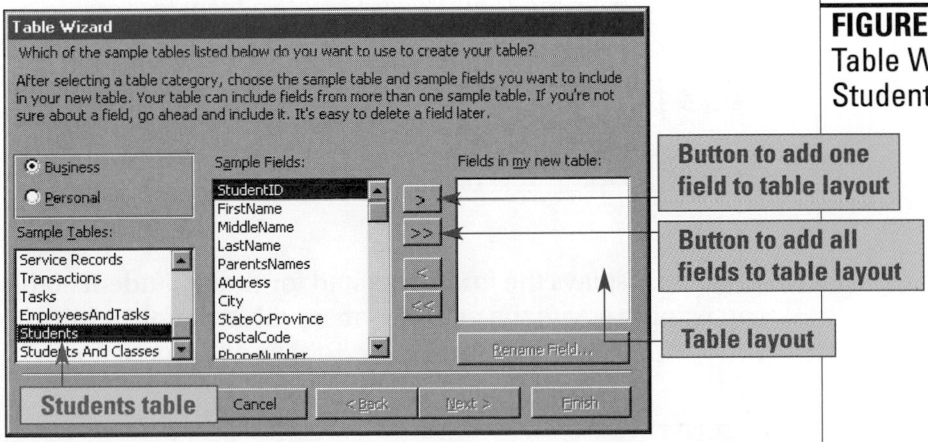

QUICK TIP

The Table Wizard includes two separate lists of table templates; the default is the Business list with 25 sample tables. To view the 20 sample tables in the Personal list, click the Personal option button above the Sample Tables: list.

Table Wizard

Which of the sample tables listed below do you want to use to create your table?

After selecting a table category, choose the sample table and sample fields you want to include in your new table. Your table can include fields from more than one sample table. If you're not sure about a field, go ahead and include it. It's easy to delete a field later.

- Business
- Personal

Sample Tables:
Service Records
Transactions
Tasks
EmployeesAndTasks
Students
Students And Classes

Sample Fields:
StudentID
FirstName
MiddleName
LastName
ParentsNames
Address
City
StateOrProvince
PostalCode
PhoneNumber

Fields in my new table:

Button to add one field to table layout

Button to add all fields to table layout

Table layout

Rename Field...

Students table   Cancel   < Back   Next >   Finish

FIGURE 2-2
Table Wizard for Students Table

Access displays the selected table templates fields in the Sample Fields: list.

Step 3	*Click*	StudentID in the Sample Fields: list, if necessary
Step 4	*Click*	the [>] button to move the selected field to the Fields in my new table: list
Step 5	*Follow*	Steps 3 and 4 until you move all the field names listed below to the Fields in my new table: list:

		StudentID	ParentsNames	PhoneNumber
		FirstName	Address	EmailName
		MiddleName	City	Major
		LastName	StateOrProvince	

| Step 6 | *Click* | Next > |

To set the primary key and name the table in the Table Wizard:

Step 1	*Key*	tblStudents in the What do you want to name your table? text box
Step 2	*Click*	No, I'll set the primary key. option button
Step 3	*Click*	Next >

Access displays the StudentID field as a candidate for the primary key because this field uniquely identifies each record. The wizard asks if you want Access to supply consecutive numbers in this field or if you want to key the values as you add new records. You accept the default choice, so Access assigns consecutive numbers to new records.

| Step 4 | *Click* | Next > |

You now have the Table Wizard create a form for you.

| Step 5 | *Click* | the Enter data into the table using a form the wizard creates for me. option button |
| Step 6 | *Click* | Finish |

Access displays the form it created for the tblStudents table. Because you want to create the other database tables before entering records, you save and close the form now. To save and close a form:

| Step 1 | *Click* | the Close button [X] on the tblStudents form title bar |
| Step 2 | *Click* | Yes to save the changes |

Step 3	*Key*	frmStudents in the Form <u>N</u>ame: text box in the Save As dialog box
Step 4	*Click*	OK
Step 5	*Click*	Forms on the Objects bar
Step 6	*Observe*	that the frmStudents form appears on the list of forms for this database

MENU TIP

You can change the default data type and the default field size for text fields in the Options dialog box.

2.d Creating a Table in Design View

Design view gives you complete control over the contents of your tables. You add fields and then assign a data type to each field. A **data type** determines what kind of information each field can contain, such as text, a number, or a date. You then can set properties, or characteristics, for each field, such as the number of characters it can contain or whether the field is required. You can also set a primary key to use when sorting records. Finally, you can customize the design of your table by changing its column widths so you can see necessary information.

Using Multiple Data Types

You select a data type for each field to determine the kind of information the field contains. Most databases contain multiple data types; the more specific you are when selecting a data type for a field, the more likely your database is to include the correct input.

Text

Use the **Text data type**, the default in Access, to enter the following in a field: text; numbers that do not require any calculations, such as phone numbers or ZIP codes; or a combination of text, numbers, and symbols. A text field can contain up to 255 characters per record. Usually you need to change the default size of 50. Don't use a text field for dates or times—Access has a special data type for them.

Memo

Use the **Memo data type** for lengthy text or combinations of text and numbers or symbols. Memo fields can contain up to 65,535 characters per record, including returns or tabs. Use memo fields for long responses or when you cannot predict the amount of information.

Number

Use the **Number data type** to include simple numbers, such as those that identify a record, and numeric data in mathematical calculations.

QUICK TIP

The Table Wizard uses the underlying table name as the form name. To follow the LNC naming convention, you name the form frmStudents.

CAUTION TIP

You cannot search a memo field in the criteria of a query. In addition, sorting on a memo field is more difficult. It is better to use text fields when you need to search, sort, or group within the database.

chapter two

You can further optimize data type use by specifying the type of number to be entered in the Field Size property. Specifying the appropriate number type can save space in the database if you do not need larger numbers or more decimal places. Table 2-4 shows the number types as indicated by the Field Size property. If you change the field size in a number field to one with fewer decimal places, any data loss is permanent.

Field Size	Explanation	Storage Size	Example
Byte	no decimals, range 0 to 255	1 byte	65
Integer	no decimals, range -32,768 to 32, 767	2 bytes	-17234
Long Integer	no decimals, range -2.1B to 2.1B	4 bytes	982615241
Single	7 digits, range $-3.4*10^{38}$ to $3.4*10^{38}$	4 bytes	-3.14159
Double	15 digits, range $-1.8*10^{308}$ to $1.8*10^{308}$	8 bytes	12838716.6353456

TABLE 2-4
Number Types and Storage Size

Date/Time

Use the **Date/Time data type** to include the date and time values for the year 100 through the year 9999. The Date/Time data type is useful for calendar or clock data. It also lets you calculate seconds, minutes, hours, days, months, and years. You can display a date/time field as a date, as a time, or as both. The format property determines how the date/time appears.

Currency

Use the **Currency data type** to insert the currency symbol and calculate numeric data with one to four decimal places. This data also is accurate to 15 digits to the left of the decimal point. Currency is useful for money fields, because they are not rounded off internally, maintaining accuracy to the penny and beyond.

AutoNumber

The **AutoNumber data type** is a unique number Access automatically inserts each time you add a new record to a table. These numbers follow a consecutive number sequence, such as 1, 2, 3, and so on.

Yes/No

The **Yes/No data type** can contain only information that uses Yes/No, True/False, or On/Off values. A check mark within a check box in a table indicates the Yes value; an empty check box implies the value No.

OLE Object

The **OLE Object data type** contains a pointer to an object (an Excel workbook, a Word document, or a graphic image) embedded in an Access table. You can display the object in Access by double-clicking it in the table. An Access form can display the object automatically.

Hyperlink

The **Hyperlink data type** stores the path and filename to a Web page URL on your computer, another computer, or a Web address. This provides a link to a customer's home page or to a file on the intranet that provides additional information about a product or service. When you enter or select the hyperlink, you "jump" to the associated location.

Lookup Wizard

Use the **Lookup Wizard data type** to choose a value for this field from another table or from a list of values. This is useful for an order form—you can then select a product from a list or key the first letters of the product name to insert the complete name in the field.

To create the tblDepartments table in Design view:

Step 1	*Click*	Tables ▦ Tables on the Objects bar in the Database window, if necessary
Step 2	*Double-click*	Create table in Design view

Your screen should look similar to Figure 2-3.

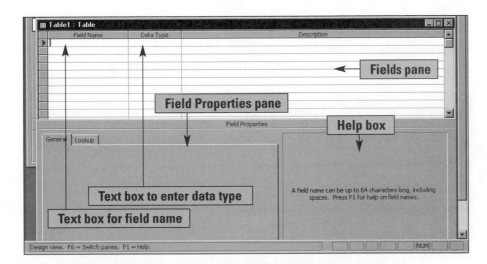

FIGURE 2-3
New Table in Design View

Using Design View to Add Fields

The Design View window contains two panes: the Fields pane at the top and the Field Properties pane at the bottom. You add field names

---

CAUTION TIP

You cannot change or update an AutoNumber field. Access uses the AutoNumber data type to generate the primary key value. You can include only one field using the AutoNumber data type in a table. Once Access generates a number for an AutoNumber field, it cannot duplicate that field value in the same table. If you delete a record that contains an AutoNumber field, its value is not reused.

QUICK TIP

Selecting the Lookup Wizard data type starts the Lookup Wizard, which guides you through the steps of creating the list box or combo box. Once you create Lookup fields, you can also modify them in Design view by changing their properties.

**chapter
two**

and data type information in the Fields pane and then set individual field properties in the Field Properties pane. The Help box in the lower-right corner displays help text for the column where your insertion point is located. You are now ready to add fields to your new table. To begin adding fields to the table:

Step 1	*Verify*	that the insertion point is in the first row of the Field Name column
Step 2	*Key*	DeptID
Step 3	*Press*	the TAB key to move the insertion point to the Data Type column

The Text data type (the default) appears in the Data Type column. You can select a different data type from a list box by clicking the Data Type list arrow. Because the DeptID field will contain a short text code, you change its field size to 3 characters.

Step 4	*Press*	the F6 key to move the insertion point to the Field Properties pane
Step 5	*Observe*	that the contents of the Help box now explain that the maximum field size is 255 characters
Step 6	*Key*	3 in the Field Size text box
Step 7	*Press*	the F6 key to return to the Fields pane
Step 8	*Press*	the TAB key to move to the Description column

The text in the Help box defines a field description. The **field description** is optional information for a text field that appear on the status bar when you select the field in a table, query, or form.

Step 9	*Key*	3-character department identifier
Step 10	*Press*	the TAB key
Step 11	*Follow*	Steps 2 through 8 to create a field named DeptName, with data type Text, a field size of 25, and the description Department name
Step 12	*Press*	the TAB key
Step 13	*Follow*	Steps 2 through 8 to create a field named DeptAddress, with data type Text, a field size of 25, and the description Building and room number

This completes the field names for the tblDepartments table. Your screen should look similar to Figure 2-4.

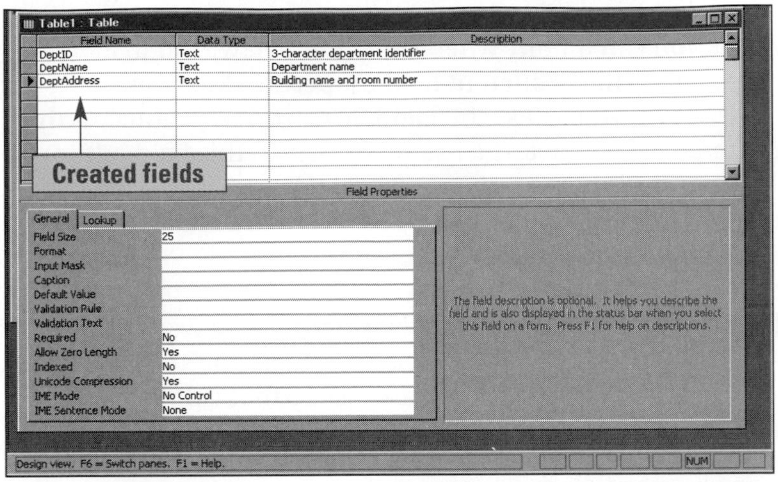

FIGURE 2-4
Completed tblDepartments
Table Design

> **QUICK TIP**
>
> **Ascending order** lists data from A to Z or from 1 to 100. **Descending order** lists data from Z to A or from 100 to 1.

Setting Primary Keys

Recall that a primary key represents the field(s) you designate to uniquely identify a record. Primary keys prevent duplication of an entry in that field. When you open a table that has a primary key field, Access sorts its records by the field in ascending order. Every table should have at least one field used as the primary key. The field you want to use as the primary key should be a field with no duplicates, such as the DeptID field. To select the DeptID field as a primary key in Table Design view:

Step 1	**Right-click**	the DeptID field name
Step 2	**Click**	Primary Key
Step 3	**Observe**	the key icon, indicating the DeptID field is set as the primary key
Step 4	**Click**	the Save button on the Table Design toolbar
Step 5	**Key**	tblDepartments in the Table Name: text box in the Save As dialog box
Step 6	**Click**	OK to save the table structure in the database

You created a simple table in Design view using the Fields pane to enter fields. If you need to change the information, you can do so in Design view. For example, you can change the properties of a field so it only contains certain kinds of information.

Modifying Field Properties

Field properties are characteristics of a field, such as its length or format. Selecting properties for your fields ensures that the information in your records is consistent—every state field, for example, contains

> **MOUSE TIP**
>
> You can set the primary key for the selected field by clicking the Primary key button on the Table Design toolbar.
>
> You can combine several fields for the primary key. For example, in the Course table you might want DeptPrefix and CourseNumber to be the primary key, as in a course called MIS 320. In Table Design view, hold down the CTRL key and click the field selector for each field you want to include in the primary key. Then click the Primary Key button on the Table Design toolbar to complete your choice.

chapter two

two uppercase characters. The General tab in Design view groups the field properties you can modify when you enter a new field in a table.

Each data type may have different field properties. Most data types share the next seven properties. The **Field Size property** indicates the maximum number of characters a user can enter in this field. Although the default size is 50 characters, a Text field can have up to 255 characters. If you reduce the field size of a field that contains data, any data loss is permanent; you cannot undo this operation.

The **Format property** indicates how you want the information to appear when it's displayed or printed. For example, if a text field should contain all uppercase text, as in a state abbreviation, choose All Uppercase for this field property. You can specify that a dollar sign be added to number fields. The Format property only affects the display of data, not how it is stored in the table.

The **Input Mask property** defines a standard pattern for helping you enter data in this field. For example, if the field is a Social Security number, you can have Access insert the hyphens in the correct places (e.g., 123-45-6789), which makes entering accurate data easier. You can decide whether to store the hyphens in the field or store only the digits. You can use this property for Text, Number, Date/Time, and Currency data types. You create an input mask later in this chapter.

The **Caption property** appears as the column header in the table and overrides the field name you entered in the Fields pane. For example, if you enter the caption "Department Number," the caption appears on the table, form, or report instead of the field name DeptID. When you build a form or a report, the field name becomes the label for a field unless you entered a caption.

The **Default Value property** is information Access automatically enters in the field when you add a new record. For example, if you almost always enter "CA" in the State field, you could enter "CA" as the Default Value property for that field. Access then inserts CA in the State field of every new record. Users can enter values other than CA if necessary.

Define data validation criteria when creating a database table. For example, you can set the criteria for a date to be after January 1, 2003, or require that a category value be within a set of choices. You can then set validation text that indicates how to correct the mistake. Note that an input mask is the preferred way to control data entry in certain common fields like phone numbers, Social Security numbers, and so forth.

The **Validation Rule property** is an expression that limits what information you can enter in a field. An **expression** is a set of specific instructions. Access only accepts information that fulfills the expression's requirements. For example, if a salary cannot be greater than $50 per hour, Access does not allow you to key $60. The validation rule expression in this case would be <=50. The **Validation Text property** is the error message that appears when an entry breaks the validation rule.

The **Required property** indicates whether you must complete the field for all records. For required fields, change this property to Yes; Access does not save the record until a user enters information in this field.

In contrast to the Required property, the **Allow Zero Length property**, when set to Yes, tells Access that a zero-length string ("") is acceptable in this field. You can use this option in only Text, Memo, or Hyperlink data types.

The **Indexed property** creates an index for a field; the primary key is automatically indexed. For example, if you search for a specific department in the tblDepartments table, you can create an index to speed sorting and searching. Keep in mind, however, that including several indexes in a table may slow data entry.

The **Unicode Compression property** tells Access to compress the Unicode file format, which lets you code data so it can be used in the world's major languages. A Unicode file format makes document sharing among multinational organizations easier, because it prevents font compatibility issues.

You want to change the field properties for the DeptName field. To modify the DeptName Required and Indexed field properties:

Step 1	*Click*	the DeptName field name
Step 2	*Press*	the F6 key to move the insertion point to the Field Properties pane
Step 3	*Observe*	the new help text in the Help box
Step 4	*Move*	the insertion point to the Required text box
Step 5	*Click*	the Required list arrow
Step 6	*Click*	Yes
Step 7	*Move*	the insertion point to the Indexed text box
Step 8	*Click*	the Indexed list arrow
Step 9	*Click*	Yes (No Duplicates)
Step 10	*Click*	the Save button on the Table Design toolbar to save the changes to the design of this table

You want to see how table looks in Datasheet view to check that column widths are correct. To open the tblDepartments table in Datasheet view:

| Step 1 | *Click* | the Datasheet View button on the Table Design toolbar |

Looking at the table, you notice you need to add space to the DeptName and DeptAddress fields. You can create more space by increasing the column width. Changing column width only affects the display of a field; it does not change the field size of data stored in that field.

chapter
two

QUICK TIP

You can move the insertion point to the Field Properties pane by clicking in the pane or by pressing the F6 key. To move from one text box to another, press the UP ARROW, DOWN ARROW, TAB, or SHIFT + TAB keys. As you move the insertion point to a different text box, the Help box displays text describing the property.

For help about any property in a table, click the property and press the F1 key. The Help window opens with help that pertains to the selected property.

MENU TIP

You can change column width by clicking the Column Width command on the Format menu and keying the column width you want.

Changing Column Widths

Access uses the same column width for every field you enter in a table. But often, as in the tblDepartments table, one or more columns are too narrow to display the entire field name. This text is not lost, just hidden. If you widen the column, you can see the full field value.

To change column widths:

Step 1	*Point to*	the right edge of the DeptName column in the field labels row, so that the mouse pointer changes to a double-headed arrow you use to adjust the column width in the table
Step 2	*Drag*	the column boundary to the right until the field is about twice as wide as it was
Step 3	*Follow*	Steps 1 and 2 to increase the width of the DeptAddress column to about the same size as the DeptName column
Step 4	*Click*	the Close button ☒ on the table title bar
Step 5	*Click*	Yes to save your changes to the table layout

You created two tables for your database, one with the Table Wizard and the other in Design view. Once the table exists, you can modify its design in Design view, regardless of how you created the table.

C 2.e Modifying a Table in Design View

Once you create a table, you should carefully review it to ensure you designed it accurately. If you need to make changes, modifying a table (using Design view) is simple as long as you haven't entered any data. Once you start entering data, modifying table design becomes more difficult.

Switching Between Object Views

It is easy to open a table in Datasheet view with the Open button in the Database window or to open a database in Design view with the Design button in the Database window. After you open a table, you can easily switch from Datasheet to Design view, or vice versa, with the View button on the Table Datasheet toolbar or the Table Design toolbar.

To switch between Datasheet view and Design view:

Step 1	*Click*	the tblDepartments table in the Database window, if necessary
Step 2	*Click*	the Open button  in the Database window to open the table in Datasheet view
Step 3	*Click*	the Design View button on the Table Datasheet toolbar to switch to Design view
Step 4	*Click*	the Datasheet View button on the Table Design toolbar to switch back to Datasheet view

MOUSE TIP

You can right-click an object in the Database window and then select the desired view from the shortcut menu.

Adding Fields

Even after you save a table, you can still enter new fields anywhere in the table by inserting a row where you want the field. To add the phone number field to the tblDepartments table:

Step 1	*Click*	the Design View button on the Table Datasheet toolbar
Step 2	*Click*	in the first blank row in the Field Name column
Step 3	*Key*	DeptPhone
Step 4	*Press*	the TAB key to move to the Data Type column, which displays the Text data type by default
Step 5	*Press*	the F6 key to move to the Field Properties pane
Step 6	*Key*	15 in the Field Size text box
Step 7	*Press*	the F6 key to move to the Fields pane
Step 8	*Press*	the TAB key to move to the Description field
Step 9	*Key*	Department telephone number
Step 10	*Click*	the Save button on the Table Design toolbar to save the table

CAUTION TIP

Although deleting a field is easy, be careful before you do so. If you delete a field that contains any information, you cannot reverse your action.

Deleting Fields

It is sometimes necessary to delete a field from a table. The parents' names are not necessary in the student table. To delete the ParentsNames field from the tblStudents table:

| Step 1 | *Press* | the F11 key to display the Database window |

Step 2	*Open*	the tblStudents table in Design view
Step 3	*Click*	the record selector to the left of the ParentsNames row to select the entire ParentsNames row
Step 4	*Click*	<u>E</u>dit
Step 5	*Click*	<u>D</u>elete

Whenever a field is deleted that contains data, you see a warning that you are about to delete the field and all its data, and a question asking if you want to proceed. In this case, no warning appears because the table has no records.

Rearranging Fields

After you add fields, you can rearrange them so they appear in a logical order. For the tblStudents table, it makes sense to move the EmailName field before the Address field based on the order of those fields on a paper form. To rearrange a field:

Step 1	*Verify*	that the tblStudents table is open in Design view
Step 2	*Click*	the record selector to the left of the row that contains the EmailName field information to select the row containing that field
Step 3	*Move*	the mouse pointer to the record selector for the EmailName field to view the left-pointing arrow mouse pointer
Step 4	*Drag*	the EmailName field before the Address field
Step 5	*Click*	the Save button 🖫 on the Table Design toolbar to save the layout change to this table

Inserting a Field

You did not add the PostalCode field when you created the tblStudents table with the Table Wizard. To add the field in Table Design view:

Step 1	*Verify*	that the tblStudents table is open in Design view
Step 2	*Click*	the record selector for the PhoneNumber field
Step 3	*Click*	<u>I</u>nsert
Step 4	*Click*	<u>R</u>ows

QUICK TIP

You can delete a field by selecting the field in Design view and then pressing the DELETE key.

MENU TIP

You can delete fields in Datasheet view by selecting the column and then selecting the Delete Column command from the <u>E</u>dit menu.

Access inserts a blank row before PhoneNumber in the table design. Now you can add the PostalCode field.

Step 5	*Click*	in the blank field name text box in the new row
Step 6	*Key*	PostalCode in the Field name text box
Step 7	*Press*	the TAB key to move to the Data Type column
Step 8	*Press*	the F6 key to move to the Field Properties pane
Step 9	*Key*	9 in the Field Size property text box
Step 10	*Press*	the F6 key to move to the Fields pane
Step 11	*Press*	the TAB key to move to the Description column
Step 12	*Key*	Zip+4 as the description of this field
Step 13	*Click*	the Save button 🖫 on the Table Design toolbar
Step 14	*Close*	the tblStudents table

MOUSE TIP

When you drag a field to a new location, Access displays a horizontal black line to indicate the new placement of the field when you release the mouse button.

To rearrange field order, you can select the entire column in Datasheet view and drag it to the new location.

You can insert a row by clicking the Insert Rows button on the Table Design toolbar.

To make it easier to enter data in the PhoneNumber field you added to the tblDepartments table, you can use the Input Mask Wizard.

2.f Using the Input Mask Wizard

Recall that the Input Mask property sets the display format and limits the type of data that users can enter, making data entry faster and more precise. The **Input Mask Wizard** guides you through the task of creating an input mask. Because phone numbers follow the same pattern, (000) 000-0000, you choose the Input Mask property for this field in tblDepartments. You use the Input Mask Wizard to set the Input Mask property. To use the Input Mask Wizard in Design view:

QUICK TIP

Once you create an input mask, you can modify it. Click the ellipsis icon in the Input Mask text box to open and modify the input mask.

Step 1	*Switch to*	the tblDepartments table in Design view
Step 2	*Click*	the DeptPhone field
Step 3	*Click*	the Input Mask text box in the Field Properties pane
Step 4	*Click*	the ellipsis icon [···] that appears on the right side of the text box to start the Input Mask Wizard

The Input Mask Wizard should look similar to Figure 2-5. Access displays the input mask for various common fields. You can test the mask by entering a value in the Try It: text box to make sure you want the selected option.

Step 5	*Verify*	that the Phone Number input mask is selected
Step 6	*Click*	the left side of the Try It: text box
Step 7	*Key*	your phone number in the Try It: text box
Step 8	*Click*	Next >

Access displays a suggested mask: !(999) 000-0000. Each 9 represents an optional digit, and each 0 a required digit. The literal characters (parentheses, space, hyphen) are part of the mask when you enter or view data in this field. For now, you accept the default mask.

| Step 9 | *Click* | Next > |

Access asks how you want to save the data. You can save the data with or without the placeholders. If you save the placeholders, you must allow for extra characters in the field size. For example, a telephone number requires at least 14 characters for the field size: 10 for the digits and 4 for the parentheses, space, and hyphen. These extra characters can use extra disk space, which is important in a large database. You can have Access include the characters with the field so that the field always looks like a phone number, even if it is exported outside Access.

QUICK TIP

The underscore placeholder may make it hard to see the number of digits required. You can select # as the placeholder character to show individual positions.

Step 10	*Click*	the With the symbols in the mask, like this: option button
Step 11	*Click*	Finish to complete the mask
Step 12	*Click*	the Save button  on the Table Design toolbar to save the table design and then close the table

2.g Creating a Lookup Field

At times, choosing the value of a field from a group of choices is more useful than keying a value. A **lookup field** displays a set of values from another table or query or from a list of fixed choices. A lookup field can help ensure data accuracy by restricting users' choices to an approved list.

You can use a lookup field in a table or in a form. You can display data in a list box or a combo box. The list box forces the user to choose one of the choices listed; a combo box lets the user select an item from the list or key a new value. The list box is already "dropped down" to show the lookup choices, whereas a combo box features a list arrow, saving space on the form.

For OLU, selecting the major by name is easier and more accurate than remembering a code. You still store the MajorCode, but the lookup field displays the name of the major. To convert an existing field to a lookup field by using the Lookup Wizard:

Step 1	*Open*	the tblStudents table in Design view
Step 2	*Click*	the Major field name (scroll to view the field)
Step 3	*Click*	the Data Type text box for the Major field
Step 4	*Click*	the list arrow
Step 5	*Click*	Lookup Wizard

Access opens the Lookup Wizard dialog box.

Step 6	*Click*	Next > to accept the default choice of the lookup column coming from values in a table or query
Step 7	*Click*	Next > to accept tblDepartments to provide values for the lookup column
Step 8	*Double-click*	DeptName in Available Fields to add this to the lookup combo box
Step 9	*Click*	Next >
Step 10	*Double-click*	the right border of the DeptName field to widen it enough to display the full department names

chapter
two

QUICK TIP

By adjusting its Limit To List property, you can force a combo box to disallow new, unlisted entries.

The combo box defaults to the list of choices from the other table or query. In this case, the list of departments comes from the tblDepartments table.

You can click the list arrow to the right of the text box to select the row source form the tables and queries in this database.

Step 11	*Click*	Next >
Step 12	*Click*	Finish to accept the default name of Major for this field
Step 13	*Click*	Yes to save the table
Step 14	*Click*	the Lookup tab in the Field Properties pane to view the changes the Lookup Wizard made

Your screen should look similar to Figure 2-6. The lookup field displays two fields from the tblDepartments table: DeptID and DeptName. The Bound Column property is 1, indicating the first column in the tblDepartments table (DeptID) provides the value for this field. Showing the department name allows the user to verify the correct choice. The Column Width property of 0,1.3125" indicates the first field is hidden (0") and the second field is 1.3125" wide.

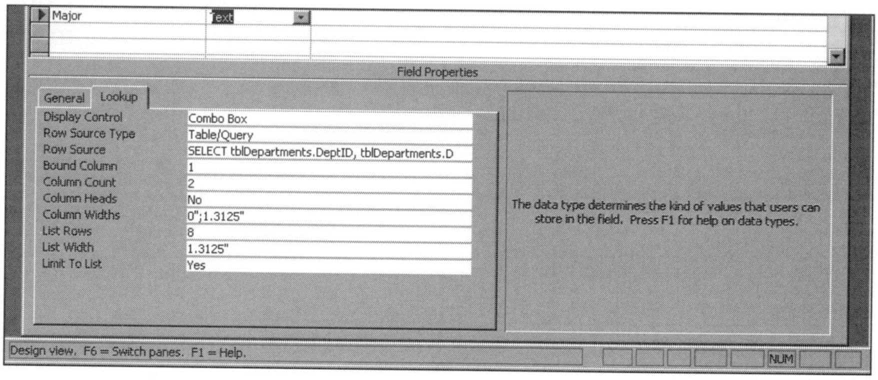

FIGURE 2-6
Combo Box Properties for the Major Field

Before you can see how the lookup field appears, you need to enter some data into the tblDepartments table.

Step 15	*Close*	the tblStudents table

2.h Importing Data into a Table

Sometimes you need data that is stored in another data file. The Import Spreadsheet Wizard guides you in both selecting the information to import from an Excel workbook and determining how you want it to appear in your Access database.

The data you need is stored in an Excel workbook. Rather than rekeying the data, you want to import it. To import Excel data into Access:

Step 1	***Verify***	that *mdbOnlineU2-1* is open and that the tblDepartments table is closed
Step 2	***Click***	File
Step 3	***Point to***	Get External Data
Step 4	***Click***	Import to open the Import dialog box
Step 5	***Switch to***	the drive and folder that contain the Data Disk

No Excel workbook files appear in the dialog box because you need to change the Files of type: list box to Microsoft Excel.

Step 6	***Click***	Microsoft Excel in the Files of type: list box
Step 7	***Double-click***	*Departments* to open the workbook

Import Spreadsheet Wizard dialog box on your screen should look similar to Figure 2-7. The Show Worksheets option is the default; The Show Named Ranges option is used to import specific named parts of large worksheets.

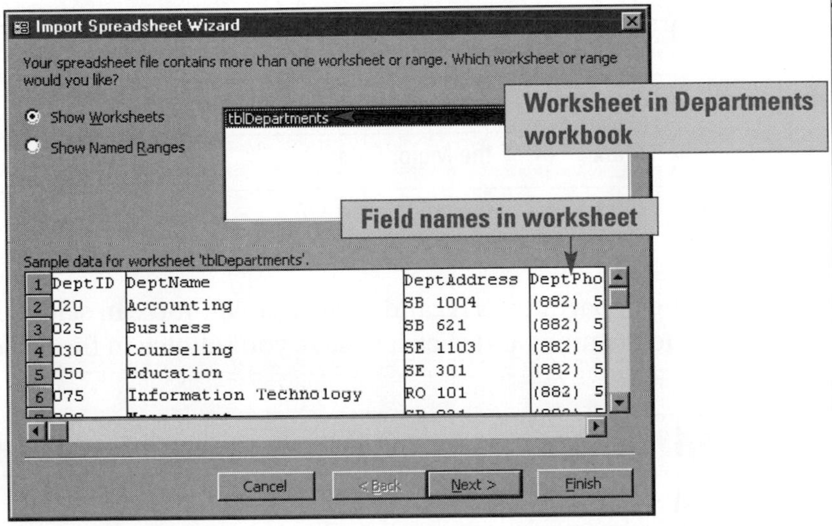

FIGURE 2-7
Import Spreadsheet Wizard Dialog Box

Step 8	***Click***	Next >

QUICK TIP

When you import an Excel workbook with the column headings in the first row, Access automatically selects the appropriate fields. This is particularly helpful for entering large amounts of data.

Once you import a table, it becomes an Access object. You then can use Access commands to change the table.

CAUTION TIP

You may get an error message during the import if the field names in the workbook file don't match those in the tblDepartments table. Double-check the names in your table.

You can now select the fields you want to import. You want to select all fields. You also want to specify that the first row of the worksheet contains field names.

Step 9	*Click*	the First Row Contains Column Headings check box to insert a check mark
Step 10	*Click*	Next >
Step 11	*Click*	the In an Existing Table: option button

Access adds these records to a table that already exists on the database. The In a New Table option places the records into a new table.

Step 12	*Click*	tblDepartments in the In an Existing Table: list
Step 13	*Click*	Next >
Step 14	*Click*	Finish
Step 15	*Click*	OK to complete the import

Access imports nine department records into the tblDepartments table. Next you can see how the Lookup field works with data from the tblStudents table. To verify the operation of the lookup field:

Step 1	*Open*	the tblStudents table in Datasheet view
Step 2	*Scroll*	right until the Major field appears
Step 3	*Click*	the Major field
Step 4	*Click*	the field list arrow

Both the department's ID and name appear. You can select the desired department and click it to save your choice in the Major field.

Step 5	*Widen*	the field until you can see the full list of departments
Step 6	*Save*	the table and close it
Step 7	*Close*	the database

You now know the basics of effective database design, and have designed and created a database with two tables.

Summary

▶ When designing a database, you need to determine the fields to include in a table, what type of information appears in each field, and how to arrange the fields in each record.

▶ Access offers field data types to help make tables unique and descriptive.

▶ Each field in a table has properties such as the field size or format. You can control data entry by choosing appropriate properties for each field. For example, you can require that fields contain data and that the data is unique to that record.

▶ You create table fields and modify properties in Design view. You enter data in a table in Datasheet view.

▶ You can set a primary key in a table, which Access can use to identify each unique record.

▶ You should select and size columns in Datasheet view to view all of the data without wasting screen space.

▶ After you create a table and enter data, you can modify the table by adding new fields and changing the names of existing fields.

▶ You can delete fields that you no longer need.

▶ You can create a lookup field that provides a list of values to choose from.

▶ Access can import data into a table from a workbook, a text file, or a database.

Commands Review

Action	Menu Bar	Shortcut Menu	Toolbar	Task Pane	Keyboard
Create a new database	File, New			Click the Blank database link in the New section in the New File task pane	ALT + F, N CTRL + N
Create a new table	Insert, Table		New		ALT + I, T
Open a table in Datasheet view		Right-click table name, click Open	Open		
Open a table in Design view		Right-click table name, click Design View			
Switch between panes in Design view			Click in the pane		F6

chapter two

Action	Menu Bar	Shortcut Menu	Toolbar	Task Pane	Keyboard
Select a field property in Design view			Click in the Field Properties pane		UP or DOWN ARROW, TAB or SHIFT + TAB
Set a primary key in Design view	Edit, Primary Key	Right-click field, click Primary Key	🔑		ALT + E, K
Resize columns in a table in Datasheet view	Format, Column Width	Right-click column, click Column Width	Drag column boundary		ALT + O, C
Delete a field in Design view	Edit, Delete Rows	Right-click field, click Delete Rows			ALT + E, R
Insert a field in Design view	Insert, Rows	Right-click field, click Insert Rows			ALT + I, R
Close and save a table	File, Close		✕		ALT + F, C
Import data into a new table	File, Get External Data, Import	Right-click Database window, click Import			ALT + F, G, I
Display Database window			📰		F11

Concepts Review

Circle the correct answer.

1. **Which of the following data types should you use for a Phone Number field?**
   [a] text
   [b] currency
   [c] date/time
   [d] number

2. **To move the insertion point forward in Design view, you can press the:**
   [a] TAB key.
   [b] F1 key.
   [c] BACKSPACE key.
   [d] CTRL + TAB keys.

3. **You can change the Field Size property in:**
   [a] Datasheet view.
   [b] the table pane.
   [c] the query pane.
   [d] Design view.

4. **To move from the Fields pane to the Field Properties pane in Design view, you press the:**
   [a] F6 key.
   [b] SHIFT + F6 keys.
   [c] F1 key.
   [d] ENTER key.

5. **The field property that you can use to control the pattern for how data should be entered in the field is:**
   [a] Field Size.
   [b] Default Value.
   [c] Validation Text.
   [d] Input Mask.

6. **You can add a field to a table:**
   [a] in Design view.
   [b] by dragging it out of Datasheet view.
   [c] by highlighting the field text and pressing the INSERT key.
   [d] only at the end of the table.

7. **Access provides a list of choices for a field in a(n):**
   [a] primary key.
   [b] validation rule.
   [c] input mask.
   [d] lookup field.

8. Once you know which objects you want to store in a database, the next step in designing a database is to determine the:
[a] data type for each field.
[b] purpose of the database.
[c] field properties you will use.
[d] fields you need.

9. A Table Wizard is a:
[a] tool for creating a new database.
[b] tool that guides you through the steps of creating a table.

[c] way to modify the fields in a table after you enter data.
[d] shortcut for saving data.

10. A primary key:
[a] must be the first field in a table.
[b] uniquely defines a record.
[c] is always chosen for you.
[d] is the default data type.

Circle **T** if the statement is true or **F** is the statement is false.

T   F   1. A student identification number must be an AutoNumber field.

T   F   2. You should set a primary key for each table.

T   F   3. The default field type is AutoNumber.

T   F   4. You cannot change the name of a field in a table after you have saved the table.

T   F   5. If a field's Required property is set to Yes, you must enter data in that field before moving to another record.

T   F   6. You can choose from five different field sizes for the Number data type.

T   F   7. Press the F5 key to move from the Fields pane to the Field Properties pane in Table Design view.

T   F   8. You cannot add a new field to a table after you place data in the table.

T   F   9. You can change the column width of a field in a table.

T   F   10. You can change the data type of a field without losing data stored in the field.

Skills Review

Exercise 1

1. Create a new, blank database named *mdbFanTours2-1* for Fantastic Sports Tours (FST).

2. Use Design view to create a new table to store information about the sporting events FST serves.

3. Add the following fields to the new table:

Field	Field Type
EventID	AutoNumber
EventName	Text
EventDate	Date/Time

4. Make EventID the primary key

5. Save the table as "tblEvents" and close it.

6. Close the database.

chapter two

Exercise 2 C

1. Open the *mdbFanTours2-1* database you created in Exercise 1.

2. Open the tblEvents table in Design view.

3. Add the following fields to the tblEvents table:

Field	Field Type	Field Size
Description	Text	30
Location	Text	25
Notes	Memo	

4. Rearrange the field list so that Description is the third field.

5. Save and close the table. Close the database.

Exercise 3 C

1. Open the *mdbFanTours2-1* database you modified in Exercise 2.

2. Use Design view to create a new employees table.

3. Add the following fields to the table:

Field	Field Type	Field Size
EmplID	Text	11
FName	Text	25
LName	Text	25

4. Set the EmplID field as the primary key.

5. Save the table as "tblEmployees" and close it. Close the database.

Exercise 4 C

1. Open the *mdbFanTours2-1* database you modified in Exercise 3.

2. Create a new table using the Table Wizard based on the Tasks sample table. Use all fields.

3. Name the table "tblTasks" and let Access set a primary key for the table. The table is not related to others.

4. Open the table in Design view to modify its design.

5. Delete the Notes field.

6. Add an EventID numeric field that is Long Integer.

7. Save the table, switch to Datasheet view, and then resize the column widths to accommodate the expected length of entries.

8. Save the tblTasks table and close it. Close the database.

Exercise 5 C

1. Open the *mdbFanTours2-1* database you modified in Exercise 4.

2. Open the tblEmployees table in Design view that you created in Exercise 3.

3. Change the Required property of the EmplID field so that it must be completed for all records.

4. Change the name of the EmplID field to EmployeeID.

5. Save the table.

6. Use the Input Mask Wizard to set the standard pattern for the Employee ID field. Use Social Security number field as xxx-xx-xxxx, where x is a number. Use # as the placeholder. Save the symbols in the mask.

7. Save the tblEmployees table and close it. Close the database.

Exercise 6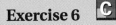

1. From the General Templates link in the New from template section of the New File task pane, create a new database based on the *Event Management* database template. (*Hint:* The *Event Management* database template is accessible through the Databases tab in the Templates dialog box.)

2. Name the database *mdbEventManagement2-1*.

3. In a Word document, prepare a list of the dialog boxes that you see as the wizard creates your database. Accept the default choices in each dialog box.

4. Click OK in the Confirmation dialog box, and then close the Company Info dialog box and close any other dialog boxes that open.

5. Close the database.

Exercise 7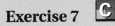

1. Open the *mdbEventManagement2-1* database you created in Exercise 6.

2. Click the Enter/View Other Information button. Click the Enter/View My Company Information button. (*Hint:* Both buttons are on the Switchboard.)

3. Using the My Company Information form, enter the following information as requested by the wizard.

Company Name:	My Company, Inc.
Address:	1234 First Street
City:	Terre Haute
State/Province:	IN
Postal Code:	47803-2080
Country/Region:	United States
Phone Number:	812-555-1312
Fax Number:	812-555-1313
Sales Tax Rate:	.05
Payment Terms:	2/10 Net 30
Invoice Descr:	Thanks for doing business with My Company

4. Make a copy of the values you entered. (*Hint:* First enter your values. Press the PRINTSCRN or (PRINTSCREEN) key near the BACKSPACE key to copy the screen with your responses to the Clipboard. Open a blank document in Word, and then paste the contents of the Clipboard. Save and print the Word document.)

5. Save the information in the database by closing the form. Close the database.

Exercise 8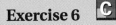

1. Open the *mdbEventManagement2-1* database you modified in Exercise 7.

2. Open the Employees table in Design view.

3. Use the Input Mask Wizard to create an input mask for the phone number for the WorkPhone field. Use the default placeholder and do not save the data with symbols.

4. Save the table and close it. Close the database.

chapter two

Case Projects

Project 1

Connect to the Internet, and then click the Templates on Microsoft.com link in the New from template section of the New File task pane. Use the Search for templates: text box on the Microsoft Web site to search for templates containing the keyword "database." Remember to look for the Access key icon when selecting a template. In a Word document, make a list of the Access templates available on the Microsoft Web site. Save, print, and close the document.

Project 2 C

Open the *mdbEventManagement2-2* database located on the Data Disk. Open the Switchboard form and describe the functions of this Event Management database. Enter the information in a Word document, then save, print, and close the document. Close the database.

Project 3 C

Open the *mdbEventManagement2-2* database located on the Data Disk. Create a Word document and prepare a list of all tables in the database; include a short definition of the purpose of each table based on the fields in the table. Save, print, and close the document. Close the database.

Project 4 C

Open the *mdbEventManagement2-2* database located on the Data Disk. Create a Word document and prepare a list of all forms in the database; include a short definition of the purpose of each form. Save, print, and close the document. Close the database.

Project 5 C

Open the *mdbEventManagement2-2* database located on the Data Disk. Starting at the Switchboard form, click the Enter/View Other Information button, and then click Enter/View Employee. Next click the Add Employee button and enter appropriate information about four employees. Close the database.

Project 6 C

Open the *mdbEventManagement2-2* database located on the Data Disk. Starting at the Switchboard form, add information about three events, using fictional but relevant information. For each event, select an employee to serve as event director. How do you think this form provides the list of employees for the Event Director field? Enter the information in a Word document, and then save, print, and close the document. Close the database.

Project 7 C

Open the *mdbEventManagement2-2* database located on the Data Disk. You want to make it simple for users to enter valid data. Define a validation rule for the StartDate and EndDate fields in the Events table. The dates should be no earlier than 1/1/2003. The Access expression to represent this is >=#1/1/2003#. Create appropriate validation text to warn a user who enters a date earlier than January 1, 2003, in that field. Open the table and key an invalid value in the field. How does Access respond to your actions? Save the information in a Word document and then save, print, and close the document. Close the database.

Project 8 C

Connect to the Internet. Then use the Database Wizard to create a database using one of the templates at Microsoft.com in the New File task pane. Look for templates in the Personal Interests, Community, and Policies groups. Close the database. Then create a Word file that documents your actions.

Entering and Editing Data into Tables

Chapter **Overview**

Once you design your database, create its tables, and define the tables' fields, you're ready to enter records. In this chapter, you enter, navigate through, and edit data in tables. In addition, you delete and sort records, and learn how to find and filter records in Access. You also print a table and insert a picture into a data field.

LEARNING OBJECTIVES

- Enter records using a datasheet
- Navigate through records
- Modify records
- Delete a record from a table
- Find records that match criteria
- Sort records in a datasheet
- Filter records
- Print a table
- Add pictures to records

Case profile

Constance Tucker, provost of Online University, approves the design of the tables in the database you created for her. She gives you the go-ahead to begin the next phase: entering the data in the database and locating records in tables. You work closely with the registrar on these tasks. Some data is available now from other records, and she wants you to investigate using photographs of instructors in the database.

chapter three

3.a Entering Records Using a Datasheet

Recall that a record is a row in a table that contains specific information about the table's subject. You can enter values for each record directly into the table datasheet, that is, into the columns of your table. (Remember that entering records directly into a table is a good choice when you have only a few records.) A **value** is the data in each field of the record. For example, Moreno would be the value of the LastName field for Maria Moreno. A **cell** is where the column and row intersect, similar to a cell in a worksheet.

You need to enter data about majors in the DegreeID and DegreeName fields in the tblDegrees table of the OLU database. To open the tblDegrees table and enter data:

Step 1	*Create*	a copy of the *mdbOnlineU3-* database located on the Data Disk
Step 2	*Click*	Tables ▦ Tables on the Objects bar in the Database window, if necessary
Step 3	*Double-click*	tblDegrees
Step 4	*Key*	1 in the DegreeID field in the first row
Step 5	*Press*	the TAB key
Step 6	*Key*	Certificate in the DegreeName field

Your screen should look similar to Figure 3-1.

FIGURE 3-1
tblDegrees Table with One Record Entered

Step 7	*Press*	the TAB key to move to the second row of the table
Step 8	*Key*	2 in the DegreeID field
Step 9	*Press*	the TAB key to move to the DegreeName field
Step 10	*Key*	Associate

| Step 11 | **Follow** | Steps 7 through 10 to enter DegreeIDs and DegreeNames in the following pairs: 3, Bachelor; 4, Master; and 5, Doctoral |
| Step 12 | **Close** | the tblDegrees table |

Next you enter degree delivery data in the tblModes table. OLU has four modes, three of which are already in the table. In this database, the word *mode* describes how a course is offered—in a classroom, on the Web, or elsewhere. To enter data in the tblModes table:

Step 1	**Double-click**	tblModes to open it in Datasheet view
Step 2	**Click**	in the ClassMode field in the first empty row in the table
Step 3	**Key**	1 in the ClassMode field
Step 4	**Key**	Classroom in the ClassModeName field
Step 5	**Close**	the tblModes table

Access automatically sorts the table by its primary key, ClassMode. Remember that sorting data rearranges the rows of data so that you can view the information that is relevant at the moment. The record you just entered appears first when you open the table again.

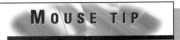

> **M O U S E   T I P**
>
> After you enter data, you might find using the mouse more effective for navigating a table. You can click directly in a cell at any time to move the insertion point to that cell.

3.b Navigating Through Records

It is efficient to use the TAB key to move around an Access datasheet as you enter records. When you use the TAB key, you need not move your hand from the keyboard to use the mouse. You also can use other keys to navigate. Table 3-1 lists keys you can use to move around a table.

TABLE 3-1
Shortcut Navigational Keys

To Move To The	Press
Next field	TAB
Previous field	SHIFT + TAB
Last field of a record	END
First field of a record	HOME
Same field in the next record	DOWN ARROW
Same field in the previous record	UP ARROW
Same field in the last record	CTRL + DOWN ARROW
Same field in the first record	CTRL + UP ARROW
Last field in the last record	CTRL + END
First field in the first record	CTRL + HOME

chapter
three

To navigate through a table using keyboard shortcuts:

Step 1	**Open**	the tblInstructors table in Datasheet view
Step 2	**Press**	the END key to move the insertion point to the last field of the first record
Step 3	**Press**	the HOME key to move the insertion point to the first field of the first record
Step 4	**Continue**	to navigate around the tblInstructors table using the keyboard shortcuts listed in Table 3-1

3.c Modifying Records

You can edit table data easily. You can correct text, add and copy data, and delete information as necessary.

Correcting Data in a Table

When you review the tblInstructors table in *mdbOnlineU3-1*, you notice Sarah Sinclair's last name listed incorrectly as Lawrence. The most efficient method of correcting it is to reenter the entire field. You can double-click a cell to move the insertion point to the cell and select the cell's data. To replace data by reentering it:

Step 1	**Verify**	that the tblInstructors table is open
Step 2	**Double-click**	the cell containing the last name Lawrence
Step 3	**Key**	Sinclair
Step 4	**Observe**	that the new data then replaces the old data in the cell

You can use the mouse to click in the appropriate place within a cell, or you can use the keyboard commands shown in Table 3-2 to move within a cell.

To Move	Press
One character to the right	RIGHT ARROW
One character to the left	LEFT ARROW
One word to the right	CTRL + RIGHT ARROW
One word to the left	CTRL + LEFT ARROW
To the end of the field	END
To the beginning of the field	HOME

MOUSE TIP

To select a single record, click the record selector, which is the gray box to the left of the record. To select more than one adjacent record at a time, select the first record, press and hold down the SHIFT key, and then select the other records. To select all the records in a table, click the blank box next to the first field name in the upper-left corner of the datasheet or press the CTRL + A keys.

QUICK TIP

You can select the contents of a cell by clicking in the cell and then pressing the F2 key.

TABLE 3-2
Shortcut Keys for
Navigating Within a Cell

If you need to make a minor change in a field, you can edit the data rather than rekeying all the information. For example, Samuel Lister's e-mail address has changed. You can edit the text of his current e-mail address to match the new address. To edit a cell's contents:

Step 1	*Click*	the cell containing Samuel Lister's e-mail address
Step 2	*Move*	the insertion point to the right of the letter c using the shortcut keys
Step 3	*Press*	the BACKSPACE key to delete the letter c from olc.edu
Step 4	*Key*	u
Step 5	*Close*	the table

Copying Data

You can use the Cut, Copy, and Paste commands on the Edit menu or the Cut, Copy, and Paste buttons on the Table Design toolbar to move or copy data within records. This is a convenient method because you don't risk making new errors by rekeying.

The tblStudents table includes a StreetAddress field. Chang mentioned that he needs a second field to enter complete address information. You can save time by copying a field and all its attributes instead of creating a new field from scratch. You want to add a second address field, copy the StreetAddress field, and rename it StreetAddress2. To open the tblStudents table:

Step 1	*Open*	the tblStudents table in Design view
Step 2	*Observe*	the StreetAddress field

Placing the StreetAddress2 field immediately after the StreetAddress field makes sense. To do this, you must insert a new row. By default, the Insert Rows command inserts a blank row before the selected field, so you need to select the City field. To insert a new row below the City field:

Step 1	*Click*	the City field name (you may need to scroll)
Step 2	*Click*	Insert
Step 3	*Click*	Rows
Step 4	*Observe*	the new row before the City field and after the StreetAddress field

MENU TIP

To select all records in a table, click Select All Records on the Edit menu. All the records are selected with dark shading.

You can undo the last change you made by clicking the Undo Saved Record command on the Edit menu or by pressing the CTRL + Z keys.

CAUTION TIP

If you select several records, only the first record has the triangle symbol next to it. The triangle symbol indicates that the record next to it is the current record.

**chapter
three**

You are ready to copy and paste the information from the StreetAddress field into the blank row. To copy and paste a field and rename the field:

Step 1	Double-click	the StreetAddress field name to select it
Step 2	Click	the Copy button 📋 on the Table Design toolbar
Step 3	Click	the blank field name
Step 4	Click	the Paste button 📋 on the Table Design toolbar
Step 5	Key	2 at the end of the field name
Step 6	Press	the TAB key to accept the Text data type
Step 7	Key	Street address for mailing purposes in the Description text box
Step 8	Click	the Save button 💾 on the Table Design toolbar to save the changes to the table structure

Your screen should look similar to Figure 3-2.

FIGURE 3-2
Inserted Address Field

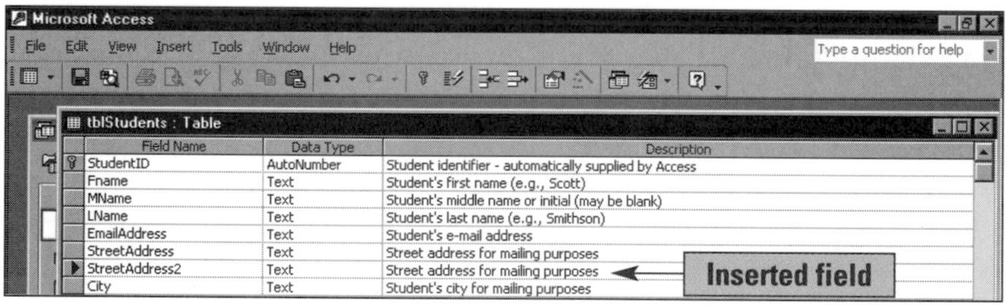

| Step 9 | Close | the tblStudents table |

You can use the same copy-and-paste process when copying records, cells, or database objects. You also can move and copy objects, such as tables or queries, between databases.

Undoing a Change

To undo changes made to a record in the table currently open, you click the Undo button on the Table Datasheet toolbar. This restores the data you most recently changed. If you already saved changes to the current record or moved to another record, you still can undo your last change.

3.d Deleting a Record from a Table

When you want to delete data, consider whether you need to remove part of a record or the entire record. To delete selected parts of the record, use the Delete command on the Edit menu. To delete the entire record, use the Delete Record command. You want to delete the record of Jillian Mellow, who left OLU last week, from the tblInstructors table.

To delete a record from a table:

Step 1	*Open*	the tblInstructors table in Datasheet view
Step 2	*Click*	the record selector for Jillian Mellow's record
Step 3	*Click*	Edit
Step 4	*Click*	Delete Record

A dialog box opens, confirming that you want to delete this record and reminding you that you won't be able to retrieve it.

| Step 5 | *Click* | Yes |
| Step 6 | *Close* | the tblInstructors table |

3.e Finding Records That Match Criteria

You can use the Find feature to perform simple searches, such as when you want to locate a record that contains a particular word or value. You can use the Replace feature to quickly find text or other values in your records and replace them with different text or values. Access also has more sophisticated tools for finding data: **Sorting** rearranges data on the screen in the order you specify, so that it is easier to scan records to find the one you want. **Filtering** narrows a list of records to eliminate the data you don't want. **Querying** creates a more formal filter with complex criteria. **Reporting** creates a printed report containing only the records that you want to see.

The registrar asks you to locate all prospects in California. To open the Find and Replace dialog box:

| Step 1 | *Open* | the tblStudents table in Datasheet view |

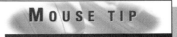

MOUSE TIP

If you inadvertently undo a change that you want to keep, you can redo the change by clicking the Redo button on the Standard toolbar or by using the Redo command on the Edit menu. The Redo command appears on the Edit menu only when the respective action is one that can be undone.

QUICK TIP

You can undo changes made to the current record (before those changes are committed to the database) by pressing the ESCAPE key.

chapter
three

| Step 2 | *Click* | the State field header (you may need to scroll) |

| Step 3 | *Click* | the Find button 🔍 on the Table Datasheet toolbar |

MENU TIP

You can open the Find and Replace dialog box by clicking the <u>F</u>ind command on the <u>E</u>dit menu from Datasheet or Form view.

Your Find and Replace dialog box should look similar to Figure 3-3.

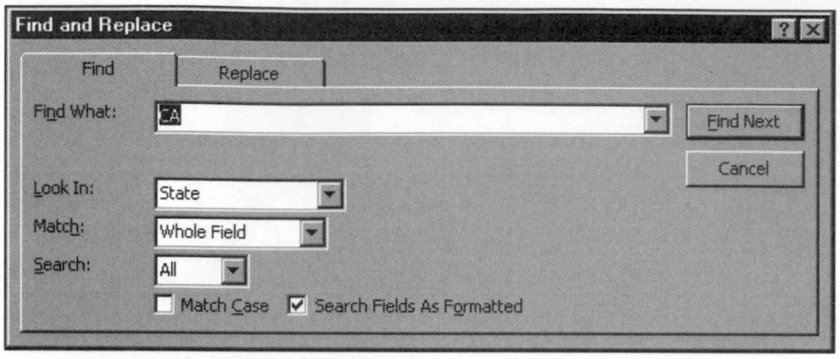

Find and Replace	? ✕
Find	Replace
Fi<u>n</u>d What:	CA ▼	<u>F</u>ind Next
		Cancel
<u>L</u>ook In:	State ▼	
Mat<u>c</u>h:	Whole Field ▼	
<u>S</u>earch:	All ▼	
	☐ Match <u>C</u>ase ☑ Search Fields As <u>F</u>ormatted	

FIGURE 3-3
Find and Replace
Dialog Box

The Find and Replace dialog box lets you specify the information you want Access to locate in the database. You can do a broad search, such as looking for all records that include the abbreviation CA in the State field, or you can be more specific, and look everywhere in the tblStudents table for a record that includes the abbreviation CA. To specify search requirements in the Find and Replace dialog box:

QUICK TIP

You can open the Find and Replace dialog box by pressing the CTRL + F keys.

| Step 1 | *Key* | CA in the Fi<u>n</u>d What: text box, if necessary |

| Step 2 | *Click* | the Mat<u>c</u>h: list arrow |

You have three options: Whole Field searches for data that matches what you key in the Fi<u>n</u>d What: text box. Start of Field finds data that begins with the letters you key in the Fi<u>n</u>d What: text box; for example, key "C" in the text box to find CA, CO, and CT. Any Part of Field finds data that includes the characters you key in the Fi<u>n</u>d What: text box anywhere in a field; for example, key "CA" to find "Cat" or "Orca."

| Step 3 | *Click* | Any Part of Field |

You can enter other specific search requirements. In the <u>S</u>earch: list box, you can choose to search Up, Down, or All of the current table. Up searches all records before the current one. For example, if you are working with record 15, select Up to search only records 1 through 15. Down searches all records after the current one. For example, if you are working in record 15, select Down to search from record 15 to the last record. All, the default, searches all records.

You can limit your search by matching the letter case or searching fields as formatted when you search. If the Match Case check box contains a check mark, Access finds CA but not ca. If the Search Fields As Formatted check box contains a check mark, Access does not find **CA** because it is boldfaced. For the CA state search, you use the defaults.

Step 4	*Click*	Find Next to find the first occurrence of CA
Step 5	*Drag*	the Find and Replace dialog box out of the way, if necessary, so you can see the table window
Step 6	*Click*	Find Next to find the next occurrence of CA in the State field

Replacing Text

The Replace tab in the Find and Replace dialog box enables you to replace text that you find. There is an Ontario, California, address that is incorrectly labeled as CAL in the *mdbOnlineU3-1* database. You can correct the mistake by replacing the text. To replace text using the Find and Replace dialog box:

Step 1	*Click*	the Replace tab in the Find and Replace dialog box
Step 2	*Key*	CAL in the Find What: text box
Step 3	*Key*	CA in the Replace With: text box

If you click Replace, Access substitutes CA for the next occurrence of CAL that it locates in the database. If you click Replace All, Access substitutes CA for all occurrences of CAL. Clicking Find Next locates the next occurrence of CA.

| Step 4 | *Click* | Find Next to move the record pointer to the first matching record |
| Step 5 | *Click* | Replace |

Even if you think the database has no other mistakes, continuing to look for other occurrences of the incorrect text is a good idea.

Step 6	*Click*	Find Next to look for another matching record
Step 7	*Click*	OK to acknowledge that no other records match
Step 8	*Cancel*	the Find and Replace dialog box
Step 9	*Close*	the tblStudents table

M O U S E   T I P

The Find and Replace dialog box remains open so that you can continue using its features. You can drag it by its title bar to view the table window.

Q U I C K   T I P

If you need to find several records at once, you can filter the data.

chapter three

3.f Sorting Records in a Datasheet

QUICK TIP

The Find command is a quick way to locate a record or a value in one or more records. However, sometimes you may want to read through a table to find a record or value. Doing so is easier if you sort the records first.

MENU TIP

You can click the Sort command on the Records menu to begin a sort.

When you add records to a database, you do not necessarily enter them in a logical order for viewing. Often, you enter information as you receive it. After you enter records, you can sort them to find those you want for a particular purpose. An **ascending order** sorts fields from A to Z or 1 to 9. A **descending order** sorts fields from Z to A or 9 to 1. You can sort in Datasheet view, and you can rearrange the records according to any fields you like.

Sorting Records on a Single Field

The registrar asks you to sort the OLU instructors' records according to department to display information on all instructors in a particular department. Grouping the instructors logically helps the registrar review staffing levels and future requirements of each department. You start by sorting the records on a single field; that is, you are sorting the records based on the contents of a particular field.

To sort records on a single field:

Step 1	*Open*	the tblInstructors table in Datasheet view
Step 2	*Click*	the first row under the DeptID field
Step 3	*Click*	the Sort Ascending button on the Table Datasheet toolbar

Access rearranges the records by the DeptID field. Your screen should look similar to Figure 3-4.

FIGURE 3-4
Records Sorted in Ascending Order by Department

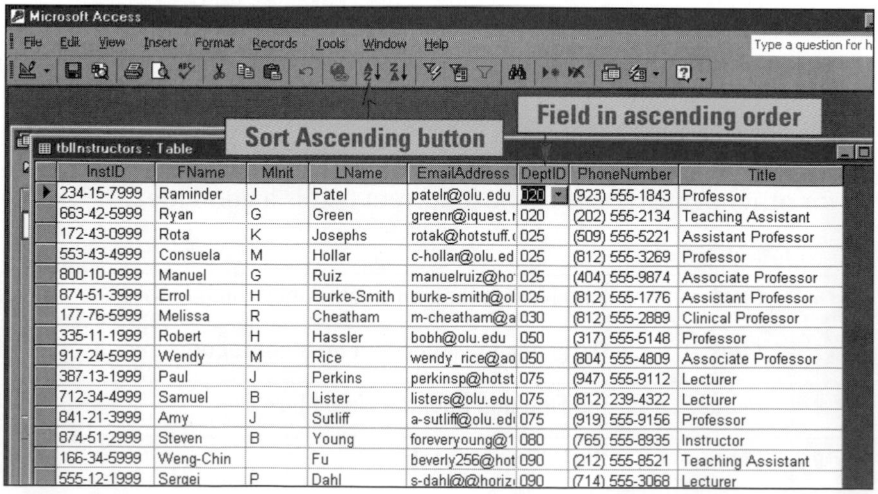

The original record order is based on the primary key. To restore the original order, select the Remove Filter/Sort command on the Records menu. Otherwise, you save the sort order when you save the form or datasheet.

Step 4	*Click*	Records
Step 5	*Click*	Remove Filter/Sort
Step 6	*Close*	the table without saving changes

Sorting Records on Multiple Fields

You also can perform a more in-depth sort using multiple fields. You can select two or more adjacent columns in a datasheet and then sort them. Access sorts the records starting with the left selected column.

You want to sort the table on the course title to change the order, and then sort on two adjacent fields. To sort records on multiple fields:

Step 1	*Open*	the tblCourses table in Datasheet view
Step 2	*Click*	the CourseTitle column header to select that column
Step 3	*Click*	the Sort Ascending button 🔼 on the Table Datasheet toolbar
Step 4	*Drag*	the mouse pointer over the DeptPrefix and Course column headers to select those columns
Step 5	*Click*	the Sort Ascending button 🔼 on the Table Datasheet toolbar

Access rearranges the records according to the chosen fields. Your screen should look similar to Figure 3-5.

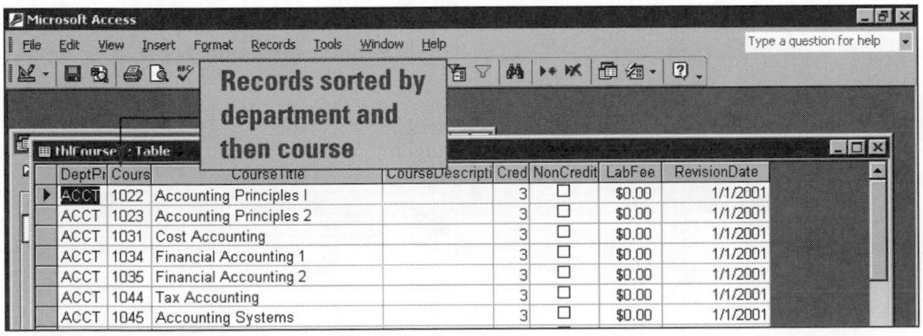

FIGURE 3-5
Records Sorted Alphabetically by Multiple Fields

Step 6	*Close*	the tblCourses table, saving the changes

MENU TIP

When you close the datasheet, Access saves the sort order. You can restore the original sort order before you close a datasheet by clicking the Remove Filter/Sort command on the Records menu.

CAUTION TIP

When dragging the mouse pointer over a column heading, the entire field name may not be visible.

QUICK TIP

Although sorting helps to modify the order of all records, it is not useful for displaying only records that match a certain condition.

chapter
three

C **3.g Filtering Records**

You should filter data when you want to view only specific records. When you specify criteria for a filter, Access shows only those records that meet the criteria. Filtering temporarily narrows the number of displayed records.

Applying Filters by Selection

Filtering by selection, the easiest method of filtering, requires that you define a value; Access then finds all records that include that value. For example, suppose you want to find all records of students from California and view them as a group. You start by examining the values in a record that meet this criterion. To filter by selection:

Step 1	*Open*	the tblStudents table in Datasheet view
Step 2	*Scroll*	to view the State field for the first record

This record is for a student from California; you establish the value of the State field as a filter condition.

Step 3	*Right-click*	the State field of this record
Step 4	*Click*	Filter By Selection

Access extracts only those records whose State field contains CA. Your screen should look similar to Figure 3-6. The word (Filtered) appears in the navigation area and FLTR appears in the status bar to indicate a filter is in place.

MOUSE **TIP**

You can filter by excluding records by right-clicking the field, and then clicking Filter Excluding Selection. You then see all records in the current list that do not include the selected text.

FIGURE 3-6
Filtered Records for
California Students

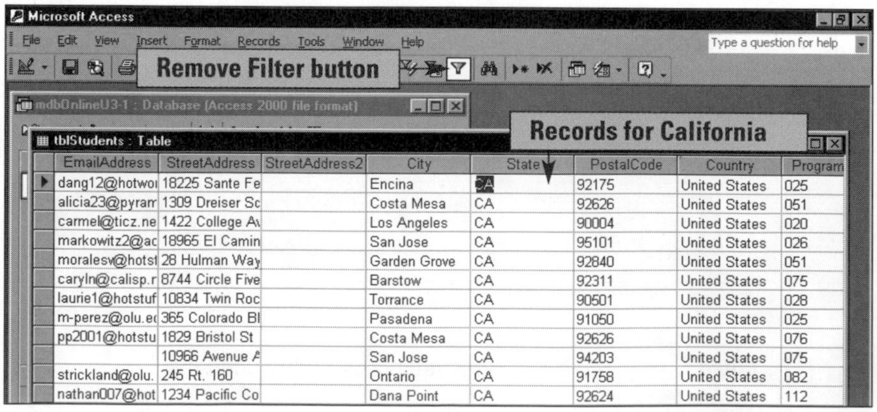

EmailAddress	StreetAddress	StreetAddress2	City	State	PostalCode	Country	Program
dang12@hotwor	18225 Sante Fe		Encina	CA	92175	United States	025
alicia23@pyram	1309 Dreiser Sc		Costa Mesa	CA	92626	United States	051
carmel@ticz.ne	1422 College Av		Los Angeles	CA	90004	United States	020
markowitz2@ac	18965 El Camin		San Jose	CA	95101	United States	026
moralesw@hotst	28 Hulman Way		Garden Grove	CA	92840	United States	051
caryln@calisp.r	8744 Circle Five		Barstow	CA	92311	United States	075
laurie1@hotstuf	10834 Twin Roc		Torrance	CA	90501	United States	028
m-perez@olu.ed	365 Colorado Bl		Pasadena	CA	91050	United States	025
pp2001@hotstu	1829 Bristol St		Costa Mesa	CA	92626	United States	076
	10966 Avenue A		San Jose	CA	94203	United States	075
strickland@olu.	245 Rt. 160		Ontario	CA	91758	United States	082
nathan007@hot	1234 Pacific Co		Dana Point	CA	92624	United States	112

Microsoft Access
File Edit View Insert Format Records Tools Window Help
Type a question for help
Remove Filter button
mdbOnlineU3-1 : Database (Access 2000 file format)
tblStudents : Table
Records for California

After filtering, Access displays the records that match the selection criterion that you entered—you don't see the other records.

| Step 5 | Close | the table, but do not save the changes |

Applying Filters by Form

Filtering by form is more powerful than filtering by selection. **Filter by form** allows you to select several criteria to filter in one step. The criteria can be, for example, an OR filter or a logical expression. OR filters find records that match any one of several criteria. Logical filters create filters based on the result of logical expressions; for instance, you can search for records having an ID number greater than 3456.

The registrar thinks staff incorrectly entered some MIS certificate majors as Management Information Systems majors. You can filter by form to find all records that describe a student's major as either 075 or as 076. To filter by form:

| Step 1 | Open | the tblStudents table in Datasheet view |
| Step 2 | Click | the Filter By Form button ⊞ on the Table Datasheet toolbar |

The tblStudents: Filter By Form dialog box on your screen should look similar to Figure 3-7. In this dialog box, you can establish filter criteria in any field. You can select the field values from a list or key the exact value in the field text box.

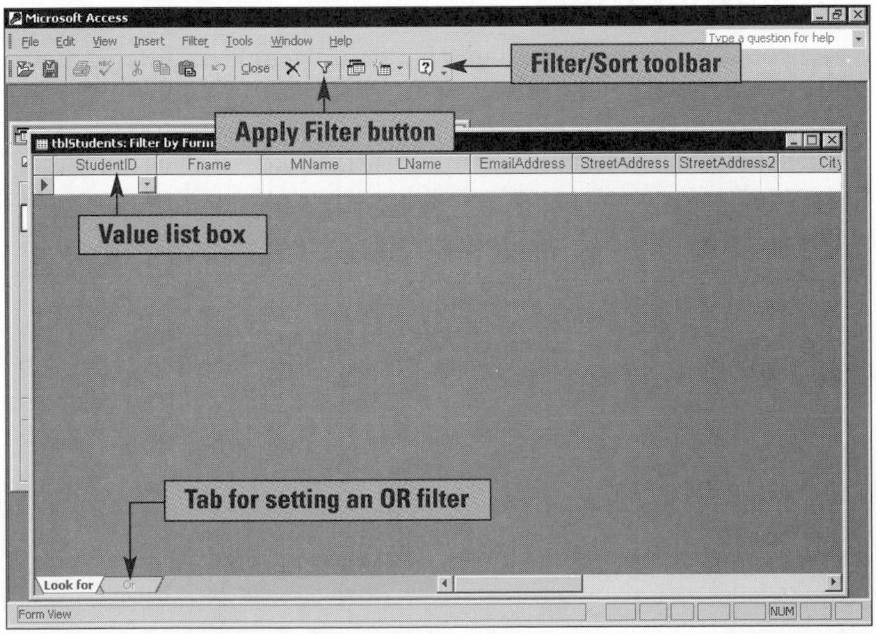

QUICK TIP

If you save a table or form, Access saves the filters you created. You can reapply the filters, if necessary, the next time you open the table or form.

MENU TIP

To select the data you want to use as the criterion, position the insertion point in the column of the field and move to a record containing the desired value for the field. Click the Filter command on the Records menu, and then click Filter by Selection.

FIGURE 3-7
Blank Filter By Form Window

chapter three

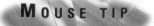

| Step 3 | *Scroll* | to the right to the ProgramCode field |
| Step 4 | *Click* | the first row under the ProgramCode field |

This is the field you want to use to set the criteria. A list arrow appears.

| Step 5 | *Click* | the ProgramCode field list arrow |
| Step 6 | *Click* | 075 in the list of program codes |

You can enter as many criteria as you like in various fields. Because you want to find either 075 or 076, you set an OR criterion. As you fill in the fields that you wish to filter, another Or tab appears at the bottom of the page.

Step 7	*Click*	the Or tab at the bottom of the tblStudents table
Step 8	*Click*	the ProgramCode field list arrow
Step 9	*Click*	076
Step 10	*Click*	the Apply Filter button [⧩] on the Filter/Sort toolbar

Sixteen records appear in the table instead of the original 54. You can scroll to confirm that only records with the program codes 075 and 076 appear.

Removing Filters

When you want to return a filtered list to its original, unfiltered state, you need to remove the filter. When you remove a filter, you don't delete it—you merely stop showing records based on the criteria defined in a filter. If you save the table or form, Access saves the filters you create. You then can reapply the filters the next time you open the table or form. When you close a table containing a filter (even if you removed the filter), Access asks whether you want to save the changes to the table. If you click the No button, the filter is *not* saved in the table and you must recreate the filter if you want to apply it again. To remove the filter from the tblStudents table:

Step 1	*Click*	the Remove Filter button [⧩] on the Filter/Sort toolbar
Step 2	*Close*	the tblStudents table
Step 3	*Click*	No when asked if you want to save the changes to the table design

The records display as they were before you applied the filter. If you apply more than one filter to the same table, all filters are removed when you use the Remove Filter command or the Remove Filter button.

3.h Printing a Table

C

A printed copy of a table, with or without data, can be useful. For example, you can print a copy of a table to check its structure and field order before entering data, or you can verify data in a table. Constance wants to see the fields you created for the tblInstructors table. You print a copy for her. To print the tblInstructors table:

Step 1	***Open***	the tblInstructors table in Datasheet view
Step 2	***Click***	the Print Preview button on the Table Datasheet toolbar
Step 3	***Click***	the zoom pointer on the data to enlarge the view

Your Print Preview view of the table on your screen should look similar to Figure 3-8. You are ready to print.

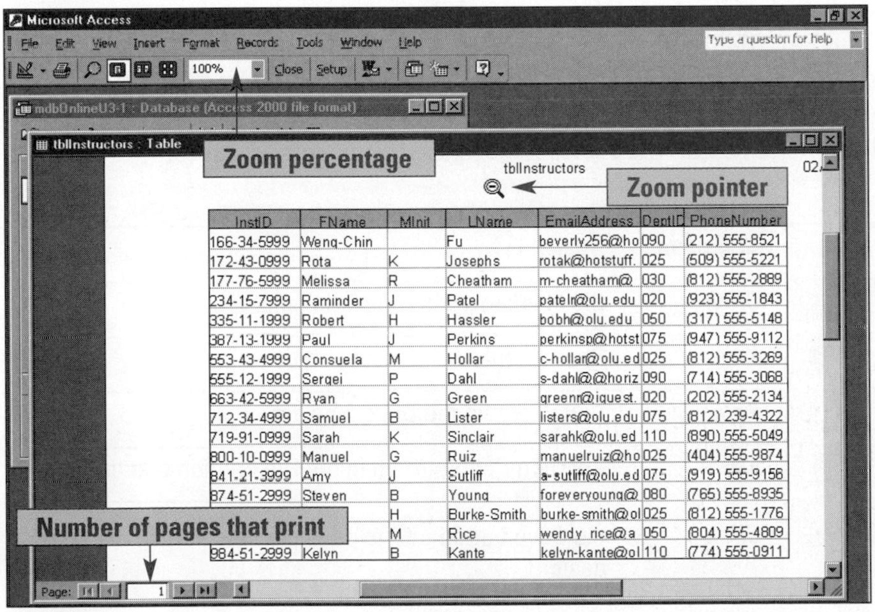

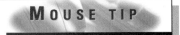

FIGURE 3-8
tblInstructors Table in Print Preview

Step 4	***Click***	the Print button on the Print Preview toolbar
Step 5	***Click***	the Close button on the Print Preview toolbar

MENU TIP

You can open the Filter By Form dialog box by clicking the Filter command on the Records menu and then clicking Filter by Form.

You can remove a filter by selecting the Remove Filter/Sort command on the Records menu.

MOUSE TIP

In the preview of the datasheet, the mouse pointer appears as a magnifying glass and is called the zoom pointer. You can use the zoom pointer to zoom in and out of the data.

chapter three

The Print Preview window closes. Your last task is to add photographs of OLU's employees to the database.

C **3.i** Adding Pictures to Records

You can add pictures and clip art to records. Access saves each image as an **OLE object**, which means the image was created using another application but appears as a separate object in Access. There are two types of OLE objects: linked and embedded. A **linked object** is not saved as part of a database but instead includes a reference to the file's location, so that Access can find it. An **embedded object** is stored as part of the database.

You should link an object if you want to keep the database small, if the object being linked is still under construction, if you are sure that a computer containing the file is stable, or if you do not plan to send the file by e-mail. (A linked file is associated with a specific computer or location; if you e-mail the file, that location is not available to the recipient.) You should embed an object if you have enough room for a large database, if you do not need to keep the file as a separate document, or if you plan to send the document by e-mail or disk.

Photographs can be added to a record only if they are first saved as bitmap images. You can do this by scanning photographs with a scanner or by using a digital camera. Some photo processors make CD-ROMs with bitmap-image copies of your photographs. These tools produce excellent images for an Access database.

You have the bitmap image containing the photograph of Sarah Sinclair, Associate Professor at OLU. You are ready to add it to the tblInstructors table. Before you can add a picture to a table record, you must create the Photo field. To add the Photo field to the tblInstructors table:

Step 1	*Switch to*	Design view
Step 2	*Click*	the blank row after the Title field
Step 3	*Key*	Photo in the Field Name text box
Step 4	*Select*	OLE Object in the Data Type list
Step 5	*Key*	Instructor photograph in the Description text box
Step 6	*Click*	the Save button to save the new field in the table's design

The new field in Design view on your screen should look similar to Figure 3-9.

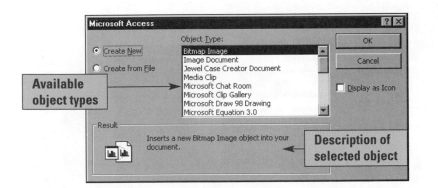

FIGURE 3-9
New Photo OLE Object Field

CAUTION TIP

Some bitmap images are very large, particularly those with high resolution or a large number of colors. For most database purposes, low resolution and a few colors are satisfactory. A database with a large bitmap image can require a lot of space on your disk drive and cause slow response times when you open records in forms or tables.

To switch to Datasheet view and insert the photograph:

Step 1	*Switch to*	Datasheet view for the tblInstructors table
Step 2	*Click*	the Photo field for Sarah Sinclair's record
Step 3	*Click*	Insert
Step 4	*Click*	Object

The Insert Object dialog box on your screen should look similar to Figure 3-10.

FIGURE 3-10
Insert Object Dialog Box

Step 5	*Click*	Bitmap Image in the Object Type: list, if necessary
Step 6	*Click*	the Create from File option button
Step 7	*Click*	Browse
Step 8	*Switch to*	the drive and folder containing the Data Disk
Step 9	*Double-click*	SSinclair.bmp
Step 10	*Click*	OK

chapter
three

You embedded the image in the Access database. You are now looking at the Datasheet view of the table, and the Photograph cell lets you know you have a bitmap image in this record. You can view the photograph only in Form view of the tblInstructors table. To do so, you first need to close the table.

Step 11	*Close*	the tblInstructors table

The tblInstructors table has an associated frmInstrPhotos form. You need to open that form to view the photograph. To view the image in the frmInstrPhotos form:

Step 1	*Click*	Forms  on the Objects bar in the Database window
Step 2	*Double-click*	frmInstrPhotos
Step 3	*Click*	the Next Record button ▶ until you see Sarah Sinclair's record

Your screen should look similar to Figure 3-11.

FIGURE 3-11
frmInstrPhotos Form with
Bitmap Image

After you view Sinclair's record and the photo, you can close the form.

Step 4	*Close*	the frmInstrPhotos form and the database

As you can see, you can enter photographs in a database table just as easily as you enter text.

Summary

▶ A cell is the intersection between a row and a column.

▶ To navigate through records, you can use the mouse, the TAB key, and a variety of other keys.

▶ To replace text in a cell, click in the cell and rekey the information.

▶ You can copy a field, include attributes, and then paste the field. This saves time when you create new fields.

▶ The Office Clipboard stores up to 24 items that you cut or copy. You can paste these items into your current file.

▶ You can undo some mistakes made when entering data.

▶ The Delete command deletes the item you are working with; the Delete Record command deletes the entire record.

▶ Use the Find command in Access to perform simple searches, such as those that find a word or a particular value in your records. You can also replace values in your records.

▶ Sorting rearranges data on the screen, so that it is easier to scan records to find the one that you want. You can sort in ascending order (from A to Z or 1 to 9) or descending order (from Z to A or 9 to 1) on a single field or multiple fields in adjacent columns of the table. Access sorts the records starting with the leftmost selected column.

▶ When you save a sorted datasheet or form, Access saves the sort order. When you open that table again, it remains in sorted order. Removing a sort on a datasheet returns the information to its original state.

▶ Filtering temporarily narrows a list of records to eliminate the data you don't want. Filter data when you want to view only specific records. You specify criteria and Access shows only those records that meet the criteria. You can filter by selection and by form.

▶ When you filter by selection, you define a value and Access finds all the records that include that value. When you filter by form, you can select several criteria to filter.

▶ When you save a table or form, Access saves the filter you created. You can reapply a filter the next time you open the database. If you no longer need it, you can remove the filter.

▶ Before printing, you can view a table datasheet in the Print Preview window and use the zoom pointer to see the data in the window more clearly. Or you can send the datasheet directly to the printer.

▶ To insert a picture in a table, use the Object command on the Insert menu. However, you can only view the picture on the screen in Form view.

chapter three

Commands Review

Action	Menu Bar	Shortcut Menu	Toolbar	Task Pane	Keyboard
Select cell contents					F2
Undo a change	Edit, Undo		↰		ESC CTRL + Z ALT + E, U
Redo a change	Edit, Redo		↱		CTRL + Y ALT + E, R
Delete a record	Edit, Delete Record	Right-click record, Delete			DELETE ALT + E, R
Display the Office Clipboard	Edit, Office Clipboard				ALT + E, B
Copy data to Clipboard	Edit, Copy	Right-click item, Copy	▣		CTRL + C ALT + E, C
Paste data from Clipboard	Edit, Paste	Right-click location, Paste	▣		CTRL + V ALT + E, P
Insert a row in Design view	Insert, Rows	Right-click row, Insert Rows			Alt + I, R
Find data	Edit, Find		🔍		CTRL + F ALT + E, F
Replace data	Edit, Replace				CTRL + H ALT + E, E
Sort records In ascending or descending	Records, Sort, Sort Ascending or Sort Descending	Right-click record, Sort Ascending or Sort Descending	↓AZ or ↓ZA		ALT + R, S, A or D
Filter by form	Records, Filter, Filter by Form	Right-click field, Filter By Form	▤		ALT + R, F, F
Filter by selection	Records, Filter, Filter by Selection	Right-click field, Filter By Selection	▼		ALT + R, F, S
Apply a filter	Records, Apply Filter/Sort	Right-click record, Apply Filter/Sort	▽		ALT + R, Y
Remove a filter or sort	Records, Remove Filter/Sort	Right-click field, Remove Filter/Sort	▽		ALT + R, R
Print a table	File, Print		🖨		ALT + F, P CTRL + P
Insert a bitmap image	Insert, Object	Right-click field, Insert Object			ALT + I, O

Concepts Review

SCANS

Circle the correct answer.

1. When you enter a single value, you enter data in a:
[a] cell.
[b] record.
[c] picture.
[d] query.

2. A value is the:
[a] data in each field of the record.
[b] field in each piece of data in the record.
[c] cell in each field in the record.
[d] value in each field in the cell.

3. **A cell is where a:**
   [a] value and a cell intersect.
   [b] column and a row intersect.
   [c] row and a record intersect.
   [d] datasheet and a row intersect.

4. **To locate a particular value in a table, use the:**
   [a] Locate command.
   [b] Repeat command.
   [c] Find command.
   [d] Sort command.

5. **To move the insertion point to the next field in a table, press the:**
   [a] TAB key.
   [b] INSERT key.
   [c] F10 key.
   [d] CTRL + TAB keys.

6. **The pencil icon in the record selection area means that you:**
   [a] saved the record.
   [b] committed the record to the database.
   [c] did not commit the record to the database.
   [d] marked the record for deletion.

7. **The type of filter for which you choose a field value from a particular record as the criteria is a:**
   [a] filter by selection.
   [b] filter by form.
   [c] filter by criteria.
   [d] query.

8. **If you sort on more than one field in a table, Access first sorts the field that is the:**
   [a] one you chose first.
   [b] leftmost field.
   [c] rightmost field.
   [d] field you chose last.

9. **If you select several records in a table, a triangle marks:**
   [a] all the selected records.
   [b] the first and last records.
   [c] the first record.
   [d] the last record.

10. **When you add a picture to a record, Access saves the image as a:**
   [a] photograph.
   [b] form or table.
   [c] linked or embedded object.
   [d] hypertext link.

Circle **T** if the statement is true or **F** if the statement is false.

T   F   1. You can enter data in a table or a form.

T   F   2. You can move to the last field in the last record by pressing the ALT + END keys.

T   F   3. The Clipboard task pane lets you review the last 24 items copied to the Clipboard.

T   F   4. You can delete a record by pressing the BACKSPACE key.

T   F   5. When you close a table with a filter, Access does not store the filter with the table.

T   F   6. The pencil icon in the record selection area of a table means that you committed the changes to the database.

T   F   7. You cannot undo the results of a filter.

T   F   8. You can print the contents of a table with the Print Preview command.

T   F   9. You can view a picture within a table in Datasheet view.

T   F   10. You can reverse your last change to a field value in a table by using the Undo option.

chapter three

Skills Review

Exercise 1 [C]

1. Create a copy of the *mdbFanTours3-* database located on the Data Disk.

2. Open the tblEvents table in Datasheet view.

3. Key the following event names in the EventName field of this table: "Rose Bowl," "Orange Bowl," "Super Bowl," "The Masters," and "PGA."

4. Close the table, and then close the database.

Exercise 2 [C]

1. Open the *mdbFanTours3-1* database you created in Exercise 1.

2. Open the tblEvents table.

3. Update the information in the table by entering the following information.

EventName	EventDate	Description	DetailedDescription	Location
Rose Bowl	1/2/2003	The Rose Bowl	Tournament of Roses Parade and Rose Bowl game	Pasadena, CA
Orange Bowl	1/4/2003	Orange Bowl game		Miami, FL
Super Bowl	1/26/2003	Super Bowl XXXVIII game		New Orleans, LA
The Masters	4/2/2003	The Masters golf tournament	Augusta National Golf Club	Augusta, GA
PGA	8/13/2003	PGA Championship	Willowbrook Golf Club	Indianapolis, IN

4. Close the table, and then close the database.

Exercise 3 [C]

1. Open the *mdbFanTours3-1* database you modified in Exercise 2.

2. Open the tblEmployees table.

3. Add three employee records using the following information.

EmployeeID	First Name	Last Name
123-41-7999	Juan	Hectorez
876-34-1999	Eileen	Raptor
714-33-8999	David	Washington

4. Close the table, and then close the database.

Exercise 4 [C]

1. Open the *mdbFanTours3-1* database you modified in Exercise 3.

2. Open the tblEmployees table in Design view.

3. Insert new text fields called "Address," "City," "State," and "Zip" after the LastName field. Field sizes are 25, 25, 2, and 5, respectively.

4. Switch to Datasheet view and key the values shown below in the new fields.

EmployeeID	Address	City	State	Zip
123-41-7999	121 8th Ave	Terre Haute	IN	47805
876-34-1999	4809 Westbourne Dr.	Indianapolis	IN	46226
714-33-8999	11820 Pendleton	Indianapolis	IN	46228

5. Save and close the tblEmployees table, and then close the database.

Exercise 5

1. Open the *mdbFanTours3-1* database you modified in Exercise 4.

2. Open the tblProspects table in Datasheet view.

3. Sort this table by the last name in ascending order.

4. Close the tblProspects table, saving the changes to its design. Close the database.

Exercise 6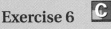

1. Open the *mdbFanTours3-1* database you modified in Exercise 5.

2. Open the tblProspects table in Design view and review the description for ContactType.

3. Switch to Datasheet view. Use Filter By Selection on the ContactType field to learn how many prospects responded by e-mail.

4. Remove the filter.

5. Using Filter By Form, filter each value in the ContactType field, so that you can count the number of records for each type. Don't forget the blank (missing) field value. (*Hint:* You can use the expression IS NULL in the ContactType criteria to count the missing records.)

6. Remove the filters.

7. Close the tblProspects table without saving the changes to the design. Close the database.

Exercise 7

1. Open the *mdbFanTours3-1* database you modified in Exercise 6.

2. Open the tblEmployees table.

3. Insert the *Photo01.bmp* photograph located on the Data Disk in the Photo field in the first employee's record.

4. Close the tblEmployees table.

5. View the image in the frmEmplPhotos form.

6. Close the form, and then close the database.

Exercise 8

1. Open the *mdbFanTours3-1* database you modified in Exercise 7.

2. Open the tblEmployees table in Datasheet view.

3. Add two more employee records using the following information.

chapter three

EmployeeID	First Name	Last Name	Address	City	State	Zip
111-22-3333	Ming	Lui	56 Winding Way	Chicago Heights	IL	60411
222-33-4444	Alicia	Ohara	864 1st St	Chicago Heights	IL	60411

4. Close the table, and then close the database.

Case Projects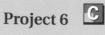

Project 1

Using the *mdbFanTours3-2* database located on the Data Disk, enter information for two new customers in the tblCustomers table. Use a keyboard shortcut to enter some data. Close the database.

Project 2

Using the *mdbFanTours3-2* database you modified in Project 1, enter information for two new employees in the frmEmplPhotos form. Use keyboard shortcuts to navigate the form. Close the database.

Project 3

Using the *mdbFanTours3-2* database you modified in Project 2, add a field to the tblEvents table that gives the cost of the tour. Assume that most tours cost around $1,000, excluding airfare. Add appropriate costs to this table, and print a copy with your changes. Save your work in a Word document. Close the database.

Project 4

Using the *mdbFanTours3-2* database you modified in Project 3, open the tblEmployees table and create a new field for phone numbers. Enter data for two records. Then create a field for a second phone number, such as the number for a fax machine or mobile phone. Copy the design from the first Phone Number field, and modify it to fit. Close the database.

Project 5

Using the *mdbFanTours3-2* database you modified in Project 4, create a new table called "tblInvoices." Add appropriately named fields for Invoice ID, Invoice Date, Customer ID, and Tour Cost. Add two records to the new table that match customers already in the tblCustomers table. Close the database.

Project 6

Using the *mdbFanTours3-2* database you modified in Project 5, open the tblEmployees table. Add a photograph to the second record using the bitmap image *Photo02.bmp* located on the Data Disk. Close the table. Open the frmEmplPhotos form and use it to edit the first record's data, but undo all your changes. Close the database.

Project 7

Using the *mdbFanTours3-2* database you modified in Project 6, open the tblProspects table. Filter the table to find how many prospects from California contacted Fantastic Sports Tours via the Web or e-mail. Save the table with your changes to its design. Close the database.

Project 8

Connect to the Internet and search for a Web site that offers copyright-free clip art. Locate an image that would be useful for Fantastic Sports Tours. Download one small bitmap file, remembering to save it as a .bmp file. Add it to an appropriate table in the *mdbFanTours3-2* database you modified in Project 7. Close the database.

Establishing Relationships Between Tables

Chapter Overview

When you relate tables in Access, Access links the information in them for use in queries. The queries then become the data source for forms and reports. When properly designed, relationships make the database easier to maintain. In this chapter, you learn how to plan relationships and then join the tables in the Relationships window. You also learn how to enforce and verify referential integrity.

Case profile

Online University stores student and course information in Access database tables. Hector Guarez, the assistant admissions officer, maintains student data in one table. Michael Golden, the associate provost, tracks course offerings data in a second table. Jung Me, the assistant registrar, keeps data on classes and registrations in other tables. Academic affairs personnel store information about instructors in still another table. They ask you to create an efficient way for them to use one another's information. To do this, you create relationships among the tables.

chapter four **4**

4.a Establishing Table Relationships

Recall that no one table in the OLU relational database contains all the information about the university. There are tables for students, courses, classes, instructors, class registrations, departments, and other OLU entities. For instance, instructor information appears in the tblInstructors table, not in the tblClasses table, for each class that each instructor teaches. This separation of information is similar to sorting the information, on paper, in two different binders. You can certainly access and read information in both binders, but you can't do so simultaneously. The same data item is often named differently, depending on its use. For instance, in the tblClasses table, the ClassInstructorCode field describes the ID for the person assigned to teach that class; in the tblInstructors table, the primary key field is InstID; and in the tblStudents table, the AdvisorID field describes a student's academic advisor.

To overcome the limitation of not being able to read the two "binders" simultaneously, fields that contain common values relate—or link—the tblInstructors table to the tblClasses table. A common value that resides in *both* tables links related tables. In this case, the instructor ID, the value (or content) of which appears under two different field names, links the two tables. InstID and ClassInstructorCode are the link fields.

When two tables are related, one table becomes the primary table and one table becomes the related table. The **primary table** is the table in which the link field is the primary key. Recall that a primary key uniquely identifies each record in the table. In this example, the primary table is tblInstructors. The primary table contains the information you want to relate or look up.

The **related table**, sometimes called the secondary or child table, is the table in which the link field is a foreign key. In this case, the tblClasses table is the related table and the ClassInstructorCode field is the foreign key. A **foreign key** is a field in the related table that matches a primary key in the primary table.

You create a relationship between two tables to organize the records shared in those tables. When you organize records, you combine the related information from the tables in a temporary table that you can use in a form or report. It is easier to maintain the information in separate tables, yet be able to link the information when necessary.

Types of Relationships

Once you determine that you want to relate tables in a database, you start by defining the kind of relationship(s) you want to establish.

- A **one-to-one relationship** means that any record in the primary table can have one or no related records. For instance, a department has a single department head. One-to-one relationships are least common.
- A **one-to-many relationship** means that any one record in the primary table can have more than one related record in the related table. This is the most common type of relationship. For instance, an instructor can teach many classes, but each class is taught by only one instructor. A one-to-many relationship may also have no related records.
- A **many-to-many relationship** means each table can have many related records. For instance, a student is enrolled in many classes and each class has many students.

QUICK TIP

You cannot establish a relationship with a table open in Access.

Access supports one-to-one and one-to-many relationships. It indirectly supports many-to-many relationships through the use of a linking table, called a junction table. For a many-to-many relationship (such as the relationship between students and classes), the **junction table** (like the tblRegistration table) contains the primary keys from both related tables. Using the junction table, you must create two one-to-many relationships. For instance, in the OLU junction table tblRegistration: the tblStudents table relates to the tblRegistration table through the StudentID field, and the tblClasses table relates to the tblRegistration table through the ClassID field. Each record in the tblRegistration table refers to a student enrolled in a specific class section.

Examining Tables and Fields

To determine which relationship you want to establish in your database tables, first look at the fields of your tables and how you use the data in the tables. For the OLU database, Hector, Michael, and Jung maintain the data for their departments. At times, they want to access information in each other's tables, especially when they want to avoid entering information already contained in another table. To meet their needs, first determine the relationships for the tables. You can examine the fields in the tables so you can decide which fields you can use to link the tables. You view the fields for each table in the Relationships window.

To create a copy of the OLU database and open the Relationships window to view the fields for each table:

Step 1	*Create*	a copy of the *mdbOnlineU4-* database located on the Data Disk
Step 2	*Close*	any open tables, if necessary
Step 3	*Right-click*	the Database window
Step 4	*Click*	Relationships

**chapter
four**

QUICK TIP

The tblClasses table shown in Figure 4-1 also has primary key fields, which reflect the table's relationships with other tables. Because these relationships are outside the current topic, they are not boldface in the figure.

The Relationships window and the Show Table dialog box open. Using the dialog box, you can add the tables to the Relationships window and establish relationships among the tables.

Step 5	*Click*	the Tables tab, if necessary
Step 6	*Double-click*	tblCourses
Step 7	*Follow*	Steps 5 and 6 to add the tblClasses, tblRegistration, and tblStudents tables to the Relationships window
Step 8	*Close*	the Show Table dialog box
Step 9	*Resize*	the four tables in the Relationships window by dragging each bottom boundary with the mouse pointer so that you can see the field names, if necessary

Your screen should look similar to Figure 4-1. The boldface field names are the primary keys for each table.

FIGURE 4-1
Tables in the Relationships Window

MOUSE TIP

You can click the Relationships button on the Database toolbar to open the Relationships window.

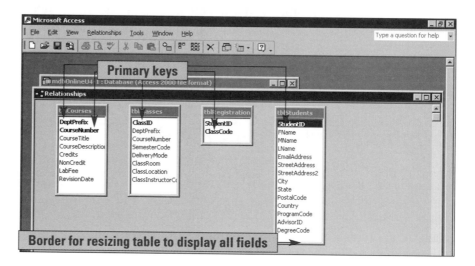

The fact that some of the tables include identical or similar field names reflects an important principle: The existence of identical or similar field names should immediately make you think that these fields contain common values and are candidates for a relationship. For example, both the tblStudents and tblRegistration tables include a StudentID field, which you can use to relate the two tables. That is, you can match records from both tables that have the same StudentID field value. You can also relate the tblClasses table with the tblRegistration table based on the ClassID and ClassCode fields. Finally, you can relate the tblClasses table to the tblCourses table based on the DeptPrefix and CourseNumber fields. You can therefore establish three different relationships for these tables. These three relationships let you use related information from the three tables in forms and reports.

Creating the Relationship

You establish database relationships by linking the common fields in two tables. You do this by dragging the common field from the primary table to the common field in the related table. The drag direction is significant, because the operation establishes the role of each table. For example, in the relationship between the tblRegistration and tblStudents tables, the latter is the primary table. To join two tables:

| Step 1 | *Drag* | the StudentID field in the tblStudents table to the StudentID field in the tblRegistration table |
| Step 2 | *Release* | the mouse button when the mouse pointer changes to a small box |

The Edit Relationships dialog box on your screen should look similar to Figure 4-2. For now, you accept the default settings for the join. This is a one-to-many join; one record in the tblStudents table may relate to many records in the tblRegistration table.

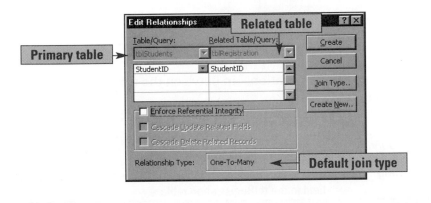

| Step 3 | *Click* | Create |

Access creates a relationship between these tables. The Relationships window on your screen should look similar to Figure 4-3. The **join line** between the tblRegistration and tblStudents tables indicates the relationship.

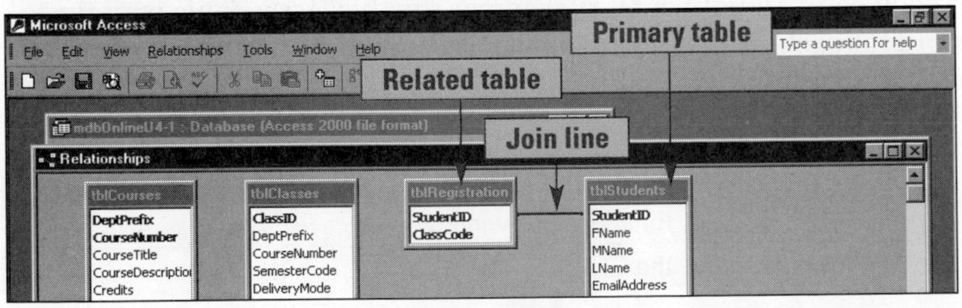

QUICK TIP

You may need to move the Show Table dialog box to see the tables you added. Drag its title bar to move it.

Remember that the primary table is the one that has the join field as its primary key. In the related table, the join field is the foreign key. A join field contains the common value in both tables.

FIGURE 4-2
Edit Relationships
Dialog Box

FIGURE 4-3
Relationships Window with
One Join

chapter
four

4.b Establishing Other One-to-Many Relationships

There are many other potential relationships in the OLU database. For example, one class could have many students. For this relationship, you would set the relationship for the tblClasses table with the tblRegistration table based on the ClassID and ClassCode fields. Another potential relationship is that between the tblDepartments and tblInstructors tables through the DeptID field. Table 4-1 summarizes the potential relationships in the database.

TABLE 4-1
Potential Relationships in the OLU Database

Primary Table	Primary Key	Related Table	Foreign Key
tblStudents	StudentID	tblRegistration	StudentID
tblClasses	ClassID	tblRegistration	ClassCode
tblCourses	DeptPrefix	tblClasses	DeptPrefix
	CourseNumber		CourseNumber
tblInstructors	InstID	tblClasses	ClassInstructorCode
tblDepartments	DeptID	tblInstructors	DeptID

To create a one-to-many relationship between the tblClasses and tblRegistration tables:

Step 1	**Verify**	that the Relationships window is open
Step 2	**Drag**	the ClassID field in the tblClasses table to the ClassCode field in the tblRegistration table
Step 3	**Release**	the mouse button when the mouse pointer changes to a small box
Step 4	**Click**	Create

Creating a relationship by joining on more than one field is a little trickier. The relationship between the tblCourses and tblClasses tables is an example of this. Recall that the tblCourses table contains entries for each *course* taught at OLU, whereas the tblClasses table contains a record for each *class section*. You can create the relationships between the tblCourses and tblClasses tables. To create the relationship:

Step 1	**Click**	the DeptPrefix field in the tblCourses table in the Relationships window
Step 2	**Press & hold**	the CTRL key

| Step 3 | *Click* | the CourseNumber field in the tblCourses table |
| Step 4 | *Release* | the CTRL key |

Both the DeptPrefix and CourseNumber fields are selected in the tblCourses table. You use them together as the join field.

| Step 5 | *Drag* | to the DeptPrefix field in the tblClasses table |
| Step 6 | *Release* | the mouse button when the mouse pointer changes to several small boxes |

The mouse pointer shape indicates that Access uses more than one field to link these tables. The Edit Relationships dialog box opens so you can identify the related fields in the tblClasses table.
To identify the two related fields:

Step 1	*Click*	in the text box in the first row under tblClasses
Step 2	*Click*	the list arrow in the text box
Step 3	*Click*	DeptPrefix
Step 4	*Click*	in the text box in the second row under tblClasses
Step 5	*Click*	the list arrow in the text box
Step 6	*Click*	CourseNumber
Step 7	*Click*	Create to complete the relationship

You can print the Relationships window with the Print Relationships command on the File menu. You may find this useful when discussing the database structure with others. To print the Relationships window:

| Step 1 | *Click* | File |
| Step 2 | *Click* | Print Relationships |

Access creates a report that displays the Relationships window in Print Preview. You can click the Print button on the Print Preview toolbar to send the report to the printer.

| Step 3 | *Click* | the Print button  on the Print Preview toolbar |

chapter
four

You can save the report in the database or delete it when you close the Print Preview window.

Step 4	*Close*	the Print Preview window
Step 5	*Click*	Yes to save the changes
Step 6	*Click*	OK to accept the default name for the report

You created several relationships in the database. It's important for each foreign key to have a matching primary key; without it, matching information from the primary table is lost. You can solve this problem by enforcing referential integrity.

C 4.c Enforcing Referential Integrity

Databases that contain related tables need to guarantee the integrity of the relationships. That is, the related tables need to stay related—or connected—to one another, even if the data changes. For example, suppose Hector deletes the student A. Z. Delta from the tblStudents table. Remember that the tblStudents table is related to the tblRegistration table. Because of this relationship, what happens to the classes for which A. Z. registered? Those records in the tblRegistration table are no longer related to a record in the tblStudents table and are considered **orphans**. The classes A. Z. took are orphaned because her StudentID number is no longer valid.

Access helps to avoid orphans by letting you enforce **referential integrity**. This means you cannot delete a record from the primary table that has an existing relationship unless you first delete the relationship. Referential integrity is a system of rules Access uses to ensure that relationships between records in related tables are valid (foreign key matches a primary key in the primary table) and that you don't accidentally delete or change related data. Setting referential integrity does not prevent you from deleting a record from the related table.

To set referential integrity for the relationships that you created:

Step 1	*Double-click*	the join line between the tblStudents and tblRegistration tables to open the Edit Relationships dialog box
Step 2	*Click*	the Enforce Referential Integrity check box to insert a check mark
Step 3	*Click*	OK

The Relationships window on your screen should look similar to Figure 4-4. Observe the infinity symbol next to the tblRegistration table (the "many" side) and the 1 symbol next to the tblStudents table (the "one" side) on the join line.

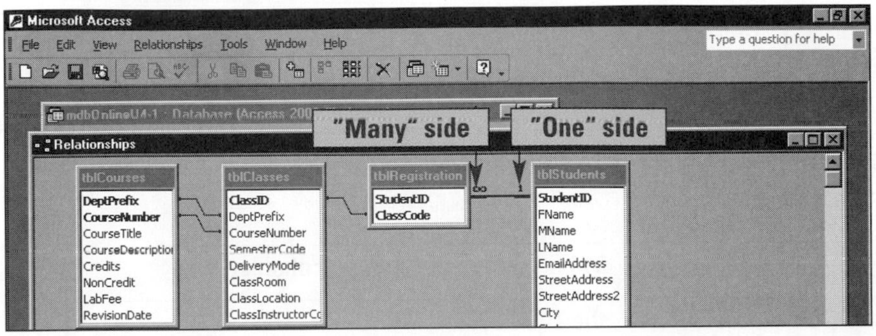

FIGURE 4-4
Referential Integrity Is
Enforced

Access checks the contents of your related tables when you enforce referential integrity. If it finds a referential integrity violation, it displays a warning message. Access does not let you enforce referential integrity until you repair the primary key or foreign key that does not match. Therefore, it is better to set relationships *before* you add data to the tables.

C AUTION TIP

Remember that the direction makes a relationship unique. Referential integrity between the tblRegistration and tblStudents tables is not the same as referential integrity between the tblStudents and tblRegistration tables.

Step 4	*Follow*	Steps 1 though 3 to enforce referential integrity between the tblRegistration and tblClasses tables
Step 5	*Click*	the Save button 🖫 on the Relationship toolbar to save the layout
Step 6	*Close*	the Relationships window

Next you want to verify that the referential integrity you created works for the OLU database.

4.d Verifying Referential Integrity

You enforced referential integrity between the tblRegistration table and its two primary tables: tblStudents and tblClasses. That means that *each record* in the tblRegistrations table must have a matching student record and a matching class record. The easiest way to check whether Access will enforce this condition is by adding a record to the tblRegistrations table that has no matching primary record.

chapter
four

To add a record without a matching primary record:

Step 1	*Double-click*	tblRegistration to open the table
Step 2	*Observe*	the zero placeholder in the last row of the table
Step 3	*Click*	the StudentID field in the last row of the table

A list arrow appears in this lookup field. You can click the list arrow to view the available choices from the tblStudents table.

Step 4	*Key*	114 to replace the zero placeholder
Step 5	*Press*	the TAB key
Step 6	*Key*	00142 in the ClassCode field in the same row
Step 7	*Press*	the ENTER key

The warning dialog box on your screen should look similar to Figure 4-5. Because your record's student identification does not exist in the tblStudents table, Access does not let you add this record to the tblRegistration table.

FIGURE 4-5
Message Warning New
Record Violates
Referential Integrity

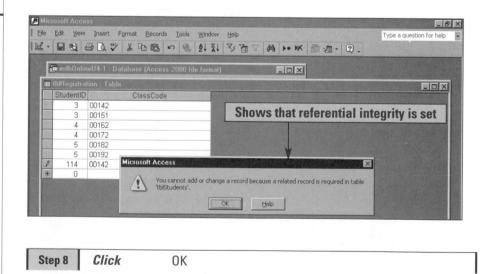

| Step 8 | *Click* | OK |

You must provide a correct value for StudentID or cancel the entire record before you can leave this record.

Step 9	**Click**	the StudentID field
Step 10	**Click**	the list arrow
Step 11	**Click**	14
Step 12	**Close**	the tblRegistration table

Access does not let you enter a record value for the foreign key in the tblRegistration table unless it matches the primary key in another table. Next you try to delete a related record from one of the primary tables. To attempt to delete a related record:

Step 1	**Double-click**	the tblStudents table in the Database window
Step 2	**Click**	the record selector for the record with StudentID 14
Step 3	**Click**	the Delete Record button ▶✕ on the Table Datasheet toolbar

Access again warns you that you cannot delete this record, because you enforced referential integrity. Your screen should look similar to Figure 4-6.

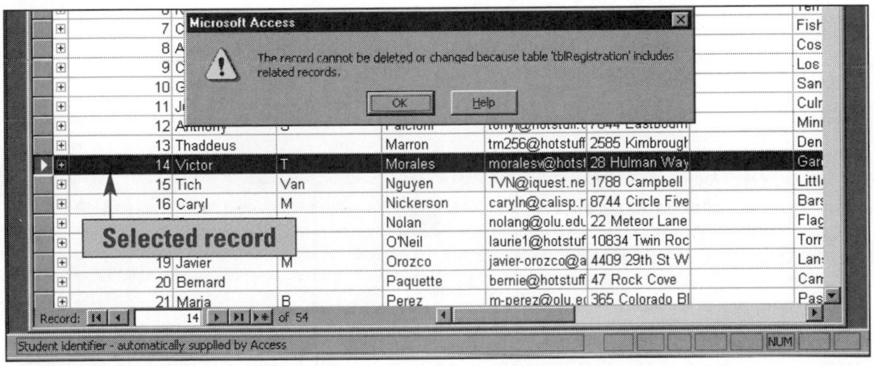

FIGURE 4-6
Message Warning Deletion Violates Referential Integrity

| Step 4 | **Click** | OK |
| Step 5 | **Close** | the tblStudents table and the database |

You established relationships for several tables in the OLU database and enforced referential integrity. This assures that the data in the relational database remains synchronized.

chapter
four

Summary

▶ A relationship links common fields in separate tables. These fields must be of the same data type and have the same value, but they don't need to have the same name.

▶ All values in the related key must match a value in the primary key. It is not necessary for a primary key value to match a related key value.

▶ You can define three kinds of relationships among tables. A one-to-one relationship means each table has only one related field. A one-to-many relationship means the primary table can have more than one related record in the secondary table. A many-to-many relationship means each table can have many related records.

▶ To create a relationship between tables, draw a join line between the common fields. Drag from the primary table to the related table in the Relationships window.

▶ A join line indicates that two fields in separate tables are related. A join is the actual link that defines the relationship between related tables.

▶ Enforce referential integrity to ensure that related records stay related: you cannot delete a primary record with a matching related record, and you cannot add a related record whose foreign key does not match the primary key in the related table.

Commands Review

Action	Menu Bar	Shortcut Menu	Toolbar	Task Pane	Keyboard
Open Relationships window	Tools, Relationships	Right-click window, click Relationships	[icon]		ALT + T, R
View a relationship (in the Relationships window)	Relationships, Edit Relationship	Right-click, click Edit Relationship	Double-click the join line		ALT + R, R
Create a relationship (in the Relationships window)			Drag field between tables		
View a join (when the Relationships window is open)	Relationships, Edit Relationship	Right-click join line, click Edit Relationship	Double-click the join line		ALT + R, R
Create a join (when the Relationships window is open)			Click join type		
Add a table to the Relationships window	Relationships, Show Table	Right-click, click Show Table	[icon]		ALT + R, T
Set referential integrity	Relationships, Edit Relationship	Double-click the join line			ALT + R, R, E
Print Relationships window	File, Print Relationships				ALT + F, R

Concepts Review

Circle the correct answer.

1. A relationship is a:
[a] way to print reports.
[b] combination of two tables.
[c] connection between two tables based on data in a common field.
[d] referential integrity definition.

2. You should identify relationships to:
[a] coordinate information between two tables.
[b] uniquely identify a row in a table.
[c] make finding duplicate records easier.
[d] relate tables in two different databases.

3. A one-to-many relationship links:
[a] one table with many other tables.
[b] one field with many possible fields.
[c] one record with many other records in another table.
[d] one database with many tables.

4. Referential integrity refers to the:
[a] accuracy of data entry.
[b] system of rules that ensures you have matching data in the primary table.
[c] database design.
[d] data validity.

5. To create a relationship:
[a] drag the join line out of the way.
[b] drag the foreign key in the related table to the primary key in the primary table.
[c] drag the primary key in the primary table to the foreign key in the related table.
[d] click the Join button in the Database toolbar.

6. To edit a join, you must:
[a] open the Join Properties dialog box.
[b] double-click the table you want.
[c] click the referential integrity button.
[d] draw a line between two fields.

7. Creating a junction table is useful when you:
[a] want a table to update independently.
[b] want to link tables that have different fields with the same type of information.
[c] have a many-to-one relationship.
[d] have a many-to-many relationship.

8. The field that uniquely identifies a row in the table is the:
[a] primary key.
[b] foreign key.
[c] join type.
[d] record selector.

9. In the Relationships window, a join:
[a] also appears in the Database window under Joins objects.
[b] eliminates referential integrity.
[c] is indicated by a dotted line.
[d] is indicated by a solid line.

10. Set referential integrity to:
[a] check each relationship in the database.
[b] avoid orphaned records.
[c] join fields of those records that match exactly.
[d] link common fields in separate tables.

Circle **T** if the statement is true or **F** if the statement is false.

T   F   1. A relationship is the linking of two tables by a common field.

T   F   2. The most common relationship is a many-to-many relationship.

T   F   3. Referential integrity checks the accuracy of the data you enter.

T   F   4. Referential integrity does not let you delete a record in the primary table that has a related record.

T   F   5. You can create a relationship using more than one field from a table.

T   F   6. A foreign key uniquely identifies a row in a table.

chapter four

T F   7. By default, you enforce referential integrity when you create a relationship.

T F   8. In a one-to-one relationship, a record in one table is related to exactly one record in another table.

T F   9. To create a relationship between tables, you must close them.

T F   10. In a one-to-many relationship, one student record may be related to many class records.

Skills Review

Exercise 1 C

1. Create a new database from the *mdbFanTours4-* database located on the Data Disk.

2. Open the Relationships window and add the tblEmployees, tblEventDetails, tblEvents, tblVCategories, and tblVendors tables to the relationship. Close the Show Table dialog box.

3. Examine the tblEvents and tblEventDetails tables. Determine which fields you can use to establish a relationship.

4. Relate the tblEvents and tblEventDetails tables based on the EventID field.

5. Save and close the Relationships window, and then close the database.

Exercise 2 C

1. Open the *mdbFanTours4-1* database you created in Exercise 1.

2. Open the Relationships window, and examine the relationship between the tblEvents and tblEventDetails tables.

3. Enforce referential integrity between the tables.

4. Save and close the Relationships window, and then close the database.

Exercise 3 C

1. Open the *mdbFanTours4-1* database you modified in Exercise 2.

2. Open the Relationships window, and examine the fields in the tblEmployees and tblEventDetails tables.

3. Set a one-to-many relationship between the EmployeeID field in the tblEmployees table and the StaffID field in the tblEventDetails table.

4. Enforce referential integrity between the tables.

5. Save and close the Relationships window, and then close the database.

Exercise 4 C

1. Open *the mdbFanTours4-1* database you modified in Exercise 3.

2. Open the Relationships window, and then examine the fields in the tblVendors and tblEventDetails tables.

3. Set a one-to-many relationship between the tblVendors and tblEventDetails tables using the VendorID field.

4. Enforce referential integrity for the relationship between the tblVendors and tblEventDetails table.

5. Save and close the Relationships window, and then close the database.

Exercise 5   C

1. Open the *mdbFanTours4-1* database you modified in Exercise 4.

2. Open the Relationships window, and then examine the fields in the tblVendors and tblVCategories tables.

3. Set a one-to-many relationship between the tblVendors and tblVCategories tables using the VendorCatID and VendorType fields.

4. Enforce referential integrity.

5. Save and close the Relationships window, and then close the database.

Exercise 6

1. Open the *mdbFanTours4-1* database you modified in Exercise 5.

2. Open the tblEventDetails table in Datasheet view.

3. Several fields in this table are used as foreign keys for other tables. List each field and describe the matching primary table and primary key. Put your answer in a Word document.

4. Close the table, and then close the database.

Exercise 7

1. Open the *mdbFanTours4-1* database you modified in Exercise 6.

2. Open the tblEvents table in Datasheet view. Note that the sixth record describes the Indy 500 automobile race.

3. Select the Indy 500 record, and press the DELETE key to delete this record.

4. Describe the result of deleting this record. Put your answer in a Word document.

5. Close the tblEvents table, and then close the database.

Exercise 8

1. Open the *mdbFanTours4-1* database you modified in Exercise 7.

2. Open the tblEventDetails table in Datasheet view, and select record 11, Indy 500 test record.

3. Delete record 11, which is related to Event 6, the Indy 500.

4. Explain why can you delete *this* record but cannot delete record 6 from tblEvents. Put your answer in a Word document, print the document, and then save and close the document.

5. Close the tblEventDetails table, and then close the database.

chapter four

Case Projects

Project 1 C

Open the *mdbFanTours4-2* database located on the Data Disk. There is a many-to-many relationship between the tblEvents and tblVendors tables. How is this implemented in the Fan Tours database? Save your answer in a Word document. Use the Show Table dialog box to add the remaining tables to the Relationships window, and see if any other relationships are appropriate in this database. Close the database.

Project 2 C

Open the *mdbFanTours4-2* database you modified in Project 1. Add four event-detail records about the Super Bowl tour, which is event 3, using real or fictional data values. Describe your actions. Save your answer in a Word document. Close the database.

Project 3 C

Open the *mdbFanTours4-2* database you modified in Project 2. Consider the event-details records that you entered in Project 2. Which fields are the foreign keys? How could you simplify entering valid data for the foreign key fields in the tblEventDetails table? Save your answer in a Word document. Close the database.

Project 4 C

Open the *mdbFanTours4-2* database from Project 3. You know that Access queries use the relationships established in the Relationships window to link tables together. Open the qryEventDetails query in the database, and print the resulting datasheet. In Query Design view, determine which tables this query involves. Save your answer in a Word document. Close the database.

Project 5 C

Open the *mdbFanTours4-2* database you modified in Project 4. Print the Relationships window. What other relationships should you establish for this database? Should you establish referential integrity for any other relationships? Save your answers in a Word document. Close the database.

Project 6 C

Project 6 requires the Northwind sample database, which is installed with the complete installation of Access. If you are not working with the complete installation, you may need to install the database.

Use the Sample <u>D</u>atabases command on the <u>H</u>elp menu to open the Northwind sample database packaged with Access. Close the welcome screen and open the Relationships window. Prepare a list of the relationships depicted in this database, and describe the type of relationship for each join. Save your work in a Word document. Close the database.

Project 7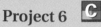

Connect to the Internet and search the Web for an online computer dictionary or encyclopedia. Find definitions for terms used in this chapter, such as *referential integrity*, *relationships*, *one-to-many relationship*, and *joins*. For each term, print at least two definitions or explanations. Save your work in a Word document.

Project 8

Using the Office on the <u>W</u>eb command on the <u>H</u>elp menu, connect to the Microsoft Web site and look for tips and basic information about defining relationships in Access. Print at least two Web pages.

Creating and Modifying Basic Queries

Chapter Overview

Like a filter, a query uses criteria you specify to select and display records. However, a filter works with one table, but a query can work with many tables. It also can perform actions on your data, such as updating or deleting records. In this chapter, you create a simple query, modify the query, and then print the query results.

LEARNING OBJECTIVES

- ▷ Create a multi-table select query
- ▷ Specify query criteria
- ▷ Modify a multi-table select query
- ▷ Add a calculated field to the query
- ▷ Print query results

Case profile

An upcoming meeting in the admissions office concerns OLU's enrollment. One admissions counselor, Juanita Chavez, has been asked to prepare a presentation showing enrollment data. Although the OLU database contains all the information Juanita needs for her presentation, she is unsure how to locate it quickly. She asks you to help her find the information she needs. To do this, you create queries.

chapter
five
5

C 5.a Creating a Multi-Table Select Query

A **query** is a question you ask about the data stored in your tables or a request you make to perform an action on the data, such as to calculate the sum of records. You can create different types of queries. The most common is the **select query**, which retrieves data from one or more tables using criteria you specify and then displays records in a datasheet in the order you want. An **action query** makes changes in the database to records that meet the criteria you specify. There are four types of action queries. A **make-table query** places records that meet the criteria in a new table. An **append query** adds the records that meet the criteria to an existing table in the database. An **update query** changes one or more fields for all records that meet the criteria. A **delete query** permanently deletes the records that meet the criteria.

Juanita asks you to identify the students majoring in Management Information Systems. To find this data, you create a select query. You can use the Query Wizard to create a simple query, such as a select query. A select query can select records that meet Juanita's request to see majors that attract the most students. An OLU staff member established relationships for most—but not all—tables in the OLU database. Access automatically recognizes these relationships when you add the tables to the query design; that is, you need not re-establish them. To create a simple query using the Query Wizard:

Step 1	**Create**	a copy of the *mdbOnlineU5-* database located on your Data Disk
Step 2	**Click**	Queries on the Objects bar
Step 3	**Double-click**	Create query by using wizard to open the Simple Query Wizard
Step 4	**Click**	Table: tblStudents in the Tables/Queries list box
Step 5	**Move**	the FName, LName, and ProgramCode fields from the Available Fields: list box to the Selected Fields: list box

The tblStudents table includes part of the information you want to see—student names and program codes. Because Juanita wants to see the program name as well as student information, include a field from the tblPrograms table in the query.

| Step 6 | **Click** | Table: tblPrograms in the Tables/Queries list box |
| Step 7 | **Move** | the ProgramName field from the Available Fields: list box to the Selected Fields: list box |

Step 8	**Click**	<u>N</u>ext >
Step 9	**Key**	qryStudentMajors as the query title
Step 10	**Click**	Finish to accept the default option to open the query to view information

The Query Wizard automatically saves the query under the name you provide. The query datasheet holds 54 records, one per student. Access inserted the ProgramName field from the tblPrograms table that corresponds to the ProgramCode field in the tblStudents table.

| Step 11 | **Leave** | the Query window open |

You see all the records the query selected from the tblStudents and tblPrograms tables. However, for each record, you see only the FName, LName, ProgramCode, and ProgramName fields. The records appear in alphabetical order by major. The relationship between the tblPrograms and tblStudents tables causes the records in the query to appear in order by the ProgramName, the primary key of the primary table.

5.b Specifying Query Criteria C

If you do not provide criteria, Access retrieves all records for the query's datasheet. By specifying conditions for fields in the query, you restrict the results of the query to matching records. In addition to student name and major, Juanita wants to know the name of students' academic advisors. You can provide this information by adding a field to the query.

Adding Fields

After you create a query, you can add only those fields whose data you want to view, set criteria for, group by, update, or sort. Because Juanita wants to see the academic advisors' names, you add the FName and LName fields from the tblInstructors table to the qryStudentMajors query. To add fields from other tables to an existing query:

Step 1	**Switch to**	Design view
Step 2	**Click**	the Show Table button on the Query Design toolbar
Step 3	**Double-click**	tblInstructors in the Show Table dialog box to add this table to the query design

MENU TIP

You can save a query with a new name by using the Save <u>A</u>s command on the <u>F</u>ile menu.

QUICK TIP

You can create a new query with multiple criteria using the Query Wizard, or you can modify an existing query to include additional criteria, or additional fields and criteria.

chapter
five

Step 4	*Click*	<u>C</u>lose to close the Show Table window
Step 5	*Drag*	the FName field from the tblInstructors table to the first row of the blank column that is to the right of the ProgramName column in the design grid in the bottom half of the Select Query window
Step 6	*Follow*	Step 5 to move LName from the tblInstructors table to the design grid

Notice that all Show box fields are checked. Because the relationship between the tblInstructors and tblStudents tables was not established earlier, you must add it to the query design. You need to establish the join relationship before you can access fields from both tables in the query.

Joining Tables in a Query

If you create a relationship in the Access Relationships window, Access automatically recognizes that relationship whenever you add tables to a query design or use the Query Wizard while still in that same database. Although you can join tables and create a relationship within the query in the same manner as you did in the Relationships window, that relationship is only available within the query. If you reuse the tables in another query, you need to recreate the relationship. Creating the relationship in the Relationships window before building queries saves time. To join tables within the Query Design window:

Step 1	*Verify*	that the qryStudentMajors query is open in Design view
Step 2	*Scroll*	the tblStudents table in the top pane until you see the AdvisorID field
Step 3	*Drag*	the InstID field in the tblInstructors table to the AdvisorID field in the tblStudents table

Access creates a one-to-many relationship between the tblInstructors and tblStudents tables.

Running a Query

While you develop a query, it is customary to test it by running the query manually. When a select query runs, no changes to the database take place. However, when an action query runs, changes to the database do occur. As you develop the criteria and polish the query's design, you can run the query as often as you wish.

The query runs automatically when you use it as a data source for another query, a form, or a report. In other words, when you open a form or print a report based on a query, Access runs the query first in the background and saves the results in a temporary datasheet. Then Access uses records from that datasheet for the form or report.

To run the query from Query Design view:

Step 1	*Click*	the Run button 🔲 on the Query Design toolbar

Access creates a datasheet that contains the records from the query that match the specified criteria. Some columns are not wide enough to display all information or the column name. To widen the columns:

Step 1	*Position*	the mouse pointer at the right border of the first column, until it changes to a double-headed arrow
Step 2	*Double-click*	the column border to widen the column to display the entire column header or the data in the widest cell
Step 3	*Follow*	Steps 1 and 2 for the tblStudents.LName, tblInstructors.FName, and tblInstructorsLName fields

Notice that Access changed the column names for the FName and LName student fields, because you added fields with the same names from the tblInstructors table.

Setting Criteria

Criteria are restrictions you place on a query to identify the records you want to work with. You set criteria when you want to refine your queries to show specific information. For example, to create a list of OLU students, majoring in Management Information Systems you set one criterion in the Criteria row of the design grid to limit the records the query retrieves to those with the ProgramCode 075.

The **design grid** shows the fields for your query, sorting instructions, and criteria. You set criteria in the query's design grid by entering an expression in the Criteria row for a field. An **expression** in a query usually combines field names, symbols, values, words, and operators that indicate what action to take. An expression can be as simple as one word or more complex.

You can use **comparison criteria** to find records by comparing their values. For example, you can find instructors hired before January 1, 2001 or courses with lab fees of more than $5. Use **OR** or **AND** to show records based on multiple criteria, such as those students whose major is Management Information Systems or Business Administration (using the OR operator) or those who major in Management Information Systems and share a particular academic advisor (using the AND operator). You can also use **NULL** to retrieve records that have a field with no value, such as a record of a student without a major. Use **wildcard characters** to search for text patterns in your records, such as fields containing words that start with *Mac*.

CAUTION TIP

If you use the Query Wizard to create a query with more than one table, each table used must be related to at least one other table. If the tables are not related, Access cannot build an accurate query. You can relate tables in the Relationships window or in the Query Design window.

QUICK TIP

There are several ways to run a query manually. In Query Design view, you can switch to Datasheet view by clicking the Datasheet View button, click the Run button on the Query Design toolbar, or use the Run command on the Query menu. From the Database window, you can select the query and click the Open button in the Database window or right-click the query and click Open on the shortcut menu.

chapter
five

Setting Comparison Criteria

Use comparison criteria when you want to retrieve records with values greater than, greater than or equal to, less than, less than or equal to, or between values you specify. Table 5-1 provides comparison examples, showing you what criteria to enter to find certain dates.

TABLE 5-1
Date Comparison
Expressions

Enter	For This Result
8/5/03	The exact date
<8/5/03	Before 8/5/03
>8/5/03	After 8/5/03
>=8/5/03	On or after 8/5/03
<=8/5/03	On or before 8/5/03
Not <8/5/03	Not before 8/5/03
Not >8/5/03	Not after 8/5/03

Juanita now wants information on students with a Management Information Systems major, identified by ProgramCode 075. You need to set the criteria accordingly. To set criteria for a query:

Step 1	*Switch to*	Design view
Step 2	*Click*	in the Criteria: row for the ProgramCode field
Step 3	*Key*	075
Step 4	*Press*	the ENTER key to complete the entry

You selected all records with ProgramCode 075. Your screen should look similar to Figure 5-1. Notice that Access changed your criterion to "075" because ProgramCode is a text field that is enclosed in quotes.

FIGURE 5-1
Query Design Grid
with Criteria

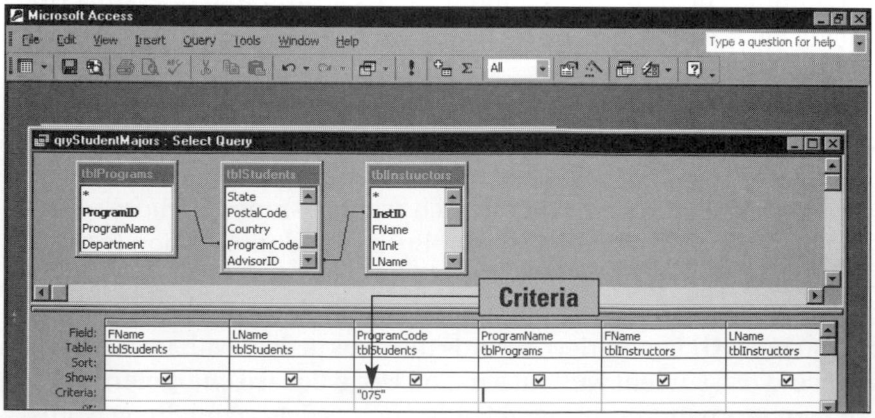

Step 5	***Switch to***	Datasheet view to see the query results
Step 6	***Observe***	that 12 records match the criteria—Management Information Systems majors

Specifying Criteria in Multiple Fields

Use the AND expression when you want to select records to which both conditions apply. Use OR when you want to select records that meet either condition. In general, OR expands your selection—you choose records that contain one value or another. AND narrows your selection—you choose only those records that contain both values.

Juanita wants to find all the students majoring in Business Administration or Accounting. Use the OR criteria because you want to select records that contain the ProgramCode field 025 or 020. Start by removing the criterion that you already applied. To clear current criterion:

Step 1	***Switch to***	Design view
Step 2	***Select***	"075" in the ProgramCode Criteria: text box
Step 3	***Press***	the DELETE key

You're ready to create new criteria to retrieve records based on the ProgramCode field. To expand a query selection with an OR expression:

Step 1	***Click***	in the Criteria: row of the ProgramCode field, if necessary
Step 2	***Key***	020 or 025 (key both numbers and the word)
Step 3	***Press***	the ENTER key

Access formats the criteria to build an expression—it includes quotation marks around "025" and "020" after you press the TAB or ENTER key. Your screen should look similar to Figure 5-2.

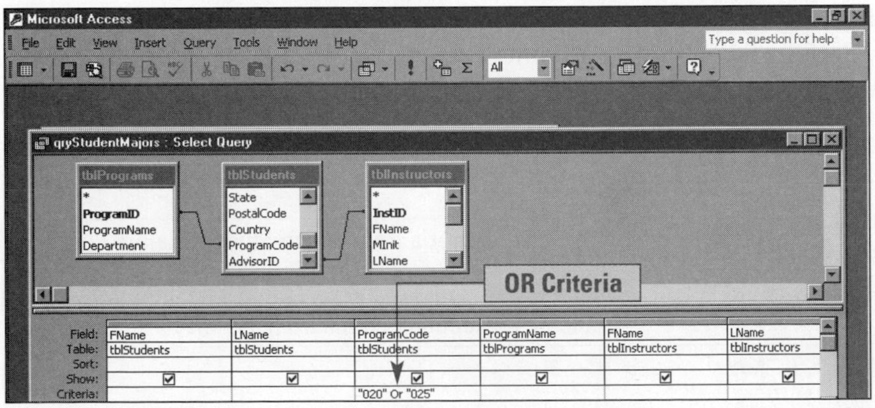

FIGURE 5-2
OR Criteria in Query Design Grid

CAUTION TIP

Double-clicking the "075" criterion does not select the quotation marks, so you cannot delete the entire expression this way.

QUICK TIP

Instead of keying the OR expression in the Criteria: row, you can key the first criterion in the Criteria: row and key the second criterion in the "or:" row of the design grid.

chapter five

Step 4	*Run*	the query

Step 5	*Observe*	the 12 students with Business Administration or Accounting majors

Using the NULL Criterion

Use the NULL criterion when you want to find records with fields that contain no values. You can set a NULL criterion to find students who have no e-mail address in the database. Before you set a NULL criterion, clear all criteria from the qryStudentMajors query. Then add the EmailAddress field to the query. To add the EmailAddress field:

Step 1	*Switch to*	Design view
Step 2	*Clear*	the current criteria by using the previous method
Step 3	*Double-click*	the EmailAddress field in the tblStudents table to add the field at the end of the query grid
Step 4	*Click*	in the Criteria: row of the EmailAddress field (scroll right to view the field)
Step 5	*Key*	Is Null
Step 6	*Run*	the query
Step 7	*Observe*	the list of two students whose records have no EmailAddress value

The comparison AND, OR, and NULL criteria retrieve records based on the complete information in a record. You use wildcards to retrieve records by specifying only partial information.

Using Wildcards in Queries

Use wildcard characters in query criteria to search for records if you only know part of the information or if you want to find data patterns. A wildcard symbol (*) stands for one or more unknown characters. With a wildcard character, you can, for example, search for students whose names begin with *Mac* or end in *son*. Juanita wants to contact a student but can only recall that the first letter in his last name is *H*. You can use a wildcard to find his record. To use wildcards in a query:

Step 1	*Switch to*	Design view
Step 2	*Clear*	the current criteria from the qryStudentMajors query
Step 3	*Click*	in the Criteria: row of the LName field in the tblStudents table in the second column from the left
Step 4	*Key*	H*

CAUTION TIP

If you use the AND criteria, you do not retrieve any records— no record includes both 025 and 020 in its ProgramCode field.

QUICK TIP

If you want to list students who have an EmailAddress, use the NOT NULL criterion, which has the opposite effect of the IS NULL criterion.

Step 5	Press	the ENTER key to complete the expression
Step 6	Observe	that Access changes the wildcard expression to Like "H*"
Step 7	Run	the query
Step 8	Observe	the two records of students whose last names start with H

5.c Modifying a Multi-Table Select Query

C

Once you create a select query, you can then modify it so that it produces different information in Datasheet view.

Sorting Records in a Query

You already created the qryStudentMajors query to generate a subset of the data in your database. This subset lists students, their majors, and their academic advisors. You now can sort the list alphabetically by major to see which programs attract the most students. To sort the records in a query datasheet:

Step 1	Switch to	Design view
Step 2	Clear	the criteria in the query grid for the LName field in the tblStudents table
Step 3	Run	the query
Step 4	Click	in the ProgramName column in the datasheet
Step 5	Click	the Sort Ascending button 🔼 on the Query Datasheet toolbar

Your screen should look similar to Figure 5-3.

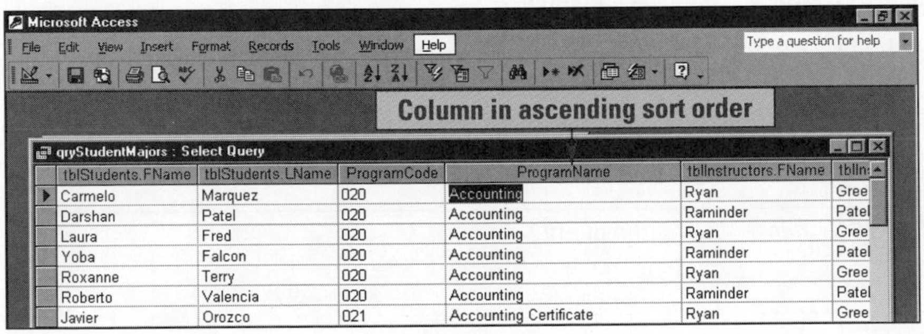

FIGURE 5-3
Sorted Query Datasheet

chapter
five

You can quickly scan the list to see which majors attract the most students. Juanita wants to see which students in which majors are generating the most demand. To see the information Juanita needs, you sort on multiple fields.

To sort on more than one field, you first arrange the sort fields in the design grid in the order you want the sort performed. Access sorts on the leftmost field first, then on the next field to the right, and so on. To see an alphabetical list of students in each major, sort first on ProgramCode, then on student's LName. To sort on multiple fields in a query:

Step 1	**Switch to**	Design view
Step 2	**Click**	the selection bar above the ProgramCode field to select the ProgramCode field
Step 3	**Drag**	the selection bar above the ProgramCode field to the left of the FName field from tblStudents

Your screen should look similar to Figure 5-4.

FIGURE 5-4
Reordered Query Grid

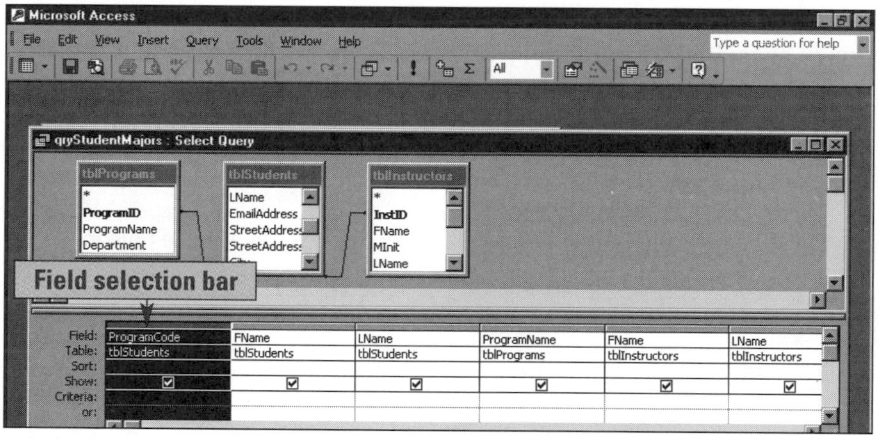

Step 4	**Click**	the Sort row for the ProgramCode field
Step 5	**Click**	the list arrow
Step 6	**Click**	Ascending
Step 7	**Click**	the Sort row for the LName field from the tblStudents table
Step 8	**Click**	the list arrow
Step 9	**Click**	Ascending
Step 10	**Run**	the query

Removing Fields from a Query

If your query shows information you don't need, you can remove a field. When you remove a field, you only remove it from the query. You do not delete the field or its data from the table on which your query is based. Juanita wants you to remove the EmailAddress field from the query. To delete a field from a query:

Step 1	*Switch to*	Design view
Step 2	*Click*	the selection bar above the EmailAddress field (you may need to scroll)
Step 3	*Press*	the DELETE key

You deleted the EmailAddress field from the query. Now that you created a query to find exactly the information Juanita needs, you save it.

Saving the Query

Access begins to save the query when you close the Query window. You then see the query name in the Queries list in the Database window. To save and close the query:

Step 1	*Click*	the Close button ⊠ on the Select Query window title bar
Step 2	*Click*	Yes to save the query, if prompted

5.d Adding a Calculated Field to a Select Query

You can add a calculated field to the query that performs some sort of calculation, such as determining the cost of a class based upon the number of credit hours and lab fee. You also can calculate with a date to determine, for example, how long a particular instructor has worked for Online University. To add a calculated field by creating a new query in Design view:

Step 1	*Double-click*	Create query in Design view in the Queries window
Step 2	*Double-click*	tblInstructors in the Show Table dialog box to add it to the Queries window
Step 3	*Close*	the Show Table dialog box

chapter
five

CAUTION TIP

You cannot create a calculated field in a table.

Step 4	*Key*	FName&" "&LName in the Field row of the first column
Step 5	*Press*	the ENTER key to complete the entry

Access inserts the following expression: Expr1:[FName]&" "&[LName]. The & (ampersand) is the **concatenation operator** that merges two text strings into one character string.

Step 6	*Double-click*	the first column's right border to widen the column to see the expression
Step 7	*Double-click*	DeptID in tblInstructors in the top pane
Step 8	*Double-click*	HireDate in tblInstructors in the top pane

Your screen should look similar to Figure 5-5.

FIGURE 5-5
Calculated Field in Query Grid

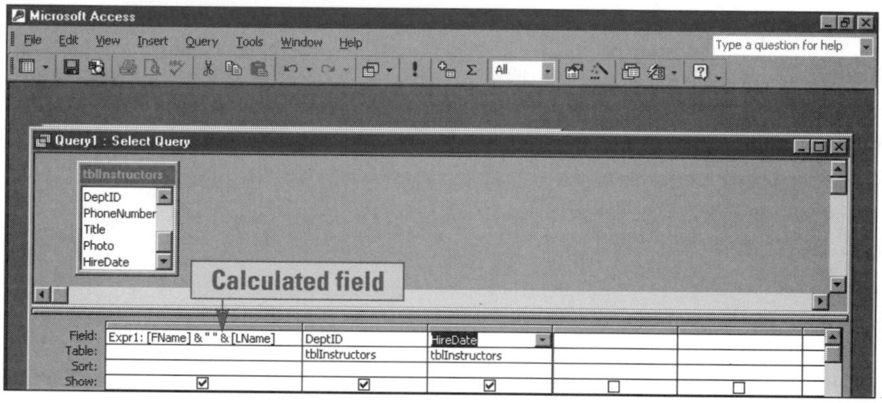

Before you run the query, clean up the calculated field by naming it. This makes it easier to recognize the data in this column. Select the Expr1 label, and key the new label over it.

Step 9	*Double-click*	the "Expr1" text in the field column to select it
Step 10	*Key*	Instructor
Step 11	*Run*	the query

Access displays three fields—Instructor, DeptID, and HireDate—in the query datasheet. Juanita wants to show those instructors hired on or after January 1, 2001.

Step 12	*Switch to*	Design view to add criteria to this query

Step 13	*Click*	in the Criteria row beneath the HireDate column
Step 14	*Key*	>=1/1/2001
Step 15	*Run*	the query

Five records qualify. Your screen should look similar to Figure 5-6.

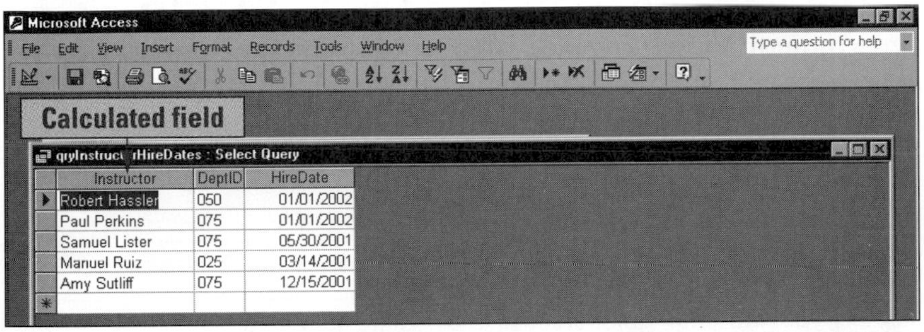

FIGURE 5-6
Query Datasheet for
Calculated Field

Finally, you save and close this query. To save and close the query:

Step 1	*Click*	the Save button 🖫 on the Query Datasheet toolbar
Step 2	*Key*	qryInstructorHireDates as the name
Step 3	*Click*	OK
Step 4	*Close*	the query

5.e Printing Query Results

The query results print like a datasheet—Access prints the query data in a table, similar to the one you see on your screen. Juanita wants to print the results of the qryStudentMajors query, so that she can show the data to her colleagues. If the data changed since the last time you ran the query, Access automatically updates the query datasheet when you open the query. To print the query results:

Step 1	*Double-click*	qryStudentMajors in the Database window
Step 2	*Click*	File
Step 3	*Click*	Print

The Print dialog box opens. You can select print options, such as the number of copies. Juanita wants to print all records, so you accept the defaults in the dialog box.

QUICK TIP

To save time, you can print the results of a query that meet the criteria rather than printing *all* records in a large table.

You can print certain records by selecting the records in the datasheet first, and then clicking the Selected Records option button in the Print dialog box.

Step 4	*Click*	OK
Step 5	*Close*	the query

Juanita knows that applying some formatting to query datasheets can improve their printed appearance.

Formatting the Results for Printing

One common formatting task is adjusting column widths. To do so, you drag the column border left or right to display the right amount of information. You also can adjust the row height to display the fields' full contents. To create a query for courses and adjust cell size:

Step 1	*Double-click*	Create query in Design view
Step 2	*Double-click*	tblCourses to add it to the query grid
Step 3	*Close*	the Show Table dialog box

Access displays the tblCourses table in the top portion of the Query Design window. Notice the asterisk (*) above the primary key field. The * is the shorthand notation for all fields. It helps you quickly select all fields. Although this is useful, when you add fields to the query with *, the individual fields do not appear in Query Design view. Thus, you cannot provide criteria or sort instructions for those fields.

Step 4	*Drag*	the asterisk (*) from the tblCourses table to the first column in the query grid

Access displays tblCourses.* in the Field row of query grid to signify all fields. Your screen should look similar to Figure 5-7. When you run the query, each field appears in the datasheet.

MOUSE TIP

Like fields in a table, fields in a query have properties. You can right-click the field, click Properties, and then assign a format or an input mask to the field.

QUICK TIP

To establish criteria for these fields, add them to the query grid and assign criteria, but uncheck the Show: box for each field so that they don't appear twice.

FIGURE 5-7
Design Grid for All Fields Query

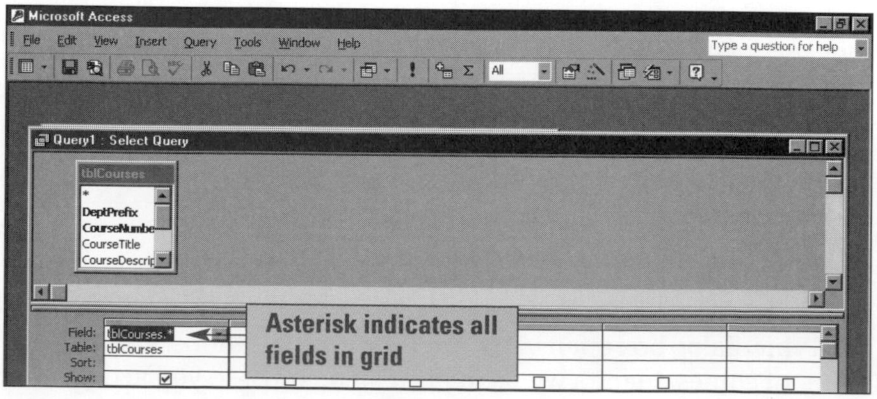

Step 5	*Run*	the query

To improve readability, you can widen columns and change row height.

Step 6	*Point to*	the border between the CourseDescription and Credits columns, until the mouse pointer changes to a two-headed (horizontal) arrow
Step 7	*Drag*	the CourseDescription column to the right until it is approximately 3 inches wide
Step 8	*Point to*	the border between the first and second row selectors, until the mouse pointer changes to a two-headed (vertical) arrow
Step 9	*Drag*	the row border down until the row is about four times as tall as it was originally, so it can hold up to four rows of information

Your screen should look similar to Figure 5-8.

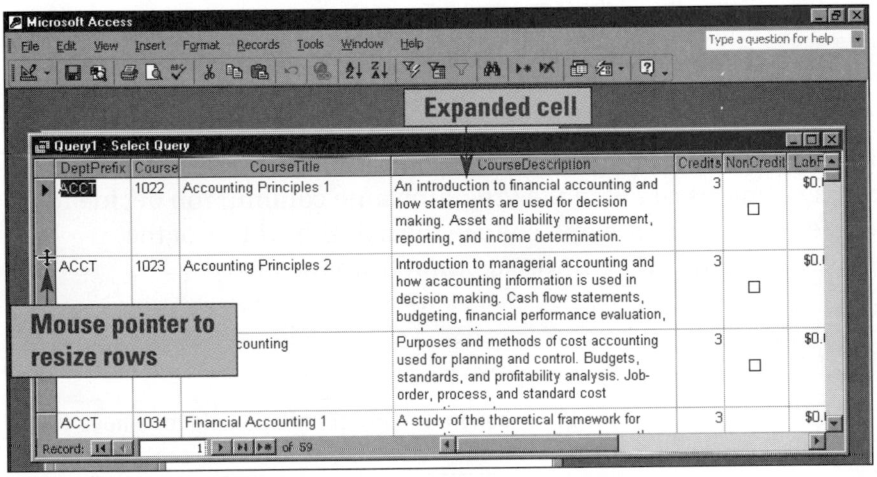

FIGURE 5-8
Reformatted Query Datasheet

Step 10	*Save*	the query as qryCourses and close it

Juanita knows what to do with the qryStudentMajors query. Several columns are too wide and need renaming. To adjust the columns:

Step 1	*Open*	qryStudentMajors in Design view
Step 2	*Right-click*	the FName field for tblStudents in the second column

chapter
five

Step 3	*Click*	Properties

Access opens the Field Properties dialog box for this field in the query. You want to give this column a new name using the Caption property.

Step 4	*Click*	the Caption text box on the General tab in the Field Properties dialog box
Step 5	*Key*	First Name
Step 6	*Run*	the query
Step 7	*Switch to*	Design view
Step 8	*Click*	the LName field in the third column of the lower pane
Step 9	*Click*	the Caption text box
Step 10	*Key*	Last Name
Step 11	*Follow*	Steps 9 and 10 for the advisor's FName and LName fields, naming them Adv First Name and Adv Last Name
Step 12	*Close*	the Properties dialog box
Step 13	*Run*	the query

Notice that some columns are too wide and the ProgramCode column is not necessary with the ProgramName column. You decide to remove the first column and change the column widths of the renamed columns. To remove a column from the query:

Step 1	*Switch to*	Design view
Step 2	*Click*	the Show box for the ProgramCode field to remove the check mark that removes this field from the query
Step 3	*Run*	the query
Step 4	*Double-click*	the border between the First Name and Last Name columns to resize the first column
Step 5	*Double-click*	the border between the Last Name and ProgramName columns to resize the second column
Step 6	*Observe*	that all columns fit on the screen
Step 7	*Save*	the query and close it
Step 8	*Close*	the database

Juanita will use the qryStudentMajors query results in her presentation.

Summary

▶ A query is a question you ask about the data stored in your tables or a request you make to perform a calculation on the data, such as restricting records to a certain date. A query can find and filter records in a number of tables.

▶ A select query, the most common query, retrieves data from one or more tables using criteria you specify and then displays the data in the order you want.

▶ You can use the Query Wizard to create a simple select query.

▶ Once you run a query to generate a subset of the data in your database, you can sort the list in ascending or descending order. To sort on more than one field, first arrange the fields in the design grid in the order you want to perform the sort. Access sorts the leftmost sort field first, then the next sort field to the right, and so on.

▶ Access can save a query when you close the Queries window. You then see the query name in the Queries list in the Database window.

▶ You can run a query at any time by opening it, which displays the results in Datasheet view. If the underlying data changed since the last time you ran the query, the query datasheet shows the latest results.

▶ You can modify an existing query to include additional criteria by adding other fields. Add only those fields whose data you want to view, set criteria on, group by, update, or sort.

▶ Criteria are restrictions you place on a query to identify the records you want to work with. Set criteria when you want to refine your queries to show specific information.

▶ You set criteria in the query's design grid by entering expressions in the Criteria row for a field. An expression in a query combines field names, symbols, values, words, and operators that indicate what action to take. An expression can be as simple as one word or more complex.

▶ You can use comparison criteria to find records by comparing their values.

▶ Use AND or OR to show records based on multiple criteria. In general, OR expands your selection—you choose records that contain one value or another. AND narrows your selection—you choose only those records that contain both values.

▶ You can use IS NULL to retrieve records that have fields with no values.

chapter five

► Use wildcards to search for text patterns in your records or to find values that contain certain characters. A wildcard symbol (*) stands for unknown characters.

► The & concatenation operator can merge two text strings into one text string.

► The query results print like a datasheet—Access prints the query data in a table, similar to the one you see on your screen when viewing a query in Datasheet view.

► If your query shows information you don't need, you can remove a field. When you do, you only remove it from the query. You do not delete the field or its data from the table that is the basis of your query.

Commands Review

Action	Menu Bar	Shortcut Menu	Toolbar	Task Pane	Keyboard
Sort a query in ascending order	Records, Sort, Ascending	Sort Ascending			ALT + R, S, A
Sort a query in descending order	Records, Sort, Descending	Sort Descending			ALT + R, S, D
Add a table to a query	Query, Show Table	Show Table			ALT + Q, H
Run a query	Query, Run View, Datasheet View	Datasheet View			ALT + Q, R ALT + V, S
Open a query in Design view	View, Design View	Query Design			ALT + V, D
Print a query datasheet	File, Print				ALT + F, P CTRL + P

Concepts Review

SCANS

Circle the correct answer.

1. A select query is a:
[a] way to display related records from one or more tables.
[b] the only type of query that Access provides.
[c] tool that selects data and writes it to an Access table.
[d] tool that deletes information from your database.

2. Use a select query to:
[a] update records that match the criteria.
[b] accept data.

[c] extract information from one or more tables.
[d] insert information in a table.

3. Saving a query is:
[a] part of backing up your data.
[b] necessary if you want to run the query in the future.
[c] required before printing.
[d] something Access does automatically when you close the query.

4. The Query Wizard:
  [a] requires that tables be related if more than one is used.
  [b] performs the same function as a Table Wizard.
  [c] checks your query for errors.
  [d] analyzes your data before performing a query.

5. To see the results of a query:
  [a] switch to Datasheet view.
  [b] click the Results button.
  [c] sort or filter it first.
  [d] click the Close button.

6. Add fields to a query when you want to:
  [a] find records by comparing values.
  [b] view, set criteria on, or sort the data in the fields.
  [c] modify the table the fields come from.
  [d] quickly scan the data in the fields.

7. When you drag the * field to the query grid:
  [a] an asterisk appears in the query datasheet.
  [b] you multiply two adjacent number fields.
  [c] anything matches in that field.
  [d] you place all fields in the query datasheet.

8. To join two tables in a query:
  [a] use the Join command.
  [b] the tables must have identical field names.
  [c] place them side-by-side in the Query Design window.
  [d] relate the appropriate field names in the table area by dragging them together.

9. Use the OR criteria when you want to:
  [a] narrow your selection.
  [b] expand your selection.
  [c] know a field's entire name.
  [d] find records with a field that does not contain a value.

10. When you sort records in the query design grid:
  [a] Access sorts the leftmost sort column first.
  [b] Access also sorts the records in the underlying tables in the same way.
  [c] Access sorts the leftmost sort column last.
  [d] you cannot sort records in the query datasheet.

Circle **T** if the statement is true or **F** if the statement is false.

T F 1. You can expand the size of rows and columns to display data better.

T F 2. A query lets you view or enter data in one table while working in another related table.

T F 3. The criteria *H includes records in which the field begins with *H*.

T F 4. You can use comparison criteria to find records by comparing their values.

T F 5. A query runs automatically when you open the report for which the query is the data source.

T F 6. Use the IS NULL criterion to enter zero values in your tables.

T F 7. Access inserts quotation marks around text you enter unless the text is a key word or a field name.

T F 8. A select query does not change any values in the database.

T F 9. You can use the AND expression to find students majoring in Nursing or Accounting, for example.

T F 10. A query can display records from one or more tables.

chapter five

Skills Review

SCANS

Exercise 1 [C]

1. Create the *mdbFanTours5-1* database from the *mdbFanTours5-* database located on the Data Disk.

2. Use the Query Wizard to create a simple select query that selects the EventName, EventDate, and Location fields from the tblEvents table; DetailName from the tblEventDetails table; and VendorName from the tblVendors table.

3. Save the query as "qryEventDetails."

4. Print a copy of the query datasheet.

5. Close the query and the database.

Exercise 2 [C]

1. Open the *mdbFanTours5-1* database you created in Exercise 1.

2. Run the qryEventDetails query you created in Exercise 1.

3. Sort the records alphabetically (ascending) by vendor name.

4. Print a copy of the query datasheet.

5. Save and close the query, and close the database.

Exercise 3 [C]

1. Open the *mdbFanTours5-1* database you modified in Exercise 2.

2. Open in Design view the qryEventDetails query you modified in Exercise 2.

3. Add the LastName field from the tblEmployees table to the query.

4. Run the query.

5. Print a copy of the query datasheet.

6. Save and close the query, and close the database.

Exercise 4 [C]

1. Open the *mdbFanTours5-1* database you modified in Exercise 3.

2. Create a query in Design view that uses these fields from the tblProspects table: FName, LName, ContactType, and ContactDate.

3. Use the IS NULL expression to retrieve records of prospects whose ContactType is missing.

4. Run the query.

5. Save the query as "qryProspects."

6. Print a copy of the query datasheet.

7. Close the query and the database.

Exercise 5 [C]

1. Open the *mdbFanTours5-1* database you modified in Exercise 4.

2. Open in Design view the qryProspects query you created in Exercise 4.

3. Clear all current criteria.

4. Use the OR criteria to retrieve records where the ContactType is E or W.

5. Run the query.

6. Print a copy of the query datasheet.

7. Save and close the query, and close the database.

Exercise 6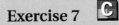

1. Open the *mdbFanTours5-1* database you modified in Exercise 5.

2. Open in Design view the qryProspects query you modified in Exercise 5.

3. Clear all current criteria.

4. Create a calculated field that concatenates the first and last name fields and leaves a space between them. Change the name of the expression to *Prospect*.

5. Remove the check from the Show box for the FName and LName fields, so these fields don't appear in the query datasheet. The calculated field should appear first.

6. Run the query.

7. Widen the Prospect column, and then print a copy of the query datasheet.

8. Save and close the query, and close the database.

Exercise 7 C

1. Open the *mdbFanTours5-1* database you modified in Exercise 6.

2. Open in Design view the qryProspects query you modified in Exercise 6.

3. Add the StreetAddress, City, State, and PostalCode fields. Remove the ContactType field.

4. Sort the query in ascending order by postal code.

5. Run the query. Print a copy of the query datasheet.

6. Using the Save As command on the File menu, save the query as "qryProspectsZipOrder."

7. Close the query and the database.

Exercise 8 C

1. Open the *mdbFanTours5-1* database you modified in Exercise 7.

2. Use the Simple Query Wizard to create a new query called "qryVendorCategories."

3. Add the tblVCategories and tblVendors tables to the query grid.

4. Add the following fields: VendorCategory, VendorName, and Vendor Contact.

5. Sort first by VendorCategory and then by Vendor Name, both in ascending order.

6. Run the query.

7. Save, print, and close the query, and then close the database.

chapter five

Case Projects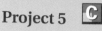

Project 1 C

Open the *mdbFanTours5-2* database located on the Data Disk. Catherine Emmen needs a list of tours that customers ordered. Create a query in the *mdbFanTours5-2* database called "qryTours" that shows the CustID, EventID, DateRegistered, FName, LName, Description, and EventCost fields from the tblBookings, tblCustomers, and tblEvents tables. You must create the query in Design view, because the Relationships window shows no relationship between the tblBookings and tblCustomers tables. Save the query and close the database.

Project 2 C

Open the *mdbFanTours5-2* database you modified in Project 1. Catherine wants to see the bookings first sorted by EventID and then by DateRegistered. Rearrange the fields and then sort the qryTours query to provide the information Catherine wants. The sort should show Description but *not* EventID. Save the query and close the database.

Project 3 C

Open the *mdbFanTours5-2* database you modified in Project 2. Catherine needs to know which customers booked more than one trip. Use the tblCustomers, tblBookings, and tblEmployees tables, and create a new query called "qryCustomerBookings" that displays the customer's full name in a single field, the last name of the employee who booked that customer, and the date of the booking. Sort by customer last name, but don't display the last name in the datasheet. Save the query and close the database.

Project 4 C

Open the *mdbFanTours5-2* database you modified in Project 3. Catherine wants a list of all the prospects who contacted FST in 2001. Create a query called "qry2001Prospects" using criteria to list all 2001 contacts. (*Hint:* Use AND criteria to list

those on or after 1/1/2001 and on or before 12/31/2001.) Sort the query in chronological order. Save the query and close the database.

Project 5 C

Open the *mdbFanTours5-2* database you modified in Project 4. Catherine also needs a list of all vendors participating in tours using the tblVendors and tblEventDetails tables. Create a query called "qryVendorActivity" that shows the vendor name, contact person, contact person's phone number, the detail name associated with it, the date, and the time for the event. Sort first by vendor, then by date and time. Save the query and close the database.

Project 6 C

Open the *mdbFanTours5-2* database you modified in Project 5. Open the qryVendorActivity query you created in Project 5. Catherine wants to print the contents of that query. She wants it to fit nicely on the page, so resize columns and/or rows so that they display the entire contents of each field. The report may take more than one page. Save the query and close the database.

Project 7

Using the Office on the Web command on the Help menu, connect to the Microsoft Web site and look for information on queries. Print at least one article that explains the basic concepts of queries. Save the article in a Word document, and then close the Word document.

Project 8

Using the Office on the Web command on the Help menu, connect to the Microsoft Web site and look for information on criteria in queries. Print at least one article about setting criteria, including using expressions or operators. Save the article in a Word document, and then close the Word document.

Creating and Modifying Forms

Chapter Overview

Forms simplify data entry and viewing. In this chapter, you explore how to design and create forms using the Form Wizard and AutoForm. You learn why forms are useful, what they look like, and how to use them. You also modify your form designs in Design view. You then enter and modify records with a form and learn how to print a form.

LEARNING OBJECTIVES

- ▶ Create a form with the Form Wizard and AutoForm
- ▶ Modify a form in Design view
- ▶ Create a calculated control on a form
- ▶ Enter and modify records using a form
- ▶ Print a form

Case profile

Tyler Leving, an admissions advisor, and Elsa Higgins, the personnel manager, ask you to make the Online University database easy for their departments' personnel to use. You create several Access forms to meet their needs. Elsa's staff can use your forms to enter new employee information efficiently, and Tyler's admissions staff can use the forms to enter and track student records.

chapter
six

C 6.a Creating a Form with the Form Wizard and AutoForm

> **QUICK TIP**
>
> Well-designed forms make entering data easy by using clear field labels (text that describes the field) and including only the necessary fields. They also make viewing data easy by arranging fields in appealing, logical ways.

Most people prefer to use forms when they enter or view information in a database. Like paper-based forms, electronic forms can be visually appealing and guide users through the process of entering data. You can use Access forms to accomplish the following tasks:

- **Enter, view, and modify data.** The most common use of forms is to enter and view data in records. When two tables are related, a well-designed form often presents another form (called a **subform**) that displays data from the related table.
- **Automate your tasks.** Forms can work to automate certain actions. With macros and Visual Basic, you can open other forms, run queries, and restrict the data you display. You also can use macros or modules in forms to provide data values, which let you perform calculations quickly and accurately.
- **Provide instructions.** You can include instructions, tips, notes, and other information on forms that provide information for the user about how to use Access or the special features of your database.
- **Print information.** You can use forms to increase your flexibility when printing information. For example, you can design a registration form with two sets of headers and footers: one for entering data and the other for printing a student invoice based on the registration information.

> **CAUTION TIP**
>
> Although the Form Wizard saves you time, it limits your design options. Because of these limitations, use it only in those situations that require simple forms with a moderate number of fields.

Elsa wants a form so that her staff can efficiently enter, update, and maintain information for new employees. You create the form using the Form Wizard. Like other Access wizards, the **Form Wizard** guides you through the steps of creating a form. You can use it to create a simple form that includes all fields from a related table, or you can select the fields to include in a form. Once you create a form with the Form Wizard, you can customize it in Design view.

Using the Form Wizard

As you step through a Form Wizard, you locate and select the information to include in the form, and then Access creates the form for you. In the process, you answer a series of questions about the content and appearance of the form. To start the Form Wizard:

Step 1	*Create*	a copy of the *mdbOnlineU6-* database located on the Data Disk
Step 2	*Click*	Forms ⊞ Forms on the Objects bar in the Database window, if necessary

| **Step 3** | ***Double-click*** | Create form by using wizard to start the Form Wizard |

The Form Wizard can create a simple columnar form that contains all fields in the tblInstructors table. You also can select only specific fields from the tblInstructors table. For your form, you use all fields, except for the Photo field. At this time, Elsa is not sure if her department wants to include photographs.

| **Step 4** | ***Click*** | Table: tblInstructors in the Table/Queries list box |

The Available Fields: list box displays the fields you can use. Your Form Wizard dialog box should look similar to Figure 6-1.

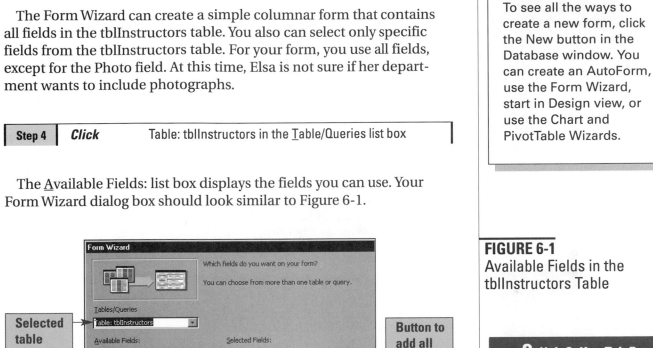

FIGURE 6-1
Available Fields in the tblInstructors Table

Step 5	***Click***	>> in the Form Wizard to add all fields
Step 6	***Click***	Photo in the Selected Fields: list box
Step 7	***Click***	< in the Form Wizard to remove the selected field
Step 8	***Click***	Next >

The next Form Wizard dialog box enables you to choose a form layout. You can choose a columnar, tabular, datasheet, or justified layout. For Elsa's form, you use the default columnar layout.

| **Step 9** | ***Click*** | the Columnar option button, if necessary |
| **Step 10** | ***Click*** | Next > |

chapter
six

QUICK TIP

Although you can change the Caption property for a label in a form, changing the Caption property in the table design makes more sense, because this makes the caption available wherever other objects subsequently use the respective field.

CAUTION TIP

If you change a field property table design *after* using that field in a form, Access does not automatically reapply the property change to the form.

In the next Form Wizard dialog box you select the background design of your form. Notice the samples of each background. Because you want to keep Elsa's form as simple as possible, you choose Standard style.

Step 11	*Click*	Standard, if necessary
Step 12	*Click*	Next >

The last Form Wizard dialog box asks you for a form title and asks whether you want to open the form in Form view at this time or modify it in Design view. You want to open it in Form view.

Step 13	*Key*	frmInstructors as the name of the form
Step 14	*Click*	Finish

Each field provides information to two places on the form—a label with the field's name and a text box or combo box for the field value. A **combo box** is a drop-down list that displays multiple choices.

Step 15	*Close*	the frmInstructors form

Before creating the next form, you add captions for each field in the tblDepartments table.

Adding Field Captions

Form fields that that get their information from existing fields are called **bound controls**. Bound controls inherit most of the field properties from the underlying table or query. By default, the Form Wizard uses the field name in the table as a label *unless* you set the Caption property for the fields in Table Design view. To set the Caption property in Table Design view:

Step 1	*Click*	Tables ⊞ Tables on the Objects bar, if necessary
Step 2	*Open*	the tblDepartments table in Design view
Step 3	*Click*	the Caption text box in the Field Properties pane of the DeptID field
Step 4	*Key*	Dept ID

Your screen should look similar to Figure 6-2.

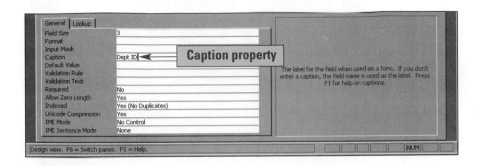

FIGURE 6-2
Caption Property for the
tblDepartments Table

Step 5	*Click*	the DeptName field
Step 6	*Key*	Dept Name in the Caption text box in the Field Properties pane
Step 7	*Click*	the DeptAddress field
Step 8	*Key*	Dept Address in the Caption text box in the Field Properties pane
Step 9	*Click*	the DeptPhone field
Step 10	*Key*	Dept Phone in the Caption text box in the Field Properties pane
Step 11	*Save*	the tblDepartments table and close it

Now that you have established captions for the fields in the tblDepartments table, you can create an AutoForm for this table.

Using AutoForm

The **AutoForm** procedure produces a columnar form automatically from a given table. An AutoForm form is useful in certain situations, such as creating a small table. To use it, you simply select a table or query in the Database window, and then click the AutoForm button on the Database toolbar. OLU needs a simple form to enter department information. You use an AutoForm. To create an AutoForm in the Tables window:

Step 1	*Click*	tblDepartments in the Database window, if necessary
Step 2	*Click*	the New Object: AutoForm button list arrow 📋 ▾ on the Database toolbar
Step 3	*Click*	AutoForm

Access generates a columnar form for the tblDepartments table. Your screen should look similar to Figure 6-3. Because the tblDepartments and tblInstructors tables are related in the Relationships window, Access also creates a subform to show the Instructors in that department.

QUICK TIP

Like the Form Wizard, AutoForm uses the field name or the Caption property as the label for each field. It includes all fields in the same order in which they appear in the table or query design.

MENU TIP

To create an AutoForm, you can click the AutoForm command on the Insert menu.

CAUTION TIP

Although AutoForm is quick, the Form Wizard lets you choose which fields to add to the form in which sequence. This is important because you might need to display fields in a different order than they appear in the data source.

chapter
six

FIGURE 6-3
tblDepartments AutoForm

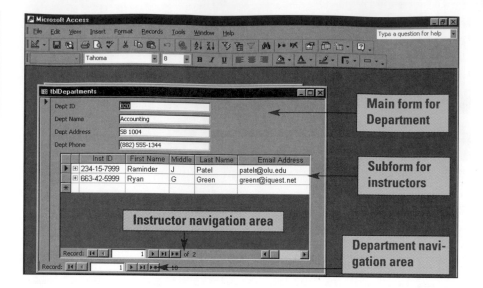

MOUSE TIP

You can modify the form's properties by right-clicking the appropriate object in Form Design view and then clicking Properties on the shortcut menu. You can display the Properties box with the Properties command on the View menu.

Step 4	*Close*	the AutoForm
Step 5	*Click*	Yes to save the form design
Step 6	*Key*	frmDepartments
Step 7	*Click*	OK to close the form

6.b Modifying a Form in Design View

After you create a form, you can modify its design to fit the requirements for that form. You may need to widen or move some fields. After viewing the frmDepartments form, you decide to resize the form's fields, and delete the inappropriate tblInstructors subform.

Using Controls

Controls are graphical representations of text, data, and images on your form. When you add a field to a form, you also add a text box and a label. The text box is a **bound control**, meaning it takes its value from the control source, a field in the underlying data source for the form. The label is an **unbound control**, meaning it does not take its value from any underlying data source. Other controls include option buttons, check boxes, toggle buttons, and option groups.

A **check box** control displays information that can have two valid choices. For example, you use a check box for a Yes or No choice. A check box with a check mark means yes and without means no. **Option group** controls provide option button controls for two or more choices

QUICK TIP

You use a combo box to conserve space on the form or to let the user enter a value not on the list. You can, however, set properties for a combo box to limit choices to those listed.

from which users select one option. A **list box** control lets users select from a list of values. A **combo box** control is a list box with drop-down options. The combo box takes only as much space as a text box, until it drops down. You use the **line** control to draw a straight line on the form, and you use the **rectangle** control to draw boxes on the form. Clicking a **command button** control runs a macro or module.

Using the Toolbox

You can add controls to the form design from the **Toolbox**, which contains a button for each type of control. Although there are many control types, you typically use only three or four types on most forms. For the frmInstructors form, you want to add a combo box with a list of available departments. To create a combo box control:

Step 1	*Click*	Forms  on the Objects bar
Step 2	*Open*	the frmInstructors form in Design view
Step 3	*Verify*	that the Toolbox is displayed
Step 4	*Click*	the DeptID text box (*not* the Dept ID label) to select it and its matching label
Step 5	*Press*	the DELETE key to remove the text box and its matching label
Step 6	*Verify*	that the Control Wizards button ▨ in the Toolbox is selected (appears white)
Step 7	*Click*	the Combo Box button ▦ in the Toolbox
Step 8	*Click*	the blank space where the upper-left corner of the DeptID text box used to be to start the Combo Box Wizard

The upper-left corner of the control is placed at the insertion point indicated by the mouse pointer. Access creates a label to the left of the control. You want to provide values from the tblDepartments table. To use the Combo Box Wizard to complete your combo box:

Step 1	*Click*	the I want the combo box to look up values in a table or a query option button, if necessary
Step 2	*Click*	Next >
Step 3	*Click*	the Tables option button, if necessary, to restrict the list to tables
Step 4	*Click*	tblDepartments in the list box
Step 5	*Click*	Next >

MENU TIP

To display the Toolbox in Form Design view, click the Toolbox command on the View menu.

MOUSE TIP

To display the Toolbox, you can click the Toolbox button on the Form Design toolbar.

If you inadvertently delete the wrong control(s), you can click the Undo button to replace the control.

When the Control Wizards button is selected (appears white) in the Toolbox, the Control Wizard starts when you add a control button to the form design.

chapter six

CAUTION TIP

Be careful when positioning the mouse over a selected field. If you click a selection handle, the mouse pointer changes to a pointing hand, which lets you move only the text box or the label, whichever one is selected. If the mouse pointer changes to a hand with all fingers outstretched, you move *both* controls at once.

Step 6	*Double-click*	the DeptName field to add it to the Selected Fields: list
Step 7	*Click*	Next >
Step 8	*Verify*	that the Hide key column (recommended) check box contains a check mark

The DeptName field appears. By hiding the key column, you do not display the redundant DeptID field. The wizard hides the DeptID field and makes it 0 inches wide.

| Step 9 | *Double-click* | the right border of the Dept Name column heading to resize the column to display the widest name |
| Step 10 | *Click* | Next > |

You can have the combo box value (DeptID) stored in the corresponding row of the underlying table. This enables you to assign or change the department name when you enter or modify an instructor's record. To complete the Combo Box Wizard:

QUICK TIP

When a form's tab order matches a source document, the person entering the data doesn't need to use the mouse to move between controls.

The horizontal black line shows you the control's place in the tab order.

Step 1	*Click*	the Store that value in this field: option button
Step 2	*Click*	DeptID in the list in the combo box
Step 3	*Click*	Next >
Step 4	*Key*	Department as the label for the combo box
Step 5	*Click*	Finish
Step 6	*Drag*	the combo box label's move handle to reposition the label so that it aligns with the other label controls
Step 7	*Drag*	the combo box text box's move handle, to reposition the combo box so that it aligns with the other text boxes

The form on your screen should look similar to Figure 6-4.

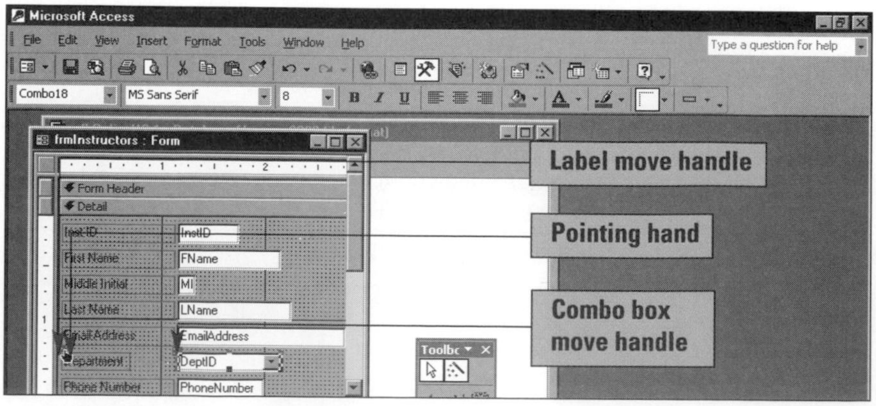

FIGURE 6-4
Finished frmInstructors
Form in Design View

Elsa tests the form by entering data. She notices when she presses the TAB or ENTER key after entering a field, she skips around the form instead of moving in logical order from one field to another. You can change the **tab order** of the form to define the sequence in which fields become active when the user presses the TAB key. The tab order should match the order of fields' appearance in the source document. To change the tab order of a form in Design view:

Step 1	*Right-click*	the form
Step 2	*Click*	Tab Order
Step 3	*Click*	the record selector next to Combo18
Step 4	*Drag*	the Combo18 field selection box above the PhoneNumber field, using the horizontal black line to determine the control's placement
Step 5	*Click*	OK

MENU TIP

You can open the Tab Order dialog box with the Tab Order command on View menu.

Next you view the form with the combo box field and see how the tab order works. To view the form:

Step 1	*Click*	the Form View button [icon] to switch to Form view and observe the finished form

You want to check the tab order of your form.

CAUTION TIP

The number of the combo box might vary, depending on whether you attempted some steps more than once.

Step 2	*Press*	the TAB key repeatedly to verify that you move through the fields from top to bottom, in order
Step 3	*Save*	the frmInstructors form

Adding Fields

You can use Design view to add (and delete) fields in a form. Elsa is ready to add a photograph to the record of each employee. The images are stored in OLE Object fields. You need to add an OLE Object field to the form's design. To add a field to the frmInstructors form:

Step 1	*Switch to*	Design view
Step 2	*Point to*	the right edge of the window until the mouse pointer becomes a two-headed arrow
Step 3	*Drag*	the right edge of the Form window until the window is about 5 inches wide

QUICK TIP

You can tell that the focus, or active control, moves when you press the TAB key because you see the mouse pointer move to a different control box.

**chapter
six**

Step 4	*Drag*	the right edge of the Detail section of the form until the section fills the Form window
Step 5	*Click*	View
Step 6	*Click*	Field List, if necessary, to open the Field List

The Field List dialog box contains a list of all fields in the underlying data source. You can drag fields from the field list to the form in Design view.

Step 7	*Drag*	the Photo field to the top right side of the Detail area of the form to place the photo's left corner at the 3-inch mark
Step 8	*Scroll*	the form to the right using the horizontal scroll bar
Step 9	*Drag*	the middle sizing handle on the right border of the Photo field to the 5-inch mark
Step 10	*Save*	the form
Step 11	*Close*	the Field List

Using Form Sections

A **Form Header** appears at the top of a form page, and a **Form Footer** appears at the bottom of a form page in Form view. The **Detail section** contains the data values in bound controls that correspond to each field in the underlying data source. To add a header to a form:

Step 1	*Verify*	that the frmInstructors form is open in Design view
Step 2	*Point to*	the boundary between the Form Header and Detail section of the form until the mouse pointer changes to a double-headed arrow
Step 3	*Drag*	the boundary down about 1.5 inches
Step 4	*Click*	the Label button *Aa* in the Toolbox
Step 5	*Drag*	in the Form Header section from the upper-left corner to the 3-inch mark on the horizontal ruler to create a label control approximately 3 inches wide and almost 0.5 inches tall
Step 6	*Key*	Online University Instructors
Step 7	*Press*	the ENTER key to complete the entry
Step 8	*Click*	the Font Size button list arrow 8 ▼ on the Formatting toolbar
Step 9	*Click*	14

Modifying Control Format Properties

You can enhance a form's design by modifying format properties, such as the form's font, font size, style, theme, and color. To select a theme for the frmInstructors form:

Step 1	*Click*	the Select All button ▣
Step 2	*Click*	For̲mat
Step 3	*Click*	AutoF̲ormat
Step 4	*Click*	Sumi Painting
Step 5	*Click*	OK
Step 6	*Change*	the font size of the Online University Instructors label to 14 point

Inserting a Graphic on a Form

Inserting a graphic often improves a form's appearance and makes it more user friendly. When the image is in the form's header sections and not from the underlying data source, you use an image control. To insert a graphic in the Form Header section using the Toolbox:

Step 1	*Click*	the Image button 🖾 in the Toolbox
Step 2	*Click*	in the Header section below the title to open the Insert Picture dialog box
Step 3	*Select*	*Employee.bmp* located on the Data Disk
Step 4	*Click*	OK to place the image on the form
Step 5	*Resize*	the image as necessary to fit within the header
Step 6	*Save*	the form

Your screen should look similar to Figure 6-5.

CAUTION TIP

One principle of good design is consistency. You should use the same format for each form in a database.

QUICK TIP

An image associated with a field in a data source is stored in a bound object control. Thus, each record displays its own image in the control on the form. With an unbound object control, the image does not change as you navigate the records.

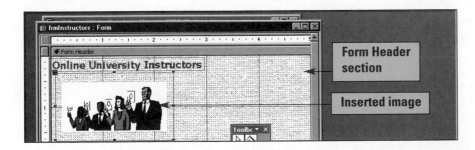

FIGURE 6-5
Modified frmInstructors Form

chapter
six

6.c Creating a Calculated Control on a Form

A calculated control uses the result of a calculation or expression as its data source. For instance, you could concatenate text fields such as FName and LName to produce one name. You could calculate the tuition and fees due from an OLU student; the calculation results appear on the form but are not added to the underlying table. To use a calculated control, you add an unbound text box using the Toolbox and then open the properties for that control. An unbound control does not take its value from a field in an underlying table and does not update the value of any field in an underlying table. In the Control Source property of the text box, you place an equal sign (=) and then key the expression for that control. To add a calculated field to a form:

| Step 1 | *Verify* | that the frmInstructors form is open in Design view |

You must resize the Detail section to hold the new controls.

Step 2	*Scroll*	down to view the lower parts of the form in Design view
Step 3	*Drag*	the lower edge of the form to about .5 inches below the Hire Date controls at the bottom of the form
Step 4	*Display*	the Toolbox, if necessary
Step 5	*Click*	the Text Box button ab| in the Toolbox
Step 6	*Click*	two grid lines below the left corner of the Hire Date text box

Access adds two controls—a label and the unbound text box—at the location you clicked. Next you adjust the properties of these controls.

Step 7	*Click*	the Properties button on the Form Design toolbar to display the Properties box, if necessary
Step 8	*Click*	the Control Source text box in the All tab of the Properties box
Step 9	*Key*	=FName&" "&MInit&" "&LName
Step 10	*Press*	the ENTER key
Step 11	*Close*	the Properties box
Step 12	*Switch to*	Form view and observe how the form looks

Notice that the label control shows Text23 or some similar term. You need to return to Design view and give the label an appropriate caption.

In Design view, Access displays the text box names in the Object window of the Formatting toolbar.

Step 13	*Switch to*	Design view
Step 14	*Select*	the contents of the label control
Step 15	*Key*	Full Name
Step 16	*Press*	the ENTER key
Step 17	*Move*	the label to align with the other label controls
Step 18	*Switch to*	Form view and observe the form
Step 19	*Save*	the form

6.d   Entering and Modifying Records Using a Form

A form is often created to view the contents of a datasheet. Some datasheets are overwhelming, especially to novice users, and the form provides a user-friendly interface for data entry. Elsa wants to demonstrate how to enter data for a new instructor. To add a new record to a form:

Step 1	*Verify*	that the frmInstructors form is open in Form view
Step 2	*Click*	the New Record button ▶✳ on the Form View toolbar
Step 3	*Key*	the data shown in Table 6-1 to complete the record

Field	Data	Field	Data
Inst ID	546-58-2139	**Department**	Business
First Name	Marcia	**Phone Number**	(425) 555-6897
Middle Initial	L	**Title**	Instructor
Last Name	Wilson	**Hire Date**	2/19/2001
E-mail Address	mwilson@dyn.com		

TABLE 6-1
Data for New Record Entry

Access displays the pencil icon in the record selector box until you move to another record. Access automatically saves the data after you move to a new record. Some of the form's fields are too narrow.

chapter
six

Step 4	*Switch to*	Design view
Step 5	*Widen*	the InstID, DeptID, and PhoneNumber text boxes so that all their contents are visible
Step 6	*Switch to*	Form view and observe the changes you made in the text boxes
Step 7	*Click*	Save

Your screen should look similar to Figure 6-6.

FIGURE 6-6
frmInstructors Form with
New Record

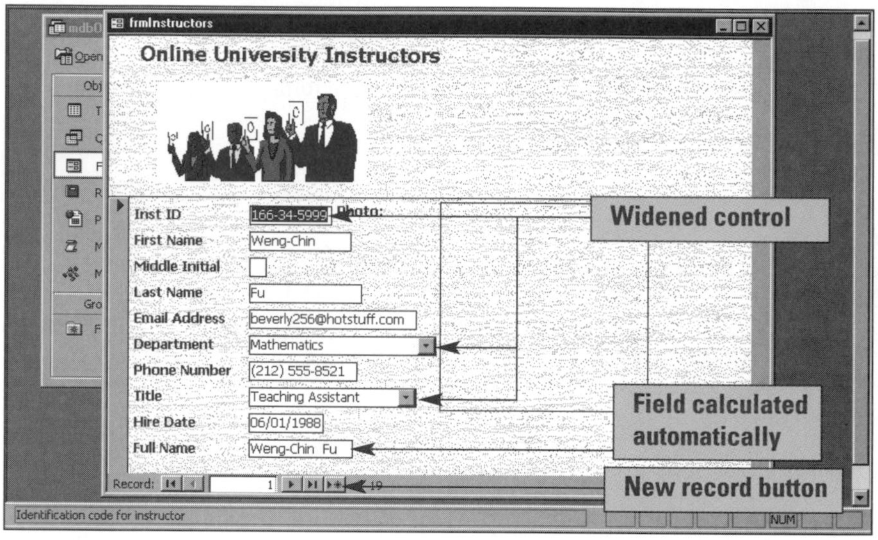

Modifying an Existing Record Using a Form

To modify a record in a form, first locate the record in Form view. Then edit the record as you would edit any other item. To find and modify Marcia Wilson's record in the Form window in Form view:

Step 1	*Click*	<u>E</u>dit
Step 2	*Click*	<u>F</u>ind
Step 3	*Key*	Marcia in the Fi<u>n</u>d What: text box
Step 4	*Click*	frmInstructors in the <u>L</u>ook In: list box
Step 5	*Click*	<u>F</u>ind Next

You see Marcia's record. You need to change her department to Information Technology.

Step 6	*Click*	Cancel to close the Find and Replace dialog box
Step 7	*Click*	the Department field list arrow
Step 8	*Click*	Information Technology

You completed the frmInstructors form for Elsa's department. You now make a permanent record by printing the form.

6.e Printing a Form

Elsa wants a copy of the frmInstructors form to show to her department when she explains how to use the form for data entry. You can print a single page, a range of pages, or all pages. To print the frmInstructors form:

Step 1	*Verify*	the frmInstructors form is open in Form view
Step 2	*Click*	the Print Preview button ▣ on the Form View toolbar
Step 3	*Review*	the form in Print Preview

When you are satisfied with the form's appearance, you can print it from the Print Preview window.

Step 4	*Click*	the Print button 🖨 on the Print Preview toolbar
Step 5	*Close*	the frmInstructors form and the database
Step 6	*Click*	Yes to save the changes

You can use forms to simplify data entry and display data in an attractive format.

**chapter
six**

Summary

► You create an Access form to enter and view data in records, control application flow, automate your application, provide instructions, and print the record and its data.

► You can use the Form Wizard to create a simple form that contains all fields in the related table or only selected fields. AutoForm can create a simple form.

► In Design view, you can add, delete, rearrange fields, add controls, insert pictures, change background color, and choose a theme to improve your form's appearance and usefulness.

► After you create a form, you test it by using it to enter data and create records. To modify an existing record, click the navigation buttons or the Find button to locate the field, click in the field, and key the modified data.

► Form controls let you select options, as you do on a standard Windows dialog box. You can include text boxes, option buttons, check boxes, toggle buttons, option groups, list boxes, and combo boxes.

► One principle of good design is consistency. You can keep the design of all forms in your database consistent by setting a theme using AutoFormat.

► You can add a header to a form to let users know its topic. You can include text and graphics in the form's header.

► If a form contains information you want to print, you can specify the form's printed layout and print it.

Commands Review

Action	Menu Bar	Shortcut Menu	Toolbar	Task Pane	Keyboard
When entering or editing form data:					
Open a combo box or a drop-down list			Click the drop-down arrow		F4 ALT + DOWN ARROW
Move up or down one line			Click the line		UP or DOWN ARROW
Move to the previous or next page			Click the scroll arrows		PAGEUP PAGEDOWN
Move to the next field			Click the next field		TAB
Find a record	Edit, Find Edit, Go To		🔍		CTRL + F ALT + E, F ALT + E, G
Print Preview a form	File, Print Preview		🔍		ALT + F, V
Change page layout	File, Page Setup				ALT + F, U
When designing a form:					
Create AutoForm (in Tables window)	Insert, AutoForm		🗐		ALT + I, O
Select a field			Click to see selection handles		TAB
Select more than one field			SHIFT + Click to select adjacent fields; CTRL + Click to select nonadjacent fields; double-click field list title bar to select all fields		SHIFT + ARROW CTRL + ARROW
Display fields list	View, Field List		🗒		ALT + V, L
Display the Toolbox	View, Toolbox		🛠		ALT + V, X
Display properties	View, Properties	Right-click object, click Properties	🗐		ALT + V, P F4
Apply theme	Format, AutoFormat				ALT + O, F
View tab order	View, Tab Order	Right-click form, Tab Order			ALT + V, B

Concepts Review

Circle the correct answer.

1. The quickest way to create a form is:
  [a] to build a custom form.
  [b] with the Form Wizard.
  [c] with AutoForm.
  [d] with AutoReport.

2. Which of the following is not a purpose of a form?
  [a] print information
  [b] enter and view data
  [c] provide instructions
  [d] design a layout for your tables

chapter six

3. **To hide the details of the database from the user, the form acts like a:**
   [a] tool.
   [b] mask.
   [c] creator.
   [d] wizard.

4. **When you edit records in a form:**
   [a] you also edit the corresponding records in the underlying table.
   [b] the underlying table opens automatically.
   [c] you do not change the corresponding records in the underlying table.
   [d] the underlying table is unaffected because you cannot edit records in a form.

5. **To view data in a form:**
   [a] you must be in Form view.
   [b] you must be in Design view.
   [c] use the Form Wizard.
   [d] you need to know advanced Access techniques.

6. **When you want to create a simple form using all fields in the underlying table use:**
   [a] Design view.
   [b] the Form Wizard.
   [c] the Table Wizard.
   [d] AutoReport.

7. **To give the user a list of choices for a field, you use a:**
   [a] text box control.
   [b] macro button.
   [c] combo box.
   [d] command button.

8. **You place a form's title in the:**
   [a] Form Header section.
   [b] Detail section.
   [c] Form Footer section.
   [d] Form Title section.

9. **An unbound control in a form:**
   [a] assumes the value from a field in the underlying table.
   [b] has no limited maximum value.
   [c] assumes the value from another control in the form.
   [d] can be used to display calculated values.

10. **You can enhance the design of a form by:**
    [a] modifying it in Datasheet view.
    [b] choosing a theme.
    [c] entering all required data.
    [d] creating a custom form.

Circle **T** if the statement is true or **F** if the statement is false.

T F   1. A control determines how the form opens.

T F   2. You can use a table or a query as the data source for a form.

T F   3. You can change the tab order of a form, so that users can move logically from one form to another.

T F   4. You can create a form in the Forms window using AutoForm.

T F   5. With the Form Wizard, you can create forms that let you enter information from several different tables.

T F   6. A combo control offers you a choice of values for a field.

T F   7. To find a record you want to edit, you can use the Find command.

T F   8. Tab order determines the sequence of fields as you tab through a form.

T F   9. The Combo Box Wizard guides you through the steps of including a combo box in your form.

T F   10. One principle of good design is to create a form that resembles the paper document used to collect the data entered in the form.

Skills Review

Exercise 1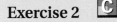

1. Create a copy of the *mdbFanTours6-* database located on the Data Disk.

2. Use the AutoForm to create a new form based on the tblVendors table.

3. Save the form as "frmVendors" and close it.

4. Close the database.

Exercise 2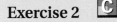

1. Open the *mdbFanTours6-1* database you created in Exercise 1.

2. Use the Form Wizard to create a new form based on the tblCustomers table. Use only the following fields in the form: CustID, FName, MName, LName, StreetAddress, City, State, and PostalCode.

3. Choose the justified layout and Standard style for the form.

4. Save the new form as "frmCustomers."

5. Close the frmCustomers form and close the database.

Exercise 3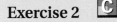

1. Open the *mdbFanTours6-1* database you modified in Exercise 2.

2. Open the frmCustomers form you modified in Exercise 2 in Form view.

3. Enter the following data in new records in the form. Remember to press the TAB key to move past CustID, which is an AutoNumber field.

Bryce Alan Preformo, 12 N. Ontario, Lawrence, IN 46227
Heime M. Esperante, 4445 Brenton St., Tucson, AZ 85715
Toru C. Nagaro, 9784 Glommer Blvd, Kent, WA 98032

4. Print the frmCustomers form with the data.

5. Save and close the frmCustomers form, and then close the database.

Exercise 4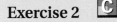

1. Open the *mdbFanTours6-1* database you modified in Exercise 3.

2. Open the frmCustomers form in Design view. Display the Toolbox and the Field List box.

3. Drag the EmailAddress field from the Field List box to the form. Place the control at the end of the form, next to the PostalCode control. Align the label control with the Postal Code label; align the text box control with the PostalCode text box. Do not change any other properties of these controls.

4. Switch to Form view and add the following e-mail addresses to the three records you entered in Exercise 3.

bryceboy@aol.com
esper56@hotstuff.com
torun@olu.edu

5. Print the frmCustomers form, and then save and close the form.

6. Close the database.

chapter six

Exercise 5 C

1. Open the *mdbFanTours6-1* database you modified in Exercise 4.

2. Open the frmVendors form you created in Exercise 1.

3. In Design view, replace the text box for VendorType with a combo box, getting values from the tblVCategories table. Use VendorCategory as the field that contains the values. Store the values in the VendorType field. The label for the combo box is "Type." Align the label with other label controls. Save the form design.

4. Swtich to Form view and maximize the form, if necessary, to view the navigation area. View the combo box by scrolling through the vendor records using the navigation area at the bottom of the form. Notice how the combo box changes for each vendor.

5. If you maximized the form, restore it to its former size.

6. Close the frmVendors form, and then close the database.

Exercise 6 C

1. Open the *mdbFanTours6-1* database you modified in Exercise 5.

2. Open the frmVendors form you modified in Exercise 5 in Design view.

3. Change the tab order of the form, so that you progress from top to bottom of the main form (*Hint:* Drag the combo box below the Vender Contact field.)

4. Test the tab order in the main form in Form view.

5. Save and close the frmVendors form, and then close the database.

Exercise 7

1. Open the *mdbFanTours6-1* database you modified in Exercise 6.

2. Open the frmVendors form you modified in Exercise 6 in Design view.

3. Assign the Sumi Painting theme for the form's design using AutoFormat command on the Format menu.

4. Save and close the frmVendors form, and then close the database.

Exercise 8 C

1. Open the *mdbFanTours6-1* database you modified in Exercise 7.

2. Open the frmCustomers form you modified in Exercise 4 in Design view.

3. Add a header to the form. In the header, place a 14-point, bold label control that reads "FST Customers."

4. Switch to Form view and view the form. Print a copy of the form.

5. Save and close the frmCustomers form, and then close the database.

Case Projects

Project 1

Using the Office on the <u>W</u>eb command on the <u>H</u>elp menu, open the Microsoft home page and then link to pages that provide basic information about Access forms. Print at least two Web pages. Save the pages in a Word document, and then save and close the document.

Project 2

Connect to the Internet and search the Web for sites that provide principles of good design of paper-based publications, such as a newsletter, or electronic publications. Print at least two of the Web pages. You use this information in Projects 3 through 8. Save the pages in a Word document, and then save and close the document.

Project 3

Open the *mdbFanTours6-2* database located on the Data Disk. The owner of Fantastic Sports Tours asks you to create four forms for the tables in the database. Start by creating a simple form for the tblVCategories table. Choose a theme for the form. Modify and enhance the form to conform to good design principles. Save the form as "frmVendor Categories." Close the database.

Project 4

Open the *mdbFanTours6-2* database you modified in Project 3. Use the Form Wizard to create the second form based on the tblEvents, tblEventDetails, and tblVendors tables. Use the same theme for the frmEventDetails form as you did for the frmVendor Categories form. Resize the controls as needed to display information in the form and subform. Close the database.

Project 5

Open the *mdbFanTours6-2* database you modified in Project 4. Create the third form based on the tblBookings table. Use the same design you used for the other forms. Check the tab order to make sure users can complete the fields in logical order. Add an input mask for the EmplID field. Close the database.

Project 6

Open the *mdbFanTours6-2* database you modified in Project 5. In Design view, create the fourth form based on the tblProspects table. Place the two contact fields, Type and Contact Date, right after the ProspectID field. Use the columnar layout for this form. Use the same style you used for the other forms. Close the database.

Project 7

Open the *mdbFanTours6-2* database you modified in Project 6. Open the frmBookings form you created in Project 5. Modify all labels to display information in the space available. Modify the Caption property of the underlying tblBookings table to match, so that the next form created with this table has the updated captions. Close the database.

Project 8

Open the *mdbFanTours6-2* database you modified in Project 7. Open the frmVendors form. Test the form design by entering data. Enhance the design by adding a graphic (search the Office clip art using the Microsoft Clip Organizer command, which is located in the Microsoft Office Tools folder in the Start menu) or a header, or by changing the font styles of the field labels. Close the database.

chapter six

Creating a Report

Chapter Overview

You often may need to present to others information you store in Access. A report is an effective way to present data in printed format. You can create and modify the appearance of reports to suit your needs. In this chapter, you learn how to use AutoReport and the Report Wizard. You also learn how to modify a report, use the Print Preview toolbar, print a report, and create labels.

LEARNING OBJECTIVES

- ► **Understand report types**
- ► **Create a report with AutoReport**
- ► **Create a report with the Report Wizard**
- ► **Modify a report in Design view**
- ► **Preview and print a report**
- ► **Create labels with the Label Wizard**

Case profile

The administrators of Online University ask you to produce reports for the annual trustees meeting. Elsa Higgins, OLU's personnel manager, wants to provide a general report listing OLU employees. Michael Golden from the provost's office wants a student report that displays students' names and their academic advisors. The provost's office also needs a set of mailing labels for all students.

chapter
seven

7.a Understanding Report Types

A **report** is an Access database object that presents detailed information in a printed format. Reports include a class roster, a phone list, and a set of mailing labels. You can control the size and appearance of everything on the report. Most information in a report comes from an underlying table or query, where the report finds its data.

Access provides a variety of report types. A **columnar report** arranges each record's data vertically—each field for each record appears on a line by itself. A **tabular report** arranges the data for each record horizontally, with each field appearing in a column. A **detail report** lists record details, and a **grouped report** organizes records into groups and then subtotals the groups. A **label report** creates multiple-column reports suitable for mailing labels, and a **chart report** includes a chart or graph comparing numeric data.

You use **AutoReport** to create a simple report based on a single table or query, and you use the **Report Wizard** to specify the kind of report you want to create, and then have Access guide you step by step. You can modify the report later in Design view.

7.b Creating a Report with AutoReport

You use AutoReport to create the report for Elsa that lists OLU's employees and their departments. Because you do not want to include all the data from the tblInstructors table, you base the report on the qryInstructors query, which contains lists of certain fields related to the instructors and their departments. To create a report using AutoReport:

Step 1	*Create*	a copy of the *mdbOnlineU7-* database located on the Data Disk
Step 2	*Click*	Reports [Reports] on the Objects bar
Step 3	*Click*	the New button [New] in the Database window

The New Report dialog box opens, providing options to use the Report Wizard, create an AutoReport, use the Chart Wizard for graphs, create Labels with the Label Wizard, or start in Design view and build the custom report piece by piece. You want to create a simple, tabular

chapter
seven

report based on the qryInstructors query. You select the query rather than the tblInstructors table to exclude the Photo field from the report. In a tabular report, fields in each record appear on one line, and the labels print once at the top of each page.

Step 4	*Click*	AutoReport: Tabular
Step 5	*Click*	the Choose the table or query where the object's data comes from: list arrow
Step 6	*Click*	qryInstructors
Step 7	*Click*	OK

Access automatically creates the report. Notice that the report title is the title of the underlying query (which, in this case, is based on the tblInstructors table) and the report is in landscape orientation.

Step 8	*Click*	the Close button ☒ on the Report window title bar
Step 9	*Click*	Yes to open the Save As dialog box
Step 10	*Key*	rptInstructors as the report's name
Step 11	*Click*	OK

You use AutoReport to create a report from one table or query. If you want to create a report from more than one source or choose the fields to include, you should use the Report Wizard.

C 7.c Creating a Report with the Report Wizard

Like the Form Wizard, the Report Wizard lets you choose the tables and queries for the underlying data, the fields, grouping levels, sort order, and more options. You can use the Report Wizard to create the report for Michael that shows the students currently in the database. To create a report using the Report Wizard:

Step 1	*Click*	Reports 📄 Reports on the Objects bar, if necessary
Step 2	*Double-click*	Create report by using wizard

The first Report Wizard dialog box opens. You select the fields you want in the report from one or more tables or queries.

Step 3	*Click*	Table: tblStudents in the Tables/Queries list box
Step 4	*Move*	the StudentID, FName, and LName fields into the Selected Fields: text box
Step 5	*Click*	Table: tblInstructors in the Tables/Queries list box
Step 6	*Move*	the FName and LName fields into the Selected Fields: text box
Step 7	*Click*	Table: tblPrograms in the Tables/Queries list box
Step 8	*Move*	the ProgramName field into the Selected Fields: text box
Step 9	*Click*	Next > to complete this phase of the Report Wizard's work

You next select how you want to view your data. You want to follow Michael's suggestion to group together all the data. When you add multiple tables or queries to the report, the Report Wizard asks which table you want to use to organize the records in the report. Because you want records to appear in student order, you select the tblStudents table. To complete the Report Wizard:

| Step 1 | *Click* | by tblStudents, if necessary |

You can add your own grouping levels, if you like. A **group report** groups records that share the same group field value and displays counts and subtotals for that group. For now, you create a simple report with no grouping.

| Step 2 | *Click* | Next > |
| Step 3 | *Click* | Next > to begin the sorting steps of the Report Wizard |

You can choose how to sort the information in the report, using up to four sort fields, in ascending or descending order. By default, no sorting is specified. Michael wants the records sorted by student name, so you sort first by the tblStudents_LName field in ascending order and then by tblStudent_FName in ascending order.

| Step 4 | *Click* | the list arrow in the first list box |
| Step 5 | *Click* | tblStudents_LName |

MOUSE TIP

You can click the Show Me More Information button in the Report Wizard dialog box to read tips on grouping your data.

QUICK TIP

To uniquely identify fields, the Report Wizard adds a table name as a prefix to each duplicate field name.

You can customize field widths in Design view after the Report Wizard finishes its work.

chapter
seven

Step 6	*Click*	tblStudents_FName in the second list box
Step 7	*Click*	Next >

You can choose a layout for your report. The default layout, tabular and portrait, is fine for Michael's report. The Preview window shows examples of the other layout choices.

> **CAUTION TIP**
>
> Use a descriptive report name that tells readers the report's subject at a glance.

Step 8	*Verify*	that Tabular and Portrait are selected, and that the Adjust the field width so all fields fit on a page check box contains a check mark
Step 9	*Click*	Next > to accept the default layout

Now you choose a style for the report. The Report Wizard shows a preview of each style. The style you choose sets options such as the font, font style, and line spacing for the report.

> **QUICK TIP**
>
> Once you select a report style (or form style) in the Report Wizard, it becomes the default style of subsequent Report Wizard reports.

Step 10	*Click*	Corporate, if necessary, to give the report a crisp, business style
Step 11	*Click*	Next >
Step 12	*Key*	rptStudent Advisor List as the report's title

The last step in the Report Wizard lets you select how the report opens—in Print Preview view or in Design view. Print Preview view is the default.

Step 13	*Click*	Finish to complete the wizard and open the report in Print Preview view

Your report should look similar to Figure 7-1. Although the report contains the information that you want, it lacks visual appeal.

FIGURE 7-1
Report Wizard Report in Print Preview View

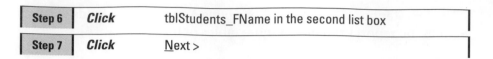

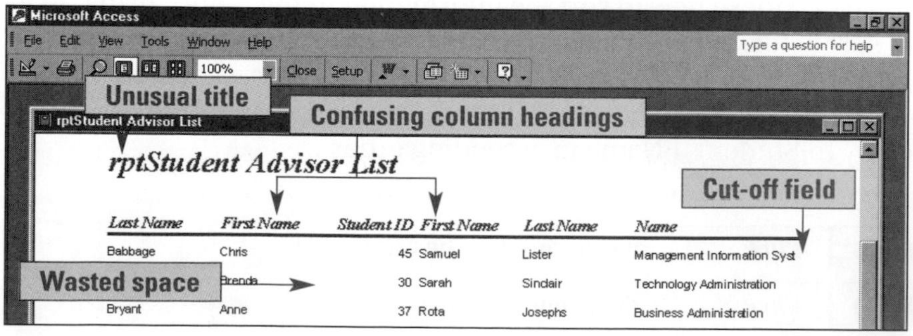

7.d Modifying a Report in Design View

C

Once you create a report, you can modify it in Design view. You also can customize headers and footers for both the page and the report. You want to improve the content and format of Michael's report.

Using Report Sections

The information in a report is divided into sections. Each section has a different purpose and prints in a particular order. First, Access displays the **Report Header** section at the top of the report's first page. This section is usually the report's cover page or title page. Next, Access displays the **Page Header** section, which appears at the top of each page of the report. This section usually includes the column headings. Below the page header, Access inserts the **Detail** section, which displays the data from the fields for each record. The **Page Footer** section appears at the bottom of each page of the report and usually shows the page number. You also can include a **Report Footer** section, which appears at the bottom of the report's last page, to display items such as report subtotals and grand totals for numeric fields or counts of the number of records included. The **horizontal ruler** and **vertical ruler** help you size and place controls in Design view.

You determine where information appears in every section by including controls such as labels and text boxes. A **label** shows the name of an item, such as a field. Fields values are usually shown in text boxes. To modify the Report Header label to remove the "rpt" text:

Step 1	*Switch to*	Design view
Step 2	*Display*	the Toolbox, if necessary
Step 3	*Click*	the rptStudent Advisor List label in the Report Header section
Step 4	*Select*	rpt in the label
Step 5	*Press*	the DELETE key

Michael's report includes fields with the same label—Last Name, which refers to the student's last name and the advisor's last name. You can modify the labels for these fields and then adjust the labels' positions so that they align with the other labels in the report. To remove a label control:

| Step 1 | *Click* | the student's First Name label in the Page Header section to select it |

QUICK TIP

By default, the Report Wizard places only the report title in the Report Header section. To display the title on every page of the report, you move the title to the Page Header section.

chapter seven

| Step 2 | *Press* | the DELETE key |

Access removes the label. Now you can resize the remaining label and modify its caption. To adjust the size of a label:

Step 1	*Click*	the student's Last Name label to select it
Step 2	*Select*	Last in the label
Step 3	*Key*	Student
Step 4	*Press*	the ENTER key to complete the entry

Access displays the changes. Next you modify the labels over the instructor name fields. First, you delete both labels. To modify the labels:

Step 1	*Click*	the instructor's First Name label
Step 2	*Shift + Click*	the instructor's Last Name label
Step 3	*Press*	the DELETE key to remove both controls

Your screen should look similar to Figure 7-2.

FIGURE 7-2
Modified Report in
Design View

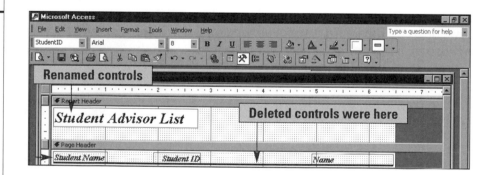

Using the Control Toolbox to Add Controls

As you modify the report in Design view, you usually need to add controls. When you add a field to the report, you actually add two controls—a label control containing the field's caption (if one exists) or its name, and a text box control containing the value of the field. To add a new label control to the report:

| Step 1 | *Click* | the Label button Aa in the Toolbox |

Step 2	Click	in the Page Header section above the tblInstructors_FName field to create a thin box that expands as you key an expression
Step 3	Key	Academic Advisor
Step 4	Press	the ENTER key to complete the entry

Notice that you need to align the new control. Once you add a label, you can move it. You want to align the Academic Advisor label with the other labels in the Page Header section. To move a label control:

Step 1	Verify	that the Academic Advisor label is selected
Step 2	Point to	the move handle at the upper-left corner of the label until the pointer becomes a hand with a single pointing finger
Step 3	Drag	the label to align it with the other labels in the Page Header section
Step 4	Click	the Name label above the ProgramName field
Step 5	Select	Name in the label
Step 6	Key	Major

You need to reduce the size of the Student ID field, so that the report can display other information. To reduce the width of a control:

Step 1	Click	the Student ID label in the Page Header section
Step 2	Drag	the right sizing handle to the left, so that the control ends at the 2.5-inch mark on the horizontal ruler
Step 3	Follow	Steps 1 and 2 for the StudentID field in the Detail section
Step 4	Select	the text in the Student ID label in the Page Header section
Step 5	Key	ID as the new label

You need to move the advisor fields and widen the ProgramName field, so its contents appear on the report. To move a group of fields:

Step 1	Click	the tblInstructors_FName field in the Detail section
Step 2	Shift + Click	the tblInstructors_LName field in the Detail section
Step 3	Observe	that you selected both fields and can move them as a block
Step 4	Drag	the two fields about .5 inches to the left

**chapter
seven**

Step 5	*Click*	the ProgramName field in the Detail section
Step 6	*Drag*	its left sizing handle about .5 inches to the left
Step 7	*Drag*	the Academic Advisor label to about the 2.75-inch mark on the horizontal ruler
Step 8	*Switch to*	Print Preview view

Your screen should look similar to Figure 7-3.

FIGURE 7-3
Modified Report in Print Preview View

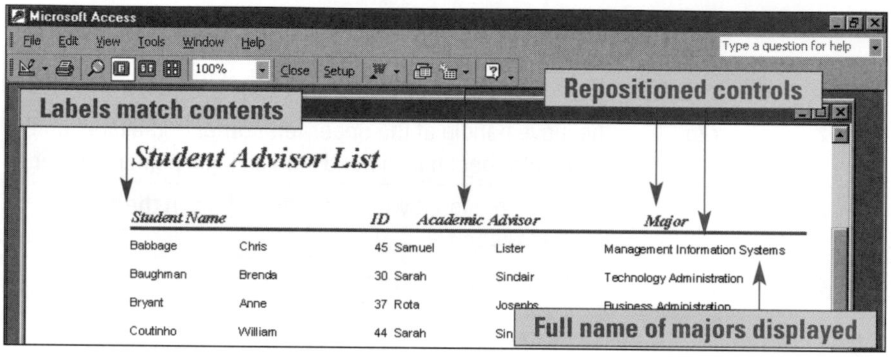

CAUTION TIP

Printing a large report with background color uses a lot of ink in an ink jet printer.

MOUSE TIP

If the Formatting toolbar does not appear in Report Design view, right-click a toolbar and then click Formatting (Form/Report).

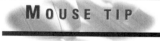

Modifying Control Format Properties

Report control properties are very similar to form control properties. You can change the font type, size, and color; add boldface or italic; and adjust spacing for label and text box controls. In addition, you can add background color to report sections. To change font size:

Step 1	*Switch to*	Design view
Step 2	*Click*	the Student Advisor List label in the Report Header section
Step 3	*Click*	the Font Size button list arrow [8] on the Formatting toolbar
Step 4	*Click*	24
Step 5	*Right-click*	the Student Advisor List label
Step 6	*Point to*	Size
Step 7	*Click*	To Fit

Access enlarges the label control to fit the length of text already there. You also can change the font color for the label. To change the font color:

Step 1	*Right-click*	the label in the Report Header section

Step 2	*Point to*	Fo<u>n</u>t/Fore Color
Step 3	*Click*	the red color (first color, third row)

Using a Calculated Control in a Report

A **calculated control** displays the result of a count. In your current report, you add a text box that calculates the records by counting all the StudentID fields listed in the report. No record has this field blank, so the count accurately indicates the number of students listed in this report.

You start by opening the hidden Report Footer section. To open the hidden section:

Step 1	*Point to*	the bottom border of the Report Footer section until the mouse pointer changes to a double-headed arrow
Step 2	*Drag*	the Report Footer bottom border downward approximately ½ inch to increase the size of the footer area

To add the calculated control to the report footer:

Step 1	*Click*	the Text Box button [ab] on the Toolbox
Step 2	*Click*	below the ProgramName field in the Report Footer section

When you insert a text box from the Toolbox, you insert a **compound control**, that is, a control that has two parts—an attached label for the text and text itself. The label's text is boldfaced, such as **Text11**. The text *Unbound* in the text box means the label does not take the value of any control source in the underlying table or query.

Step 3	*Select*	the new label's text
Step 4	*Key*	Number of Students
Step 5	*Press*	the ENTER key
Step 6	*Drag*	the label to the left until it no longer overlaps the Report Footer section the text box
Step 7	*Click*	twice in the unbound text box to position the insertion point in the control (do not double-click)

You can enter a value in the text box, or you can enter an expression that calculates a value for you. If you enter an expression, the text box becomes a calculated control—it calculates values in your report. If you don't enter an expression, the text box displays nothing.

MOUSE TIP

Although you can use the Properties box to change formatted items, using the Formatting toolbar buttons is much simpler, because they generally provide lists from which you can select options.

CAUTION TIP

Access ignores a blank field when counting the number of records.

QUICK TIP

A bound label takes its value from an underlying table or query.

chapter
seven

| Step 8 | *Key* | =Count([StudentID]) |
| Step 9 | *Press* | the ENTER key |

Your screen should look similar to Figure 7-4.

FIGURE 7-4
Expression for Unbound
Text Box

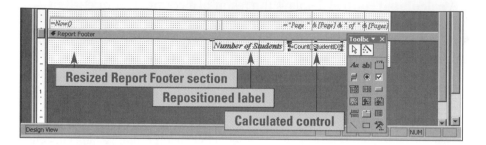

Now you can see the results of your changes. To preview a report two pages at a time:

| Step 1 | *Switch to* | Print Preview |
| Step 2 | *Click* | the Two Pages button 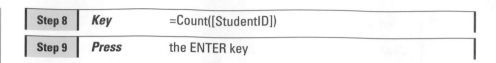 on the Print Preview toolbar |

Notice that the report title appears only on the report's first page. For the report's title to appear on each page, you must place this control in the Page Header section. To move the title into the Page Header section:

Step 1	*Switch to*	Design view
Step 2	*Maximize*	the Report window to see the entire width of the Page Header section
Step 3	*Drag*	the lower border of the Page Header section down about .5 inches to make room for the title
Step 4	*Click + Drag*	in an empty space to the left (or right) of the Page Header section to create a rectangle that touches all controls in the Page Header section, making sure that you include the horizontal line object in the box
Step 5	*Drag*	the entire group of controls down to the bottom of the Page Header section
Step 6	*Right-click*	the Student Advisor List label in the Report Header section
Step 7	*Click*	Cu_t to move the title onto the Clipboard
Step 8	*Click*	in the Page Header section above the Student Name label
Step 9	*Click*	the Paste button to paste the Student Advisor List label into the Page Header section

MOUSE TIP

You can use the Format Painter feature to copy a control's color, style, and font, and apply it to another control. Click the control you want to duplicate, click the Format Painter button on the Formatting toolbar, and then click the control you want to format.

QUICK TIP

If only every other page displays after clicking the Two Pages button, resize the page width in Design view.

Step 10	*Drag*	the lower border of the Report Header section all the way up, closing this section
Step 11	*Switch to*	Print Preview
Step 12	*Observe*	that the report title now appears on every page

To close and save the report:

Step 1	*Click*	the Close button <u>Close</u> on the Print Preview toolbar
Step 2	*Close*	the Report window
Step 3	*Click*	<u>Y</u>es to save the report

7.e Previewing and Printing a Report

Before printing a report, you can preview it to see how it looks on the printed page. Michael wants to see the report's content and layout of the report before printing, especially because his report is longer than one page. To preview a report from the Database window:

Step 1	*Click*	rptStudent Advisor List in the Database window
Step 2	*Click*	the Preview button in the Database window
Step 3	*Click*	the Two Pages button on the Print Preview toolbar
Step 4	*Click*	the Zoom button on the Print Preview toolbar to increase the magnification of the report
Step 5	*Click*	the Zoom button again to decrease the magnification

You see that the Report Wizard creates a useful report for Michael's department. However, occasionally, you need to change the report's margins or page orientation so that it better fits the page. For this, you can use the Page Setup dialog box. To modify the report's page setup:

Step 1	*Click*	the <u>S</u>etup button <u>Setup</u> on the Print Preview toolbar

MOUSE TIP

From Design view, you can view a report in Print Preview by clicking the Print Preview button on the Report Design toolbar.

C

QUICK TIP

Clicking the Print Preview button has the same effect as clicking the View button and selecting Print Preview view.

Clicking the Zoom button has the same effect as clicking the zoom mouse pointer.

chapter
seven

The Page Setup dialog box opens. You set margins on the Margins tab, select page orientation on the Page tab, and configure grid settings for multicolumn or label reports on the Columns tab.

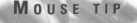
Step 2	*Click*	the Page tab
Step 3	*Click*	the Landscape option button
Step 4	*Click*	OK

Access displays the report in landscape orientation. Because you changed column widths earlier, you do not need to use landscape orientation for this report. So you change the report's orientation back to portrait.

Step 5	*Follow*	Steps 1 though 4, selecting the Portrait option button
Step 6	*Click*	the Close button Close on the Print Preview toolbar to close Print Preview

Printing a Report

After you create a report, you can print it. Because you already saved and closed Michael's report, you select it first in the Database window. To print a report from the Database window:

Step 1	*Select*	the rptStudent Advisor List report in the Database window, if necessary
Step 2	*Click*	File
Step 3	*Click*	Print

The Print dialog box opens, so you can specify a printer, the range of pages and number of copies you want to print, and whether to collate them. You accept the defaults, because they fit your print requirements.

Step 4	*Click*	OK

7.f Creating Labels with the Label Wizard

Michael wants to print student mailing labels from the database. To create mailing labels using the Label Wizard:

Step 1	*Click*	the Reports button [Reports] on the Objects bar, if necessary
Step 2	*Click*	the New button [New] in the Database window
Step 3	*Click*	Label Wizard in the New Report dialog box
Step 4	*Click*	tblStudents in the Choose the table or query where the object's data comes from: text box
Step 5	*Click*	OK
Step 6	*Verify*	that Avery is selected in the Filter by manufacturer: list box and English is the Unit of Measure
Step 7	*Click*	5160 in the Product Number: column (scroll to view the product number)

These are 1 × 2 ⅝ inch labels placed in three columns across the page. So you create a three-column label report. The dialog box on your screen should look similar to Figure 7-5.

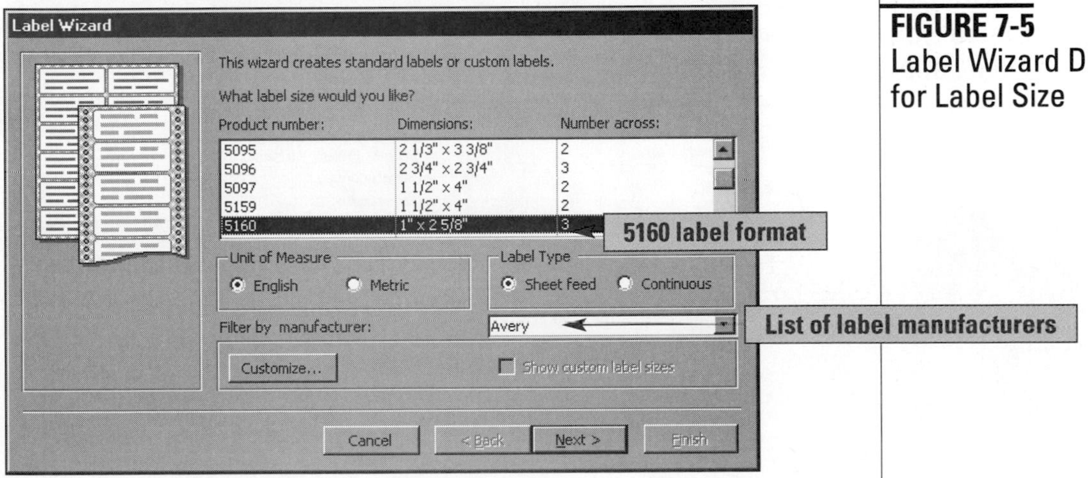

FIGURE 7-5
Label Wizard Dialog Box for Label Size

Step 8	*Click*	Next >
Step 9	*Verify*	that 8-point Arial font is selected

QUICK TIP

The Label Wizard can assist you in preparing the labels as a report. In the wizard, you select the label style, specify the data source, and enter the fields and appropriate spacing and punctuation from which the label report is created.

| Step 10 | *Click* | Next > |

As you did when you worked with the Report Wizard, you move fields from the Available fields column to the Prototype label: text box. You also can key punctuation, spaces, and line breaks as needed. To build the prototype label layout:

Step 1	*Double-click*	FName in the Available fields: list to add it to the prototype label
Step 2	*Press*	the SPACEBAR to add a space after the first name field
Step 3	*Double-click*	MName
Step 4	*Press*	the SPACEBAR
Step 5	*Double-click*	LName
Step 6	*Press*	the ENTER key
Step 7	*Enter*	the rest of the label layout, moving fields and keying the punctuation, spaces, and line breaks as shown: StreetAddress StreetAddress2 City, State PostalCode

The completed Label Wizard dialog box on your screen should look similar to Figure 7-6.

FIGURE 7-6
Label Wizard Dialog Box
Prototype Label

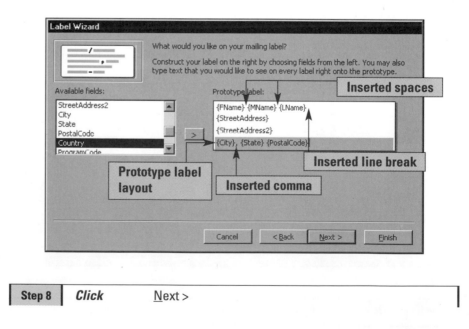

| Step 8 | *Click* | Next > |

Because OLU can take advantage of lower mailing rates for presorted mail, you need to sort by PostalCode.

Step 9	***Double-click***	PostalCode (scroll to view this option)
Step 10	***Click***	Next >
Step 11	***Key***	lblStudents in the What name would you like for your report? text box

You can preview the labels or modify their design. You want to preview the labels in the Print Preview window.

Step 12	***Verify***	that See the labels as they will look printed option is checked
Step 13	***Click***	Finish to complete the label report
Step 14	***Click***	OK to acknowledge that some data might not be displayed

The label preview on your screen should look similar to Figure 7-7. This type of report is called a **multi-column report**, because its records appear in three columns.

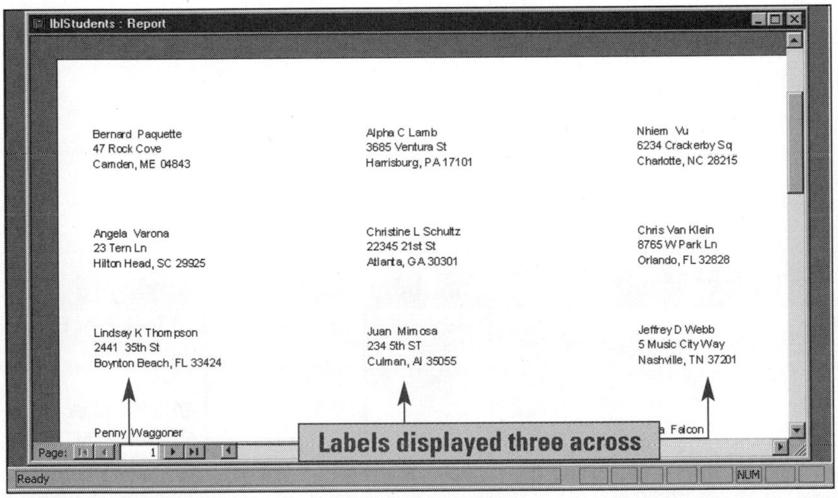

FIGURE 7-7
Print Preview of Finished Labels

Step 15	***Close***	the Print Preview window
Step 16	***Close***	the database

With your reports in hand, the OLU administrators are ready for the annual trustees meeting.

QUICK TIP

You can adjust the label formatting in the Page Setup dialog box. For the Avery 5160 labels, Access set 2.625" as the Width in the Column Size section and 0.125" for Column Spacing in the Grid Settings section of the Columns tab. Slightly reducing the left or right margins in the Margins tab can accommodate the width of these labels.

Summary

► A report is an Access database object that presents information in a printed format.

► Most information in a report comes from an underlying table or query where the report finds its data.

► A columnar report arranges each record's data vertically—each field for each record appears on a line by itself. A tabular report arranges the data for each record horizontally, with each field appearing in a column.

► You use AutoReport to create a simple report based on a single table or query. You use the Report Wizard to specify the kind of report you want to create and let the wizard guide you step by step, or to gain more control over what data the report includes.

► Once you create a report, you can modify it in Design view by changing its labels (the descriptions of each field), customizing its headers and footers, and changing its overall format.

► After you create and save a report, you can print it. Before you print a report for the first time, check the report's appearance in Print Preview.

► You can create mailing label reports with the Label Wizard. The wizard helps you create the prototype label layout and establish sort fields.

Commands Review

Action	Menu Bar	Shortcut Menu	Toolbar	Task Pane	Keyboard
Create a report	Insert, Report or AutoReport				ALT + I, R or E
Preview a report	File, Print Preview	Right-click report, Print Preview	🔍		ALT + F, V
Select several controls					SHIFT + Click or drag a rectangle to include them
Adjust control size	Format, Size, To Fit	Right-click report, Size, To Fit			ALT + O, S, F
Change font size			8 ▾		
Change font color		Right-click report, Font/Fore Color	A ▾		
Save a report	File, Save		💾		CTRL + S ALT + F, S
Print a report	File, Print	Right-click report, Print Preview	🖨		CTRL + P ALT + F, P

Concepts Review

Circle the correct answer.

1. A report is:
[a] the same as a form.
[b] a way of sorting and filtering data.
[c] an Access feature similar to tables.
[d] a way of displaying information from queries and tables.

2. A tabular report displays data from records in:
[a] vertical columns.
[b] horizontal rows.
[c] charts.
[d] columns like mailing labels.

3. Which of the following report types is *not* available in the Report Wizard?
[a] tabular report
[b] columnar report
[c] group report
[d] filter report

4. Use the Report Wizard to:
[a] create a report based on one or more tables or queries.
[b] set the properties of the report's header.
[c] create a report by starting with a blank design.
[d] modify the layout of an existing report.

5. Use AutoReport to:
[a] create a simple report based on a single table or query.
[b] set the properties of the report's footer.
[c] create a report by starting with a blank design.
[d] choose a number of options to determine your report's format and content.

6. Use the Setup button on the Print Preview toolbar to:
[a] change the report margins.
[b] choose a theme for the report.
[c] see the report's content and layout before you print it.
[d] change the printer name.

7. To add a label control in a report, use the:
[a] Control toolbar.
[b] Database window.
[c] Form Design view.
[d] Toolbox.

8. A report title from the Report Wizard customarily appears in the:
[a] Detail section.
[b] Report Header section.
[c] Page Header section.
[d] Group Header section.

9. Column headings usually appear in the:
[a] Detail section.
[b] Report Header section.
[c] Page Header section.
[d] Group Header section.

10. You normally place a calculated value in a:
[a] label control.
[b] calculation control.
[c] unbound text box control.
[d] calculation box control.

Circle **T** if the statement is true or **F** if the statement is false.

T   F   1. You can press the ALT + P keys to create an AutoReport.

T   F   2. AutoReport helps you create a report based on a single table or query.

T   F   3. You can choose portrait or landscape orientation for a report in the Report Wizard.

T   F   4. Click the Setup button in Print Preview to see two adjacent pages in a multi-page report.

chapter seven

T   F   5. The Detail section presents information about each record in the report.

T   F   6. You can direct the Report Wizard to fit all fields on a page.

T   F   7. The most common type of report is the tabular report where each record appears horizontally.

T   F   8. Material in the Report Header section appears on the top of each page of the report.

T   F   9. Once you insert a label and text box in one section, you cannot move it to another section.

T   F   10. You can set the background color of a report section.

Skills Review

Exercise 1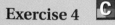

1. Create a copy of the *mdbFanTours7-* database located on the Data Disk.

2. Click the New Report button, and then create a columnar AutoReport based on the tblVendors table.

3. Save the report, naming the new report "rptVendors."

4. Print and close the new report, and then close the database.

Exercise 2

1. Open the *mdbFanTours7-1* database you created in Exercise 1.

2. In Design View, open the rptVendors report you created in Exercise 1.

3. Preview the report in Print Preview. Increase and decrease the magnification. Choose the two-page view, and then return to the one-page view.

4. Close the report and the database.

Exercise 3

1. Open the *mdbFanTours7-1* database you modified in Exercise 2.

2. Use the Report Wizard to create a new report based on the tblEvents, tblEventDetails, and tblEmployees tables. Use only the following fields in the report: EventName, EventDate, Description, and EventCost from the tblEvents table; DetailName, DetailDate, and DetailTime from the tblEventDetails table; and LastName from the tblEmployees table.

3. Choose to view the data by tblEvents. Do not choose grouping levels or sorting.

4. Choose the <u>A</u>lign Left 1 layout, the Corporate format, and Portrait orientation for the report.

5. Save the new report as "rptEvents."

6. Print the report.

7. Close the report and the database.

Exercise 4

1. Open the *mdbFanTours7-1* database you modified in Exercise 3.

2. In Design View, open the rptEvents report you created in Exercise 3.

3. Change the report's title to "Fantastic Sports Tour Events." Change the employee Last label to "FST Employee."

4. Resize any labels as necessary to display the entire contents of the column heading.

5. Save and print the rptEvents report.

6. Close the report and the database.

Exercise 5 [C]

1. Open the *mdbFanTours7-1* database you modified in Exercise 4.

2. In Design view, open the rptVendors report.

3. Add a control to the report footer to calculate the total number of vendors. Label it "Number of Vendors." The calculated field should be =Count([VendorName]).

4. Preview the report, scrolling to the end to view the Total Vendors controls at the end of the report.

5. Save and print the report.

6. Close the report and the database.

Exercise 6 [C]

1. Open the *mdbFanTours7-1* database you modified in Exercise 5.

2. Create a Tabular AutoReport for the qryProspectsZipOrder query.

3. Examine the report in Print Preview. What is the orientation of this report?

4. In Design view, change the report's title to "Prospect List."

5. Preview the report, save it as "rptProspectList," and print it.

6. Close the report and the database.

Exercise 7 [C]

1. Open the *mdbFanTours7-1* database you modified in Exercise 6.

2. In Design View, open the rptProspectList report you created in Exercise 6.

3. Enlarge the Page Header section by dragging down the top edge of the Detail section.

4. Move the report title label to the Page Header section, so that it appears once on every page. (*Hint:* You must move down all labels in the Page Header section to make room for this control.)

5. Center the title above the other fields in the Page Header section.

6. Preview, save, and print the report.

7. Close the report and the database.

Exercise 8 [C]

1. Open the *mdbFanTours7-1* database you modified in Exercise 7.

2. In Design view, open the rptProspectList report you modified in Exercise 7.

3. Create a calculated control in the Report Footer section that gives the total number of records in the report.

4. Use No of Prospects as the label for the calculated control. The calculated field should be =Count([Prospect]).

5. Preview the report, scrolling to the end to view the calculated field in the Report Footer section.

6. Save and print the report.

7. Close the report and the database.

chapter seven

Case Projects

Project 1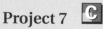

Using the Office on the Web command on the Help menu to connect to the Microsoft Web page and open the Office home page, and then link to pages that provide basic information about Access reports. Print at least one of the Web pages.

Project 2

Search online Help for information about creating and modifying reports. Connect to the Internet, and search for a Microsoft Web page that provides more information or examples. Print at least one page from the site.

Project 3

Open the *mdbFanTours7-2* database located on the Data Disk. Create a report with the Report Wizard for the tblEmployees table. Use all fields except the Photo field. Title the report "Employee List," and name the report itself "rptEmployees." Save the report, and close the database.

Project 4

Open the *mdbFanTours7-2* database you modified in Project 3. You received a request to add a graphic image to the Report Header section of the rptEmployees report. This procedure is very similar to inserting a graphic image in a form. Insert the *Employee.bmp* graphic file located on the Data Disk into the rptEmployees report. Open the report in Design view, and then click the Unbound Object Frame button in the Toolbox. Click where you want to insert the graphic, and then select the *Employee.bmp*. Save the report, and close the database.

Project 5

Open the *mdbFanTours7-2* database you modified in Project 4. Fantastic Sports Tours wants to create a report that sorts employees by hire date, from earliest to latest. You can do this in the Report Wizard. Run the Report Wizard and create a report named "rptEmployees By Hire Date." Use all fields but reduce the size of the Photo field, so that it is very small. Resize the Detail section to minimal height. Save the report, and close the database.

Project 6

Open the *mdbFanTours7-2* database you modified in Project 5. Elsa wants you to create a report showing a list of Fantastic Sports Tours' vendors. Create that report and include each vendor's category name. Save the report as "rptVendor Categories." Print a copy of the report. Close the report, and close the database.

Project 7

Open the *mdbFanTours7-2* database you modified in Project 6. In Design view, open the rptVendor Categories report you modified in Project 6. Enlarge the Detail section enough so that you can move the Fax field from the top line to right below the telephone number field. Enlarge the two fields so that the entire phone number appears. Delete the Fax label. Change the Phone label to "Phone/Fax." Print a copy of the report, and save the report. Close the report, and close the database.

Project 8

Open the *mdbFanTours7-2* database you modified in Project 6. With the Report Wizard, create a report that shows customers' names, customers' e-mail addresses, the tours each customer booked, and the cost of each tour. You can pull the fields from the tblBookings, tblCustomers, and tblEvents tables. Organize the report by customer. Adjust field widths and locations as necessary. Save this report as "rptCustomer Bookings." Print a copy of the report. Save the report, and close the database.

Importing and Exporting Access Data

Chapter Overview

I t is often helpful to use data from one application in documents you create in other applications. In Access, you can import and export data so that the information is where you need it, when you need it, without your needing to rekey it. In this chapter, you learn to use an Access database with Word and Excel. In addition, you learn to save Access objects as Web pages and create a simple data access page, so that you and others can view information on the Web.

Case profile

Administrators at Online University want to use information from other Microsoft Office applications, such as Word and Excel, with Access data. The Admissions Office wants a report about students and majors. Michael Golden, the associate provost, wants to send letters to students using information from an Access table. Jung Me, the assistant registrar, wants to use information from Excel workbooks to create new Access tables. The Human Resources Office wants to view information about instructors on the school's intranet.

Learning Objectives

► **Integrate Access with Word using Office Links**
► **Integrate Access with Excel**
► **Import Access data from another database**
► **Save a table, query, form, or report as a Web page**
► **Create a simple DAP**

chapter eight

C 8.a Integrating Access with Word Using Office Links

Rather than rekeying Access data in other Office applications, you can export or import it. In this context, **exporting** means transferring data from Access to a file format that other applications, such as Word and Excel, can read, and **importing** means transferring data from an Office application, such as Word and Excel, to a file format that Access can read.

Exporting Query Results to Word

The Office Links button on the Database toolbar has two exporting options. The Merge It with Microsoft Word option lets you insert data from Access fields into Word documents to create personalized letters, labels, and envelopes. The Publish It with Microsoft Word choice creates and opens a Word Rich Text Format (RTF) document using the table or query name followed by the .rtf filename extension. To publish a query datasheet to Word:

Step 1	*Create*	a copy of the *mdbOnlineU8-* database located on the Data Disk
Step 2	*Click*	Queries [Queries] on the Objects bar
Step 3	*Click*	qryStudentMajors, if necessary
Step 4	*Click*	the Office Links button list arrow [icon] on the Database toolbar
Step 5	*Click*	Publish It with Microsoft Word

Word starts and displays the query results in an RTF document, which is saved as *qryStudentMajors* in the same folder as *mdbOnlineU8-1*.

| Step 6 | *Click* | the Word button on the taskbar, if necessary, to display the document |
| Step 7 | *Click* | the Close button [X] on the Word title bar to close the document and exit Word |

Merging an Access Table with a Word Document

Michael wrote a letter to OLU's students using Word, and he wants you to add the most current information to each letter. You can export the data from an Access table to the Word document. You can use the Merge It with Microsoft Word option to accomplish this task.

When you're ready to merge, Word finds the table, records, and fields you specified, and merges that information in the main document. To merge data with a Microsoft Word document, you first select the Access data source (in this case, a query) and then use the Office Links button on the Database toolbar. You are using a query so that you include only the appropriate records of the database. To merge the data:

Step 1	*Select*	qryStudentAdvisors in the Database window
Step 2	*Click*	the Office Links button list arrow [W ▼] on the Database toolbar
Step 3	*Click*	Merge It with Microsoft Word

The Mail Merge Wizard asks whether you want to use an existing document or create a new one. Although you could select the first option and use the letter Michael wrote, you choose to create a new one so you can see the process of entering merge fields.

Step 4	*Click*	the Create a new document and then link data to it option button
Step 5	*Click*	OK to start Word and display the Mail Merge task pane
Step 6	*Maximize*	the Word application window, if necessary

Your screen should look similar to Figure 8-1.

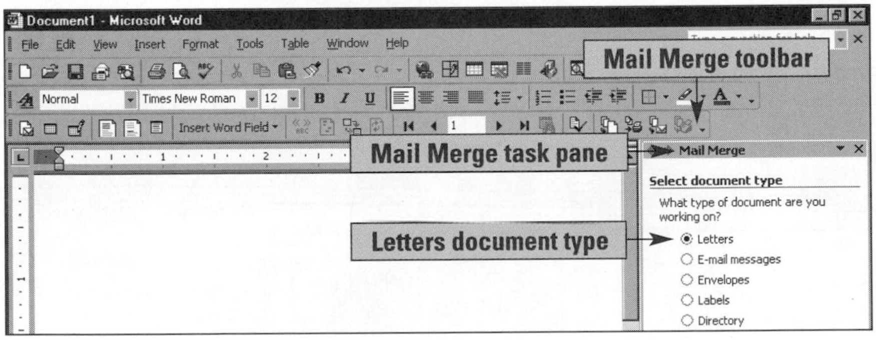

FIGURE 8-1
Step 1 - Select Document Type

Word contains preprogrammed formats for several document types. The formats provide you with sample merge fields and page layouts for

chapter
eight

each document type, from letters to labels to envelopes and more. To select the main document type:

| Step 1 | *Verify* | that the Letters option button is selected in the Select document type section of the Mail Merge task pane |
| Step 2 | *Click* | the Next: Starting document link in the Mail Merge task pane |

Your screen should look similar to Figure 8-2.

FIGURE 8-2
Step 2 - Select Starting Document

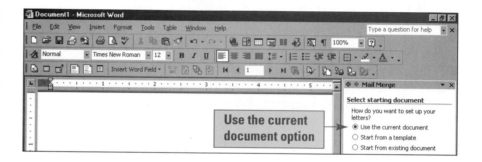

To set up the main document for merging:

| Step 1 | *Verify* | that the Use the current document option button is selected in the Select starting document section of the Mail Merge task pane |
| Step 2 | *Click* | the Next: Select recipients link in the Mail Merge task pane |

Your screen should look similar to Figure 8-3.

FIGURE 8-3
Step 3 - Select Recipients

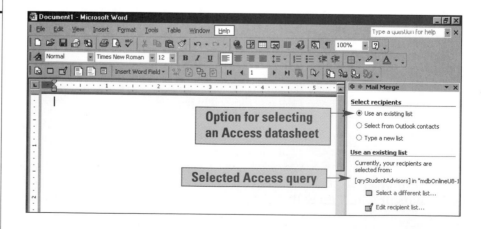

To select the letter recipients from the Access query:

| Step 1 | *Verify* | that the Use an existing list option button is selected in the Select recipients section of the Mail Merge task pane |
| Step 2 | *Click* | the Next: Write your letter link in the Mail Merge task pane |

Michael already keyed the letter into a Word document. You insert this document now to save keying time. To insert the document:

Step 1	*Click*	<u>I</u>nsert
Step 2	*Click*	Fi<u>l</u>e
Step 3	*Switch to*	the drive and folder that contains the Data Disk
Step 4	*Double-click*	*Student Advisor Letter*

Word inserts this file to which you add the merge codes. Your screen should look similar to Figure 8-4.

Welcome to the Spring semester at Online University. We are pleased that you
your college studies at OLU. Your faculty advisor is able to answer most of yo
the curriculum, the registration process, and your academic progress. Your fac
NNN with phone number PPP and e-mail address EEE.

Step 5	*Select*	the AAA text beneath the date
Step 6	*Click*	the Address block link in the Write your letter section of the Mail Merge task pane
Step 7	*Observe*	the sample data in the Insert Address Block dialog box
Step 8	*Click*	OK to accept the default address block format that appears in the preview
Step 9	*Observe*	the << <<AddressBlock>> >> merge field in the main document
Step 10	*Select*	GGG beneath the address block

FIGURE 8-4
Step 4 - Write Your Letter

chapter
eight

Step 11	*Click*	the Greeting line link in the Mail Merge task pane to open the Greeting Line dialog box
Step 12	*Click*	OK to accept the default greeting format commonly used in letters
Step 13	*Select*	NNN
Step 14	*Click*	the More items link in the Write your letter section of the Mail Merge task pane

The Insert Merge Fields dialog box opens, so you can select a merge field to insert into the letter.

Step 15	*Click*	Advisor in the Fields: list box (making sure the Database Fields option button is selected)
Step 16	*Click*	Insert
Step 17	*Close*	the Insert Merge Field dialog box

Word inserts the <<Advisor>> merge field, which represents the value of the advisor's name for this student.

| Step 18 | *Follow* | Steps 13 through 17 to insert the Adv Phone merge field for the PPP block |
| Step 19 | *Follow* | Steps 13 through 17 to insert the Adv Email merge field for the EEE block |

Angle bracket characters (<< >>) surround all fields you selected for merging. The Access data source supplies the information that eventually replaces the brackets in each individual letter. Although you don't want to save the document that contains the letters, you do want to save the main document with the merge codes, so that you don't need to create it the next time you send Michael's letters. In this case, you save the Student Advisor Main Document. To save the main document:

Step 1	*Click*	the Save button 🖫 on the Standard toolbar
Step 2	*Key*	Student Advisor Main Document in the File name: text box
Step 3	*Click*	Save

The *Student Advisor Main Document* contains the letter and the merge codes. The *Student Advisor Letter* document contains only the letter.

MOUSE **TIP**

You can double-click a field name in the Insert Merge Field dialog box to place a merge field in your document.

QUICK **TIP**

When you merge, Word replaces merge fields (the <<*text*>> items) with the corresponding data from each record in the data source.

After you select and set up the main document, you're ready to merge information from the data source. To merge the data:

Step 1	Click	the Next: Preview your letters link in the Mail Merge task pane
Step 2	Observe	that Access inserts the data from the first record in the qryStudentAdvisors datasheet into the letter
Step 3	Click	the Next: Complete the merge link in the Mail Merge task pane

Your screen should look similar to Figure 8-5.

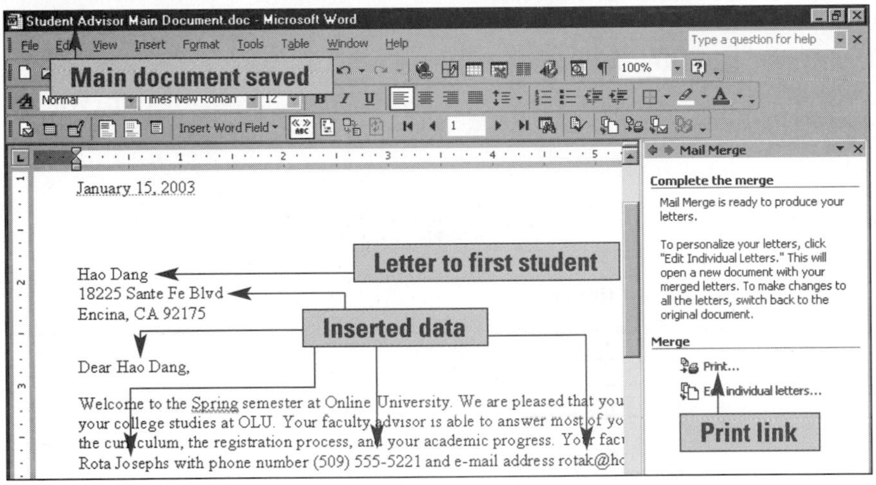

FIGURE 8-5
Step 6 - Complete the Merge

QUICK TIP

Before you print merged letters, it is good practice to preview them to make sure that the merge occurred properly.

You have to choose the destination for your letters. Access can create the letters for printing or place them in one document. To merge the data and create the letters in a new document:

| Step 1 | Click | the Edit individual letters link in the Mail Merge task pane |

The Merge to New Document dialog box opens. You can choose to create all records, the current record, or a range of records.

Step 2	Verify	that the All records option is selected
Step 3	Click	OK
Step 4	Observe	that a new Word document opens, containing the 54 letters
Step 5	Scroll	through the merged letters

chapter
eight

You can print the merged letters, save them in a file, or discard them. You discard them because you can easily recreate the letters from the main document you created.

Step 6	*Close*	the document containing the merged letters, without saving the letters
Step 7	*Exit*	Word without saving changes to the main document

C 8.b Integrating Access with Excel

If you want to integrate Access data with Excel, you can export the Access data to Excel, with or without formatting. Exporting data without formatting speeds the export process. To export a table to Excel:

Step 1	*Click*	Tables on the Objects bar in Access
Step 2	*Click*	tblCourses
Step 3	*Click*	File
Step 4	*Click*	Export

The Export Table To dialog box opens, where you can specify the name, location, and type of file you want to export. You also have an option to save any Access table formatting, including field widths, fonts, colors, or data from Lookup fields. You saved the field widths in the tblCourses table.

Step 5	*Key*	tblCourses
Step 6	*Click*	the Save as type: list arrow
Step 7	*Click*	Microsoft Excel 97-2002
Step 8	*Click*	the Save formatted check box to insert a check mark
Step 9	*Click*	Export

Access creates the workbook containing the records from the tblCourses table and puts the field names in the first row of the first worksheet. You can select a few records from the tblCourses table and export them directly to a new Excel worksheet using an Office Links command.

To export selected records and open an Excel workbook:

Step 1	**Double-click**	tblCourses in the Database window
Step 2	**Drag**	to select the first three records
Step 3	**Click**	Tools
Step 4	**Point to**	Office Links
Step 5	**Click**	Analyze It with Microsoft Excel
Step 6	**Click**	No so that Access creates a new workbook
Step 7	**Key**	Courses in the File name: text box in the Output To dialog box
Step 8	**Click**	OK

Access saves the records as an Excel workbook, and then Excel automatically starts and opens the workbook.

| Step 9 | **Exit** | Excel |
| Step 10 | **Close** | the tblCourses table in Access |

Using the Clipboard to Copy Data to Excel

You can use the Clipboard to copy a table or a query datasheet into Excel. The copying process also automatically translates the data—or makes it readable in Excel. This copying procedure requires that both Excel and Access be open. To copy an entire table and paste it in Excel:

Step 1	**Start**	Microsoft Excel and create a blank workbook, if necessary
Step 2	**Click**	the Access button on the taskbar to switch back to Access
Step 3	**Click**	tblPrograms in the Database window
Step 4	**Click**	the Copy button 🖺 on the Database toolbar
Step 5	**Switch to**	Excel and click cell A1, if necessary
Step 6	**Click**	the Paste button 🖺 on the Excel Standard toolbar

Access inserts the data into Excel. If the datasheet has wide fields, Excel adjusts row height so the data fits on more than one line.

chapter eight

MOUSE TIP

Instead of using the Clipboard, you can drag and drop data to or from Excel. To drag and drop efficiently, open both Access and Excel and resize the application windows so that they fit side by side on your desktop. Then you can drag data from one application and drop it in the other.

QUICK TIP

Linking data from Excel to Access inserts an object in the database that names an Excel workbook and its location. If you change the original workbook, the database reflects those changes and *vice versa*—changing the linked data changes the original workbook. Because you are inserting a link, and not the data itself, you do not need extra disk space.

| Step 7 | *Close* | Excel without saving the workbook |

Importing an Excel List into an Access Table

When you import structured data, you take information from Excel and copy it to an Access table, retaining the Excel formatting and data types. The Excel data becomes part of your Access database—you can change the imported data without affecting the original file. When you copy information from an Excel workbook to your database, you use extra disk space. After you import the data, you can change all properties and structures. If you delete the database object, you also delete the data.

When you link data from Excel to Access, Access must be able to find the Excel workbook, so that it can display up-to-date information. The Excel data remains in its original format but acts like an Access database. You can change properties that affect the way the data appears in Access, but you cannot change the data structure. Linking data makes Access work more slowly than importing data does.

Importing Data to a New Table

OLU recently developed an articulation agreement with a junior college system. The registrar asks you to add the course information from the junior college system to your database from an Excel worksheet. To begin importing Excel data into Access:

Step 1	*Click*	File
Step 2	*Point to*	Get External Data
Step 3	*Click*	Import
Step 4	*Switch to*	the drive and folder containing the Data Disk
Step 5	*Click*	Microsoft Excel in the Files of type: list box
Step 6	*Double-click*	*Transfer Courses* to open the Excel workbook

The Import Worksheet Wizard opens to guide you both in selecting the information to import from the Excel workbook and in determining its appearance in the Access database. In the first dialog box, you select and preview the worksheet or ranges to use. To use the Import Worksheet Wizard:

| Step 1 | *Click* | Next > to take information from Sheet1 |

The second wizard dialog box asks you if the first row contains the column headings.

Step 2	*Verify*	that the First Row Contains Column Headings check box contains a check mark
Step 3	*Click*	Next >
Step 4	*Click*	Next > to import the information into a new table

When you import an Excel worksheet with column headings in the first row, Access automatically selects the appropriate fields.

| Step 5 | *Click* | Next > to accept all the fields |

Access asks if you want to select the primary key. Because you need to select two fields as the primary key, you don't select a primary key during the import process.

Step 6	*Click*	No primary key
Step 7	*Click*	Next >
Step 8	*Key*	tblTransferCourses
Step 9	*Click*	Finish
Step 10	*Click*	OK

Access imports the data, and it becomes an Access object. You open the table to check it. You can modify the data or the table design as you would any Access table.

Step 11	*Double-click*	tblTransferCourses
Step 12	*Switch to*	Design view
Step 13	*Select*	the Dept row selector
Step 14	*CTRL + Click*	the Number row selector to select it
Step 15	*Click*	the Primary Key button 🔑 to make these fields the primary key
Step 16	*Close*	the tblTransferCourses table, saving the changes to its design

> **QUICK TIP**
>
> Although Access usually uses the same name as the original table, you can change the name if necessary.

chapter
eight

Linking an Excel Workbook to an Access Database

Jung has an Excel workbook that lists the online courses available at another university. Jung asks you to add this information to your database. Because this information changes periodically, you link the data. This way, any changes to the original Excel workbook are reflected in your database. To start the Link Worksheet Wizard to link an Excel workbook to an Access database:

Step 1	*Click*	File
Step 2	*Point to*	Get External Data
Step 3	*Click*	Link Tables to open the Link dialog box
Step 4	*Click*	Microsoft Excel in the Files of type: list box
Step 5	*Double-click*	CCC Courses

The Link Worksheet Wizard starts. To use the Link Worksheet Wizard:

Step 1	*Click*	Next > to accept the tblCourses worksheet

The next dialog box asks if the first row contains the column headings. In this worksheet, the first row does contain the column headings.

Step 2	*Click*	the First Row Contains Column Headings check box to insert a check mark
Step 3	*Click*	Next >

Although Access gives the table the same name as the original table, you change the name because a table with that name already exists.

Step 4	*Key*	tblCCC Courses in the Linked Table Name: text box
Step 5	*Click*	Finish
Step 6	*Click*	OK

The table appears in the Database window. To open the table:

Step 1	*Double-click*	tblCCC Courses in the Database window

| Step 2 | **Double-click** | the right border of the CourseTitle column header to widen the field |

Your screen should look similar to Figure 8-6.

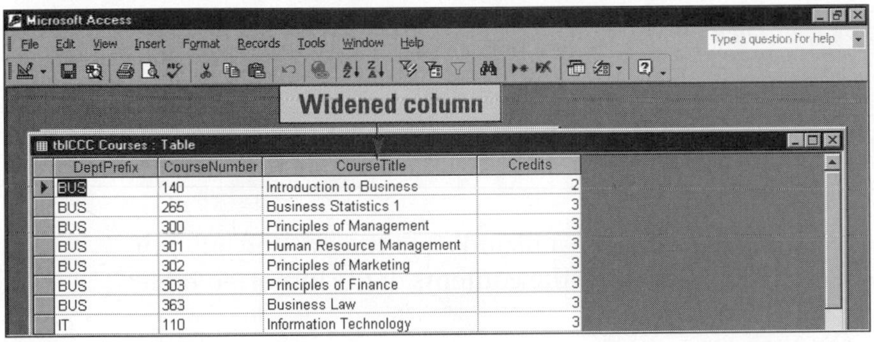

FIGURE 8-6
Table with Linked Data

> **QUICK TIP**
>
> In the Database window, a small arrow and the Excel icon in front of a table name signify a linked Excel table.

The Link Worksheet Wizard creates the tblCCC Courses table with a link to the *CCC Courses* workbook. To change a value in the linked table:

Step 1	**Click**	the CourseNumber cell of the MATH 120 row
Step 2	**Key**	121 in place of 120 in this cell
Step 3	**Close**	the table in Access, clicking Yes to save changes to the table
Step 4	**Start**	Microsoft Excel
Step 5	**Open**	the *CCC Courses* workbook that you linked to Access earlier
Step 6	**Verify**	that the MATH 120 row has been changed to MATH 121
Step 7	**Close**	Excel

8.c Importing Access Data from Another Database

You can import any database object (table, query, form, report, page, macro, or module) from another Access database or export objects to another database. To import an object into an open Access database:

| Step 1 | **Click** | File |
| Step 2 | **Point to** | Get External Data |

chapter
eight

Step 3	*Click*	Import
Step 4	*Switch to*	the drive and folder containing the Data Disk
Step 5	*Click*	Microsoft Access in the Files of type: list box, if necessary
Step 6	*Double-click*	mdbOnlineU8-2
Step 7	*Click*	the Tables tab in the Import Objects dialog box
Step 8	*Click*	tblTransferStudents
Step 9	*Click*	OK

Access imports the table and adds it to the existing tables in *mdbOnlineU8-1*. To verify the contents of the imported table:

Step 1	*Double-click*	tblTransferStudents
Step 2	*Observe*	the contents of the imported table
Step 3	*Close*	the tblTransferStudents table

C 8.d Saving a Table, Query, Form, or Report as a Web Page

Access lets you save results from a table, query, form, or report in a static HTML page that can be read on the Web. A **static HTML page** contains HTML commands and data that was present when the Web page was created. The Web page is *not* updated when you make subsequent changes to the Access object. To update the content of Web page, you need to re-save the Access object to the HTML page.

A static Web page displays tables, queries, and forms in a datasheet format and displays reports in a report format.

For OLU, you decide to make the class offerings available as a static Web page. You save it on your own computer for now, so that you can view it with your computer's Web browser. Later you can **publish** (or save) this file on a Web server on the Internet so others can view it. A query in *mdbOnlineU8-1*, qryClassOfferings, contains the information you need. To create a static Web page:

INTERNET TIP

To make static HTML files available on the Web, you save them on a Web server on the Internet. A **Web server** is a computer on the Internet (or an intranet) that sends HTML files to your browser when the browser requests that file.

Step 1	*Click*	Queries 📇 Queries on the Objects bar
Step 2	*Right-click*	qryClassOfferings

Step 3	*Click*	Export
Step 4	*Key*	classofferings in the File name: text box
Step 5	*Click*	HTML Documents in the Save as type: list
Step 6	*Click*	Export

Access might display the HTML Output Options dialog box where you can specify an HTML template to format the data in a predetermined way. If you don't specify an HTML template, the data appears in a table.

| Step 7 | *Click* | OK to create the HTML file, if the HTML Output Options dialog box opens |

Access creates the file *classofferings.htm* and saves it in the same folder as *mdbOnlineU8-1*. You can preview this Web page by opening it in your Web browser. To preview a Web page in your browser:

Step 1	*Start*	Internet Explorer
Step 2	*Click*	File
Step 3	*Click*	Open
Step 4	*Click*	Browse
Step 5	*Switch to*	the drive and folder where you store *mdbOnlineU8-1*
Step 6	*Double-click*	*classofferings.htm* in the Look in: list
Step 7	*Click*	OK to open the Web page in the browser window
Step 8	*Observe*	that the blank cells correspond to classes that have no instructor listed in the database
Step 9	*Close*	Internet Explorer

8.e Creating a Simple DAP

A **data access page (DAP)** is a dynamic HTML file that contains pointers to data in an Access database. Unlike a static Web page, the DAP displays up-to-date values from the current Access database. The Human Resources Office needs a way to view information about instructors on the school's intranet. A simple DAP can display this information. To create a simple DAP:

| Step 1 | *Click* | Pages on the Objects bar |

chapter eight

Step 2	*Double-click*	Create data access page by using wizard to start the Page Wizard
Step 3	*Click*	tblInstructors in the <u>T</u>ables/Queries list box
Step 4	*Click*	the `>>` button to select all fields
Step 5	*Click*	<u>N</u>ext >
Step 6	*Click*	<u>N</u>ext > to not select any grouping levels
Step 7	*Click*	<u>N</u>ext > to not set any sort fields for this page
Step 8	*Key*	dapInstructors in the What title do you want for your page? text box
Step 9	*Click*	the Open the page. option button
Step 10	*Click*	<u>F</u>inish

The telephone number field does not display the full number. To modify a DAP in Design view:

Step 1	*Switch to*	Design view
Step 2	*Click*	the PhoneNumber text box (not the label)
Step 3	*Drag*	the right sizing handle approximately four grid lines to the right
Step 4	*Click*	the Page View button 🖳 on the Page Design View toolbar

Your screen should look similar to Figure 8-7. You can see the database values in the browser.

FIGURE 8-7
dapInstructors Data
Access Page in Page View

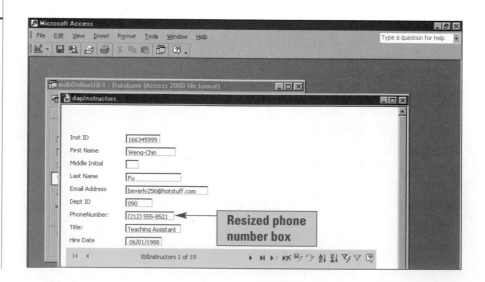

The Page Wizard does not save the HTML file automatically when you close the page. To save and close a DAP:

Step 1	Click	the Save button 🔲 on the Page View toolbar
Step 2	Key	dapInstructors in the File name: text box, if necessary
Step 3	Click	Save

Access saves your page in a separate file, *dapInstructors.htm*, and places it in the same folder as the database file. It also saves the design as dapInstructors in the Pages tab of the Database window. You can modify the design by opening dapInstructors in Design view in Access.

You receive a message warning that your connection string specifies an absolute path. The *dapInstructors.htm* file contains a **connection string** that gives the explicit path (including drive, folder, and filename) of the Access database. A DAP works only if the database is located on the same path and has the same name as those given by the connection string property. You can test your DAP by viewing the HTML file directly in a browser. You don't have to close Access to view the HTML file.

Step 4	Click	OK to acknowledge the absolute path warning message
Step 5	Close	the DAP window
Step 6	Start	Internet Explorer
Step 7	Click	File
Step 8	Click	Open
Step 9	Click	Browse
Step 10	Switch to	the drive and folder where you store *mdbOnlineU8-1*
Step 11	Double-click	dapInstructors in the Look in: list
Step 12	Click	OK

Access opens the DAP in the browser window. This view is identical to the one you saw in the Access Page view.

| Step 13 | Close | Internet Explorer and the database |

A DAP is a great way to share current Access data with others over the Internet or an intranet.

> **CAUTION TIP**
>
> To view a DAP you must use Microsoft's Internet Explorer browser version 5.0 or later. DAPs do not work with Netscape Navigator.

chapter
eight

Summary

▶ You can merge Access data to a Word document using the Access Office Links command and the Word Mail Merge Wizard.

▶ You can include Excel data in an Access table by importing or linking an Excel workbook to a new or existing Access table. When you import from an Excel workbook, you copy the Excel data to an Access table.

▶ When you link an Excel workbook to an Access table, you insert a reference to the workbook, so Access can display the information in the worksheet.

▶ You can import any database object (table, query, form, report, page, macro, or module) from another Access database or export objects from one database to another.

▶ You can save tables, queries, forms, and reports as static HTML files for viewing in a Web browser. The HTML file does not reflect subsequent changes in the database.

▶ A DAP is a dynamic HTML file that gets its data directly from the Access database. The DAP reflects subsequent changes to the database.

Commands Review

Action	Menu Bar	Shortcut Menu	Toolbar	Task Pane	Keyboard
Start Word Mail Merge Wizard	Tools, Letters and Mailings, Mail Merge Wizard				ALT + T, E, M
Import a table	File, Get External Data, Import	Right-click table, Import			ALT + F, G, I
Link to a table	File, Get External Data, Link tables	Right-click table, Link Tables			ALT + F, G, L
Export records	File, Export	Right-click record, Export			ALT + F, E
Export records and open in Excel	Tools, Office Links, Analyze It with Excel		🖼		ALT + T, L, A
Export records and open in Word	Tools, Office Links, Publish It with Word		🖼		ALT + T, L, P
Export records and merge in Word	Tools, Office Links, Merge It with Word		🖼		ALT + T, L, M
Repair and compact a database	Tools, Database Utilities, Compact and Repair Database				ALT + T, D, C

Concepts Review

Circle the correct answer.

1. To display Access data in a Word table, use the:
[a] Merge It option.
[b] Mail Merge option.
[c] Analyze It option.
[d] Publish It option.

2. To create letters that contain data from an Access datasheet, use the:
[a] Merge It option.
[b] Format It option.
[c] Analyze It option.
[d] Publish It option.

3. In a Word document, the code <<field>> means:
[a] enclose the field value in angle brackets.
[b] insert the name of the field instead of its value.
[c] insert the value of the field.
[d] insert the literal characters, <<field>>.

4. Which one of these is *not* a way to export a datasheet to an Excel worksheet?
[a] export
[b] drag-and-drop method
[c] copy and paste method
[d] link the datasheet to the workbook

5. Merge Access data into Word when you want to:
[a] insert a reference to Access within a Word document.
[b] create Word documents customized with Access information.
[c] copy an entire Access table into a Word document.
[d] change fields frequently.

6. Which one of these objects cannot be imported from another Access database?
[a] table
[b] page
[c] macro
[d] wizard

7. When you need data in a Web page to change when the database changes:
[a] use a data access page.
[b] use static HTML file.
[c] export to Excel.
[d] export to a text file.

8. Imported data does *not*:
[a] change when the external table changes.
[b] convert to Access format.
[c] work faster with Access.
[d] allow data type translation.

9. A linked table generally:
[a] requires extra storage space.
[b] lets you delete information.
[c] works slower with Access.
[d] lets you change any properties.

10. A data access page is:
[a] stored in a database file.
[b] a static HTML file.
[c] a dynamic HTML file.
[d] only accessible when viewed within Access.

Circle **T** if the statement is true or **F** if the statement is false.

T   F   1. When you publish an Access datasheet in Word, Access creates a .doc file.

T   F   2. You should identify a main Word document as well as the Access data source to merge print information from the Access database.

T   F   3. The merge fields you insert in a Word document are indicated by [[field]].

chapter eight

T   F   4. Linked tables appear in the Database window with a large *L* icon.

T   F   5. Access works somewhat slower with a linked table than with an imported table.

T   F   6. If you need to update data that changes frequently, you should link the data.

T   F   7. You can add data in Access to a linked Excel workbook.

T   F   8. You can change all properties of data that you link from an Excel workbook.

T   F   9. A DAP is an HTML file saved outside of Access.

T   F   10. It is good to avoid using an absolute connection string with a data access page.

Skills Review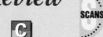

Exercise 1

1. Create a copy of the *mdbFanTours8-* database located on the Data Disk.

2. Use the OfficeLinks button on the Database toolbar to publish the tblEmployees table from the *mdbFanTours8-1* database in Word.

3. Verify that the document now exists as *tblEmployees.rtf.*

4. Print the document, exit Word, and close the database.

Exercise 2

1. Open the *mdbFanTours8-1* database you created in Exercise 1. Select the tblProspects table.

2. Use the Office Links button on the Database toolbar and select Merge It with Microsoft Word, creating a new document.

3. Create Letters in Step 1 of the Word Mail Merge task pane.

4. Accept the default choices for Steps 2 and 3 of the Mail Merge task pane.

5. Text for the letter appears in *Prospect Letter Text.doc.* Use the Insert, File command to insert this text at Step 4 in the Mail Merge task pane.

6. At Step 4, use the More items command on the Mail Merge task pane to insert the individual FName, MName, LName, StreetAddress, City, State, and PostalCode merge fields where indicated in the text. Adjust spacing as necessary after you insert the merge fields.

7. Save the main document as *Prospect Letter Main Document.*

8. Preview the letters in Step 5. Print the first letter, by specifying the print range as the first record.

9. Close Word and close the database.

Exercise 3

1. Open the *mdbFanTours8-1* database you modified in Exercise 2.

2. Use the Get External Data command to import the *FST Salary* Excel workbook from the Data Disk into a new table named tblSalary. Use Employee ID as the primary key. Click OK to any dialog boxes that appear.

3. Open the imported table and navigate through its records.

4. Close the table and the database.

Exercise 4   C

1. Open the *mdbFanTours8-1* database you modified in Exercise 3.

2. Export the qryCustomerBookings query to a Microsoft Excel 97-2002 workbook named "qryCustomerBookings." Use the Save Formatted option.

3. Open the *qryCustomerBookings* workbook in Excel.

4. Widen the columns if necessary in Excel. Print a copy of the worksheet.

5. Close Excel, saving the workbook, and close the database.

Exercise 5   C

1. Open the *mdbFanTours8-1* database you modified in Exercise 4.

2. Use the Get External Data command to link the *Temporary Staff* Excel workbook from the Data Disk. The first row contains column headings. Use all fields.

3. Save the linked table as "tblTemporaryStaff" in the database.

4. Print a copy of the Database window showing the linked table. (*Hint:* Switch to Tables, press the PrintScrn key, and then paste the contents of the Clipboard in a Word document.) Print the Word document.

5. Close the database.

Exercise 6   C

1. Open the *mdbFanTours8-1* database you modified in Exercise 5.

2. Import the tblInstructors table from the *mdbOnlineU8-* database on the Data Disk. Because you are importing from another Access database, you must select Microsoft Access in the Files of type: list box in the Import dialog box.

3. Print a copy of the table, and then close the database.

Exercise 7   C   [internet]

1. Open the *mdbFanTours8-1* database you modified in Exercise 6.

2. Select the tblEvents table from the database.

3. Export the tblEvents table to an HTML document named *fstevents.htm*.

4. Open *fstevents.htm* in your Web browser to check its appearance.

5. Close the browser and the database.

Exercise 8   C

1. Open the *mdbFanTours8-1* database you modified in Exercise 7.

2. Switch to Pages in the Database window.

3. Using the Page Wizard, create a data access page for the qryVendorActivity query. Use all fields.

4. Accept all default choices in the wizard, and select tblVendors as the unique table. Name this page "dapVendorActivity."

5. Open the page in your browser. Navigate to different records.

6. Print a copy of the page that shows the first record.

7. Close the page. Save the page as *dapVendorActivity.htm*. Close the database.

chapter eight

Case Projects

Project 1

The owner of Fantastic Sports Tours asks you to determine if you can convert an Access 2002 database so someone with a previous version of Access can use it. You know that Access 2002 uses the Access 2000 file version as the default format but wonder if Access can convert to Access 97. Search online Help for information on converting an Access 2002 database to a previous version. Use Word to create a document that provides the information. Print and save the document as a Word file.

Project 2

The marketing manager wants you to find a quick way to use Access tables and queries in an Excel worksheet. Open the *mdbFanTours8-2* database located on the Data Disk. Open Microsoft Excel and resize Excel and Access so you can see both windows on your desktop. In the Access Database window, click the qryTours query and drag it from Access to a blank worksheet in Excel. Save and print the new worksheet. Save the Excel workbook as *qryTours.xls*. Close the database.

Project 3

Open the *mdbFanTours8-2* database you modified in Project 2. Catherine Emmen, marketing manager, asks you to create a set of customized letters to prospective customers about upcoming events. Use the <u>M</u>erge It with Microsoft Word option to create the letter. Using the name and address information in the tblProspects table, write a business letter that describes the three football bowl games found in the first three records of the tblEvents table. Because the football game information does not change for each letter, just key it into the letter as text. Save the main document as *Prospect Letter Main Document*, and print a copy of the preview of the first letter. Save the merged document as *Prospect Letters*. Close Word and close the database.

Project 4

Open the *mdbFanTours8-2* database you modified in Project 2. The managing partner thinks some information in the database is appropriate for the FST Web site. Export the tblCustomers table in *mdbFanTours8-2* as a static HTML file named *customers.htm*. Open your browser and view the HTML file. Close the browser. Close the database.

Project 5

Open the *mdbFanTours8-2* database you modified in Project 4. Open the tblTemporaryStaff linked table in the *mfbFanTours8-2* database. Add a new record to it with information about a new temporary employee. Try to delete the record you just added. Open the workbook in Excel to verify that you added the record, and then print the table. Close Excel and then close the database.

Project 6

Open the *mdbFanTours8-2* database you modified in Project 5. Before you created the database for Fantastic Sports Tours, the marketing manager stored important customer information in a text file in which commas separate each field. Now she wants you to import this text file—*Best Customers*—into the tblCustomers table. Search online Help for instructions on importing a text file to Access using the Import Text Wizard. Then follow these instructions to import the text into new table called "tblBestCustomers." The field names appear in the first row. Use CustID as the primary key. Print a copy of the table in Access, and then close the database.

Project 7

Open *mdbFanTours8-2* you modified in Project 6. Create a DAP for the tblInstructors table. Save the page as *dapInstructor.htm*. Open the *dapInstructor.htm* page in Internet Explorer, and print a copy of the *last* instructor's information. Close Internet Explorer. Close the database.

Project 8

Connect to the Internet and search the Web for information about creating and using DAPs. Look for topics dealing with Design view, record navigation in a DAP, or sections in the DAP. Print at least one page of information.

Working with Windows 2000

Appendix Overview

The Windows 2000 operating system creates a workspace on your computer screen, called the desktop. The desktop is a graphical environment that contains icons you click with the mouse pointer to access your computer system resources or to perform a task such as opening a software application. This appendix introduces you to the Windows 2000 desktop by describing the default desktop icons and showing how to access your computer resources, use menu commands and toolbar buttons to perform a task, and review and select dialog box options.

LEARNING OBJECTIVES

- ▶ Review the Windows 2000 desktop
- ▶ Access your computer system resources
- ▶ Use menu commands and toolbar buttons
- ▶ Use the Start menu
- ▶ Review dialog box options
- ▶ Use Windows 2000 shortcuts
- ▶ Understand the Recycle Bin
- ▶ Shut down Windows 2000

appendix

 Reviewing the Windows 2000 Desktop

Whenever you start your computer, the Windows 2000 operating system automatically starts. You are prompted to log on with your user name and password, which identify your account. Then the Windows 2000 desktop appears on your screen. To view the Windows 2000 desktop:

Step 1	*Turn on*	your computer and monitor

The Log On to Windows dialog box opens, as shown in Figure A-1.

FIGURE A-1
Log On to Windows
Dialog Box

Text boxes for
your account info

Step 2	*Key*	your user name in the User name: text box
Step 3	*Key*	your password in the Password: text box
Step 4	*Click*	OK
Step 5	*Click*	the Exit button in the Getting Started with Windows 2000 dialog box, if necessary
Step 6	*Observe*	the Windows 2000 desktop work area, as shown in Figure A-2

The Windows 2000 desktop contains three elements: icons, background, and taskbar. The icons represent Windows objects and shortcuts to opening software applications or performing tasks. Table A-1 describes some of the default icons. The taskbar, at the bottom of the window, contains the Start button and the Quick Launch toolbar, and tray. The icon types and arrangement, desktop background, or Quick Launch toolbar on your screen might be different.

QUICK TIP

If you don't see the Log On to Windows dialog box, you can open the Windows Security window at any time by pressing the CTRL + ALT + DELETE keys. From this window, you can log off the current user and log back on as another user. You can also change passwords, shut down Windows 2000 and your computer, and use the Task Manager to shut down a program.

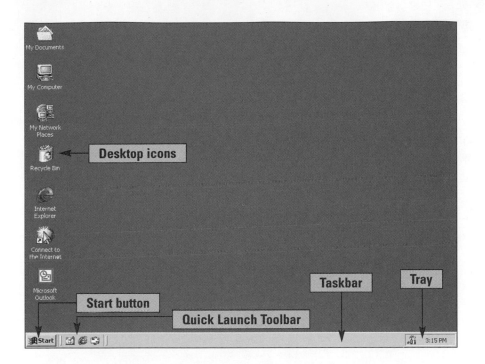

Desktop icons

Taskbar

Tray

Start button

Quick Launch Toolbar

TABLE A-1
Common Desktop Icons

Icon	Name	Description
	My Computer	Provides access to computer system resources
	My Documents	Stores Office documents (by default)
	Internet Explorer	Opens Internet Explorer Web browser
	Microsoft Outlook	Opens Outlook 2002 information manager software
	Recycle Bin	Temporarily stores folders and files deleted from the hard drive
	My Network Places	Provides access to computers and printers net worked in your workgroup

The Start button on the taskbar displays the Start menu, which you can use to perform tasks. By default, the taskbar also contains the **Quick Launch toolbar**, which has shortcuts to open the Internet Explorer Web browser and Outlook Express e-mail software, and to switch between the desktop and open application windows. You can customize the Quick Launch toolbar to include other shortcuts.

appendix
A

Q U I C K   T I P

An **active desktop** can contain live Web content. You can create an active desktop by adding windows to the desktop that contain automatically updated Web pages. To add Web pages to your desktop, right-click the desktop, point to Active Desktop, click Customize my Desktop, and click the Web tab in the Display Properties dialog box. For more information on Active Desktop features, see online Help.

A.b Accessing Your Computer System Resources

The My Computer window provides access to your computer system resources. Double-click the My Computer desktop icon to open the window. To open the My Computer window:

Step 1	*Point to*	the My Computer icon 🖥 on the desktop
Step 2	*Observe*	a brief description of the icon in the box, called a ScreenTip
Step 3	*Double-click*	the My Computer icon 🖥 to open the My Computer window shown in Figure A-3

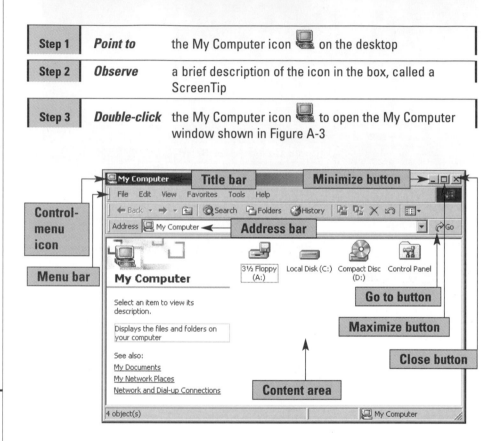

FIGURE A-3
My Computer window

A window is a rectangular area on your screen in which you view operating system options or a software application, such as Internet Explorer. Windows 2000 has some common window elements. The **title bar**, at the top of the window, includes the window's Control-menu icon, the window name, and the Minimize, Restore (or Maximize), and Close buttons. The **Control-menu icon**, in the upper-left corner of the window, accesses the Control menu that contains commands for restoring, moving sizing, minimizing, maximizing, and closing the window. The **Minimize** button, near the upper-right corner of the window, reduces the window to a taskbar button. The **Maximize** button, to the right of the Minimize button, enlarges the window to fill the entire screen viewing area above the taskbar. If the window is already maximized, the Restore button appears in its place. The **Restore** button reduces the window size. The **Close** button, in the upper-right corner, closes the window. To maximize the My Computer window:

Step 1	*Click*	the Maximize button 🗖 on the My Computer window title bar
Step 2	*Observe*	that the My Computer window completely covers the desktop

When you want to leave a window open, but do not want to see it on the desktop, you can minimize it. To minimize the My Computer window:

Step 1	*Click*	the Minimize button 🗕 on the My Computer window title bar
Step 2	*Observe*	that the My Computer button remains on the taskbar

The minimized window is still open but not occupying space on the desktop. To view the My Computer window and then restore it to a smaller size:

Step 1	*Click*	the My Computer button on the taskbar to view the window
Step 2	*Click*	the Restore button 🗗 on the My Computer title bar
Step 3	*Observe*	that the My Computer window is reduced to a smaller window on the desktop

You can move and size a window with the mouse pointer. To move the My Computer window:

Step 1	*Position*	the mouse pointer on the My Computer title bar
Step 2	*Drag*	the window down and to the right approximately ½ inch
Step 3	*Drag*	the window back to the center of the screen

Several Windows 2000 windows—My Computer, My Documents, and Windows Explorer—have the same menu bar and toolbar features. When you size a window too small to view all its icons, a vertical or horizontal scroll bar may appear. A scroll bar includes scroll arrows and a scroll box for viewing different parts of the window contents.

QUICK TIP

This book uses the following notations for mouse instructions. **Point** means to place the mouse pointer on the command or item. **Click** means to press the left mouse button and then release it. **Right-click** means to press the right mouse button and then release it. **Double-click** means to press the left mouse button twice very rapidly. **Drag** means to hold down the left mouse button as you move the mouse pointer on the mouse pad. **Right-drag** means to hold down the right mouse button as you move the mouse pointer on the mouse pad. **Scroll** means to use the application scroll bar features or the IntelliMouse scrolling wheel.

**appendix
A**

You can display four taskbar toolbars: Address, Links, Desktop, and Quick Launch. The Quick Launch toolbar appears on the taskbar by default. You can also create additional toolbars from other folders or subfolders and you can add folder or file shortcuts to an existing taskbar toolbar. To view other taskbar toolbars, right-click the taskbar, point to Toolbars, and then click the desired toolbar name.

To size the My Computer window:

Step 1	*Position*	the mouse pointer on the lower-right corner of the window
Step 2	*Observe*	that the mouse pointer becomes a black, double-headed sizing pointer
Step 3	*Drag*	the lower-right corner boundary diagonally up until the horizontal scroll bar appears and release the mouse button
Step 4	*Click*	the right scroll arrow on the horizontal scroll bar to view hidden icons
Step 5	*Size*	the window to a larger size to remove the horizontal scroll bar

You can open the window associated with any My Computer icon by double-clicking it. The windows open in the same window, not separate windows. To open the Control Panel Explorer-style window:

| Step 1 | *Double-click* | the Control Panel icon |
| Step 2 | *Observe* | that the Address bar displays the Control Panel icon and name, and the content area displays the Control Panel icons for accessing computer system resources |

A.c Using Menu Commands and Toolbar Buttons

You can click a menu command or toolbar button to perform specific tasks in a window. The **menu bar** is a special toolbar located below the window title bar that contains the File, Edit, View, Favorites, Tools, and Help menus. The **Standard Buttons toolbar**, located below the menu bar, contains shortcut "buttons" you click with the mouse pointer to execute a variety of commands. You can use the Back and Forward buttons on the Standard Buttons toolbar to switch between My Computer and the Control Panel. To view My Computer:

Step 1	*Click*	the Back button ⬅ on the Standard Buttons toolbar to view My Computer
Step 2	*Click*	the Forward button ➡ on the Standard Buttons toolbar to view the Control Panel
Step 3	*Click*	View on the menu bar
Step 4	*Point to*	Go To
Step 5	*Click*	the My Computer command to view My Computer

| Step 6 | *Click* | the Close button ⊠ on the My Computer window title bar |

A.d Using the Start Menu

The **Start button** on the taskbar opens the Start menu. You use this menu to access several Windows 2000 features and to open software applications, such as Word or Excel. To open the Start menu:

| Step 1 | *Click* | the Start button 🏴Start on the taskbar to open the Start menu, as shown in Figure A-4 |

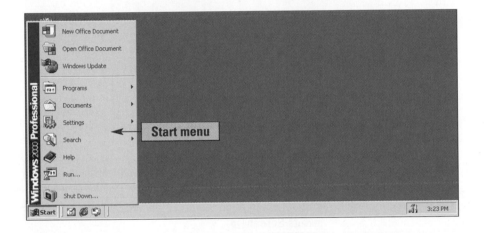

| Step 2 | *Point to* | Programs to view the software applications installed on your computer |
| Step 3 | *Click* | the desktop outside the Start menu and Programs menu to close them |

A.e Reviewing Dialog Box Options

A **dialog box** is a window that contains options you can select, turn on, or turn off to perform a task. To view a dialog box:

| Step 1 | *Right-click* | the desktop |
| Step 2 | *Point to* | Active Desktop |

QUICK TIP

You can use Start menu commands to create or open Office XP documents, connect to the Microsoft Web site to download operating system updates, open software applications, open a favorite folder or file, or open one of the last fifteen documents you worked on. You can also change the Windows 2000 settings, search for files, folders, and resources on the Internet, get online Help, run software applications, log off a network, and shut down Windows 2000.

FIGURE A-4
Start Menu

appendix
A

| Step 3 | *Click* | Customize My Desktop to open the Display Properties dialog box |
| Step 4 | *Click* | the Effects tab (see Figure A-5) |

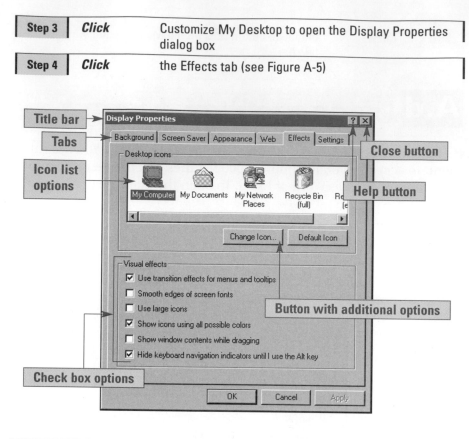

FIGURE A-5
Effects Tab in the Display Properties Dialog Box

Step 5	*Click*	each tab and observe the different options available (do not change any options unless directed by your instructor)
Step 6	*Right-click*	each option on each tab and then click What's This? to view its ScreenTip
Step 7	*Click*	Cancel to close the dialog box without changing any options

A.f Using Windows 2000 Shortcuts

You can use the drag-and-drop method to reposition or remove Start menu commands. You can also right-drag a Start menu command to the desktop to create a desktop shortcut. To reposition the Windows Update item on the Start menu:

Step 1	*Click*	the Start button [Start] on the taskbar
Step 2	*Point to*	the Windows Update item
Step 3	*Drag*	the Windows Update item to the top of the Start menu

To remove the Windows Update shortcut from the Start menu and create a desktop shortcut:

Step 1	*Drag*	the Windows Update item to the desktop
Step 2	*Observe*	that the desktop shortcut appears after a few seconds
Step 3	*Verify*	that the Windows Update item no longer appears on the Start menu

To add a Windows Update shortcut back to the Start menu and delete the desktop shortcut:

Step 1	*Drag*	the Windows Update shortcut to the Start button 🔳Start on the taskbar and then back to its original position when the Start menu appears
Step 2	*Close*	the Start menu
Step 3	*Drag*	the Windows Update shortcut on the desktop to the Recycle Bin

You can close multiple application windows at one time from the taskbar using the CTRL key and a shortcut menu. To open two applications and then use the taskbar to close them:

Step 1	*Open*	the Word and Excel applications (in this order) from the Programs menu on the Start menu
Step 2	*Observe*	the Word and Excel buttons on the taskbar (Excel is the selected, active button)
Step 3	*Press & hold*	the CTRL key
Step 4	*Click*	the Word application taskbar button (the Excel application taskbar button is already selected)
Step 5	*Release*	the CTRL key
Step 6	*Right-click*	the Word or Excel taskbar button
Step 7	*Click*	Close to close both applications

You can use the drag-and-drop method to add a shortcut to the Quick Launch toolbar for folders and documents you have created. To create a new subfolder in the My Documents folder:

| Step 1 | *Double-click* | the My Documents icon on the desktop to open the window |
| Step 2 | *Right-click* | the contents area (but not a file or folder) |

appendix
A

Step 3	*Point to*	New
Step 4	*Click*	Folder
Step 5	*Key*	Example
Step 6	*Press*	the ENTER key to name the folder
Step 7	*Drag*	the Example folder to the end of the Quick Launch toolbar (a black vertical line indicates the drop position)
Step 8	*Observe*	the new icon on the toolbar
Step 9	*Close*	the My Documents window
Step 10	*Position*	the mouse pointer on the Example folder shortcut on the Quick Launch toolbar and observe the ScreenTip

You remove a shortcut from the Quick Launch toolbar by dragging it to the desktop and deleting it, or dragging it directly to the Recycle Bin. To remove the Example folder shortcut and then delete the folder:

Step 1	*Drag*	the Example folder icon to the Recycle Bin
Step 2	*Open*	the My Documents window
Step 3	*Delete*	the Example folder icon using the shortcut menu
Step 4	*Click*	Yes
Step 5	*Close*	the My Documents window

A.g Understanding the Recycle Bin

The **Recycle Bin** is an object that temporarily stores folders, files, and shortcuts you delete from your hard drive. If you accidentally delete an item, you can restore it to its original location on your hard drive if it is still in the Recycle Bin. Because the Recycle Bin takes up disk space you should review and empty it regularly. When you empty the Recycle Bin, its contents are removed from your hard drive and can no longer be restored.

MENU TIP

You can open the Recycle Bin by right-clicking the Recycle Bin icon on the desktop and clicking Open. To restore an item to your hard drive after opening the Recycle Bin, click the item to select it and then click the Restore command on the File menu. You can also restore an item by opening the Recycle Bin, right-clicking an item, and clicking Restore.

To empty the Recycle Bin, right-click the Recycle Bin icon and then click Empty Recycle Bin.

A.h Shutting Down Windows 2000

It is very important that you follow the proper procedures for shutting down the Windows 2000 operating system when you are finished, to allow the operating system to complete its internal "housekeeping" properly. To shut down Windows 2000 correctly:

Step 1	*Click*	the Start button 🔲 Start on the taskbar
Step 2	*Click*	Shut Down to open the Shut Down Windows dialog box shown in Figure A-6

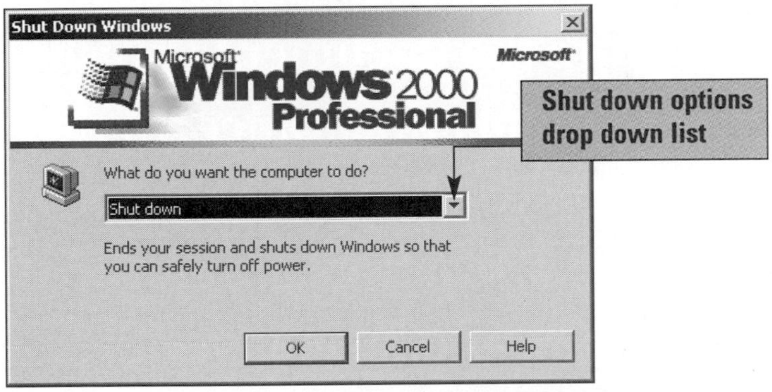

FIGURE A-6
Shut Down Windows
Dialog Box

You can log off, shut down, and restart from this dialog box. You want to shut down completely.

Step 3	*Click*	the Shut down option from the drop-down list, if necessary
Step 4	*Click*	OK

appendix
A

Formatting Tips for Business Documents

Appendix Overview

Most organizations follow specific formatting guidelines when preparing letters, envelopes, memorandums, and other documents to ensure the documents present a professional appearance. In this appendix you learn how to format different size letters, interoffice memos, envelopes, and formal outlines. You also review a list of style guides and learn how to use proofreader's marks.

LEARNING OBJECTIVES

▶ Format letters
▶ Insert mailing notations
▶ Format envelopes
▶ Format interoffice memorandums
▶ Format formal outlines
▶ Use style guides
▶ Use proofreader's marks

B.a Formatting Letters

Most companies use special letter paper with the company name and address (and sometimes a company logo or picture) preprinted on the paper. The preprinted portion is called a **letterhead** and the paper is called **letterhead paper.** When you create a letter, the margins vary depending on the style of your letterhead and the length of your letter. Most letterheads use between 1 inch and 2 inches of the page from the top of the sheet. There are two basic business correspondence formats: block format and modified block format. When you create a letter in **block format**, all the text is placed flush against the left margin. This includes the date, the letter address information, the salutation, the body, the complimentary closing, and the signature information. The body of the letter is single spaced with a blank line between paragraphs.[1] Figure B-1 shows a short letter in the block format with standard punctuation.

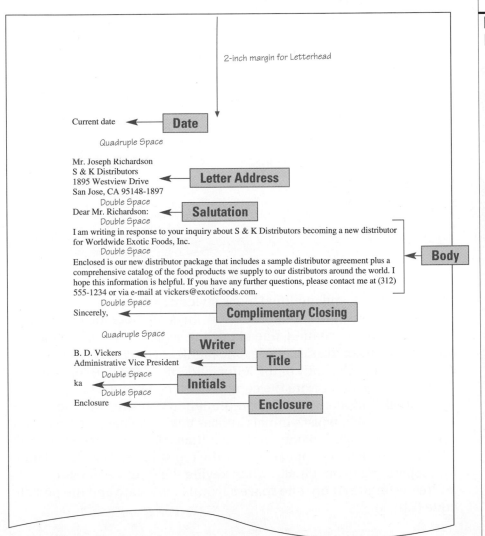

FIGURE B-1
Block Format Letter

> ### QUICK TIP
>
> The quality and professionalism of a company's business correspondence can affect how customers, clients, and others view a company. That correspondence represents the company to those outside it. To ensure a positive and appropriate image, many companies set special standards for margins, typeface, and font size for their business correspondence. These special standards are based on the common letter styles illustrated in this section.

appendix
B

In the **modified block format**, the date begins near the center of the page or near the right margin. The closing starts near the center or right margin. Paragraphs can be either flush against the left margin or indented. Figure B-2 shows a short letter in the modified block format with standard punctuation.

FIGURE B-2
Modified Block
Format Letter

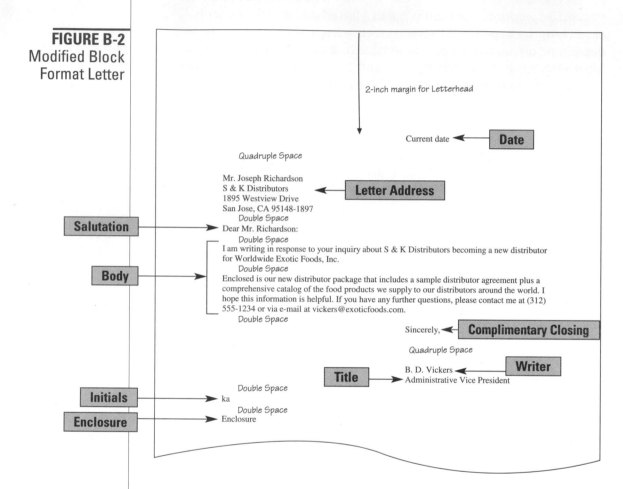

Both the block and modified block styles use the same spacing for the non-body portions. Three blank lines separate the date from the addressee information, one blank line separates the addressee information from the salutation, one blank line separates the salutation from the body of the letter, and one blank line separates the body of the letter from the complimentary closing. There are three blank lines between the complimentary closing and the writer's name. If a typist's initials appear below the name, a blank line separates the writer's name from the initials. If an enclosure is noted, the word "Enclosure" appears below the typist's initials with a blank line separating them. Finally, when keying the return address or addressee information, one space separates the state and the postal code (ZIP+4).

QUICK TIP

When you key a letter on plain paper in the modified block format, the return address usually appears near the right margin and above the date, with one blank line between the return address and the date.

B.b Inserting Mailing Notations

Mailing notations add information to a business letter. For example, the mailing notations CERTIFIED MAIL or SPECIAL DELIVERY indicate how a business letter was sent. The mailing notations CONFIDENTIAL or PERSONAL indicate how the person receiving the letter should handle the letter contents. Mailing notations should be keyed in uppercase characters at the left margin two lines below the date.[2] Figure B-3 shows a mailing notation added to a block format business letter.

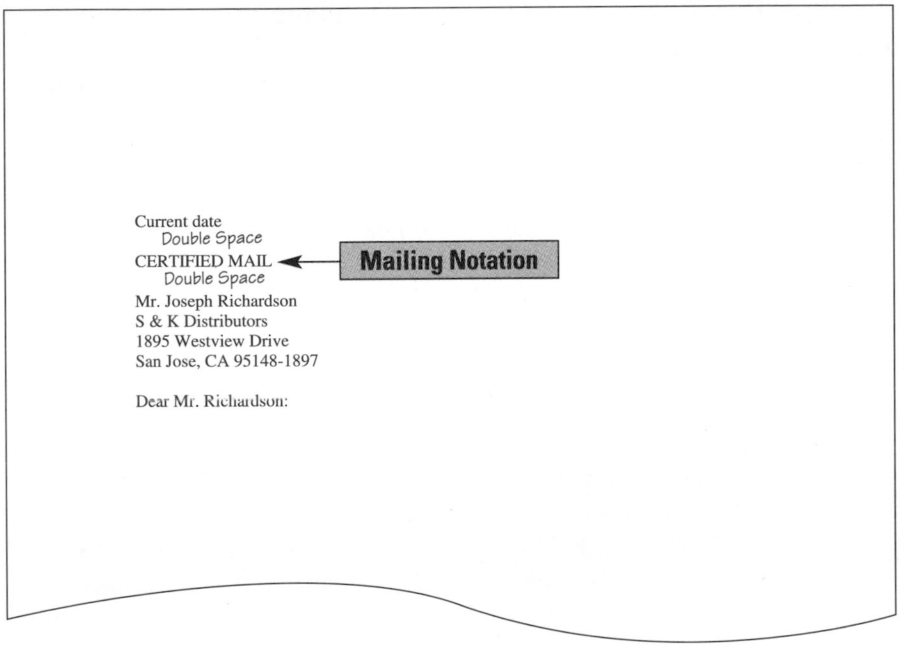

Current date
    Double Space
CERTIFIED MAIL ◄—— **Mailing Notation**
    Double Space
Mr. Joseph Richardson
S & K Distributors
1895 Westview Drive
San Jose, CA 95148-1897

Dear Mr. Richardson:

FIGURE B-3
Mailing Notation on Letter

B.c Formatting Envelopes

Two U.S. Postal Service publications, *The Right Way* (Publication 221), and *Postal Addressing Standards* (Publication 28) available from the U.S. Post Office, provide standards for addressing letter envelopes. The U.S. Postal Service uses optical character readers (OCRs) and barcode sorters (BCSs) to increase the speed, efficiency, and accuracy in processing mail. To get a letter delivered more quickly, envelopes should be addressed to take advantage of this automation process.

appendix
B

Table B-1 lists the minimum and maximum size for letters. The post office cannot process letters smaller than the minimum size. Letters larger than the maximum size cannot take advantage of automated processing and must be processed manually.

TABLE B-1
Minimum and Maximum
Letter Dimensions

Dimension	Minimum	Maximum
Height	3½ inches	6⅛ inches
Length	5 inches	11½ inches
Thickness	.007 inch	¼ inch

The delivery address should be placed inside a rectangular area on the envelope that is approximately ⅝ inch from the top and bottom edge of the envelope and ½ inch from the left and right edge of the envelope. This is called the **OCR read area**. All the lines of the delivery address must fit within this area and no lines of the return address should extend into this area. To assure the delivery address is placed in the OCR read area, begin the address approximately ½ inch left of center and on approximately line 14.[3]

The lines of the delivery address should be in this order:

1. any optional nonaddress data, such as advertising or company logos, must be placed above the delivery address
2. any information or attention line
3. the name of the recipient
4. the street address
5. the city, state, and postal code (ZIP+4)

The delivery address should be complete, including apartment or suite numbers and delivery designations, such as RD (road), ST (street), or NW (northwest). Leave the area below and on both sides of the delivery address blank. Use uppercase characters and a sans serif font (such as Arial) for the delivery address. Omit all punctuation except the hyphen in the ZIP+4 code.

Figure B-4 shows a properly formatted business letter envelope.

QUICK TIP

Foreign addresses should include the country name in uppercase characters as the last line of the delivery address. The postal code, if any, should appear on the same line as the city.

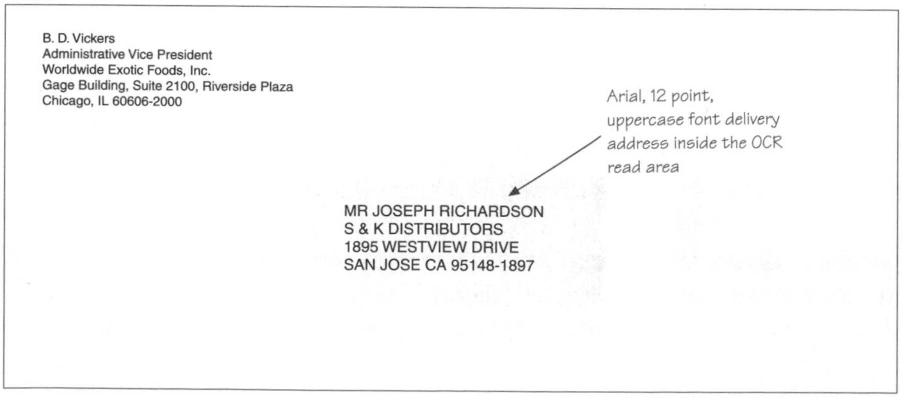

FIGURE B-4
Business Letter Envelope

B. D. Vickers
Administrative Vice President
Worldwide Exotic Foods, Inc.
Gage Building, Suite 2100, Riverside Plaza
Chicago, IL 60606-2000

Arial, 12 point, uppercase font delivery address inside the OCR read area

MR JOSEPH RICHARDSON
S & K DISTRIBUTORS
1895 WESTVIEW DRIVE
SAN JOSE CA 95148-1897

B.d Formatting Interoffice Memorandums

Business correspondence that is sent within a company is usually prepared as an **interoffice memorandum**, also called a **memo**, rather than a letter. There are many different interoffice memo styles used in offices today, and word processing applications usually provide several memo templates based on different memo styles. Also, just as with business letters that are sent outside the company, many companies set special standards for margins, typeface, and font size for their interoffice memos.

A basic interoffice memo should include lines for "TO:", "FROM:", "DATE:", and "SUBJECT:" followed by the body text. Memos can be prepared on blank paper or on paper that includes a company name and even a logo. The word MEMORANDUM is often included. Figure B-5 shows a basic interoffice memorandum.

FIGURE B-5
Interoffice Memorandum

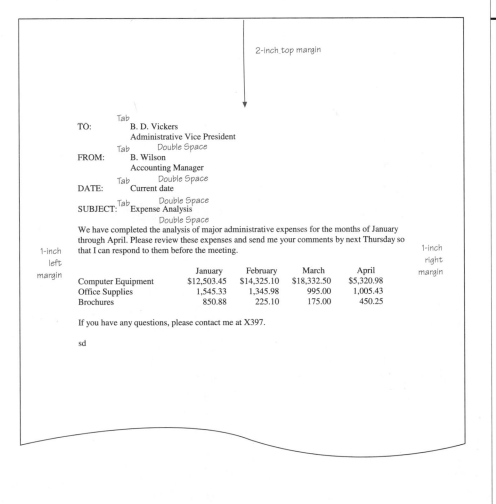

appendix
B

B.e Formatting Formal Outlines

Companies use outlines to organize data for a variety of purposes, such as reports, meeting agenda, and presentations. Word processing applications usually offer special features to help you create an outline. If you want to follow a formal outline format, you may need to add formatting to outlines created with these special features.

Margins for a short outline of two or three topics should be set at 1½ inches for the top margin and 2 inches for the left and right margins. For a longer outline, use a 2-inch top margin and 1-inch left and right margins.

The outline level-one text should be in uppercase characters. Second-level text should be treated like a title, with the first letter of the main words capitalized. Capitalize only the first letter of the first word at the third level. Double space before and after level one and single space the remaining levels.

Include at least two parts at each level. For example, you must have two level-one entries in an outline (at least I. and II.). If there is a second level following a level-one entry, it must contain at least two entries (at least A. and B.). All numbers must be aligned at the period and all subsequent levels must begin under the text of the preceding level, not under the number.[4]

Figure B-6 shows a formal outline prepared using the Word Outline Numbered list feature with additional formatting to follow a formal outline.

B.f Using Style Guides

A **style guide** provides a set of rules for punctuating and formatting text. There are a number of style guides used by writers, editors, business document proofreaders, and publishers. You can purchase style guides at a commercial bookstore, an online bookstore, or a college bookstore. Your local library likely has copies of different style guides and your instructor may have copies of several style guides for reference. Some popular style guides are *The Chicago Manual of Style* (The University of Chicago Press), *The Professional Secretary's Handbook* (Barron's), *The Holt Handbook* (Harcourt Brace College Publishers), and the *MLA Style Manual and Guide to Scholarly Publishing* (The Modern Language Association of America).

FIGURE B-6
Formal Outline

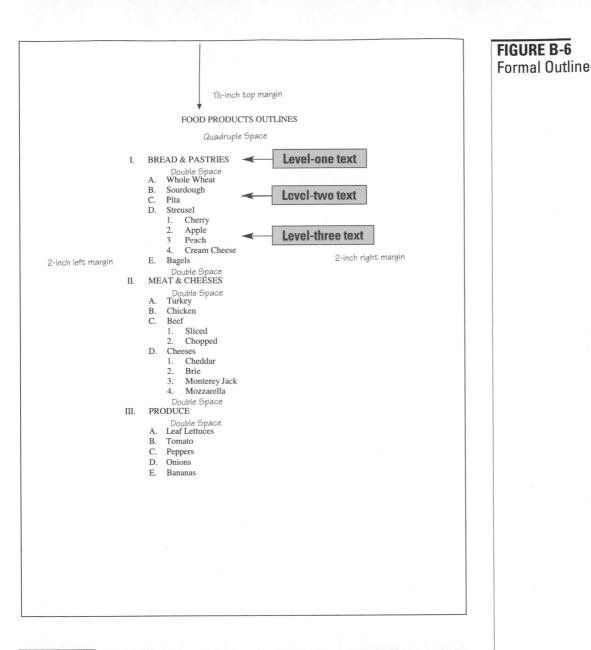

B.g   Using Proofreader's Marks

Standard proofreader's marks enable an editor or proofreader to make corrections or change notations in a document that can be recognized by anyone familiar with the marks. The following list illustrates standard proofreader's marks.

appendix
B

Defined		Examples
Paragraph	¶	¶ Begin a new paragraph at this
Insert a character	∧	point. Insert a letter here.
Delete	ℓ	Delete ~~these words.~~ ℓ Disregard
Do not change	*stet* or . . .	the previous correction. To
Transpose	*tr*	transpose is to around turn.
Move to the left	[	[Move this copy to the left.
Move to the right	]	Move this copy to the right.
No paragraph	*No* ¶	*No* ¶ Do not begin a new paragraph
Delete and close up	(symbol)	here. Delete the hyphen from
		pre-empt and close up the space.
Set in caps	*Caps* or ≡	a sentence begins with a capital
Set in lower case	*lc* or /	letter. This Word should not
Insert a period	⊙	be capitalized. Insert a period⊙
Quotation marks	⌄⌄ ⌄⌄	Quotation marks and a comma
Comma	∧	should be placed here he said.
Insert space	#	Space between these words. An
Apostrophe	⌄	apostrophe is whats needed here.
Hyphen	=	Add a hyphen to Kilowatt hour. Close
Close up	⌣	up the extra spa ce.
Use superior figure	⌄	Footnote this sentence. Set
Set in italic	*Ital.* or —	the words, <u>sine qua non</u>, in italics.
Move up	⊓	This word is too low. That word is
Move down	⊔	too high.

Endnotes

[1] Jerry W. Robinson et al., *Keyboarding and Information Processing* (Cincinnati: South-Western Educational Publishing, 1997).

[2] Ibid.

[3] Ibid.

[4] Ibid.

Using Office XP Speech Recognition

Appendix Overview

You are familiar with using the keyboard and the mouse to key text and select commands. With Office XP, you also can use your voice to perform these same activities. Speech recognition enables you to use your voice to perform keyboard and mouse actions without ever lifting a hand. In this appendix, you learn how to set up Speech Recognition software and train the software to recognize your voice. You learn how to control menus, navigate dialog boxes, and open, save, and close a document. You then learn how to dictate text, including lines and punctuation, correct errors, and format text. Finally, you learn how to turn off and on Speech Recognition.

LEARNING OBJECTIVES

- ▶ Train your speech software
- ▶ Use voice commands
- ▶ Dictate, edit, and format by voice
- ▶ Turn Microsoft Speech Recognition on and off

appendix C

C.a Training Your Speech Software

Speech recognition is an exciting new technology that Microsoft has integrated into its XP generation of products. Microsoft has been working on speech recognition for well over a decade. The state-of-the-art is advancing. If you haven't tried it before, this is a great time for you to experience this futuristic technology.

Voice recognition has important benefits:

- Microsoft's natural speech technologies can make your computer experience more enjoyable.
- Speech technology can increase your writing productivity.
- Voice recognition software can greatly reduce your risk for keyboard- and mouse-related injuries.

In the following activities, you learn to use your voice like a mouse and to write without the aid of the keyboard.

Connecting and Positioning Your Microphone

Start your speech recognition experience by setting up your microphone. There are several microphone styles used for speech recognition. The most common headset microphone connects to your computer's sound card, as shown in Figure C-1. Connect the microphone end to your computer's microphone audio input port. Connect the speaker end into your speech output port.

FIGURE C-1
Standard Sound Card Headset (Courtesy Plantronics Inc.)

USB speech microphones, such as the one shown in Figure C-2, are becoming very popular because they normally increase performance and accuracy. USB is short for Universal Serial Bus. USB microphones bypass the sound card and input speech with less distortion into your system.

USB microphones are plugged into the USB port found in the back of most computers. Windows automatically installs the necessary USB drivers after you start your computer with the USB microphone plugged into its slot.

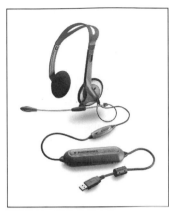

FIGURE C-2
A USB Headset (Courtesy Plantronics Inc.)

After your headset has been installed, put on your headset and position it comfortably. Remember these two important tips:

- Place the speaking side of your microphone about a thumb's width away from the side of your mouth, as shown in Figure C-3.
- Keep your microphone in the same position every time you speak. Changing your microphone's position can decrease your accuracy.

Position your headset within an inch of the side of your mouth

FIGURE C-3
Proper Headset Position

CAUTION TIP

If you see additional buttons on the Language Bar than shown in Figure C-4, click the Microphone button to hide them.

Installing Microsoft Speech Recognition

Open Microsoft Word and see if your speech software has already been installed. As Word opens, you should see either the floating Language Bar, shown in Figure C-4, or the Language Bar icon in the Windows Taskbar tray, as shown in Figure C-5.

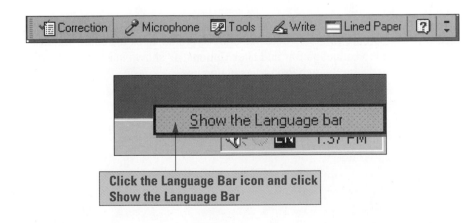

Correction | Microphone | Tools | Write | Lined Paper | ? |

Show the Language bar

Click the Language Bar icon and click Show the Language Bar

FIGURE C-4
Floating Language Bar

FIGURE C-5
Language Bar Icon

appendix
C

If you can open and see the Language Bar, jump to Step-by-Step C.2. However, if this essential tool is missing, proceed with Step-by-Step C.1.

Step-by-Step C.1

Step 1	To install Microsoft speech recognition, open Microsoft Word by clicking **Start**, **Programs**, **Microsoft Word**.
Step 2	Click **Tools**, **Speech** from the Word menu bar, as shown in Figure C-6.

FIGURE C-6
Click Speech from the
Tools menu

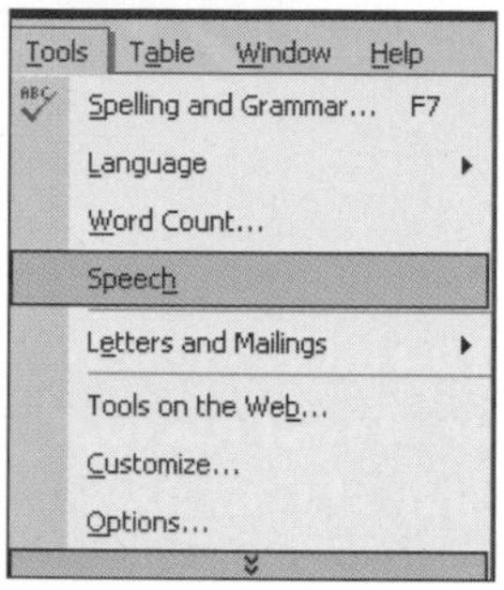

Step 3	You are prompted through the installation procedure. The process is a simple one. Follow the onscreen instructions.

Training Your System

Microsoft speech recognition can accommodate many different voices on the same computer. In order to work properly, your Microsoft Office Speech Recognition software must create a user **profile** for each voice it hears—including your voice.

If you are the first user and have just installed your speech software, chances are the system is already prompting you through the training steps. Skip to Step 3 in Step-by-Step C.2 for hints and help as you continue. However, if you are the second or later user of the system, you need to create a new profile by starting with Step 1.

Step-by-Step C.2

Step 1	To create your own personal speech profile, click the **Tools** button on the Language Bar and click **Options**, as shown in Figure C-7. This opens the Speech Properties dialog box.

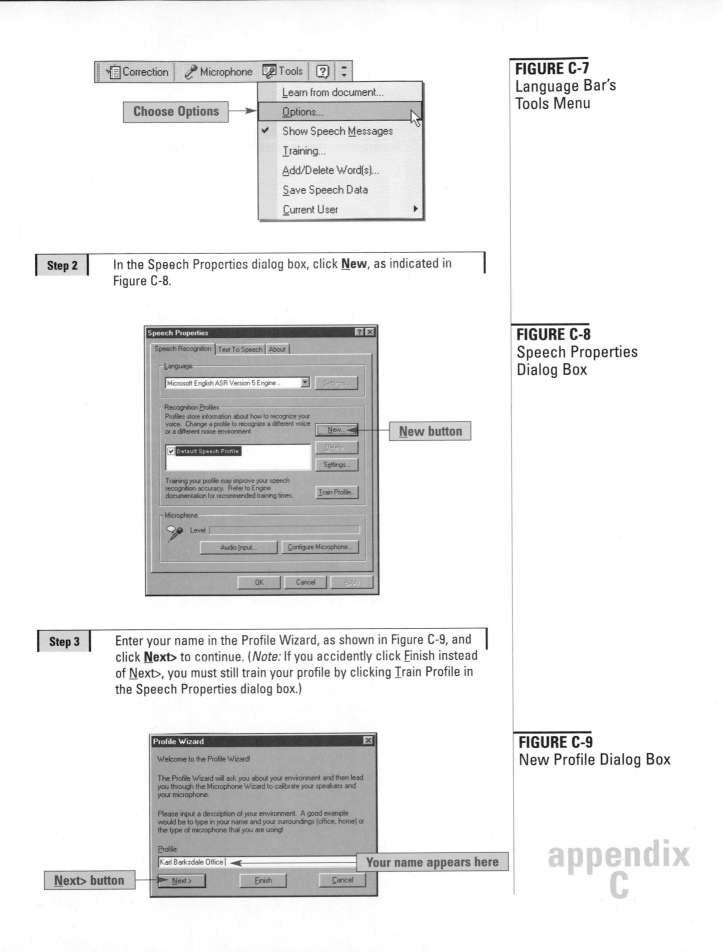

FIGURE C-7
Language Bar's
Tools Menu

Choose Options

| **Step 2** | In the Speech Properties dialog box, click **New**, as indicated in Figure C-8. |

FIGURE C-8
Speech Properties
Dialog Box

New button

| **Step 3** | Enter your name in the Profile Wizard, as shown in Figure C-9, and click **Next>** to continue. (*Note:* If you accidently click Finish instead of Next>, you must still train your profile by clicking Train Profile in the Speech Properties dialog box.) |

FIGURE C-9
New Profile Dialog Box

Next> button

Your name appears here

appendix
C

Step 4 Adjust your microphone, as explained on the Microphone Wizard Welcome dialog box, as shown in Figure C-10. Click **Next>** to begin adjusting your microphone.

FIGURE C-10
Correctly Position Your
Microphone

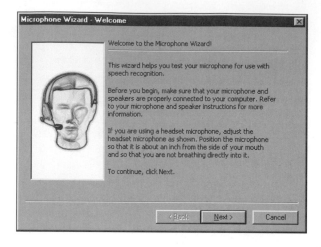

Step 5 Read the test sentence indicated in Figure C-11 until the volume adjustment settings appear consistently in the green portion of the volume adjustment meter. Your volume settings are adjusted automatically as you speak. Click **Next>** to continue.

FIGURE C-11
Read Aloud to Adjust Your
Microphone Volume

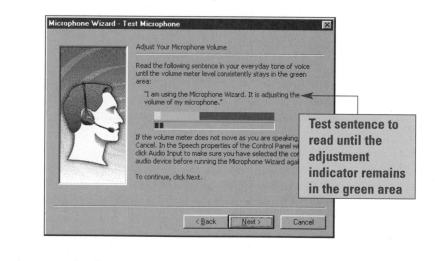

Test sentence to read until the adjustment indicator remains in the green area

> ## QUICK TIP
>
> Microsoft Office Speech Recognition tells you if your microphone is not adequate for good speech recognition. You may need to try a higher quality microphone, install a compatible sound card, or switch to a USB microphone. Check the Microsoft Windows Help files for assistance with microphone problems.

Step 6 The next audio check tests the output of your speakers. Read the test sentence indicated in Figure C-12 and then listen. If you can hear your voice, your speakers are connected properly. Click **Finish** and continue.

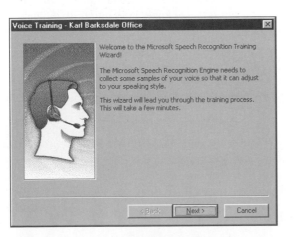

Microphone Wizard - Test Positioning

Position Your Microphone

If you do not have a headset microphone, click Finish.

Read the following sentence in your everyday tone of voice:

"This papaya tastes perfect"

Test sentence

After a pause, a recording will be played back to you. If it sounds like you are blowing into the microphone, reposition the microphone, and repeat the above sentence.

When you have adjusted the microphone so that it does not sound as though you are blowing into it, click Finish.

< Back   Finish   Cancel

FIGURE C-12
Read Aloud to Test Your
Sound Output

QUICK TIP

Your user file will remember your microphone settings from session to session. However, if others use the system before you, you may need to readjust the audio settings by clicking **Tools**, **Options**, **Configure Microphone**.

CAUTION TIP

Never touch any part of your headset or microphone while speaking. Holding or touching the microphone creates errors.

Training Your Software

Next, you are asked to train your software. During the training session, you read a training script or story for about 10 to 15 minutes. As you read, your software gathers samples of your speech. These samples help the speech software customize your speech recognition profile to your way of speaking. As you read, remember to:

- Read clearly.
- Use a normal, relaxed reading voice. Don't shout, but don't whisper softly either.
- Read at your normal reading pace. Do not read slowly and do not rush.

Step-by-Step C.3

| Step 1 | Microsoft Office Speech Recognition prepares you to read a story or script. Read the instruction screen shown in Figure C-13 and click **Next>** to continue. |

Voice Training - Karl Barksdale Office

Welcome to the Microsoft Speech Recognition Training Wizard!

The Microsoft Speech Recognition Engine needs to collect some samples of your voice so that it can adjust to your speaking style.

This wizard will lead you through the training process. This will take a few minutes.

< Back   Next >   Cancel

FIGURE C-13
Read the Onscreen
Instructions Carefully

| Step 2 | Enter your gender and age information (see Figure C-14) to help the system calibrate its settings to your voice. Click **Next>** to continue. |

**appendix
C**

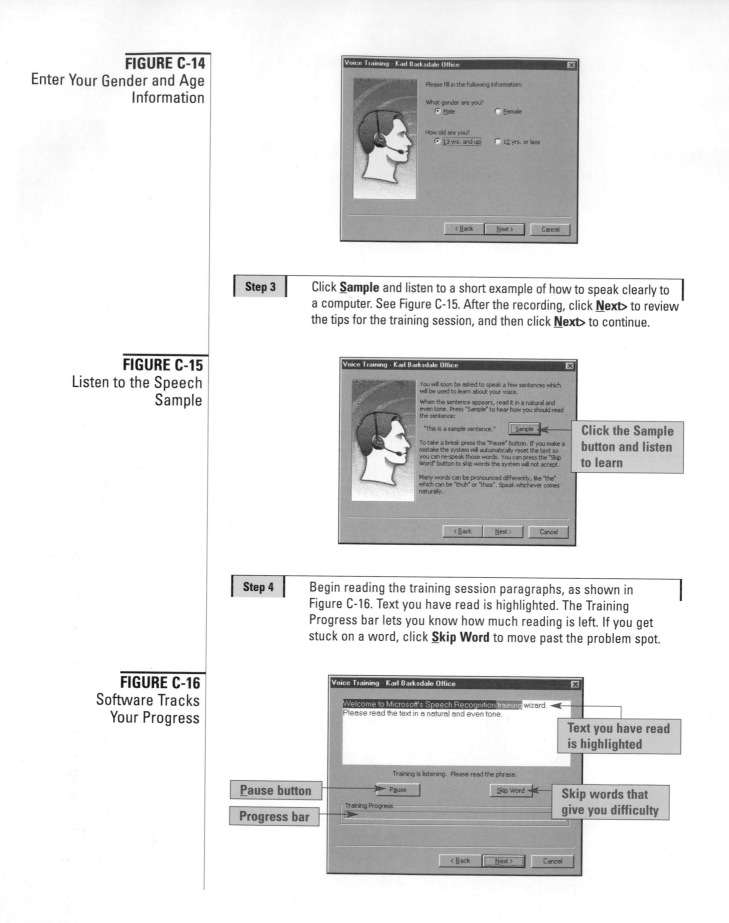

FIGURE C-14
Enter Your Gender and Age
Information

| **Step 3** | Click **Sample** and listen to a short example of how to speak clearly to a computer. See Figure C-15. After the recording, click **Next>** to review the tips for the training session, and then click **Next>** to continue. |

FIGURE C-15
Listen to the Speech
Sample

Click the Sample button and listen to learn

| **Step 4** | Begin reading the training session paragraphs, as shown in Figure C-16. Text you have read is highlighted. The Training Progress bar lets you know how much reading is left. If you get stuck on a word, click **Skip Word** to move past the problem spot. |

FIGURE C-16
Software Tracks
Your Progress

Text you have read is highlighted

Pause button

Progress bar

Skip words that give you difficulty

Step 5 The screen shown in Figure C-17 appears after you have finished reading the entire first story or training session script. You now have a couple of choices. Click **More Training**, click **Next>**, and continue reading additional scripts as explained in Step 6 (or you can click Finish and quit for the day).

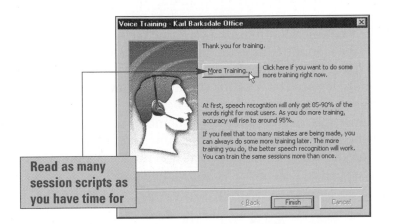

Read as many session scripts as you have time for

Step 6 Choose another training session story or script from the list, as shown in Figure C-18, and then click **Next>**.

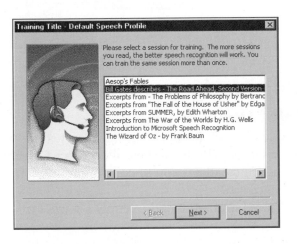

Step 7 At the end of the training process, Microsoft Office Speech Recognition shows you a multimedia training tutorial (you may need to install Macromedia Flash to view the tutorial). Enjoy the tutorial before continuing.

QUICK TIP

The more stories you read, the better. Users with thick accents, or accuracy below 90 percent, must read additional stories. You can read additional training session scripts at any time by clicking **Tools**, **Training** on the Language Bar.

FIGURE C-17
First Training Script Completed

FIGURE C-18
Choose Another Story or Training Script to Read

CAUTION TIP

You must read until Microsoft Office Speech Recognition has a large enough sample of your voice to process and adjust to your unique way of speaking. Click **Pause** to take a break. However, it is best to read the entire session training script in one sitting.

appendix C

C.b Using Voice Commands

Microsoft makes it easy to replace mouse clicks with voice commands. The voice commands are very intuitive. In most cases, you simply say what you see. For example, to open the File menu, you can simply say **File**.

Microsoft Office XP voice commands allow you to control dialog boxes and menu bars, and to format documents by speaking. You can give your hands a rest by speaking commands instead of clicking them. This can help reduce your risk for carpal tunnel syndrome and other serious injuries.

Before you begin using voice commands, remember that if more than one person is using speech recognition on the same computer, you must select your user profile from the Current Users list. The list is found by clicking the Language Bar Tools menu, as shown in Figure C-19.

FIGURE C-19
Current Users List

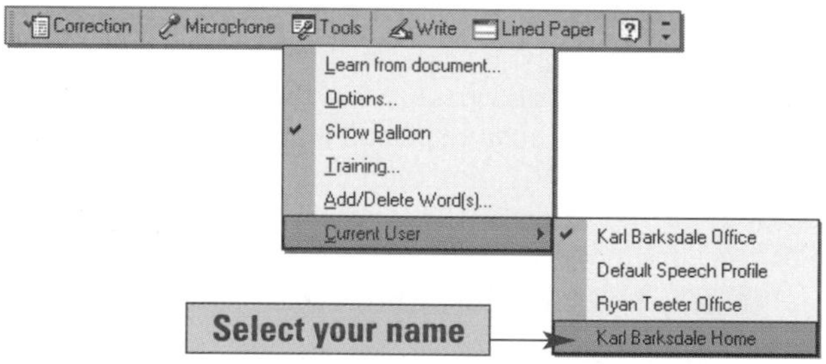

Switching Modes and Moving the Language Bar

Microsoft Office Speech Recognition works in two modes. The first is called **Dictation mode**. The second is called **Voice Command mode**. Voice Command mode allows you to control menus, give commands, and format documents.

When using Voice Command mode, simply *say what you see on the screen or in dialog boxes.* You see how this works in the next few exercises. In Step-by-Step C.4, you learn how to switch between the two modes.

Step-by-Step C.4

Step 1	Open **Microsoft Word** and the **Language Bar**, if necessary.
Step 2	The Language Bar can appear collapsed (see Figure C-20) or expanded (see Figure C-21). You can switch between the two options by clicking the **Microphone** button.

MENU TIP

After you have selected your user profile, you may wish to refresh your audio settings by clicking **Tools, Options, Configure Microphone**. This will help adjust the audio settings to the noise conditions in your current dictation environment.

> **Microphone button**

FIGURE C-20
Collapsed Language Bar

Clicking the Microphone button with your mouse turns on the microphone and expands the Language Bar.

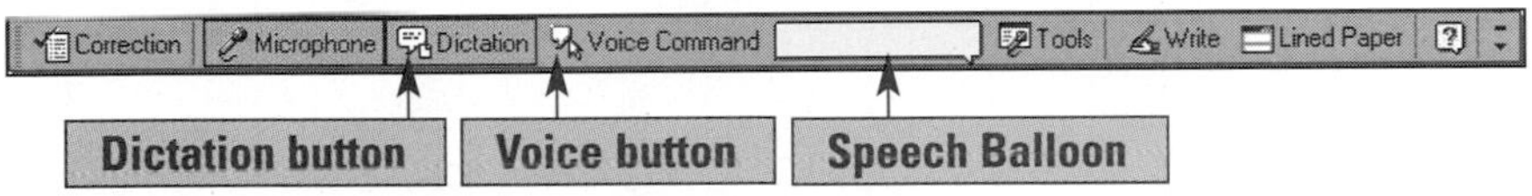

| Correction | Microphone | Dictation | Voice Command | | Tools | Write | Lined Paper | ? |

> **Dictation button**   **Voice button**   **Speech Balloon**

FIGURE C-21
Expanded Language Bar

Step 3	Compare the tools found on the expanded Language Bar with those in the collapsed Language Bar. You see several new features on the expanded bar, including the Dictation, Voice Command, and Speech Balloon options.

Step 4	Switch between **Dictation** mode (used for dictating words) and **Voice Command** mode (used for giving commands) by saying the following commands clearly. Make sure you pause momentarily after you say each command.
	Turn on the Microphone and say:
	    Voice Command *\<pause\>*
	    Dictation *\<pause\>*
	    Voice Command *\<pause\>*
	    Dictation *\<pause\>*

Step 5	Practice turning off the microphone with your voice (thereby collapsing the Language Bar) by saying: ***Microphone***
Step 6	Click and drag the Language Bar to various parts of the screen by clicking the markers found on the left end of the Language Bar (see Figure C-22).

> **QUICK TIP**
>
> The Language Bar can float anywhere on the screen. Move the Language Bar to a spot that is convenient and out of the way. Most users position the Language Bar in the title bar or status bar when using speech with Microsoft Word.

| Correction | Microphone | Tools | Write | Lined Paper | ? |

> **Click and drag the Language Bar marker**

FIGURE C-22
Move the Language Bar to a Convenient Spot

Giving Menu Commands

When you use Microsoft Office Voice Commands, your word will be obeyed. Before you begin issuing commands, take a few seconds and analyze Figure C-23. The toolbars you will be working with in the next few activities are identified in the figure.

appendix
C

FIGURE C-23
Customize Microsoft Word
with Your Voice

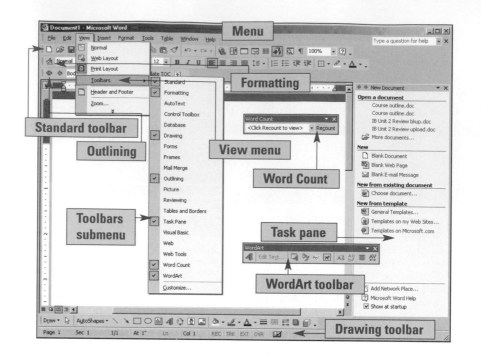

Step-by-Step C.5

Step 1	Switch on the **Microphone** from the Language Bar.
Step 2	Switch to Voice Command mode by saying: **Voice Command**
Step 3	Open and close several menus by saying: **File** *(Pause briefly between commands)* **Escape** **Edit** **Cancel** **View** **Escape**
Step 4	Close or display a few of the popular toolbars found in Microsoft Word by saying the following commands: **View** **Toolbars** **Standard** **View** **Toolbars** **Formatting** **View** **Toolbars** **Drawing**

Step 5	Close or redisplay the toolbars by saying the following commands: *View* *Toolbars* *Drawing* *View* *Toolbars* *Formatting* *View* *Toolbars* *Standard*
Step 6	Practice giving voice commands by adding and removing the Task Pane and WordArt toolbar. Try some other options. When you are through experimenting, turn off the microphone and collapse the Language Bar by saying: *Microphone*

Navigating Dialog Boxes

Opening files is one thing you do nearly every time you use Microsoft Office. To open files, you need to manipulate the Open dialog box (Figure C-24). A dialog box allows you to make decisions and execute voice commands. For example, in the Open dialog box you can switch folders and open files by voice.

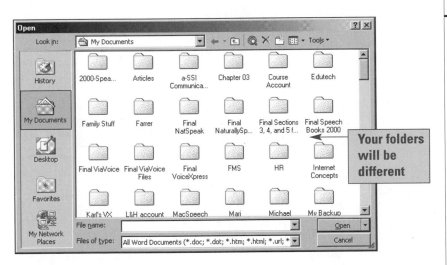

FIGURE C-24
Open Dialog Box

Step-by-Step C.6

Step 1	Turn on the **Microphone**, switch to Voice Command mode, and access the Open dialog box, as shown in Figure C-25, using the following commands: *Voice Command* *File* *Open*

appendix
C

FIGURE C-25
Say File, Open

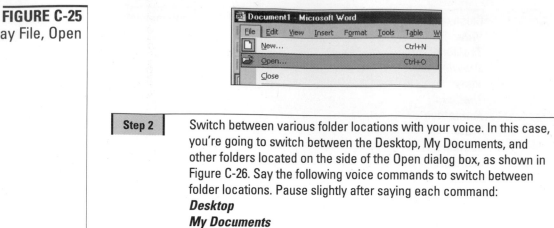

Step 2 Switch between various folder locations with your voice. In this case, you're going to switch between the Desktop, My Documents, and other folders located on the side of the Open dialog box, as shown in Figure C-26. Say the following voice commands to switch between folder locations. Pause slightly after saying each command:
Desktop
My Documents
History
Desktop
Favorites
My Documents

FIGURE C-26
Switch Between Various
Folder Locations

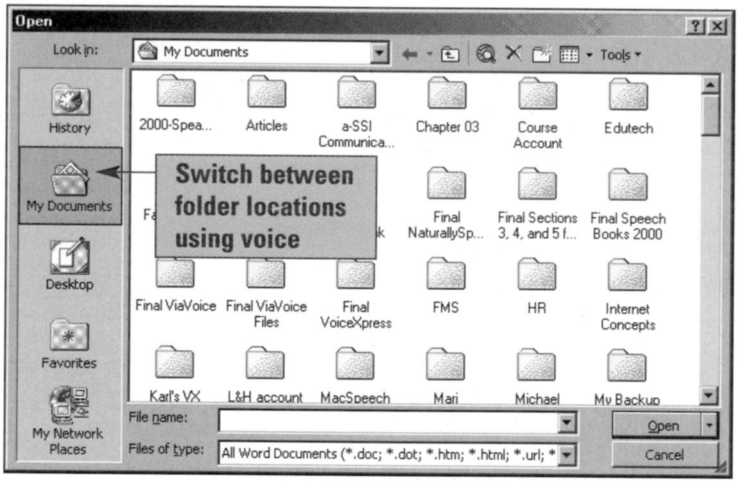

QUICK TIP

Any time a button in a dialog box appears dark around the edges, the button is active. You can access active buttons at any time by saying the name of the button or by saying **Enter**. You can also move around dialog boxes using the **Tab** or **Shift Tab** voice commands, or move between folders and files by saying **Up Arrow**, **Down Arrow**, **Left Arrow**, and **Right Arrow**. When selecting files, you'll probably find it much easier to use your mouse instead of your voice.

Step 3 You can change how your folders and files look in the Open dialog box by manipulating the Views menu, as shown in Figure C-27. Say the following voice commands to change the look of your folders and files:
Views
Small Icons
Views
List
Views
Details
Views
Thumbnails
Views
Large icons
Views
List

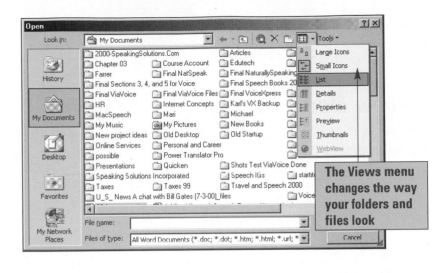

FIGURE C-27
Change the Look of Folders with the Views Menu

| Step 4 | Close the Open dialog box by using the Cancel command. Say:
Cancel |

Open and Count a Document

In Step-by-Step C.7, you combine your traditional mouse skills with voice skills to accomplish tasks more conveniently. Use your skills to open a file. Then, use your menu selecting technique to open the Word Count toolbar and count the number of words in a document.

Step-by-Step C.7

Step 1	Using your voice, say *File*, *Open* and select the **My Documents** folder (or the location of your Data Disk). View the folders and files in **List** view. (Review Step-by-Step C.6 if you have forgotten how to make these changes in the Open dialog box.)
Step 2	Scroll through the list of files with your mouse until you see the file called *Prevent Injury*. To open the file, select it with your mouse and say: *Open* (or you also may say *Enter*)
Step 3	As the file opens, notice that the document title is PREVENT INJURY WITH SPEECH. Speech recognition can help you avoid serious keyboarding and mouse injuries. Count the words in the article. Open the Word Count toolbar by saying the following: *View* *Toolbars* *Word Count*
Step 4	With the Word Count toolbar open, say the following command to count the words: *Recount*

QUICK TIP

To complete Step-by-Step C.7, the *Prevent Injury* document should be moved from the Data Disk to the My Documents folder on your computer.

appendix
C

Step 5	How many words are contained in the article?

Step 6	Leave the *Prevent Injury* document open for the next activity.

Save a Document and Exit Word

Saving a file will give you a chance to practice manipulating dialog boxes. Switching from the keyboard and mouse to your voice has several benefits. For example, have you heard of carpal tunnel syndrome and other computer keyboard-related injuries caused by repetitive typing and clicking? By using your speech software even part of the time, you can reduce your risk for these long-term and debilitating nerve injuries.

In Step-by-Step C.8, you change the filename *Prevent Injury* to *My prevent injury file* using the Save As dialog box.

Step-by-Step C.8

Step 1	Make sure the **Prevent Injury** document appears on your screen. If you closed the document, repeat Step-by-Step C.7.
Step 2	Open the **Save As** dialog box. Notice that it is a lot like the Open dialog box. Try the following commands: ***Voice Command*** *(if necessary)* ***File*** ***Save as***
Step 3	Switch to the **My Documents** folder and display the folder in **List** view as you learned to do in Step-by-Step C.7.
Step 4	Click your mouse in the **File name:** text box and type the filename or switch to Dictation mode and name the file with your voice by saying: ***Dictation*** ***My prevent injury file***
Step 5	Save your document and close the Save As the box by saying: ***Voice Command*** ***Save***
Step 6	Close the **Word Count** toolbar using the steps you learned earlier.
Step 7	Close Microsoft Word and collapse the Language Bar with the following commands: (When asked whether to save other open documents, say ***No***.) ***File*** ***Close*** ***Microphone***

C.c Dictating, Editing, and Formatting by Voice

If you have always dreamed of the day when you could sit back, relax, and write the next great American novel by speaking into a microphone, well, that day has arrived. It is possible to write that novel, a report, or even a simple e-mail message at speeds of 130–160 words per minute. However, it takes practice to achieve an acceptable level of accuracy. This section is designed to help you build accuracy.

Microsoft Office Speech Recognition is not made for complete handsfree use. You still need to use your keyboard and mouse much of the time. But, if you're willing to put in some effort, you can improve your speaking accuracy to the point that you can dramatically improve your output.

Dictating

Microsoft Speech Recognition allows you to work in **Dictation** mode when voice writing words into your documents. Switching from Voice Command mode to Dictation mode is as easy as saying ***Dictation***.

In Dictation mode, don't stop speaking in the middle of a sentence—even if your words don't appear immediately. The software needs a few seconds to process what you're saying. Microsoft Office Speech Recognition lets you know it is working by placing a highlighted bar with dots in your document, as shown in Figure C-28. A few seconds later, your words appear.

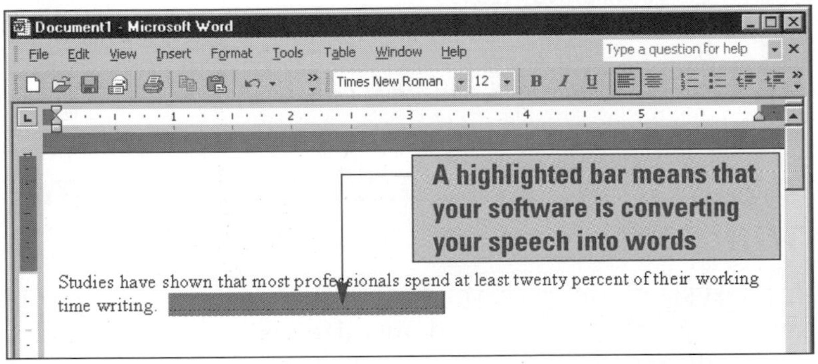

FIGURE C-28
Continue Talking Even If Your Words Don't Appear Instantly

QUICK TIP

The best way to improve dictation accuracy is to read additional training session stories to your computer. You should read at least three to five stories. Do this by clicking **Tools, Current User**, and double-checking to see if your user profile name has a check mark by it. Then, click **Tools, Training** from the Language Bar and follow the onscreen instructions.

appendix C

QUICK TIP

Think about the following as you begin voice writing:
- Speak naturally, without stopping in the middle of your sentences.
- Don't speak abnormally fast or slow.
- Say each word clearly. Don't slur your words or leave out sounds.

QUICK TIP

You'll need to dictate punctuation marks. Say the word *Period* to create a (.), say *Comma* to create a (,), say *Question Mark* for a (?), and *Exclamation Mark/Point* for (!).

During the next steps, don't be overly concerned about making mistakes. You learn some powerful ways to correct mistakes in the next few exercises. For now, experiment and see what happens.

Step-by-Step C.9

Step 1	Open **Microsoft Word** and the **Language Bar**, if necessary. Don't forget to select your user profile.
Step 2	Turn on the **Microphone**, switch to **Dictation mode**, and read this short selection into Microsoft Word. *Dictation* *Studies have shown that most professionals spend at least twenty percent of their working time writing <period> You can use speech recognition software to help you in any career you choose <period> Microsoft speech can be used in the medical <comma> legal <comma> financial <comma> and educational professions <period>* *Microphone*
Step 3	Examine your paragraph. How well did you do? Count the mistakes or word errors. How many errors did you make?
Step 4	Now delete all the text on your screen. Start by turning on the **Microphone** and then switching to **Voice Command** mode by saying (remember to pause briefly after each command): *Voice Command* *Edit* *Select All* *Backspace*
Step 5	Repeat the selection from Step 2. This time, say any word that gave you difficulty a little more clearly. See if your computer understands more of what you say this time around.
Step 6	Did you improve? Yes/No
Step 7	Delete all the text on your screen again before you continue, using the *Voice Command, Edit, Select All, Backspace* commands.

Using the New Line and New Paragraph Commands

In this next set of exercises, you have a chance to use the New Line and New Paragraph commands to organize text. These essential commands allow you to control the look and feel of your documents. (See Figure C-29.) It helps to pause briefly before and after you say each command.

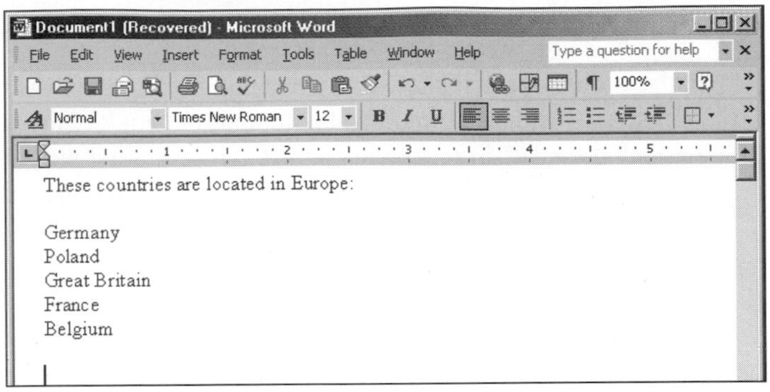

FIGURE C-29
New Line and New
Paragraph Commands
Organize Text

Step-by-Step C.10

Step 1	The New Line and New Paragraph commands help organize lists of information. Dictate the following list of European countries. Turn on the **Microphone**, if necessary, and say: **Dictation** **These countries are located in Europe <colon> <New Paragraph>** **Germany <New Line>** **Poland <New Line>** **Great Britain <New Line>** **France <New Line>** **Belgium <New Paragraph>**
Step 2	Save the file in the Save As dialog box with the **Voice Command**, **File**, **Save As** commands.
Step 3	Click your mouse in the **File name:** text box and enter **Countries of Europe** as the filename. (*Note:* If you speak the filename, remember to switch to Dictation mode.)
Step 4	Close the Save As dialog box with the **Voice Command**, **Save** commands, and then clear your screen by saying **Edit**, **Select All**, **Backspace**.

Using Undo

Microsoft Office Speech Recognition offers powerful ways to make corrections and train the software to recognize difficult words, so they appear correctly when you say them again. For example, erasing mistakes is easy with the Undo command. That's the first trick you learn in this section.

The Undo command works like pressing the Undo button or clicking Edit, Undo with your mouse. You can quickly erase the problem when you misspeak. All you need to do is switch to Voice Command mode and say **Undo**.

QUICK TIP

Say the word *Colon* to create a (:).

QUICK TIP

When dictating words in a list, it helps to pause slightly before and after saying the commands, as in *<pause> New Line <pause>* and *<pause> New Paragraph <pause>*.

appendix
C

CAUTION TIP

A common speech mistake occurs when speakers break words into syllables. For example, they may say **speak keen clear lee** instead of **speaking clearly.**

QUICK TIP

A key to great accuracy in speech recognition is to speak in complete phrases and sentences. Complete sentences and phrases make it easier for the software to understand what you're trying to say. The software makes adjustments based on the context of the words that commonly appear together. The more words you say as a group or phrase, the more information your software has to work with.

Step-by-Step C.11

Step 1	In this step, say the name of the academic subject, then erase it immediately with the Undo command and replace it with the next subject in the list. Erase the subject regardless of whether it is correct. Switch to Voice Command mode before saying Undo.

Dictation

Biology	*Voice Command*	*Undo*	*Dictation*
French	*Voice Command*	*Undo*	*Dictation*
American history	*Voice Command*	*Undo*	*Dictation*

Step 2	The Undo command deletes the last continuous phrase you have spoken. Say each of the following phrases, then use Undo to erase them.

To infinity and beyond	*Voice Command*	*Undo*	*Dictation*
The check is in the mail	*Voice Command*	*Undo*	*Dictation*
Money isn't everything	*Voice Command*	*Undo*	
Microphone			

Correcting Errors

Correcting mistakes is obviously important. There are several ways to make corrections effectively.

Because speech recognition software recognizes phrases better than individual words, one of the best ways to correct a mistake is to use your mouse to select the phrase where the mistake occurs and then repeat the phrase. For example, in the sentence below the software has keyed the word *share* instead of the word *sure*. Select the phrase (like the boldface example) with your mouse, then say the phrase again:

What you should select: You sound **very share of yourself**.
What you would repeat: **very sure of yourself**

If you still make a mistake, select the misspoken word with your mouse and take advantage of the power of the **Correction** button on the Language Bar. Carefully read through these steps and then practice what you learned in Step 5.

Step-by-Step C.12

Step 1	If you make an error, select the mistake, as shown in Figure C-30.
Step 2	With your microphone on, say *Correction* or click the Correction button with your mouse.
Step 3	If the correct alternative appears in the correction list, click the correct alternative with your mouse.

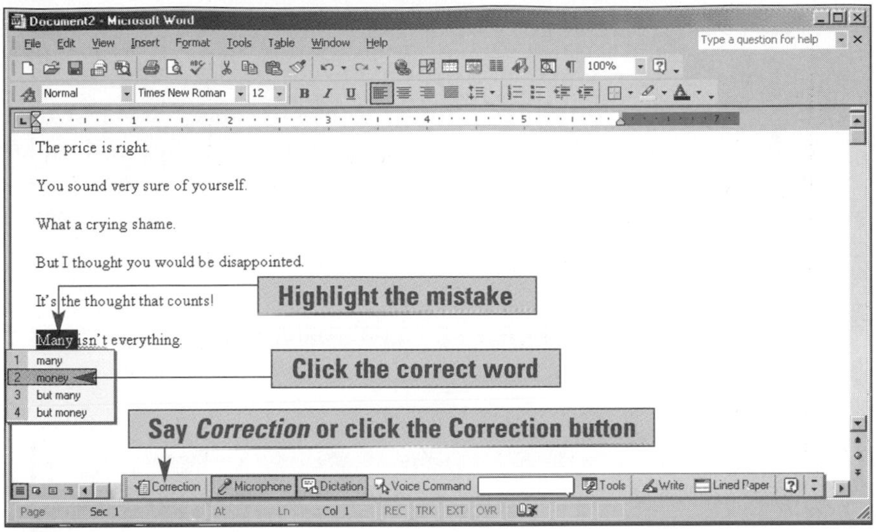

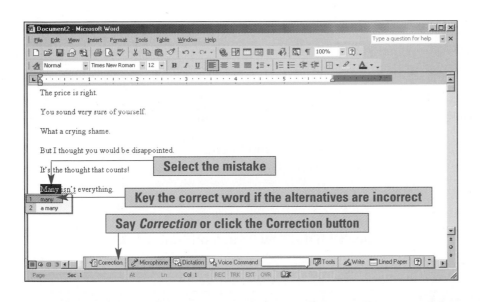

FIGURE C-30
Select the Mistake and
Say *Correction*

Step 4 | If the correct word does not appear, as in Figure C-31, key the correct response with your keyboard.

FIGURE C-31
If the Correct Word Doesn't
Appear, Key the Word

Step 5 | Now give it a try. Speak the following sentences. (*Hint:* Say the complete sentence before you make any corrections.) Try to correct the error first by repeating the phrase. Then, select individual word errors and use the Correction button to help you fix any remaining mistakes:
The price is right.
You sound very sure of yourself.
What a crying shame.
But, I thought you would be disappointed.
It's the thought that counts!
Money isn't everything.

appendix
C

Formatting Sentences

After you dictate text, you can format it, copy it, paste it, and manipulate it just like you would with a mouse. In this exercise, you dictate a few sentences, and then you change the font styles and make a copy of the sentences. That is a lot to remember, so take a look at what you are about to accomplish. Review Figure C-32 to get a sneak preview of this activity.

FIGURE C-32
Dictate, Format, and Copy and Paste These Lines

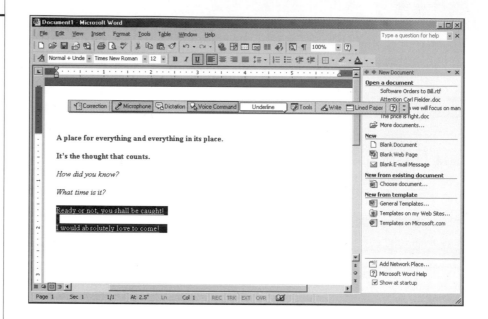

M O U S E   T I P

When you correct a mistake using the Correction button, Microsoft Office Speech Recognition plays back what you said and remembers any corrections that you make. This helps to ensure that the software won't make the same mistake the next time you say the same word or phrase. Use the Correction button as often as you can. This helps to improve your speech recognition accuracy.

A few quick reminders before you begin:

- Use your mouse and voice together to bold, italicize, and underline text.
- Say the basic punctuation marks, exclamation point/mark (!), period (.), comma (,), question mark (?), semicolon (;), colon (:).
- Start a new line with the New Paragraph command.

Step-by-Step C.13

Step 1	Speak the following sentences, using the New Paragraph command to space between each. Do not pause in the middle of any sentence. If you make mistakes, correct them using the Correction button, as explained in Step-by-Step C.12.

Dictation
A place for everything and everything in its place.
It's the thought that counts.
How did you know?
What time is it?
Ready or not, you shall be caught!
I would absolutely love to come!

Step 2	With your mouse, select the first two sentences and make them bold with the following commands: ***Voice Command*** ***Bold***
Step 3	Select the two questions and italicize them by saying: ***Italic***
Step 4	Select the final two exclamatory sentences and underline them by saying: ***Underline***
Step 5	Copy all the text on your screen and paste a copy at the bottom of your document by saying: ***Edit*** ***Select All*** ***Copy*** ***Down Arrow*** ***Paste***
Step 6	Print your document with the following commands: ***File*** ***Print*** ***OK***
Step 7	Close your document without saving using the ***File***, ***Close*** command and then say ***No*** when you are asked to save.
Step 8	Open a new document with your voice with the ***File***, ***New***, ***Blank Document*** commands and turn off your ***Microphone*** before you continue.

Adding and Training Names

Your speech software can remember what you teach it as long as you follow these simple steps. When you click <u>A</u>dd/Delete Word(s) from the Tools menu, the Add/Delete Word(s) dialog box opens. This is a very powerful tool. It allows you to enter a name or any other word or phrase, click the **<u>R</u>ecord pronunciation** button, and record your pronunciation of the word or phrase.

Step-by-Step C.14

Step 1	Click **Tools**, **<u>A</u>dd/Delete Word(s)** from the Language Bar, as shown in Figure C-33.

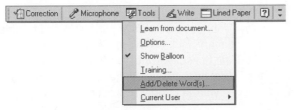

FIGURE C-33
Click the Add/Delete Word(s) Option

appendix
C

Step 2 | Enter your name into the **Word** text box as shown in Figure C-34.

FIGURE C-34
Enter Your Name in the
Word Text Box

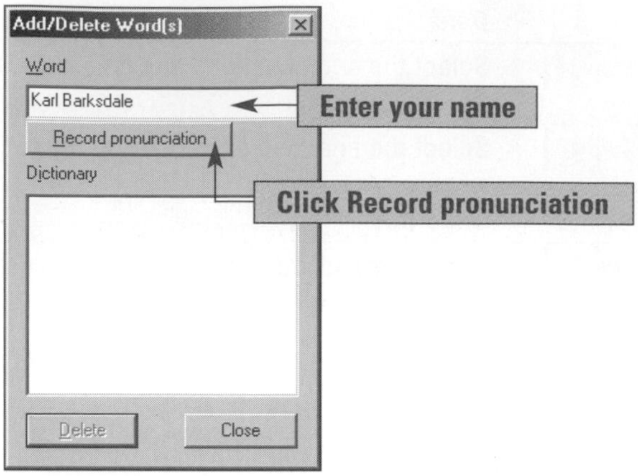

Add/Delete Word(s)

Word
Karl Barksdale ← **Enter your name**
Record pronunciation
Click Record pronunciation
Dictionary

Delete   Close

Step 3 | Click the **Record pronunciation** button and say your name aloud.

Step 4 | Your name appears in the Dictionary list. Double-click your name to hear a digitized voice repeat your name. (See Figure C-35.)

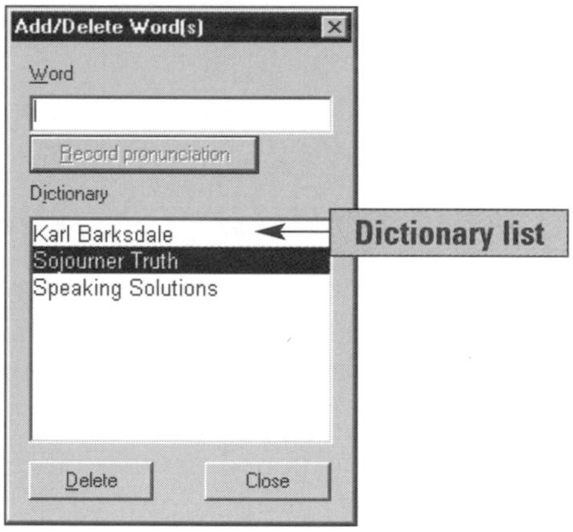

Add/Delete Word(s)

Word

Record pronunciation

Dictionary

Karl Barksdale ← **Dictionary list**
Sojourner Truth
Speaking Solutions

Delete   Close

FIGURE C-35
Add/Delete Word(s)
Dialog Box

Step 5 | Close the Add/Delete Word(s) dialog box by clicking the **Close** button.

Step 6 | Return to Microsoft Word, turn on your **Microphone**, switch to **Dictation** mode. Say your name several times and see if it appears correctly.

Step 7 | To improve your accuracy, it's important to add troublesome words to your dictionary. Pick five words that have given you difficulty in the past. Train the software to recognize these words as explained in Steps 1 through 6. As you add and train for the pronunciation of those words, your accuracy improves bit by bit.

C.d Turning Microsoft Speech Recognition On and Off

Microsoft Office Speech Recognition isn't for everybody—at least not in its present form. It requires a powerful CPU and a lot of RAM. It also takes a quality headset. If you don't have the necessary hardware, chances are speech recognition isn't working very well for you.

Perhaps you are simply uncomfortable using speech software. You may be an expert typist with no sign of carpal tunnel syndrome or any other repetitive stress injury. Whatever your reason for choosing not to use Microsoft speech software, it is important to know how to disable the feature.

There are two ways to turn off your speech software. You can minimize the toolbar and place it aside temporarily, or you can turn it off entirely. If you decide you want to use speech recognition at a later time, you can always turn it back on again.

Turning Off Speech Recognition

Microsoft Speech Recognition allows you to minimize the Language Bar, putting it aside temporarily. Minimizing places the Language Bar in the taskbar tray in the form of the Language Bar icon. After the Language Bar has been minimized, it is then possible to turn the system off altogether. To see how this is accomplished, follow Step-by-Step C.15.

Step-by-Step C.15

| Step 1 | Open **Microsoft Word** and the **Language Bar**, if necessary. |
| Step 2 | Click the **Minimize** button on the Language Bar, as shown in Figure C-36. |

FIGURE C-36
Click the Minimize Button on the Language Bar

appendix
C

Step 3   When you minimize for the first time, a dialog box explains what is going to happen to your Language Bar, as shown in Figure C-37. Read this dialog box carefully, then click **OK**.

FIGURE C-37
Read This
Information Carefully

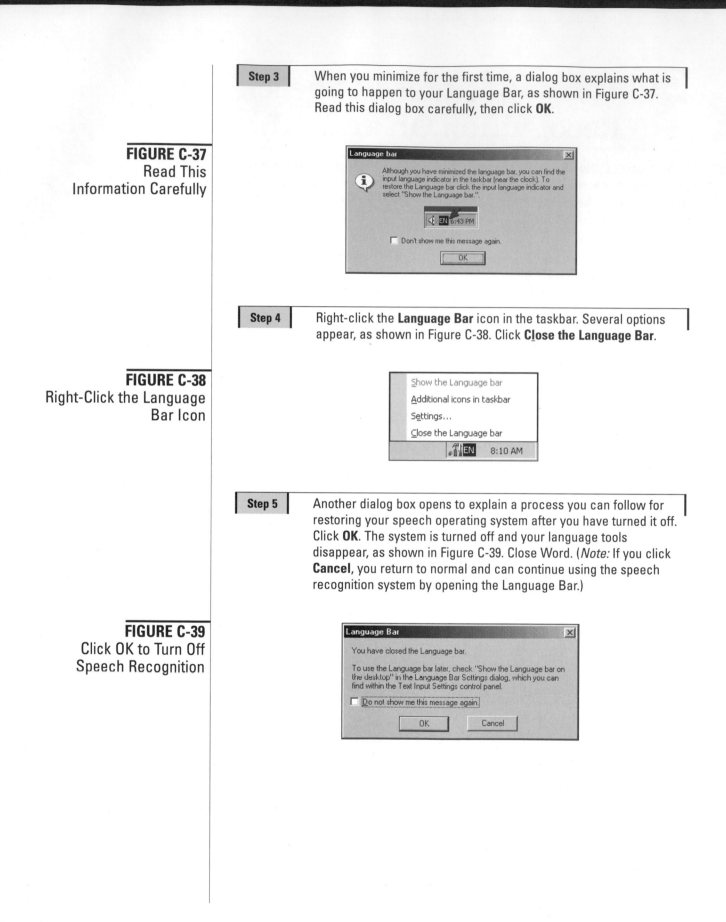

Step 4   Right-click the **Language Bar** icon in the taskbar. Several options appear, as shown in Figure C-38. Click **Close the Language Bar**.

FIGURE C-38
Right-Click the Language
Bar Icon

Step 5   Another dialog box opens to explain a process you can follow for restoring your speech operating system after you have turned it off. Click **OK**. The system is turned off and your language tools disappear, as shown in Figure C-39. Close Word. (*Note:* If you click **Cancel**, you return to normal and can continue using the speech recognition system by opening the Language Bar.)

FIGURE C-39
Click OK to Turn Off
Speech Recognition

Turning On Speech Recognition

There are several ways to turn your speech recognition system back on. Follow Step-by-Step C.16.

Step-by-Step C.16

| Step 1 | Open **Microsoft Word** and click **Speech** on the **Tools** menu, as shown in Figure C-40. Your speech recognition software is restored and you can begin using it again. |

FIGURE C-40
Click Speech on the Tools Menu

If your speech software did not restore itself after Step 1, continue with Steps 2 through 5.

| Step 2 | Click the **Start** button, **Settings**, **Control Panel**. Then double-click the **Text Services** icon to open the Text Services dialog box, as shown in Figure C-41. |

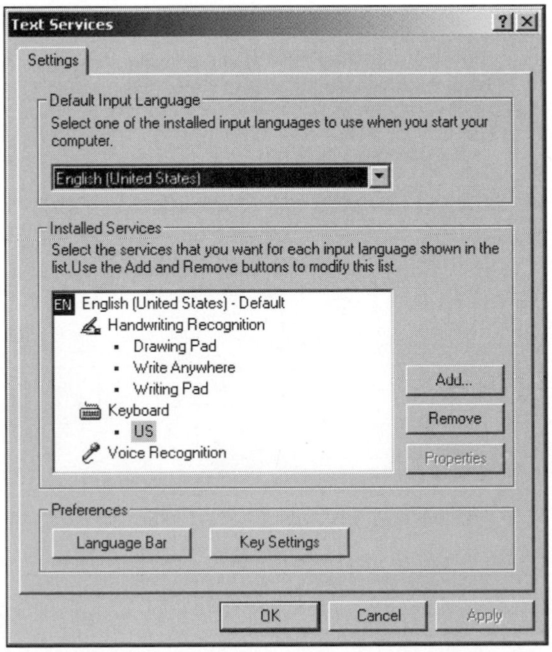

FIGURE C-41
Click Language Bar in the Text Input Settings Dialog Box

appendix
C

| Step 3 | Click **Language Bar** in the Text Services dialog box. |

| Step 4 | In the Language Bar Settings dialog box, click the **Show the Language bar on the desktop** check box to insert a check mark, as shown in Figure C-42. |

FIGURE C-42
Language Bar Settings
Dialog Box

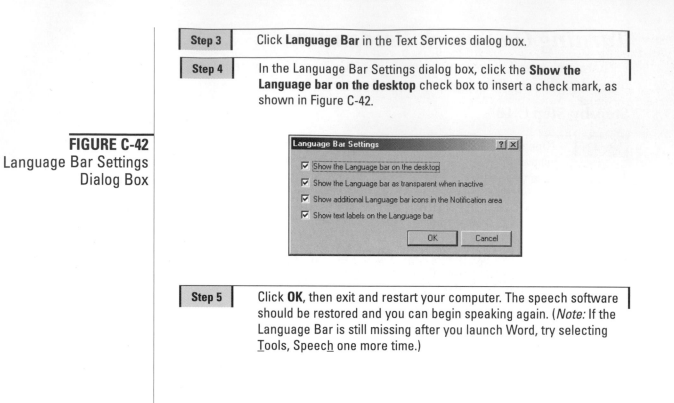

| Step 5 | Click **OK**, then exit and restart your computer. The speech software should be restored and you can begin speaking again. (*Note:* If the Language Bar is still missing after you launch Word, try selecting Tools, Speech one more time.) |

Mastering and Using Office XP

APPROVED COURSEWARE

Core MOUS Objectives

Microsoft Word 2002

Standardized Coding Number	Skill Sets and Skills Being Measured	Chapter Number	Chapter Pages	Exercise Pages	Exercises
W2002-1	**Inserting and Modifying Text**				
W2002-1-1	Insert, modify, and move text and symbols	1	WI 6, 7	WI 23–27	Skills Review 1–7, 9 Case Projects 1–8
		2	WI 34, 38	WI 50	Skills Review 5
		3	WI 59, 63, 68	WI 75–78	Skills Review 3–6, 8, 9 Case Projects 1–3, 5–8
		4 and throughout text	WI 96		
W2002-1-2	Apply and modify text formats	4 and throughout text	WI 81, 82, 83, 84, 86, 92	WI 101–104	Skills Review 1–8 Case Projects 1–8
W2002-1-3	Correct spelling and grammar usage	3	WI 55, 58	WI 74–78	Skills Review 1–3, 7, 8 Case Projects 1–3, 5–8
W2002-1-4	Apply font and text effects	4	WI 88, 90, 95	WI 102–104	Skills Review 6, 7 Case Projects 1, 2, 5
W2002-1-5	Enter and format date and time	2 and throughout text	WI 33	WI 48–53	Skills Review 1, 3, 5, 6, 7 Case Projects 1, 4–6, 8, 9
W2002-1-6	Apply character styles	4 and throughout text	WI 86	WI 101–104	Skills Review 1–5, 7, 8 Case Projects 1, 2, 4, 5, 7, 8

Standardized Coding Number	Skill Sets and Skills Being Measured	Chapter Number	Chapter Pages	Exercise Pages	Exercises
W2002-2	***Creating and Modifying Paragraphs***				
W2002-2-1	Modify paragraph formats	6 and throughout text	WI 125, 127, 129, 132	WI 151–155	Skills Review 1–8 Case Projects 1, 4, 6, 7
W2002-2-2	Set and modify tabs	5 and throughout text	WI 109, 111, 112, 113, 114	WI 118–122	Skills Review 1–8 Case Projects 1–6, 8
W2002-2-3	Apply bullet, outline, and numbering formats to paragraphs	6	WI 124, 142, 143	WI 151–155	Skills Review 1–3, 5, 7, 8 Case Project 8
W2002-2-4	Apply paragraph styles	6 and throughout text	WI 140	WI 152–155	Skills Review 4, 5 Case Project 4
W2002-3	***Formatting Documents***				
W2002-3-1	Create and modify a header and footer	6	WI 139	WI 151–154	Skills Review 1, 5, 6, 7
W2002-3-2	Apply and modify column settings	9	WI 191, 192, 193	WI 209–212	Skills Review 1, 3, 5, 6, 7 Case Projects 1, 2, 3, 7
W2002-3-3	Modify document layout and Page Setup options	2	WI 30, 32	WI 48–53	Skills Review 1, 3, 6, 7 Case Projects 1, 4–6, 8, 9
		6 and throughout text	WI 136, 137	WI 151–154	Skills Review 1–7
W2002-3-4	Create and modify tables	10	WI 214, 219, 222, 224	WI 228–233	Skills Review 1–8 Case Projects 1–8
W2002-3-5	Preview and print documents, envelopes, and labels	1	WI 10	WI 23–27	Skills Review 1–7, 9 Case Projects 1–8
		2		WI 48–53	Skills Review 1–8 Case Projects 1, 2, 4–6, 8, 9
		7	WI 157, 162	WI 169–172	Skills Review 1–8 Case Projects 1–8
		8 and throughout text	WI 174, 180	WI 186–189	Skills Review 1–8 Case Projects 1–5

Standardized Coding Number	Skill Sets and Skills Being Measured	Chapter Number	Chapter Pages	Exercise Pages	Exercises
W2002-4	**Managing Documents**				
W2002-4-1	Manage files and folders for documents	1	WI 18	WI 25	Skills Review 9
W2002-4-2	Create documents using templates	1	WI 18	WI 23–27	Skills Review 1, 3, 5, 7, 9 Case Projects 1–8
		11	WI 235	WI 244–247	Skills Review 1–3, 5–8 Case Projects 1–8
		and throughout text			
W2002-4-3	Save documents using different names and file formats	1	WI 8, 17, 18	WI 23–27	Skills Review 1–7, 9 Case Projects 1–8
		and throughout text			
W2002-5	**Working with Graphics**				
W2002-5-1	Insert images and graphics	9	WI 194	WI 210, 212	Skills Review 3, 6 Case Projects 3, 5, 6, 7
W2002-5-2	Create and modify diagrams and charts	9	WI 198, 201	WI 209–212	Skills Review 2, 4, 7, 8 Case Projects 4, 8
W2002-6	**Workgroup Collaboration**				
W2002-6-1	Compare and merge documents	12	WI 254	WI 261–263	Skills Review 4, 7 Case Projects 1, 6
W2002-6-2	Insert, view, and edit comments	12	WI 253	WI 261–263	Skills Review 6 Case Project 7
W2002-6-3	Convert documents into Web pages	12	WI 255	WI 260–263	Skills Review 1, 5, 8 Case Project 4

Microsoft Excel 2002

Standardized Coding Number	Skill Sets and Skills Being Measured	Chapter Number	Chapter Pages	Exercise Pages	Exercises
Ex2002-1	**Working with Cells and Cell Data**				
Ex2002-1-1	Insert, delete, and move cells	3 4	EI 46–49 EI 68, 84	EI 66 EI 91–96	Skills Review 8 Skills Review 1, 2, 4, 6, 7 Case Projects 1, 3–7
Ex2002-1-2	Enter and edit cell data including text, numbers, and formulas	2 3 4	EI 28–32 EI 43–44, 50, 52, 53–57 EI 72–75	EI 38–41 EI 62–66 EI 91–96	Skills Review 1, 2, 4–8 Case Projects 1–8 Skills Review 1–4, 6, 7 Case Projects 1, 2, 5, 6, 8 Skills Review 1–4, 6, 7 Case Projects 1, 3–7
Ex2002-1-3	Check spelling	5	EI 99–101	EI 117	Skills Review 3
Ex2002-1-4	Find and replace cell data and formats	5 6	EI 98–99 EI 136–137	EI 117 EI 141–142	Skills Review 3 Skills Review 1, 3
Ex2002-1-5	Work with a subset of data by filtering lists	4	EI 86–87	EI 91, 96	Skills Review 1 Case Project 6
Ex2002-2	**Managing Workbooks**				
Ex2002-2-1	Manage workbook files and folders	1	EI 6–7, 13	EI 23–25	Skills Review 1, 2, 4–8 Case Project 2
Ex2002-2-2	Create workbooks using templates	1	EI 17–19	EI 23, 25	Skills Review 3 Case Project 4
Ex2002-2-3	Save workbooks using different names and file formats	1	EI 14–15, 17	EI 23–25	Skills Review 1–8 Case Project 4
Ex2002-3	**Formatting and Printing Worksheets**				
Ex2002-3-1	Apply and modify cell formats	4	EI 70–79	EI 91–96	Skills Review 1–8 Case Projects 1–7
Ex2002-3-2	Modify row and column settings	4	EI 82, 84–86	EI 92, 94–96	Skills Review 2, 7 Case Projects 3, 4, 6
Ex2002-3-3	Modify row and column formats	4	EI 72, 82–84	EI 91–96	Skills Review 1, 2, 4–8 Case Projects 1–7
Ex2002-3-4	Apply styles	4	EI 80–82	EI 94–95	Skills Review 8
Ex2002-3-5	Use automated tools to format worksheets	4	EI 70–71	EI 92	Skills Review 3
Ex2002-3-6	Modify Page Setup options for worksheets	5	EI 102–112	EI 116–119	Skills Review 1–4, 6–8 Case Projects 2–4, 6–8
Ex2002-3-7	Preview and print worksheets and workbooks	1 5	EI 16–17 EI 102, 108–113	EI 23–24 EI 116–119	Skills Review 1–5, 8 Skills Review 1–4 Case Projects 2–4, 6–8

Standardized Coding Number	Skill Sets and Skills Being Measured	Chapter Number	Chapter Pages	Exercise Pages	Exercises
Ex2002-4	**Modifying Workbooks**				
Ex2002-4-1	Insert and delete worksheets	1	EI 11, 13	EI 23–24	Skills Review 4, 5, 6
Ex2002-4-2	Modify worksheet names and positions	1 2	EI 11–13 EI 34–35	EI 23–24 EI 39–41	Skills Review 2, 6 Skills Review 3, 6, 7 Case Projects 3, 4, 8
Ex2002-4-3	Use 3-D references	3	EI 58–59	EI 64–65	Skills Review 7, 8
Ex2002-5	**Creating and Revising Formulas**				
Ex2002-5-1	Create and revise formulas	3	EI 43–44, 49–51	EI 62–66	Skills Review 1, 4, 7 Case Projects 1, 8
Ex2002-5-2	Use statistical, date and time, financial, and logical functions in formulas	3	EI 50–59	EI 62–66	Skills Review 1, 7 Case Projects 1, 2, 6
Ex2002-6	**Creating and Modifying Graphics**				
Ex2002-6-1	Create, modify, position, and print charts	6	EI 121–127, 129–132	EI 141–144	Skills Review 1, 3–8 Case Projects 1, 3–8
Ex2002-6-2	Create, modify, and position graphics	6	EI 127–128	EI 141–144	Skills Review 3 Case Project 3
Ex2002-7	**Workgroup Collaboration**				
Ex2002-7-1	Convert worksheets into Web pages	6	EI 135–136	EI 142, 144	Skills Review 6 Case Project 7
Ex2002-7-2	Create hyperlinks	6	EI 133–134	EI 143, 144	Skills Review 8 Case Project 4
Ex2002-7-3	View and edit comments	6	EI 132–133, 134–135	EI 143–144	Skills Review 7 Case Projects 1, 8

Microsoft Access 2002

Standardized Coding Number	Skill Sets and Skills Being Measured	Chapter Number	Chapter Pages	Exercise Pages	Exercises
Ac2002-1	**Creating and Using Databases**				
Ac2002-1-1	Create Access databases	2	AI 24	AI 47–50	Skills Review 1, 6 Case Project 8
Ac2002-1-2	Open database objects in multiple views	2	AI 36	AI 48–50	Skills Review 2, 4, 5, 7, 8 Case Projects 2–7
Ac2002-1-3	Move among records	3	AI 53	AI 72–74	Skills Review 1–4, 8 Case Projects 1–6
Ac2002-1-4	Format datasheets	5	AI 104	AI 110–112	Skills Review 2–8 Case Projects 1–6
Ac2002-2	**Creating and Modifying Tables**				
Ac2002-2-1	Create and modify tables	2	AI 27, 29, 36	AI 47–50	Skills Review 1–5, 8 Case Project 7
Ac2002-2-2	Add a predefined input mask to a field	2	AI 39	AI 48–49	Skills Review 5, 8
Ac2002-2-3	Create Lookup fields	2	AI 41		
Ac2002-2-4	Modify field properties	2	AI 33, 39	AI 47–50	Skills Review 1–5, 8 Case Project 7
Ac2002-3	**Creating and Modifying Queries**				
Ac2002-3-1	Create and modify Select queries	5	AI 92, 99	AI 110–112	Skills Review 1, 8 Case Projects 1, 2, 3
Ac2002-3-2	Add calculated fields to Select queries	5	AI 101, 104	AI 111–112	Skills Review 6, 7 Case Projects 4, 5, 6
Ac2002-4	**Creating and Modifying Forms**				
Ac2002-4-1	Create and display forms	6	AI 114, 125	AI 131–133	Skills Review 1, 2 Case Projects 3–6
Ac2002-4-2	Modify form properties	6	AI 118	AI 131–133	Skills Review 4–8 Case Projects 3–5, 7, 8
Ac2002-5	**Viewing and Organizing Information**				
Ac2002-5-1	Enter, edit, and delete records	3	AI 52, 55, 57, 66	AI 72–74	Skills Review 1–4, 7, 8 Case Projects 1-6, 8
		6	AI 125	AI 131, 133	Skills Review 2–4 Case Projects 4, 8
Ac2002-5-2	Create queries	5	AI 92	AI 110–112	Skills Review 1, 8 Case Projects 1, 3, 4, 5

Standardized Coding Number	Skill Sets and Skills Being Measured	Chapter Number	Chapter Pages	Exercise Pages	Exercises
Ac2002-5-3	Sort records	3	AI 60	AI 73	Skills Review 5
Ac2002-5-4	Filter records	3	AI 62	AI 73–74	Skills Review 6 Case Project 7
Ac2002-6	*Defining Relationships*				
Ac2002-6-1	Create one-to-many relationships	4	AI 76, 80	AI 88–90	Skills Review 1, 3, 4, 5 Case Projects 1, 4, 5, 6
Ac2002-6-2	Enforce referential integrity	4	AI 82, 83	AI 88–90	Skills Review 2, 3, 4, 5 Case Project 5
Ac2002-7	*Producing Reports*				
Ac2002-7-1	Create and format reports	7	AI 136, 139	AI 152–154	Skills Review 1, 3, 4, 6, 7 Case Projects 3, 5, 6, 7, 8
Ac2002-7-2	Add calculated controls to reports	7	AI 143	AI 153, 154	Skills Review 5, 8 Case Project 6
Ac2002-7-3	Preview and print reports	7	AI 145	AI 152–154	Skills Review 1–8 Case Projects 6, 7, 8
Ac2002-8	*Integrating with Other Applications*				
Ac2002-8-1	Import data to Access	2 8	AI 42 AI 162, 167	AI 174–176	Skills Review 3, 5, 6 Case Project 6
Ac2002-8-2	Export data from Access	8	AI 156, 162, 168	AI 174–176	Skills Review 1, 2, 4, 7 Case Projects 2, 3, 4
Ac2002-8-3	Create a simple data access page	8	AI 169	AI 175, 176	Skills Review 8 Case Projects 7, 8

Index